Contents

D0365991

Preface

This new edition of the Oxford German Mini Dictionary provides a handy and up-to-date reference work for tourists, students, and business people. It fully reflects recent changes to the spelling of German.

The dictionary also includes an easy-to-use Phrasefinder, which groups together essential phrases you will need for everyday conversation. The section is thematically arranged and covers key topics including: going places, keeping in touch, food and drink, places to stay, shopping and money, sports and leisure, time and dates, and conversion charts.

Proprietary terms

This dictionary includes some words which are, or are asserted to be, proprietary names or trademarks. Their inclusion does not imply that they have acquired for legal purposes a non-proprietary or general significance, nor is any other judgement implied concerning their legal status. In cases where the editor has some evidence that a word is used as a proprietary name or trademark this is indicated by the symbol ®, but no judgement concerning the legal status of such words is made or implied thereby.

Symbols used in this dictionary

familiar	▯	familiär
slang	▣	Slang
old spelling	*	alte Schreibung
proprietary term	®	Markenzeichen

Mathematics	*Math*	Mathematik
Medicine	*Med*	Medizin
Military	*Mil*	Militär
Music	*Mus*	Musik
noun	*n*	Substantiv
Nautical	*Naut*	nautisch
nominative	*nom*	Nominativ
neuter	*nt*	Neutrum
or	*od*	oder
pejorative	*pej*	abwertend
Photography	*Phot*	Fotografie
Physics	*Phys*	Physik
plural	*pl*	Plural
Politics	*Pol*	Politik
possessive	*poss*	Possessiv-
past participle	*pp*	zweites Partizip
predicative	*pred*	prädikativ
prefix	*pref*	Präfix, Vorsilbe
preposition	*prep*	Präposition
present	*pres*	Präsens
present participle	*pres p*	erstes Partizip
pronoun	*pron*	Pronomen
past tense	*pt*	Präteritum
Railway	*Rail*	Eisenbahn
regular	*reg*	regelmäßig
relative	*rel*	Relativ-
Religion	*Relig*	Religion
see	*s.*	siehe
School	*Sch*	Schule
separable	*sep*	trennbar
singular	*sg*	Singular
someone	*s.o.*	jemand
Technical	*Techn*	Technik
Telephone	*Teleph*	Telefon
Theatre	*Theat*	Theater
University	*Univ*	Universität
intransitive verb	*vi*	intransitives Verb
reflexive verb	*vr*	reflexives Verb
transitive verb	*vt*	transitives Verb
Zoology	*Zool*	Zoologie

Oxford
German
Mini Dictionary

FIFTH EDITION

German–English
English–German

Deutsch–Englisch
Englisch–Deutsch

OXFORD
UNIVERSITY PRESS

OXFORD
UNIVERSITY PRESS

Great Clarendon Street, Oxford OX2 6DP

Oxford University Press is a department of the University of Oxford.
It furthers the University's objective of excellence in research, scholarship,
and education by publishing worldwide in

Oxford New York

Auckland Cape Town Dar es Salaam Hong Kong Karachi Kuala Lumpur
Madrid Melbourne Mexico City Nairobi New Delhi Shanghai Taipei
Toronto

With offices in
Argentina Austria Brazil Chile Czech Republic France Greece
Guatemala Hungary Italy Japan South Korea Poland Portugal
Singapore Switzerland Thailand Turkey Ukraine Vietnam

Oxford is a registered trade mark of Oxford University Press
in the UK and in certain other countries

First edition published 1993
Second edition published 1997
Third edition published 2002
Fourth edition published 2005
This edition published 2008

British Library Cataloguing in Publication Data

Data available

Library of Congress Cataloging in Publication Data
Data available

ISBN 978-0-19-953437-1
ISBN 978-0-19-954125-6 (US edition)

10 9 8 7 6 5 4

Typeset by Interactive Sciences Ltd, Gloucester
Printed and bound in Italy by Legoprint S.p.A.

1552898338157552

List of contributors

Fifth Edition

Editors
Joanna Rubery
Nicholas Rollin

Supplementary Material
Eva Vennebusch
Inge Milfull

Fourth Edition

Editors
Nicholas Rollin
Roswitha Morris
Eva Vennebusch

Data Capture
Susan Wilkin
Anne McConnell

Proof-reading
Katrin Thier
Stephen Curtis

Third Edition

Editors
Gunhild Prowe
Jill Schneider

Second Edition

Editors
Roswitha Morris
Robin Sawers

Supplementary Material
Robin Sawers
Neil and Roswitha Morris
Valerie Grundy
Eva Vennebusch

First Edition

Editors
Gunhild Prowe
Jill Schneider

Introduction

The text of this dictionary reflects changes to the spelling of German ratified in July 1996. The symbol * has been introduced to refer from the old spelling to the new, preferred one:

> **As*** *nt* **-ses, -se** *s.* **Ass**
>
> **dasein*** *vi sep (sein)* **da-sein,** *s.* **da**
>
> **Schiffahrt*** *f s.* **Schifffahrt**

Where both the old and new forms are valid, an equals sign = is used to refer to the preferred form:

> **aufwändig** *adj* = **aufwendig**
>
> **Tunfisch** *m* = **Thunfisch**

When such forms follow each other alphabetically, they are given with commas, with the preferred form in first place:

> **Panther, Panter** *m* **-s, -** panther

In phrases, od (oder) is used:

> **...deine(r,s)** *poss pron* yours;
>
> **die D∼en** *od* **d∼en** *pl* your family *sg*

On the English–German side, only the preferred German form is given.

- A swung dash ∼ represents the headword or that part of the headword preceding a vertical bar |. The initial letter of a German headword is given to show whether or not it is a capital.

- The vertical bar | precedes the part of the headword which is not repeated in compounds or derivatives.

- Square brackets [ ] are used for optional material.

- Parentheses are used after a verb translation to indicate the object; before a verb translation to indicate the subject; before an adjective to indicate a typical noun which it qualifies.

- Parentheses are also used for field or style labels (see the inside covers), and for explanatory matter.

- A bold bullet indicates a new part of speech within an entry.

- *od* (oder) and *or* denote that words or portions of a phrase are synonymous. An oblique stroke / is used where there is a difference in usage or meaning.

- ≈ is used where no exact equivalent exists in the other language.

- A dagger † indicates that a German verb is irregular and that the parts can be found in the verb table on pages 604–608. Compound verbs are not listed there as they follow the pattern of the basic verb.

- The stressed vowel is marked in a German headword by _ (long) or . (short). A phonetic transcription is only given for words which do not follow the normal rules of pronunciation. A guide to German pronunciation rules can be found on pages ix–x.

- Phonetics are given for all English headwords. In blocks of compounds, if no stress is shown, it falls on the first element.

- A change in pronunciation or stress shown within a block of compounds applies only to that particular word (subsequent entries revert to the pronunciation and stress of the headword).

- German headword nouns are followed by the gender and, with the exception of compound nouns, by the genitive and plural. These are only given at compound nouns if they present some difficulty. Otherwise the user should refer to the final element.

- Nouns that decline like adjectives are entered as follows: **-e(r)** *m/f,* **-e(s)** *nt.*

- Adjectives which have no undeclined form are entered in the feminine form with the masculine and neuter in brackets **-e(r,s)**.

- The reflexive pronoun sich is accusative unless marked (*dat*).

Phonetic symbols used for German words

a	Hand	hant	ŋ	lang	laŋ
aː	Bahn	baːn	o	Moral	moˈraːl
ɐ	Ober	ˈoːbɐ	oː	Boot	boːt
ɐ̯	Uhr	uːɐ̯	ǫ	loyal	lǫaˈjaːl
ã	Conférencier	kõferãˈsje	õ	Konkurs	kõˈkʊrs
ãː	Abonnement	abɔnəˈmãː	õ	Ballon	baˈlõː
ai̯	weit	vai̯t	ɔ	Post	pɔst
au̯	Haut	hau̯t	ø	Ökonom	økoˈnoːm
b	Ball	bal	øː	Öl	øːl
ç	ich	ɪç	œ	göttlich	ˈɡœtlɪç
d	dann	dan	ɔy̯	heute	ˈhɔy̯tə
dʒ	Gin	dʒɪn	p	Pakt	pakt
e	Metall	meˈtal	r	Rast	rast
eː	Beet	beːt	s	Hast	hast
ɛ	mästen	ˈmɛstən	ʃ	Schal	ʃaːl
ɛː	wählen	ˈvɛːlən	t	Tal	taːl
ə	Cousin	kuˈzɛ̃ː	ts	Zahl	tsaːl
ə	Nase	ˈnaːzə	tʃ	Couch	kau̯tʃ
f	Faß	fas	u	Kupon	kuˈpõː
ɡ	Gast	ɡast	uː	Hut	huːt
h	haben	ˈhaːbən	ǫ	aktuell	akˈtǫɛl
i	Rivale	riˈvaːlə	ʊ	Pult	pʊlt
iː	viel	fiːl	v	was	vas
i̯	Aktion	akˈtsi̯oːn	x	Bach	bax
ɪ	Birke	ˈbɪrkə	y	Physik	fyˈziːk
j	ja	jaː	yː	Rübe	ˈryːbə
k	kalt	kalt	ỹ	Nuance	ˈnỹãːsə
l	Last	last	ʏ	Fülle	ˈfʏlə
m	Mast	mast	z	Nase	ˈnaːzə
n	Naht	naːt	ʒ	Regime	reˈʒiːm

ʔ Glottal stop, e.g. Koordination /koʔɔrdinaˈtsion/.

ː length sign after a vowel, e.g. Chrom /kroːm/.

ˈ Stress mark before stressed syllable, e.g. Balkon /balˈkõː/.

Guide to German pronunciation

Consonants

Pronounced as in English with the following exceptions:

b	as	p	
d	as	t	} *at the end of a word or syllable*
g	as	k	
ch	as in Scottish lo<u>ch</u>		*after a, o, u, au*
	like an exaggerated h as in <u>h</u>uge		*after i, e, ä, ö, ü, eu, ei*
-chs	as	x	(as in bo<u>x</u>)
-ig	as	-ich / ɪç /	*when a suffix*
j	as	y	(as in <u>y</u>es)
ps			the p is pronounced
pn	}		
qu	as	k + v	
s	as	z	(as in <u>z</u>ero) *at the beginning of a word*
	as	s	(as in bu<u>s</u>) *at the end of a word or syllable, before a consonant (except p and t), or when doubled*
sch	as	sh	
sp	as	shp	*at the beginning of a word or syllable*
st	as	sht	*at the beginning of a word or syllable*
v	as	f	(as in <u>f</u>or)
	as	v	(as in <u>v</u>ery) *within a word*
w	as	v	(as in <u>v</u>ery)
z	as	ts	

Guide to German pronunciation

· ·

Vowels

Approximately as follows:

a	short	as	u	(as in but)
	long	as	a	(as in car)
e	short	as	e	(as in pen)
	long	as	a	(as in paper)
i	short	as	i	(as in bit)
	long	as	ee	(as in queen)
o	short	as	o	(as in hot)
	long	as	o	(as in pope)
u	short	as	oo	(as in foot)
	long	as	oo	(as in boot)

Vowels are always short before a double consonant, and long when followed by an h or when double

ie	is pronounced	ee	(as in keep)

Diphthongs

au	as	ow	(as in how)
ei	as	y	(as in my)
ai			
eu	as	oy	(as in boy)
äu			

Die für das Englische verwendeten Zeichen der Lautschrift

ɑ:	barn	bɑːn	l	lot	lɒt
ɑ̃	nuance	'njuːɑ̃s	m	mat	mæt
æ	fat	fæt	n	not	nɒt
æ̃	lingerie	'læ̃ʒərɪ	ŋ	sing	sɪŋ
aɪ	fine	faɪn	ɒ	got	gɒt
aʊ	now	naʊ	ɔ:	paw	pɔː
b	bat	bæt	ɔɪ	boil	bɔɪl
d	dog	dɒg	p	pet	pet
dʒ	jam	dʒæm	r	rat	ræt
e	met	met	s	sip	sɪp
eɪ	fate	feɪt	ʃ	ship	ʃɪp
eə	fairy	'feərɪ	t	tip	tɪp
əʊ	goat	gəʊt	tʃ	chin	tʃɪn
ə	ago	ə'gəʊ	θ	thin	θɪn
ɜ:	fur	fɜː(r)	ð	the	ðə
f	fat	fæt	u:	boot	buːt
g	good	gʊd	ʊ	book	bʊk
h	hat	hæt	ʊə	tourism	'tʊərɪzm
ɪ	bit, happy	bɪt, 'hæpɪ	ʌ	dug	dʌg
ɪə	near	nɪə(r)	v	van	væn
i:	meet	miːt	w	win	wɪn
j	yet	jet	z	zip	zɪp
k	kit	kɪt	ʒ	vision	'vɪʒn

:   bezeichnet Länge des vorhergehenden Vokals, z. B. boot /buːt/.

'   Betonung, steht unmittelbar vor einer betonten Silbe, z. B. ago /ə'gəʊ/.

(r)   Ein „r" in runden Klammern wird nur gesprochen, wenn im Textzusammenhang ein Vokal unmittelbar folgt, z. B. fire /'faɪə(r)/; fire at /'faɪər æt/.

Pronunciation of the alphabet/ Aussprache des Alphabets

English/Englisch		German/Deutsch
eɪ	**a**	a:
biː	**b**	be:
siː	**c**	tseː
diː	**d**	deː
iː	**e**	eː
ef	**f**	ɛf
dʒiː	**g**	geː
eɪtʃ	**h**	haː
aɪ	**i**	iː
dʒeɪ	**j**	jɔt
keɪ	**k**	kaː
el	**l**	ɛl
em	**m**	ɛm
en	**n**	ɛn
əʊ	**o**	oː
piː	**p**	peː
kjuː	**q**	kuː
aː(r)	**r**	ɛr
es	**s**	ɛs
tiː	**t**	teː
juː	**u**	uː
viː	**v**	fau
'dʌbljuː	**w**	veː
eks	**x**	ɪks
waɪ	**y**	'ʏpsilɔn
zed	**z**	tsɛt
eɪ umlaut	**ä**	ɛː
əʊ umlaut	**ö**	ø
juː umlaut	**ü**	yː
es'zed	**ß**	ɛs'tsɛt

Aal m -[e]s,-e eel

Aas nt -es carrion; ⊠ swine

ab prep (+ dat) from ● adv off; (weg) away; (auf Fahrplan) departs; ab und zu now and then; auf und ab up and down

abändern vt sep alter; (abwandeln) modify

Abbau m dismantling; (Kohlen-) mining. **a~en** vt sep dismantle; mine (Kohle)

abbeißen† vt sep bite off

abbeizen vt sep strip

abberufen† vt sep recall

abbestellen vt sep cancel; jdn a~ put s.o. off

abbiegen† vi sep (sein) turn off; [nach] links a~ turn left

Abbildung f -,-en illustration

abblättern vi sep (sein) flake off

abblend|en vt/i sep (haben) [die Scheinwerfer] a~en dip one's headlights. **A~licht** nt dipped headlights pl

abbrechen† v sep ● vt break off; (abreißen) demolish; (Computer) cancel ● vi (sein/haben) break off

abbrennen† v sep ● vt burn off; (niederbrennen) burn down ● vi (sein) burn down

abbringen† vt sep dissuade (von from)

Abbruch m demolition; (Beenden) breaking off

abbuchen vt sep debit

abbürsten vt sep brush down; (entfernen) brush off

abdanken vi sep (haben) resign; (Herrscher:) abdicate

abdecken vt sep uncover; (abnehmen) take off; (zudecken) cover; den Tisch a~ clear the table

abdichten vt sep seal

abdrehen vt sep turn off

Abdruck m (pl =e) impression. **a~en** vt sep print

abdrücken vt/i sep (haben) fire; sich a~ leave an impression

Abend m -s,-e evening; am A~ in the evening; heute A~ this evening, tonight; gestern A~ yesterday evening, last night. **A~brot** nt supper; (einfacher) supper. **A~essen** nt dinner; (einfacher) supper. **A~mahl** nt (Relig) [Holy] Communion. **a~s** adv in the evening

Abenteuer nt -s,- adventure; (Liebes-) affair. **a~lich** adj fantastic

aber conj but; oder a~ or else ● adv (wirklich) really

Aber|glaube m superstition. **a~gläubisch** adj superstitious

abfahr|en† v sep ● vi (sein) leave; (Auto:) drive off ● vt take away; (entlangfahren) drive along; use (Fahrkarte); abgefahrene Reifen worn tyres. **A~t** f (Abfahrt); (Tal-fahrt) descent; (Piste) run; (Ausfahrt) exit

Abfall m refuse, rubbish; (auf der Straße) litter; (Industrie-) waste

abfallen† vi sep (sein) drop, fall; (übrig bleiben) be left (für for); (sich neigen) slope away. **a~d** adj sloping

Abfallhaufen m rubbish-dump

abfällig adj disparaging

abfangen† vt sep intercept

abfärben vi sep (haben) (Farbe:)

a

run; (*Stoff:*) not be colour-fast

abfassen *vt sep* draft

abfertigen *vt sep* attend to; (*zollamtlich*) clear; jdn kurz a~ 🗊 give s.o. short shrift

abfeuern *vt sep* fire

abfind|en† *vt sep* pay off; (*entschädigen*) compensate; sich a~en mit come to terms with. **A~ung** *f* -,-en compensation

abfliegen† *vi sep* (*sein*) fly off; (*Aviat*) take off

abfließen† *vi sep* (*sein*) drain or run away

Abflug *m* (*Aviat*) departure

Abfluss *m* drainage; (*Öffnung*) drain. **A~rohr** *nt* drain-pipe

abfragen *vt sep* jdn od jdm Vokabeln a~ test s.o. on vocabulary

Abfuhr *f* - removal; (*fig*) rebuff

abführ|en *vt sep* take or lead away. **A~mittel** *nt* laxative

abfüllen *vt sep* auf od in Flaschen a~ bottle

Abgase *ntpl* exhaust fumes

abgeben† *vt sep* hand in; (*abliefern*) deliver; (*verkaufen*) sell; (*zur Aufbewahrung*) leave; (*Fußball*) pass; (*ausströmen*) give off; (*abfeuern*) fire; (*verlauten lassen*) give; cast (*Stimme*); jdm etw a~ give s.o. a share of sth

abgehen† *v sep* ● *vi* (*sein*) leave; (*Theat*) exit; (*sich lösen*) come off; (*abgezogen werden*) be deducted ● *vt* walk along

abgehetzt *adj* harassed. **abgelegen** *adj* remote. **abgeneigt** *adj* etw (*dat*) nicht abgeneigt sein not be averse to sth. **abgeneigt** *adj* worn. **Abgeordnete(r)** *m/f* deputy; (*Pol*) Member of Parliament. **abgepackt** *adj* pre-packed. **abgeschieden** *adj* secluded **abgeschlossen** *adj* (*fig*) com-

plete; (*Wohnung*) self-contained. **abgesehen** *prep* apart (from von). **abgespannt** *adj* exhausted. **abgestanden** *adj* stale. **abgestorben** *adj* dead; (*Glied*) numb. **abgetragen** *adj* worn. **abgewetzt** *adj* threadbare

abgewinnen† *vt sep* win (jdm from s.o.); etw (*dat*) Geschmack a~ get a taste for sth

abgewöhnen *vt sep* jdm/sich das Rauchen a~ cure s.o. of/give up smoking

abgießen† *vt sep* pour off; drain (*Gemüse*)

Abgott *m* idol

abgöttisch *adv* a~ lieben idolize

abgrenz|en *vt sep* divide off; (*fig*) define. **A~ung** *f* - demarcation

Abgrund *m* abyss; (*fig*) depths *pl*

abgucken *vt sep* 🗊 copy

Abguss *m* cast

abhacken *vt sep* chop off

abhaken *vt sep* tick off

abhalten† *vt sep* keep off; (*hindern*) keep, prevent (von from); (*veranstalten*) hold

abhanden *adv* a~ kommen get lost

Abhandlung *f* treatise

Abhang *m* slope

abhängen¹ *vt sep* (*reg*) take down; (*abkuppeln*) uncouple

abhäng|en²† *vi sep* (*haben*) depend (von on). **a~ig** *adj* dependent (von on). **A~igkeit** *f* - dependence

abhärten *vt sep* toughen up

abheben† *v sep* ● *vt* take off; (*vom Konto*) withdraw; sich a~ stand out (gegen against) ● *vi* (*haben*) (*Cards*) cut [the cards]; (*Aviat*) take off; (*Rakete:*) lift off

abheften *vt sep* file

Abhilfe *f* remedy

abholen vt sep collect

abhör|en vt sep listen to; (*überwachen*) tap; **jdn od jdm Vokabeln a~en** test s.o. on vocabulary. **A~gerät** nt bugging device

Abitur nt -s ≈ A levels pl

Abitur The *Abitur*, or *Matura* in Austria, is the final exam taken by pupils at a ▷GYMNASIUM or comprehensive school. The result is based on continuous assessment during the last two years before the *Abitur*, plus examinations in four subjects. The *Abitur* is an obligatory qualification for university entrance.

---

abkaufen vt sep buy (*dat* from)

abklingen† vi sep (sein) die away; (*nachlassen*) subside

abkochen vt sep boil

abkommen† vi sep (sein) **a~ von** stray from; (*aufgeben*) give up. **A~** nt -s,- agreement

Abkömmling m -s,-e descendant

abkratzen vt sep scrape off

abkühlen vt/i sep (sein) cool; **sich a~** cool [down]

Abkunft f - origin

abkuppeln vt sep uncouple

abkürz|en vt sep shorten; abbreviate (*Wort*). **A~ung** f short cut; (*Wort*) abbreviation

abladen† vt sep unload

Ablage f shelf; (*für Akten*) tray

ablager|n vt sep deposit. **A~ung** f -,-en deposit

ablassen† vt sep drain [off]; let off (*Dampf*)

Ablauf m drain; (*Verlauf*) course; (*Ende*) end; (*einer Frist*) expiry. **a~en†** v sep ● vi (sein) run or drain off; (*verlaufen*) go off; (*enden*) ex-

pire; (*Zeit*) run out; (*Uhrwerk*) run down ● vt walk along; (*absuchen*) scour (nach for)

ableg|en v sep ● vt put down; discard (*Karte*); (*abheften*) file; (*ausziehen*) take off; sit, take (*Prüfung*); **abgelegte Kleidung** cast-offs pl ● vi (haben) take off one's coat; (*Naut*) cast off. **A~er** m -s,- (*Bot*) cutting; (*Schössling*) shoot

ablehn|en vt sep refuse; (*missbilligen*) reject. **A~ung** f -,-en refusal; rejection

ableit|en vt sep divert; **sich a~en** be derived (von/aus from). **A~ung** f derivation; (*Wort*) derivative

ablenk|en vt sep deflect; divert (*Aufmerksamkeit*). **A~ung** f -,-en distraction

ablesen† vt sep read

ablicht|en vt sep photocopy. **A~ung** f photocopy

abliefern vt sep deliver

ablös|en vt sep detach; (*abwechseln*) relieve; **sich a~en** come off; (*sich abwechseln*) take turns. **A~ung** f relief

abmach|en vt sep remove; (*ausmachen*) arrange; (*vereinbaren*) agree. **A~ung** f -,-en agreement

abmager|n vi sep (sein) lose weight. **A~ungskur** f slimming diet

abmelden vt sep cancel; **sich a~** (*im Hotel*) check out; (*Computer*) log off

abmessen† vt sep measure

abmühen (sich) vr sep struggle

Abnäher m -s,- dart

abnehmen† v sep ● vt take off, remove; pick up (*Hörer*); **jdm etw a~en** take/(*kaufen*) buy sth from s.o. ● vi (haben) decrease; (*nachlassen*) decline; (*Person*:) lose weight; (*Mond*:) wane. **A~er** m -s,- buyer

a

Abneigung f dislike (gegen of)

abnorm adj abnormal

abnutz|en vt sep wear out.
A~ung f - wear [and tear]

Abon|nement /abɔnəˈmãː/ nt
-s,-s subscription. A~nent m -en,
-en subscriber. a~nieren vt take
out a subscription to

Abordnung f -,-en deputation

abpassen vt sep wait for; gut a~
time well

abraten† vt sep (haben) jdm von
etw a~ advise s.o. against sth

abräumen vt/i (haben) clear away

abrechn|en v sep • vt deduct • vi
(haben) settle up. A~ung f settlement; (Rechnung) account

Abreise f departure. a~n vi sep
(sein) leave

abreißen† v sep • vt tear off; (demolieren) pull down • vi (sein)
come off

abrichten vt sep train

Abriss m demolition; (Übersicht)
summary

abrufen† vt sep call away; (Computer) retrieve

abrunden vt sep round off

abrüst|en vi sep (haben) disarm.
A~ung f disarmament

abrutschen vi sep (sein) slip

Absage f -,-n cancellation; (Ablehnung) refusal. a~n v sep • vt cancel
• vi (haben) [jdm] a~n cancel an
appointment [with s.o.]; (auf Einladung) refuse [s.o.'s invitation]

Absatz m heel; (Abschnitt) paragraph; (Verkauf) sale

abschaffen vt sep abolish; get rid
of (Auto, Hund)

abschalten vt/i sep (haben)
switch off

Abscheu m - revulsion

abscheulich adj revolting

abschicken vt sep send off

Abschied m -[e]s,-e farewell;
(Trennung) parting; A~ nehmen
say goodbye (von to)

abschießen† vt sep shoot down;
(abfeuern) fire; launch (Rakete)

abschirmen vt sep shield

abschlagen† vt sep knock off;
(verweigern) refuse

Abschlepp|dienst m break-
down service. A~en vt sep tow
away. A~seil nt tow-rope

abschließen† v sep • vt lock; (beenden, abmachen) conclude; make
(Wette); balance (Bücher) • vi
(haben) lock up; (enden) end. a~d
adv in conclusion

Abschluss m conclusion.
A~zeugnis nt diploma

abschmecken vt sep season

abschmieren vt sep lubricate

abschneiden† v sep • vt cut off
• vi (haben) gut/schlecht a~ do
well/badly

Abschnitt m section; (Stadium)
stage; (Absatz) paragraph

abschöpfen vt sep skim off

abschrauben vt sep unscrew

abschreck|en vt sep deter;
(Culin) put in cold water (Ei).
a~end adj repulsive. A~ungsmit-
tel nt deterrent

abschreib|en† v sep • vt copy;
(Comm & fig) write off • vi (haben)
copy. A~ung f (Comm) depre-
ciation

Abschrift f copy

Abschuss m shooting down; (Abfeuern) firing; (Raketen-) launch

abschüssig adj sloping;
(steil) steep

abschwellen† vi sep (sein)
go down

absehbar adj in a~barer Zeit in

5 abseits | abtragen

the foreseeable future. a~ent *vt/i sep* (haben) copy; (voraussehen) foresee; a~en von disregard; (aufgeben) refrain from

abseits *adv* apart; (Sport) offside ● *prep* (+ gen) away from. **A~ nt** – (Sport) offside

absend|en† *vt sep* send off. **A~er** *m* sender

absetzen *v sep* ● *vt* put or set down; (ablagern) deposit; (abnehmen) take off; (abbrechen) stop; (entlassen) dismiss; (verkaufen) sell; (abziehen) deduct ● *vi* (haben) pause

Absicht *f* -,-en intention; mit A~ intentionally, on purpose

absichtlich *adj* intentional

absitzen *v sep* ● *vi* (sein) dismount ● *vt* 🄵 serve (Strafe)

absolut *adj* absolute

absolvieren *vt* complete; (bestehen) pass

absonder|n *vt sep* separate; (ausscheiden) secrete. **A~ung** *f* -,-en secretion

absorbieren *vt* absorb

abspeisen *vt sep* fob off (mit with)

absperr|en *vt sep* cordon off; (abstellen) turn off; (SGer) lock. **A~ung** *f* -,-en barrier

abspielen *vt sep* play; (Fußball) pass; sich a~ take place

Absprache *f* agreement

absprechen† *vt sep* arrange; sich a~ agree

abspringen† *vi sep* (sein) jump off; (mit Fallschirm) parachute; (abgehen) come off

Absprung *m* jump

abspülen *vt sep* rinse

abstammen *vi sep* (haben) be descended (von from). **A~ung** *f* -

descent

Abstand *m* distance; (zeitlich) interval; A~ halten keep one's distance

abstatten *vt sep* jdm einen Besuch a~ pay s.o. a visit

Abstecher *m* -s,- detour

abstehen† *vi sep* (haben) stick out

absteigen *vi sep* (sein) dismount; (niedersteigen) descend; (Fußball) be relegated

abstell|en *vt sep* put down; (lagern) store; (parken) park; (abschalten) turn off. **A~gleis** *nt* siding. **A~raum** *m* box-room

absterben† *vi sep* (sein) die; (gefühllos werden) go numb

Abstieg *m* -[e]s,-e descent; (Fußball) relegation

abstimmen *v sep* ● *vi* (haben) vote (über + acc on) ● *vt* coordinate (auf + acc with). **A~ung** *f* vote

Abstinenzler *m* -s,- teetotaller

abstoßen† *vt sep* knock off; (verkaufen) sell; (fig: ekeln) repel. **a~d** *adj* repulsive

abstreiten† *vt sep* deny

Abstrich *m* (Med) smear

abstufen *vt sep* grade

Absturz *m* fall; (Aviat) crash

abstürzen *vi sep* (sein) fall; (Aviat) crash

absuchen *vt sep* search

absurd *adj* absurd

Abszess *m* -es,-e abscess

Abt *m* -[e]s,-e abbot

abtasten *vt sep* feel; (Techn) scan

abtauen *vt/i sep* (sein) thaw; (entfrosten) defrost

Abtei *f* -,-en abbey

Abteil *nt* compartment

Abteilung *f* -,-en section; (Admin, Comm) department

abtragen† *vt sep* clear; (einebnen)

a level; (*abnutzen*) wear out

abträglich *adj* detrimental (*dat* to)

abtreib|en† *vt sep* (*Naut*) drive off course; ein Kind a~en lassen have an abortion. A~ung f -,-en abortion

abtrennen *vt sep* detach; (*abteilen*) divide off

Abtreter m -s,- doormat

abtrocknen *vt/i sep* (*haben*) dry; sich a~ dry oneself

abtropfen *vi sep* (*sein*) drain

abtun† *vt sep* (*fig*) dismiss

abwägen† *vt sep* (*fig*) weigh

abwandeln *vt sep* modify

abwarten *v sep* ●*vt* wait for ●*vi* (*haben*) wait [and see]

abwärts *adv* down[wards]

Abwasch m -[e]s washing-up; (*Geschirr*) dirty dishes *pl*. a~en *v sep* ●*vt* wash; wash up (*Geschirr*); (*entfernen*) wash off ●*vi* (*haben*) wash up. **A~lappen** m dishcloth

Abwasser nt -s,⁻ sewage. **A~kanal** m sewer

abwechseln *vi/r sep* (*haben*) [sich] a~ alternate; (*Personen:*) take turns. a~d *adj* alternate

Abwechslung f -,-en change; zur A~ for a change

abwegig *adj* absurd

Abwehr f - defence; (*Widerstand*) resistance; (*Pol*) counter-espionage. a~en *vt sep* ward off. **A~system** nt immune system

abweich|en† *vi sep* (*sein*) deviate/(*von Regel*) depart (*von* from); (*sich unterscheiden*) differ (*von* from). a~end *adj* divergent; (*verschieden*) different. **A~ung** f -,-en deviation

abweis|en† *vt sep* turn down; turn away (*Person*). a~end *adj* un-

friendly. **A~ung** f rejection

abwenden† *vt sep* turn away; (*verhindern*) avert

abwerfen† *vt sep* throw off; throw (*Reiter*); (*Aviat*) drop; (*Kartenspiel*) discard; shed (*Haut, Blätter*); yield (*Gewinn*)

abwert|en *vt sep* devalue. **A~ung** f -,-en devaluation

Abwesenheit f - absence; absent-mindedness

abwickeln *vt sep* unwind; (*erledigen*) settle

abwischen *vt sep* wipe

abzahlen *vt sep* pay off

abzählen *vt sep* count

Abzahlung f instalment

Abzeichen nt badge

abzeichnen *vt sep* copy

Abzieh|bild nt transfer. a~en† *v sep* ●*vt* pull off; take off (*Laken*); strip (*Bett*); (*häuten*) skin; (*Phot*) print; run off (*Kopien*); (*zurückziehen*) withdraw; (*abrechnen*) deduct ●*vi* (*sein*) go away, (*Rauch:*) escape

Abzug m (*withdrawal*; (*Abrechnung*) deduction; (*Phot*) print (*Korrektur-*) proof; (*am Gewehr*) trigger; (*A~söffnung*) vent; **A~e** *pl* deductions

abzüglich *prep* (+ *gen*) less

Abzugshaube f (*cooker*) hood

abzweig|en *v sep* ●*vi* (*sein*) branch off ●*vt* divert. **A~ung** f -,-en junction; (*Gabelung*) fork

ach *int* oh; a~ je! oh dear! a~ so I see

Achse f -,-n axis; (*Rad-*) axle

Achsel f -,-n shoulder. **A~höhle** f armpit. **A~zucken** nt -s shrug

acht *inv adj*. **A~¹** f -,-en eight

Acht² f **A~ geben** be careful; **A~ geben auf** (+ *acc*) look after; **A~ lassen** disregard; sich in **A~ nehmen** be careful

acht|e(r,s) *adj* eighth. **a~eckig**
adj octagonal. **A~el** *nt* -s,- eighth

achten *vt* respect ●*vi* (*haben*) **a~**
auf (+ *acc*) pay attention to; (*auf-*
passen) look after

Achterbahn *f* roller-coaster

achtlos *adj* careless

achtsam *adj* careful

Achtung *f* - respect (vor + *dat*
for); **A~!** look out!

acht|zehn *inv adj* eighteen.
a~zehnte(r,s) *adj* eighteenth.
a~zig *a inv* eighty. **a~zigste(r,s)**
adj eightieth

Acker *m* -s,⁼ field. **A~bau** *m* agriculture. **A~land** *nt* arable land

addieren *vt/i* (*haben*) add

Addition /-ˈtsjoːn/ *f* -,-en addition

ade *int* goodbye

Adel *m* -s nobility

Ader *f* -,-n vein

Adjektiv *nt* -s,-e adjective

Adler *m* -s,- eagle

adlig *adj* noble. **A~e(r)** *m*
nobleman

Administration /-ˈtsjoːn/ *f* -
administration

Admiral *m* -s,⁼e admiral

adop|tieren *vt* adopt. **A~tion** *f*
-,-en adoption. **A~tiveltern** *pl*
adoptive parents. **A~tivkind** *nt* ad-
opted child

Adrenalin *nt* -s adrenalin

Adres|se *f* -,-n address. **a~sieren**
vt address

Adria *f* - Adriatic

Adverb *nt* -s,-ien adverb

Affäre *f* -,-n affair

Affe *m* -n,-n monkey; (*Men-*
schen-) ape

affektiert *adj* affected

affig *adj* affected; (*eitel*) vain

Afrika *nt* -s Africa

Afrikan|er(in) *m* -s,- (*f* -,-nen)
African. **a~isch** *adj* African

After *m* -s,- anus

Agen|t(in) *m* -en,-en (*f* -,-nen)
agent. **A~tur** *f* -,-en agency

Aggres|sion *f* -,-en aggression.
a~siv *adj* aggressive

Agnostiker *m* -s,- agnostic

Ägypten /ɛˈɡʏptən/ *nt* -s Egypt.
Ä~er(in) *m* -s,- (*f* -,-nen) Egyptian. **ä~isch** *adj* Egyptian

ähneln *vi* (*haben*) (+ *dat*) resemble;
sich ä~ be alike

ahnen *vt* have a presentiment of;
(*vermuten*) suspect

Ahnen *mpl* ancestors. **A~for-**
schung *f* genealogy

ähnlich *adj* similar; jdm ä~ sehen
resemble s.o. **Ä~keit** *f* -,-en simi-
larity; resemblance

Ahnung *f* -,-en premonition; (*Ver-*
mutung) idea, hunch

Ahorn *m* -s,-e maple

Ähre *f* -,-n ear [of corn]

Aids /eːts/ *nt* - Aids

Airbag /ˈɛːɡbɛk/ *m* -s, -s (*Auto*)
air bag

Akademie *f* -,-n academy

Akadem|iker(in) *m* -s,- (*f*
-,-nen) university graduate. **a~isch**
adj academic

akklimatisieren (sich) *vr* become acclimatized

Akkord *m* -[e]s,-e (*Mus*) chord.
A~arbeit *f* piecework

Akkordeon *nt* -s,-s accordion

Akkumulator *m* -s,-en (*Electr*)
accumulator

Akkusativ *m* -s,-e accusative.
A~objekt *nt* direct object

Akrobat|(in) *m* -en,-en (*f*
-,-nen) acrobat. **a~isch** *adj*
acrobatic

Akt *m* -[e]s,-e act; (*Kunst*) nude

a

Akte f-,-n file; **A~n** documents. **A~ntasche** f briefcase

Aktie /ˈaktsjə/ f-,-n (Comm) share. **A~ngesellschaft** f joint-stock company

Aktion /akˈtsjoːn/ f-,-en action. **A~är** m-s,-e shareholder

aktiv adj active

aktuell adj topical; (gegenwärtig) current

Akupunktur f- acupuncture

Akustik f- acoustics pl.

akut adj acute

Akzent m-[e]s,-e accent

akzept|abel adj acceptable. **a~ieren** vt accept

Alarm m-s alarm; (Mil) alert. **a~ieren** vt alert; (beunruhigen) alarm

Albdruck m nightmare

albern adj silly ● vi (haben) play the fool

Albtraum m nightmare

Al|bum nt-s,-ben album

Algebra f- algebra

Algen fpl algae

Algerien /-jən/ nt-s Algeria

Alibi nt-s,-s alibi

Alimente pl maintenance sg

Alkohol m-s alcohol. **A~frei** adj non-alcoholic

Alkohol|iker(in) m-s,- (f-,-nen) alcoholic. **a~isch** adj alcoholic

Alkopop nt-(s), -s alcopop

All inv pron all das/mein Geld all the/my money; all dies all this

All nt-s universe

alle pred adj finished

all|e(r,s) pron all; (jeder) every; **a~es** everything, all; (alle Leute) everyone; **a~e** pl all; **a~es Geld** all the money; **a~e beide** both [of them/us]; **a~e Tage** every day; **a~e drei Jahre** every three years; **ohne a~en Grund** without any reason; **vor a~em** above all; **a~es in a~em** all in all; **a~es aussteigen!** all change!

Allee f-,-n avenue

allein adv alone; (nur) only; **a~stehend** single; **a~ der Gedanke** the mere thought; **von a~[e]** of its/(Person) one's own accord; (automatisch) automatically ● conj but. **A~erziehende(r)** m/f single parent. **a~ig** adj sole. **A~stehende** pl single people

allemal adv every time; (gewiss) certainly

allenfalls adv at most; (eventuell) possibly

aller|beste(r,s) adj very best; **am a~besten** best of all. **a~dings** adv indeed; (zwar) admittedly. **a~erste(r,s)** adj very first

Allergie f-,-n allergy

allergisch adj allergic (gegen to)

Aller|heiligen nt-s All Saints Day. **a~höchstens** adv at the very most. **a~lei** inv adj all sorts of ● pron all sorts of things. **a~letzte(r,s)** adj very last. **a~liebste(r,s)** adj favourite ● adv am a~liebsten for preference; am a~liebsten haben like best of all. **a~meiste(r,s)** adj most ● adv am a~meisten most of all. **a~seelen** nt-s All Souls Day. **a~wenigste(r,s)** adj very least ● adv am a~wenigste least of all

allgemein adj general; im A~en (a~en) in general. **A~heit** f- community; (Öffentlichkeit) general public

Allianz f-,-en alliance

Alligator m-s,-en alligator

alliiert adj allied; die A~en pl

the Allies

all|jährlich adj annual. **a~mäh-lich** adj gradual

Alltag m working day; der A~ (fig) everyday life

alltäglich adj daily; (gewöhnlich) everyday; (Mensch) ordinary

alltags adv on weekdays

allzu adv [far] too; a~ oft all too often; a~ vorsichtig over-cautious

Alm f -,-en alpine pasture

Almosen ntpl alms

Alpdruck* m = Albdruck

Alpen pl Alps

Alphabet nt -[e]s,-e alphabet. **a~isch** adj alphabetical

Alptraum* m = Albtraum

als conj as; (zeitlich) when; (mit Komparativ) than; nichts als nothing but; als ob as if or though

also adv & conj so; a~ gut all right then; na a~! there you are!

alt adj old; (gebraucht) second-hand; (ehemalig) former; alt werden grow old

Alt m -s, -e (Mus) contralto

Altar m -s,⸚e altar

Alt|e(r) m/f old man/woman; die A~en old people. **A~eisen** nt scrap iron. **A~enheim** nt old people's home

Alter nt -s,- age; (Bejahrtheit) old age; im A~ von at the age of

älter adj older; mein ä~er Bruder my elder brother

altern vi (sein) age

Alternative f -,-n alternative

Alters|grenze f age limit. **A~heim** nt old people's home. **A~rente** f old-age pension. **a~schwach** adj old and infirm. **A~vorsorge** f provision for old age

Alter|tum nt -s,⸚er antiquity.

a~tümlich adj old; (altmodisch) old-fashioned

altklug adj precocious

alt|modisch adj old-fashioned. **A~papier** nt waste paper. **A~wa-renhändler** m second-hand dealer

Alufolie f [aluminium] foil

Aluminium nt -s aluminium, (Amer) aluminum

am prep = an dem; am Montag on Monday; am Morgen in the morning; am besten [the] best

Amateur /-'tø:ɐ̯/ m -s,-e amateur

Ambition /-'tsi̯o:n/ f -,-en ambition

Amboss m -es,-e anvil

ambulan|t adj out-patient ● adv a~t behandeln treat as an out-patient. **A~z** f -,-en out-patients' department

Ameise f -,-n ant

amen int, A~ nt -s amen

Amerika nt -s America

Amerikan|er(in) m -s,- (f -,-nen) American. **a~isch** adj American

Ammoniak nt -s ammonia

Amnestie f -,-n amnesty

amoralisch adj amoral

Ampel f -,-n traffic lights pl

Amphitheater nt amphitheatre

Amput|ation /-'tsi̯o:n/ f -,-en amputation. **a~ieren** vt amputate

Amsel f -,-n blackbird

Amt nt -[e]s, ⸚er office; (Aufgabe) task; (Teleph) exchange. **a~lich** adj official. **A~szeichen** nt dialling tone

Amulett nt -[e]s,-e [lucky] charm

amüs|ant adj amusing. **a~ieren** vt amuse; sich a~ieren be amused (über + acc at); (sich vergnügen) enjoy oneself

an

● *preposition (+ dative)*

! Note that an plus dem can become am

····▸ *(räumlich)* on; *(Gebäude, Ort)* at. **an der Wand** on the wall. **Frankfurt an der Oder** Frankfurt an der [the] Oder. **an der Ecke** at the corner. **am Bahnhof** at the station. **an uns vorbei** past. **am 24. Mai** on May 24th

····▸ *(zeitlich)* on. **am Montag** on Monday. **an jedem Sonntag** every Sunday

····▸ *(sonstige Verwendungen)* **arm/reich an Vitaminen** low/ rich in vitamins. **jdn an etw erkennen** recognize s.o. by sth. **an etw leiden** suffer from sth. **an einer Krankheit sterben** die of a disease. **an [und für] sich** actually

● *preposition (+ accusative)*

! Note that an plus das can become ans

····▸ to. **schicke es an deinen Bruder** send it to your brother. **er ging ans Fenster** he went to the window

····▸ *(auf, gegen)* on. **etw an die Wand hängen** to hang sth on the wall. **lehne es an den Baum** lean it on or against the tree

····▸ *(sonstige Verwendungen)* **an etw glauben** believe in sth/s.o. **an etw denken** think of sth. **sich an etw erinnern** remember sth

● *adverb*

····▸ *(auf Fahrplan)* **Köln an: 9.15** arriving Cologne 09.15

····▸ *(angeschaltet)* on. **die Waschmaschine/der Fernseher/das Licht/das Gas ist an** the washing machine/television/light/gas is on

····▸ *(ungefähr)* around; about. **an [die] 20000 DM** around or about 20,000 DM

····▸ *(in die Zukunft)* **von heute an** from today (onwards)

analog *adj* analogous; *(Computer)* analog. **A~ie** *f* -,-n analogy

Analphabet *m* -en,-en illiterate person. **A~entum** *nt* -s illiteracy

Analy|se *f* -,-n analysis. **a~sieren** *vt* analyse. **A~tiker** *m* -s,- analyst. **a~tisch** *adj* analytical

Anämie *f* - anaemia

Ananas *f* -,-[se] pineapple

Anatomie *f* - anatomy

Anbau *m* cultivation; *(Gebäude)* extension. **a~en** *vt sep* build on; *(anpflanzen)* cultivate, grow

anbei *adv* enclosed

anbeißen† *v sep* ● *vt* take a bite of ● *vi (haben) (Fisch:)* bite

anbeten *vt sep* worship

Anbetracht *m* **in A~** *(+ gen)* in view of

anbieten† *vt sep* offer; **sich a~** offer (zu to)

anbinden† *vt sep* tie up

Anblick *m* sight. **a~en** *vt sep* look at

anbrechen† *v sep* ● *vt* start on; break into *(Vorräte)* ● *vi (sein)* begin; *(Tag:)* break; *(Nacht:)* fall

anbrennen† *v sep* ● *vt* light ● *vi (sein)* burn

anbringen† *vt sep* bring [along]; *(befestigen)* fix

Anbruch *m (fig)* dawn; **bei A~ des Tages/der Nacht** at daybreak/nightfall

Andacht f -,-en reverence; (Gottesdienst) prayers pl

andächtig adj reverent; (fig) rapt

andauern vi sep (haben) last; (anhalten) continue. a~d adj persistent; (ständig) constant

Andenken nt -s,- memory; (Souvenir) souvenir

ander|e(r,s) adj other; (verschie-
den) different; (nächste) next; ein
a~er, eine a~e another ● pron
der a~e/die a~en the other/
others; ein a~er another [one];
(Person) someone else; kein a~er
no one else; einer nach dem a~en
one after the other; alles a~e/
nichts a~es everything/nothing
else; unter a~em among other
things. a~enfalls adv otherwise.
a~erseits adv on the other hand.
a~mal ein a~mal an-
other time

ändern vt alter; (wechseln) change;
sich ä~ change

anders pred adj different; a~ werden change ● adv differently; (riechen, schmecken) different; (sonst)
else; jemand a~ someone else

andersherum adv the other
way round

anderthalb inv adj one and a
half; a~ Stunden an hour and
a half

Änderung f -,-en alteration;
(Wechsel) change

andeut|en vt sep indicate; (anspie-
len) hint at. A~ung f -,-en indication; hint

Andrang m rush (nach for); (Gedränge) crush

androhen vt sep jdm etw a~
threaten s.o. with sth

aneignen vt sep sich (dat) a~ appropriate; (lernen) learn

aneinander adv & prefix together;
(denken) of one another; a~ vorbei
past one another; a~ geraten
quarrel

Anekdote f -,-n anecdote

anerkannt adj acknowledged

anerkenn|en† vt sep acknow-
ledge, recognize; (würdigen) appreciate. a~end adj approving.
A~ung f -,- acknowledgement, recognition; appreciation

anfahren† v sep ● vt deliver; (streifen) hit ● vi (sein) start

Anfall m fit, attack. a~en† v sep
● vt attack ● vi (sein) arise; (Zinsen:)
accrue

anfällig adj susceptible (für to);
(zart) delicate

Anfang m -s,ⁿe beginning, start;
zu od am A~ at the beginning;
(anfangs) at first. a~en† vt/i sep
(haben) begin, start; (tun) do

Anfänger(in) m -s,- (f -,-nen)
beginner

anfangs adv at first. A~buch-
stabe m initial letter. A~gehalt nt
starting salary

anfassen vt sep touch; (behandeln)
treat; tackle (Arbeit); sich a~
hold hands

anfechten† vt sep contest

anfertigen vt sep make

anfeuchten vt sep moisten

anflehen vt sep implore, beg

Anflug m (Avia) approach

anforder|n vt sep demand;
(Comm) order. A~ung f demand

Anfrage f enquiry. a~n vi sep
(haben) enquire, ask

anfreunden (sich) vr sep make
friends (mit with)

anfügen vt sep add

anfühlen vt sep feel; sich weich
a~ feel soft

a **anführ|en** vt sep lead; (zitieren) quote; (angeben) give. A~er m leader. A~ungszeichen ntpl quotation marks

Angabe f statement; (Anweisung) instruction; (Tennis) service; nähere A~n particulars

angeb|en† v sep ●vt state; give (Namen, Grund); (anzeigen) indicate; set (Tempo) ●vi (Tennis) serve; (ⅰ: protzen) show off. A~er(in) m -s,- (f -,-nen) ⅰ show-off. A~erei f - ⅰ showing-off

angeblich adj alleged

angeboren adj innate; (Med) congenital

Angebot nt offer; (Auswahl) range; A~ und Nachfrage supply and demand

angebracht adj appropriate

angeheiratet adj (Onkel, Tante) by marriage

angeheitert adj ⅰ tipsy

angehen† v sep ●vi (sein) begin, start; (Licht, Radio:) come on; (anwachsen) take root; a~ gegen fight ●vt attack; tackle (Arbeit); (betreffen) concern

angehör|en vi sep (haben) (+ dat) belong to. A~ige(r) m/f relative

Angeklagte(r) m/f accused

Angel f -,-n fishing-rod; (Tür-) hinge

Angelegenheit f matter

Angel|haken m fish-hook. a~n vi (haben) fish (nach for); a~n gehen go fishing ●vt (fangen) catch. A~rute f fishing-rod

angelsächsisch adj Anglo-Saxon

angemessen adj commensurate (dat with); (passend) appropriate

angenehm adj pleasant; (bei Vorstellung) a~! delighted to meet you!

angeregt adj animated

angesehen adj respected; (Firma) reputable

angesichts prep (+ gen) in view of

angespannt adj intent; (Lage) tense

Angestellte(r) m/f employee

angewandt adj applied

angewiesen adj dependent (auf + acc on); auf sich selbst a~ on one's own

angewöhnen vt sep jdm etw a~ get s.o. used to sth; sich (dat) etw a~ get into the habit of doing sth

Angewohnheit f habit

Angina f - tonsillitis

angleichen† vt sep adjust (dat to)

anglikanisch adj Anglican

Anglistik f - English [language and literature]

Angorakatze f Persian cat

angreif|en† vt sep attack; tackle (Arbeit); (schädigen) damage. A~er m -s,- attacker; (Pol) aggressor

angrenzen vi sep (haben) adjoin (an etw acc sth). a~d adj adjoining

Angriff m attack; in A~ nehmen tackle. a~slustig adj aggressive

Angst f -,-̈e fear; (Psychology) anxiety; (Sorge) worry (um about); A~ haben be afraid (vor + dat of); (sich sorgen) be worried (um about); jdm A~ machen frighten s.o.

ängstigen vt frighten; (Sorge machen) worry; sich ä~ be frightened; be worried (um about)

ängstlich adj nervous; (scheu) timid; (verängstigt) frightened, scared; (besorgt) anxious

angucken vt sep ⅰ look at

angurten (sich) vr sep fasten one's seat belt

anhaben† vt sep have on; er/es kann mir nichts a~ (fig) he/it cannot hurt me

anhalt|en v sep ● vt stop; hold (Atem); jdn zur Arbeit a~en urge s.o. to work ● vi (haben) stop; (andauern) continue. **a~end** adj persistent. **A~er(in)** m s,- (f -,-nen) hitchhiker; per a~er fahren hitchhike. **A~spunkt** m clue

anhand prep (+ gen) with the aid of

Anhang m (zu Buch) appendix; (zu E-mail) attachment

anhäng|en[1] vt sep (reg) hang up; (befestigen) attach

anhäng|en[2]† vi (haben) be a follower of. **A~er** m s,- follower; (Auto) trailer; (Schild) [tie-on] label; (Schmuck) pendant. **A~erin** f -,-nen follower. **a~lich** adj affectionate

anhäufen vt sep pile up

Anhieb m auf A~ straight away

Anhöhe f hill

anhören vt sep listen to; sich gut a~ sound good

animieren vt encourage (zu to)

Anis m -es aniseed

Anker m -s,- anchor; vor A~ gehen drop anchor. **a~n** vi (haben) anchor; (liegen) be anchored

anketten vt sep chain up

Anklage f accusation; (Jur) charge; (Ankläger) prosecution. **A~bank** f dock. **a~n** vt sep accuse (gen of); (Jur) charge (gen with)

Ankläger m accuser; (Jur) prosecutor

anklammern vt sep clip on; sich a~ cling (an + acc to)

ankleben v sep ● vt stick on ● vi (sein) stick (an + dat to)

anklicken vt sep click on

anklopfen vi sep (haben) knock

anknipsen vt sep [🔌] switch on

ankommen† vi sep (sein) arrive; (sich nähern) approach; gut a~ arrive safely; (fig) go down well (bei with); nicht a~ gegen (fig) be no match for (+ acc) depend on; das kommt darauf an it [all] depends

ankreuzen vt sep mark with a cross

ankündig|en vt sep announce. **A~ung** f announcement

Ankunft f - arrival

ankurbeln vt sep (fig) boost

anlächeln vt sep smile at

anlachen vt sep smile at

Anlage f -,-n installation; (Industrie-) plant; (Komplex) complex; (Geld-) investment; (Plan) layout; (Beilage) enclosure; (Veranlagung) aptitude; (Neigung) predisposition; [öffentliche] A~n [public] gardens; als A~ enclosed

Anlass m -es,-ᵉe reason; (Gelegenheit) occasion; A~ geben zu give cause for

anlass|en† vt sep (Auto) start; [🔌] leave on (Licht); keep on (Mantel). **A~er** m -s,- starter

anlässlich prep (+ gen) on the occasion of

Anlauf m (Sport) run-up; (fig) attempt. **a~en**† v sep ● vi (sein) start; (beschlagen) mist up; (Metall:) tarnish; rot a~en blush ● vt (Naut) call at

anlegen v sep ● vt put (an + acc against); put on (Kleidung, Verband); lay back (Ohren); aim (Gewehr); (investieren) invest; (ausgeben) spend (für on); draw up (Liste); es darauf a~ (fig) aim (zu to) ● vi (haben) (Schiff:) moor; an~ auf (+ acc) aim at

anlehnen vt sep lean (an + acc against); sich a~ lean (an + acc on)

Anleihe f -,-n loan

a

anleit|en vt sep instruct. **A∼ung** f instructions pl

anlernen vt sep train

Anliegen nt -s,- request; (Wunsch) desire

anlieg|en vi sep (haben) [eng] a∼en fit closely; [eng] a∼end close-fitting. **A∼er** mpl residents; 'A∼er frei' access for residents only'

anlügen† vt sep lie to

anmachen vt sep ⏺ fix; (anschalten) turn on; dress (Salat)

anmalen vt sep paint

Anmarsch m (Mil) approach

anmeld|en vt sep announce; (Admin) register; **sich a∼en** say that one is coming; (Admin) register; (Sch) enrol; (im Hotel) check in; (beim Arzt) make an appointment; (Computer) log on. **A∼ung** f announcement; (Admin) registration; (Sch) enrolment; (Termin) appointment

anmerk|en vt sep mark; **sich** (dat) etw a∼en lassen show sth. **A∼ung** f -,-en note

Anmut f - grace; (Charme) charm

anmutig adj graceful

annähen vt sep sew on

annäher|nd adj approximate. **A∼ungsversuche** mpl advances

Annahme f -,-n acceptance; (Adoption) adoption; (Vermutung) assumption

annehm|bar adj acceptable. **a∼en†** vt sep accept; (adoptieren) adopt; acquire (Gewohnheit); (sich zulegen, vermuten) assume; angenommen, dass assuming that. **A∼lichkeiten** fpl comforts

Anno adv A∼ 1920 in the year 1920

Annon|ce /a'nõ:sə/ f -,-n advertisement. **a∼cieren** vt/i (haben) advertise

annullieren vt annul; cancel

Anomalie f -,-n anomaly

anonym adj anonymous

Anorak m -s,-s anorak

anordn|en vt sep arrange; (befehlen) order. **A∼ung** f arrangement; order

anorganisch adj inorganic

anormal adj abnormal

anpass|en vt sep try on; (angleichen) adapt (dat to); **sich a∼** adapt (dat to). **A∼ung** f - adaptation. **a∼ungsfähig** adj adaptable. **A∼ungsfähigkeit** f adaptability

Anpfiff m (Sport) kick-off

Anprall m -[e]s impact. **a∼en** vi sep (sein) strike (an etw acc sth)

anpreisen† vt sep commend

Anprob|e f fitting. **a∼ieren** vt sep try on

anrechnen vt sep count (als as); (berechnen) charge for; (verrechnen) allow (Summe)

Anrecht nt right (auf + acc to)

Anrede f [form of] address. **a∼n** vt sep address; speak to

anreg|en vt sep stimulate; (ermuntern) encourage (zu to); (vorschlagen) suggest. **a∼end** adj stimulating. **A∼ung** f stimulation; (Vorschlag) suggestion

Anreise f journey; (Ankunft) arrival. **a∼n** vi sep (sein) arrive

Anreiz m incentive

Anrichte f -,-n sideboard. **a∼n** vt sep (Culin) prepare; (garnieren) garnish (mit with); (verursachen) cause

anrüchig adj disreputable

Anruf m call. **A∼beantworter** m -s,- answering machine. **a∼en†** vt sep ⏺vt call to; (bitten) call on (um for); (Teleph) ring ⏺vi (haben) ring (bei jdm s.o.)

anrühren vt sep touch; (verrühren) mix

ans prep = an das

Ansage f announcement. **a~n** vt sep announce

ansamm|eln vt sep collect; (anhäufen) accumulate; **sich a~eln** collect; (sich häufen) accumulate; (Leute:) gather. **A~lung** f collection; (Menschen-) crowd

ansässig adj resident

Ansatz m beginning; (Versuch) attempt

anschaffen vt sep [sich dat] etw **a~en** acquire/(kaufen) buy sth

anschalten vt sep switch on

anschau|en vt sep look at. **a~lich** adj vivid. **A~ung** f -,-en (fig) view

Anschein m appearance. **a~end** adv apparently

anschirren vt sep harness

Anschlag m notice; (Vor-) estimate; (Überfall) attack (auf + acc on); (Mus) touch; (Techn) stop. **a~en†** v sep ● vt put up (Aushang); strike (Note, Taste); cast on (Masche); (beschädigen) chip ● vi (haben) strike/(stoßen) knock (an + acc against); (wirken) be effective ● vi (sein) knock (an + acc against)

anschließen† v sep ● vt connect (an + acc to); (zufügen) add; **sich a~ an** (+ acc) (anstoßen) adjoin; (folgen) follow; (sich anfreunden) become friendly with; **sich jdm a~** join s.o. ● vi (haben) an (+ acc) adjoin; (folgen) follow. **a~d** adj adjoining; (zeitlich) following ● adv afterwards

Anschluss m connection; (Kontakt) contact; **A~ finden** make friends; **im A~ an** (+ acc) after

anschmiegsam adj affectionate

anschmieren vt sep smear

anschnallen vt sep strap on; **sich a~** fasten one's seat-belt

anschneiden† vt sep cut into; broach (Thema)

anschreiben† vt sep write (an + acc on); (Comm) put on s.o.'s account; (sich wenden) write to

Anschrift f address

anschuldig|en vt sep accuse. **A~ung** f -,-en accusation

anschwellen† vi sep (sein) swell

ansehen† vt sep look at; (einschätzen) regard (als as); [sich dat] etw **a~** look at sth; (TV) watch sth. **A~** nt -s respect; (Ruf) reputation

ansehnlich adj considerable

ansetzen v sep ● vt join (an + acc to); (veranschlagen) estimate ● vi (haben) (anbrennen) burn; **zum Sprung a~** get ready to jump

Ansicht f view; **meiner A~ nach** in my view; **zur A~** (Comm) on approval. **A~s[post]karte** f picture postcard. **A~ssache** f matter of opinion

ansiedeln (sich) vr sep settle

ansonsten adv apart from that

anspannen vt sep hitch up; (anstrengen) strain; tense (Muskel)

Anspielung f -,-en allusion; hint

Anspitzer m -s,- pencil-sharpener

Ansprache f address

ansprechen† v sep ● vt speak to; (fig) appeal to ● vi (haben) respond (auf + acc to)

anspringen† v sep ● vt jump at ● vi (sein) (Auto) start

Anspruch m claim/(Recht) right (auf + acc to); **A~ haben** be entitled (auf + acc to); **in A~ nehmen** make use of; (erfordern) demand; take up (Zeit); occupy (Person); **hohe A~e stellen** be very demanding. **a~slos** adj undemanding. **a~svoll** adj demanding; (kri-

a tisch) discriminating; (vornehm) up-market

anstacheln vt sep (fig) spur on

Anstalt f -,-en institution

Anstand m decency; (Benehmen) [good] manners pl

anständig adj decent; (ehrbar) respectable; (richtig) proper

anstandslos adv without any trouble

anstarren vt sep stare at

anstatt conj & prep (+ gen) instead of

msteck|en v sep ● vt pin (an + acc to/on); put on (Ring); (anzünden) light; (in Brand stecken) set fire to; (Med) infect; sich a∼en catch an infection (bei from) ● vi (haben) be infectious. **a∼end** adj infectious. **A∼ung** f -,-en infection

anstehen† vi sep (haben) queue

anstelle prep (+ gen) instead of

anstell|en vt sep put, stand (an + acc against); (einstellen) employ; (anschalten) turn on; (tun) do; sich a∼en queue [up]. **A∼ung** f employment; (Stelle) job

Anstieg m -[e]s,-e climb; (fig) rise

anstiften vt sep cause; (anzetteln) instigate

Anstoß m (Anregung) impetus; (Stoß) knock; (Fußball) kick-off; a∼ erregen give offence. **a∼en†** v sep ● vt knock; (mit dem Ellbogen) nudge ● vi (sein) knock (an + acc against) and adjoin (an etw acc sth); a∼en auf (+ acc) drink to; mit der Zunge a∼en lisp

anstößig adj offensive

anstrahlen vt sep floodlight

anstreichen† vt sep paint; (anmerken) mark

anstreng|en vt sep strain; (ermüden) tire; sich a∼en exert oneself; (sich bemühen) make an effort (zu

to). **a∼end** adj strenuous; (ermüdend) tiring. **A∼ung** f -,-en strain; (Mühe) effort

Anstrich m coat [of paint]

Ansturm m rush; (Mil) assault

Ansuchen nt -s,- request

Antarktis f - Antarctic

Anteil m share; A∼ nehmen take an interest (an + dat in). **A∼nahme** f - interest (an + dat in); (Mitgefühl) sympathy

Antenne f -,-n aerial

Anthologie f -,-n anthology

Anthrax m - anthrax

Anthropologie f - anthropology

Anti|alkoholiker m teetotaller. **A∼biotikum** nt -s,-ka antibiotic

antik adj antique. **A∼e** f - [classical] antiquity

Antikörper m antibody

Antilope f -,-n antelope

Antipathie f - antipathy

Antiquariat nt -[e]s,-e antiquarian bookshop

Antiquitäten fpl antiques. **A∼händler** m antique dealer

Antrag m -[e]s,∸e proposal; (Pol) motion; (Gesuch) application. **A∼steller** m -s,- applicant

antreffen† vt sep find

antreten† v sep ● vt start; take up (Amt) ● vi (sein) line up

Antrieb m urge; (Techn) drive; aus eigenem A∼ of one's own accord

Antritt m start; bei A∼ eines Amtes when taking office

antun† vt sep jdm etw a∼ do sth to s.o.; sich (dat) etwas a∼ take one's own life

Antwort f -,-en answer, reply (auf + acc to). **a∼en** vt/i (haben) answer (jdm s.o.)

anvertrauen vt sep entrust/(mitteilen) confide (jdm to s.o.)

Anwalt m -[e]s, ːe, **Anwältin** f -,-nen lawyer; (vor Gericht) counsel

Anwandlung f -,-en fit (von of)

anweis|en† vt sep assign (dat to); (beauftragen) instruct. **A∼ung** f instruction; (Geld-) money order

anwend|en vt sep apply (auf + acc to); (gebrauchen) use. **A∼ung** f application; use

anwerben† vt sep recruit

Anwesen nt -s,- property

anwesen|d adj present (bei at); die A∼den those present. **A∼heit** f -presence

anwidern vt sep disgust

Anwohner mpl residents

Anzahl f number

anzahl|en vt sep pay a deposit on. **A∼ung** f deposit

anzapfen vt sep tap

Anzeichen nt sign

Anzeige f -,-n announcement; (Inserat) advertisement; A∼ erstatten gegen jdn report s.o. to the police. **a∼n** vt sep announce; (inserieren) advertise; (melden) report [to the police]; (angeben) indicate

anzieh|en† vt sep ● vt attract; (festziehen) tighten; put on (Kleider, Bremse); (ankleiden) dress; sich a∼en get dressed. **a∼end** adj attractive. **A∼ungskraft** f attraction; (Phys) gravity

Anzug m suit

anzüglich adj suggestive

anzünden vt sep light; (in Brand stecken) set fire to

anzweifeln vt sep question

apart adj striking

Apathie f - apathy

apathisch adj apathetic

Aperitif m -s,-s aperitif

Apfel m -s, ː apple

Apfelsine f -,-n orange

Apostel m -s,- apostle

Apostroph m -s,-e apostrophe

Apotheke| f -,-n pharmacy. **A∼r(in)** m -s,- (f -,-nen) pharmacist, [dispensing] chemist

Apparat m -[e]s,-e device; (Phot) camera; (Radio, TV) set; (Teleph) telephone; am A∼! speaking!

Appell m -s,-e appeal; (Mil) roll-call. **a∼ieren** vi (haben) appeal (an + acc to)

Appetit m -s appetite; guten A∼! enjoy your meal! **a∼lich** adj appetizing

Applaus m -es applause

Aprikose f -,-n apricot

April m -[s] April

Aquarell nt -s,-e water-colour

Aquarium nt -s,-ien aquarium

Äquator m -s equator

Ära f - era

Araber(in) m -s,- (f -,-nen) Arab

arabisch adj Arab; (Geog) Arabian; (Ziffer) Arabic

Arbeit f -,-en work; (Anstellung) employment, job; (Aufgabe) task; (Sch) [written] test; (Abhandlung) treatise; (Qualität) workmanship; sich an die A∼ machen set to work; sich (dat) viel A∼ machen go to a lot of trouble. **a∼en** v sep ● vi (haben) work (an + dat on) ● vt make. **A∼er(in)** m -s,- (f -,-nen) worker; (Land-, Hilfs-) labourer. **A∼erklasse** f working class

Arbeit|geber m -s,- employer. **A∼nehmer** m -s,- employee

Arbeits|amt nt employment exchange. **A∼erlaubnis, A∼genehmigung** f work permit. **A∼kraft** f worker. **a∼los** adj unemployed;

~los sein be out of work. A~lo-
se(r) m/f unemployed person; die
A~losen the unemployed pl.
A~losenunterstützung f unemployment benefit. A~losigkeit f -
unemployment

arbeitsparend adj labour-saving

Arbeitsplatz m job

Archäologe m -n,-n archaeolo-
gist. A~logie f - archaeology

Arche f - die A~ Noah Noah's Ark

Architekt(in) m -en,-en (f
-,-nen) architect. A~tonisch adj
architectural. A~tur f - architecture

Archiv nt -s,-e archives pl

Arena f -,-nen arena

arg adj bad; (groß) terrible

Argentinien /-jən/ nt -s Argentina. a~isch adj Argentinian

Ärger m -s annoyance; (Unannehm-
lichkeit) trouble. ä~lich adj annoyed; (leidig) annoying; ä~lich
sein be annoyed. ä~n vt annoy;
(necken) tease; sich ä~n get annoyed (über jdn/etw with s.o./
about sth). Ä~nis nt -ses,-se annoyance; öffentliches Ä~nis public
nuisance

Arglist f - malice

arglos adj unsuspecting

Argument nt -[e]s,-e argument.
a~ieren vi (haben) argue
(dass that)

Arie /'a:rjə/ f -,-n aria

Aristokrat m -en,-en aristocrat.
A~kratie f - aristocracy. a~kra-
tisch adj aristocratic

Arktis f - Arctic. a~isch adj Arctic

arm adj poor

Arm m -[e]s,-e arm; jdn auf den
Arm nehmen ⏰ pull s.o.'s leg

Armaturenbrett nt instrument
panel; (Auto) dashboard

Armband nt (pl -bänder) bracelet; (Uhr-) watch-strap. A~uhr f
wrist-watch

Arm|e(r) m/f poor man/woman;
die A~en the poor pl

Armee f -,-n army

Ärmel m -s,- sleeve. Ä~kanal m
[English] Channel. ä~los adj
sleeveless

Armlehne f arm. A~leuchter m
candelabra

ärmlich adj poor; (elend) miserable

armselig adj miserable

Armut f - poverty

Arrangement /arãʒə'mã:/ nt
-s,-s arrangement. a~gieren vt
arrange

arrogant adj arrogant

Arsch m -[e]s,ⁱe (vulgar) arse

Arsen nt -s arsenic

Art f -,-en manner; (Weise) way;
(Natur) nature; (Sorte) kind; (Biology)
species; auf diese Art in this way

Arterie /-jə/ f -,-n artery

Arthritis f - arthritis

artig adj well-behaved

Artikel m -s,- article

Artillerie f - artillery

Artischocke f -,-n artichoke

Arznei f -,-en medicine

Arzt m -[e]s,ⁱe doctor

Ärztin f -,-nen [woman] doctor.
ä~lich adj medical

As* nt -ses,-se = Ass

Asbest m -[e]s asbestos

Asche f - ash. A~nbecher m ashtray. A~rmittwoch m Ash Wednesday

Asiat(in) m -en,-en (f -,-nen)
Asian. a~isch adj Asian

Asien /'a:zjən/ nt -s Asia

asozial adj antisocial

Aspekt m -[e]s,-e aspect

Asphalt m -[e]s asphalt. **a~ieren** vt asphalt

Ass nt -es,-e ace

Assistent(in) m -en,-en (f -,-nen) assistant

Ast m -[e]s,-̈e branch

ästhetisch adj aesthetic

Asth|ma nt -s asthma. **a~matisch** adj asthmatic

Astro|loge m -n,-n astrologer. **A~logie** f - astrology. **A~naut** m -en,-en astronaut. **A~nomie** f - astronomy

Asyl nt -s,-e home; (Pol) asylum. **A~bewerber(in)** m -e, - (f -en, -en) asylum seeker

Atelier /-'lje:/ nt -s,-s studio

Atem m -s breath. **a~los** adj breathless. **A~zug** m breath

Atheist m -en,-en atheist

Äther m -s ether

Äthiopien /-jən/ nt -s Ethiopia

Athlet|(in) m -en,-en (f -,-nen) athlete. **a~isch** adj athletic

Atlant|ik m -s Atlantic. **a~isch** adj Atlantic; der A~ische Ozean the Atlantic Ocean

Atlas m -lasses,-lanten atlas

atmen vt/i (haben) breathe

Atmosphäre f -,-n atmosphere

Atmung f - breathing

Atom nt -s,-e atom. **A~bombe** f atom bomb. **A~krieg** m nuclear war

Atten|tat nt -[e]s,-e assassination attempt. **A~täter** m assassin

Attest nt -[e]s,-e certificate

Attrak|tion /-'tsjoːn/ f -,-en attraction. **a~tiv** adj attractive

Attribut nt -[e]s,-e attribute

ätzen vt corrode; (Med) cauterize; (Kunst) etch. **ä~d** adj corrosive; (Spott) caustic

au int ouch; au fein! oh good!

Aubergine /ober'ʒiːnə/ f -,-n aubergine

auch adv & conj also, too; (außerdem) what's more; (selbst) even; a~ wenn even if; sie weiß es a~ nicht she doesn't know either; wer/ wie/was a~ immer whoever/however/whatever

Audienz f -,-en audience

audiovisuell adj audio-visual

Auditorium nt -s,-ien (Univ) lecture hall

auf

● preposition (+ dative)

⋯▸ (nicht unter) on. auf dem Tisch on the table. auf Deck on deck. auf der Erde on earth. auf der Welt in the world. auf der Straße in the street

⋯▸ (bei Institution, Veranstaltung usw.) in. auf dem Gebäude, Zimmer) in. auf der Schule/Uni at school/university. auf einer Party/Hochzeit at a party/wedding. Geld auf der Bank haben have money in the bank. sie ist auf ihrem Zimmer she's in her room. auf einem Lehrgang on a course. auf Urlaub on holiday

● preposition (+ accusative)

⋯▸ (nicht unter) on[to]. er legte das Buch auf den Tisch he laid the book on the table. auf eine Mauer steigen climb onto a wall. auf die Straße gehen go [out] into the street

⋯▸ (bei Institution, Veranstaltung usw.) to. auf eine Party/die Toilette gehen go to a party/the toilet. auf die Schule/Uni gehen go to school/university. auf einen Lehrgang/auf Urlaub gehen go on a course/on holiday

····▸ *(bei Entfernung)* auf 10 km [Entfernung] zu sehen/hören visible/audible for [a distance of] 10 km

····▸ *(zeitlich)* (wie lange) for; (bis) until; (wann) on. auf Jahre [hinaus] for years [to come]. auf ein paar Tage for a few days. etw auf nächsten Mittwoch verschieben postpone sth until next Wednesday. das fällt auf einen Montag it falls on a Monday

····▸ *(Art und Weise)* in. auf diese [Art und] Weise in this way. auf Deutsch/Englisch in German/English

····▸ *(aufgrund)* auf Wunsch on request. auf meine Bitte on or at my request. auf Befehl on command

····▸ *(Proportion)* to. ein Teelöffel auf einen Liter Wasser one teaspoon to one litre of water. auf die Sekunde/den Millimeter [genau] [precise] to the nearest second/millimetre

····▸ *(Toast)* to. auf deine Gesundheit! to your health!

● *adverb*

····▸ *(aufgerichtet, aufgestanden)* up. auf! (steh auf!) up you get! auf und ab (hin und her) up and down

····▸ *(aufsetzen)* Helm/Hut/Brille auf! helmet/hat/glasses on!

····▸ *(geöffnet, offen)* open. Fenster/Mund auf! open the window/your mouth!

aufatmen vi sep (haben) heave a sigh of relief

aufbahren vt sep lay out

Aufbau m construction; (Struktur)

structure. **a~en** v sep ● vt construct, build; (errichten) erect; (schaffen) build up; (arrangieren) arrange; sich a~en (fig) be based (auf + dat on) ● vi (haben) be based (auf + dat on)

aufbauschen vt sep puff out; (fig) exaggerate

aufbekommen† vt sep get open; (Sch) be given [as homework]

aufbessern vt sep improve; (erhöhen) increase

aufbewahr|en vt sep keep; (lagern) store. A~ung f - safe keeping; storage; (Gepäck-) left-luggage office

aufblas|bar adj inflatable. a~en† vt sep inflate

aufbleiben† vi sep (sein) stay open; (Person:) stay up

aufblenden vt/i sep (haben) (Auto) switch to full beam

aufblühen vi sep (sein) flower

aufbocken vt sep jack up

aufbrauchen vt sep use up

aufbrechen† v sep ● vt break open ● vi (sein) (Knospe:) open; (sich aufmachen) set out, start

aufbringen† vt sep raise (Geld); find (Kraft)

Aufbruch m start, departure

aufbrühen vt sep make (Tee)

aufbürden vt sep jdm etw a~ (fig) burden s.o. with sth

aufdecken vt sep (auflegen) put on; (abdecken) uncover; (fig) expose

aufdrehen vt sep turn on

aufdringlich adj persistent

aufeinander adv one on top of the other; (schießen) at each other; (warten) for each other; a~ folgend successive; (Tage) consecutive.

Aufenthalt m stay; 10 Minuten A~ haben (Zug:) stop for 10 minutes. A~serlaubnis, A~sgenehmigung f residence permit. A~sraum m recreation room; (im Hotel) lounge

Auferstehung f - resurrection

aufessen† vt sep eat up

auffahr|en† vi sep (sein) drive up; (aufprallen) crash, run (auf + acc into). A~t f drive; (Autobahn-) access road, slip road; (Bergfahrt) ascent

auffallen† vi sep (sein) be conspicuous; unangenehm a~ make a bad impression

auffällig adj conspicuous

auffangen† vt sep catch; pick up

auffass|en† vt sep understand; (deuten) take. A~ung f understanding; (Ansicht) view

auffordern| vt sep ask; (einladen) invite. A~ung f request; invitation

auffrischen v sep ● vt freshen up; revive (Erinnerung); seine Englischkenntnisse a~ brush up one's English

aufführ|en vt sep perform; (angeben) list; sich a~en behave. A~ung f performance

auffüllen vt sep fill up

Aufgabe f task; (Rechen-) problem; (Verzicht) giving up; A~n (Sch) homework sg

Aufgang m way up; (Treppe) stairs pl; (der Sonne) rise

aufgeben† vt sep ● vt give up; post (Brief); send (Telegramm); place (Bestellung); register (Gepäck); put in the paper (Annonce); jdm eine Aufgabe a~ set s.o. a task; jdm Suppe a~ serve s.o. with soup ● vi (haben) give up

Aufgebot nt contingent (an + dat of); (Relig) banns pl

aufgedunsen adj bloated

aufgehen† vi sep (sein) open; (sich

lösen) come undone; (Teig, Sonne:) rise; (Saat:) come up; (Math) come out exactly; in Flammen a~ go up in flames

aufgelegt adj gut/schlecht a~ sein be in a good/bad mood

aufgeregt adj excited; (erregt) agitated

aufgeschlossen adj (fig) open-minded

aufgeweckt adj (fig) bright

aufgießen† vt sep pour on; (aufbrühen) make (Tee)

aufgreifen† vt sep pick up; take up (Vorschlag, Thema)

aufgrund prep (+ gen) on the strength of

Aufguss m infusion

aufhaben† v sep ● vt have on; den Mund a~ have one's mouth open; viel a~ (Sch) have a lot of homework ● vi (haben) be open

aufhalten† vt sep hold up; (anhalten) stop; (abhalten) keep; (offenhalten) hold open; hold out (Hand); sich a~ stay; (sich befassen) spend one's time (mit on)

aufhäng|en vt/i sep (haben) hang up; (henken) hang; sich a~en hang oneself. A~er m -s,- loop

aufheben† vt sep pick up; (hochheben) raise; (aufbewahren) keep; (beenden) end; (rückgängig machen) lift; (abschaffen) abolish; (Jur) quash (Urteil); repeal (Gesetz); (ausgleichen) cancel out; gut aufgehoben sein be well looked after

aufheitern vt sep cheer up; sich a~ (Wetter:) brighten up

aufhellen vt sep lighten; sich a~ (Himmel:) brighten

aufhetzen vt sep incite

aufholen v sep ● vt make up ● vi (haben) catch up; (zeitlich) make up time

a

aufhören vi sep (haben) stop

aufklappen vt/i sep (sein) open

aufklär|en vt sep solve; jdn a~en enlighten s.o.; sich a~en be solved; (Wetter:) clear up. **A~ung** f solution; enlightenment; (Mil) reconnaissance; sexuelle A~ung sex education

aufkleb|en vt sep stick on. **A~er** m -s,- sticker

aufknöpfen vt sep unbutton

aufkochen v sep ●vt bring to the boil ●vi (sein) come to the boil

aufkommen† vi sep (sein) start; (Wind:) spring up; (Mode:) come in

aufkrempeln vt sep roll up

aufladen† vt sep load; (Electr) charge

Auflage f impression; (Ausgabe) edition; (Zeitungs-) circulation

auflassen† vt sep leave open; leave on (Hut)

Auflauf m crowd; (Culin) ≈ soufflé

auflegen v sep ●vt apply (auf + acc to); put down (Hörer); neu a~ reprint ●vi (haben) ring off

auflehn|en (sich) vr sep (fig) rebel. **A~ung** f - rebellion

auflesen† vt sep pick up

aufleuchten vi sep (haben) light up

auflös|en vt sep dissolve; close (Konto); sich a~en dissolve; (Nebel:) clear. **A~ung** f dissolution; (Lösung) solution

aufmach|en v sep ●vt open; (lösen) undo; sich a~en set out (nach for) ●vi (haben) open; jdm a~en open the door to s.o. **A~ung** f -,-en get-up

aufmerksam adj attentive; a~ werden auf (+ acc) notice; jdn a~ machen auf (+ acc) draw s.o.'s attention to. **A~keit** f -,-en attention; (Höflichkeit) courtesy

aufmuntern vt sep cheer up

Aufnahme f -,-n acceptance; (Empfang) reception; (in Klub, Krankenhaus) admission; (Einbeziehung) inclusion; (Beginn) start; (Foto) photograph; (Film-) shot; (Mus) recording; (Band-) tape recording. a~fähig adj receptive. **A~prüfung** f entrance examination

aufnehmen† vt sep pick up; (absorbieren) absorb; take (Nahrung, Foto); (fassen) hold; (annehmen) accept; (leihen) borrow; (empfangen) receive; (in Klub, Krankenhaus) admit; (beherbergen, geistig erfassen) take in; (einbeziehen) include; (beginnen) take up; (niederschreiben) take down; (filmen) film, shoot; (Mus) record; auf Band a~ tape[-record]

aufopfer|n vt sep sacrifice; sich a~n sacrifice oneself. **A~ung** f self-sacrifice

aufpassen vi sep (haben) pay attention; (sich vorsehen) take care; a~ auf (+ acc) look after

Aufprall m -[e]s impact. a~en vi sep (sein) a~en auf (+ acc) hit

aufpumpen vt sep pump up, inflate

aufputsch|en vt sep incite. **A~mittel** nt stimulant

aufquellen† vi sep (sein) swell

aufraffen vt sep pick up; sich a~en pick oneself up; (fig) pull oneself together

aufragen vi sep (sein) rise [up]

aufräumen vt/i sep (haben) tidy up; (wegräumen) put away

aufrecht adj & adv upright. a~erhalten† vt sep (fig) maintain

aufreg|en vt sep excite; (beunruhigen) upset; (ärgern) annoy; sich a~en get excited; (sich erregen) get worked up. a~end adj exciting. **A~ung** f excitement

aufreiben† vt sep chafe; (fig) wear down. **a~d** adj trying

aufreißen† v sep ●vt tear open; dig up (Straße); open wide (Augen, Mund) ●vi (sein) split open

aufrichtig adj sincere. **A~keit** f - sincerity

aufrollen vt sep roll up; (entrollen) unroll

aufrücken vi sep (sein) move up; (fig) be promoted

Aufruf m appeal (an + dat to); a~en† vt sep call out (Namen); jdn a~en call s.o.'s name

Aufruhr m -s,-e turmoil; (Empörung) revolt

aufrühr|en vt sep stir up. **A~er** m -s,- rebel. **a~erisch** adj inflammatory; (rebellisch) rebellious

aufrunden vt sep round up

aufrüsten vi sep arm

aufsagen vt sep recite

aufsässig adj rebellious

Aufsatz m top; (Sch) essay

aufsaugen† vt sep soak up

aufschauen vi sep (haben) look up (zu at/(fig) to)

aufschichten vt sep stack up

aufschieben† vt sep slide open; (verschieben) put off, postpone

Aufschlag m impact; (Tennis) service; (Hosen-) turn-up; (Ärmel-) upturned cuff; (Revers) lapel; (Comm) surcharge. a~en† v sep ●vt open; crack (Ei); (hochschlagen) turn up; (errichten) put up; (erhöhen) increase; cast on (Masche); **sich** (dat) das Knie a~en cut [open] one's knee ●vi (haben) hit (auf etw acc/ dat sth); (Tennis) serve; (teurer werden) go up

aufschließen† v sep ●vt unlock ●vi (haben) unlock the door

aufschlussreich adj revealing

(lehrreich) informative

aufschneiden† v sep ●vt cut open; (in Scheiben) slice ●vi (haben) ⯈ exaggerate

Aufschnitt m sliced sausage, cold meat [and cheese]

aufschrauben vt sep screw on; (abschrauben) unscrew

Aufschrei m [sudden] cry

aufschreiben† vt sep write down; jdn a~ (Polizist:) book s.o.

Aufschrift f inscription; (Etikett) label

Aufschub m delay; (Frist) grace

aufschürfen vt sep sich (dat) das Knie a~ graze one's knee

aufschwingen† (sich) vr sep find the energy (zu for)

Aufschwung m (fig) upturn

aufsehen† vi sep (haben) look up (zu at/(fig) to). **A~** nt -s **A~** erregen cause a sensation; **A~** erregend sensational

Aufseher(in) m -s,- (f -,-nen) supervisor; (Gefängnis-) warder

aufsetzen vt sep put on; (verfassen) draw up; (entwerfen) draft; sich a~ sit up

Aufsicht f supervision; (Person) supervisor. **A~srat** m board of directors

aufsperren vt sep open wide

aufspielen v sep (haben) play ●vr sich a~ show off

aufspießen vt sep spear

aufspringen† vi sep (sein) jump up; (aufprallen) bounce; (sich öffnen) burst open

aufspüren vt sep track down

aufstacheln vt sep incite

Aufstand m uprising, rebellion

aufständisch adj rebellious

aufstehen† vi sep (sein) get up; (offen sein) be open; (fig) rise up

aufsteigen† vi sep (sein) get on; (Reiter:) mount; (Bergsteiger:) climb up; (hochsteigen) rise [up]; (fig: befördert werden) rise (zu to); (Sport) be promoted

aufstell|en vt sep put up; (Culin) put on; (postieren) post; (in einer Reihe) line up; (nominieren) nominate; (Sport) select (Mannschaft); make out (Liste); lay down (Regel); make (Behauptung); set up (Rekord). A~ung f nomination; (Liste) list

Aufstieg m -[e]s, -e ascent; (fig) rise; (Sport) promotion

Aufstoßen nt -s burping

aufstrebend adj (fig) ambitious

Aufstrich m [sandwich] spread

aufstützen vt sep rest (auf + acc on); sich a~ lean (auf + acc on)

Auftakt m (fig) start

auftauchen vi sep (sein) emerge; (fig) turn up; (Frage:) crop up

auftauen vt/i sep (sein) thaw

aufteil|en vt sep divide [up]. A~ung f division

auftischen vt sep serve [up]

Auftrag m -[e]s, ⸚e task; (Kunst) commission; (Comm) order; im A~ (+ gen) on behalf of. a~en† vt sep apply; (servieren) serve; (abtragen) wear out; jdm a~en instruct s.o. (zu to). A~geber m -s,- client

auftrennen vt sep unpick, undo

auftreten† vi sep (sein) tread; (sich benehmen) behave, act; (Theat) appear; (die Bühne betreten) enter; (vorkommen) occur

Auftrieb m buoyancy; (fig) boost

Auftritt m (Theat) appearance; (auf die Bühne) entrance; (Szene) scene

aufwachen vi sep (sein) wake up

aufwachsen† vi sep (sein) grow up

Aufwand m -[e]s expenditure; (Luxus) extravagance; (Mühe) trouble; A~ treiben be extravagant

aufwändig adj = aufwendig

aufwärmen vt sep heat up; (fig) rake up; sich a~ warm oneself; (Sport) warm up

Aufwartefrau f cleaner

aufwärts adv upwards; (bergauf) uphill; es geht a~ mit jdm/etw someone/something is improving

Aufwartung f - cleaner

aufwecken vt sep wake up

aufweichen v sep ● vt soften ● vi (sein) become soft

aufweisen† vt sep have, show

aufwend|en† vt sep spend; Mühe a~en take pains. a~ig adj lavish; (teuer) expensive

aufwert|en vt sep revalue. A~ung f revaluation

aufwickeln vt sep roll up; (auswickeln) unwrap

Aufwiegler m -s,- agitator

aufwisch|en vt sep wipe up; wash (Fußboden). A~lappen m floorcloth

aufwühlen vt sep churn up

aufzähl|en vt sep enumerate, list. A~ung f list

aufzeichn|en vt sep record; (zeichnen) draw. A~ung f recording; A~ungen notes

aufziehen v sep ● vt pull up; hoist (Segel); (öffnen) open; draw (Vorhang); (großziehen) bring up; rear (Tier); mount (Bild); thread (Perlen); wind up (Uhr); (fig: necken) tease ● vi (sein) approach

Aufzug m hoist; (Fahrstuhl) lift; (Amer) elevator; (Prozession) procession; (Theat) act

Augapfel m eyeball

Auge nt -s,-n eye; (Punkt) spot;

vier A∼n werfen throw a four;
gute A∼n good eyesight; unter
vier A∼n in private; im A∼ behalten keep in sight; (fig) bear in mind

Augenblick m moment; A∼! just
a moment! a∼lich adj immediate;
(derzeitig) present ● adv immediately; (derzeit) at present

Augen|braue f eyebrow.
A∼höhle f eye socket. A∼licht nt
sight. A∼lid nt eyelid

August m -[s] August

Auktion /'tsĭoːn/ f -,-en auction

Aula f -,-len (Sch) [assembly] hall

Au-pair-Mädchen /oˈpɛːr-/ nt
aupair

aus prep (+ dat) out of; (von) from;
(bestehend) [made] of; aus Angst
from or out of fear; aus Spaß for
fun ● adv out of; (Licht, Radio) off; aus
sein auf (+ acc) be after; aus und
ein in and out; von etw aus of
one's own accord; von mir aus as
far as I'm concerned

ausarbeiten vt sep work out

ausarten vi sep (sein) degenerate
(in + acc into)

ausatmen vt/i sep (haben)
breathe out

ausbauen vt sep remove; (vergrößern) extend; (fig) expand

ausbedingen† vt sep sich (dat)
a∼ insist on; (zur Bedingung machen) stipulate

ausbesser|n vt sep mend, repair.
A∼ung f repair

ausbeulen vt sep remove the
dents from; (dehnen) make baggy

ausbild|en vt sep train; (formen)
form; (entwickeln) develop; sich
a∼en train (als/zu as); (entstehen)
develop. A∼ung f training; (Sch)
education

ausbitten† vt sep sich (dat) a∼
ask for; (verlangen) insist on

ausblasen† vt sep blow out

ausbleiben† vi sep (sein) fail to
appear/ (Erfolg): materialize; (nicht
heimkommen) stay out

Ausblick m view

ausbrech|en vi sep (sein) break
out; (Vulkan): erupt; (fliehen) escape; in Tränen a∼en burst into
tears. A∼er m runaway

ausbreiten vt sep spread [out].
A∼ung f spread

Ausbruch m outbreak; (Vulkan-)
eruption; (Wut-) outburst; (Flucht)
escape, break-out

ausbrüten vt sep hatch

Ausdauer f perseverance; (körperlich) stamina. a∼nd adj persevering; (unermüdlich) untiring

ausdehnen vt sep stretch; (fig)
extend; sich a∼ stretch; (Phys & fig)
expand; (dauern) last

ausdenken† vt sep sich (dat) a∼
think up; (sich vorstellen) imagine

Ausdruck m expression; (Fach-)
term; (Computer) printout. a∼en vt
sep print

ausdrücken vt sep squeeze out;
squeeze (Zitrone); stub out (Zigarette); (äußern) express

ausdrucks|los adj expressionless.
a∼voll adj expressive

auseinander adv apart; (entzwei)
in pieces; a∼ falten unfold; a∼
gehen part; (Linien, Meinungen): diverge; (Ehe): break up; a∼ halten
tell apart; a∼ nehmen take apart
or to pieces; a∼ setzen explain
(jdm to s.o.); sich a∼ setzen sit
apart; (sich aussprechen) have it out
(mit jdm with s.o.); come to grips
(mit einem Problem with a problem). A∼setzung f -,-en discussion; (Streit) argument

auserlesen adj select, choice

Ausfahrt f drive; (Autobahn-,

a

Garagen-) exit

Ausfall m failure; (Absage) cancellation; (Comm) loss. a~en† vi sep (sein) fall out; (versagen) fail; (abgesagt werden) be cancelled; gut/schlecht a~en turn out to be good/bad

ausfallend, ausfällig adj abusive

ausfertig|en vt sep make out. A~ung f-, sep in doppelter A~ung in duplicate

ausfindig adj a~ machen find

Ausflug m excursion, outing

Ausflügler m -s,- [day-]tripper

Ausfluss m outlet; (Abfluss) drain; (Med) discharge

ausfragen vt sep question

Ausfuhr f -,-en (Comm) export

ausführ|en vt sep take out; (Comm) export; (erklären) explain. a~lich adj detailed ● adv in detail. A~ung f execution; (Comm) version; (äußere) finish; (Qualität) workmanship; (Erklärung) explanation

Ausgabe f issue; (Buch-) edition; (Comm) version

Ausgang m way out, exit; (Flugsteig) gate; (Ende) end; (Ergebnis) outcome. A~spunkt m starting point. A~sperre f curfew

ausgeben† vt sep give out; issue (Fahrkarten); spend (Geld); sich a~ als pretend to be

ausgebildet adj trained

ausgebucht adj fully booked; (Vorstellung) sold out

ausgefallen adj unusual

ausgefranst adj frayed

ausgeglichen adj [well-]balanced

ausgeh|en† vi sep (sein) go out; (Haare:) fall out; (Vorräte, Geld:) run out; (verblassen) fade; gut/schlecht a~en end well/badly; davon a~en, dass assume that. A~ver-

bot nt curfew

ausgelassen adj high-spirited

ausgemacht adj agreed

ausgenommen conj except; a~ wenn unless

ausgeprägt adj marked

ausgeschlossen pred adj out of the question

ausgeschnitten adj low-cut

ausgesprochen adj marked ● adv decidedly

ausgestorben adj extinct; [wie] a~ (Straße:) deserted

Ausgestoßene(r) m/f outcast

ausgezeichnet adj excellent

ausgiebig adj extensive; (ausgedehnt) long; a~ Gebrauch machen von make full use of

ausgießen† vt sep pour out

Ausgleich m -[e]s balance; (Entschädigung) compensation. a~en† v sep ● vt balance; even out (Höhe); (wettmachen) compensate for; sich a~en balance out ● vi (haben) (Sport) equalize. A~streffer m equalizer

ausgrab|en† vt sep dig up; (Archaeology) excavate. A~ung f -,-en excavation

Ausguss m [kitchen] sink

aushaben† vt sep have finished (Buch)

aushalten† vt sep bear, stand; hold (Note); (Unterhalt zahlen für) keep; nicht auszuhalten, nicht zum A~ unbearable

aushändigen vt sep hand over

aushängen¹ vt sep (reg) display; take off its hinges (Tür)

aushäng|en²† vi sep (haben) be displayed. A~eschild nt sign

ausheben† vt sep excavate

aushecken vt sep (fig) hatch

aushelfen† vi sep (haben)

help out (jdm s.o.)

Aushilf|**e** f [temporary] assistant; zur A~e to help out. A~**skraft** f temporary worker. **a~sweise** adv temporarily

aushöhlen vt sep hollow out

auskennen† **(sich)** vr sep know one's way around; **sich mit/in etw** (dat) a~ know all about sth

auskommen vi sep (sein) manage (mit/ohne with/without); (sich vertragen) get on (gut well)

auskugeln vt sep sich (dat) den Arm a~ dislocate one's shoulder

auskühlen vt/i sep (sein) cool

auskundschaften vt sep spy out

Auskunft f -,⸚e information; (A~sstelle) information desk/ (Büro) bureau; (Teleph) enquiries pl; **eine A~** a piece of information

auslachen vt sep laugh at

Auslage f [window] display; A~n expenses

Ausland nt im/ins A~ abroad

Ausländ|**er(in)** m -s,- (f -,-nen) foreigner. **a~isch** adj foreign

Auslandsgespräch nt international call

auslass|**en**† vt sep let out; let down (Saum); (weglassen) leave out; (versäumen) miss; (Culin) melt; (fig) vent (Ärger) (an + dat on). A~**ungszeichen** nt apostrophe

Auslauf m run. **a~en**† vi sep (sein) run out; (Farbe:) run; (Naut) put to sea; (Modell:) be discontinued

ausleeren vt sep empty [out]

ausleg|**en** vt sep lay out; display (Waren); (auskleiden) line (mit with); (bezahlen) pay; (deuten) interpret. A~**ung** f -,-en interpretation

ausleihen† vt sep lend; **sich** (dat) a~ borrow

Auslese f - selection; (fig) pick; (Elite) elite

ausliefer|**n** vt sep hand over; (Jur) extradite. A~**ung** f handing over; (Jur) extradition; (Comm) distribution

ausloggen vi sep log off or out

auslosen vt sep draw lots for

auslös|**en** vt sep set off, trigger; (fig) cause; arouse (Begeisterung); (einlösen) redeem; pay a ransom for (Gefangene). A~**er** m -s,- trigger; (Phot) shutter release

Auslosung f draw

auslüften vt/i sep (haben) air

ausmachen vt sep put out; (abschalten) turn off; (abmachen) arrange; (erkennen) make out; (betragen) amount to; (wichtig sein) matter

Ausmaß nt extent; A~e dimensions

Ausnahm|**e** f -,-n exception. A~**ezustand** m state of emergency. **a~slos** adv without exception. **a~sweise** adv as an exception

ausnehmen† vt sep take out; gut (Fisch); **sich gut** a~ look good. **a~d** adv exceptionally

ausnutz|**en, ausnütz**|**en** vt sep exploit. A~**ung** f exploitation

auspacken vt sep unpack; (auswickeln) unwrap

ausplaudern vt sep let out, blab

ausprobieren vt sep try out

Auspuff m -s exhaust [system]. A~**gase** ntpl exhaust fumes. A~**rohr** nt exhaust pipe

auspusten vt sep blow out

ausradieren vt sep rub out

ausrauben vt sep rob

ausräuchern vt sep smoke out; fumigate (Zimmer)

ausräumen vt sep clear out

a **ausrechnen** vt sep work out

Ausrede f excuse. a~n v sep ● vi (haben) finish speaking ● vt jdm etw a~n talk s.o. out of sth

ausreichen vi sep (haben) be enough. a~d adj adequate

Ausreise f departure. a~n vi sep (sein) leave the country. A~visum nt exit visa

ausreißen† v sep ● vt pull or tear out ● vi (sein) 1 run away

ausrenken vt sep dislocate

ausrichten vt sep align; (bestellen) deliver; (erreichen) achieve; jdm a~ tell s.o. (dass that); ich soll Ihnen Grüße von X a~ X sends [you] his regards

ausrotten vt sep exterminate; (fig) eradicate

Ausruf m exclamation. a~en† vt sep exclaim; call out (Namen); (verkünden) proclaim; jdn a~en lassen put out a call for s.o. A~ezeichen nt exclamation mark

ausruhen vt/i sep (haben) rest; sich a~ have a rest

ausrüst|en vt sep equip. A~ung f equipment; (Mil) kit

ausrutschen vi sep (sein) slip

Aussage f -,-n statement; (Jur) testimony, evidence; (Gram) predicate. a~n vt/i sep (haben) state; (Jur) give evidence, testify

ausschalten vt sep switch off

Ausschank m sale of alcoholic drinks; (Bar) bar

Ausschau f - A~ halten nach look out for

ausscheiden† vi sep (sein) leave; (Sport) drop out; (nicht in Frage kommen) be excluded

ausschenken vt sep pour out

ausscheren vi sep (sein) (Auto) pull out

ausschildern vt sep signpost

ausschimpfen vt sep tell off

ausschlafen† vi/r sep (haben) [sich] a~ get enough sleep; (morgens) sleep late

Ausschlag m (Med) rash; den A~ geben (fig) tip the balance. a~gebend adj decisive

ausschließ|en† vt sep lock out; (fig) exclude; (entfernen) expel. a~lich adj exclusive

ausschlüpfen vi sep (sein) hatch

Ausschluss m exclusion; expulsion; unter A~ der Öffentlichkeit in camera

ausschneiden† vt sep cut out

Ausschnitt m excerpt, extract; (Zeitungs-) cutting; (Hals-) neckline

ausschöpfen vt sep ladle out; (Naut) bail out; exhaust (Möglichkeiten)

ausschreiben† vt sep write out; (ausstellen) make out; (bekanntgeben) announce; put out to tender (Auftrag)

Ausschreitungen fpl riots; (Exzesse) excesses

Ausschuss m committee; (Comm) rejects pl

ausschütten vt sep tip out; (verschütten) spill; (leeren) empty

aussehen† vi sep (haben) look; wie sieht er aus? what does he/it look like? A~ nt -s appearance

außen adv [on the] outside; nach a~ outwards. A~bordmotor m outboard motor. A~handel m foreign trade. A~minister m Foreign Minister. A~politik f foreign policy. A~seite f outside. A~seiter m -s,- outsider; (fig) misfit. A~stände mpl outstanding debts

außer prep (+ dat) except [for], apart from; (außerhalb) out of; a~

sich (*fig*) beside oneself ● *conj* except; a~ wenn unless. a~dem *adv* in addition, as well ● *conj* moreover

äußer|e(r,s) *adj* external; (*Teil, Schicht*) outer. Ä~e(s) *nt* exterior; (*Aussehen*) appearance

außer|ehelich *adj* extramarital. a~gewöhnlich *adj* exceptional. a~halb *prep* (+ *gen*) outside ● *adv* a~halb wohnen live outside town

äußer|lich *adj* external; (*fig*) outward. ä~n *vt* express; sich ä~n comment; (*sich zeigen*) manifest itself

außerordentlich *adj* extraordinary

äußerst *adv* extremely

äußerste|(r,s) *adj* outermost; (*weiteste*) furthest; (*höchste*) utmost, extreme; (*letzte*) last; (*schlimmste*) worst. Ä~(s) *nt* das Ä~e the limit; (*Schlimmste*) the worst; sein Ä~s tun do one's utmost; aufs Ä~ extremely

Äußerung *f* -,-en comment; (*Bemerkung*) remark

aussetzen *v sep* ● *vt* expose (*dat* to); abandon (*Kind*); launch (*Boot*); offer (*Belohnung*); etwas auszusetzen haben an (+ *dat*) find fault with ● *vi* (*haben*) stop; (*Motor*:) cut out

Aussicht *f* -,-en view/(*fig*) prospect (auf + *acc* of); weitere A~en (*Meteorology*) further outlook *sg*. a~slos *adj* hopeless

ausspannen *v sep* ● *vt* spread out; unhitch (*Pferd*) ● *vi* (*haben*) rest

aussperren *vt sep* lock out

ausspielen *v sep* ● *vt* play (*Karte*); (*fig*) play off (*gegen against*) ● *vi* (*haben*) (*Kartenspiel*) lead

Aussprache *f* pronunciation; (*Gespräch*) talk

aussprechen† *vt sep* pronounce; (*äußern*) express; sich a~ talk;

come out (für/gegen in favour of/against)

Ausspruch *m* saying

ausspucken *v sep* ● *vt* spit out ● *vi* (*haben*) spit

ausspülen *vt sep* rinse out

ausstatten *vt sep* equip. A~ung *f* -,-en equipment; (*Innen-*) furnishings *pl*; (*Theat*) scenery and costumes *pl*

ausstehen *v sep* ● *vt* suffer; Angst a~ be frightened; ich kann sie nicht a~ I can't stand her ● *vi* (*haben*) be outstanding

aussteigen† *vi sep* (*sein*) get out; (*aus Bus, Zug*) get off; alles a~! all change!

ausstell|en *vt sep* exhibit; (*Comm*) display; (*ausfertigen*) make out; issue (*Pass*). A~ung *f* exhibition; (*Comm*) display

aussterben† *vi sep* (*sein*) die out; (*Biology*) become extinct

Aussteuer *f* trousseau

Ausstieg *m* -[e]s,-e exit

ausstopfen *vt sep* stuff

ausstoßen† *vt sep* emit; utter (*Fluch*); heave (*Seufzer*); (*ausschließen*) expel

ausstrahl|en *vt/i sep* (*sein*) radiate, emit; (*Radio, TV*) broadcast. A~ung *f* radiation

ausstrecken *vt sep* stretch out; put out (*Hand*)

ausstreichen† *vt sep* cross out

ausströmen *v sep* ● *vi* (*sein*) pour out; (*entweichen*) escape ● *vt* emit; (*ausstrahlen*) radiate

aussuchen *vt sep* pick, choose

Austausch *m* exchange. a~bar *adj* interchangeable. a~en *vt sep* exchange; (*auswechseln*) replace

austeilen *vt sep* distribute

Auster *f* -,-n oyster

a

austragen† vt sep deliver; hold (Wettkampf); play (Spiel)

Austral|ien /-jən/ nt -s Australia. **A~ier(in)** m -s,- (f -,-nen) Australian. **a~isch** adj Australian

austreiben† vt sep drive out; (Relig) exorcize

austreten† v sep ● vt stamp out; (abnutzen) wear down ● vi (sein) come out; (ausscheiden) leave (aus etw sth); [mal] a~ 🔲 go to the loo

austrinken† vt/i sep (haben) drink up; (leeren) drain

Austritt m resignation

austrocknen vt/i sep (sein) dry out

ausüben vt sep practise; carry on (Handwerk); exercise (Recht); exert (Druck, Einfluss)

Ausverkauf m [clearance] sale. **a~t** adj sold out

Auswahl f choice, selection; (Comm) range; (Sport) team

auswählen vt sep choose, select

Auswander|er m emigrant. **a~n** vi sep (sein) emigrate. **A~ung** f emigration

auswärt|ig adj non-local; (ausländisch) foreign. **a~s** adv outwards; (Sport) away. **A~sspiel** nt away game

auswaschen† vt sep wash out

auswechseln vt sep change; (ersetzen) replace; (Sport) substitute

Ausweg m (fig) way out

ausweichen† vi sep (sein) get out of the way; jdm/etw a~en avoid; (sich entziehen) evade someone/ something

Ausweis m -es,-e pass; (Mitglieds-, Studenten-) card. a~en† vt sep deport; sich a~en prove one's identity. **A~papiere** ntpl identification papers. **A~ung** f deportation

auswendig adv by heart

auswerten vt sep evaluate

auswickeln vt sep unwrap

auswirk|en (sich) vr sep have an effect (auf + acc on). **A~ung** f effect; (Folge) consequence

auswringen vt sep wring out

auszahlen vt sep pay out; (entlohnen) pay off; (abfinden) buy out; sich a~ (fig) pay off

auszählen vt sep count; (Boxen) count out

Auszahlung f payment

auszeichn|en vt sep (Comm) price; (ehren) honour; (mit einem Preis) award a prize to; (Mil) decorate; sich a~en distinguish oneself. **A~ung** f honour; (Preis) award; (Mil) decoration; (Sch) distinction

ausziehen† v sep ● vt pull out; (auskleiden) undress; take off (Mantel, Schuhe) ● vi (sein) move out; (sich aufmachen) set out

Auszug m departure; (Umzug) move; (Ausschnitt) extract; (Bank-) statement

Auto nt -s,-s car; A~ fahren drive; (mitfahren) go in the car. **A~bahn** f motorway

Autobiographie f autobiography

Auto|bus m bus. **A~fahrer(in)** m(f) driver, motorist. **A~fahrt** f drive

Autogramm nt -s,-e autograph

Automat m -en,-en automatic device; (Münz-) slot-machine; (Verkaufs-) vending-machine; (Fahrkarten-) machine; (Techn) robot. **A~ik** f - automatic mechanism; (Auto) automatic transmission

automatisch adj automatic

Autonummer f registration number

Autopsie f -,-n autopsy

31

Autor | Balsam

Autor *m* -s,-en author

Auto|reisezug *m* Motorail.
A~rennen *nt* motor race

Autorin *f* -,-nen author[ess]

Autori|sation /-'tsjo:n/ *f* - authorization. **A~tät** *f* -,-en authority

Auto|schlosser *m* motor mechanic. **A~skooter** *m* -s,- dodgem. **A~stopp** *m* -s per A~stopp fahren hitch-hike. **A~verleih** *m* car hire [firm]. **A~waschanlage** *f* car wash

autsch *int* ouch

Axt *f* -,⁻e axe

Bb

B, b /be:/ *nt* - (*Mus*) B flat

Baby /'be:bi/ *nt* -s,-s baby. **B~ausstattung** *f* layette. **B~sitter** *m* -s,- babysitter

Bach *m* -[e]s,⁻e stream

Backbord *nt* -[e]s port [side]

Backe *f* -,-n cheek

backen *vt/i* (*haben*) bake; (*braten*) fry

Backenzahn *m* molar

Bäcker *m* -s,- baker. **B~ei** *f* -,-en, **B~laden** *m* baker's shop

Back|obst *nt* dried fruit. **B~ofen** *m* oven. **B~pfeife** 🔲 slap in the face. **B~pflaume** *f* prune. **B~pulver** *nt* baking-powder. **B~stein** *m* brick

Bad *nt* -[e]s,⁻er bath; (*Zimmer*) bathroom; (*Schwimm-*) pool; (*Ort*) spa

Bade|anstalt *f* swimming baths *pl*. **B~anzug** *m* swim-suit. **B~hose** *f* swimming trunks *pl*. **B~kappe** *f*

bathing-cap. **B~mantel** *m* bathrobe. **b~n** *vi* (*haben*) have a bath; (*im Meer*) bathe ● *vt* bath; (*waschen*) bathe. **B~ort** *m* seaside resort. **B~wanne** *f* bath. **B~zimmer** *nt* bathroom

Bagger *m* -s,- excavator; (*Nass-*) dredger. **B~see** *m* flooded gravel-pit

Bahn *f* -,-en path; (*Astronomy*) orbit; (*Sport*) track; (*einzelne*) lane; (*Rodel-*) run; (*Stoff-*) width; (*Eisen-*) railway; (*Zug*) train; (*Straßen-*) tram. **b~brechend** *adj* (*fig*) pioneering. **B~hof** *m* [railway] station. **B~steig** *m* -s,-e platform. **B~übergang** *m* level crossing

Bahre *f* -,-n stretcher

Baiser /bɛ'ze:/ *nt* -s,-s meringue

Bake *f* -,-n (*Naut, Aviat*) beacon

Bakterien /-jən/ *fpl* bacteria

Balance /ba'lãsə/ *f* - balance.
b~ieren *vt/i* (*haben/sein*) balance

bald *adv* soon; (*fast*) almost

Baldachin /-xin/ *m* -s,-e canopy

bald|ig *adj* early; (*Besserung*) speedy. **b~möglichst** *adv* as soon as possible

Balg *nt* & *m* -[e]s,⁻er 🔲 brat

Balkan *m* -s Balkans *pl*

Balken *m* -s,- beam

Balkon /bal'kõ:/ *m* -s,-e balcony; (*Theat*) circle

Ball¹ *m* -[e]s,⁻e ball

Ball² *m* -[e]s,⁻e (*Tanz*) ball

Ballade *f* -,-n ballad

Ballast *m* -[e]s ballast. **B~stoffe** *mpl* roughage *sg*

Ballen *m* -s,- bale; (*Anat*) ball of the hand/(*Fuß-*) foot; (*Med*) bunion

Ballerina *f* -,-nen ballerina

Ballett *nt* -s,-e ballet

Ballon /ba'lõ:/ *m* -s,-s balloon

Balsam *m* -s balm

Balt|ikum nt -s Baltic States pl.
b~isch adj Baltic

b

Bambus m -ses,-se bamboo

banal adj banal

Banane f -,-n banana

Banause m -n,-n philistine

Band[1] nt -[e]s,=er ribbon; (Naht-, Ton-, Ziel-) tape; am laufenden B~ non-stop

Band[2] m -[e]s,=e volume

Band[3] nt -[e]s,-e (fig) bond

Band[4] /bænt/ f -,-s [jazz] band

Bandag|e /ban'da:ʒə/ f -,-n bandage. **b~ieren** vt bandage

Bande f -,-n gang

bändigen vt control, restrain; (zähmen) tame

Bandit m -en,-en bandit

Band|maß nt tape-measure. B~scheibe f (Anat) disc. B~wurm m tapeworm

Bang|e f B~e haben be afraid; jdm B~e machen frighten s.o. **b~en** vi (haben) fear (um for)

Banjo nt -s,-s banjo

Bank[1] f -,=e bench

Bank[2] f -,-en (Comm) bank. B~einzug m direct debit

Bankett nt -s,-e banquet

Bankier /baŋˈkjeː/ m -s,-s banker

Bankkonto nt bank account

Bankrott m -s,-e bankruptcy. **b~** adj bankrupt

Bankwesen nt banking

Bann m -[e]s,-e (fig) spell. **b~en** vt exorcize; (abwenden) avert; [wie] gebannt spellbound

Banner nt -s,- banner

bar adj (rein) sheer; (Gold) pure; **b~es** Geld cash; [in] bar bezahlen pay cash

Bar f -,-s bar

Bär m -en,-en bear

Baracke f -,-n (Mil) hut

Barb|ar m -en,-en barbarian.
b~arisch adj barbaric

bar|fuß adv barefoot. B~geld nt cash

barmherzig adj merciful

barock adj baroque. B~ nt & m -[s] baroque

Barometer nt -s,- barometer

Baron m -s,-e baron. B~in f -,-nen baroness

Barren m -s,- (Gold-) bar, ingot; (Sport) parallel bars pl. B~gold nt gold bullion

Barriere f -,-n barrier

Barrikade f -,-n barricade

barsch adj gruff

Barsch m -[e]s,-e (Zool) perch

Bart m -[e]s,=e beard; (der Katze) whiskers pl

bärtig adj bearded

Barzahlung f cash payment

Basar m -s,-e bazaar

Base[1] f -,-n [female] cousin

Base[2] f -,-n (Chemistry) alkali, base

Basel nt -s Basle

basieren vi (haben) be based (auf + dat on)

Basilikum nt -s basil

Basis f -,Basen base; (fig) basis

basisch adj (Chemistry) alkaline

Bask|enmütze f beret. **b~isch** adj Basque

Baß m -sses,=e bass

Bassin /ba'sɛ̃:/ nt -s,-s pond; (Brunnen-) basin; (Schwimm-) pool

Bassist m -en,-en bass player; (Sänger) bass

Bast m -[e]s raffia

basteln vt make ● vi (haben) do handicrafts

Batterie f -,-n battery

Bau¹ m -[e]s,-e burrow; (*Fuchs-*) earth

Bau² m -[e]s,-ten construction; (*Gebäude*) building; (*Auf-*) structure; (*Körper-*) build; (*B~stelle*) building site. **B~arbeiten** fpl building work sg; (*Straßen-*) roadworks

Bauch m -[e]s, Bäuche abdomen, belly; (*Magen*) stomach; (*Bauchung*) bulge. **b~ig** adj bulbous. **B~nabel** m navel. **B~redner** m ventriloquist. **B~schmerzen** mpl stomach-ache sg. **B~speicheldrüse** f pancreas

bauen vt build; (*konstruieren*) construct ● vi (*haben*) build (an etw dat sth); b~ auf (+ acc) (fig) rely on

Bauer¹ m -n,-n farmer; (*Schach*) pawn

Bauer² nt -s,- [bird]cage

bäuerlich adj rustic

Bauern|haus nt farmhouse. **B~hof** m farm

bau|fällig adj dilapidated. **B~genehmigung** f planning permission. **B~gerüst** nt scaffolding. **B~jahr** nt year of construction. **B~kunst** f architecture. **b~lich** adj structural

Baum m -[e]s, Bäume tree

baumeln vi (*haben*) dangle

bäumen (sich) vr rear [up]

Baum|schule f [tree] nursery. **B~wolle** f cotton

Bausch m -[e]s, Bäusche wad; in **B~** und Bogen (fig) wholesale. **b~en** vt puff out

Bau|sparkasse f building society. **B~stein** m building brick. **B~stelle** f building site; (*Straßen-*) roadworks pl. **B~unternehmer** m building contractor

Bayer|(in) m -n,-n (f -,-nen) Bavarian. **B~n** nt -s Bavaria

bay[e]risch adj Bavarian

Bazillus m -,-llen bacillus

beabsichtig|en vt intend. **b~t** adj intended; intentional

beacht|en vt take notice of; (*einhalten*) observe; (*folgen*) follow; nicht b~en ignore. **b~lich** adj considerable. **B~ung** f - observance; etw (dat) keine B~ung schenken take no notice of sth

Beamte(r) m, **Beamtin** f -,-nen official; (*Staats-*) civil servant; (*Schalter-*) clerk

beanspruchen vt claim; (*erfordern*) demand

beanstand|en vt find fault with; (*Comm*) make a complaint about. **B~ung** f -,-en complaint

beantragen vt apply for

beantworten vt answer

bearbeiten vt work; (*weiter-*) process; (*behandeln*) treat (mit with); (*Admin*) deal with; (*redigieren*) edit; (*Theat*) adapt; (*Mus*) arrange

Beatmungsgerät nt ventilator

beaufsichtig|en vt supervise. **B~ung** f - supervision

beauftragen vt instruct; commission (*Künstler*)

bebauen vt build on; (*bestellen*) cultivate

beben vi (*haben*) tremble

Becher m -s,- beaker; (*Henkel-*) mug; (*Joghurt-*, *Sahne-*) carton

Becken nt -s,- basin; pool; (*Mus*)

cymbals pl; (Anat) pelvis
bedacht adj careful; darauf b∼
anxious (zu to)
bedächtig adj careful; slow
bedanken (sich) vr thank (bei
jdm s.o.)
Bedarf m -s need/(Comm) demand
(an + dat for); bei B∼ if required.
B∼shaltestelle f request stop
bedauer|lich adj regrettable.
b∼licherweise adv unfortunately.
b∼n vt regret; (bemitleiden) feel
sorry for; bedauere! sorry!
b∼nswert adj pitiful; (bedauerlich)
regrettable
bedeckt adj covered; (Himmel)
overcast
bedenken† vt consider; (überlegen) think over. B∼ pl misgivings;
ohne B∼ without hesitation
bedenklich adj doubtful; (verdächtig) dubious; (ernst) serious
bedeut|en vi (haben) mean.
b∼end adj important; (beträchtlich)
considerable. B∼ung f -,-en meaning; (Wichtigkeit) importance.
b∼ungslos adj meaningless; (unwichtig) unimportant. b∼ungsvoll
adj significant; (vielsagend) meaningful
bedien|en vt serve; (betätigen) op-
erate; sich [selbst] b∼en help oneself. B∼ung f -,-en service; (Betätigung) operation; (Kellner) waiter;
(Kellnerin) f waitress. B∼ungsgeld
nt service charge
Bedingung f -,-en condition;
B∼en conditions; (Comm) terms.
b∼slos adj unconditional
bedrohen vt threaten. b∼lich
adj threatening. B∼ung f threat
bedrücken vt depress
bedruckt adj printed
bedürf|en† vi (haben) (+ gen)
need. B∼nis nt -ses,-se need

Beefsteak /'bi:fste:k/ nt -s,-s
steak; deutsches B∼ hamburger
beeilen (sich) vr hurry; hasten
(zu to)
beeindrucken vt impress
beeinflussen vt influence
beeinträchtigen vt mar; (schädigen) impair
beengen vt restrict
beerdig|en vt bury. B∼ung f
-,-en funeral
Beere f -,-n berry
Beet nt -[e]s,-e (Horticulture) bed
Beete f -,-n Rote B∼ beetroot
befähig|en vt enable; (qualifizie-
ren) qualify. B∼ung f - qualification; (Fähigkeit) ability
befahrbar adj passable
befallen† vt attack; (Angst:) seize
befangen adj shy; (gehemmt) self-
conscious; (Jur) biased. B∼heit f -
shyness; self-consciousness; bias
befassen (sich) vr concern one-
self/(behandeln) deal (mit with)
Befehl m -[e]s,-e order; (Leitung)
command (über + acc of). b∼en †
vt jdm etw b∼en order s.o. to do
sth ●vi (haben) give the orders.
B∼sform f (Gram) imperative.
B∼shaber m -s,- commander
befestigen vt fasten (an + dat
to); (Mil) fortify
befeuchten vt moisten
befinden† (sich) vr be. B∼ nt -s
[state of] health
beflecken vt stain
befolgen vt follow
beförder|n vt transport; (im
Rang) promote. B∼ung f -,-en
transport; promotion
befragen vt question
befrei|en vt free; (räumen) clear
(von of); (freistellen) exempt (von
from); sich b∼en free oneself.

B~er m -s, liberator. B~ung f - liberation; exemption

befreunden (sich) vr make friends; befreundet sein be friends

befriedig|en vt satisfy. **b~end** adj satisfying; (zufrieden stellend) satisfactory. B~ung f - satisfaction

befrucht|en vt fertilize. B~ung f - fertilization; künstliche B~ung artificial insemination

Befugnis f -,-se authority

Befund m result

befürcht|en vt fear. B~ung f -,-en fear

befürworten vt support

begab|t adj gifted. B~ung f -,-en gift, talent

begeben† (sich) vr go; sich in Gefahr b~ expose oneself to danger

begegn|en vi (sein) jdm/etw b~en meet someone/something. B~ung f -,-en meeting

begehr|en vt desire. **b~t** adj sought-after

begeister|n vt jdn b~n arouse someone's enthusiasm. **b~t** adj enthusiastic; (eifrig) keen. B~ung f - enthusiasm

Begierde f -,-n desire

Beginn m -s beginning. **b~en†** vt/i (haben) start, begin

beglaubigen vt authenticate

begleichen† vt settle

begleit|en vt accompany. B~er m -s, companion; (Mus) accompanist. B~ung f -,-en company; (Mus) accompaniment

beglück|en vt make happy. b~wünschen vt congratulate (zu to)

begnadigen vt (Jur) pardon. B~ung f -,-en (Jur) pardon

begraben† vt bury

Begräbnis n -ses,-se burial; (Feier) funeral

begreif|en† vt understand; nicht zu b~en incomprehensible. **b~lich** adj understandable

begrenz|en vt form the boundary of; (beschränken) restrict. **b~t** adj limited. B~ung f -,-en restriction; (Grenze) boundary

Begriff m -[e]s,-e concept; (Ausdruck) term; (Vorstellung) idea

begründ|en vt give one's reason for. **b~et** adj justified. B~ung f -,-en reason

begrüß|en vt greet; (billigen) welcome. **b~enswert** adj welcome. B~ung f - greeting; welcome

begünstigen vt favour

begütert adj wealthy

behaart adj hairy

behäbig adj portly

behag|en vi (haben) please (jdm s.o.). **B~en** nt -s contentment; (Genuss) enjoyment. **b~lich** adj comfortable. B~lichkeit f - comfort

behalten† vt keep; (sich merken) remember

Behälter m -s, container

behand|eln vt treat; (sich befassen) deal with. B~lung f treatment

beharr|en vi (haben) persist (auf + dat in). **b~lich** adj persistent

behaupt|en vt maintain; (vorgeben) claim; (sagen) say; (bewahren) retain; sich b~en hold one's own. B~ung f -,-en assertion; claim; (Äußerung) statement

beheben† vt remedy

behelf|en† (sich) vr make do (mit with). **b~smäßig** adj makeshift ●adv provisionally

beherbergen vt put up

beherrsch|en vt rule over; (dominieren) dominate; (meistern, zügeln) control; (*können*) know. **b∼t** *adj* self-controlled. **B∼ung** *f* - control

beherzigen *vt* heed

behilflich *adj* jdm **b∼** sein help s.o.

behinder|n *vt* hinder; (*blockieren*) obstruct. **b∼t** *adj* handicapped; (*schwer*) disabled. **B∼te(r)** *m/f* handicapped/disabled person. **B∼ung** *f* -,-en obstruction; (*Med*) handicap; disability

Behörde *f* -,-n [public] authority

behüte|n *vt* protect. **b∼t** *adj* sheltered

behutsam *adj* careful; (*zart*) gentle

---

bei

● preposition (+ *dative*)

! Note that bei plus dem can become beim

····▶ (*nahe*) near; (*dicht an, neben*) by; (*als Begleitung*) with. wer steht da bei ihm? who is standing there next to or with him? etw bei sich haben have sth with or on one. bleiben Sie beim Gepäck/bei den Kindern stay with the luggage/the children. war heute ein Brief für mich bei der Post? was there a letter for me in the post today?

····▶ (*an*) by. jdn bei der Hand nehmen take s.o. by the hand

····▶ (*in der Wohnung von*) at ... 's home or house/flat. bei mir [zu Hause] at my home or [T] place. bei seinen Eltern leben live with one's parents. wir sind bei Ulrike eingeladen we have been invited to Ulrike's. bei Schmidt at the Schmidts';

(*Geschäft*) at Schmidts'; (*auf Briefen*) c/o Schmidt. bei jdm/ einer Firma arbeiten work for s.o./a firm. bei uns tut man das nicht we don't do that where I come from.

····▶ (*gegenwärtig*) at; (*verwickelt*) in. bei einer Hochzeit/einem Empfang at a wedding/reception. bei einem Unfall in an accident

····▶ (*im Falle von*) in the case of, with; (*bei Wetter*) in. wie bei den Römern as with the Romans. bei Nebel in fog, if there is fog. bei dieser Hitze in this heat

····▶ (*angesichts*) with; (*trotz*) in spite of. bei deinen guten Augen with your good eyesight. bei all seinen Bemühungen in spite of or despite all his efforts

····▶ (*Zeitpunkt*) at, on. bei diesen Worten errötete er he blushed at this or on hearing this. bei seiner Ankunft on his arrival. bei Tag/Nacht by day/night.

····▶ (*Gleichzeitigkeit, mit Verbalsubstantiv*) beim ... en while or when ... ing. beim Spaziergehen im Walde while walking in the woods. beim Überqueren der Straße when crossing the road. sie war beim Lesen she was reading. wir waren beim Frühstück we were having breakfast

beibehalten† *vt sep* keep

beibringen† *vt sep* jdm etw **b∼** teach s.o. sth; (*mitteilen*) break sth to s.o.; (*zufügen*) inflict sth on s.o.

Beicht|e *f* -,-n confession. **b∼en** *vt/i* (*haben*) confess. **B∼stuhl** *m* confessional

beide *adj & pron* both; **b∼s** both; dreißig **b∼** (*Tennis*) thirty all.

b~rseitig adj mutual. **b~rseits** adv & prep (+ gen) on both sides (of)

beieinander adv together

Beifahrer(in) m(f) [front-seat] passenger; (Motorrad) pillion passenger

Beifall m -[e]s applause; (Billigung) approval; **B~ klatschen** applaud

beifügen vt sep add; (beilegen) enclose

beige /beːʒ/ inv adj beige

beigeben† vt sep add

Beihilfe f financial aid; (Studien-) grant; (Jur) aiding and abetting

Beil nt -[e]s,-e hatchet, axe

Beilage f supplement; (Gemüse) vegetable

beiläufig adj casual

beilegen vt sep enclose; (schlichten) settle

Beileid nt condolences pl. **B~sbrief** m letter of condolence

beiliegend adj enclosed

beim prep = bei dem; **b~ Militär** in the army; **b~ Frühstück** at breakfast

beimessen† vt sep (fig) attach (dat to)

Bein nt -[e]s,-e leg; **jdm ein B~ stellen** trip s.o. up

beinah[e] adv nearly, almost

Beiname m epithet

beipflichten vi sep (haben) agree (dat with)

Beirat m advisory committee

beisammen adv together; **b~ sein** be together

Beisein nt presence

beiseite adv aside; (abseits) apart; **b~ legen** put aside; (sparen) put by

beisetzen vt sep bury. **B~ung** f -,-en funeral

Beispiel nt example; **zum B~** for

example. **b~sweise** adv for example

beißen† vt/i (haben) bite; (brennen) sting; **sich b~** (Farben:) clash

Beistand m -[e]s help. **b~stehen†** vi sep (haben) **jdm b~stehen** help s.o.

beistimmen vi sep (haben) agree

Beistrich m comma

Beitrag m -[e]s,-e contribution; (Mitglieds-) subscription; (Versicherungs-) premium; (Zeitungs-) article. **b~en†** vt/i sep (haben) contribute

beitreten† vi sep (sein) (+ dat) join. **B~tritt** m joining

Beize f -,-n (Holz-) stain

beizeiten adv in good time

beizen vt stain (Holz)

bejahen vt answer in the affirmative; (billigen) approve of

bejahrt adj aged, old

bekämpf|en vt fight. **B~ung** f fight (gegen against)

bekannt adj well-known; (vertraut) familiar; **jdn b~ machen** introduce s.o.; **etw b~ machen od geben** announce sth; **b~ werden** become known. **B~e(r)** m/f acquaintance; (Freund) friend. **B~gabe** f announcement. **b~lich** adv as is well known. **B~machung** f -,-en announcement; (Anschlag) notice. **B~schaft** f - acquaintance; (Leute) acquaintances pl; (Freunde) friends pl

bekehr|en vt convert. **B~ung** f -,-en conversion

bekenn|en† vt confess, profess (Glauben); **sich [für] schuldig b~en** admit one's guilt. **B~tnis** nt -ses,-se confession; (Konfession) denomination

beklag|en vt lament; (bedauern) deplore; **sich b~en** complain. **b~enswert** adj unfortunate.

B∼te(r) *m/f* (*Jur*) defendant
bekleid|en *vt* hold (*Amt*). **B∼ung**
f clothing

Beklemmung *f* -,-en feeling of
oppression

bekommen† *vt* get; have (*Baby*);
catch (*Erkältung*) ● *vi* (*sein*) jdm gut
b∼ do s.o. good; (*Essen:*) agree
with s.o.

beköstig|en *vt* feed. **B∼ung** *f* -
board; (*Essen*) food

bekräftigen *vt* reaffirm

bekreuzigen (**sich**) *vr* cross
oneself

bekümmert *adj* troubled; (*besorgt*) worried

bekunden *vt* show

Belag *m* -[e]s,-e coating; (*Fußbo-
den-*) covering; (*Brot-*) topping;
(*Zahn-*) tartar; (*Brems-*) lining

belager|n *vt* besiege. **B∼ung** *f*
-,-en siege

Belang *m* von B∼ of importance;
B∼e *pl* interests. b∼los *adj* irrelevant; (*unwichtig*) trivial

belassen† *vt* leave; es dabei b∼
leave it at that

belasten *vt* load; (*fig*) burden; (*beanspruchen*) put a strain on; (*Comm*)
debit; (*Jur*) incriminate

belästigen *vt* bother; (*bedrängen*)
pester; (*unsittlich*) molest

Belastung *f* -,-en load; (*fig*)
strain; (*Comm*) debit. **B∼smaterial**
nt incriminating evidence.
B∼szeuge *m* prosecution witness

belaufen† (**sich**) *vr* amount (auf +
acc to)

belauschen *vt* eavesdrop on

beleb|en *vt* (*fig*) revive; (*lebhaft
machen*) enliven. **b∼t** *adj* lively;
(*Straße*) busy

Beleg *m* -[e]s,-e evidence; (*Beispiel*)
instance (für of); (*Quittung*) receipt.

b∼en *vt* cover/(*garnieren*) garnish
(mit with); (*besetzen*) reserve; (*Univ*)
enrol for; (*nachweisen*) provide evidence for; den ersten Platz b∼en
(*Sport*) take first place. **B∼schaft** *f*
-,-en workforce. **b∼t** *adj* occupied;
(*Zunge*) coated; (*Stimme*) husky;
b∼te Brote open sandwiches

belehren *vt* instruct

beleidig|en *vt* offend; (*absichtlich*)
insult. **B∼ung** *f* -,-en insult

belesen *adj* well-read

beleucht|en *vt* light; (*anleuchten*)
illuminate. **B∼ung** *f* -,-en illu-
mination

Belg|ien /-ĭən/ *nt* -s Belgium.
B∼ier(in) *m* -s,- (*f* -,-nen) Belgian.
b∼isch *adj* Belgian

belicht|en *vt* (*Phot*) expose.
B∼ung *f* - exposure

Belieb|en *nt* -s nach B∼en [just]
as one likes. **b∼ig** *adj* eine b∼ige
Zahl any number you like ● *adv*
b∼ig oft as often as one likes. **b∼t**
adj popular

bellen *vi* (*haben*) bark

belohn|en *vt* reward. **B∼ung** *f*
-,-en reward

belustig|en *vt* amuse. **B∼ung** *f*
-,-en amusement

bemalen *vt* paint

bemängeln *vt* criticize

bemannt *adj* manned

bemerk|bar *adj* sich b∼bar ma-
chen attract attention. **b∼en** *vt* notice; (*äußern*) remark. **b∼enswert**
adj remarkable. **B∼ung** *f* -,-en
remark

bemitleiden *vt* pity

bemüh|en *vt* trouble; sich b∼en
try (zu to; um etw to get sth); (*sich
kümmern*) attend (um to); b∼t sein
endeavour (zu to). **B∼ung** *f* -,-en
effort

benachbart *adj* neighbouring

benachrichtig|en vt inform; (amtlich) notify. B~ung f -,-en notification

benachteiligen vt discriminate against; (ungerecht sein) treat unfairly

benehmen† (sich) vr behave. B~ nt -s behaviour

beneiden vt envy (um etw sth)

Bengel m -s,- boy; (Rüpel) lout

benötigen vt need

benutz|en, (SGer) **benütz|en** vt use; take (Bahn) B~ung f use

Benzin nt -s petrol

beobacht|en vt observe. B~er m -s,- observer. B~ung f -,-en observation

bequem adj comfortable; (mühelos) easy; (faul) lazy. b~en (sich) vr deign (zu to). B~lichkeit f -,-en comfort; (Faulheit) laziness

berat|en† vt advise; (überlegen) discuss; sich b~en confer ● vi (haben) discuss (über etw acc sth); (beratschlagen) confer. B~er(in) m -s,- (f -,-nen) adviser. B~ung f -,-en guidance; (Rat) advice; (Besprechung) discussion; (Med, Jur) consultation

berechn|en vt calculate; (anrechnen) charge for; (abfordern) charge. B~ung f calculation

berechtig|en vt entitle; (befugen) authorize; (fig) justify. b~t adj justified, justifiable. B~ung f -,-en authorization; (Recht) right; (Rechtmäßigkeit) justification

bered|en vt talk about; sich b~en talk. B~samkeit f - eloquence

beredt adj eloquent

Bereich m -[e]s,-e area; (fig) realm; (Fach-) field

bereichern vt enrich

bereit adj ready. b~en vt prepare;

(verursachen) cause; give (Überraschung). b~halten† vt sep have/(ständig) keep ready. b~legen vt sep put out [ready]. b~machen vt sep get ready. b~s adv already

Bereitschaft f -,-en readiness; (Einheit) squad. B~sdienst m B~sdienst haben (Mil) be on stand-by; (Arzt:) be on call. B~spolizei f riot police

bereit|stehen† vi sep (haben) be ready. b~stellen vt sep put out ready; (verfügbar machen) make available. B~ung f - preparation. b~willig adj willing

bereuen vt regret

Berg m -[e]s,-e mountain; (Anhöhe) hill; in den B~en in the mountains. B~ab adv downhill. B~arbeiter m miner. b~auf adv uphill. B~bau m -[e]s mining

bergen† vt recover; (Naut) salvage; (retten) rescue

Berg|führer m mountain guide. b~ig adj mountainous. B~kette f mountain range. B~mann m (pl -leute) miner. B~steiger(in) m -s,- (f -,-nen) mountaineer, climber

Bergung f - recovery; (Naut) salvage; (Rettung) rescue

Berg|wacht f mountain rescue service. B~werk nt mine

Bericht m -[e]s,-e report; (Reise-) account. b~en vt/i (haben) report; (erzählen) tell (von of). B~erstatter(in) m -s,- (f -,-nen) reporter

berichtigen vt correct

beriesel|n vt irrigate. B~ungsanlage f sprinkler system

Berlin nt -s Berlin. B~er m -s,- Berliner

Bernhardiner m -s,- St Bernard

Bernstein m amber

berüchtigt adj notorious

berücksichtig|en vt take into

consideration. B~ung f - consideration

Beruf m profession; (*Tätigkeit*) occupation; (*Handwerk*) trade. b~en† vt appoint; sich b~en refer (auf + acc to); (*vorgeben*) plead (auf etw acc sth). • adj competent; b~en sein be destined (zu to). b~lich adj professional; (*Ausbildung*) vocational • adv professionally; b~lich tätig sein work, have a job. B~sberatung f vocational guidance. B~sausbildung f professional training. b~smäßig adv professionally. B~sschule f vocational school. B~ssoldat m regular soldier. b~stätig adj working; b~stätig sein work, have a job. B~stätige(r) m/f working man/woman. B~ung f -,-en appointment; (*Bestimmung*) vocation; (*Jur*) appeal; B~ung einlegen appeal. B~ungsgericht nt appeal court

beruhen vi (haben) be based (auf + dat on)

beruhig|en vt calm [down]; (*zuversichtlich machen*) reassure. b~end adj calming; (*tröstend*) reassuring; (*Med*) sedative. B~ung f - calming; reassurance; (*Med*) sedation. B~ungsmittel nt sedative; (*bei Psychosen*) tranquillizer

berühmt adj famous. B~heit f -,-en fame; (*Person*) celebrity

berühr|en vt touch; (*erwähnen*) touch on. B~ung f -,-en touch; (*Kontakt*) contact

besänftigen vt soothe

Besatz m -es,¨e trimming

Besatzung f -,-en crew; (*Mil*) occupying force

beschädig|en vt damage. B~ung f -,-en damage

beschaffen vt obtain, get • adj so b~ sein, dass be such that. B~heit f - consistency

beschäftig|en vt occupy; (*Arbeitgeber:*) employ; sich b~en occupy oneself. b~t adj busy; (*angestellt*) employed (bei at). B~ung f -,-en occupation; (*Anstellung*) employment

beschämt adj ashamed; (*verlegen*) embarrassed

beschatten vt shade; (*überwachen*) shadow

Bescheid m -[e]s information; jdm B~ sagen od geben let s.o. know; B~ wissen know

bescheiden adj modest. B~heit f - modesty

bescheinen† vt shine on; von der Sonne beschienen sunlit

bescheinig|en vt certify. B~ung f -,-en (*written*) confirmation; (*Schein*) certificate

beschenken vt give a present/presents to

Bescherung f -,-en distribution of Christmas presents

beschildern vt signpost

beschimpf|en vt abuse, swear at. B~ung f -,-en abuse

beschirmen vt protect

Beschlag m in B~ nehmen monopolize. b~en† vt shoe • vi (sein) steam or mist up • adj steamed or misted up. B~nahme f -,-n confiscation; (*Jur*) seizure. b~nahmen vt confiscate; (*Jur*) seize

beschleunig|en vt hasten; (*schneller machen*) speed up (*Schritt*) • vi (haben) accelerate. B~ung f - acceleration

beschließen† vt decide; (*beenden*) end • vi (haben) decide (über + acc about)

Beschluss m decision

beschmutzen vt make dirty

beschneid|en† vt trim; (*Horticulture*) prune; (*Relig*) circumcise.

B~ung f - circumcision

beschnüffeln vt sniff at

beschönigen vt (fig) gloss over

beschränken vt limit, restrict; sich b~ auf (+ acc) confine oneself to

beschrankt adj (Bahnübergang) with barrier[s]

beschränk|t adj limited; (geistig) dull-witted. B~ung f -,-en limitation, restriction

beschreib|en† vt describe. B~ung f -,-en description

beschuldig|en vt accuse. B~ung f -,-en accusation

beschummeln vt 🗊 cheat

Beschuss m (Mil) fire; (Artillerie-) shelling

beschütz|en vt protect. B~er m -s,- protector

Beschwer|de f -,-n complaint; B~den (Med) trouble sg. b~en vt weight down; sich b~en complain. b~lich adj difficult

beschwindeln vt cheat (um out of); (belügen) lie to

beschwipst adj 🗊 tipsy

beseitig|en vt remove. B~ung f - removal

Besen m -s,- broom

ℹ️ **Besenwirtschaft** An inn set up by a local winegrower for a few weeks after the new wine has been made. An inflated pig's bladder is hung up outside the door to show that the new vintage may be sampled there. This is mainly found in Southern Germany. ▷**HEURIGE.**

---

besessen adj obsessed (von by)

besetz|en vt occupy; fill (Posten); (Theat) cast (Rolle); (verzieren) trim (mit with). b~t adj occupied; (Toi-lette, Leitung) engaged; (Zug, Bus) full up; der Platz ist b~t this seat is taken. B~zeichen nt engaged tone. B~ung f -,-en occupation; (Theat) cast

besichtig|en vt look round (Stadt); (prüfen) inspect; (besuchen) visit. B~ung f -,-en visit; (Prüfung) inspection; (Stadt-) sightseeing

besiedelt adj dünn/dicht b~ sparsely/densely populated

besiegen vt defeat

besinn|en† (sich) vr think, reflect; (sich erinnern) remember (auf jdn/ etw someone/something). B~ung f - reflection; (Bewusstsein) consciousness; bei/ohne B~ung conscious/unconscious. b~ungslos adj unconscious

Besitz m possession; (Eigentum, Land-) property; (Gut) estate. b~en† vt own, possess; (haben) have. B~er(in) m -s,- (f -,-nen) owner; (Comm) proprietor

besoffen adj 🗷 drunken; b~ sein be drunk

besonder|e(r,s) adj special; (bestimmt) particular; (gesondert) separate. b~s adv [e]specially, particularly; (gesondert) separately

besonnen adj calm

besorg|en vt get; (kaufen) buy; (erledigen) attend to; (versorgen) look after. b~t adj worried/(bedacht) concerned (um about). B~ung f -,-en errand; B~ungen machen do shopping

bespitzeln vt spy on

besprech|en† vt discuss; (rezensieren) review. B~ung f -,-en discussion; review; (Konferenz) meeting

besser adj & adv better. b~n vt improve; sich b~n get better. B~ung f - improvement; gute B~ung! get well soon!

Bestand m -[e]s, ⸚e existence; (Vorrat) stock (an + dat of)

beständig adj constant; (Wetter) settled; b~ gegen resistant to

Bestand|saufnahme f stocktaking. **B~teil** m part

bestätig|en vt confirm; acknowledge (Empfang); sich b~en prove to be true. **B~ung** f -,-en confirmation

bestatt|en vt bury. **B~ung** f -,-en funeral

Bestäubung f - pollination

bestaunen vt gaze at in amazement; (bewundern) admire

best|e(r,s) adj best; b~en Dank! many thanks! **B~e(r,s)** m/f/nt best; sein B~es tun do one's best

bestech|en† vt bribe; (bezaubern) captivate. **b~end** adj captivating. **b~lich** adj corruptible. **B~ung** f - bribery. **B~ungsgeld** nt bribe

Besteck nt -[e]s,-e [set of] knife, fork and spoon; (coll) cutlery

bestehen† vi (Probe) exist; (fortdauern) last; (bei Prüfung) pass; ~ aus consist/(gemacht sein) be made of; ~ auf (+ dat) insist on ● vt pass (Prüfung)

besteigen† vt climb; (aufsteigen) mount; ascend (Thron). **B~ung** f ascent

bestell|en vt order; (vor-) book; (ernennen) appoint; (bebauen) cultivate; (ausrichten) tell; zu sich b~en send for; b~t sein have an appointment; kann ich etwas b~en? can I take a message? **B~schein** m order form. **B~ung** f order; (Botschaft) message; (Bebauung) cultivation

besteuer|n vt tax. **B~ung** f - taxation

Bestie /ˈbɛstjə/ f -,-n beast

bestimm|en vt fix; (entscheiden)

decide; (vorsehen) intend; (ernennen) appoint; (ermitteln) determine; (definieren) define; (Gram) qualify ● vi (haben) be in charge (über + acc of). ~t adj definite; (gewiss) certain; (fest) firm. **B~ung** f fixing; (Vorschrift) regulation; (Ermittlung) determination; (Definition) definition; (Zweck) purpose; (Schicksal) destiny. **B~ungsort** m destination

Bestleistung f (Sport) record

bestrafen vt punish. **B~ung** f -,-en punishment

Bestrahlung f radiotherapy

Bestreb|en nt -s endeavour; (Absicht) aim. **B~ung** f -,-en effort

bestreiten† vt dispute; (leugnen) deny; (bezahlen) pay for

bestürz|t adj dismayed; (erschüttert) stunned. **B~ung** f - dismay, consternation

Bestzeit f (Sport) record [time]

Besuch m -[e]s,-e visit; (kurz) call; (Schul-) attendance; (Gast) visitor; (Gäste) visitors pl; **B~ haben** have a visitor/visitors; **bei jdm zu od auf B~ sein** be staying with s.o. **~en** vt visit; (kurz) call on; (teilnehmen) attend; go to (Schule, Ausstellung). **B~er(in)** m -s,- (f -,-nen) visitor; caller. **B~szeit** f visiting hours pl

betagt adj aged, old

betätig|en vt operate; sich b~en work (als as). **B~ung** f -,-en operation; (Tätigkeit) activity

betäub|en vt stun; (Lärm:) deafen; (Med) anaesthetize; (lindern) ease; deaden (Schmerz); **wie b~t** dazed. **B~ung** f - daze; (Med) anaesthesia. **B~ungsmittel** nt anaesthetic

Bete f -,-n Rote B~ beetroot

beteilig|en vt give a share to; sich b~en take part (an + dat in); (beitragen) contribute (an + dat to). **b~t** adj b~t sein take part/(an Un-

fall) be involved/(*Comm*) have a share (**an** + *dat* in); **alle B~ten** all those involved. **B~ung** *f* -,-en participation; involvement; (*Anteil*) share

beten *vi* (*haben*) pray

Beton /be'tɔŋ/ *m* -s concrete

betonen *vt* stressed, emphasize

beton|t *adj* stressed; (*fig*) pointed. **B~ung** *f* -,-en stress

Betracht *m* **in B~ ziehen** consider; **außer B~ lassen** disregard; **nicht in B~ kommen** be out of the question. **b~en†** *vt* look at; (*fig*) regard (**als** as)

beträchtlich *adj* considerable

Betrachtung *f* -,-en contemplation; (*Überlegung*) reflection

Betrag *m* -[e]s,ᵉe amount. **b~en†** *vt* amount to; **sich b~en** behave. **B~en** *nt* -s behaviour; (*Sch*) conduct

betreff|en† *vt* affect; (*angehen*) concern. **b~end** *adj* relevant. **b~s** *prep* (+ *gen*) concerning

betreiben† *vt* (*leiten*) run; (*ausüben*) carry on

betreten† *vt* step on; (*eintreten*) enter; 'B~ verboten' 'no entry'; (*bei Rasen*) 'keep off [the grass]'

betreuen *vt* look after. **B~er(in)** *m* -s,- (*f* -,-nen) helper; (*Kranken-*) nurse. **B~ung** *f* - care

Betrieb *m* business; (*Firma*) firm; (*Treiben*) activity; (*Verkehr*) traffic; **außer B~** not in use; (*defekt*) out of order

Betriebs|anleitung, B~anweisung *f* operating instructions *pl*. **B~ferien** *pl* firm's holiday. **B~leitung** *f* management. **B~rat** *m* works committee. **B~störung** *f* breakdown

betrinken† (sich) *vr* get drunk

betroffen *adj* disconcerted; **b~**

sein be affected (**von** by)

betrüb|en *vt* sadden. **b~t** *adj* sad

Betrug *m* -[e]s deception; (*Jur*) fraud

betrüg|en† *vt* cheat, swindle; (*Jur*) defraud; (*in der Ehe*) be unfaithful to. **B~er(in)** *m* -s,- (*f* -,-nen) swindler. **B~erei** *f* -,-en fraud

betrunken *adj* drunken; **b~ sein** be drunk. **B~e(r)** *m* drunk

Bett *nt* -[e]s,-en bed. **B~couch** *f* sofa-bed. **B~decke** *f* blanket; (*Tages-*) bedspread

Bettel|ei *f* - begging. **b~n** *vi* (*haben*) beg

Bettler(in) *m* -s,- (*f* -,-nen) beggar

Bettpfanne *f* bedpan

Betttuch (Bettuch) *nt* sheet

Bett|wäsche *f* bed linen. **B~zeug** *nt* bedding

betupfen *vt* dab (**mit** with)

beug|en *vt* bend; (*Gram*) decline; conjugate (*Verb*); **sich b~en** bend; (*lehnen*) lean; (*sich fügen*) submit (**dat** to). **B~ung** *f* -,-en (*Gram*) declension; conjugation

Beule *f* -,-n bump; (*Delle*) dent

beunruhig|en *vt* worry; **sich b~en** worry. **B~ung** *f* - worry

beurlauben *vt* give leave to

beurteil|en *vt* judge. **B~ung** *f* -,-en judgement; (*Ansicht*) opinion

Beute *f* - booty, haul; (*Jagd-*) bag; (*eines Raubtiers*) prey

Beutel *m* -s,- bag; (*Tabak- & Zool*) pouch. **B~tier** *nt* marsupial

Bevölkerung *f* -,-en population

bevollmächtigen *vt* authorize

bevor *conj* before; **b~ nicht** not until

bevormunden *vt* treat like a child

bevorstehen† *vi sep* (*haben*) approach; (*unmittelbar*) be imminent.

b~d adj approaching, forthcoming; unmittelbar b~d imminent

bevorzug|en vt prefer; (begünstigen) favour. **b~t** adj privileged; (Behandlung) preferential

bewachen vt guard

Bewachung f- guard; unter B~ under guard

bewaffn|en vt arm. **b~et** adj armed. **B~ung** f- armament; (Waffen) arms pl

bewahren vt protect (vor + dat from); (behalten) keep; die Ruhe b~ keep calm

bewähren (sich) vr prove one's/(Ding:) its worth; (erfolgreich sein) prove a success

bewähr|t adj reliable; (erprobt) proven. **B~ung** f- (Jur) probation. **B~ungsfrist** f [period of] probation. **B~ungsprobe** f (fig) test

bewältigen vt cope with; (überwinden) overcome

bewässer|n vt irrigate. **B~ung** f- irrigation

bewegen¹ vt (reg) move; sich b~ move; (körperlich) take exercise

bewegen²† vt jdn dazu b~, etw zu tun induce s.o. to do sth

Beweg|grund m motive. **b~lich** adj movable, mobile; (wendig) agile. **B~lichkeit** f- mobility; agility. **B~ung** f-,-en movement; (Phys) motion; (Rührung) emotion; (Gruppe) movement; körperliche B~ung physical exercise. **b~ungslos** adj motionless

Beweis m -es,-e proof; (Zeichen) token; B~e evidence sg. **b~en**† vt prove; (zeigen) show; sich b~en prove oneself/(Ding:) itself. **B~material** nt evidence

bewerb|en† (sich) vr apply (um for; bei to). **B~er(in)** m -s,- (f -,-nen) applicant. **B~ung** f-,-en application

bewerten vt value; (einschätzen) rate; (Sch) mark, grade

bewilligen vt grant

bewirken vt cause; (herbeiführen) bring about

bewirt|en vt entertain. **B~ung** f - hospitality

bewohn|bar adj habitable. **b~en** vt inhabit, live in. **B~er(in)** m -s,- (f-,-nen) resident, occupant; (Einwohner) inhabitant

bewölk|en (sich) vr cloud over; **b~t** cloudy. **B~ung** f- clouds pl

bewunder|n vt admire. **b~nswert** adj admirable. **B~ung** f - admiration

bewusst adj conscious (gen of); (absichtlich) deliberate. **b~los** adj unconscious. **B~losigkeit** f- unconsciousness. **B~sein** nt -s consciousness; (Gewissheit) awareness; bei **b~sein** conscious

bezahl|en vt/i (haben) pay; pay for (Ware, Essen). **B~ung** f- payment; (Lohn) pay. **B~fernsehen** nt pay television; pay TV

bezaubern vt enchant

bezeichn|en vt mark; (bedeuten) denote; (beschreiben, nennen) describe (als as). **b~end** adj typical. **B~ung** f marking; (Beschreibung) description (als as); (Ausdruck) term; (Name) name

bezeugen vt testify to

bezichtigen vt accuse (gen of)

bezieh|en† vt cover; (einziehen) move into; (beschaffen) obtain; (erhalten) get; (in Verbindung bringen) relate (auf + acc to); sich b~en (bewölken) cloud over; sich b~en auf (+ acc) refer to; das Bett frisch b~en put clean sheets on the bed. **B~ung** f-,-en relation; (Verhältnis) relationship; (Bezug) respect; B~un-

gen haben have connections.
b~ungsweise adv respectively;
(vielmehr) or rather

Bezirk m -[e]s,-e district

Bezug m cover; (Kissen-) case; (Be-schaffung) obtaining; (Kauf) purchase; (Zusammenhang) reference;
B~e pl earnings; **B~** nehmen refer (auf + acc to); in **B~** auf (+ acc) regarding

bezüglich prep (+ gen) regarding
● adj relating (auf + acc to)

bezwecken vt (fig) aim at

bezweifeln vt doubt

BH /beːˈhaː/ m -[s],-[s] bra

Bibel f -,-n Bible

Biber m -s,- beaver

Biblio|thek f -,-en library.
B~thekar(in) m -s,- (f -,-nen) librarian

biblisch adj biblical

bieg|en† vt bend; sich b~en bend
● vi (sein) curve (nach to); um die Ecke b~en turn the corner.
b~sam adj flexible, supple. **B~ung** f -,-en bend

Biene f -,-n bee. **B~nstock** m beehive. **B~nwabe** f honey-comb

Bier nt -s,-e beer. **B~deckel** m beer-mat. **B~krug** m beer-mug

bieten† vt offer; (bei Auktion) bid

Bifokalbrille f bifocals pl

Bigamie f - bigamy

bigott adj over-pious

Bikini m -s,-s bikini

Bilanz f -,-en balance sheet; (fig) result; die **B~** ziehen (fig) draw conclusions (aus from)

Bild nt -[e]s,-er picture; (Theat) scene

bilden vt form; (sein) be; (erziehen) educate

Bild|erbuch nt picture-book.
B~fläche f screen. **B~hauer** m -s,- sculptor. **B~lich** adj pictorial; (figurativ) figurative. **B~nis** nt -ses,-se portrait. **B~punkt** m pixel.
B~schirm m (TV) screen.
B~schirmgerät nt visual display unit, VDU. **b~schön** adj very beautiful

Bildung f - formation; (Erziehung) education; (Kultur) culture

Billard /ˈbɪljart/ nt -s billiards sg.
B~tisch m billiard table

Billett /bɪlˈjɛt/ nt -[e]s-e & -s ticket

Billiarde f -,-n thousand million million

billig adj cheap; (dürftig) poor; recht und **b~** right and proper.
b~en vt approve. **B~flieger** m low-cost airline. **B~ung** f - approval

Billion /bɪlˈjoːn/ f -,-en million million, billion

Bimsstein m pumice stone

Binde f -,-n band; (Verband) bandage; (Damen-) sanitary towel.
B~hautentzündung f conjunctiv-

b

itis. b∼n† *vt* tie (an + *acc* to); make
(Strauß) bind (Buch); (*fesseln*) tie
up; (Culin) thicken; sich b∼n commit oneself. B∼**strich** *m* hyphen.
B∼**wort** *nt* (*pl* -wörter) (Gram)
conjunction

Bind|faden *m* string. B∼**ung** *f*
-,-en (*fig*) tie; (Beziehung) relationship; (Verpflichtung) commitment;
(Ski-) binding; (Textiles) weave

binnen *prep* (+ *dat*) within.
B∼**handel** *m* home trade

Bio- *prefix* organic

Bio|chemie *f* biochemistry.
b∼**dynamisch** *m* organic. B∼**gra-
phie**, B∼**grafie** *f* -,-n biography

Bio|hof *m* organic farm. B∼**laden**
m health-food store

Biokraftstoff *m* biofuel

Biolog|e *m* -n,-n biologist. B∼**ie** *f*
- biology. b∼**isch** *adj* biological;
b∼ischer Anbau organic farming;
b∼isch angebaut organically
grown

Bioterrorismus *m* bioterrorism

Birke *f* -,-n birch [tree]

Birma *nt* -s Burma. b∼**anisch** *adj*
Burmese

Birn|baum *m* pear-tree. B∼**e** *f*
-,-n pear; (Electr) bulb

bis *prep* (+ *acc*) as far as, [up] to;
(zeitlich) until, till; (spätestens) by;
bis zu up to; bis auf (+ *acc*) (einschließlich) [down] to; (ausgenommen) except [for]; drei bis vier Minuten three to four minutes; bis
morgen! see you tomorrow!
● *conj* until

Bischof *m* -s,ᵉe bishop

bisher *adv* so far, up to now

Biskuit|rolle /bɪsˈkviːt-/ *f* Swiss
roll. B∼**teig** *m* sponge mixture

Biss *m* -es,-e bite

bisschen *inv pron* ein b∼ a bit, a
little; kein b∼ not a bit

Biss|en *m* -s,- bite, mouthful.
b∼**ig** *adj* vicious; (*fig*) caustic

bisweilen *adv* from time to time

bitt|e *adv* please; (nach Klopfen)
come in; (als Antwort auf 'danke')
don't mention it, you're welcome;
wie b∼e? pardon? B∼**e** *f* -,-n re-
quest/(dringend) plea (um for).
b∼**en** *vt/i* (haben) ask/(dringend)
beg (um for); (einladen) invite, ask.
b∼**end** *adj* pleading

bitter *adj* bitter. B∼**keit** *f* - bitter-
ness. b∼**lich** *adv* bitterly

Bittschrift *f* petition

bizarr *adj* bizarre

bläh|en *vt* swell; (Vorhang, Segel:)
billow ● *vi* (haben) cause flatulence.
B∼**ungen** *fpl* flatulence *sg*, Ⓣ
wind *sg*

Blamage /blaˈmaːʒə/ *f* -,-n humili-
ation; (Schande) disgrace

blamieren *vt* disgrace; sich b∼
disgrace oneself; (sich lächerlich machen) make a fool of oneself

blanchieren /blãˈʃiːrən/ *vt* (Culin)
blanch

blank *adj* shiny. B∼**oscheck** *m*
blank cheque

Blase *f* -,-n bubble; (Med) blister;
(Anat) bladder. b∼n† *vt/i* (haben)
blow; play (Flöte). B∼**nentzündung**
f cystitis

Blas|instrument *nt* wind instru-
ment. B∼**kapelle** *f* brass band

blass *adj* pale; (schwach) faint

Blässe *f* - pallor

Blatt *nt* -[e]s,ᵉer (Bot) leaf; (Papier)
sheet; (Zeitung) paper

Blattlaus *f* greenfly

blau *adj*, B∼ *nt* -s,- blue; b∼er
Fleck bruise; b∼es Auge black eye;
b∼ sein Ⓣ be tight; Fahrt ins B∼e
mystery tour. B∼**beere** *f* bilberry.
B∼**licht** *nt* blue flashing light

Blech *nt* -[e]s,-e sheet metal;
(Weiß-) tin; (Platte) metal sheet;

(Back-) baking sheet; (Mus) brass; (🔟: Unsinn) rubbish. **B~schaden** m (Auto) damage to the bodywork

Blei nt ~[e]s lead

Bleibe f ~ place to stay. **b~n†** vi (sein) remain, stay; (übrig-) be left; ruhig **b~n** keep calm; bei etw **b~n** (fig) stick to sth; **b~n Sie** am Apparat hold the line; etw **b~n lassen** not do sth. **b~nd** adj permanent; (anhaltend) lasting

bleich adj pale. **b~en** vt/i (sein) bleach; (ver-) fade ● vt (reg) bleach. **B~mittel** nt bleach

blei|ern adj leaden. **~frei** adj unleaded. **B~stift** m pencil. **B~stiftabsatz** m stiletto heel. **B~stiftspitzer** m -s,- pencil sharpener

Blende f ~,-n shade, shield; (Sonnen-) [sun] visor; (Phot) diaphragm; (Öffnung) aperture; (an Kleid) facing. **b~n** vt dazzle, blind

Blick m -[e]s,-e look; (kurz) glance; (Äussic) view; auf den ersten **B~** at first sight. **b~en** vi (haben) look/(kurz) glance (auf + acc at). **B~punkt** m (fig) point of view

blind adj blind; (trübe) dull; **b~er** Alarm false alarm; **b~er** Passagier stowaway. **B~darm** m appendix. **B~darmentzündung** f appendicitis. **B~e(r)** m/f blind man/woman; die **B~en** the blind pl. **B~enhund** m guidedog. **B~enschrift** f braille. **B~gänger** m -s,- (Mil) dud. **B~heit** f ~ blindness

blink|en vi (haben) flash; (funkeln) gleam; (Auto) indicate. **B~er** m -s,- (Auto) indicator. **B~licht** nt flashing light

blinzeln vi (haben) blink

Blitz m -es,-e [flash of] lightning; (Phot) flash. **B~ableiter** m lightning-conductor. **b~artig** adj lightning ● adv like lightning. **B~en** vi (haben) flash; (funkeln) sparkle; es

hat geblitzt there was a flash of lightning. **B~eis** nt black ice. **B~licht** nt (Phot) flash. **b~sauber** adj spick and span. **b~schnell** adj lightning ● adv like lightning

Block m -[e]s,ˉe block ● -[e]s,-s & ˉe pad; (Häuser-) block

Blockade f ~,-n blockade

Blockflöte f recorder

blockieren vt block; (Mil) blockade

Blockschrift f block letters pl

blöd[e] adj feeble-minded; (dumm) stupid

Blödsinn m -[e]s idiocy; (Unsinn) nonsense

Blog nt/m blog

blöken vi (haben) bleat

blond adj fair-haired; (Haar) fair

bloß adj bare; (alleinig) mere ● adv only, just

bloß|legen vt sep uncover. **b~stellen** vt sep compromise

Bluff m -s,-s bluff. **b~en** vt/i (haben) bluff

blühen vi (haben) flower; (fig) flourish. **b~d** adj flowering; (fig) flourishing, thriving

Blume f ~,-n flower; (vom Wein) bouquet. **B~nbeet** nt flower-bed. **B~ngeschäft** nt flower-shop, florist's. **B~nkohl** m cauliflower. **B~nmuster** nt floral design. **B~nstrauß** m bunch of flowers. **B~ntopf** m flowerpot; (Pflanze) pot plant. **B~nzwiebel** f bulb

blumig adj flowery

Bluse f ~,-n blouse

Blut nt -[e]s blood. **b~arm** adj anaemic. **B~bahn** f blood-stream. **B~bild** nt blood count. **B~druck** m blood pressure. **b~dürstig** adj bloodthirsty

Blüte f ~,-n flower, bloom; (vom Baum) blossom; (B~zeit) flowering period; (Baum-) blossom time;

(*Höhepunkt*) peak, prime

Blut|egel m -s,- leech. **b~en** vi (*haben*) bleed

Blüten|blatt nt petal. **B~staub** m pollen

Blut|er m -s,- haemophiliac. **B~er-guss** m bruise. **B~gefäß** nt blood-vessel. **B~gruppe** f blood group. **b~ig** adj bloody. **B~körperchen** nt -s,- corpuscle. **B~probe** f blood test. **b~rünstig** adj (fig) bloody, gory. **B~schande** f incest. **B~spender** m blood donor. **B~sturz** m haemorrhage. **B~transfusion,** **B~übertragung** f blood transfusion. **B~ung** f -,-en bleeding; (Med) haemorrhage; (Regel-) period. **b~unterlaufen** adj bruised; (Auge) bloodshot. **B~ver-giftung** f blood-poisoning. **B~wurst** f black pudding

Bö f -,-en gust; (Regen-) squall

Bob m -s,-s bob[-sleigh]

Bock m -[e]s, ⸚e buck; (Ziege) billy goat; (Schaf) ram; (Gestell) support. **b~ig** adj Ⓣ stubborn. **B~sprin-gen** nt leap-frog

Boden m -s,⸚ ground; (Erde) soil; (Fuß-) floor; (Grundfläche) bottom; (Dach-) loft, attic. **B~satz** m sediment. **B~schätze** mpl mineral deposits. **B~see** (der) Lake Constance

Bogen m -s,- & ⸚ curve; (Geometrie) arc; (beim Skilauf) turn; (Architecture) arch; (Waffe, Geigen-) bow; (Papier) sheet; einen großen **B~** um jdn/etw machen Ⓣ give s.o./sth a wide berth. **B~schießen** nt archery

Bohle f -,-n [thick] plank

Böhm|en nt -s Bohemia. **b~isch** adj Bohemian

Bohne f -,-n bean; grüne **B~n** French beans

bohner|n vt polish. **B~wachs** nt

floor-polish

bohr|en vt/i (haben) drill (nach for); drive (Tunnel); sink (Brunnen); (Insekt:) bore. **B~er** m -s,- drill. **B~insel** f [offshore] drilling rig. **B~turm** m derrick

Boje f -,-n buoy

Böllerschuss m gun salute

Bolzen m -s,- bolt; (Stift) pin

bombardieren vt bomb; (fig) bombard (mit with)

Bombe f -,-n bomb. **B~nangriff** m bombing raid. **B~nerfolg** m huge success

Bon /bɔŋ/ m -s,-s voucher; (Kassen-) receipt

Bonbon /bɔŋˈbɔŋ/ m & nt -s,-s sweet

Bonus m -[ses],-[se] bonus

Boot nt -[e]s,-e boat. **B~ssteg** m landing-stage

Bord[1] nt -[e]s,-e shelf

Bord[2] m (Naut) an **B~** aboard, on board; über **B~** overboard. **B~buch** nt log[-book]

Bordell nt -s,-e brothel

Bordkarte f boarding-pass

borgen vt borrow; jdm etw **b~** lend s.o. sth

Borke f -,-n bark

Börse f -,-n purse; (Comm) stock exchange. **B~nmakler** m stockbroker

Borst|e f -,-n bristle. **b~ig** adj bristly

Borte f -,-n braid

Böschung f -,-en embankment

böse adj wicked, evil; (unartig) naughty; (schlimm) bad; (zornig) cross; jdm od auf jdn **b~** sein be cross with s.o.

bos|haft adj malicious, spiteful. **B~heit** f -,-en malice; spite; (Handlung) spiteful act/(Bemerkung) remark

böswillig adj malicious

Botani|k f - botany. **B~ker(in)** m -s,- (f -,-nen) botanist

Bot|e m -n,-n messenger. **B~engang** m errand. **B~schaft** f -,-en message; (Pol) embassy. **B~schafter** m -s,- ambassador

Bouillon /'bʊljɔŋ/ f -,-s clear soup. **B~würfel** m stock cube

Bowle /'boːlə/ f -,-n punch

Box f -,-en box; (Pferde-) loose box; (Lautsprecher-) speaker; (Autorennen) pit

box|en vi (haben) box ● vt punch. **B~en** nt -s boxing. **B~enluder** nt pit babe. **B~er** m -s,- boxer. **B~stopp** m pit stop

brachliegen† vi sep (haben) lie fallow

Branche /'brãːʃə/ f -,-n [line of] business. **B~nverzeichnis** nt (Teleph) classified directory

Brand m -[e]s,ˇe fire; (Med) gangrene; (Bot) blight; in B~ geraten catch fire; in B~ setzen od stecken set on fire. **B~bombe** f incendiary bomb

Brand|stifter m arsonist. **B~stiftung** f arson

Brandung f - surf

Brand|wunde f burn. **B~zeichen** nt brand

Branntwein m spirit; (coll) spirits pl. **B~brennerei** f distillery

brasilianisch adj Brazilian. **B~ilien** nt -s Brazil

Brat|apfel m baked apple. **b~en**† vt/i (haben) roast; (in der Pfanne) fry. **B~en** m -s,- roast; (B~stück) joint. **b~fertig** adj oven-ready. **B~hähnchen** nt roasting chicken. **B~kartoffeln** fpl fried potatoes. **B~pfanne** f frying-pan

Bratsche f -,-n (Mus) viola

Bratspieß m spit

Brauch m -[e]s,Bräuche custom. **b~bar** adj usable; (nützlich) useful. **b~en** vt need; (ge-, verbrauchen) use; take (Zeit); er b~t es nur zu sagen he only has to say

Braue f -,-n eyebrow

brau|en vt brew. **B~er** m -s,- brewer. **B~erei** f -,-en brewery

braun adj, **B~** nt -s,- brown; b~ werden (Person:) get a tan; b~ [gebrannt] sein be [sun-]tanned

Bräune f - [sun-]tan. **b~n** vt/i (haben) brown; (in der Sonne) tan

Braunschweig nt -s Brunswick

Brause f -,-n (Dusche) shower; (an Gießkanne) rose; (B~limonade) fizzy drink

Braut f -,ˇe bride; (Verlobte) fiancée

Bräutigam m -s,-e bridegroom; (Verlobter) fiancé

Brautkleid nt wedding dress

Brautpaar nt bridal couple; (Verlobte) engaged couple

brav adj good; (redlich) honest ● adv dutifully; (redlich) honestly

bravo int bravo!

BRD abbr (Bundesrepublik Deutschland) FRG

Brech|eisen nt jemmy; (B~stange) crowbar. **b~en**† vt break; (Phys) refract (Licht); (erbrechen) vomit; sich b~en (Wellen:) break; (Licht:) be refracted; sich (dat) den Arm b~en break one's arm ● vi (sein) break ● vi (haben) vomit, be sick. **B~reiz** m nausea. **B~stange** f crowbar

Brei m -[e]s,-e paste; (Culin) purée; (Hafer-) porridge

breit adj wide; (Schultern, Grinsen) broad. **B~band** nt broadband. **B~e** f -,-n width; breadth; (Geog) latitude. **b~en** vt spread (über + acc over). **B~engrad** m [degree of] latitude. **B~enkreis** m parallel

Bremse¹ f -,-n horsefly

Bremse² f -,-n brake. **b~n** vt
slow down; (fig) restrain ● vi
(haben) brake

Bremslicht nt brake-light

brenn|bar adj combustible; leicht
b~bar highly [in]flammable.
b~en† vi (haben) burn; (Licht:) be
on; (Zigarette:) be alight; (weh tun)
smart, sting ● vt burn; (rösten)
roast; (im Brennofen) fire; (destillieren) distil. **b~end** adj burning; (an-
gezündet) lighted; (fig) fervent.
B~er m -s,- burner. **B~erei** f
-,-en distillery

Brennnessel† f = Brennnessel

Brenn|holz nt firewood. **B~ofen**
m kiln. **B~nessel** f stinging nettle.
B~punkt m (Phys) focus. **B~spiri-
tus** m methylated spirits. **B~stoff**
m fuel. **B~stoffzelle** f fuel cell

Bretagne /bre'tanjə/ (die) -
Brittany

Brett nt -[e]s,-er board; (im Regal)
shelf; schwarzes B~ notice board.
B~spiel nt board game

Brezel f -,-n pretzel

Bridge /brɪtʃ/ nt - (Spiel) bridge

Brief m -[e]s,-e letter. **B~be-
schwerer** m -s,- paperweight.
B~freund(in) m (f) pen-friend.
B~kasten m letter-box. **B~kopf** m
letter-head. **b~lich** adj & adv by
letter. **B~marke** f [postage] stamp.
B~öffner m paper-knife. **B~pa-
pier** nt notepaper. **B~tasche** f wallet. **B~träger** m postman. **B~um-
schlag** m envelope. **B~wahl** f
postal vote. **B~wechsel** m correspondence

Brikett nt -s,-s briquette

Brillant m -en,-en [cut] diamond

Brille f -,-n glasses pl, spectacles pl;
(Schutz-) goggles pl; (Klosett-) toi-

let seat

bringen† vt bring; (fort-) take;
(ein-) yield; (veröffentlichen) publish;
(im Radio) broadcast; show (Film);
ins Bett b~ put to bed; jdn nach
Hause b~ take/(begleiten) see s.o.
home; um etw b~ deprive of sth;
jdn dazu b~, etw zu tun get s.o. to
do sth; es weit b~ (fig) go far

Brise f -,-n breeze

Brit|e m -n,-n, **B~in** f -,-nen
Briton. **b~isch** adj British

Bröck|chen nt -s,- (Culin) crou-
ton. **b~elig** adj crumbly; (Gestein)
friable. **b~eln** vt/i (haben/sein)
crumble

Brocken m -s,- chunk; (Erde,
Kohle) lump

Brokat m -[e]s,-e brocade

Brokkoli pl broccoli sg

Brombeere f blackberry

Bronchitis f - bronchitis

Bronze /'brõːsə/ f -,-n bronze

Brosch|e f -,-n brooch. **b~iert** adj
paperback. **B~üre** f -,-n brochure;
(Heft) booklet

Brösel mpl (Culin) breadcrumbs

Brot nt -[e]s,-e bread; ein B~ a
loaf [of bread]; (Scheibe) a slice
of bread

Brötchen nt -s,- [bread] roll

Brotkrümel m breadcrumb

Bruch m -[e]s,ᵉe break; (Brechen)
breaking; (Rohr-) burst; (Med) fracture; (Eingeweide-) rupture, hernia;
(Math) fraction; (fig) breach; (in Beziehung) break-up

brüchig adj brittle

Bruch|landung f crash-landing.
B~rechnung f fractions pl.
B~stück nt fragment. **B~teil** m
fraction

Brücke f -,-n bridge; (Teppich) rug

Bruder m -s,ᵉ brother

brüderlich adj brotherly, fraternal

Brügge nt -s Bruges

Brüh|e f -,-n broth, stock. B~**würfel** m stock cube

brüllen vt/i (haben) roar

brumm|eln vt/i (haben) mumble. b~**en** vi (haben) (Insekt:) buzz; (Bär:) growl; (Motor:) hum; (murren) grumble. B~**er** m -s,- 🔲 bluebottle. b~**ig** adj 🔲 grumpy

brünett adj dark-haired

Brunnen m -s,- well; (Spring-) fountain; (Heil-) spa water

brüsk adj brusque

Brüssel nt -s Brussels

Brust f -,ːe chest; (weibliche, Culin: B~stück) breast. B~**bein** nt breastbone

brüsten (sich) vr boast

Brust|fellentzündung f pleurisy. B~**schwimmen** nt breaststroke

Brüstung f -,-en parapet

Brustwarze f nipple

Brut f -,-en incubation

brutal adj brutal

brüten vi (haben) sit (on eggs); (fig) ponder (über + dat over)

Brutkasten m (Med) incubator

brutto adv, B~- prefix gross

BSE f - BSE

Bub m -en,-en (SGer) boy. B~**e** m -n,-n (Karte) jack, knave

Buch nt -[e]s,ːer book; B~ führen keep a record (über + acc of); die B~er führen keep the accounts

Buche f -,-n beech

buchen vt book; (Comm) enter

Bücher|ei f -,-en library. B~**regal** nt bookcase, bookshelves pl. B~**schrank** m bookcase

Buchfink m chaffinch

Buch|führung f bookkeeping. B~**halter(in)** m -s,- (f -,-nen) bookkeeper, accountant. B~**hal-**

tung f bookkeeping, accountancy; (Abteilung) accounts department. B~**handlung** f bookshop

Büchse f -,-n box; (Konserven-) tin, can

Buch|stabe m -n,-n letter. b~**stabieren** vt spell [out]. b~**stäblich** adv literally

Bucht f -,-en (Geog) bay

Buchung f -,-en booking, reservation; (Comm) entry

Buckel m -s,- hump; (Beule) bump; (Hügel) hillock

bücken (sich) vr bend down

bucklig adj hunchbacked

Bückling m -s,-e smoked herring

Buddhis|mus m - Buddhism. B~t(in) m -en,-en (f -,-nen) Buddhist. b~**tisch** adj Buddhist

Bude f -,-n hut; (Kiosk) kiosk; (Markt-) stall; (🔲: Zimmer) room

Budget /byˈdʒeː/ nt -s,-s budget

Büfett nt -[e]s,-e sideboard; (Theke) bar; kaltes B~ cold buffet

Büffel m -s,- buffalo

Bügel m -s,- frame; (Kleider-) coathanger; (Steig-) stirrup; (Brillen-) sidepiece. B~**brett** nt ironingboard. B~**eisen** nt iron. B~**falte** f crease. b~**frei** adj non-iron. b~**n** vt/i (haben) iron

Bühne f -,-n stage. B~**nbild** nt set. B~**neingang** m stage door

Buhrufe mpl boos

Bukett nt -[e]s,-e bouquet

Bulgarien /-jən/ nt -s Bulgaria

Bull|auge nt (Naut) porthole. B~**dogge** f bulldog. B~**dozer** m -s,- bulldozer. B~**e** m -n,-n bull; (sl: Polizist) cop

Bummel m -s,- 🔲 stroll. B~**lei** f - 🔲 dawdling

bummel|ig adj 🔲 slow; (nachläs-

sig) careless. **b~n** *vi (sein)* ⓣ stroll
● **vi (haben)** ⓣ dawdle. **B~streik** *m*
go-slow. **B~zug** *m* ⓣ slow train
Bums *m -es,-e* ⓣ bump, thump
Bund¹ *nt -[e]s,-e* bunch
Bund² *m -[e]s,≃e* association;
(Bündnis) alliance; *(Pol)* federation;
(Rock-, Hosen-) waistband; **der B~**
the Federal Government
Bündel *nt -s,-* bundle. **b~n** *vt*
bundle [up]
Bundes|- *prefix* Federal. **B~ge-
nosse** *m* ally. **B~kanzler** *m* Federal
Chancellor. **B~land** *nt* [federal]
state; *(Aust)* province. **B~liga** *f* Ger-
man national league. **B~rat** *m*
Upper House of Parliament. **B~re-
gierung** *f* Federal Government.
B~republik *f* **die B~republik
Deutschland** the Federal Republic
of Germany. **B~tag** *m* Lower House
of Parliament. **B~wehr** *f* [Federal
German] Army

bünd|ig *adj & adv* kurz und b~ig
short and to the point. **B~nis** *nt
-ses,-se* alliance
Bunker *m -s,-* bunker; *(Luftschutz-)*
shelter

bunt *adj* coloured; *(farbenfroh)* col-
ourful; *(grell)* gaudy; *(gemischt)* varied; *(wirr)* confused; **b~e Platte** assorted cold meats. **B~stift** *m*
crayon
Bürde *f -,-n (fig)* burden
Burg *f -,-en* castle
Bürge *m -n,-n* guarantor. **b~n** *vi
(haben)* **b~n für** vouch for; *(fig)*
guarantee
Bürger|(in) *m -s,- (f -,-nen)* citi-
zen. **B~krieg** *m* civil war. **b~lich**
adj (civ) *(Pflicht)* civic; *(mittelstän-
disch)* middle-class. **B~liche(r)** *m/f*
commoner. **B~meister** *m* mayor.
B~rechte *npl* civil rights. **B~steig**
m -[e]s,-e pavement
Bürgschaft *f -,-en* surety
Burgunder *m -s,- (Wein)*
Burgundy
Büro *nt -s,-s* office. **B~angestell-
te(r)** *m/f* office worker. **B~klam-
mer** *f* paper clip. **B~kratie** *f -,-n*
bureaucracy. **b~kratisch** *adj* bur-
eaucratic
Bursche *m -n,-n* lad, youth
Bürste *f -,-n* brush. **b~n** *vt* brush.
B~nschnitt *m* crew cut
Bus *m -ses,-se* bus; *(Reise-)* coach
Busch *m -[e]s,≃e* bush
Büschel *nt -s,-* tuft
buschig *adj* bushy
Busen *m -s,-* bosom
Bussard *m -s,-e* buzzard
Buße *f -,-n* penance; *(Jur)* fine
Bußgeld *nt (Jur)* fine
Büste *f -,-n* bust; *(Schneider-)*
dummy. **B~nhalter** *m -s,-* bra
Butter *f -* butter. **B~blume** *f* but-
tercup. **B~brot** *nt* slice of bread
and butter. **B~milch** *f* buttermilk.
b~n *vt* butter
b.w. *abbr* (bitte wenden) P.T.O.

Cc

ca. *abbr* (circa) about

Café /kaˈfeː/ *nt* -s,-s café

Camcorder /ˈkamkɔrdɐ/ *m* -s, - camcorder

camp|en /ˈkɛmpən/ *vi* (haben) go camping. **C~ing** *nt* -s camping. **C~ingplatz** *m* campsite

Caravan /ˈka(ˌ)ravan/ *m* -s, - (Auto) caravan; (Kombi) estate car

CD /tseːˈdeː/ *f* -,-s compact disc, CD. **CD-ROM** *f* -,-(s) CD-ROM

Cell|ist(in) /tʃɛˈlɪst(ɪn)/ *m* -en,-en (*f* -,-nen) cellist. **C~o** *nt* -,-los & -li cello

Celsius /ˈtsɛlzjʊs/ *inv* Celsius, centigrade

Cent /tsɛnt/ *m* -[s], -[s] cent

Champagner /ʃamˈpanjɐ/ *m* -s champagne

Champignon /ˈʃampɪnjɔn/ *m* -s,-s (field) mushroom

Chance /ˈʃãːs[ə]/ *f* -,-n chance

Chaos /ˈkaːɔs/ *nt* - chaos

Charakter /kaˈrakteɐ/ *m* -s,-e character. **c~isieren** *vt* characterize. **c~istisch** *adj* characteristic (für of)

charm|ant /ʃarˈmant/ *adj* charming. **C~e** *m* -s charm

Charter|flug /ˈtʃ-, ˈʃartɐ-/ *m* charter flight. **c~n** *vt* charter

Chassis /ʃaˈsiː/ *nt* -,- chassis

Chauffeur /ʃɔˈføːɐ/ *m* -s,-e chauffeur; (Taxi-) driver

Chauvinist /ʃoviˈnɪst/ *m* -en,-en chauvinist

Chef /ʃɛf/ *m* -s,-s head; 🔲 boss

Chemie /çeˈmiː/ *f* - chemistry

Chem|iker(in) /ˈçeː-/ *m* -s,- (*f*

-,-nen) chemist. **c~isch** *adj* chemical; **c~ische Reinigung** dry-cleaning; (Geschäft) dry-cleaner's

Chicorée /ˈʃikoreː/ *m* -s chicory

Chiffre /ˈʃifə, ˈʃifrə/ *f* -,-n cipher

Chile /ˈçiːle/ *nt* -s Chile

China /ˈçiːna/ *nt* -s China. **C~ese** *m* -n,-n, **C~esin** *f* -,-nen Chinese. **c~esisch** *adj* Chinese. **C~esisch** *nt* -[s] (Lang) Chinese

Chip /tʃɪp/ *m* -s,-s [micro]chip. **C~s** *pl* crisps

Chirurg /çiˈrʊrk/ *m* -en,-en surgeon. **C~ie** *f* - surgery

Chlor /kloːɐ/ *nt* -s chlorine

Choke /tʃoːk/ *m* -s,-s (Auto) choke

Cholera /ˈkoːlera/ *f* - cholera

cholerisch /koˈleːrɪʃ/ *adj* irascible

Cholesterin /ço-, kolɛsteˈriːn/ *nt* -s cholesterol

Chor /koːɐ/ *m* -[e]s, ⸚e choir

Choreographie, Choreografie /koreograˈfiː/ *f* -,-n choreography

Christ /krɪst/ *m* -en,-en Christian. **C~baum** *m* Christmas tree. **C~entum** *nt* -s Christianity **c~lich** *adj* Christian

Christus /ˈkrɪstʊs/ *m* -ti Christ

Chrom /kroːm/ *nt* -s chromium

Chromosom /kromoˈzoːm/ *nt* -s,-en chromosome

Chronik /ˈkroːnɪk/ *f* -,-en chronicle

chronisch /ˈkroːnɪʃ/ *adj* chronic

Chrysantheme /kryzanˈteːmə/ *f* -,-n chrysanthemum

circa /ˈtsɪrka/ *adv* about

Clique /ˈklɪka/ *f* -,-n clique

Clou /kluː/ *m* -s,-s highlight, 🔲 high spot

Clown /klaʊn/ *m* -s,-s clown

Club /klʊp/ *m* -s,-s club

Co₂-Fußabdruck *m* carbon footprint

Cocktail /ˈkɔkteːl/ *m* -s,-s cocktail

Code /ˈkoːt/ *m* -s,-s code

Comic-Heft /'kɔmɪk-/ nt comic

Computer /kɔm'pjuːtɐ/ m -s,-
computer. c~**isieren** vt computer-
ize. C~**spiel** nt computer game

Conférencier /kõferã'sjeː/ m -s,-
compère

Cord /kɔrt/ m -s, C~**samt** m -s,-
corduroy

Couch /kautʃ/ f -,-s settee

Cousin /ku'zɛ̃/ m -s,-s [male]
cousin. C~e f -,-n [female] cousin

Creme /kreːm/ f -s,-s cream;
(Speise) cream dessert

Curry /'kari, 'kœri/ nt & m -s curry
powder ● nt -s,-s (Gericht) curry

Cursor /'kɛːɐsɐ/ m -s, - cursor

Cyberspace /'sajbɐspeːs/ m -
cyberspace

• •

Dd

• •

da adv there; (hier) here; (zeitlich)
then; (in dem Fall) in that case; von
da an from then on; da sein be
there/(hier) here; (existieren) exist;
wieder da sein be back ● conj
as, since

dabei (emphatic: dabei) adv
nearby; (daran) with it; (eingeschlossen) included; (hinsichtlich) about it;
(während dem) during this; (gleichzeitig) at the same time; (doch) and
yet; dicht d~ close by; d~ sein be
present; (mitmachen) be involved;
d~ sein, etw zu tun be just
doing sth

Dach nt -[e]s, ⸚er roof. D~**boden**
m loft. D~**luke** f skylight.
D~**rinne** f gutter

Dachs m -es,-e badger

Dachsparren m -s,- rafter

Dackel m -s,- dachshund

dadurch (emphatic: dadurch) adv
through it/them; (Ursache) by it;
(deshalb) because of that; d~, dass
because

dafür (emphatic: dafür) adv for
it/them; (anstatt) instead; (als Ausgleich) but [on the other hand];
d~, dass considering that; ich
kann nichts dafür it's not my fault

dagegen (emphatic: dagegen) adv
against it/them; (Mittel, Tausch) for
it; (verglichen damit) by comparison;
(jedoch) however; hast du was
d~? do you mind?

daheim adv at home

daher (emphatic: daher) adv from
there; (deshalb) for that reason; das
kommt d~, weil that's because
● conj that is why

dahin (emphatic: dahin) adv there;
bis d~ up to there; (bis dann)
until/(Zukunft) by then; jdn d~
bringen, dass er etw tut get s.o.
to do sth

dahinten adv back there

dahinter (emphatic: dahinter) adv
behind it/them; d~ kommen (fig)
get to the bottom of it

Dahlie /-jə/ f -,-n dahlia

dalassen† vt sep leave there

daliegen† vi sep (haben) lie there

damalig adj at that time; der
d~e Minister the then minister

damals adv at that time

Damast m -es,-e damask

Dame f -,-n lady; (Karte, Schach)
queen; (D~spiel) draughts sg.
d~**haft** adj ladylike

damit (emphatic: damit) adv with
it/them; (dadurch) by it; hör auf
d~! stop it! ● conj so that

Damm m -[e]s,⸚e dam

dämmerig adj dim. D~**licht** nt
twilight. d~**n** vi (haben) (Morgen:)

dawn; es d~t it is getting light;(abends) dark. D~ung f dawn; (Abend-) dusk

Dämon m -s,-en demon

Dampf m -es, ⸚e steam; (Chemistry) vapour. **d~en** vi (haben) steam

dämpfen vt (Culin) steam; (fig) muffle (Ton); lower (Stimme)

Dampf|er m -s,- steamer. **D~kochtopf** m pressure-cooker. **D~maschine** f steam engine. **D~walze** f steamroller

danach (emphatic: danach) adv after it/them; (suchen) for it/them; (riechen) of it; (später) afterwards; (entsprechend) accordingly; es sieht d~ aus it looks like it

Däne m -n,-n Dane

daneben (emphatic: daneben) adv beside it/them; (außerdem) in addition; (verglichen damit) by comparison

Dän|emark nt -s Denmark. **D~in** f -,-nen Dane. **d~isch** adj Danish

Dank m -es thanks pl; vielen D~! thank you very much! **d~** prep (+ dat or gen) thanks to. **d~bar** adj grateful; (erleichtert) thankful; (lohnend) rewarding. **D~barkeit** f -gratitude. **d~e** adv d~e [schön od sehr]! thank you [very much]! **d~en** vi (haben) thank (jdm s.o.); (ablehnen) decline; nichts zu d~en! don't mention it!

dann adv then; selbst d~, wenn even if

daran (emphatic: daran) adv on it/them; to it/them; (denken) of it; nahe d~ on the point (etw zu tun of doing sth). **d~setzen** vt sep alles d~setzen do one's utmost (zu to)

darauf (emphatic: darauf) adv on it/them; (warten) for it; (antworten) to it; (danach) after that; (d~hin) as

a result. **d~hin** adv as a result

daraus (emphatic: daraus) adv out of or from it/them; er macht sich nichts d~ he doesn't care for it

darlegen vt sep expound; (erklären) explain

Darlehen nt -s,- loan

Darm m -[e]s, ⸚e intestine

darstell|en vt sep represent; (bildlich) portray; (Theat) interpret; (spielen) play; (schildern) describe. **D~er** m -s,- actor. **D~erin** f -,-nen actress. **D~ung** f representation; interpretation; description

darüber (emphatic: darüber) adv over it/them; (höher) above it/them; (sprechen, lachen, sich freuen) about it; (mehr) more; d~ hinaus beyond [it]; (dazu) on top of that

darum (emphatic: darum) adv round it/them; (bitten, kämpfen) for it; (deshalb) that is why; d~, weil because

darunter (emphatic: darunter) adv under it/them; (tiefer) below it/them; (weniger) less; (dazwischen) among them

das def art & pron s. der

dasein* vi sep (sein) = da sein, s. da. **D~** nt -s existence

dass conj that

dasselbe pron s. derselbe

Daten|sichtgerät nt visual display unit, VDU. **D~verarbeitung** f data processing

datieren vt/i (haben) date

Dativ m -s,-e dative. **D~objekt** nt indirect object

Dattel f -,-n date

Datum nt -s,-ten date; Daten dates; (Angaben) data

Dauer f - duration, length; (Jur) term; auf die D~ in the long run. **D~auftrag** m standing order. **d~haft** adj lasting, enduring; (fest) durable. **D~karte** *f* season ticket. **d~n** *vi* (*haben*) last; **lange d~n** take a long time. **d~nd** *adj* lasting; (*ständig*) constant. **D~welle** *f* perm

Daumen *m* -s, -, thumb; **jdm den D~ drücken** *od* **halten** keep one's fingers crossed for s.o.

Daunen *fpl* down *sg*. **D~decke** *f* [down-filled] duvet

davon (*emphatic*: davon) *adv* from it/them; (*dadurch*) by it; (*damit*) with it/them; (*darüber*) about it; (*Menge*) of it/them; **das kommt d~!** it serves you right! **d~kommen†** *vi sep* (*sein*) escape (**mit dem Leben** with one's life). **d~laufen†** *vi sep* (*sein*) run away. **d~machen (sich)** *vr sep* ⊥ make off. **d~tragen†** *vt sep* carry off; (*erleiden*) suffer; (*gewinnen*) win

davor (*emphatic*: davor) *adv* in front of it/them; (*sich fürchten*) of it; (*zeitlich*) before it/them

dazu (*emphatic*: dazu) *adv* to it/them; (*damit*) with it/them; (*dafür*) for it; **noch d~** in addition to that; **jdn d~ bringen, etw zu tun** get s.o. to do sth; **ich kam nicht d~** I didn't get round to [doing] it. **d~kommen†** *vi sep* (*sein*) arrive [on the scene]; (*hinzukommen*) be added. **d~rechnen†** *vt sep* add to it/them

dazwischen (*emphatic*: dazwischen) *adv* between them; in between; (*darunter*) among them. **d~kommen†** *vi sep* (*sein*) (*fig*) crop up; **wenn nichts d~kommt** if all goes well

Debat|te *f* -,-n debate; **zur D~ stehen** be at issue. **d~tieren** *vt/i* (*haben*) debate

Debüt /de'by:/ *nt* -s,-s début

Deck *nt* -[e]s,-s (*Naut*) deck; **an D~** on deck. **D~bett** *nt* duvet

Decke *f* -,-n cover; (*Tisch-*) table-

cloth; (*Bett-*) blanket; (*Reise-*) rug; (*Zimmer-*) ceiling; **unter einer D~ stecken** ⊥ be in league

Deckel *m* -s,-, lid; (*Flaschen-*) top; (*Buch-*) cover

decken *vt* cover; tile (*Dach*); lay (*Tisch*); (*schützen*) shield; (*Sport*) mark; meet (*Bedarf*); **jdn d~** (*fig*) cover up for s.o.; **sich d~** (*fig*) cover oneself (**gegen** against); (*übereinstimmen*) coincide

Deckname *m* pseudonym

Deckung *f* - (*Mil*) cover; (*Sport*) defence; (*Mann-*) marking; (*Boxen*) guard; (*Sicherheit*) security; **in D~ gehen** take cover

defin|ieren *vt* define. **D~ition** *f* -,-en definition

Defizit *nt* -s,-e deficit

deformiert *adj* deformed

deftig *adj* ⊥ (*Mahlzeit*) hearty; (*Witz*) coarse

Degen *m* -s,-, sword; (*Fecht-*) épée

degeneriert *adj* (*fig*) degenerate

degradieren *vt* (*Mil*) demote; (*fig*) degrade

dehn|bar *adj* elastic. **d~en** *vt* stretch; lengthen (*Vokal*); **sich d~en** stretch

Deich *m* -[e]s,-e dike

dein *poss pron* your. **d~e(r,s)** *poss pron* yours; **die D~en** *od* **d~en** *pl* your family *sg*. **d~erseits** *adv* for your part. **d~etwegen** *adv* for your sake; (*wegen dir*) because of you, on your account. **d~etwillen** *adv* **um d~etwillen** for your sake. **d~ige** *poss pron* **der/die/das d~ige** yours. **d~s** *poss pron* yours

Dekan *m* -s,-e dean

Deklin|ation /-'tsjo:n/ *f* -,-en declension. **d~ieren** *vt* decline

Dekolleté, Dekolletee /dekɔl'te:/ *nt* -s,-s low neckline

Dekor *m* & *nt* -s decoration. **D~**

ateur m -s,-e interior decorator; (Schaufenster-) window-dresser. **D~ation** f -,-en decoration; (Schaufenster-) window-dressing; (Auslage) display. **d~ativ** adj decorative. **d~ieren** vt decorate; dress (Schaufenster)

Delegation /-'tsjo:n/ f -,-en delegation. **D~ierte(r)** m/f delegate

delikat adj delicate; (lecker) delicious; (taktvoll) tactful. **D~essengeschäft** nt delicatessen

Delikt nt -[e]s,-e offence

Delinquent m -en,-en offender

Delle f -,-n dent

Delphin m -s,-e dolphin

Delta nt -s,-s delta

dem def art & pron s. der

dementieren vt deny

dem|entsprechend adj corresponding; (passend) appropriate ● adv accordingly; (passend) appropriately. **d~nächst** adv soon; (in Kürze) shortly

Demokrat m -en,-en democrat. **D~ie** f -,-n democracy. **d~isch** adj democratic

demolieren vt wreck

Demonstr|ant m -en,-en demonstrator. **D~ation** f -,-en demonstration. **d~ieren** vt/i (haben) demonstrate

demontieren vt dismantle

Demoskopie f - opinion research

Demut f - humility

den def art & pron s. der. **d~en** pron s. der

denk|bar adj conceivable. **d~en†** vt/i (haben) think (an + acc of); (sich erinnern) remember (an etw acc sth); das kann ich mir d~en I can imagine [that]; ich d~e nicht daran I have no intention of doing it. **D~mal** nt memorial; (Monument) monument. **d~würdig**

adj memorable

denn conj for; besser/mehr d~ je better/more than ever ● adv wie/wo d~? but how/where? warum d~ nicht? why ever not? es sei d~ [, dass] unless

dennoch adv nevertheless

Denunz|iant m -en,-en informer. **d~ieren** vt denounce

Deodorant nt -s,-s deodorant

deplaciert, deplatziert /-'tsi:ɐt/ adj (fig) out of place

Deponie f -,-n dump. **d~ren** vt deposit

deportieren vt deport

Depot /de'po:/ nt -s,-s depot; (Lager) warehouse; (Bank-) safe deposit

Depression f -,-en depression

deprimieren vt depress

---

der, **die, das,** pl **die**

● definite article

> | acc den, die, das, pl die; gen des, der, des, pl der; dat dem, der, dem, pl den |

····▸ the. der Mensch the person; (als abstrakter Begriff) man. die Natur nature. das Leben life. das Lesen/Tanzen reading/dancing. sich (dat) das Gesicht/die Hände waschen wash one's face/hands. 3 Euro das Pfund 3 euros a pound

● pronoun

> | acc den, die, das, pl die; gen dessen, deren, dessen, pl deren; dat dem, der, dem, pl denen |

● demonstrative pronoun
····▸ that; (pl) those

‹···▸ (attributiv) der Mann war es
it was 'that man

‹···▸ (substantivisch) he, she, it;
(pl) they. der war es it was
'him. die da (a person) that
woman/girl; (thing) that one

● relative pronoun

‹···▸ (Person) who. der Mann,
der/dessen Sohn hier arbeitet
the man who/whose son works
here. die Frau, mit der ich Tennis spiele the woman with
whom I play tennis, the woman
I play tennis with. das Mädchen, das ich gestern sah the
girl I saw yesterday

‹···▸ (Ding) which, that. ich sah
ein Buch, das mich interes-
sierte I saw a book that interested me. die CD, die ich mir
anhöre the CD I am listening to.
das Auto, mit dem wir nach
Deutschland fahren the car we
are going to Germany in or in
which we are going to Germany

derb adj tough; (kräftig) strong;
(grob) coarse; (unsanft) rough

deren pron s. der

dergleichen inv adj such ● pron
such a thing/such things

der-/die-/dasselbe, pl dieselben pron the same; ein- und dasselbe one and the same thing

derzeit adv at present

des def art s. der

Desert|eur /-'tø:ɐ/ m -s,-e de-
serter. **d~ieren** vi (sein/haben)
desert

desgleichen adv likewise ● pron
the like

deshalb adv for this reason; (also)
therefore

Design nt -s, -s design

Designer(in) /di'zaɪnɐ, -nərɪn/ m

-s,- (f -,-nen) designer

Desin|fektion /dɛsʔɪnfɛk'tsɪo:n/ f
disinfecting. **D~fektionsmittel** nt
disinfectant. **d~fizieren** vt disinfect

dessen pron s. der

Destill|ation /-'tsɪo:n/ f - distilla-
tion. **d~ieren** vt distil

desto adv je mehr **d~besser** the
more the better

deswegen adv = deshalb

Detektiv m -s,-e detective

Deton|ation /-'tsɪo:n/ f -,-en ex-
plosion. **d~ieren** vi (sein) explode

deut|en vt interpret; predict (Zu-
kunft) ● vi (haben) point (auf + acc
at/(fig) to). **d~lich** adj clear; (eindeutig) plain

deutsch adj German. **D~** nt -[s]
(Lang) German; auf **D~** in German.
D~e(r) m/f German. **D~land** nt -s
Germany

Deutung f -,-en interpretation

Devise f -,-n motto. **D~n** pl foreign currency or exchange sg

Dezember m -s,- December

dezent adj unobtrusive; (diskret)
discreet

Dezernat nt -[e]s,-e department

Dezimalzahl f decimal

d.h. abbr (das heißt) i.e.

Dia nt -s,-s (Phot) slide

Diabet|es m - diabetes. **D~iker**
m -s,- diabetic

Diadem nt -s,-e tiara

Diagnose f -,-n diagnosis

diagonal adj diagonal. **D~e** f -,-n
diagonal

Diagramm nt -s,-e diagram; (Kur-
ven-) graph

Diakon m -s,-e deacon

Dialekt m -[e]s,-e dialect

Dialog m -[e]s,-e dialogue

Diamant m -en,-en diamond

Diapositiv nt -s,-e (Phot) slide

Diaprojektor m slide projector

Diät f -,-en (Med) diet; **D~ leben** be on a diet

dich pron (acc of du) you; (reflexive) yourself

dicht adj dense; (dick) thick; (undurchlässig) airtight; (wasser-) watertight ●adv densely; (nahe) close (bei to). **D~e** density. **d~en¹** vt make watertight

dicht|en² vi (haben) write poetry. ●vt write. **D~er(in)** m -s,- (f -,-nen) poet. **d~erisch** adj poetic. **D~ung¹** f -,-en poetry; (Gedicht) poem

Dichtung² f -,-en seal; (Ring) washer; (Auto) gasket

dick adj thick; (beleibt) fat; (geschwollen) swollen; (fam: eng) close; **d~ machen** be fattening. **D~flüssig** adj thick; (Phys) viscous. **D~kopf** m 🗓 stubborn person; **einen D~kopf haben** be stubborn

die def art & pron s. der

Dieb|(in) m -[e]s,-e (f -,-nen) thief. **d~isch** adj thieving; (Freude) malicious. **D~stahl** m -[e]s,ˉe theft

Diele f -,-n floorboard; (Flur) hall

dien|en vi (haben) serve. **D~er** m -s,- servant; (Verbeugung) bow. **D~erin** f -,-nen maid, servant

Dienst m -[e]s,-e service; (Arbeit) work; (Amtsausübung) duty; **außer D~** off duty; (pensioniert) retired; **D~ haben** work; (Soldat, Arzt:) be on duty

Dienstag m Tuesday. **d~s** adv on Tuesdays

Dienst|bote m servant. **d~frei** adj **d~freier Tag** day off; **d~frei haben** have time off; (Soldat, Arzt:) be off duty. **D~grad** m rank. **D~leistung** f service. **d~lich** adj

official ●adv **d~lich verreist** away on business. **D~mädchen** nt maid. **D~reise** f business trip. **D~stelle** f office. **D~stunden** fpl office hours

dies inv pron this. **D~bezüglich** adj relevant ●adv regarding this matter. **d~e(r,s)** pron this; (pl) these; (substantivisch) this [one]; (pl) these; **d~e Nacht** tonight; (letzte) last night

dieselbe pron s. derselbe

Dieselkraftstoff m diesel [oil]

diesmal adv this time

Dietrich m -s,-e skeleton key

Diffamation /-'tsio:n/ f - defamation

Differential° /-'tsia:l/ nt -s,-e = Differenzial

Differenz f -,-en difference. **D~ial** nt -s,-e differential. **d~ieren** vt/i (haben) differentiate (zwischen + dat between)

digital adj digital

Digital- prefix digital. **D~kamera** f digital camera. **D~uhr** f digital clock/watch

digitalisieren vt digitize

Dikt|at nt -[e]s,-e dictation. **D~ator** m -s,-en dictator. **D~atur** f -,-en dictatorship. **d~ieren** vt/i (haben) dictate

Dill m -s dill

Dimension f -,-en dimension

Ding nt -[e]s,-e & 🗓 -er thing; **guter D~e sein** be cheerful; **vor allen D~en** above all

Dinosaurier /-ȝǝ/ m -s,- dinosaur

Diözese f -,-n diocese

Diphtherie f - diphtheria

Diplom nt -s,-e diploma; (Univ) degree

Diplomat m -en,-en diplomat

dir pron (dat of du) [to] you; (reflexive) yourself; **ein Freund von dir** a friend of yours

direkt adj direct ● adv directly; (wirklich) really. **D~ion** f - management; (Vorstand) board of directors. **D~or** m -s,-en, **D~orin** f -,-nen director; (Bank-, Theater-) manager; (Sch) head; (Gefängnis) governor. **D~übertragung** f live transmission

Dirig|ent m -en,-en (Mus) conductor. **d~ieren** vt direct; (Mus) conduct

Dirndl nt -s,- dirndl [dress]

Discounter m -s, - discount supermarket

Diskette f -,-n floppy disc

Disko f -,-s 🛈 disco. **D~thek** f -,-en discothèque

diskret adj discreet

Diskus m -,-se & Disken discus

Disku|ssion f -,-en discussion. **d~tieren** vt/i (haben) discuss

disponieren vi (haben) make arrangements; **d~** [können] über (+ acc) have at one's disposal

Disqualifi|kation /-tsio:n/ f disqualification. **d~zieren** vt disqualify

Dissertation /-tsio:n/ f -,-en dissertation

Dissident m -en,-en dissident

Distanz f -,-en distance. **d~ieren (sich)** vr dissociate oneself (von from). **d~iert** adj aloof

Distel f -,-n thistle

Disziplin f -,-en discipline. **d~arisch** adj disciplinary. **d~iert** adj disciplined

dito adv ditto

diverse attrib a pl various

Divid|ende f -,-en dividend. **d~ieren** vt divide (durch by)

Division f -,-en division

DJH abbr (Deutsche Jugendherberge) [German] youth hostel

DM abbr (Deutsche Mark) DM

doch conj & adv but; (dennoch) yet; (trotzdem) after all; wenn **d~** ... ! if only ... ! nicht **d~**! don't!

Docht m -[e]s,-e wick

Dock nt -s,-s dock. **d~en** vt/i (haben) dock

Dogge f -,-n Great Dane

Dogma nt -s,-men dogma. **d~a-tisch** adj dogmatic

Dohle f -,-n jackdaw

Doktor m -s,-en doctor. **D~ar-beit** f [doctoral] thesis

Dokument nt -[e]s,-e document. **D~arbericht** m documentary. **D~arfilm** m documentary film

Dolch m -[e]s,-e dagger

Dollar m -s,- dollar

dolmetsch|en vt/i (haben) interpret. **D~er(in)** m -s,- (f -,-nen) interpreter

Dom m -[e]s,-e cathedral

Domino nt -s,-s dominoes sg. **D~stein** m domino

Dompfaff m -en,-en bullfinch

Donau f - Danube

Donner m -s,- thunder. **d~n** vi (haben) thunder

Donnerstag m Thursday. **d~s** adv on Thursdays

doof adj 🛈 stupid

Doppel nt -s,- duplicate; (Tennis) doubles pl. **D~bett** nt double bed. **D~decker** m -s,- doubledecker [bus]. **d~deutig** adj ambiguous.

D~gänger m -s,- double. D~kinn nt double chin. D~klicken vi (haben) double-click (auf + acc on). D~name m double-barrelled name. D~punkt m (Gram) colon. D~stecker m two-way adaptor. d~t adj double; (Boden) false; in d~ter Ausfertigung in duplicate; die d~te Menge twice the amount ●adv doubly; (zweimal) twice; d~t so viel twice as much. D~zimmer nt double room

Dorf nt -[e]s, ⸚er village. D~bewohner m villager

dörflich adj rural

Dorn m -[e]s,-en thorn. d~ig adj thorny

Dorsch m -[e]s,-e cod

dort adv there. d~ig adj local

Dose f -,-n tin, can

dösen vi (haben) doze

Dosen|milch f evaporated milk. D~öffner m tin or can opener. D~pfand nt deposit (on beer cans etc)

dosieren vt measure out

Dosis f -, Dosen dose

Dotter m & nt -s,- [egg] yolk

Dozent(in) m -en,-en (f -,-nen) (Univ) lecturer

Dr. abbr (Doktor) Dr

Drache m -n,-n dragon. D~n m -s,- kite. D~nfliegen nt hang-gliding

Draht m -[e]s, ⸚e wire; auf D~ 🄵 on the ball. D~seilbahn f cable railway

Dram|a nt -s,-men drama. D~atik f - drama. D~atiker m -s,- dramatist. d~atisch adj dramatic

dran adv 🄵 = daran; gut/schlecht d~ sein be well/in a bad way; ich bin d~ it's my turn

Drang m -[e]s urge; (Druck) pressure

dräng|eln vt/i (haben) push; (bedrängen) pester. d~en vt push; (bedrängen) urge; sich d~en crowd (um round) ●vi (haben) push; (eilen) be urgent; d~en auf (+ acc) press for

dran|halten (sich) vr sep hurry. d~kommen vi sep (sein) have one's turn

drauf adv 🄵 = darauf; d~ und dran sein be on the point (etw zu tun of doing sth). D~gänger m -s,- daredevil

draußen adv outside; (im Freien) out of doors

drechseln vt (Techn) turn

Dreck m -s dirt; (Morast) mud

Dreh m -s 🄵 knack; den D~ heraushaben have got the hang of it. D~bank f lathe. D~bleistift m propelling pencil. D~buch nt screenplay, script. d~en vt turn; (im Kreis) rotate; (verschlingen) twist; roll (Zigarette); shoot (Film); lauter/leiser d~en turn up/down; sich d~en turn; (im Kreis) rotate; (schnell) spin; (Wind:) change; sich d~en um revolve around; (sich handeln) be about ●vi (haben) turn; (Wind:) change; an etw (dat) d~en turn sth. D~stuhl m swivel chair. D~tür f revolving door. D~ung f -,-en turn; (im Kreis) rotation. D~zahl f number of revolutions

drei inv adj, D~ f -,-en three; (Sch) ≈ pass. D~eck nt -[e]s,-e triangle. d~eckig adj triangular. d~erlei inv adj three kinds of ●pron three things. d~fach adj triple. d~mal adv three times. D~rad nt tricycle

dreißig inv adj thirty. d~ste(r,s) adj thirtieth

dreiviertel[1] inv adj = drei viertel, s. viertel. D~stunde f three-quarters of an hour

dreizehn inv adj thirteen

d~te(r,s) adj thirteenth

dreschen† vt thresh

dress|ieren vt train. D~ur f- training

dribbeln vi (haben) dribble

Drill m -[e]s (Mil) drill. **d~en** vt drill

Drillinge mpl triplets

dringlich adj urgent

Drink m -[s],-s [alcoholic] drink

drinnen adv inside

dritt adv zu d~ in threes; wir waren zu d~ there were three of us. **d~e(r,s)** adj third; ein D~er a third person. **D~el** nt -s,- inv adj third. **D~ens** adv thirdly. **d~rangig** adj third-rate

Droge f-,-n drug. **D~enabhängige(r)** m/f drug addict. **D~erie** f -,-n chemist's shop. **D~ist** m -en, -en chemist

drohen vi (haben) threaten (jdm s.o.)

dröhnen vi (haben) resound; (tönen) boom

Drohung f-,-en threat

drollig adj funny; (seltsam) odd

Drops m -,- [fruit] drop

Drossel f -,-n thrush

drosseln vt (Techn) throttle; (fig) cut back

drüben adv over there

Druck¹ m -[e]s,¨e pressure; unter D~ setzen (fig) pressurize

Druck² m -[e]s,-e printing; (Schrift, Reproduktion) print. **D~buchstabe** m block letter

drucken vt print

drücken vt/i (haben) press; (aus-) squeeze; (Schuh:) pinch; (umarmen) hug; Preise d~ force down prices; (an Tür) d~ push; sich d~ make oneself scarce; sich d~ vor (+ dat) 🔲 shirk. **d~d** adj heavy; (schwül) oppressive

Drucker m -s,- printer

Druckerei f-,-en printing works

Druck|fehler m misprint. **D~knopf** m press-stud. **D~luft** f compressed air. **D~sache** f printed matter. **D~schrift** f type; (Veröffentlichung) publication; in D~schrift in block letters pl

Druckstelle f bruise

Drüse f-,-n (Anat) gland

Dschungel m -s,- jungle

du pron (familiar address) you; auf Du und Du on familiar terms

Dübel m -s,- plug

Dudelsack m bagpipes pl

Duell nt -s,-e duel

Duett nt -s,-e [vocal] duet

Duft m -[e]s,¨e fragrance, scent; (Aroma) aroma. **d~en** vi (haben) smell (nach of)

dulden vt tolerate; (erleiden) suffer ● vi (haben) suffer

dumm adj stupid; (unklug) foolish; (🔲: lästig) awkward; wie d~! unfortunately. **d~erweise** adv stupidly; (leider) unfortunately. **D~heit** f-,-en stupidity; (Torheit) foolishness; (Handlung) folly. **D~kopf** m 🔲 fool.

dumpf adj dull

Düne f-,-n dune

Dung m -s manure

Dünge|mittel nt fertilizer. **d~n** vt fertilize. **D~r** m -s,- fertilizer

dunk|el adj dark; (vage) vague; (fragwürdig) shady; d~les Bier brown ale; im D~eln in the dark

Dunkel|heit f- darkness. **D~kammer** f dark-room. **d~n** vi (haben) get dark

dünn adj thin; (Buch) slim; (spärlich) sparse; (schwach) weak

Dunst m -es,¨e mist, haze; (Dampf) vapour

dünsten vt steam

dunstig adj misty, hazy

Duo nt -s,-s [instrumental] duet

Duplikat nt -[e]s,-e duplicate

Dur nt - (Mus) major [key]

durch prep (+ acc) through; (mittels) by; [geteilt] d~ (Math) divided by ● adv die Nacht d~ throughout the night; d~ und d~ nass wet through

durchaus adv absolutely; d~nicht by no means

durchblättern vt sep leaf through

durchblicken vi sep (haben) look through; d~ lassen (fig) hint at

Durchblutung f circulation

durchbohren vt insep pierce

durchbrechen[1]† vt/i sep (haben) break [in two]

durchbrechen[2]† vt insep break through; break (Schallmauer)

durchbrennen† vi sep (sein) burn through; (Sicherung:) blow

Durchbruch m breakthrough

durchdrehen v sep ● vt mince ● vi (haben/sein) 🔲 go crazy

durchdringen† vi sep (sein) penetrate; (sich durchsetzen) get one's way. d~d adj penetrating; (Schrei) piercing

durcheinander adv in a muddle; (Person) confused; d~ bringen muddle [up]; confuse (Person); d~ geraten get mixed up; d~ reden all talk at once. D~ nt -s muddle

durchfahren† vi sep (sein) drive through; (Zug:) go through

Durchfahrt f journey/drive through; auf der D~ passing through; 'D~ verboten' 'no thoroughfare'

Durchfall m diarrhoea. d~en/vi sep (sein) fall through; (🔲: versagen)

flop; (bei Prüfung) fail

Durchfuhr f - (Comm) transit

durchführ|bar adj feasible. d~en vt sep carry out

Durchgang m passage; (Sport) round; 'D~ verboten' 'no entry'. D~sverkehr m through traffic

durchgeben† vt sep pass through; (übermitteln) transmit; (Radio, TV) broadcast

durchgebraten adj gut d~ well done

durchgehen† vi sep (sein) go through; (davonlaufen) run away; (Pferd:) bolt; jdm etw d~ lassen let s.o. get away with sth. d~d adj continuous; d~d geöffnet open all day; d~der Zug through train

durchgreifen† vi sep (haben) reach through; (vorgehen) take drastic action. d~d adj drastic

durchhalte|n† v sep (fig) ● vi (haben) hold out ● vt keep up. D~vermögen nt stamina

durchkommen† vi sep (sein) come through; (gelangen, am Telefon) get through

durchlassen† vt sep let through

durchlässig adj permeable; (undicht) leaky

Durchlauferhitzer m -s,- geyser

durchlesen† vt sep read through

durchleuchten vt insep X-ray

durchlöchert adj riddled with holes

durchmachen vt sep go through; (erleiden) undergo

Durchmesser m -s,- diameter

durchnässt adj wet through

durchnehmen† vt sep (Sch) do

durchnummeriert adj numbered consecutively

durchpausen vt sep trace

durchqueren vt insep cross

Durchreiche f -,-n hatch

Durchreise f journey through; auf der D~ passing through. **d~n** vi sep (sein) pass through

durchreißen† vt/i sep (sein) tear

Durchsage f -,-n announcement. **d~n** vt sep announce

Durchschlag m carbon copy; (Culin) colander. **d~en†** v sep ● vt (Culin) rub through a sieve; sich **d~en** (fig) struggle through ● vi (sein) (Sicherung:) blow

durchschlagend adj (fig) effective; (Erfolg) resounding

durchschneiden† vt sep cut

Durchschnitt m average; im D~ on average. **d~lich** adj average ● adv on average. **D~s-** prefix average

Durchschrift f carbon copy

durchsehen† v sep ● vi (haben) see through ● vt look through

durchseihen vt sep strain

durchsetzen vt sep force through; sich **d~** assert oneself; (Mode:) catch on

Durchsicht f check

durchsichtig adj transparent

durchsickern vi sep (sein) seep through; (Neuigkeit:) leak out

durchstehen† vt sep (fig) come through

durchstreichen† vt sep cross out

durchsuch|en vt insep search. **D~ung** f -,-en search

durchwachsen adj (Speck) streaky; (🗓: gemischt) mixed

durchwählen vi sep (haben) (Teleph) dial direct

durchweg adv without exception

durchwühlen vt insep rummage through; ransack (Haus)

Durchzug m through draught

---

dürfen†

● transitive & auxiliary verb

····▸ (Erlaubnis haben zu) be allowed; may, can. etw [tun] dürfen be allowed to do sth. darf ich das tun? may or can I do that? nein, das darfst du nicht no you may not or cannot [do that]. er sagte mir, ich dürfte sofort gehen he told me I could go at once. hier darf man nicht rauchen smoking is prohibited here. sie darf/durfte es nicht sehen she must not/was not allowed to see it.

····▸ (in Höflichkeitsformeln) may. darf ich rauchen? may I smoke? darf/dürfte ich um diesen Tanz bitten? may/might I have the pleasure of this dance?

····▸ dürfte (sollte) should, ought. jetzt dürften sie dort angekommen sein they should or ought to be there by now. das dürfte nicht allzu schwer sein that should not be too difficult. ich hätte es nicht tun/sagen dürfen I ought not to have done/said it

● intransitive verb

····▸ (irgendwohin gehen dürfen) be allowed to go; may go; can go. darf ich nach Hause? may or can I go home? sie durfte nicht ins Theater she was not allowed to go the theatre

---

dürftig adj poor; (Mahlzeit) scanty

dürr adj dry; (Boden) arid; (mager) skinny. **D~e** f -,- drought

Durst m -[e]s thirst; D~ haben be thirsty. **d~ig** adj thirsty

Dusche f -,-n shower. **d~n** vi/r (haben) [sich] **d~n** have a shower

Düse f -,-n nozzle. **D∼nflugzeug** nt jet

Dutzend nt -s,-e dozen. **d∼weise** adv by the dozen

duzen vt jdn d∼ call s.o. 'du'

DVD f -, -s DVD

Dynam|ik f - dynamics sg; (fig) dynamism. **d∼isch** adj dynamic; (Rente) index-linked

Dynamit nt -es dynamite

Dynamo m -s,-s dynamo

Dynastie f -,-n dynasty

D-Zug /'de:-/ m express [train]

• •

Ee

• •

Ebbe f -,-n low tide

eben adj level; (glatt) smooth; zu e∼er Erde on the ground floor • adv just; (genau) exactly; e∼ noch only just; (gerade vorhin) just now; das ist es e∼! that's just it! **E∼bild** nt image

Ebene f -,-n (Geog) plain; (Geometry) plane; (fig: Niveau) level

eben|falls adv also; danke, e∼falls thank you, [the] same to you. **E∼holz** nt ebony. **e∼so** adv just the same; (ebenso sehr) just as much; **e∼so gut** just as good; adv just as well; **e∼so sehr** just as much; **e∼so viel** just as much/ many; **e∼so wenig** just as little/ few; (noch) no more

Eber m -s,- boar

ebnen vt level; (fig) smooth

Echo nt -s,-s echo

echt adj genuine, real; authentic • adv 🆃 really; typically. **E∼heit** f - authenticity

Eck|ball m (Sport) corner. **E∼e** f -,-n corner; **um die E∼e bringen** 🆃 bump off. **e∼ig** adj angular; (Klammern) square; (unbeholfen) awkward. **E∼zahn** m canine tooth

Ecu, ECU /e'ky:/ m -[s],-[s] ecu

edel adj noble; (wertvoll) precious; (fein) fine. **e∼mütig** adj magnanimous. **E∼stahl** m stainless steel. **E∼stein** m precious stone

Efeu m -s ivy

Effekt m -[e]s,-e effect. **E∼en** pl securities. **e∼iv** adj actual; (wirksam) effective

EG f - abbr (Europäische Gemeinschaft) EC

egal adj das ist mir e∼ 🆃 it's all the same to me • adv e∼ wie/wo no matter how/where

Egge f -,-n harrow

Ego|ismus m - selfishness. **E∼ist(in)** m -en,-en (f -,-nen) egoist. **e∼istisch** adj selfish

eh adv (Aust, 🆃) anyway

ehe conj before; ehe nicht until

Ehe f -,-n marriage. **E∼bett** nt double bed. **E∼bruch** m adultery. **E∼frau** f wife. **e∼lich** adj marital; (Recht) conjugal; (Kind) legitimate

ehemalig adj former. **e∼s** adv formerly

Ehe|mann m (pl -männer) husband. **E∼paar** nt married couple

eher adv earlier, sooner; (lieber, vielmehr) rather; (mehr) more

Ehering m wedding ring

Ehr|e f -,-n honour. **e∼en** vt honour. **e∼enamtlich** adj honorary • adv in an honorary capacity. **E∼engast** m guest of honour. **e∼enhaft** adj honourable. **E∼ensache** f point of honour. **E∼enwort** nt word of honour. **e∼erbietig** adj deferential. **E∼furcht** f reverence; (Scheu) awe. **e∼fürchtig** adj reverent. E~gefühl nt sense of honour. E~geiz m ambition. e~geizig adj ambitious. e~lich adj honest; e~lich gesagt to be honest. E~lichkeit f - honesty. e~los adj dishonourable. e~würdig adj venerable; (als Anrede) Reverend

Ei nt -[e]s,-er egg

Eibe f -,-n yew

Eiche f -,-n oak. **E~l** f -,-n acorn

eichen vt standardize

Eichhörnchen nt -s,- squirrel

Eid m -[e]s,-e oath

Eidechse f -,-n lizard

eidlich adj sworn ● adv on oath

Eidotter m & nt egg yolk

Eier|becher m egg-cup. E~kuchen m pancake; (Omelett) omelette. E~schale f eggshell. E~schnee m beaten egg-white. E~stock m ovary

Eifer m -s eagerness. E~sucht f jealousy. e~süchtig adj jealous

eifrig adj eager

Eigelb nt -[e]s,-e [egg] yolk

eigen adj own; (typisch) characteristic (dat of); (seltsam) odd; (genau) particular. E~art f peculiarity. e~artig adj peculiar. e~händig adj personal; (Unterschrift) own. E~heit f -,-en peculiarity. E~name m proper name. e~nützig adj selfish. e~s adv specially. E~schaft f -,-en quality; (Phys) property; (Merkmal) characteristic; (Funktion) capacity. E~schaftswort nt (pl -wörter) adjective. E~sinn m obstinacy. e~sinnig adj obstinate

eigentlich adj actual, real; (wahr) true ● adv actually, really; (streng genommen) strictly speaking

Eigen|tor nt own goal. E~tum nt -s property. E~tümer(in) m -s,- (f -,-nen) owner. E~tumswohnung f

freehold flat. e~willig adj self-willed; (Stil) highly individual

eignen (sich) vr be suitable

Eil|brief m express letter. E~e f -hurry; E~e haben be in a hurry; (Sache) be urgent. e~en vi (sein) hurry ● (haben) (drängen) be urgent. e~ig adj hurried; (dringend) urgent; es e~ig haben be in a hurry. E~zug m semi-fast train

Eimer m -s,- bucket; (Abfall-) bin

ein

● indefinite article

····▸ a, (vor Vokal) an. ein Kleid/ Apfel/Hotel/Mensch a dress/an apple/a[n] hotel/a human being. so ein such a. was für ein ... (Frage) what kind of a ... ? (Ausruf) what a ... !

● adjective

····▸ (Ziffer) one. eine Minute one minute. wir haben nur eine Stunde we only have an/(betont) one hour. eines Tages/Abends one day/evening

····▸ (derselbe) the same. einer Meinung sein be of the same opinion. mit jdm in einem Zimmer schlafen sleep in the same room as s.o.

einander pron one another

Einäscherung f -,-en cremation

einatmen vt/i sep (haben) inhale, breathe in

Einbahnstraße f one-way street

einbalsamieren vt sep embalm

Einband m binding

Einbau m installation; (Montage) fitting. e~en vt sep install; (montieren) fit. E~küche f fitted kitchen

einbegriffen pred adj included

Einberufung f call-up

Einbettzimmer nt single room

einbeulen vt sep dent

einbeziehen† vt sep [mit] e~in‑ clude; (berücksichtigen) take into account

einbiegen† vi sep (sein) turn

einbild|en vt sep sich (dat) etw e~en imagine sth; sich (dat) viel e~en be conceited. **E~ung** f im‑ agination; (Dünkel) conceit. **E~ungskraft** f imagination

einblenden vt sep fade in

Einblick m insight

einbrech|en vi sep (haben/sein) break in; bei uns ist eingebrochen worden we have been burgled. **E~er** m burglar

einbringen† vt sep get in; bring in (Geld)

Einbruch m burglary; bei E~ der Nacht at nightfall

einbürger|n vt sep naturalize. **E~ung** f - naturalization

einchecken /-tʃɛkn/ vt/i sep (haben) check in

eindecken (sich) vr sep stock up

eindeutig adj unambiguous; (deutlich) clear

eindicken vt sep (Culin) thicken

eindringen† vi sep (sein) e~en in (+ acc) penetrate into; (mit Gewalt) force one's/(Wasser:) its way into; (Mil) invade

Eindruck m impression

eindrücken vt sep crush

eindrucksvoll adj impressive

ein|e(r,s) pron one; (jemand) someone; (man) one, you

einebnen vt sep level

eineiig adj (Zwillinge) identical

eineinhalb inv adj one and a half; e~ Stunden an hour and a half

Einelternfamilie f one-parent family

einengen vt sep restrict

Einer m -s,- (Math) unit. **e~** pron s. **eine(r,s).** **e~** adj one kind of; (eintönig, einheitlich) the same ●pred adj 1 immaterial; es ist mir e~lei it's all the same to me. **e~seits** adv on the one hand

einfach adj simple; (Essen) plain; (Faden, Fahrt) single; **e~er Soldat** private. **E~heit** f - simplicity

einfädeln vt sep thread; (fig: ar‑ rangieren) arrange

einfahr|en† v sep ●vi (sein) arrive; (Zug:) pull in ●vt (Auto) run in. **E~t** f arrival; (Eingang) entrance, way in; (Auffahrt) drive; (Autobahn:) access road; **keine E~t** no entry

Einfall m idea; (Mil) invasion. **e~en**† vi sep (sein) collapse; (ein‑ dringen) invade; **jdm e~en** occur to s.o.; **was fällt ihm ein!** what does he think he is doing!

Einfalt f - naïvety

einfarbig adj of one colour; (Stoff, Kleid) plain

einfass|en vt sep edge; set (Edel‑ stein). **E~ung** f border, edging

einfetten vt sep grease

Einfluss m influence. **e~reich** adj influential

einförmig adj monotonous. **E~keit** f - monotony

einfrieren† vt/i sep (sein) freeze

einfügen vt sep insert; (einschie‑ ben) interpolate; **sich e~** fit in

einfühlsam adj sensitive

Einfuhr f -,-en import

einführ|en vt sep introduce; (ein‑ stecken) insert; (einweisen) initiate; (Comm) import. **e~end** adj intro‑ ductory. **E~ung** f introduction; (Einweisung) initiation

Eingabe f petition; (Compu‑ ter) input

Eingang m entrance, way in; (An‑ kunft) arrival

eingebaut adj built-in; (Schrank) fitted

eingeben† vt sep hand in; (Computer) feed in

eingebildet adj imaginary; (überheblich) conceited

Eingeborene(r) m/f native

eingehen† v sep ● vi (sein) come in; (ankommen) arrive; (einlaufen) shrink; (sterben) die; (Zeitung, Firma:) fold; auf etw (acc) e~ go into sth; (annehmen) agree to sth ● vt enter into; contract (Ehe); make (Wette) ● vt (Risiko)

eingemacht adj (Culin) bottled

eingenommen pred adj (fig) taken (von with); prejudiced (gegen against)

eingeschneit adj snowbound

eingeschrieben adj registered

Einge|ständnis nt admission. e~stehen† vt sep admit

eingetragen adj registered

Eingeweide pl bowels, entrails

eingewöhnen (sich) vr sep settle in

eingießen† vt sep pour in; (einschenken) pour

eingleisig adj single-track

einglieder|n vt sep integrate. E~ung f integration

eingravieren vt sep engrave

eingreifen† vi sep (haben) intervene. E~ nt -s intervention

Eingriff m intervention; (Med) operation

einhaken vt/r sep jdn e~ od sich bei jdm e~ take someone's arm

einhalten† v sep ● vt keep; (befolgen) observe ● vi (haben) stop

einhändigen vt sep hand in

einhängen vt sep hang; put down (Hörer)

einheimisch adj local; (eines Lan-

des) native; (Comm) homeproduced. E~e(r) m/f local, native

Einheit f -,-en unity; (Maß-, Mil) unit. e~lich adj uniform. E~spreis m standard price; (Fahrpreis) flat fare

einholen vt sep catch up with; (aufholen) make up for; (erbitten) seek; (einkaufen) buy

einhüllen vt sep wrap

einhundert inv adj one hundred

einig adj united; [sich (dat)] e~ sein be in agreement

einig|e(r,s) pron some; (ziemlich viel) quite a lot of; (substantivisch) e~e pl some; (mehrere) several; (ziemlich viele) quite a lot; e~es sg some things; vor e~er Zeit some time ago

einigen vt unite; unify (Land); sich e~ come to an agreement

einigermaßen adv to some extent; (ziemlich) fairly; (ziemlich gut) fairly well

Einigkeit f - unity; (Übereinstimmung) agreement

einjährig adj one-year-old; e~e Pflanze annual

einkalkulieren vt sep take into account

einkassieren vt sep collect

Einkauf m purchase; (Einkaufen) shopping; Einkäufe machen do some shopping. e~en vt sep buy; e~en gehen go shopping. E~swagen m shopping trolley

einklammern vt sep bracket

Einklang m harmony; im e~ stehen be in accord (mit with)

einkleben vt sep stick in

einkleiden vt sep fit out

einklemmen vt sep clamp

einkochen v sep ● vi (sein) boil down ● vt preserve, bottle

Einkommen nt -s income. **E∼[s]steuer** f income tax

Einkünfte pl income sg; (Einnahmen) revenue sg

einlad|en† vt sep load; (auffordern) invite; (bezahlen für) treat. **E∼ung** f invitation

Einlage f enclosure; (Schuh-) arch support; (Programm-) interlude; (Comm) investment; (Bank-) deposit; Suppe mit E∼ soup with noodles/dumplings

Ein|lass m -es admittance. e∼lassen† vt sep let in; run (Bad, Wasser); sich auf etw (acc) e∼lassen get involved in sth

einleben (sich) vr sep settle in

Einlege|arbeit f inlaid work. e∼n vt sep put in; lay in (Vorrat); lodge (Protest); (einfügen) insert; (Auto) engage (Gang); (Culin) pickle; (marinieren) marinade; eine Pause e∼n have a break. **E∼sohle** f insole

einleit|en vt sep initiate; (eröffnen) begin. **E∼ung** f introduction

einleuchten vi sep (haben) be clear (dat to). e∼d adj convincing

einliefer|n vt sep take (ins Krankenhaus to hospital). **E∼ung** f admission

einlösen vt sep cash (Scheck); redeem (Pfand); (fig) keep

einmachen vt sep preserve

einmal adv once; (eines Tages) one or some day; noch/schon e∼ again/before; noch e∼ so teuer twice as expensive; auf e∼ at the same time; (plötzlich) suddenly; nicht e∼ not even. **E∼eins** nt -[multiplication] tables pl. e∼ig adj (einzigartig) unique; (fam: großartig) fantastic

einmarschieren vi sep (sein) march in

einmisch|en (sich) vr sep interfere. **E∼ung** f interference

Einnahme f -,-n taking; (Mil) capture; **E∼n** pl income sg; (Einkünfte) revenue sg; (Comm) receipts; (eines Ladens) takings

einnehmen† vt sep take; have (Mahlzeit); (Mil) capture; take up (Platz)

einordnen vt sep put in its proper place; (klassifizieren) classify; sich e∼ fit in; (Auto) get in lane

einpacken vt sep pack

einparken vt sep park

einpflanzen vt sep plant; implant (Organ)

einplanen vt sep allow for

einprägen vt sep impress (jdm [up]on s.o.); sich (dat) etw e∼en memorize sth

einrahmen vt sep frame

einrasten vi sep (sein) engage

einräumen vt sep put away; (zugeben) admit; (zugestehen) grant

einrechnen vt sep include

einreden v sep ● vt jdm/sich etw e∼ persuade s.o./oneself of sth

einreiben† vt sep rub (mit with)

einreichen vt sep submit; die Scheidung e∼ file for divorce

Einreih|er m -s,- single-breasted suit. e∼ig adj single-breasted

Einreise f entry. e∼n vi sep (sein) enter (nach Irland Ireland)

einrenken vt sep (Med) set

einricht|en vt sep fit out; (möblieren) furnish; (anordnen) arrange; (Med) set (Bruch); (eröffnen) set up; sich e∼en furnish one's home; (sich einschränken) economize; (sich vorbereiten) prepare (auf + acc for). **E∼ung** f furnishing; (Möbel) furnishings pl; (Techn) equipment; (Vor-

richtung) device; *(Eröffnung)* setting up; *(Institution)* institution; *(Gewohnheit)* practice

einrosten *vi sep (sein)* rust; *(fig)* get rusty

eins *inv adj & pron* one; noch e~ one other thing; mir ist alles e~ 🔟 it's all the same to me. **E~** *f* -, -en one; *(Sch)* ≈ A

einsam *adj* lonely; *(allein)* solitary; *(abgelegen)* isolated. **E~keit** *f* - loneliness; solitude; isolation

einsammeln *vt sep* collect

Einsatz *m* use; *(Mil)* mission; *(Wett-)* stake; *(E~teil)* insert; im E~ in action

einschalten *vt sep* switch on; *(einschieben)* interpolate; *(fig: beteiligen)* call in; sich e~en *(fig)* intervene. **E~quote** *f (TV)* viewing figures *pl*; ≈ ratings *pl*

einschätzen *vt sep* assess; *(bewerten)* rate

einschenken *vt sep* pour

einscheren *vi sep (sein)* pull in

einschicken *vt sep* send in

einschieben† *vt sep* push in; *(einfügen)* insert

einschiffen (sich) *vr sep* embark. **E~ung** *f* - embarkation

einschlafen† *vi sep (sein)* go to sleep; *(aufhören)* peter out

einschläfern *vt sep* lull to sleep; *(betäuben)* put out; *(töten)* put to sleep. **e~d** *adj* soporific

Einschlag *m* impact. **e~en**† *v sep* •*vt* knock in; *(zerschlagen)* smash; *(drehen)* turn; take *(Weg)*; take up *(Laufbahn)* •*vi (haben)* hit/*(Blitz:)* strike *(in etw acc* sth); *(Erfolg haben)* be a hit

einschleusen *vt sep* infiltrate

einschließen† *vt sep* lock in; *(umgeben)* enclose; *(einkreisen)* surround; *(einbeziehen)* include; sich

e~en lock oneself in; Bedienung eingeschlossen service included. **e~lich** *adv* inclusive •*prep (+ gen)* including

einschneiden† *vt/i sep (haben)* [in] etw *acc* e~ cut into sth. **e~d** *adj (fig)* drastic

Einschnitt *m* cut; *(Med)* incision; *(Lücke)* gap; *(fig)* decisive event

einschränken *vt sep* restrict; *(reduzieren)* cut back; sich e~en economize. **E~ung** *f* -, -en restriction; *(Reduzierung)* reduction; *(Vorbehalt)* reservation

Einschreib[e]brief *m* registered letter. **e~en**† *vt sep* enter; register *(Brief)*; sich e~en put one's name down; *(sich anmelden)* enrol. **E~en** *nt* registered letter/ packet; als od per E~en by registered post

einschüchtern *vt sep* intimidate

Einsegnung *f* -, -en confirmation

einsehen† *vt sep* inspect; *(lesen)* consult; *(begreifen)* see

einseitig *adj* one-sided; *(Pol)* unilateral •*adv* on one side; *(fig)* onesidedly; *(Pol)* unilaterally

einsenden† *vt sep* send in

einsetzen *v sep* •*vt* put in; *(einfügen)* insert; *(verwenden)* use; put on *(Zug)*; call out *(Truppen)*; *(Mil)* deploy; *(ernennen)* appoint; *(wetten)* stake; *(riskieren)* risk •*vi (haben)* start; *(Winter, Regen:)* set in

Einsicht *f* insight; *(Verständnis)* understanding; *(Vernunft)* reason. **e~ig** *adj* understanding

Einsiedler *m* hermit

einsinken† *vi sep (sein)* sink in

einspannen *vt sep* harness; jdn e~ 🔟 rope s.o. in

einsparen *vt sep* save

einsperren *vt sep* shut/*(im Gefängnis)* lock up

einsprachig adj monolingual

einspritzen vt sep inject

Einspruch m objection; E~ erheben object; (Jur) appeal

einspurig adj single-track; (Auto) single-lane

einst adv once; (Zukunft) one day

Einstand m (Tennis) deuce

einstecken vt sep put in; post (Brief); (Electr) plug in; (☐: behalten) pocket; (☐: hinnehmen) take; suffer (Niederlage); etw e~ put sth in one's pocket

einsteigen† vi sep (sein) get in; (in Bus/Zug) get on

einstellen vt sep put in; (anstellen) employ; (aufhören) stop; (regulieren) adjust, set; (Optik) focus; tune (Motor, Zündung); tune to (Sender); sich e~en turn up; (Schwierigkeiten:) arise; sich e~en auf (+ acc) adjust to; (sich vorbereiten) prepare for. E~ung f employment; (Regulierung) adjustment; (TV, Auto) tuning; (Haltung) attitude

einstig adj former

einstimmig adj unanimous. E~keit f - unanimity

einstöckig adj single-storey

einstudieren vt sep rehearse

einstufen vt sep classify

Einsturz m collapse. e~stürzen vi sep (sein) collapse

einstweilen adv for the time being; (inzwischen) meanwhile

eintasten vt sep key in

eintauchen vt/i sep (sein) dip in

eintauschen vt sep exchange

eintausend inv adj one thousand

einteilen vt sep divide (in + acc into); (Biology) classify; sich (dat) seine Zeit gut e~en organize one's time well. e~ig adj one-piece. E~ung f division

eintönig adj monotonous. E~keit f - monotony

Eintopf m, E~gericht nt stew

Eintracht f - harmony

Eintrag m -[e]s, ⸚e entry. e~en† vt sep enter; (Admin) register; sich e~en put one's name down

einträglich adj profitable

Eintragung f -,-en registration

eintreffen† vi sep (sein) arrive; (fig) come true

eintreiben† vt sep drive in; (einziehen) collect

eintreten v sep ● vi (sein) enter; (geschehen) occur; in einen Klub e~ join a club; e~ für (fig) stand up for ● vt kick in

Eintritt m entrance; (zu Veranstaltung) admission; (Beitritt) joining; (Beginn) beginning. E~skarte f [admission] ticket

einüben vt sep practise

einundachtzig inv adj eighty-one

Einvernehmen nt -s understanding; (Übereinstimmung) agreement

einverstanden adj e~ sein agree

Einverständnis nt agreement; (Zustimmung) consent

Einwand m -[e]s, ⸚e objection

Einwander|er m immigrant. e~n vi sep (sein) immigrate. E~ung f immigration

einwandfrei adj perfect

einwärts adv inwards

einwechseln vt sep change

einwecken vt sep preserve, bottle

Einweg- prefix non-returnable

einweichen vt sep soak

einweih|en vt sep inaugurate; (Relig) consecrate; (einführen) initiate; in ein Geheimnis e~en let into a secret. **E~ung** f -,-en inauguration; consecration; initiation

einweisen† vt sep direct; (einführen) initiate; ins Krankenhaus e~ send to hospital

einwerfen† vt sep insert; post (Brief); (Sport) throw in

einwickeln vt sep wrap [up]

einwillig|en vi sep (haben) consent, agree (in + acc to). **E~ung** f consent

Einwohner|(in) m -s,- (f -,-nen) inhabitant. **E~zahl** f population

Einwurf m interjection; (Einwand) objection; (Sport) throw-in; (Münz-) slot

Einzahl f (Gram) singular

einzahl|en vt sep pay in. **E~ung** f payment; (Einlage) deposit

einzäunen vt sep fence in

Einzel nt -s,- (Tennis) singles pl. **E~bett** nt single bed. **E~gänger** m -s,- loner. **E~haft** f solitary confinement. **E~handel** m retail trade. **E~händler** m retailer. **E~haus** nt detached house. **E~heit** f -,-en detail. **E~karte** f single ticket. **E~kind** nt only child

einzeln adj single; (individuell) individual; (gesondert) separate; odd (Handschuh, Socken); e~e Fälle some cases. **E~e(r,s)** pron der/die/das e~e the individual; **E~e** pl some; im **E~en** in detail

Einzel|teil nt [component] part. **E~zimmer** nt single room

einziehen† v sep ● vt pull in; draw in (Atem, Krallen); (Zool, Techn) retract; indent (Zeile); (aus dem Verkehr ziehen) withdraw; (beschlagnahmen) confiscate; (eintreiben) collect; make (Erkundigungen); (Mil) call up ● vi (sein) enter; (umziehen) move in; (eindringen) penetrate

einzig adj only; (einmalig) unique;

eine e~e Frage a a single question ● adv only; e~ und allein solely. **E~e(r,s)** pron der/die/das e~e the only one; ein/kein **E~er** a/not a single one; das **E~e**, was mich stört the only thing that bothers me

Eis nt -es ice; (Speise-) ice-cream; Eis am Stiel ice lolly; Eis laufen skate. **E~bahn** f ice rink. **E~bär** m polar bear. **E~becher** m ice-cream sundae. **E~berg** m iceberg. **E~diele** f ice-cream parlour

Eisen nt -s,- iron. **E~bahn** f railway

eisern adj iron; (fest) resolute; e~er Vorhang (Theat) safety curtain; (Pol) Iron Curtain

Eis|fach nt freezer compartment. **e~gekühlt** adj chilled. **e~ig** adj icy. **E~kaffee** m iced coffee. **E~lauf** m skating. **E~läufer(in)** m(f) skater. **E~pickel** m ice-axe. **E~scholle** f ice-floe. **E~vogel** m kingfisher. **E~würfel** m ice-cube. **E~zapfen** m icicle. **E~zeit** f ice age

eitel adj vain; (rein) pure. **E~keit** f - vanity

Eiter m -s pus. **e~n** vi (haben) discharge pus

Eiweiß nt -es,-e egg-white

Ekel m -s disgust; (Widerwille) revulsion. **e~haft** adj nauseating; (widerlich) repulsive. **e~n** vt/i (haben) mich od mir e~t [es] davor it makes me feel sick ● vr sich e~n vor (+ dat) find repulsive

eklig adj disgusting, repulsive

Ekzem nt -s,-e eczema

elastisch adj elastic; (federnd) springy; (fig) flexible

Elch m -[e]s,-e elk

Elefant m -en,-en elephant

elegan|t adj elegant.

E~z f - elegance

Elektri|ker m -s,- electrician.
e~**sch** adj electric

Elektrizität f - electricity.
E~**swerk** nt power station

Elektr|oartikel mpl electrical appliances. E~**ode** f -,-n electrode.
E~**onik** f - electronics sg.
e~**onisch** adj electronic

Elend nt -s misery; (Armut) poverty. e~ adj miserable; (krank) poorly; (gemein) contemptible.
E~**sviertel** nt slum

elf inv adj. E~ f -,-en eleven

Elfe f -,-n fairy

Elfenbein nt ivory

Elfmeter m (Fußball) penalty

elfte(r,s) adj eleventh

Ell[en]bogen m elbow

Ellip|se f -,-n ellipse. e~**tisch** adj
elliptical

Elsass nt - Alsace

elsässisch adj Alsatian

Elster f -,-n magpie

elter|lich adj parental. E~**n** pl
parents. e~**nlos** adj orphaned.
E~**nteil** m parent

Email /e'mai/ nt -s,-s, E~**le** f -,-n
enamel

E-Mail /'i:me:l/ f -,-s e-mail

Emanzi|pation /-'tsio:n/ f -
emancipation. e~**piert** adj emancipated

Embargo nt -s,-s embargo

Embryo m -s,-s embryo

Emigr|ant(in) m -en,-en (f
-,-nen) emigrant. E~**ation** f -
emigration. e~**ieren** vi (sein)
emigrate

Empfang m -[e]s, ̈ e reception;
(Erhalt) receipt; in E~ nehmen receive; (annehmen) accept. e~**en**† vt
receive; (Biology) conceive

Empfäng|er m -s,- recipient;

(Post-) addressee; (Zahlungs-) payee;
(Radio, TV) receiver. E~**nis** f - (Biology) conception

Empfängnisverhütung f contraception. E~**smittel** nt contraceptive

Empfangs|bestätigung f receipt. E~**dame** f receptionist.
E~**halle** f [hotel] foyer

empfehl|en† vt recommend.
E~**ung** f -,-en recommendation;
(Gruß) regards pl

empfind|en† vt feel. e~**lich** adj
sensitive (gegen to); (zart) delicate.
E~**lichkeit** f - sensitivity; delicacy;
tenderness; touchiness. E~**ung** f
-,-en sensation; (Regung) feeling

empor adv (literarisch) up[wards]

empören vt incense; sich e~ be
indignant; (sich auflehnen) rebel

Emporkömmling m -s,-e
upstart

empör|t adj indignant. E~**ung** f -
indignation; (Auflehnung) rebellion

Ende nt -s,-n end; (eines Films, Romans) ending; (⊡: Stück) bit; zu E~
sein be finished; etw zu E~ schreiben finish writing sth; am E~ at
the end; (schließlich) in the end; (⊡:
vielleicht) perhaps; (⊡: erschöpft) at
the end of one's tether

end|en vi (haben) end. e~**gültig**
adj final; (bestimmt) definite

Endivie /-jə/ f -,-n endive

endlich adv at last, finally;
(schließlich) in the end. e~**los** adj
endless. E~**station** f terminus.
E~**ung** f -,-en (Gram) ending

Energie f - energy

energieeffizient adj energy-efficient

energisch adj resolute; (nachdrücklich) vigorous

eng adj narrow; (beengt) cramped;
(anliegend) tight; (nah) close; e~
anliegend tight-fitting

Engagement /ãgaʒə'mãː/ *nt* -s,-s (*Theat*) engagement; (*fig*) commitment

Engel *m* -s,- angel

England *nt* -s England

Engländer *m* -s,- Englishman; (*Techn*) monkey-wrench; **die E~** the English *pl.* **E~in** *f* -,-nen Englishwoman

englisch *adj* English. **E~** *nt* -[s] (*Lang*) English; **auf E~** in English

Engpass *m* (*fig*) bottleneck

en gros /ã'gro:/ *adv* wholesale

Enkel *m* -s,- grandson; **E~** *pl* grandchildren. **E~in** *f* -,-nen granddaughter. **E~kind** *nt* grandchild. **E~sohn** *m* grandson. **E~tochter** *f* granddaughter

Ensemble /ã'sã:bəl/ *nt* -s,-s ensemble; (*Theat*) company

entarten *vi* (*sein*) degenerate. **e~et** *adj* degenerate

entbehren *vt* do without; (*vermissen*) miss

entbind|en† *vt* release (von from); (*Med*) deliver (von of) ● *vi* (*haben*) give birth. **E~ung** *f* delivery. **E~ungsstation** *f* maternity ward

entdeck|en *vt* discover. **E~er** *m* -s,- discoverer; (*Forscher*) explorer. **E~ung** *f* -,-en discovery

Ente *f* -,-n duck

entehren *vt* dishonour

enteignen *vt* dispossess; expropriate (*Eigentum*)

enterben *vt* disinherit

Enterich *m* -s,-e drake

entfallen† *vi* (*sein*) not apply; **auf jdn e~** be s.o.'s share

entfern|en *vt* remove; sich e~en leave. **e~t** *adj* distant; (*schwach*) vague; **2 Kilometer e~t** 2 kilometres away; **e~t verwandt** distantly related. **E~ung** *f* -,-en removal; (*Abstand*) distance; (*Reichweite*) range

entfliehen† *vi* (*sein*) escape

entfremden *vt* alienate

entfrosten *vt* defrost

entführ|en *vt* abduct, kidnap; hijack (*Flugzeug*). **E~er** *m* abductor, kidnapper; hijacker. **E~ung** *f* abduction, kidnapping; hijacking

entgegen *adv* towards ● *prep* (+ *dat*) contrary to. **e~gehen†** *vi sep* (*sein*) (+ *dat*) go to meet; (*fig*) be heading for. **e~gesetzt** *adj* opposite; (*gegensätzlich*) opposing. **e~kommen†** *vi sep* (*sein*) (+ *dat*) come to meet; (*zukommen auf*) come towards; (*fig*) oblige. **E~kommen** *nt* -s helpfulness; (*Zugeständnis*) concession. **e~kommend** *adj* approaching; (*Verkehr*) oncoming; (*fig*) obliging. **e~nehmen†** *vt sep* accept. **e~wirken** *vi sep* (*haben*) (+ *dat*) counteract; (*fig*) oppose

entgegn|en *vt* reply (auf + *acc* to). **E~ung** *f* -,-en reply

entgehen† *vi sep* (*sein*) (+ *dat*) escape; **jdm e~** (*unbemerkt bleiben*) escape s.o.'s notice; **sich** (*dat*) **etw e~ lassen** miss sth

Entgelt *nt* -[e]s payment; **gegen E~** for money

entgleis|en *vi* (*sein*) be derailed; (*fig*) make a gaffe. **E~ung** *f* -,-en derailment; (*fig*) gaffe

entgräten *vt* fillet, bone

Enthaarungsmittel *nt* depilatory

enthalt|en† *vt* contain; **in etw** (*dat*) **e~en sein** be contained; (*eingeschlossen*) included in sth; **sich der Stimme e~en** (*Pol*) abstain. **e~sam** *adj* abstemious. **E~ung** *f* (*Pol*) abstention

enthaupten *vt* behead

entheben† vt jdn seines Amtes e~ relieve s.o. of his post

Enthüllung f -,-en revelation

Enthusias|mus m - enthusiasm. E~t m -en,-en enthusiast

entkernen vt stone; core (Apfel)

entkleiden vt undress; sich e~en undress

entkommen† vi (sein) escape

entkorken vt uncork

entladen† vt unload; (Electr) discharge; sich e~ discharge; (Gewitter:) break; (Zorn:) explode

entlang adv & prep (+ preceding acc or following dat) along; die Straße e~ along the road; an etw (dat) e~ along sth. e~fahren† vi sep (sein) drive along. e~gehen† vi sep (sein) walk along

entlarven vt unmask

entlass|en† vt dismiss; (aus Krankenhaus) discharge; (aus der Haft) release. E~ung f -,-en dismissal; discharge; release

entlast|en vt relieve the strain on; ease (Gewissen, Verkehr); relieve (von of); (Jur) exonerate. E~ung f - relief; exoneration

entlaufen† vi (sein) run away

entleeren vt empty

entlegen adj remote

entlohnen vt pay

entlüft|en vt ventilate. E~er m -s,- extractor fan. E~ung f ventilation

entmündigen vt declare incapable of managing his own affairs

entmutigen vt discourage

entnehmen† vt take (dat from); (schließen) gather (dat from)

entpuppen (sich) vr (fig) turn out (als etw to be sth)

entrahmt adj skimmed

entrichten vt pay

entrinnen† vi (sein) escape

entrüst|en vt fill with indignation; sich e~en be indignant (über + acc at). e~et adj indignant. E~ung f - indignation

entsaft|en vt extract the juice from. E~er m -s,- juice extractor

entsagen vi (haben) (+ dat) renounce

entschädig|en vt compensate. E~ung f -,-en compensation

entschärfen vt defuse

entscheid|en† vt/i (haben) decide; sich e~en decide; (Sache:) be decided. e~end adj decisive; (kritisch) crucial. E~ung f decision

entschließen (sich)† vr decide, make up one's mind; sich anders e~ change one's mind

entschlossen adj determined; (energisch) resolute; kurz e~ without hesitation. E~heit f - determination

Entschluss m decision

entschlüsseln vt decode

entschuld|bar adj excusable. e~igen vt excuse; sich e~igen apologize (bei to); e~igen Sie [bitte]! sorry! (bei Frage) excuse me. E~igung f -,-en apology; (Ausrede) excuse; um E~igung bitten apologize

entsetz|en vt horrify. E~en nt -s horror. e~lich adj horrible; (schrecklich) terrible

Entsorgung f - waste disposal

entspann|en vt relax; sich e~en relax; (Lage:) ease. E~ung f - relaxation; easing; (Pol) détente

entsprech|en† vi (haben) (+ dat) correspond to; (übereinstimmen) agree with. e~end adj corresponding; (angemessen) appropriate; (zuständig) relevant ● adv correspondingly; appropriately; (demgemäß)

accordingly ● prep (+ dat) in accordance with

entspringen† vi (sein) (Fluss:) rise; (fig) arise, spring (dat from)

entstammen vi (sein) come-/(abstammen) be descended (dat from)

entsteh|en† vi (sein) come into being; (sich bilden) form; (sich entwickeln) develop; (Brand:) start; (stammen) originate. E~ung f - origin; formation; development

entstell|en vt disfigure; (verzerren) distort. E~ung f disfigurement; distortion

entstört adj (Electr) suppressed

enttäusch|en vt disappoint. E~ung f disappointment

entwaffnen vt disarm

entwässer|n vt drain. E~ung f - drainage

entweder conj & adv either

entwerfen† vt design; (aufsetzen) draft; (skizzieren) sketch

entwert|en vt devalue; (ungültig machen) cancel. E~er m -s,- ticket-cancelling machine. E~ung f devaluation; cancelling

entwick|eln vt develop; sich e~eln develop. E~lung f -,-en development; (Biology) evolution. E~lungsland nt developing country

entwöhnen vt wean (gen from); cure (Süchtige)

entwürdigend adj degrading

Entwurf m design; (Konzept) draft; (Skizze) sketch

entwurzeln vt uproot

entzie|hen† vt take away (dat from); jdm den Führerschein e~hen disqualify s.o. from driving; sich e~hen (+ dat) withdraw from. E~hungskur f treatment for drug/alcohol addiction

entziffern vt decipher

Entzug m withdrawal; (Vorenthaltung) deprivation

entzünd|en vt ignite; (anstecken) light; (fig: erregen) inflame; sich e~en ignite; (Med) become inflamed. e~et adj (Med) inflamed. e~lich adj inflammable. E~ung f (Med) inflammation

entzwei adj broken

Enzian m -s,-e gentian

Enzyklo|pädie f -,-en encyclopaedia. e~pädisch adj encyclopaedic

Enzym nt -s,-e enzyme

Epidemie f -,-n epidemic

Epi|lepsie f - epilepsy. E~leptiker(in) m -s,- (f -,-nen) epileptic. e~leptisch adj epileptic

Epilog m -s,-e epilogue

Episode f -,-n episode

Epoche f -,-n epoch

Epos nt -, Epen epic

er pron he; (Ding, Tier) it

erachten vt consider (für nötig necessary). E~ nt -s meines E~s in my opinion

erbarmen (sich) vr have pity-/(Gott:) mercy (gen on). E~ nt -s pity; mercy

erbärmlich adj wretched

erbauen vt build; (fig) edify; nicht e~t von 🔲 not pleased about

Erbe¹ m -n,-n heir

Erbe² nt -s inheritance; (fig) heritage. e~n vt inherit

erbeuten vt get; (Mil) capture

Erbfolge f (Jur) succession

erbieten† (sich) vr offer (zu to)

Erbin f -,-nen heiress

erbitten† vt ask for

erbittert adj bitter; (heftig) fierce

erblassen vi (sein) turn pale

erblich *adj* hereditary

erblicken *vt* catch sight of

erblinden *vi* (sein) go blind

erbrechen† *vt* vomit ● e~/*vir* [sich] e~ vomit. E~ *nt* -s vomiting

Erbschaft *f* -,-en inheritance

Erbse *f* -,-n pea

Erb|stück *nt* heirloom. E~teil *nt* inheritance

Erd|apfel *m* (Aust) potato. E~beben *nt* -s,- earthquake. E~beere *f* strawberry

Erde *f* -,-n earth; (Erdboden) ground; (Fußboden) floor. e~n *vt* (Electr) earth

erdenklich *adj* imaginable

Erd|gas *nt* natural gas. E~geschoss *nt* ground floor. E~kugel *f* globe. E~kunde *f* geography. E~nuss *f* peanut. E~öl *nt* [mineral] oil

erdrosseln *vt* strangle

erdrücken *vt* crush to death

Erd|rutsch *m* landslide. E~teil *m* continent

erdulden *vt* endure

ereignen (sich) *vr* happen

Ereignis *nt* -ses,-se event. e~los *adj* uneventful. e~reich *adj* eventful

Eremit *m* -en,-en hermit

erfahren† *vt* learn, hear; (erleben) experience ● *adj* experienced. E~ung *f* -,-en experience; in E~ung bringen find out

erfassen *vt* seize; (begreifen) grasp; (einbeziehen) include; (aufzeichnen) record

erfind|en† *vt* invent. E~er *m* -s,- inventor. e~erisch *adj* inventive. E~ung *f* -,-en invention

Erfolg *m* -[e]s,-e success; (Folge) result; E~ haben be successful. e~en *vi* (sein) take place; (geschehen) happen. e~los *adj* unsuccessful. e~reich *adj* successful

erforder|lich *adj* required, necessary. e~n *vt* require, demand

erforsch|en *vt* explore; (untersuchen) investigate. E~ung *f* exploration; investigation

erfreu|en *vt* please. e~lich *adj* pleasing. e~licherweise *adv* happily. e~t *adj* pleased

erfrier|en† *vi* (sein) freeze to death; (Glied:) become frostbitten; (Pflanze:) be killed by the frost. E~ung *f* -,-en frostbite

erfrisch|en *vt* refresh. E~ung *f* -,-en refreshment

erfüll|en *vt* fill; (nachkommen) fulfil; serve (Zweck); discharge (Pflicht:) sich e~en come true. E~ung *f* fulfilment

erfunden invented

ergänz|en *vt* complement; (hinzufügen) add. E~ung *f* complement; supplement; (Zusatz) addition

ergeben† *vt* produce; (zeigen) show, establish; sich e~en result; (Schwierigkeit:) arise; (kapitulieren) surrender; (sich fügen) submit ● *adj* devoted; (resigniert) resigned

Ergebnis *nt* -ses,-se result. e~los *adj* fruitless

ergiebig *adj* productive; (fig) rich

ergreifen† *vt* seize; take (Maßnahme, Gelegenheit); take up (Beruf); (rühren) move; die Flucht e~ flee. e~d *adj* moving

ergriffen *adj* deeply moved. E~heit *f* - emotion

ergründen *vt* (fig) get to the bottom of

erhaben *adj* raised; (fig) sublime

Erhalt *m* -[e]s receipt. e~en† *vt* receive, get; (gewinnen) obtain; (bewahren) preserve, keep; (instand halten) maintain; (unterhalten) support;

am Leben e~en keep alive ● adj
gut/schlecht e~en in good/bad
condition; e~en bleiben survive

erhältlich adj obtainable

Erhaltung f - preservation; maintenance

erhängen (sich) vr hang oneself

erheb|en† vt raise; levy (Steuer);
charge (Gebühr); Anspruch e~en
lay claim (auf + acc to); Protest
e~en protest; sich e~en rise;
(Frage:) arise. e~lich adj considerable. E~ung f -,-en elevation; (Anhöhe) rise; (Aufstand) uprising; (Ermittlung) survey

erheiter|n vt amuse. E~ung f -
amusement

erhitzen vt heat

erhöh|en vt raise; (fig) increase;
sich e~en rise, increase. E~ung f
-,-en increase

erhol|en (sich) vr recover (von
from); (nach Krankheit) convalesce;
(sich ausruhen) have a rest. e~sam
adj restful. E~ung f - recovery;
(Ruhe) rest

erinner|n vt remind (an + acc of);
sich e~n remember (an jdn/etw
s.o./sth). E~ung f -,-en memory;
(Andenken) souvenir

erkält|en (sich) vr catch a cold;
e~et sein have a cold. E~ung f
-,-en cold

erkenn|bar adj recognizable;
(sichtbar) visible. e~en† vt recognize; (wahrnehmen) distinguish.
E~tnis f -,-se recognition; realization; (Wissen) knowledge; die neuesten E~tnisse the latest findings

Erker m -s,- bay

erklär|en vt declare; (erläutern) ex-
plain; sich bereit e~en agree (zu
to). e~end adj explanatory. e~lich
adj explicable; (verständlich) understandable. e~licherweise adv

understandably. E~ung f -,-en declaration; explanation; öffentliche
E~ung public statement

erkrank|en vi (sein) fall ill; be
taken ill (an + dat with). E~ung f
-,-en illness

erkundig|en (sich) vr enquire
(nach jdm/etw after s.o./about
sth). E~ung f -,-en enquiry

erlangen vt attain, get

Erlass m -es,-e (Admin) decree;
(Befreiung) exemption; (Straf-) re-
mission

erlassen† vt (Admin) issue; jdm
etw e~ exempt s.o. from sth; let
s.o. off (Strafe)

erlauben vt allow, permit; ich
kann es mir nicht e~ I can't afford it

Erlaubnis f - permission.
E~schein m permit

erläutern vt explain

Erle f -,-n alder

erleb|en vt experience; (mit-) see;
have (Überraschung). E~nis nt
-ses,-se experience

erledigen vt do; (sich befassen
mit) deal with; (beenden) finish; (entscheiden) settle; (töten) kill

erleichter|n vt lighten; (vereinfa-
chen) make easier; (befreien) relieve;
(lindern) ease. e~t adj relieved.
E~ung f - relief

erleiden† vt suffer

erleuchten vt illuminate; hell
e~et brightly lit

erlogen adj untrue, false

Erlös m -es proceeds pl

erlöschen† vi (sein) go out; (vergehen) die; (aussterben) die out; (ungültig werden) expire; erloschener
Vulkan extinct volcano

erlös|en vt save; (befreien) release
(von from); (Relig) redeem. e~t adj
relieved. E~ung f release; (Erleichte-

*rung) relief; (*Relig*) redemption
ermächtig|en *vt* authorize.
E~**ung** *f* -,-en authorization

Ermahnung *f* exhortation; admonition

ermäßig|en *vt* reduce. E~**ung** *f* -,-en reduction

ermessen† *vt* judge; (*begreifen*) appreciate. E~ *nt* -s discretion; (*Urteil*) judgement; **nach eigenem** E~ at one's own discretion

ermitt|eln *vt* establish; (*herausfinden*) find out ● *vi* (*haben*) investigate (**gegen** jdn s.o.). E~**lungen** *fpl* investigations. E~**lungsverfahren** *nt* (*Jur*) preliminary inquiry

ermöglichen *vt* make possible

ermord|en *vt* murder. E~**ung** *f* -,-en murder

ermüd|en *vt* tire ● *vi* (*sein*) get tired. E~**ung** *f* - tiredness

ermutigen *vt* encourage. e~**d** *adj* encouraging

ernähr|en *vt* feed; (*unterhalten*) support, keep; **sich** e~**en von** live/(*Tier:*) feed on. E~**er** *m* -s,- breadwinner. E~**ung** *f* - nourishment; nutrition; (*Kost*) diet

ernenn|en† *vt* appoint. E~**ung** *f* -,-en appointment

erneu|ern *vt* renew; (*auswechseln*) replace; change (*Verband*); (*renovieren*) renovate. E~**erung** *f* renewal; replacement; renovation. e~**t** *adj* renewed; (*neu*) new ● *adv* again

ernst *adj* serious; e~ **nehmen** take seriously. E~ *m* -es seriousness; **im** E~ seriously; **mit einer Drohung** E~ **machen** carry out a threat; **ist das dein** E~? are you serious? e~**haft** *adj* serious. e~**lich** *adj* serious

Ernte *f* -,-n harvest; (*Ertrag*) crop. E~**dankfest** *nt* harvest festival. e~**n** *vt* harvest; (*fig*) reap, win

ernüchter|n *vt* sober up; (*fig*) bring down to earth. e~**nd** *adj* (*fig*) sobering

Erober|er *m* -s,- conqueror. e~**n** *vt* conquer. E~**ung** *f* -,-en conquest

eröffn|en *vt* open; **jdm etw** e~**en** announce sth to s.o. E~**ung** *f* opening; (*Mitteilung*) announcement

erörter|n *vt* discuss. E~**ung** *f* -,-en discussion

Erot|ik *f* - eroticism. e~**isch** *adj* erotic

Erpel *m* -s,- drake

erpicht *adj* e~ **auf** (+ *acc*) keen on

erpress|en *vt* extort; blackmail (*Person*). E~**er** *m* -s,- blackmailer. E~**ung** *f* - extortion; blackmail

erprob|en *vt* test. e~**t** *adj* proven

erraten† *vt* guess

erreg|bar *adj* excitable. e~**en** *vt* excite; (*hervorrufen*) arouse; **sich** e~**en** get worked up. e~**end** *adj* exciting. E~**er** *m* -s,- (*Med*) germ. e~**t** *adj* agitated; (*hitzig*) heated. E~**ung** *f* - excitement

erreich|bar *adj* within reach; (*Ziel*) attainable; (*Person*) available. e~**en** *vt* reach; catch (*Zug*); live to (*Alter*); (*durchsetzen*) achieve

errichten *vt* erect

erringen† *vt* gain, win

erröten *vi* (*sein*) blush

Errungenschaft *f* -,-en achievement; (🄘: *Anschaffung*) acquisition

Ersatz *m* -es replacement, substitute; (*Entschädigung*) compensation. E~**reifen** *m* spare tyre. E~**teil** *nt* spare part

erschaffen† *vt* create

erschein|en *vi* (*sein*) appear; (*Buch:*) be published. E~**ung** *f* -,-en appearance; (*Person*) figure; (*Phänomen*) phenomenon; (*Symptom*) symptom; (*Geist*) apparition

erschieß|en† vt shoot [dead].
E~ungskommando nt firing squad

erschlaffen vi (sein) go limp

erschlagen† vt beat to death;
(tödlich treffen) strike dead; vom
Blitz e~ werden be killed by
lightning

erschließen† vt develop

erschöpf|en vt exhaust. e~t adj
exhausted. E~ung f - exhaustion

erschrecken† vi (sein) get a
fright ● vt (reg) startle; (beunruhigen) alarm; du hast mich e~t you
gave me a fright

erschrocken adj frightened; (er-
schreckt) startled

erschütter|n vt shake; (ergreifen)
upset deeply. E~ung f -,-en shock

erschwinglich adj affordable

ersehen† vt (fig) see (aus from)

ersetzen vt replace; make good
(Schaden); refund (Kosten); jdm etw
e~ compensate s.o. for sth

ersichtlich adj obvious, apparent

erspar|en vt save. E~nis f -,-se
saving; E~nisse savings

erst adv (zuerst) first; (noch nicht
mehr als) only; (nicht vor) not until;
e~ dann only then; eben e~
[only] just

erstarren vi (sein) solidify; (gefrieren) freeze; (steif werden) go stiff;
(vor Schreck) be paralysed

erstatten vt (zurück-) refund; Bericht e~ report (jdm to s.o.)

Erstaufführung f first performance, première

erstaun|en vt amaze, astonish.
E~en nt amazement, astonish-
ment. e~lich adj amazing

Erst|ausgabe f first edition.
e~e(r,s) adj first; (beste) best; e~e
Hilfe first aid. E~e(r) m/f first;
(Beste) best; fürs E~e for the time
being; als E~es first of all; er kam

als E~er he arrived first

erstechen† vt stab to death

ersteigern ● vt buy at an auction

erst|ens adv firstly, in the first
place. e~ere(r,s) adj the former;
der/die/das E~ere the former

ersticken vt suffocate; smother
(Flammen) ● vi (sein) suffocate. E~
nt -s suffocation; zum E~ stifling

erstklassig adj first-class

ersuchen vt ask, request. E~ nt
-s request

ertappen vt 🗉 catch

erteilen vt give (jdm s.o.)

ertönen vi (sein) sound; (erschal-
len) ring out

Ertrag m -[e]s, ⸚e yield. e~en†
vt bear

erträglich adj bearable; (leidlich)
tolerable

ertränken vt drown

ertrinken† vi (sein) drown

erübrigen (sich) vr be unnecessary

erwachsen adj grown-up.
E~e(r) m/f adult, grown-up

erwäg|en† vt consider. E~ung f
-,-en consideration; in E~ung ziehen consider

erwähn|en vt mention. E~ung f
-,-en mention

erwärmen vt warm; sich e~
warm up; (fig) warm (für to)

erwart|en vt expect; (warten auf)
wait for. E~ung f -,-en expectation

erweisen† vt prove; (bezeigen) do
(Gefallen, Dienst, Ehre); sich e~ als
prove to be

erweiter|n vt widen; dilate (Pu-
pille); (fig) extend, expand

Erwerb m -[e]s acquisition; (Kauf)
purchase; (Brot-) livelihood; (Verdienst) earnings pl. e~en† vt acquire; (kaufen) purchase. e~slos adj

unemployed. **e~stätig** adj employed

erwider|n vt reply; return (Besuch, Gruß). **E~ung** f -,-en reply

erwirken vt obtain

erwürgen vt strangle

Erz nt -es,-e ore

erzähl|en† vt tell (jdm s.o.) ● vi (haben) talk (von about). **E~er** m -s,- narrator. **E~ung** f -,-en story, tale

Erzbischof m archbishop

erzeug|en vt produce; (Electr) generate. **E~er** m -s,- producer. **E~nis** nt -ses,-se product; landwirtschaftliche **E~nisse** farm produce sg.

erzieh|en† vt bring up; (Sch) educate. **E~er** m -s,- [private] tutor. **E~erin** f -,-nen governess. **E~ung** f - upbringing; education

erzielen vt achieve; score (Tor)

erzogen adj gut/schlecht e~ well/badly brought up

es
● pronoun
····▸ (Sache) it; (weibliche Person) she/her; (männliche Person) he/him. ich bin es it's me. wir sind traurig, ihr seid es auch we are sad, and so are you. er ist es, der ... he is the one who ... es sind Studenten they are students

····▸ (impers) it. es hat geklopft there was a knock. es klingelt someone is ringing. es wird schöner the weather is improving. es geht ihm gut/schlecht he is well/unwell. es lässt sich aushalten it is bearable. es gibt there is or (pl) are

····▸ (als formales Objekt) er hat es

gut he has it made; he's well off. er meinte es gut he meant well. ich hoffe/glaube es I hope/think so

Esche f -,-n ash

Esel m -s,- donkey; (ⅠⅠ: Person) ass

Eskimo m -[s],-[s] Eskimo

Eskorte f -,-n (Mil) escort. **e~ieren** vt escort

essbar adj edible

essen† vt/i (haben) eat; zu Mittag/ Abend e~ have lunch/supper; e~ gehen eat out. **E~** nt -s,- food; (Mahl) meal; (festlich) dinner

Esser(in) m -s,- (f -,-nen) eater

Essig m -s vinegar. **E~gurke** f [pickled] gherkin

Esslöffel m ≈ dessertspoon. **Essstäbchen** ntpl chopsticks. **Esstisch** m dining-table. **Esswaren** fpl food sg; (Vorräte) provisions. **Esszimmer** nt dining-room

Estland nt -s Estonia

Estragon m -s tarragon

etablieren (sich) vr establish oneself/(Geschäft:) itself

Etage /e'taːʒə/ f -,-n storey. **E~nbett** nt bunk-beds pl. **E~nwohnung** f flat

Etappe f -,-n stage

Etat /e'taː/ m -s,-s budget

Eth|ik f - ethic; (Sittenlehre) ethics sg. **e~isch** adj ethical

ethnisch adj ethnic; e~e Säuberung ethnic cleansing

Etikett nt -[e]s,-e[n] label; (Preis-) tag. **e~ieren** vt label

Etui /e'tviː/ nt -s,-s case

etwa adv (ungefähr) about; (zum Beispiel) for instance; (womöglich) perhaps; nicht e~, dass ... not that ... ; denkt nicht e~ ... don't imagine ...

etwas pron something; (fragend/

verneint) anything; (ein bisschen) some, a little; sonst noch e~? anything else? so e~ Ärgerliches! what a nuisance! ● adv a bit

Etymologie f - etymology

euch pron (acc of **ihr** pl) you; (dat) [to] you; (reflexive) yourselves; (einander) each other

euer poss pron pl your. e~e, e~t-s. eure, euret-

Eule f -,-n owl

Euphorie f - euphoria

eur|e poss pron pl your. e~e(r,s) poss pron yours. e~etwegen adv for your sake; (wegen euch) because of you, on your account. e~etwillen adv um e~etwillen for your sake. e~ige poss pron der/die/das e~ige yours

Euro m -[s],[-s] euro. E~- prefix Euro-

Europa n -s Europe. E~- prefix European

Europäer(in) m -s,- (f -,-nen) European. E~isch adj European

Euter nt -s,- udder

evakuier|en vt evacuate. E~ung f - evacuation

evangelisch adj Protestant. E~gelium nt -s,-ien gospel

eventuell adj possible ● adv possibly; (vielleicht) perhaps

Evolution /-'tsio:n/ f - evolution

ewig adj eternal; (endlos) neverending; e~ dauern 🔲 take ages. E~keit f - eternity

Examen nt -s,- & -mina (Sch) examination

Exemplar nt -s,-e specimen; (Buch) copy. e~isch adj exemplary

exerzieren vt/i (haben) (Mil) drill; (üben) practise

exhumieren vt exhume

Exil nt -s exile

Existenz f -,-en existence; (Lebensgrundlage) livelihood

existieren vi (haben) exist

exklusiv adj exclusive. e~e prep (+ gen) excluding

exkommunizieren vt excommunicate

Exkremente npl excrement sg

Expedition /-'tsio:n/ f -,-en expedition

Experiment nt -[e]s,-e experiment. e~ieren vi (haben) experiment

Experte m -n,-n expert

explo|dieren vi (sein) explode. E~sion f -,-en explosion

Expor|t m -[e]s,-e export. E~teur m -s,-e exporter. e~tieren vt export

extra adv separately; (zusätzlich) extra; (eigens) specially; (🔲: absichtlich) on purpose

extravagan|t adj flamboyant; (übertrieben) extravagant

extravertiert adj extrovert

extrem adj extreme. E~ist m -en,-en extremist

Exzellenz f - (title) Excellency

Exzentr|iker m -s,- eccentric. e~isch adj eccentric

....

Ff

....

Fabel f -,-n fable. f~haft 🔲 fantastic

Fabrik f -,-en factory. F~ant m -en,-en manufacturer. F~at nt -[e]s,-e product; (Marke) make. F~ation f - manufacture

Fach nt -[e]s,⸚er compartment;

(*Schub-*) drawer; (*Gebiet*) field; (*Sch*) subject. **F~arbeiter** m skilled worker. **F~arzt** m, **F~ärztin** f specialist. **F~ausdruck** m technical term

Fächer m -s,- fan

Fach|gebiet nt field. **f~kundig** adj expert. **f~lich** adj technical; (*beruflich*) professional. **F~mann** m (pl -leute) expert. **f~männisch** adj expert. **F~schule** f technical college. **F~werkhaus** nt half-timbered house. **F~wort** nt (pl -wörter) technical term

Fackel f -,-n torch

fade adj insipid; (*langweilig*) dull

Faden m -s,- thread; (*Bohnen-*) string; (*Naut*) fathom

Fagott nt -[e]s,-e bassoon

fähig adj capable (zu/gen of); (*tüchtig*) able, competent. **F~keit** f -,-en ability; competence

fahl adj pale

fahnd|en vi (haben) search (nach for). **F~ung** f -,-en search

Fahne f -,-n flag; (*Druck-*) galley [proof]; **eine F~ haben** ☐ reek of alcohol. **F~nflucht** f desertion

Fahr|ausweis m ticket. **F~bahn** f carriageway; (*Straße*) road. **f~bar** adj mobile

Fähre f -,-n ferry

fahr|en† vi (sein) go, travel; (*Fahrer:*) drive; (*Radfahrer:*) ride; (*verkehren*) run, (ab-) leave; (*Schiff:*) sail; **mit dem Auto/Zug f~en** go by car/train; **was ist in ihn gefahren?** ☐ what has got into him? ● vt drive; ride (*Fahrrad*); take (*Kurve*). **f~end** adj moving; (*f~bar*) mobile; (*nicht sesshaft*) travelling. **F~er** m -s,- driver. **F~erflucht** f failure to stop after an accident. **F~erhaus** nt driver's cab. **F~erin** f -,-nen woman driver. **F~gast** m passen-

ger. **F~geld** nt fare. **F~gestell** nt chassis; (*Aviat*) undercarriage. **F~karte** f ticket. **F~kartenschalter** m ticket office. **f~lässig** adj negligent. **F~lässigkeit** f -, negligence. **F~lehrer** m driving instructor. **F~plan** m timetable. **f~planmäßig** adj scheduled ● adv according to/(pünktlich) on schedule. **F~preis** m fare. **F~prüfung** f driving test. **F~rad** nt bicycle. **F~schein** m ticket. **F~schule** f driving school. **F~schüler(in)** m (f) learner driver. **F~stuhl** m lift

Fahrt f -,-en journey; (*Auto*) drive; (*Ausflug*) trip; (*Tempo*) speed

Fährte f -,-n track; (*Witterung*) scent

Fahrt|kosten pl travelling expenses. **F~werk** nt undercarriage. **F~zeug** nt -[e]s,-e vehicle; (*Wasser-*) craft, vessel

fair /fɛːɐ̯/ adj fair

Fakultät f -,-en faculty

Falke m -n,-n falcon

Fall m -[e]s,-e fall; (*Jur, Med, Gram*) case; **im F~[e]** in case (gen of); **auf jeden F~** in any case; (*bestimmt*) definitely; **für alle F~e** just in case; **auf keinen F~** on no account

Falle f -,-n trap

fallen† vi (sein) fall; (*sinken*) go down; **[im Krieg] f~** be killed in the war; **f~ lassen** drop (etw, fig: Plan, jdn); make (Bemerkung)

fällen vt fell; (fig) pass (Urteil)

fällig adj due; (*Wechsel*) mature; **längst f~** long overdue. **F~keit** f - (Comm) maturity

falls conj in case; (wenn) if

Fallschirm m parachute. **F~jäger** m paratrooper. **F~springer** m parachutist

Falltür f trapdoor

falsch adj wrong; (nicht echt, unauf-

fälschen | fassen

84

richtig) false; (*gefälscht*) forged; (*Geld*) counterfeit; (*Schmuck*) fake ● *adv* wrongly; falsely; (*singen*) out of tune; **f~ gehen** (*Uhr.:*) be wrong

fälschen *vt* forge, fake

Falschgeld *nt* counterfeit money

fälschlich *adj* wrong; (*irrtümlich*) mistaken

Falsch|meldung *f* false report; (*absichtlich*) hoax report. **F~münzer** *m* -s,- counterfeiter

Fälschung *f* -,-en forgery, fake

Falte *f* -,-n fold; (*Rock-*) pleat; (*Knitter-*) crease; (*im Gesicht*) line; wrinkle

falten *vt* fold

Falter *m* -s,- butterfly; moth

faltig *adj* creased; (*Gesicht*) lined; wrinkled

familiär *adj* family ; (*vertraut, zudringlich*) familiar; (*zwanglos*) informal

Famili|e /-jə/ *f* -,-n family. **F~nforschung** *f* genealogy. **F~nname** *m* surname. **F~nplanung** *f* family planning. **F~nstand** *m* marital status

Fan /fɛn/ *m* -s,-s fan

Fana|tiker *m* -s,- fanatic. **f~tisch** *adj* fanatical

Fanfare *f* -,-n trumpet; (*Signal*) fanfare

Fang *m* -[e]s, ⸚e capture; (*Beute*) catch; **F~e** (*Krallen*) talons; (*Zähne*) fangs. **f~arm** *m* tentacle. **f~en†** *vt* catch; (*ein-*) capture; **gefangen nehmen** take prisoner. **F~en** *nt* -s **F~en spielen** play tag. **F~frage** *f* catch question

Fantasie *f* -,-n = Phantasie

Farb|aufnahme *f* colour photograph. **F~band** *nt* (*pl* -bänder) typewriter ribbon. **F~e** *f* -,-n colour; (*Maler-*) paint; (*zum Färben*) dye; (*Karten*) suit. **f~echt** *adj* colour-fast

färben *vt* colour; dye (*Textilien, Haare*) ● *vi* (*haben*) not be colour-fast

farb|enblind *adj* colour-blind. **f~enfroh** *adj* colourful. **F~film** *m* colour film. **f~ig** *adj* coloured ● *adv* in colour. **F~ige(r)** *m/f* coloured man/woman. **F~kasten** *m* box of paints. **F~los** *adj* colourless. **F~stift** *m* crayon. **F~stoff** *m* dye; (*Lebensmittel-*) colouring. **F~ton** *m* shade

Färbung *f* -,-en colouring

Farn *m* -[e]s,-e fern

Färse *f* -,-n heifer

Fasan *m* -[e]s,-e[n] pheasant

Faschierte(s) *nt* (*Aust*) mince

Fasching *m* -s (*SGer*) carnival

Fasching, Fastnachtszeit
The carnival season begins at Epiphany and ends on *Aschermittwoch* (Ash Wednesday) for Lent. Depending on the region, it is also called *Karneval* or *Fasnet*, and is celebrated in Germany, Austria and Switzerland. Celebrations reach a climax on *Faschingsdienstag*, or *Rosenmontag* in the Rhineland, when there are street processions.

Faschis|mus *m* - fascism. **F~t** *m* -en,-en fascist. **f~tisch** *adj* fascist

Faser *f* -,-n fibre

Fass *nt* -es, ⸚er barrel, cask; **Bier vom F~** draught beer

Fassade *f* -,-n façade

fassbar *adj* comprehensible; (*greifbar*) tangible

fassen *vt* take [hold of], grasp; (*ergreifen*) seize; (*fangen*) catch; (*ein-*) set; (*enthalten*) hold; (*fig: begreifen*) take in, grasp; conceive (*Plan*); make (*Entschluss*); **sich f~** compose oneself; **sich kurz f~** be brief; **nicht zu f~** (fig) unbelievable ● **vi** (haben) **f~ an** (+ acc) touch

Fassung f -,-en mount; (Edelstein-) setting; (Electr) socket; (Version) version; (Beherrschung) composure; **aus der F~ bringen** disconcert. **F~slos** adj shaken; (erstaunt) flabbergasted. **F~svermögen** nt capacity

fast adv almost, nearly; **f~ nie** hardly ever

fasten vi (haben) fast. **F~enzeit** f Lent. **F~nacht** f Shrovetide; (Karneval) carnival. **F~nachtsdienstag** m Shrove Tuesday

fatal adj fatal; (peinlich) embarrassing

Fata Morgana f -,- -nen mirage

fauchen vi (haben) spit, hiss ● vt snarl

faul adj lazy; (verdorben) rotten, bad; (Ausrede) lame

faulen vi (sein) rot; (Zahn:) decay; (verwesen) putrefy. **f~enzen** vi (haben) be lazy. **F~enzer** m -s,- lazy-bones sg. **F~heit** f - laziness

Fäulnis f - decay

Fauna f - fauna

Faust f -,Fäuste fist; **auf eigene F~** (fig) off one's own bat. **F~handschuh** m mitten. **F~schlag** m punch

Fauxpas /foˈpa/ m -,- gaffe

Favorit(in) /favoˈriːt(m)/ m -en, -en (f -,-nen) (Sport) favourite

Fax nt -,-[e] fax. **f~en** vt fax

Faxen fpl 🗊 antics; **F~ machen** fool about

Faxgerät nt fax machine

Februar m -s,-e February

fechten† vi (haben) fence. **F~er** m -s,- fencer

Feder f -,-n feather; (Schreib-) pen;

(Spitze) nib; (Techn) spring. **F~ball** m shuttlecock; (Spiel) badminton. **F~busch** m plume. **f~leicht** adj as light as a feather. **f~n** vi (haben) be springy; (nachgeben) give; (hoch-) bounce. **f~nd** adj springy; (elastisch) elastic. **F~ung** f - (Techn) springs pl; (Auto) suspension

Fee f -,-n fairy

Fegefeuer nt purgatory

fegen vt sweep

Fehde f -,-n feud

fehl adj **f~ am Platze** out of place. **F~betrag** m deficit. **f~en** vi (haben) be missing/(Sch) absent; (mangeln) be lacking; **mir f~t die Zeit** I haven't got the time; **was f~t ihm?** what's the matter with him? **das hat uns noch gefehlt!** that's all we need! **f~end** adj missing; (Sch) absent

Fehler m -s,- mistake, error; (Sport & fig) fault; (Makel) flaw. **f~frei** adj faultless. **f~haft** adj faulty. **f~los** adj flawless

Fehl|geburt f miscarriage. **F~griff** m mistake. **F~kalkulation** f miscalculation. **F~schlag** m failure. **f~schlagen†** vi sep (sein) fail. **F~start** m (Sport) false start. **F~zündung** f (Auto) misfire

Feier f -,-n celebration; (Zeremonie) ceremony; (Party) party. **F~abend** m end of the working day; **F~abend machen** stop work. **f~lich** adj solemn; (förmlich) formal. **f~n** vt celebrate; hold (Fest) ● vi (haben) celebrate. **F~tag** m [public] holiday; (kirchlicher) feastday; **erster/zweiter F~tag** Christmas Day / Boxing Day. **F~tags** adv on public holidays

feige adj cowardly; **f~ sein** be a coward ● adv in a cowardly way

Feige f -,-n fig

Feig|heit f - cowardice. **F~ling** m -s,-e coward

Feile f -,-n file. **F~n** vt/i (haben) file

feilschen vi (haben) haggle

fein adj fine; (zart) delicate; (Strümpfe) sheer; (Unterschied) subtle; (scharf) keen; (vornehm) refined; (prima) great; **sich f~ machen** dress up. **F~arbeit** f precision work

Feind(in) m -es,-e (f -,-nen) enemy. **f~lich** adj enemy; (f~selig) hostile. **F~schaft** f -,-en enmity

fein|fühlig adj sensitive. **F~gefühl** nt sensitivity; (Takt) delicacy. **F~heit** f -,-en fineness; delicacy; subtlety; refinement. **F~heiten** subtleties. **F~kostgeschäft** nt delicatessen [shop]

feist adj fat

Feld nt -[e]s,-er field; (Fläche) ground; (Sport) pitch; (Schach-) square; (auf Formular) box. **F~bett** nt camp-bed. **F~forschung** f fieldwork. **F~herr** m commander. **F~stecher** m -s,- field-glasses pl. **F~webel** m -s,- (Mil) sergeant. **F~zug** m campaign

Felge f -,-n [wheel] rim

Fell nt -[e]s,-e (Zool) coat; (Pelz) fur; (abgezogen) skin, pelt

Fels m -en,-en rock. **F~block** m boulder. **F~en** m -s,- rock

Femininum nt -s,-na (Gram) feminine

Feminist|(in) m -en,-en (f -,-nen) feminist. **f~isch** adj feminist

Fenchel m -s fennel

Fenster nt -s,- window. **F~brett** nt window sill. **F~scheibe** f [window-]pane

Ferien /ˈfeːriən/ pl holidays; (Univ) vacation sg; **F~ haben** be on holiday. **F~ort** m holiday resort

Ferkel nt -s,- piglet

fern adj distant; **der F~e Osten** the Far East; **sich f~ halten** keep away ●adv far away; **von f~** from a distance ●prep (+ dat) far [away] from. **F~bedienung** f remote control. **F~e** f - distance; **in weiter F~e** far away; (zeitlich) in the distant future. **f~er** adj further ●adv (außerdem) furthermore; (in Zukunft) in future. **f~gelenkt** adj remote-controlled; (Rakete) guided. **F~gespräch** nt long-distance call. **F~glas** nt binoculars pl. **F~kurs[us]** m correspondence course. **F~licht** nt (Auto) full beam. **F~meldewesen** nt telecommunications pl. **F~rohr** nt telescope. **F~schreiben** nt telex

Fernseh|apparat m television set. **f~en†** vi sep (haben) watch television. **F~en** nt -s television. **F~er** m -s,- [television] viewer; (Gerät) television set

Fernsprech|amt nt telephone exchange. **F~er** m telephone

Fern|steuerung f remote control. **F~studium** nt distance learning

Ferse f -,-n heel

fertig adj finished; (bereit) ready; (Comm) ready-made; (Gericht) ready-to-serve; **f~ werden** mit finish; (bewältigen) cope with; **f~ sein** have finished; (fig) be through (mit jdm with s.o.); (⊡: erschöpft) be all in/(seelisch) shattered; **etw f~ bringen** manage to do sth; (beenden) finish sth; **etw/jdn f~ machen** finish sth; (bereitmachen) get sth/s.o. ready; (⊡: erschöpfen) wear s.o. out; (seelisch) shatter s.o.; **sich f~ machen** get ready; **etw f~ stellen** complete sth ●adv **f~ essen/lesen** finish eating/reading. **F~bau** m (pl -bauten) prefabricated building. **f~en** vt make. **F~gericht** nt ready-to-serve meal. **F~haus** nt prefabricated house. **F~keit** f -,-en skill. **F~stellung** f completion. **F~ung** f - manufacture

fesch adj ① attractive

Fessel f -,-n ankle

fesseln vt tie up; tie (an + acc to); (fig) fascinate

fest adj firm; (nicht flüssig) solid; (erstarrt) set; (haltbar) strong; (nicht locker) tight; (feststehend) fixed; (ständig) steady; (Anstellung) permanent; (Schlaf) sound; (Blick, Stimme) steady; **f~** werden harden; (Gelee:) set; **f~e** Nahrung solids pl ● adv firmly; tightly; steadily; soundly; (kräftig, tüchtig) hard; **f~** schlafen be fast asleep; **f~** angestellt be permanent

Fest nt -[e]s,-e celebration; (Party) party; (Relig) festival; frohes **F~!** happy Christmas!

fest|binden† vt sep tie (an + dat to). **f~bleiben** vi sep (sein) (fig) remain firm. **f~halten**† v sep ● vt hold on to; (aufzeichnen) record; sich **f~halten** hold on ● vi (haben) **f~halten an** (+ dat) (fig) stick to; cling to (Tradition). **f~igen** vt strengthen. **F~iger** m -s,- styling lotion/(Schaum-) mousse. **F~igkeit** f - (s. fest) firmness; solidity; strength; steadiness. **F~land** nt mainland; (Kontinent) continent. **f~legen** v sep (fig) fix, settle; lay down (Regeln); tie up (Geld); sich **f~legen** commit oneself

festlich adj festive. **F~keiten** fpl festivities

fest|liegen† vi sep (haben) be fixed, settled. **f~machen** v sep ● vt fasten/(binden) tie (an + dat to); (f~legen) fix, settle ● vi (haben) (Naut) moor. **F~nahme** f -,-n arrest. **f~nehmen**† vt sep arrest. **f~netz** nt land-

line network. **F~platte** f hard disk. **f~setzen** vt sep fix, settle; (inhaftieren) gaol; sich **f~setzen** collect. **f~sitzen**† vi sep (haben) be firm/(Schraube:) tight; (haften) stick; (nicht weiterkommen) be stuck. **F~spiele** npl festival sg. **f~stehen**† vi sep (haben) be certain. **f~stellen** vt sep (ermitteln) establish; (bemerken) notice; (sagen) state. **F~tag** m special day

Festung f -,-en fortress

Festzug m [grand] procession

Fete /ˈfeːtə, ˈfɛːtə/ f -,-n party

fett adj fat; fatty; (fettig) greasy; (üppig) rich; (Druck) bold. **F~** nt -[e]s,-e fat; (flüssig) grease. **f~arm** adj low-fat. **f~en** vt grease ● vi (haben) be greasy. **F~fleck** m grease mark. **f~ig** adj greasy.

Fetzen m -s,- scrap; (Stoff) rag

feucht adj damp, moist; (Luft) humid. **F~igkeit** f - dampness; (Nässe) moisture; (Luft-) humidity. **F~igkeitscreme** f moisturizer

Feuer nt -s,- fire; (für Zigarette) light; (Begeisterung) passion; **F~** machen light a fire. **F~alarm** m fire alarm. **f~gefährlich** adj [in]flammable. **F~leiter** f fire escape. **F~löscher** m -s,- fire extinguisher. **F~melder** m -s,- fire alarm. **f~n** vi (haben) fire (auf + acc on). **F~probe** f (fig) test. **f~rot** adj crimson. **F~stein** m flint. **F~stelle** f hearth. **F~treppe** f fire escape. **F~wache** f fire station. **F~waffe** f firearm. **F~wehr** f -,-en fire brigade. **F~wehrauto** nt fire engine. **F~wehrmann** m (pl -männer od -leute) fireman. **F~werk** nt firework display, fireworks pl. **F~zeug** nt lighter

feurig adj fiery; (fig) passionate

Fiaker m -s,- (Aust) horse-drawn cab

Fichte f -,-n spruce

Fieber nt -s [raised] temperature. F~ haben have a temperature. f~n vi (haben) be feverish. F~ **thermometer** nt thermometer

fiebrig adj feverish

Figur f -,-en figure; (Roman-, Film-) character; (Schach-) piece

Filet /fi'le:/ nt -s,-s fillet

Filiale f -,-n (Comm) branch

Filigran nt -s filigree

Film m -[e]s,-e film; (Kino-) film; (Schicht) coating. f~en vt/i (haben) film. F~kamera f cine/ (für Kinofilm) film camera

Filt|er m & (Techn) nt -s,- filter; (Zigaretten-) filter-tip. f~ern vt filter. F~erzigarette f filter-tipped cigarette. f~rieren vt filter

Filz m -es felt. F~stift m felttipped pen

Fimmel m -s,- ⚇ obsession

Finale nt -s,- (Mus) finale; (Sport) final

Finanz f -,-en finance. F~amt nt tax office. f~iell adj financial. f~ie ren vt finance. F~minister m minister of finance

find|en† vt find; (meinen) think; den Tod ~ meet one's death; wie f~est du das? what do you think of that? es wird sich f~en it'll turn up; (fig) it'll be all right ● vi (haben) find one's way. F~er m -s,- finder. F~erlohn m reward. f~ig adj resourceful

Finesse f -,-n (Kniff) trick; F~n (Techn) refinements

Finger m -s,- finger; die F~ las sen von ⚇ leave alone. F~ab druck m finger mark; (Admin) fingerprint. F~hut m thimble. F~nagel m fingernail. F~spitze f fingertip. F~zeig m -[e]s,-e hint

Fink m -en,-en finch

Finn|e m -n,-n, F~in f -,-nen Finn. f~isch adj Finnish. F~land nt -s Finland

finster adj dark; (düster) gloomy; (unheildrohend) sinister. F~nis f darkness; (Astronomy) eclipse

Firm|a f -,-men firm, company

Firmen|wagen m company car. F~zeichen nt trade mark, logo

Firmung f -,-en (Relig) confirmation

Firnis m -ses,-se varnish. f~sen vt varnish

First m -[e]s,-e [roof] ridge

Fisch m -[e]s,-e fish; F~e (Astrology) Pisces. F~dampfer m trawler. f~en vt/i (haben) fish. F~er m -s,- fisherman. F~erei f - fishing. F~händler m fishmonger. F~rei her m heron

Fiskus m - der F~ the Treasury

fit adj fit. **Fitness** f - fitness

fix adj ⚇ quick; (geistig) bright; f~e Idee obsession; fix und fertig all finished; (bereit) all ready; (⚇: er schöpft) shattered. F~er m -s,- ⊠ junkie

fixieren vt stare at; (Phot) fix

Fjord m -[e]s,-e fiord

flach adj flat; (eben) level; (niedrig) low; (nicht tief) shallow

Flachbildschirm m flat screen

Fläche f -,-n (Ober-) surface; (Seite) face. F~nmaß nt square measure

Flachs m -es flax. f~blond adj flächsen-haired; (Haar) flaxen

flackern vi (haben) flicker

Flagge f -,-n flag

Flair /flɛ:ɐ/ nt -s air, aura

Flak f -,-[s] anti-aircraft artillery/(Geschütz) gun

flämisch adj Flemish

Flamme f -,-n flame;

(Koch-) burner

Flanell m -s (Textiles) flannel

Flank|e f -,-n flank. **f~ieren** vt flank

Flasche f -,-n bottle. **f~nbier** nt bottled beer. **F~nöffner** m bottle-opener. **F~npfand** nt deposit (on bottle)

flatter|haft adj fickle. **f~n** vi (sein/haben) flutter; (Segel:) flap

flau adj (schwach) faint; (Comm) slack

Flaum m -[e]s down. **f~ig** adj downy; **f~ig rühren** (Aust Culin) cream

flauschig adj fleecy; (Spielzeug) fluffy

Flausen fpl 🗌 silly ideas

Flaute f -,-n (Naut) calm; (Comm) slack period; (Schwäche) low

fläzen (sich) vr 🗌 sprawl

Flechte f -,-n (Med) eczema; (Bot) lichen; (Zopf) plait. **f~n**† vt plait; weave (Korb)

Fleck m -[e]s,-e[n] spot; (größer) patch; (Schmutz-) stain, mark; **blauer F~** bruise. **f~en** vi (haben) stain. **f~enlos** adj spotless. **F~entferner** m -s,- stain remover. **f~ig** adj stained

Fledermaus f bat

Flegel m -s,- lout. **f~haft** adj loutish

flehen vi (haben) beg (um for)

Fleisch nt -[e]s flesh; (Culin) meat; (Frucht-) pulp; **F~ fressend** (Culin) carnivorous. **F~er** m -s,- butcher. **F~fresser** m carnivore. **f~ig** adj fleshy. **f~lich** adj carnal. **F~wolf** m mincer

Fleiß m -es diligence; **mit F~** diligently; (absichtlich) on purpose. **f~ig** adj diligent; (arbeitsam) industrious

fletschen vt die Zähne f~ (Tier:)

bare its teeth

flex|ibel adj flexible; (Einband) limp. **F~ibilität** f - flexibility

flicken vt mend; (mit Flicken) patch. **F~** m -s,- patch

Flieder m -s lilac

Fliege f -,-n fly; (Schleife) bow-tie. **f~n**† vi (sein) fly; (geworfen werden) be thrown; (🗌: fallen) fall; (🗌: entlassen werden) be fired/(von der Schule) expelled; **in die Luft f~n** blow up ● vt fly. **f~nd** adj flying. **F~r** m -s,- airman; (Pilot) pilot; (🗌: Flugzeug) plane. **F~rangriff** m air raid

flieh|en† vi (sein) flee (vor + dat from); (entweichen) escape ● vt shun. **f~end** adj fleeing; (Kinn, Stirn) receding

Fliese f -,-n tile

Fließ|band nt assembly line. **f~en**† vi (sein) flow; (aus Wasserhahn) run. **f~end** adj flowing; (Wasser) running; (Verkehr) moving; (geläufig) fluent

flimmern vi (haben) shimmer; (TV) flicker

flink adj nimble; (schnell) quick

Flinte f -,-n shotgun

Flirt /flœɐt/ m -s,-s flirtation. **f~en** vi (haben) flirt

Flitter m -s sequins pl. **f~wochen** fpl honeymoon sg

flitzen vi (sein) 🗌 dash

Flock|e f -,-n flake; (Wolle) tuft. **f~ig** adj fluffy

Floh m -[e]s,ꞏe flea. **F~spiel** nt tiddly-winks sg

Flora f - flora

Florett nt -[e]s,-e foil

florieren vi (haben) flourish

Floskel f -,-n [empty] phrase

Floß nt -es,ꞏe raft

Flosse f -,-n fin; (Seehund-, Gum-

mi-) flipper; (*sl:* Hand) paw

Flöt|e *f* -,-n flute; (*Block-*) recorder. **f~en** *vi* (haben) play the flute/recorder; (**!**: *pfeifen*) whistle ● *vt* play on the flute/recorder. **F~ist(in)** *m* -en,-en (*f* -,-nen) flautist

flott *adj* quick; (*lebhaft*) lively; (*schick*) smart

Flotte *f* -,-n fleet

flottmachen *vt sep* wieder f~ (*Naut*) refloat; get going again (*Auto*); put back on its feet (*Unternehmen*)

Flöz *nt* -es,-e [coal] seam

Fluch *m* -[e]s,ᵉe curse. **f~en** *vi* (haben) curse, swear

Flucht *f* -,- flight; (*Entweichen*) escape; die F~ ergreifen take flight. **f~artig** *adj* hasty

flücht|en *vi* (sein) flee (vor + *dat* from); (*entweichen*) escape ● *vr* sich f~en take refuge. **f~ig** *adj* fugitive; (*kurz*) brief; (*Blick*) fleeting; (*Bekanntschaft*) passing; (*oberflächlich*) cursory; (*nicht sorgfältig*) careless. **f~ig kennen** know slightly. **F~igkeitsfehler** *m* slip. **F~ling** *m* -s,-e fugitive; (*Pol*) refugee

Fluchwort *nt* (*pl* -wörter) swear word

Flug *m* -[e]s,ᵉe flight. **F~abwehr** *f* anti-aircraft defence

Flügel *m* -s,- wing; (*Fenster-*) casement; (*Mus*) grand piano

Fluggast *m* [air] passenger

flügge *adj* fully-fledged

Flug|gesellschaft *f* airline. **F~hafen** *m* airport. **F~lotse** *m* air-traffic controller. **F~platz** *m* airport; (*klein*) airfield. **F~preis** *m* air fare. **F~schein** *m* air ticket. **F~schneise** *f* flight path. **F~schreiber** *m* -s,- flight recorder. **F~schrift** *f* pamphlet. **F~steig** *m* -[e]s,-e gate. **F~zeug** *nt* -[e]s,-e

aircraft, plane

Flunder *f* -,-n flounder

flunkern *vi* (haben) **!** tell fibs

Flur *m* -[e]s,-e [entrance] hall; (*Gang*) corridor

Fluss *m* -es,ᵉe river; (*Fließen*) flow; im F~ (*fig*) in a state of flux. **f~abwärts** *adv* downstream. **f~aufwärts** *adv* upstream

flüssig *adj* liquid; (*Lava*) molten; (*fließend*) fluent; (*Verkehr*) freely moving. **F~keit** *f* -,-en liquid; (*Anat*) fluid

Flusspferd *nt* hippopotamus

flüstern *vt/i* (haben) whisper

Flut *f* -,-en high tide; (*fig*) flood

Föderation /-'tsio:n/ *f* -,-en federation

Fohlen *nt* -s,- foal

Föhn *m* -s föhn [wind]; (*Haartrockner*) hairdrier. **f~en** *vt* [blow-]dry

Folge *f* -,-n consequence; (*Reihe*) succession; (*Fortsetzung*) instalment; (*Teil*) part. **f~n** *vi* (sein) follow (jdm/etw s.o./sth); (*zuhören*) listen (dat to); wie f~t as follows ● (haben) (*gehorchen*) obey (jdm s.o.). **f~end** *adj* following; **F~** endes the following

folger|n *vt* conclude (aus from). **F~ung** *f* -,-en conclusion

folg|lich *adv* consequently. **f~sam** *adj* obedient

Folie /'fo:liə/ *f* -,-en foil; (*Plastik-*) film

Folklore *f* folklore

Folter *f* -,-n torture. **f~n** *vt* torture

Fön ® *m* -s,-e hairdrier

Fonds /fõ:/ *m* -,- fund

fönen* *vt* = föhnen

Förder|band *nt* (*pl* -bänder) conveyor belt. **f~lich** *adj* beneficial

fordern *vt* demand; (*beanspruchen*) claim; (*zum Kampf*) challenge

fördern vt promote; (unterstützen) encourage; (finanziell) sponsor; (gewinnen) extract

Forderung f -,-en demand; (Anspruch) claim

Förderung f - promotion; encouragement; (Techn) production

Forelle f -,-n trout

Form f -,-en form; (Gestalt) shape; (Culin, Techn) mould; (Back-) tin; [gut] in F~ in good form

Formalität f -,-en formality

Format nt -[e]s,-e format; (Größe) size; (fig: Bedeutung) stature

formatieren vt format

Formel f -,-n formula

formen vt shape, mould; (bilden) form; sich f~ take shape

förmlich adj formal

form|los adj shapeless; (zwanglos) informal. **F~sache** f formality

Formular nt -s,-e [printed] form

formulier|en vt formulate, word. **F~ung** f -,-en wording

forsch|en vi (haben) search (nach for). **f~end** adj searching. **F~er** m -s,- research scientist; (Reisender) explorer. **F~ung** f -,-en research

Forst m -[e]s,-e forest

Förster m -s,- forester

Forstwirtschaft f forestry

Fort nt -s,-s (Mil) fort

fort adv away; **f~ sein** be away; (gegangen/verschwunden) have gone; **und so f~** and so on; **in einem f~** continuously. **F~bewegung** f locomotion. **F~bildung** f further education/training. **f~bleiben†** vi sep (sein) stay away. **f~bringen†** vt sep take away. **f~fahren†** vi sep (sein) go away • (haben/sein) continue (zu to). **f~fallen†** vi sep (sein) be dropped/(ausgelassen) omitted; (ent-

fallen) no longer apply; (aufhören) cease. **f~führen** vt sep continue. **f~gehen†** vi sep (sein) leave, go away; (ausgehen) go out; (andauern) go on. **f~geschritten** adj advanced; (spät) late. **F~geschrittene(r)** m/f advanced student. **f~lassen†** vt sep let go; (auslassen) omit. **f~laufen†** vi sep (sein) run away; (sich f~setzen) continue. **f~laufend** adj consecutive. **f~pflanzen (sich)** vr sep reproduce; (Ton, Licht:) travel. **F~pflanzung** f - reproduction. **F~pflanzungsorgan** nt reproductive organ. **f~schicken** vt sep send away; (abschicken) send off. **f~schreiten†** vi sep (sein) continue; (Fortschritte machen) progress, advance. **f~schreitend** adj progressive; (Alter) advancing. **F~schritt** m progress; **F~schritte machen** make progress. **f~schrittlich** adj progressive. **f~setzen** vt sep continue; sich **f~setzen** continue. **F~setzung** f -,-en continuation; (Folge) instalment; **F~setzung folgt** to be continued. **F~setzungsroman** m serialized novel, serial. **f~während** adj constant. **f~ziehen†** vt sep move • vt pull away • vi (sein) move away

Fossil nt -s,-ien fossil

Foto nt -s,-s photo. **F~apparat** m camera. **f~gen** adj photogenic

Fotograf(in) m -en,-en (f -,-nen) photographer. **F~ie** f -,-n photography; (Bild) photograph. **f~ieren** vt take a photo[graph] • vi (haben) take photographs. **f~isch** adj photographic

Fotohandy nt camera phone

Fotokopie f photocopy. **F~ren** vt photocopy. **F~rgerät** nt photocopier

Fötus m -,-ten foetus

Foul /faul/ nt -s,-s (Sport) foul.

f~en vt foul

Fracht f -,-en freight. F~er m -s,- freighter. F~gut nt freight. F~schiff nt cargo boat

Frack m -[e]s,=e & -s tailcoat

Frage f -,-n question; nicht in F~ kommen s. infrage. F~bogen m questionnaire. f~n vt (haben) ask; sich f~n wonder (ob whether). f~nd adj questioning. F~zeichen nt question mark

frag|lich adj doubtful; (Person, Sache) in question. f~los adv undoubtedly

Fragment nt -[e]s,-e fragment

fragwürdig adj questionable; (verdächtig) dubious

Fraktion /-'tsio:n/ f -,-en parliamentary party

Franken¹ m -s,- (Swiss) franc

Franken² nt -s Franconia

frankieren vt stamp, frank

Frankreich nt -s France

Fransen fpl fringe sg

Franz|ose m -n,-n Frenchman; die F~osen the French pl. F~ösin f -,-nen Frenchwoman. f~ösisch adj French. F~ösisch nt -[s] (Lang) French

Fraß m -es feed; (pej: Essen) muck

Fratze f -,-n grotesque face; (Grimasse) grimace

Frau f -,-en woman; (Ehe-) wife; F~ Thomas Mrs Thomas; Unsere Liebe F~ (Relig) Our Lady

Frauen|arzt m gynaecologist. F~rechtlerin f -,-nen feminist

Fräulein nt -s,- single woman; (jung) young lady; (Anrede) Miss

frech adj cheeky; (unverschämt) impudent. F~heit f -,-en cheekiness; impudence; (Äußerung) impertinence

frei adj free; (freischaffend) freelance; (Künstler) independent; (nicht besetzt) vacant; (offen) open; (bloß) bare; f~er Tag day off; sich (dat) f~ nehmen take time off; f~ machen (räumen) clear; vacate (Platz); (befreien) liberate; f~ lassen leave free; ist dieser Platz f~? is this seat taken? 'Zimmer f~' 'vacancies' ● adv freely; (ohne Notizen) without notes; (umsonst) free

Frei|bad nt open-air swimming pool. f~beruflich adj & adv freelance. F~e nt im F~en in the open air, out of doors. F~gabe f release. f~geben† v sep ● vt release; (eröffnen) open; jdm einen Tag f~geben give s.o. a day off ● vi (haben) jdm f~geben give s.o. time off. f~gebig adj generous. F~gebigkeit f - generosity. f~haben† v sep ● vt eine Stunde f~haben have an hour off; (Sch) have a free period ● vi (haben) be off work/(Sch) school; (beurlaubt sein) have time off. f~händig adv without holding on

Freiheit f -,-en freedom, liberty. F~strafe f prison sentence

Frei|herr m baron. F~körperkultur f naturism. F~lassung f - release. f~lauf m free-wheel. f~legen vt sep expose. f~lich adv admittedly; (natürlich) of course. F~lichttheater nt open-air theatre. f~machen vt sep (frankieren) frank; (entkleiden) bare; einen Tag f~machen take a day off. F~maurer m Freemason. f~schaffend adj freelance. F~schwimmen (sich) v sep pass one's swimming test. f~sprechen† vt sep acquit. F~spruch m acquittal. f~stehen† vi sep (haben) stand empty; es steht ihm f~ (fig) he is free (zu to). f~stellen vt sep exempt (von from); jdm etw f~stellen leave sth

up to s.o. **F~stil** m freestyle.
F~stoß m free kick

Freitag m Friday. **f~s** adv on
Fridays

Frei|tod m suicide. **F~umschlag**
m stamped envelope. **f~weg** adv
freely; (*offen*) openly. **f~willig** adj
voluntary. **F~willige(r)** m/f volunteer. **F~zeichen** nt ringing tone;
(*Rufzeichen*) dialling tone. **F~zeit** f
free or spare time; (*Muße*) leisure.
F~zeit- prefix leisure... **F~zeitbe-
kleidung** f casual wear. **f~zügig**
adj unrestricted; (*großzügig*) liberal

fremd adj foreign; (*unbekannt*)
strange; (*nicht das eigene*) other
people's; **ein f~er Mann** a stranger; **f~e Leute** strangers; **unter
f~em Namen** under an assumed
name; **ich bin hier f~** I'm a stranger here. **F~e** f - in der **F~e** away
from home; (*im Ausland*) in a foreign country. **F~e(r)** m/f stranger;
(*Ausländer*) foreigner; (*Tourist*) tourist. **F~enführer** m [tourist] guide.
F~enverkehr m tourism. **F~en-
zimmer** nt room [to let]; (*Gäste-*)
guest room. **f~gehen**† vi sep (*sein*)
🔒 be unfaithful. **F~sprache** f foreign language. **F~wort** nt (pl
-wörter) foreign word

Freske f -,-n, **Fresko** nt s,-ken
fresco

Fresse f -,-n 🔲 (*Mund*) gob; (*Gesicht*) mug. **f~n**† vt/i (*haben*) eat.
F~n nt -s feed; (*sl: Essen*) grub

Fressnapf m feeding bowl

Freud|e f -,-n pleasure; (*innere*)
joy; **mit F~en** with pleasure; **jdm
eine F~e machen** please s.o. **f~ig**
adj joyful

freuen vt please; **sich f~** be
pleased (*über + acc* about); **sich f~
auf (+ acc)** look forward to; **es
freut mich** I'm glad (*dass* that)

Freund m -es,-e friend; (*Verehrer*)

boyfriend. **F~in** f -,-nen friend;
(*Liebste*) girlfriend. **f~lich** adj kind;
(*umgänglich*) friendly; (*angenehm*)
pleasant. **f~licherweise** adv kindly.
F~lichkeit f -,-en kindness; friend-
liness; pleasantness

Freundschaft f -,-en friendship;
F~ schließen become friends.
f~lich adj friendly

Frieden m -s peace; **F~ schließen**
make peace; **im F~** in peacetime;
lass mich in F~! leave me alone!
F~svertrag m peace treaty

Fried|hof m cemetery. **f~lich** adj
peaceful

frieren† vi (*haben*) (Person:) be
cold; *impers* **es friert mich**; **gefroren**
it is freezing/there has been a frost;
frierst du? are you cold? ● adv
(*sein*) (*gefrieren*) freeze

Fries m -es,-e frieze

frisch adj fresh; (*sauber*) clean;
(*leuchtend*) bright; (*munter*) lively;
(*rüstig*) fit; **sich f~ machen** freshen
up ● adv freshly, newly; **im Bett
f~ beziehen** put clean sheets on a
bed; **f~ gestrichen!** wet paint!
F~e f - freshness; brightness; liveliness; fitness. **F~haltepackung** f
vacuum pack

Fri|seur /friˈzøːɐ̯/ m -s,-e hair-
dresser; (*Herren-*) barber. **F~seur-
salon** m hairdressing salon.
F~seuse f -,-n hairdresser

frisier|en vt jdn/sich **f~en** do
someone's/one's hair; **die Bilanz/
einen Motor f~en** 🔲 fiddle the ac-
counts/soup up an engine

Frisör m -s, -e = Friseur

Frist f -,-en period; (*Termin*) dead-
line; (*Aufschub*) time; **drei Tage F~**
three days' grace. **f~los** adj instant

Frisur f -,-en hairstyle

frittieren vt deep-fry

frivol /friˈvoːl/ adj frivolous

froh adj happy; (freudig) joyful; (erleichtert) glad

fröhlich adj cheerful; (vergnügt) merry. **F~keit** f - cheerfulness; merriment

fromm adj devout; (gutartig) docile

Frömmigkeit f - devoutness

Fronleichnam m Corpus Christi

Front f -,-en front. **f~al** adj frontal; (Zusammenstoß) head-on ● adv from the front; (zusammenstoßen) head-on. **F~alzusammenstoß** m head-on collision

Frosch m -[e]s,¨e frog. **F~laich** m frog-spawn. **F~mann** m (pl -männer) frogman

Frost m -[e]s,¨e frost. **F~beule** f chilblain

frösteln vi (haben) shiver

frost|ig adj frosty. **F~schutzmittel** nt antifreeze

Frottee nt & m -s towelling; **F~[hand]tuch** nt terry towel

frottieren vt rub down

Frucht f -,¨e fruit; (fig) fruit. **f~ tragen** bear fruit. **f~bar** adj fertile; (fig) fruitful. **F~barkeit** f - fertility

früh adj early ● adv early; (morgens) in the morning; **heute f~** this morning; **von f~ an** od **auf** from an early age. **f~aufsteher** m -s,- early riser. **F~e** f - in aller **F~e** bright and early; in der **F~e** (SGer) in the morning. **f~er** adv earlier; (eher) sooner; (ehemals) formerly; (vor langer Zeit) in the old days; **f~er oder später** sooner or later; **ich wohnte f~er in X** I used to live in X. **f~ere(r,s)** adj earlier; (ehemalig) former; (vorige) previous; in **f~eren Zeiten** in former times. **f~estens** adv at the earliest. **F~geburt** f premature birth/(Kind) baby. **F~jahr** nt spring. **F~ling** m -s,-e spring. **f~morgens** adv early

in the morning. **f~reif** adj precocious

Frühstück nt breakfast. **f~en** vi (haben) have breakfast

frühzeitig adj & adv early; (vorzeitig) premature

Frustr|ation /-'tsjo:n/ f -,-en frustration. **f~ieren** vt frustrate

Fuchs m -es,¨e fox; (Pferd) chestnut. **f~en** vt (fam) annoy

Füchsin f -,-nen vixen

Fuge[1] f -,-n joint

Fuge[2] f -,-n (Mus) fugue

füg|en vt fit (in + acc into); (an-) join (an + acc on to); (dazu-) add (zu to); **sich f~en** fit (in + acc into); adjoin/(folgen) follow (an etw acc sth); (fig: gehorchen) submit (dat to). **f~sam** adj obedient.

F~ung f -,-en eine **F~ung des Schicksals** a stroke of fate

fühl|bar adj noticeable. **f~en** vt/i (haben) feel; **sich f~en** feel (krank/einsam ill/lonely); (☐: stolz sein) fancy oneself. **F~er** m -s,- feeler. **F~ung** f - contact

Fuhre f -,-n load

führ|en vt lead; guide (Tourist); (geleiten) take; (leiten) run; (befehligen) command; (verkaufen) stock; bear (Namen); keep (Liste, Bücher); bei od mit sich **f~en** carry ● vi (haben) lead; (verlaufen) go, run; zu etw **f~en** lead to sth. **f~end** adj leading. **F~er** m -s,- leader; (Fremden-) guide; (Buch) guide[book]. **F~erhaus** nt driver's cab. **F~erschein** m driving licence; den **F~erschein machen** take one's driving test. **F~erscheinentzug** m disqualification from driving.

F~ung f -,-en leadership; (Leitung) management; (Mil) command; (Betragen) conduct; (Besichtigung) guided tour; (Vorsprung) lead; in **F~ung gehen** go into the lead

Fuhr|unternehmer *m* haulage contractor. **F~werk** *nt* cart

Fülle *f* -,-n abundance, wealth (an + *dat* of); (*Körper:*) plumpness. **f~n** *vt* fill; (*Culin*) stuff

Füllen *nt* -s,- foal

Füll|er *m* -s,- [T], **F~federhalter** *m* fountain pen. **F~ung** *f* -,-en filling; (*Braten-*) stuffing

fummeln *vi* (haben) fumble (an + *dat* with)

Fund *m* -[e]s,-e find

Fundament *nt* -[e]s,-e foundations *pl.* **f~al** *adj* fundamental

Fundbüro *nt* lost-property office

fünf *inv adj.* **F~** *f* -,-en five; (*Sch*) ≈ fail mark. **F~linge** *mpl* quintuplets. **f~te(r,s)** *adj* fifth. **f~zehn** *inv adj* fifteen. **f~zehnte(r,s)** *adj* fifteenth. **f~zig** *inv adj* fifty. **f~zigste(r,s)** *adj* fiftieth

fungieren *vi* (haben) act (als as)

Funk *m* -s radio. **F~e** *m* -n,-n spark. **f~eln** *vi* (haben) sparkle; (*Stern:*) twinkle. **F~en** *m* -s,- spark. **f~en** *vt* radio. **F~gerät** *nt* walkie-talkie. **F~spruch** *m* radio message. **F~streife** *f* [police] radio patrol

Funktion /-'tsjo:n/ *f* -,-en function; (*Stellung*) position; (*Funktionieren*) working; außer **F~** out of action. **f~är** *m* -s,-e official. **f~ieren** *vi* (haben) work

für *prep* (+ *acc*) for; Schritt für Schritt step by step; was für [ein] what [a]! (*fragend*) what sort of [a]? **F~** *nt* das **Für** und **Wider** the pros and cons *pl*

Furche *f* -,-n furrow

Furcht *f* - fear (vor + *dat* of); **F~** erregend terrifying. **f~bar** *adj* terrible

fürcht|en *vt/i* (haben) fear; sich **f~en** be afraid (vor + *dat* of).

f~erlich *adj* dreadful

füreinander *adv* for each other

Furnier *nt* -s,-e veneer. **F~t** *adj* veneered

Fürsorg|e *f* care; (*Admin*) welfare; ([T]: *Geld*) ≈ social security. **F~er(in)** *m* -s,- (*f* -,-nen) social worker. **f~lich** *adj* solicitous

Fürst *m* -en,-en prince. **F~entum** *nt* -s, ᵉr principality. **F~in** *f* -,-nen princess

Furt *f* -,-en ford

Furunkel *m* -s,- (*Med*) boil

Fürwort *nt* (*pl* -wörter) pronoun

Furz *m* -es,-e (*vulgar*) fart

Fusion *f* -,-en fusion; (*Comm*) merger

Fuß *m* -es,ᵉe foot; (*Aust: Bein*) leg; (*Lampen-*) base; (*von Weinglas*) stem; zu Fuß on foot; zu Fuß gehen walk; auf freiem Fuß free. **F~abdruck** *m* footprint. **F~abtreter** *m* -s,- doormat. **F~ball** *m* football. **F~ballspieler** *m* footballer. **F~balltoto** *nt* football pools *pl.* **F~bank** *f* footstool. **F~boden** *m* floor

Fussel *f* -,-n & *m* -s,-[n] piece of fluff; **F~n** fluff *sg.* **f~n** *vi* (haben) shed fluff

fußen *vi* (haben) be based (auf + *dat* on)

Fußgänger|(in) *m* -s,- (*f* -,-nen) pedestrian. **F~brücke** *f* footbridge. **F~zone** *f* pedestrian precinct

Fuß|geher *m* -s,- (*Aust*) = **F~gänger. F~gelenk** *nt* ankle. **F~hebel** *m* pedal. **F~nagel** *m* toenail. **F~note** *f* footnote. **F~pflege** *f* chiropody. **F~rücken** *m* instep. **F~sohle** *f* sole of the foot. **F~tritt** *m* kick. **F~weg** *m* footpath; eine Stunde **F~weg** an hour's walk

futsch *pred adj* [T] gone

Futter¹ *nt* -s feed; (*Trocken-*)

fodder

Futter² nt -s, - (Kleider-) lining

Futteral nt -s, -e case

füttern¹ vt feed

füttern² vt line

Futur nt -s (Gram) future

Gg

Gabe f -,-n gift; (Dosis) dose

Gabel f -,-n fork. **g~n (sich)** vr fork. **G~stapler** m -s, - fork-lift truck. **G~ung** f -,-en fork

gackern vi (haben) cackle

gaffen vi (haben) gape, stare

Gage /'ga:ʒə/ f -,-n (Theat) fee

gähnen vi (haben) yawn

Gala f - ceremonial dress

Galavorstellung f gala performance

Galerie f -,-en gallery

Galgen m -s, - gallows sg. **G~frist** f 🔟 reprieve

Galionsfigur f figurehead

Galle f - bile; (G~nblase) gall-bladder. **G~nblase** f gall-bladder. **G~nstein** m gallstone

Galopp m -s gallop; im G~ at a gallop. **g~ieren** vi (sein) gallop

gamm|eln vi (haben) 🔟 loaf around. **G~ler(in)** m -s, - (f -,-nen) drop-out

Gams f -,-en (Aust) chamois

Gämse f -,-n chamois

Gang m -[e]s, ⁼e walk; (G~art) gait; (Boten-) errand; (Funktionieren) running; (Verlauf, Culin) course; (Durch-) passage; (Korridor) corridor; (zwischen Sitzreihen) aisle, gangway;

(Anat) duct; (Auto) gear; in G~ bringen get going; im G~e sein be in progress; Essen mit vier G~en four-course meal

gängig adj common; (Comm) popular

Gangschaltung f gear change

Gangster /'gɛŋstɐ/ m -s, - gangster

Ganove m -n,-n 🔟 crook

Gans f -, ⁼e goose

Gänse|blümchen nt -s, - daisy. **G~füßchen** ntpl inverted commas. **G~haut** f goose-pimples pl. **G~rich** m -s,-e gander

ganz adj whole, entire; (vollständig) complete; (🔟: heil) undamaged, intact; (bis auf) die ganze Zeit all the time, the whole time; eine g~e Weile/Menge quite a while/lot; inv g~ Deutschland the whole of Germany; wieder g~ machen 🔟 mend; im Großen und G~en on the whole ● adv quite; (völlig) completely, entirely; (sehr) very; nicht g~ not quite; g~ allein all on one's own; g~ und gar completely, totally; g~ und gar nicht not at all. **G~e(s)** nt whole. **g~jährig** adv all the year round. **g~tägig** adj & adv full-time; (geöffnet) all day. **g~tags** adv all day; (arbeiten) full-time

gar¹ adj done, cooked

gar² adv gar nicht/nichts/niemand not/nothing/no one at all

Garage /ga'ra:ʒə/ f -,-n garage

Garantie f -,-n guarantee. **g~ren** vt/i (haben) [für] etw g~ren guarantee sth. **G~schein** m guarantee

Garderobe f -,-n (Kleider) wardrobe; (Ablage) cloakroom; (Künstler-) dressing-room. **G~nfrau** f cloakroom attendant

Gardine f -,-n curtain

garen vt/i (haben) cook

gären† vi (haben) ferment; (fig) seethe

Garn nt -[e]s,-e yarn; (Näh-) cotton

Garnele f -,-n shrimp; prawn

garnieren vt decorate; (Culin) garnish

Garnison f -,-en garrison

Garnitur f -,-en set; (Möbel-) suite

Garten m -s,:̈ garden. **G~arbeit** f gardening. **G~bau** m horticulture. **G~haus** nt, **G~laube** f summerhouse. **G~schere** f secateurs pl

Gärtner|(in) m -s,- (f -,-nen) gardener. **G~ei** f -,-en nursery

Gärung f - fermentation

Gas nt -es,-e gas; Gas geben 1 accelerate. **G~maske** f gas mask. **G~pedal** nt (Auto) accelerator

Gasse f -,-n alley; (Aust) street

Gast m -[e]s,:̈e guest; (Hotel-) visitor; (im Lokal) patron; zum Mittag G~e haben have people to lunch; bei jdm zu G~ sein be staying with s.o. **G~arbeiter** m foreign worker. **G~bett** nt spare bed

Gäste|bett nt spare bed. **G~buch** nt visitors' book. **G~zimmer** nt [hotel] room; (privat) spare room

gast|freundlich adj hospitable. **G~freundschaft** f hospitality. **G~geber** m -s,- host. **G~geberin** f -,-nen hostess. **G~haus** nt, **G~hof** m inn, hotel

gastlich adj hospitable

Gastronomie f - gastronomy

Gast|spiel nt guest performance. **G~spielreise** f (Theat) tour. **G~stätte** f restaurant. **G~wirt** m landlord. **G~wirtin** f landlady. **G~wirtschaft** f restaurant

Gas|werk nt gasworks sg. **G~zähler** m gas meter

Gatte m -n,-n husband

Gattin f -,-nen wife

Gattung f -,-en kind; (Biology) genus; (Kunst) genre

Gaudi f - (Aust, 1) fun

Gaumen m -s,- palate

Gauner m -s,- crook, swindler. **G~ei** f -,-en swindle

Gaze /'ga:zə/ f - gauze

Gazelle f -,-n gazelle

Gebäck nt -s [cakes and] pastries pl; (Kekse) biscuits pl

Gebälk nt -s timbers pl

geballt adj (Faust) clenched

Gebärde f -,-n gesture

gebär|en† vt give birth to, bear; geboren werden be born. **G~mutter** f womb, uterus

Gebäude nt -s,- building

Gebeine ntpl [mortal] remains

Gebell nt -s barking

geben† vt give; (tun, bringen) put; (Karten) deal; (aufführen) perform; (unterrichten) teach; etw verloren g~ give sth up as lost; viel/wenig g~ auf (+ acc) set great/little store by; sich g~ (nachlassen) wear off; (besser werden) get better; (sich verhalten) behave ● impers es gibt there is/are; was gibt es Neues/ zum Mittag/im Kino? what's the news/for lunch/on at the cinema? es wird Regen g~ it's going to rain ● vi (haben) (Karten) deal

Gebet nt -[e]s,-e prayer

Gebiet nt -[e]s,-e area; (Hoheits-) territory; (Sach-) field

gebieten† vt command; (erfordern) demand ● vi (haben) rule

Gebilde nt -s,- structure

gebildet adj educated; (kultiviert) cultured

Gebirg|e nt -s,- mountains pl. **g~ig** adj mountainous

g

Gebiss nt -es,-e teeth pl; (künstliches) false teeth pl; dentures pl, (des Zaumes) bit

geblümt adj floral, flowered

gebogen adj curved

geboren adj born; g~er Deutscher German by birth; Frau X, g~e Y Mrs X, née Y

Gebot nt -[e]s,-e rule

gebraten adj fried

Gebrauch m use; (Sprach-) usage; Gebräuche customs; in G~ in use; G~ machen von make use of. g~en vt use; zu nichts zu g~en useless

gebräuchlich adj common; (Wort) in common use

Gebrauch|sanleitung, G~sanweisung f directions pl for use. g~t adj used; (Comm) secondhand. G~twagen m used car

gebrechlich adj frail, infirm

gebrochen adj broken ● adv g~Englisch sprechen speak broken English

Gebrüll nt -s roaring

Gebühr f -,-en charge, fee; über G~ excessively. g~end adj due; (geziemend) proper. g~enfrei adj free ● adv free of charge. g~enpflichtig adj & adv subject to a charge; g~enpflichtige Straße toll road

Geburt f -,-en birth; von G~ by birth. G~enkontrolle, G~enregelung f birth control. G~enziffer f birth rate

gebürtig adj native (aus of); g~er Deutscher German by birth

Geburts|datum nt date of birth. G~helfer m obstetrician. G~hilfe f obstetrics sg. G~ort m place of birth. G~tag m birthday. G~urkunde f birth certificate

Gebüsch nt -[e]s,-e bushes pl

Gedächtnis nt -ses memory; aus dem G~ from memory

Gedanke m -ns,-n thought (an + acc of); (Idee) idea; sich (dat) G~n machen worry (über + acc about). g~nlos adj thoughtless; (zerstreut) absent-minded. G~nstrich m dash

Gedärme ntpl intestines; (Tier-) entrails

Gedeck nt -[e]s,-e place setting; (auf Speisekarte) set meal

gedeihen† vi (sein) thrive, flourish

gedenken† vi (haben) propose (etw zu tun to do sth); jds g~ remember s.o. G~ nt -s memory

Gedenk|feier f commemoration. G~gottesdienst m memorial service

Gedicht nt -[e]s,-e poem

Gedräng|e nt -s crush, crowd. g~t adj (knapp) concise ● adv g~t voll packed

Geduld f - patience; G~ haben be patient. g~en (sich) vr be patient. g~ig adj patient. G~[s]spiel nt puzzle

gedunsen adj bloated

geehrt adj honoured; Sehr g~er Herr X Dear Mr X

geeignet adj suitable; im g~en Moment at the right moment

Gefahr f -,-en danger; in G~ in danger; auf eigene G~ at one's own risk; G~ laufen run the risk (etw zu tun of doing sth)

gefähr|den vt endanger; (fig) jeopardize. g~lich adj dangerous

gefahrlos adj safe

Gefährt nt -[e]s,-e vehicle

Gefährte m -n,-n, **Gefährtin** f -,-nen companion

gefahrvoll adj dangerous, perilous

Gefälle nt -s,- slope;

(Straßen-) gradient

gefallen† vi (haben) jdm g~ please s.o.; er/es gefällt mir I like him/it; sich (dat) etw g~ lassen put up with sth

Gefallen¹ m -s,- favour

Gefallen² nt -s pleasure (an + dat in); dir zu G~ to please you

Gefallene(r) m soldier killed in the war

gefällig adj pleasing; (hübsch) attractive; (hilfsbereit) obliging; noch etwas g~? will there be anything else? G~keit f -,-en favour; (Freundlichkeit) kindness

Gefangene|(r) m/f prisoner. G~nahme f - capture. g~nehmen* vt sep = g~ nehmen, s. fangen. G~schaft f - captivity

Gefängnis nt -ses,-se prison; (Strafe) imprisonment. G~strafe f imprisonment; (Urteil) prison sentence. G~wärter m [prison] warder

Gefäß nt -es,-e container; (Blut-) vessel

gefasst adj composed; (ruhig) calm; g~ sein auf (+ acc) be prepared for

gefedert adj sprung

gefeiert adj celebrated

Gefieder nt -s plumage

gefleckt adj spotted

Geflügel nt -s poultry. G~klein nt -s giblets pl. g~t adj winged

Geflüster nt -s whispering

Gefolge nt -s retinue, entourage

gefragt adj popular

Gefreite(r) m lance corporal

gefrier|en† vi (sein) freeze. G~fach nt freezer compartment. G~punkt m freezing point. G~schrank m upright freezer. G~truhe f chest freezer

gefroren adj frozen

gefügig adj compliant; (gehorsam) obedient

Gefühl nt -[e]s,-e feeling; (Empfindung) sensation; (G~sregung) emotion; im G~ haben know instinctively. g~los adj insensitive; (herzlos) unfeeling; (taub) numb. g~smäßig adj emotional; (instinktiv) instinctive. G~sregung f emotion. g~voll adj sensitive; (sentimental) sentimental

gefüllt adj filled; (voll) full

gefürchtet adj feared, dreaded

gefüttert adj lined

gegeben adj given; (bestehend) present; (passend) appropriate. g~enfalls adv if need be

gegen prep (+ acc) against; (Sport) versus; (g~über) to[-wards]; (Vergleich) compared with; (Richtung, Zeit) towards; (ungefähr) around; ein Mittel g~ a remedy for ● adv g~ 100 Leute about 100 people. G~angriff m counter-attack

Gegend f -,-en area, region; (Umgebung) neighbourhood

gegeneinander adv against/(gegenüber) towards one another

Gegen|fahrbahn f opposite carriageway. G~gift nt antidote. G~maßnahme f countermeasure. G~satz m contrast; (Widerspruch) contradiction; (G~teil) opposite; im G~satz zu unlike. g~seitig adj mutual; sich g~seitig hassen hate one another. G~stand m object; (Gram, Gesprächs-) subject. G~stück nt counterpart; (G~teil) opposite. G~teil nt opposite, contrary; im G~teil on the contrary. g~teilig adj opposite

gegenüber prep (+ dat) opposite; (Vergleich) compared with; jdm g~ höflich sein be polite to s.o. ● adv opposite. G~ nt -s person opposite.

g

g~**liegend** adj opposite. g~**stehen†** vi sep (haben) (+ dat) face; **feindlich g~stehen** (+ dat) be hostile to. g~**stellen** vt sep confront; (vergleichen) compare

Gegen|verkehr m oncoming traffic. **G~vorschlag** m counterproposal. **G~wart** f - present; (Anwesenheit) presence. g~**wärtig** adj present ● adv at present. **G~wehr** f - resistance. **G~wert** m equivalent. **G~wind** m head wind. g~**zeichnen** vt sep countersign

geglückt adj successful

Gegner|(in) m -s,- (f -,-nen) opponent. g~**isch** adj opposing

Gehabe nt -s affected behaviour

Gehackte(s) nt mince

Gehalt nt -[e]s, ̈er salary. **G~serhöhung** f rise

gehässig adj spiteful

gehäuft adj heaped

Gehäuse nt -s,- case; (TV, Radio) cabinet; (Schnecken-) shell

Gehege nt -s,- enclosure

geheim adj secret; g~ **halten** keep secret; im g~**en** secretly. **G~dienst** m Secret Service. **G~nis** nt -ses,-se secret. g~**nisvoll** adj mysterious. **G~nummer** f PIN

gehemmt adj (fig) inhibited

---

gehen†

● intransitive verb (sein)

····▸ (sich irgendwohin begeben) go; (zu Fuß) walk. **tanzen/schwimmen/einkaufen gehen** go dancing/swimming/shopping. **schlafen gehen** go to bed. **zum Arzt gehen** go to the doctor's. **in die Schule gehen** go to school. **auf und ab gehen** walk up and down. **über die Straße gehen** cross the street

····▸ (weggehen; fam: abfahren) go; leave. **ich muss bald gehen** I must go soon. **Sie können gehen** you may go. **der Zug geht um zehn Uhr** ⊺ the train leaves or goes at ten o'clock

····▸ (funktionieren) work. **der Computer geht wieder/nicht mehr** the computer is working again/has stopped working. **meine Uhr geht falsch/richtig** my watch is wrong/right

····▸ (möglich sein) be possible. **ja, das geht** yes, I or we can manage that. **das geht nicht** that can't be done; (⊺: ist nicht akzeptabel) it's not on ⊺. **es geht einfach nicht, dass du so spät nach Hause kommst** it simply won't do for you to come home so late

····▸ (⊺: gerade noch angehen) **es geht [so]** it is all right. **Wie war die Party? — Es ging so** How was the party? — Not bad or So-so

····▸ (sich entwickeln) do; go. **der Laden geht gut** the shop is doing well. **es geht alles nach Wunsch** everything is going to plan

····▸ (impers) **wie geht es Ihnen?** how are you? **jdm geht es gut/schlecht** (gesundheitlich) s.o. is doing well/badly

····▸ (impers; sich um etw handeln) **es geht um** it concerns. **worum geht es hier?** what is this all about? **es geht ihr nur ums Geld** she is only interested in money

---

Geheul nt -s howling

Gehilfe m -n,-n, **Gehilfin** f -,-nen trainee; (Helfer) assistant

Gehirn nt -s brain; (Verstand) brains pl **G~erschütterung** f concussion. **G~hautentzündung** f meningitis. **G~wäsche** f brainwashing

gehoben adj (fig) superior

Gehöft nt -[e]s,-e farm

Gehör nt -s hearing

gehorchen vi (haben) (+ dat) obey

gehören vi (haben) belong (dat to); dazu gehört Mut that takes courage; es gehört sich nicht it isn't done

gehörlos adj deaf

Gehörn nt -s,-e horns pl; (Geweih) antlers pl

gehorsam adj obedient. **G~** m -s obedience

Geh|steig m -[e]s,-e pavement. **G~weg** m = Gehsteig; (Fußweg) footpath

Geier m -s,- vulture

Geig|e f -,-n violin. **g~en** vi (haben) play the violin • vt play on the violin. **G~er(in)** m -s,- (f -,-nen) violinist

geil adj lecherous; randy; (🔲: toll) great

Geisel f -,-n hostage

Geiß f -,-en (SGer) [nanny-]goat. **G~blatt** nt honeysuckle

Geist m -[e]s,-er mind; (Witz) wit; (Gesinnung) spirit; (Gespenst) ghost; der Heilige **G~** the Holy Ghost or Spirit

geistes|abwesend adj absentminded. **G~blitz** m brainwave. **g~gegenwärtig** adv with great presence of mind. **g~gestört** adj [mentally] deranged. **g~krank** adj mentally ill. **G~krankheit** f mental illness. **G~wissenschaften** fpl arts. **G~zustand** m mental state

geist|ig adj mental; (intellektuell)

intellectual. **g~lich** adj spiritual; (religiös) religious; (Musik) sacred; (Tracht) clerical. **G~liche(r)** m clergyman. **G~lichkeit** f - clergy. **g~reich** adj clever; (witzig) witty

Geiz m -es meanness. **g~en** vi (haben) be mean (mit with). **G~hals** m 🔲 miser. **g~ig** adj mean, miserly. **G~kragen** m 🔲 miser

Gekicher nt -s giggling

geknickt adj 🔲 dejected

gekonnt adj accomplished • adv expertly

gekränkt adj offended, hurt

Gekritzel nt -s scribble

Gelächter nt -s laughter

geladen adj loaded

gelähmt adj paralysed

Geländer nt -s,- railings pl; (Treppen-) banisters

gelangen vi (sein) reach/(fig) attain (zu etw/an etw acc sth)

gelassen adj composed; (ruhig) calm. **G~heit** f - equanimity; (Fassung) composure

Gelatine /ʒela-/ f - gelatine

geläufig adj common, current; (fließend) fluent; jdm g~ sein be familiar to s.o.

gelaunt adj gut/schlecht g~ sein be in a good/bad mood

gelb adj yellow; (bei Ampel) amber; das G~ vom Ei the yolk of the egg. **G~** nt -s,- yellow. **g~lich** adj yellowish. **G~sucht** f jaundice

Geld nt -es,-er money; öffentliche **G~er** public funds. **G~automat** m cashpoint machine. **G~beutel** m, **G~börse** f purse. **G~geber** m -s,- backer. **g~lich** adj financial. **G~mittel** ntpl funds. **G~schein** m banknote. **G~schrank** m safe. **G~strafe** f fine. **G~stück** nt coin

Gelee /ʒe'le:/ nt -s,-s jelly

gelegen adj situated; (passend) convenient

Gelegenheit f -,-en opportunity, chance; (Anlass) occasion; (Comm) bargain; bei G~ some time. G~sarbeit f casual work. G~skauf m bargain

gelegentlich adj occasional ● adv occasionally; (bei Gelegenheit) some time

Gelehrte(r) m/f scholar

Geleit nt -[e]s escort; freies G~ safe conduct. g~en vt escort

Gelenk nt -[e]s,-e joint. g~ig adj supple (Techn) flexible

gelernt adj skilled

Geliebte(r) m/f lover

gelingen† vi (sein) succeed, be successful. G~ nt -s success

gellend adj shrill

geloben vt promise [solemnly]; das Gelobte Land the Promised Land

Gelöbnis nt -ses,-se vow

gelöst adj (fig) relaxed

gelten† vi (haben) be valid; (Regel:) apply; g~ als be regarded as; etw nicht g~ lassen not accept sth; wenig/viel g~ be worth/(fig) count for little/a lot; jdm g~ be meant for s.o.; das gilt nicht that doesn't count. g~d adj valid; (Preise) current; (Meinung) prevailing; g~d machen assert (Recht, Forderung); bring to bear (Einfluss)

Geltung f - validity; (Ansehen) prestige; zur G~ bringen set off

Gelübde nt -s,- vow

gelungen adj successful

Gelüst nt -[e]s,-e desire

gemächlich adj leisurely ● adv in a leisurely manner

Gemahl m -s,-e husband. G~in f -,-nen wife

Gemälde nt -s,- painting. G~galerie f picture gallery

gemäß prep (+ dat) in accordance with

gemäßigt adj moderate; (Klima) temperate

gemein adj common; (unanständig) vulgar; (niederträchtig) mean; g~er Soldat private

Gemeinde f -,-n [local] community; (Admin) borough; (Pfarr-) parish; (bei Gottesdienst) congregation. G~rat m local council/(Person) councillor. G~wahlen fpl local elections

gemein|gefährlich adj dangerous. G~heit f -,-en commonness; vulgarity; meanness; (Bemerkung, Handlung) mean thing [to say/do]; so eine G~heit! how mean! G~kosten pl overheads. g~nützig adj charitable. g~sam adj common ● adv together

Gemeinschaft f -,-en community. g~lich adj joint; (Besitz) communal ● adv jointly; (zusammen) together. G~sarbeit f team work

Gemenge nt -s,- mixture

Gemisch nt -[e]s,-e mixture. g~t adj mixed

Gemme f -,-n engraved gem

Gemse* f -,-n = Gämse

Gemurmel nt -s murmuring

Gemüse nt -s,- vegetable; (coll) vegetables pl. G~händler m greengrocer

gemustert adj patterned

Gemüt nt -[e]s,-er nature, disposition; (Gefühl) feelings pl

gemütlich adj cosy; (gemächlich) leisurely; (zwanglos) informal; (Person) genial; es sich (dat) g~ machen make oneself comfortable. G~keit f - cosiness

Gen nt -s,-e gene

genau adj exact, precise; (Waage, Messung) accurate; (sorgfältig) meticulous; (ausführlich) detailed; nichts G~es wissen not know any details; g~ genommen strictly speaking; g~! exactly! **G~igkeit** f – exactitude; precision; accuracy; meticulousness

genauso adv just the same; (g~sehr) just as much; g~ teuer just as expensive; g~ gut just as good; adv just as well; g~ sehr just as much; g~ viel just as much/ many; g~ wenig just as little/few; (noch) no more

Gendarm /ʒã'darm/ m -en,-en (Aust) policeman

Genealogie f – genealogy

genehmig|en vt grant; approve (Plan). **G~ung** f –,-en permission; (Schein) permit

geneigt adj sloping, inclined; (fig) well-disposed (dat towards)

General m -s,-e general. **G~direktor** m managing director. **G~probe** f dress rehearsal. **G~streik** m general strike

Generation /-'tsio:n/ f –,-en generation

Generator m -s,-en generator

generell adj general

genes|en vi (sein) recover. **G~ung** f – recovery; (Erholung) convalescence

Genetik f – genetics sg

genetisch adj genetic

Genf nt -s Geneva. **G~er** adj Geneva ; **G~er See** Lake Geneva

genial adj brilliant. **G~ität** f genius

Genick nt -s,-e [back of the] neck; sich (dat) das G~ brechen break one's neck

Genie /ʒe'ni:/ nt -s,-s genius

genieren /ʒe'ni:rən/ vt embarrass; sich g~ feel or be embarrassed

genieß|bar adj fit to eat/drink. **g~en†** vt enjoy; (verzehren) eat/drink

Genitiv m -s,-e genitive

genmanipuliert adj genetically modified

Genom nt -s, -e genome

Genosse m -n,-n (Pol) comrade. **G~nschaft** f –,-en cooperative

Gentechnologie f genetic engineering

genug inv adj & adv enough

Genüge f zur G~ sufficiently. **g~n** vi (haben) be enough. **g~nd** inv adj sufficient, enough; (Sch) fair ● adv sufficiently, enough

Genuss m -es, ̈e enjoyment; (Vergnügen) pleasure; (Verzehr) consumption

geöffnet adj open

Geo|graphie, G~grafie f geography. **g~graphisch, g~grafisch** adj geographical. **G~logie** f – geology. **g~logisch** adj geological. **G~meter** m -s,- surveyor. **G~metrie** f – geometry. **g~metrisch** adj geometric[al]

geordnet adj well-ordered; (stabil) stable; alphabetisch g~ in alphabetical order

Gepäck nt -s luggage, baggage. **G~ablage** f luggage-rack. **G~aufbewahrung** f left-luggage office. **G~schein** m left-luggage ticket; (Aviat) baggage check. **G~träger** m porter; (Fahrrad-) luggage carrier; (Dach-) roof-rack

Gepard m -s,-e cheetah

gepflegt adj well-kept; (Person) well-groomed; (Hotel) first-class

gepunktet adj spotted

gerade adj straight; (direkt) direct; (aufrecht) upright; (aufrichtig) straightforward; (Zahl) even ● adv straight; directly; (eben) just;

(*genau*) exactly; (*besonders*) especially; g~ sitzen/stehen sit/stand [up] straight; g~ erst only just. G~ f -,-n straight line. g~aus adv straight ahead/on. g~heraus adv (*fig*) straight out. g~so adv just the same; g~so gut just as good; adv just as well. g~stehen† vi sep (*haben*) (*fig*) accept responsibility (für for). g~zu adv virtually; (*wirklich*) absolutely

Geranie /-jə/ f -,-n geranium

Gerät nt -[e]s,-e tool; (*Acker-*) implement; (*Küchen-*) utensil; (*Elektro-*) appliance; (*Radio-, Fernseh-*) set; (*Turn-*) piece of apparatus; (*coll*) equipment

geraten† vi (*sein*) get; in Brand g~ catch fire; in Wut g~ get angry; gut g~ turn out well

Geratewohl nt aufs G~ at random

geräuchert adj smoked

geräumig adj spacious, roomy

Geräusch nt -[e]s,-e noise. g~los adj noiseless

gerben vt tan

gerecht adj just; (*fair*) fair. g~fertigt adj justified. G~igkeit f - justice; fairness

Gerede nt -s talk

geregelt adj regular

gereizt adj irritable

Geriatrie f - geriatrics sg

Gericht[1] nt -[e]s,-e (*Culin*) dish

Gericht[2] nt -[e]s,-e court [of law]; vor G~ in court; das Jüngste G~ the Last Judgement. g~lich adj judicial; (*Verfahren*) legal ● adv g~lich vorgehen take legal action. G~shof m court of justice. G~smedizin f forensic medicine. G~ssaal m court room. G~svollzieher m -s,- bailiff

gerieben adj grated; (□:

schlau) crafty

gering adj small; (*niedrig*) low; (*g~fügig*) slight. g~fügig adj slight. g~schätzig adj contemptuous; (*Bemerkung*) disparaging. g~ste(r,s) f least; nicht im G~sten not in the least

gerinnen† vi (*sein*) curdle; (*Blut:*) clot

Gerippe nt -s,- skeleton; (*fig*) framework

gerissen adj □ crafty

Germ m -[e]s & (*Aust*) f - yeast

German|e m -n,-n [ancient] German. g~isch adj Germanic. G~istik f - German [language and literature]

gern[e] adv gladly; g~ haben like; (*lieben*) be fond of; ich tanze g~ I like dancing; willst du mit?—g~! do you want to come?—I'd love to!

Gerste f - barley. G~nkorn nt (*Med*) stye

Geruch m -[e]s,:e smell (von/nach of). g~los adj odourless. G~ssinn m sense of smell

Gerücht nt -[e]s,-e rumour

gerührt adj (*fig*) moved, touched

Gerümpel nt -s lumber, junk

Gerüst nt -[e]s,-e scaffolding; (*fig*) framework

gesammelt adj collected; (*gefasst*) composed

gesamt adj entire, whole. G~ausgabe f complete edition. G~eindruck m overall impression. G~heit f - whole. G~schule f comprehensive school. G~summe f total

Gesandte(r) m/f envoy

Gesang m -[e]s,:e singing; (*Lied*) song; (*Kirchen-*) hymn. G~verein m choral society

Gesäß nt -es buttocks pl

Geschäft nt -[e]s,-e business; (Laden) shop, store; (Transaktion) deal; schmutzige G~e shady dealings; ein gutes G~ machen do very well (mit out of). g~ig adj busy; (Treiben) bustling. G~igkeit f - activity. g~lich adj business ● adv on business

Geschäfts|brief m business letter. G~führer m manager; (Vereins-) secretary. G~mann m (pl -leute) businessman. G~stelle f office; (Zweigstelle) branch. G~tüchtig adj g~tüchtig sein be a good businessman/-woman. G~zeiten pl hours of business

geschehen† vi (sein) happen (dat to); das geschieht dir recht! it serves you right! gern g~! you're welcome! G~ nt -s events pl

gescheit adj clever

Geschenk nt -[e]s,-e present, gift

Geschichte f -,-n history; (Erzählung) story; (**ᵻ**: Sache) business. g~lich adj historical

Geschick nt -[e]s fate; (Talent) skill. G~lichkeit f - skilfulness, skill. g~t adj skilful; (klug) clever

geschieden adj divorced

Geschirr nt -s,-e (coll) crockery; (Porzellan) china; (Service) service; (Pferde-) harness; schmutziges G~ dirty dishes pl. G~spülmaschine f dishwasher. G~tuch nt tea towel

Geschlecht nt -[e]s,-er sex; (Gram) gender; (Generation) generation. g~lich adj sexual. G~skrankheit f venereal disease. G~steile ntpl genitals. G~sverkehr m sexual intercourse. G~swort nt (pl -wörter) article

geschliffen adj (fig) polished

Geschmack m -[e]s,-e taste; (Aroma) flavour; (G~ssinn) sense of taste; einen guten G~ haben (fig) have good taste. g~los adj taste-

less; g~los sein (fig) be in bad taste. g~voll adj (fig) tasteful

Geschoss nt -es,-e missile; (Stockwerk) storey, floor

Geschrei nt -s screaming; (fig) fuss

Geschütz nt -es,-e gun, cannon

geschützt adj protected; (Stelle) sheltered

Geschwader nt -s,- squadron

Geschwätz nt -es talk

geschweige conj g~ denn let alone

Geschwindigkeit f -,-en speed; (Phys) velocity. G~sbegrenzung, G~sbeschränkung f speed limit

Geschwister pl brother[s] and sister[s]; siblings

geschwollen adj swollen; (fig) pompous

Geschworene|(r) m/f juror; die G~n the jury sg

Geschwulst f -,-e swelling; (Tumor) tumour

geschwungen adj curved

Geschwür nt -s,-e ulcer

gesellig adj sociable; (Zool) gregarious; (unterhaltsam) convivial; g~er Abend social evening

Gesellschaft f -,-en company; (Veranstaltung) party; die G~ society; jdm G~ leisten keep s.o. company. g~lich adj social. G~sspiel nt party game

Gesetz nt -es,-e law. G~entwurf m bill. g~gebend adj legislative. G~gebung f - legislation. g~lich adj legal. g~mäßig adj lawful; (gesetzlich) legal. g~widrig adj illegal

gesichert adj secure

Gesicht nt -[e]s,-er face; (Aussehen) appearance. G~sfarbe f complexion. G~spunkt m point of view. G~szüge mpl features

g

Gesindel nt -s riff-raff

Gesinnung f -,-en mind; (Einstellung) attitude

gesondert adj separate

Gespann nt -[e]s,-e team; (Wagen) horse and cart/carriage

gespannt adj taut; (fig) tense; (Beziehungen) strained; (neugierig) eager; (erwartungsvoll) expectant; g~ sein, ob wonder whether; auf etw g~ sein look forward eagerly to sth

Gespenst nt -[e]s,-er ghost. g~isch adj ghostly; (unheimlich) eerie

Gespött nt -[e]s mockery; zum G~ werden become a laughing stock

Gespräch nt -[e]s,-e conversation; (Telefon-) call; ins G~ kommen get talking; im G~ sein be under discussion. g~ig adj talkative G~sthema nt topic of conversation

Gestalt f -,-en figure; (Form) shape, form; G~ annehmen (fig) take shape. g~en vt shape; (organisieren) arrange; (schaffen) create; (entwerfen) design; sich g~en turn out

Geständnis nt -ses,-se confession

Gestank m -s stench, [bad] smell

gestatten vt allow, permit; nicht gestattet prohibited; g~ Sie? may I?

Geste /'gɛ-, 'gɛːstə/ f -,-n gesture

Gesteck nt -[e]s,-e flower arrangement

gestehen† vt/i (haben) confess; confess to (Verbrechen)

Gestein nt -[e]s,-e rock

Gestell nt -[e]s,-e stand; (Flaschen-) rack; (Rahmen) frame

gesteppt adj quilted

gestern adv yesterday; g~ Nacht last night

gestrandet adj stranded

gestreift adj striped

gestrichelt adj (Linie) dotted

gestrichen adj g~er Teelöffel level teaspoon[ful]

gestrig /'gɛstrɪç/ adj yesterday's; am g~en Tag yesterday

Gestrüpp nt -s,-e undergrowth

Gestüt nt -[e]s,-e stud [farm]

Gesuch nt -[e]s,-e request; (Admin) application. g~t adj sought-after

gesund adj healthy; g~ sein be in good health; (Sport, Getränk:) be good for one; wieder g~ werden get well again

Gesundheit f - health; G~! (bei Niesen) bless you! g~lich adj health; g~licher Zustand state of health ● adv es geht ihm g~lich gut/ schlecht he is in good/poor health. g~sschädlich adj harmful

getäfelt adj panelled

Getöse nt -s racket, din

Getränk nt -[e]s,-e drink. G~ekarte f wine-list

getrauen v sich (dat) etw g~ dare [to] do sth; sich g~ dare

Getreide nt -s (coll) grain

getrennt adj separate; g~ leben live apart; g~ schreiben write as two words

getreu adj faithful ● prep (+ dat) true to. g~lich adv faithfully

Getriebe nt -s,- bustle; (Techn) gear; (Auto) transmission; (Gehäuse) gearbox

getrost adv with confidence

Getto nt -s,-s ghetto

Getue nt -s Ⓣ fuss

Getümmel nt -s tumult

geübt adj skilled

Gewächs nt -es,-e plant

gewachsen adj jdm g~ sein be

a match for s.o.
Gewächshaus nt greenhouse
gewagt adj daring
gewählt adj refined
gewahr adj g~ werden become aware (acc/gen of)
Gewähr f- guarantee
gewähr|en vt grant; (geben) offer. **g~leisten** vt guarantee
Gewahrsam m -s safekeeping; (Haft) custody
Gewalt f-,-en power; (Kraft) force; (Brutalität) violence; mit G~ by force. **G~herrschaft** f tyranny. **g~ig** adj powerful; (ﬁ: groß) enormous; (stark) tremendous. **g~sam** adj forcible; (Tod) violent. **g~tätig** adj violent. **G~tätigkeit** f-,-en violence; (Handlung) act of violence
Gewand nt -[e]s,¨er robe
gewandt adj skilful. **G~heit** f - skill
Gewebe nt -s,- fabric; (Anat) tissue
Gewehr nt -s,-e rifle, gun
Geweih nt -[e]s,-e antlers pl
Gewerb|e nt -s,- trade. **g~lich** adj commercial. **g~smäßig** adj professional
Gewerkschaft f-,-en trade union. **G~ler(in)** m -s,- (f -,-nen) trade unionist
Gewicht nt -[e]s,-e weight; (Bedeutung) importance. **G~heben** nt -s weight lifting
Gewinde nt -s,- [screw] thread
Gewinn m -[e]s,-e profit; (fig) gain, benefit; (beim Spiel) winnings pl; (Preis) prize; (Los) winning ticket. **G~beteiligung** f profit-sharing. **g~en†** vt win; (erlangen) gain; (fördern) extract ● vi (haben) win; **g~en an** (+ dat) gain in. **g~end** adj engaging. **G~er(in)** m -s,- (f -,-nen) winner

Gewirr nt -s,-e tangle; (Straßen-) maze
gewiss adj certain
Gewissen nt -s,- conscience. **g~haft** adj conscientious. **g~los** adj unscrupulous. **G~sbisse** mpl pangs of conscience
gewissermaßen adv to a certain extent; (sozusagen) as it were
Gewissheit f- certainty
Gewitt|er nt -s,- thunderstorm. **g~rig** adj thundery
gewogen adj (fig) well-disposed (dat towards)
gewöhnen vt jdn/sich g~ an (+ acc) get s.o. used to/get used to; [an] jdn/etw gewöhnt sein be used to s.o./sth
Gewohnheit f-,-en habit. **G~srecht** nt common law
gewöhnlich adj ordinary; (üblich) usual; (ordinär) common
gewohnt adj customary; (vertraut) familiar; (üblich) usual; etw (acc) g~ sein be used to sth
Gewölbe nt -s,- vault
Gewühl nt -[e]s crush
gewunden adj winding
Gewürz nt -es,-e spice. **G~nelke** f clove
gezackt adj serrated
gezähnt adj serrated; (Säge) toothed
Gezeiten fpl tides
gezielt adj specific; (Frage) pointed
geziert adj affected
gezwungen adj forced. **g~ermaßen** adv of necessity
Gicht f- gout
Giebel m -s,- gable
Gier f- greed (nach for). **g~ig** adj greedy
gieß|en† vt pour; water (Blumen, Garten); (Techn) cast ● v impers es

Gift | gleichermaßen

g~t it is pouring [with rain].
G~kanne f watering can

Gift nt -[e]s,-e poison; (*Schlangen-*) venom; (*Med*) toxin. **g~ig** adj poisonous; (*Schlange*) venomous; (*Med, Chemistry*) toxic; (*fig*) spiteful. **G~müll** m toxic waste. **G~pilz** m toadstool

Gilde f -,-n guild

Gin /dʒin/ m -s gin

Ginster m -s (*Bot*) broom

Gipfel m -s,- summit, top; (*fig*) peak. **G~konferenz** f summit conference. **g~n** vi (*haben*) culminate (in + *dat* in)

Gips m -es plaster. **G~verband** m (*Med*) plaster cast

Giraffe f -,-n giraffe

Girlande f -,-n garland

Girokonto /ˈʒiːro-/ nt current account

Gischt m -[e]s & f - spray

Gitar|re f -,-n guitar. **G~rist(in)** m -en,-en (f -,-nen) guitarist

Gitter nt -s,- bars pl; (*Rost*) grating, grid; (*Geländer, Zaun*) railings pl; (*Fenster-*) grille; (*Draht-*) wire screen

Glanz m -es shine; (*von Farbe, Papier*) gloss; (*Seiden-*) sheen; (*Politur*) polish; (*fig*) brilliance; (*Pracht*) splendour

glänzen vi (*haben*) shine. **g~d** adj shining, bright; (*Papier*) glossy; (*fig*) brilliant

glanz|los adj dull. **G~stück** nt masterpiece

Glas nt -es,-̈er glass; (*Brillen-*) lens; (*Fern-*) binoculars pl; (*Marmeladen-*) [glass] jar. **G~er** m -s,- glazier

glasieren vt glaze, ice (*Kuchen*)

glas|ig adj glassy; (*durchsichtig*) transparent. **G~scheibe** f pane

Glasur f -,-en glaze; (*Culin*) icing

glatt adj smooth; (*eben*) even;

(*Haar*) straight; (*rutschig*) slippery; (*einfach*) straightforward; (*Absage*) flat; **g~** streichen smooth out; **g~** rasiert clean-shaven; **g~** gehen go off smoothly; **das ist g~** gelogen it's a downright lie

Glätte f - smoothness; (*Rutschigkeit*) slipperiness

Glatt|eis nt [black] ice. **g~weg** adv 🆃 outright

Glatz|e f -,-n bald patch; (*Voll-*) bald head; **eine G~e bekommen** go bald. **g~köpfig** adj bald

Glaube m -ns belief (an + *acc* in); (*Relig*) faith; **G~n schenken** (+ *dat*) believe. **g~n** vt/i (*haben*) believe (an + *acc* in); (*vermuten*) think; **jdm g~n** believe s.o.; **nicht zu g~n** unbelievable, incredible. **G~nsbekenntnis** nt creed

gläubig adj religious; (*vertrauend*) trusting. **G~e(r)** m/f (*Relig*) believer; **die G~en** the faithful. **G~er** m -s,- (*Comm*) creditor

glaub|lich adj kaum g~lich scarcely believable. **g~würdig** adj credible; (*Person*) reliable

gleich adj same; (*identisch*) identical; (*g~wertig*) equal; **g~** bleibend constant; **2 mal 5** [ist] **g~** 10 two times 5 equals 10; **das ist mir g~** it's all the same to me; **ganz g~,** wo/wer no matter where/who ● *adv* equally; (*übereinstimmend*) identically, the same; (*sofort*) immediately; (*in Kürze*) in a minute; (*fast*) nearly; (*direkt*) right. **g~altrig** adj [of] the same age. **g~bedeutend** adj synonymous. **g~berechtigt** adj equal. **G~berechtigung** f equality

gleichen† vi (*haben*) jdm/etw g~ be like or resemble s.o./something

gleich|ermaßen adv equally. **g~falls** adv also, likewise; **danke g~falls** thank you, the same to you. **G~gewicht** nt balance; (Phys & fig) equilibrium. **g~gültig** adj indifferent; (unwichtig) unimportant. **G~gültigkeit** f indifference. **g~machen** vt sep make equal; **dem Erdboden g~machen** raze to the ground. **g~mäßig** adj even, regular; (beständig) constant. **G~mäßigkeit** f - regularity

Gleichnis nt -ses,-se parable

Gleich|schritt m im **G~schritt** in step. **g~setzen** vt sep equate/(g~stellen) place on a par (dat/mit with). **g~stellen** vt sep place on a par (dat with). **G~strom** m direct current

Gleichung f -,-en equation

gleichwertig adv adj of equal value. **g~zeitig** adj simultaneous

Gleis nt -es,-e track; (Bahnsteig) platform; **G~ 5** platform 5

gleiten† vi (sein) glide; (rutschen) slide. **g~d** adj sliding; **g~de Arbeitszeit** flexitime

Gleitzeit f flexitime

Gletscher m -s,- glacier

Glied nt -[e]s,-er limb; (Teil) part; (Ketten-) link; (Mitglied) member; (Mil) rank. **g~ern** vt arrange; (einteilen) divide. **G~maßen** fpl limbs

glitschig adj slippery

glitzern vi (haben) glitter

global adj global

globalisier|en vt globalize. **G~ung** f -,-en globalization

Globus m - & -busses,-ben & -busse globe

Glocke f -,-n bell. **G~nturm** m bell tower, belfry

glorreich adj glorious

Glossar nt -s,-e glossary

Glosse f -,-n comment

glotzen vi (haben) stare

Glück nt -[e]s [good] luck; (Zufrie- denheit) happiness; **G~ bringend** lucky; **G~/kein G~ haben** be lucky/unlucky; **zum G~** luckily, fortunately; **auf gut G~** on the off chance; (wahllos) at random. **g~en** vi (sein) succeed

glücklich adj lucky, fortunate; (zufrieden) happy; (sicher) safe ● adv happily; safely. **g~erweise** adv luckily, fortunately

Glücksspiel nt game of chance; (Spielen) gambling

Glückwunsch m good wishes pl; (Gratulation) congratulations pl; **herzlichen G~!** congratulations! (zum Geburtstag) happy birthday! **G~karte** f greetings card

Glüh|birne f light bulb. **g~en** vi (haben) glow. **g~end** adj glowing; (rot-) red-hot; (Hitze) scorching; (leidenschaftlich) fervent. **G~faden** m filament. **G~wein** m mulled wine. **G~würmchen** nt -s,- glow-worm

Glukose f - glucose

Glut f - embers pl; (Röte) glow; (Hitze) heat; (fig) ardour

Glyzinie f -/a/ f -,-n wisteria

GmbH abbr (Gesellschaft mit beschränkter Haftung) ≈ plc

Gnade f - mercy; (Gunst) favour; (Relig) grace. **G~nfrist** f reprieve

gnädig adj gracious; (mild) lenient; **g~e Frau** Madam

Gnom m -en,-en gnome

Gobelin /gobəˈlɛ̃/ m -s,-s tapestry

Gold nt -[e]s gold. **g~en** adj gold; (g~farben) golden. **G~fisch** m goldfish. **g~ig** adj sweet, lovely. **G~lack** m wallflower. **G~regen** m laburnum. **G~schmied** m goldsmith

Golf[1] m -[e]s,-e (Geog) gulf

Golf[2] nt -s golf. **G~platz** m golf course. **G~schläger** m golf club. **G~spieler(in)** m(f) golfer

Gondel f -,-n gondola; (Kabine) cabin

gönnen vt jdm etw g~ not begrudge s.o. sth; jdm etw nicht g~ begrudge s.o. sth

googeln vt/i ® google

Gör nt -s,-en, **Göre** f -,-n [!] kid

Gorilla m -s,-s gorilla

Gosse f -,-n gutter

Got|ik f - Gothic. **g~isch** adj Gothic

Gott m -[e]s,-er God; (Myth) god

Götterspeise f jelly

Gottes|dienst m service. **G~lästerung** f blasphemy

Gottheit f -,-en deity

Göttin f -,-nen goddess

göttlich adj divine

gottlos adj ungodly; (atheistisch) godless

Grab nt -[e]s,-er grave

graben† vi (haben) dig

Graben m -s,- ditch; (Mil) trench

Grab|mal nt tomb. **G~stein** m gravestone, tombstone

Grad m -[e]s,-e degree

Graf m -en,-en count

Grafik f -,-en graphics sg; (Kunst) graphic arts pl; (Druck) print

Gräfin f -,-nen countess

grafisch adj graphic; **g~e** Darstellung graphics

Grafschaft f -,-en county

Gram m -s grief

grämen (sich) vr grieve

Gramm nt -s,-e gram

Gram|matik f -,-en grammar. **g~matikalisch** adj grammatical

Granat m -[e]s,-e garnet. **G~e** f -,-n shell; (Hand-) grenade

Granit m -s,-e granite

Gras nt -es,-er grass. **g~en** vi (haben) graze. **G~hüpfer** m -s,- grasshopper

grässlich adj dreadful

Grat m -[e]s,-e [mountain] ridge

Gräte f -,-n fishbone

Gratifikation /-'tsio:n/ f -,-en bonus

gratis adv free [of charge]. **G~probe** f free sample

Gratu|lant(in) m -en,-en (f -,-nen) well-wisher. **G~lation** f -,-en congratulations pl; (Glückwünsche) best wishes pl. **g~lieren** vi (haben) jdm g~lieren congratulate s.o. (zu on); (zum Geburtstag) wish s.o. happy birthday

grau adj, **G~** nt -s,- grey

Gräuel m -s,- horror

grauen v impers mir graut [es] davor I dread it. **G~** nt -s dread. **g~haft** adj gruesome; (grässlich) horrible

gräulich adj horrible

grausam adj cruel. **G~keit** f -,-en cruelty

graus|en v impers mir graust davor I dread it. **G~en** nt -s horror, dread. **g~ig** adj gruesome

gravieren vt engrave. **g~d** adj (fig) serious

graziös adj graceful

greifen† vt take hold of; (fangen) catch ● vi (haben) reach (nach for); um sich g~ (fig) spread

Greis m -es,-e old man. **G~in** f -,-nen old woman

grell adj glaring; (Farbe) garish; (schrill) shrill

Gremium nt -s,-ien committee

Grenz|e f -,-n border; (Staats-) frontier; (Grundstücks-) boundary; (fig) limit. **g~en** vi (haben) border (an + acc on). **g~enlos** adj boundless; (maßlos) infinite

Griech|e m -n,-n Greek. **G~en-**

land nt -s Greece. **G~in** f -,-nen Greek woman. **g~isch** adj Greek. **G~isch** nt -[s] (Lang) Greek

Grieß m -es semolina

Griff m -[e]s,-e grasp, hold; (Hand-) movement of the hand; (Tür-, Mes-ser-) handle; (Schwert-) hilt. **g~bereit** adj handy

Grill m -s,-s grill; (Garten-) barbecue

Grille f -,-n (Zool) cricket

grillen vt grill; (im Freien) barbecue ● vi (haben) have a barbecue. **G~fest** nt barbecue

Grimasse f -,-n grimace; **G~n** schneiden pull faces

grimmig adj furious; (Kälte) bitter

grinsen vi (haben) grin

Grippe f -,-n influenza, 🔟 flu

grob adj coarse; (unsanft, ungefähr) rough; (unhöflich) rude; (schwer) gross; (Fehler) bad; **g~** geschätzt roughly. **G~ian** m -s,-e brute

Groll m -[e]s resentment. **g~en** vi (haben) be angry (dat with); (Donner:) rumble

Grönland nt -s Greenland

Gros nt -es,- (Maß) gross

Groschen m -s,- (Aust) groschen; 🔟 ten-pfennig piece

groß adj big; (Anzahl, Summe) large; (bedeutend, stark) great; (g~artig) grand; (Buchstabe) capital; **g~e** Ferien summer holidays; der größte Teil the majority or bulk; **g~** werden (Person:) grow up; **g~** in etw (dat) sein be good at sth; **G~** und Klein young and old; im **G~en** und Ganzen on the whole ● adv (feiern) in style; (🔟: viel) much

groß|artig adj magnificent. **G~aufnahme** f close-up. **G~britannien** nt -s Great Britain. **G~buchstabe** m capital letter. **G~e(r)** m/f unser **G~er** our eldest;

die **G~en** the grown-ups; (fig) the great pl

Größe f -,-n size; (Ausmaß) extent; (Körper-) height; (Bedeutsamkeit) greatness; (Math) quantity; (Person) great figure

Großeltern pl grandparents

Groß|handel m wholesale trade. **G~händler** m wholesaler. **G~macht** f superpower. **g~mütig** adj magnanimous. **G~mutter** f grandmother. **G~schreibung** f capitalization. **g~spurig** adj pompous; (überheblich) arrogant. **G~stadt** f [large] city. **g~städtisch** adj city; **G~teil** m large proportion; (Haupt-teil) bulk

größtenteils adv for the most part

groß|tun† (sich) vr sep brag. **G~vater** m grandfather. **g~zie-hen†** vt sep bring up; rear (Tier). **g~zügig** adj generous. **G~zügig-keit** f -generosity

Grotte f -,-n grotto

Grübchen nt -s,- dimple

Grube f -,-n pit

grübeln vi (haben) brood

Gruft f -,ːe [burial] vault

grün adj green; im **G~en** out in the country; die **G~en** the Greens

Grund m -[e]s,ːe ground; (Boden) bottom; (Hinter-) background; (Ursa-che) reason; aus diesem **G~e** for this reason; im **G~e** [genommen] basically; auf **G~** laufen (Naut) run aground; zu **G~e** richten/gehen s. zugrunde. **G~begriffe** mpl basics. **G~besitzer** m landowner

gründ|en vt found, set up; start (Familie), (fig) base (auf + acc on); sich **g~en** be based (auf + acc on). **G~er(in)** m -s,- (f -,-nen) founder

Grund|farbe f primary colour. **G~form** f (Gram) infinitive. **G~**

gesetz nt (Pol) constitution.
G~lage f basis, foundation

> **Grundgesetz** The written German constitution, or 'basic law', which came into force in May 1949. It lays down the basic rights of German citizens and the legal framework of the German state.

g **gründlich** adj thorough. **G~keit** f - thoroughness

Gründonnerstag m Maundy Thursday

Grund|regel f basic rule. **G~riss** m ground plan; (fig) outline. **G~satz** m principle. **g~sätzlich** adj fundamental; (im Allgemeinen) in principle; (prinzipiell) on principle. **G~schule** f primary school. **G~stück** nt plot [of land]

Gründung f -,-en foundation

Grün|span m verdigris. **G~streifen** m grass verge; (Mittel-) central reservation

grunzen vi (haben) grunt

Gruppe f -,-n group; (Reise-) party

gruppieren vt group

Grusel|geschichte f horror story. **g~ig** adj creepy

Gruß m -es, ː e greeting; (Mil) salute; einen schönen G~ an X give my regards to X; viele/herzliche G~e regards; Mit freundlichen G~en Yours sincerely/faithfully

grüßen vt/i (haben) say hello (jdn to s.o.); (Mil) salute; g~ Sie X von mir give my regards to X; grüß Gott! (SGer, Aust) good morning/afternoon/evening!

gucken vi (haben) 🗊 look

Guerilla /ge'rɪlja/ f - guerrilla warfare. **G~kämpfer** m guerrilla

Gulasch nt & m -[e]s goulash

gültig adj valid

Gummi m & nt -s,-[s] rubber; (Harz) gum. **G~band** nt (pl -bänder) elastic or rubber band

gummiert adj gummed

Gummi|knüppel m truncheon. **G~stiefel** m gumboot, wellington. **G~zug** m elastic

Gunst f - favour

günstig adj favourable; (passend) convenient

Gurgel f -,-n throat. **g~n** vi (haben) gargle

Gurke f -,-n cucumber; (Essig-) gherkin

Gurt m -[e]s,-e strap; (Gürtel) belt; (Auto) safety belt. **G~band** nt (pl -bänder) waistband

Gürtel m -s,- belt. **G~linie** f waistline. **G~rose** f shingles sg

Guss m -es, ː e (Techn) casting; (Strom) stream; (Regen-) downpour; (Torten-) icing. **G~eisen** nt cast iron

gut adj good; (Gewissen) clear; (gütig) kind (zu to); jdm gut sein be fond of s.o.; im G~en amicably; schon gut that's all right ● adv well; (schmecken, riechen) good; (leicht) easily; gut zu sehen clearly visible; gut drei Stunden a good three hours

Gut nt -[e]s,ː er possession, property; (Land-) estate; Gut und Böse good and evil; Güter (Comm) goods

Gutacht|en nt -s,- expert's report. **G~er** m -s,- expert

gutartig adj good-natured; (Med) benign

Gute|(s) nt etwas/nichts G~s something/nothing good; G~s tun do good; alles G~! all the best!

Güte f -,-n goodness, kindness; (Qualität) quality

Güterzug m goods train

gut|gehen* vi sep (sein) gut

gehen, s. gehen. **g~gehend*** adj
gut gehend, s. gehen. **g~gläubig**
adj trusting. **g~haben†** vt sep fünfzig Euro g~haben have fifty euros
credit (bei with). **G~haben** nt -s,-
[credit] balance; (Kredit) credit

gut|machen vt sep make up for;
make good (Schaden). **g~mütig**
adj good-natured. **G~mütigkeit** f -
good nature. **G~schein** m credit
note; (Bon) voucher; (Geschenk-) gift
token. **g~schreiben†** vt sep credit.
G~schrift f credit

Guts|haus nt manor house
gut|tun† vi sep (haben) gut tun, s.
tun. **g~willig** adj willing
Gymnasium nt -s,-ien ≈ grammar school

Gymnastik f -[keep-fit] exercises
pl; (Turnen) gymnastics sg
Gynäko|loge m -n,-n gynaecolo-
gist. **G~logie** f - gynaecology

Hh

H, h /ha:/ nt -,- (Mus) B, b
Haar nt -[e]s,-e hair; sich (dat) die
Haare od das H~ waschen wash
one's hair; um ein H~ 🔟 very
nearly. **H~bürste** f hairbrush.

h~en vi (haben) shed hairs; (Tier:)
moult ● vr sich h~en moult. **h~ig**
adj hairy; 🔟 tricky. **H~klemme** f
hair grip. **H~nadelkurve** f hairpin
bend. **H~schnitt** m haircut.
H~spange f slide. **H~waschmit-
tel** nt shampoo
Habe f - possessions pl

Habgier f greed. **h~ig** adj greedy
Habicht m -s,-e hawk
Hachse f -,-n (Culin) knuckle
Hackbraten m meat loaf
Hacke¹ f -,-n hoe; (Spitz-) pick

Hacke² f -,-n, **Hacken** m -s,- heel

hack|en vt hoe; (schlagen, zerkleinern) chop; (Vogel:) peck. **H~fleisch** nt mince

Hafen m -s,∵ harbour; (See:) port. **H~arbeiter** m docker. **H~stadt** f port

Hafer m -s oats pl. **H~flocken** fpl [rolled] oats

Haft f - (Jur) custody; (H~strafe) imprisonment. **h~bar** adj (Jur) liable. **H~befehl** m warrant

haften vi (haben) cling; (kleben) stick; (bürgen) vouch/(Jur) be liable (für for)

Häftling m -s,-e detainee

Haftpflicht f (Jur) liability. **H~versicherung** f (Auto) third-party insurance

Haftung f - (Jur) liability

Hagebutte f -,-n rose hip

Hagel m -s hail. **h~n** vi (haben) hail

hager adj gaunt

Hahn m -[e]s,∵e cock; (Techn) tap

Hähnchen nt -s,- (Culin) chicken

Hai[fisch] m -[e]s,-e shark

Häkchen nt -s,- tick

häkel|n vt/i (haben) crochet. **H~nadel** f crochet hook

Haken m -s,- hook; (Häkchen) tick; (◻: Schwierigkeit) snag. **h~** vt hook (an + acc to). **H~kreuz** nt swastika

halb adj half; auf h~em Weg half-way ● adv half; **h~** drei half past two; **fünf** [Minuten] vor/nach **h~** vier twenty-five [minutes] past three/to four. **H~e(r,s)** f/m/nt half [a litre]

halber prep (+ gen) for the sake of; Geschäfte h~ on business

Halbfinale nt semifinal

halbieren vt halve, divide in half; (Geometry) bisect

Halb|insel f peninsula. **H~kreis** m semicircle. **H~kugel** f hemisphere. **h~laut** adj low ● adv in an undertone. **h~mast** adv at half-mast. **H~mond** m half moon. **H~pension** f half board. **h~rund** adj semicircular. **H~schuh** m [flat] shoe. **h~tags** adv [for] half a day; **h~tags arbeiten** ≈ work part-time. **H~ton** m semitone. **h~wegs** adv half-way; (ziemlich) more or less. **h~wüchsig** adj adolescent. **H~zeit** f (Sport) half-time; (Spielzeit) half

Halde f -,-n dump, tip

Hälfte f -,-n half; zur H~ half

Halfter f -,-n & nt -s,- holster

Halle f -,-n hall; (Hotel-) lobby; (Bahnhofs-) station concourse

hallen vi (haben) resound; (wider-) echo

Hallen- prefix indoor

hallo int hallo

Halluzination /-'tsio:n/ f -,-en hallucination

Halm m -[e]s,-e stalk; (Gras-) blade

Hals m -es,∵e neck; (Kehle) throat; aus vollem H~e at the top of one's voice; (lachen) out loud. **H~band** nt (pl -bänder) collar. **H~schmerzen** mpl sore throat sg

halt int stop! (Mil) halt!; ◻ wait a minute!

Halt m -[e]s,-e hold; (Stütze) support; (innerer) stability; (Anhalten) stop; **H~** machen stop. **h~bar** adj durable; (Textiles) hard-wearing; (fig) tenable; **h~bar bis** (Comm) use by

halten† vt hold; make (Rede); give (Vortrag); (einhalten, bewahren) keep; [sich (dat)] etw h~ keep (Hund); take (Zeitung); be liable with regard as; **viel h~ von** think highly of; sich links h~ keep left; sich

h~an (+ acc) (fig) keep to ●**vi** (haben) hold; (haltbar sein, bestehen bleiben) keep; (Freundschaft, Blumen:) last; (Halt machen) stop; auf sich (acc) h~ take pride in oneself; zu jdm h~ be loyal to s.o.

Halte|stelle f stop. **H~verbot** nt waiting restriction; 'H~verbot' 'no waiting'

Haltung f -,-en (Körper-) posture; (Verhalten) manner; (Einstellung) attitude; (Fassung) composure; (Halten) keeping

Hammel m -s,- ram; (Culin) mutton. **H~fleisch** nt mutton.

Hammer m -s,⁼ hammer

hämmern vt/i (haben) hammer

Hamster m -s,- hamster. **h~n** vt/i 🔊 hoard

Hand f -,⁼e hand; jdm die H~ geben shake hands with s.o.; rechter/linker H~ on the right/left; zweiter H~ second-hand; unter der H~ unofficially; (geheim) secretly; H~ und Fuß haben (fig) be sound. **H~arbeit** f manual work; (handwerklich) handicraft; (Nadelarbeit) needlework; (Gegenstand) hand-made article. **H~ball** m [German] handball. **H~bewegung** f gesture. **H~bremse** f handbrake. **H~buch** nt handbook, manual

Händedruck m handshake

Handel m -s trade, commerce; (Unternehmen) business; (Geschäft) deal; H~ treiben trade. **h~n** vi (haben) act; (Handel treiben) trade (mit in); von etw od über etw (acc) h~n deal with sth; sich h~n um be about, concern. **H~smarine** f merchant navy. **H~sschiff** nt merchant vessel. **H~sschule** f commercial college. **H~sware** f merchandise

Hand|feger m -s,- brush. **H~fläche** f palm. **H~gelenk** nt wrist.

H~gemenge nt -s,- scuffle. **H~gepäck** nt hand luggage. **h~geschrieben** adj hand-written. **h~greiflich** adj tangible; h~greiflich werden become violent. **H~griff** m handle

handhaben vt insep (reg) handle

Handikap /ˈhɛndikɛp/ nt -s,-s handicap

Handkuss m kiss on the hand

Händler m -s,- dealer, trader

handlich adj handy

Handlung f -,-en act; (Handeln) action; (Roman-) plot; (Geschäft) shop. **H~sweise** f conduct

Hand|schellen fpl handcuffs. **H~schlag** m handshake. **H~schrift** f handwriting; (Text) manuscript. **H~schuh** m glove. **H~stand** m handstand. **H~tasche** f handbag. **H~tuch** nt towel

Handwerk nt craft, trade. **H~er** m -s,- craftsman; (Arbeiter) workman

Handy /ˈhɛndi/ nt -s,-s mobile phone, cell phone Amer

Hanf m -[e]s hemp

Hang m -[e]s,⁼e slope; (fig) inclination

Hänge|brücke f suspension bridge. **H~matte** f hammock

hängen¹ vt (reg) hang

hängen² vi (reg) vi (haben) hang; h~ an (+ dat) (fig) be attached to; h~ lassen leave

Hannover nt -s Hanover

hänseln vt tease

hantieren vi (haben) busy oneself

Happen m -s,- mouthful; einen H~ essen have a bite to eat

Harfe f -,-n harp

Harke f -,-n rake. **h~n** vt/i (haben) rake

harmlos adj harmless;

(*arglos*) innocent

Harmonie *f* -,-n harmony

Harmonika *f* -,-s accordion; (*Mund*-) mouth organ

harmonisch *adj* harmonious

Harn *m* -[e]s urine. **H~blase** *f* bladder

Harpune *f* -,-n harpoon

hart *adj* hard; (*heftig*) violent; (*streng*) harsh

Härte *f* -,-n hardness; (*Strenge*) harshness; (*Not*) hardship. **h~n** *vt* harden

Hart|faserplatte *f* hardboard. **h~näckig** *adj* stubborn; (*ausdauernd*) persistent. **H~näckigkeit** *f* - stubbornness; persistence

Harz *nt* -es,-e resin

Haschee *nt* -s,-s (*Culin*) hash

Haschisch *nt* & *m* -[s] hashish

Hase *m* -n,-n hare

Hasel *f* -,-n hazel. **H~maus** *f* dormouse. **H~nuss** *f* hazel nut

Hass *m* -es hatred

hassen *vt* hate

hässlich *adj* ugly; (*unfreundlich*) nasty. **H~keit** *f* - ugliness; nastiness

Hast *f* - haste. **h~ig** *adj* hasty, *adv* -ily, hurried

hast, hat, hatte, hätte *s.* haben

Haube *f* -,-n cap; (*Trocken*-) drier; (*Kühler*-) bonnet

Hauch *m* -[e]s breath; (*Luft*-) breeze; (*Duft*) whiff; (*Spur*) tinge. **h~dünn** *adj* very thin

Haue *f* -,-n pick; (⊞: *Prügel*) beating. **h~n†** *vt* beat; (*hämmern*) knock; (*meißeln*) hew; sich **h~n** fight; übers Ohr **h~n** ⊞ cheat • *vi* (*haben*) bang (auf + *acc* on); jdm ins Gesicht **h~n** hit s.o. in the face

Haufen *m* -s,- heap, pile; (*Leute*) crowd

häufen *vt* heap or pile [up]; sich **h~** pile up; (*zunehmen*) increase

häufig *adj* frequent

Haupt *nt* -[e]s, Häupter head. **H~bahnhof** *m* main station. **H~fach** *nt* main subject. **H~gericht** *nt* main course

Häuptling *m* -s,-e chief

Haupt|mahlzeit *f* main meal **H~mann** *m* (*pl* -leute) captain. **H~post** *f* main post office. **H~quartier** *nt* headquarters *pl*. **H~rolle** *f* lead; (*fig*) leading role. **H~sache** *f* main thing; in der **H~sache** in the main. **h~sächlich** *adj* main. **H~satz** *m* main clause. **H~stadt** *f* capital. **H~verkehrsstraße** *f* main road. **H~verkehrszeit** *f* rush hour. **H~wort** *nt* (*pl* -wörter) noun

Haus *nt* -es, Häuser house; (*Gebäude*) building; (*Schnecken*-) shell; zu **H~e** at home; nach **H~e** home. **H~arbeit** *f* housework; (*Sch*) homework. **H~arzt** *m* family doctor. **H~aufgaben** *fpl* homework *sg*. **H~besetzer** *m* -s,- squatter

hausen *vi* (*haben*) live; (*wüten*) wreak havoc

Haus|frau *f* housewife. **h~gemacht** *adj* home-made. **H~halt** *m* -[e]s,-e household; (*Pol*) budget. **h~halten†** *vi sep* (*haben*) **h~halten** mit manage carefully; conserve (*Kraft*). **H~hälterin** *f* -,-nen housekeeper. **H~haltsgeld** *nt* housekeeping [money]. **H~haltsplan** *m* budget. **H~herr** *m* head of the household; (*Gastgeber*) host

Hausierer *m* -s,- hawker

Hauslehrer *m* [private] tutor. **H~in** *f* governess

häuslich *adj* domestic, (*Person*) domesticated

Haus|meister *m* caretaker. **H~ordnung** *f* house rules *pl.*

H~putz m cleaning. **H~rat** m -[e]s household effects pl. **H~schlüssel** m front-door key. **H~schuh** m slipper. **H~suchung** f [police] search. **H~suchungsbefehl** m search warrant. **H~tier** nt domestic animal; (Hund, Katze) pet. **H~tür** f front door. **H~wirt** m landlord. **H~wirtin** f landlady

Haut f -,Häute skin; (Tier-) hide. **H~arzt** m dermatologist

häuten vt skin; sich h~ moult

haut|eng adj skin-tight. **H~farbe** f colour; (Teint) complexion

Hebamme f -,-n midwife

Hebel m -s,- lever

heben† vt lift; (hoch-, steigern) raise; sich h~ rise; (Nebel:) lift; (sich verbessern) improve

hebräisch adj Hebrew

hecheln vi (haben) pant

Hecht m -[e]s,-e pike

Heck nt -s,-s (Naut) stern; (Aviat) tail; (Auto) rear

Hecke f -,-n hedge

Heck|fenster nt rear window. **H~tür** f hatchback

Heer nt -[e]s,-e army

Hefe f - yeast

Heft nt -[e]s,-e booklet; (Sch) exercise book; (Zeitschrift) issue. **h~en** vt (nähen) tack; (stecken) pin/ (klammern) clip/(mit Heftmaschine) staple (an + acc to). **H~er** m -s,- file

heftig adj fierce, violent; (Regen) heavy; (Schmerz, Gefühl) intense

Heft|klammer f staple; (Büro-) paper clip. **H~maschine** f stapler. **H~zwecke** f -,-n drawing pin

Heide¹ m -n,-n heathen

Heide² f -,-n heath; (Bot) heather. **H~kraut** nt heather

Heidelbeere f bilberry

Heidin f -,-nen heathen

heikel adj difficult, tricky

heil adj undamaged, intact; (Person) unhurt; mit h~er Haut 🔢 unscathed

Heil nt -s salvation

Heiland m -s (Relig) Saviour

Heil|anstalt f sanatorium; (Nerven-) mental hospital. **H~bad** nt spa. **H~bar** adj curable

Heilbutt m -[e]s,-e halibut

heilen vt cure; heal (Wunde) • vi (sein) heal

Heilgymnastik f physiotherapy

heilig adj holy; (geweiht) sacred; der H~e Abend Christmas Eve; die h~e Anna Saint Anne; (Feiertag); h~ sprechen canonize. **H~abend** m Christmas Eve. **H~e(r)** m/f saint. **H~enschein** m halo. **H~keit** f - sanctity, holiness. **H~tum** nt -s,-̈er shrine

heil|kräftig adj medicinal. **H~kräuter** ntpl medicinal herbs. **H~mittel** nt remedy. **H~praktiker** m -s,- practitioner of alternative medicine. **H~sarmee** f Salvation Army. **H~ung** f - cure

Heim nt -[e]s,-e home; (Studenten-) hostel. **h~** adv home

Heimat f -,-en home; (Land) native land. **H~stadt** f home town

heim|begleiten vt sep see home. **H~computer** m home computer. **h~fahren†** v sep • vi (sein) go/drive home • vt take/drive home. **H~fahrt** f way home. **h~gehen†** vi sep (sein) go home

heimisch adj native, indigenous; (Pol) domestic

Heim|kehr f - return [home]. **h~kehren** vi sep (sein) return home. **h~kommen†** vi sep (sein) come home

heimlich adj secret; etw h~ tun

do sth secretly. **H~keit** f -,-en secrecy; **H~keiten** secrets

Heim|reise f journey home. **H~spiel** nt home game. **h~suchen** vt sep afflict. **h~tückisch** adj treacherous; (Krankheit) insidious. **h~wärts** adv home. **H~weg** m way home. **H~weh** nt -s homesickness; **H~weh haben** be homesick. **H~werker** m -s,- [home] handyman. **h~zahlen** vt sep jdm etw **h~zahlen** (fig) pay s.o. back for sth

Heirat f -,-en marriage. **h~en** vt/i (haben) marry. **H~santrag** m proposal; **jdm einen H~santrag machen** propose to s.o.

heiser adj hoarse. **H~keit** f - hoarseness

heiß adj hot; (hitzig) heated; (leidenschaftlich) fervent

heißen† vi (haben) be called; (bedeuten) mean; **ich heiße ...** my name is ...; **wie heißt du?** what is your name? **wie heißt ... auf Englisch?** what's the English for ...? ● vt call; **jdn etw tun h~** tell s.o. to do sth

heiter adj cheerful; (Wetter) bright; (amüsant) amusing; **aus h~em Himmel** (fig) out of the blue

Heiz|anlage f heating; (Auto) heater. **H~decke** f electric blanket. **h~en** vt heat; light (Ofen) ● vi (haben) put the heating on; (Ofen:) give out heat. **H~gerät** nt heater. **H~kessel** m boiler. **H~körper** m radiator. **H~lüfter** m -s,- fan heater. **H~material** nt fuel. **H~ung** f -,-en heating; (Heizkörper) radiator

Hektar nt & m -s,- hectare

Held m -en,-en hero. **h~enhaft** adj heroic. **H~entum** nt -s heroism. **H~in** f -,-nen heroine

helfen† vi (haben) help (jdm s.o.);

(nützen) be effective; **sich (dat) nicht zu h~en wissen** not know what to do; **es hilft nichts** it's no use. **H~er(in)** m -s,- (f -,-nen) helper, assistant

hell adj light; (Licht ausstrahlend, klug) bright; (Stimme) clear; (🗆: völlig) utter; **h~es Bier** ≈ lager ● adv brightly

Hell|igkeit f - brightness. **H~seher(in)** m -s,- (f -,-nen) clairvoyant

Helm m -[e]s,-e helmet

Hemd nt -[e]s,-en vest; (Ober-) shirt

Hemisphäre f -,-n hemisphere

hemm|en vt check; (verzögern) impede; (fig) inhibit. **H~ung** f -,-en (fig) inhibition; (Skrupel) scruple; **H~ungen haben** be inhibited. **h~ungslos** adj unrestrained

Hendl nt -s,-[n] (Aust) chicken

Hengst m -[e]s,-e stallion

Henkel m -s,- handle

Henne f -,-n hen

her adv here; (zeitlich) ago; **her mit ...!** give me ...! **von Norden/weit her** from the north/far away; **vom Thema her** as far as the subject is concerned; **her sein** come (von from); **es ist schon lange her** it was a long time ago

herab adv down [here]; **von oben h~** from above; (fig) condescending

herablassen† vt sep let down; **sich h~** condescend (zu to)

herab|sehen† vi sep (haben) look down (auf + acc on). **h~setzen** vt sep reduce, cut; (fig) belittle

Heraldik f - heraldry

heran adv near; [bis] **h~ an** (+ acc) up to. **h~kommen†** vi sep (sein) approach; **h~kommen an** (+ acc) come up to; (erreichen) get at; (fig) measure up to. **h~machen**

(sich) *vr sep* sich h∼machen an (+ *acc*) approach; get down to (*Arbeit*). h∼wachsen† *vi sep* (*sein*) grow up. h∼ziehen† *v sep* ● *vt* pull up (an (+ *acc* to); (*züchten*) raise; (h∼bilden) train; (*hinzuziehen*) call in ● *vi* (*sein*) approach

herauf *adv sep* [here]; die Treppe h∼ up the stairs. h∼setzen *vt sep* raise, increase

heraus *adv sep* (aus of); h∼ damit o du mit der Sprache! out with it! h∼bekommen† *vt sep* get out; (*ausfindig machen*) find out; (*lösen*) solve; Geld h∼bekommen get change. h∼finden† *v sep* ● *vt* find out ● *vi* (*haben*) find one's way out. h∼fordern *vt sep* provoke; challenge (*Person*). H∼forderung *f* provocation; challenge. H∼gabe *f* handing over; (*Admin*) issue; (*Veröffentlichung*) publication. h∼geben† *vt sep* hand over; (*Admin*) issue; (*veröffentlichen*) publish; edit (*Zeitschrift*); jdm Geld h∼geben give s.o. change ● *vi* (*haben*) give change (auf + *acc* for). H∼geber *m* -s,- publisher; editor. h∼halten† (sich) *vr sep* keep out (aus of). h∼kommen† *vi sep* (*sein*) come out; (*aus Schwierigkeit, Takt*) get out; auf eins o dasselbe h∼kommen 🔢 come to the same thing. h∼lassen† *vt sep* let out. h∼nehmen† *vt sep* take out; sich zu viel h∼nehmen (*fig*) take liberties. h∼reden (sich) *vr sep* make excuses. h∼rücken *v sep* ● *vt* move out; (*hergeben*) hand over ● *vi* (*sein*) h∼rücken mit hand over; (*fig: sagen*) come out with. h∼schlagen† *vt sep* knock out; (*fig*) gain. h∼stellen *vt sep* put out; sich h∼stellen turn out (als to be; dass that). h∼ziehen† *vt sep* pull out

herb *adj* sharp; (*Wein*) dry; (*fig*) harsh

herbei *adv* here. h∼führen *vt sep* (*fig*) bring about. h∼schaffen *vt sep* get. h∼sehnen *vt sep* long for

Herberg|e *f* -,-n (*youth*) hostel; (*Unterkunft*) lodging. H∼svater *m* warden

herbestellen *vt sep* summon

herbitten† *vt sep* ask to come

herbringen† *vt sep* bring [here]

Herbst *m* -[e]s,-e autumn. h∼lich *adj* autumnal

Herd *m* -[e]s,-e stove, cooker

Herde *f* -,-n herd; (*Schaf-*) flock

herein *adv* in [here]; h∼! come in! h∼bitten† *vt sep* ask in. h∼fallen† *vi sep* (*sein*) 🔢 be taken in (auf + *acc* by). h∼kommen† *vi sep* (*sein*) come in. h∼lassen† *vt sep* let in. h∼legen *vt sep* 🔢 take for a ride

Herfahrt *f* journey/drive here

herfallen† *vi sep* (*sein*) ∼ über (+ *acc*) attack; fall upon (*Essen*)

hergeben† *vt sep* hand over; (*fig*) give up

hergehen† *vi sep* (*sein*) h∼ vor (+ *dat*) walk along in front of; es ging lustig her 🔢 there was a lot of merriment

herholen *vt sep* fetch; weit hergeholt (*fig*) far-fetched

Hering *m* -s,-e herring; (*Zeltpflock*) tent peg

her|kommen† *vi sep* (*sein*) come here; wo kommt das her? where does it come from? h∼kömmlich *adj* traditional. H∼kunft *f* - origin

herleiten *vt sep* derive

hermachen *vt sep* viel/wenig h∼ be impressive/unimpressive; (*wichtig nehmen*) make a lot of/little fuss (von of); sich h∼ über (+ *acc*) fall upon; tackle (*Arbeit*)

Hermelin¹ *nt* -s,-e (*Zool*) stoat

Hermelin² *m* -s,-e (*Pelz*) ermine

Hernie /ˈhɛrnjə/ f -,-n hernia
Heroin nt -s heroin
heroisch adj heroic
Herr m -n,-en gentleman; (Gebieter) master (über + acc of); [Gott,] der H∼ the Lord [God]; Herr Meier Mr Meier; Sehr geehrte H∼en Dear Sirs. H∼enhaus nt manor [house]. h∼enlos adj ownerless; (Tier) stray
Herrgott m der H∼ the Lord
herrichten vt sep prepare; wieder h∼ renovate
Herrin f -,-nen mistress
herrlich adj marvellous; (großartig) magnificent
Herrschaft f -,-en rule; (Macht) power; (Kontrolle) control; meine H∼en! ladies and gentlemen!
herrsch|en vi (haben) rule; (verbreitet sein) prevail; es h∼te Stille there was silence. H∼er(in) m -s,- (f -,-nen) ruler
herrühren vi sep (haben) stem (von from)
herstammen vi sep (haben) come (aus/von from)
herstell|en vt sep establish; (Comm) manufacture, make. H∼er m -s,- manufacturer, maker. H∼ung f - establishment; manufacture
herüber adv over [here]
herum adv im Kreis h∼ [round] in a circle; falsch h∼ the wrong way round; um ... h∼ round ... ; (ungefähr) [round] about ; h∼ sein be over. h∼drehen vt sep turn round/ (wenden) over; turn (Schlüssel). h∼gehen† vi sep (sein) walk around/ (Zeit:) pass; h∼gehen um go round. h∼kommen† vi sep (sein) get about; come round (Ecke); um etw [nicht] h∼kommen† (fig) [not] get out of sth. h∼sitzen† vi sep

(haben) sit around; h∼sitzen um sit round. h∼sprechen† (sich) vr sep (Gerücht:) get about. h∼treiben† (sich) vr sep hang around. h∼ziehen† vi sep (sein) move around; (ziellos) wander about
herunter adv down [here]; die Treppe h∼ down the stairs. h∼fallen† vi fall off. h∼gekommen adj (fig) run-down; (Gebäude) dilapidated; (Person) down-at-heel. h∼kommen† vi sep (sein) come down; (fig) go to rack and ruin; (Firma, Person:) go downhill; (gesundheitlich) get run down. h∼laden vt † download. h∼lassen† vt sep let down, lower. h∼machen† vt sep † reprimand; (herabsetzen) run down. h∼spielen vt sep (fig) play down
hervor adv out (aus of). h∼bringen† vt sep produce; utter (Wort). h∼gehen† vi sep (sein) come/(sich ergeben) emerge/(folgen) follow (aus from). h∼heben† vt sep (fig) stress, emphasize. h∼ragen vi sep (haben) jut out; (fig) stand out. h∼ragend adj (fig) outstanding. h∼rufen† vt sep (fig) cause. h∼stehen† vi sep (haben) protrude. h∼treten† vi sep (sein) protrude, bulge; (fig) stand out. h∼tun† (sich) vr sep (fig) distinguish oneself; (angeben) show off
Herweg m way here
Herz nt -ens,-en heart; (Kartenspiel) hearts pl; sich (dat) ein H∼ fassen pluck up courage. H∼anfall m heart attack
herzhaft adj hearty; (würzig) savoury
herziehen† v sep ● vt hinter sich (dat) h∼ pull along [behind one] ● vi sep hinter jdm h∼ follow along behind s.o.; über jdn h∼ run s.o. down

herz|ig *adj* sweet, adorable. **H~in-farkt** *m* heart attack. **H~klopfen** *nt* -s palpitations *pl*

herzlich *adj* cordial; (*warm*) warm; (*aufrichtig*) sincere; **h~en Dank!** many thanks! **h~e Grüße** kind regards

herzlos *adj* heartless

Herzog *m* -s, ⸚e duke. **H~in** *f* -,-nen duchess. **H~tum** *nt* -s, ⸚er duchy

Herzschlag *m* heartbeat; (*Med*) heart failure

Hessen *nt* -s Hesse

heterosexuell *adj* heterosexual

Hetze *f* - rush; (*Kampagne*) virulent campaign (**gegen** against). **h~n** *vt* chase; **sich h~n** hurry

Heu *nt* -s hay

Heuchelei *f* - hypocrisy

heuch|eln *vt* feign ● *vi* (*haben*) pretend. **H~ler(in)** *m* -s,- (*f* -,-nen) hypocrite. **h~lerisch** *adj* hypocritical

heuer *adv* (*Aust*) this year

heulen *vi* (*haben*) howl; (⯅: *wei-nen*) cry

> *i* **Heurige** This is an Austrian term for both a new wine and an inn with new wine on tap, especially an inn with its own vineyard in the Vienna region. A garland of pine twigs outside the gates of the *Heurige* shows that the new barrel has been tapped.

Heu|schnupfen *m* hay fever. **H~schober** *m* -s,- haystack. **H~schrecke** *f* -,-n grasshopper

heut|e *adv* today; (*heutzutage*) nowadays; **h~e früh** od **Morgen** this morning; **von h~e auf mor-gen** from one day to the next.

h~ig *adj* today's; (*gegenwärtig*) present; **der h~ige Tag** today. **h~zutage** *adv* nowadays

Hexe *f* -,-n witch. **h~n** *vi* (*haben*) work magic. **H~nschuss** *m* lumbago

Hieb *m* -[e]s,-e blow; (*Peitschen-*) lash; **H~e** hiding *sg*

hier *adv* here; **h~ sein/bleiben/las-sen/behalten** be/stay/leave/keep here; **h~ und da** here and there; (*zeitlich*) now and again

hier|auf *adv* on this/these; (*ant-worten*) to this; (*zeitlich*) after this. **h~aus** *adv* out of or from this/these. **h~durch** *adv* through this/these; (*Ursache*) as a result of this. **h~her** *adv* here. **h~hin** *adv* here. **h~in** *adv* in this/these. **h~mit** *adv* with this/these; (*Comm*) herewith; (*Admin*) hereby. **h~nach** *adv* after this/these; (*demgemäß*) according to this/these. **h~über** *adv* over/(*höher*) above this/these; (*spre-chen, streiten*) about this/these. **h~von** *adv* from this/these; (*h~über*) about this/these; (*Menge*) of this/these. **h~zu** *adv* to this/these; (*h~für*) for this/these. **h~zulande** *adv* here

hiesig *adj* local. **H~e(r)** *m/f* local

Hilf|e *f* -,-n help, aid; **um H~e rufen** call for help. **h~los** *adj* helpless. **H~losigkeit** *f* - helplessness. **h~reich** *adj* helpful

Hilfs|arbeiter *m* unskilled labourer. **h~bedürftig** *adj* needy; **h~bedürftig sein** be in need of help. **h~bereit** *adj* helpful. **H~kraft** *f* helper. **H~mittel** *nt* aid. **h~verb** *nt* auxiliary verb

Himbeere *f* raspberry

Himmel *m* -s,- sky; (*Relig & fig*) heaven; (*Bett-*) canopy; **unter freiem H~** in the open air. **H~bett** *nt* four-poster [bed].

H~fahrt f Ascension

himmlisch adj heavenly

hin adv there; **hin und her** to and fro; **hin und zurück** there and back; (*Rail*) return; **hin und wieder** now and again; **an** (+ *dat*) ... **hin** along; **auf** (+ *acc*) ... **hin** in reply to (*Brief, Anzeige*); **on** (*jds Rat*); **zu od nach** ... **hin** towards; **hin sein** 🄵 be gone; **es ist noch lange hin** it's a long time yet

hinauf adv up [there]. **h~gehen†** vi sep (sein) go up. **h~setzen** vt sep raise

hinaus adv out [there]; (*nach draußen*) outside; **zur Tür h~** out of the door; **auf Jahre h~** for years to come; **über etw** (+ *acc*) **h~** beyond sth; (*Menge*) [over and] above sth; **über etw** (+ *acc*) **h~ sein** (*fig*) be past sth. **h~gehen†** vi sep (sein) go out; (*Zimmer:*) face (nach Norden north); **h~gehen über** (+ *acc*) go beyond, exceed. **h~laufen†** vi sep (sein) run out; **h~laufen auf** (+ *acc*) (*fig*) amount to. **h~lehnen (sich)** vr sep lean out. **h~schieben†** vt sep push out; (*fig*) put off. **h~werfen†** vt sep throw out; (🄵: *entlassen*) fire. **h~wollen†** vi sep (haben) want to go out; **h~wollen auf** (+ *acc*) (*fig*) aim at. **h~ziehen†** v sep ●vt pull out; (*in die Länge ziehen*) drag out; (*verzögern*) delay; **sich h~ziehen** drag on; be delayed ●vi (sein) move out. **h~zögern** vt delay; **sich h~zögern** be delayed

Hinblick m im H~ **auf** (+ *acc*) in view of; (*hinsichtlich*) regarding

hinder|lich adj awkward; **jdm h~lich sein** hamper s.o. **h~n** vt hamper; (*verhindern*) prevent. **H~nis** nt -ses,-se obstacle. **H~nisrennen** nt steeplechase

Hindu m -s,-s Hindu.

hindurch adv through it/them

hinein adv in [there]; (*nach drinnen*) inside; **h~ in** (+ *acc*) into. **h~fallen†** vi sep (sein) fall in. **h~gehen†** vi sep (sein) go in; **h~gehen in** (+ *acc*) go into. **h~reden** vi sep (haben) jdm h~reden interrupt s.o.; (*sich einmischen*) interfere in s.o.'s affairs. **h~versetzen (sich)** vr sep sich in jds Lage h~versetzen put oneself in s.o.'s position. **h~ziehen†** vt sep pull in; **h~ziehen in** (+ *acc*) pull into; in etw (acc) h~gezogen werden (*fig*) become involved in sth

hin|fahren† v sep ●vi (sein) go/drive there ●vt take/drive there. **H~fahrt** f journey/drive there; (*Rail*) outward journey. **h~fallen†** vi sep (sein) fall. **h~fliegen†** v sep ●vi (sein) fly there; 🄵 fall ●vt fly there. **H~flug** m flight there; (*Aviat*) outward flight

Hingeb|ung f - devotion. **h~ungsvoll** adj devoted

hingehen† vi sep (sein) go/(zu Fuß) walk there; (*vergehen*) pass; **h~ zu go up to**; **wo h~?** where are you going?

hingerissen adj rapt; **h~ sein** be carried away (von by)

hinhalten† vt sep hold out; (*warten lassen*) keep waiting

hinken vi (haben/sein) limp

hin|knien (sich) vr sep kneel down. **h~kommen†** vi sep (sein) get there; (*h~gehören*) belong, go; (🄵: *auskommen*) manage (mit with); (🄵: *stimmen*) be right. **h~laufen†** vi sep (sein) run/(gehen) walk there. **h~legen** vt sep lay or put down; **sich h~legen** lie down. **h~nehmen†** vt sep (*fig*) accept

hinreichen v sep ●vt hand (dat to) ●vi (haben) extend (bis to); (*ausreichen*) be adequate. **h~d** adj adequate

Hinreise f journey there; (Rail) outward journey

hinreißen† vt sep (fig) carry away; **sich h~ lassen** get carried away. **h~d** adj ravishing

hinrichten vt sep execute. **H~ung** f execution

hinschreiben† vt sep write there; (aufschreiben) write down

hinsehen† vi sep (haben) look

hinsetzen vt sep put down; **sich h~** sit down

Hinsicht f - in dieser **H~** in this respect; in finanzieller **H~** financially. **h~lich** prep (+ gen) regarding

hinstellen vt sep put or set down; park (Auto)

hinstrecken vt sep hold out; **sich h~** extend

hinten adv at the back; dort **h~** back there; nach/von **h~** to the back/from behind. **h~herum** adv round the back; ⊤ by devious means

hinter prep (+ dat/acc) behind; (nach) after; **h~ jdm/etw herlaufen** run after s.o./something; **h~ etw** (dat) **stecken** (fig) be behind sth; **h~ etw** (acc) **kommen** (fig) get to the bottom of sth; **etw h~ sich** (acc) **bringen** get sth over [and done] with

Hinterbliebene pl (Admin) surviving dependants; **die H~n** the bereaved family sg

hintere|(r,s) adj back, rear; **h~s Ende** far end

hintereinander adv one behind/(zeitlich) after the other; dreimal **h~** three times in succession

Hintergedanke m ulterior motive

hintergehen† vt deceive

Hinter|grund m background.

H~halt m -[e]s,-e ambush. **h~hältig** adj underhand

hinterher adv behind, after; (zeitlich) afterwards

Hinter|hof m back yard. **H~kopf** m back of the head

hinterlassen† vt leave [behind]; (Jur) leave, bequeath (dat to). **H~schaft** f -,-en (Jur) estate

hinterlegen vt deposit

Hinter|leib m (Zool) abdomen. **H~list** f deceit. **h~listig** adj deceitful. **H~n** m -s,- ⊤ bottom, backside. **h~rad** nt rear or back wheel. **h~rücks** adv from behind. **h~ste(r,s)** adj last; **h~ste Reihe** back row. **H~teil** nt ⊤ behind. **H~treppe** f back stairs pl

hinterziehen† vt (Admin) evade

hinüber adv over or across [there]; **h~ sein** (⊤: unbrauchbar, tot) have had it. **h~gehen†** vi sep (sein) go over or across; **h~gehen über** (+ acc) cross

hinunter adv down [there]. **h~gehen†** vi sep (sein) go down. **h~schlucken** vt sep swallow

Hinweg m way there

hinweg adv away, off; **h~ über** (+ acc) over; **über eine Zeit h~** over a period. **h~kommen** vt sep (sein) **h~kommen über** (+ acc) (fig) get over. **h~sehen** vi sep (haben) **h~sehen über** (+ acc) see over; (fig) overlook. **h~setzen** (sich) vr sep **sich h~setzen über** (+ acc) ignore

Hinweis m -es,-e reference; (Andeutung) hint; (Anzeichen) indication; **unter H~ auf** (+ acc) with reference to. **h~en†** v sep ●vi (haben) point (**auf** + acc to) ●vt **jdn auf etw** (acc) **h~en** point sth out to s.o.

hinwieder adv on the other hand

hin|zeigen vi sep (haben) point (auf + acc to). **h~ziehen†** vt sep pull; (fig: in die Länge ziehen) drag out; (verzögern) delay; **sich h~zie-hen** drag on

hinzu adv in addition. **h~fügen** vt sep add. **h~kommen†** vt sep (sein) be added; (ankommen) arrive [on the scene]; join (**zu jdm** s.o.). **h~ziehen†** vt sep call in

Hiobsbotschaft f bad news sg

Hirn nt -s brain; **h~ziehen†** brains pl. **H~hautentzündung** f meningitis

Hirsch m -[e]s,-e deer; (männlich) stag; (Culin) venison

Hirse f - millet

Hirt m -en,-en, **Hirte** m -n,-n shepherd

hissen vt hoist

Histor|iker m -s,- historian. **h~isch** adj historical; (bedeutend) historic

Hitze f - heat. **h~ig** adj (fig) heated; (Person) hot-headed; (jäh-zornig) hot-tempered. **H~schlag** m heat-stroke

H-Milch /ˈhaː-/ f long-life milk

Hobby nt -s,-s hobby

Hobel m -s,- (Techn) plane; (Culin) slicer. **h~n** vt/i (haben) plane. **H~späne** mpl shavings

hoch adj (attrib hohe(r,s) high; (Baum, Mast) tall; (Offizier) high-ranking; (Alter) great; (Summe) large; (Strafe) heavy; **hohe Schuhe** ankle boots ● adv high; (sehr) highly; **h~ gewachsen** tall; **h~be-gabt** highly gifted; **h~gestellte Persönlichkeit** important person; **die Treppe h~** up the stairs; **sechs Mann h~** six of us/them. **H~** nt -s,-s cheer; (Meteorology) high

Hoch|achtung f high esteem. **H~achtungsvoll** adv Yours faith-fully. **H~betrieb** m great activity;

in den Geschäften herrscht **H~betrieb** the shops are terribly busy. **H~deutsch** nt High German. **H~druck** m high pressure. **H~ebene** f plateau. **h~fahren†** vi sep (sein) go up; (auffahren) start up; (aufbrausen) flare up. **h~gehen†** vi sep (sein) go up; (explodieren) blow up; (aufbrausen) flare up. **h~ge-stellt** attrib adj (Zahl) superior; (fig) **ʰh~ gestellt**, s. hoch. **H~glanz** m high gloss. **h~gradig** adj extreme. **h~hackig** adj high-heeled. **h~hal-ten†** vt sep hold up; (fig) uphold. **H~haus** nt high-rise building. **h~heben†** vt sep lift up; raise (Hand). **h~kant** adv on end. **h~kommen†** vi sep (sein) come up; (aufstehen) get up; (fig) get on [in the world]. **H~konjunktur** f boom. **h~krempeln** vt sep roll up. **h~leben** vi sep (haben) **h~leben lassen** give three cheers for; **H~mut** m pride, arrogance. **h~nä-sig** adj 🗹 snooty. **H~ofen** m blast-furnace. **h~ragen** vi sep rise [up]; (Turm:) soar. **H~ruf** m cheer. **H~saison** f high season. **h~schla-gen†** vt sep turn up (Kragen). **H~schule** f university; (Musik-, Kunst-) academy. **H~sommer** m midsummer. **H~spannung** f high/(fig) great tension. **h~spielen** vt sep (fig) magnify. **H~sprung** m high jump

---

Hochdeutsch There are many regional dialects in Germany, Austria and Switzerland. *Hochdeutsch* (High German) is the standard language that can be understood by all German speakers. Newspapers and books are generally printed in *Hochdeutsch*.

---

höchst adv extremely, most

Hochstapler m -s,- confidence trickster

höchst|e(r,s) adj highest; (Baum, Turm) tallest; (oberste, größte) top; es ist h~e Zeit it is high time. **h~ens** adv at most; (es sei denn) except perhaps. **H~geschwindigkeit** f top or maximum speed. **H~maß** nt maximum. **H~persönlich** adv in person. **H~preis** m top price. **H~temperatur** f maximum temperature

Hoch|verrat m high treason. **H~wasser** nt high tide; (Überschwemmung) floods pl. **H~würden** m -s Reverend; (Anrede) Father

Hochzeit f -,-en wedding. **H~skleid** nt wedding dress. **H~sreise** f honeymoon [trip]. **H~stag** m wedding day/(Jahrestag) anniversary

Hocke f - in der H~ sitzen squat. **h~n** vi (haben) squat ● vr sich **h~n** squat down

Hocker m -s,- stool

Höcker m -s,- bump; (Kamel-) hump

Hockey /hɔki/ nt -s hockey

Hode f -,-n, **Hoden** m -s,- testicle

Hof m -[e]s,ᵉe [court]yard; (Bauern-) farm; (Königs-) court; (Schul-) playground; (Astronomy) halo

hoffen vt/i (haben) hope (auf + acc for). **h~tlich** adv I hope so, hopefully

Hoffnung f -,-en hope. **h~slos** adj hopeless. **h~svoll** adj hopeful

höflich adj polite. **H~keit** f -,-en politeness, courtesy

hohe(r,s) adj s. hoch

Höhe f -,-n height; (Aviat, Geog) altitude; (Niveau) level; (einer Summe) size; (An-) hill

Hoheit f -,-en (Staats-) sovereignty; (Titel) Highness. **H~sgebiet** nt

[sovereign] territory. **H~szeichen** nt national emblem

Höhe|nlinie f contour line. **H~nsonne** f sun lamp. **H~punkt** m (fig) climax, peak. **h~r** adj & adv higher; **h~re Schule** secondary school

hohl adj hollow; (leer) empty

Höhle f -,-n cave; (Tier-) den; (Hohlraum) cavity; (Augen-) socket

Hohl|maß nt measure of capacity. **H~raum** m cavity

Hohn m -s scorn, derision

höhnen vt deride

holen vt fetch, get; (kaufen) buy; (nehmen) take (aus from)

Holland nt -s Holland

Hollän|der m -s,- Dutchman; die **H~er** the Dutch pl. **H~erin** f -,-nen Dutchwoman. **h~isch** adj Dutch

Hölle f - hell. **h~isch** adj infernal; (schrecklich) terrible

Holunder m -s (Bot) elder

Holz nt -es,ᵉe wood; (Nutz-) timber. **H~blasinstrument** nt woodwind instrument

hölzern adj wooden

Holz|hammer m mallet. **~ig** adj woody. **H~kohle** f charcoal. **H~schnitt** m woodcut. **H~wolle** f wood shavings pl

Homöopathie f - homoeopathy

homöopathisch adj homoeopathic

homosexuell adj homosexual. **H~e(r)** m/f homosexual

Honig m -s honey. **H~wabe** f honeycomb

Hono|rar nt -s,-e fee. **h~rieren** vt remunerate; (fig) reward

Hopfen m -s hops pl; (Bot) hop

hopsen vi (sein) jump

horchen vi (haben) listen (auf +

acc to); *(heimlich)* eavesdrop

hören *vt* hear; *(an-)* listen to ● *vi* *(haben)* hear; *(horchen)* listen; *(gehorchen)* obey; **h~ auf** *(+ acc)* listen to

Hör|er *m* -s,- listener; *(Teleph)* receiver. **H~funk** *m* radio. **H~gerät** *nt* hearing aid

Horizont *m* -[e]s horizon. **h~tal** *adj* horizontal

Hormon *nt* -s,-e hormone

Horn *nt* -s,ˉer horn. **H~haut** *f* hard skin; *(Augen-)* cornea

Hornisse *f* -,-n hornet

Horoskop *nt* -[e]s,-e horoscope

Horrorfilm *m* horror film

Hör|saal *m* *(Univ)* lecture hall. **H~spiel** *nt* radio play

Hort *m* -[e]s,-e *(Schatz)* hoard; *(fig)* refuge. **h~en** *vt* hoard

Hortensie *f* -/a/ *f* -,-n hydrangea

Hose *f* -,-n, **Hosen** *pl* trousers *pl*. **H~nrock** *m* culottes *pl*. **H~nschlitz** *m* fly, flies *pl*. **H~nträger** *mpl* braces

Hostess *f* -,-tessen hostess; *(Aviat)* air hostess

Hostie /ˈhɔstjə/ *f* -,-n *(Relig)* host

Hotel *nt* -s,-s hotel

hübsch *adj* pretty; *(nett)* nice

Hubschrauber *m* -s,- helicopter

Huf *m* -[e]s,-e hoof. **H~eisen** *nt* horseshoe

Hüft|e *f* -,-n hip. **H~gürtel** *m* -s,- girdle

Hügel *m* -s,- hill. **h~ig** *adj* hilly

Huhn *nt* -s,ˉer chicken; *(Henne)* hen

Hühn|chen *nt* -s,- chicken. **H~erauge** *nt* corn **H~erstall** *m* henhouse

Hülle *f* -,-n cover; *(Verpackung)* wrapping; *(Platten-)* sleeve. **h~n** *vt* wrap

Hülse *f* -,-n *(Bot)* pod; *(Etui)* case. **H~nfrüchte** *fpl* pulses

human *adj* humane. **H~ität** *f* humanity

Hummel *f* -,-n bumble bee

Hummer *m* -s,- lobster

Hum|or *m* -s humour; **H~or haben** have a sense of humour. **h~orvoll** *adj* humorous

humpeln *vi* *(sein/haben)* hobble

Humpen *m* -s,- tankard

Hund *m* -[e]s,-e dog; *(Jagd-)* hound. **H~ehütte** *f* kennel

hundert *inv adj* one/a hundred. **H~** *nt* -s,-e hundred; **H~e od h~e** von hundreds of. **H~jahrfeier** *f* centenary. **h~prozentig** *adj & adv* one hundred per cent. **h~ste(r,s)** *adj* hundredth. **H~stel** *nt* -s,- hundredth

Hündin *f* -,-nen bitch

Hüne *m* -n,-n giant

Hunger *m* -s hunger; **H~ haben** be hungry. **h~n** *vi* *(haben)* starve. **H~snot** *f* famine

hungrig *adj* hungry

Hupe *f* -,-n *(Auto)* horn. **h~n** *vi* *(haben)* sound one's horn

hüpfen *vi* *(sein)* skip; *(Frosch:)* hop; *(Grashüpfer:)* jump

Hürde *f* -,-n *(Sport & fig)* hurdle; *(Schaf-)* pen, fold

Hure *f* -,-n whore

hurra *int* hurray

husten *vi* *(haben)* cough. **H~** *m* -s cough. **H~saft** *m* cough mixture

Hut¹ *m* -[e]s,ˉe hat; *(Pilz-)* cap

Hut² *f* - auf der H~ sein be on one's guard *(vor + dat* against)

hüten *vt* watch over; tend *(Tiere)*; *(aufpassen)* look after; **das Bett h~ müssen** be confined to bed; **sich h~** be on one's guard *(vor + dat* against); sich h~, etw zu tun take care not to do sth

Hütte f -,-n hut; (Hunde-) kennel; (Techn) iron and steel works. **H~nkäse** m cottage cheese. **H~nkunde** f metallurgy

Hyäne f -,-n hyena

hydraulisch adj hydraulic

Hygien|e /hy'gje:nə/ f - hygiene. **h~isch** adj hygienic

Hypno|se f - hypnosis. **h~tisch** adj hypnotic. **H~tiseur** m -s,-e hypnotist. **h~tisieren** vt hypnotize

Hypochonder /hypo'xɔndɐ/ m -s,- hypochondriac

Hypothek f -,-en mortgage

Hypothese f -,-n hypothesis

Hys|terie f - hysteria. **h~terisch** adj hysterical

i

ich pron I; ich bins it's me. **Ich** nt -[s],-[s] self; (Psychology) ego

IC-Zug /i'tse:-/ m inter-city train

ideal adj ideal. **I~** nt -s,-e ideal. **I~ismus** m - idealism. **I~ist(in)** m -en,-en (f -,-nen) idealist. **i~istisch** adj idealistic

Idee f -,-n idea; fixe I~ obsession

identifizieren vt identify

identisch adj identical

Identität f -, -en identity

Ideo|logie /-'gi:/ n ideology. **i~logisch** adj ideological

idiomatisch adj idiomatic

Idiot m -en,-en idiot. **i~isch** adj idiotic

idyllisch /i'dylıʃ/ adj idyllic

Igel m -s,- hedgehog

ihm pron (dat of er, es) [to] him; (Ding, Tier) [to] it

ihn pron (acc of er) him; (Ding, Tier) it. **I~en** pron (dat of sie pl) [to] them. **I~en** pron (dat of Sie) [to] you

ihr pron (2nd pers pl) you ● (dat of sie sg) [to] her; (Ding, Tier) [to] it ● poss pron their; (Ding, Tier) its; (pl) their. **Ihr** poss pron your. **I~e(r,s)** poss pron hers; (pl) theirs. **I~e(r,s)** poss pron yours. **I~erseits** adv for her/(pl) their part. **I~erseits** adv on your part. **i~etwegen** adv for her/(Ding, Tier) its/(pl) their sake; (wegen) because of her/it/them, on her/its/their account. **I~etwegen** adv for your sake; (wegen) because of you, on your account. **I~ige** poss pron der/die/das i~ige hers; (pl) theirs. **I~ige** poss pron der/die/das I~ige yours. **I~s** poss pron hers; (pl) theirs. **I~s** poss pron yours

Ikone f -,-n icon

illegal adj illegal

Illus|ion f -,-en illusion. **i~orisch** adj illusory

Illustr|ation /-'tsjo:n/ f -,-en illustration. **i~ieren** vt illustrate. **I~ierte** f -n,-[n] [illustrated] magazine

Iltis m -ses,-se polecat

im prep = in dem

Imbiss m snack. **I~stube** f snack bar

Imit|ation /-'tsjo:n/ f -,-en imitation. **i~ieren** vt imitate

Imker m -s,- bee-keeper

immatrikul|ation /-'tsjo:n/ f -,-en (Univ) enrolment. **i~ieren** vt (Univ) enrol; sich i~ieren enrol

immer adv always; für i~ for ever;

Immobilien | Inhalt

(*endgültig*) for good; i~ noch still; i~ mehr more and more; was i~ whatever. i~hin *adv* (*wenigstens*) at least; (*trotzdem*) all the same; (*schließlich*) after all. i~zu *adv* all the time

Immobilie /-jən/ *pl* real estate *sg*. i~makler *m* estate agent

immun *adj* immune (gegen to)

Imperialismus *m* - imperialism

impf|en *vt* vaccinate, inoculate. I~stoff *m* vaccine. I~ung *f* -,-en vaccination, inoculation

imponieren *vi* (*haben*) impress (jdm s.o.)

Impor|t *m* -[e]s,-e import. I~teur *m* -s,-e importer. i~tieren *vt* import

impoten|t *adj* (*Med*) impotent. I~z *f* - (*Med*) impotence

imprägnieren *vt* waterproof

Impressionismus *m* - impressionism

improvisieren *vt/i* (*haben*) improvise

imstande *pred adj* able (zu to); capable (etw zu tun of doing sth)

in *prep* (+ *dat*) in; (+ *acc*) into, in; (*bei Bus, Zug*) on; in der Schule at school; in die Schule to school ● *adj* in sein be in

Inbegriff *m* embodiment

indem *conj* (*während*) while; (*dadurch*) by (+ -ing)

Inder(in) *m* -s,- (*f* -,-nen) Indian

indessen *conj* while ● *adv* (*unterdessen*) meanwhile

Indian|er(in) *m* -s,- (*f* -,-nen) (American) Indian. i~isch *adj* Indian

Indien /'ɪndjən/ *nt* -s India

indirekt *adj* indirect

indisch *adj* Indian

indiskret *adj* indiscreet

indiskutabel *adj* out of the question

Individu|alist *m* -en,-en individualist. I~alität *f* - individuality. i~ell *adj* individual

Indizienbeweis /ɪn'diːtsjən-/ *m* circumstantial evidence

industrialisiert *adj* industrialized. I~ie *f* -,-n industry. i~iell *adj* industrial

ineinander *adv* in/into one another

Infanterie *f* - infantry

Infektion /-'tsio:n/ *f* -,-en infection. I~skrankheit *f* infectious disease

infizieren *vt* infect; sich i~ become/ (*Person:*) be infected

Inflation /-'tsio:n/ *f* - inflation. i~är *adj* inflationary

infolge *prep* (+ *gen*) as a result of. i~dessen *adv* consequently

Inform|atik *f* - information science. I~ation *f* -,-en information; I~ationen information *sg*. i~ieren *vt* inform; sich i~ieren find out (über + *acc* about)

Infrage *adv* etw i~ stellen question sth; (*ungewiss machen*) make sth doubtful; nicht i~ kommen be out of the question

infrarot *adj* infra-red

Ingenieur /ɪnʒe'njøːɐ/ *m* -s,-e engineer

Ingwer *m* -s ginger

Inhaber(in) *m* -s,- (*f* -,-nen) holder; (*Besitzer*) proprietor; (*Scheck-*) bearer

inhaftieren *vt* take into custody

inhalieren *vt/i* (*haben*) inhale

Inhalt *m* -[e]s,-e contents *pl*; (*Bedeutung, Gehalt*) content; (*Ge-*

schichte) story. I**~sangabe** f summary. I**~sverzeichnis** nt list/(in Buch) table of contents

Initiative /initsja'ti:və/ f -,-n initiative

inklusive prep (+ gen) including ● adv inclusive

inkonsequent adj inconsistent

inkorrekt adj incorrect

Inkubationszeit /-'tsjo:ns-/ f (Med) incubation period

Inland nt -[e]s home country; (Binnenland) interior. I**~sgespräch** nt inland call

inmitten prep (+ gen) in the middle of; (unter) amongst

innen adv inside; nach i**~** inwards. I**~architekt(in)** m(f) interior designer. I**~minister** m Minister of the Interior; (in UK) Home Secretary. I**~politik** f domestic policy. I**~stadt** f town centre

inner|e(r,s) adj inner; (Med, Pol) internal. I**~e(s)** nt interior; (Mitte) centre; (fig: Seele) inner being. I**~eien** fpl (Culin) offal sg. I**~halb** prep (+ gen) inside; (zeitlich & fig) within; (während) during ● adv i**~halb** von within. I**~lich** adj internal

innig adj sincere

innovativ adj innovative

Innung f -,-en guild

ins prep = in das

Insasse m -n,-n inmate; (im Auto) occupant; (Passagier) passenger

insbesondere adv especially

Inschrift f inscription

Insekt nt -[e]s,-en insect. I**~envertilgungsmittel** nt insecticide

Insel f -,-n island

Inser|at nt -[e]s,-e [newspaper] advertisement. I**~ieren** vt/i

(haben) advertise

insge|heim adv secretly. I**~samt** adv [all] in all

insofern, **insoweit** adv in this respect; i**~** als in as much as

Insp|ektion /mspɛk'tsjo:n/ f -,-en inspection. I**~ektor** m -en,-en inspector

Install|ateur /mstala'tø:ɐ/ m -s,-e fitter; (Klempner) plumber. I**~ieren** vt install

instand adv i**~** halten maintain; (pflegen) look after. I**~haltung** f maintenance, upkeep

Instandsetzung f - repair

Instanz /-st-/ f -,-en authority

Instinkt /-st-/ m -[e]s,-e instinct. I**~iv** adj instinctive

Institut /-st-/ nt -[e]s,-e institute

Instrument /-st-/ nt -[e]s,-e instrument. I**~almusik** f instrumental music

Insulin nt -s insulin

inszenier|en vt (Theat) produce. I**~ung** f -,-en production

Integr|ation /-'tsjo:n/ f - integration. I**~ieren** vt integrate; sich i**~ieren** integrate

Intellekt m -[e]s intellect. I**~uell** adj intellectual

intelligen|t adj intelligent. I**~z** f - intelligence

Intendant m -en,-en director

Intensivstation f intensive-care unit

interaktiv adj interactive

inter|essant adj interesting. I**~esse** nt -s,-n interest; I**~esse** haben be interested (an + dat in). I**~essengruppe** f pressure group. I**~essent** m -en,-en interested party; (Käufer) prospective buyer. I**~essieren** vt interest; sich i**~es-**

sieren be interested (für in)

Inter|nat nt -[e]s,-e boarding school. **I~national** adj international. **I~nist** m -en,-en specialist in internal diseases. **I~pretation** /-'tsi̯oːn/ f -,-en interpretation. **i~pretieren** vt interpret. **I~vall** nt -s,-e interval. **I~vention** /-'tsi̯oːn/ f -,-en intervention

Internet nt -s,-s Internet; im I~ on the Internet

Interview /'ɪntevju:/ nt -s,-s interview. **i~en** vt interview

intim adj intimate

intolerant adj intolerant. **I~z** f -intolerance

intravenös adj intravenous

Intrige f -,-n intrigue

introvertiert adj introverted

Invalidenrente f disability pension

Invasion f -,-en invasion

Inven|tar nt -s,-e furnishings and fittings pl; (Techn) equipment; (Bestand) stock; (Liste) inventory. **I~tur** f -,-en stock-taking

investieren vt invest

inwie|fern adv in what way. **i~weit** adv how far, to what extent

Inzest m -[e]s incest

inzwischen adv in the meantime

Irak (der) -[s] Iraq. **i~isch** adj Iraqi

Iran (der) -[s] Iran. **i~isch** adj Iranian

irdisch adj earthly

Ire m -n,-n Irishman; die I~n the Irish pl

irgend adv wenn i~ möglich if at all possible. **i~ein** indefinite article some/any; i~ein anderer someone/anyone else. **i~eine(r,s)** pron any one; (jemand) someone/anyone. **i~etwas** pron something;

anything. **i~jemand** pron someone; anyone. **i~wann** pron at some time [or other]/at any time. **i~was** pron ⓣ something [or other]/anything. **i~welche(r,s)** pron any. **i~wer** pron someone/anyone. **i~wie** adv somehow [or other]. **i~wo** adv somewhere

Irin f -,-nen Irishwoman

irisch adj Irish

Irland nt -s Ireland

Ironie f - irony

ironisch adj ironic

irre adj mad, crazy; (ⓣ: gewaltig) incredible. **I~(r)** m/f lunatic. **i~führen** vt sep (fig) mislead

irre|machen vt sep confuse. **i~n** vi/r (haben) [sich] i~n be mistaken ● vi (sein) wander. **I~nanstalt** f, **I~nhaus** nt lunatic asylum. **i~werden†** vi sep (sein) get confused

Irrgarten m maze

irritieren vt irritate

Irr|sinn m madness, lunacy. **i~sinnig** adj mad; (ⓣ: gewaltig) incredible. **I~tum** m -s,⸚er mistake

Ischias m & nt - sciatica

Islam m -[s] -[s] Islam. **islamisch** adj Islamic

Island nt -s Iceland

Isolier|band nt insulating tape. **i~en** vt isolate; (Phys, Electr) insulate; (gegen Schall) soundproof. **I~ung** f - isolation; insulation; soundproofing

Israel /'ɪsraeːl/ nt -s Israel. **I~eli** m -[s],-s & f -,-[s] Israeli. **i~elisch** adj Israeli

ist s. sein; er ist he is

Ital|ien /-i̯ən/ nt -s Italy. **I~iener(in)** m -s,- (f -,-nen) Italian. **i~ienisch** adj Italian. **I~ienisch** nt -[s] (Lang) Italian

Jj

ja adv, **Ja** nt -[s] yes; **ich glaube ja** I think so; **ja nicht!** not on any account! **da seid ihr ja!** there you are!

Jacht f -,-en yacht

Jacke f -,-n jacket; (Strick-) cardigan

Jackett /ʒa'kɛt/ nt -s,-s jacket

Jade m -[s] & f - jade

Jagd f -,-en hunt; (Schießen) shoot; (Jagen) hunting; (fig) pursuit (nach of); **auf die J~ gehen** go hunting/shooting. **J~gewehr** nt sporting gun. **J~hund** m gun-dog; (Hetzhund) hound

jagen vt hunt; (schießen) shoot; (verfolgen, wegjagen) chase; (treiben) drive; **sich j~** chase each other; **in die Luft j~** blow up ●vi (haben) hunt, go hunting/shooting; (fig) chase (nach after) ●vi (sein) race, dash

Jäger m -s,- hunter

Jahr nt -[e]s,-e year. **J~elang** adv for years. **J~eszahl** f year. **J~eszeit** f season. **J~gang** m year; (Wein) vintage. **J~hundert** nt century

jährlich adj annual, yearly

Jahr|markt m fair. **J~tausend** nt millennium. **J~zehnt** nt -[e]s,-e decade

Jähzorn m violent temper. **j~ig** adj hot-tempered

Jalousie /ʒalu'ziː/ f -,-n venetian blind

Jammer m -s misery

jämmerlich adj miserable; (Mitleid erregend) pitiful

jammern vi (haben) lament ●vt **jdn j~n** arouse s.o.'s pity

Jänner m -s,- (Aust) January

Januar m -s,-e January

Japan nt -s Japan. **J~aner(in)** m -s,- / f -,-nen) Japanese. **j~anisch** adj Japanese. **J~anisch** nt -[s] (Lang) Japanese

jäten vt/i (haben) weed

jaulen vi (haben) yelp

Jause f -,-n (Aust) snack

jawohl adv yes

Jazz /jats, dʒɛs/ m - jazz

je adv (jemals) ever; (jeweils) each; (pro) per; **je nach** according to; **seit eh und je** always ●conj **je mehr, desto besser** the more the better ●prep (+ acc) per

Jeans /dʒiːns/ pl jeans

jed|e(r,s) pron every; (j~er Einzelne) each; (j~er Beliebige) any; (substantivisch) everyone; each one; anyone; **ohne j~en Grund** without any reason. **j~enfalls** adv in any case; (wenigstens) at least. **j~ermann** pron everyone. **j~erzeit** adv at any time. **j~esmal** adv every time

jedoch adv & conj however

jemals adv ever

jemand pron someone, somebody; (fragend, verneint) anyone, anybody

jen|e(r,s) pron that; (pl) those; (substantivisch) that one; (pl) those. **j~seits** prep (+ gen) [on] the other side of

jetzt adv now

jiddisch adj, **J~** nt -[s] Yiddish

Job /dʒɔp/ m -s,-s job. **J~ben** vi (haben) 🗓 work

Joch nt -[e]s,-e yoke

Jockei, Jockey /'dʒɔki/ m -s,-s jockey

Jod nt -[e]s iodine

jodeln vi (haben) yodel

Joga m & nt -[s] yoga

joggen /'dʒɔgən/ vi (haben)

sein) jog

Joghurt, **Jogurt** m & nt -[s] yoghurt

Johannisbeere f redcurrant

Joker m -s,- (*Karte*) joker

Jolle f -,-n dinghy

Jongleur /ʒɔ̃'gløːɐ̯/ m -s,-e juggler

Jordanien nt -s Jordan

Journalis|mus /ʒʊrna'lɪsmʊs/ m - journalism. **J~t(in)** m -en,-en (f -,-nen) journalist

Jubel m -s rejoicing, jubilation. **j~n** vi (*haben*) rejoice

Jubiläum nt -s,-äen jubilee; (*Jahrestag*) anniversary

jucken vi (*haben*) itch; sich **j~en** scratch; es **j~t** mich I have an itch

Jude m -n,-n Jew. **J~ntum** nt -s judaism; (*Juden*) Jewry

Jüd|in f -,-nen Jewess. **j~isch** adj Jewish

Judo nt -[s] judo

Jugend f - youth; (*junge Leute*) young people pl. **J~herberge** f youth hostel. **J~kriminalität** f juvenile delinquency. **j~lich** adj youthful. **J~liche(r)** m/f young man/woman. **J~liche** pl young people. **J~stil** m art nouveau

Jugoslaw|ien /-jan/ nt -s Yugoslavia. **j~isch** adj Yugoslav

Juli m -s,-s July

jung adj young; (*Wein*) new ● pron **J~** und Alt young and old. **J~e** m -n,-n boy. **J~e(s)** nt young animal/bird; (*Katzen-*) kitten; (*Bären-*) cub; (*Hunde-*) pup; die **J~en** the young pl

Jünger m -s,- disciple

Jung|frau f virgin; (*Astrology*) Virgo. **J~geselle** m bachelor

Jüngling m -s,-e youth

jüngst|e(r,s) adj youngest; (*neueste*) latest; in **j~er** Zeit recently

Juni m -[s],-s June

Jura pl law sg

Jurist|(in) m -en,-en (f -,-nen) lawyer. **j~isch** adj legal

Jury /ʒy'riː/ f -,-s jury; (*Sport*) judges pl

Justiz f - die **J~** justice

Juwel m & nt -s,-en & (fig) -e jewel. **J~ier** m -s,-e jeweller

Jux m -es,-e 🗊 joke; aus **Jux** for fun

Kk

Kabarett nt -s,-s & -e cabaret

Kabel nt -s,- cable. **K~fernsehen** nt cable television

Kabeljau m -s,-e & -s cod

Kabine f -,-n cabin; (*Umkleide-*) cubicle; (*Telefon-*) booth; (*einer K~nbahn*) car. **K~nbahn** f cable-car

Kabinett nt -s,-s (*Pol*) Cabinet

Kabriolett nt -s,-s convertible

Kachel f -,-n tile. **k~n** vt tile

Kadenz f -,-en (*Mus*) cadence

Käfer m -s,- beetle

Kaffee /'kafeː, ka'feː/ m -s,-s coffee. **K~kanne** f coffee pot. **K~maschine** f coffee maker. **K~mühle** f coffee grinder

Käfig m -s,-e cage

kahl adj bare; (*haarlos*) bald; **k~geschoren** shaven

Kahn m -s,-̈e boat; (*Last-*) barge

Kai m -s,-s quay

Kaiser m -s,- emperor. **K~in** f -,-nen empress. **k~lich** adj imperial. **K~reich** nt empire. **K~schnitt**

m Caesarean [section]

Kajüte f -,-n (Naut) cabin

Kakao /ka'kaʊ/ m -s cocoa

Kakerlak m -s & -en,-en cockroach

Kaktus m -,-teen cactus

Kalb nt -[e]s, ⸚er calf. **K~fleisch** nt veal

Kalender m -s,- calendar; (Termin-) diary

Kaliber nt -s,- calibre; (Gewehr-) bore

Kalium nt -s potassium

Kalk m -[e]s,-e lime; (Kalzium) calcium. **k~en** vt whitewash. **K~stein** m limestone

Kalkul|ation /-'tsjoːn/ f -,-en calculation. **k~ieren** vt/i (haben) calculate

Kalorie f -,-ie calorie

kalt adj cold; **mir ist k~** I am cold

Kälte f - cold; (Gefühls-) coldness; 10 Grad K~ 10 degrees below zero

Kalzium nt -s calcium

Kamel nt -s,-e camel

Kamera f -,-s camera

Kamerad(in) m -en,-en (f -,-nen) companion; (Freund) mate; (Mil, Pol) comrade

Kameramann m (pl -männer & -leute) cameraman

Kamille f - chamomile

Kamin m -s,-e fireplace; (SGer: Schornstein) chimney

Kamm m -[e]s, ⸚e comb; (Berg-) ridge; (Zool, Wellen-) crest

kämmen vt comb; **jdn/sich k~** comb someone's/one's hair

Kammer f -,-n small room; (Techn, Biology, Pol) chamber. **K~musik** f chamber music

Kammgarn nt (Textiles) worsted

Kampagne /kam'panjə/ f -,-n (Pol, Comm) campaign

Kampf m -es, ⸚e fight; (Schlacht) battle; (Wett-) contest; (fig) struggle

kämpf|en vi (haben) fight; sich k~en durch fight one's way through. **K~er(in)** m -s,- (f -,-nen) fighter

Kampfrichter m (Sport) judge

Kanada nt -s Canada

Kanad|ier(in) /-jɐ, -jɐrɪn/ m -s,- (f -,-nen) Canadian. **k~isch** adj Canadian

Kanal m -s, ⸚e canal; (Abfluss-) drain, sewer; (Radio, TV) channel; der K~ the [English] Channel

Kanalisation /-'tsjoːn/ f - sewerage system, drains pl

Kanarienvogel /-jən-/ m canary

Kanarisch adj K~e Inseln Canaries

Kandidat(in) m -en,-en (f -,-nen) candidate

kandiert adj candied

Känguru nt -s,-s kangaroo

Kaninchen nt -s,- rabbit

Kanister m -s,- canister; (Benzin-) can

Kännchen nt -s,- [small] jug; (Kaffee-) pot

Kanne f -,-n jug; (Tee-) pot; (Öl-) can; (große Milch-) churn

Kannibal|e m -n,-n cannibal. **K~ismus** m - cannibalism

Kanon m -s,-s canon; (Lied) round

Kanone f -,-n cannon, gun

kanonisieren vt canonize

Kantate f -,-n cantata

Kante f -,-n edge

Kanten m -s,- crust [of bread]

Kanter m -s,- canter

kantig adj angular

Kantine f -,-n canteen

Kanton m -s,-e (Swiss) canton

Kanton The name for the individual autonomous states that make up Switzerland. There are 26 cantons, each with its own government and constitution.

Kanu nt -s,-s canoe
Kanzel f -,-n pulpit; (Aviat) cockpit
Kanzler m -s,- chancellor
Kap nt -s,-s (Geog) cape
Kapazität f -,-en capacity
Kapelle f -,-n chapel; (Mus) band
kapern vt (Naut) seize
kapieren vt ⒤ understand
Kapital nt -s, Kapitalien or -e capital. K~ismus m - capitalism. K~ist m -en,-en capitalist. k~istisch adj capitalist
Kapitän m -s,-e captain
Kapitel nt -s,- chapter
Kaplan m -s,⁻e curate
Kappe f -,-n cap
Kapsel f -,-n capsule; (Flaschen-) top
kaputt adj ⒤ broken; (zerrissen) torn; (defekt) out of order; (ruiniert) ruined; (erschöpft) worn out. k~gehen† vi sep (sein) ⒤ break; (zerreißen) tear; (defekt werden) pack up; (Ehe, Freundschaft) break up. k~lachen (sich) vr sep ⒤ be in stitches. k~machen vt sep ⒤ break; (zerreißen) tear; (defekt machen) put out of order; (erschöpfen) wear out; sich k~machen wear oneself out
Kapuze f -,-n hood
Kapuzinerkresse f nasturtium
Karaffe f -,-n carafe; (mit Stöpsel) decanter
Karamell m -s caramel. K~bonbon m & nt ≈ toffee
Karat nt -[e]s,-e carat
Karawane f -,-n caravan

Kardinal m -s,⁻e cardinal. K~zahl f cardinal number
Karfreitag m -s Good Friday
karg adj meagre; (frugal) frugal; (spärlich) sparse; (unfruchtbar) barren; (gering) scant
Karibik f - Caribbean
kariert adj check[ed]; (Papier) squared; schottisch k~ tartan
Karik|atur f -,-en caricature; (Journalism) cartoon. k~ieren vt caricature
Karneval m -s,-e & -s carnival
Kärnten nt -s Carinthia
Karo nt -s,-s (Raute) diamond; (Viereck) square; (Muster) check (Kartenspiel) diamonds pl
Karosserie f -,-n bodywork
Karotte f -,-n carrot
Karpfen m -s,- carp
Karren m -s,- cart; (Hand-) barrow. k~ vt cart
Karriere /kaˈrjɛːrə/ f -,-n career; K~ machen get to the top
Karte f -,-n card; (Eintritts-, Fahr-) ticket; (Speise-) menu; (Land-) map
Kartei f -,-en card index
Karten|spiel nt card game; (Spielkarten) pack of cards. K~vorverkauf m advance booking
Kartoffel f -,-n potato. K~brei m mashed potatoes
Karton /karˈtɔŋ/ m -s,-s cardboard; (Schachtel) carton
Karussell nt -s,-s & -e roundabout
Käse m -s,- cheese
Kaserne f -,-n barracks pl
Kasino nt -s,-s casino
Kasperle m & nt -s,- Punch. K~theater nt Punch and Judy show
Kasse f -,-n till; (Registrier-) cash register; (Zahlstelle) cash desk; (im Supermarkt) check out; (Theater-)

Kasserolle | Keim

box office; (Geld) pool [of money], 🎲 kitty; (Kranken-) health insurance scheme; **knapp bei K~ sein** 🎲 be short of cash. **K~nwart** m -[e]s,-e treasurer. **K~nzettel** m receipt

Kasserolle f -,-n saucepan

Kassette f -,-n cassette; (Film-, Farbband-) cartridge. **K~nrekorder** m -s,- cassette recorder

kassier|en vi (haben) collect the money/(im Bus) the fares ● vt collect. **K~er(in)** m -s,- (f -,-nen) cashier

Kastanie /kas'ta:nja/ f -,-n [horse] chestnut, 🎲 conker

Kasten m -s,- box; (Brot-) bin; (Flaschen-) crate; (Brief-) letter box; (Aust: Schrank) cupboard

kastrieren vt castrate; neuter

Katalog m -[e]s,-e catalogue

Katalysator m -s,-en catalyst; (Auto) catalytic converter

Katapult nt -[e]s,-e catapult

Katarrh, Katarr m -s,-e catarrh

Katastrophe f -,-n catastrophe

Katechismus m - catechism

Kategorie f -,-n category

Kater m -s,- tom cat; (🎲: Katzenjammer) hangover

Kathedrale f -,-n cathedral

Kath|olik(in) m -en,-en (f -,-nen) Catholic. **k~olisch** adj Catholic. **K~olizismus** m - Catholicism

Kätzchen nt -s,- kitten; (Bot) catkin

Katze f -,-n cat. **K~njammer** m 🎲 hangover. **K~nsprung** m ein K~nsprung 🎲 a stone's throw

Kauderwelsch nt -[s] gibberish

kauen vt/i (haben) chew; bite (Nägel)

Kauf m -[e]s, Käufe purchase; **guter K~** bargain; **in K~ nehmen**

(fig) put up with. **k~en** vt/i (haben) buy; (im Geschäft) shop at

Käufer(in) m -s,- (f -,-nen) buyer; (im Geschäft) shopper

Kauf|haus nt department store. **K~laden** m shop

käuflich adj saleable; (bestechlich) corruptible; **k~ erwerben** buy

Kauf|mann m (pl -leute) businessman; (Händler) dealer; (Dialekt) grocer. **K~preis** m purchase price

Kaugummi m chewing gum

Kaulquappe f -,-n tadpole

kaum adv hardly

Kaution /-'tsjo:n/ f -,-en surety; (Jur) bail; (Miet-) deposit

Kautschuk m -s rubber

Kauz m -es, Käuze owl

Kavalier m -s,-e gentleman

Kavallerie f - cavalry

Kaviar m -s caviare

keck adj bold; cheeky

Kegel m -s,- skittle; (Geometry) cone. **K~bahn** f skittle-alley. **k~n** vi (haben) play skittles

Kehl|e f -,-n throat; **aus voller K~e** at the top of one's voice. **K~kopf** m larynx. **K~kopfentzündung** f laryngitis

Kehr|e f -,-n [hairpin] bend. **k~en** vt/i (haben) (fegen) sweep ● vt sweep; (wenden) turn; **sich nicht k~en an** (+ acc) not care about. **K~icht** m -[e]s sweepings pl. **K~reim** m refrain. **K~seite** f (fig) drawback. **k~tmachen** vi sep (haben) turn back; (sich umdrehen) turn round

Keil m -[e]s,-e wedge

Keilriemen m fan belt

Keim m -[e]s,-e (Bot) sprout; (Med) germ. **k~en** vi (haben) germinate; (austreiben) sprout. **k~frei** adj sterile

kein pron no; not a; k~e fünf Minuten less than five minutes. k~e(r,s) pron no one, nobody; (Ding) none, not one. k~esfalls adv on no account. k~eswegs adv by no means. k~mal adv not once. k~s pron none, not one

Keks m -[es],-[e] biscuit

Kelch m -[e]s,-e goblet, cup; (Relig) chalice; (Bot) calyx

Kelle f -,-n ladle; (Maurer) trowel

Keller m -s,- cellar. K~ei f -,-en winery. K~wohnung f basement flat

Kellner m -s,- waiter. K~in f -,-nen waitress

keltern vt press

keltisch adj Celtic

Kenia nt -s Kenya

kennen† vt know; k~en lernen get to know; (treffen) meet; sich k~en lernen meet; (näher) get to know one another. K~er m -s,-. K~erin f -,-nen connoisseur; (Experte) expert. k~tlich adj recognizable; k~tlich machen mark. K~tnis f -,-se knowledge; zur K~tnis nehmen take note of; in K~tnis setzen inform (von of). K~wort nt (pl -wörter) reference; (geheimes) password. K~zeichen nt distinguishing mark or feature; (Merkmal) characteristic; (Markierung) marking; (Auto) registration. k~zeichnen vt distinguish; (markieren) mark

kentern vi (sein) capsize

Keramik f -,-en pottery

Kerbe f -,-n notch

Kerker m -s,- dungeon; (Gefängnis) prison

Kerl m -s,-e & -s [T] fellow, bloke

Kern m -s,-e pip; (Kirsch-) stone; (Nuss-) kernel; (Techn) core; (Atom-, Zell- & fig) nucleus; (Stadt-) centre;

(einer Sache) heart. K~energie f nuclear energy. K~gehäuse nt core. k~los adj seedless. K~physik f nuclear physics sg

Kerze f -,-n candle. K~nhalter m -s,- candlestick

kess adj pert

Kessel m -s,- kettle

Kette f -,-n chain; (Hals-) necklace. k~n vt chain (an + acc to). K~nladen m chain store

Ketze|r(in) m -s,- (f -,-nen) heretic. K~rei f - heresy

keuch|en vi (haben) pant. K~husten m whooping cough

Keule f -,-n club; (Culin) leg; (Hühner-) drumstick

keusch adj chaste

Khaki nt - khaki

kichern vi (haben) giggle

Kiefer¹ f -,-n pine[-tree]

Kiefer² m -s,- jaw

Kiel m -s,-e (Naut) keel

Kiemen fpl gills

Kies m -es gravel. K~el m -s,-. K~elstein m pebble

Kilo nt -s,-[s] kilo. K~gramm nt kilogram. K~hertz nt kilohertz. K~meter m kilometre. K~meterstand m ≈ mileage. K~watt nt kilowatt

Kind nt -es,-er child; von K~ auf from childhood

Kinder|arzt m, K~ärztin f paediatrician. K~bett nt child's cot. K~garten m nursery school. K~geld nt child benefit. K~lähmung f polio. k~leicht adj very easy. K~los adj childless. K~mädchen nt nanny. K~reim m nursery rhyme. K~spiel nt children's game. K~tagesstätte f day nursery. K~teller m children's menu. K~wagen m pram. K~zimmer nt child's/children's room; ((für

Baby) nursery

Kind|heit f - childhood. **k~isch** adj childish. **k~lich** adj childlike

kinetisch adj kinetic

Kinn nt -[e]s,-e chin. **K~lade** f jaw

Kino nt -s,-s cinema

Kiosk m -[e]s,-e kiosk

Kippe f -,-n (Müll-) dump; (☐: Zigaretten-) fag end. **k~n** vt tilt; (schütten) tip (in + acc into) ● vi (sein) topple

Kirch|e f -,-n church. **K~enbank** f pew. **K~endiener** m verger. **K~enlied** nt hymn. **K~enschiff** nt nave. **K~hof** m churchyard. **k~lich** adj church ● adv **k~lich getraut werden** be married in church. **K~turm** m church tower, steeple. **K~weih** f -,-en [village] fair

Kirmes f -,-sen = Kirchweih

Kirsche f -,-n cherry

Kissen nt -s,- cushion; (Kopf-) pillow

Kiste f -,-n crate; (Zigarren-) box

Kitsch m -es sentimental rubbish; (Kunst) kitsch

Kitt m -s [adhesive] cement; (Fenster-) putty

Kittel m -s,- overall, smock

Kitz nt -es,-e (Zool) kid

Kitz|el m -s,- tickle; (Nerven-) thrill. **k~eln** vt/i (haben) tickle. **k~lig** adj ticklish

kläffen vi (haben) yap

Klage f -,-n lament; (Beschwerde) complaint; (Jur) action. **k~n** vi (haben) lament; (sich beklagen) complaint; (Jur) sue

Kläger(in) m -s,- (f -,-nen) (Jur) plaintiff

klamm adj cold and damp; (steif) stiff. **K~** f -,-en (Geog) gorge

Klammer f -,-n (Wäsche-) peg; (Büro-) paper clip; (Heft-) staple;

(Haar-) grip; (für Zähne) brace; (Techn) clamp; (Typography) bracket. **k~n (sich)** vr cling (an + acc to)

Klang m -[e]s,ˆe sound; (K~farbe) tone

Klapp|e f -,-n flap; (☐: Mund) trap. **k~en** vt fold; (hoch-) tip up ● vi (haben) ☐ work out. **Klapphandy** nt folding mobile phone

Klapper f -,-n rattle. **k~n** vi (haben) rattle. **K~schlange** f rattlesnake

klapp|rig adj rickety; (schwach) decrepit. **K~stuhl** m folding chair

Klaps m -es,-e pat, smack

klar adj clear; **sich** (dat) **k~ werden** make up one's mind; (erkennen) realize (dass that); **sich** (dat) **k~ od im K~en sein** realize (dass that) ● adv clearly; (☐: natürlich) of course

klären vt clarify; **sich k~** clear; (fig: sich lösen) resolve itself

Klarheit f -,- clarity

Klarinette f -,-n clarinet

klar|machen vt sep make clear (dat to); **sich** (dat) **etw k~machen** understand sth. **k~stellen** vt sep clarify

Klärung f - clarification

Klasse f -,-n class; (Sch) class, form; (Zimmer) classroom. **k~** inv adj ☐ super. **K~narbeit** f [written] test. **K~nzimmer** nt classroom

Klassik f - classicism; (Epoche) classical period. **K~iker** m -s,- classical author/(Mus) composer. **k~isch** adj classical; (typisch) classic

Klatsch m -[e]s gossip. **K~base** f ☐ gossip. **k~en** vt slap; Beifall **k~en** applaud ● vi (haben) make a slapping sound; (im Wasser) splash; (tratschen) gossip; (applaudieren) clap. **k~nass** adj ☐ soaking wet

klauen vt/i (haben) ☐ steal

Klausel f -,-n clause

Klaustrophobie f - claustrophobia

Klausur f -,-en (*Univ*) paper

Klavier nt -s,-e piano. **K~spieler(in)** m(f) pianist

kleb|en vt stick/(*mit Klebstoff*) glue (an + acc to) ● vi (haben) stick (an + dat to). **k~rig** adj sticky. **K~stoff** m adhesive, glue. **K~streifen** m adhesive tape

Klecks m -es,-e stain; (*Tinten-*) blot; (*kleine Menge*) dab. **k~en** vi (haben) make a mess

Klee m -s clover

Kleid nt -[e]s,-er dress; **K~er** dresses; (*Kleidung*) clothes. **k~en** vt dress; (*gut stehen*) suit. **K~erbügel** m coat hanger. **K~erbürste** f clothes brush. **K~erhaken** m coathook. **K~erschrank** m wardrobe. **k~sam** adj becoming. **K~ung** f -clothes pl, clothing. **K~ungsstück** nt garment

Kleie f - bran

klein adj small, little; (*von kleinem Wuchs*) short; **k~ schneiden** cut up small. **von k~ auf** from childhood. **K~arbeit** f painstaking work. **K~e(r,s)** m/f/nt little one. **K~geld** nt [small] change. **K~handel** m retail trade. **K~heit** f - smallness; (*Wuchs*) short stature. **K~holz** nt firewood. **K~igkeit** f -,-en trifle; (*Mahl*) snack. **K~kind** nt infant. **k~laut** adj subdued. **k~lich** adj petty

klein|schreiben† vt sep write with a small [initial] letter. **K~stadt** f small town. **k~städtisch** adj provincial

Kleister m -s paste. **k~n** vt paste

Klemme f -,-n (*hair-*)grip. **k~n** vt jam; **sich** (dat) **den Finger k~n** get one's finger caught ● vi (haben) jam

Klempner m -s,- plumber

Klerus (der) - the clergy

Klette f -,-n burr

kletter|n vi (sein) climb. **K~pflanze** f climber

Klettverschluss m Velcro ® fastening

klicken vi (haben) click

Klient(in) /kliˈɛnt(m)/ m -en,-en (f -,-nen) (*Jur*) client

Kliff nt -[e]s,-e cliff

Klima nt -s climate. **K~anlage** f air conditioning. **K~wandel** m climate change

klimat|isch adj climatic. **k~isiert** adj air-conditioned

klimpern vi (haben) jingle; **k~ auf** (+ dat) tinkle on (*Klavier*); strum (*Gitarre*)

Klinge f -,-n blade

Klingel f -,-n bell. **k~n** vi (haben) ring; **es k~t** there's a ring at the door

klingen† vi (haben) sound

Klinik f -,-en clinic

Klinke f -,-n [door] handle

Klippe f -,-n [submerged] rock

Klips m -es,-e clip; (*Ohr-*) clip-on ear ring

klirren vi (haben) rattle; (*Glas:*) chink

Klo nt -s,-s 🔲 loo

Klon m -s,-e clone. **k~en** vt clone

klopfen vi (haben) knock; (*leicht*) tap; (*Herz:*) pound; **es k~te** there was a knock at the door

Klops m -es,-e meatball

Klosett nt -s,-s lavatory

Kloß m -es,ⁱe dumpling

Kloster nt -s,ⁱ monastery; (*Nonnen-*) convent

klösterlich adj monastic

Klotz m -es,ⁱe block

Klub m -s,-s club

Kluft f -,=e cleft; (fig: Gegensatz) gulf

klug adj intelligent; (schlau) clever. **K~heit** f -cleverness

Klump|en m -s,- lump

knabbern vt/i (haben) nibble

Knabe m -n,-n boy. **k~nhaft** adj boyish

Knäckebrot nt crispbread

knack|en vt/i (haben) crack. **K~s** m -es,-e crack

Knall m -[e]s,-e bang. **K~bonbon** m cracker. **k~en** vi (haben) go bang; (Peitsche:) crack ●vt (🔟: werfen) chuck; jdm eine **k~en** 🔟 clout s.o. **k~ig** adj 🔟 gaudy

knapp adj (gering) scant; (kurz) short; (mangelnd) scarce; (gerade ausreichend) bare; (eng) tight. **K~heit** f -scarcity

knarren vi (haben) creak

Knast m -[e]s 🔟 prison

knattern vi (haben) crackle; (Gewehr:) stutter

Knäuel m & nt -s,- ball

Knauf m -[e]s, Knäufe knob

knauserig adj 🔟 stingy

knautschen vt 🔟 crumple ●vi (haben) crease

Knebel m -s,- gag. **k~n** vt gag

Knecht m -[e]s,-e farm-hand; (fig) slave

kneif|en† vt pinch ●vi (haben) pinch; (🔟: sich drücken) chicken out. **K~zange** f pincers pl

Kneipe f -,-n 🔟 pub

knet|en vt knead; (formen) mould. **K~masse** f Plasticine®

Knick m -[e]s,-e bend; (Kniff) crease. **k~en** vt bend; (kniffen) fold; geknickt sein to be dejected

Knicks m -es,-e curtsy. **k~en** vi (haben) curtsy

Knie nt -s,- knee

knien /'kni:ən/ vi (haben) kneel ●vr sich **k~** kneel [down]

Kniescheibe f kneecap

Kniff m -[e]s,-e pinch; (Falte) crease; (🔟: Trick) trick. **k~en** vt fold

knipsen vt (lochen) punch; (Phot) photograph ●vi (haben) take a photograph/photographs

Knirps m -es,-e 🔟 little chap; ® (Schirm) telescopic umbrella

knirschen vi (haben) grate; (Schnee, Kies:) crunch

knistern vi (haben) crackle; (Papier:) rustle

Knitter|falte f crease. **k~frei** adj crease-resistant. **k~n** vi (haben) crease

knobeln vi (haben) toss (um for)

Knoblauch m -s garlic

Knöchel m -s,- ankle; (Finger-) knuckle

Knochen m -s,- bone. **K~mark** nt bone marrow

knochig adj bony

Knödel m -s,- (SGer) dumpling

Knolle f -,-n tuber

Knopf m -[e]s,=e button; (Griff) knob

knöpfen vt button

Knopfloch nt buttonhole

Knorpel m -s gristle; (Anat) cartilage

Knospe f bud

Knoten m -s,- knot; (Med) lump; (Haar-) bun, chignon. **k~** vt knot. **K~punkt** m junction

knüll|en vt crumple ●vi (haben) crease. **K~er** m -s,- 🔟 sensation

knüpfen vt knot; (verbinden) attach (an + acc to)

Knüppel m -s,- club; (Gummi-) truncheon

knurren vi (haben) growl; (Magen:) rumble

knusprig adj crunchy, crisp

knutschen vi (haben) 🔤 smooch

k.o. /kaːˈoː/ adj k.o. schlagen knock out; **k.o. sein** 🔤 be worn out

Koalition /koaliˈtsjoːn/ f -,-en coalition

Kobold m -[e]s,-e goblin, imp

Koch m -[e]s, ⸚e cook; (im Restaurant) chef. **K~buch** nt cookery book. **k~en** vt cook; (sieden) boil; make (Kaffee, Tee); hart gekochtes Ei hard-boiled egg ● vi (haben) cook; (sieden) boil; 🔤 seethe (vor + dat with). **K~en** nt -s cooking; (Sieden) boiling. **k~end** adj boiling. **K~herd** m cooker, stove

Köchin f -,-nen [woman] cook

Koch|löffel m wooden spoon. **K~nische** f kitchenette. **K~platte** f hotplate. **K~topf** m saucepan

Köder m -s,- bait

Koffein /kɔfeˈiːn/ nt -s caffeine. **k~frei** adj decaffeinated

Koffer m -s,- suitcase. **K~kuli** m luggage trolley. **K~raum** m (Auto) boot

Kognak /ˈkɔnjak/ m -s,-s brandy

Kohl m -[e]s cabbage

Kohle f -,-n coal. **K~[n]hydrat** nt -[e]s,-e carbohydrate. **K~nbergwerk** nt coal mine, colliery. **K~ndioxid** nt carbon dioxide. **K~nsäure** f carbon dioxide. **K~nstoff** m carbon

Koje f -,-n (Naut) bunk

Kokain /koˈkaˈiːn/ nt -s cocaine

kokett adj flirtatious. **k~ieren** vi (haben) flirt

Kokon /koˈkõː/ m -s,-s cocoon

Kokosnuss f coconut

Koks m -es coke

Kolben m -s,- (Gewehr-) butt; (Mais-) cob; (Techn) piston; (Chemistry) flask

Kolibri m -s,-s humming bird

Kolik f -,-en colic

Kollaborateur /-ˈtøːg/ m -s,-e collaborator

Kolleg nt -s,-s & -ien (Univ) course of lectures

Kolleg|e m -n,-n, **K~in** f -,-nen colleague. **K~ium** nt -s,-ien staff

Kollek|te f -,-n (Relig) collection. **K~tion** /-ˈtsːiˌoːn/ f -,-en collection

Köln nt -s Cologne. **K~ischwasser, K~isch Wasser** nt eau-de-Cologne

Kolonie f -,-n colony

Kolonne f -,-n column; (Mil) convoy

Koloss m -es,-e giant

Koma nt -s,-s coma

Kombi m -s,-s = **K~wagen**. **K~nation** /-tsˈiːfoːn/ f -,-en combination; (Folgerung) deduction; (Kleidung) co-ordinating outfit. **k~nieren** vt combine; (fig) reason; (folgern) deduce. **K~wagen** m estate car

Kombüse f -,-n (Naut) galley

Komet m -en,-en comet

Komfort /kɔmˈfoːg/ m -s comfort; (Luxus) luxury

Komik f - humour. **K~er** m -s,- comic, comedian

komisch adj funny; (Oper) comic; (sonderbar) odd, funny. **k~erweise** adv funnily enough

Komitee nt -s,-s committee

Komma nt -s & -ta comma; (Dezimal-) decimal point; drei **K~** fünf three point five

Kommando nt -s,-s order; (Befehlsgewalt) command; (Einheit) detachment. **K~brücke** f bridge

kommen† vi (sein) come; (eintref-

fen) arrive; (*gelangen*) get (nach to);
k∼ lassen send for; auf/hinter etw
(*acc*) k∼ think of/find out about
sth; um/zu etw k∼ lose/acquire
sth; wieder zu sich k∼ come
round; wie kommt das? why is
that? k∼d *adj* coming; k∼den
Montag next Monday

Kommen|tar *m* -s,-e commentary; (*Bemerkung*) comment. **k∼tieren** *vt* comment on

kommerziell *adj* commercial

Kommissar *m* -s,-e commissioner; (*Polizei*) superintendent

Kommission *f* -,-en commission; (*Gremium*) committee

Kommode *f* -,-n chest of drawers

Kommunalwahlen *fpl* local elections

Kommunion *f* -,-en [Holy] Communion

Kommun|ismus *m* - Communism. **K∼ist(in)** *m* -en,-en (*f* -,-nen) Communist. **k∼istisch** *adj* Communist

kommunizieren *vi* (*haben*) receive [Holy] Communion

Komödie /koˈmøːdjə/ *f* -,-n comedy

Kompagnon /ˈkɔmpanjõ:/ *m* -s,-s (*Comm*) partner

Kompanie *f* -,-n (*Mil*) company

Komparse *m* -n,-n (*Theat*) extra

Kompass *m* -es,-e compass

komplett *adj* complete

Komplex *m* -es,-e complex

Komplikation /-ˈtsioːn/ *f* -,-en complication

Kompliment *nt* -[e]s,-e compliment

Komplize *m* -n,-n accomplice

komplizier|en *vt* complicate.
k∼t *adj* complicated

Komplott *nt* -[e]s,-e plot

kompo|nieren *vt/i* (*haben*) compose. **K∼nist** *m* -en,-en composer

Kompost *m* -[e]s compost

Kompott *nt* -[e]s,-e stewed fruit

Kompromiss *m* -es,-e compromise; einen K∼ schließen compromise. **k∼los** *adj* uncompromising

Konden|sation /-ˈtsioːn/ *f* - condensation. **k∼sieren** *vt* condense

Kondensmilch *f* - evaporated/(*gesüßt*) condensed milk

Kondition /-ˈtsioːn/ *f* - (*Sport*) fitness; in K∼ in form

Konditor *m* -s,-en confectioner.
K∼ei *f* -,-en patisserie

Kondo|lenzbrief *m* letter of condolence. **k∼lieren** *vi* (*haben*) express one's condolences

Kondom *nt* & *m* -s,-e condom

Konfekt *nt* -[e]s confectionery; (*Pralinen*) chocolates *pl*

Konfektion /-ˈtsioːn/ *f* - readyto-wear clothes *pl*

Konferenz *f* -,-en conference; (*Besprechung*) meeting

Konfession *f* -,-en [religious] denomination. **k∼ell** *adj* denominational

Konfetti *nt* -s confetti

Konfirm|and(in) *m* -en,-en (*f* -,-nen) candidate for confirmation.
K∼ation *f* -,-en (*Relig*) confirmation. **k∼ieren** *vt* (*Relig*) confirm

Konfitüre *f* -,-n jam

Konflikt *m* -[e]s,-e conflict

Konföderation /-ˈtsioːn/ *f* confederation

konfus *adj* confused

Kongress *m* -es,-e congress

König *m* -s,-e king. **K∼in** *f* -,-nen queen. **k∼lich** *adj* royal; (*hoheitsvoll*) regal; (*großzügig*) handsome.
K∼reich *nt* kingdom

Konjunktiv *m* -s,-e subjunctive

Konjunktur f - economic situation; (Hoch-) boom

konkret adj concrete

Konkurren|t(in) (m) -en,-en (f -,-nen) competitor, rival. K~z f - competition; jdm K~z machen compete with s.o. K~zkampf m competition, rivalry

konkurrieren vi (haben) compete

Konkurs m -es,-e bankruptcy

---

können†

● auxiliary verb

····▸ (vermögen) be able to; (Präsens) can; (Vergangenheit, Konditional) could. ich kann nicht schlafen I cannot or can't sleep. kann ich Ihnen helfen? can I help you? kann/könnte das explodieren? can/could this explode? es kann sein, dass er kommt he may come

! Distinguish konnte and könnte (both can be 'could'): er konnte sie nicht retten he couldn't or was unable to rescue them. er konnte sie noch retten he was able to rescue them. er könnte sie noch retten, wenn ... he could still rescue them if ...

····▸ (dürfen) can, may. kann ich gehen? can or may I go? können wir mit[kommen]? can or may we come too?

● transitive verb

····▸ (beherrschen) know (language); be able to play (game). können Sie Deutsch? do you know any German? sie kann das [gut] she can do that [well]. ich kann nichts dafür

can't help that, I'm not to blame

● intransitive verb

····▸ (fähig sein) ich kann [heute] nicht I can't [today]. er kann nicht anders there's nothing else he can do; (es ist seine Art) he can't help it. er kann nicht mehr Ⓘ he can't go on; (nicht mehr essen) he can't eat any more

····▸ (irgendwohin gehen können) be able to go; can go. ich kann nicht ins Kino I can't go to the cinema. er konnte endlich nach Florenz at last he was able to go to Florence

konsequen|t adj consistent; (logisch) logical. K~z f -,-en consequence

konservativ adj conservative

Konserv|en fpl tinned or canned food sg. K~endose f tin, can. K~ierungsmittel nt preservative

Konsonant m -en,-en consonant

Konstitution /-'tsjo:n/ f -,-en constitution. k~ell adj constitutional

konstruieren vt construct; (entwerfen) design

Konstruk|tion /-'tsjo:n/ f -,-en construction; (Entwurf) design. k~tiv adj constructive

Konsul m -s,-n consul. K~at nt -[e]s,-e consulate

Konsum m -s consumption. K~güter npl consumer goods

Kontakt m -[e]s,-e contact. K~linsen fpl contact lenses. K~person f contact

kontern vt/i (haben) counter

Kontinent /'kon-, kɔnti'nɛnt/ m -[e]s,-e continent

Konto nt -s,-s account. K~auszug

m [bank] statement. **K∼nummer** *f* account number. **K∼stand** *m* [bank] balance

Kontrabass *m* double bass

Kontroll|abschnitt *m* counterfoil. **K∼e** *f* -,-n control; (*Prüfung*) check. **K∼eur** *m* -s,-e [ticket] inspector. **K∼ieren** *vt* check; inspect (*Fahrkarten*); (*beherrschen*) control

Kontroverse *f* -,-n controversy

Kontur *f* -,-en contour

konventionell *adj* conventional

Konversationslexikon *nt* encyclopaedia

konvert|ieren *vi* (haben) (*Relig*) convert. **K∼it** *m* -en,-en convert

Konzentration /-'tsio:n/ *f* -,-en concentration. **K∼slager** *nt* concentration camp

konzentrieren *vt* concentrate; sich **k∼** concentrate (auf + *acc* on)

Konzept *nt* -[e]s,-e [rough] draft; jdn aus dem **K∼bringen** put s.o. off his stroke

Konzern *m* -s,-e (*Comm*) group [of companies]

Konzert *nt* -[e]s,-e concert; (*Klavier-*) concerto

Konzession *f* -,-en licence; (*Zugeständnis*) concession

Konzil *nt* -s,-e (*Relig*) council

Kooperation /ko?opera'tsio:n/ *f* co-operation

Koordin|ation /ko?ordina'tsio:n/ *f* -,-en co-ordination. **k∼ieren** *vt* co-ordinate

Kopf *m* -[e]s,¨e head; ein **K∼** Kohl/Salat a cabbage/lettuce; aus dem **K∼** from memory; (*auswendig*) by heart; auf dem **K∼** (*verkehrt*) upside down; **K∼** stehen stand on one's head; sich (*dat*) den **K∼** waschen wash one's hair; sich (*dat*) den **K∼** zerbrechen rack one's brains. **K∼ball** *m* header

köpfen *vt* behead; (*Fußball*) head

Kopf|ende *nt* head. **K∼haut** *f* scalp. **K∼hörer** *m* headphones *pl*. **K∼kissen** *nt* pillow. **k∼los** *adj* panic-stricken. **K∼rechnen** *nt* mental arithmetic. **K∼salat** *m* lettuce. **K∼schmerzen** *mpl* headache *sg*. **K∼sprung** *m* header, dive. **K∼stand** *m* headstand. **K∼steinpflaster** *nt* cobblestones *pl*. **K∼tuch** *nt* headscarf. **k∼über** *adv* head first; (*fig*) headlong. **K∼wäsche** *f* shampoo. **K∼weh** *nt* headache

Kopie *f* -,-n copy. **k∼ren** *vt* copy. **K∼rschutz** *m* copy protection

Koppel[1] *f* -,-n enclosure; (*Pferde-*) paddock

Koppel[2] *nt* -s,- (*Mil*) belt. **k∼n** *vt* couple

Koralle *f* -,-n coral

Korb *m* -[e]s,¨e basket; jdm einen **K∼** geben (*fig*) turn s.o. down. **K∼ball** *m* [kind of] netball

Kord *m* -s (*Textiles*) corduroy

Kordel *f* -,-n cord

Korinthe *f* -,-n currant

Kork *m* -s,-e cork. **K∼en** *m* -s,- cork. **K∼enzieher** *m* -s,- corkscrew

Korn *nt* -[e]s,¨er grain, (*Samen-*) seed; (*am Visier*) front sight

Körn|chen *nt* -s,- granule. **k∼ig** *adj* granular

Körper *m* -s,- body; (*Geometry*) solid. **K∼bau** *m* build, physique. **k∼behindert** *adj* physically disabled. **k∼lich** *adj* physical; (*Strafe*) corporal. **K∼pflege** *f* personal hygiene. **K∼schaft** *f* -,-en corporation, body

korrekt *adj* correct. **K∼or** *m* -s,-en proof reader. **K∼ur** *f* -,-en correction. **K∼urabzug** *m* proof

Korrespon|dent(in) *m* -en,-en (*f* -,-nen) correspondent. **K∼denz** *f*

-,-en correspondence

Korridor m -s,-e corridor

korrigieren vt correct

Korrosion f - corrosion

korrupt adj corrupt. **K~tion** f - corruption

Korsett nt -[e]s,-e corset

koscher adj kosher

Kosename m pet name

Kosmet|ik f - beauty culture. **K~ika** ntpl cosmetics. **K~ikerin** f -,-nen beautician. **k~isch** adj cosmetic; (Chirurgie) plastic

kosm|isch adj cosmic. **K~o-naut(in)** m -en,-en (f -,-nen) cosmonaut

Kosmos m - cosmos

Kost f - food; (Ernährung) diet; (Ver-pflegung) board

kostbar adj precious. **K~keit** f -,-en treasure

kosten[1] vt/i (haben) [von] etw k~ taste sth

kosten[2] vt cost; (brauchen) take; wie viel kostet es? how much is it? **K~** pl expense sg, cost sg; (Jur) costs; auf meine **K~** at my expense. **K~[vor]anschlag** m estimate. **k~los** adj free ● adv free [of charge]

köstlich adj delicious; (entzückend) delightful

Kostprobe f taste; (fig) sample

Kostüm nt -s,-e (Theat) costume; (Verkleidung) fancy dress; (Schneider-) suit. **k~iert** adj **k~iert** sein be in fancy dress

Kot m - excrement

Kotelett /kɔtˈlɛt/ nt -s,-s chop, cutlet. **K~en** pl sideburns

Köter m -s,- (pej) dog

Kotflügel m (Auto) wing

kotzen vi (haben) 🗵 throw up

Krabbe f -,-n crab, shrimp

krabbeln vi (sein) crawl

Krach m -[e]s, ̈e din, racket; (Knall) crash; (🗵: Streit) row; (🗵: Ruin) crash. **k~en** vi (haben) crash; es hat gekracht there was a bang/(🗵: Unfall) a crash ● (sein) break, crack; (auftreffen) crash (gegen into)

krächzen vi (haben) croak

Kraft f -, ̈e strength; (Gewalt) force; (Arbeits-) worker; in/außer **K~** in/no longer in force. **K~fah-rer** m driver. **K~fahrzeug** nt motor vehicle. **K~fahrzeugbrief** m [vehicle] registration document

kräftig adj strong; (gut entwickelt) sturdy; (nahrhaft) nutritious; (heftig) hard

kraft|los adj weak. **K~probe** f trial of strength. **K~stoff** m (Auto) fuel. **K~wagen** m motor car. **K~werk** nt power station

Kragen m -s,- collar

Krähe f -,-n crow

krähen vi (haben) crow

Kralle f -,-n claw

Kram m -s 🗵 things pl, 🗵 stuff; (Angelegenheiten) business. **k~en** vi (haben) rummage about (in + dat; nach for)

Krampf m -[e]s, ̈e cramp. **K~a-dern** pl varicose veins. **k~haft** adj convulsive; (verbissen) desperate

Kran m -[e]s, ̈e (Techn) crane

Kranich m -s,-e (Zool) crane

krank adj sick; (Knie, Herz) bad; **k~ sein/werden** be/fall ill. **K~e(r)** m/f sick man/woman, invalid; der **K~en** the sick pl

kränken vt offend, hurt

Kranken|bett nt sick bed. **K~geld** nt sickness benefit. **K~gymnast|in** m -en,-en (f -,-nen) physiotherapist. **K~gym-nastik** f physiotherapy. **K~haus** nt hospital. **K~kasse** *f* health insurance scheme/(*Amt*) office. **K~pflege** *f* nursing. **K~saal** *m* [hospital] ward. **K~schein** *m* certificate of entitlement to medical treatment. **K~schwester** *f* nurse. **K~versicherung** *f* health insurance. **K~wagen** *m* ambulance

Krankheit *f* -,-en illness, disease

kränklich *adj* sickly

krank|melden *vt sep* **jdn k~melden** report s.o. sick; **sich k~melden** report sick

Kranz *m* -es,⸚e wreath

Krapfen *m* -s,- doughnut

Krater *m* -s,- crater

kratzen *vt/i* (*haben*) scratch. **K~er** *m* -s,- scratch

Kraul *nt* -s (*Sport*) crawl. **k~en**[1] *vi* (*haben/sein*) (*Sport*) do the crawl

kraulen[2] *vt* tickle; **sich am Kopf k~** scratch one's head

kraus *adj* wrinkled; (*Haar*) frizzy; (*verworren*) muddled. **K~e** *f* -,-n frill

kräuseln *vt* wrinkle; frizz (*Haar-*); gather (*Stoff*); **sich k~** wrinkle; (*sich kringeln*) curl; (*Haar:*) go frizzy

Kraut *nt* -[e]s, **Kräuter** herb; (*SGer*) cabbage; (*Sauer-*) sauerkraut

Krawall *m* -s,-e riot; (*Lärm*) row

Krawatte *f* -,-n [neck]tie

krea|tiv /krea'ti:f/ *adj* creative. **K~tur** *f* -,-en creature

Krebs *m* -es,-e crayfish; (*Med*) cancer; (*Astrology*) Cancer

Kredit *m* -s,-e credit; (*Darlehen*) loan; **auf K~** on credit. **K~karte** *f* credit card

Kreid|e *f* - chalk. **k~ig** *adj* chalky

kreieren /kre'i:rən/ *vt* create

Kreis *m* -es,-e circle; (*Admin*) district

kreischen *vt/i* (*haben*) screech; (*schreien*) shriek

Kreisel *m* -s,- [spinning] top

kreis|en *vi* (*haben*) circle; revolve (um around). **k~förmig** *adj* circular. **K~lauf** *m* cycle; (*Med*) circulation. **K~säge** *f* circular saw. **K~verkehr** *m* [traffic] roundabout

Krem *f* -,-s & *m* -s,-e cream

Krematorium *nt* -s,-ien crematorium

Krempe *f* -,-n [hat] brim

krempeln *vt* turn (**nach oben** up)

Krepp *m* -s,-s & -e crêpe

Kreppapier *nt* crêpe paper

Kresse *f* -,-n cress; (*Kapuziner-*) nasturtium

Kreta *nt* -s Crete

Kreuz *nt* -es,-e cross; (*Kreuzung*) intersection; (*Mus*) sharp; (*Kartenspiel*) clubs *pl*; (*Anat*) small of the back; **über K~** crosswise; **das K~ schlagen** cross oneself. **k~en** *vt* cross; **sich k~en** cross; (*Straßen:*) intersect; (*Meinungen:*) clash ● *vi* (*haben/sein*) cruise. **K~fahrt** *f* (*Naut*) cruise. **K~gang** *m* cloister

kreuzig|en *vt* crucify. **K~ung** *f* -,-en crucifixion

Kreuz|otter *f* adder, common viper. **K~ung** *f* -,-en intersection; (*Straßen-*) crossroads *sg*. **K~verhör** *nt* cross-examination. **k~weise** *adv* crosswise. **K~worträtsel** *nt* crossword [puzzle]. **K~zug** *m* crusade

kribbel|ig *adj* 🅸 edgy. **k~n** *vi* (*haben*) tingle; (*kitzeln*) tickle

kriech|en† *vi* (*sein*) crawl; (*fig*) grovel (**vor** + *dat* to). **K~spur** *f* (*Auto*) crawler lane. **K~tier** *nt* reptile

Krieg *m* -[e]s,-e war

kriegen *vt* 🅸 get; **ein Kind k~** have a baby

kriegs|beschädigt *adj* war-disabled. **K~dienstverweigerer** *m*

k

-s,- conscientious objector. **K~ge-fangene(r)** *m* prisoner of war. **K~gefangenschaft** *f* captivity. **K~gericht** *nt* court martial. **K~list** *f* stratagem. **K~rat** *m* council of war. **K~recht** *nt* martial law

Krimi *m* -s,-s 𝕋 crime story/film. **K~nalität** *f* - crime; (*Vorkommen*) crime rate. **K~nalpolizei** *f* criminal investigation department. **K~nal-roman** *m* crime novel. **k~nell** *adj* criminal

Krippe *f* -,-n manger; (*Weihnachts-*) crib; (*Kinder-*) crèche. **K~nspiel** *nt* Nativity play

Krise *f* -,-n crisis

Kristall *nt* -s crystal; (*geschliffen*) cut glass

Kritik *f* -,-en criticism; (*Rezension*) review; unter aller K~ 𝕋 abysmal

Kriti|ker *m* -s,- critic; (*Rezensent*) reviewer. **k~sch** *adj* critical. **k~sieren** *vt* criticize; review

kritzeln *vt/i* (*haben*) scribble

Krokodil *nt* -s,-e crocodile

Krokus *m* -,-[se] crocus

Krone *f* -,-n crown; (*Baum-*) top

krönen *vt* crown

Kronleuchter *m* chandelier

Krönung *f* -,-en coronation; (*fig: Höhepunkt*) crowning event

Kropf *m* -[e]s,ːe (*Zool*) crop; (*Med*) goitre

Kröte *f* -,-n toad

Krücke *f* -,-n crutch

Krug *m* -[e]s,ːe jug; (*Bier-*) tankard

Krümel *m* -s,- crumb. **k~ig** *adj* crumbly. **k~n** *vt* crumble ● *vi* (*haben*) be crumbly

krumm *adj* crooked; (*gebogen*) curved; (*verbogen*) bent

krümmen *vt* bend; crook (*Finger*); sich k~ bend; (*sich winden*) writhe; (*vor Lachen*) double up

Krümmung *f* -,-en bend, curve

Krüppel *m* -s,- cripple

Kruste *f* -,-n crust; (*Schorf*) scab

Kruzifix *nt* -es,-e crucifix

Kuba *nt* -s Cuba. **k~anisch** *adj* Cuban

Kübel *m* -s,- tub; (*Eimer*) bucket; (*Techn*) skip

Küche *f* -,-n kitchen; (*Kochkunst*) cooking; kalte/warme K~ cold/hot food

Kuchen *m* -s,- cake

Küchen|herd *m* cooker, stove. **K~maschine** *f* food processor, mixer. **K~schabe** *f* -,-n cockroach

Kuckuck *m* -s,-e cuckoo

Kufe *f* -,-n [sledge] runner

Kugel *f* -,-n ball; (*Geometry*) sphere; (*Gewehr-*) bullet; (*Sport*) shot. **k~förmig** *adj* spherical. **K~lager** *nt* ball-bearing. **k~n** *vt/i* (*haben*) roll; sich k~n (*vor Lachen*) fall about. **K~schreiber** *m* -s,- ballpoint [pen]. **k~sicher** *adj* bulletproof. **K~stoßen** *nt* -s shot-putting

Kuh *f* -,ːe cow

kühl *adj* cool; (*kalt*) chilly. **K~box** *f* -,-en cool box. **K~e** *f* - coolness; chilliness. **k~en** *vt* cool; refrigerate (*Lebensmittel*); chill (*Wein*). **K~er** *m* -s,- (*Auto*) radiator. **K~erhaube** *f* bonnet. **K~fach** *nt* frozen-food compartment. **K~raum** *m* cold store. **K~schrank** *m* refrigerator. **K~truhe** *f* freezer. **K~wasser** *nt* [radiator] water

kühn *adj* bold

Kuhstall *m* cowshed

Küken *nt* -s,- chick; (*Enten-*) duckling

Kulissen *fpl* (*Theat*) scenery *sg*; (*seitlich*) wings; hinter den K~ (*fig*) behind the scenes

Kult *m* -[e]s,-e cult

kultivier|en vt cultivate. **k~t** adj cultured

Kultur f -,-en culture. **K~beutel** m toilet bag. **k~ell** adj cultural. **K~film** m documentary film. **K~tourismus** m cultural tourism

Kultusminister m Minister of Education and Arts

Kümmel m -s caraway; (Getränk) kümmel

Kummer m -s sorrow, grief; (Sorge) worry; (Ärger) trouble

kümmer|lich adj puny; (dürftig) meagre; (armselig) wretched. **k~n** vt concern; **sich k~n um** look after; (sich befassen) concern oneself with; (beachten) take notice of

kummervoll adj sorrowful

Kumpel m -s,- 🅣 mate

Kunde m -n,-n customer. **K~ndienst** m [after-sales] service

Kundgebung f -,-en (Pol) rally

kündig|en vt cancel (Vertrag); give notice of withdrawal for (Geld); give notice to quit (Wohnung); **seine Stellung k~en** give [in one's] notice ● vi (haben) give [in one's] notice; **jdm k~en** give s.o. notice. **K~ung** f -,-en cancellation; notice [of withdrawal/dismissal/to quit]; (Entlassung) dismissal. **K~ungsfrist** f period of notice

Kund|in f -,-nen [woman] customer. **K~schaft** f - clientele, customers pl

künftig adj future ● adv in future

Kunst f -,ˆe art; (Können) skill. **K~faser** f synthetic fibre. **K~galerie** f art gallery. **K~geschichte** f history of art. **K~gewerbe** nt arts and crafts pl. **K~griff** m trick

Künstler m -s,- artist; (Könner) master. **K~in** f -,-nen [woman] artist. **k~isch** adj artistic

künstlich adj artificial

Kunst|stoff m plastic. **K~stück** nt trick; (große Leistung) feat. **k~voll** adj artistic; (geschickt) skilful

kunterbunt adj multicoloured; (gemischt) mixed

Kupfer nt -s copper

Kupon /ku'põ:/ m -s,-s voucher; (Zins-) coupon; (Stoff-) length

Kuppe f -,-n [rounded] top

Kuppel f -,-n dome

kupp|eln vt couple (an + acc to) ● vi (haben) (Auto) operate the clutch. **K~lung** f -,-en coupling; (Auto) clutch

Kur f -,-en course of treatment, cure

Kur A health cure in a spa town may last up to 6 weeks and usually involves a special diet, exercise programmes, physiotherapy and massage. The cure is intended for people with minor complaints or who are recovering from illness, and it plays an important role in preventative medicine in Germany.

Kür f -,-en (Sport) free exercise; (Eislauf) free programme

Kurbel f -,-n crank. **K~welle** f crankshaft

Kürbis m -ses,-se pumpkin

Kurier m -s,-e courier

kurieren vt cure

kurios adj curious, odd. **K~ität** f -,-en oddness; (Objekt) curiosity

Kurort m health resort; (Bade-ort) spa

Kurs m -es,-e course; (Aktien-) price. **K~buch** nt timetable

kursieren vi (haben) circulate

kursiv adj italic ● adv in italics. **K~schrift** f italics pl

Kursus m -,-Kurse course
Kurswagen m through carriage
Kurtaxe f visitors' tax
Kurve f -,-n curve; (Straßen-) bend
kurz adj short; (knapp) brief; (rasch) quick; (schroff) curt; k~e Hosen shorts; vor k~em a short time ago; seit k~em lately; den Kürzeren ziehen get the worst of it; k~ vor shortly before; sich k~ fassen be brief; k~ und gut in short; zu k~ kommen get less than one's fair share. k~ärmelig adj short-sleeved. k~atmig adj k~atmig sein be short of breath
Kürze f - shortness; (Knappheit) brevity; in k~ shortly. k~n vt shorten; (verringern) cut
kurzfristig adj short-term ● adv at short notice
kürzlich adv recently
Kurz|meldung f newsflash. K~schluss m short circuit. K~schrift f shorthand. k~sichtig adj short-sighted. K~sichtigkeit f - short-sightedness. K~streckenrakete f short-range missile
Kürzung f -,-en shortening; (Verringerung) cut (gen in)
Kurz|waren fpl haberdashery sg. K~welle f short wave
kuscheln (sich) vr snuggle (an + acc up to)
Kusine f -,-n (female) cousin
Kuss m -es,-e kiss
küssen vt/i (haben) kiss; sich k~ kiss
Küste f -,-n coast
Küster m -s,- verger
Kutsch|e f -,-n (horse-drawn) carriage/(geschlossen) coach. K~er m -s,- coachman, driver
Kutte f -,-n (Relig) habit
Kutter m -s,- (Naut) cutter

Kuvert /ku'veːɐ̯/ nt -s,-s envelope

L

Labor nt -s,-s & -e laboratory. L~ant(in) m -en,-en (f -,-nen) laboratory assistant
Labyrinth nt -[e]s,-e maze, labyrinth
Lache f -,-n puddle; (Blut-) pool
lächeln vi (haben) smile. L~ nt -s smile. l~d adj smiling
lachen vi (haben) laugh. L~ nt -s laugh; (Gelächter) laughter
lächerlich adj ridiculous; sich l~ machen make a fool of oneself. L~keit f -,-en ridiculousness; (Kleinigkeit) triviality
Lachs m -es,-e salmon
Lack m -[e]s,-e varnish; (Japan-) lacquer; (Auto) paint. l~en vt varnish. l~ieren vt varnish; (spritzen) spray. L~schuhe mpl patent-leather shoes
laden† vt load; (Electr) charge; (Jur: vor-) summon
Laden m -s,: shop; (Fenster-) shutter. L~dieb m shoplifter. L~schluss m [shop] closing time. L~tisch m counter
Laderaum m (Naut) hold
lädieren vt damage
Ladung f -,-en load; (Naut, Aviat) cargo; (elektrische) charge
Lage f -,-n position, situation; (Schicht) layer; nicht in der L~ sein not be in a position (zu to)
Lager nt -s,- camp; (L~haus) warehouse; (Vorrat) stock; (Techn) bearing; (Erz-, Ruhe-) bed; (eines Tieres)

lair; [nicht] auf L~ [not] in stock.
L~haus nt warehouse. **l~en** vt
store; (legen) lay; **sich l~en** settle.
L~raum m store-room. **L~ung** f -
storage

Lagune f -,-n lagoon

lahm adj lame. **l~en** vi (haben)
be lame

lähmen vt paralyse

Lähmung f -,-en paralysis

Laib m -[e]s,-e loaf

Laich m -[e]s (Zool) spawn

Laie m -n,-n layman; (Theat) amateur. **l~nhaft** adj amateurish

Laken nt -s,- sheet

Lakritze f - liquorice

lallen vt/i (haben) mumble; (Baby:)
babble

Lametta nt -s tinsel

Lamm nt -[e]s,⸚er lamb

Lampe f -,-n lamp; (Decken-,
Wand-) light; (Glüh-) bulb. **L~n-
fieber** nt stage fright

Lampion /lamˈpjɔŋ/ m -s,-s
Chinese lantern

Land nt -[e]s,⸚er country; (Fest-)
land; (Bundes-) state, Land; (Aust)
province; **auf dem L~e** in the
country; **an L~ gehen** (Naut) go
ashore. **L~arbeiter** m agricultural
worker. **L~ebahn** f runway. **l~en**
vt/i (sein) land; (①: gelangen)
end up

Ländereien pl estates

Länderspiel nt international

Landesverrat m treason

Landkarte f map

ländlich adj rural

Landschaft f -,-en scenery;
(Geog, Kunst) landscape; (Gegend)
country[side]. **l~schaftlich** adj
scenic; (regional) regional. **L~strei-
cher** m -s,- tramp. **L~tag** m
state/(Aust) provincial parliament

Landung f -,-en landing

Land|vermesser m -s,- sur-
veyor. **L~weg** m country lane; **auf
dem L~weg** overland. **L~wirt** m
farmer. **L~wirtschaft** f agriculture;
(Hof) farm. **l~wirtschaftlich** adj
agricultural

lang[1] adv & prep (+ preceding acc or
preceding an + dat) along; **den od
am Fluss l~** along the river

lang[2] adj long; (groß) tall; **seit
l~em** for a long time ● adv **eine
Stunde l~** for an hour; **mein
Leben l~** all my life. **l~ärmelig**
adj long-sleeved. **l~atmig** adj long-
winded. **l~e** adv a long time;
(schlafen) late; **schon l~e** [for] a
long time; (zurückliegend) a long
time ago; **l~e nicht** not for a long
time; (bei weitem nicht) nowhere near

Länge f -,-n length; (Geog) longitude; **der L~ nach** lengthways

Länge|ngrad m degree of longi-
tude. **l~er** adj & adv longer; (län-
gere Zeit) [for] some time

Langeweile f - boredom; **L~
haben** be bored

lang|fristig adj long-term; (Vor-
hersage) long-range. **l~jährig** adj
long-standing; (Erfahrung) long

länglich adj oblong; **l~ rund** oval

längs adv & prep (+ gen/dat) along;
(der Länge nach) lengthways

lang|sam adj slow. **L~samkeit** f -

slowness

längst adv [schon] I~ for a long time; (zurückliegend) a long time ago; I~ nicht nowhere near

Lang|strecken- prefix long-distance; (Mil, Aviat) long-range. I~weilen vt bore; sich I~weilen be bored. I~weilig adj boring

Lanze f -,-n lance

Lappalie f -,-n [trifle

Lappen m -s,- cloth; (Anat) lobe

Laptop m -s,-s laptop

Lärche f -,-n larch

Lärm m -s noise. I~end adj noisy

Larve /'larfə/ f -,-n larva; (Maske) mask

lasch adj listless; (schlaff) limp

Lasche f -,-n tab, flap

Laser /'le:-, 'la:zɐ/ m -s,- laser

---

lassen†

● transitive verb

····▸ (+ infinitive; veranlassen) etw tun lassen have or get sth done. jdn etw tun lassen make s.o. do sth; get s.o. to do sth sich dat die Haare schneiden lassen have or get one's hair cut. jdn warten lassen make or let s.o. wait; keep s.o. waiting. jdn grüßen lassen send one's regards to s.o. jdn kommen/rufen lassen send for s.o.

····▸ (+ infinitive; erlauben) let; allow; (hineinlassen/herauslassen) let or allow (in + acc into, aus + dat out of). jdn etw tun lassen let s.o. do sth; allow s.o. to do sth. er ließ mich nicht ausreden he didn't let me finish [what I was saying]

····▸ (belassen, bleiben lassen) leave. jdn in Frieden lassen leave s.o. in peace. etw ungesagt lassen leave sth unsaid

····▸ (unterlassen) stop. das Rauchen lassen stop smoking. er kann es nicht lassen, sie zu quälen he can't stop or he is forever tormenting her

····▸ (überlassen) jdm etw lassen let s.o. have sth

····▸ (als Aufforderung) lass/lasst uns gehen/fahren! let's go!

● reflexive verb

····▸ das lässt sich machen that can be done. das lässt sich nicht beweisen it can't be proved. die Tür lässt sich leicht öffnen the door opens easily

● intransitive verb

····▸ ① Lass mal. Ich mache das schon Leave it. I'll do it

---

lässig adj casual. L~keit f - casualness

Lasso nt -s,-s lasso

Last f -,-en load; (Gewicht) weight; (fig) burden; L~en charges; (Steuern) taxes. L~auto nt lorry. I~en vi (haben) weigh heavily/(liegen) rest (auf + dat on)

Laster¹ m -s,- ① lorry

Laster² nt -s,- vice

läster|n vt blaspheme ● vi (haben) make disparaging remarks (über + acc about). L~ung f -,-en blasphemy

lästig adj troublesome; I~ sein/ werden be/become a nuisance

Last|kahn m barge. L~[kraft]wagen m lorry

Latein nt -[s] Latin. L~amerika nt Latin America. I~isch adj Latin

Laterne f -,-n lantern; (Straßen-) street lamp. L~npfahl m lamp-post

latschen vi (sein) ① traipse

Latte f -,-n slat; (Tor-, Hochsprung-) bar

Latz m -es, ̈-e bib

Lätzchen nt -s,- [baby's] bib

Latzhose f dungarees pl

Laub nt -[e]s leaves pl; (L∼werk) foliage. **L∼baum** m deciduous tree

Laube f -,-n summer-house

Laub|säge f fretsaw. **L∼wald** m deciduous forest

Lauch m -[e]s leeks pl

Lauer f auf der L∼ liegen lie in wait. **l∼n** vi (haben) lurk; **l∼n auf** (+ acc) lie in wait for

Lauf m -[e]s, Läufe run; (Laufen) running; (Laufen) course; (Wett-race; (Sport: Durchgang) heat; (Gewehr-) barrel; im L∼e (+ gen) in the course of. **L∼bahn** f career. **l∼en†** vi (sein) run; (zu Fuß gehen) walk; (gelten) be valid; Ski/Schlittschuh l∼en ski/skate. **l∼end** adj running; (gegenwärtig) current; (regelmäßig) regular; auf dem l∼enden sein be up to date ● adv continually

Läufer m -s,- (Person, Teppich) runner; (Schach) bishop

Lauf|gitter nt play-pen. **L∼masche** f ladder. **L∼text** m marquee text. **L∼zettel** m circular

Lauge f -,-n soapy water

Laun|e f -,-n mood; (Einfall) whim; guter L∼e sein, gute L∼e haben be in a good mood. **l∼isch** adj moody

Laus f -,Läuse louse; (Blatt-) greenfly

lauschen vi (haben) listen

laut adj loud; (geräuschvoll) noisy; l∼ lesen read aloud; l∼er stellen turn up ● prep (+ gen/dat) according to. **L∼** m -es,-e sound

Laute f (Mus) lute

lauten vi (haben) (Text:) run, read

läuten vt/i (haben) ring

lauter adj pure; (ehrlich) honest;

(Wahrheit) plain ● adj inv sheer; (nichts als) nothing but

laut|hals adv at the top of one's voice, (lachen) out loud. **l∼los** adj silent, (Stille) hushed. **L∼schrift** f phonetics pl. **L∼sprecher** m loudspeaker. **L∼stärke** f volume

lauwarm adj lukewarm

Lava f -,-ven lava

Lavendel m -s lavender

lavieren vi (haben) manœuvre

Lawine f -,-n avalanche

Lazarett nt -[e]s,-e military hospital

leasen /'li:sən/ vt rent

Lebehoch nt cheer

leben vt/i (haben) live (von on); leb wohl! farewell! **L∼** nt -s,- life, (Treiben) bustle; am L∼ alive. **l∼d** adj living

lebendig adj live; (lebhaft) lively; (anschaulich) vivid; l∼ sein be alive. **L∼keit** f - liveliness; vividness

Lebens|abend m old age. **L∼alter** nt age. **L∼fähig** adj viable. **L∼gefahr** f mortal danger; in L∼gefahr in mortal danger; (Patient) critically ill. **L∼gefährlich** adj extremely dangerous; (Verletzung) critical. **L∼haltungskosten** pl cost of living sg. **L∼länglich** adj life-long ● adv for life. **L∼lauf** m curriculum vitae. **L∼mittel** ntpl food sg. **L∼mittelgeschäft** nt food shop. **L∼mittelhändler** m grocer. **L∼partnerschaft** f civil partnership. **L∼retter** m rescuer; (beim Schwimmen) life-guard. **L∼unterhalt** m livelihood; seinen L∼unterhalt verdienen earn one's living. **L∼versicherung** f life assurance. **L∼wandel** m conduct. **l∼wichtig** adj vital. **L∼zeit** f auf L∼zeit for life

Leber f -,-n liver. **L∼fleck** m mole

Lebe|wesen nt living being.

L~wohl nt -s,-s & -e farewell

leb|haft adj lively; (Farbe) vivid. **L~kuchen** m gingerbread. **L~los** adj lifeless. **L~zeiten** fpl zu jds **L~zeiten** in s.o.'s lifetime

leck adj leaking. **L~** nt -s,-s leak. **l~en¹** vi (haben) leak

lecken² vi (haben) lick

lecker adj tasty. **L~bissen** m delicacy

Leder nt -s,- leather

ledig adj single, unmarried

leer adj empty; (unbesetzt) vacant; **l~ laufen** (Auto) idle. **l~en** vt empty; sich **l~en** empty. **L~lauf** m (Auto) neutral. **L~ung** f -,-en (Post) collection

legal adj legal. **l~isieren** vt legalize. **L~ität** f - legality

Legasthenie f - dyslexia **L~theniker** m -s,- dyslexic

legen vt put; (hin-, ver-) lay; set (Haare); sich **l~** lie down; (nachlassen) subside

Legende f -,-n legend

leger /le'ʒɛːɐ/ adj casual

Legierung f -,-en alloy

Legion f -,-en legion

Legislative f - legislature

legitim adj legitimate. **L~ität** f - legitimacy

Lehm m -s clay

Lehne f -,-n (Rücken-) back; (Arm-) arm. **l~en** vt lean (an + acc against); sich **l~en** lean (an + acc against) ● vi (haben) be leaning (an + acc against)

Lehr|buch nt textbook. **L~e** f -,-n apprenticeship; (Anschauung) doctrine; (Theorie) theory; (Wissenschaft) science; (Erfahrung) lesson. **l~en** vt/i (haben) teach. **L~er** m -s,- teacher; (Fahr-) instructor. **L~erin** f -,-nen teacher. **L~erzim-**

mer nt staff-room. **L~fach** nt (Sch) subject. **L~gang** m course. **L~kraft** f teacher. **L~ling** m -s,-e apprentice; (Auszubildender) trainee. **L~plan** m syllabus. **l~reich** adj instructive. **L~stelle** f apprenticeship. **L~stuhl** m (Univ) chair. **L~zeit** f apprenticeship

Leib m -es,-er body; (Bauch) belly. **L~eserziehung** f (Sch) physical education. **L~gericht** nt favourite dish. **l~lich** adj physical; (blutsverwandt) real, natural. **L~wächter** m bodyguard

Leiche f -,-n [dead] body; corpse. **L~nbestatter** m -s,- undertaker. **L~nhalle** f mortuary. **L~nwagen** m hearse. **L~nzug** m funeral procession, cortège

Leichnam m -s,-e [dead] body

leicht adj light; (Stoff) lightweight; (gering) slight; (mühelos) easy; jdm **l~ fallen** be easy for s.o.; etw **l~ machen** make sth easy (dat for); es sich (dat) **l~ machen** take the easy way out; etw **l~ nehmen** (fig) take sth lightly. **L~athletik** f [track and field] athletics sg. **L~gewicht** nt (Boxen) lightweight. **l~gläubig** adj gullible. **l~hin** adv casually. **L~igkeit** f - lightness; (Mühelosigkeit) ease; (L~sein) easiness; mit **L~igkeit** with ease. **L~sinn** m carelessness; recklessness; (Frivolität) frivolity. **l~sinnig** adj careless; (unvorsichtig) reckless

Leid nt -[e]s sorrow, grief; (Böses) harm; es tut mir **L~** I am sorry; er tut mir **L~** I feel sorry for him. **l~** adj jdn/etw **l~ sein/werden** be/get tired of s.o./something

Leide|form f passive. **l~n†** vt/i (haben) suffer (an + dat from); jdn/ etw nicht **l~n können** dislike s.o./ something. **L~n** nt -s,- suffering; (Med) complaint; (Krankheit) dis-

ease. l∼nd adj suffering.
L∼nschaft f -,-en passion.
l∼nschaftlich adj passionate

leider adv unfortunately; l∼er ja-/nicht I'm afraid so/not

Leier|kasten m barrel-organ.
l∼n vt/i (haben) wind; (herunter-) drone out

Leih|e f -,-n loan. l∼en† vt lend; sich (dat) etw l∼en borrow sth.
L∼gabe f loan. L∼gebühr f rental; lending charge. L∼haus nt pawnshop. L∼wagen m hire-car.
l∼weise adv on loan

Leim m -s glue. l∼en vt glue

Leine f -,-n rope; (Wäsche-) line; (Hunde-) lead, leash

Lein|en nt -s linen. L∼wand f linen; (Kunst) canvas; (Film-) screen

leise adj quiet; (Stimme, Berührung) soft; (schwach) faint; (leicht) light; l∼r stellen turn down

Leiste f -,-n strip; (Holz-) batten; (Anat) groin

leist|en vt achieve, accomplish; sich (dat) etw l∼en treat oneself to sth; (T: anstellen) get up to sth; ich kann es mir nicht l∼en I can't afford it. L∼ung f -,-en achievement; (Sport, Techn) performance; (Produktion) output; (Zahlung) payment

Leit|artikel m leader, editorial.
l∼en vt run, manage; (an-/hinführen) lead; (Mus, Techn, Phys) conduct; (lenken, schicken) direct.
l∼end adj leading; (Posten) executive

Leiter[1] f -,-n ladder

Leit|er[2] m -s,- director; (Comm) manager; (Führer) leader; (Mus, Phys) conductor; L∼erin f -,-nen director; manageress; leader.
L∼planke f crash barrier.
L∼spruch m motto. L∼ung f -,-en

(Führung) direction; (Comm) management; (Aufsicht) control; (Electr: Schnur) lead, flex; (Kabel) cable; (Telefon-) line; (Rohr-) pipe; (Haupt-) main. L∼ungswasser nt tap water

Lektion /-'tsio:n/ f -,-en lesson

Lekt|or m -s,-en, L∼orin f -,-nen (Univ) assistant lecturer; (Verlags-) editor. L∼üre f -,-n reading matter

Lende f -,-n loin

lenken vt guide; (steuern) steer; (regeln) control; jds Aufmerksamkeit auf sich (acc) l∼en attract s.o.'s attention. L∼rad nt steering-wheel. L∼stange f handlebars pl.
L∼ung f -,-en steering

Leopard m -en,-en leopard

Lepra f - leprosy

Lerche f -,-n lark

lernen vt/i (haben) learn; (für die Schule) study

Lernkurve f learning curve

Lesb|ierin /'lɛsbjərin/ f -,-nen lesbian. l∼isch adj lesbian

les|en† vt/i (haben) read; (Univ) lecture ● vt pick, gather. L∼en nt -s reading. L∼er(in) m -s,- (f -,-nen) reader. l∼erlich adj legible. L∼e-zeichen nt bookmark

lethargisch adj lethargic

Lettland nt -s Latvia

letzt|e(r,s) adj last; (neueste) latest; in l∼er Zeit recently; l∼en Endes in the end. l∼ens adv recently; (zuletzt) lastly. l∼ere(r,s) adj the latter; der/die/das L∼ere (l∼ere) the latter

Leucht|e f -,-n light. l∼en vi (haben) shine. l∼end adj shining.
L∼er m -s,- candlestick. L∼feuer nt beacon. L∼rakete f flare. L∼re-klame f neon sign. L∼röhre f fluorescent tube. L∼turm m lighthouse

leugnen vt deny

Leukämie f - leukaemia

Leumund m -s reputation

Leute pl people; (Mil) men; (Arbeiter) workers

Leutnant m -s,-s second lieutenant

Lexikon nt -s,-ka encyclopaedia; (Wörterbuch) dictionary

Libanon (der) -s Lebanon

Libelle f -,-n dragonfly

liberal adj (Pol) liberal

Libyen nt -s Libya

Licht nt -[e]s,-er light; (Kerze) candle; L~ machen turn on the light. l~ adj bright; (Med) lucid; (spärlich) sparse. L~bild nt [passport] photograph; (Dia) slide. L~blick m (fig) ray of hope. l~en vt thin out; den Anker l~en (Naut) weigh anchor; sich l~en become less dense; thin. L~hupe f headlight flasher; die L~hupe betätigen flash one's headlights. L~maschine f dynamo. L~ung f -,-en clearing

Lid nt -[e]s,-er [eye]lid. L~schatten m eye-shadow

lieb adj dear; (nett) nice; (artig) good; jdn l~ haben be fond of s.o.; (lieben) love s.o.; es wäre mir l~er I should prefer it (wenn if)

Liebe f -,-n love. l~n vt love; (mögen) like; sich l~n love each other; (körperlich) make love. l~nd adj loving. l~nswert a lovable. l~nswürdig adj kind. l~nswürdigerweise adv very kindly

lieber adv rather; (besser) better; l~ mögen like better; ich trinke l~ Tee I prefer tea

Liebes|brief m love letter. L~dienst m favour. L~kummer m heartache. L~paar nt [pair of] lovers pl

lieb|evoll adj loving, affectionate. L~haber m -s,- lover; (Sammler)

collector. L~haberei f -,-en hobby. L~kosung f -,-en caress. l~lich adj lovely; (sanft) gentle; (süß) sweet. L~ling m -s,-e darling; (Bevorzugte) favourite. L~lings- prefix favourite. L~los adj loveless; (Eltern) uncaring; (unfreundlich) unkind. L~schaft f -,-en [love] affair. l~ste(r,s) adj dearest; (bevorzugt) favourite ● adv am l~sten best [of all]; jdn/etw am l~sten mögen like s.o./something best [of all]. L~ste(r) m/f beloved; (Schatz) sweetheart

Lied nt -[e]s,-er song

liederlich adj slovenly; (unordentlich) untidy. L~keit f - slovenliness; untidiness

Lieferant m -en,-en supplier

liefer|bar adj (Comm) available. l~n vt supply; (zustellen) deliver; (hervorbringen) yield. L~ung f -,-en delivery; (Sendung) consignment

Liege f -,-n couch. l~n vi (haben) lie; (gelegen sein) be situated; l~n bleiben remain lying [there]; (im Bett) stay in bed; (Ding:) be left; (Schnee:) settle; (Arbeit:) remain undone; (zurückgelassen werden) be left behind; l~n lassen leave; (zurücklassen) leave behind; (nicht fortführen) leave undone; l~n an (+ dat) (fig) be due to; (abhängen) depend on; jdm [nicht] l~n [not] suit s.o.; mir liegt viel daran it is very important to me. L~stuhl m deckchair. L~stütz m -es,-e press-up, (Amer) push-up. L~wagen m couchette car

Lift m -[e]s,-e & -s lift

Liga f -,-gen league

Likör m -s,-e liqueur

lila inv adj mauve; (dunkel) purple

Lilie /'liːli̯ə/ f -,-n lily

Liliputaner(in) m -s,- (f -,-nen) dwarf

Limo f -,-[s] 🄵, **L∼nade** f -,-n fizzy drink; lemonade

Limousine /limu'zi:nə/ f -,-n saloon

lind adj mild

Linde f -,-n lime tree

linder|n vt relieve, ease. **L∼ung** f - relief

Lineal nt -s,-e ruler

Linie /-jə/ f -,-n line; (Zweig) branch; (Bus-) route; **L∼ 4** number 4 [bus/tram]; **in erster L∼** primarily. **L∼nflug** m scheduled flight. **L∼nrichter** m linesman

lin[i]iert adj lined, ruled

Link|e f -n,-n left side; (Hand) left hand; (Boxen) left; **die L∼e** (Pol) the left. **I∼e(r,s)** adj left; (Pol) leftwing; **l∼e Masche** purl

links adv on the left; (bei Stoff) on the wrong side; (verkehrt) inside out; **l∼stricken** purl. **L∼händer(in)** m -s,- (f -,-nen) lefthander. **l∼händig** adj & adv lefthanded

Linoleum /-leʊm/ nt -s lino, linoleum

Linse f -,-n lens; (Bot) lentil

Lippe f -,-n lip. **L∼nstift** m lipstick

Liquid|ation /-'tsjo:n/ f -,-en liquidation. **l∼ieren** vt liquidate

lispeln vt/i (haben) lisp

List f -,-en trick, ruse

Liste f -,-n list

listig adj cunning, crafty

Litanei f -,-en litany

Litauen nt -s Lithuania

Liter m & nt -s,- litre

Literatur f - literature

Liturgie f -,-n liturgy

Litze f -,-n braid

Lizenz f -,-en licence

Lob nt -[e]s praise

Lobby /'lɔbi/ f - (Pol) lobby

loben vt praise

löblich adj praiseworthy

Lobrede f eulogy

Loch nt -[e]s,⸚er hole. **l∼en** vt punch a hole/holes in; punch (Fahrkarte). **L∼er** m -s,- punch

löcherig adj full of holes

Locke f -,-n curl. **l∼n¹** vt curl; **sich l∼n** curl

locken² vt lure, entice; (reizen) tempt. **l∼d** adj tempting

Lockenwickler m -s,- curler; (Rolle) roller

locker adj loose; (Seil) slack; (Erde) light; (zwanglos) casual; (zu frei) lax. **l∼n** vt loosen; slacken (Seil); break up (Boden); relax (Griff); **sich l∼n** become loose; (Seil:) slacken; (sich entspannen) relax

lockig adj curly

Lockmittel nt bait

Loden m -s (Textiles) loden

Löffel m -s,- spoon; (L∼ voll) spoonful. **l∼n** vt spoon up

Logarithmus m -,-men logarithm

Logbuch nt (Naut) log-book

Loge /'lo:ʒə/ f -,-n lodge; (Theat) box

Log|ik f - logic. **l∼isch** adj logical

Logo nt -s,-s logo

Lohn m -[e]s,⸚e wages pl, pay; (fig) reward. **L∼empfänger** m wage-earner. **l∼en** v[i]r (haben) [sich] l∼en be worth it or worth while ● vt be worth. **l∼end** adj worthwhile; (befriedigend) rewarding. **L∼erhöhung** f [pay] rise. **L∼steuer** f income tax

Lok f -,-s 🄵 = Lokomotive

Lokal nt -s,-e restaurant; (Trink-) bar

Lokomotiv|e f -,-n engine, locomotive. **L∼führer** m engine driver

London nt -s London. **L~er** adj London ● m -s,- Londoner

Lorbeer m -s,-en laurel. **L~blatt** nt (Culin) bay-leaf

Lore f -,-n (Rail) truck

Los nt -es,-e lot; (Lotterie-) ticket; (Schicksal) fate

los pred adj los sein be loose; jdn/etw los sein be rid of s.o./something; was ist [mit ihm] los? what's the matter [with him]? ● adv los! go on! Achtung, fertig, los! ready, steady, go!

lösbar adj soluble

losbinden† vt sep untie

Lösch|blatt nt sheet of blotting-paper. **l~en** vt put out, extinguish; quench (Durst); blot (Tinte); (tilgen) cancel; (streichen) delete

Löschfahrzeug nt fire-engine

lose adj loose

Lösegeld nt ransom

losen vt (haben) draw lots (um for)

lösen vt undo; (lockern) loosen; (entfernen) detach; (klären) solve; (auflösen) dissolve; cancel (Vertrag); break off (Beziehung); (kaufen) buy; sich l~ come off; (sich trennen) detach oneself/itself; (lose werden) come undone; (sich klären) resolve itself; (sich auflösen) dissolve

los|fahren† vi sep (sein) start; (Auto:) drive off; **l~fahren nach** (+ dat) head for. **l~gehen†** vi sep (sein) set off; (⚡: anfangen) start; (Bombe:) go off; **l~gehen nach** (+ dat) head for; (fig: angreifen) go for. **l~kommen†** vt sep get away (von from). **l~lassen†** vt sep let go of; (freilassen) release

löslich adj soluble

los|lösen vt sep detach; sich **l~lösen** become detached; (fig) break away (von from). **l~machen†** vt sep detach; untie. **l~reißen†** vt sep tear

off; sich **l~reißen** break free; (fig) tear oneself away. **l~schicken** vt sep send off. **l~sprechen†** vt sep absolve (von from)

Losung f -,-en (Pol) slogan; (Mil) password

Lösung f -,-en solution. **L~smittel** nt solvent

loswerden† vt sep get rid of

Lot nt -[e]s,-e perpendicular; (Blei-) plumb[-bob]. **l~en** vt plumb

löt|en vt solder. **L~lampe** f blow-lamp

lotrecht adj perpendicular

Lotse m -n,-n (Naut) pilot. **l~n** vt (Naut) pilot; (fig) guide

Lotterie f -,-n lottery

Lotto nt -s,-s lotto; (Lotterie) lottery

Love Parade A techno music and dance festival, which takes place in Berlin every summer. Originally a celebration of youth culture and very popular with young people, this festival has become a major tourist attraction.

Löw|e m -n,-n lion; (Astrology) Leo. **L~enzahn** m (Bot) dandelion. **L~in** f -,-nen lioness

loyal /loa'ja:l/ adj loyal. **L~ität** f - loyalty

Luchs m -es,-e lynx

Lücke f -,-n gap. **l~nhaft** adj incomplete; (Wissen) patchy. **l~nlos** adj complete; (Folge) unbroken

Luder nt -s,- ✗ (Frau) bitch

Luft f -,ˮe air; tief **L~** holen take a deep breath; in die **L~** gehen explode. **L~angriff** m air raid. **L~aufnahme** f aerial photograph. **L~ballon** m balloon. **L~blase** f air bubble. **L~druck** m atmospheric pressure

lüften vt air; raise (Hut); reveal (Geheimnis)

Luft|fahrt f aviation. L~**fahrtgesellschaft** f airline. L~**gewehr** nt airgun. l~**ig** adj airy; (Kleid) light. L~**kissenfahrzeug** nt hovercraft. L~**krieg** m aerial warfare. l~**leer** adj l~**leerer Raum** vacuum. L~**linie** f 100 km L~**linie** 100 km as the crow flies. L~**matratze** f airbed, inflatable mattress. L~**pirat** m hijacker. L~**post** f airmail. L~**röhre** f windpipe. L~**schiff** nt airship. L~**schlange** f [paper] streamer. L~**schutzbunker** m air-raid shelter

Lüftung f - ventilation

Luft|veränderung f change of air. L~**waffe** f air force. L~**zug** m draught

Lüg|e f -,-n lie. l~**en†** vt/i (haben) lie. L~**ner(in)** m -s,- (f -,-nen) liar. l~**nerisch** adj untrue; (Person) untruthful

Luke f -,-n hatch; (Dach-) skylight

Lümmel m -s,- lout

Lump m -en,-en scoundrel. L~**en** m -s,- rag; in L~**en** in rags. L~**enpack** nt riff-raff. L~**ensammler** m rag-and-bone man. l~**ig** adj mean, shabby

Lunge f -,-n lungs pl; (L~**flügel**) lung. L~**nentzündung** f pneumonia

Lupe f -,-n magnifying glass

Lurch m -[e]s,-e amphibian

Lust f -,-¨e pleasure; (Verlangen) desire; (sinnliche Begierde) lust; L~ **haben** feel like (auf etw acc sth); **ich habe keine** L~ I don't feel like it; (will nicht) I don't want to

lustig adj jolly; (komisch) funny; **sich** l~ **machen über** (+ acc) make fun of

Lüstling m -s,-e lecher

lust|los adj listless. L~**mörder** m sex killer. L~**spiel** nt comedy

lutsch|en vt/i (haben) suck. L~**er** m -s,- lollipop

Lüttich nt -s Liège

Luv f & nt - **nach Luv** (Naut) to windward

luxuriös adj luxurious

Luxus m - luxury

Lymph|drüse /'lymf-/ f, L~**knoten** m lymph gland

lynchen /'lynçən/ vt lynch

Lyr|ik f - lyric poetry. L~**iker** m -s,- lyric poet. l~**isch** adj lyrical

Mm

Machart f style

---

machen

● **transitive verb**

····▸ (herstellen, zubereiten) make (money, beds, music, exception, etc). **aus Plastik/Holz gemacht** made of plastic/wood. **etw machen lassen** have sth made. **etw aus jdm machen** make s.o. into sth. **jdn zum Präsidenten machen** make s.o. president. **er machte sich** (dat) **viele Freunde/Feinde** he made a lot of friends/enemies. **jdm/sich** (dat) **[einen] Kaffee machen** make [some] coffee for s.o./oneself. **ein Foto machen** take a photo

····▸ (verursachen) make, cause (difficulties); cause (pain, anxiety). **jdm Arbeit machen** make [extra] work for s.o., cause s.o. extra work. **jdm Mut/Hoffnung machen** give s.o. courage/hope.

das macht Hunger/Durst this
makes you hungry/thirsty. das
macht das Wetter that's [be-
cause of] the weather

····▸ (ausführen, ordnen) do (job,
repair, fam: room, washing, etc.);
take (walk, trip, exam, course).
sie machte mir die Haare 🛈
she did my hair for me. einen
Besuch [bei jdm] machen pay
[s.o.] a visit

····▸ (tun) do (nothing, everything).
was machst du [da]? what are
you doing? so etwas macht
man nicht that [just] isn't done

····▸ was macht ... ? (wie ist es
um bestellt?) how is ...? was
macht die Gesundheit/Arbeit?
how are you keeping/how is the
job [getting on]?

····▸ (Math: ergeben) be. zwei mal
zwei macht vier two times two
is four. das macht 6 Euro [zu-
sammen] that's or that comes
to six euros [altogether]

····▸ (schaden) was macht das
schon? what does it matter?
[das] macht nichts! 🛈 it
doesn't matter

····▸ mach's gut! 🛈 look after
yourself!; (auf Wiedersehen) so
long!

● reflexive verb

····▸ sich machen 🛈 do well

····▸ sich an etw (acc) machen
get down to sth. sie machte
sich an die Arbeit she got
down to work

● intransitive verb

····▸ das macht hungrig/durstig
it makes you hungry/thirsty. das
macht dick it's fattening

Macht f -,⸚e power. **M~haber** m
-s,- ruler

mächtig adj powerful ● adv 🛈

terribly

machtlos adj powerless
Mädchen nt -s,- girl; (Dienst-)
maid. **m~haft** adj girlish.
M~name m girl's name; (vor der
Ehe) maiden name
Made f -,-n maggot
madig adj maggoty
Madonna f -,-nen madonna
Magazin nt -s,-e magazine;
(Lager) warehouse; store-room
Magd f -,⸚e maid
Magen m -s,⸚ stomach. **M~ver-
stimmung** f stomach upset
mager adj thin; (Fleisch) lean;
(Boden) poor; (dürftig) meagre.
M~keit f - thinness; leanness.
M~sucht f anorexia
Magie f - magic
Magier /'ma:giɐ/ m -s,- magician.
m~isch adj magic
Magistrat m -s,-e city council
Magnet m -en & -[e]s,-e magnet.
m~isch adj magnetic
Mahagoni nt -s mahogany
Mäh|drescher m -s,- combine
harvester. **m~en** vt/i (haben) mow
Mahl nt -[e]s,⸚er & -e meal
mahlen† vt grind
Mahlzeit f meal; **M~!** enjoy
your meal!
Mähne f -,-n mane
mahn|en vt/i (haben) remind
(wegen about); (ermahnen) admon-
ish; (auffordern) urge (zu to).
M~ung f -,-en reminder; ad-
monition
Mai m -[e]s,-e May; der Erste Mai
May Day. **M~glöckchen** nt -s,- lily
of the valley
Mailand nt -s Milan
Mais m -es maize; (Culin)
sweet corn
Majestät f -,-en majesty.

m~isch adj majestic

Major m -s,-e major

Majoran m -s marjoram

makaber adj macabre

Makel m -s,- blemish; (Defekt) flaw

Makkaroni pl macaroni sg

Makler m -s,- (Comm) broker

Makrele f -,-n mackerel

Makrone f -,-n macaroon

mal adv (Math) times; (bei Maßen) by; (①: einmal) once; (eines Tages) one day; nicht mal not even

Mal nt -[e]s,-e time; zum ersten/ letzten Mal for the first/last time; ein für alle Mal once and for all; jedes Mal every time; jedes Mal, wenn whenever

Mal|buch nt colouring book. m~en vt/i (haben) paint. M~er m -s,- painter. M~erei f -,-en painting. M~erin f -,-nen painter. m~erisch adj picturesque

Mallorca /ma'lorka, -'jorka/ nt -s Majorca

malnehmen† vt sep multiply (mit by)

Malz nt -es malt

Mama /'mama, ma'ma:/ f -s mummy

Mammut nt -s,-e & -s mammoth

mampfen vt ① munch

man pron one, you; (die Leute) people, they; man sagt they say, it is said

manch|e(r,s) pron many a; [so] m~es Mal many a time; m~e Leute some people ● (substantivisch) m~er/m~e many a man/ woman; m~e pl some; (Leute) some people; (viele) many [people]; m~es some things; (vieles) many things. m~erlei inv adj various ● pron various things

manchmal adv sometimes

Mandant(in) m -en,-en (f -,-nen) (Jur) client

Mandarine f -,-n mandarin

Mandat nt -[e]s,-e mandate; (Jur) brief; (Pol) seat

Mandel f -,-n almond; (Anat) tonsil. M~entzündung f tonsillitis

Manege /ma'ne:ʒə/ f -,-n ring; (Reit-) arena

Mangel¹ m -s,= lack; (Knappheit) shortage; (Med) deficiency; (Fehler) defect

Mangel² f -,-n mangle

mangel|haft adj faulty, defective; (Sch) unsatisfactory. m~n¹ vi (haben) es m~t an (+ dat) there is a lack/(Knappheit) shortage of

mangeln² vt put through the mangle

Manie f -,-n mania

Manier f -,-en manner; M~en manners. m~lich adj well-mannered ● adv properly

Manifest nt -[e]s,-e manifesto

Maniküre f -,-n manicure; (Person) manicurist. m~n vt manicure

Manko nt -s,-s disadvantage; (Fehlbetrag) deficit

Mann m -[e]s,=er man; (Ehe-) husband

Männchen nt -s,- little man; (Zool) male

Mannequin /'manakɛ̃/ nt -s model

männlich adj male; (Gram & fig) masculine; (mannhaft) manly; (Frau) mannish. M~keit f - masculinity; (fig) manhood

Mannschaft f -,-en team; (Naut) crew

Manöver nt -s,- manœuvre; (Winkelzug) trick. m~rieren vt/i (haben) manœuvre

Mansarde f -,-n attic room;

(*Wohnung*) attic flat

Manschette f -,-n cuff. **M~nknopf** m cuff-link

Mantel m -s, ⁼ coat; overcoat

Manuskript nt -[e]s,-e manuscript

Mappe f -,-n folder; (*Akten-*) briefcase; (*Schul-*) bag

Märchen nt -s,- fairy-tales

Margarine f - margarine

Marienkäfer /maˈriːən-/ m ladybird

Marihuana nt -s marijuana

Marine f marine; (*Kriegs-*) navy. **m~blau** adj navy [blue]

marinieren vt marinade

Marionette f -,-n puppet, marionette

Mark[1] f -,- (*alte Währung*) mark; drei M~ three marks

Mark[2] nt -[e]s (*Knochen-*) marrow (*Bot*)pith; (*Frucht-*) pulp

markant adj striking

Marke f -,-n token; (*rund*) disc; (*Erkennungs-*) tag; (*Brief-*) stamp; (*Lebensmittel-*) coupon; (*Spiel-*) counter; (*Markierung*) mark; (*Fabrikat*) make; (*Tabak-*) brand. **M~nartikel** m branded article

markieren vt mark; (🗵: *vortäuschen*) fake

Markise f -,-n awning

Markstück nt one-mark piece

Markt m -[e]s, ⁼e market; (*M~platz*) market-place. **M~forschung** f market research

Marmelade f -,-n jam; (*Orangen-*) marmalade

Marmor m -s marble

Marokko nt -s Morocco

Marone f -,-n [sweet] chestnut

Marsch m -[e]s, ⁼e march. **m~** int (*Mil*) march!

Marschall m -s, ⁼e marshal

marschieren vi (*sein*) march

Marter f -,-n torture. **m~n** vt torture

Märtyrer(in) m -s,- (f -,-nen) martyr

Marxismus m - Marxism

März m -,-e March

Marzipan nt -s marzipan

Masche f -,-n stitch; (*im Netz*) mesh; (🗵: *Trick*) dodge. **M~ndraht** m wire netting

Maschin|e f -,-n machine; (*Flugzeug*) plane; (*Schreib-*) typewriter; **M~e** schreiben type. **m~egeschrieben** adj typewritten, typed. **m~ell** adj machine ● adv by machine. **M~enbau** m mechanical engineering. **M~engewehr** nt machine-gun. **M~ist** m -en,-en machinist; (*Naut*) engineer

Masern pl measles sg

Maserung f -,-en [wood] grain

Maske f -,-n mask; (*Theat*) make-up

maskieren vt mask; sich m~ dress up (als as)

maskulin adj masculine

Masochist m -en,-en masochist

Maß[1] nt -es,-e measure; (*Abmessung*) measurement; (*Grad*) degree; (*Mäßigung*) moderation; in hohem Maße to a high degree

Maß[2] f -,- (*SGer*) litre [of beer]

Massage /maˈsaːʒə/ f -,-n massage

Massaker nt -s,- massacre

Maßband nt (pl -bänder) tape-measure

Masse f -,-n mass; (*Culin*) mixture; (*Menschen-*) crowd; eine M~ Arbeit 🗵 masses of work. **m~nhaft** adv in huge quantities. **M~nproduktion** f mass production. **M~nvernichtungswaffen** fpl weapons of

mass destruction. **m~nweise** *adv*
in huge numbers

Masseu|r /ma'søːɐ/ *m* -s,-e masseur. **M~se** *f* -,-n masseuse

maß|gebend *adj* authoritative;
(*einflussreich*) influential. **m~geblich** *adj* decisive. **m~geschneidert** *adj* made-to-measure

massieren *vt* massage

massig *adj* massive

mäßig *adj* moderate; (*mittelmäßig*)
indifferent. **m~en** *vt* moderate;
sich **m~en** (*sich beherrschen*) restrain oneself. **M~ung** *f* -
moderation

massiv *adj* solid; (*stark*) heavy

Maß|krug *m* beer mug. **m~los**
adj excessive; (*grenzenlos*) boundless; (*äußerst*) extreme. **M~nahme**
f -,-n measure

Maßstab *m* scale; (*Norm & fig*)
standard. **m~sgerecht**, **m~sgetreu** *adj* scale ● *adv* to scale

Mast¹ *m* -[e]s,-e[n] pole; (*Überland-*)
pylon; (*Naut*) mast

Mast² *f* - fattening

mästen *vt* fatten

masturbieren *vi* (*haben*) masturbate

Material *nt* -s,-ien material; (*coll*)
materials *pl*. **M~ismus** *m* - materialism. **m~istisch** *adj* materialistic

Mathe *f* - 🔲 maths *sg*

Mathe|matik *f* - mathematics *sg*.
M~matiker *m* -s,- mathematician.
m~matisch *adj* mathematical

Matinee *f* -,-n (*Theat*) morning
performance

Matratze *f* -,-n mattress

Matrose *m* -n,-n sailor

Matsch *m* -[e]s mud; (*Schnee-*) slush

matt *adj* weak; (*gedämpft*) dim;
(*glanzlos*) dull; (*Politur, Farbe*) matt.

M~ *nt* -s (*Schach*) mate

Matte *f* -,-n mat

Mattglas *nt* frosted glass

Matura *f* - (*Aust*) ≈ A levels *pl*

Matura ▷ ABITUR

Mauer *f* -,-n wall. **M~werk** *nt*
masonry

Maul *nt* -[e]s, Mäuler (*Zool*)
mouth; halts **M~!** 🔲 shut up!
M~- und Klauenseuche *f* foot-and-mouth disease. **M~korb** *m*
muzzle. **M~tier** *nt* mule. **M~wurf**
m mole

Maurer *m* -s,- bricklayer

Maus *f* -,Mäuse mouse

Maut *f* -,-en (*Aust*) toll. **M~straße**
f toll road

maximal *adj* maximum

Maximum *nt* -s,-ma maximum

Mayonnaise /majo'nɛːzə/ *f* -,-n
mayonnaise

Mechan|ik /me'çaːnɪk/ *f* - mechanics *sg*; (*Mechanismus*) mechanism.
M~iker *m* -s,- mechanic. **m~isch**
adj mechanical. **m~isieren** *vt*
mechanize. **M~ismus** *m* -,-men
mechanism

meckern *vi* (*haben*) bleat; (🔲: *nörgeln*) grumble

Medaill|e /me'daljə/ *f* -,-n medal.
M~on *nt* -s,-s medallion (*Schmuck*)
locket

Medikament *nt* -[e]s,-e
medicine

Medit|ation /-'tsjoːn/ *f* -,-en
meditation. **m~ieren** *vi* (*haben*)
meditate

Medium *nt* -s,-ien medium; die
Medien the media

Medizin *f* -,-en medicine. **M~er**
m -s,- doctor; (*Student*) medical student. **m~isch** *adj* medical;

m

(heilkräftig) medicinal

Meer nt -[e]s,-e sea. **M~busen** m gulf. **M~enge** f strait. **M~esspiegel** m sea-level. **M~jungfrau** f mermaid. **M~rettich** m horseradish. **M~schweinchen** nt -s,- guinea-pig

Mehl nt -[e]s flour. **M~schwitze** f (Culin) roux

mehr pron & adv more; nicht m~ no more; (zeitlich) no longer; nichts m~ no more; (nichtsweiter) nothing else; nie m~ never again. **m~eres** pron several things pl. **m~fach** adj multiple; (mehrmalig) repeated ● adv several times. **M~fahrtenkarte** f book of tickets. **M~heit** f -,-en majority. **m~malig** adj repeated. **m~mals** adv several times. **m~sprachig** adj multilingual. **M~wertsteuer** f value-added tax, VAT. **M~zahl** f majority; (Gram) plural. **M~zweck-** prefix multipurpose

meiden† vt avoid, shun

Meile f -,-n mile. **m~nweit** adv [for] miles

mein poss pron my. **m~e(r,s)** poss pron mine; die **M~en** od **m~en** pl my family sg

Meineid m perjury

meinen vt mean; (glauben) think; (sagen) say

mein|erseits adv for my part. **m~etwegen** adv for my sake; (wegen mir) because of me; (🔲: von mir aus) as far as I'm concerned

Meinung f -,-en opinion; jdm die **M~** sagen give s.o. a piece of one's mind. **M~sumfrage** f opinion poll

Meise f -,-n (Zool) tit

Meißel m -s,- chisel. **m~n** vt/i (haben) chisel

meist adv mostly; (gewöhnlich)

usually. **m~e** adj der/die/das m~e most; die m~en Leute most people; am m~en [the] most ● pron das m~e most [of it]; die m~en most. **m~ens** adv mostly; (gewöhnlich) usually

Meister m -s,- master craftsman; (Könner) master; (Sport) champion. **m~n** vt master. **M~schaft** f -,-en mastery; (Sport) championship

meld|en vt report; (anmelden) register; (ankündigen) announce; sich m~en report (bei to); (zum Militär) enlist; (freiwillig) volunteer; (Teleph) answer; (Sch) put up one's hand; (von sich hören lassen) get in touch (bei with). **M~ung** f -,-en report; (Anmeldung) registration

melken† vt milk

Melodie f -,-n tune, melody

melodisch adj melodic

Melone f -,-n melon

Memoiren /me'mǫa:rən/ pl memoirs

Memorystick m memory stick

Menge f -,-n amount, quantity; (Menschen-) crowd; (Math) set; eine **M~** Geld a lot of money. **m~n** vt mix

Mensa f -,-sen (Univ) refectory

Mensch m -en,-en human being; der **M~** man; die m~en people; jeder/kein **M~** everybody/nobody. **M~enaffe** m ape. **m~enfeindlich** adj antisocial. **M~enfresser** m -s,- cannibal; (Zool) man-eater. **m~enfreundlich** adj philanthropic. **M~enleben** nt human life; (Lebenszeit) lifetime. **m~enleer** adj deserted. **M~enmenge** f crowd. **M~enraub** m kidnapping. **M~enrechte** ntpl human rights. **m~enscheu** adj unsociable. **m~enwürdig** adj humane. **M~heit** f - die **M~heit** mankind, humanity. **m~lich** adj human; (human) hu-

mane. **M~lichkeit** f - humanity
Menstru|ation /-'tsjo:n/ f - menstruation. **m~ieren** vi (haben) menstruate
Mentalität f -,-en mentality
Menü nt -s,-s menu; (festes M~) set meal
Meridian m -s,-e meridian
merk|bar adj noticeable. **M~blatt** nt [explanatory] leaflet. **m~en** vt notice; **sich** (dat) **etw m~en** remember sth. **M~mal** nt feature
merkwürdig adj odd, strange
Messe¹ f -,-n (Relig) mass; (Comm) [trade] fair
Messe² f -,-n (Mil) mess
messen† vt/i (haben) measure; (ansehen) look at; **[bei jdm] Fieber m~** take s.o.'s temperature; **sich mit jdm m~ können** be a match for s.o.
Messer nt -s,- knife
Messias m - Messiah
Messing nt -s brass
Messung f -,-en measurement
Metabolismus m - metabolism
Metall nt -s,-e metal. **m~isch** adj metallic
Metamorphose f -,-n metamorphosis
metaphorisch adj metaphorical
Meteor m -s,-e meteor. **M~ologie** f - meteorology
Meter m & nt -s,- metre. **M~maß** nt tape-measure
Method|e f -,-n method. **m~isch** adj methodical
Metropole f -,-n metropolis
Metzger m -s,- butcher. **M~ei** f -,-en butcher's shop
Meuterei f -,-en mutiny
meutern vi (haben) mutiny; (🗊: schimpfen) grumble

Mexikan|er(in) m -s,- (f -,-nen) Mexican. **m~isch** adj Mexican
Mexiko nt -s Mexico
miauen vi (haben) mew, miaow
mich pron (acc of ich) me; (reflexive) myself
Mieder nt -s,- bodice
Miene f -,-n expression
mies adj 🗊 lousy
Miet|e f -,-n rent; (Mietgebühr) hire charge; **zur M~e wohnen** live in rented accommodation. **m~en** vt rent (Haus, Zimmer); hire (Auto, Boot). **M~er(in)** m -s,- (f -,-nen) tenant. **M~frei** adj & adv rent-free. **M~shaus** nt block of rented flats. **M~vertrag** m lease. **M~wagen** m hire-car. **M~wohnung** f rented flat; (zu vermieten) flat to let
Migräne f -,-n migraine
Mikro|chip m microchip. **M~computer** m microcomputer. **M~film** m microfilm
Mikro|fon, M~phon nt -s,-e microphone. **M~skop** nt -s,-e microscope. **m~skopisch** adj microscopic
Mikrowelle f microwave. **M~nherd** m microwave oven
Milbe f -,-n mite
Milch f - milk. **M~glas** nt opal glass. **m~ig** adj milky. **M~mann** m (pl -männer) milkman. **M~straße** f Milky Way
mild adj mild; (nachsichtig) lenient. **M~e** f - mildness; leniency. **m~ern** vt make milder; (mäßigen) moderate; (lindern) ease; **sich m~ern** become milder; (sich mäßigen) moderate; (Schmerz:) ease; **m~ernde Umstände** mitigating circumstances
Milieu /mi'ljø:/ nt -s,-s [social] environment
Militär nt -s army; (Soldaten)

troops pl; **beim M~** in the army.
m~isch adj military

Miliz f -,-en militia

Milliarde /mɪˈljardə/ f -,-n thousand million, billion

Milli|gramm nt milligram.
M~meter m & nt millimetre.
M~meterpapier nt graph paper

Million /mɪˈljoːn/ f -,-en million.
M~är m -s,-e millionaire

Milz f - (Anat) spleen. **~brand** m anthrax

mimen vt (🇮: vortäuschen) act

Mimose f -,-n mimosa

Minderheit f -,-en minority

minderjährig adj (Jur) underage. **M~e(r)** m/f (Jur) minor

mindern vt diminish; decrease

minderwertig adj inferior.
M~keit f - inferiority. **M~keitskomplex** m inferiority complex

Mindest- prefix minimum. **m~e** adj & pron der/die/das **M~e** of m~e the least; **nicht im M~en** not in the least. **m~ens** adv at least. **M~lohn** m minimum wage. **M~maß** nt minimum

Mine f -,-n mine; (Bleistift-) lead; (Kugelschreiber-) refill. **M~nräumboot** nt minesweeper

Mineral nt -s,-e & -ien mineral. **m~isch** adj mineral. **M~wasser** nt mineral water

Miniatur f -,-en miniature

Minigolf nt miniature golf

minimal adj minimal

Minimum nt -s,-ma minimum

Mini|ster m -s,- minister. **m~steriell** adj ministerial. **M~sterium** nt -s,-ien ministry

minus conj, adv & prep (+ gen) minus. **M~** nt - deficit; (Nachteil) disadvantage. **M~zeichen** nt minus [sign]

Minute f -,-n minute

mir pron (dat of ich) [to] me; (reflexive) myself

Misch|ehe f mixed marriage.
m~en vt mix; blend (Tee, Kaffee); toss (Salat); shuffle (Karten); sich **m~en** mix; (Person:) mingle (unter + acc with); sich **m~en in** (+ acc) join in (Gespräch); meddle in (Angelegenheit) ● vi (haben) shuffle the cards. **M~ung** f -,-en mixture; blend

miserabel adj abominable

missachten vt disregard

Miss|achtung f disregard.
M~billigung f deformity

missbilligen vt disapprove of

Miss|billigung f disapproval.
M~brauch m abuse

missbrauchen vt abuse; (vergewaltigen) rape

Misserfolg m failure

Misse|tat f misdeed. **M~täter** m 🇮 culprit

missfallen† vi (haben) displease (jdm s.o.)

Miss|fallen nt -s displeasure; (Missbilligung) disapproval. **M~geburt** f freak; (fig) monstrosity. **M~geschick** nt mishap; (Unglück) misfortune

miss|glücken vi (sein) fail.
m~gönnen vt begrudge

misshandeln vt ill-treat

Misshandlung f ill-treatment

Mission f -,-en mission

Missionar(in) m -s,-e (f -,-nen) missionary

Missklang m discord

misslingen† vi (sein) fail; es misslang ihr she failed. **M~** nt -s failure

Missmut m ill humour. **m~ig** adj morose

missraten† vi (sein) turn

Miss|stand m abuse; (Zustand) undesirable state of affairs. **M~stimmung** f discord; (Laune) bad mood

misstrauen vi (haben) jdm/etw m~ mistrust s.o./sth; (Argwohn hegen) distrust s.o./sth

Misstrau|en nt -s mistrust; (Argwohn) distrust. **M~ensvotum** nt vote of no confidence. **m~isch** adj distrustful; (argwöhnisch) suspicious

Miss|verständnis nt misunderstanding. **m~verstehen**† vt misunderstand. **M~wirtschaft** f mismanagement

Mist m -[e]s manure; 🟦 rubbish

Mistel f -,-n mistletoe

Misthaufen m dungheap

mit prep (+ dat) with; (sprechen) to; (mittels) by; (inklusive) including; (bei) at; mit Bleistift in pencil; mit lauter Stimme in a loud voice; mit drei Jahren at the age of three ● adv (auch) as well; mit anfassen (fig) lend a hand

Mitarbeit f collaboration. **m~en** vi sep collaborate (an + dat on). **M~er(in)** m(f) collaborator; (Kollege) colleague; employee

Mitbestimmung f co-determination

mitbringen† vt sep bring [along]

miteinander adv with each other

Mitesser m (Med) blackhead

mitfahren† vi sep (sein) come along; mit jdm m~ go with s.o.; (mitgenommen werden) be given a lift by s.o.

mitfühlen vi sep (haben) sympathize

mitgeben† vt sep jdm etw m~ give s.o. sth to take with him

Mitgefühl nt sympathy

mitgehen† vi sep (sein) mit jdm m~ go with s.o.

Mitgift f -,-en dowry

Mitglied nt member. **M~schaft** f - membership

mithilfe prep (+ gen) with the aid of

Mithilfe f assistance

mitkommen† vi sep (sein) come [along] too; (fig: folgen können) keep up; (verstehen) follow

Mitlaut m consonant

Mitleid nt pity, compassion; **M~erregend** adj pitiful. **m~ig** adj pitying; (mitfühlend) compassionate. **m~slos** adj pitiless

mitmachen v sep ● vt take part in; (erleben) go through ● vi (haben) join in

Mitmensch m fellow man

mitnehmen† vt sep take along; (mitfahren lassen) give a lift to; (fig: schädigen) affect badly; (erschöpfen) exhaust; 'zum M~' 'to take away'

mitreden vi sep (haben) join in [the conversation]; (mit entscheiden) have a say (bei in)

mitreißen† vt sep sweep along; (fig: begeistern) carry away; **m~d** rousing

mitsamt prep (+ dat) together with

mitschreiben† vt sep (haben) take down

Mitschuld f partial blame. **m~ig** adj m~ig sein be partly to blame

Mitschüler(in) m(f) fellow pupil

mitspielen vi sep (haben) join in; (Theat) be in the cast; (beitragen) play a part

Mittag m midday, noon; (Mahlzeit) lunch; (Pause) lunch-break; heute/ gestern M~ at lunch-time today/ yesterday; [zu] M~ essen have lunch. **M~essen** nt lunch. **m~s** adv at noon; (als Mahlzeit) for lunch; **um 12 Uhr m~s** at noon. **M~spause** f lunch-hour; (Pause) lunch-break. **M~sschlaf** m afterlunch nap

Mittäter|(in) m(f) accomplice. **M~schaft** f - complicity

Mitte f -,-n middle; (Zentrum) centre; **die goldene M~** the golden mean; **M~ Mai** in mid-May; **in unserer M~** in our midst

mitteil|en vt sep jdm etw m~en tell s.o. sth; (amtlich) inform s.o. of sth. **M~ung** f -,-en communication; (Nachricht) piece of news

Mittel nt -s,- means sg; (Heil-) remedy; (Medikament) medicine; (M~wert) mean; (Durchschnitt) average; **m~pl** (Geld-) funds, resources. **m~** pred adj medium; (m~mäßig) middling. **M~alter** nt Middle Ages pl. **m~alterlich** adj medieval. **M~ding** nt (fig) cross. **m~europäisch** adj Central European. **M~finger** m middle finger. **m~los** adj destitute. **m~mäßig** adj middling; [nur] m~mäßig mediocre. **M~meer** nt Mediterranean. **M~punkt** m centre; (fig) centre of attention

mittels prep (+ gen) by means of
Mittel|schule f = Realschule. **M~smann** m (pl -männer) intermediary, go-between. **M~stand** m middle class. **M~ste(r,s)** adj middle. **M~streifen** m (Auto) central reservation. **M~stürmer** m centreforward. **M~welle** f medium wave. **M~wort** nt (pl -wörter) participle

mitten adv m~ in/auf (dat/acc) in the middle of. **m~durch** adv [right] through the middle

Mitternacht f midnight
mittler|e(r,s) adj middle; (Größe,

Qualität) medium; (durchschnittlich) mean, average. **m~weile** adv meanwhile; (seitdem) by now

Mittwoch m -s,-e Wednesday. **m~s** adv on Wednesdays

mitunter adv now and again
mitwirk|en vi sep (haben) take part; (helfen) contribute. **M~ung** f participation

mix|en vt mix. **M~er** m -s,- (Culin) liquidizer, blender

mobb|en vt bully, harass. **M~ing** nt -s bullying, harassment

Möbel pl furniture sg. **M~stück** nt piece of furniture. **M~wagen** m removal van

Mobiliar nt -s furniture
mobilisier|en vt mobilize. **M~ung** f - mobilization

Mobil|machung f - mobilization. **M~telefon** nt mobile phone

möblier|en vt furnish; **m~tes Zimmer** furnished room

möchte, möchte s. mögen
Mode f -,-n fashion; **M~ sein** be fashionable

Modell nt -s,-e model. **m~ieren** vt model

Modenschau f fashion show
Modera|tor m -s,-en, **M~torin** f -,-nen (TV) presenter

modern adj modern; (modisch) fashionable. **m~isieren** vt modernize

Mode|schmuck m costume jewellery. **M~schöpfer** m fashion designer

modisch adj fashionable
Modistin f -,-nen milliner
modrig adj musty
modulieren vt modulate
Mofa nt -s,-s moped
mogeln vi (haben) 🔲 cheat

mögenf

● *transitive verb*

‥‥▸ like. sie mag ihn sehr [gern] she likes him very much. möchten Sie ein Glas Wein? would you like a glass of wine? lieber mögen prefer. ich möchte lieber Tee I would prefer tea

● *auxiliary verb*

‥‥▸ (wollen) want to. sie mochte nicht länger bleiben she didn't want to stay any longer. ich möchte ihn [gerne] sprechen I'd like to speak to him. möchtest du nach Hause? do you want to go home? or would you like to go home?

‥‥▸ (Vermutung, Möglichkeit) may. ich mag irren I may be wrong. wer/was mag das sein? whoever/whatever can it be? [das] mag sein that may well be. mag kommen, was da will come what may

möglich adj possible; alle m~en all sorts of; über alles M~e sprechen talk about all sorts of things. m~erweise adv possibly. M~keit f -,-en possibility. M~keitsform f subjunctive. m~st adv if possible; m~st viel as much as possible

Mohammedan|er(in) m -s,- (f -,-nen) Muslim. m~isch adj Muslim

Mohn m -s poppy

Möhre, Mohrrübe f -,-n carrot

Mokka m -s mocha; (Geschmack) coffee

Molch m -[e]s,-e newt

Mole f -,-n (Naut) mole

Molekül nt -s,-e molecule

Molkerei f -,-en dairy

Moll nt - (Mus) minor

mollig adj cosy; (warm) warm; (rundlich) plump

Moment m -s,-e moment;

M~[mal]! just a moment! **m~an** adj momentary; (gegenwärtig) at the moment

Monarch m -en,-en monarch. M~ie f -,-n monarchy

Monat m -s,-e month. m~elang adv for months. m~lich adj & adv monthly

Mönch m -[e]s,-e monk

Mond m -[e]s,-e moon

mondän adj fashionable

Mond|finsternis f lunar eclipse. m~hell adj moonlit. M~sichel f crescent moon. M~schein m moonlight

monieren vt criticize

Monitor m -s,-en (Techn) monitor

Monogramm nt -s,-e monogram

Mono|log m -s,-e monologue. M~pol nt -s,-e monopoly. m~ton adj monotonous

Monster nt -s,- monster

Monstrum nt -s,-stren monster

Monsun m -s,-e monsoon

Montag m Monday

Montage /mɔnˈtaːʒə/ f -,-n fitting; (Zusammenbau) assembly; (Film-) editing; (Kunst) montage

montags adv on Mondays

Montanindustrie f coal and steel industry

Monteur /mɔnˈtøːɐ/ m -s,-e fitter. M~anzug m overalls pl

montieren vt fit; (zusammenbauen) assemble

Monument nt -[e]s,-e monument. m~al adj monumental

Moor nt -[e]s,-e bog; (Heide-) moor

Moos nt -es,-e moss. m~ig adj mossy

Moped nt -s,-s moped

Mopp m -s,-s mop

Moral f - morals pl, (Selbstvertrauen) morale; (Lehre) moral. **m~isch** adj moral

Mord m -[e]s,-e murder, (Pol) assassination. **M~anschlag** m murder/assassination attempt. **m~en** vt/i (haben) murder, kill

Mörder m -s,- murderer, (Pol) assassin. **M~in** f -,-nen murderess. **m~isch** adj murderous; (☐: schlimm) dreadful

morgen adv tomorrow; m~ Abend tomorrow evening

Morgen m -s,- morning; (Maß) ≈ acre; am M~ in the morning; heute/Montag M~ this/Monday morning. **M~dämmerung** f dawn. **M~rock** m dressing-gown. **M~rot** nt red sky in the morning. **m~s** adj in the morning

morgig adj tomorrow's; der m~e Tag tomorrow

Morphium nt -s morphine

morsch adj rotten

Morsealphabet nt Morse code

Mörtel m -s mortar

Mosaik /moza'i:k/ nt -s,-e[n] mosaic

Moschee f -,-n mosque

Mosel f - Moselle

Moskau nt -s Moscow

Moskito m -s,-s mosquito

Moslem m -s,-s Muslim

Motiv nt -s,-e motive; (Kunst) motif

Motor /'mo:tɔr, mo'to:ɐ/ m -s,-en engine; (Elektro-) motor. **M~boot** nt motor boat

motorisieren vt motorize

Motor|rad nt motor cycle. **M~roller** m motor scooter

Motte f -,-n moth. **M~nkugel** f mothball

Motto nt -s,-s motto

Möwe f -,-n gull

Mücke f -,-n gnat; (kleine) midge; (Stech-) mosquito

müd|e adj tired; es m~e sein to be tired (etw zu tun of doing sth). **M~igkeit** f - tiredness

muffig adj musty; (☐: mürrisch) grumpy

Mühe f -,-n effort; (Aufwand) trouble; sich (dat) M~ geben make an effort; (sich bemühen) try; nicht der M~ wert not worth while; mit M~ und Not with great difficulty; (gerade noch) only just. **m~los** adj effortless

muhen vi (haben) moo

Mühl|e f -,-n mill; (Kaffee-) grinder. **M~stein** m millstone

Müh|sal f -,-e (literarisch) toil; (Mühe) trouble. **m~sam** adj laborious; (beschwerlich) difficult

Mulde f -,-n hollow

Müll m -s refuse. **M~abfuhr** f refuse collection

Mullbinde f gauze bandage

Mülleimer m waste bin; (Mülltonne) dustbin

Müller m -s,- miller

Müll|halde f [rubbish] dump. **M~schlucker** m refuse chute. **M~tonne** f dustbin

multi|national adj multinational. **M~plikation** f -,-en multiplication. **m~plizieren** vt multiply

Mumie /'mu:miə/ f -,-n mummy

Mumm m -s ☐ energy

Mumps m - mumps

Mund m -[e]s,ᵉer mouth; ein M~ voll Suppe a mouthful of soup; halt den M~! ☒ shut up! **M~art** f dialect. **m~artlich** adj dialect

Mündel nt & m -s,- (Jur) ward. **m~sicher** adj gilt-edged

münden vi (sein) flow/(Straße:) lead (in + acc into)

Mundharmonika f
mouth-organ

mündig adj m~ sein/werden
(Jur) be/come of age. **M~keit** f
(Jur) majority

mündlich adj verbal; m~e
Prüfung oral

Mündung f -,-en (Fluss-) mouth;
(Gewehr-) muzzle

Mundwinkel m corner of
the mouth

Munition /-'tsjo:n/ f - ammunition

munkeln vt/i (haben) talk (von
of); es wird gemunkelt rumour has
it (dass that)

Münster nt -s,- cathedral

munter adj lively; (heiter) merry;
m~ sein (wach) be wide awake;
gesund und m~ fit and well

Münze f -,-n coin; (M~stätte)
mint. **M~fernsprecher** m
payphone

mürbe adj crumbly; (Obst) mellow;
(Fleisch) tender. **M~teig** m short
pastry

Murmel f -,-n marble

murmeln vt/i (haben) murmur;
(undeutlich) mumble

Murmeltier nt marmot

murren vt/i (haben) grumble

mürrisch adj surly

Mus nt -es purée

Muschel f -,-n mussel; [sea] shell

Museum /mu'ze:ʊm/ nt -s,-seen
museum

Musik f - music. **m~alisch** adj
musical

Musiker(in) m -s,- (f -,-nen)
musician

Musik|instrument nt musical
instrument. **M~kapelle** f band.
M~pavillon m bandstand

musisch adj artistic

musizieren vi (haben)
make music

Muskat m -[e]s nutmeg

Muskel m -s,-n muscle. **M~kater**
m stiff and aching muscles pl

muskulös adj muscular

muss s. müssen

Muße f - leisure

müßig adj idle

musste, müsste s. müssen

Muster nt -s,- pattern; (Probe)
sample; (Vorbild) model. **M~bei-
spiel** nt typical example; (Vorbild)
perfect example. **m~gültig,
m~haft** adj exemplary. **m~n** vt
eye; (inspizieren) inspect. **M~ung** f

-,-en inspection; (*Mil*) medical; (*Muster*) pattern

Mut *m* -[e]s courage; jdm Mut machen encourage s.o.; zu M~e sein feel like it; s. zumute

mut|ig *adj* courageous. **m~los** *adj* despondent

mutmaßen *vt* presume; (*Vermutungen anstellen*) speculate

Mutprobe *f* test of courage

Mutter[1] *f* -,⸚ mother

Mutter[2] *f* -,-n (*Techn*) nut

Muttergottes *f* - madonna

Mutterland *nt* motherland

mütterlich *adj* maternal; (*fürsorglich*) motherly. **m~erseits** *adv* on one's/the mother's side

Mutter|mal *nt* birthmark; (*dunkel*) mole. **M~schaft** *f* - motherhood. **m~seelenallein** *adj* & *adv* all alone. **M~sprache** *f* mother tongue. **M~tag** *m* Mother's Day

Mütze *f* -,-n cap; wollene M~ woolly hat

MwSt. *abbr* (Mehrwertsteuer) VAT

mysteriös *adj* mysterious

Mystik /ˈmʏstɪk/ *f* - mysticism

myth|isch *adj* mythical. **M~ologie** *f* - mythology

Nn

na *int* well; na gut all right then

Nabel *m* -s,- navel. **N~schnur** *f* umbilical cord

nach

● preposition (+ dative)

····▸ (*räumlich*) to. nach London fahren go to London. der Zug

nach München the train to Munich; (*noch nicht abgefahren*) the train for Munich; the Munich train. nach Hause gehen go home. nach Osten [zu] eastwards; towards the east

····▸ (*zeitlich*) after; (*Uhrzeit*) past. nach fünf Minuten/dem Frühstück after five minutes/breakfast. zehn [Minuten] nach zwei ten [minutes] past two

····▸ ([*räumliche und zeitliche*] *Reihenfolge*) after. nach Ihnen! after you!

····▸ (*mit bestimmten Verben*) for. greifen/streben/schicken nach grasp/strive/send for

····▸ (*gemäß*) according to. nach der neuesten Mode gekleidet dressed in [accordance with] the latest fashion. dem Gesetz nach in accordance with the law; by law. nach meiner Ansicht od Meinung, meiner Ansicht od Meinung nach in my view or opinion. nach etwas schmecken/riechen taste/smell of sth

● adverb

····▸ (*zeitlich*) nach und nach little by little; gradually. nach wie vor still

nachahm|en *vt sep* imitate. **N~ung** *f* -,-en imitation

Nachbar|(in) *m* -n,-n (*f* -,-nen) neighbour. **N~haus** *nt* house next door. **n~lich** *adj* neighbourly; (*Nachbar-*) neighbouring. **N~schaft** *f* - neighbourhood

nachbestell|en *vt sep* reorder. **N~ung** *f* repeat order

nachbild|en *vt sep* copy, reproduce. **N~ung** *f* copy, reproduction

nachdatieren *vt sep* backdate

nachdem *conj* after; je n~ it depends

nachdenk|en† vi sep (haben) think (über + acc about). **n~lich** adj thoughtful

nachdrücklich adj emphatic

nacheinander adv one after the other

Nachfahre m -n,-n descendant

Nachfolg|e f succession. **N~er(in)** m -s,- (f -,-nen) successor

nachforsch|en vi sep (haben) make enquiries. **N~ung** f enquiry

Nachfrage f (Comm) demand. **n~n** vi sep (haben) enquire

nachfüllen vt sep refill

nachgeben† v sep ● vi (haben) give way: (sich fügen) give in, yield ● vt jdm Suppe n~ give s.o. more soup

Nachgebühr f surcharge

nachgehen† vi sep (sein) (Uhr:) be slow; jdm/etw n~ follow s.o./ something; follow up (Spur, Angelegenheit); pursue (Angelegenheit)

Nachgeschmack m after-taste

nachgiebig adj indulgent; (gefällig) compliant. **N~keit** f - indulgence; compliance

nachgrübeln vi sep (haben) ponder (über + acc on)

nachhaltig adj lasting

nachhelfen† vi sep (haben) help

nachher adv later; (danach) afterwards; bis n~! see you later!

Nachhilfeunterricht m coaching

Nachhinein adv im N~ afterwards

nachhinken vi sep (sein) (fig) lag behind

nachholen vt sep (später holen) fetch later; (mehr holen) get more; (später machen) do later; (aufholen) catch up on

Nachkomme m -n,-n descendant. **n~n**† vi sep (sein) follow [later], come later; etw (dat) n~n (fig) comply with (Bitte); carry out (Pflicht). **N~nschaft** f - descendants pl, progeny

Nachkriegszeit f post-war period

Nachlass m -es,-̈e discount; (Jur) [deceased's] estate

nachlassen† v sep ● vi (haben) decrease; (Regen, Hitze:) let up; (Schmerz:) ease; (Sturm:) abate; (Augen, Leistungen:) deteriorate ● vt etw vom Preis n~ take sth off the price

nachlässig adj careless; (leger) casual; (unordentlich) sloppy. **N~kt** f - carelessness; sloppiness

nachlesen† vt sep look up

nachlöse|n vt sep (haben) pay one's fare on the train/on arrival. **N~schalter** m excess-fare office

nachmachen vt sep (später machen) do later; (imitieren) imitate, copy; (fälschen) forge

Nachmittag m afternoon; heute/ gestern N~ this/yesterday afternoon. **n~s** adv in the afternoon

Nachnahme f etw per N~ schicken send sth cash on delivery or COD

Nachname m surname

Nachporto nt excess postage

nachprüfen vt sep check, verify

Nachricht f -,-en [piece of] news sg; **N~en** news sg; eine N~ hinterlassen leave a message; jdm N~ geben inform s.o. **N~endienst** m (Mil) intelligence service

nachrücken vi sep (sein) move up

Nachruf m obituary

nachsagen vt sep repeat (jdm after s.o.); jdm Schlechtes/Gutes n~ speak ill/well of s.o.

Nachsaison f late season
nachschicken vt sep (später schicken) send later; (hinterher-) send after (jdm s.o.); send on (Post) (jdm to s.o.)

nachschlagen† v sep ●vt look up ●vi (haben) in einem Wörterbuch n∼en consult a dictionary; jdm n∼en take after s.o.

Nachschrift f transcript; (Nachsatz) postscript

Nachschub m (Mil) supplies pl

nachsehen† v sep ●vt (prüfen) check; (nachschlagen) look up; (hinwegsehen über) overlook ●vi (haben) have a look; (prüfen) check; im Wörterbuch n∼ consult a dictionary

nachsenden† vt sep forward (Post) (jdm to s.o.); 'bitte n∼' 'please forward'

nachsichtig adj forbearing; lenient; indulgent

Nachsilbe f suffix

nachsitzen† vi sep (haben) n∼ müssen be kept in [after school]; jdn n∼ lassen give s.o. detention. N∼ nt -s (Sch) detention

Nachspeise f dessert, sweet
nachsprechen† vt sep repeat (jdm after s.o.)

nachspülen vt sep rinse

nächst /-çst/ prep (+ dat) next to. n∼beste(r,s) adj first [available]; (zweitbeste) next best. n∼e(r,s) adj next; (nächstgelegene) nearest; (Verwandte) closest; in n∼er Nähe close by; am n∼en sein be nearest or closest ●pron der/die/das N∼e (n∼e) the next; den N∼en (n∼e) bitte next please; als N∼es (n∼es) next; fürs n∼e (n∼e) for the time being. N∼e(r) m fellow man

nachstehend adj following
●adv below

Nächst|enliebe f charity. n∼ens adv shortly. n∼gelegen adj nearest
nachsuchen vi sep (haben) search; n∼ um request

Nacht f -,∸e night; über/bei N∼ overnight/at night; morgen N∼ tomorrow night; heute N∼ tonight; (letzte Nacht) last night; gestern N∼ last night; (vorletzte Nacht) the night before last. N∼dienst m night duty

Nachteil m disadvantage; zum N∼ to the detriment (gen of)

Nacht|falter m moth. N∼hemd nt night-dress; (Männer-) night-shirt
Nachtigall f -,-en nightingale
Nachtisch m dessert
Nachtklub m night-club
nächtlich adj nocturnal, night
Nacht|lokal nt night-club. N∼mahl nt (Aust) supper

Nachtrag m postscript; (Ergänzung) supplement. n∼en† vt sep add; jdm etw n∼en (fig) bear a grudge against s.o. for sth. n∼end adj vindictive; n∼end sein bear grudges

nachträglich adj subsequent, later; (verspätet) belated ●adv later; (nachher) afterwards; (verspätet) belatedly

Nacht|ruhe f night's rest; angenehme N∼ruhe! sleep well! n∼s adv at night; 2 Uhr n∼s 2 o'clock in the morning. N∼schicht f night-shift. N∼tisch m bedside table. N∼tischlampe f bedside lamp. N∼topf m chamber-pot. N∼wächter m night-watchman. N∼zeit f night-time

Nachuntersuchung f check-up
Nachwahl f by-election
Nachweis m -es,-e proof. n∼bar adj demonstrable. n∼en† vt sep prove; (aufzeigen) show; (vermitteln)

give details of; jdm nichts n~en können have no proof against s.o.

Nachwelt f posterity

Nachwirkung f after-effect

Nachwuchs m new generation; (ⓘ: *Kinder*) offspring. **N~spieler** m young player

nachzahlen vt/i sep (haben) pay extra; (*später zahlen*) pay later; Steuern n~ pay tax arrears

nachzählen vt/i sep (haben) count again; (*prüfen*) check

Nachzahlung f extra/later payment; (*Gehalts-*) back-payment

nachzeichnen vt sep copy

Nachzügler m -s,- late-comer; (*Zurückgebliebener*) straggler

Nacken m -s,- nape or back of the neck

nackt adj naked; (*bloß, kahl*) bare; (*Wahrheit*) plain. **N~heit** f - nakedness, nudity. **N~kultur** f nudism. **N~schnecke** f slug

Nadel f -,-n needle; (*Häkel-*) hook; (*Schmuck-, Hut-*) pin. **N~arbeit** f needlework. **N~baum** m conifer. **N~stich** m stitch; (*fig*) pinprick. **N~wald** m coniferous forest

Nagel m -,= nail. **N~haut** f cuticle. **N~lack** m nail varnish. **n~n** vt nail. **n~neu** adj brand-new

nagen vt/i (haben) gnaw (an + dat at); **n~d** (fig) nagging

Nagetier nt rodent

nah adj, adv & prep = nahe

Näharbeit f sewing

Nahaufnahme f close-up

nahe adj nearby; (*zeitlich*) imminent; (*eng*) close; der N~ Osten the Middle East; in n~r Zukunft in the near future; von n~m [from] close to; n~ sein be close (dat to) ● prep near, close; (*verwandt*) closely; n~ an (+ acc/dat) near [to], close to; n~ daran sein, etw zu tun

nearly do sth; n~ liegen be close; (fig) be highly likely; n~ legen (fig) recommend (dat to); jdm n~ legen, etw zu tun urge s.o. to do sth; jdm n~ gehen (fig) affect s.o. deeply; jdm zu n~ treten (fig) offend s.o. ● prep (+ dat) near [to], close to

Nähe f - nearness, proximity; aus der N~ [from] close to; in der N~ near or close by

nahe|gehen* vi sep (sein) n~gehen, s. nahe. **n~legen*** vt sep n~ legen, s. nahe. **n~liegen*** vi sep (haben) n~ liegen, s. nahe

nähen vt/i (haben) sew; (*anfertigen*) make; (*Med*) stitch [up]

näher adj closer; (*Weg*) shorter; (*Einzelheiten*) further ● adv closer; (*genauer*) more closely; n~ kommen come closer; (fig) get closer (dat to); sich n~ erkundigen make further enquiries; n~an (+ acc/dat) nearer [to], closer to ● prep (+ dat) nearer [to], closer to. **N~e[s]** nt [further] details pl. **n~n** (sich) vr approach

nahezu adv almost

Nähgarn nt [sewing] cotton

Nahkampf m close combat

Näh|maschine f sewing machine. **N~nadel** f sewing-needle

nähren vt feed; (fig) nurture

nahrhaft adj nutritious

Nährstoff m nutrient

Nahrung f - food, nourishment. **N~smittel** nt food

Nährwert m nutritional value

Naht f -,=e seam; (*Med*) suture. **n~los** adj seamless

Nahverkehr m local service

Nähzeug nt sewing; (*Zubehör*) sewing kit

naiv /naˈiːf/ adj naïve. **N~ität** f - naïvety

Name m -ns,-n name; im N~n (+ gen) in the name of; (handeln) on behalf of. **n~los** adj nameless; (unbekannt) unknown, anonymous. **N~nstag** m name-day. **N~nsvetter** m namesake. **N~nszug** m signature. **n~ntlich** adv by name; (besonders) especially

namhaft adj noted; (ansehnlich) considerable; n~ machen name

nämlich adv (und zwar) namely; (denn) because

Nanotechnologie f nanotechnology

nanu int hallo

Napf m -[e]s,⸚e bowl

Narbe f -,-n scar

Narkose f -,-n general anaesthetic. **N~arzt** m anaesthetist. **N~mittel** nt anaesthetic

Narr m -en,-en fool; zum N~en halten make a fool of. **n~en** vt fool

Närr|in f -,-nen fool. **n~isch** adj foolish; (fig: verrückt) crazy (auf + acc about)

Narzisse f -,-n narcissus

naschen vt/i (haben) nibble (an + dat at)

Nase f -,-n nose

näseln vi (haben) speak through one's nose; n~d nasal

Nasen|bluten nt -s nosebleed. **N~loch** nt nostril

Nashorn nt rhinoceros

nass adj wet

Nässe f - wet; wetness. **n~n** vt wet

Nation /natsi̯oːn/ f -,-en nation. **n~al** adj national. **N~alhymne** f national anthem. **N~alismus** m - nationalism. **N~alität** f -,-en nationality. **N~alspieler** m international

Nationalrat In Austria the Nationalrat is the Federal Assembly's lower house, whose 183 members are elected for four years under a system of proportional representation. In Switzerland, the Nationalrat is made up of 200 representatives.

Natrium nt -s sodium

Natron nt -s doppeltkohlensaures N~ bicarbonate of soda

Natter f -,-n snake; (Gift-) viper

Natur f -,-n nature; von N~ aus by nature. **n~alisieren** vt naturalize. **N~alisierung** f -,-en naturalization

Naturell nt -s,-e disposition

Natur|erscheinung f natural phenomenon. **N~forscher** m naturalist. **N~heilkunde** f natural medicine. **N~kunde** f natural history

natürlich adj natural ●adv naturally; (selbstverständlich) of course. **N~keit** f - naturalness

natur|rein adj pure. **N~schutz** m nature conservation; unter N~schutz stehen be protected. **N~schutzgebiet** nt nature reserve. **N~wissenschaft** f [natural] science. **N~wissenschaftler** m scientist

nautisch adj nautical

Navigation /-'tsi̯oːn/ f - navigation

Nazi m -s,-s Nazi

n.Chr. abbr (nach Christus) AD

Nebel m -s,- fog; (leicht) mist

neben prep (+ dat/acc) next to, beside; (+ dat) (außer) apart from. **n~an** adv next door

Neben|anschluss m (Teleph) extension. **N~ausgaben** fpl incidental expenses

nebenbei adv in addition; (*beiläufig*) casually

Neben|bemerkung f passing remark. **N~beruf** m second job

nebeneinander adv next to each other, side by side

Neben|eingang m side entrance. **N~fach** nt (*Univ*) subsidiary subject. **N~fluss** m tributary

nebenher adv in addition

nebenhin adv casually

Neben|höhle f sinus. **N~kosten** pl additional costs. **N~produkt** nt by-product. **N~rolle** f supporting role; (*Kleine*) minor role. **N~sache** f unimportant matter. **n~sächlich** adj unimportant. **N~satz** m subordinate clause. **N~straße** f minor road; (*Seiten-*) side street. **N~wirkung** f side-effect. **N~zimmer** nt room next door

neblig adj foggy; (*leicht*) misty

neck|en vt tease. **N~erei** f - teasing. **n~isch** adj teasing

Neffe m -n,-n nephew

negativ adj negative. **N~** nt -s,-e (*Phot*) negative

Neger m -s,- Negro

nehmen† vt take (*dat* from); sich (*dat*) etw n~ take sth; help oneself to (*Essen*)

Neid m -[e]s envy, jealousy. **n~isch** adj envious, jealous (*auf* + *acc* of); **auf jdn n~isch sein** envy s.o.

neig|en vt incline; (*zur Seite*) tilt; (*beugen*) bend; sich n~en incline; (*Boden:*) slope; (*Person:*) bend (*über* + *acc* over) ● vi (*haben*) n~en zu (*fig*) have a tendency towards; be prone to (*Krankheit*); incline towards (*Ansicht*); **dazu n~en, etw zu tun** tend to do sth. **N~ung** f -,-en inclination; (*Gefälle*) slope; (*fig*) tendency

nein adv, **N~** nt -s no

Nektar m -s nectar

Nelke f -,-n carnation; (*Culin*) clove

nenn|en† vt call; (*taufen*) name; (*angeben*) give; (*erwähnen*) mention; sich n~en call oneself. **n~enswert** adj significant

Neon nt -s neon. **N~beleuchtung** f fluorescent lighting

Nerv m -s,-en nerve; **die N~en verlieren** lose control of oneself. **n~en** vt jdn n~en ⊠ get on s.o.'s nerves. **N~enarzt** m neurologist. **n~enaufreibend** adj nerve-racking. **N~enkitzel** m ⊡ thrill. **N~ensystem** nt nervous system. **N~enzusammenbruch** m nervous breakdown

nervös adj nervy, edgy; (*Med*) nervous; n~ sein be on edge

Nervosität f - nerviness, edginess

Nerz m -es,-e mink

Nessel f -,-n nettle

Nest nt -[e]s,-er nest; (⊡: *Ort*) small place

nett adj nice; (*freundlich*) kind

netto adv net

Netz nt -es,-e net; (*Einkaufs-*) string bag; (*Spinnen-*) web; (*auf Landkarte*) grid; (*System*) network; (*Electr*) mains pl. **N~haut** f retina. **N~karte** f area season ticket. **N~werk** nt network

neu adj new; (*modern*) modern; **wie neu** as good as new; **das ist mir neu** it's news to me; **von n~em** all over again ● adv newly; (*gerade erst*) only just; (*erneut*) again; **etw neu schreiben** rewrite sth; **neu vermähltes Paar** newly-weds pl. **N~auflage** f new edition; (*unveränder*) reprint. **N~bau** m (pl -ten) new house/building

Neu|e(r) m/f new person, newcomer; (*Schüler*) new boy/girl.

N~e(s) nt das N~e the new; etwas N~es something new; (Neuigkeit) a piece of news; was gibt's N~es? what's the news?

neuerdings adv [just] recently

neuest|e(r,s) adj newest; (letzte) latest; seit n~em just recently. N~e nt das N~e the latest thing: (Neuigkeit) the latest news sg

neugeboren adj newborn

Neugier, Neugierde f - curiosity; (Wissbegierde) inquisitiveness

neugierig adj curious (auf + acc about); (wissbegierig) inquisitive

Neuheit f -,-en novelty; newness

Neuigkeit f -,-en piece of news; N~en news sg

Neujahr nt New Year's Day; über N~ over the New Year

neulich adv the other day

Neumond m new moon

neun inv adj, N~ f -,-en nine. n~te(r,s) adj ninth. n~zehn inv adj nineteen. n~zehnte(r,s) adj nineteenth. n~zig inv adj ninety. n~zigste(r,s) adj ninetieth

Neuralgie f -,-n neuralgia

neureich adj nouveau riche

Neurologe m -n,-n neurologist

Neurose f -,-n neurosis

Neuschnee m fresh snow

Neuseeland nt -s New Zealand

neuste(r,s) adj = neueste(r,s)

neutral adj neutral. N~ität f - neutrality

Neutrum nt -s,-tra neuter noun

neu|vermählt† adj newly married, s. neu. N~zeit f modern times pl

nicht adv not; ich kann n~ I cannot or can't; er ist n~ gekommen he hasn't come; bitte n~! please don't! n~ berühren! do not touch! du kennst ihn doch, n~? you do

know him, don't you?

Nichte f -,-n niece

Nichtraucher m non-smoker

nichts pron & a nothing; n~ mehr no more; n~ ahnend unsuspecting; n~ sagend meaningless; (uninteressant) nondescript. N~ nt - nothingness; (fig: Leere) void

Nichtschwimmer m non-swimmer

nichts|nutzig adj good-for-nothing; ([T]: unartig) naughty. n~sagend* adj n~ sagend, s. nichts. N~tun nt -s idleness

Nickel nt -s nickel

nicken vi (haben) nod

Nickerchen nt -s,-, [T] nap

nie adv never

nieder adj low ● adv down. n~brennen vt/i sep (sein) burn down. N~deutsch nt Low German. N~gang m (fig) decline. n~gedrückt adj (fig) depressed. n~schlagen adj dejected, despondent. N~kunft f -,⁀e confinement. N~lage f defeat

Niederlande (die) pl the Netherlands

Niederländ|er m -s,- Dutchman; die N~er the Dutch pl. N~erin f -,-nen Dutchwoman. n~isch adj Dutch

nieder|lassen† vt sep let down; sich n~lassen settle; (sich setzen) sit down. N~lassung f -,-en settlement; (Zweigstelle) branch. n~legen vt sep put or lay down; resign (Amt); die Arbeit n~legen go on strike. n~metzeln vt sep massacre. N~sachsen nt Lower Saxony. N~schlag m precipitation; (Regen) rainfall; (radioaktiver) fallout. n~schlagen† vt sep knock down; lower (Augen); (unterdrücken) crush. n~schmettern vt sep (fig) shatter.

n~setzen vt sep put or set down; sich n~setzen sit down. **n~strecken** vt sep fell; (durch Schuss) gun down. **n~trächtig** adj base, vile. **n~walzen** vt sep flatten

niedlich adj pretty; sweet

niedrig adj low; (fig: gemein) base ● adv low

niemals adv never

niemand pron nobody, no one

Niere f -,-n kidney; künstliche N~ kidney machine

niesel|n vi (haben) drizzle. **N~regen** m drizzle

niesen vi (haben) sneeze. **N~** nt -s sneezing; (Nieser) sneeze

Niete[1] f -,-n rivet; (an Jeans) stud

Niete[2] f -,-n blank; ⊤ failure

nieten vt rivet

Nikotin nt -s nicotine

Nil m -[s] Nile. **N~pferd** nt hippopotamus

nimmer adv (SGer) not any more; nie und n~ never

nirgend|s, n~wo adv nowhere

Nische f -,-n recess, niche

nisten vi (haben) nest

Nitrat nt -[e]s,-e nitrate

Niveau /ni'voː/ nt -s,-s level; (geistig, künstlerisch) standard

nix adv ⊤ nothing

Nixe f -,-n mermaid

nobel adj noble; (⊤: luxuriös) luxurious; (⊤: großzügig) generous

noch adv still; (zusätzlich) in addition; (mit Komparativ) even; n~ nicht not yet; gerade n~ only just; n~ immer od immer n~ still; n~ letzte Woche only last week; wer n~? who else? n~ etwas something else; (Frage) anything else? n~ einmal again; n~ ein Bier another beer; n~ größer even bigger; n~ so sehr however much

● conj weder n~ ... neither nor ...

nochmals adv again

Nomad|e m -n,-n nomad. **n~isch** adj nomadic

nominier|en vt nominate. **N~ung** f -,-en nomination

Nonne f -,-n nun. **N~nkloster** nt convent

Nonstopflug m direct flight

Nord m -[e]s north. **N~amerika** nt North America

Norden m -s north

nordisch adj Nordic

nördlich adj northern; (Richtung) northerly ● adv & prep (+ gen) n~ [von] der Stadt [to the] north of the town

Nordosten m north-east

Nord|pol m North Pole. **N~see** f - North Sea. **N~westen** m north-west

Nörgelei f -,-en grumbling

nörgeln vi (haben) grumble

Norm f -,-en norm; (Techn) standard; (Soll) quota

normal adj normal. **n~erweise** adv normally

normen vt standardize

Norwegen nt -s Norway. **N~ger(in)** m -s,- (f -,-nen) Norwegian. **n~gisch** adj Norwegian

Nost|algie f - nostalgia. **n~algisch** adj nostalgic

Not f -,-ᵉe need; (Notwendigkeit) necessity; (Entbehrung) hardship; (seelisch) trouble; Not leiden be in need, suffer hardship; Not leidende Menschen needy people; zur Not if need be; (äußerstenfalls) at a pinch

Notar m -s,-e notary public

Not|arzt m emergency doctor. **N~ausgang** m emergency exit. **N~behelf** m -[e]s,-e makeshift. **N~bremse** f emergency brake.

n

N~dienst m N~dienst haben be on call

Note f -,-n note; (Zensur) mark; ganze/halbe N~ (Mus) semi-breve/minim; N~n lesen read music; persönliche N~ personal touch. **N~nblatt** nt sheet of music. **N~nschlüssel** m clef

Notfall m emergency; für den N~ just in case. N~ if need be

notieren vt note down; (Comm) quote; sich (dat) etw n~ make a note of sth

nötig adj necessary; n~ haben need; das N~ste the essentials pl ● adv urgently. **N~enfalls** adv if need be. **N~ung** f - coercion

Notiz f -,-en note; (Zeitungs-) item; [keine] N~ nehmen von take [no] notice of. **N~buch** nt notebook. **N~kalender** m diary

Not|lage f plight. **n~landen** vi (sein) make a forced landing. **N~landung** f forced landing. **n~leidend*** adj Not leidend, s. Not. **N~lösung** f stopgap

Not|ruf m emergency call; (Naut, Aviat) distress call; (Nummer) emergency services number. **N~signal** nt distress signal. **N~stand** m state of emergency. **N~unterkunft** f emergency accommodation. **N~wehr** f - (Jur) self-defence

notwendig adj necessary; essential ● adv urgently. **N~keit** f -,-en necessity

Notzucht f - (Jur) rape

Nougat /'nu:gat/ m & nt -s nougat

Novelle f -,-n novella; (Pol) amendment

November m -s,- November

Novize m -n,-n, **Novizin** f -,-nen (Relig) novice

Nu m im Nu ⚡ in a flash

nüchtern adj sober; (sachlich)

matter-of-fact; (schmucklos) bare; (ohne Würze) bland; auf n~en Magen on an empty stomach

Nudel f -,-n piece of pasta; N~n pasta sg; (Band-) noodles. **N~holz** nt rolling-pin

Nudist m -en,-en nudist

nuklear adj nuclear

null inv adj zero, nought; (Teleph) O; (Sport) nil; (Tennis) love; n~ Fehler no mistakes; n~ und nichtig (Jur) null and void. **N~** f -,-en nought, zero; (fig: Person) nonentity. **N~punkt** m zero

numerieren* vt = nummerieren

Nummer f -,-n number; (Ausgabe) issue; (Darbietung) item; (Zirkus-) act; (Größe) size. **n~ieren** vt number. **N~nschild** nt number-plate

nun adv now; (na) well; (halt) just; nun gut! very well then!

nur adv only, just; wo kann sie nur sein? wherever can she be? er soll es nur versuchen! just let him try!

Nürnberg nt -s Nuremberg

nuscheln vt/i (haben) mumble

Nuss f -,⁼e nut. **N~knacker** m -s,- nutcrackers pl

Nüstern fpl nostrils

Nut f -,-en, **Nute** f -,-n groove

Nutte f -,-n tart ⚡

nutz|bar adj usable; n~bar machen utilize; cultivate (Boden). **n~bringend** adj profitable

nutzen vt use, utilize; (aus-) take advantage of ● vi (haben) = nützen. **N~** m -s benefit; (Comm) profit; N~ ziehen aus benefit from; von N~ sein be useful

nützen vi (haben) be useful or of use (dat to); (Mittel:) be effective; nichts n~ be useless or no use; was nützt mir das? what good is that to me? ● vt = nutzen

nützlich adj useful. **N~keit** f -

usefulness

nutz|los adj useless; (vergeblich) vain. **N~losigkeit** f - uselessness. **N~ung** f - use, utilization

Nylon /ˈnaɪlɔn/ nt -s nylon

Nymphe /ˈnʏmfə/ f -,-n nymph

Oo

o int o ja/nein! oh yes/no!

Oase f -,-n oasis

ob conj whether; ob reich, ob arm rich or poor; und ob! 🗉 you bet!

Obacht f O~ geben pay attention; O~! look out!

Obdach nt -[e]s shelter. **o~los** adj homeless. **O~lose(r)** m/f homeless person; **die O~losen** the homeless pl

Obduktion /-ˈtsioːn/ f -,-en post-mortem

O-Beine ntpl 🗉 bow-legs, bandy legs

oben adv at the top; (auf der Oberseite) on top; (eine Treppe hoch) upstairs; (im Text) above; **da o~** up there; **o~ im Norden** up in the north; **siehe o~** see above; **nach o~** auf (+ acc/dat) on top of; **nach o~** up[wards]; (die Treppe hinauf) upstairs; **von o~** from above/upstairs; **von o~ bis unten** from top to bottom/(Person) to toe; **jdn von o~ bis unten mustern** look s.o. up and down; **o~ erwähnt** od genannt above-mentioned. **o~drein** adv on top of that

Ober m -s,- waiter

Ober|arm m upper arm. **O~arzt** m ≈ senior registrar. **O~deck** nt

upper deck. **o~e(r,s)** adj upper; (höhere) higher. **O~fläche** f surface. **o~flächlich** adj superficial. **O~geschoss** nt upper storey. **o~halb** adv & prep (+ gen) above. **O~haupt** nt (fig) head. **O~haus** nt (Pol) upper house; (in UK) House of Lords. **O~hemd** nt [man's] shirt. **o~irdisch ●** adv above ground. **O~kiefer** m upper jaw. **O~körper** m upper part of the body. **O~leutnant** m lieutenant. **O~lippe** f upper lip

Obers nt - (Aust) cream

Ober|schenkel m thigh. **O~schule** f grammar school. **O~seite** f upper/(rechte Seite) right side

Oberst m -en & -s,-en colonel

oberste(r,s) adj top; (höchste) highest; (Befehlshaber, Gerichtshof) supreme; (wichtigste) first

Ober|stimme f treble. **O~teil** nt top. **O~weite** f chest/(der Frau) bust size

obgleich conj although

Obhut f - care

obig adj above

Objekt nt -[e]s,-e object; (Haus, Grundstück) property

Objektiv nt -s,-e lens. **o~** adj objective. **O~ität** f - objectivity

Oblate f -,-n (Relig) wafer

Obmann m (pl -männer) [jury] foreman; (Sport) referee

Oboe /oˈboːə/ f -,-n oboe

Obrigkeit f - authorities pl

obschon conj although

Observatorium nt -s,-ien observatory

obskur adj obscure; dubious

Obst nt -es (coll) fruit. **O~baum** m fruit-tree. **O~garten** m orchard. **O~händler** m fruiterer

n

o

obszön adj obscene

O-Bus m trolley bus

obwohl conj although

Ochse m -n,-n ox

öde adj desolate; (unfruchtbar) barren; (langweilig) dull. **Öde** f - desolation; barrenness; dullness

oder conj or; du kennst ihn doch, o~? you know him, don't you?

Ofen m -s, = stove; (Heiz-) heater; (Back-) oven; (Techn) furnace

offen adj open; (Haar) loose; (Flamme) naked; (o~herzig) frank; (o~ gezeigt) overt; (unentschieden) unsettled; o~ Stelle vacancy; Wein o~ verkaufen sell wine by the glass; o~ bleiben remain open; o~ halten hold open (Tür); keep open (Mund, Augen); o~ lassen leave open; leave vacant (Stelle); o~ stehen be open; (Rechnung:) be outstanding; jdm o~ stehen (fig) be open to s.o.; adv o~ gesagt od gestanden to be honest. **o~bar** adj obvious ● adv apparently. **o~baren** vt reveal. **O~barung** f -,-en revelation. **O~heit** f -, frankness, openness. **o~sichtlich** adj obvious

offenstehen* vi sep (haben) offen stehen, s. offen

öffentlich adj public. **Ö~keit** f - public; in aller Ö~keit in public, publicly

Offerte f -,-n (Comm) offer

offiziell adj official

Offizier m -s,-e (Mil) officer

öffn|en vt/i (haben) open; sich ö~en open. **Ö~er** m -s,- opener. **Ö~ung** f -,-en opening. **Ö~ungszeiten** fpl opening hours

oft adv often

öfter adv quite often. **ö~e(r,s)** adj frequent; des Ö~en (ö~en) frequently. **ö~s** adv 🆅 quite often

oh int oh!

ohne prep (+ acc) without; o~ mich! count me out! oben o~ topless ● conj so zu überlegen without thinking; o~ dass ich es merkte he did it without my noticing it. **o~dies** adv anyway. **o~gleichen** pred adj unparalleled. **o~hin** adv anyway

Ohn|macht f -,-en faint; (fig) powerlessness; in O~macht fallen faint. **o~mächtig** adj unconscious; (fig) powerless; o~mächtig werden faint

Ohr nt -[e]s,-en ear

Öhr nt -[e]s,-e eye (of needle)

Ohrenschmalz nt ear-wax. **O~schmerzen** mpl earache sg

Ohrfeige f slap in the face. **o~n** vt jdn o~n slap s.o.'s face

Ohr|läppchen nt -s,- ear-lobe. **O~ring** m ear-ring. **O~wurm** m earwig

oje int oh dear!

okay /o'ke:/ adj & adv 🆅 OK

Öko|logie f - ecology. **ö~logisch** adj ecological. **Ö~nomie** f - economy; (Wissenschaft) economics sg. **ö~nomisch** adj economic; (sparsam) economical

Oktave f -,-n octave

Oktober m -s,- October

> **Oktoberfest** Germany's biggest beer festival and funfair, which takes place every year in Munich. Over 16 days more than 5 million litres of beer are drunk in marquees erected by the major breweries. The festival goes back to 1810, when a horse race was held to celebrate the wedding of Ludwig, Crown Prince of Bavaria.

ökumenisch adj ecumenical

Öl nt -[e]s,-e oil; in Öl malen paint

in oils. **Ölbaum** m olivetree. **ölen** vt oil. **Ölfarbe** f oil-paint. **Ölfeld** nt oilfield. **Ölgemälde** nt oil-painting. **ölig** adj oily

Oliv|e f -,-n olive. **O~enöl** nt olive oil

Ölmessstab m dip-stick. **Ölsardinen** fpl sardines in oil. **Ölstand** m oil-level. **Öltanker** m oil-tanker. **Ölteppich** m oil-slick

Olympiade f -,-n Olympic Games pl

Olymp|iasieger(in) /o'lympia-/ m(f) Olympic champion. **o~isch** adj Olympic; **O~ische Spiele** Olympic Games

Ölzeug nt oilskins pl

Oma f -,-s 🔲 granny

Omnibus m bus; (Reise-) coach

onanieren vi (haben) masturbate

Onkel m -s,- uncle

Online-Tagebuch nt blog

Opa m -s,-s 🔲 grandad

Opal m -s,-e opal

Oper f -,-n opera

Operation /-'tsio:n/ f -,-en operation. **O~ssaal** m operating theatre

Operette f -,-n operetta

operieren vt operate on (Patient, Herz); **sich o~ lassen** have an operation ● vi (haben) operate

Opernglas nt opera-glasses pl

Opfer nt -s,- sacrifice; (eines Unglücks) victim; **ein O~ bringen** make a sacrifice; **jdm etw zum O~ fallen** fall victim to s.o./something. **o~n** vt sacrifice

Opium nt -s opium

Opposition /-'tsio:n/ f - opposition. **O~spartei** f opposition party

Optik f - optics sg, (🔲: Objektiv) lens. **O~er** m -s,- optician

optimal adj optimum

Optimi|smus m - optimism. **O~t** m -en,-en optimist. **o~tisch**

adj optimistic

optisch adj optical; (Eindruck) visual

Orakel nt -s,- oracle

Orange /o'rã:ʒə/ f -,-n orange. **o~** inv adj orange. **O~ade** f -,-n orangeade. **O~nmarmelade** f [orange] marmalade

Oratorium nt -s,-ien oratorio

Orchester /ɔr'kɛstə/ nt -s,- orchestra

Orchidee /ɔrçi'de:ə/ f -,-n orchid

Orden m -s,- (Ritter-, Kloster-) order; (Auszeichnung) medal, decoration

ordentlich adj neat. tidy; (anständig) respectable; (ordnungsgemäß, fam: richtig) proper; (Mitglied, Versammlung) ordinary; (🔲: gut) decent; (🔲: gehörig) good

Order f -,-s & -n order

ordinär adj common

Ordination /-'tsio:n/ f -,-en (Relig) ordination; (Aust) surgery

ordn|en vt put in order; tidy; (anarrange. **O~er** m -s,- steward; (Akten-) file

Ordnung f - order; **O~ machen** tidy up; **in O~ bringen** put in order; (aufräumen) tidy; (reparieren) mend; (fig) put right; **in O~ sein** be in order; (ordentlich sein) be tidy; (fig) be all right; [geht] in O~! OK! **o~sgemäß** adj proper. **O~sstrafe** f (Jur) fine. **o~swidrig** adj improper

Ordonnanz. Ordonanz f -,-en (Mil) orderly

Organ nt -s,-e organ; voice

Organisation /-'tsio:n/ f -,-en organization

organisch adj organic

organisieren vt organize; (🔲: beschaffen) get [hold of]

o

Organismus m -,-men organism; (*System*) system

Organspenderkarte f donor card

Orgasmus m -,-men orgasm

Orgel f -,-n (*Mus*) organ. **O~pfeife** f organ-pipe

Orgie /ˈɔrgiə/ f -,-n orgy

Orient /ˈoːriɛnt/ m -s Orient. **o~talisch** adj Oriental

orientier|en /oriɛnˈtiːrən/ vt inform (über + acc about); sich **o~en** get one's bearings, orientate oneself; (*unterrichten*) inform oneself (über + acc about). **O~ung** f - orientation; die **O~ung** verlieren lose one's bearings

original adj original. **O~** nt -s,-e original. **O~übertragung** f live transmission

originell adj original; (*eigenartig*) unusual

Orkan m -s,-e hurricane

Ornament nt -[e]s,-e ornament

Ort m -[e]s,-e place; (*Ortschaft*) [small] town; am **O~** locally; am **Ort des Verbrechens** at the scene of the crime

ortho|dox adj orthodox. **O~graphie, O~grafie** f - spelling. **O~päde** m -n,-n orthopaedic specialist

örtlich adj local

Ortschaft f -,-en [small] town; (*Dorf*) village; geschlossene **O~** (*Auto*) built-up area

Orts|gespräch nt (*Teleph*) local call. **O~verkehr** m local traffic. **O~zeit** f local time

Öse f -,-n eyelet; (*Schlinge*) loop; **Haken und Öse** hook and eye

Ost m -[e]s east

Osten m -s east; nach **O~** east

ostentativ adj pointed

Osteopath m -en,-en osteopath

Oster|ei /ˈoːstɐʔai/ nt Easter egg. **O~fest** nt Easter. **O~glocke** f daffodil. **O~n** nt -,- Easter; frohe **O~n!** happy Easter!

Österreich nt -s Austria. **Ö~er** m, -s,-, **Ö~erin** f -,-nen Austrian. **ö~isch** adj Austrian

östlich adj eastern; (*Richtung*) easterly ●adv & prep (+ gen) **ö~** [von] der Stadt [to the] east of the town

Ostsee f Baltic [Sea]

Otter¹ m -s,- otter

Otter² f -,-n adder

Ouverture /uvɛrˈtyːrə/ f -,-n overture

oval adj oval. **O~** nt -s,-e oval

Oxid, Oxyd nt -[e]s,-e oxide

Ozean m -s,-e ocean

Ozon nt -s ozone. **O~loch** nt hole in the ozone layer. **O~schicht** f ozone layer

Pp

paar pron inv **ein p~** a few; **ein p~ Mal** a few times; **alle p~ Tage** every few days. **P~** nt -[e]s,-e pair; (*Ehe-, Liebes-*) couple. **p~en** vt mate; (*verbinden*) combine; sich **p~en** mate. **P~ung** f -,-en mating. **p~weise** adv in pairs, in twos

Pacht f -,-en lease; (*P~summe*) rent. **p~en** vt lease

Pächter m -s,- lessee; (*eines Hofes*) tenant

Pachtvertrag m lease

Päckchen nt -s,- package, small packet

pack|en vt/i (haben) pack; (*ergrei-*

fen) seize; (fig: fesseln) grip. **P~en**
m -s,- bundle. **P~end** adj (fig)
gripping. **P~papier** nt [strong]
wrapping paper. **P~ung** f -,-en
packet; (Med) pack

Pädagoge|e m -n,-n educational-
ist; (Lehrer) teacher. **P~ik** f - educa-
tional science

Paddel nt -s,- paddle. **P~boot** nt
canoe. **p~n** vt/i (haben/sein) paddle. **P~sport** m canoeing

Page /'pa:ʒə/ m -n,-n page

Paillette /pai'jɛtə/ f -,-n sequin

Paket nt -[e]s,-e packet; (Post-)
parcel

Pakist|an nt -s Pakistan. **P~ane-**
r(in) m -s,- (f -,-nen) Pakistani.
p~anisch adj Pakistani

Palast m -[e]s,ᵉe palace

Paläst|ina nt -s Palestine. **P~i-**
nenser(in) m -s,- (f -,-nen) Palestinian. **p~inensisch** adj Palestinian

Palette f -,-n palette

Palme f -,-n palm[-tree]

Pampelmuse f -,-n grapefruit

Panier|mehl nt (Culin) bread-
crumbs pl. **p~t** adj (Culin) breaded

Panik f - panic

Panne f -,-n breakdown; (Reifen-)
flat tyre; (Missgeschick) mishap

Panter, Panther m -s,- panther

Pantine f -,-n [wooden] clog

Pantoffel m -s,- slipper; mule

Pantomime¹ f -,-n mime

Pantomime² m -n,-n mime
artist

Panzer m -s,- armour; (Mil) tank;
(Zool) shell. **p~n** vt armourplate.
P~schrank m safe

Papa /'papa, pa'pa:/ m -s,-s daddy

Papagei m -s & -en,-en parrot

Papier nt -[e]s,-e paper. **P~korb**
m waste-paper basket. **P~schlange**
f streamer. **P~waren** fpl

stationery sg

Pappe f - cardboard

Pappel f -,-n poplar

pappig adj ⓘ sticky

Papp|karton m, **P~schachtel** f
cardboard box

Paprika m -s,-[s] [sweet] pepper;
(Gewürz) paprika

Papst m -[e]s,ᵉe pope

päpstlich adj papal

Parade f -,-n parade

Paradies nt -es,-e paradise

Paraffin nt -s paraffin

Paragraf, Paragraph m -en,-en
section

parallel adj & adv parallel. **P~e** f
-,-n parallel

Paranuss f Brazil nut

Parasit m -en,-en parasite

parat adj ready

Parcours /par'ku:ɐ̯/ m -,- /-[s],-s/
(Sport) course

Pardon /par'dõ:/ int sorry!

Parfüm nt -s,-e & -s perfume,
scent. **p~iert** adj perfumed,
scented

parieren vi (haben) ⓘ obey

Park m -s,-s park. **p~en** vt/i
(haben) park. **P~en** nt -s parking;
'P~en verboten' 'no parking'

Parkett nt -[e]s, -e parquet floor;
(Theat) stalls pl

Park|haus nt multi-storey car
park. **P~kralle** f wheel clamp.
P~lücke f parking space. **P~platz**
m car park; parking space.
P~scheibe f parking-disc.
P~schein m car-park ticket.
P~uhr f parking-meter. **P~verbot**
nt parking ban; 'P~verbot' 'no
parking'

Parlament nt -[e]s,-e parliament.
p~arisch adj parliamentary

Parodie f -,-n parody

p

Parole f -,-n slogan; (Mil) password

Partei f -,-en (Pol, Jur) party; (Miet-) tenant; für jdn P~ ergreifen take s.o.'s part. **p~isch** adj biased

Parterre /par'tɛr/ nt -s,-s ground floor; (Theat) rear stalls pl

Partie f -,-n part; (Tennis, Schach) game; (Golf) round; (Comm) batch; eine gute P~ machen marry well

Partikel nt -s,- particle

Partitur f -,-en (Mus) full score

Partizip nt -s,-ien participle

Partner|(in) m -s,- (f -,-nen) partner. **P~schaft** f -,-en partnership. **P~stadt** f twin town

Party /'pa:ɐ̯ti/ f -,-s party

Parzelle f -,-n plot [of ground]

Pass m -es, ̈e passport; (Geog, Sport) pass

Passage /pa'sa:ʒə/ f -,-n passage; (Einkaufs-) shopping arcade

Passagier /pasa'ʒi:ɐ̯/ m -s,-e passenger

Passant(in) m -en,-en (f -,-nen) passer-by

Passe f -,-n yoke

passen vi (haben) fit; (geeignet sein) be right (für for); (Sport) pass the ball; (aufgeben) pass; p~ zu go [well] with; (übereinstimmen) match; jdm p~ fit s.o.; (gelegen sein) suit s.o.; [ich] passe pass. **p~d** adj suitable; (angemessen) appropriate; (günstig) convenient; (übereinstimmend) matching

passier|en vt pass; cross (Grenze); (Culin) rub through a sieve ● vi (sein) happen (jdm to s.o.); es ist ein Unglück p~t there has been an accident. **P~schein** m pass

Passiv nt -s,-e (Gram) passive

Passstraße f pass

Paste f -,-n paste

Pastell nt -[e]s,-e pastel

Pastete f -,-n pie; (Gänseleber-) pâté

pasteurisieren /pastøri'zi:rən/ vt pasteurize

Pastor m -s,-en pastor

Pate m -n,-n godfather; (fig) sponsor; P~n godparents. **P~nkind** nt godchild

Patent nt -[e]s,-e patent; (Offiziers-) commission. **p~** adj (fam) clever; (Person) resourceful. **p~ieren** vt patent

Pater m -s,- (Relig) Father

Patholog|e m -n,-n pathologist. **p~isch** adj pathological

Patience /pa'sjã:s/ f -,-n patience

Patient(in) /pa'tsjɛnt(ɪn)/ m -en,-en (f -,-nen) patient

Patin f -,-nen godmother

Patriot|(in) m -en,-en (f -,-nen) patriot. **p~isch** adj patriotic. **P~ismus** m - patriotism

Patrone f -,-n cartridge

Patrouille /pa'trʊljə/ f -,-n patrol

Patsch|e f in der P~e sitzen (fam) be in a jam. **p~nass** adj (fam) soaking wet

Patt nt -s stalemate

Patz|er m -s,- (fam) slip. **p~ig** adj (fam) insolent

Pauk|e f -,-n kettledrum; auf die P~e hauen (fam) have a good time; (prahlen) boast. **p~en** vt/i (haben) (fam) swot

pauschal adj all-inclusive; (einheitlich) flat-rate; (fig) sweeping (Urteil). **p~e** Summe lump sum. **P~e** f -,-n lump sum. **P~reise** f package tour. **P~summe** f lump sum

Pause¹ f -,-n break; (beim Sprechen) pause; (Theat) interval; (im Kino) intermission; (Mus) rest; P~ machen have a break

Pause² f -,-n tracing. p~n vt trace

pausenlos adj incessant

pausieren vi (haben) have a break; (ausruhen) rest

Pauspapier nt tracing-paper

Pavian m -s,-e baboon

Pavillon /'pavɪljõ/ m -s,-s pavilion

Pazifik|k m -s Pacific (Ocean). p~sch adj Pacific

Pazifist m -en,-en pacifist

Pech nt -s pitch; (Unglück) bad luck; P~ haben be unlucky

Pedal nt -s,-e pedal

Pedant m -en,-en pedant

Pediküre f -,-n pedicure

Pegel m -s,- level; (Gerät) water-level indicator. P~stand m [water] level

peilen vt take a bearing on

peinigen vt torment

peinlich adj embarrassing, awkward; (genau) scrupulous; es war mir sehr p~ I was very embarrassed

Peitsche f -,-n whip. p~n vt whip; (fig) lash ● vi (sein) lash (an + acc against). P~nhieb m lash

Pelikan m -s,-e pelican

Pell|e f -,-n skin. p~en vt peel; shell (Ei); sich p~en peel

Pelz m -es,-e fur

Pendel nt -s,- pendulum. p~n vi (haben) swing ● vi (sein) commute. P~verkehr m shuttle-service; (für Pendler) commuter traffic

Pendler m -s,- commuter

penetrant adj penetrating; (fig) obtrusive

Penis m -,-se penis

Penne f -,-n 🄸 school

Pension /pãˈzjoːn/ f -,-en pension; (Hotel) guest-house; bei voller/halber P~ with full/half board. P~är(in) m -s,-e (f -,-nen) pen-

sioner. P~at nt -[e]s,-e boarding-school. p~ieren vt retire. P~ierung f - retirement

Pensum nt -s [allotted] work

Peperoni f -,- chilli

per prep (+ acc) by

Perfekt nt -s (Gram) perfect

Perfektion /-ˈtsjoːn/ f - perfection

perforiert adj perforated

Pergament nt -[e]s,-e parchment. P~papier nt grease-proof paper

Period|e f -,-n period. p~isch adj periodic

Perl|e f -,-n pearl; (Glas-, Holz-) bead; (Sekt-) bubble. P~mutt nt -s mother-of-pearl

Pers|ien /-jən/ nt -s Persia. p~isch adj Persian

Person f -,-en person; (Theat) character; für vier P~en for four people

Personal nt -s personnel, staff. P~ausweis m identity card. P~chef m personnel manager. P~ien pl personal particulars. P~mangel m staff shortage

persönlich adj personal ● adv personally, in person. P~keit f -,-en personality

Perücke f -,-n wig

pervers adj [sexually] perverted. P~ion f -,-en perversion

Pessimis|mus m - pessimism. P~t m -en,-en pessimist. p~tisch adj pessimistic

Pest f - plague

Petersilie /-jə/ f - parsley

Petroleum /-leʊm/ nt -s paraffin

Petze f -,-n 🄸 sneak. p~n vi (haben) 🄸 sneak

Pfad m -[e]s,-e path. P~finder m -s,- [Boy] Scout. P~finderin f -,-nen [Girl] Guide

p

Pfahl m -[e]s,-̈e stake, post

Pfalz (die) - the Palatinate

Pfand nt -[e]s,-̈er pledge; (beim Spiel) forfeit; (Flaschen-) deposit

pfänd|en vt (Jur) seize. **P~erspiel** nt game of forfeits

Pfandleiher m -s,- pawnbroker

Pfändung f -,-en (Jur) seizure

Pfanne f -,-n (frying-)pan. **P~kuchen** m pancake

Pfarr|er m -s,- vicar, parson; (katholischer) priest. **P~haus** nt vicarage

Pfau m -s,-en peacock

Pfeffer m -s pepper. **P~kuchen** m gingerbread. **P~minze** f - (Bot) peppermint. **P~n** vt pepper; (fam: schmeißen) chuck. **P~streuer** m -s,- pepperpot

Pfeife f -,-n whistle; (Tabak-, Orgel-) pipe. **P~n†** vt/i (haben) whistle; (als Signal) blow the whistle

Pfeil m -[e]s,-e arrow

Pfeiler m -s,- pillar; (Brücken-) pier

Pfennig m -s,-e pfennig

Pferch m -[e]s,-e [sheep] pen

Pferd nt -es,-e horse; zu P~e on horseback. **P~erennen** nt horse-race; (als Sport) [horse-]racing. **P~eschwanz** m horse's tail; (Frisur) pony-tail. **P~estall** m stable. **P~estärke** f horsepower

Pfiff m -[e]s,-e whistle

Pfifferling m -s,-e chanterelle

pfiffig adj 🗊 smart

Pfingst|en nt - Whitsun. **P~rose** f peony

Pfirsich m -s,-e peach

Pflanz|e f -,-n plant. **p~en** vt plant. **P~enfett** nt vegetable fat. **p~lich** adj vegetable

Pflaster nt -s,- pavement; (Heft-) plaster. **p~n** vt pave

Pflaume f -,-n plum

Pflege f - care; (Kranken-) nursing; in P~ nehmen look after; (Admin) foster (Kind). **p~bedürftig** adj in need of care. **P~kind** nt foster-child. **p~leicht** adj easy-care. **p~n** vt look after, care for; nurse (Kranke); cultivate (Künste, Freundschaft). **P~r(in)** m -s,- (f -,-nen) nurse; (Tier-) keeper

Pflicht f -,-en duty; (Sport) compulsory exercise/routine. **p~bewusst** adj conscientious. **P~gefühl** nt sense of duty

pflücken vt pick

Pflug m -[e]s,-̈e plough

pflügen vt/i (haben) plough

Pforte f -,-n gate

Pförtner m -s,- porter

Pfosten m -s,- post

Pfote f -,-n paw

Pfropfen m -s,- stopper; (Korken) cork. **p~** vt graft (auf + acc on [to]); (🗊: pressen) cram (in + acc into)

pfui int ugh

Pfund nt -[e]s,-e & - pound

Pfusch|arbeit f 🗊 shoddy work. **p~en** vi (haben) 🗊 botch one's work. **P~erei** f -,-en 🗊 botch-up

Pfütze f -,-n puddle

Phantasie f -,-n imagination; **P~n** fantasies; (Fieber-) hallucinations. **p~los** adj unimaginative. **p~ren** vi (haben) fantasize; (im Fieber) be delirious. **p~voll** adj imaginative

phantastisch adj fantastic

pharma|zeutisch adj pharmaceutical. **P~zie** f - pharmacy

Phase f -,-n phase

Philologie f - [study of] language and literature

Philosoph m -en,-en philosopher.

P~ie f -,-n philosophy

philosophisch adj philosophical

Phobie f -,-n phobia

Phonet|ik f - phonetics sg. **p~isch** adj phonetic

Phosphor m -s phosphorus

Photo nt, Photo- = Foto-, Foto-

Phrase f -,-n empty phrase

Physik f - physics sg. **p~alisch** adj physical

Physiker(in) m -s,- (f -,-nen) physicist

Physiologie f - physiology

physisch adj physical

Pianist(in) m -en,-en (f -,-nen) pianist

Pickel m -s,- pimple, spot; (Spitzhacke) pick. **p~ig** adj spotty

Picknick nt -s,-s picnic

piep[s]|en vi (haben) (Vogel:) cheep; (Maus:) squeak; (Techn) bleep. **P~er** m -s,- bleeper

Pier m -s,-e [harbour] pier

Pietät /piε'tε:t/ f - reverence. **p~los** adj irreverent

Pigment nt -[e]s,-e pigment. **P~ierung** f - pigmentation

Pik nt -s,-s (Karten) spades pl

pikant adj piquant; (gewagt) racy

piken vt 🔲 prick

pikiert adj offended, hurt

Pilger|(in) m -s,- (f -,-nen) pilgrim. **P~fahrt** f pilgrimage. **p~n** vi (sein) make a pilgrimage

Pille f -,-n pill

Pilot m -en,-en pilot

Pilz m -es,-e fungus; (essbarer) mushroom

PIN f PIN

pingelig adj 🔲 fussy

Pinguin m -s,-e penguin

Pinie /-jə/ f -,-n stone-pine

pinkeln vi (haben) 🔲 pee

Pinsel m -s,- [paint]brush

Pinzette f -,-n tweezers pl

Pionier m -s,-e (Mil) sapper; (fig) pioneer

Pirat m -en,-en pirate

Piste f -,-n (Ski-) run, piste; (Renn-) track; (Aviat) runway

Pistole f -,-n pistol

pitschnass adj 🔲 soaking wet

pittoresk adj picturesque

Pizza f -,-s pizza

Pkw /'pe:kave:/ m -s,-s car

plädieren vi (haben) plead (für for); auf Freispruch p~ (Jur) ask for an acquittal

Plädoyer /plεdoa'je:/ nt -s,-s (Jur) closing speech; (fig) plea

Plage f -,-n [hard] labour; (Mühe) trouble; (Belästigung) nuisance. **p~n** vt torment, plague; (bedrängen) pester; sich p~n struggle

Plakat nt -[e]s,-e poster

Plakette f -,-n badge

Plan m -[e]s,⁻e plan

Plane f -,-n tarpaulin; (Boden-) groundsheet

planen vt/i (haben) plan

Planet m -en,-en planet

planier|en vt level. **P~raupe** f bulldozer

Planke f -,-n plank

plan|los adj unsystematic. **p~mäßig** adj systematic; (Ankunft) scheduled

Plansch|becken nt paddling pool. **p~en** vi (haben) splash about

Plantage /plan'ta:ʒə/ f -,-n plantation

Planung f - planning

plappern vi (haben) chatter ● vt talk (Unsinn)

plärren vi (haben) bawl

Plasma nt -s plasma

Plastik¹ f -,-en sculpture

Plast|ik² nt -s plastic. **p~isch** adj three-dimensional; (formbar) plastic; (anschaulich) graphic

Plateau /pla'to:/ nt -s,-s plateau

Platin nt -s platinum

platonisch adj platonic

plätschern vi (haben) splash; (Bach:) babble ●vi (sein) (Bach:) babble along

platt adj & adv flat. **P~** nt -[s] (Lang) Low German

Plättbrett nt ironing-board

Platte f -,-n slab; (Druck-) plate; (Metall-, Glas-) sheet; (Fliese) tile; (Koch-) hotplate; (Tisch-) top; (Schall-) record, disc; (zum Servieren) [flat] dish, platter; kalte P~ assorted cold meats and cheeses pl

Plätt|eisen nt iron. **p~en** vt/i (haben) iron

Plattenspieler m record-player

Platt|form f -,-en platform. **P~füße** mpl flat feet

Platz m -es, ⸚e place; (von Häusern umgeben) square; (Sitz-) seat; (Sport-) ground; (Fußball-) pitch; (Tennis-) court; (Golf-) course; (freier Raum) room, space; P~ nehmen take a seat; P~ machen make room; vom P~ stellen (Sport) send off. **P~anweiserin** f -,-nen usherette

Plätzchen nt -s,- spot; (Culin) biscuit

platzen vi (sein) burst; (auf-) split; (⊡: scheitern) fall through; (Verlobung:) be off

Platz|karte f seat reservation ticket. **P~mangel** m lack of space. **P~patrone** f blank. **P~verweis** m (Sport) sending off. **P~wunde** f laceration

Plauderei f -,-en chat

plaudern vi (haben) chat

plausibel adj plausible

pleite adj ⊡ **p~ sein** be broke: (Firma:) be bankrupt. **P~** f -,-n ⊡ bankruptcy; (Misserfolg) flop; **p~ gehen od machen** go bankrupt

plissiert adj [finely] pleated

Plomb|e f -,-n seal; (Zahn-) filling. **p~ieren** vt seal; fill (Zahn)

plötzlich adj sudden

plump adj plump; clumsy

plumpsen vi (sein) ⊡ fall

plündern vt/i (haben) loot

Plunderstück nt Danish pastry

Plural m -s,-e plural

plus adv, conj & prep (+ dat) plus. **P~** nt - surplus; (Gewinn) profit (Vorteil) advantage, plus. **P~punkt** m (Sport) point; (fig) plus

Po m -s,-s ⊡ bottom

Pöbel m -s mob, rabble. **p~haft** adj loutish

pochen vi (haben) knock, (Herz:) pound; **p~ auf** (+ acc) (fig) insist on

pochieren /po'ʃi:rən/ vt poach

Pocken pl smallpox sg

Podest nt -[e]s,-e rostrum

Podium nt -s,-ien platform; (Podest) rostrum

Poesie /poe'zi:/ f - poetry

poetisch adj poetic

Pointe /'pɛ̃:tə/ f -,-n punchline (of a joke)

Pokal m -s,-e goblet; (Sport) cup

pökeln vt (Culin) salt

Poker nt -s poker

Pol m -s,-e pole. **p~ar** adj polar

Polarstern m pole-star

Pole m, -n,-n Pole. **P~n** nt -s Poland

Police /po'li:sə/ f -,-n policy

Polier m -s,-e foreman

polieren vt polish

Polin f -,-nen Pole

Politesse f -,-n [woman] traffic warden

Politik f - politics sg; (Vorgehen, Maßnahme) policy

Polit|iker(in) m -s,- (f. -,-nen) politician. **p~isch** adj political

Politur f -,-en polish

Polizei f - police pl. **p~lich** adj police ● adv by the police; (sich anmelden) with the police. **P~streife** f police patrol. **P~stunde** f closing time. **P~wache** f police station

Polizist m -en,-en policeman. **P~in** f -,-nen policewoman

Pollen m -s pollen

polnisch adj Polish

Polster nt -s,- pad; (Kissen) cushion; (Möbel-) upholstery. **P~n** vt pad; upholster (Möbel). **P~ung** f - padding; upholstery

Polter|abend m eve-of-wedding party. **p~n** vi (haben) thump bang

---

Polterabend This is Germany's equivalent of pre-wedding stag and hen nights. The *Polterabend* is a party for family and friends of both bride and groom. It is held a few days before the wedding, and guests traditionally smash crockery to bring good luck to the happy couple.

Polyäthylen nt -s polythene

Polyester m -s polyester

Polyp m -en,-en polyp. **P~en** adenoids pl

Pommes frites /pɔmˈfriːt/ pl chips; (dünner) French fries

Pomp m -s pomp

Pompon /pɔ̃ˈpɔ̃/ m -s,-s pompon

pompös adj ostentatious

Pony[1] nt -s,-s pony

Pony[2] m -s,-s fringe

Pop m -[s] pop

Popo m -s,-s 🔢 bottom

populär adj popular

Pore f -,-n pore

Porno|grafie, Pornographie f - pornography. **p~grafisch, p~graphisch** adj pornographic

Porree m -s leeks pl

Portal nt -s,-e portal

Portemonnaie /portmɔˈneː/ nt -s,-s purse

Portier /porˈtjeː/ m -s,-s doorman, porter

Portion /-ˈtsjoːn/ f -,-en helping, portion

Portmonee nt -s,-s = **Portemonnaie**

Porto nt -s postage. **p~frei** adv post free, post paid

Porträt /porˈtrɛː/ nt -s,-s portrait. **p~tieren** vt paint a portrait of

Portugal nt -s Portugal

Portugies|e m -n,-n, **P~in** f -,-nen Portuguese. **p~isch** adj Portuguese

Portwein m port

Porzellan nt -s china, porcelain

Posaune f -,-n trombone

Position /-ˈtsjoːn/ f -,-en position

positiv adj positive. **P~** nt -s,-e (Phot) positive

Post f - post office; (Briefe) mail, post; mit der P~ by post

postalisch adj postal

Post|amt nt post office. **P~anweisung** f postal money order. **P~bote** m postman

Posten m -s,- post; (Wache) sentry; (Waren-) batch; (Rechnungs-) item, entry

Poster nt & m -s,- poster

Postfach nt post-office or PO box

Post|karte f postcard. **p~lagernd** adv poste restante. **P~leit-**

P

zahl f postcode. **P~scheckkonto** nt ≈ National Girobank account. **P~stempel** m postmark

postum adj posthumous

post|wendend adv by return of post. **P~wertzeichen** nt [postage] stamp

Potenz f -,-en potency; (Math & fig) power

Pracht f - magnificence, splendour

prächtig adj magnificent; splendid

prachtvoll adj magnificent

Prädikat nt -[e]s,-e rating; (Comm) grade; (Gram) predicate

prägen vt stamp (auf + acc on); emboss (Leder); mint (Münze); coin (Wort); (fig) shape

prägnant adj succinct

prähistorisch adj prehistoric

prahl|en vi (haben) boast, brag (mit about)

Prakti|k f -,-en practice. **P~kant(in)** m -en,-en (f -,-nen) trainee

Prakti|kum nt -s,-ka practical training. **p~sch** adj practical; (nützlich) handy; (tatsächlich) virtual; **p~scher Arzt** general practitioner ● adv practically; virtually; (in der Praxis) in practice. **p~zieren** vt/i (haben) practise; (anwenden) put into practice; (🔲: bekommen) get

Praline f -,-n chocolate

prall adj bulging; (dick) plump; (Sonne) blazing ● adv **p~ gefüllt** full to bursting. **p~en** vi (sein) **p~ auf** (+ acc)/**gegen** collide with, hit; (Sonne) blaze down on

Prämie f -,-n premium; (Preis) award

präm[i]ieren vt award a prize to

Pranger m -s,- pillory

Pranke f -,-n paw

Präparat nt -[e]s,-e preparation

Präsens nt - (Gram) present

präsentieren vt present

Präsenz f - presence

Präservativ nt -s,-e condom

Präsident|(in) m -en,-en (f -,-nen) president. **P~schaft** f - presidency

Präsidium nt -s presidency; (Gremium) executive committee; (Polizei-) headquarters pl

prasseln vi (haben) (Regen:) beat down; (Feuer:) crackle

Prater Vienna's largest amusement park was a private game reserve for the Austrian royal family until 1766. The Prater is famous for its old-fashioned carousels. A Riesenrad, big wheel or Ferris wheel, with a diameter of 67 metres was built there for the World Exhibition of 1897.

i

Präteritum nt -s imperfect

Praxis f -,-xen practice; (Erfahrung) practical experience; (Arzt-) surgery; **in der P~** in practice

Präzedenzfall m precedent

präzis[e] adj precise

predig|en vt/i (haben) preach. **P~t** f -,-en sermon

Preis m -es,-e price; (Belohnung) prize. **P~ausschreiben** nt competition

Preiselbeere f (Bot) cowberry; (Culin) ≈ cranberry

preisen† vt praise

preisgeben† vt sep abandon (dat to); reveal (Geheimnis)

preis|gekrönt adj award-winning. **p~günstig** adj reasonably priced ● adv at a reasonable price. **P~lage** f price range. **p~lich** adj price ● adv in price. **P~richter** m judge. **P~schild** nt price-tag. **P~träger(in)** m(f) prize-winner.

p~wert adj reasonable

Prell|bock m buffers pl. **p~en** vt bounce; (verletzen) bruise; (🔟: betrügen) cheat. **P~ung** f -,-en bruise

Premiere /prə'mjeːrə/ f -,-n première

Premierminister(in) /prə'mjeː-/ m(f) Prime Minister

Presse f -,-n press. **p~n** vt press

Pressluftbohrer m pneumatic drill

Preuß|en nt -s Prussia. **p~isch** adj Prussian

prickeln vi (haben) tingle

Priester m -s,- priest

prima inv adj 🔟 first-class, first-rate; (toll) fantastic

primär adj primary

Primel f -,-n primula

primitiv adj primitive

Prinz m -en,-en prince. **P~essin** f -,-nen princess

Prinzip nt -s,-ien principle. **p~iell** adj (Frage) of principle ● adv on principle

Prise f -,-n P~ Salz pinch of salt

Prisma nt -s,-men prism

privat adj private, personal. **P~adresse** f home address. **p~isieren** vt privatize

Privileg nt -[e]s,-ien privilege. **p~iert** adj privileged

pro prep (+ dat) per. **Pro** nt - das Pro und Kontra the pros and cons pl

Probe f -,-n test, trial; (Menge, Muster) sample; (Theat) rehearsal; auf die P~ stellen put to the test; ein Auto P~ fahren test-drive a car. **p~n** vt/i (haben) (Theat) rehearse. **p~weise** adv on a trial basis. **P~zeit** f probationary period

probieren vt/i (haben) try; (kosten) taste; (proben) rehearse

Problem nt -s,-e problem. **p~atisch** adj problematic

problemlos adj problem-free ● adv without any problems

Produkt nt -[e]s,-e product

Produk|tion /-'tsjoːn/ f -,-en production. **p~tiv** adj productive

Produ|zent m -en,-en producer. **p~zieren** vt produce

Professor m -s,-en professor

Profi m -s,-s (Sport) professional

Profil nt -s,-e profile; (Reifen-) tread; (fig) image

Profit m -[e]s,-e profit. **p~ieren** vi (haben) profit (von from)

Prognose f -,-n forecast; (Med) prognosis

Programm nt -s,-e programme; (Computer-) program; (TV) channel; (Comm: Sortiment) range. **p~ieren** vt/i (haben) (Computer) program. **P~ierer(in)** m -s,- (f -,-nen) [computer] programmer

Projekt nt -[e]s,-e project

Projektor m -s,-en projector

Prolet m -en,-en boor. **P~ariat** nt -[e]s proletariat

Prolog m -s,-e prologue

Promenade f -,-n promenade

Promille pl 🔟 alcohol level sg in the blood; zu viel P~ haben 🔟 be over the limit

Prominenz f - prominent figures pl

Promiskuität f - promiscuity

promovieren vi (haben) obtain one's doctorate

prompt adj prompt

Pronomen nt -s,- pronoun

Propaganda f - propaganda; (Reklame) publicity

Propeller m -s,- propeller

Prophet m -en,-en prophet

prophezei|en vt prophesy

P~ung f -,-en prophecy

Proportion /-'tsjo:n/ f -,-en proportion

Prosa f - prose

prosit int cheers!

Prospekt m -[e]s,-e brochure; (Comm) prospectus

prost int cheers!

Prostitu|ierte f -n,-n prostitute. P~tion f - prostitution

Protest m -[e]s,-e protest

Protestant|(in) m -en,-en (f -,-nen) (Relig) Protestant. p~isch adj (Relig) Protestant

protestieren vi (haben) protest

Prothese f -,-n artificial limb; (Zahn-) denture

Protokoll nt -s,-e record; (Sitzungs-) minutes pl; (diplomatisches) protocol

protz|en vi (haben) show off (mit etw sth). p~ig adj ostentatious

Proviant m -s provisions pl

Provinz f -,-en province

Provision f -,-en (Comm) commission

provisorisch adj provisional, temporary

Provokation /-'tsjo:n/ f -,-en provocation

provozieren vt provoke

Prozedur f -,-en [lengthy] business

Prozent nt -[e]s,-e & - per cent; 5 P~ 5 per cent. P~satz m percentage. p~ual adj percentage

Prozess m -es,-e process; (Jur) lawsuit; (Kriminal-) trial

Prozession f -,-en procession

Prozessor m -s,-en processor

prüde adj prudish

prüf|en vt test/(über-) check (auf + acc for); audit (Bücher); (Sch) examine; p~ender Blick searching look.

P~er m -s,- inspector; (Buch-) auditor; (Sch) examiner. P~ling m -s,-e examination candidate. P~ung f -,-en examination; (Test) test; (Bücher-) audit; (fig) trial

Prügel m -s,- cudgel; P~ pl hiding sg, beating sg. P~ei f -,-en brawl, fight. p~n vt beat, thrash

Prunk m -[e]s magnificence, splendour

Psalm m -s,-en psalm

Pseudonym nt -s,-e pseudonym

pst int shush!

Psychi|ater m -s,- psychiatrist. P~atrie f - psychiatry. p~atrisch adj psychiatric

psychisch adj psychological

Psycho|analyse f psychoanalysis. P~loge m -n,-n psychologist. P~logie f - psychology. p~logisch adj psychological

Pubertät f - puberty

Publi|kum nt -s public; (Zuhörer) audience; (Zuschauer) spectators pl. p~zieren vt publish

Pudding m -s,-s blancmange; (im Wasserbad gekocht) pudding

Pudel m -s,- poodle

Puder m & 🆃 nt -s,- powder. P~dose f [powder] compact. p~n vt powder. P~zucker m icing sugar

Puff m & nt -s,-s 🅧 brothel

Puffer m -s,- (Rail) buffer; (Culin) pancake. P~zone f buffer zone

Pull|i m -s,-s jumper. P~over m -s,- jumper; (Herren-) pullover

Puls m -es pulse. P~ader f artery

Pult nt -[e]s,-e desk

Pulver nt -s,- powder. p~ig adj powdery

Pulverkaffee m instant coffee

pummelig adj 🆃 chubby

Pumpe f -,-n pump. p~n vt/i (haben) pump; (🆃: leihen) lend;

[sich (*dat*)] etw p∼n (🗉: *borgen*) borrow sth

Pumps /pœmps/ *pl* court shoes

Punkt *m* -[e]s,-e dot; (*Textiles*) spot; (*Geometry, Sport & fig*) point; (*Gram*) full stop, period; P∼ **sechs Uhr** at six o'clock sharp

pünktlich *adj* punctual. **P∼keit** *f* - punctuality

Pupille *f* -,-n (*Anat*) pupil

Puppe *f* -,-n doll; (*Marionette*) puppet; (*Schaufenster-, Schneider-*) dummy; (*Zool*) chrysalis

pur *adj* pure; (🗉: *bloß*) sheer

Püree *nt* -s,-s purée; (*Kartoffel-*) mashed potatoes *pl*

purpurrot *adj* crimson

Purzel|baum *m* somersault. **p∼n** *vi* (*sein*) 🗉 tumble

Puste *f* - 🗉 breath. **p∼n** *vt/i* (*haben*) 🗉 blow

Pute *f* -,-n turkey

Putsch *m* -[e]s,-e coup

Putz *m* -es plaster; (*Staat*) finery. **p∼en** *vt* (*bloß*) dry-clean; (*zieren*) adorn; **sich p∼en** dress up; **sich** (*dat*) **die Zähne/Nase p∼en** clean one's teeth/blow one's nose. **P∼frau** *f* cleaner, charwoman. **p∼ig** *adj* amusing, cute; (*seltsam*) odd

Puzzlespiel /'pazl-/ *nt* jigsaw

Pyramide *f* -,-n pyramid

Qq

Quacksalber *m* -s,- quack

Quadrat *nt* -[e]s,-e square. **q∼isch** *adj* square

quaken *vi* (*haben*) quack; (*Frosch:*) croak

Quäker(in) *m* -s,- (*f* -,-nen) Quaker

Qual *f* -,-en torment; (*Schmerz*) agony

quälen *vt* torment; (*foltern*) torture; (*bedrängen*) pester; **sich q∼** torment oneself; (*leiden*) suffer; (*sich mühen*) struggle

Quälerei *f* -,-en torture

Qualifi|kation /-'tsio:n/ *f* -,-en qualification. **q∼zieren** *vt* qualify. **q∼ziert** *adj* qualified; (*fähig*) competent; (*Arbeit*) skilled

Qualität *f* -,-en quality

Qualle *f* -,-n jellyfish

Qualm *m* -s [thick] smoke

qualvoll *adj* agonizing

Quantum *nt* -s,-ten quantity; (*Anteil*) share, quota

Quarantäne *f* - quarantine

Quark *m* -s quark, ≈ curd cheese

Quartal *nt* -s,-e quarter

Quartett *nt* -[e]s,-e quartet

Quartier *nt* -s,-e accommodation; (*Mil*) quarters *pl*

Quarz *m* -es quartz

quasseln *vi* (*haben*) 🗉 jabber

Quaste *f* -,-n tassel

Quatsch *m* -[e]s 🗉 nonsense, rubbish; Q∼ **machen** (*Unfug machen*) fool around; (*etw falsch machen*) do a silly thing. **q∼en** 🗉 *vi* (*haben*) talk; (*Wasser, Schlamm:*) squelch ● *vt* talk

Quecksilber *nt* mercury

Quelle *f* -,-n spring; (*Fluss- & fig*) source

quengeln *vi* 🗉 whine

quer *adv* across, crosswise; (*schräg*) diagonally; q∼ **gestreift** horizontally striped

Quere *f* - der Q∼ **nach** across, crosswise; jdm **in die Q∼ kommen** get in s.o.'s way

p
q

Quer|latte f crossbar. **Q~schiff** nt transept. **Q~schnitt** m cross-section. **q~schnittsgelähmt** adj paraplegic. **Q~straße** f side-street. **Q~verweis** m cross-reference

quetschen vt squash; (drücken) squeeze; (zerdrücken) crush; (Culin) mash; **sich q~** in (+ acc) squeeze into

Queue /køː/ nt -s,-s cue

quieken vi (haben) squeal; (Maus:) squeak

quietschen vi (haben) squeal; (Tür, Dielen:) creak

Quintett nt -[e]s,-e quintet

quirlen vt mix

Quitte f -,-n quince

quittieren vt receipt (Rechnung); sign for (Geldsumme, Sendung); den Dienst q~ resign

Quittung f -,-en receipt

Quiz /kvɪs/ nt -,- quiz

Quote f -,-n proportion

Rr

Rabatt m -[e]s,-e discount

Rabatte f -,-n (Horticulture) border

Rabattmarke f trading stamp

Rabbiner m -s,- rabbi

Rabe m -n,-n raven

Rache f - revenge, vengeance

Rachen m -s,- pharynx

rächen vt avenge; **sich r~** take revenge (an + dat on); (Fehler:) cost s.o. dear

Rad nt -[e]s,ⁿer wheel; (Fahr-) bicycle, 🔲 bike; **Rad fahren** cycle

Radar m & nt -s radar

Radau m -s 🔲 din, racket

radeln vi (sein) 🔲 cycle

Rädelsführer m ringleader

radfahr|en* vi sep (sein) Rad fahren, s. Rad. **R~er(in)** m(f) -s,- (f -,-nen) cyclist

radier|en vt/i (haben) rub out; (Kunst) etch. **R~gummi** m eraser, rubber. **R~ung** f -,-en etching

Radieschen /-'diːsçən/ nt -s,- radish

radikal adj radical, drastic

Radio nt -s,-s radio

radioaktiv adj radioactive. **R~ität** f - radioactivity

Radius m -,-ien radius

Rad|kappe f hub-cap. **R~ler** m -s,- cyclist; (Getränk) shandy

raffen vt grab; (kräuseln) gather; (kürzen) condense

Raffin|ade f - refined sugar. **R~erie** f -,-n refinery. **R~esse** f -,-n refinement; (Schlauheit) cunning. **r~iert** adj ingenious; (durchtrieben) crafty

ragen vi (haben) rise [up]

Rahm m -s (SGer) cream

rahmen vt frame. **R~** m -s,- frame; (fig) framework; (Grenze) limits pl; (einer Feier:) setting

Rakete f -,-n rocket; (Mil) missile

Rallye /'ralɪ/ nt -s,-s rally

rammen vt ram

Rampe f -,-n ramp; (Theat) front of the stage

Ramsch m -[e]s junk

ran adv = heran

Rand m -[e]s,ⁿe edge; (Teller-, Gläser-, Brillen-) rim; (Zier-) border, edging; (Brief-) margin; (Stadt-) outskirts pl; (Ring) ring

randalieren vi (haben) rampage

Randstreifen m (Auto) hard shoulder

Rang m -[e]s,ⁿe rank; (Theat) tier:

erster/zweiter R~ (Theat) dress/
upper circle; ersten R~es first-class

rangieren /raŋ'ʒi:rən/ vt shunt
●vi (haben) rank (**vor** + dat before)

Rangordnung f order of importance; (Hierarchie) hierarchy

Ranke f -,-n tendril; (Trieb) shoot

ranken (sich) vr (Bot) trail; (in die
Höhe) climb

Ranzen m -s,- (Sch) satchel

ranzig adj rancid

Rappe m -n,-n black horse

Raps m -es (Bot) rape

rar adj rare; er macht sich rar ①
we don't see much of him. **R~ität**
f -,-en rarity

rasant adj fast; (schnittig, schick)
stylish

rasch adj quick

rascheln vi (haben) rustle

Rasen m -s,- lawn

rasen vi (sein) tear [along]; (Puls:)
race; (Zeit:) fly; gegen eine Mauer
r~ career into a wall ●vi (haben)
rave; (Sturm:) rage. **r~d** adj furious;
(tobend) raving; (Sturm, Durst:) ra-
ging; (Schmerz) excruciating; (Beifall) tumultuous

Rasenmäher m lawn-mower

Rasier|apparat m razor. **r~en**
vt shave; **sich r~en** shave.
R~klinge f razor blade. **R~wasser**
nt aftershave [lotion]

Raspel f -,-n rasp; (Culin) grater.
r~n vt grate

Rasse f -,-n race. **R~hund** m pedigree dog

Rassel f -,-n rattle. **r~n** vi (haben)
rattle; (Schlüssel:) jangle;
(Kette:) clank

Rassendiskriminierung f racial discrimination

Rassepferd nt thoroughbred. **rassisch** adj racial

Rassis|mus m - racism. **r~tisch**
adj racist

Rast f -,-en rest. **R~platz** m picnic
area. **R~stätte** f motorway restaurant [and services]

Rasur f -,-en shave

Rat m -[e]s [piece of] advice; **sich**
(dat) keinen Rat wissen not know
what to do; zu Rat[e] ziehen = zurate ziehen, s. zurate

Rate f -,-n instalment

raten† vt guess; (empfehlen) advise
●vi (haben) guess; jdm r~ advise s.o.

Ratenzahlung f payment by in-
stalments

Rat|geber m -s,- adviser; (Buch)
guide. **R~haus** nt town hall

ratifizier|en vt ratify. **R~ung** f
-,-en ratification

Ration /ra'tsi̯o:n/ f -,-en ration.
r~ell adj efficient. **r~ieren** vt
ration

rat|los adj helpless; **r~los sein** not
know what to do. **r~sam** pred adj
advisable; prudent. **R~schlag** m
piece of advice; **R~schläge** advice sg

Rätsel nt -s,- riddle; (Kreuzwort)
puzzle; (Geheimnis) mystery. **r~haft**
adj puzzling, mysterious. **R~n** vi
(haben) puzzle

Ratte f -,-n rat

rau adj rough; (unfreundlich) gruff;
(Klima) harsh, raw; (heiser) husky;
(Hals) sore

Raub m -[e]s robbery; (Menschen-)
abduction; (Beute) loot, booty.
r~en vt steal; abduct (Menschen)

Räuber m -s,- robber

Raub|mord m robbery with mur-
der. **R~tier** nt predator. **R~vogel**
m bird of prey

Rauch m -[e]s smoke. **r~en** vt/i
(haben) smoke. **R~en** nt -s smok-

ing; 'R~en verboten' 'no smoking'.
R~er m -s,-smoker

Räucher|lachs m smoked sal-
mon. r~n vt (Culin) smoke

rauf adv = herauf, hinauf

rauf|en vt pull ● vr/i (haben) [sich]
r~en fight. R~erei f -,-en fight

rauh ' adj = rau

Raum m -[e]s, Räume room; (Gebiet) area; (Welt-) space

räumen vt clear; vacate (Wohnung); evacuate (Gebäude, Gebiet,
(Mil) Stellung); (bringen) put (in/auf
+ acc into/on); (holen) get (aus
out of)

Raum|fahrer m astronaut.
R~fahrt f space travel. R~inhalt
m volume

räumlich adj spatial

Raum|pflegerin f cleaner.
R~schiff nt spaceship

Räumung f - clearing; vacating;
evacuation. R~sverkauf m clear-
ance/closing-down sale

Raupe f -,-n caterpillar

raus adv = heraus, hinaus

Rausch m -[e]s, Räusche intoxica-
tion; (fig) exhilaration; einen
R~haben be drunk

rauschen vi (haben) (Wasser,
Wind:) rush; (Bäume Blätter:) rustle
● vi Ⓣ (sein) rush [along]

Rauschgift nt [narcotic] drug;
(coll) drugs pl. R~süchtige(r) m/f
drug addict

räuspern (sich) vr clear one's
throat

rausschmeißen† vt sep Ⓣ
throw out; (entlassen) sack

Raute f -,-n diamond

Razzia f -, [en [police] raid

Reagenzglas nt test-tube

reagieren vi (haben) react (auf +
acc to)

Reaktion /-'tsjo:n/ f -,-en reac-
tion. r~är adj reactionary

Reaktor m -s,-en reactor

realisieren vt realize

Realis|mus m - realism. R~t m
-en,-en realist. r~tisch adj realistic

Realität f -,-en reality

Realschule f ≈ secondary modern school

Rebe f -,-n vine

Rebell m -en,-en rebel. r~ieren vi
(haben) rebel. R~ion f -,-en rebellion

rebellisch adj rebellious

Rebhuhn nt partridge

Rebstock m vine

Rechen m -s,- rake

Rechen|aufgabe f arithmetical
problem; (Sch) sum. R~maschine f
calculator

recherchieren /refer'fi:rən/ vt/i
(haben) investigate; (Journalism) research

rechnen vi (haben) do arithmetic;
(schätzen) reckon; (zählen) count (zu
among; auf + acc on); r~ mit
reckon with; (erwarten) expect ● vt
calculate, work out; (fig) count (zu
among). R~ nt -s arithmetic

Rechner m -s,- calculator; (Computer) computer

Rechnung f -,-en bill; (Comm) invoice; (Berechnung) calculation; R~
führen über (+ acc) keep account
of. R~sjahr nt financial year.
R~sprüfer m auditor

Recht nt -[e]s,-e law; (Berechtigung) right (auf + acc to); im R~
sein be in the right; R~ haben/be-
halten be right; R~ bekommen be
proved right; jdm R~ geben agree
with s.o.; mit od zu R~ rightly

recht adj (richtig), (wirklich) real; ich
habe keine r~e Lust I don't really
feel like it; es jdm r~ machen

please s.o.; **jdm r~ sein** be all right with s.o. **r~ vielen Dank** many thanks

Recht|**e** f -n,-[n] right side; (Hand) right hand; (Boxen) right; **die R~e** (Pol) the right; **zu meiner R~en** on my right. **r~e(r,s) adj** right; (Pol) right-wing; **r~e Masche** plain stitch. **R~e(r)** m/f der/die **R~e** the right man/woman; **R~e(s)** nt das **R~e** the right thing; **etwas R~es lernen** learn something useful; **nach dem R~en sehen** see that everything is all right

Rechteck nt -[e]s,-e rectangle. **r~ig** adj rectangular

rechtfertigen vt justify; **sich r~en** justify oneself

recht|**haberisch** adj opinionated. **r~lich** adj legal. **r~mäßig** adj legitimate

rechts adv on the right; (bei Stoff) on the right side; **von/nach r~** from/to the right; **zwei r~, zwei links stricken** knit two, purl two. **R~anwalt** m, **R~anwältin** f lawyer

Rechtschreib|**programm** nt spell checker. **R~ung** f - spelling

Rechts|**händer(in)** m -s,- (f -,-nen) right-hander. **r~händig** adj & adv right-handed. **r~kräftig** adj legal. **R~streit** m law suit. **R~verkehr** m driving on the right. **r~widrig** adj illegal. **R~wissenschaft** f jurisprudence

rechtzeitig adj & adv in time

Reck nt -[e]s,-e horizontal bar

recken vt stretch

Redakteur /redak'tø:ɐ/ m -s,-e editor; (Radio, TV) producer

Redaktion /-'tsjo:n/ f -,-en editing; (Radio, TV) production; (Abteilung) editorial/production department

Rede f -,-n speech; **zur R~stellen** demand an explanation from; **nicht der R~ wert** not worth mentioning

reden vi (haben) talk (von about; mit to); (eine Rede halten) speak ● vt talk; speak (Wahrheit). **R~sart** f saying

Redewendung f idiom

redigieren vt edit

Redner m -s,- speaker

reduzieren vt reduce

Reeder m -s,- shipowner. **R~ei** f -,-en shipping company

Refer|**at** nt -[e]s,-e report; (Abhandlung) paper; (Abteilung) section. **R~ent(in)** m -en,-en (f -,-nen) speaker; (Sachbearbeiter) expert. **R~enz** f -,-en reference

Reflex m -es,-e reflex; (Widerschein) reflection. **R~ion** f -,-en reflection. **r~iv** adj reflexive

Reform f -,-en reform. **R~ation** f - (Relig) Reformation

Reform|**haus** nt health-food shop. **r~ieren** vt reform

Refrain /rə'frɛ̃:/ m -s,-s refrain

Regal nt -s,-e [set of] shelves pl

Regatta f -,-ten regatta

rege adj active; (lebhaft) lively; (geistig) alert; (Handel) brisk

Regel f -,-n rule; (Monats-) period. **r~mäßig** adj regular. **r~n** vt regulate; direct (Verkehr); (erledigen) settle. **r~recht** adj real, proper ● adv really. **R~ung** f -,-en regulation; settlement

regen vt move; **sich r~** move; (wach werden) stir

Regen m -s,- rain. **R~bogen** m rainbow. **R~bogenhaut** f iris

Regener|**ation** /-'tsjo:n/ f - regeneration. **r~ieren** vt regenerate

Regen|**mantel** m raincoat.

r

R~schirm *m* umbrella. R~tag *m* rainy day. R~wetter *nt* wet weather. R~wurm *m* earthworm

Regie /reˈʒiː/ *f* direction; R~ führen direct

regier|en *vt/i (haben)* govern, rule; *(Monarch:)* reign [over]; *(Gram)* take. R~ung *f*,-en government; *(Herrschaft)* rule; *(eines Monarchen)* reign

Regiment *nt* -[e]s,-er regiment

Region *f* -,-en region. **r~al** *adj* regional

Regisseur /reʒɪˈsøːɐ̯/ *m* -s,-e director

Register *nt* -s,- register; *(Inhaltsverzeichnis)* index; *(Orgel-)* stop

Regler *m* -s,- regulator

reglos *adj & adv* motionless

regn|en *vi (haben)* rain; es r~et it is raining. **r~erisch** *adj* rainy

regul|är *adj* normal; *(rechtmäßig)* legitimate. **r~ieren** *vt* regulate

Regung *f* -,-en movement; *(Gefühls-)* emotion. **r~slos** *adj & adv* motionless

Reh *nt* -[e]s,-e roe-deer; *(Culin)* venison

Rehbock *m* roebuck

reib|en† *vt* rub; *(Culin)* grate ● *vi (haben)* rub. R~ung *f* friction. **r~ungslos** *adj (fig)* smooth

reich *adj* rich (an + *dat* in)

Reich *nt* -[e]s,-e empire; *(König-)* kingdom; *(Bereich)* realm

Reiche(r) *m/f* rich man/woman; die R~en the rich *pl*

reichen *vt* hand; *(anbieten)* offer ● *vi (haben)* be enough; *(in der Länge)* be long enough; r~ bis zu reach [up to]; *(sich erstrecken)* extend to; mit dem Geld r~ have enough money

reich|haltig *adj* extensive, large *(Mahlzeit)* substantial. **r~lich** *adj*

ample; *(Vorrat)* abundant. R~tum *m* -s,-tümer wealth (an + *dat* of); *(Techn, Mil)* range

---

Reichstag This historic building in the centre of Berlin was Germany's parliament building until 1945. It became the seat of the enlarged ▷**BUNDESTAG** in 1999. The refurbishment of the *Reichstag* in the 1990s included the building of a glass cupola, with a walkway and viewing platform providing spectacular views over the city.

Reif *m* -[e]s [hoar-]frost

reif *adj* ripe; *(fig)* mature; r~ für ready for. **r~en** *vi (sein)* ripen; *(Wein, Käse & fig)* mature

Reifen *m* -s,- hoop; *(Arm-)* bangle; *(Auto-)* tyre. R~druck *m* tyre pressure. R~panne *f* puncture, flat tyre

reiflich *adj* careful

Reihe *f* -,-n row; *(Anzahl & Math)* series; der R~ nach in turn; wer ist an der R~? whose turn is it? r~n *(sich)* *vr* sich r~n an *(+ acc)* follow. R~nfolge *f* order. R~nhaus *nt* terraced house

Reiher *m* -s,- heron

Reim *m* -[e]s,-e rhyme. r~en *vt* rhyme; sich r~en rhyme

rein¹ *adj* pure; *(sauber)* clean; *(Unsinn, Dummheit)* sheer; ins R~e *(r~e)* schreiben make a fair copy of

rein² *adv* = herein, hinein

Reineclaude /rɛːnəˈkloːdə/ *f* -,-n greengage

Reinfall *m* 🄵 let-down; *(Misserfolg)* flop

Rein|gewinn *m* net profit. R~heit *f* - purity

reinig|en *vt* clean; *(chemisch)* dry-

clean. R~**ung** f -,-en cleaning; (chemische) dry-cleaning; (Geschäft) dry
cleaner's

reinlegen vt sep put in; T dupe;
(betrügen) take for a ride

reinlich adj clean. R~**keit** f -
cleanliness

Reis m -es rice

Reise f -,-n journey; (See-) voyage;
(Urlaubs-, Geschäfts-) trip. R~**andenken** nt souvenir. R~**büro** nt
travel agency. R~**bus** m coach.
R~**führer** m tourist guide; (Buch)
guide. R~**gesellschaft** f tourist
group. R~**leiter(in)** m(f) courier.
r~**n** vi (sein) travel. R~**nde(r)** m/f
traveller. R~**pass** m passport.
R~**scheck** m traveller's cheque.
R~**veranstalter** m -s,- tour operator. R~**ziel** nt destination

Reisig nt -s brushwood

Reißaus m R~ nehmen T
run away

Reißbrett nt drawing-board

reißen† vt tear; (weg-) snatch;
(töten) kill; Witze r~ crack jokes;
an sich (acc) r~snatch; seize
(Macht); sich r~ um T fight for
● vi (sein) tear; (Seil, Faden:) break
● vi (haben) r~ an (+ dat) pull at

Reißer m -s,- T thriller; (Erfolg)
big hit

Reiß|nagel m = R~zwecke.
R~**verschluss** m zip (fastener).
R~**wolf** m shredder. R~**zwecke** f
-,-n drawing-pin

reit|en† vt/i (sein) ride. R~**er(in)**
m -s,- (f -,-nen) rider. R~**hose** f
riding breeches pl. R~**pferd** nt sad-
dle-horse. R~**weg** m bridle-path

Reiz m -es,-e stimulus; (Anziehungskraft) attraction, appeal; (Charme)
charm. r~**bar** adj irritable. R~**bar-
keit** f - irritability. r~**en** vt provoke; (Med) irritate; (interessieren,

locken) appeal to, attract; arouse
(Neugier); (beim Kartenspiel) bid.
R~**ung** f -,-en (Med) irritation.
r~**voll** adj attractive

rekeln (sich) vr T stretch

Reklamation /-'tsi̯oːn/ f -,-en
(Comm) complaint

Reklam|e f -,-n advertising, pub-
licity; (Anzeige) advertisement; (TV,
Radio) commercial; R~ machen
advertise (für etw sth). r~**ieren** vt
complain about; (fordern) claim ● vi
(haben) complain

Rekord m -[e]s,-e record

Rekrut m -en,-en recruit

Rek|tor m -s,-en head[mas-
ter]; (Univ) vice-chancellor. R~**torin**
f -,-nen head, headmistress; vice-
chancellor

Relais /rəˈlɛː/ nt -,- /-,-s,-s/
(Electr) relay

relativ adj relative

Religi|on f -,-en religion; (Sch) reli-
gious education. r~**ös** adj religious

Reling f -,-s (Naut) rail

Reliquie /reˈliːkvi̯ə/ f -,-n relic

rempeln vt jostle; (stoßen) push

Reneklode f -,-n greengage

Rennbahn f race-track; (Pferde-)
racecourse. R~**boot** nt speed-boat.
r~**en†** vi (sein) run; um die Wette
r~**en** have a race. R~**en** nt -s,-
race. R~**pferd** nt racehorse.
R~**sport** m racing. R~**wagen** m
racing car

renommiert adj renowned;
(Hotel, Firma) of repute

renovier|en vt renovate; redecor-
ate (Zimmer). R~**ung** f - renova-
tion; redecoration

rentabel adj profitable

Rente f -,-n pension; in R~ gehen
T retire. R~**nversicherung** f pension scheme

Rentier nt reindeer

rentieren (sich) vr be profitable; (sich lohnen) be worth while

Rentner(in) m -s,- (f -,-nen) [old-age] pensioner

Reparatur f -,-en repair. **R~werkstatt** f repair workshop; (Auto) garage

reparieren vt repair, mend

Reportage /-'ta:ʒə/ f -,-n report

Reporter(in) m -s,- (f -,-nen) reporter

repräsentativ adj representative (für of); (eindrucksvoll) imposing

Reprodukltion /-'tsjo:n/ f -,-en reproduction. **r~zieren** vt reproduce

Reptil nt -s,-ien reptile

Republik f -,-en republic. **r~a‌nisch** adj republican

Requisiten pl (Theat) properties, 🄳 props

Reservat nt -[e]s,-e reservation

Reserve f -,-n reserve; (Mil, Sport) reserves pl. **R~rad** nt spare wheel

reservierlen vt reserve; **r~en lassen** book. **r~t** adj reserved. **R~ung** f -,-en reservation

Reservoir /rezer'voa:ɐ/ nt -s,-s reservoir

Residenz f -,-en residence

Resignlation /-'tsjo:n/ f - resignation. **r~ieren** vi (haben) (fig) give up. **r~iert** adj resigned

resolut adj resolute

Resonanz f -,-en resonance

Respekt /-sp-, -ʃp-/ m -[e]s respect (vor + dat for). **r~ieren** vt respect

respektlos adj disrespectful

Ressort /rε'so:ɐ/ nt -s,-s department

Rest m -[e]s,-e remainder, rest; **R~e** remains; (Essens-) leftovers

Restaurant /rεsto'rã:/ nt -s,-s restaurant

Restaurlation /rεstaura'tsjo:n/ f - restoration. **r~ieren** vt restore

Restlbetrag m balance. **r~lich** adj remaining

Resultat nt -[e]s,-e result

rettlen vt save (vor + dat from); (aus Gefahr befreien) rescue; **sich r~en** save oneself; (flüchten) escape. **R~er** m -s,- rescuer; (fig) saviour

Rettich m -s,-e white radish

Rettung f -,-en rescue; (fig) salvation; **jds letzte R~** s.o.'s last hope. **R~sboot** nt lifeboat. **R~sdienst** m rescue service. **R~sgürtel** m lifebelt. **r~slos** adv hopelessly. **R~sring** m lifebelt. **R~ssanitä‌ter(in)** m(f) paramedic. **R~swagen** m ambulance

retuschieren vt (Phot) retouch

Reue f - remorse; (Relig) repentance

Revanchle /re'vã:ʃə/ f -,-n revenge; **R~e fordern** (Sport) ask for a return match. **r~ieren (sich)** vr take revenge; (sich erkenntlich zeigen) reciprocate (mit with)

Revers /re've:ɐ/ nt -,- /-[s],-s/ lapel

Revier nt -s,-e district; (Zool & fig) territory; (Polizei-) [police] station

Revision f -,-en revision; (Prüfung) check; (Jur) appeal

Revolution /-'tsjo:n/ f -,-en revolution. **r~är** adj revolutionary. **r~ieren** vt revolutionize

Revolver m -s,- revolver

rezenlsieren vt review. **R~sion** f -,-en review

Rezept nt -[e]s,-e prescription; (Culin) recipe

Rezession f -,-en recession

R-Gespräch nt reverse-charge call

Rhabarber m -s rhubarb

Rhein m -s Rhine. **R~land** nt -s

Rhineland. R~wein m hock

Rhetorik f - rhetoric

Rheum|a nt -s rheumatism. r~a-tisch adj rheumatic. R~atismus m - rheumatism

Rhinozeros nt -[ses],-se rhinoceros

rhyth|misch /'ryt-/ adj rhythmic[al]. R~mus m -,-men rhythm

richten vt direct (auf + acc at); address (Frage) (an + acc to); aim (Waffe) (auf + acc at); (einstellen) set; (vorbereiten) prepare; (reparieren) mend; in die Höhe r~ raise [up]; sich r~ be directed (auf + acc at; gegen against); (Blick:) turn (auf + acc on); sich r~nach comply with (Vorschrift); fall in with (jds Plänen); (abhängen) depend on • vi (haben) r~ über (+ acc) judge

Richter m -s,- judge

richtig adj right, correct; (wirklich, echt) real; das R~e the right thing • adv correctly; really; r~ stellen put right (Uhr); (fig) correct (Irrtum); die Uhr geht r~ the clock is right

Richtlinien fpl guidelines

Richtung f -,-en direction

riechen† vt/i (haben) smell (nach of; an etw dat sth)

Riegel m -s,- bolt; (Seife) bar

Riemen m -s,- strap; (Ruder) oar

Riese m -n,-n giant

rieseln vi (sein) trickle; (Schnee:) fall lightly

riesengroß adj huge, enormous

riesig adj huge; (gewaltig) enormous • adv 🆃 terribly

Riff nt -[e]s,-e reef

Rille f -,-n groove

Rind nt -es,-er ox; (Kuh) cow; (Stier) bull; (R~fleisch) beef; R~er cattle pl

Rinde f -,-n bark; (Käse-) rind; (Brot-) crust

Rinder|braten m roast beef. R~wahnsinn m 🆃 mad cow disease

Rindfleisch nt beef

Ring m -[e]s,-e ring

ringeln (sich) vr curl

ring|en† vi (haben) wrestle; (fig) struggle (um/nach for) • vt wring (Hände). R~er m -s,- wrestler. R~kampf m wrestling match; (als Sport) wrestling

ringsherum, r~um adv all around

Rinn|e f -,-n channel; (Dach-) gutter. r~en† vi (sein) run; (Sand:) trickle. R~stein m gutter

Rippe f -,-n rib. R~nfellentzündung f pleurisy

Risiko nt -s,-s & -ken risk

risk|ant adj risky. r~ieren vt risk

Riss m -es,-e tear; (Mauer-) crack; (fig) rift

rissig adj cracked; (Haut) chapped

Rist m -[e]s,-e instep

Ritt m -[e]s,-e ride

Ritter m -s,- knight

Ritual nt -s,-e ritual

Ritz m -es,-e scratch. R~e f -,-n crack; (Fels-) cleft; (zwischen Betten, Vorhängen) gap. r~en vt scratch

Rival|e m -n,-n, R~in f -,-nen rival. R~ität f -,-en rivalry

Robbe f -,-n seal

Robe f -,-n gown; (Talar) robe

Roboter m -s,- robot

robust adj robust

röcheln vi (haben) breathe noisily

Rock¹ m -[e]s,⸚e skirt; (Jacke) jacket

Rock² m -[s] (Mus) rock

rodel|n vi (sein/haben) toboggan. R~schlitten m toboggan

roden vt clear (Land); grub up (Stumpf)

Rogen m -s,- [hard] roe

Roggen m -s rye

roh adj rough; (ungekocht) raw; (Holz) bare; (brutal) brutal. R~bau m -[e]s,-ten shell. R~kost f raw [vegetarian] food. R~ling m -s,-e brute. R~öl nt crude oil

Rohr nt -[e]s,-e pipe; (Geschütz-) barrel; (Bot) reed; (Zucker-, Bambus-) cane

Röhre f -,-n tube; (Radio-) valve; (Back-) oven

Rohstoff m raw material

Rokoko nt -s rococo

Roll|bahn f taxiway; (Start-/Landebahn) runway. R~balken m scroll bar

Rolle f -,-n roll; (Garn-) reel; (Draht-) coil; (Techn) roller; (Seil-) pulley; (Lauf-) castor; (Theat) part, role; das spielt keine R~ (fig) that doesn't matter. r~n vt (roll; (auf-) roll up; (Computer) scroll; sich r~n roll ●vi (sein) roll; (Flugzeug:) taxi. R~r m -s,- scooter. R~rblades® /-ble:ds/ mpl Rollerblades®

Roll|feld nt airfield. R~kragen m polo-neck. R~mops m roll-mop[s] sg

Rollo nt -s,-s [roller] blind

Roll|schuh m roller-skate; R~schuh laufen roller-skate. R~stuhl m wheelchair. R~treppe f escalator

Rom nt -s Rome

Roman m -s,-e novel. r~isch adj Romanesque; (Sprache) Romance

Romant|ik f - romanticism. r~isch adj romantic

Röm|er(in) m -s,- (f -,-nen) Roman. r~isch adj Roman

Rommé, Rommee /'rɔme:/ nt -s rummy

röntgen vt X-ray. R~aufnahme f, R~bild nt X-ray. R~strahlen mpl X-rays

rosa inv adj. R~ nt -[s],- pink

Rose f -,-n rose. R~nkohl m [Brussels] sprouts pl. R~nkranz m (Relig) rosary

Rosine f -,-n raisin

Rosmarin m -s rosemary

Ross nt -es, ̈er horse

Rost¹ m -[e]s,-e grating; (Kamin-) grate; (Brat-) grill

Rost² m -[e]s rust. r~en vi (haben) rust

rösten vt roast; toast (Brot)

rostfrei adj stainless

rostig adj rusty

rot adj, Rot nt -s,- red; rot werden turn red; (erröten) go red, blush

Röte f - redness; (Scham-) blush

Röteln pl German measles sg

röten vt redden; sich r~ turn red

rothaarig adj red-haired

rotieren vi (haben) rotate

Rot|kehlchen nt -s,- robin. R~kohl m red cabbage

rötlich adj reddish

Rotwein m red wine

Roulade /ru'la:də/ f -,-n beef olive. R~leau nt -s,-s [roller] blind

Routine /ru'ti:nə/ f -,-n routine; (Erfahrung) experience. r~emäßig adj routine ●adv routinely. r~iert adj experienced

Rowdy /'raudi/ m -s,-s hooligan

Rübe f -,-n beet; rote R~ beetroot

Rubin m -s,-e ruby

Rubrik f -,-en column

Ruck m -[e]s,-e jerk

ruckartig adj jerky

rück|bezüglich adj (Gram) re-

flexive. **R~blende** f flashback.
R~blick m (fig) review (auf + acc
of). **r~blickend** adv in retrospect.
r~datieren vt (infinitive & pp only)
backdate

Rücken m -s,- back; (Buch-) spine;
(Berg-) ridge. **R~lehne** f back.
R~mark nt spinal cord.
R~schwimmen nt backstroke.
R~wind m following wind; (Aviat)
tail wind

rückerstatten vt (infinitive & pp
only) refund

Rückfahr|karte f return ticket.
R~t f return journey

Rück|fall m relapse. **R~flug** m return flight. **R~frage** f [further]
query. **r~fragen** vi (haben) (infinitive & pp only) check (bei with).
R~gabe f return. **r~gängig** adj
r~gängig machen cancel; break
off (Verlobung). **R~grat** nt -[e]s,-e
spine, backbone. **R~hand** f backhand. **R~kehr** return. **R~lagen** fpl
reserves. **R~licht** nt rear-light.
R~reise f return journey

Rucksack m rucksack

Rück|schau f review. **R~schlag**
m (Sport) return; (fig) set-back.
r~schrittlich adj retrograde.
R~seite f back; (einer Münze)
reverse

Rücksicht f -,-en consideration.
R~nahme f - consideration.
r~slos adj inconsiderate; (schonungslos) ruthless. **r~svoll** adj considerate

Rück|sitz m back seat; (Sozius) pillion. **R~spiegel** m rear-view mirror.
R~spiel nt return match. **R~stand**
m (Chemistry) residue; (Arbeits-)
backlog; **im R~stand sein** be behind. **r~ständig** adj (fig) backward. **R~stau** m (Auto) tailback.
R~strahler m -s,- reflector.
R~tritt m resignation; (Fahrrad)

back pedalling

rückwärt|ig adj back, rear. **r~s**
adv backwards. **R~sgang** m reverse [gear]

Rückweg m way back

rück|wirkend adj retrospective.
R~wirkung f retrospective force;
mit R~wirkung vom backdated
to. **R~zahlung** f repayment

Rüde m -n,-n [male] dog

Rudel nt -s,- herd; (Wolfs-) pack;
(Löwen-) pride

Ruder nt -s,- oar; (Steuer-) rudder;
am R~ (Naut & fig) at the helm.
R~boot nt rowing boat. **r~n** vt/i
(haben/sein) row

Ruf m -[e]s,-e call; (laut) shout; (Telefon) telephone number; (Ansehen)
reputation. **r~en†** vt/i (haben) call
(nach for); **r~en lassen** send for

Ruf|name m forename by which
one is known. **R~nummer** f telephone number. **R~zeichen** nt dialling tone

Rüge f -,-n reprimand. **r~n** vt reprimand; (kritisieren) criticize

Ruhe f - rest; (Stille) quiet; (Frieden)
peace; (innere) calm; (Gelassenheit)
composure; **R~ [da]!** quiet! **r~los**
adj restless. **r~n** vi (haben) rest
(auf + dat on); (Arbeit, Verkehr)
have stopped. **R~pause** f rest,
break. **R~stand** m retirement; **im
R~stand** retired. **R~störung** f disturbance of the peace. **R~tag** m
day of rest; 'Montag R~tag'
'closed on Mondays'

ruhig adj quiet; (erholsam) restful;
(friedlich) peaceful; (unbewegt, gelassen) calm; **man kann r~ darüber sprechen** there's no harm in
talking about it

Ruhm m -[e]s fame; (Ehre) glory

rühmen vt praise

ruhmreich adj glorious

Ruhr f - (Med) dysentery

Rühr|ei nt scrambled eggs pl. **r~en** vt move; (Culin) stir; sich **r~en** move ● vi (haben) stir; **r~en an** (+ acc) touch; (fig) touch on. **r~end** adj touching

Rührung f - emotion

Ruin m -s ruin. **R~e** f -,-n ruin; ruins pl (gen of). **r~ieren** vt ruin

rülpsen vi (haben) [] belch

Rum m -s rum

Rumän|ien /-iən/ nt -s Romania. **r~isch** adj Romanian

Rummel m -s [] hustle and bustle; (Jahrmarkt) funfair

Rumpelkammer f junk-room

Rumpf m -[e]s, ⸚e body, trunk; (Schiffs-) hull; (Aviat) fuselage

rund adj ● adv approximately; **r~ um** [a]round. **R~blick** m panoramic view. **R~brief** m circular [letter]

Runde f -,-n round; (Kreis) circle; (eines Polizisten) beat; (beim Rennen) lap; eine **R~** Bier a round of beer

Rund|fahrt f tour. **R~frage** f poll

Rundfunk m radio; im **R~** on the radio. **R~gerät** nt radio [set]

Rund|gang m round; (Spaziergang) walk (durch round). **r~heraus** adv straight out. **r~herum** adv all around. **r~lich** adj rounded; (mollig) plump. **R~reise** f [circular] tour. **R~schreiben** nt circular. **r~um** adv all round. **R~ung** f -,-en curve

Runzel f -,-n wrinkle

runzlig adj wrinkled

Rüpel m -s,- [] lout

rupfen vt pull out; pluck (Geflügel)

Rüsche f -,-n frill

Ruß m -es soot

Russe m -n,-n Russian

Rüssel m -s,- (Zool) trunk

Russ|in f -,-nen Russian. **r~isch** adj Russian. **R~isch** nt -[s] (Lang) Russian

Russland nt -s Russia

rüsten vi (haben) prepare (zu/für for) ● vr sich **r~** get ready

rüstig adj sprightly

rustikal adj rustic

Rüstung f -,-en armament; (Harnisch) armour. **R~skontrolle** f arms control

Rute f -,-n twig; (Angel-, Wünschel-) rod; (zur Züchtigung) birch; (Schwanz) tail

Rutsch m -[e]s,-e slide. **R~bahn** f slide. **R~e** f -,-n chute. **r~en** vi (haben) slide; (rücken) move ● vi (sein) slide; (aus-, ab-) slip; (Auto) skid. **r~ig** adj slippery

rütteln vt shake ● vi (haben) **r~ an** (+ dat) rattle

Ss

Saal m -[e]s,Säle hall; (Theat) auditorium; (Kranken-) ward

Saat f -,-en seed; (Säen) sowing; (Gesätes) crop

sabbern vi (haben) [] slobber; (Baby:) dribble; (reden) jabber

Säbel m -s,- sabre

Sabo|tage /zabo'ta:ʒə/ f - sabotage. **S~teur** m -s,-e saboteur. **s~tieren** vt sabotage

Sach|bearbeiter m expert. **S~buch** nt non-fiction book

Sache f -,-n matter, business; (Ding) thing; (fig) cause

Sach|gebiet nt (fig) area, field. **s~kundig** adj expert. **s~lich** adj factual; (*nüchtern*) matter-of-fact

sächlich *adj* (*Gram*) neuter

Sachse *m* -n,-n Saxon. **S~n** *nt* -s Saxony

sächsisch *adj* Saxon

Sach|verhalt *m* -[e]s facts *pl*.
S~verständige(r) *m/f* expert

Sack *m* -[e]s,ᵉe sack

Sack|gasse *f* cul-de-sac; (*fig*) impasse. **S~leinen** *nt* sacking

Sadis|mus *m* - sadism. **S~t** *m* -en,-en sadist

säen *vt/i* (*haben*) sow

Safe /zeːf/ *m* -s,-s safe

Saft *m* -[e]s,ᵉe juice; (*Bot*) sap.
s~ig *adj* juicy

Sage *f* -,-n legend

Säge *f* -,-n saw. **S~mehl** *nt* sawdust

sagen *vt* say; (*mitteilen*) tell; (*bedeuten*) mean

sägen *vt/i* (*haben*) saw

sagenhaft *adj* legendary

Säge|späne *mpl* wood shavings.
S~werk *nt* sawmill

Sahne *f* - cream. **S~bonbon** *m & nt* ≈ toffee. **s~ig** *adj* creamy

Saison /zɛˈzõː/ *f* -,-s season

Saite *f* -,-n (*Mus, Sport*) string.
S~ninstrument *nt* stringed instrument

Sakko *m & nt* -s,-s sports jacket

Sakrament *nt* -[e]s,-e sacrament

Sakristei *f* -,-en vestry

Salat *m* -[e]s,-e salad. **S~soße** *f* salad-dressing

Salbe *f* -,-n ointment

Salbei *m* -s & *f* - sage

salben *vt* anoint

Saldo *m* -s,-dos & -den balance

Salon /zaˈlõː/ *m* -s,-s salon

salopp *adj* casual; (*Benehmen*) informal

Salto *m* -s,-s somersault

Salut *m* -[e]s,-e salute. **s~ieren** *vi* (*haben*) salute

Salve /-və/ *f* -,-n volley; (*Geschütz-*) salvo, (*von Gelächter*) burst

Salz *nt* -es,-e salt. **s~en†** *vt* salt.
S~fass *nt* salt-cellar. **s~ig** *adj* salty.
S~kartoffeln *fpl* boiled potatoes.
S~säure *f* hydrochloric acid

Salzburger Festspiele   *i*

The Austrian city of Salzburg, the home of Wolfgang Amadeus Mozart (1756-91), hosts this annual festival as a tribute to the great composer. Every summer since 1920, Mozart-lovers have enjoyed his music at the Salzburg Festival.

Samen *m* -s,- seed; (*Anat*) semen, sperm

Sammel|becken *nt* reservoir.
s~n *vt/i* (*haben*) collect; (*suchen, versammeln*) gather; sich **s~n** collect; (*sich versammeln*) gather; (*sich fassen*) collect oneself. **S~name** *m* collective noun

Samm|ler(in) *m* -s,- (*f* -,-nen) collector. **S~lung** *f* -,-en collection; (*innere*) composure

Samstag *m* -s Saturday. **s~s** *adv* on Saturdays

samt *prep* (+ *dat*) together with

Samt *m* -[e]s velvet

sämtlich indefinite pronoun inv all.
s~e(r,s) indefinite pronoun all the; **s~e Werke** complete works

Sanatorium *nt* -s,-ien sanatorium

Sand *m* -[e]s sand

Sandale *f* -,-n sandal

Sand|bank *f* sandbank. **S~kasten** *m* sand-pit. **S~papier** *nt* sandpaper

s

sanft *adj* gentle

Sänger(in) *m* -s,-(*f* -,-nen) singer

sanieren *vt* clean up; redevelop (*Gebiet*); (*modernisieren*) modernize; make profitable (*Industrie, Firma*); **sich s~** become profitable

sanitär *adj* sanitary

Sanität|er *m* -s,- first-aid man; (*Fahrer*) ambulance man; (*Mil*) medical orderly. **S~swagen** *m* ambulance

Sanktion /zaŋkˈtsjoːn/ *f* -,-en sanction. **s~ieren** *vt* sanction

Saphir *m* -s,-e sapphire

Sardelle *f* -,-n anchovy

Sardine *f* -,-n sardine

Sarg *m* -[e]s,ᵉe coffin

Sarkasmus *m* - sarcasm

Satan *m* -s Satan; (℞: *Teufel*) devil

Satellit *m* -en,-en satellite. **S~enfernsehen** *nt* satellite television. **S~enschüssel** *f* satellite dish. **S~entelefon** *nt* satphone

Satin /zaˈtɛ̃ː/ *m* -s satin

Satire *f* -,-n satire

satt *adj* full; (*Farbe*) rich; **s~ sein** have had enough [to eat]; **etw s~ haben** 🔢 be fed up with sth

Sattel *m* -s,ᵉ saddle. **s~n** *vt* saddle. **S~zug** *m* articulated lorry

sättigen *vt* satisfy; (*Chemistry & fig*) saturate ● *vi* (*haben*) be filling

Satz *m* -es,ᵉe sentence; (*Teil-*) clause; (*These*) proposition; (*Math*) theorem; (*Mus*) movement; (*Tennis, Zusammengehöriges*) set; (*Boden-*) sediment; (*Kaffee-*) grounds *pl*; (*Steuer-, Zins-*) rate; (*Druck-*) setting; (*Schrift-*) type; (*Sprung*) leap, bound. **S~aussage** *f* predicate. **S~gegenstand** *m* subject. **S~zeichen** *nt* punctuation mark

Sau *f* -,Säue sow

sauber *adj* clean; (*ordentlich*) neat;

(*anständig*) decent; **s~ machen** clean. **S~keit** *f* - cleanliness; neatness

säuberlich *adj* neat

Sauce /ˈzoːsə/ *f* -,-n sauce; (*Braten-*) gravy

Saudi-Arabien /-jən/ *nt* -s Saudi Arabia

sauer *adj* sour; (*Chemistry*) acid; (*eingelegt*) pickled; (*schwer*) hard; **saurer Regen** acid rain

Sauerkraut *nt* sauerkraut

säuerlich *adj* slightly sour

Sauerstoff *m* oxygen

saufen† *vt/i* (*haben*) drink; ℞ booze

Säufer *m* -s,- ℞ boozer

saugen† *vt/i* (*haben*) suck; (*staub-*) vacuum, hoover; **sich voll Wasser s~** soak up water

säugen *vt* suckle

Säugetier *nt* mammal

saugfähig *adj* absorbent

Säugling *m* -s,-e infant

Säule *f* -,-n column

Saum *m* -[e]s,Säume hem; (*Rand*) edge

säumen *vt* hem; (*fig*) line

Sauna *f* -,-nas & -nen sauna

Säure *f* -,-n acidity; (*Chemistry*) acid

sausen *vi* (*haben*) rush; (*Ohren:*) buzz ● *vi* (*sein*) rush [along]

Saxophon, Saxofon *nt* -s,-e saxophone

S-Bahn *f* city and suburban railway

Scanner *m* -s,- scanner

sch *int* shush! (*fort*) shoo!

Schabe *f* -,-n cockroach

schaben *vt/i* (*haben*) scrape

schäbig *adj* shabby

Schablone *f* -,-n stencil; (*Muster*) pattern; (*fig*) stereotype

Schach nt -s chess; S~! check! S~brett nt chessboard

Schachfigur f chess-man

schachmatt adj s~ setzen checkmate; s~! checkmate!

Schachspiel nt game of chess

Schacht m -[e]s,⸚e shaft

Schachtel f -,-n box; (Zigaretten-) packet

Schachzug m move

schade adj s~ sein be a pity or shame: zu s~ für too good for

Schädel m -s, skull. S~bruch m fractured skull

schaden vi (haben) (+ dat) damage; (nachteilig sein) hurt. S~ m -s,⸚ damage; (Defekt) defect; (Nachteil) disadvantage. S~ersatz m damages pl. S~freude f malicious glee. s~froh adj gloating

schädig|en vt damage, harm. S~ung f -,-en damage

schädlich adj harmful

Schädling m -s,-e pest. S~sbekämpfungsmittel nt pesticide

Schaf nt -[e]s,-e sheep. S~bock m ram

Schäfer m -s, shepherd. S~hund m sheepdog; Deutscher S~hund alsatian

schaffen¹† vt create; (herstellen) establish; make (Platz)

schaffen² v (reg) ● vt manage [to do]; pass (Prüfung); catch (Zug); (bringen) take

Schaffner m -s, conductor; (Zug-) ticket-inspector

Schaffung f - creation

Schaft m -[e]s,⸚e shaft; (Gewehr-) stock; (Stiefel-) leg

Schal m -s,-s scarf

Schale f -,-n skin; (abgeschält) peel; (Eier-, Nuss-, Muschel-) shell; (Schüssel) dish

schälen vt peel; sich s~ peel

Schall m -[e]s sound. S~dämpfer m silencer. s~dicht adj soundproof. s~en vi (haben) ring out: (nachhallen) resound. S~platte f record, disc

schalt|en vt switch ● vi (haben) switch/(Ampel:) turn (auf + acc to); (Auto) change gear; (□: begreifen) catch on. S~er m -s, switch; (Post-, Bank-) counter; (Fahrkarten-) ticket window. S~hebel m switch; (Auto) gear lever. S~jahr nt leap year. S~ung f -,-en circuit; (Auto) gear change

Scham f - shame; (Anat) private parts pl

schämen (sich) vr be ashamed

scham|haft adj modest. s~los adj shameless

Schampon nt -s shampoo. s~ieren vt shampoo

Schande f - disgrace, shame

schändlich adj disgraceful

Schanktisch m bar

Schanze f, -,-n [ski-]jump

Schar f -,-en crowd; (Vogel-) flock

Scharade f -,-n charade

scharen vt um sich s~ gather round one; sich s~ um flock round. s~weise adv in droves

scharf adj sharp; (stark) strong; (stark gewürzt) hot; (Geruch) pungent; (Wind, Augen, Verstand) keen; (streng) harsh; (Galopp) hard; (Munition) live; (Hund) fierce; s~ einstellen (Phot) focus; s~ sein (Phot) be in focus; s~ sein auf (+ acc) □ be keen on

Schärfe f sharpness; strength; hotness; pungency; keenness; harshness. s~n vt sharpen

Scharf|richter m executioner. S~schütze m marksman. S~sinn m astuteness

Scharlach m -s scarlet fever

Scharlatan m -s,-e charlatan

Scharnier nt -s,-e hinge

Schärpe f -,-n sash

scharren vi (haben) scrape; (Huhn) scratch ● vt scrape

Schaschlik m & nt -s,-e kebab

Schatten m -s, - shadow; (schattige Stelle) shade. **S~riss** m silhouette. **S~seite** f shady side; (fig) disadvantage

schattier|en vt shade. **S~ung** f -,-en shading

schattig adj shady

Schatz m -es,-̈e treasure; (Freund, Freundin) sweetheart

schätzen vt estimate; (taxieren) value; (achten) esteem; (würdigen) appreciate

Schätzung f -,-en estimate; (Taxierung) valuation

Schau f -,-en show. **S~bild** nt diagram

Schauder m -s shiver; (vor Abscheu) shudder. **s~haft** adj dreadful. **s~n** vi (haben) shiver; (vor Abscheu) shudder

schauen vi (haben) (SGer, Aust) look; s~, dass make sure that

Schauer m -s, - shower; (Schauder) shiver. **S~geschichte** f horror story. **s~lich** adj ghastly

Schaufel f -,-n shovel; (Kehr-) dustpan. **s~n** vt shovel; (graben) dig

Schaufenster nt shop-window. **S~puppe** f dummy

Schaukel f -,-n swing. **s~n** vt rock ● vi (haben) rock; (auf einer Schaukel) swing; (schwanken) sway. **S~pferd** nt rocking-horse. **S~stuhl** m rocking-chair

Schaum m -[e]s foam; (Seifen-) lather; (auf Bier) froth; (als Frisier-, Rasiermittel) mousse

schäumen vi (haben) foam, froth; (Seife:) lather

Schaum|gummi m foam rubber. **s~ig** frothy; **s~ig** rühren (Culin) cream. **S~stoff** m [synthetic] foam. **S~wein** m sparkling wine

Schauplatz m scene

schaurig adj dreadful; (unheimlich) eerie

Schauspiel nt play; (Anblick) spectacle. **S~er** m actor. **S~erin** f actress

Scheck m -s,-s cheque. **S~buch**, **S~heft** nt cheque-book. **S~karte** f cheque card

Scheibe f -,-n disc; (Schieß-) target; (Glas-) pane; (Brot-, Wurst-) slice. **S~nwischer** m -s, - windscreen-wiper

Scheich m -s,-e & -s sheikh

Scheide f -,-n sheath; (Anat) vagina

scheid|en vt separate; (unterscheiden) distinguish; dissolve (Ehe); sich s~en lassen get divorced ● vi (sein) leave; (voneinander) part. **S~ung** f -,-en divorce

Schein m -[e]s,-e light; (Anschein) appearance; (Bescheinigung) certificate; (Geld-) note. **s~bar** adj apparent. **s~ent** vi (haben) shine; (den Anschein haben) seem, appear

scheinheilig adj hypocritical

Scheinwerfer m -s, - floodlight; (Such-) searchlight; (Auto) headlight; (Theat) spotlight

Scheiße f - (vulgar) shit. **s~nt** vi (haben) (vulgar) shit

Scheit nt -[e]s,-e log

Scheitel m -s, - parting

scheitern vi (sein) fail

Schelle f -,-n bell. **s~n** vi (haben) ring

Schellfisch m haddock

Schelm m -s,-e rogue

Schelte f - scolding

Schema nt -s,-mata model, pattern; (Skizze) diagram

Schemel m -s,- stool

Schenke f -,-n tavern

Schenkel m -s,- thigh

schenken vt give [as a present]; jdm Vertrauen s~ trust s.o.

Scherbe f -,-n [broken] piece

Schere f -,-n scissors pl; (Techn) shears pl; (Hummer-) claw. s~n¹† vt shear; crop (Haar)

scheren² vt (reg) ⊥ bother; sich nicht s~ um not care about

Scherenschnitt m silhouette

Scherereien fpl ⊥ trouble sg

Scherz m -es,-e joke; im/zum S~ as a joke. s~en vi (haben) joke

scheu adj shy; (Tier) timid; s~ werden (Pferd:) shy

scheuchen vt shoo

scheuen vt be afraid of; (meiden) shun; keine Mühe/Kosten s~ spare no effort/expense; sich s~ be afraid (vor + dat of); shrink (etw zu tun from doing sth)

scheuern vt scrub; (reiben) rub; [wund] s~n chafe ● vi (haben) rub, chafe

Scheuklappen fpl blinkers

Scheune f -,-n barn

Scheusal nt -s,-e monster

scheußlich adj horrible

Schi m -s,-er ski; S~ fahren od laufen ski

Schicht f -,-en layer; (Geology) stratum; (Gesellschafts-) class; (Arbeits-) shift. S~arbeit f shift work. s~en vt stack [up]

schick adj stylish; (Frau) chic. S~ m -[e]s style

schicken vt/i (haben) send;

s~ nach send for

Schicksal nt -s,-e fate. S~sschlag m misfortune

Schieb|edach nt (Auto) sun-roof. s~en† vt push; (gleitend) slide; (⊥: handeln mit) traffic in; etw s~en auf (+ acc) (fig) put sth down to; shift (Schuld) on to ● vi (haben) push. S~etür f sliding door. S~ung f -,-en ⊥ illicit deal; (Betrug) rigging, fixing

Schieds|gericht nt panel of judges; (Jur) arbitration tribunal. S~richter m referee; (Tennis) umpire; (Jur) arbitrator

schief adj crooked; (unsymmetrisch) lopsided; (geneigt) slanting, sloping; (nicht senkrecht) leaning; (Winkel) oblique; (fig) false; suspicious ● adv not straight; s~ gehen ⊥ go wrong

Schiefer m -s slate

schielen vi (haben) squint

Schienbein nt shin

Schiene f -,-n rail; (Gleit-) runner; (Med) splint. s~n vt (Med) put in a splint

Schieß|bude f shooting-gallery. s~en† vt shoot; fire (Kugel); score (Tor) ● vi (haben) shoot, fire (auf + acc at). S~scheibe f target. S~stand m shooting-range

Schifahr|en nt skiing. S~er(in) m(f) skier

Schiff nt -[e]s,-e ship; (Kirchen-) nave; (Seiten-) aisle

Schiffahrt* f = Schifffahrt

schiff|bar adj navigable. S~bruch m shipwreck. s~brüchig adj shipwrecked. S~fahrt f shipping

Schikan|e f -,-n harassment; mit allen S~en ⊥ with every refinement. s~ieren vt harass

Schi|laufen nt -s skiing. S~läufer(in) m(f) (-s,- (f -,-nen)) skier

s

Schild¹ m -[e]s,-e shield

Schild² nt -[e]s,-er sign; (Nummern-) plate; (Mützen-) badge; (Etikett) label

Schilddrüse f thyroid [gland]

schilder|n vt describe. **S∼ung** f -,-en description

Schild|kröte f tortoise; (See-) turtle. **S∼patt** nt -[e]s tortoiseshell

Schilf nt -[e]s reeds pl

schillern vi (haben) shimmer

Schimmel m -s,- mould; (Pferd) white horse. **s∼n** vi (haben/sein) go mouldy

schimmern vi (haben) gleam

Schimpanse m -n,-n chimpanzee

schimpf|en vi (haben) grumble (mit at; über + acc about); scold (mit jdm s.o.). ●vt call. **S∼wort** nt (pl -wörter) swear-word

Schinken m -s,- ham. **S∼speck** m bacon

Schippe f -,-n shovel. **s∼n** vt shovel

Schirm m -[e]s,-e umbrella; (Sonnen-) sunshade; (Lampen-) shade; (Augen-) visor; (Mützen-) peak; (Ofen-, Bild-) screen; (fig: Schutz) shield. **S∼herrschaft** f patronage. **S∼mütze** f peaked cap

schizophren adj schizophrenic. **S∼ie** f - schizophrenia

Schlacht f -,-en battle

schlachten vt slaughter, kill

Schlacht|feld nt battlefield. **S∼hof** m abattoir

Schlacke f -,-n slag

Schlaf m -[e]s sleep; im S∼ in one's sleep. **S∼anzug** m pyjamas pl

Schläfe f -,-n (Anat) temple

schlafen† vi (haben) sleep; s∼ gehen go to bed; er schläft noch he is still asleep

schlaff adj limp; (Seil) slack;

(Muskel) flabby

Schlaf|lied nt lullaby. **s∼los** adj sleepless. **S∼losigkeit** f - insomnia. **S∼mittel** nt sleeping drug

schläfrig adj sleepy

Schlaf|saal m dormitory. **S∼sack** m sleeping-bag. **S∼tablette** f sleeping-pill. **S∼wagen** m sleeping-car, sleeper. **s∼wandeln** vi (haben/ sein) sleep-walk. **S∼zimmer** nt bedroom

Schlag m -[e]s,ᵉe blow; (Faust-) punch; (Herz-, Puls-, Trommel-) beat; (einer Uhr) chime; (Glocken-, Gong- & Med) stroke; (elektrischer) shock; (Art) type; S∼e bekommen get a beating; S∼ auf S∼ in rapid succession. **S∼ader** f artery. **S∼anfall** m stroke. **S∼baum** m barrier

schlagen† vt hit, strike; (fällen) fell; knock (Loch, Nagel) (in + acc into); (prügeln, besiegen) beat; (Culin) whisk (Eiweiß); whip (Sahne); (legen) throw; (wickeln) wrap; sich s∼ fight ●vi (haben) beat; (Tür:) bang; (Uhr:) strike; (melodisch) chime; mit den Flügeln s∼ flap its wings ●vi sein (schlug) in etw (acc) s∼ (Blitz, Kugel:) strike; nach jdm s∼ (fig) take after s.o.

Schlager m -s,- popular song; (Erfolg) hit

Schläger m -s,- racket; (Tischtennis-) bat; (Golf-) club; (Hockey-) stick. **S∼ei** f -,-en fight, brawl

schlagfertig adj quick-witted. **S∼loch** nt pot-hole. **S∼sahne** f whipped cream; (ungeschlagen) whipping cream. **S∼seite** f (Naut) list. **S∼stock** m truncheon. **S∼wort** nt (pl -worte) slogan. **S∼zeile** f headline. **S∼zeug** nt (Mus) percussion. **S∼zeuger** m -s,- percussionist; (in Band) drummer

Schlamm m -[e]s mud. **s∼ig** adj muddy

Schlampe f -,-n 🔲 slut. **s~en** vi (haben) 🔲 be sloppy (bei in). **s~ig** adj slovenly; (Arbeit) sloppy

Schlange f -,-n snake; (Menschen-, Auto-) queue; **s~ stehen** queue

schlängeln (sich) vr wind; (Person:) weave (durch through)

schlank adj slim. **S~heitskur** f slimming diet

schlapp adj tired; (schlaff) limp

schlau adj clever; (gerissen) crafty; ich werde nicht **s~** daraus I can't make head or tail of it

Schlauch m -[e]s,Schläuche tube; (Wasser-) hose[pipe]. **S~boot** nt rubber dinghy

Schlaufe f -,-n loop

schlecht adj bad; (böse) wicked; (unzulänglich) poor; **s~** werden go bad; (Wetter:) turn bad; mir ist **s~** I feel sick; **s~** machen 🔲 run down. **s~gehen** vi sep (sein) **s~** gehen, s. **gehen**

schlecken vt/i (haben) lick (an etw dat sth); (auf-) lap up

Schlegel m -s,- (SGer: Keule) leg; (Hühner-) drumstick

schleichen vi (sein) creep; (langsam gehen/fahren) crawl ●vr sich **s~** creep. **s~d** adj creeping

Schleier m -s,- veil; (fig) haze

Schleife f -,-n bow; (Fliege) bowtie; (Biegung) loop

schleifen[1] v (reg) ●vt drag ●vi (haben) trail, drag

schleifen[2]† vt grind; (schärfen) sharpen; cut (Edelstein, Glas)

Schleim m -[e]s slime; (Anat) mucus; (Med) phlegm. **s~ig** adj slimy

schlendern vi (sein) stroll

schlenkern vt/i (haben) swing; **s~** mit swing; dangle (Beine)

Schlepp|dampfer m tug. **S~e** f

-,-n train. **s~en** vt drag; (tragen) carry; (ziehen) tow; **sich s~en** drag oneself; (sich hinziehen) drag on; **sich s~en** mit carry. **S~er** m -s,-n tug; (Traktor) tractor. **S~kahn** m barge. **S~lift** m T-bar lift. **S~tau** nt tow-rope; **ins S~tau nehmen** take in tow

Schleuder f -,-n catapult; (Wäsche-) spin-drier. **s~n** vt hurl; spin (Wäsche) ●vi (sein) skid; **ins S~n geraten** skid. **S~sitz** m ejector seat

Schleuse f -,-n lock; (Sperre) sluice[-gate]. **s~n** vt steer

Schliche pl tricks

schlicht adj plain; simple

Schlichtung f - settlement; (Jur) arbitration

schließen v tr clasp; buckle

schließen† vt close (ab-) lock; fasten (Kleid, Verschluss); (stilllegen) close down; (beenden, folgern) conclude; enter into (Vertrag); **sich s~** close; etw aus (+ acc) conclude sth to; **sich s~** an (+ acc) follow ●vi (haben) close, (den Betrieb einstellen) close down; (den Schlüssel drehen) turn the key; (enden, folgern) conclude

Schließ|fach nt locker. **s~lich** adv finally, in the end; (immerhin) after all. **S~ung** f -,-en closure

Schliff m -[e]s cut; (Schleifen) cutting; (fig) polish

schlimm adj bad

Schlinge f -,-n loop; (Henkers-) noose; (Med) sling; (Falle) snare

Schlingel m -s,- 🔲 rascal

schlingen† vt wind, wrap; tie (Knoten) ●vt/i (haben) bolt one's food

Schlips m -es,-e tie

Schlitten m -s,- sledge; (Rodel-) toboggan; (Pferde-) sleigh; **s~ fahren** toboggan

schlittern vi (haben/sein) slide

Schlittschuh m skate; **S∼** laufen skate. **S∼läufer(in)** m(f) -s,- (f -,-nen) skater

Schlitz m -es,-e slit; (für Münze) slot; (Jacken-) vent; (Hosen-) flies pl. **s∼en** vt slit

Schloss nt -es,-er lock; (Vorhänge-) padlock; (Verschluss) clasp; (Gebäude) castle; palace

Schlosser m -s,- locksmith; (Auto-) mechanic

Schlucht f -,-en ravine, gorge

schluchzen vi (haben) sob

Schluck m -[e]s,-e mouthful; (klein) sip

Schluckauf m -s hiccups pl

schlucken vt/i (haben) swallow

Schlummer m -s slumber

Schlund m -[e]s [back of the] throat; (fig) mouth

schlüpf|en vi (sein) slip; [aus dem Ei] **s∼en** hatch. **S∼er** m -s,- knickers pl. **s∼rig** adj slippery

schlürfen vt/i (haben) slurp

Schluss m -es,-e end; (S∼folgerung) conclusion; zum S∼ finally; S∼ machen stop (mit etw sth); finish (mit jdm with s.o.)

Schlüssel m -s,- key; (Schrauben-) spanner; (Geheim-) code; (Mus) clef. **S∼bein** nt collar-bone. **S∼bund** m & nt bunch of keys. **S∼loch** nt keyhole

Schlussfolgerung f conclusion

schlüssig adj conclusive

Schluss|licht nt rear-light. **S∼verkauf** m sale

schmächtig adj slight

schmackhaft adj tasty

schmal adj narrow; (dünn) thin; (schlank) slender; (karg) meagre

schmälern vt diminish; (herabsetzen) belittle

Schmalz¹ nt -es lard; (Ohren-) wax

Schmalz² m -es 🆃 schmaltz

Schmarotzer m -s,- parasite; (Person) sponger

schmatzen vi (haben) eat noisily

schmausen vi (haben) feast

schmecken vi (haben) taste (nach of); (gut) s∼ taste good ● vt taste

Schmeichelei f -,-en flattery; (Kompliment) compliment

schmeichel|haft adj complimentary, flattering. **s∼n** vi (haben) (+ dat) flatter

schmeißen† vt/i (haben) s∼ [mit] 🆃 chuck

Schmeißfliege f bluebottle

schmelz|en† vt/i (sein) melt; smelt (Erze). **S∼wasser** nt melted snow and ice

Schmerbauch m 🆃 paunch

Schmerz m -es,-en pain; (Kummer) grief; S∼en haben be in pain. **s∼en** vt hurt; (fig) grieve ● vi (haben) hurt, be painful. **S∼engeld** nt compensation for pain and suffering. **s∼haft** adj painful. **s∼los** adj painless **s∼stillend** adj pain-killing; **s∼stillendes Mittel** analgesic, pain-killer. **S∼tablette** f pain-killer

Schmetterball m (Tennis) smash

Schmetterling m -s,-e butterfly

schmettern vt hurl; (Tennis) smash; (singen) sing ● vi (haben) sound

Schmied m -[e]s,-e blacksmith

Schmiede f -,-n forge. **S∼eisen** nt wrought iron. **s∼n** vt forge

Schmier|e f -,-n grease; (Schmutz) mess. **s∼en** vt lubricate; (streichen) spread; (schlecht schreiben) scrawl ● vi (haben) smudge; (schreiben) scrawl. **S∼geld** nt 🆃 bribe. **s∼ig** adj greasy; (schmutzig) grubby. **S∼mittel** nt lubricant

Schminke f -,-n make-up. **s~n** vt make up; **sich** ~ put on make-up; **sich** (dat) **die Lippen s~n** put on lipstick

schmirgel|n vt sand down. **S~papier** nt emery-paper

schmollen vi (haben) sulk

schmor|en vt/i (haben) braise. **S~topf** m casserole

Schmuck m -[e]s jewellery; (Verzierung) ornament, decoration

schmücken vt decorate, adorn

schmuck|los adj plain. **S~stück** nt piece of jewellery

Schmuggel m smuggling. **s~n** vt smuggle. **S~ware** f contraband

Schmuggler m -s,- smuggler

schmunzeln vi (haben) smile

schmusen vi (haben) cuddle

Schmutz m -es dirt. **s~en** vi (haben) get dirty. **s~ig** adj dirty

Schnabel m -s, beak, bill; (eines Kruges) lip; (Tülle) spout

Schnalle f -,-n buckle. **s~n** vt strap; (zu-) buckle

schnalzen vi (haben) mit der Zunge **s~** click one's tongue

schnapp|en vi (haben) **s~en nach** snap at; gasp for (Luft) ● vt snatch, grab; (🄸: festnehmen) nab. **S~schloss** nt spring lock. **S~schuss** m snapshot

Schnaps m -es, snaps

schnarchen vi (haben) snore

schnaufen vi (haben) puff, pant

Schnauze f -,-n muzzle; (eines Kruges) lip; (Tülle) spout

schnäuzen (sich) vr blow one's nose

Schnecke f -,-n snail; (Nackt-) slug; (Spirale) scroll. **S~nhaus** nt snail-shell

Schnee m -s snow; (Eier-) beaten egg-white. **S~besen** m whisk.

S~brille f snow-goggles pl. **S~fall** m snow-fall. **S~flocke** f snowflake. **S~glöckchen** nt -s,- snowdrop. **S~kette** f snow chain. **S~mann** m (pl -männer) snowman. **S~pflug** m snowplough. **S~schläger** m whisk. **S~sturm** m snowstorm, blizzard. **S~wehe** f -,-n snowdrift

Schneide f -,-n [cutting] edge; (Klinge) blade

schneiden† vt cut; (in Scheiben) slice; (kreuzen) cross; (nicht beachten) cut dead; **Gesichter s~** pull faces; **sich s~** cut oneself; (über-) intersect

Schneider m -s,- tailor. **S~in** f -,-nen dressmaker. **s~n** vt make (Anzug, Kostüm)

Schneidezahn m incisor

schneien vi (haben) snow; **es schneit** it is snowing

Schneise f -,-n path

schnell adj quick; (Auto, Tempo) fast ● adv quickly; (in s~em Tempo) fast; (bald) soon; **mach s~!** hurry up! **S~igkeit** f -, rapidity; (Tempo) speed. **S~kochtopf** m pressure-cooker. **s~stens** adv as quickly as possible. **S~zug** m express [train]

schnetzeln vt cut into thin strips

Schnipsel m & nt -s,- scrap

Schnitt m -[e]s,-e cut; (Film-) cutting; (S~muster) [paper] pattern; **im S~** (durchschnittlich) on average

Schnitte f -,-n slice [of bread]

schnittig adj stylish; (stromlinienförmig) streamlined

Schnitt|lauch m chives pl. **S~muster** nt [paper] pattern. **S~punkt** m [point of] intersection. **S~stelle** f interface. **S~wunde** f cut

Schnitzel nt -s,- scrap; (Culin) escalope. **s~n** vt shred

schnitzen vt/i (haben) carve

schnodderig adj 🔳 brash

Schnorchel m -s,- snorkel

Schnörkel m -s,- flourish; (Kunst) scroll. **s~ig** adj ornate

schnüffeln vi (haben) sniff (an etw dat sth); (🔳: spionieren) snoop [around]

Schnuller m -s,- [baby's] dummy

Schnupf|en m -s,- [head] cold. **S~tabak** m snuff

schnuppern vt/i (haben) sniff (an etw dat sth)

Schnur f -,ꞏe string; (Kordel) cord; (Electr) flex

schnüren vt tie; lace [up] (Schuhe)

Schnurr|bart m moustache. **s~en** vi (haben) hum; (Katze:) purr

Schnürsenkel m [shoe-]lace

Schock m -[e]s,-e shock. **s~en** vt 🔳 shock. **s~ieren** vt shock

Schöffe m -n,-n lay judge

Schokolade f - chocolate

Scholle f -,-n clod [of earth]; (Eis-) [ice-]floe; (Fisch) plaice

schon adv already; (allein) just; (sogar) even; (ohnehin) anyway; **s~ einmal** before; (jemals) ever; **s~ immer/oft/wieder** always/often/ again; **s~** deshalb for that reason alone; das ist **s~ möglich** that's quite possible; ja **s~,** aber well yes, but

schön adj beautiful; (Wetter) fine; (angenehm, nett) nice; (gut) good; (🔳: beträchtlich) pretty; **s~en** Dank! thank you very much!

schonen vt spare; (gut behandeln) look after. **s~d** adj gentle

Schönheit f -,-en beauty. **S~sfehler** m blemish. **S~skonkurrenz** f beauty contest

Schonung f -,-en gentle care; (nach Krankheit) rest; (Baum-) plantation. **s~slos** adj ruthless

Schonzeit f close season

schöpf|en vt scoop [up]; ladle (Suppe); Mut **s~en** take heart. **s~erisch** adj creative. **S~kelle** f. **S~löffel** m ladle. **S~ung** f -,-en creation

Schoppen m -s,- (SGer) ≈ pint

Schorf m -[e]s scab

Schornstein m chimney. **S~feger** m -s,- chimney sweep

Schoß m -es,ꞏe lap; (Frack-) tail

Schössling m -s,-e (Bot) shoot

Schote f -,-n pod; (Erbse) pea

Schotte m -n,-n Scot, Scotsman

Schotter m -s gravel

Schottin f -nen Scot, Scotswoman

schott|isch adj Scottish, Scots. **S~land** nt -s Scotland

schraffieren vt hatch

schräg adj diagonal; (geneigt) sloping; **s~** halten tilt. **S~strich** m oblique stroke

Schramme f -,-n scratch

Schrank m -[e]s,ꞏe cupboard; (Kleider-) wardrobe; (Akten-, Glas-) cabinet

Schranke f -,-n barrier

Schraube f -,-n screw; (Schiffs-) propeller. **s~n** vt screw; (ab-) unscrew; (drehen) turn. **S~nschlüssel** m spanner. **S~nzieher** m -s,- screwdriver

Schraubstock m vice

Schreck m -[e]s,-e fright. **S~en** m -s,- fright; (Entsetzen) horror

Schreck|gespenst nt spectre. **s~haft** adj easily frightened; (nervös) jumpy. **s~lich** adj terrible.

Schrei m -[e]s,-e cry, shout; (gellend) scream; der letzte **S~** 🔳 the latest thing

schreib|en† vt/i (haben) write; (auf der Maschine) type; richtig/ falsch **s~en** spell right/wrong; sich

s~en (Wort:) be spelt; (korrespondieren) correspond. **S~en** nt -s,- writing; (Brief) letter. **S~fehler** m spelling mistake. **S~heft** nt exercise book. **S~kraft** f clerical assistant; (für Maschineschreiben) typist. **S~maschine** f typewriter. **S~tisch** m desk. **S~ung** f -,-en spelling. **S~waren** fpl stationery sg.

schreien† vt/i (haben) cry; (gellend) scream; (rufen, laut sprechen) shout

Schreiner m -s,- joiner

schreiten† vi (sein) walk

Schrift f -,-en writing; (Druck-) type; (Abhandlung) paper; die Heilige S~ the Scriptures pl. **S~führer** m secretary. **s~lich** adj written ● adv in writing. **S~sprache** f written language. **S~steller(in)** m -s,- (f -,-nen) writer. **S~stück** nt document. **S~zeichen** nt character

schrill adj shrill

Schritt m -[e]s,-e step; (Entfernung) pace; (Gangart) walk; (der Hose) crotch. **S~macher** m -s,- pace-maker. **s~weise** adv step by step

schroff adj precipitous; (abweisend) brusque; (unvermittelt) abrupt; (Gegensatz) stark

Schrot m & nt -[e]s coarse meal; (Blei-) small shot. **S~flinte** f shotgun

Schrott m -[e]s scrap[-metal]; zu S~ fahren Ⅰ write off. **S~platz** m scrap-yard

schrubben vt/i (haben) scrub

Schrull|e f -,-n whim; alte S~e old crone. **s~ig** adj cranky

schrumpfen vi (sein) shrink

schrumpf[el]ig adj wrinkled

Schub m -[e]s,=e (Phys) thrust; (S~fach) drawer; (Menge) batch. **S~fach** nt drawer. **S~karre** f,

S~karren m wheelbarrow. **S~lade** f drawer

Schubs m -es,-e push, shove **s~en** vt push, shove

schüchtern adj shy. **S~heit** f - shyness

Schuft m -[e]s,-e (pej) swine

Schuh m -[e]s,-e shoe. **S~anzieher** m -s,- shoehorn. **S~band** nt (pl -bänder) shoe-lace. **S~creme** f shoe-polish. **S~löffel** m shoehorn. **S~macher** m -s,- shoemaker

Schul|abgänger m -s,- schoolleaver. **S~arbeiten, S~aufgaben** fpl homework sg.

Schuld f -,-en guilt; (Verantwortung) blame; (Geld-) debt; S~en machen get into debt; S~ haben be to blame (an + dat for); jdm S~ geben blame s.o. ● s~ sein be to blame (an + dat for). **s~en** vt owe

schuldig adj guilty (gen of); (gebührend) due; jdm etw s~sein owe s.o. sth. **S~keit** f - duty

schuldlos adj innocent. **S~ner** m -s,- debtor. **S~spruch** m guilty verdict

Schule f -,-n school; in der/die S~ at/to school. **s~n** vt train

Schüler(in) m -s,- (f -,-nen) pupil

schul|frei adj s~freier Tag day without school; wir haben morgen s~frei there's no school tomorrow. **S~hof** m [school] playground. **S~jahr** nt school year; (Klasse) form. **S~kind** nt schoolchild. **S~stunde** f lesson

Schulter f -,-n shoulder. **S~blatt** nt shoulder-blade

Schulung f - training

schummeln vi (haben) Ⅰ cheat

Schund m -[e]s trash

Schuppe f -,-n scale; **S~n** pl dandruff sg. **s~n (sich)** vr flake [off]

Schuppen m -s,- shed

schürf|en vt mine; sich (dat) das Knie ~en graze one's knee ● vi (haben) ~en nach prospect for. **S~wunde** f abrasion, graze

Schürhaken m poker

Schurke m -n,-n villain

Schürze f -,-n apron

Schuss m -es,·̈e shot; (kleine Menge) dash

Schüssel f -,-n bowl; (TV) dish

Schuss|fahrt f (Ski) schuss. **S~waffe** f firearm

Schuster m -s, = Schuhmacher

Schutt m -[e]s rubble. **S~ablade- platz** m rubbish dump

Schüttel|frost m shivering fit. **s~n** vt shake; sich ~n shake one- self/itself; (vor Ekel) shudder; jdm die Hand s~n shake s.o.'s hand

schütten vt pour; (kippen) tip; (ver-) spill ● vi (haben) es schüttet it is pouring [with rain]

Schutz m -es protection; (Zuflucht) shelter; (Techn) guard; **S~ suchen** take refuge. **S~anzug** m protective suit. **S~blech** nt mudguard. **S~brille** f goggles pl

Schütze m -n,-n marksman; (Tor-) scorer; (Astrology) Sagittarius

schützen vt protect; (Zuflucht ge- währen) shelter (vor + dat from) ● vi (haben) give protection/shelter (vor + dat from)

Schutz|engel m guardian angel. **S~heilige(r)** m/f patron saint

Schützling m -s,-e charge

schutz|los adj defenceless, help- less. **S~mann** m (pl -männer & -leute) policeman. **S~umschlag** m dust-jacket

Schwaben nt -s Swabia

schwäbisch adj Swabian

schwach adj weak; (nicht gut; ge- ring) poor; (leicht) faint

Schwäche f -,-n weakness. **s~n** vt weaken

schwäch|lich adj delicate. **S~ling** m -s,-e weakling

Schwachsinn m mental defi- ciency. **s~ig** adj mentally deficient; 🗓 idiotic

Schwager m -s,·̈ brother-in-law

Schwägerin f -,-nen sister-in-law

Schwalbe f -,-n swallow

Schwall m -[e]s torrent

Schwamm m -[e]s,·̈e sponge; (SGer: Pilz) fungus; (essbar) mush- room. **s~ig** adj spongy

Schwan m -[e]s,·̈e swan

schwanger adj pregnant

Schwangerschaft f -,-en pregnancy

Schwank m -[e]s,·̈e (Theat) farce

schwank|en vi (haben) sway; (Boot:) rock; (sich ändern) fluctuate; (unentschieden sein) be undecided ● (sein) stagger. **S~ung** f -,-en fluc- tuation

Schwanz m -es,·̈e tail

schwänzen vt 🗓 skip; die Schule s~ play truant

Schwarm m -[e]s,·̈e swarm; (Fisch-) shoal; (🗓: Liebe) idol

schwärmen vi (haben) swarm; **s~ für** 🗓 adore; (verliebt sein) have a crush on

Schwarte f -,-n (Speck-) rind

schwarz adj black; (🗓: illegal) il- legal; **s~er Markt** black market; **s~ gekleidet** dressed in black; **s~ auf weiß** in black and white; **s~ sehen** (fig) be pessimistic; **ins S~e treffen** score a bull's-eye. **S~** nt -[e]s,- black. **S~arbeit** f moon- lighting. **s~arbeiten** vi sep (haben) moonlight. **S~e(r)** m/f black

Schwärze f - blackness. **s~n** vt blacken

Schwarz|fahrer m fare-dodger. **S~handel** m black market (mit in). **S~händler** m black marketeer. **S~markt** m black market. **S~wald** m Black Forest. **S~weiß** adj black and white

schwatzen, (SGer) **schwätzen** (haben) chat; (klatschen) gossip; (Sch) talk [in class] • vt talk

Schwebe f - in der S~ (fig) undecided. **S~bahn** f cable railway. s~n vi (haben) float; (fig) be undecided; (Verfahren:) be pending; in Gefahr s~n be in danger • (sein) float

Schwed|e m -n,-n Swede. **S~en** nt -s Sweden. **S~in** f -,-nen Swede. s~isch adj Swedish

Schwefel m -s sulphur

schweigen† vi (haben) be silent; ganz zu s~ von let alone. **S~** nt -s silence; zum S~ bringen silence

schweigsam adj silent; (wortkarg) taciturn

Schwein nt -[e]s,-e pig; (Culin) pork; (⚠ Schuft) swine; **S~haben** 🄫 be lucky. **S~ebraten** m roast pork. **S~efleisch** nt pork. **S~erei** f -,-en ⚠ [dirty] mess; (Gemeinheit) dirty trick. **S~estall** m pigsty. **S~sleder** nt pigskin

Schweiß m -es sweat

schweißen vt weld

Schweiz (die) - Switzerland. **S~er** adj & m -s,-, **S~erin** f -,-nen Swiss. s~erisch adj Swiss

Schweizerische Eidgenossenschaft The Swiss Confederation is the official name for Switzerland. The confederation was established in 1291 when the cantons (▶KANTON) of Uri, Schwyz and Unterwalden swore to defend their traditional rights against the Habsburg Empire. The unified federal state as it is known today was formed in 1848.

Schwelle f -,-n threshold; (Eisenbahn-) sleeper

schwell|en† vi (sein) swell. **S~ung** f -,-en swelling

schwer adj heavy; (schwierig) difficult; (mühsam) hard; (ernst) serious; (schlimm) bad; 2 Pfund s~ sein weigh 3 pounds • adv heavily; with difficulty; (mühsam) hard; (schlimm, sehr) badly, seriously; s~ krank/verletzt seriously ill/injured; s~ hören be hard of hearing; etw s~ nehmen take sth seriously; jdm s~ fallen be hard for s.o.; es jdm s~ machen make it hard or things difficult for s.o.; sich s~ tun have difficulty (mit with); s~ zu sagen difficult or hard to say

Schwere f - heaviness; (Gewicht) weight; (Schwierigkeit) difficulty; (Ernst) gravity. **S~losigkeit** f - weightlessness

schwer|fällig adj ponderous, clumsy. **S~gewicht** nt heavyweight. **S~hörig** adj s~hörig sein be hard of hearing. **S~kraft** f (Phys) gravity. **s~mütig** adj melancholic. **S~punkt** m centre of gravity; (fig) emphasis

Schwert nt -[e]s,-er sword. **S~lilie** f iris

Schwer|verbrecher m serious offender. **s~wiegend** adj weighty

Schwester f -,-n sister; (Kranken-) nurse. **s~lich** adj sisterly

Schwieger|eltern pl parents-in-law. **S~mutter** f mother-in-law. **S~sohn** m son-in-law. **S~tochter** f daughter-in-law. **S~vater** m father-in-law

schwierig adj difficult. **S~keit** f

-,-en difficulty

Schwimm|bad nt swimming-baths pl. **S~becken** nt swimming-pool. **s~en†** vt/i (sein/haben) swim; (auf dem Wasser treiben) float. **S~weste** f life-jacket

Schwindel m -s dizziness, vertigo; (①: Betrug) fraud; (Lüge) lie. **S~anfall** m dizzy spell. **s~frei** adj **s~frei sein** have a good head for heights. **s~n** vi (haben) lie

Schwindl|er m -s,- liar; (Betrüger) fraud, con-man. **s~ig** adj dizzy; mir ist od wird **s~ig** I feel dizzy

schwing|en† vi (haben) swing; (Phys) oscillate; (vibrieren) vibrate ● vt swing; wave (Fahne); (drohend) brandish. **S~ung** f -,-en oscillation; vibration

Schwips m -es,-e einen **S~** haben ① be tipsy

schwitzen vi (haben) sweat; ich **s~e** I am hot

schwören† vt/i (haben) swear (auf + acc by)

schwul adj (①: homosexuell) gay

schwül adj close. **S~e** f - closeness

Schwung m -[e]s,ᵉe swing; (Bogen) sweep; (Schnelligkeit) momentum; (Kraft) vigour. **s~los** adj dull. **s~voll** adj vigorous; (Bogen, Linie) sweeping; (mitreißend) spirited

Schwur m -[e]s,ᵉe vow; (Eid) oath. **S~gericht** nt jury [court]

sechs inv adj six. **S~** f -,-en six; (Sch) ≈ fail mark. **s~eckig** adj hexagonal. **s~te(r,s)** adj sixth

sech|zehn inv adj sixteen. **s~zehnte(r,s)** adj sixteenth. **s~zig** inv adj sixty. **s~zigste(r,s)** adj sixtieth

See¹ m -s,-n lake

See² f -s,-n sea; an die/der See to/at the seaside; auf See at sea. **S~fahrt** f [sea] voyage; (Schifffahrt)

navigation. **S~gang** m schwerer **S~gang** rough sea. **S~hund** m seal. **s~krank** adj seasick

Seele f -,-n soul

seelisch adj psychological; (geistig) mental

See|macht f maritime power. **S~mann** m (pl -leute) seaman, sailor. **S~not** f in **S~not** in distress. **S~räuber** m pirate. **S~reise** f [sea] voyage. **S~rose** f water-lily. **S~sack** m kitbag. **S~stern** m starfish. **S~tang** m seaweed. **s~tüchtig** adj seaworthy. **S~zunge** f sole

Segel nt -s,- sail. **S~boot** nt sailing-boat. **S~flugzeug** nt glider. **s~n** vt/i (sein/haben) sail. **S~schiff** nt sailing-ship. **S~sport** m sailing. **S~tuch** nt canvas

Segen m -s blessing

Segler m -s,- yachtsman

segnen vt bless

sehen† vt see; watch (Fernsehsendung); jdn/etw wieder **s~** see s.o./ sth again; sich **s~ lassen** show oneself ● vi (haben) see; (blicken) look (auf + acc at); (ragen) show (aus above); gut/schlecht **s~** have good/bad eyesight; vom **S~** kennen know by sight; **s~** nach keep an eye on; (betreuen) look after; (suchen) look for. **s~swert**, **s~swürdig** adj worth seeing. **S~swürdigkeit** f -,-en sight

Sehne f -,-n tendon; (eines Bogens) string

sehnen (sich) vr long (nach for)

Sehn|sucht f - longing (nach for). **s~süchtig** adj longing; (Wunsch) dearest

sehr adv very; (mit Verb) very much; so **s~**, dass so much that

seicht adj shallow

seid s. sein¹

Seide f -,-n silk

Seidel nt -s,- beer-mug

seiden adj silk **S~papier** nt tissue paper. **S~raupe** f silk-worm

seidig adj silky

Seife f -,-n soap. **S~npulver** nt soap powder. **S~nschaum** m lather

Seil nt -[e]s,-e rope; (Draht-) cable. **S~bahn** f cable railway. **s~springen** vi (sein) (infinitive & pp only) skip. **S~tänzer(in)** m(f) tightrope walker

sein¹

● intransitive verb (sein)

‥‥▸ be. ich bin glücklich I am happy. er ist Lehrer/Schwede he is a teacher/Swedish. bist du es? is that you? sei still! be quiet! sie waren in Paris they were in Paris. morgen bin ich zu Hause I shall be at home tomorrow. er ist aus Berlin he is or comes from Berlin

‥‥▸ (impers + dat) mir ist kalt/ besser I am cold/better. ihr ist schlecht she feels sick

‥‥▸ (existieren) es ist/sind ‥ there is/are ‥. es ist keine Hoffnung mehr there is no more hope. es sind vier davon there are four of them. es war einmal ein Prinz once upon a time there was a prince

● auxiliary verb

‥‥▸ (zur Perfektumschreibung) have. er ist gestorben he has died. sie sind angekommen they have arrived. sie war dort gewesen she had been there. ich wäre gefallen I would have fallen

‥‥▸ (zur Bildung des Passivs) be. wir sind gerettet worden/wir waren gerettet we were saved

‥‥▸ (+ zu + Infinitiv) be to be. es

war niemand zu sehen there was no one to be seen. das war zu erwarten that was to be expected. er ist zu bemitleiden he is to be pitied. die Richtlinien sind strengstens zu beachten the guidelines are to be strictly followed

sein² poss pron his; (Ding, Tier) its; (nach man) one's. **s~** Glück versuchen try one's luck. **s~e(r,s)** poss pron his; (nach man) one's own; das **S~e** tun do one's share. **s~erseits** adv for his part. **s~erzeit** adv in those days. **s~etwegen** adv for his sake; (wegen ihm) because of him, on his account. **s~ige** poss pron der/die/das **s~ige** his

seins poss pron his; (nach man) one's own

seit conj & prep (+ dat) since; **s~** einiger Zeit for some time [past]; ich wohne **s~** zehn Jahren hier I've lived here for ten years. **s~dem** conj since ● adv since then

Seite f -,-n side; (Buch-) page; zur **S~** treten step aside; auf der einen/anderen **S~** (fig) on the one/other hand

seitens prep (+ gen) on the part of

Seiten|schiff nt [side] aisle. **S~sprung** m infidelity. **S~stechen** nt -s (Med) stitch. **S~straße** f side-street. **S~streifen** m verge; (Autobahn-) hard shoulder

seither adv since then

seit|lich adj side ● adv at/on the side; **s~lich von** to one side of ● prep (+ gen) to one side of. **s~wärts** adv on/to one side; (zur Seite) sideways

Sekret|är m -s,-e secretary; (Schrank) bureau. **S~ariat** nt -[e]s,-e secretary's office. **S~ärin** f -,-nen secretary

Sekt m -[e]s [German] sparkling wine

Sekte f -,-n sect

Sektor m -s,-en sector

Sekunde f -,-n second

Sekundenschlaf m microsleep

selber pron ⓘ = selbst

selbst pron oneself; ich/du/er/sie
s~ I myself /you yourself/ he him-
self/she herself; wir/ihr/sie s~ we
ourselves/you yourselves/they themselves; ich schneide mein Haar s~
I cut my own hair; von s~ of one's
own accord; (automatisch) automatically; s~ gemacht ,home-made
● adv even

selbständig adj = selbstständig.
S~keit f - = Selbstständigkeit

Selbst|bedienung f self-service.
S~befriedigung f masturbation.
s~bewusst adj self-confident.
S~bewusstsein nt self-confidence.
S~bildnis nt self-portrait. S~er-
haltung f self-preservation. s~ge-
macht* adj = s~ gemacht, s.
selbst. s~haftend adj self-adhesive. S~hilfe f self-help. s~kle-
bend adj self-adhesive. S~kosten-
preis m cost price. S~laut m
vowel. s~los adj selfless. S~mord
m suicide. S~mordattentat nt suicide attack. S~mörder(in) m(f)
suicide. s~mörderisch adj suicidal.
S~porträt nt self-portrait. s~si-
cher adj self-assured. s~ständig
adj independent; self-employed
(Handwerker); sich s~ständig machen set up on one's own. s~stän-
digkeit f - independence. s~süch-
tig adj selfish. s~tanken nt
self-service (for petrol). s~tätig adj
automatic. s~versorgung f self-
catering. s~verständlich adj natural; etw für s~ halten take sth
for granted; das ist s~ that goes

without saying; s~! of course!
S~verteidigung f self-defence.
S~vertrauen nt self-confidence.
S~verwaltung f self-government

selig adj blissfully happy; (Relig)
blessed; (verstorben) late. S~keit f
- bliss

Sellerie m -s,-s & f -,- celeriac;
(Stangen-) celery

selten adj rare ● adv rarely, seldom; (besonders) exceptionally.
S~heit f -,-en rarity

seltsam adj odd, strange. s~er-
weise adv oddly

Semester nt -s,- (Univ) semester

Semikolon nt -s,-s semicolon

Seminar nt -s,-e seminar; (Institut)
department; (Priester-) seminary

Semmel f -,-n (Aust, SGer) [bread]
roll. S~brösel pl breadcrumbs

Senat m -[e]s,-e senate. S~or m
-s,-en senator

senden¹† vt send

sende|n² vt (reg) broadcast; (über
Funk) transmit, send. S~r m -s,-
[broadcasting] station; (Anlage)
transmitter. S~reihe f series

Sendung f -,-en consignment,
shipment; (TV) programme

Senf m -s mustard

senil adj senile. S~ität f - senility

Senior m -s,-en senior; S~en senior citizens. S~enheim nt old
people's home

senken vt lower; bring down (Fieber, Preise); bow (Kopf); sich s~
come down, fall; (absinken) subside

senkrecht adj vertical. S~e f
-n,-n perpendicular

Sensation /-'tsjo:n/ f -,-en sensation. s~ell adj sensational

Sense f -,-n scythe

sensibel adj sensitive

sentimental adj sentimental

September m -s,- September

Serie /ˈzeːrjə/ f -,-n series; (Briefmarken) set; (Comm) range.
S~nnummer f serial number

seriös adj respectable; (zuverlässig) reliable

Serpentine f -,-n winding road; (Kehre) hairpin bend

Serum nt -s,Sera serum

Server m -s,- server

Service[1] /ˈzɛrviːs/ nt -[s],- service, set

Service[2] /ˈzøːɐvɪs/ m & nt -s (Comm, Tennis) service

servier|en vt/i (haben) serve.
S~erin f -,-nen waitress

Serviette f -,-n napkin, serviette

Servus int (Aust) cheerio; (Begrüßung) hallo

Sessel m -s,- armchair. **S~bahn** f, **S~lift** m chairlift

sesshaft adj settled

Set /zɛt/ nt & m -[s],-s set; (Deckchen) place-mat

setz|en vt put; (abstellen) set down; (hin-) sit down (Kind); (Spielstein) (pflanzen) plant; (schreiben, wetten) put; **sich s~en** sit down; (sinken) settle ● vi (sein) leap ● vi (haben) **s~en auf** (+ acc) back

Seuche f -,-n epidemic

seufz|en vi (haben) sigh. **S~er** m -s,- sigh

Sex /zɛks/ m -[es] sex

Sexualität f - sexuality. **s~ell** adj sexual

sezieren vt dissect

Shampoo /ʃamˈpuː/, **Shampoon** /ʃamˈpoːn/ nt -s shampoo

siamesisch adj Siamese

sich reflexive pron oneself; (mit er/sie/es) himself/herself/itself; (mit sie pl) themselves; (mit Sie) yourself; (pl) yourselves; (einander) each

other; **s~ kennen** know oneself/(einander) each other; **s~ waschen** have a wash; **s~** (dat) **die Haare kämmen** comb one's hair; **s~ wundern** be surprised; **s~ gut verkaufen** sell well; **von s~ aus** of one's own accord

Sichel f -,-n sickle

sicher adj safe; (gesichert) secure; (gewiss) certain; (zuverlässig) reliable; sure (Urteil); steady (Hand); (selbstbewusst) self-confident; **bist du s~?** are you sure? ● adv safely; securely; certainly; reliably; self-confidently; (wahrscheinlich) most probably; **s~!** certainly! **s~gehent** vi sep (sein) (fig) be sure

Sicherheit f - safety; (Pol, Psych, Comm) security; (Gewissheit) certainty; (Zuverlässigkeit) reliability; (des Urteils) surety; (Selbstbewusstsein) self-confidence. **S~sgurt** m safety belt; (Auto) seat belt. **S~snadel** f safety pin

sicherlich adv certainly; (wahrscheinlich) most probably

sicher|n vt secure; (garantieren) safeguard; (schützen) protect; put the safety catch on (Pistole).
S~ung f -,-en safeguard, protection; (Gewehr-) safety catch; (Electr) fuse

Sicht f - view; (S~weite) visibility; **auf lange S~** in the long term.
s~bar adj visible. **S~vermerk** m visa. **S~weite** f visibility; **außer S~weite** out of sight

sie pron (nom) (sg) she; (Ding, Tier) it; (pl) they; (acc) (sg) her; (Ding, Tier) it; (pl) them

Sie pron you; gehen/warten Sie! go/wait!

Sieb nt -[e]s,-e sieve; (Tee-) strainer.
s~en[1] vt sieve, sift

sieben[2] inv adj seven, **S~** f -,-en seven.
S~sachen fpl 🛈 belongings.

s ◾

s~te(r,s) *adj* seventh
sieb|te(r,s) *adj* seventh. **s~zehn**
inv adj seventeen. **s~zehnte(r,s)**
adj seventeenth. **s~zig** *inv adj* seventy. **s~zigste(r,s)** *adj* seventieth
siede|n† *vt/i* (haben) boil.
S~punkt *m* boiling point
Siedlung *f* -,-en [housing] estate;
(*Niederlassung*) settlement
Sieg *m* -[e]s,-e victory
Siegel *nt* -s,- seal. **S~ring** *m* signet-ring
sieg|en *vi* (haben) win. **S~er(in)** *m*
-s,- (f -,-nen) winner. **s~reich** *adj*
victorious
siezen *vt* jdn s~ call s.o. 'Sie'
Signal *nt* -s,-e signal
Silbe *f* -,-n syllable
Silber *nt* -s silver. **s~n** *adj* silver
Silhouette /zɪˈlʊɛtə/ *f* -,-n silhouette
Silizium *nt* -s silicon
Silo *m* & *nt* -s,-s silo
Silvester *nt* -s New Year's Eve
SIM-Karte *f* SIM card
Sims *m* & *nt* -es,-e ledge
simsen *vi* send a text
simultan *adj* simultaneous
sind *s.* sein¹
Sinfonie *f* -,-n symphony
singen† *vt/i* (haben) sing
Singvogel *m* songbird
sinken† *vi* (sein) sink; (*nieder-*)
drop; (*niedriger werden*) go down,
fall; **den Mut s~ lassen** lose
courage
Sinn *m* -[e]s,-e sense; (*Denken*)
mind; (*Zweck*) point; in gewissem
S~e in a sense; es hat keinen S~
it is pointless. **S~bild** *nt* symbol
sinnlich *adj* sensory; (*sexuell*) sensual; (*Genüsse*) sensuous. **S~keit** *f*
sensuality; sensuousness
sinn|los *adj* senseless; (*zwecklos*)

pointless. **s~voll** *adj* meaningful;
(*vernünftig*) sensible
Sintflut *f* flood
Siphon /ˈziːfõ/ *m* -s,-s siphon
Sippe *f* -,-n clan
Sirene *f* -,-n siren
Sirup *m* -s,-e syrup; treacle
Sitte *f* -,-n custom; **S~n** manners
sittlich *adj* moral. **S~keit** *f* - morality. **S~keitsverbrecher** *m* sex offender
sittsam *adj* well-behaved; (*züchtig*)
demure
Situation /-ˈtsi̯oːn/ *f* -,-en situation. **s~iert** *adj* gut/schlecht
s~iert well/badly off
Sitz *m* -es,-e seat; (*Passform*) fit
sitzen† *vi* (haben) sit; (*sich befinden*) be; (*passen*) fit; (⊡: *treffen*) hit
home; [im Gefängnis] s~ ⊡ be in
jail; s~ bleiben remain seated; ⊡
(*Sch*) stay or be kept down; (*nicht
heiraten*) be left on the shelf; s~
bleiben auf (+ *dat*) be left with
Sitz|gelegenheit *f* seat.
S~platz *m* seat. **S~ung** *f* -,-en
session
Sizilien /-i̯ən/ *nt* -s Sicily
Skala *f* -,-len scale; (*Reihe*) range
Skalpell *nt* -s,-e scalpel
skalpieren *vt* scalp
Skandal *m* -s,-e scandal. **s~ös** *adj*
scandalous
Skandinav|ien /-i̯ən/ *nt* -s Scandinavia. **s~isch** *adj* Scandinavian
Skat *m* -s skat
Skateboard /ˈskeːtbɔːɐt/ *nt* -s,-s
skateboard
Skelett *nt* -[e]s,-e skeleton
Skep|sis *f* - scepticism. **s~tisch**
adj sceptical
Ski /ʃiː/ *m* -s,-er ski; **Ski fahren** or
laufen ski. **S~fahrer(in)**, **S~läufer(in)** *m(f)* -s,- (f -,-nen) skier.

S~sport m skiing

Skizz|e f ~,-n sketch. **s~ieren** vt sketch

Sklav|e m -n,-n slave. **S~erei** f - slavery. **S~in** f ~,-nen slave

Skorpion m -s,-e scorpion; (Astrology) Scorpio

Skrupel m -s,- scruple. **s~los** adj unscrupulous

Skulptur f ~,-en sculpture

Slalom m -s,-s slalom

Slaw|e m -n,-n, **S~in** f ~,-nen Slav. **s~isch** adj Slav; (Lang) Slavonic

Slip m -s,-s briefs pl

Smaragd m -[e]s,-e emerald

Smoking m -s,-s dinner jacket

SMS-Nachricht f text message

Snob m -s,-s snob. **S~ismus** f - snobbery **s~istisch** adj snobbish

so adv so; (so sehr) so much; (auf diese Weise) like this/that; (solch) such; (⊞: sowieso) anyway; (⊞: umsonst) free; (⊞: ungefähr) about; so viel so much; so gut/bald wie as good/soon as; so ein Zufall! what a coincidence! mir ist so, als ob I feel as if; so oder so in any case; so um zehn Euro ⊞ about ten euros; so? really? ● conj (also) so; (dann) then; so dass = sodass

sobald conj as soon as

Söckchen nt -s,- [ankle] sock

Socke f ~,-n sock

Sockel m -s,- plinth, pedestal

Socken m -s,- sock

sodass conj so that

Sodawasser nt soda water

Sodbrennen nt -s heartburn

soeben adv just [now]

Sofa nt -s,-s settee, sofa

sofern adv provided [that]

sofort adv at once, immediately; (auf der Stelle) instantly

Software /ˈzɔftvɛːɐ̯/ f - software

sogar adv even

sogenannt adj so-called

sogleich adv at once

Sohle f ~,-n sole; (Tal-) bottom

Sohn m -[e]s,ᵉe son

Sojabohne f soya bean

solange conj as long as

solch inv pron such; **s~ ein(e)** such a; **s~ einer/eine/eins** one/(Person) someone like that. **s~e(r,s)** pron such ● (substantivisch) **ein s~er/ eine s~e/ein s~es** one/(Person) someone like that; **s~e** pl those; (Leute) people like that

Soldat m -en,-en soldier

Söldner m -s,- mercenary

Solidarität f - solidarity

solide adj solid; (haltbar) sturdy; (sicher) sound; (anständig) respectable

Solist(in) m -en,-en (f -,-nen) soloist

Soll nt -s (Comm) debit; (Produktions-) quota

sollen†

● auxiliary verb

···▸ (Verpflichtung) be [supposed or meant] to. er soll morgen zum Arzt gehen he is [supposed] to go to the doctor tomorrow. die beiden Flächen sollen fluchten the two surfaces are meant to be or should be in alignment. du solltest ihn anrufen you were meant to phone him or should have phoned him

···▸ (Befehl) du sollst sofort damit aufhören you're to stop that at once. er soll hereinkommen he is to come in; (sagen Sie es ihm) tell him to come in

···▸ sollte (subjunctive) should;

ought to. **wir sollten früher aufstehen** we ought to or should get up earlier. **das hätte er nicht tun/sagen sollen** he shouldn't have done/ said that

····▸ *(Zukunft, Geplantes)* be to. **ich soll die Abteilung übernehmen** I am to take over the department. **du sollst das Geld zurückbekommen** you are to or shall get your money back. **es soll nicht wieder vorkommen** it won't happen again. **sie sollten ihr Reiseziel nie erreichen** they were never to reach their destination

····▸ *(Ratlosigkeit)* be to; shall. **was soll man nur machen?** what is one to do?; what shall I/we do? **ich weiß nicht, was ich machen soll** I don't know what I should do or what to do

····▸ *(nach Bericht)* be supposed to. **er soll sehr reich sein** he is supposed or is said to be very rich. **sie soll geheiratet haben** they say or I gather she has got married

····▸ *(Absicht)* be meant or supposed to. **was soll dieses Bild darstellen?** what is this picture supposed to represent? **das sollte ein Witz sein** that was meant or supposed to be a joke

····▸ *(in Bedingungssätzen)* should. **sollte er anrufen, falls** *od* **wenn er anrufen sollte** should he or if he should telephone

● *intransitive verb*

····▸ *(irgendwohin gehen sollen)* be [supposed] to go. **er soll morgen zum Arzt/nach Berlin** he is [supposed] to go to the doctor/ to Berlin tomorrow. **ich sollte ins Theater** I was supposed to

go to the theatre

····▸ *(sonstige Wendungen)* **soll er doch!** let him! **was soll das?** what's that in aid of? [1]

Solo *nt* -s,-los & -li solo

somit *adv* therefore, so

Sommer *m* -s,- summer. **s~lich** *adj* summery; *(Sommer-)* summer ● *adv* **s~lich warm** as warm as summer. **S~sprossen** *fpl* freckles

Sonate *f* -,-n sonata

Sonde *f* -,-n probe

Sonder|angebot *nt* special offer. **s~bar** *adj* odd. **S~fahrt** *f* special excursion. **S~fall** *m* special case. **s~gleichen** *adv* **eine Gemeinheit s~gleichen** unparalleled meanness. **S~ ling** *m* -s,-e crank. **S~marke** *f* special stamp

sondern *conj* but; **nicht nur ... s~ auch** not only ... but also

Sonder|preis *m* special price. **S~schule** *f* special school

Sonett *nt* -[e]s,-e sonnet

Sonnabend *m* -s,-e Saturday. **s~s** *adv* on Saturdays

Sonne *f* -,-n sun. **s~n (sich)** *vr* sun oneself

Sonnen|aufgang *m* sunrise. **s~baden** *vi (haben)* sunbathe. **S~bank** *f* sun-bed. **S~blume** *f* sunflower. **S~brand** *m* sunburn. **S~brille** *f* sunglasses *pl.* **S~energie** *f* solar energy. **S~finsternis** *f* solar eclipse. **S~milch** *f* sun-tan lotion. **S~öl** *nt* sun-tan oil. **S~schein** *m* sunshine. **S~schirm** *m* sunshade. **S~stich** *m* sunstroke. **S~uhr** *f* sundial. **S~untergang** *m* sunset. **S~wende** *f* solstice

sonnig *adj* sunny

Sonntag *m* -s,-e Sunday. **s~s** *adv* on Sundays

sonst *adv (gewöhnlich)* usually; (im

Übrigen) apart from that; *(andernfalls)* otherwise, or [else]; wer/was/wie/wo s~? who/what/how/where else? s~ **niemand** no one else; s~ **noch etwas?** anything else? s~ **noch Fragen?** any more questions? s~ **jemand** *od* wer someone/(*fragend, verneint)* anyone else; *(irgendjemand)* [just] anyone; s~ **wo** somewhere/(*fragend, verneint)* anywhere else; *(irgendwo)* [just] anywhere. s~**ig** *adj* other

sooft *conj* whenever

Sopran *m* -s,-e soprano

Sorge f -,-n worry (um about); *(Fürsorge)* care; **sich** *(dat)* **S~n machen** worry. **s~n** *vi (haben)* **s~n für** look after, care for; *(vorsorgen)* provide for; *(sich kümmern)* see to; **dafür s~n, dass** see or make sure that ● *vr* **sich s~n** worry. **s~nfrei** *adj* carefree. **s~nvoll** *adj* worried. **S~recht** *nt (Jur)* custody

Sorg|falt f - care. **s~fältig** *adj* careful

Sorte f -,-n kind, sort; *(Comm)* brand

sort|ieren *vt* sort [out]; *(Comm)* grade. **S~iment** *nt* -[e]s,-e range

sosehr *conj* however much

Soße f -,-n sauce; *(Braten-)* gravy; *(Salat-)* dressing

Souvenir /zuvə'ni:ɐ̯/ *nt* -s,-s souvenir

souverän /zuvə'rɛ:n/ *adj* sovereign

soviel *conj* however much; s~ **ich weiß** as far as I know ● *adv* *so viel, *s.* viel

soweit *conj* as far as; *(insoweit)* [in] so far as ● *adv** so weit, *s.* weit

sowenig *conj* however little ● *adv* *so wenig, *s.* wenig

sowie *conj* as well as; *(sobald)* as soon as

sowieso *adv* anyway, in any case

sowjet|isch *adj* Soviet. **S~union** f - Soviet Union

sowohl *adv* s~ ... **als** *od* **wie auch** as well as ...

sozial *adj* social; *(Einstellung, Beruf)* caring. **S~arbeit** f social work. **S~demokrat** *m* social democrat. **S~hilfe** f social security

Sozialis|mus *m* - socialism. **S~t** *m* -en,-en socialist

Sozial|versicherung f National Insurance. **S~wohnung** f ≈ council flat

Soziologie f - sociology

Sozius *m* -,-se *(Comm)* partner; *(Beifahrersitz)* pillion

Spachtel *m* -s,- & f -,-n spatula

Spagat *m* -[e]s,-e *(Aust)* string; **s~ machen** do the splits *pl*

Spaghetti, Spagetti *pl* spaghetti *sg*

Spalier *nt* -s,-e trellis

Spalt|e f -,-n crack; *(Gletscher-)* crevasse; *(Druck-)* column; *(Orangen-)* segment. **s~en†** *vt* split. **S~ung** f -,-en splitting; *(Kluft)* split; *(Phys)* fission

Span *m* -[e]s, ̈e [wood] chip

Spange f -,-n clasp; *(Haar-)* slide; *(Zahn-)* brace

Span|ien /-jən/ *nt* -s Spain. **S~ier** *m* -s,-, **S~ierin** f -,-nen Spaniard. **s~isch** *adj* Spanish. **S~isch** *nt* -[s] *(Lang)* Spanish

Spann *m* -[e]s instep

Spanne f -,-n span; *(Zeit-)* space; *(Comm)* margin

spann|en *vt* stretch; put up *(Leine)*; *(straffen)* tighten; *(an-)* harness (**an** + *acc* to); **sich s~en** tighten ● *vi (haben)* be too tight. **s~end** *adj* exciting. **S~ung** f -,-en tension; *(Erwartung)* suspense; *(Electr)* voltage

s

Spar|buch nt savings book.
S~büchse f money-box. s~en vt/i
(haben) save; (sparsam sein) economize (mit/an + dat on). S~er m
-s,- saver

Spargel m -s,- asparagus

Spar|kasse f savings bank.
S~konto nt deposit account

sparsam adj economical; (Person)
thrifty. S~keit f - economy; thrift

Sparschwein nt piggy bank

Sparte f -,-n branch; (Zeitungs-)
section; (Rubrik) column

Spaß m -es,ˀe fun; (Scherz) joke;
im/aus/zum S~ for fun; S~ machen be fun; (Person): be joking;
viel S~! have a good time! s~en
vi (haben) joke. S~vogel m joker

Spastiker m -s,- spastic

spät adj & adv late; wie s~ ist es?
what time is it? zu s~ kommen
be late

Spaten m -s,- spade

später adj later; (zukünftig) future
● adv later

spätestens adv at the latest

Spatz m -en,-en sparrow

Spätzle pl (Culin) noodles

spazieren vi (sein) stroll; s~
gehen go for a walk

Spazier|gang m walk; einen
S~gang machen go for a walk.
S~gänger(in) m -s,- (f -,-nen)
walker. S~stock m walking-stick

Specht m -[e]s,-e woodpecker

Speck m -s bacon. s~ig adj greasy

Spedi|teur /ʃpedi'tøːɐ/ m -s,-e
haulage/(für Umzüge) removals con-
tractor. S~tion f -,-en carriage,
haulage; (Firma) haulage/(für Umzüge) removals firm

Speer m -[e]s,-e spear; (Sport)
javelin

Speiche f -,-n spoke

Speichel m -s saliva

Speicher m -s,- warehouse; (Dialekt: Dachboden) attic; (Computer)
memory. s~n vt store

Speise f -,-n food; (Gericht) dish;
(Pudding) blancmange. S~eis nt
ice-cream. S~kammer f larder.
S~karte f menu. s~n vi (haben)
eat ● vt feed. S~röhre f oesopha-
gus. S~saal m dining room.
S~wagen m dining car

Spektrum nt -s,-tra spectrum

Spekul|ant m -en,-en speculator.
s~ieren vi (haben) speculate;
s~ieren auf (+ acc) I hope to get

Spelze f -,-n husk

spendabel adj generous

Spende f -,-n donation. s~n vt
donate; give (Blut, Schatten); Beifall
s~n applaud. S~r m -s,- donor;
(Behälter) dispenser

spendieren vt pay for

Sperling m -s,-e sparrow

Sperre f -,-n barrier; (Verbot) ban;
(Comm) embargo. s~n vt close;
(ver-) block; (verbieten) ban; cut off
(Strom, Telefon); stop (Scheck, Kredit); s~n in (+ acc) put in (Gefängnis, Käfig)

Sperr|holz nt plywood. S~müll
m bulky refuse. S~stunde f closing time

Spesen pl expenses

spezial|isieren (sich) vr special-
ize (auf + acc in). S~ist m -en,-en
specialist. S~ität f -,-en speciality

speziell adj special

spicken vt (Culin) lard; gespickt
mit (fig) full of ● vi (haben) I crib
(bei from)

Spiegel m -s,- mirror; (Wasser-, Al-
kohol-) level. S~bild nt reflection.
S~ei nt fried egg. s~n vt reflect;
sich s~n be reflected ● vi (haben)
reflect [the light]; (glänzen) gleam.
S~ung f -,-en reflection

Spiel nt -[e]s,-e game; (Spielen) playing; (Glücks-) gambling; (Schau-) play; (Satz) set; auf dem S~ stehen be at stake; aufs S~ setzen risk. **S~automat** m fruit machine. **S~bank** f casino. **S~dose** f musical box. **s~en** vt/i (haben) play; (im Glücksspiel) gamble; (vortäuschen) act; (Roman:) be set (**in** + dat in); **s~en mit** (fig) toy with

Spieler(in) m -s,- (f -,-nen) player; (Glücks-) gambler

Spiel|feld nt field, pitch. **S~marke** f chip. **S~plan** m programme. **S~platz** m playground. **S~raum** m (fig) scope; (Techn) clearance. **S~regeln** fpl rules [of the game]. **S~sachen** fpl toys. **S~verderber** m -s,- spoilsport. **S~waren** fpl toys. **S~warengeschäft** nt toyshop. **S~zeug** nt toy; (S~sachen) toys pl

Spieß m -es,-e spear; (Brat-) spit; skewer; (Fleisch-) kebab. **S~er** m -s,- [petit] bourgeois. **s~ig** adj bourgeois

Spike[s]reifen /ˈʃpaik[s]-/ m studded tyre

Spinat m -s spinach

Spindel f -,-n spindle

Spinne f -,-n spider

spinn|en† vt/i (haben) spin; er spinnt 𝔽 he's crazy. **S~[en]gewebe** nt, **S~webe** f -,-n cobweb

Spion m -s,-e spy

Spionage /ʃpioˈnaːʒə/ f espionage, spying. **S~abwehr** f counterespionage

spionieren vi (haben) spy

Spionin f -,-nen [woman] spy

Spirale f -,-n spiral. **s~ig** adj spiral

Spirituosen pl spirits

Spiritus m -alcohol; (Brenn-) methylated spirits pl. **S~kocher** m

spirit stove

spitz adj pointed; (scharf) sharp; (schrill) shrill; (Winkel) acute. **S~bube** m scoundrel

Spitze f -,-n point; (oberer Teil) top; (vorderer Teil) front; (Pfeil-, Finger-, Nasen-) tip; (Schuh-, Strumpf-) toe; (Zigarren-, Zigaretten-) holder; (Höchstleistung) maximum; (Textiles) lace; (𝔽: Anspielung) dig; **an der S~ liegen** be in the lead

Spitzel m -s,- informer

spitzen vt sharpen; purse (Lippen); prick up (Ohren). **S~geschwindigkeit** f top speed

Spitzname m nickname

Spleen /ʃpliːn/ m -s,-e obsession

Splitter m -s,- splinter. **s~n** vi (sein) shatter

sponsern vt sponsor

Spore f -,-n (Biology) spore

Sporn m -[e]s, **Sporen** spur

Sport m -s; (Hobby) hobby. **S~art** f sport. **S~ler** m -s,- sportsman. **S~lerin** f -,-nen sportswoman. **s~lich** adj sports; (fair) sporting; (schlank) sporty. **S~platz** m sports ground. **S~verein** m sports club. **S~wagen** m sports car; (Kinder-) push-chair, (Amer) stroller

Spott m -[e]s mockery

spotten vi (haben) mock; **s~ über** (+ acc) make fun of; (höhnend) ridicule

spöttisch adj mocking

Sprach|e f -,-n language; (Sprechfähigkeit) speech; **zur S~e bringen** bring up. **S~fehler** m speech defect. **S~labor** nt language laboratory. **s~lich** adj linguistic. **s~los** adj speechless

Spray /ʃpreː/ nt & m -s,-s spray. **S~dose** f aerosol [can]

Sprechanlage f intercom

sprechen† vi (haben) speak/(sich unterhalten) talk (über + acc/von about/of); Deutsch s~ speak German ● vt speak; (sagen) say; (pronounce (Urteil); schuldig s~ find guilty; Herr X ist nicht zu s~ Mr X is not available

Sprecher(in) m -s,- (f -,-nen) speaker; (Radio, TV) announcer; (Wortführer) spokesman, f spokeswoman

Sprechstunde f consulting hours pl; (Med) surgery. **S~nhilfe** f (Med) receptionist

Sprechzimmer nt consulting room

spreizen vt spread

spreng|en vt blow up; blast (Felsen); (fig) burst; (begießen) water; (mit Sprenger) sprinkle; dampen (Wäsche). **S~er** m -s,- sprinkler. **S~kopf** m warhead. **S~körper** m explosive device. **S~stoff** m explosive

Spreu f- chaff

Sprich|wort nt (pl -wörter) proverb. **s~wörtlich** adj proverbial

Springbrunnen m fountain

spring|en† vi (sein) jump; (Schwimmsport) dive; (Ball:) bounce; (spritzen) spurt; (zer-) break; (rissig werden) crack; (SGer: laufen) run. **S~er** m -s,- jumper; (Kunst-) diver; (Schach) knight. **S~reiten** nt showjumping

Sprint m -s,-s sprint

Spritz|e f -,-n syringe; (Injektion) injection; (Feuer-) hose. **s~en** vt spray; (be-, ver-) splash; (Culin) pipe; (Med) inject ● vi (haben) splash; (Fett:) spit ● vi (sein) splash; (hervor-) spurt. **S~er** m -s,- splash; (Schuss) dash

spröde adj brittle; (trocken) dry

Sprosse f -,-n rung

Sprotte f-,-n sprat

Spruch m -[e]s, ̈e saying; (Denk-) motto; (Zitat) quotation. **S~band** nt (pl -bänder) banner

Sprudel m -s,- sparkling mineral water. **s~n** vi (haben/sein) bubble

Sprüh|dose f aerosol [can]. **s~en** vt spray ● vi (sein) (Funken:) fly; (fig) sparkle

Sprung m -[e]s, ̈e jump, leap; (Schwimmsport) dive; (⊤: Katzen-) stone's throw; (Riss) crack. **S~brett** nt springboard. **S~schanze** f skijump. **S~seil** nt skipping rope

Spucke f- spit. **s~n** vt/i (haben) spit; (sich übergeben) be sick

Spuk m -[e]s,-e [ghostly] apparition. **s~en** vi (haben) (Geist:) walk; in diesem Haus s~t es this house is haunted

Spülbecken nt sink

Spule f -,-n spool

Spüle f -,-n sink

spulen vt spool

spül|en vt rinse; (schwemmen) wash; Geschirr s~en wash up ● vi (haben) flush (the toilet). **S~kasten** m cistern. **S~mittel** nt washing-up liquid

Spur f -,-en track; (Fahr-) lane; (Fährte) trail; (Anzeichen) trace; (Hinweis) lead

spürbar adj noticeable

spür|en vt feel; (seelisch) sense. **S~hund** m tracker dog

spurlos adv without trace

spurten vi (sein) put on a spurt

sputen (sich) vr hurry

Staat m -[e]s,-en state; (Land) country; (Putz) finery. **s~lich** adj state ● adv by the state

Staatsangehörige(r) m/f national. **S~keit** f - nationality

Staats|anwalt m state prosecutor. **S~beamte(r)** m civil servant. **S~besuch** m state visit. **S~bürger(in)** m(f) national. **S~mann** m (pl -männer) statesman. **S~streich** m coup

Stab m -[e]s, ⸚e rod; (Gitter-) bar (Sport) baton; (Mil) staff

Stäbchen ntpl chopsticks

Stabhochsprung m pole-vault

stabil adj stable; (gesund) robust; (solide) sturdy

Stachel m -s,-n spine; (Gift-) sting; (Spitze) spike. **S~beere** f gooseberry. **S~draht** m barbed wire. **S~schwein** nt porcupine

Stadion nt -s,-ien stadium

Stadium nt -s,-ien stage

Stadt f -,⸚e town; (Groß-) city

städtisch adj urban; (kommunal) municipal

Stadt|mitte f town centre. **S~plan** m street map. **S~teil** m district

Staffel f -,-n team; (S~lauf) relay; (Mil) squadron

Staffelei f -,-en easel

Staffel|lauf m relay race. **s~n** vt stagger; (abstufen) grade

Stahl m -s steel. **S~beton** m reinforced concrete

Stall m -[e]s,⸚e stable; (Kuh-) shed; (Schweine-) sty; (Hühner-) coop; (Kaninchen-) hutch

Stamm m -[e]s⸚e trunk; (Sippe) tribe; (Wort-) stem. **S~baum** m family tree; (eines Tieres) pedigree

stammeln vt/i (haben) stammer

stammen vi (haben) come; (zeitlich) date (von/aus from)

stämmig adj sturdy

Stamm|kundschaft f regulars pl. **S~lokal** nt favourite pub

Stammtisch A large table reserved for regulars in most German Kneipen (pubs). The word is also used to refer to the group of people who meet around this table for a drink and lively discussion.

stampfen vi (haben) stamp; (Maschine) pound ● vi (sein) tramp ● vt pound; mash (Kartoffeln)

Stand m -[e]s,⸚e standing position; (Zustand) state; (Spiel-) score; (Höhe) level; (gesellschaftlich) class; (Verkaufs-) stall; (Messe-) stand; (Taxi-) rank; auf den neuesten S~ bringen up-date

Standard m -s,-s standard

Standbild nt statue

Ständer m -s,- stand; (Geschirr-) rack; (Kerzen-) holder

Standes|amt nt registry office. **S~beamte(r)** m registrar

standhaft adj steadfast

ständig adj constant; (fest) permanent

Stand|licht nt sidelights pl. **S~ort** m position; (Firmen-) location; (Mil) garrison. **S~punkt** m point of view. **S~uhr** f grandfather clock

Stange f -,-n bar; (Holz-) pole; (Gardinen-) rail; (Hühner-) perch; (Zimt-) stick; von der S~ 🔲 off the peg

Stängel m -s,- stalk, stem

Stangenbohne f runner bean

Stanniol nt -s tin foil. **S~papier** nt silver paper

stanzen vt stamp; punch (Loch)

Stapel m -s,- stack, pile. **S~lauf** m launch[ing]. **s~n** vt stack or pile up

Star[1] m -[e]s,-e starling

Star[2] m -[e]s (Med) [grauer] S~ cataract; grüner S~ glaucoma

s

Star³ m -s,-s (Theat, Sport) star

stark adj strong; (Motor) powerful; (Verkehr, Regen) heavy; (Hitze, Kälte) severe; (groß) big; (schlimm) bad; (dick) thick; (korpulent) stout ● adv (sehr) very much

Stärk|e f -,-n strength; power; thickness; stoutness; (Größe) size; (Mais-, Wäsche-) starch. **S~emehl** nt cornflour. **s~en** vt strengthen; starch (Wäsche); **sich s~en** fortify oneself. **S~ung** f -,-en strengthening; (Erfrischung) refreshment

starr adj rigid; (steif) stiff

starren vi (haben) stare

Starr|sinn m obstinacy. **s~sinnig** adj obstinate

Start m -s,-s start; (Aviat) take-off. **S~bahn** f runway. **s~en** vt/i (haben) start; (Aviat) take off ● vt start; (fig) launch

Station /-'tsjo:n/ f -,-en station; (Haltestelle) stop; (Abschnitt) stage; (Med) ward; **S~ machen** break one's journey. **s~är** adv as an inpatient. **s~ieren** vt station

statisch adj static

Statist(in) m -en,-en (f -,-nen) (Theat) extra

Statisti|k f -,-en statistics sg; (Aufstellung) statistics pl. **s~sch** adj statistical

Stativ nt -s,-e (Phot) tripod

statt prep (+ gen) instead of; an seiner s~ in his place; an Kindes s~ annehmen adopt ● conj s~ etw zu tun instead of doing sth. **s~dessen** adv instead

statt|finden† vi sep (haben) take place. **s~haft** adj permitted

Statue /'∫ta:tuə/ f -,-n statue

Statur f - build, stature

Status m - status. **S~symbol** nt status symbol

Statut nt -[e]s,-en statute

Stau m -[e]s,-s congestion; (Auto) [traffic] jam; (Rück-) tailback

Staub m -[e]s dust; **s~ wischen** dust; **S~ saugen** vacuum, hoover

Staubecken nt reservoir

staub|ig adj dusty. **s~saugen** vt/i (haben) vacuum, hoover. **S~sauger** m vacuum cleaner, Hoover®

Staudamm m dam

stauen vt dam up; **sich s~** accumulate; (Autos:) form a tailback

staunen vi (haben) be amazed or astonished

Stau|see m reservoir. **S~ung** f -,-en congestion; (Auto) [traffic] jam

Steak /∫te:k, ste:k/ nt -s,-s steak

stechen† vt stick (in + acc in); (verletzen) prick; (mit Messer) stab; (Insekt:) sting; (Mücke:) bite ● vi (haben) prick; (Insekt:) sting; (Mücke:) bite; (mit Stechuhr) clock in/out; in See s~ put to sea

Stech|ginster m gorse. **S~kahn** m punt. **S~palme** f holly. **S~uhr** f time clock

Steck|brief m 'wanted' poster. **S~dose** f socket. **s~en** vt put; (mit Nadel, Reißzwecke) pin; (pflanzen) plant ● vi (haben) be; (fest-) be stuck; **s~ bleiben** get stuck; den Schlüssel **s~ lassen** leave the key in the lock

Steckenpferd nt hobby-horse

Steck|er m -s,- (Electr) plug. **S~nadel** f pin

Steg m -[e]s,-e foot-bridge; (Boots-) landing-stage; (Brillen-) bridge

stehen† vi (haben) stand; (sich befinden) be; (still-) be stationary; (Maschine, Uhr:) have stopped; **s~ bleiben** remain standing; (gebäude:) be left standing; (anhalten) stop; (Motor:) stall; (Zeit:) stand still; vor dem Ruin **s~** face ruin; zu jdm/ etw **s~** (fig) stand by s.o./sth

jdm [gut] s~ suit s.o.; **sich gut s~** be on good terms; **es steht 3 zu 1 the score is 3–1. s~d** adj standing; (sich nicht bewegen) stationary; (Gewässer) stagnant

Stehlampe f standard lamp

stehlen† vt/i (haben) steal; **sich s~** steal, creep

Steh|platz m standing place. **S~vermögen** nt stamina, staying-power

steif adj stiff

Steig|bügel m stirrup. **S~eisen** nt crampon

steigen† vi (sein) climb; (hochgehen) rise, go up; (Schulden, Spannung): mount; **s~ auf** (+ acc) climb on [to] (Stuhl); climb (Berg, Leiter); get on (Pferd, Fahrrad); **s~ in** (+ acc) climb into; get in (Auto); get on (Bus, Zug); **s~ aus** climb out of; get out of (Bett, Auto); get off (Bus, Zug); **s~de Preise** rising prices

steiger|n vt increase; **sich s~n** increase; (sich verbessern) improve. **S~ung** f -,-en increase; improvement; (Gram) comparison

steil adj steep. **S~küste** f cliffs pl

Stein m -[e]s,-e (Ziegel-) brick; (Spiel-) piece. **S~bock** m ibex; (Astrology) Capricorn. **S~bruch** m quarry. **S~garten** m rockery. **S~gut** nt earthenware. **s~ig** adj stony. **s~igen** vt stone. **S~kohle** f [hard] coal. **S~schlag** m rock fall

Stelle f -,-n place; (Fleck) spot; (Abschnitt) passage; (Stellung) position; (Behörde) authority; **auf der S~** immediately

stellen vt put; (aufrecht) stand; set (Wecker, Aufgabe); ask (Frage); make (Antrag, Forderung, Diagnose); zur Verfügung **s~** provide; lauter/leiser **s~** turn up/down; kalt/warm **s~** chill/keep hot; **sich s~** [go and]

stand; give oneself up (der Polizei to the police); **sich tot s~** pretend to be dead; **gut gestellt sein** be well off

Stellen|anzeige f job advertisement. **S~vermittlung** f employment agency. **s~weise** adv in places

Stellung f -,-en position; (Arbeit) job; **S~nehmen** make a statement (zu on). **S~suche** f job-hunting

Stellvertreter m deputy

Stelzen fpl stilts. **s~** vi (sein) stalk

stemmen vt press; lift (Gewicht)

Stempel m -s,- stamp; (Post-) post-mark; (Präge-) die; (Feingehalts-) hallmark. **s~n** vt stamp; hallmark (Silber); cancel (Marke)

Stengel m -s,- * **Stängel**

Steno f - ⓘ shorthand

Steno|gramm nt -[e]s,-e shorthand text. **S~grafie** f - shorthand. **s~grafieren** vt take down in shorthand ● vi (haben) do shorthand

Steppdecke f quilt

Steppe f -,-n steppe

Stepptanz m tap-dance

sterben† vi (sein) die (an + dat of); **im S~ liegen** be dying

sterblich adj mortal. **S~keit** f - mortality

stereo adv in stereo. **S~anlage** f stereo [system]

steril adj sterile. **s~isieren** vt sterilize. **S~ität** f - sterility

Stern m -[e]s,-e star. **S~bild** nt constellation. **S~chen** nt -s,- asterisk. **S~kunde** f astronomy. **S~schnuppe** f -,-n shooting star. **S~warte** f -,-n observatory

stets adv always

Steuer¹ nt -s,- steering-wheel; (Naut) helm; **am S~** at the wheel

Steuer² f -,-n tax

Steuer|bord nt -[e]s starboard [side]. **s~erklärung** f tax return. **s~frei** adj & adv tax-free. **S~mann** m (pl -leute) helmsman; (beim Rudern) cox. **s~n** vi steer; (Aviat) pilot; (Techn) control ● vi (haben) be at the wheel/(Naut) helm.
s~pflichtig adj taxable. **S~rad** nt steering-wheel. **S~ruder** nt helm. **S~ung** f - steering; (Techn) controls pl. **S~zahler** m -s,- taxpayer

Stewardess /'stjuːɐdɛs/ f -,-en air hostess, stewardess

Stich m -[e]s,-e prick; (Messer-) stab; (S~wunde) stab wound; (Bienen-) sting; (Mücken-) bite; (Schmerz) stabbing pain; (Näh-) stitch; (Kupfer-) engraving; (Kartenspiel) trick

stick|en vt/i (haben) embroider. **S~erei** f - embroidery

Stickstoff m nitrogen

Stiefel m -s,- boot

Stief|kind nt stepchild. **S~mutter** f stepmother. **S~mütterchen** nt -s,- pansy. **S~sohn** m stepson. **S~tochter** f stepdaughter. **S~vater** m stepfather

Stiege f -,-n stairs pl

Stiel m -[e]s,-e handle; (Blumen-, Gläser-) stem; (Blatt-) stalk

Stier m -[e]s,-e bull; (Astrology) Taurus

Stierkampf m bullfight

Stift[1] m -[e]s,-e pin; (Nagel) tack; (Blei-) pencil; (Farb-) crayon

Stift[2] nt -[e]s,-e [endowed] foundation. **s~en** vt endow; (spenden) donate; create (Unheil, Verwirrung); bring about (Frieden). **S~ung** f -,-en foundation; (Spende) donation

Stil m -[e]s,-e style

still adj quiet; (reglos, ohne Kohlensäure) still; (heimlich) secret; der S~e Ozean the Pacific; im S~en

secretly. **S~e** f - quiet; (Schweigen) silence

Stilleben* nt = Stillleben

stillen vt satisfy; quench (Durst); stop (Schmerzen, Blutung); breast-feed (Kind)

still|halten† vi sep (haben) keep still. **S~leben** nt still life. **S~legen** vt sep close down. **S~schweigen** nt silence. **S~stand** m standstill; zum S~stand bringen/kommen stop. **s~stehen**† vi sep (haben) stand still; (anhalten) stop; (Verkehr:) be at a standstill

Stimm|bänder ntpl vocal cords. **s~berechtigt** adj entitled to vote. **S~bruch** m er ist im S~bruch his voice is breaking

Stimme f -,-n voice; (Wahl-) vote

stimmen vi (haben) be right; (wählen) vote ● vt tune

Stimmung f -,-en mood; (Atmosphäre) atmosphere

Stimmzettel m ballot-paper

stink|en† vi (haben) smell/(stark) stink (nach of). **S~tier** nt skunk

Stipendium nt -s,-ien scholarship; (Beihilfe) grant

Stirn f -,-en forehead

stochern vi (haben) s~ in (+ dat) poke (Feuer); pick at (Essen)

Stock[1] m -[e]s,ːe stick; (Ski-) pole; (Bienen-) hive; (Rosen-) bush; (Reb-) vine

Stock[2] m -[e]s,- storey, floor. **S~bett** nt bunk-beds pl.

stock|en vi (haben) stop; (Verkehr:) come to a standstill; (Person:) falter. **S~ung** f -,-en hold-up

Stockwerk nt storey, floor

Stoff m -[e]s,-e substance; (Textiles) fabric, material; (Thema) subject [matter]; (Gesprächs-) topic. **S~wechsel** m metabolism

stöhnen vi (haben) groan, moan

Stola f -,-len stole

Stollen m -s,- gallery; (Kuchen) stollen

stolpern vi (sein) stumble; s~ über (+ acc) trip over

stolz adj proud (auf + acc of). S~ m -es pride

stopfen vt stuff; (stecken) put; (ausbessern) darn ● vi (haben) be constipating

Stopp m -s,-s stop. s~ int stop!

stoppelig adj stubbly

stopp|en vt stop; (Sport) time ● vi (haben) stop. S~uhr f stop-watch

Stöpsel m -s,- plug; (Flaschen-) stopper

Storch m -[e]s,¨e stork

Store /ʃtoːɐ/ m -s,-s net curtain

stören vt disturb; disrupt (Rede); jam (Sender); (missfallen) bother ● vi (haben) be a nuisance

stornieren vt cancel

störrisch adj stubborn

Störung f -,-en disturbance; disruption; (Med) trouble; (Radio) interference; technische S~ technical fault

Stoß m -es,¨e push, knock; (mit Ellbogen) dig; (Hörner-) butt; (mit Waffe) thrust; (Schwimm-) stroke; (Ruck) jolt; (Erd-) shock; (Stapel) stack, pile. S~dämpfer m -s,- shock absorber

stoßen† vt push, knock; (mit Füßen) kick; (mit Kopf) butt; (an-) poke, nudge; (treiben) thrust; sich s~ knock oneself; sich (dat) den Kopf s~ hit one's head ● vi (haben) push; s~ an (+ acc) knock against; (angrenzen) adjoin ● vi (sein) s~ gegen knock against; bump into (Tür); s~ auf (+ acc) bump into; (entdecken) come across; strike (Öl)

Stoß|stange f bumper. S~verkehr m rush-hour traffic. S~zahn

m tusk. S~zeit f rush-hour

stottern vt/i (haben) stutter, stammer

Str. abbr (Straße) St

Strafanstalt f prison

Strafe f -,-n punishment; (Jur & fig) penalty; (Geld-) fine; (Freiheits-) sentence. s~n vt punish

straff adj tight, taut. s~en vt tighten

Strafgesetz nt criminal law

sträf|lich adj criminal. S~ling m -s,-e prisoner

Straf|mandat nt (Auto) [parking/speeding] ticket. S~porto nt excess postage. S~raum m penalty area. S~stoß m penalty. S~tat f crime

Strahl m -[e]s,-en ray; (einer Taschenlampe) beam; (Wasser-) jet. s~en vi (haben) shine; (funkeln) sparkle; (lächeln) beam. S~enbehandlung f radiotherapy. S~ung f - radiation

Strähne f -,-n strand

stramm adj tight

Strampel|höschen /-sç-/ nt -s,- rompers pl. s~n vi (haben) (Baby:) kick

Strand m -[e]s,¨e beach. s~en vi (sein) run aground

Strang m -[e]s,¨e rope

Strapaz|e f -,-n strain. s~ieren vt be hard on; tax (Nerven)

Strass m - & -es paste

Straße f -,-n road; (in der Stadt auch) street; (Meeres-) strait. S~nbahn f tram. S~nkarte f road-map. S~nsperre f road-block

Strat|egie f -,-n strategy. s~egisch adj strategic

Strauch m -[e]s, Sträucher bush

Strauß¹ m -es, Sträuße bunch [of flowers]; (Bukett) bouquet

Strauß² m -es,-e ostrich

streben vi (haben) strive (nach for) ● vi (sein) head (nach/zu for)

Streber m -s,- pushy person

Strecke f -,-n stretch, section; (Entfernung) distance; (Rail) line; (Route) route

strecken vt stretch; (aus-) stretch out; (gerade machen) straighten; (Culin) thin down; den Kopf aus dem Fenster s~ put one's head out of the window

Streich m -[e]s,-e prank, trick

streicheln vt stroke

streichen† vt spread; (weg-) smooth; (an-) paint; (aus-) delete; (kürzen) cut ● vi (haben) s~ über (+ acc) stroke

Streichholz nt match

Streich|instrument nt stringed instrument. **S~käse** m cheese spread. **S~orchester** nt string orchestra. **S~ung** f -,-en deletion; (Kürzung) cut

Streife f -,-n patrol

streifen vt brush against; (berühren) touch; (verletzen) graze; (fig) touch on (Thema)

Streifen m -s,- stripe; (Licht-) streak; (auf der Fahrbahn) line; (schmales Stück) strip

Streifenwagen m patrol car

Streik m -[e]s,-e strike; in den S~ treten go on strike. **S~brecher** m strike-breaker, (pej) scab. **s~en** vi (haben) strike; Ⓣ refuse; (versagen) pack up

Streit m -[e]s,-e quarrel; (Auseinandersetzung) dispute. **s~en†** vr/i (haben) [sich] s~en quarrel. **S~igkeiten** fpl quarrels. **S~kräfte** fpl armed forces

streng adj strict; (Blick, Ton) stern; (rau, nüchtern) severe; (Geschmack) sharp; s~ genommen strictly

speaking. **S~e** f - strictness; sternness; severity

Stress m -es,-e stress

stressig adj stressful

streuen vt (ver-) scatter; sprinkle (Zucker, Salz); die Straßen s~ grit the roads

streunen vi (sein) roam

Strich m -[e]s,-e line; (Feder-, Pinsel-) stroke; (Morse-, Gedanken-) dash. **S~kode** m bar code. **S~punkt** m semicolon

Strick m -[e]s,-e cord; (Seil) rope

strick|en vt/i (haben) knit. **S~jacke** f cardigan. **S~leiter** f rope ladder. **S~nadel** f knitting-needle. **S~waren** fpl knitwear sg. **S~zeug** nt knitting

striegeln vt groom

strittig adj contentious

Stroh nt -[e]s straw. **S~blumen** fpl everlasting flowers. **S~dach** nt thatched roof. **S~halm** m straw

Strolch m -[e]s,-e Ⓣ rascal

Strom m -[e]s,-̈e river; (Menschen-, Auto-, Blut-) stream; (Tränen-) flood; (Schwall) torrent; (Electr) current, power; gegen den S~ (fig) against the tide. **s~abwärts** adv downstream. **s~aufwärts** adv upstream

strömen vi (sein) flow; (Menschen, Blut:) stream, pour

Strom|kreis m circuit. **s~linienförmig** adj streamlined. **S~sperre** f power cut

Strömung f -,-en current

Strophe f -,-n verse

Strudel m -s,- whirlpool; (SGer Culin) strudel

Strumpf m -[e]s,-̈e stocking; (Knie-) sock. **S~band** nt (pl -bänder) suspender. **S~hose** f tights pl

Strunk m -[e]s,-̈e stalk

struppig adj shaggy

Stube f -,-n room. s~nrein adj
house-trained

Stuck m -s stucco

Stück nt -[e]s,-e piece; (Zucker-)
lump; (Seife) tablet; (Theater-)
play; (Gegenstand) item; (Exemplar) specimen; ein S~ (Entfernung) some
way. S~chen nt -s,- [little] bit.
s~weise adv bit by bit; (einzeln)
singly

Student|(in) m -en,-en (f -,-nen)
student. s~isch adj student

Studie /-jə/ f -,-n study

studieren vt/i (haben) study

Studio nt -s,-s studio

Studium nt -s,-ien studies pl

Stufe f -,-n step; (Treppen-) stair;
(Raketen-) stage; (Niveau) level. s~n
vt terrace; (staffeln) grade

Stuhl m -[e]s,-e chair; (Med) stools
pl. S~gang m bowel movement

stülpen vt put (über + acc over)

stumm adj dumb; (schweigsam)
silent

Stummel m -s,- stump; (Zigaret-
ten-) butt; (Bleistift-) stub

Stümper m -s,- bungler

stumpf adj blunt; (Winkel) obtuse;
(glanzlos) dull; (fig) apathetic. S~
m -[e]s,-e stump

Stumpfsinn m apathy; tedium

Stunde f -,-n hour; (Sch) lesson

stunden vt jdm eine Schuld s~
give s.o. time to pay a debt

Stunden|kilometer mpl kilo-
metres per hour. s~lang adj for
hours. S~lohn m hourly rate.
S~plan m timetable. s~weise adv
by the hour

stündlich adj & adv hourly

stur adj pigheaded

Sturm m -[e]s,-e gale; storm; (Mil)
assault

stürm|en vi (haben) (Wind:) blow

hard ● vi (sein) rush ● vt storm; (bedrängen) besiege. S~er m -s,- forward. s~isch adj stormy; (Überfahrt) rough

Sturz m -es,-e [heavy] fall; (Preis-)
sharp drop; (Pol) overthrow

stürzen vi (sein) fall [heavily]; (in
die Tiefe) plunge; (Preise:) drop
sharply; (Regierung:) fall; (eilen) rush
● vt throw; (umkippen) turn upside
down; turn out (Speise, Kuchen);
(Pol) overthrow, topple; sich s~
throw oneself (aus/in + acc out
of/into)

Sturzhelm m crash-helmet

Stute f -,-n mare

Stütze f -,-n support

stützen vt support; (auf-) rest;
sich s~ auf (+ acc) lean on

stutzig adj puzzled; (misstrauisch)
suspicious

Stützpunkt m (Mil) base

Substantiv nt -s,-e noun

Substanz f -,-en substance

Subvention /-'tsio:n/ f -,-en subsidy. s~ieren vt subsidize

Suche f - search; auf der S~e
nach looking for. s~en vt look for;
(intensiv) search for; seek (Hilfe, Rat);
'Zimmer gesucht' 'room wanted'
● vi (haben) look, search (nach for).
S~er m -s,- (Phot) viewfinder.
S~maschine f search engine

Sucht f -,-e addiction; (fig) mania

süchtig adj addicted. S~e(r) m/f
addict

Süd m -[e]s south. S~afrika nt
South Africa. S~amerika nt South
America. s~deutsch adj South
German

Süden m -s south; nach S~ south

Südfrucht f tropical fruit. s~lich
adj southern; (Richtung) southerly
● adv & prep (+ gen) s~lich der
Stadt south of the town. S~pol m

South Pole. s~wärts adv southwards

Sühne f -,-n atonement; (*Strafe*) penalty. s~n vt atone for

Sultanine f -,-n sultana

Sülze f -,-n [meat] jelly

Summe f -,-n sum

summen vi (*haben*) hum; (*Biene:*) buzz ● vt hum

summieren (sich) vr add up

Sumpf m -[e]s, ̈e marsh, swamp

Sünd|e f -,-n sin. S~enbock m scapegoat. S~er(in) m -s,- (f -,-nen) sinner. s~igen vi (*haben*) sin

super inv adj 🆃 great. S~markt m supermarket

Suppe f -,-n soup. S~nlöffel m soup-spoon. S~nteller m soup plate. S~nwürfel m stock cube

Surf|brett /'sœgf-/ nt surfboard. s~en vi (*haben*) surf. S~en nt -s surfing

surren vi (*haben*) whirr

süß adj sweet. S~e f - sweetness. s~en vt sweeten. S~igkeit f -,-en sweet. s~lich adj sweetish; (*fig*) sugary. S~speise f sweet. S~stoff m sweetener. S~waren fpl confectionery sg, sweets pl. S~wasser- prefix freshwater

Sylvester nt -s = Silvester

Symbol nt -s,-e symbol. S~ik f - symbolism. s~isch adj symbolic

Sym|metrie f - symmetry. s~metrisch adj symmetrical

Sympathie f -,-n sympathy

sympathisch adj agreeable; (*Person*) likeable

Symptom nt -s,-e symptom. s~atisch adj symptomatic

Synagoge f -,-n synagogue

synchronisieren /zynkroni'zi:rən/ vt synchronize; dub (*Film*)

Syndikat nt -[e]s,-e syndicate

Syndrom nt -s,-e syndrome

synonym adj synonymous

Synthese f -,-n synthesis

Syrien /-jan/ nt -s Syria

System nt -s,-e system. s~atisch adj systematic

Szene f -,-n scene

Tt

Tabak m -s,-e tobacco

Tabelle f -,-n table; (*Sport*) league table

Tablett nt -[e]s,-s tray

Tablette f -,-n tablet

tabu adj taboo. T~ nt -s,-s taboo

Tacho m -s,-s, **Tachometer** m & nt speedometer

Tadel m -s,- reprimand; (*Kritik*) censure; (*Sch*) black mark. t~los adj impeccable. t~n vt reprimand; censure

Tafel f -,-n (*Tisch, Tabelle*) table; (*Platte*) slab; (*Anschlag-, Hinweis-*) board; (*Gedenk-*) plaque; (*Schiefer-*) slate; (*Wand-*) blackboard; (*Bild-*) plate; (*Schokolade*) bar

Täfelung f - panelling

Tag m -[e]s,-e day; unter T~e underground; es wird Tag it is getting light; guten Tag! good morning/afternoon!

Tage|buch nt diary. t~lang adv for days

Tages|anbruch m daybreak. T~ausflug m day trip. T~decke f bedspread. T~karte f day ticket; (*Speise-*) menu of the day. T~licht nt daylight. T~mutter f child-

minder. T∼ordnung f agenda.
T∼rückfahrkarte f day return
[ticket]. T∼zeit f time of the day.
T∼zeitung f daily [news]paper

täglich adj & adv daily; zweimal
t∼ twice a day

tags adv by day; t∼ zuvor/darauf
the day before/after

tagsüber adv during the day

tag|täglich adj daily ● adv every
single day. T∼ung f, -en meeting;
conference

Taill|e /'taljə/ f, -n waist. t∼iert
adj fitted

Takt m -[e]s, -e tact; (Mus) bar;
(Tempo) time; (Rhythmus) rhythm;
im T∼ in time

Taktik f - tactics pl.

takt|los adj tactless. T∼losigkeit
f - tactlessness. T∼stock m baton.
t∼voll adj tactful

Tal nt -[e]s, ̈er valley

Talar m -s, -e robe; (Univ) gown

Talent nt -[e]s, -e talent. t∼iert
adj talented

Talg m -s tallow; (Culin) suet

Talsperre f dam

Tampon /tam'pō:/ m -s, -s tampon

Tank m -s, -s tank. t∼en vi fill up
with (Benzin) ● vi (haben) fill up
with petrol; (Aviat) refuel. T∼er m
-s, - tanker. T∼stelle f petrol station. T∼wart m -[e]s, -e petrol-
pump attendant

Tanne f, -n fir [tree]. T∼nbaum
m fir tree; (Weihnachtsbaum) Christmas tree. T∼nzapfen m fir cone

Tante f, -n aunt

Tantiemen /tan'tje:mən/ pl roy-
alties

Tanz m -es, ̈e dance. t∼en vt/i
(haben) dance

Tänzer(in) m -s, - (f, -nen)
dancer

Tapete f, -n wallpaper

tapezieren vt paper

tapfer adj brave. T∼keit f -
bravery

Tarif m -s, -e rate; (Verzeichnis) tariff

tarn|en vt disguise; (Mil) camou-
flage. T∼ung f - disguise; camouflage

Tasche f, -n bag; (Hosen-, Mantel-)
pocket. T∼nbuch nt paperback.
T∼ndieb m pickpocket. T∼ngeld
nt pocket-money. T∼nlampe f
torch. T∼nmesser nt penknife.
T∼ntuch nt handkerchief

Tasse f, -n cup

Tastatur f, -en keyboard

Tast|e f, -n key; (Druck-) push but-
ton. t∼en vi (haben) feel, grope
(nach für) ● vt key in (Daten); sich
t∼en feel one's way (zu to)

Tat f, -en action; (Helden-) deed;
(Straf-) crime; auf frischer Tat er-
tappt caught in the act

Täter(in) m -s, - (f, -nen) culprit;
(Jur) offender

tätig adj active; t∼ sein work.
T∼keit f, -en activity; (Arbeit)
work, job

Tatkraft f energy

Tatort m scene of the crime

tätowier|en vt tattoo. T∼ung f
-, -en tattooing; (Bild) tattoo

Tatsache f fact. T∼nbericht m
documentary

tatsächlich adj actual

Tatze f, -n paw

Tau[1] m -[e]s dew

Tau[2] nt -[e]s, -e rope

taub adj deaf; (gefühllos) numb

Taube f, -n pigeon; dove.
T∼nschlag m pigeon loft

Taub|heit f - deafness. t∼stumm
adj deaf and dumb

tauch|en vt dip, plunge; (unter-)

duck ●*vi* (haben/sein) dive/(ein-) plunge (in + *acc* into); (auf-) appear (aus out of). T~er *m* -s,- diver. T~eranzug *m* diving-suit

tauen *vi* (sein) melt, thaw ● *v impers* es taut it is thawing

Tauf|becken *nt* font. T~e *f* -,-n christening, baptism. t~en *vt* christen, baptize. T~pate *m* godfather

taugen *vi* (haben) etwas/nichts t~n be good/no good

tauglich *adj* suitable; (*Mil*) fit

Tausch *m* -[e]s,-e exchange, 🔲 swap. t~en *vt* exchange/(handeln) barter (gegen for) ● *vi* (haben) swap (mit etw *sth*; mit jdm with s.o.)

täuschen *vt* deceive, fool; betray (Vertrauen); **sich t~** delude oneself; (sich irren) be mistaken ● *vi* (haben) be deceptive. t~d *adj* deceptive; (Ähnlichkeit) striking

Täuschung *f* -,-en deception; (Irrtum) mistake; (Illusion) delusion

tausend *inv adj* one/a thousand. T~ *nt* -s,-e thousand. T~füßler *m* -s,- centipede. t~ste(r, s) *adj* thousandth. T~stel *nt* -s,- thousandth

Tau|tropfen *m* dewdrop. T~wetter *nt* thaw

Taxe *f* -,-n charge; (Kur-) tax; (Taxi) taxi

Taxi *nt* -s,-s taxi, cab

Taxi|fahrer *m* taxi driver. T~stand *m* taxi rank

Teakholz /ˈtiːk-/ *nt* teak

Team /tiːm/ *nt* -s,-s team

Techni|k *f* -,-en technology; (Methode) technique. T~ker *m* -s,- technician. t~sch *adj* technical; (technologisch) technological. T~sche Hochschule Technical University

Techno|logie *f* -,-n technology. t~logisch *adj* technological

Teddybär *m* teddy bear

Tee *m* -s,-s tea. T~beutel *m* tea-bag. T~kanne *f* teapot. T~löffel *m* teaspoon

Teer *m* -s tar. t~en *vt* tar

Tee|sieb *nt* tea strainer. T~wagen *m* [tea] trolley

Teich *m* -[e]s,-e pond

Teig *m* -[e]s,-e pastry; (Knet-) dough; (Rühr-) mixture; (Pfannkuchen-) batter. T~rolle *f* rolling-pin. T~waren *fpl* pasta *sg*

Teil *m* -[e]s,-e part; (Bestand-) component; (Jur) party; zum T~ partly; zum großen/größten T~ for the most part ● *m* & *nt* -[e]s (Anteil) share; ich für mein[en] T~ for my part ● *nt* -[e]s,-e part; (Ersatz-) spare part; (Anbau-) unit

teil|bar *adj* divisible. T~chen *nt* -s,- particle. t~en *vt* divide; (auf-) share out; (gemeinsam haben) share; (Pol) partition (Land); sich t~en divide; (sich gabeln) fork; (Meinungen:) differ ● *vi* (haben) share

Teilhaber *m* -s,- (Comm) partner

Teilnahme *f* - participation; (innere) interest; (Mitgefühl) sympathy

teilnehm|en|t *vi sep* (haben) t~en an (+ *dat*) take part in; (mitfühlen) share [in]. T~er(in) *m* -s,- (*f* -,-nen) participant; (an Wettbewerb) competitor

teils *adv* partly. T~ung *f* -,-en division; (Pol) partition. t~weise *adj* partial ● *adv* partially, partly. T~zahlung *f* part payment; (Rate) instalment. T~zeitbeschäftigung *f* part-time job

Teint /tɛ̃/ *m* -s,-s complexion

Telearbeit *f* teleworking

Telefax *nt* fax

Telefon *nt* -s,-e [tele]phone. T~anruf *m*, T~at *nt* -[e]s,-e

[tele]phone call. **T~buch** nt [tele-] phone book. **t~ieren** vi (haben) [tele]phone

telefon|isch adj [tele]phone ● adv by [tele]phone. **T~ist(in)** m -en,-en (f -,-nen) telephonist. **T~karte** f phone card. **T~nummer** f [tele]phone number. **T~zelle** f [tele]phone box

Telegraf m -en,-en telegraph. **T~enmast** m telegraph pole. **t~ieren** vi (haben) send a telegram. **t~isch** adj telegraphic ● adv by telegram

Telegramm nt -s,-e telegram

Teleobjektiv nt telephoto lens

Telepathie f - telepathy

Teleskop nt -s,-e telescope

Telex nt -,-[e] telex. **t~en** vt telex

Teller m -s,- plate

Tempel m -s,- temple

Temperament nt -s,-e temperament; (Lebhaftigkeit) vivacity

Temperatur f -,-en temperature

Tempo nt -s,-s speed; **T~ [T~]!** hurry up!

Tendenz f -,-en trend; (Neigung) tendency

Tennis nt - tennis. **T~platz** m tennis-court. **T~schläger** m tennis-racket

Teppich m -s,-e carpet. **T~boden** m fitted carpet

Termin m -s,-e date; (Arzt-) appointment. **T~kalender** m [appointments] diary

Terpentin nt -s turpentine

Terrasse f -,-n terrace

Terrier /ˈtɛriɐ/ m -s,- terrier

Terrine f -,-n tureen

Territorium nt -s,-ien territory

Terror m -s terror. **t~isieren** vt terrorize. **T~ismus** m - terrorism. **T~ist** m -en,-en terrorist

Tesafilm® m ≈ Sellotape®

Test m -[e]s,-s & -e test

Testament nt -[e]s,-e will; Altes/ Neues T~ Old/New Testament. **T~svollstrecker** m -s,- executor

testen vt test

Tetanus m - tetanus

teuer adj expensive; (lieb) dear; wie t~? how much?

Teufel m -s,- devil. **T~skreis** m vicious circle

teuflisch adj fiendish

Text m -[e]s,-e text; (Passage) passage; (Bild-) caption; (Lied-) lyrics pl. **T~er** m -s,- copywriter; (Schlager-) lyricist

Textilien /-iən/ pl textiles; (Textilwaren) textile goods

Text|nachricht f text message. **T~verarbeitungssystem** nt word processor

Theater nt -s,- theatre; (①: Getue) fuss. **T~kasse** f box-office. **T~stück** nt play

Theke f -,-n bar; (Ladentisch) counter

Thema nt -s,-men subject

Themse f - Thames

Theolo|ge m -n,-n theologian. **T~gie** f - theology

theor|etisch adj theoretical. **T~ie** f -,-n theory

Therapeut(in) m -en,-en (f -,-nen) therapist

Therapie f -,-n therapy

Thermalbad nt thermal bath

Thermometer nt -s,- thermometer

Thermosflasche® f Thermos flask®

Thermostat m -[e]s,-e thermostat

These f -,-n thesis

Thrombose f -,-n thrombosis

Thron m -[e]s,-e throne. **t~en** vi
(haben) sit [in state]. **T~folge** f
succession. **T~folger** m -s,- heir to
the throne

Thunfisch m tuna

Thymian m -s thyme

ticken vi (haben) tick

tief adj deep; (t~ liegend, niedrig)
low; (t~gründig) profound; **t~er**
Teller** soup-plate ● adv deep; low;
(sehr) deeply, profoundly; (schlafen)
soundly. **T~** nt -s,-s (Meteorology)
depression. **T~bau** m civil engineering. **T~e** f -,-n depth. **T~ga-
rage** f underground car park.
t~gekühlt adj [deep-]frozen

Tiefkühl|fach nt freezer com-
partment. **T~kost** f frozen food.
T~truhe f deep-freeze

Tiefsttemperatur f minimum
temperature

Tier nt -[e]s,-e animal. **T~arzt** m,
T~ärztin f vet, veterinary surgeon.
T~garten m zoo. **T~kreis** m zodiac. **T~kunde** f zoology. **T~quä-
lerei** f cruelty to animals

Tiger m -s,- tiger

tilgen vt pay off (Schuld); (streichen) delete; (fig: auslöschen)
wipe out

Tinte f -,-n ink. **T~nfisch** m squid

Tipp (Tip) m -s,-s tip

tipp|en vt (I) type ● vi (haben) (be-
rühren) touch (auf/an etw acc sth);
(I: Maschine schreiben) type; **t~en
auf** (+ acc) (I: wetten) bet on.
T~schein m pools/lottery coupon

tipptopp adj (I) immaculate

Tirol nt -s [the] Tyrol

Tisch m -[e]s,-e table; (Schreib-)
desk; nach **T~** after the meal.
T~decke f table-cloth. **T~gebet** nt
grace. **T~ler** m -s,- joiner; (Möbel-)
cabinet-maker. **T~rede** f after-din-
ner speech. **T~tennis** nt

table tennis

Titel m -s,- title

Toast /to:st/ m -[e]s,-e toast;
(Scheibe) piece of toast. **T~er** m
-s,- toaster

toben vi (haben) rave; (Sturm:)
rage; (Kinder:) play boisterously

Tochter f -,= daughter. **T~gesell-
schaft** f subsidiary

Tod m -es death

Todes|angst f mortal fear. **T~an-
zeige** f death announcement; (Zei-
tungs-) obituary. **T~fall** m death.
T~opfer nt fatality, casualty.
T~strafe f death penalty. **T~urteil**
nt death sentence

todkrank adj dangerously ill

tödlich adj fatal; (Gefahr) mortal

Toilette /toa'lɛtə/ f -,-n toilet.
T~npapier nt toilet paper

toler|ant adj tolerant. **T~anz** f
tolerance. **t~ieren** vt tolerate

toll adj crazy, mad; (I: prima) fantastic; (schlimm) awful ● adv (sehr)
very; (schlimm) badly. **t~kühn** adj
foolhardy. **T~wut** f rabies. **t~wü-
tig** adj rabid

Tölpel m -s,- fool

Tomate f -,-n tomato. **T~nmark**
nt tomato purée

Tombola f -,-s raffle

Ton¹ m -[e]s clay

Ton² m -[e]s,=e tone; (Klang)
sound; (Note) note; (Betonung)
stress; (Farb-) shade; der gute Ton
(fig) good form. **T~abnehmer** m
-s,- pick-up. **t~angebend** adj (fig)
leading. **T~art** f tone [of voice];
(Mus) key. **T~band** nt (pl -bänder)
tape. **T~bandgerät** nt tape recorder

tönen vi (haben) sound ● vt tint

Tonleiter f scale

Tonne f -,-n barrel, cask; (Müll-)

bin; (Maß) tonne, metric ton

Topf m -[e]s, ‥e pot; (Koch-) pan

Töpfen m -s (Aust) ≈ curd cheese

Töpferei f -,-en pottery

Topf|lappen m oven-cloth. T~pflanze f potted plant

Tor nt -[e]s,-e gate; (Einfahrt) gateway; (Sport) goal

Torf m -s peat

torkeln vi (sein/habe) stagger

Tornister m -s,- knapsack; (Sch) satchel

Torpedo m -s,-s torpedo

Torpfosten m goal-post

Torte f -,-n gateau; (Obst-) flan

Tortur f -,-en torture

Torwart m -s,-e goalkeeper

tot adj dead; tot geboren stillborn; sich tot stellen pretend to be dead

total adj total. T~schaden m ≈ write-off

Tote(r) m/f dead man/woman; (Todesopfer) fatality; die T~n the dead pl

töten vt kill

Toten|gräber m -s,- grave-digger. T~kopf m skull. T~schein m death certificate

totfahren† vt sep run over and kill

Toto nt & m -s football pools pl. T~schein m pools coupon

tot|schießen† vt sep shoot dead. T~schlag m (Jur) manslaughter. t~schlagen† vt sep kill

Tötung f -,-en killing; fahrlässige T~ (Jur) manslaughter

Toup|et /tu'pe:/ nt -s,-s toupee. t~ieren vt back-comb

Tour /tu:ɐ̯/ f -,-en tour; (Ausflug) trip; (Auto-) drive; (Rad-) ride; (Strecke) distance; (Techn) revolution; (ſ: Weise) way

Touris|mus /tu'rɪsmʊs/ m - tourism. **T~t** m -en,-en tourist

Tournee /tʊr'ne:/ f -,-n tour

Trab m -[e]s trot

Trabant m -en,-en satellite

traben vi (haben/sein) trot

Tracht f -,-en (national) costume

Tradition /-'tsjoːn/ f -,-en tradition. t~ell adj traditional

Trag|bahre f stretcher. t~bar adj portable; (Kleidung) wearable

tragen† vt carry; (an-/aufhaben) wear; (fig) bear ● vi (Baum:) produce a good crop

Träger m -s,- porter; (Inhaber) bearer; (eines Ordens) holder; (Bau-) beam; (Stahl-) girder; (Achsel-) [shoulder] strap. T~kleid nt pinafore dress

Trag|etasche f carrier bag. T~flächenboot, T~flügelboot nt hydrofoil

Trägheit f - sluggishness; (Faulheit) laziness; (Phys) inertia

Trag|ik f - tragedy. t~isch adj tragic

Tragödie /-jə/ f -,-n tragedy

Train|er /'trɛːnɐ/ m -s,- trainer; (Tennis-) coach. t~ieren vt/i (haben) train

Training /'trɛːnɪŋ/ nt -s training. T~sanzug m tracksuit. T~schuhe mpl trainers

Traktor m -s,-en tractor

trampeln vi (haben) stamp one's feet ● vi (sein) trample (auf + acc on) ● vt trample

trampen /'trɛmpən/ vi (sein) Ⓔ hitch-hike

Tranchiermesser /trɑ̃'ʃiːɐ̯-/ nt carving knife

Träne f -,-n tear. t~n vi (haben) water. T~ngas nt tear-gas

Tränke f -,-n watering place; (Trog) drinking trough. t~n vt water

(*Pferd*); (*nässen*) soak (mit with)

Trans|formator *m* -s,-en transformer. **T~fusion** *f* -,-en [blood] transfusion

Transit /tranˈziːt/ *m* -s transit

Transparent *nt* -[e]s,-e banner; (*Bild*) transparency

transpirieren *vi* (*haben*) perspire

Transport *m* -[e]s,-e transport; (*Güter-*) consignment. **t~ieren** *vt* transport

Trapez *nt* -es,-e trapeze

Tratte *f* -,-n (*Comm*) draft

Traube *f* -,-n bunch of grapes; (*Beere*) grape; (*fig*) cluster. **T~nzucker** *m* glucose

trauen *vi* (*haben*) (+ *dat*) trust ● *vt* marry; **sich t~** dare (etw zu tun [to] do sth); venture (in + *acc*/aus into/out of)

Trauer *f* - mourning; (*Schmerz*) grief (um for); **T~** tragen be [dressed] in mourning. **T~fall** *m* bereavement. **T~feier** *f* funeral service. **t~n** *vi* (*haben*) grieve; **t~n um** mourn [for]. **T~spiel** *nt* tragedy. **T~weide** *f* weeping willow

Traum *m* -[e]s, Träume dream

Trauma *nt* -s,-men trauma

träumen *vt/i* (*haben*) dream

traumhaft *adj* dreamlike; (*schön*) fabulous

traurig *adj* sad; (*erbärmlich*) sorry. **T~keit** *f* - sadness

Trau|ring *m* wedding-ring. **T~schein** *m* marriage certificate. **T~ung** *f* -,-en wedding [ceremony]

Treff *nt* -s,-e (*Karten*) spades *pl*

treff|en *vt* hit; (*Blitz:*) strike; (*fig: verletzen*) hurt; (*zusammenkommen mit*) meet; take (*Maßnahme*); **sich t~en** meet (mit jdm s.o.); **sich gut t~en** be convenient; **sich gut/ schlecht t~en** be lucky/unlucky ● *vi* (*haben*) hit the target; **t~en**

auf (+ *acc*) meet; (*fig*) meet with. **T~en** *nt* -s,- meeting. **T~er** *m* -s,- hit; (*Los*) winner. **T~punkt** *m* meeting-place

treiben *vt* drive; (*sich befassen mit*) do; carry on (*Gewerbe*); indulge in (*Luxus*); get up to (*Unfug*); **Handel t~** trade ● *vi* (*sein*) drift; (*schwimmen*) float ● *vi* (*haben*) (*Bot*) sprout. **T~** *nt* -s activity

Treib|haus *nt* hothouse. **T~hauseffekt** *m* greenhouse effect. **T~holz** *nt* driftwood. **T~riemen** *m* transmission belt. **T~sand** *m* quicksand. **T~stoff** *m* fuel

trenn|bar *adj* separable. **t~en** *vt* separate/(*abtrennen*) detach (von from); divide, split (*Wort*); **sich t~en** separate; (*auseinander gehen*) part; (*sich von etw*) leave; (*fortgeben*) part with. **T~ung** *f* -,-en separation; (*Silben-*) division. **T~ungsstrich** *m* hyphen. **T~wand** *f* partition

trepp|ab *adv* downstairs. **t~auf** *adv* upstairs

Treppe *f* -,-n stairs *pl*; (*Außen-*) steps *pl*. **T~ngeländer** *nt* banisters *pl*

Tresor *m* -s,-e safe

Tresse *f* -,-n braid

Treteimer *m* pedal bin

treten *vi* (*sein/haben*) step; (*versehentlich*) tread; (*ausschlagen*) kick (nach at); **in Verbindung t~** get in touch ● *vt* tread; (*mit Füßen*) kick

treu *adj* faithful; (*fest*) loyal. **T~e** *f* - faithfulness; loyalty; (*eheliche*) fidelity. **T~ekarte** *f* loyalty card. **T~händer** *m* -s,- trustee. **t~los** *adj* disloyal; (*untreu*) unfaithful

Tribüne *f* -,-n platform; (*Zuschauer-*) stand

Trichter *m* -s,- funnel; (*Bomben-*) crater

Trick m -s,-s trick. **T~film** m cartoon. **t~reich** adj clever

Trieb m -[e]s,-e drive, urge; (Instinkt) instinct; (Bot) shoot. **T~verbrecher** m sex offender. **T~werk** nt (Aviat) engine; (Uhr-) mechanism

triefen† vi (haben) drip; (nass sein) be dripping (von/vor + dat with)

Trigonometrie f - trigonometry

Trikot¹ /'tri:ko:/ m -s (Textiles) jersey

Trikot² nt -s,-s (Sport) jersey; (Fußball-) shirt

Trimester nt -s,- term

Trimm-dich nt -s,- keep-fit

trimmen vt trim; tune (Motor); sich t~ keep fit

trink|en† vt/i (haben) drink. **T~er(in)** m -s,- (f -,-nen) alcoholic. **T~geld** nt tip. **T~spruch** m toast

trist adj dreary

Tritt m -[e]s,-e step; (Fuß-) kick. **T~brett** nt step

Triumph m -s,-e triumph. **t~ieren** vi (haben) rejoice

trocken adj dry. **T~haube** f drier. **T~heit** f -,-en dryness; (Dürre) drought. **t~legen** vt sep change (Baby); drain (Sumpf). **T~milch** f powdered milk

trockn|en vt/i (sein) dry. **T~er** m -s,- drier

Trödel m -s 🔲 junk. **t~n** vi (haben) dawdle

Trödler m -s,- 🔲 slowcoach; (Händler) junk-dealer

Trog m -[e]s,-e trough

Trommel f -,-n drum. **T~fell** nt ear-drum. **t~n** vi (haben) drum

Trommler m -s,- drummer

Trompete f -,-n trumpet. **T~r** m -s,- trumpeter

Tropen pl tropics

Tropf m -[e]s,-e (Med) drip

tröpfeln vt/i (sein/haben) drip

tropfen vt/i (sein/haben) drip. **T~** m -s,- drop; (fallend) drip. **t~weise** adv drop by drop

Trophäe /tro'fɛ:ə/ f -,-n trophy

tropisch adj tropical

Trost m -[e]s consolation, comfort

tröst|en vt console, comfort; sich t~en console oneself. **t~lich** adj comforting

trost|los adj desolate; (elend) wretched; (reizlos) dreary. **T~preis** m consolation prize

Trott m -s amble; (fig) routine

Trottel m -s,- 🔲 idiot

Trottoir /trɔ'toa:ɐ/ nt -s,-s pavement

trotz prep (+ gen) despite, in spite of. **T~** m -es defiance. **t~dem** adv nevertheless. **t~ig** adj defiant; stubborn

trübe adj dull; (Licht) dim; (Flüssigkeit) cloudy; (fig) gloomy

Trubel m -s bustle

trüben vt dull; make cloudy (Flüssigkeit); (fig) spoil; strain (Verhältnis); sich t~ (Flüssigkeit) become cloudy; (Himmel:) cloud over; (Augen:) dim

Trüb|sal f - misery. **T~sinn** m melancholy. **t~sinnig** adj melancholy

trügen† vt deceive ● vi (haben) be deceptive

Trugschluss m fallacy

Truhe f -,-n chest

Trümmer pl rubble sg; (T~teile) wreckage sg, (fig) ruins

Trumpf m -[e]s,-e trump [card]. **t~en** vi (haben) play trumps

Trunk m -[e]s drink. **T~enheit** f -

drunkenness; T~enheit am Steuer drink-driving

Trupp m -s,-s group; (Mil) squad. T~e f -,-n (Mil) unit; (Theat) troupe; T~en troops

Truthahn m turkey

Tschech|e m -n,-n, T~in f -,-nen Czech. t~isch adj Czech. T~oslowakei (die) Czechoslovakia

tschüs, tschüss int bye, cheerio

Tuba f -,-ben (Mus) tuba

Tube f -,-n tube

Tuberkulose f - tuberculosis

Tuch nt -[e]s, ̈er cloth; (Hals-, Kopf-) scarf; (Schulter-) shawl

tüchtig adj competent; (reichlich, beträchtlich) good; (groß) big ● adv competently; (ausreichend) well

Tück|e f -,-n malice. t~isch adj malicious; (gefährlich) treacherous

Tugend f -,-en virtue. t~haft adj virtuous

Tülle f -,-n spout

Tulpe f -,-n tulip

Tümmler m -s,- porpoise

Tumor m -s,-en tumour

Tümpel m -[e]s,- pond

Tumult m -[e]s,-e commotion; (Aufruhr) riot

tun† vt do; take (Schritt, Blick); work (Wunder); (bringen) put (in + acc into); tun hurt so.; jdm etwas tun hurt s.o.; das tut nichts it doesn't matter ● vi (haben) act (als ob as if); er tut nur so he's just pretending; jdm/etw gut tun do s.o./sth good; zu tun haben have things/work to do; [es] zu tun haben mit have to deal with. **Tun** nt -s actions pl

Tünche f -,-n whitewash; (fig) veneer. t~n vt whitewash

Tunesien /-iən/ nt -s Tunisia

Tunfisch m Thunfisch

Tunnel m -s,- tunnel

tupf|en vt dab ● vi (haben) t~en an/auf (+ acc) touch. T~en m -s,- spot. T~er m -s,- spot; (Med) swab

Tür f -,-en door

Turban m -s,-e turban

Turbine f -,-n turbine

Türk|e m -n,-n Turk. T~ei (die) Turkey. T~in f -,-nen Turk

türkis inv adj turquoise

türkisch adj Turkish

Turm m -[e]s, ̈e tower; (Schach) rook, castle

Türm|chen nt -s,- turret. t~en vt pile [up]; sich t~en pile up

Turmspitze f spire

turn|en vi (haben) do gymnastics. T~en nt -s gymnastics sg; (Sch) physical education, [1] gym. T~er(in) m -s,- (f -,-nen) gymnast. T~halle f gymnasium

Turnier nt -s,-e tournament; (Reit-) show

Turnschuhe mpl gym shoes; trainers

Türschwelle f doorstep, threshold

Tusche f -,-n [drawing] ink

tuscheln vt/i (haben) whisper

Tüte f -,-n bag; (Comm) packet; (Eis-) cornet; in die T~ blasen [1] be breathalysed

TÜV m - ≈ MOT [test]

Typ m -s,-en type; ([1]: Kerl) bloke. T~e f -,-n type

Typhus m - typhoid

typisch adj typical (für of)

Typus m -, Typen type

Tyrann m -en,-en tyrant. T~ei f - tyranny. t~isch adj tyrannical. t~isieren vt tyrannize

Uu

U-Bahn f underground
übel adj bad; (hässlich) nasty; mir ist ü~ I feel sick; jdm etw ü~ nehmen hold sth against s.o. **Ü~keit** f - nausea
üben vt/i (haben) practise
über prep (+ dat/acc) over; (höher als) above; (betreffend) about; (Buch, Vortrag) on; (Scheck, Rechnung) for; (quer ü~) across; ü~ Köln fahren go via Cologne; ü~ Ostern over Easter; die Woche ü~ during the week; Fehler ü~ Fehler mistake after mistake ● adv ü~ und ü~ all over; jdm ü~ sein be better/(stärker) stronger than s.o. ● adj [1] ü~ sein be left over; etw ü~ sein be fed up with sth
überall adv everywhere
überanstrengen vt insep overtax; strain (Augen)
überarbeiten vt insep revise; sich ü~en overwork
überbieten† vt insep outbid; (übertreffen) surpass
Überblick m overall view; (Abriss) summary
überblicken vt insep overlook; (abschätzen) assess
überbringen† vt insep deliver
überbrücken vt insep (fig) bridge
überbuchen vt insep overbook
überdies adv moreover
überdimensional adj oversized
Überdosis f overdose
überdrüssig adj ü~ sein/werden be/grow tired (gen of)
übereignen vt insep transfer

übereilt adj over-hasty
übereinander adv one on top of/above the other; (sprechen) about each other
überein|kommen vi sep (sein) agree. **Ü~kunft** f - agreement. **ü~stimmen** vi sep (haben) agree; (Zahlen:) tally; (Ansichten:) coincide; (Farben:) match. **Ü~stimmung** f agreement
überfahren† vt insep run over
Überfahrt f crossing
Überfall m attack; (Bank-) raid
überfallen† vt insep attack; raid (Bank); (bestürmen) bombard (mit with)
Überfluss m abundance; (Wohlstand) affluence
überflüssig adj superfluous
überfordern vt insep overtax
überführ|en vt insep transfer; (Jur) convict (gen of). **Ü~ung** f transfer; (Straße) flyover; (Fußgänger-) foot-bridge
überfüllt adj overcrowded
Übergabe f handing over; transfer
Übergang m crossing; (Wechsel) transition
übergeben† vt insep hand over; (übereignen) transfer; sich ü~ be sick
übergehen† vt insep (fig) pass over; (nicht beachten) ignore; (auslassen) leave out
Übergewicht nt excess weight; (fig) predominance; Ü~ haben be overweight
über|greifen† vi sep (haben) spread (auf + acc to). **Ü~griff** m infringement
über|groß adj outsize; (übertrieben) exaggerated. **Ü~größe** f outsize
überhand adv ü~ nehmen

u

increase alarmingly

überhäufen vt insep inundate
(mit with)

überhaupt adv (im Allgemeinen)
altogether; (eigentlich) anyway;
(überdies) besides; ü~ nicht/nichts
not/nothing at all

überheblich adj arrogant.
Ü~keit f - arrogance

überholen† vt insep overtake; (reparieren) overhaul. ü~t adj outdated. Ü~ung f -,-en overhaul.
Ü~verbot nt 'Ü~verbot' 'no overtaking'

überhören vt insep fail to hear;
(nicht beachten) ignore

überirdisch adj supernatural

überkochen vi sep (sein)
boil over

überlassen† vt insep jdm etw
ü~ leave sth to s.o.; (geben) let s.o.
have sth; sich (dat) selbst ü~ sein
be left to one's own devices

Überlauf m overflow

überlaufen† vi sep (sein) overflow; (Mil, Pol) defect

Überläufer m defector

überleben vt/i insep (haben) survive. Ü~de(r) m/f survivor

überlegen[1] vt sep put over

überlegen[2] v insep ● vt [sich dat]
ü~ think over, consider; sich (dat) anders ü~ change one's mind ● vi (haben) think, reflect

überlegen[3] adj superior. Ü~heit
f - superiority

Überlegung f -,-en reflection

überliefern vt insep hand down.
Ü~ung f tradition

überlisten vt insep outwit

Übermacht f superiority

übermäßig adj excessive

Übermensch m superman.
ü~lich adj superhuman

übermitteln vt insep convey;
(senden) transmit

übermorgen adv the day after
tomorrow

übermüdet adj overtired

Über|mut m high spirits pl. ü~mütig adj high-spirited

übernächst|e(r,s) adj next but
one; ü~es Jahr the year after next

übernacht|en vi insep (haben)
stay overnight. Ü~ung f -,-en overnight stay; Ü~ung und Frühstück
bed and breakfast

Übernahme f - taking over;
(Comm) take-over

übernatürlich adj supernatural

übernehmen† vt insep take over;
(annehmen) take on; sich ü~
overdo things; (finanziell) overreach oneself

überqueren vt insep cross

überrasch|en vt insep surprise.
ü~end adj surprising; (unerwartet)
unexpected. Ü~ung f -,-en
surprise

überreden vt insep persuade

Überreste mpl remains

Überschall- prefix supersonic

überschätzen vt insep overestimate

Überschlag m rough estimate;
(Sport) somersault

überschlagen[1]† vt sep cross
(Beine)

überschlagen[2]† vt insep estimate roughly; (auslassen) skip; sich
ü~ somersault; (Ereignisse:) happen
fast ● adj tepid

überschneiden† (sich) vr insep
intersect, cross; (zusammenfallen)
overlap

überschreiten† vt insep cross;
(fig) exceed

Überschrift f heading; (Zeitungs-)

Über|schuss m surplus.
ü~schüssig adj surplus

überschwemm|en vt insep
flood; (fig) inundate. **Ü~ung** f
-,-en flood

Übersee in/nach Ü~ overseas;
aus/von Ü~ from overseas.
Ü~dampfer m ocean liner. **ü~isch**
adj overseas

übersehen† vt insep look out
over; (abschätzen) assess; (nicht
sehen) overlook, miss; (ignorieren)
ignore

übersenden† vt insep send

übersetzen¹ vi sep (haben/sein)
cross [over]

übersetz|en² vt insep translate.
Ü~er(in) m -s,- (f -,-nen) transla-
tor. **Ü~ung** f -,-en translation

Übersicht f overall view; (Abriss)
summary; (Tabelle) table. **ü~lich**
adj clear

Übersiedlung f move

überspielen vt insep (fig) cover
up; auf Band ü~ tape

überstehen† vt insep come
through; get over (Krankheit); (überleben) survive

übersteigen† vt insep climb
[over]; (fig) exceed

überstimmen vt insep outvote

Überstunden fpl overtime sg;
Ü~ machen work overtime

überstürz|en vt insep rush; sich
ü~en (Ereignisse:) happen fast. **ü~t**
adj hasty

übertrag|bar adj transferable;
(Med) infectious. **ü~en**† vt insep
transfer; (übergeben) assign (dat to);
(Techn, Med) transmit; (Radio, TV)
broadcast; (übersetzen) translate;
(anwenden) apply (auf + acc to)
● adj transferred, figurative.
Ü~ung f -,-en transfer; transmis-

sion; broadcast; translation; application

übertreffen† vt insep surpass;
(übersteigen) exceed; sich selbst ü~
excel oneself

übertreib|en† vt insep exagger-
ate; (zu weit treiben) overdo.
Ü~ung f -,-en exaggeration

übertreten¹† vi sep (sein) step
over the line; (Pol) go over/(Relig)
convert (zu to)

übertret|en²† vt insep infringe,
break (Gesetz). **Ü~ung** f -,-en infringement; breach

übertrieben adj exaggerated

übervölkert adj overpopulated

überwachen vt insep supervise;
(kontrollieren) monitor; (bespitzeln)
keep under surveillance

überwältigen vt insep over-
power; (fig) overwhelm

überweis|en† vt insep transfer;
refer (Patienten). **Ü~ung** f transfer;
(ärztliche) referral

überwiegen† v insep ● vi (haben)
predominate. ● vt outweigh

überwind|en† vt insep overcome;
sich ü~en force oneself. **Ü~ung** f
effort

Über|zahl f majority. **ü~zählig**
adj spare

überzeug|en vt insep convince;
sich [selbst] ü~ satisfy oneself.
ü~end adj convincing. **Ü~ung** f
-,-en conviction

überziehen¹† vt sep put on

überziehen²† vt insep cover;
overdraw (Konto)

Überzug m cover; (Schicht)
coating

üblich adj usual; (gebräuchlich) customary

U-Boot nt submarine

übrig adj remaining; (andere) other;

alles Ü~e [all] the rest; im Ü~en besides; (ansonsten) apart from that; ü~ sollte od bleiben be left [over]; etw ü~ lassen leave sth [over]; uns blieb nichts anderes ü~ we had no choice

Übung f -,-en exercise; (Üben) practice; außer od aus der Ü~ out of practice

Ufer nt -s,-. shore; (Fluss-) bank

Uhr f -,-en clock; (Armband-) watch; (Zähler) meter; um ein U~ at one o'clock; wie viel U~ ist es? what's the time? U~macher m -s,-. watch and clockmaker. U~werk nt clock/watch mechanism. U~zeiger m [clock-/watch-]hand. U~zeit f time

Uhu m -s,-s eagle owl

UKW abbr (Ultrakurzwelle) VHF

ulkig adj funny; (seltsam) odd

Ulme f -,-n elm

Ultimatum nt -s,-ten ultimatum

Ultra|kurzwelle f very high frequency. U~leichtflugzeug nt microlight [aircraft]

Ultraschall m ultrasound

ultraviolett adj ultraviolet

um prep (+ acc) [a]round; (Uhrzeit) at; (bitten) for; (streiten) over; (sich sorgen) about; (betrügen) out of; (bei Angabe einer Differenz) by; um [... herum] around, [round] about; Tag um Tag day after day; um seinetwillen for his sake ● adv (ungefähr) around, about; um sein □ be over; (Zeit) be up ● conj um zu to; (Absicht) [in order] to; zu müde, um zu ... too tired to ...

umarm|en vt insep embrace, hug. U~ung f -,-en embrace, hug

Umbau m rebuilding; conversion (zu into). u~en vt sep rebuild; convert (zu into)

Umbildung f reorganization; (Pol) reshuffle

umbinden† vt sep put on

umblättern v sep ● vt turn [over] ● vi (haben) turn the page

umbringen† vt sep kill; sich u~ kill oneself

umbuchen v sep ● vt change; (Comm) transfer ● vi (haben) change one's booking

umdrehen v sep ● vt turn round/(wenden) over; turn (Schlüssel); (umkrempeln) turn inside out; sich u~ turn round; (im Liegen) turn over ● vi (haben/sein) turn back

Umdrehung f turn; (Motor-) revolution

umeinander adv around each other; sich u~ sorgen worry about each other

umfahren¹† vt sep run over

umfahren²† vt insep go round; bypass (Ort)

umfallen† vi sep (sein) fall over; (Person) fall down

Umfang m girth; (Geometry) circumference; (Größe) size

umfangreich adj extensive; (dick) big

umfassen vt insep consist of, comprise; (umgeben) surround. u~d adj comprehensive

Umfrage f survey, poll

umfüllen vt sep transfer

umfunktionieren vt sep convert

Umgang m [social] contact; (Umgehen) dealing (mit with)

Umgangssprache f colloquial language

umgeb|en† vt insep (haben) surround ● adj u~en von surrounded by. U~ung f -,-en surroundings pl

umgehen† vt insep avoid; (nicht beachten) evade; (Straße:) bypass

umgehend adj immediate

Umgehungsstraße f bypass
umgekehrt adj inverse; (Reihenfolge) reverse; es war u~ it was
the other way round
umgraben† vt sep dig [over]
Umhang m cloak
umhauen† vt sep knock down;
(fällen) chop down
umhören (sich) vr sep ask around
Umkehr f - turning back. **u~en** v
sep ● vi (sein) turn back ● vt turn
round; turn inside out (Tasche); (fig)
reverse
umkippen v sep ● vt tip over;
(versehentlich) knock over ● vi (sein)
fall over; (Boot:) capsize
Umkleide|kabine f changing-
cubicle. **u~n** (sich) vr sep change.
U~raum m changing-room
umknicken v sep ● vt bend; (falten) fold ● vi (sein) bend; (mit dem
Fuß) go over on one's ankle
umkommen† vi sep (sein) perish
Umkreis m surroundings pl; im
U~ von within a radius of
umkreisen vt insep circle; (Astronomy) revolve around; (Satellit:)
orbit
umkrempeln vt sep turn up;
(von innen nach außen) turn inside
out; (ändern) change radically
Umlauf m circulation; (Astronomy)
revolution. **U~bahn** f orbit
Umlaut m umlaut
umlegen vt sep lay or put down;
flatten (Getreide); turn down (Kragen); put on (Schal); throw (Hebel);
(verlegen) transfer; (🔲: töten) kill
umleit|en vt sep divert. **U~ung** f
diversion
umliegend adj surrounding
umpflanzen vt sep transplant
umranden vt insep edge
umräumen vt sep rearrange

umrechn|en vt sep convert.
U~ung f conversion
umreißen† vt insep outline
Umriss m outline
umrühren vt/i sep (haben) stir
ums pron = um das
Umsatz m (Comm) turnover
umschalten vt sep (haben)
switch over; auf Rot u~ (Ampel:)
change to red
Umschau f U~ halten nach look
out for
Umschlag m cover; (Schutz-)
jacket; (Brief-) envelope; (Med) compress; (Hosen-) turn-up. **u~en†** vt
sep ● vt turn up; turn down (Seite);
(fällen) chop down ● vi (sein) topple
over; (Wetter:) change; (Wind:) veer
umschließen† vt insep enclose
umschreib|en vt insep define;
(anders ausdrücken) paraphrase
umschulen vt sep retrain; (Sch)
transfer to another school
Umschwung m (fig) change;
(Pol) U-turn
umseh|en† (sich) vr sep look
round; (zurück) look back; sich u~
nach look for
umsein* vi sep (sein) um sein,
s. um
umseitig adj & adv overleaf
umsetzen vt sep move; (umpflanzen) transplant; (Comm) sell
umsied|eln vt sep resettle ● vi
(sein) move. **U~lung** f resettlement
umso conj u~ besser/mehr all the
better/more; je mehr, ~ besser
the more the better
umsonst adv in vain; (grundlos)
without reason; (gratis) free
Umstand m circumstance; (Tatsache) fact; (Aufwand) fuss; (Mühe)
trouble; unter U~en possibly; jdm
U~e machen put s.o. to trouble; in

u

andern U~en pregnant

umständlich adj laborious; (kompliziert) involved

Umstands|kleid nt maternity dress. **U~wort** nt (pl -wörter) adverb

Umstehende pl bystanders

umsteigen† vi sep (sein) change

umstellen¹ vt insep surround

umstell|en² vt sep rearrange; transpose (Wörter); (anders einstellen) reset; (Techn) convert; (ändern) change; sich u~en adjust. **U~ung** f rearrangement; transposition; resetting; conversion; change; adjustment

umstritten adj controversial; (ungeklärt) disputed

umstülpen vt sep turn upside down; (von innen nach außen) turn inside out

Um|sturz m coup. **u~stürzen** v sep ● vt overturn; (Pol) overthrow ● vi (sein) fall over

umtaufen vt sep rename

Umtausch m exchange. **u~en** vt sep change; exchange (gegen for)

umwechseln vt sep change

Umweg m detour; auf U~en (fig) in a roundabout way

Umwelt f environment. **u~freundlich** adj environmentally friendly. **U~schutz** m protection of the environment

umwerfen† vt sep knock over; (fig) upset (Plan)

umziehen† v sep ● vi (sein) move ● vt change; sich u~ change

umzingeln vt insep surround

Umzug m move; (Prozession) procession

unabänderlich adj irrevocable; (Tatsache) unalterable

unabhängig adj independent;

u~ davon, ob irrespective of whether. **U~keit** f - independence

unablässig adj incessant

unabsehbar adj incalculable

unabsichtlich adj unintentional

unachtsam adj careless

unangebracht adj inappropriate

unangenehm adj unpleasant; (peinlich) embarrassing

Unannehmlichkeiten fpl trouble sg

unansehnlich adj shabby

unanständig adj indecent

unappetitlich adj unappetizing

Unart f -,-en bad habit. **u~ig** adj naughty

unauffällig adj inconspicuous; unobtrusive

unaufgefordert adv without being asked

unauf|haltsam adj inexorable. **u~hörlich** adj incessant

unaufmerksam adj inattentive

unaufrichtig adj insincere

unausbleiblich adj inevitable

unausstehlich adj insufferable

unbarmherzig adj merciless

unbeabsichtigt adj unintentional

unbedenklich adj harmless ● adv without hesitation

unbedeutend adj insignificant; (geringfügig) slight

unbedingt adj absolute; nicht u~ not necessarily

unbefriedig|end adj unsatisfactory. **u~t** adj dissatisfied

unbefugt adj unauthorized ● adv without authorization

unbegreiflich adj incomprehensible

unbegrenzt adj unlimited ● adv indefinitely

unbegründet *adj* unfounded

Unbehagen *nt* unease; (*körperlich*) discomfort

unbekannt *adj* unknown; (*nicht vertraut*) unfamiliar. **U~e(r)** *m/f* stranger

unbekümmert *adj* unconcerned; (*unbeschwert*) carefree

unbeliebt *adj* unpopular. **U~heit** *f* unpopularity

unbemannt *adj* unmanned

unbemerkt *adj & adv* unnoticed

unbenutzt *adj* unused

unbequem *adj* uncomfortable; (*lästig*) awkward

unberechenbar *adj* unpredictable

unberechtigt *adj* unjustified; (*unbefugt*) unauthorized

unberührt *adj* untouched; (*fig*) virgin; (*Landschaft*) unspoilt

unbescheiden *adj* presumptuous

unbeschrankt *adj* unguarded

unbeschränkt *adj* unlimited
● *adv* without limit

unbeschwert *adj* carefree

unbesiegt *adj* undefeated

unbespielt *adj* blank

unbeständig *adj* inconsistent; (*Wetter*) unsettled

unbestechlich *adj* incorruptible

unbestimmt *adj* indefinite; (*Alter*) indeterminate; (*ungewiss*) uncertain; (*unklar*) vague

unbestritten *adj* undisputed
● *adv* indisputably

unbeteiligt *adj* indifferent; **u~ an** (+ *dat*) not involved in

unbetont *adj* unstressed

unbewacht *adj* unguarded

unbewaffnet *adj* unarmed

unbeweglich *adj & adv* motionless, still

unbewohnt *adj* uninhabited

unbewusst *adj* unconscious

unbezahlbar *adj* priceless

unbrauchbar *adj* useless

und *conj* and; **und so weiter** and so on; **nach und nach** bit by bit

Undank *m* ingratitude. **u~bar** *adj* ungrateful; (*nicht lohnend*) thankless. **U~barkeit** *f* ingratitude

undeutlich *adj* indistinct; vague

undicht *adj* leaking; **u~e Stelle** leak

Unding *nt* absurdity

undiplomatisch *adj* undiplomatic

unduldsam *adj* intolerant

undurch|dringlich *adj* impenetrable; (*Miene*) inscrutable. **u~führbar** *adj* impracticable

undurch|lässig *adj* impermeable. **u~sichtig** *adj* opaque; (*fig*) doubtful

uneben *adj* uneven. **U~heit** *f* -,-en unevenness; (*Buckel*) bump

unecht *adj* false; **u~er Schmuck** imitation jewellery

unehelich *adj* illegitimate

uneinig *adj* (*fig*) divided; [*sich* (*dat*)] **u~ sein** disagree

uneins *adj* **~ sein** be at odds

unempfindlich *adj* insensitive (*gegen* to); (*widerstandsfähig*) tough; (*Med*) immune

unendlich *adj* infinite; (*endlos*) endless. **U~keit** *f* - infinity

unentbehrlich *adj* indispensable

unentgeltlich *adj* free, (*Arbeit*) unpaid ● *adv* free of charge

unentschieden *adj* undecided; (*Sport*) drawn; **u~ spielen** draw. **U~** *nt* -s,- draw

unentschlossen *adj* indecisive; (*unentschieden*) undecided

unentwegt *adj* persistent; (*unauf-*

*hörlich) incessant

unerfahren adj inexperienced.
U~heit f - inexperience
unerfreulich adj unpleasant
unerhört adj enormous; (*empörend*) outrageous
unerklärlich adj inexplicable
unerlässlich adj essential
unerlaubt adj unauthorized ● adv without permission
unerschwinglich adj prohibitive
unersetzlich adj irreplaceable; (*Verlust*) irreparable
unerträglich adj unbearable
unerwartet adj unexpected
unerwünscht adj unwanted; (*Besuch*) unwelcome

unfähig adj incompetent; u~, etw zu tun incapable of doing sth; (*nicht in der Lage*) unable to do sth. **U~keit** f incompetence; inability (zu to)
unfair adj unfair
Unfall m accident. **U~flucht** f failure to stop after an accident. **U~station** f casualty department
unfassbar adj incomprehensible
Unfehlbarkeit f - infallibility
unfolgsam adj disobedient
unförmig adj shapeless
unfreiwillig adj involuntary; (*unbeabsichtigt*) unintentional
unfreundlich adj unfriendly; (*unangenehm*) unpleasant. **U~keit** f unfriendliness; unpleasantness
Unfriede[n] m discord
unfruchtbar adj infertile; (*fig*) unproductive. **U~keit** f infertility
Unfug m -s mischief; (*Unsinn*) nonsense
Ungar|(in) m -n,-n (f -,-nen) Hungarian. **u~isch** adj Hungarian. **U~n** nt -s Hungary

ungeachtet prep (+ gen) in spite of; dessen u~ notwithstanding [this]. **ungebraucht** adj unused.
ungedeckt adj uncovered; (*Sport*) unmarked; (*Tisch*) unlaid
Ungeduld f impatience. **u~ig** adj impatient
ungeeignet adj unsuitable
ungefähr adj approximate, rough
ungefährlich adj harmless
ungeheuer adj enormous. **U~** nt -s,- monster
ungehorsam adj disobedient.
U~ m disobedience
ungeklärt adj unsolved; (*Frage*) unsettled; (*Ursache*) unknown
ungelegen adj inconvenient
ungelernt adj unskilled
ungemütlich adj uncomfortable; (*unangenehm*) unpleasant
ungenau adj inaccurate; vague.
U~igkeit f -,-en inaccuracy
ungeniert /'ʊnʒeniːɐt/ adj uninhibited ● adv openly
ungenießbar adj inedible; (*Getränk*) undrinkable. **ungenügend** adj inadequate; (*Sch*) unsatisfactory.
ungepflegt adj neglected; (*Person*) unkempt. **ungerade** adj (*Zahl*) odd
ungerecht adj unjust. **U~igkeit** f -,-en injustice
ungern adv reluctantly
ungesalzen adj unsalted
Ungeschick|lichkeit f clumsiness. **u~t** adj clumsy
ungeschminkt adj without make-up; (*Wahrheit*) unvarnished.
ungesetzlich adj illegal. **ungestört** adj undisturbed. **ungesund** adj unhealthy. **ungesüßt** adj unsweetened. **ungetrübt** adj perfect
Ungetüm nt -s,-e monster
ungewiss adj uncertain; im Ungewissen sein/lassen be/leave in

the dark. **U~heit** f uncertainty
ungewöhnlich adj unusual. **ungewohnt** adj unaccustomed; (nicht vertraut) unfamiliar
Ungeziefer nt -s vermin
ungezogen adj naughty
ungezwungen adj informal; (natürlich) natural
ungläubig adj incredulous
unglaublich adj incredible, unbelievable
ungleich adj unequal; (verschieden) different. **U~heit** f - inequality. **u~mäßig** adj uneven
Unglück nt -s,-e incurable (Pech) bad luck; (Missgeschick) mishap; (Unfall) accident. **u~lich** adj unhappy; (ungünstig) unfortunate. **u~licherweise** adv unfortunately
ungültig adj invalid; (Jur) void
ungünstig adj unfavourable; (unpassend) inconvenient
Unheil nt -s disaster; **U~ anrichten** cause havoc
unheilbar adj incurable
unheimlich adj eerie; (gruselig) creepy; (🅵: groß) terrific ● adv eerily; (🅵: sehr) terribly
unhöflich adj rude. **U~keit** f rudeness
unhygienisch adj unhygienic
Uni f -,-s 🅵 university
uni /yˈniː/ inv adj plain
Uniform f -,-en uniform
uninteressant adj uninteresting
Union f -,-en union
universell adj universal
Universität f -,-en university
Universum nt -s universe
unkenntlich adj unrecognizable
unklar adj unclear; (ungewiss) uncertain; (vage) vague; **im U~en (u~en) sein** be in the dark
unkompliziert adj un-

complicated
Unkosten pl expenses
Unkraut nt weed; (coll) weeds pl; **U~ jäten** weed. **U~vertilgungsmittel** nt weed-killer
unlängst adv recently
unlauter adj dishonest; (unfair) unfair
unleserlich adj illegible
unleugbar adj undeniable
unlogisch adj illogical
Unmenge f enormous amount/(Anzahl) number
Unmensch m 🅵 brute. **u~lich** adj inhuman
unmerklich adj imperceptible
unmittelbar adj immediate; (direkt) direct
unmöbliert adj unfurnished
unmodern adj old-fashioned
unmöglich adj impossible. **U~keit** f - impossibility
Unmoral f immorality. **u~isch** adj immoral
unmündig adj under-age
Unmut m displeasure
unnatürlich adj unnatural
unnormal adj abnormal
unnötig adj unnecessary
unord|entlich adj untidy; (nachlässig) sloppy. **U~nung** f disorder; (Durcheinander) muddle
unorthodox adj unorthodox ● adv in an unorthodox manner
unparteiisch adj impartial
unpassend adj inappropriate; (Moment) inopportune
unpersönlich adj impersonal
unpraktisch adj impractical
unpünktlich adj unpunctual ● adv late
unrealistisch adj unrealistic
unrecht adj wrong ● n jdm u~

u

tun do s.o. an injustice. **U~nt** wrong; **zu U~** wrongly; **U~ haben** be wrong; **jdm U~ geben** disagree with s.o. **u~mäßig** adj unlawful

unregelmäßig adj irregular

unreif adj unripe; (fig) immature

unrein adj impure; (Luft) polluted; (Haut) bad; **ins U~e schreiben** make a rough draft of

unrentabel adj unprofitable

Unruhe f -,-n restlessness; (Erregung) agitation; (Besorgnis) anxiety; **U~en** (Pol) unrest sg. **u~ig** adj restless; (laut) noisy; (besorgt) anxious

uns pron (acc/dat of **wir**) us; (reflexive) ourselves; (einander) each other

unsauber adj dirty; (nachlässig) sloppy

unschädlich adj harmless

unscharf adj blurred

unschätzbar adj inestimable

unscheinbar adj inconspicuous

unschlagbar adj unbeatable

unschlüssig adj undecided

Unschuld f - innocence; (Jungfräulichkeit) virginity. **u~ig** adj innocent

unselbständig,
unselbständig adj dependent
● adv **u~ denken** not think for oneself

unser poss pron **u.** **u~e(r,s)** poss pron ours. **u~erseits** adv for our part. **u~twegen** adv for our sake; (wegen uns) because of us, on our account

unsicher adj unsafe; (ungewiss) uncertain; (nicht zuverlässig) unreliable; (Schritte, Hand) unsteady; (Person) insecure ● adv unsteadily. **U~heit** f uncertainty; unreliability; insecurity

unsichtbar adj invisible

Unsinn m nonsense. **u~ig** adj nonsensical, absurd

Unsitt|e f bad habit. **u~lich** adj indecent

unsportlich adj not sporty; (unfair) unsporting

uns|re(r,s) poss pron = **unsere(r,s). u~rige** poss pron **der/die/das u~rige** ours

unsterblich adj immortal. **U~keit** f immortality

Unsumme f vast sum

unsympathisch adj unpleasant; **er ist mir u~** I don't like him

untätig adj idle

untauglich adj unsuitable; (Mil) unfit

unten adv at the bottom; (auf der Unterseite) underneath; (eine Treppe tiefer) downstairs; (im Text) below; **hier/da u~** down here/there; **nach u~** down[wards]; (die Treppe hinunter) downstairs; **siehe u~** see below

unter prep (+ dat/acc) under; (niedriger als) below; (inmitten, zwischen) among; **u~ anderem** among other things; **u~ der Woche** during the week; **u~ sich** by themselves

Unter|arm m forearm. **U~bewusstsein** nt subconscious

unterbieten† vt insep undercut; beat (Rekord)

unterbinden† vt insep stop

unterbrech|en† vt insep interrupt; break (Reise). **U~ung** f -,-en interruption, break

unterbringen† vt sep put; (beherbergen) put up

unterdessen adv in the meantime

Unterdrückung f - suppression; oppression

untere(r,s) adj lower

untereinander adv one below the other; (miteinander) among ourselves/yourselves/themselves

unterernähr|t adj undernourished. **U~ung** f malnutrition

Unterführung f underpass; (Fußgänger-) subway

Untergang m (der Sonne) setting; (Naut) sinking; (Zugrundegehen) disappearance; (der Welt) end

Untergebene(r) m/f subordinate

untergehen vi sep (sein) (Astronomy) set; (versinken) go under; (Schiff:) go down, sink; (zugrunde gehen) disappear; (Welt:) come to an end

Untergeschoss nt basement

Untergrund m foundation; (Hintergrund) background. **U~bahn** f underground [railway]

unterhaken vt sep jdn u~ take s.o.'s arm; untergehakt arm in arm

unterhalb adv & prep (+ gen) below

Unterhalt m maintenance

unterhalt|en vt insep maintain; (ernähren) support; (betreiben) run; (erheitern) entertain; **sich u~en** talk; (sich vergnügen) enjoy oneself. **U~ung** f -,-en maintenance; (Gespräch) conversation; (Zeitvertreib) entertainment

Unter|haus nt (Pol) lower house; (in UK) House of Commons. **U~hemd** nt vest. **U~hose** f underpants pl. **u~irdisch** adj & adv underground

Unterkiefer m lower jaw

unterkommen vi sep (sein) find accommodation; (eine Stellung finden) get a job

Unterkunft f -,-künfte accommodation

Unterlage f pad; **U~n** papers

Unterlass m ohne U~ incessantly

Unterlassung f -,-en omission

unterlegen adj inferior; (Sport) losing; zahlenmäßig u~ out-numbered (dat by). **U~e(r)** m/f loser

Unterleib m abdomen

unterliegen vi insep (sein) lose (dat to); (unterworfen sein) be subject (dat to)

Unterlippe f lower lip

Untermiete f zur U~ wohnen be a lodger. **U~r(in)** m(f) lodger

unternehm|en vt insep undertake; take (Schritte); **etw/nichts u~en** do sth/nothing. **U~en** nt -s,- undertaking, enterprise (Betrieb) concern. **U~er** m -s,- employer; (Bau-) contractor; (Industrieller) industrialist. **u~ungslustig** adj enterprising

Unteroffizier m non-commissioned officer

unterordnen vt sep subordinate

Unterredung f -,-en talk

Unterricht m -[e]s teaching; (Privat-) tuition; (U~sstunden) lessons pl

unterrichten vt/i insep (haben) teach; (informieren) inform; **sich u~** inform oneself

Unterrock m slip

untersagen vt insep forbid

Untersatz m mat; (mit Füßen) stand; (Gläser-) coaster

unterscheid|en vt/i insep (haben) distinguish; (auseinander halten) tell apart; **sich u~en** differ. **U~ung** f distinction

Unterschied m -[e]s,-e difference; (Unterscheidung) distinction; im U~ zu ihm unlike him. **u~lich** adj different; (wechselnd) varying

unterschlagen vt insep embezzle; (verheimlichen) suppress. **U~ung** f -,-en embezzlement;

suppression

Unterschlupf m -[e]s shelter; (Versteck) hiding-place

unterschreiben† vt/i insep (haben) sign

Unter|schrift f signature; (Bild-) caption. **U~seeboot** nt submarine

Unterstand m shelter

unterste(r,s) adj lowest, bottom

unterstehen† v insep ● vi (haben) be answerable (dat to); (unterliegen) be subject (dat to)

unterstellen¹ vt sep put underneath; (abstellen) store; sich u~ shelter

unterstellen² vt insep place under the control (dat of); (annehmen) assume; (fälschlich zuschreiben) impute (dat to)

unterstreichen† vt insep underline

unterstütz|en vt insep support; (helfen) aid. **U~ung** f -,-en support; (finanziell) aid; (regelmäßiger Betrag) allowance; (Arbeitslosen-) benefit

untersuch|en vt insep examine; (Jur) investigate; (prüfen) test; (überprüfen) check; (durchsuchen) search. **U~ung** f -,-en examination; investigation; test; check; search. **U~ungshaft** f detention on remand

Untertan m -s & -en,-en subject

Untertasse f saucer

Unterteil nt bottom (part)

Untertitel m subtitle

untervermieten vt/i insep (haben) sublet

Unterwäsche f underwear

unterwegs adv on the way; (außer Haus) out; (verreist) away

Unterwelt f underworld

unterzeichnen vt insep sign

unterziehen† vt insep etw einer Untersuchung/Überprüfung u~ examine/ check sth; sich einer Operation/Prüfung u~ have an operation/take a test

Untier nt monster

untragbar adj intolerable

untrennbar adj inseparable

untreu adj disloyal; (in der Ehe) unfaithful. **U~e** f disloyalty; infidelity

untröstlich adj inconsolable

unübersehbar adj obvious; (groß) immense

ununterbrochen adj incessant

unveränderlich adj invariable; (gleichbleibend) unchanging

unverändert adj unchanged

unverantwortlich adj irresponsible

unverbesserlich adj incorrigible

unverbindlich adj non-committal; (Comm) not binding ● adv without obligation

unverdaulich adj indigestible

unver|gesslich adj unforgettable. **u~gleichlich** adj incomparable. **u~heiratet** adj unmarried. **u~käuflich** adj not for sale; (Muster) free

unverkennbar adj unmistakable

unverletzt adj unhurt

unvermeidlich adj inevitable

unver|mindert adj & adv undiminished. **u~mutet** adj unexpected

Unver|nunft f folly. **u~nünftig** adj foolish

unverschämt adj insolent; (ஊ: ungeheuer) outrageous. **U~heit** f -,-en insolence

unver|sehens adv suddenly. **u~sehrt** adj unhurt; (unbeschädigt) intact

unverständlich adj incomprehensible; (undeutlich) indistinct

unverträglich adj incompatible; (Person) quarrelsome; (unbekömmlich) indigestible

unver|wundbar adj invulnerable. **u~wüstlich** adj indestructible; (Person, Humor) irrepressible; (Gesundheit) robust. **u~zeihlich** adj unforgivable

unverzüglich adj immediate

unvollendet adj unfinished

unvollkommen adj imperfect; (unvollständig) incomplete

unvollständig adj incomplete

unvor|bereitet adj unprepared. **u~hergesehen** adj unforeseen

unvorsichtig adj careless

unvorstellbar adj unimaginable

unvorteilhaft adj unfavourable; (nicht hübsch) unattractive

unwahr adj untrue. **U~heit** f -,-en untruth. **u~scheinlich** adj unlikely; (unglaublich) improbable; (ↄ: groß) incredible

unweit adv & prep (+ gen) not far

unwesentlich adj unimportant

Unwetter nt -s,- storm

unwichtig adj unimportant

unwider|legbar adj irrefutable. **u~stehlich** adj irresistible

Unwill|e m displeasure. **u~ig** adj angry; (widerwillig) reluctant

unwirklich adj unreal

unwirksam adj ineffective

unwirtschaftlich adj uneconomic

unwissen|d adj ignorant. **U~heit** f - ignorance

unwohl adj unwell; (unbehaglich) uneasy

unwürdig adj unworthy (gen of)

Unzahl f vast number. **unzählig** adj innumerable, countless

unzerbrechlich adj unbreakable

unzerstörbar adj indestructible

unzertrennlich adj inseparable

Unzucht f sexual offence; gewerbsmäßige U~ prostitution

unzüchtig adj indecent; (Schriften) obscene

unzufrieden adj dissatisfied; (innerlich) discontented. **U~heit** f dissatisfaction

unzulässig adj inadmissible

unzurechnungsfähig adj insane. **U~keit** f insanity

unzusammenhängend adj incoherent

unzutreffend adj inapplicable; (falsch) incorrect

unzuverlässig adj unreliable

unzweifelhaft adj undoubted

üppig adj luxuriant; (überreichlich) lavish

uralt adj ancient

Uran nt -s uranium

Uraufführung f first performance

Urenkel m great-grandson; (pl) great-grandchildren

Urgroß|mutter f great-grandmother. **U~vater** m great-grandfather

Urheber m -s,- originator; (Verfasser) author. **U~recht** nt copyright

Urin m -s,-e urine

Urkunde f -,-n certificate; (Dokument) document

Urlaub m -s holiday; (Mil, Admin) leave; auf U~ on holiday/leave; U~ haben be on holiday/leave. **U~er(in)** m -s,- (f -,-nen) holidaymaker. **U~sort** m holiday resort

Urne f -,-n urn; (Wahl-) ballot-box

Ursache f cause; (Grund) reason; keine U~! I don't mention it!

Ursprung m origin

ursprünglich adj original; (anfänglich) initial; (natürlich) natural

Urteil nt -s,-e judgement; (Meinung) opinion; (U~sspruch) verdict; (Strafe) sentence. **u~en** vi (haben) judge

Urwald m primeval forest; (tropischer) jungle

Urzeit f primeval times pl

USA pl USA sg

usw. abbr (und so weiter) etc.

utopisch adj Utopian

Vv

Vakuum /'va:kuʊm/ nt -s vacuum. **v~verpackt** adj vacuum-packed

Vanille /va'nɪljə/ f - vanilla

variieren vt/i (haben) vary

Vase /'va:zə/ f -,-n vase

Vater m -s, ⸚ father. **V~land** nt fatherland

väterlich adj paternal; (fürsorglich) fatherly. **v~erseits** adv on one's/ the father's side

Vater|schaft f - fatherhood; (Jur) paternity. **V~unser** nt -s,- Lord's Prayer

v. Chr. abbr (vor Christus) BC

Vegetar|ier(in) /vege'ta:rje, -jərɪn/ m(f) -s,- (f -,-nen) vegetarian. **v~isch** adj vegetarian

Veilchen nt -s,- violet

Vene /'ve:nə/ f -,-n vein

Venedig /ve'ne:dɪç/ nt -s Venice

Ventil /vɛn'ti:l/ nt -s,-e valve. **V~ator** m -s,-en fan

verabred|en vt arrange; sich [mit jdm] v~en arrange to meet [s.o.]. **V~ung** f -,-en arrangement; (Treffen) appointment

verabschieden vt say goodbye to; (aus dem Dienst) retire; pass (Gesetz); sich v~ say goodbye

verachten vt despise

Verachtung f - contempt

verallgemeinern vt/i (haben) generalize

veränder|lich adj changeable; (Math) variable. **v~n** vt change; sich v~n change; (beruflich) change one's job. **V~ung** f change

verängstigt adj frightened, scared

verankern vt anchor

veranlag|t adj künstlerisch/musikalisch v~t sein have an artistic/a musical bent; praktisch v~t practically minded. **V~ung** f -,-en disposition; (Neigung) tendency; (künstlerisch) bent

veranlassen vt (reg) arrange for; (einleiten) institute; jdn v~ prompt s.o. (zu to)

veranschlagen vt (reg) estimate

veranstalt|en vt organize; hold, give (Party); make (Lärm). **V~er** m -s,- organizer. **V~ung** f -,-en event

verantwort|lich adj responsible; v~lich machen hold responsible. **V~ung** f - responsibility. **v~ungsbewusst** adj responsible. **v~ungslos** adj irresponsible. **v~ungsvoll** adj responsible

verarbeiten vt use; (Techn) process; (verdauen & fig) digest

verärgern vt annoy

verausgaben (sich) vr spend all one's money (or) strength

veräußern vt sell

Verb /vɛrp/ nt -s,-en verb

Verband m -[e]s, ⸚e association; (Mil) unit; (Med) bandage; (Wund-) dressing. **V~szeug** nt first-aid kit

verbann|en vt exile; (fig) banish. **V~ung** f - exile

verbergen† vt hide; **sich v~** hide

verbesser|n vt improve; (berichtigen) correct. **V~ung** f -,-en improvement; correction

verbeug|en (sich) vr bow. **V~ung** f bow

verbeulen vt dent

verbiegen† vt bend

verbieten† vt forbid; (Admin) prohibit, ban

verbillig|en vt reduce [in price]. **v~t** adj reduced

verbinden† vt connect (mit to); (zusammenfügen) join; (verknüpfen) combine; (in Verbindung bringen) associate; (Med) bandage; dress (Wunde); **jdm verbunden sein** (fig) be obliged to s.o.

verbindlich adj friendly; (bindend) binding

Verbindung f connection; (Verknüpfung) combination; (Kontakt) contact; (Vereinigung) association; chemiche **V~** chemical compound; **in V~ stehen/sich in V~ setzen** be/get in touch

verbissen adj grim

verbitter|n vt make bitter. **v~t** adj bitter. **V~ung** f - bitterness

verblassen vi (sein) fade

Verbleib m -s whereabouts pl

verbleit adj (Benzin) leaded

verblüff|en vt amaze, astound. **V~ung** f - amazement

verblühen vi (sein) wither, fade

verbluten vi (sein) bleed to death

verborgen vt lend

Verbot nt -[e]s,-e ban. **v~en** adj forbidden; (Admin) prohibited

Verbrauch m -[e]s consumption. **v~en** vt use; consume (Lebensmittel); (erschöpfen) use up. **V~er** m -s,- consumer

Verbrechen† nt -s,- crime

Verbrecher m -s,- criminal

verbreit|en vt spread. **v~et** adj widespread. **V~ung** f - spread; (Verbreiten) spreading

verbrenn|en vt/i (sein) burn; cremate (Leiche). **V~ung** f -,-en burning; cremation; (Wunde) burn

verbringen† vt spend

verbrühen vt scald

verbuchen vt enter

verbünd|en (sich) vr form an alliance. **V~ete(r)** m/f ally

verbürgen vt guarantee; **sich v~ für** vouch for

Verdacht m -[e]s suspicion; **in or im V~ haben** suspect

verdächtig adj suspicious. **v~en** vt suspect (gen of). **V~te(r)** m/f suspect

verdamm|en vt condemn; (Relig) damn. **v~t** adj & adv 🗶 damned; **v~t!** damn!

verdampfen vt/i (sein) evaporate

verdanken vt owe (dat to)

verdau|en vt digest. **v~lich** adj digestible. **V~ung** f - digestion

Verdeck nt -[e]s,-e hood; (Oberdeck) top deck

verderb|en† vi (sein) spoil (Lebensmittel); go bad ● vt spoil; **ich habe mir den Magen verdorben** I have an upset stomach. **V~en** nt -s ruin. **v~lich** adj perishable; (schädlich) pernicious

verdien|en vt/i (haben) earn; (fig) deserve. **V~er** m -s,- wage-earner

Verdienst[1] m -[e]s earnings pl

Verdienst[2] nt -[e]s,-e merit

verdient adj well-deserved

verdoppeln vt double

verdorben adj spoilt, ruined; (Magen) upset; (moralisch) corrupt; (verkommen) depraved

verdrehen vt twist; roll (Augen)

(fig) distort. v~t adj 🔟 crazy

verdreifachen vt treble, triple

verdrücken vt crumple; (🔟: essen) polish off; sich v~ 🔟 slip away

Verdruss m -es annoyance

verdünnen vt dilute; sich v~ taper off

verdunst|en vi (sein) evaporate. V~ung f - evaporation

verdursten vi (sein) die of thirst

veredeln vt refine; (Horticulture) graft

verehr|en vt revere; (Relig) worship; (bewundern) admire; (schenken) give. V~er(in) m -s,- (f -,-nen) admirer. V~ung f - veneration; worship; admiration

vereidigen vt swear in

Verein m -s,-e society; (Sport-) club

vereinbar adj compatible. v~en vt arrange. V~ung f -,-en agreement

vereinfachen vt simplify

vereinheitlichen vt standardize

vereinig|en vt unite; merge (Firmen); wieder v~en reunite; reunify (Land); sich v~en unite; V~te Staaten [von Amerika] United States sg (of America). V~ung f -,-en union; (Organisation) organization

vereinzelt adj isolated ● adv occasionally

vereist adj frozen; (Straße) icy

vereitert adj septic

verenden vi (sein) die

verengen vt restrict; sich v~ narrow; (Pupille:) contract

vererb|en vt leave (dat to); (Biology & fig) pass on (dat to). V~ung f - heredity

verfahren† vi (sein) proceed; v~

mit deal with ● vr sich v~ lose one's way ● adj muddled. V~ nt -s,- procedure; (Techn) process; (Jur) proceedings pl

Verfall m decay; (eines Gebäudes) dilapidation; (körperlich & fig) decline; (Ablauf) expiry. v~en† vi (sein) decay; (Person, Sitten:) decline; (ablaufen) expire; v~en in (+ acc) lapse into; v~en auf (+ acc) hit on (Idee)

verfärben (sich) vr change colour; (Stoff:) discolour

verfass|en vt write; (Jur) draw up; (entwerfen) draft. V~er m -s,- author. V~ung f (Pol) constitution; (Zustand) state

verfaulen vi (sein) rot, decay

verfechten† vt advocate

verfehlen vt miss

verfeinde|n (sich) vr become enemies; v~t sein be enemies

verfeinern vt refine; (verbessern) improve

verfilmen vt film

verfluch|en vt curse. v~t adj & adv 🔟 damned; v~t! damn!

verfolg|en vt pursue; (folgen) follow; (bedrängen) pester; (Pol) persecute; strafrechtlich v~en prosecute. V~er m -s,- pursuer. V~ung f - pursuit; persecution

verfrüht adj premature

verfügbar adj available

verfüg|en vt order; (Jur) decree ● vi (haben) v~en über (+ acc) have at one's disposal. V~ung f -,-en order; (Jur) decree; jdm zur V~ung stehen be at s.o.'s disposal

verführ|en vt seduce; tempt. V~ung f seduction; temptation

vergangen adj past; (letzte) last. V~heit f - past; (Gram) past tense

vergänglich adj transitory

vergas|en vt gas. V~er m -s,-

carburettor

vergeb|en† *vt* award (an + *dat* to); (*weggeben*) give away; (*verzeihen*) forgive. **v~lich** *adj* futile, vain ● *adv* in vain. **V~ung** *f* - forgiveness

vergehen *vi* (*sein*) pass; sich v~ violate (gegen etw sth). **V~** *nt* -s,- offence

vergelt|en† *vt* repay. **V~ung** *f* - retaliation; (*Rache*) revenge

vergessen† *vt* forget; (*liegen lassen*) leave behind

vergesslich *adj* forgetful. **V~keit** *f* - forgetfulness

vergeuden *vt* waste, squander

vergewaltig|en *vt* rape. **V~ung** *f* -,-en rape

vergießen† *vt* spill; shed (*Tränen, Blut*)

vergift|en *vt* poison. **V~ung** *f* -,-en poisoning

Vergissmeinnicht *nt* -[e]s,-[e] forget-me-not

vergittert *adj* barred

verglasen *vt* glaze

Vergleich *m* -[e]s,-e comparison; (*Jur*) settlement. **v~bar** *adj* comparable. **v~en**† *vt* compare (mit with/to)

vergnüg|en (sich) *vr* enjoy oneself. **V~en** *nt* -s,- pleasure; (*Spaß*) fun; viel V~en! have a good time! **v~t** *adj* cheerful; (*zufrieden*) happy. **V~ungen** *fpl* entertainments

vergolden *vt* gild; (*plattieren*) gold-plate

vergraben† *vt* bury

vergriffen *adj* out of print

vergrößer|n *vt* enlarge; (*Linse:*) magnify; (*vermehren*) increase; (*erweitern*) extend; expand (*Geschäft*); sich v~n grow bigger; (*Firma:*) expand; (*zunehmen*) increase. **V~ung** *f* -,-en magnification; increase; ex-

pansion; (*Phot*) enlargement.
V~ungsglas *nt* magnifying glass

vergüt|en *vt* pay for; jdm etw v~en reimburse s.o. for sth.
V~ung *f* -,-en remuneration; (*Erstattung*) reimbursement

verhaft|en *vt* arrest. **V~ung** *f* -,-en arrest

verhalten (sich) *vr* behave; (*handeln*) act; (*beschaffen sein*) be. **V~** *nt* -s behaviour, conduct

Verhältnis *nt* -ses,-se relationship; (*Liebes-*) affair; (*Math*) ratio; **V~se** circumstances; conditions. **v~mäßig** *adv* comparatively, relatively

verhand|eln *vt* discuss; (*Jur*) try ● *vi* (*haben*) negotiate. **V~lung** *f* (*Jur*) trial; **V~lungen** negotiations

Verhängnis *nt* -ses fate, doom

verhärten *vt/i* (*sein*) harden

verhasst *adj* hated

verhätscheln *vt* spoil

verhauen† *vt* ① beat; make a mess of (*Prüfung*)

verheilen *vi* (*sein*) heal

verheimlichen *vt* keep secret

verheirat|en (sich) *vt* get married (mit to); sich wieder v~en remarry. **v~et** *adj* married

verhelfen† *vi* (*haben*) jdm zu etw v~ help s.o. get sth

verherrlichen *vt* glorify

verhexen *vt* bewitch

verhindern *vt* prevent; **v~t** sein be unable to come

Verhör *nt* -s,-e interrogation; ins V~ nehmen interrogate. **v~en** *vt* interrogate; sich v~en mishear

verhungern *vi* (*sein*) starve

verhüt|en *vt* prevent. **V~ung** *f* - prevention. **V~ungsmittel** *nt* contraceptive

verirren (sich) *vr* get lost

verjagen vt chase away

verjüngen vt rejuvenate

verkalkt adj 🇮 senile

verkalkulieren (sich) vr miscalculate

Verkauf m sale; **zum V~** for sale. **v~en** vt sell; **zu v~en** for sale

Verkäufer(in) m(f) seller; (im Geschäft) shop assistant

Verkehr m -s traffic; (Kontakt) contact; (Geschlechts~) intercourse; **aus dem V~ ziehen** take out of circulation. **v~en** vi (haben) operate; (Bus, Zug:) run; (Umgang haben) associate, mix (mit with); (Gast sein) visit (bei jdm s.o.)

Verkehrs|**ampel** f traffic lights pl. **V~unfall** m road accident. **V~verein** m tourist office. **V~zeichen** nt traffic sign

verkehrt adj wrong; **v~ herum** adv the wrong way round; (links) inside out

verklagen vt sue (auf + acc for)

verkleid|**en** vt disguise; (Techn) line; **sich v~en** disguise oneself; (für Kostümfest) dress up. **V~ung** f -,-en disguise; (Kostüm) fancy dress; (Techn) lining

verkleiner|n vt reduce [in size]. **V~ung** f - reduction

verknittern vt/i (sein) crumple

verknüpfen vt knot together

verkommen† vi (sein) be neglected; (sittlich) go to the bad; (verfallen) decay; (Haus:) fall into disrepair; (Gegend:) become run-down; (Lebensmittel:) go bad ●adj neglected; (sittlich) depraved; (Haus) dilapidated; (Gegend:) run-down

verkörpern vt embody, personify

verkraften vt cope with

verkrampft adj (fig) tense

verkriechen† (sich) vr hide

verkrümmt adj crooked, bent

verkrüppelt adj crippled; (Glied) deformed

verkühl|**en (sich)** vr catch a chill. **V~ung** f -,-en chill

verkümmern vi (sein) waste-/(Pflanze:) wither away

verkünden vt announce; pronounce (Urteil)

verkürzen vt shorten; (verringern) reduce; (abbrechen) cut short; while away (Zeit)

Verlag m -[e]s,-e publishing firm

verlangen vt ask for; (fordern) demand; (berechnen) charge. **V~** nt -s desire; (Bitte) request

verlänger|n vt extend; lengthen (Kleid); (zeitlich) prolong; renew (Pass, Vertrag); (Culin) thin down. **V~ung** f -,-en extension; renewal. **V~ungsschnur** f extension cable

verlassen† vt leave; (im Stich lassen) desert; **sich v~ auf** (+ acc) rely or depend on ●adj deserted. **V~heit** f - desolation

verlässlich adj reliable

Verlauf m course; **im V~** (+ gen) in the course of. **v~en**† vi (sein) run; (ablaufen) go; **gut v~en** go [off] well ●vr **sich v~en** lose one's way

verlegen vt move; (verschieben) postpone; (vor-) bring forward; (verlieren) mislay; (versperren) block; (legen) lay (Teppich, Rohre); (veröffentlichen) publish; **sich v~ auf** (+ acc) take up (Beruf); resort to (Bitten) ●adj embarrassed. **V~heit** f - embarrassment

Verleger m -s,- publisher

verleihen† vt lend; (gegen Gebühr) hire out; (überreichen) award, confer; (fig) give

verlernen vt forget

verletz|en vt injure; (kränken)

hurt; (verstoßen gegen) infringe; violate (Grenze). **V~end** adj hurtful, wounding. **V~te(r)** m/f injured person; (bei Unfall) casualty. **V~ung** f -,-en (Verstoß) infringement; violation

verleugnen vt deny; disown (Freund)

verleumd|en vt slander; (schriftlich) libel. **v~erisch** adj slanderous; libellous. **V~ung** f -,-en slander; (schriftlich) libel

verlieben (sich) vr fall in love (in + acc with); **verliebt sein** be in love (in + acc with)

verlier|en† vt lose; shed (Laub) ●vi (haben) lose (an etw dat sth). **V~er** m -s,- loser

verlob|en (sich) vr get engaged (mit to); **v~t sein** be engaged. **V~te** f fiancée. **V~te(r)** m fiancé. **V~ung** f -,-en engagement

verlock|en vt tempt. **V~ung** f -,-en temptation

verloren adj lost; **v~ gehen** get lost

verlos|en vt raffle. **V~ung** f -,-en raffle; (Ziehung) draw

Verlust m -[e]s,-e loss

vermachen vt leave, bequeath

Vermächtnis nt -ses,-se legacy

vermähl|en (sich) vr marry. **V~ung** f -,-en marriage

vermehren vt increase; propagate (Pflanzen); **sich v~** increase; (sich fortpflanzen) breed

vermeiden† vt avoid

Vermerk m -[e]s,-e note. **v~en** note [down]

vermessen† vt measure; survey (Gelände) ●adj presumptuous

vermiet|en vt let, rent [out]; hire out (Boot, Auto); **zu v~en** to let; (Boot:) for hire. **V~er** m landlord. **V~erin** f landlady

vermindern vt reduce

vermischen vt mix

vermissen vt miss

vermisst adj missing

vermitteln vi (haben) mediate ●vt arrange; (beschaffen) find; place (Arbeitskräfte)

Vermittl|er m -s,- agent; (Schlichter) mediator. **V~ung** f -,-en arrangement; (Agentur) agency; (Teleph) exchange; (Schlichtung) mediation

Vermögen nt -s,- fortune. **v~d** adj wealthy

vermut|en vt suspect; (glauben) presume. **v~lich** adj probable ●adv presumably. **V~ung** f -,-en supposition; (Verdacht) suspicion

vernachlässigen vt neglect

vernehm|en† vt hear; (verhören) question; (Jur) examine. **V~ung** f -,-en questioning

verneigen (sich) vr bow

vernein|en vt answer in the negative; (ablehnen) reject. **v~end** adj negative. **V~ung** f -,-en negative answer

vernicht|en vt destroy; (ausrotten) exterminate. **V~ung** f - destruction; extermination

Vernunft f - reason

vernünftig adj reasonable, sensible

veröffentlich|en vt publish. **V~ung** f -,-en publication

verordn|en vt prescribe (dat for). **V~ung** f -,-en prescription; (Verfügung) decree

verpachten vt lease [out]

verpack|en vt pack; (einwickeln) wrap. **V~ung** f packaging; wrapping

verpassen vt miss; (①: geben) give

verpfänden vt pawn

verpflanzen vt transplant

verpfleg|en vt feed: sich selbst v~en cater for oneself. V~ung f-board; (Essen) food; Unterkunft und V~ung board and lodging

verpflicht|en vt oblige; (einstellen) engage; (Sport) sign; sich v~en undertake/(versprechen) promise (zu to); (vertraglich) sign a contract. V~ung f-,-en obligation, commitment

verprügeln vt beat up, thrash

Verputz m -es plaster. v~en vt plaster

Verrat m -[e]s betrayal, treachery. v~en† vt betray; give away (Geheimnis)

Verräter m -s,- traitor

verrechn|en vt settle; clear (Scheck); sich v~nen make a mistake; (fig) miscalculate. V~nungsscheck m crossed cheque

verreisen vi (sein) go away; verreist sein be away

verrenken vt dislocate

verrichten vt perform, do

verriegeln vt bolt

verringer|n vt reduce; sich v~n decrease. V~ung f - reduction; decrease

verrost|en vi (sein) rust. v~et adj rusty

verrückt adj crazy, mad. V~e(r) m/f lunatic. V~heit f -,-en madness; (Torheit) folly

v **verrühren** vt mix

verrunzelt adj wrinkled

verrutschen vi (sein) slip

Vers /fɛrs/ m -es,-e verse

versag|en vi (haben) fail ● vt sich etw v~en deny oneself sth. V~en nt -s,- failure. V~er m -s,- failure

versalzen† vt put too much salt

in/on; (fig) spoil

versamm|eln vt assemble. V~lung f assembly, meeting

Versand m -[e]s dispatch. V~haus nt mail-order firm

versäumen vt miss; lose (Zeit); (unterlassen) neglect; [es] v~en, etw zu tun fail to do sth

verschärfen vt intensify; tighten (Kontrolle); increase (Tempo); aggravate (Lage); sich v~ intensify; increase; (Lage:) worsen

verschätzen (sich) vr sich v~ in (+ dat) misjudge

verschenken vt give away

verscheuchen vt shoo/(jagen) chase away

verschicken vt send; (Comm) dispatch

verschieb|en† vt move; (aufschieben) put off, postpone; sich v~en move, shift; (verrutschen) slip; (zeitlich) be postponed. V~ung f shift; postponement

verschieden adj different; v~e pl different; (mehrere) various; (v~es some things; (dieses und jenes) various things; das ist v~ it varies ● adv differently; v~ groß of different sizes. v~artig adj diverse

verschimmeln vi (sein) go mouldy. v~t adj mouldy

verschlafen† vi (haben) oversleep ● vt sleep through (Tag); sich v~ oversleep ● adj sleepy

verschlagen† vt lose (Seite); jdm die Sprache/den Atem v~ leave s.o. speechless/take s.o.'s breath away ● adj sly

verschlechter|n vt make worse; sich v~n get worse, deteriorate. V~ung f -,-en deterioration

Verschleiß m -es wear and tear

verschleppen vt carry off; (entführen) abduct; spread (Seuche);

neglect (*Krankheit*); (*hinausziehen*) delay

verschleudern vt sell at a loss

verschließen† vt close; (*abschließen*) lock; (*einschließen*) lock up

verschlimmer|n vt make worse; aggravate (*Lage*); **sich v~n** get worse, deteriorate. **V~ung** f -,-en deterioration

verschlossen adj reserved. **V~heit** f - reserve

verschlucken vt swallow; **sich v~** choke (an + dat on)

Verschluss m -es, ⸚e fastener, clasp; (*Koffer-*) catch; (*Flaschen-*) top; (*luftdicht*) seal; (*Phot*) shutter

verschlüsselt adj coded

verschmelzen† vt/i (sein) fuse

verschmerzen vt get over

verschmutz|en vt soil; pollute (*Luft*) ● vi (sein) get dirty. **V~ung** f - pollution

verschneit adj snow-covered

verschnörkelt adj ornate

verschnüren vt tie up

verschollen adj missing

verschonen vt spare

verschossen adj faded

verschränken vt cross

verschreiben† vt prescribe; **sich v~** make a slip of the pen

verschulden vt be to blame for. **V~** nt -s fault

verschuldet adj v~ sein be in debt

verschütten vt spill; (*begraben*) bury

verschweigen† vt conceal, hide

verschwend|en vt waste. **V~ung** f - extravagance; (*Vergeudung*) waste

verschwiegen adj discreet

verschwinden† vi (sein) disappear; [mal] v~ 🚹 spend a penny

verschwommen adj blurred

verschwör|en† (sich) vr conspire. **V~ung** f -,-en conspiracy

versehen† vt perform; hold (*Posten*); keep (*Haushalt*); **v~ mit** provide with; **sich v~** make a mistake. **V~** nt -s,- oversight; (*Fehler*) slip; **aus V~** by mistake. **v~tlich** adv by mistake

Versehrte(r) m disabled person

versengen vt singe; (*stärker*) scorch

versenken vt sink

versessen adj keen (auf + acc on)

versetz|en vt move; transfer (*Person*); (*Sch*) move up; (*verpfänden*) pawn; (*verkaufen*) sell; (*vermischen*) blend; **jdn v~en** (🚹: *warten lassen*) stand s.o. up; **jdm in Angst/Erstaunen v~en** frighten/astonish s.o.; **sich in jds Lage v~en** put oneself in s.o.'s place. **V~ung** f -,-en move; transfer; (*Sch*) move to a higher class

verseuchen vt contaminate

versicher|n vt insure; (*bekräftigen*) affirm; **jdm v~n** assure s.o. (*dass* that). **V~ung** f -,-en insurance; assurance

versiegeln vt seal

versiert /vɛrˈziːɐt/ adj experienced

versilbert adj silver-plated

Versmaß /ˈfɛrs-/ nt metre

versöhn|en vt reconcile; **sich v~en** become reconciled. **V~ung** f -,-en reconciliation

versorg|en vt provide, supply (*mit* with); provide for (*Familie*); (*betreuen*) look after. **V~ung** f - provision, supply; (*Betreuung*) care

verspät|en (sich) vr be late. **v~et** adj late; (*Zug*) delayed; (*Dank*) belated. **V~ung** f - lateness; **V~ung haben** be late

versperren vt block; bar (*Weg*)

v

verspiel|en vt gamble away. **v~t** adj playful

verspotten vt mock, ridicule

versprech|en† vt promise; sich v~en make a slip of the tongue; sich (dat) viel v~en von have high hopes of; ein viel v~ender Anfang a promising start. **V~en** nt -s,- promise. **V~ungen** fpl promises

verstaatlich|en vt nationalize. **V~ung** f - nationalization

Verstand m -[e]s mind; (Vernunft) reason; den V~ verlieren go out of one's mind

verständig adj sensible; (klug) intelligent. **v~en** vt notify, inform; sich v~en communicate; (sich verständlich machen) make oneself understood. **V~ung** f - notification; communication; (Einigung) agreement

verständlich adj comprehensible; (deutlich) clear; (begreiflich) understandable; **sich v~** machen make oneself understood. **v~erweise** adv understandably

Verständnis nt -ses understanding

verstärk|en vt strengthen, reinforce; (steigern) intensify, increase; amplify (Ton). **V~er** m -s,- amplifier. **V~ung** f reinforcement; increase; amplification; (Truppen) reinforcements pl

verstaubt adj dusty

verstauchen vt sprain

Versteck nt -[e]s,-e hiding-place; V~ spielen play hide-and-seek. **v~en** vt hide; sich v~en hide

verstehen† vt understand; (können) know; falsch v~ misunderstand; sich v~ understand one another; (auskommen) get on

versteiger|n vt auction. **V~ung** f auction

versteinert adj fossilized

verstell|en vt adjust; (versperren) block; (verändern) disguise; sich v~en pretend. **V~ung** f - pretence

versteuern vt pay tax on

verstimm|t adj disgruntled; (Magen) upset; (Mus) out of tune. **V~ung** f - ill humour; (Magen-) upset

verstockt adj stubborn

verstopf|en vt plug; (versperren) block; v~t blocked; (Person) constipated. **V~ung** f -,-en blockage; (Med) constipation

verstorben adj late, deceased. **V~e(r)** m/f deceased

verstört adj bewildered

Verstoß m infringement. **v~en†** vt disown ● vi (haben) v~en gegen contravene, infringe

verstreuen vt scatter

verstümmeln vt mutilate; garble (Text)

Versuch m -[e]s,-e attempt; (Experiment) experiment. **v~en** vt (haben) try; v~t sein be tempted (zu to). **V~ung** f -,-en temptation

vertagen vt adjourn; (aufschieben) postpone; sich v~ adjourn

vertauschen vt exchange; (verwechseln) mix up

verteidig|en vt defend. **V~er** m -s,- defender; (Jur) defence counsel. **V~ung** f -,-en defence

verteil|en vt distribute; (zuteilen) allocate; (ausgeben) hand out; (verstreichen) spread. **V~ung** f - distribution; allocation

vertief|en vt deepen; v~t sein in (+ acc) be engrossed in. **V~ung** f -,-en hollow, depression

vertikal /vɛrtiˈkaːl/ adj vertical

vertilgen vt exterminate; kill off (Unkraut)

vertippen (sich) vr make a typing mistake

vertonen vt set to music

Vertrag m -[e]s,ᵉe contract; (Pol) treaty

vertragen† vt tolerate, stand; take (Kritik, Spaß); **sich v~** get on

vertraglich adj contractual

verträglich adj good-natured; (bekömmlich) digestible

vertrauen vi (haben) trust (jdm/etw s.o./sth; auf + acc in). **V~** nt -s trust, confidence (zu in); **im V~** in confidence. **v~swürdig** adj trustworthy

vertraulich adj confidential; (intim) familiar

vertraut adj intimate; (bekannt) familiar. **V~heit** f - intimacy; familiarity

vertreiben† vt drive away; drive out (Feind); (Comm) sell; **sich** (dat) **die Zeit v~en** pass the time. **V~ung** f -,-en expulsion

vertreten† vt represent; (einspringen für) stand in or deputize for; (verfechten) support; hold (Meinung); **sich** (dat) **den Fuß v~en** twist one's ankle. **V~er** m -s,- representative; deputy; (Arzt-) locum; (Verfechter) supporter. **V~ung** f -,-en representation; (Person) deputy; (eines Arztes) locum; (Handels-) agency

Vertrieb m -[e]s (Comm) sale

vertrocknen vi (sein) dry up

verüben vt commit

verunglücken vi (sein) be involved in an accident; (🄸: missglücken) go wrong; **tödlich v~** be killed in an accident

verunreinigen vt pollute; (verseuchen) contaminate

verursachen vt cause

verurteilen vt condemn; (Jur)

convict (wegen of); sentence (zum Tode to death). **V~ung** f - condemnation; (Jur) conviction

vervielfachen vt multiply

vervielfältigen vt duplicate

vervollständigen vt complete

verwählen (sich) vr misdial

verwahren vt keep; (verstauen) put away

verwahrlost adj neglected; (Haus) dilapidated

Verwahrung f - keeping; **in V~ nehmen** take into safe keeping

verwaist adj orphaned

verwalt|en vt administer; (leiten) manage; govern (Land). **V~er** m -s,- administrator; manager. **V~ung** f -,-en administration; management; government

verwand|eln vt transform, change (in + acc into) **sich v~eln** change, turn (in + acc into). **V~lung** f transformation

verwandt adj related (mit to). **V~e(r)** m/f relative. **V~schaft** f - relationship; (Menschen) relatives pl

verwarn|en vt warn, caution. **V~ung** f warning, caution

verwechs|eln vt mix up, confuse; (halten für) mistake (mit for). **V~lung** f -,-en mix-up

verweiger|n vt/i (haben) refuse (jdm etw s.o. sth). **V~ung** f refusal

Verweis m -es,-e reference (auf + acc to); (Tadel) reprimand; **v~en†** vt refer (auf/an + acc to); (tadeln) reprimand; **von der Schule v~en** expel

verwelken vi (sein) wilt

verwend|en† vt use; spend (Zeit, Mühe). **V~ung** f use

verwerten vt utilize, use

verwesen vi (sein) decompose

verwickeln | vielleicht

verwick|eln vt involve (in + acc in); sich v~eln get tangled up. v~elt adj complicated

verwildert adj wild; (Garten) overgrown; (Aussehen) unkempt

verwinden† vt (fig) get over

verwirklichen vt realize

verwirr|en vt tangle up; (fig) confuse; sich v~en get tangled; (fig) become confused. v~t adj confused. V~ung f - confusion

verwischen vt smudge

verwittert adj weathered

verwitwet adj widowed

verwöhn|en vt spoil. v~t adj spoilt

verworren adj confused

verwund|bar adj vulnerable. v~en vt wound

verwunder|lich adj surprising. v~n vt surprise; sich v~n be surprised. V~ung f - surprise

Verwund|ete(r) m wounded soldier; die V~eten the wounded pl. V~ung f -,-en wound

verwüst|en vt devastate, ravage. V~ung f -,-en devastation

verzählen (sich) vr miscount

verzaubern vt bewitch; (fig) enchant; v~ in (+ acc) turn into

Verzehr m -s consumption. v~en vt eat

verzeih|en† vt forgive; v~en Sie! excuse me! V~ung f - forgiveness; um V~ung bitten apologize; V~ung! sorry! (bei Frage) excuse me!

Verzicht m -[e]s renunciation (auf + acc of). v~en vi (haben) do without; v~en auf (+ acc) give up; renounce (Recht, Erbe)

verziehen† vt pull out of shape; (verwöhnen) spoil; sich v~ lose shape; (Holz:) warp; (Gesicht:) twist;

(verschwinden) disappear; (Nebel:) disperse; (Gewitter:) pass ● vi (sein) move [away]

verzier|en vt decorate. V~ung f -,-en decoration

verzinsen vt pay interest on

verzöger|n vt delay; (verlangsamen) slow down. V~ung f -,-en delay

verzollen vt pay duty on; haben Sie etwas zu v~? have you anything to declare?

verzweif|eln vi (sein) despair. v~elt adj desperate. V~lung f - despair; (Ratlosigkeit) desperation

verzweigen (sich) vr branch [out]

Veto /'ve:to/ nt -s,-s veto

Vetter m -s,-n cousin

vgl. abbr (vergleiche) cf.

Viadukt /vja'dʊkt/ nt -[e]s,-e viaduct

Video /'vi:deo/ nt -s,-s video. V~handy nt vision phone. V~kassette f video cassette. V~recorder m -s,- video recorder

Vieh nt -[e]s livestock; (Rinder) cattle pl; (🔲: Tier) creature

viel pron a great deal/(🔲) a lot of; (pl) many, (🔲) a lot of; (substantivisch) v~[es] much, (🔲) a lot; nicht/ so/wie/zu v~ not/so/how/too much/ (🔲) many; v~e pl many; das v~e Geld all that money ● adv much, (🔲) a lot; v~ mehr/weniger much more/less; v~zu groß/klein much or far too big/small; so v~ wie möglich as much as possible; so/zu v~ arbeiten work so/too much

viel|deutig adj ambiguous. v~fach adj multiple ● adv many times; (🔲: oft) frequently. V~falt f - diversity, [great] variety

vielleicht adv perhaps, maybe;

(🔢: *wirklich*) really

vielmals *adv* very much

vielmehr *adv* rather; (*im Gegenteil*) on the contrary

vielseitig *adj* varied; (*Person*) versatile. **V~keit** *f* versatility

vielversprechend· *adj* viel versprechend, *s.* **versprechen**

vier *inv adj* four, **V~** *f* -,-en four; (*Sch*) ≈ fair. **V~eck** *nt* -[e]s,-e oblong, rectangle; (*Quadrat*) square. **v~eckig** *adj* oblong, rectangular; square. **V~linge** *mpl* quadruplets

viertel /'fɪrtl/ *inv adj* quarter; um v~ neun at [a] quarter past eight; um drei v~ neun at [a] quarter to nine. **V~** *nt* -s,- quarter; (*Wein*) quarter litre; **V~** vor/nach sechs [a] quarter to/past six. **V~finale** *nt* quarter-final. **V~jahr** *nt* three months *pl*; (*Comm*) quarter. **v~jährlich** *adj* & *adv* quarterly. **V~stunde** *f* quarter of an hour

vier|zehn /'fɪr-/ *inv adj* fourteen. **v~zehnte(r,s)** *adj* fourteenth. **v~zig** *inv adj* forty. **v~zigste(r,s)** *adj* fortieth

Villa /'vɪla/ *f* -,-len villa

violett /vjo'lɛt/ *adj* violet

Vio|line /vjo'li:nə/ *f* -,-n violin. **V~linschlüssel** *m* treble clef

Virus /'fɪr-/ *inv adj* -ren virus

Visier /vi'zi:ɐ/ *nt* -s,-e visor

Visite /vi'zi:tə/ *f* -,-n round; **V~** machen do one's round

Visum /'vi:zʊm/ *nt* -s,-sa visa

Vitamin /vita'mi:n/ *nt* -s,-e vitamin

Vitrine /vi'tri:nə/ *f* -,-n display cabinet/(*im Museum*) case

Vizepräsident /'fi:tsə-/ *m* vice president

Vogel *m* -s, ¨ bird; einen **V~** haben 🔢 have a screw loose. **V~scheuche** *f* -,-n scarecrow

Vokabeln /vo'ka:bəln/ *fpl* vocabulary *sg*

Vokal /vo'ka:l/ *m* -s,-e vowel

Volant /vo'lã:/ *m* -s,-s flounce

Volk *nt* -[e]s, ¨er people *sg*; (*Bevölkerung*) people *pl*

Völker|kunde *f* ethnology. **V~mord** *m* genocide. **V~recht** *nt* international law

Volks|abstimmung *f* plebiscite. **V~fest** *nt* public festival. **V~hochschule** *f* adult education classes *pl*/(*Gebäude*) centre. **V~lied** *nt* folksong. **V~tanz** *m* folk-dance. **v~tümlich** *adj* popular. **V~wirt** *m* economist. **V~wirtschaft** *f* economics *sg*. **V~zählung** *f* [national] census

voll *adj* full (von od mit of); (*Haar*) thick; (*Erfolg, Ernst*) complete; (*Wahrheit*) whole; v~ machen fill up; v~ tanken fill up with petrol ●*adv* (*ganz*) completely; (*arbeiten*) full-time; (*auszahlen*) in full; v~ und ganz completely

Vollblut *nt* thoroughbred

vollende|n *vt insep* complete. **v~t** *adj* perfect

Vollendung *f* completion; (*Vollkommenheit*) perfection

voller *inv adj* full of

Volleyball /'vɔli-/ *m* volleyball

vollführen *vt insep* perform

vollfüllen *vt sep* fill up

Vollgas *nt* **V~** geben put one's foot down; mit **V~** flat out

völlig *adj* complete

volljährig *adj* v~ sein (*Jur*) be of age. **V~keit** *f* - (*Jur*) majority

Vollkaskoversicherung *f* fully comprehensive insurance

vollkommen *adj* perfect; (*völlig*) complete

Voll|kornbrot *nt* wholemeal

v

bread. V~macht f -,-en authority; (Jur) power of attorney. V~mond m full moon. V~pension f full board

vollständig adj complete

vollstrecken vt insep execute; carry out (Urteil)

volltanken vt sep (haben) voll tanken, s. voll

Volltreffer m direct hit

vollzählig adj complete

vollziehen vt insep carry out; perform (Handlung); consummate (Ehe); sich v~ take place

Volt /vɔlt/ nt -[s],- volt

Volumen /voˈluːmən/ nt -s,- volume

vom prep = von dem

von

● preposition (+ dative)

! Note that von dem can become vom

····▸ (räumlich) from; (nach Richtungen) of. von hier an from here on[ward]. von Wien aus [starting] from Vienna. nördlich/südlich von Mannheim [to the] north/south of Mannheim. rechts/links von mir to the right/left of me; on my right/left

····▸ (zeitlich) from. von jetzt an from now on. von heute/morgen an [as] from today/tomorrow; starting today/tomorrow

····▸ (zur Angabe des Urhebers, der Ursache; nach Passiv) by. der Roman ist von Fontane the novel is by Fontane. sie hat ein Kind von ihm. she has a child

by him. er ist vom Blitz erschlagen worden he was killed by lightning

····▸ (anstelle eines Genitivs; Hingehören, Beschaffenheit, Menge etc.) of. ein Stück von dem Kuchen a piece of the cake. einer von euch one of you. eine Fahrt von drei Stunden a drive of three hours; a three-hour drive. das Brot von gestern yesterday's bread. ein Tal von erstaunlicher Schönheit a valley of extraordinary beauty

····▸ (betreffend) about. handeln/wissen/erzählen od reden von ... know/talk about ... eine Geschichte von zwei Elefanten a story about or of two elephants

voneinander adv from each other; (abhängig) on each other

vonseiten prep (+ gen) on the part of

vonstatten adv v~ gehen take place

vor prep (+ dat/acc) in front of; (zeitlich, Reihenfolge) before; (+ dat) (bei Uhrzeit) to; (warnen, sich fürchten) of; (schützen, davonlaufen) from; (Respekt haben) for; vor Angst zittern tremble with fear; vor drei Tagen three days ago; vor allen Dingen above all ● adv forward; vor und zurück backwards and forwards

Vorabend m eve

voran adv at the front; (voraus) ahead; (vorwärts) forward. v~gehen† vi sep (sein) lead the way; (Fortschritte machen) make progress. v~kommen† vi sep (sein) make progress; (fig) get on

Voranschlag m estimate. V~anzeige f advance notice. V~arbeiter m foreman

voraus adv ahead (dat of); (vorn) at the front; (vorwärts) forward ● **im Voraus** in advance. **v~bezahlen** vt sep pay in advance. **v~gehen†** vi sep (sein) go on ahead; **jdm/etw v~gehen** precede s.o./ sth. **V~sage** f -,-n prediction. **v~sagen** vt sep predict

voraussetz|en vt sep take for granted; (erfordern) require; **vorausgesetzt, dass** provided that. **V~ung** f -,-en assumption; (Erfordernis) prerequisite

voraussichtlich adj anticipated, expected ● adv probably

Vorbehalt m -[e]s,-e reservation

vorbei adv past (an etw/jdm s.o./ sth); (zu Ende) over. **v~fahren†** vi sep (sein) drive/go past. **v~gehen†** vi sep (sein) go past; (verfehlen) miss; (vergehen) pass; (ⓣ: besuchen) drop in (bei on)

vorbereit|en vt sep prepare; prepare for (Reise); **sich v~en** prepare [oneself] (auf + acc for). **V~ung** f -,-en preparation

vorbestellen vt sep order/(im Theater, Hotel) book in advance

vorbestraft adj **v~ sein** have a [criminal] record

Vorbeugung f - prevention

Vorbild nt model. **v~lich** adj exemplary, model ● adv in an exemplary manner

vorbringen† vt sep put forward; offer (Entschuldigung)

vordatieren vt sep post-date

Vorder|bein nt foreleg. **v~e(r,s)** adj front. **V~grund** m foreground. **V~rad** nt front wheel. **V~seite** f front; (einer Münze) obverse. **v~ste(r,s)** adj front, first. **V~teil** nt front

vor|drängeln (sich) vr sep ⓣ jump the queue. **v~drängen**

(sich) vr sep push forward. **v~drängen†** vi sep (sein) advance

voreilig adj rash

voreingenommen adj biased, prejudiced. **V~heit** f - bias

vorenthalten† vt sep withhold

vorerst adv for the time being

Vorfahr m -en,-en ancestor

Vorfahrt f right of way; **'V~ beachten'** 'give way'. **V~straße** f ≈ major road

Vorfall m incident. **v~en†** vi sep (sein) happen

vorfinden† vt sep find

Vorfreude f [happy] anticipation

vorführ|en vt sep present, show; (demonstrieren) demonstrate; (aufführen) perform. **V~ung** f presentation; demonstration; performance

Vor|gabe f (Sport) handicap. **V~gang** m occurrence; (Techn) process. **V~gänger(in)** m -s,- (f -,-nen) predecessor

vorgehen† vi sep (sein) go forward; (voraus-) go on ahead; (Uhr:) be fast; (wichtig sein) take precedence; (verfahren) act, proceed; (geschehen) happen, go on. **V~** nt -s -s action

vor|geschichtlich adj prehistoric. **V~geschmack** m foretaste. **V~gesetzte(r)** m/f superior. **v~gestern** adv the day before yesterday; **v~gestern Abend** the evening before last

vorhaben† vt sep propose, intend (zu to); **etw v~** have sth planned. **V~** nt -s,- plan

Vorhand f (Sport) forehand

vorhanden adj existing; **v~ sein** exist; be available

Vorhang m curtain

Vorhängeschloss nt padlock

vorher adv before[hand]

v

vorhergehend adj previous

vorherrschend adj predominant

Vorher|sage f -,-n prediction; (Wetter-) forecast. **v~sagen** vt sep predict; forecast (Wetter). **v~sehen†** vt sep foresee

vorhin adv just now

vorige(r,s) adj last, previous

Vor|kehrungen fpl precautions. **V~kenntnisse** fpl previous knowledge sg

vorkommen† vi sep (sein) happen; (vorhanden sein) occur; (nach vorn kommen) come forward; (hervorkommen) come out; (zu sehen sein) show; jdm bekannt **v~** seem familiar to s.o.

Vorkriegszeit f pre-war period

vorlad|en† vt sep (Jur) summons. **V~ung** f summons

Vorlage f model; (Muster) pattern; (Gesetzes-) bill

vorlassen† vt sep admit; jdn **v~** Ⓣ let s.o. pass; (den Vortritt lassen) let s.o. go first

Vor|lauf m (Sport) heat. **V~läufer** m forerunner. **v~läufig** adj provisional; (zunächst) for the time being. **v~laut** adj forward. **V~leben** nt past

vorleg|en vt sep put on (Kette); (unterbreiten) present; (vorzeigen) show. **V~er** m -s,- mat; (Bett-) rug

vorles|en† vt sep read [out]; jdm **v~en** read to s.o. **V~ung** f lecture

vorletzt|e(r,s) adj last ... but one; **v~es Jahr** the year before last

Vorliebe f preference

vorliegen† vt sep (haben) be present/(verfügbar) available; (bestehen) exist, be

vorlügen† vt sep lie (dat to)

vormachen vt sep put up; put on (Kette); push (Riegel); (zeigen) demonstrate; jdm etwas **v~** (Ⓣ:

täuschen) kid s.o.

Vormacht f supremacy

vormals adv formerly

vormerken vt sep make a note of; (reservieren) reserve

Vormittag m morning; gestern/ heute **V~** yesterday/this morning. **v~s** adv in the morning

Vormund m -[e]s,-munde & -münder guardian

vorn adv at the front; nach **v~** to the front; von **v~** from the front/(vom Anfang) beginning; von **v~** anfangen start afresh

Vorname m first name

vorne adv = vorn

vornehm adj distinguished; smart

vornehmen† vt sep carry out; sich (dat) **v~**, etw zu tun plan to do sth

vornherein adv von **v~herein** from the start

Vor|ort m suburb. **V~rang** m priority, precedence (vor + dat over). **V~rat** m -[e]s,-e supply, stock (an + dat of). **v~rätig** adj available; **v~rätig haben** have in stock. **V~ratskammer** f larder. **V~recht** nt privilege. **V~richtung** f device

Vorrunde f qualifying round

vorsagen vt/i sep (haben) recite; jdm **v~** tell s.o. the answer

Vor|satz m resolution. **v~sätzlich** adj deliberate; (Jur) premeditated

Vorschau f preview; (Film-) trailer

Vorschein m zum **V~kommen** appear

Vorschlag m suggestion, proposal. **v~en†** vt sep suggest, propose

vorschnell adj rash

vorschreiben† vt sep lay down; dictate (dat to); vorgeschriebene Dosis prescribed dose

Vorschrift f regulation; (*Anweisung*) instruction; **jdm V~en** tell s.o. what to do. **v~smäßig** adj correct

Vorschule f nursery school

Vorschuss m advance

vorseh|en† v sep ● vt intend (für/als for/as); (*planen*) plan; sich **v~en** be careful (vor + dat of) ● vi (haben) peep out. **V~ung** f - providence

Vorsicht f - care; (*bei Gefahr*) caution; **V~!** careful! (*auf Schild*) 'caution'. **v~ig** adj careful; cautious. **V~smaßnahme** f precaution

Vorsilbe f prefix

Vorsitz m chairmanship; den **V~** führen be in the chair. **V~ende(r)** m/f chairman

Vorsorge f **V~ treffen** take precautions; make provisions (für for). **v~n** vi sep (haben) provide (für for)

Vorspeise f starter

Vorspiel nt prelude. **v~en** v sep ● vt perform/ (*Mus*) play (dat for) ● vi (haben) audition

vorsprechen† v sep ● vt recite; (*zum Nachsagen*) say (dat to) ● vi (haben) (*Theat*) audition; bei jdm **v~** call on s.o.

Vor|sprung m projection; (*Fels-*) ledge; (*Vorteil*) lead (vor + dat over). **V~stadt** f suburb. **V~stand** m board [of directors]; (*Vereins-*) committee; (*Partei-*) executive

vorsteh|en† vi sep (haben) project, protrude; einer Abteilung **v~en** be in charge of a department. **V~er** m -s,- head

vorstell|en vt sep put forward (Bein, Uhr); (*darstellen*) represent; (*bekanntmachen*) introduce; sich **v~en** introduce oneself; (*als Bewerber*) go for an interview; sich (dat) etw **v~en** imagine sth. **V~ung** f

introduction; (*bei Bewerbung*) interview; (*Aufführung*) performance; (*Idee*) idea; (*Phantasie*) imagination. **V~ungsgespräch** nt interview

Vorstoß m advance

Vorstrafe f previous conviction

Vortag m day before

vortäuschen vt sep feign, fake

Vorteil m advantage. **v~haft** adj advantageous; flattering

Vortrag m -[e]s,-e talk; (*wissenschaftlich*) lecture. **v~en**† vt sep perform; (*aufsagen*) recite; (*singen*) sing; (*darlegen*) present (dat to)

vortrefflich adj excellent

Vortritt m precedence; **jdm den V~ lassen** let s.o. go first

vorüber adv **v~ sein** be over; an etw (dat) **v~** past sth. **v~gehend** adj temporary

Vor|urteil nt prejudice. **V~verkauf** m advance booking

vorverlegen vt sep bring forward

Vor|wahl[nummer] f dialling code. **V~wand** m -[e]s,-e pretext; (*Ausrede*) excuse

vorwärts adv forward[s]; **v~kommen** make progress; (*fig*) get on or ahead

vorwegnehmen† vt sep anticipate

vorweisen† vt sep show

vorwiegend adv predominantly

Vorwort nt (pl -worte) preface

Vorwurf m reproach; **jdm Vorwürfe machen** reproach s.o. **v~svoll** adj reproachful

Vorzeichen nt sign; (*fig*) omen

vorzeigen vt sep show

vorzeitig adj premature

vorziehen† vt sep pull forward; draw (Vorhang); (*lieber mögen*) prefer; favour

Vor|zimmer nt anteroom; (*Büro*)

outer office. **V~zug** m preference; (gute Eigenschaft) merit, virtue; (Vorteil) advantage

vorzüglich adj excellent

vulgär /vʊlˈɡɛːɐ̯/ adj vulgar ● adv in a vulgar way

Vulkan /vʊlˈkaːn/ m -s,-e volcano

Ww

Waage f -,-n scales pl; (Astrology) Libra. **w~recht** adj horizontal

Wabe f -,-n honeycomb

wach adj awake; (aufgeweckt) alert; w~ werden wake up

Wache f -,-n guard; (Posten) sentry; (Dienst) guard duty; (Naut) watch; (Polizei-) station; **W~e** halten keep watch. **W~hund** m guard-dog

Wacholder m -s juniper

Wachposten m sentry

Wachs nt -es wax

wachsam adj vigilant. **W~keit** f -vigilance

wachsen¹ vi (sein) grow

wachsen² vt (reg) wax. **W~figur** f waxwork

Wachstum nt -s growth

Wächter m -s,- guard; (Park-) keeper; (Parkplatz-) attendant

Wachtmeister m [police] constable. **W~posten** m sentry

wackelig adj wobbly; (Stuhl) rickety; (Person) shaky. **W~kontakt** m loose connection. **w~n** vi (haben) wobble; (zittern) shake

Wade f -,-n (Anat) calf

Waffe f -,-n weapon; **W~n** arms

Waffel f -,-n waffle; (Eis-) wafer

Waffenruhe f cease-fire. **W~schein** m firearms licence. **W~stillstand** m armistice

Wagemut m daring

wagen vt risk; es w~, etw zu tun dare [to] do sth; sich w~ (gehen) venture

Wagen m -s,- cart; (Eisenbahn-) carriage, coach; (Güter-) wagon; (Kinder-) pram; (Auto) car. **W~heber** m -s,- jack

Waggon /vaˈɡõ:/ m -s,-s wagon

Wahl f -,-en choice; (Pol, Admin) election; (geheime) ballot; zweite **W~** (Comm) seconds pl

wählen vt/i (haben) choose; (Pol, Admin) elect; (stimmen) vote; (Teleph) dial. **W~er(in)** m -s,- (f -,-nen) voter. **w~erisch** adj choosy, fussy

Wahlfach nt optional subject. **w~frei** adj optional. **W~kampf** m election campaign. **W~kreis** m constituency. **W~lokal** nt polling-station. **w~los** adj indiscriminate

Wahlspruch m motto. **W~urne** f ballot-box

Wahn m -[e]s delusion; (Manie) mania

Wahnsinn m madness. **w~ig** adj mad, insane; (fam: unsinnig) crazy; (fam: groß) terrible; **w~ig** werden go mad ● adv fam terribly. **W~ige(r)** m/f maniac

wahr adj true; (echt) real; du kommst doch, nicht w~? you are coming, aren't you?

während prep (+ gen) during ● conj while; (wohingegen) whereas

Wahrheit f -,-en truth. **w~sgemäß** adj truthful

wahrnehmen vt sep notice; (nutzen) take advantage of; exploit (Vorteil); look after (Interessen);

W~ung f -,-en perception
Wahrsagerin f -,-nen fortune teller
wahrscheinlich adj probable.
W~keit f probability
Währung f -,-en currency
Wahrzeichen nt symbol
Waise f -,-n orphan. **W~nhaus** nt orphanage. **W~nkind** nt orphan
Wal m -[e]s,-e whale
Wald m -[e]s,⸚er wood; (groß) forest. **w~ig** adj wooded

Waldorfschule An increasingly popular type of private school originally inspired by the Austrian educationist Rudolf Steiner (1861-1925) in the 1920s. The main aim of Waldorf schools is to develop pupils' creative and cognitive abilities through music, art and crafts.

Waliser m -s,- Welshman
Waliserin f -,-nen Welshwoman
w~isch adj Welsh
Wall m -[e]s,⸚e mound
Wallfahr|er(in) m(f) pilgrim.
W~t f pilgrimage
Walnuss f walnut
Walze f -,-n roller. **w~n** vt roll
Walzer m -s,- waltz
Wand f -,⸚e wall; (Trenn-) partition; (Seite) side; (Fels-) face
Wandel m -s change
Wander|er m -s,-, **W~in** f -,-nen hiker, rambler. **w~n** vi (sein) hike, ramble; (ziehen) travel; (gemächlich gehen) wander; (ziellos) roam. **W~schaft** f travels pl.
W~ung f -,-en hike, ramble.
W~weg m footpath
Wandlung f -,-en change, transformation
Wand|malerei f mural. **W~ta-**

fel f blackboard. **W~teppich** m tapestry
Wange f -,-n cheek
wann adv when
Wanne f -,-n tub
Wanze f -,-n bug
Wappen nt -s,- coat of arms.
W~kunde f heraldry

Bundeswappen The federal coat of arms features a heraldic eagle, which was originally the emblem of Roman emperors. It was incorporated into the coat of arms of the German Empire when it was founded in 1871. In 1950 it was revived as the official coat of arms of the Federal Republic of Germany.

---

war, wäre s. **sein**
Ware f -,-n article; (Comm) commodity; (coll) merchandise; **W~n** goods. **W~nhaus** nt department store. **W~nprobe** f sample.
W~nzeichen nt trademark
warm adj warm; (Mahlzeit) hot; **w~ machen** heat ●adv warmly; **w~ essen** have a hot meal
Wärm|e f - warmth; (Phys) heat; 10 Grad **W~e** 10 degrees above zero. **w~en** vt warm; heat (Essen, Wasser). **W~flasche** f hot-water bottle
Warn|blinkanlage f hazard [warning] lights pl. **w~en** vt/i (haben) warn (vor + dat of).
W~ung f -,-en warning
Warteliste f waiting list
warten vi (haben) wait (auf + acc for) ●vt service
Wärter(in) m -s,- (f -,-nen) keeper; (Museums-) attendant; (Gefängnis-) warder; (Kranken-) orderly
Warte|raum, W~saal m wait-

w

ing-room. **W~zimmer** nt (Med)
waiting-room

Wartung f - (Techn) service

warum adv why

Warze f -,-n wart

was pron what ● rel pron that;
alles, was ich brauche all [that] I
need ● indefinite pronoun (🄸 :
etwas) something; (fragend, verneint) anything; so was Ärgerliches! what a nuisance! ● adv (🄸)
(warum) why; (wie) how

wasch|bar adj washable. **W~**
becken nt wash-basin

Wäsche f - washing; (Unter-)
underwear

waschecht adj colour-fast

Wäscheklammer f clothes-peg

waschen† vt wash; sich w~ have
a wash; **W~** und Legen shampoo
and set ● vi (haben) do the washing

Wäscherei f -,-en laundry

Wäsche|schleuder f spin-drier.
W~trockner m tumble-drier

Wasch|küche f laundry-room.
W~lappen m face-flannel.
W~maschine f washing machine.
W~mittel nt detergent. **W~pul-**
ver m washing-powder. **W~salon**
m launderette. **W~zettel** m blurb

Wasser nt -s water. **W~ball** m
beach-ball; (Spiel) water polo.
w~dicht adj watertight; (Kleidung)
waterproof. **W~fall** m waterfall.
W~farbe f water-colour. **W~hahn**
m tap. **W~kraft** f water-power.
W~kraftwerk nt hydroelectric
power-station. **W~leitung** f water-
main; aus der W~leitung from the
tap. **W~mann** m (Astrology)
Aquarius

wässern vt soak; (begießen) water
● vi (haben) water

Wasser|ski nt -s water-skiing.
W~stoff m hydrogen. **W~straße**

f waterway. **W~waage** f spirit-level

wässrig adj watery

watscheln vi (sein) waddle

Watt nt -s,- (Phys) watt

Watt|e f - cotton wool. **w~iert**
adj padded; (gesteppt) quilted

WC /ve:'tse:/ nt -s,-s WC

Web|cam f -,-s web camera.
W~design nt web design

web|en vt/i (haben) weave. **W~er**
m -s,- weaver

Web|seite /'vep-/ f web page.
W~site f -,-s website

Wechsel m -s,- change; (Tausch)
exchange; (Comm) bill of exchange.
W~geld nt change. **w~haft** adj
changeable. **W~jahre** npl menopause sg. **W~kurs** m exchange
rate. **w~n** vt change; (tauschen) exchange ● vi (haben) change; vary.
w~nd adj changing; varying.
W~strom m alternating current.
W~stube f bureau de change

weck|en vt wake [up]; (fig)
awaken ● vi (haben) (Wecker:) go
off. **W~er** m -s,- alarm [clock]

wedeln vi (haben) wave; mit dem
Schwanz w~ wag its tail

weder conj w~ ... noch neither
... nor

Weg m -[e]s,-e way; (Fuß-) path;
(Fahr-) track; (Gang) errand; sich
auf den Weg machen set off

weg adv away, off; (verschwunden)
gone; weg sein be away; (gegan-
gen/verschwunden) have gone;
Hände weg! hands off!

wegen prep (+ gen) because of;
(um ... willen) for the sake of; (bezüglich) about

weg|fahren† vi sep (sein) go
away; (abfahren) leave. **W~fahr-**
sperre f immobilizer. **w~fallen†** vi
sep (sein) be dropped/(ausgelassen)
omitted; (entfallen) no longer apply.

w~geben† vt sep give away.
w~gehen† vi sep (sein) leave, go away; (ausgehen) go out. w~kommen† vi sep (sein) get away; (verloren gehen) disappear; schlecht w~kommen 🄸 get a raw deal. w~lassen† vt sep (auslassen) omit. w~laufen† vi sep (sein) run away. w~räumen vt sep put away; (entfernen) clear away. w~schicken vt sep send away; (abschicken) send off. w~tun† vt sep put away; (wegwerfen) throw away.

Wegweiser m -s,- signpost

weg|werfen† vt sep throw away. w~ziehen† v sep ● vt pull away ● vi (sein) move away

weh adj sore; weh tun hurt; (Kopf, Rücken:) ache; jdm weh tun hurt s.o.

wehe int alas; w~ [dir/euch]! (drohend) don't you dare!

wehen vi (haben) blow; (flattern) flutter ● vt blow

Wehen fpl contractions

Wehr¹ nt -[e]s,-e weir

Wehr² f sich zur W~ setzen resist. W~dienst m military service. W~dienstverweigerer m -s,- conscientious objector

wehren (sich) vr resist; (gegen Anschuldigung) protest; (sich sträuben) refuse

wehr|los adj defenceless. W~macht f armed forces pl. W~pflicht f conscription

Weib nt -[e]s,-er woman; (Ehe:) wife. W~chen nt -s,- (Zool) female. w~lich adj feminine; (Biology) female

weich adj soft; (gar) done

Weiche f -,-n (Rail) points pl

Weich|heit f - softness. w~lich adj soft; (Charakter:) weak. W~spüler m -s,- (Textiles) conditioner.

W~tier nt mollusc

Weide¹ f -,-n (Bot) willow

Weide² f -,-n pasture. w~n vt/i (haben) graze

weigern (sich) vr refuse. W~ung f -,-en refusal

Weihe f -,-n consecration; (Priester:) ordination. w~n vt consecrate; (zum Priester) ordain

Weiher m -s,- pond

Weihnacht|en nt -s & pl Christmas. w~lich adj Christmassy. W~sbaum m Christmas tree. W~slied nt Christmas carol. W~smann m (pl -männer) Father Christmas. W~stag m erster/zweiter W~stag Christmas Day/Boxing Day

Weihnachtsmarkt During the weeks of Advent, Christmas markets are held in most German towns. Visitors can buy Christmas decorations, handmade toys and crib figures, traditional Christmas biscuits, and mulled wine to sustain them while they shop.

Weih|rauch m incense. W~wasser nt holy water

weil conj because; (da) since

Weile f - while

Wein m -[e]s,-e wine; (Bot) vines pl; (Trauben) grapes pl. W~bau m winegrowing. W~berg m vineyard. W~brand m -[e]s brandy

weinen vt/i (haben) cry, weep

Wein|glas nt wine glass. W~karte f wine list. W~lese f grape harvest. W~liste f wine list. W~probe f wine tasting. W~rebe f, W~stock m vine. W~stube f wine bar. W~traube f bunch of grapes; (W~beere) grape

weise adj wise

w

Weise f -,-n way; (*Melodie*) tune
Weisheit f -,-en wisdom.
W~szahn m wisdom tooth
weiß adj, W~ nt -,- white
weissag|en vt/i insep (haben)
prophesy. W~ung f -,-en prophecy
Weiß|brot nt white bread.
W~e(r) m/f white man/woman.
w~en vt whitewash. W~wein m
white wine
Weisung f -,-en instruction; (*Befehl*) order
weit adj wide; (*ausgedehnt*) extensive; (*lang*) long ● adv widely;
(*offen, öffnen*) wide; (*lang*) far; von
w~em from a distance; bei
w~em by far; w~ und breit far
and wide; ist es noch w~? is it
much further? so w~ wie möglich
as far as possible; ich bin so w~
I'm ready; w~ verbreitet widespread; w~ reichende Folgen far-
reaching consequences
Weite f -,-n expanse; (*Entfernung*)
distance; (*Größe*) width. w~n vt
widen; stretch (*Schuhe*)
weiter adj further ● adv further;
(*außerdem*) in addition; (*anschließend*) then; etw w~ tun go
on doing sth; w~ nichts/niemand
nothing/no one else; und so w~
and so on
weiter|e(r,s) adj further; ohne
w~es just like that; (*leicht*) easily
weiter|erzählen vt sep go on
with; (*weitersagen*) repeat. w~fahren† vi (sein) go on. w~geben†
vt sep pass on. w~hin adv (*immer
noch*) still; (*in Zukunft*) in future;
(*außerdem*) furthermore; etw
w~hin tun go on doing sth.
w~machen vi sep (haben) carry on
weit|gehend adj extensive ● adv
to a large extent. w~sichtig adj
long-sighted; (*fig*) far-sighted.
W~sprung m long jump. w~ver-

breitet adj = w~ verbreitet,
s. weit
Weizen m -s wheat

welch inv pron what; w~ ein(e)
what a. w~e(r,s) pron which; um
w~e Zeit? at what time? ● rel pron
which; (*Person*) who ● indefinite pronoun some; (*fragend*) any; was für
w~e? what sort of?
Wellblech nt corrugated iron
Well|e f -,-n wave; (*Techn*) shaft.
W~enlänge f wavelength. W~en-
linie f wavy line. W~enreiten nt
surfing. W~ensittich m -s,-e
budgerigar. w~ig adj wavy.
Wellness f - mental and physical
wellbeing
Welt f -,-en world; auf der W~ in
the world; auf die od zur W~
kommen be born. W~all nt universe. w~berühmt adj world-fam-
ous. w~fremd adj unworldly.
W~kugel f globe. w~lich adj
worldly; (*nicht geistlich*) secular
Weltmeister(in) m(f) world
champion. W~schaft f world
championship
Weltraum m space. W~fahrer
m astronaut
Weltrekord m world record
wem pron (*dat of wer*) to whom
wen pron (*acc of wer*) whom
Wende f -,-n change. W~kreis m
(*Geog*) tropic
Wendeltreppe f spiral staircase
wenden¹ vt (*reg*) turn ● vi (*haben*)
turn [round]
wenden²† (& *reg*) vt turn; sich
w~ turn; sich an jdn w~
turn/(*schriftlich*) write to s.o.
Wend|epunkt m (*fig*) turning-
point. W~ung f -,-en turn; (*Biegung*) bend; (*Veränderung*) change
wenig pron little; (*pl*) few; so/zu
w~ so/too little/(*pl*) few; w~e pl

few ● adv little; (kaum) not much; so w~ wie möglich as little as possible. w~er pron less; (pl) fewer; immer w~er less and less ● adv less. w~ste(r,s) least; am w~sten least [of all]. w~stens adv at least

wenn conj if; (sobald) when; immer w~ whenever; w~ nicht od außer w~ unless; w~ auch even though

wer pron who; (①: jemand) someone; (fragend) anyone

Werbe|agentur f advertising agency. w~n† vt recruit; (Kunden, Besucher) ● vi (haben) w~n für advertise; canvass for (Partei). W~spot m -s,-s commercial

Werbung f - advertising

werden†

● intransitive verb (sein)
····▶ (+ adjective) become; get; (allmählich) grow. müde/alt/länger werden become or get/grow tired/old/longer. taub/blind/wahnsinnig werden become deaf/blind/mad. blass werden become or turn pale. krank werden become or fall ill. es wird warm/dunkel it is getting warm/dark. mir wurde schlecht/schwindlig I began to feel sick/dizzy

····▶ (+ noun) become. Arzt/Lehrer/Mutter werden become a doctor/teacher/mother. er will Lehrer werden he wants to be a teacher. was ist aus ihm geworden? what has become of him?

····▶ werden zu become; turn into. das Erlebnis wurde zu einem Albtraum the experience

became or turned into a nightmare. zu Eis werden turn into ice

● auxiliary verb
····▶ (Zukunft) will; shall. er wird bald hier sein he will or he'll soon be here. wir werden sehen we shall see. es wird bald regnen it's going to rain soon

····▶ (Konjunktiv) würde(n) would. ich würde es kaufen, wenn ... I would buy it if .... würden Sie so nett sein? would you be so kind?

····▶ (beim Passiv; pp worden) be. geliebt/geboren werden be loved/born. du wirst gerufen you are being called. er wurde gebeten he was asked. es wurde gemunkelt it was rumoured. mir wurde gesagt, dass ... I was told that .... das Haus ist soeben/1995 renoviert worden/1995 renovated in 1995

werfen† vt throw; cast (Blick, Schatten); sich w~ (Holz:) warp

Werft f -,-en shipyard

Werk nt -[e]s,-e work; (Fabrik) works sg, factory; (Trieb-) mechanism. W~en nt -s (Sch) handicraft. W~statt f -,̈-en workshop; (Auto-) garage. W~tag m weekday. w~tags adv on weekdays. w~tätig adj working

Werkzeug nt tool; (coll) tools pl. W~leiste f toolbar

Wermut m -s vermouth

wert adj viel w~ worth a lot; nichts w~ sein be worthless; jds w~ sein be worthy of s.o. W~ m -[e]s,-e value; (Nenn-) denomination; im W~ von worth. w~en

w

vt rate

Wert|gegenstand *m* object of value. **w~los** *adj* worthless. **W~minderung** *f* depreciation. **W~papier** *nt* (*Comm*) security. **W~sachen** *fpl* valuables. **w~voll** *adj* valuable

Wesen *nt* -s,- nature; (*Lebe-*) being; (*Mensch*) creature

wesentlich *adj* essential; (*grundlegend*) fundamental ● *adv* considerably, much

weshalb *adv* why

Wespe *f* -,-n wasp

wessen *pron* (*gen of* wer) whose

westdeutsch *adj* West German

Weste *f* -,-n waistcoat

Westen *m* -s west

Western *m* -[s],- western

Westfalen *nt* -s Westphalia

Westindien *nt* West Indies *pl*

west|lich *adj* western; (*Richtung*) westerly ● *adv & prep* (+ *gen*) **w~lich** [**von**] **der Stadt** [to the] west of the town. **w~wärts** *adv* westwards

weswegen *adv* why

Wettbewerb *m* -s,-e competition

Wette *f* -,-n bet; **um die W~ laufen race** (**mit jdm** *s.o.*)

wetten *vt/i* (*haben*) bet (**auf** + *acc* on); **mit jdm w~** have a bet with s.o.

Wetter *nt* -s,- weather; (*Un-*) storm. **W~bericht** *m* weather report. **W~vorhersage** *f* weather forecast. **W~warte** *f* -,-n meteorological station

Wett|kampf *m* contest. **W~kämpfer(in)** *m(f)* competitor. **W~lauf** *m* race. **W~rennen** *nt* race. **W~streit** *m* contest

Whisky *m* -s whisky

wichtig *adj* important; **w~ nehmen** take seriously. **W~keit** *f* - importance

Wicke *f* -,-n sweet pea

Wickel *m* -s,- compress

wickeln *vt* wind; (*ein-*) wrap; (*bandagieren*) bandage; **ein Kind frisch w~** change a baby

Widder *m* -s,- ram; (*Astrology*) Aries

wider *prep* (+ *acc*) against; (*entgegen*) contrary to; **w~ Willen** against one's will

widerlegen *vt insep* refute

wider|lich *adj* repulsive. **W~rede** *f* contradiction; **keine W~rede!** don't argue!

widerrufen† *vt insep* (*haben*) retract; revoke (*Befehl*)

Widersacher *m* -s,- adversary

widersetzen (**sich**) *vr insep* resist (**jdm/etw** s.o./sth)

widerspiegeln *vt sep* reflect

widersprechen† *vi insep* (*haben*) contradict (**jdm/etw** s.o./ something)

Wider|spruch *m* contradiction; (*Protest*) protest. **w~sprüchlich** *adj* contradictory. **w~spruchslos** *adv* without protest

Widerstand *m* resistance; **W~ leisten** resist. **w~sfähig** *adj* resistant; (*Bot*) hardy

widerstehen† *vi insep* (*haben*) resist (**jdm/etw** s.o./sth); (*anwidern*) be repugnant (**jdm** to s.o.)

Widerstreben *nt* -s reluctance

widerwärtig *adj* disagreeable

Widerwill|e *m* aversion, repugnance. **w~ig** *adj* reluctant

widm|en *vt* dedicate (*dat* to); (*verwenden*) devote (*dat* to); **sich w~en** (+ *dat*) devote oneself to. **W~ung** *f* -,-en dedication

wie adv how; **wie viel** how much/(pl) many; **um wie viel Uhr?** at what time? **wie viele?** how many? **wie ist Ihr Name?** what is your name? **wie ist das Wetter?** .what is the weather like? ● conj as; (gleich wie) like; (sowie) as well as; (als) when, as; **so gut wie** as good as; **nichts wie** nothing but

wieder adv again; **jdn/etw w∼erkennen** recognize s.o./something; **etw w∼ verwenden/verwerten** reuse/recycle sth; **etw w∼ gutmachen** make up for (Schaden); redress (Unrecht); (bezahlen) pay for sth

Wiederaufbau m reconstruction

wieder|bekommen† vt sep get back. **W∼belebung** f - resuscitation. **w∼bringen**† vt sep bring back. **w∼erkennen**† vt sep * w∼ erkennen, s. wieder. **w∼geben**† vt sep give back, return; (darstellen) portray; (ausdrücken, übersetzen) render; (zitieren) quote. **W∼geburt** f reincarnation

Wiedergutmachung f - reparation; (Entschädigung) compensation

wieder|herstellen vt sep re-establish; restore (Gebäude); restore to health (Kranke)

wiederhol|en vt insep repeat; (Sch) revise; **sich w∼en** recur; (Person:) repeat oneself. **w∼t** adj repeated. **W∼ung** f -,-en repetition; (Sch) revision

Wieder|hören nt **auf W∼hören!** goodbye! **W∼käuer** m -s,- ruminant. **W∼kehr** f - return; (W∼holung) recurrence. **w∼kommen**† vi sep (sein) come back

wiedersehen† vt sep wieder sehen, s. sehen. **W∼** nt -s,- reunion; **auf W∼!** goodbye!

wiedervereinig|en† vt sep wieder vereinigen, s. vereinigen.

W∼ung f reunification

wieder|verwenden† vt sep* w∼ verwenden, s. wieder. **w∼verwerten** * vt sep w∼ verwerten, s. wieder

Wiege f -,-n cradle

wiegen¹† vt/i (haben) weigh

wiegen² vt (reg) rock. **W∼lied** nt lullaby

wiehern vi (haben) neigh

Wien nt -s Vienna. **W∼er** adj Viennese ● m -s,- Viennese ● f -,- ≈ frankfurter. **w∼erisch** adj Viennese

Wiese f -,-n meadow

Wiesel nt -s,- weasel

wieso adv why

wieviel * pron wie viel, s. wie. **w∼te(r,s)** adj which; **der W∼te ist heute?** what is the date today?

wieweit adv how far

wild adj wild; (Stamm) savage; **w∼er Streik** wildcat strike; **w∼ wachsen** grow wild. **W∼** nt -[e]s game; (Rot-) deer; (Culin) venison. **W∼e(r)** m/f savage

Wilder|er m -s,- poacher. **w∼n** vt/i (haben) poach

Wild|heger m -s,- gamekeeper. **W∼hüter** m -s,- gamekeeper. **W∼leder** nt suede. **W∼nis** f - wilderness. **W∼schwein** nt wild boar. **W∼westfilm** m western

Wille m -ns will

Willenskraft f will-power

willig adj willing

willkommen adj welcome; w~
heißen welcome. **W~** nt -s
welcome

wimmeln vi (haben) swarm

wimmern vi (haben) whimper

Wimpel m -s, pennant

Wimper f -,-n [eye]lash; **W~**
tusche f mascara

Wind m -[e]s,-e wind

Winde f -,-n (Techn) winch

Windel f -,-n nappy

winden† vt wind; make (Kranz); in
die Höhe w~ winch up; sich w~
wind (um round); (sich krümmen)
writhe

Wind|hund m greyhound. **w~ig**
adj windy. **W~mühle** f windmill.
W~park m wind farm. **W~po-**
cken fpl chickenpox sg.
W~schutzscheibe f windscreen.
W~stille f calm. **W~stoß** m gust
of wind. **W~surfen** nt windsurfing

Windung f -,-en bend; (Spirale)
spiral

Winkel m -s,- angle; (Ecke) corner.
W~messer m -s,- protractor

winken vi (haben) wave

Winter m -s,- winter. **w~lich** adj
wintry; (Winter-) winter. **W~schlaf**
m hibernation. **W~sport** m winter
sports pl

Winzer m -s,- winegrower

winzig adj tiny, minute

Wipfel m -s,- [tree-]top

Wippe f -,-n see-saw

wir pron we; wir sind es it's us

Wirbel m -s,- eddy; (Drehung)
whirl; (Trommel-) roll; (Anat) verte-
bra; (Haar-) crown; (Aufsehen) fuss.
w~n vt/i (sein/haben) whirl.
W~säule f spine. **W~sturm** m
cyclone. **W~tier** nt vertebrate.

W~wind m whirlwind

wird s. werden

wirken vi (haben) have an effect
(auf + acc on); (zur Geltung kommen) be effective; (tätig sein) work;
(scheinen) seem ● vt (Textiles) knit

wirklich adj real. **W~keit** f -,-en
reality

wirksam adj effective

Wirkung f -,-en effect. **w~slos**
adj ineffective. **w~svoll** adj effective

wirr adj tangled; (Haar) tousled;
(verwirrt, verworren) confused

Wirt m -[e]s,-e landlord. **W~in** f
-,-nen landlady

Wirtschaft f -,-en economy;
(Gast-) restaurant; (Kneipe) pub.
w~en vi (haben) manage one's fi-
nances. **w~lich** adj economic;
(sparsam) economical. **W~flücht-**
ling m economic refugee.
W~geld nt housekeeping
[money]. **W~prüfer** m auditor

Wirtshaus nt inn; (Kneipe) pub

wischen vt/i (haben) wipe; wash
(Fußboden)

wissen† vt/i (haben) know; weißt
du noch? do you remember?
nichts w~ wollen von not want
anything to do with. **W~** nt -s
knowledge; meines W~s to my
knowledge

Wissenschaft f -,-en science.
W~ler m -s,- academic; (Natur-)
scientist. **w~lich** adj academic;
scientific

wissenswert adj worth knowing

witter|n vt scent; (ahnen) sense.
W~ung f -,-en (Wetter) weather

Witwe f -,-n widow. **W~r** m -s,-
widower

Witz m -es,-e joke; (Geist) wit.
W~bold m -[e]s,-e joker. **w~ig**
adj funny; witty

wo adv where; (als) when; (irgendwo) somewhere; **wo immer** wherever ●conj seeing that; (obwohl) although; (wenn) if

woanders adv somewhere else

wobei adv how; (relativ) during the course of which

Woche f -,-n week. **W~nende** nt weekend. **W~nkarte** f weekly ticket. **w~nlang** adv for weeks. **W~ntag** m day of the week; (Werktag) weekday. **w~tags** adv on weekdays

wöchentlich adj & adv weekly

Wodka m -s vodka

wofür adv what ... for; (relativ) for which

Woge f -,-n wave

woher adv where from; **woher weißt du das?** how do you know that? **wohin** adv where [to]; **wohin gehst du?** where are you going?

wohl adv well; (vermutlich) probably; (etwa) about; (zwar) perhaps; **w~ kaum** hardly; **sich w~ fühlen** feel well/(behaglich) comfortable; **jdm w~ tun** do s.o. good. **W~** nt -[e]s welfare, well-being; **zum W~** (+ gen) for the good of; **zum W~!** cheers!

Wohl|befinden nt well-being. **W~behagen** nt feeling of well-being. **W~ergehen** nt -s welfare. **w~erzogen** adj well brought-up

Wohlfahrt f - welfare. **W~sstaat** m Welfare State

wohl|habend adj prosperous, well-to-do. **w~ig** adj comfortable. **w~schmeckend** adj tasty

Wohlstand m prosperity. **W~sgesellschaft** f affluent society

Wohltat f [act of] kindness; (Annehmlichkeit) treat; (Genuss) bliss

Wohltät|er m benefactor. **w~ig** adj charitable

wohl|tuend adj agreeable. **w~tun†** vi sep (haben) **w~ tun**, s. **wohl**

Wohlwollen nt -s goodwill; (Gunst) favour. **W~d** adj benevolent

Wohn|block m block of flats. **w~en** vi (haben) live; (vorübergehend) stay. **W~gegend** f residential area. **w~haft** adj resident. **W~haus** nt house. **W~heim** nt hostel; (Alten-) home. **W~lich** adj comfortable. **W~mobil** nt -s,-e camper. **W~ort** m place of residence. **W~sitz** m place of residence

Wohnung f -,-en flat; (Unterkunft) accommodation. **W~snot** f housing shortage

Wohn|wagen m caravan. **W~zimmer** nt living-room

wölb|en vt curve; arch (Rücken). **W~ung** f -,-en curve; (Architecture) vault

Wolf m -[e]s, ⸚e wolf; (Fleisch-) mincer; (Reiß-) shredder

Wolke f -,-n cloud. **W~nbruch** m cloudburst. **W~nkratzer** m skyscraper. **w~nlos** adj cloudless. **w~ig** adj cloudy

Woll|decke f blanket. **W~e** f -,-n wool

wollen†¹

● auxiliary verb

┄┄▶ (den Wunsch haben) want to. **ich will nach Hause gehen** I want to go home. **ich wollte Sie fragen, ob ...** I wanted to ask you if ...

┄┄▶ (im Begriff sein) be about to. **wir wollten gerade gehen** we were just about to go

┄┄▶ (sich in der gewünschten Weise verhalten) will not refuses to.

w

der Motor will nicht anspringen the engine won't start

● *intransitive verb*

···▸ want to. ob du willst oder nicht whether you want to or not. ganz wie du willst just as you like

···▸ (ℹ: *irgendwohin zu gehen wünschen*) ich will nach Hause I want to go home. zu wem wollen Sie? who[m] do you want to see?

···▸ (ℹ: *funktionieren*) will nicht won't go. meine Beine wollen nicht mehr my legs are giving up ℹ

● *transitive verb*

···▸ want; (*beabsichtigen*) intend. er will nicht, dass du ihm hilfst he does not want you to help him. das habe ich nicht gewollt I never intended or meant that to happen

Wollsachen *fpl* woollens

womit *adv* what ... with; (*relativ*) with which. **wonach** *adv* what ... after/(*suchen*) for/(*riechen*) of; (*relativ*) after/for/of which

woran *adv* what ... on/(*denken, sterben*) of; (*relativ*) on/of which; woran hast du ihn erkannt? how did you recognize him? **worauf** *adv* what on ... /(*warten*) for; (*relativ*) on/for which; (*woraufhin*) whereupon. **woraus** *adv* what ... from; (*relativ*) from which

Wort *nt* -[e]s, ¨er & -e word; jdm ins W∼ fallen interrupt s.o.

Wörterbuch *nt* dictionary

Wort|führer *m* spokesman. **w∼getreu** *adj & adv* word-for-word. **W∼karg** *adj* taciturn. **W∼laut** *m* wording

wörtlich *adj* literal; (*wortgetreu*) word-for-word

wort|los *adj* silent ● *adv* without a word. **W∼schatz** *m* vocabulary. **W∼spiel** *nt* pun, play on words

worüber *adv* what ... over/(*lachen, sprechen*) about; (*relativ*) over/about which. **worum** *adv* what ... round/(*bitten, kämpfen*) for; (*relativ*) round/for which; worum geht es? what is it about? **wovon** *adv* what ... from/(*sprechen*) about; (*relativ*) from/about which. **wovor** *adv* what ... in front of; (*sich fürchten*) of; (*relativ*) in front of which; of which. **wozu** *adv* what ... to/(*brauchen, benutzen*) for; (*relativ*) to/for which; wozu? what for?

Wrack *nt* -s, -s wreck

wringen† *vt* wring

Wucher|preis *m* extortionate price. **W∼ung** *f* -, -en growth

Wuchs *m* -es growth; (*Gestalt*) stature

Wucht *f* - force

wühlen *vi* (*haben*) rummage; (*in der Erde*) burrow ● *vt* dig

Wulst *m* -[e]s, ¨e bulge; (*Fett-*) roll

wund *adj* sore; w∼ reiben chafe; sich w∼ liegen get bedsores. **W∼brand** *m* gangrene

Wunde *f* -, -n wound

Wunder *nt* -s, - wonder, marvel; (*übernatürliches*) miracle; kein W∼! no wonder! **w∼bar** *adj* miraculous; (*herrlich*) wonderful. **W∼kind** *nt* infant prodigy. **w∼n** *vt* surprise; sich w∼n be surprised (über + *acc* at). **w∼schön** *adj* beautiful

Wundstarrkrampf *m* tetanus

Wunsch *m* -[e]s, ¨e wish; (*Verlangen*) desire; (*Bitte*) request

wünschen *vt* want; sich (*dat*) etw w∼ want sth; (*bitten um*) ask for sth; jdm Glück/gute Nacht w∼ wish s.o. luck/good night; Sie w∼? can I help you? **w∼swert** *adj*

desirable

Wunschkonzert nt musical request programme

wurde, würde s. werden

Würde f -,-n dignity; (Ehrenrang) honour. **w~los** adj undignified. **W~nträger** m dignitary. **w~voll** adj dignified. ● adv with dignity

würdig adj dignified; (wert) worthy

Wurf m -[e]s, ⸚e throw; (Junge) litter

Würfel m -s,- cube; (Spiel-) dice; (Zucker-) lump. **w~n** vi (haben) throw the dice; **w~n um** play dice for ● vt throw; (in Würfel schneiden) dice. **W~zucker** m cube sugar

würgen vt choke ● vi (haben) retch; choke (an + dat on)

Wurm m -[e]s, ⸚er worm; (Made) maggot. **w~en** vi (haben) jdn **w~en** ⟨fig⟩ rankle [with s.o.]

Wurst f -, ⸚e sausage; das ist mir **W~** ⟨fig⟩ I couldn't care less

Würze f -,-n spice; (Aroma) aroma

Wurzel f -,-n root; **W~n schlagen** take root. **w~n** vi (haben) root

würz|en vt season. **w~ig** adj tasty; (aromatisch) aromatic; (pikant) spicy

wüst adj chaotic; (wirr) tangled; (öde) desolate; (wild) wild; (schlimm) terrible

Wüste f -,-n desert

Wut f -, rage, fury. **W~anfall** m fit of rage

wüten vi (haben) rage. **w~d** adj furious; **w~d machen** infuriate

w
x
y
z

x /ɪks/ inv adj (Math) x; ⟨fig⟩ umpteen. **X-Beine** ntpl knock-knees. **x-beinig, X-beinig** adj knock-kneed. **x-beliebig** adj ⟨fig⟩ any. **x-mal** adv ⟨fig⟩ umpteen times

Yoga /ˈjoːga/ m & nt -[s] yoga

Zacke f -,-n point; (Berg-) peak; (Gabel-) prong. **z~ig** adj jagged; (gezackt) serrated

zaghaft adj timid; (zögernd) tentative

zäh adj tough; (hartnäckig) tenacious. **z~flüssig** adj viscous; (Verkehr) slow-moving. **Z~igkeit** f - toughness; tenacity

Zahl f -,-en number; (Ziffer, Betrag) figure

zahlen vt/i (haben) pay; (bezahlen) pay for; bitte **z~!** the bill please!

zählen vi (haben) count; **z~ zu** ⟨fig⟩ be one/(pl) some of ● vt count; **z~ zu** add to; ⟨fig⟩ count among

zahlenmäßig adj numerical

Zähler m -s,- meter

Zahl|grenze f fare-stage. **Z~karte** f paying-in slip. **z~los** adj countless. **z~reich** adj numerous; (Anzahl, Gruppe) large ● adv in large numbers. **Z~ung** f -,-en payment; in Z~ung nehmen take in part-exchange

Zählung f -,-en count

Zahlwort nt (pl -wörter) numeral

zahm adj tame

zähmen vt tame; (fig) restrain

Zahn m -[e]s,ᵉe tooth; (am Zahnrad) cog. **Z~arzt** m, **Z~ärztin** f dentist. **Z~belag** m plaque. **Z~bürste** f toothbrush. **Z~fleisch** nt gums pl. **Z~los** adj toothless. **Z~pasta** f -,-en toothpaste. **Z~rad** nt cog-wheel. **Z~schmelz** m enamel. **Z~schmerzen** mpl toothache sg. **Z~spange** f brace. **Z~stein** m tartar. **Z~stocher** m -s,- toothpick

Zange f -,-n pliers pl; (Kneif-) pincers pl; (Kohlen-, Zucker-) tongs pl; (Geburts-) forceps pl

Zank m -[e]s squabble. **z~en** vr sich z~en squabble

Zäpfchen nt -s,- (Anat) uvula; (Med) suppository

zapfen vt tap, draw. **Z~streich** m (Mil) tattoo

Zapf|hahn m tap. **Z~säule** f petrol-pump

zappeln vi (haben) wriggle; (Kind:) fidget

zart adj delicate; (weich, zärtlich) tender; (sanft) gentle. **Z~gefühl** nt tact

zärtlich adj tender; (liebevoll) loving. **Z~keit** f -,-en tenderness; (Liebkosung) caress

Zauber m -s magic; (Bann) spell. **Z~er** m -s,- magician. **z~haft** adj enchanting. **Z~künstler** m con-

juror. **z~n** vi (haben) do magic; (Zaubertricks ausführen) do conjuring tricks ● vt produce as if by magic. **Z~stab** m magic wand. **Z~trick** m conjuring trick

Zaum m -[e]s,Zäume bridle

Zaun m -[e]s,Zäune fence

z.B. abbr (zum Beispiel) e.g.

Zebra nt -s,-s zebra. **Z~streifen** m zebra crossing

Zeche f -,-n bill; (Bergwerk) pit

zechen vi (haben) ⓘ drink

Zeder f -,-n cedar

Zeh m -[e]s,-en toe. **Z~e** f -,-n toe; (Knoblauch-) clove

zehn inv adj, **Z~** f -,-en ten. **z~te(r,s)** adj tenth. **Z~tel** nt -s,- tenth

Zeichen nt -s,- sign; (Signal) signal. **Z~setzung** f - punctuation. **Z~trickfilm** m cartoon

zeichn|en vt/i (haben) draw; (kenn-) mark; (unter-) sign. **Z~ung** f -,-en drawing

Zeige|finger m index finger. **z~n** vt show; sich z~n appear; (sich herausstellen) become clear ● vi (haben) point (auf + acc to). **Z~r** m -s,- pointer; (Uhr-) hand

Zeile f -,-n line; (Reihe) row

Zeit f -,-en time; sich (dat) Z~ lassen take one's time; es hat Z~ there's no hurry; mit der Z~ in time; in nächster Z~ in the near future; zur Z~ (rechtzeitig) in time; ´ (derzeit) s. zurzeit; eine Z~ lang for a time or while

Zeit|alter nt age, era. **z~gemäß** adj modern, up-to-date. **Z~genosse** m, **Z~genossin** f contemporary. **Z~genössisch** adj contemporary. **z~ig** adj & adv early

zeitlich adj (Dauer) in time; (Folge) chronological. ● adv z~ begrenzt for a limited time

zeit|los adj timeless. **Z~lupe** f slow motion. **Z~punkt** m time. **z~raubend** adj time-consuming. **Z~raum** m period. **Z~schrift** f magazine, periodical

Zeitung f -,-en newspaper. **Z~spapier** nt newspaper

Zeit|verschwendung f waste of time. **Z~vertreib** m pastime. **z~weise** adv at times. **Z~wort** (pl -wörter) verb. **Z~zünder** m time fuse

Zelle f -,-n cell; (Telefon-) box

Zelt nt -[e]s-e tent; (Fest-) marquee. **z~en** vi (haben) camp. **Z~** nt -s camping. **Z~plane** f tarpaulin. **Z~platz** m campsite

Zement m -[e]s cement

zen|sieren vt (Sch) mark; censor (Presse, Film). **Z~sur** f -,-en (Sch) mark; (Presse-) censorship

Zentimeter m & nt centimetre. **Z~maß** nt tape-measure

Zentner m -s,- [metric] hundred-weight (50 kg)

zentral adj central. **Z~e** f -,-n central office; (Partei-) headquarters pl; (Teleph) exchange. **Z~heizung** f central heating

Zentrum nt -s,-tren centre

zerbrech|en† vt/i (sein) break. **z~lich** adj fragile

zerdrücken vt crush

Zeremonie f -,-n ceremony

Zerfall m disintegration; (Verfall) decay. **z~en†** vi (sein) disintegrate; (verfallen) decay

zergehen† vi (sein) melt; (sich auf-lösen) dissolve

zerkleinern vt chop/(schneiden) cut up; (mahlen) grind

zerknüllen vt crumple [up]

zerkratzen vt scratch

zerlassen† vt melt

zerlegen vt take to pieces, dis-mantle; (zerschneiden) cut up; (tran-chieren) carve

zerlumpt adj ragged

zermalmen vt crush

zermürben vt (fig) wear down

zerplatzen vi (sein) burst

zerquetschen vt squash; crush

Zerrbild nt caricature

zerreißen† vt tear; (in Stücke) tear up; break (Faden, Seil) ● vi (sein) tear; break

zerren vt drag; pull (Muskel) ● vi (haben) pull (an + dat at)

zerrissen adj torn

zerrütten vt ruin, wreck; shatter (Nerven)

zerschlagen† vt smash; smash up (Möbel); sich z~ (fig) fall through; (Hoffnung:) be dashed

zerschmettern vt/i (sein) smash

zerschneiden† vt cut; (in Stücke) cut up

zersplittern vi (sein) splinter; (Glas:) shatter ● vt shatter

zerspringen† vi (sein) shatter; (bersten) burst

Zerstäuber m -s,- atomizer

zerstör|en vt destroy; (zunichte machen) wreck. **Z~er** m -s,- des-troyer. **Z~ung** f destruction

zerstreu|en vt scatter; disperse (Menge); dispel (Zweifel); sich z~en disperse; (sich unterhalten) amuse oneself. **z~t** adj absent-minded

Zertifikat nt -[e]s,-e certificate

zertrümmern vt smash [up]; wreck (Gebäude, Stadt)

Zettel m -s,- piece of paper; (Notiz) note; (Bekanntmachung) notice

Zeug nt -s ⚠ stuff; (Sachen) things pl; (Ausrüstung) gear; dummes Z~ nonsense

Zeuge m -n,-n witness. **z~n** vi

z

(*haben*) testify; z~n von (*fig*) show
● *vt* father. **Z~naussage** *f* testimony. **Z~nstand** *m* witness box

Zeugin *f* -,-nen witness

Zeugnis *nt* -ses,-se certificate; (*Sch*) report; (*Referenz*) reference; (*fig: Beweis*) evidence

Zickzack *m* -[e]s,-e zigzag

Ziege *f* -,-n goat

Ziegel *m* -s,- brick; (*Dach-*) tile. **Z~stein** *m* brick

ziehen† *vt* pull; (*sanfter; zücken; zeichnen*) draw; (*heraus-*) pull out; extract (*Zahn*); raise (*Hut*); put on (*Bremse*); move (*Schachfigur*); (*dehnen*) stretch; make (*Grimasse, Scheitel*); (*züchten*) breed; grow (*Rosen*); nach sich z~ (*fig*) entail ● *vr* sich z~ (*sich erstrecken*) run; (*sich verziehen*) warp ● *vi* (*haben*) pull (an + *dat* on/at); (*Tee, Ofen:*) draw; (*Culin*) simmer; es zieht there is a draught; solche Filme z~ nicht mehr films like that are no longer popular ● *vi* (*sein*) (*um-*) move (nach to); (*Menge:*) march; (*Vögel:*) migrate; (*Wolken, Nebel:*) drift

Ziehharmonika *f* accordion

Ziehung *f* -,-en draw

Ziel *nt* -[e]s,-e destination; (*Sport*) finish; (*Z~scheibe & Mil*) target; (*Zweck*) aim, goal. **z~bewusst** *adj* purposeful. **z~en** *vi* (*haben*) aim (auf + *acc* at). **z~los** *adj* aimless. **Z~scheibe** *f* target

ziemlich *adj* [1] fair ● *adv* rather, fairly

Zierde *f* -,-n ornament. **z~en** *vt* adorn

zierlich *adj* dainty

Ziffer *f* -,-n figure, digit; (*Zahlzeichen*) numeral. **Z~blatt** *nt* dial

Zigarette *f* -,-n cigarette

Zigarre *f* -,-n cigar

Zigeuner(in) *m* -s,-

(*f* -,-nen) gypsy

Zimmer *nt* -s,- room. **Z~mädchen** *nt* chambermaid. **Z~mann** *m* (*pl* -leute) carpenter. **Z~nachweis** *m* accommodation bureau. **Z~pflanze** *f* house plant

Zimt *m* -[e]s cinnamon

Zink *nt* -s zinc

Zinn *nt* -s tin; (*Gefäße*) pewter

Zins|en *mpl* interest *sg*; **Z~en tragen** earn interest. **Z~eszins** *m* -es,-e compound interest. **Z~fuß**, **Z~satz** *m* interest rate

Zipfel *m* -s,- corner; (*Spitze*) point

zirka *adv* about

Zirkel *m* -s,- [pair of] compasses *pl*; (*Gruppe*) circle

Zirkul|ation /-'tsĭo:n/ *f* - circulation. **z~ieren** *vi* (*sein*) circulate

Zirkus *m* -,-se circus

zirpen *vi* (*haben*) chirp

zischen *vi* (*haben*) hiss; (*Fett:*) sizzle ● *vt* hiss

Zit|at *nt* -[e]s,-e quotation. **z~ieren** *vt/i* (*haben*) quote

Zitr|onat *nt* -[e]s candied lemonpeel. **Z~one** *f* -,-n lemon

zittern *vi* (*haben*) tremble; (*vor Kälte*) shiver; (*beben*) shake

zittrig *adj* shaky

Zitze *f* -,-n teat

zivil *adj* civilian; (*Ehe, Recht*) civil. **Z~** *nt* -s civilian clothes *pl*. **Z~dienst** *m* community service

Zivili|sation /-'tsĭo:n/ *f* -,-en civilization. **z~ieren** *vt* civilize. **z~siert** *adj* civilized ● *adv* in a civilized manner

Zivilist *m* -en,-en civilian

zögern *vi* (*haben*) hesitate. **Z~** *nt* -s hesitation. **z~d** *adj* hesitant

Zoll¹ *m* -[e]s,- inch

Zoll² *m* -[e]s,∸e [customs] duty; (*Behörde*) customs *pl*. **Z~abferti-**

gung f customs clearance. **Z~be-amte(r)** m customs officer. **Z~frei** adj & adv duty-free. **Z~kontrolle** f customs check

Zone f -,-n zone

Zoo m -s,-s zoo

zoologisch adj zoological

Zopf m -[e]s,ꞌe plait

Zorn m -[e]s anger. **z~ig** adj angry

---

zu

● **preposition** (+ dative)

> ⚠ Note that zu dem can be-come zum and zu der, zur

····▸ (Richtung) to; (bei Beruf) into. wir gehen zur Schule we are going to school. ich muss zum Arzt I must go to the doctor's. zu ... hin towards. er geht ins Theater/Militär he is going into the theatre/army

····▸ (zusammen mit) with. zu dem Käse gab es Wein there was wine with the cheese. zu etw passen go with sth

····▸ (räumlich; zeitlich) at. zu Hause at home. zu ihren Füßen at her feet. zu Ostern at Easter. zur Zeit (+ gen) at the time of

····▸ (preislich) at; for. zum halben Preis at half price. das Stück zu zwei Euro at or for two euros each. eine Marke zu 60 Cent a 60-cent stamp

····▸ (Zweck, Anlass) for. zu diesem Zweck for this purpose. zum Spaß for fun. zum Lesen for reading. zum Geburtstag bekam ich ... for my birthday I got ... zum ersten Mal for the first time

····▸ (Art und Weise) to meinem

Erstaunen/Entsetzen to my surprise/horror. zu Fuß/Pferde on foot/horseback. zu Dutzen-den by the dozen. wir waren zu dritt/viert there were three/four of us

····▸ (Zahlenverhältnis) to. es steht 5 zu 3 the score is 5–3

····▸ (Ziel, Ergebnis) into. zu etw werden turn into sth

····▸ (gegenüber) to; towards. freundlich/hässlich zu jdm sein be friendly/nasty to s.o.

····▸ (über) on; about. sich zu etw äußern to comment on sth

● **adverb**

····▸ (allzu) too. zu groß/viel/weit too big/much/far

····▸ (Richtung) towards. nach dem Fluss zu towards the river

····▸ (geschlossen) closed; (an Schalter, Hahn) off. Augen zu! close your eyes! Tür zu! shut the door!

● **conjunction**

····▸ to. etwas zu essen some-thing to eat. nicht zu glauben unbelievable. zu erörternde Probleme problems to be dis-cussed

zuallerⅼerst adv first of all. **z~letzt** adv last of all

Zubehör nt -s accessories pl

zubereitⅼen vt sep prepare. **Z~ung** f - preparation; (in Rezept) method

zubinden† vt sep tie [up]

zubringⅼen† vt sep spend. **Z~er** m -s,- access road; (Bus) shuttle

Zucchini /tsuˈkiːni/ pl courgettes

Zucht f -,-en breeding; (von Pflanzen) cultivation; (Art, Rasse) breed; (von Pflanzen) strain; (Z~farm) farm; (Pferde-) stud

z

zücht|en vt breed; cultivate, grow (Rosen). **Z~er** m -s,- breeder; grower

Zuchthaus nt prison

Züchtung f -,-en breeding; (Pflanzen-) cultivation; (Art, Rasse) breed; (von Pflanzen) strain

zucken vi (haben) twitch; (sich z~d bewegen) jerk; (Blitz:) flash; (Flamme:) flicker ● vt **die Achseln z~** shrug one's shoulders

Zucker m -s sugar. **Z~dose** f sugar basin. **Z~guss** m icing. **z~krank** adj diabetic. **Z~krankheit** f diabetes. **Z~n** vt sugar. **Z~rohr** nt sugar cane. **Z~rübe** f sugar beet. **Z~watte** f candyfloss

zudecken vt sep cover up; (im Bett) tuck up; cover (Topf)

zudem adv moreover

zudrehen vt sep turn off

zueinander adv to one another; **z~ passen** go together; **z~ halten** (fig) stick together

zuerkennen† vt sep award (dat to)

zuerst adv first; (anfangs) at first

zufahr|en† vi sep (sein) **z~en auf** (+ acc) drive towards. **Z~t** f access; (Einfahrt) drive

Zufall m chance; (Zusammentreffen) coincidence; **durch Z~** by chance/ coincidence. **z~en**† vi sep (sein) close, shut; **jdm z~en** (Aufgabe:) fall/(Erbe:) go to s.o.

zufällig adj chance, accidental ● adv by chance

Zuflucht f refuge; (Schutz) shelter

zufolge prep (+ dat) according to

zufrieden adj contented; (befriedigt) satisfied; **sich z~ geben** be satisfied; **jdn z~ lassen** leave s.o. in peace; **jdn z~ stellen** satisfy s.o.; **z~ stellend** satisfactory. **Z~heit** f - contentment;

satisfaction

zufrieren† vi sep (sein) freeze over

zufügen vt sep inflict (dat on); do (Unrecht) (dat to)

Zufuhr f - supply

Zug m -[e]s, -e train; (Kolonne) column; (Um-) procession; (Mil) platoon; (Vogelschar) flock; (Ziehen, Zugkraft) pull; (Wandern, Ziehen) migration; (Schluck, Luft-) draught; (Atem-) breath; (beim Rauchen) puff; (Schach-) move; (beim Schwimmen, Rudern) stroke; (Gesichts-) feature; (Wesens-) trait

Zugabe f (Geschenk) [free] gift; (Mus) encore

Zugang m access

zugänglich adj accessible; (Mensch:) approachable

Zugbrücke f drawbridge

zugeben† vt sep add; (gestehen) admit; (erlauben) allow

zugehen† vi sep (sein) close; **jdm z~** be sent to s.o.; **z~ auf** (+ acc) go towards; **dem Ende z~** draw to a close; (Vorräte:) run low; **auf der Party ging es lebhaft zu** the party was pretty lively

Zugehörigkeit f - membership

Zügel m -s,- rein

zugelassen adj registered

zügel|los adj unrestrained. **z~n** vt rein in; (fig) curb

Zugeständnis nt concession. **z~stehen**† vt sep grant

zügig adj quick

Zugkraft f pull; (fig) attraction

zugleich adv at the same time

Zugluft f draught

zugreifen† vi sep (haben) grab it/them; (bei Tisch) help oneself; (bei Angebot) jump at it; (helfen) lend a hand

zugrunde adv **z~ richten** destroy; z~ **gehen** be destroyed; (*sterben*) die; z~ **liegen** form the basis (*dat* of)

zugunsten *prep* (+ *gen*) in favour of; (*Sammlung*) in aid of

zugute *adv* jdm/etw z~ **kommen** benefit s.o./sth

Zugvogel *m* migratory bird

zuhalten† *v sep* ●*vt* keep closed; (*bedecken*) cover; **sich** (*dat*) **die Nase z~** hold one's nose

Zuhälter *m* -s,- pimp

zuhause *adv* = zu Hause, s. Haus. **Z~** *nt* -s,- home

zuhör|en *vi sep* (*haben*) listen (*dat* to). **Z~er(in)** *m*(*f*) listener

zujubeln *vi sep* (*haben*) jdm z~ cheer s.o.

zukleben *vt sep* seal

zuknöpfen *vt sep* button up

zukommen† *vi sep* (*sein*) z~ **auf** (+ *acc*) come towards; (*sich nähern*) approach; z~ **lassen** send (jdm s.o.); devote (*Pflege*) (*dat* to); jdm z~ be s.o.'s right

Zukunft *f* - future. **zukünftig** *adj* future ●*adv* in future

zulächeln *vi sep* (*haben*) smile (*dat* at)

zulangen *vi sep* (*haben*) help oneself

zulassen† *vt sep* allow, permit; (*teilnehmen lassen*) admit; (*Admin*) license, register; (*geschlossen lassen*) leave closed; leave unopened (*Brief*)

zulässig *adj* permissible

Zulassung *f* -,-en admission; registration; (*Lizenz*) licence

zuleide *adv* jdm etwas z~ **tun** hurt s.o.

zuletzt *adv* last; (*schließlich*) in the end

zuliebe *adv* jdm/etw z~ for the sake of someone/something

zum *prep* = zu dem; **zum Spaß** for fun; **etw zum Lesen** sth to read

zumachen *v sep* ●*vt* close, shut; do up (*Jacke*); seal (*Umschlag*); turn off (*Hahn*); (*stilllegen*) close down ●*vi* (*haben*) close, shut; (*stillgelegt werden*) close down

zumal *adv* especially ●*conj* especially since

zumindest *adv* at least

zumutbar *adj* reasonable

zumute *adv* mir ist nicht danach z~ I don't feel like it

zumut|en *vt sep* jdm etw z~en ask or expect sth of s.o.; **sich** (*dat*) **zu viel z~en** overdo things. **Z~ung** *f* - imposition

zunächst *adv* first [of all]; (*anfangs*) at first; (*vorläufig*) for the moment ●*prep* (+ *dat*) nearest to

Zunahme *f* -,-n increase

Zuname *m* surname

zünd|en *vt/i* (*haben*) ignite. **Z~er** *m* -s,- detonator, fuse. **Z~holz** *nt* match. **Z~kerze** *f* sparking-plug. **Z~schlüssel** *m* ignition key. **Z~schnur** *f* fuse. **Z~ung** *f* -,-en ignition

zunehmen† *vi sep* (*haben*) increase (an + *dat* in); (*Mond:*) wax; (*an Gewicht*) put on weight. **z~d** *adj* increasing

Zuneigung *f* - affection

Zunft *f* -,-̈e guild

Zunge *f* -,-n tongue. **Z~nbrecher** *m* tongue-twister

zunutze *adv* **sich** (*dat*) **etw z~ machen** make use of sth; (*ausnutzen*) take advantage of sth

zuoberst *adv* right at the top

zuordnen *vt sep* assign (*dat* to)

zupfen *vt/i* (*haben*) pluck (an + *dat* at); pull out (*Unkraut*)

zur *prep* = zu der; **zur Schule** to

school; **zur Zeit** at present
zurate adv z∼ **ziehen** consult

> **Zürcher Festspiele** The
> Zurich festival in Switzer-
> land is an annual celebra-
> tion of classical music, opera,
> dance and art, with special per-
> formances held throughout the
> city. The festival concludes with a
> brilliant Midsummer Night's Ball in
> central Zurich.

zurechnungsfähig adj of
sound mind

zurecht|finden† (sich) vr sep
find one's way. **z∼kommen†** vi sep
(sein) cope (**mit** with); (rechtzeitig
kommen) be in time. **z∼legen** vt
sep put out ready; **sich** (dat) **eine
Ausrede z∼legen** have an excuse
all ready. **z∼machen** vt sep get
ready. **Z∼weisung** f reprimand

zureden vi sep (haben) **jdm** z∼
try to persuade s.o.

zurichten vt sep prepare; (beschädigen) damage; (verletzen) injure

zuriegeln vt sep bolt

zurück adv sep back; **Berlin, hin und
z∼** return to Berlin. **z∼bekom-
men†** vt sep get back. **z∼bleiben†**
vi sep (sein) stay behind; (nicht mit-
halten) lag behind. **z∼bringen†** vt
sep bring back; (wieder hinbringen)
take back. **z∼erstatten** vt sep refund. **z∼fahren†** vi sep ● vt drive
back ● vi (sein) return, go back; (im
Auto) drive back; (zu∼weichen) recoil. **z∼finden†** vi sep (haben) find
one's way back. **z∼führen** v sep
● vt take back; (fig) attribute (**auf** +
acc to) ● vi (haben) lead back.
z∼geben† vt sep give back, return.
z∼geblieben adj retarded. **z∼ge-
hen†** vi sep (sein) go back, return;
(abnehmen) go down; **z∼gehen auf**

(+ acc) (fig) go back to

zurückgezogen adj secluded.
Z∼heit f - seclusion

zurückhalt|en† vt sep hold back;
(abhalten) stop; **sich z∼en** restrain
oneself. **z∼end** adj reserved.
Z∼ung f - reserve

zurück|kehren vi sep (sein) re-
turn. **z∼kommen†** vi sep (sein)
come back, return; (ankommen) get
back. **z∼lassen†** vt sep leave behind; (z∼kehren lassen) allow back.
z∼legen vt sep (reservieren) keep; (sparen) put by; cover
(Strecke). **z∼liegen†** vi sep (haben)
be in the past; (Sport) be behind;
das liegt lange zurück that was
long ago. **z∼melden (sich)** vr sep
report back. **z∼schicken** vt sep
send back. **z∼schlagen** v sep ● vi
(haben) hit back ● vt hit back; (umschlagen) turn back. **z∼schrecken**
vi sep (sein) shrink back, recoil, (fig)
shrink (**vor** + dat from). **z∼stellen**
vt sep put back; (reservieren) keep;
(fig) put aside; (aufschieben) postpone. **z∼stoßen** v sep ● vt push
back ● vi (sein) reverse, back.
z∼treten† vi sep (sein) step back;
(vom Amt) resign; (verzichten) withdraw. **z∼weisen†** vt sep turn away;
(fig) reject. **z∼zahlen** vt sep pay
back. **z∼ziehen†** vt sep draw back;
(fig) withdraw; **sich z∼ziehen** withdraw; (vom Beruf) retire

Zuruf m shout. **z∼en†** vt sep shout
(**dat** to)

zurzeit adv at present

Zusage f -,-n acceptance; (Versprechen) promise. **z∼n** v sep ● vt
promise ● vi (haben) accept

zusammen adv together; (insgesamt) altogether; **z∼ sein** be
together. **Z∼arbeit** f co-operation.
z∼arbeiten vi sep (haben) co-oper-
ate. **z∼bauen** vt sep assemble.

z~**bleiben**† vi sep (sein) stay together. z~**brechen**† vi sep (sein) collapse. **Z~bruch** m collapse; (Nerven- & fig) breakdown. z~**fallen**† vi sep (sein) collapse; (zeitlich) coincide. z~**fassen** vt sep summarize, sum up. **Z~fassung** f summary. z~**fügen** vt sep fit together. z~**gehören** vi sep (haben) belong together; (z~passen) go together. z~**gesetzt** adj (Gram) compound. z~**halten**† v sep ● vt hold together; (beisammenhalten) keep together ● vi (haben) (fig) stick together. **Z~hang** m connection; (Kontext) context. z~**hanglos** adj incoherent. z~**klappen** v sep ● vt fold up ● vi (sein) collapse. z~**kommen**† vi sep (sein) meet; (sich sammeln) accumulate. **Z~kunft** f -,ᵉe meeting. z~**laufen**† vi sep (sein) gather; (Flüssigkeit:) collect; (Linien:) converge. z~**leben** vi sep (haben) live together. z~**legen** v sep ● vt put together; (z~falten) fold up; (vereinigen) amalgamate; pool (Geld) ● vi (haben) club together; summon up (Mut); collect (Gedanken); sich z~**nehmen** pull oneself together. z~**passen** vi sep (haben) go together, match. **Z~prall** m collision. z~**rechnen** vt sep add up. z~**schlagen**† vt sep smash up; (prügeln) beat up. z~**schließen**† (sich) vr sep join together; (Firmen:) merge. **Z~schluss** m union; (Comm) merger

Zusammensein nt -s get-together

zusammensetz|en vt sep put together; (Techn) assemble; sich z~en sit [down] together; (bestehen) be made up (aus from). **Z~ung** f -,-en composition; (Techn) assembly; (Wort) compound

zusammen|stellen vt sep put

together; (gestalten) compile. **z~stoß** m collision; (fig) clash. z~**treffen**† vi sep (sein) meet; (zeitlich) coincide ● **z~zählen** vt sep add up. z~**ziehen**† sep ● vt draw together; (addieren) add up; (konzentrieren) mass; sich z~**ziehen** contract; (Gewitter:) gather ● vi (sein) move in together; move in (mit with)

Zusatz m addition; (Jur) rider; (Lebensmittel-) additive. **zusätzlich** adj additional ● adv in addition

zuschau|en vi sep (haben) watch. **Z~er(in)** m -s,- (f -,-nen) spectator; (TV) viewer

Zuschlag m surcharge; (Zug) supplement. z~**pflichtig** adj (Zug) for which a supplement is payable

zuschließen† v sep ● vt lock ● vi (haben) lock up

zuschneiden† vt sep cut out; cut to size (Holz)

zuschreiben† vt sep attribute (dat to); jdm die Schuld z~ blame s.o.

Zuschrift f letter; (auf Annonce) reply

zuschulden adv sich (dat) etwas z~ kommen lassen do wrong

Zuschuss m contribution; (staatlich) subsidy

zusehends adv visibly

zusein° vi sep (sein) zu sein, s. zu

zusenden† vt sep send (dat to)

zusetzen v sep ● vt add; (einbüßen) lose

zusicher|n vt sep promise. **Z~ung** f promise.

zuspielen vt sep (Sport) pass

zuspitzen (sich) vr sep (fig) become critical

Zustand m condition, state

zustande adv z~ bringen/kommen bring/come about

zuständig adj competent; (verantwortlich) responsible

zustehen† vi sep (haben) jdm z~ be s.o.'s right; (Urlaub:) be due to s.o.

zusteigen† vi sep (sein) get on; noch jemand zugestiegen? ≈ tickets please; (im Bus) ≈ any more fares please?

zustell|en vt sep block; (bringen) deliver. Z~ung f delivery

zusteuern v sep ● vi (sein) head (auf + acc for) ● vt contribute

zustimm|en vi sep (haben) agree; (billigen) approve (dat of). Z~ung f consent; approval

zustoßen† vi sep (sein) happen (dat to)

Zustrom m influx

Zutat f (Culin) ingredient

zuteil|en vt sep allocate; assign (Aufgabe.). Z~ung f allocation

zutiefst adv deeply

zutragen† vt sep carry/(fig) report (dat to); sich z~ happen

zutrau|en vt sep jdm etw z~ believe s.o. capable of sth. Z~en nt -s confidence

zutreffen† vi sep (haben) be correct; z~ auf (+ acc) apply to

Zutritt m admittance

zuunterst adv right at the bottom

zuverlässig adj reliable. Z~keit f - reliability

Zuversicht f - confidence. z~lich adj confident

zuviel* pron & adv zu viel, s. viel

zuvor adv before; (erst) first

zuvorkommen† vi sep (sein) (+ dat) anticipate. z~d adj obliging

Zuwachs m -es increase

Zuwanderung f immigration

zuwege adv z~ bringen achieve

zuweilen adv now and then

zuweisen† vt sep assign

Zuwendung f donation; (Fürsorge) care

zuwenig* pron & adv zu wenig, s. wenig

zuwerfen† vt sep slam (Tür); jdm etw z~ throw s.o. sth

zuwider adj jdm z~ sein be repugnant to s.o. ● prep (+ dat) contrary to

zuzahlen vt sep pay extra

zuziehen† v sep ● vt pull tight; draw (Vorhänge); (hinzu-) call in; sich (dat) etw z~ contract (Krankheit); sustain (Verletzung); incur (Zorn) ● vi (sein) move into the area

zuzüglich prep (+ gen) plus

Zwang m -[e]s,⸚e compulsion; (Gewalt) force; (Verpflichtung) obligation

zwängen vt squeeze

zwanglos adj informal. Z~igkeit f - informality

Zwangsjacke f straitjacket

zwanzig inv adj twenty. z~ste(r,s) adj twentieth

zwar adv admittedly

Zweck m -[e]s,-e purpose; (Sinn) point. z~los adj pointless. z~mäßig adj suitable; (praktisch) functional

zwei inv adj, Z~ f -,-en two; (Sch) ≈ B. Z~bettzimmer nt twin-bedded room

zweideutig adj ambiguous

zwei|erlei inv adj two kinds of ● pron two things. z~fach adj double

Zweifel m -s,- doubt. z~haft adj doubtful; (fragwürdig) dubious. z~los adv undoubtedly. z~n vi (haben) doubt (an etw dat sth)

z

Zweig | Zyste

Zweig m -[e]s,-e branch. **Z~stelle** f branch [office]

Zwei|kampf m duel. **z~mal** adv twice. **z~reihig** adj (Anzug) double-breasted. **z~sprachig** adj bilingual

zweit adv zu z~ in twos; **wir waren zu z~** there were two of us. **z~beste(r,s)** adj second-best. **z~e(r,s)** adj second

zweitens adv secondly

Zwerchfell nt diaphragm

Zwerg m -[e]s,-e dwarf

Zwickel m -s,- gusset

zwicken vt/i (haben) pinch

Zwieback m -[e]s,⸚e rusk

Zwiebel f -,-n onion; (Blumen-)bulb

Zwielicht nt half-light; (Dämmerlicht) twilight. **z~ig** adj shady

Zwiespalt m conflict

Zwilling m -s,-e twin; **Z~e** (Astrology) Gemini

zwingen† vt force; **sich z~** force oneself. **z~d** adj compelling

Zwinger m -s,- run; (Zucht-) kennels pl

zwinkern vi (haben) blink; (als Zeichen) wink

Zwirn m -[e]s button thread

zwischen prep (+ dat/acc) between; (unter) among[st]. **Z~bemerkung** f interjection. **z~durch** adv in between; (in der Z~zeit) in the meantime. **Z~fall** m incident. **Z~landung** f stopover. **Z~raum** m gap, space. **Z~wand** f partition. **Z~zeit** f in der Z~zeit in the meantime

Zwist m -[e]s,-e discord; (Streit) feud

zwitschern vi (haben) chirp

zwo inv adj two

zwölf inv adj twelve. **z~te(r,s)** adj twelfth

Zylind|er m -s,- cylinder; (Hut) top hat. **z~risch** adj cylindrical

Zyn|iker m -s,- cynic. **z~isch** adj cynical. **Z~ismus** m - cynicism

Zypern nt -s Cyprus

Zypresse f -,-n cypress

Zyste /ˈtsʏsta/ f -,-n cyst

Phrasefinder/Sprachführer

Key phrases Nützliche Redewendungen

yes, please	ja bitte
no, thank you	nein danke
sorry!	Entschuldigung!
you're welcome	nichts zu danken
I don't understand	ich verstehe das nicht

Meeting people Wir lernen uns kennen

hello/goodbye	hallo!/auf Wiedersehen!
how are you?	wie geht es Ihnen?/wie geht's?
fine, thank you	danke, gut
see you later!	bis nachher!

Asking questions — Fragen

do you speak English/German?	sprechen Sie/sprichst du Englisch/Deutsch?
what's your name?	wie heißen Sie?/wie heißt du?
where are you from?	woher kommen Sie?/woher kommst du?
how much is it?	wie viel kostet das?
how far is it?	wie weit ist es?

About you — Alles über mich

my name is...	ich heiße...
I'm English	ich bin Engländer/Engländerin
I don't speak German/English very well	ich kann nicht gut Deutsch/Englisch sprechen
I'm here on holiday	ich bin im Urlaub hier
I live near Manchester/Hamburg	ich wohne in der Nähe von Manchester/Hamburg

Emergencies — Im Notfall

can you help me, please?	können Sie mir bitte helfen?
I'm lost	ich habe mich verlaufen
call an ambulance	rufen Sie einen Krankenwagen
get the police/a doctor	holen Sie die Polizei/einen Arzt
watch out!	Vorsicht!, Achtung!

Going Places/Unterwegs

By rail and underground	Mit Bahn und U-Bahn
where can I buy a ticket?	wo kann ich eine Fahrkarte kaufen?
what time is the next train to Berlin/New York?	wann geht der nächste Zug nach Berlin/New York?
do I have to change?	muss ich umsteigen?
can I take my bike on the train?	kann ich mein Rad im Zug mitnehmen?
which platform for the train to Cologne/Bath?	von welchem Bahnsteig fährt der Zug nach Köln/Bath ab?
a single/return, (*Amer* round trip) to Baltimore/Frankfurt, please	einmal einfach/eine Rückfahrkarte nach Baltimore/Frankfurt, bitte
I'd like a cheap day return/an all-day ticket	ich möchte eine Tagesrückfahrkarte/Tageskarte
I'd like to reserve a seat	ich möchte einen Platz reservieren
is there a student/senior citizen discount?	gibt es eine Ermäßigung für Studenten/Senioren?
is this the train for...?	ist dies der Zug nach...?
what time does the train arrive in Cologne/Washington?	wann kommt der Zug in Köln/Washington an?
have I missed the train?	habe ich den Zug verpasst?
which line do I need to take for the castle?	mit welcher Linie komme ich zum Schloss?

YOU WILL HEAR:	SIE HÖREN:
der Zug fährt auf Gleis 2 ein	the train is arriving at platform 2
um 10 Uhr fährt ein Zug nach Berlin/York	there's a train to Berlin/York at 10 o'clock
der Zug hat Verspätung/ist pünktlich	the train is delayed/on time
die nächste Haltestelle ist ...	the next stop is...
Ihre Fahrkarte ist ungültig	your ticket isn't valid

3

MORE USEFUL WORDS:	**NÜTZLICHE WÖRTER:**
underground station, (*Amer*) subway station	U-Bahnhof, U-Bahn-Station
timetable	Fahrplan
connection	Anschluss
express train	Schnellzug
local train	Nahverkehrszug
seat reservation	Platzreservierung
high-speed train	ICE, Intercity-Express

DID YOU KNOW...?	**WUSSTEN SIE SCHON...?**
At weekends and during busy times, it is advisable to get a seat reservation when you buy your train ticket. There is a small charge for this service.	Wenn Sie in Großbritannien Zugfahrkarten einige Wochen im Voraus kaufen, können Sie viel Geld sparen.

At the airport Am Flughafen

when's the next flight to Paris/Rome?	wann geht der nächste Flug nach Paris/Rom?
what time do I have to check in?	um wie viel Uhr muss ich einchecken?
where do I check in?	wo checkt man ein?
I'd like to confirm/cancel my flight	ich möchte meinen Flug bestätigen/stornieren
I'd like a window seat/an aisle seat	ich möchte einen Fensterplatz/Platz am Gang
can I change my booking?	kann ich umbuchen?
can I carry this in my hand, (*Amer*) carry-on luggage?	kann ich das im Handgepäck mitnehmen?
my luggage hasn't arrived	mein Gepäck ist nicht angekommen

YOU WILL HEAR:	SIE HÖREN:
Flug BA7057 ist zum Einsteigen bereit/ist verspätet/wurde gestrichen	flight BA7057 is now boarding/delayed/cancelled
gehen Sie bitte zum Flugsteig 29	please go to gate 29
darf ich Ihre Bordkarte sehen?	could I see your boarding card?

MORE USEFUL WORDS:	NÜTZLICHE WÖRTER:
arrivals	Ankunft
departures	Abflug
baggage claim	Gepäckausgabe

Asking how to get there Nach dem Weg fragen

how do I get to the airport/city centre, (Amer center)?	wie komme ich zum Flughafen/Stadtzentrum?
how long will it take me to walk there?	wie lange braucht man zu Fuß?
how far is it from here?	wie weit ist das von hier?
which bus do I take for the cathedral?	mit welchem Bus komme ich zum Dom?
where does this bus go?	wohin fährt dieser Bus?
where do I get the bus for...?	wo fährt der Bus nach...ab?
does this bus/train go to...?	fährt dieser Bus/Zug nach...?
which bus goes to...?	welcher Bus fährt nach...?
where do I get off?	wo muss ich aussteigen?
how much is the fare to the town centre (Amer center)?	was kostet es ins Stadtzentrum?
what time is the last bus?	wann fährt der letzte Bus?
where's the nearest underground station (Amer subway station)?	wo ist die nächste U-Bahn-Station?
is this the turning for...?	ist das die Abzweigung nach...?
can you call me a taxi?	können Sie mir ein Taxi bestellen?

YOU WILL HEAR:	SIE HÖREN:
nehmen Sie die erste Straße rechts	take the first turning (*Amer* turn) on the right
gehen Sie an der Ampel/ gleich nach der Kirche links	turn left at the traffic lights/ just past the church

Disabled travellers / Reisende mit Behinderungen

I'm disabled	ich habe eine Behinderung
is there wheelchair access?	gibt es einen stufenfreien Zugang?
are guide dogs permitted?	sind Blindenhunde zugelassen?

On the road / Auf der Straße

where's the nearest petrol station, (*Amer*) gas station?	wo ist die nächste Tankstelle?
what's the best way to get there?	wie komme ich am besten dorthin?
I've got a puncture, (*Amer*) flat tire	ich habe eine Reifenpanne
I'd like to hire, (*Amer*) rent a bike/car	ich möchte ein Rad/Auto mieten
where can I park around here?	wo kann man hier parken?
there's been an accident	es ist ein Unfall passiert
my car's broken down	mein Auto hat eine Panne
the car won't start	der Wagen springt nicht an
where's the nearest garage?	wo ist die nächste Autowerkstatt?
pump number six, please	Zapfsäule Nummer sechs, bitte
fill it up, please	bitte volltanken
can I wash my car here?	kann ich hier mein Auto waschen?
can I park here?	kann ich hier parken?
there's a problem with the brakes/lights	mit den Bremsen/der Beleuchtung stimmt etwas nicht
the clutch/gearstick isn't working	die Kupplung/Gangschaltung ist kaputt

take the third exit off the roundabout, (*Amer* traffic circle)	nehmen Sie im Kreisverkehr die dritte Ausfahrt
turn right at the next junction	biegen Sie an der nächsten Kreuzung rechts ab
slow down	fahren Sie langsamer
I can't drink, I'm driving	ich kann leider nichts trinken, ich muss noch fahren
can I buy a road map here?	kann ich hier eine Straßenkarte kaufen?

YOU WILL HEAR:	SIE HÖREN:
darf ich Ihren Führerschein sehen?	can I see your driving licence?
Sie müssen einen Unfallbericht ausfüllen	you need to fill out an accident report
dies ist eine Einbahnstraße	this road is one-way
das Tempolimit ist 50 Stundenkilometer	the speed limit is 50 kilometres per hour
Sie können hier nicht parken	you can't park here

MORE USEFUL WORDS:	NÜTZLICHE WÖRTER:
diesel	Diesel
unleaded	bleifreies Benzin
motorway, (*Amer* expressway)	Autobahn
toll/toll road	Maut/Mautstraße
satnav, (*Amer* GPS)	Satellitennavigationssystem
speed camera	Radarfalle
roundabout	Kreisverkehr
crossroads	Kreuzung
bus lane	Busspur
dual carriageway, (*Amer* divided highway)	vierspurige Schnellstraße
traffic lights	Ampel
driver	Fahrer/-in

DID YOU KNOW...? WUSSTEN SIE SCHON...?

Heavy goods vehicles over 7.5 tons are not allowed to travel on German motorways on Sundays and Bank Holidays. Exceptions apply to HGVs transporting perishable goods.

Radarfallen (Starenkästen) sind in Großbritannien meist gelb angestrichen und daher von Weitem gut zu erkennen. Oft weist ein Schild mit einem Kamera-Symbol auf Radarkontrollen hin.

COMMON ROAD SIGNS

Achtung Kinder	Careful - children
Anlieger frei	Residents only
Ausfahrt	Exit
Einbahnstraße	One-way street
Fahrradstraße	Priority for cyclists
H	Bus/tram stop
P	Car park, parking
Spielstraße	Home zone
Stop	Stop
Umleitung	Diversion

STRASSENSCHILDER

Get in lane	Einordnen
Give way	Vorfahrt gewähren
Level crossing	Bahnübergang
No overtaking (*Amer* Do not pass)	Überholverbot
No stopping/parking	Halteverbot/Parkverbot
P	Parkplatz
Reduce speed now	Jetzt das Tempo verlangsamen
Slow	Langsam
Stop	Stopp!, Halt!

Keeping in touch / In Verbindung bleiben

On the phone   Am Telefon

where can I buy a phone card?	wo kann man Telefonkarten kaufen?
may I use your phone?	darf ich Ihr Telefon benutzen?
do you have a mobile, (Amer cell phone?)	haben Sie ein Handy?
what is your phone number?	was ist Ihre Telefonnummer?
what is the area code for Leipzig/ Sheffield?	was ist die Vorwahl von Leipzig/ Sheffield?
I'd like to make a phone call	ich möchte gern telefonieren
I'd like to reverse the charges (Amer call collect)	ich möchte ein R-Gespräch anmelden
the line's engaged/busy	es ist besetzt
there's no answer	es meldet sich niemand
hello, this is Natalie	hallo, hier spricht Natalie
can I speak to Simon, please?	kann ich bitte Simon sprechen?
who's calling?	wer ist am Apparat?
sorry, I must have the wrong number	Entschuldigung, ich habe mich verwählt
just a moment, please	einen Augenblick bitte
please hold the line	bleiben Sie bitte am Apparat
it's a business/personal call	es ist ein geschäftliches/privates Gespräch
I'll put you through	ich verbinde Sie
he cannot come to the phone at the moment	er kann jetzt nicht an den Apparat kommen
please tell him/her I called	richten Sie ihm/ihr bitte aus, dass ich angerufen habe
can I leave a message for Eva?	kann ich eine Nachricht für Eva hinterlassen?
I'll try again later	ich versuche es später noch einmal
please tell her that Danielle called	sagen Sie ihr bitte, dass Danielle angerufen hat

can he/she call me back?	kann er/sie mich zurückrufen?
my home number is...	meine Privatnummer ist...
my business number is...	meine Nummer im Büro ist...
my fax number is...	meine Faxnummer ist...
can I send a fax from here?	kann ich von hier faxen?
we were cut off	wir sind unterbrochen worden
I'll call you later	ich rufe Sie später an
I need to top up my mobile phone (*Amer* cell phone)	ich muss mein Handy-Guthaben aufladen
the battery's run out	die Batterie ist leer
I'm running low on credit	mein Handy-Guthaben ist fast aufgebraucht
send me a text	schicken Sie mir eine SMS
there's no signal here	hier ist kein Empfang
you're breaking up	ich kann Sie nicht mehr hören
could you speak a little louder?	könnten Sie etwas lauter sprechen?

YOU WILL HEAR:	SIE HÖREN:
hallo	hello
rufen Sie mich auf meinem Handy an	call me on my mobile (*Amer* cell phone)
der Teilnehmer ist nicht erreichbar	the person you are calling is unavailable
bitte drücken Sie die Rautetaste	please press the hash key
möchten Sie eine Nachricht hinterlassen?	Would you like to leave a message?
Bitte hinterlassen Sie eine Nachricht nach dem Ton	please leave a message after the tone

MORE USEFUL WORDS:	NÜTZLICHE WÖRTER:
text message	SMS
top-up card	Aufladekarte
phone box, (*Amer* phone booth)	Telefonzelle
dial	wählen

Writing / Schreiben

can you give me your address?	können Sie mir Ihre/kannst du mir deine Adresse geben?
where is the nearest post office?	wo ist die nächste Post?
two one-euro stamps	zwei Briefmarken zu einem Euro
I'd like a stamp for a letter to Germany/Italy	ich hätte gern eine Briefmarke für einen Brief nach Deutschland/Italien
can I have two stamps for two postcards to England/the USA, please?	kann ich bitte Briefmarken für zwei Postkarten nach England/in die USA haben?
I'd like to send a parcel	ich möchte ein Paket abschicken
is there a postbox (*Amer* mailbox) near here?	gibt es hier in der Nähe einen Briefkasten?
dear Isabel/Fred	Liebe Isabel/Lieber Fred
dear Sir or Madam	Sehr geehrte Damen und Herren
yours sincerely	Mit freundlichen Grüßen
yours faithfully	Mit freundlichen Grüßen
best wishes	Viele Grüße

YOU WILL HEAR:	SIE HÖREN:
möchten Sie es per Luftpost schicken?	would you like to send it by air mail?
ist es wertvoll?	is it valuable?

MORE USEFUL WORDS:	NÜTZLICHE WÖRTER:
postcode (*Amer* ZIP code)	Postleitzahl
airmail	Luftpost
fragile	zerbrechlich
urgent	dringend
registered post (*Amer* mail)	Einschreiben

11

On line Online

are you on the Internet?	hast du Zugang zum Internet?
what's your e-mail address?	was ist deine E-Mail-Adresse?
I'll e-mail it to you	ich schicke es Ihnen per E-Mail
I've looked for it on the Internet	ich habe es im Internet gesucht
he found the information surfing the net	er hat die Informationen beim Surfen im Internet gefunden
my e-mail address is jane dot smith at new99 dot com	meine E-Mail-Adresse ist jane Punkt smith at-Zeichen new99 Punkt com
can I check my e-mail here?	kann ich hier meine E-Mails ansehen?
I have broadband/dial-up	ich habe Breitband/eine Einwahlverbindung
do you have wireless internet access here?	gibt es hier einen drahtlosen Internetzugang?
I spend a lot of time surfing the Net	ich surfe viel im Internet
I'll send you the file as an attachment	ich schicke Ihnen die Datei als Anhang

YOU MAY SEE:	SIE SEHEN:
Suche	search
auf das Symbol doppelklicken	double-click on the icon
Anwendung öffnen	open (up) the application
Datei herunterladen	download file

MORE USEFUL WORDS:	NÜTZLICHE WÖRTER:
subject (of an email)	Betreff
password	Passwort
social networking site	soziales Netzwerk
search engine	Suchmaschine
mouse	Maus
keyboard	Tastatur

Meeting up   Verabredungen

what shall we do this evening?	was machen wir heute Abend?
do you want to go out tonight?	möchten Sie/möchtest du heute Abend ausgehen?
where shall we meet?	wo treffen wir uns?
see you outside the cinema at 6 o'clock	ich treffe Sie/dich um sechs Uhr vor dem Kino
do you fancy joining in?	hast du/haben Sie Lust mitzumachen?
I can't today, I'm busy	ich kann heute nicht, ich habe keine Zeit
shall we go for something to eat?	sollen wir etwas essen gehen?
let's meet for a coffee in town	treffen wir uns in der Stadt zum Kaffeetrinken
would you like to see a show/film (Amer movie)?	möchten Sie/möchtest du eine Show/einen Film ansehen?
I'm sorry, I've got something planned	es tut mir leid, ich habe schon etwas vor
what about next week instead?	wie wäre es stattdessen nächste Woche?

YOU WILL HEAR:	SIE HÖREN:
freut mich, Sie kennenzulernen	nice to meet you
kann ich Sie zu einem Gläschen einladen?	can I buy you a drink?

MORE USEFUL WORDS:	NÜTZLICHE WÖRTER:
bar	Bar
bar (serving counter in a bar/pub)	Theke
meal	Essen
snack	Imbiss
date	Verabredung
cigarette	Zigarette

Food and Drink/Essen und trinken

Booking a table / Vorbestellungen

can you recommend a good restaurant?	können Sie uns/mir ein gutes Restaurant empfehlen?
I'd like to reserve a table for four	ich möchte einen Tisch für vier Personen bestellen
I booked a table for two	ich habe einen Tisch für zwei Personen bestellt

Ordering / Wir möchten bestellen

could we see the menu/wine list, please?	können wir bitte die Speisekarte/Weinkarte haben?
do you have a vegetarian/children's menu?	haben Sie vegetarische Gerichte/Kinderportionen?
could we have some more bread?	noch etwas Brot, bitte
what would you recommend?	was würden Sie mir/uns empfehlen?
I'd like a white/black coffee	ich möchte einen Kaffee mit Milch/einen Kaffee ohne Milch
... an espresso	... einen Espresso
... a decaffeinated coffee	... einen entkoffeinierten Kaffee
the bill, (*Amer*) check, please	Rechnung, bitte

YOU WILL HEAR: / SIE HÖREN:

hätten Sie gern einen Aperitif?	would you like an aperitif?
haben Sie schon bestellt?	are you ready to order?
möchten Sie eine Vorspeise?	would you like a starter?
was nehmen Sie als Hauptgericht?	what will you have for the main course?
möchten Sie eine Nachspeise?	would you like a dessert?
haben Sie noch einen Wunsch?	anything else?
guten Appetit!	enjoy your meal!
die Bedienung ist (nicht) inbegriffen	service is (not) included

The menu   Die Speisekarte

starters	Vorspeisen	Vorspeisen	starters
canapés	Häppchen	Häppchen	canapés
hors d'oeuvres	Horsd'oeuvres, Vorspeisen	Horsd'oeuvres, Vorspeisen	hors d'oeuvres
omelette	Omelett	Omelett	omelette
soup	Suppe	Suppe	soup

fish	Fisch	Fisch	fish
bass	Barsch	Aal	eel
cod	Kabeljau	Austern	oysters
eel	Aal	Barsch	bass
haddock	Schellfisch	Calamares	squid
hake	Seehecht	Forelle	trout
herring	Hering	Garnelen	prawns
monk fish	Anglerfisch	Hering	herring
mullet	Meeräsche	Kabeljau	cod
mussels	Muscheln	Krabben	shrimps
oysters	Austern	Lachs	salmon
plaice	Scholle	Meeräsche	mullet
prawns	Garnelen	Muscheln	mussels
red mullet	Meerbarbe	Sardinen	sardines
salmon	Lachs	Schellfisch	haddock
sardines	Sardinen	Scholle	plaice
shrimps	Krabben	Seehecht	hake
sole	Seezunge	Seezunge	sole
squid	Calamares	Steinbutt	turbot
trout	Forelle		
tuna	Thunfisch		
turbot	Steinbutt		

meat	Fleisch		Fleisch	meat
chicken	Hühnchen		Ente	duck
duck	Ente		Gans	goose
goose	Gans		Hase	hare
guinea fowl	Perlhuhn		Hühnchen	chicken
hare	Hase		Kalbfleisch	veal
kidneys	Nieren		Kaninchen	rabbit
lamb	Lammfleisch		Lammfleisch	lamb
liver	Leber		Leber	liver
pork	Schweinefleisch		Nieren	kidneys
rabbit	Kaninchen		Sauerbraten	braised beef
veal	Kalbfleisch		Schweinefleisch	pork
wild boar	Wildschwein		Wiener Schnitzel	breaded escalope
			Wildschwein	wild boar

vegetables	Gemüse		Gemüse	vegetables
artichokes	Artischocken		Artischocken	artichokes
asparagus	Spargel		Blaukraut (Aust.)	red cabbage
beans	Bohnen		Blumenkohl	cauliflower
cabbage	Kohl		Bohnen	beans
carrots	Möhren, Karotten		Endivie	endive
cauliflower	Blumenkohl		Erbsen	peas
celery	Sellerie		Kartoffeln	potatoes
endive	Endivie		Kohl	cabbage
mushrooms	Pilze		Möhren, Karotten	carrots
onions	Zwiebeln		Paprikaschoten	peppers
peas	Erbsen		Pilze	mushrooms
peppers	Paprikaschoten		Rotkohl	red cabbage
potatoes	Kartoffeln		Sellerie	celeriac; celery
red cabbage	Rotkohl, Blaukraut (Aust.)		Spargel	asparagus
			Zwiebeln	onions

the way it's cooked	wie es zubereitet wird	wie es zubereitet wird	the way it's cooked
boiled	gekocht	englisch gebraten	rare
fried	gebraten, in der Pfanne gebraten	gebraten, geröstet	roast
grilled	gegrillt	gebraten, in der Pfanne gebraten	fried
medium	halb durchgebraten	gegrillt	grilled
puréed	püriert	geschmort	stewed
rare	englisch gebraten, schwach gebraten	durch	well done
		halb durchgebraten	medium
roast	gebraten, geröstet	püriert	puréed
stewed	geschmort	schwach gebraten	rare
well done	durch		

desserts	Nachspeisen	Nachspeisen	desserts
cheese	Käse	Kaiserschmarren (Aust.)	pancake strips sprinkled with sugar and raisins
cheeseboard	Käseplatte		
chocolate gateau	Schokoladen-torte	Kompott	stewed fruit
fruit	Obst	Kuchen	cake
fruit tart	Obsttorte	Nockerln (Aust.)	sweet dumplings
ice cream	Eis		
pie	Obstkuchen	rote Grütze	red-berry compote

side dishes/ condiments	Beilagen/ Gewürze	Beilagen/ Gewürze	side dishes/ condiments
bread	Brot	Brot	bread
butter	Butter	Brötchen	rolls
herbs	Gewürzkräuter	Butter	butter
mayonnaise	Majonäse	Essig	vinegar
mustard	Senf	Gewürze	seasoning

17

olive oil	Olivenöl	Gewürzkräuter	herbs
pepper	Pfeffer	Majonäse	mayonnaise
rolls	Brötchen, Semmeln (*Aust.*)	Olivenöl	olive oil
		Pfeffer	pepper
salt	Salz	Salz	salt
sauce	Soße	Semmeln (*Aust.*)	rolls
seasoning	Gewürze	Senf	mustard
vinegar	Essig	Soße	sauce

drinks Getränke | ## Getränke drinks

drinks	Getränke	Getränke	drinks
beer	Bier	alkoholfreies Getränk	soft drink
bottle	Flasche	Bier	beer
carbonated	mit Kohlensäure	Bier vom Fass	draught beer
draught beer	Bier vom Fass	Flasche	bottle
half-bottle	eine halbe Flasche	Likör	liqueur
liqueur	Likör	mit Kohlensäure	carbonated
red wine	Rotwein	ohne Kohlensäure	still
rosé	Rosé	Rosé	rosé
soft drink	alkoholfreies Getränk	Rotwein	red wine
spritzer	Schorle	Schoppenwein	wine by the glass
still	ohne Kohlensäure	Schorle	spritzer
table wine	Tafelwein	Tafelwein	table wine
white wine	Weißwein	Wein	wine
wine	Wein	Weißwein	white wine

18

Places to stay/Unterkunft

Camping Camping

we're looking for a campsite	wir suchen einen Campingplatz
can we pitch our tent here?	können wir hier zelten?
can we park our caravan here?	können wir unseren Wohnwagen hier parken?
do you have space for a caravan/tent?	haben Sie Platz für einen Wohnwagen/ein Zelt?
are there shopping facilities?	gibt es Einkaufsmöglichkeiten?
how much is it per night?	was kostet es pro Nacht?

At the hotel Im Hotel ⭐⭐⭐

I'd like a double/single room with bath	ich möchte ein Doppelzimmer/Einzelzimmer mit Bad
we have a reservation in the name of Milnes	wir haben auf den Namen Milnes reservieren lassen
I reserved two rooms	ich habe zwei Zimmer reservieren lassen
for three nights, from Friday to Sunday	für drei Nächte, von Freitag bis Sonntag
how much does the room cost?	was kostet das Zimmer?
I'd like to see the room first, please	ich möchte das Zimmer erst sehen, bitte
what time is breakfast?	wann gibt es Frühstück?
can I leave this in the safe?	kann ich das im Safe lassen?
bed and breakfast	Zimmer mit Frühstück
we'd like to stay another night	wir möchten noch eine Nacht bleiben
please call me at 7:30	bitte wecken Sie mich um 7:30
are there any messages for me?	hat jemand eine Nachricht für mich hinterlassen?

19

Hostels | Jugendherbergen und Heime

could you tell me where the youth hostel is?	können Sie mir sagen, wo die Jugendherberge ist?
what time does the hostel close?	um wie viel Uhr macht das Heim zu?
I spent the night in a youth hostel	ich habe in einer Jugendherberge übernachtet
the hostel we're staying in is great value	unsere Herberge ist sehr preiswert
I'm staying in a youth hostel	ich wohne in einer Jugendherberge
I know a really good youth hostel in Dublin	ich kenne eine sehr gute Jugendherberge in Dublin
I'd like to go backpacking in Australia	ich würde gern in Australien mit dem Rucksack herum reisen

Rooms to rent | Zimmer zu vermieten

I'm looking for a room with a reasonable rent	ich suche ein preiswertes Zimmer
I'd like to rent an apartment for three weeks	ich möchte eine Wohnung für drei Wochen mieten
where do I find out about rooms to let?	wo kann man sich nach Fremdenzimmern erkundigen?
what's the weekly rent for the apartment?	was kostet die Wohnung pro Woche?
I'm staying with friends at the moment	ich wohne zur Zeit bei Freunden
I rent an apartment on the outskirts of town	ich habe eine Wohnung am Stadtrand gemietet
the room's fine—I'll take it	das Zimmer ist gut—ich nehme es

Shopping and money/Einkaufen und Geld

At the bank In der Bank

I'd like to change some money	ich möchte gern Geld wechseln
I want to change 100 euros into pounds	ich möchte 100 Euro[s] in Pfund wechseln
do you take Eurocheques?	nehmen Sie Euroschecks?
what's the exchange rate today?	wie steht der Wechselkurs heute?
I prefer traveller's cheques (*Amer* traveler's checks) to cash	mir sind Reiseschecks lieber als Bargeld
I'd like to transfer some money from my account	ich möchte Geld von meinem Konto überweisen
I'll get some money from the cash machine/ATM	ich hole mir Geld vom Automaten
a £50 cheque (*Amer* check)	ein Scheck über 50 Pfund
can I cash this cheque (*Amer* check) here?	kann ich diesen Scheck hier einlösen?
can I get some cash with my credit card?	kann ich auf meine Kreditkarte Bargeld bekommen?

Finding the right shop Das richtige Geschäft finden

where's the main shopping district?	wo ist das Haupteinkaufsviertel?
is the shopping centre (*Amer* mall) far from here?	ist das Einkaufszentrum weit von hier?
where's a good place to buy shoes/sunglasses?	wo kauft man am besten Schuhe/eine Sonnenbrille?
where can I buy batteries/postcards?	wo kann ich Batterien/Postkarten kaufen?
where's the nearest pharmacy (*Amer* drugstore)?	wo ist die nächste Apotheke?
what time do the shops open/close?	um wie viel Uhr machen die Läden auf/zu?
where did you get those?	wo hast du die her?
I'm looking for a present for my mother	ich suche ein Geschenk für meine Mutter

21

Are you being served? Werden Sie schon bedient?

how much does that cost?	was kostet das?
can I try it on?	kann ich es anprobieren?
can you keep it for me?	können Sie es mir zurücklegen?
could you gift-wrap it for me, please?	können Sie es bitte als Geschenk einpacken?
please wrap it up well	verpacken Sie es bitte gut
can I pay by credit card/cheque (*Amer* check)?	kann ich mit Kreditkarte/Scheck zahlen?
do you have this in another colour?	haben Sie das in einer anderen Farbe?
I'm just looking	ich sehe mich nur um
a receipt, please	eine Quittung, bitte
I need a bigger size	ich brauche die nächste Größe
I take a size...	ich habe Größe...
it doesn't suit me	das steht mir nicht

Changing things Umtauschen

can I have a refund?	kann ich mein Geld zurückbekommen?
can you mend it for me?	können Sie es mir reparieren?
can I speak to the manager?	kann ich den Geschäftsführer/ die Geschäftsführerin sprechen?
it doesn't work	es funktioniert nicht
I'd like to change the dress	ich möchte das Kleid umtauschen
I bought this here yesterday	ich habe das gestern hier gekauft

Currency Convertor		Währungsumrechner	
€/$	£/$	£/$	€/$
0.25		0.25	
0.50		0.50	
0.75		0.75	
1		1	
1.5		1.5	
2		2	
3		3	
5		5	
10		10	
20		20	
30		30	
40		40	
50		50	
100		100	
200		200	
1000		1000	

Sport and leisure/Freizeit und Sport

Keeping fit Wir halten uns fit

where can we play badminton/squash?	wo kann man Badminton/Squash spielen?
is there a local sports centre (*Amer* center)?	gibt es hier ein Sportzentrum?
we want to hire (*Amer* rent) skis/snowboards	wir möchten Skier/Snowboards mieten
what's the charge per day?	was kostet das pro Tag?
is there a reduction for children/a student discount?	gibt es eine Ermäßigung für Kinder/Studenten?
where can we go swimming/play football?	wo kann man schwimmen gehen/Fußball spielen?
are there any yoga/pilates classes here?	gibt es hier Yogakurse/Pilateskurse?
I want to do aerobics	ich möchte Aerobic machen
is there a hotel gym?	hat das Hotel ein Fitnesscenter?
do you have to be a member?	muss man Mitglied sein?
I would like to go fishing/riding	ich würde gern angeln gehen/reiten
I love playing baseball/tennis	ich spiele gern Baseball/Tennis
I play golf on Mondays	ich spiele jeden Montag Golf
would you like to play tennis/badminton?	möchten Sie Tennis/Badminton spielen?

Watching sport Zuschauen

is there a match (*Amer* game) on Saturday?	gibt es am Samstag ein Spiel?
who's playing?	wer spielt?
which teams are playing?	welche Mannschaften spielen?
where can I get tickets?	wo kann man Karten bekommen?
can you get me a ticket?	kannst du mir eine Karte besorgen?
I'd like to see a rugby match	ich würde gern ein Rugbyspiel sehen
let's watch the match on TV	sehen wir uns das Spiel im Fernsehen an
my favourite (*Amer* favorite) team is Bayern	ich bin ein Bayern-Fan
who's winning?	wer gewinnt?
the reds are winning 3-1	die Roten liegen 3 zu 1 in Führung

SPORTS

basketball	Basketball
cricket	Kricket
cycling	Radfahren
football/American football	American Football
football/soccer	Fußball
golf	Golf
hiking	Wandern
horse-riding	Reiten
ice-skating	Eislaufen
roller-blading	Inlineskaten
running	Laufen
skiing	Skifahren
snowboarding	Snowboarden
surfing	Surfen
swimming	Schwimmen

SPORTARTEN

Basketball	**basketball**
Bergsteigen	**climbing**
Eislaufen	**ice-skating**
Fußball	**football/soccer**
Handball	**handball**
Inlineskaten	**roller-blading**
Laufen	**running**
Leichtathlethik	**athletics**
Radfahren	**cycling**
Reiten	**horse-riding**
Schwimmen	**swimming**
Skifahren	**skiing**
Snowboarden	**snowboarding**
Surfen	**surfing**
Wandern	**hiking**

Going to the cinema/ theatre/club

Wir gehen ins Kino/ Theater/in einen Club

what's on at the cinema/ (*Amer*) at the movies?	was läuft im Kino?
what's on at the theatre?	was wird im Theater gespielt?
how long is the performance?	wie lange dauert die Vorstellung?
when does the box office open/close?	wann macht die Kasse auf/zu?
what time does the performance start?	um wie viel Uhr fängt die Aufführung an?
what time does the film (*Amer* movie) finish?	wann ist der Film zu Ende?
are there any tickets left?	gibt es noch Karten?
how much are the tickets?	was kosten die Karten?
where can I get a programme (*Amer* program)?	wo kann man ein Programm kaufen?
I want to book tickets for tonight	ich möchte für heute Abend Karten bestellen
I'd rather have seats in the stalls (*Amer* orchestra)/circle	ich hätte lieber Plätze im Parkett/ auf dem Balkon
we'd like to go to a club	wir wollen in einen Club gehen
I go clubbing every weekend	ich gehe am Wochenende immer in Clubs

Hobbies

Hobbys

do you have any hobbies?	hast du irgendwelche Hobbys?
what do you do at (*Amer* on) weekends?	was machst du/machen Sie immer am Wochenende?
I like reading/listening to music/ going out	ich lese gerne/höre gerne Musik/ gehe gerne aus
do you like watching TV/ shopping/travelling?	sehen Sie gerne fern?/gehen Sie gerne einkaufen?/verreisen Sie gerne?
I collect comics	ich sammle Comichefte/Comics

Good timing/Der richtige Zeitpunkt

Telling the time | Uhrzeit

could you tell me the time?	können Sie mir sagen, wie spät es ist?
what time is it?	wie viel Uhr ist es?
it's 2 o'clock	es ist zwei Uhr
at about 8 o'clock	gegen acht Uhr
at 9 o'clock tomorrow	morgen um neun Uhr
from 10 o'clock onwards	ab zehn Uhr
the meeting starts at 8 p.m.	die Besprechung fängt um zwanzig Uhr an/um acht Uhr abends
at 5 o'clock in the morning/afternoon	um fünf Uhr morgens/um fünf Uhr nachmittags (um siebzehn Uhr)
at exactly 1 o'clock	um Punkt eins
it's five past.../quarter past...	es ist fünf nach.../Viertel nach...
it's half past one	es ist halb zwei
it's twenty-five to one	es ist fünf nach halb eins
it's quarter to/five to one	es ist Viertel vor/fünf vor eins
a quarter of an hour	eine Viertelstunde
three quarters of an hour	eine Dreiviertelstunde

Days and dates | Wochentage und Datum

Sunday, Monday, Tuesday, Wednesday, Thursday, Friday, Saturday	Sonntag, Montag, Dienstag, Mittwoch, Donnerstag, Freitag, Samstag/Sonnabend
January, February, March, April, May, June, July, August, September, October, November, December	Januar, Februar, März, April, Mai, Juni, Juli, August, September, Oktober, November, Dezember
what's the date?	der Wievielte ist heute?

it's the second of June	heute ist der zweite Juni
we meet up every Monday	wir treffen uns jeden Montag
she comes on Tuesdays	sie kommt immer dienstags
we're going away in August	wir verreisen im August
I forgot it was the first of April today	ich habe ganz vergessen, dass heute der erste April ist
on November 8th	am achten November
about the 8th of June	um den 8. Juni

Public holidays and special days   Feste und Feiertage

Bank holiday	gesetzlicher Feiertag
New Year's Day (Jan 1)	Neujahr
Epiphany (Jan 6)	Heilige Drei Könige
St Valentine's Day (Feb 14)	Valentinstag
Shrove Tuesday	Fastnachtsdienstag/ Faschingsdienstag
Ash Wednesday	Aschermittwoch
Mothering Sunday/Mother's Day	Muttertag
Palm Sunday	Palmsonntag
Maundy Thursday	Gründonnerstag
Good Friday	Karfreitag
Easter Day	Ostersonntag
Easter Monday	Ostermontag
May Day (May 1)	der Erste Mai, Maifeiertag
Father's Day	Vatertag
Day of German Unity (Oct 3)	Tag der Deutschen Einheit
First Sunday in Advent	erster Advent
St Nicholas' Day (Dec 6)	Nikolaus
Christmas Eve	Heiligabend
Christmas Day (Dec 25)	erster Weihnachtstag
Boxing Day (Dec 26)	zweiter Weihnachtstag
New Year's Eve (Dec 31)	Silvester

Health and Beauty/
Gesundheit und Schönheit

At the doctor's Beim Arzt

can I see a doctor?	kann ich einen Arzt sehen?
I don't feel well	ich fühle mich schlecht
it hurts here	es tut hier weh
I have a migraine/headache	ich habe Migräne/Kopfschmerzen
the pain is getting worse	die Schmerzen werden immer schlimmer
I have a sore ankle/wrist/knee	mein Knöchel/Handgelenk/Knie tut weh
are there any side effects?	gibt es Nebenwirkungen?

YOU WILL HEAR: SIE HÖREN:

Sie müssen sich einen Termin geben lassen	you need to make an appointment
bitte setzen Sie sich	please take a seat
haben Sie eine Europäische Versicherungskarte?	do you have a European Health Insurance Card?
haben Sie Krankenversicherung?	do you have health insurance?
ich muss Ihren Blutdruck messen	I need to take your blood pressure

MORE USEFUL WORDS: NÜTZLICHE WÖRTER:

nurse	Krankenschwester
antibiotics	Antibiotika
medicine	Medikament
infection	Infektion
treatment	Behandlung
(bed)rest	(Bett)ruhe

At the pharmacy — In der Apotheke

can I have some painkillers?	kann ich ein Schmerzmittel haben?
I have asthma/hay fever/eczema	ich habe Asthma/Heuschnupfen/ein Ekzem
I've been stung by a wasp/bee	mich hat eine Wespe/Biene gestochen
I've got a cold/cough/the flu	ich bin erkältet/ich habe Husten/Grippe
I need something for diarrhoea/stomachache	ich brauche etwas gegen Durchfall/Magenschmerzen
I'm pregnant	ich bin schwanger

YOU WILL HEAR: — SIE HÖREN:

haben Sie diese Tabletten schon einmal eingenommen?	have you taken these tablets before?
tragen Sie diese Salbe dreimal täglich auf	apply this ointment three times a day
zu den Mahlzeiten/auf nüchternen Magen einnehmen	take at mealtimes/on an empty stomach
sind Sie gegen irgendetwas allergisch?	are you allergic to anything?
nehmen Sie andere Medikamente ein?	are you taking any other medication?

MORE USEFUL WORDS: — NÜTZLICHE WÖRTER:

plasters (*Amer* Band-Aid™)	Pflaster
insect repellent	Insektenschutzmittel
contraception	Verhütungsmittel
sun cream	Sonnencreme
aftersun	After-Sun-Produkt
dosage	Dosierung

At the hairdresser's/salon   Beim Friseur

I'd like a cut and blow dry	bitte schneiden und föhnen
just a trim please	bitte nur nachschneiden
a short back and sides	ein kurzer Haarschnitt
I'd like my hair washed first please	bitte waschen Sie mir zuerst die Haare
can I have a manicure/pedicure/facial?	kann ich eine Maniküre/Pediküre/Gesichtsbehandlung haben?
how much is a head/back massage?	was kostet eine Kopfmassage/Rückenmassage?
can I see a price list?	kann ich die Preisliste sehen?
do you offer reflexology/aromatherapy treatments?	bieten Sie Reflexzonenmassage/Aromatherapie an?

YOU WILL HEAR:	SIE HÖREN:
möchten Sie die Haare geföhnt haben?	would you like your hair blow-dried?
wo tragen Sie den Scheitel?	where is your parting (*Amer* part)?
möchten Sie die Haare stufig geschnitten haben?	would you like your hair layered?

MORE USEFUL WORDS:	NÜTZLICHE WÖRTER:
dry/greasy/fine/flyaway/frizzy	trocken/fettig/fein/fliegend/kraus
highlights	helle Strähnchen
extensions	Haarverlängerung
sunbed	Sonnenbank
leg/arm/bikini wax	Wachsbehandlung der Beine/Arme/Bikinizone

At the dentist's   Beim Zahnarzt

I have toothache	ich habe Zahnschmerzen
I'd like an emergency appointment	ich hätte gern einen Notfalltermin
I have cracked a tooth	ich habe mir einen Zahn angebrochen
my gums are bleeding	mein Zahnfleisch blutet

YOU WILL HEAR:	SIE HÖREN:
machen Sie den Mund auf	open your mouth
Sie brauchen eine Füllung	you need a filling
wir müssen eine Röntgenaufnahme machen	we need to take an X-ray
bitte den Mund ausspülen	please rinse

MORE USEFUL WORDS:	NÜTZLICHE WÖRTER:
anaesthetic	Betäubung
root canal treatment	Wurzelkanalbehandlung
injection	Spritze
floss	Zahnseide

Weights & measures/Maße u. Gewichte

Length/Längenmaße

inches/Zoll	0.39	3.9	7.8	11.7	15.6	19.7	39
cm/Zentimeter	1	10	20	30	40	50	100

Distance/Entfernungen

miles/Meilen	0.62	6.2	12.4	18.6	24.9	31	62
km/Kilometer	1	10	20	30	40	50	100

Weight/Gewichte

pounds/Pfund	2.2	22	44	66	88	110	220
kg/Kilogramm	1	10	20	30	40	50	100

Capacity/Hohlmaße

gallons/Gallonen	0.22	2.2	4.4	6.6	8.8	11	22
litres/Liter	1	10	20	30	40	50	100

Temperature/Temperatur

°C	0	5	10	15	20	25	30	37	38	40
°F	32	41	50	59	68	77	86	98.4	100	104

Clothing and shoe sizes/Kleider- und Schuhgrößen

Women's clothing sizes/Damengrößen

UK	8	10	12	14	16	18
US	6	8	10	12	14	16
Continent	36	38	40	42	44	46

Men's clothing sizes/Herrengrößen

UK/US	36	38	40	42	44	46
Continent	46	48	50	52	54	56

Men's and women's shoes/Schuhgrößen

UK women	4	5	6	7	7.5	8			
UK men			6	7	8	9	10	11	
US		6.5	7.5	8.5	9.5	10.5	11.5	12.5	13.5	14.5
Continent	37	38	39	40	41	42	43	44	45

Aa

a /ə/, betont /eɪ/

vor einem Vokal **an**

● *indefinite article*
···▸ ein (*m*), eine (*f*), ein (*nt*). **a**
problem ein Problem. **an**
apple ein Apfel. **a cat** eine
Katze. have you got a pencil?
hast du einen Bleistift? I gave
it to a beggar ich gab es
einem Bettler

! There are some cases where
a is not translated, as
when talking about people's
professions or nationalities: **she
is a lawyer** sie ist Rechtsanwäl-
tin. **he's an Italian** er ist Ita-
liener

···▸ (*with 'not'*) kein (*m*), keine
(*f*), kein (*nt*), keine (*pl*). that's
not a problem/not a good
idea das ist kein Problem/keine
gute Idee. there was not a
chance that ... es bestand
keine Möglichkeit, dass .... she
did not say a word sie sagte
kein Wort. I didn't tell a soul
ich habe es keinem Menschen
gesagt

···▸ (*per; each*) pro. £300 a
week 300 Pfund pro Woche.
30 miles an hour 30 Meilen
pro Stunde. (*in prices*) it costs
90p a pound es kostet 90
Pence das Pfund.

aback /əˈbæk/ *adv* be taken ∼
verblüfft sein

abandon /əˈbændən/ *vt* verlassen;

(*give up*) aufgeben

abate /əˈbeɪt/ *vi* nachlassen

abattoir /ˈæbətwɑː(r)/ *n* Schlacht-
hof *m*

abb|ey /ˈæbɪ/ *n* Abtei *f*. ∼**ot** *n*
Abt *m*

abbreviat|e /əˈbriːvɪeɪt/ *vt* abkür-
zen. ∼**ion** *n* Abkürzung *f*

abdicat|e /ˈæbdɪkeɪt/ *vi* abdanken.
∼**ion** *n* Abdankung *f*

abdom|en /ˈæbdəmən/ *n* Unter-
leib *m*. ∼**inal** *adj* Unterleibs-

abduct /əbˈdʌkt/ *vt* entführen.
∼**ion** *n* Entführung *f*

aberration /æbəˈreɪʃn/ *n* Abweichung *f*; (*mental*) Verwirrung *f*

abeyance /əˈbeɪəns/ *n* in ∼ [zeit-
weilig] außer Kraft

abhor /əbˈhɔː(r)/ *vt* (*pt/pp* ab-
horred) verabscheuen. ∼**rent** *adj*
abscheulich

abide /əˈbaɪd/ *vt* (*pt/pp* abided)
(*tolerate*) aushalten; ausstehen
(*person*)

ability /əˈbɪlətɪ/ *n* Fähigkeit *f*; (*talent*) Begabung *f*

abject /ˈæbdʒekt/ *adj* erbärmlich;
(*humble*) demütig

ablaze /əˈbleɪz/ *adj* in Flammen

able /ˈeɪbl/ *adj* (-r, -st) fähig; be ∼
to do sth etw tun können. ∼-ˈbod-
ied *adj* körperlich gesund

ably /ˈeɪblɪ/ *adv* gekonnt

abnormal /æbˈnɔːml/ *adj* anormal; (*Med*) abnorm. ∼**ity** *n* Abnor-
mität *f*. ∼**ly** *adv* ungewöhnlich

aboard /əˈbɔːd/ *adv & prep* an Bord
(+ *gen*)

abolish /əˈbɒlɪʃ/ *vt* abschaffen.

a

~ition n Abschaffung f
abominable /ə'bɒmɪnəbl/ adj,
-bly adv abscheulich
aborigines /æbə'rɪdʒəni:z/ npl Ureinwohner pl
abort /ə'bɔːt/ vt abtreiben. ~ion n
Abtreibung f. ~ive adj (attempt)
vergeblich
about /ə'baʊt/ adv umher, herum;
(approximately) ungefähr; be ~ (in
circulation) umgehen; (in existence)
vorhanden sein; be ~ to do sth im
Begriff sein, etw zu tun; there was
no one ~ es war kein Mensch da;
run/play ~ herumlaufen/-spielen
● prep um (+ acc) [... herum]; (concerning) über (+ acc); what is it ~?
worum geht es? (book:) wovon handelt es? I know nothing ~ it ich
weiß nichts davon; talk/know ~
reden/wissen von
about: ~-face n, ~-turn n Kehrtwendung f
above /ə'bʌv/ adv oben ● prep
über (+ dat/acc); ~ all vor allem
above: ~-board adj legal.
~-mentioned adj oben erwähnt
abrasive /ə'breɪsɪv/ adj Scheuer-;
(remark) verletzend ● n Scheuermittel nt; (Techn) Schleifmittel nt
abreast /ə'brest/ adv nebeneinander; keep ~ of Schritt halten mit
abridge /ə'brɪdʒ/ vt kürzen
abroad /ə'brɔːd/ adv im Ausland;
go ~ ins Ausland fahren
abrupt /ə'brʌpt/ adj abrupt; (sudden) plötzlich; (curt) schroff
abscess /'æbsɪs/ n Abszess m
absence /'æbsəns/ n Abwesenheit f
absent /'æbsənt/ adj abwesend; be
~ fehlen
absentee /æbsən'ti:/ n Abwesende(r) m/f
absent-minded /æbsənt

absolute /'æbsəlu:t/ adj absolut
absorb /əb'sɔːb/ vt absorbieren,
aufsaugen; ~ed in vertieft in (+
acc). ~ent adj saugfähig
absorption /əb'sɔːpʃn/ n Absorption f
abstain /əb'steɪn/ vi sich enthalten
(from gen)
abstemious /əb'sti:mɪəs/ adj enthaltsam
abstention /əb'stenʃn/ n (Pol)
[Stimm]enthaltung f
abstract /'æbstrækt/ adj abstrakt
● n (summary) Abriss m
absurd /əb'sɜːd/ adj absurd. ~ity
n Absurdität f
abundan|ce /ə'bʌndəns/ n Fülle f
(of an + dat). ~t adj reichlich
abuse[1] /ə'bju:z/ vt missbrauchen;
(insult) beschimpfen
abuse[2] /ə'bju:s/ n Missbrauch m;
(insults) Beschimpfungen pl. ~ive
adj ausfallend
abysmal /ə'bɪzml/ adj 🔢 katastrophal
abyss /ə'bɪs/ n Abgrund m
academic /ækə'demɪk/ adj, -ally
adv akademisch
academy /ə'kædəmɪ/ n Akademie f
accelerat|e /ək'seləreɪt/ vt/i beschleunigen. ~ion n Beschleunigung f. ~or n (Auto) Gaspedal nt
accent /'æksənt/ n Akzent m
accept /ək'sept/ vt annehmen;
(fig) akzeptieren ● vi zusagen.
~able adj annehmbar. ~ance n
Annahme f; (of invitation) Zusage f
access /'ækses/ n Zugang m.
~ible adj zugänglich
accessor|y /ək'sesərɪ/ n (Jur) Mitschuldige(r) m/f; ~ies pl (fashion)

Accessoires pl; (Techn) Zubehör nt

accident /'æksɪdənt/ n Unfall m; (chance) Zufall m; **by ~** zufällig; (unintentionally) versehentlich. **~al** adj zufällig; (unintentional) versehentlich

acclaim /ə'kleɪm/ vt feiern (as als)

acclimatize /ə'klaɪmətaɪz/ vt become **~d** sich akklimatisieren

accommodat|e /ə'kɒmədeɪt/ vt unterbringen. **~ing** adj entgegenkommend. **~ion** n (rooms) Unterkunft f

accompan|iment /ə'kʌmpənɪmənt/ n Begleitung f. **~ist** n (Mus) Begleiter(in) m(f)

accompany /ə'kʌmpənɪ/ vt (pt/pp -ied) begleiten

accomplice /ə'kʌmplɪs/ n Komplize/-zin m/f

accomplish /ə'kʌmplɪʃ/ vt erfüllen (task); (achieve) erreichen. **~ed** adj fähig. **~ment** n Fertigkeit f; (achievement) Leistung f

accord /ə'kɔːd/ n **of one's own ~** aus eigenem Antrieb. **~ance** n **in ~ance with** entsprechend (+ dat)

according /ə'kɔːdɪŋ/ adv **~ to** nach (+ dat). **~ly** adv entsprechend

accordion /ə'kɔːdɪən/ n Akkordeon nt

account /ə'kaʊnt/ n Konto nt; (bill) Rechnung f; (description) Darstellung f; (report) Bericht m; **~s** pl (Comm) Bücher pl; **on ~** wegen (+ gen); **on no ~** auf keinen Fall; **take into ~** in Betracht ziehen, berücksichtigen ● vi **~ for** Rechenschaft ablegen für; (explain) erklären

accountant /ə'kaʊntənt/ n Buchhalter(in) m(f); (chartered) Wirtschaftsprüfer m

accumulat|e /ə'kjuːmjʊleɪt/ vt ansammeln, anhäufen ● vi sich ansammeln, sich anhäufen. **~ion** n

Ansammlung f, Anhäufung f

accura|cy /'ækjʊrəsɪ/ n Genauigkeit f. **~te** adj genau

accusation /ækjuːˈzeɪʃn/ n Anklage f

accusative /ə'kjuːzətɪv/ adj & n **~ [case]** (Gram) Akkusativ m

accuse /ə'kjuːz/ vt (Jur) anklagen (of gen); **~ s.o.** of doing sth jdn beschuldigen, etw getan zu haben

accustom /ə'kʌstəm/ vt gewöhnen (to an + dat); **grow** or **get ~ed** to sich gewöhnen an (+ acc). **~ed** adj gewohnt

ace /eɪs/ n (Cards, Sport) Ass nt

ache /eɪk/ n Schmerzen pl ● vi weh tun, schmerzen

achieve /ə'tʃiːv/ vt leisten; (gain) erzielen; (reach) erreichen. **~ment** n (feat) Leistung f

acid /'æsɪd/ adj sauer; (fig) beißend ● n Säure f. **~ity** n Säure f. **~ rain** n saurer Regen m

acknowledge /ək'nɒlɪdʒ/ vt anerkennen; (admit) zugeben; erwidern (greeting); **~ receipt of** den Empfang bestätigen (+ gen). **~ment** n Anerkennung f; (of letter) Empfangsbestätigung f

acne /'æknɪ/ n Akne f

acorn /'eɪkɔːn/ n Eichel f

acoustic /ə'kuːstɪk/ adj, **-ally** adv akustisch. **~s** npl Akustik f

acquaint /ə'kweɪnt/ vt **be ~ed with** kennen; vertraut sein mit (fact). **~ance** n (person) Bekannte(r) m/f; **make s.o.'s ~ance** jdn kennen lernen

acquire /ə'kwaɪə(r)/ vt erwerben

acquisit|ion /ækwɪ'zɪʃn/ n Erwerb m; (thing) Erwerbung f. **~ive** adj habgierig

acquit /ə'kwɪt/ vt (pt/pp acquitted) freisprechen

acre /'eɪkə(r)/ n ≈ Morgen m

a **acrimon|ious** /ˌækrɪˈməʊnɪəs/ adj bitter

acrobat /ˈækrəbæt/ n Akrobat(in) m(f). **~ic** adj akrobatisch

across /əˈkrɒs/ adv hinüber/herüber; (wide) breit; (not lengthwise) quer; (in crossword) waagerecht; **come ~** sth auf etw (acc) stoßen; **go ~** hinübergehen; **bring ~** herüberbringen ● prep über (+ acc); (on the other side of) auf der anderen Seite (+ gen)

act /ækt/ n Tat f; (action) Handlung f; (law) Gesetz nt; (Theat) Akt m; (item) Nummer f ● vi handeln; (behave) sich verhalten; (Theat) spielen; (pretend) sich verstellen; **~ as** fungieren als ● vt spielen (role). **~ing** adj (deputy) stellvertretend ● n (Theat) Schauspielerei f

action /ˈækʃn/ n Handlung f; (deed) Tat f; (Mil) Einsatz m; (Jur) Klage f; (effect) Wirkung f; (Techn) Mechanismus m; **out of ~** (machine:) außer Betrieb; **take ~** handeln; **killed in ~** gefallen

activate /ˈæktɪveɪt/ vt betätigen

activ|e /ˈæktɪv/ adj aktiv; **on ~e** service im Einsatz. **~ity** n Aktivität f

act|or /ˈæktə(r)/ n Schauspieler m. **~ress** n Schauspielerin f

actual /ˈæktʃʊəl/ adj eigentlich; (real) tatsächlich

acupuncture /ˈækjʊ-/ n Akupunktur f

acute /əˈkjuːt/ adj scharf; (angle) spitz; (illness) akut. **~ly** adv sehr

ad /æd/ n 1 = advertisement

AD abbr (Anno Domini) n.Chr.

adamant /ˈædəmənt/ adj be ~ that darauf bestehen, dass

adapt /əˈdæpt/ vt anpassen; bearbeiten (play) ● vi sich anpassen. **~able** adj anpassungsfähig

adaptation /ædæpˈteɪʃn/ n (Theat) Bearbeitung f

add /æd/ vt hinzufügen; (Math) addieren ● vi zusammenzählen, addieren; **~ to** hinzufügen zu; (fig: increase) steigern; (compound) verschlimmern. **~ up** vt zusammenzählen (figures) ● vi zusammenzählen, addieren

adder /ˈædə(r)/ n Kreuzotter f

addict /ˈædɪkt/ n Süchtige(r) m/f

addict|ed /əˈdɪktɪd/ adj süchtig; **~ed to drugs** drogensüchtig. **~ion** n Sucht f

addition /əˈdɪʃn/ n Hinzufügung f; (Math) Addition f; (thing added) Ergänzung f; **in ~** zusätzlich. **~al** adj zusätzlich

additive /ˈædɪtɪv/ n Zusatz m

address /əˈdres/ n Adresse f, Anschrift f; (speech) Ansprache f ● vt adressieren (to an + acc); (speak to) anreden (person); sprechen vor (+ dat) (meeting). **~ee** n Empfänger m

adequate /ˈædɪkwət/ adj ausreichend

adhere /ədˈhɪə(r)/ vi kleben/(fig) festhalten (to an + dat)

adhesive /ədˈhiːsɪv/ adj klebend ● n Klebstoff m

adjacent /əˈdʒeɪsnt/ adj angrenzend

adjective /ˈædʒɪktɪv/ n Adjektiv nt

adjoin /əˈdʒɔɪn/ vt angrenzen an (+ acc). **~ing** adj angrenzend

adjourn /əˈdʒɜːn/ vt vertagen (until auf + acc) ● vi sich vertagen. **~ment** n Vertagung f

adjudicate /əˈdʒuːdɪkeɪt/ vi (in competition) Preisrichter sein

adjust /əˈdʒʌst/ vt einstellen; (alter) verstellen ● vi sich anpassen (to dat). **~able** adj verstellbar. **~ment** n Einstellung f; Anpassung f

ad lib /ædˈlɪb/ adv aus dem Stegreif ● *vi* (*pt/pp* ad libbed) ⊤ improvisieren

administer /ədˈmɪnɪstə(r)/ *vt* verwalten; verabreichen (*medicine*)

administration /ədmɪnɪˈstreɪʃn/ *n* Verwaltung *f*; (*Pol*) Regierung *f*

admirable /ˈædmərəbl/ *adj* bewundernswert

admiral /ˈædmərəl/ *n* Admiral *m*

admiration /ædməˈreɪʃn/ *n* Bewunderung *f*

admire /ədˈmaɪə(r)/ *vt* bewundern. ~**r** *n* Verehrer(in) *m*(*f*)

admission /ədˈmɪʃn/ *n* Eingeständnis *nt*; (*entry*) Eintritt *m*

admit /ədˈmɪt/ *vt* (*pt/pp* admitted) (*let in*) hereinlassen; (*acknowledge*) zugeben; ~ **to** sich etw zugeben. ~**tance** *n* Eintritt *m*. ~**tedly** *adv* zugegebenermaßen

admonish /ədˈmɒnɪʃ/ *vt* ermahnen

adolescen|ce /ædəˈlesns/ *n* Jugend *f*, Pubertät *f*. ~**t** *adj* Jugend-; (*boy, girl*) halbwüchsig ● *n* Jugendliche(r) *m*(*f*)

adopt /əˈdɒpt/ *vt* adoptieren; ergreifen (*measure*); (*Pol*) annehmen (*candidate*). ~**ion** *n* Adoption *f*

ador|able /əˈdɔːrəbl/ *adj* bezaubernd. ~**ation** *n* Anbetung *f*

adore /əˈdɔː(r)/ *vt* (*worship*) anbeten; (⊤: *like*) lieben

adorn /əˈdɔːn/ *vt* schmücken. ~**ment** *n* Schmuck *m*

Adriatic /eɪdrɪˈætɪk/ *adj* & *n* ~ [Sea] Adria *f*

adrift /əˈdrɪft/ *adj* be ~ treiben

adroit /əˈdrɔɪt/ *adj* gewandt, geschickt

adulation /ædjʊˈleɪʃn/ *n* Schwärmerei *f*

adult /ˈædʌlt/ *n* Erwachsene(r) *m*(*f*)

adulterate /əˈdʌltəreɪt/ *vt* verfälschen; panschen (*wine*)

adultery /əˈdʌltərɪ/ *n* Ehebruch *m*

advance /ədˈvɑːns/ *n* Fortschritt *m*; (*Mil*) Vorrücken *nt*; (*payment*) Vorschuss *m*; **in** ~ im Voraus ● *vi* vorankommen; (*Mil*) vorrücken; (*make progress*) Fortschritte machen ● *vt* fördern (*cause*); vorbringen (*idea*); vorschießen (*money*). ~**d** *adj* fortgeschritten; (*progressive*) fortschrittlich. ~**ment** *n* Förderung *f*; (*promotion*) Beförderung *f*

advantage /ədˈvɑːntɪdʒ/ *n* Vorteil *m*; **take** ~ **of** ausnutzen. ~**ous** *adj* vorteilhaft

adventur|e /ədˈventʃə(r)/ *n* Abenteuer *nt*. ~**er** *n* Abenteurer *m*. ~**ous** *adj* abenteuerlich; (*person*) abenteuerlustig

adverb /ˈædvɜːb/ *n* Adverb *nt*

adverse /ˈædvɜːs/ *adj* ungünstig

advert /ˈædvɜːt/ *n* ⊤ = advertisement

advertise /ˈædvətaɪz/ *vt* Reklame machen für; (*by small ad*) inserieren ● *vi* Reklame machen, inserieren

advertisement /ədˈvɜːtɪsmənt/ *n* Anzeige *f*; (*publicity*) Reklame *f*; (*small ad*) Inserat *nt*

advertis|er /ˈædvətaɪzə(r)/ *n* Inserent *m*. ~**ing** *n* Werbung *f*

advice /ədˈvaɪs/ *n* Rat *m*

advisable /ədˈvaɪzəbl/ *adj* ratsam

advis|e /ədˈvaɪz/ *vt* raten (s.o. jdm); (*counsel*) beraten; (*inform*) benachrichtigen; ~ **s.o. against sth** jdm von etw abraten ● *vi* raten. ~**er** *n* Berater(in) *m*(*f*). ~**ory** *adj* beratend

advocate¹ /ˈædvəkət/ *n* (*supporter*) Befürworter *m*

advocate² /ˈædvəkeɪt/ *vt* befürworten

aerial /ˈeərɪəl/ *adj* Luft- ● *n*

a

Antenne f

aerobics /eəˈrəʊbɪks/ n Aerobic nt

aero|drome /ˈeərədrəʊm/ n Flugplatz m. **~plane** n Flugzeug nt

aerosol /ˈeərəsɒl/ n Spraydose f

aesthetic /iːsˈθetɪk/ adj ästhetisch

affair /əˈfeə(r)/ n Angelegenheit f, Sache f; (scandal) Affäre f; [love-]~ [Liebes]verhältnis nt

affect /əˈfekt/ vt sich auswirken auf (+ acc); (concern) betreffen; (move) rühren; (pretend) vortäuschen. **~ation** n Affektiertheit f. **~ed** adj affektiert

affection /əˈfekʃn/ n Liebe f. **~ate** adj liebevoll

affirm /əˈfɜːm/ vt behaupten

affirmative /əˈfɜːmətɪv/ adj bejahend ● n Bejahung f

afflict /əˈflɪkt/ vt be ~ed with behaftet sein mit. **~ion** n Leiden nt

affluen|ce /ˈæflʊəns/ n Reichtum m. **~t** adj wohlhabend. **~t society** n Wohlstandsgesellschaft f

afford /əˈfɔːd/ vt be able to ~ sth sich (dat) etw leisten können. **~able** adj erschwinglich

affront /əˈfrʌnt/ n Beleidigung f ● vt beleidigen

afloat /əˈfləʊt/ adj be ~ (ship:) flott sein; keep ~ (person:) sich über Wasser halten

afraid /əˈfreɪd/ adj be ~ Angst haben (of vor + dat); I'm ~ not leider nicht; I'm ~ so [ja] leider

Africa /ˈæfrɪkə/ n Afrika nt. **~n** adj afrikanisch ● n Afrikaner(in) m(f)

after /ˈɑːftə(r)/ adv danach ● prep nach (+ dat); ~ that danach; ~ all schließlich; the day ~ tomorrow übermorgen; be ~ aus sein auf (+ acc) ● conj nachdem

after: **~-effect** n Nachwirkung f. **~math** /-mɑːθ/ n Auswirkungen pl. **~'noon** n Nachmittag m; good

~noon! int guten Tag! **~-sales service** n Kundendienst m. **~shave** n Rasierwasser nt. **~thought** n nachträglicher Einfall m. **~wards** adv nachher

again /əˈgen/ adv wieder; (once more) noch einmal; ~ and ~ immer wieder

against /əˈgenst/ prep gegen (+ acc)

age /eɪdʒ/ n Alter nt; (era) Zeitalter nt; ~s 🗆 ewig; under ~ minderjährig; of ~ volljährig; two years of ~ zwei Jahre alt ● v (pres p ageing) ● vt älter machen ● vi altern; (mature) reifen

aged¹ /eɪdʒd/ adj ~ two zwei Jahre alt

aged² /ˈeɪdʒɪd/ adj betagt ● n the ~ pl die Alten

ageless /ˈeɪdʒlɪs/ adj ewig jung

agency /ˈeɪdʒənsɪ/ n Agentur f; (office) Büro nt

agenda /əˈdʒendə/ n Tagesordnung f

agent /ˈeɪdʒənt/ n Agent(in) m(f); (Comm) Vertreter(in) m(f); (substance) Mittel nt

aggravat|e /ˈægrəveɪt/ vt verschlimmern; (🗆: annoy) ärgern. **~ion** 🗆 Ärger m

aggregate /ˈægrɪgət/ adj gesamt ● n Gesamtzahl f; (sum) Gesamtsumme f

aggression /əˈgreʃn/ n Aggression f. **~ive** adj aggressiv. **~or** n Angreifer(in) m(f)

aggro /ˈægrəʊ/ n 🗆 Ärger m

aghast /əˈgɑːst/ adj entsetzt

agil|e /ˈædʒaɪl/ adj flink, behände; (mind) wendig. **~ity** n Flinkheit f, Behändigkeit f

agitat|e /ˈædʒɪteɪt/ vt bewegen; (shake) schütteln ● vi (fig) ~ for agitieren für. **~ed** adj erregt. **~ion**

n Erregung *f*; (*Pol*) Agitation *f*

ago /əˈɡəʊ/ *adv* vor (+ *dat*); a long time ~ vor langer Zeit; how long ~ is it? wie lange ist es her?

agony /ˈæɡənɪ/ *n* Qual *f*; be in ~ furchtbare Schmerzen haben

agree /əˈɡriː/ *vt* vereinbaren; (*admit*) zugeben; ~ to do sth sich bereit erklären, etw zu tun ● *vi* (*people, figures*) übereinstimmen; (*reach agreement*) sich einigen; (*get on*) gut miteinander auskommen; (*consent*) einwilligen (to in + *acc*); ~ with s.o. jdm zustimmen; (*food*) jdm bekommen; ~ with sth (*approve of*) mit etw einverstanden sein

agreeable /əˈɡriːəbl/ *adj* angenehm

agreed /əˈɡriːd/ *adj* vereinbart

agreement /əˈɡriːmənt/ *n* Übereinstimmung *f*; (*consent*) Einwilligung *f*; (*contract*) Abkommen *nt*; reach ~ sich einigen

agricultur|al /æɡrɪˈkʌltʃərəl/ *adj* landwirtschaftlich. ~e *n* Landwirtschaft *f*

aground /əˈɡraʊnd/ *adj* gestrandet; run ~ (*ship*) stranden

ahead /əˈhed/ *adv* straight ~ geradeaus; be ~ of s.o./sth jdm/ etw sein; (*fig*) voraus sein; go on ~ vorgehen; go ~ vorankommen; go ~! ① bitte! look/plan ~ vorausblicken/-planen

aid /eɪd/ *n* Hilfe *f*; (*financial*) Unterstützung *f*; in ~ of zugunsten (+ *gen*) ● *vt* helfen (+ *dat*)

Aids /eɪdz/ *n* Aids *nt*

aim /eɪm/ *n* Ziel *nt*; take ~ zielen ● *vt* richten (at auf + *acc*); *vi* zielen (at auf + *acc*); ~ to do sth beabsichtigen, etw zu tun. ~less *adj* ziellos

air /eə(r)/ *n* Luft *f*; (*expression*)

Miene *f*; (*appearance*) Anschein *m*; be on the ~ (*programme*) gesendet werden; (*person*) auf Sendung sein; by ~ auf dem Luftweg; (*air-mail*) mit Luftpost ● *vt* lüften; vorbringen (*views*)

air: **~ bag** *n* (*Auto*) Airbag *m*. **~-conditioned** *adj* klimatisiert. **~-conditioning** *n* Klimaanlage *f*. **~craft** *n* Flugzeug *nt*. **~field** *n* Flugplatz *m*. **~ force** *n* Luftwaffe *f*. **~ freshener** *n* Raumspray *nt*. **~gun** *n* Luftgewehr *nt*. **~ hostess** *n* Stewardess *f*. **~ letter** *n* Aerogramm *nt*. **~line** *n* Fluggesellschaft *f*. **~mail** *n* Luftpost *f*. **~man** *n* Flieger *m*. **~plane** *n* (*Amer*) Flugzeug *nt*. **~port** *n* Flughafen *m*. **~-raid** *n* Luftangriff *m*. **~-raid shelter** *n* Luftschutzbunker *m*. **~ship** *n* Luftschiff *nt*. **~ ticket** *n* Flugticket *nt*. **~tight** *adj* luftdicht. **~-traffic controller** *n* Fluglotse *m*

airy /ˈeərɪ/ *adj* luftig; (*manner*) nonchalant

aisle /aɪl/ *n* Gang *m*

ajar /əˈdʒɑː(r)/ *adj* angelehnt

alarm /əˈlɑːm/ *n* Alarm *m*; (*device*) Alarmanlage *f*; (*clock*) Wecker *m*; (*fear*) Unruhe *f* ● *vt* erschrecken

alas /əˈlæs/ *int* ach!

album /ˈælbəm/ *n* Album *nt*

alcohol /ˈælkəhɒl/ *n* Alkohol *m*. **~ic** *adj* alkoholisch ● *n* Alkoholiker(in) *m* (*f*). **~ism** *n* Alkoholismus *m*

alert /əˈlɜːt/ *adj* aufmerksam ● *n* Alarm *m*

algebra /ˈældʒɪbrə/ *n* Algebra *f*

Algeria /ælˈdʒɪərɪə/ *n* Algerien *nt*

alias /ˈeɪlɪəs/ *n* Deckname *m* ● *adv* alias

alibi /ˈælɪbaɪ/ *n* Alibi *nt*

alien /ˈeɪlɪən/ *adj* fremd ● *n* Ausländer(in) *m* (*f*)

alienate /ˈeɪlɪəneɪt/ *vt* entfremden

a

alight¹ /ə'laɪt/ vi aussteigen (from aus)

alight² adj be ~ brennen; set ~ anzünden

align /ə'laɪn/ vt ausrichten. ~ment n Ausrichtung f

alike /ə'laɪk/ adj & adv ähnlich; (same) gleich; look ~ sich (dat) ähnlich sehen

alive /ə'laɪv/ adj lebendig; be ~ leben; be ~ with wimmeln von

---

all /ɔːl/

● adjective

····▸ (plural) alle. all [the] children alle Kinder. all our children alle unsere Kinder. all the books alle Bücher. all the others alle anderen

····▸ (singular = whole) ganz. all the wine der ganze Wein. all the town die ganze Stadt. all my money mein ganzes Geld; all mein Geld. all day den ganzen Tag. all Germany ganz Deutschland

● pronoun

····▸ (plural = all persons/things) alle. all are welcome alle sind willkommen. they all came sie sind alle gekommen. are we all here? sind wir alle da? the best pupils of all die besten Schüler (von allen). the most beautiful of all der/die/das schönste von allen

····▸ (singular = everything) alles. that is all das ist alles. all that I possess alles, was ich besitze

····▸ all of ganz; (with plural) alle. all of the money das ganze Geld. all of the paintings alle Gemälde. all of you/them Sie/sie alle

····▸ (in phrases) all in alles in

allem. in all insgesamt. most of all am meisten. once and for all ein für alle Mal. not at all gar nicht

● adverb

····▸ (completely) ganz. she was all alone sie war ganz allein. I was all dirty ich war ganz schmutzig

····▸ (in scores) four all vier zu vier

····▸ (all right (things) in Ordnung. is everything all right? ist alles in Ordnung? is that all right for you? passt das Ihnen? I'm all right mir geht es gut. did you get home all right? sind Sie gut nach Hause gekommen? is it all right to go in? kann ich reingehen? yes, all right ja, gut. work out all right gut gehen; klappen 🆃

····▸ (in phrases) all but (almost) fast. all at once auf einmal. all the better umso besser. all the same (nevertheless) trotzdem

---

allege /ə'ledʒ/ vt behaupten. ~d adj angeblich

allegiance /ə'liːdʒəns/ n Treue f

allerg|ic /ə'lɜːdʒɪk/ adj allergisch (to gegen). ~y n Allergie f

alleviate /ə'liːvɪeɪt/ vt lindern

alley /'ælɪ/ n Gasse f; (for bowling) Bahn f

alliance /ə'laɪəns/ n Verbindung f; (Pol) Bündnis nt

allied /'ælaɪd/ adj alliiert

alligator /'ælɪɡeɪtə(r)/ n Alligator m

allocat|e /'æləkeɪt/ vt zuteilen; (share out) verteilen. ~ion n Zuteilung f

allot /ə'lɒt/ vt (pt/pp allotted) zuteilen (s.o. jdm)

allow /ə'laʊ/ vt erlauben; (give)

geben; (*grant*) gewähren; (*reckon*) rechnen; (*agree, admit*) zugeben; ~ for berücksichtigen; ~ s.o. to do sth jdm erlauben, etw zu tun; be ~ed to do sth etw tun dürfen

allowance /əˈlaʊəns/ n (*finanzielle*) Unterstützung f; make ~s for berücksichtigen

alloy /ˈælɔɪ/ n Legierung f

allude /əˈluːd/ vi anspielen (to auf + acc)

allusion /əˈluːʒn/ n Anspielung f

ally[1] /ˈælaɪ/ n Verbündete(r) m/f; **the Allies** pl die Alliierten

ally[2] /əˈlaɪ/ vt (pt/pp -ied) verbinden; ~ oneself with sich verbünden mit

almighty /ɔːlˈmaɪti/ adj allmächtig; (□: big) Riesen-. ●n the A~ der Allmächtige

almond /ˈɑːmənd/ n (Bot) Mandel f

almost /ˈɔːlməʊst/ adv fast, beinahe

alone /əˈləʊn/ adj & adv allein; leave me ~ lass mich in Ruhe; leave that ~! lass die Finger davon! let ~ ganz zu schweigen von

along /əˈlɒŋ/ prep entlang (+ acc); ~ the river den Fluss entlang ●adv ~ with zusammen mit; all ~ die ganze Zeit; come ~ komm doch; I'll bring it ~ ich bringe es mit

along'side adv daneben ●prep neben (+ dat)

aloud /əˈlaʊd/ adv laut

alphabet /ˈælfəbɛt/ n Alphabet nt. ~ical adj alphabetisch

alpine /ˈælpaɪn/ adj alpin; A~ Alpen-

Alps /ælps/ npl Alpen pl

already /ɔːlˈrɛdi/ adv schon

Alsace /ælˈsæs/ n Elsass nt

Alsatian /ælˈseɪʃn/ n (dog) [deut-

scher] Schäferhund m

also /ˈɔːlsəʊ/ adv auch

altar /ˈɔːltə(r)/ n Altar m

alter /ˈɔːltə(r)/ vt ändern ●vi sich verändern. ~ation n Änderung f

alternate[1] /ˈɔːltəneɪt/ vi [sich] abwechseln ●vt abwechseln

alternate[2] /ɔːlˈtɜːnət/ adj abwechselnd; on ~ days jeden zweiten Tag

alternative /ɔːlˈtɜːnətɪv/ adj andere(r,s); ~ medicine Alternativmedizin f ●n Alternative f. ~ly adv oder aber

although /ɔːlˈðəʊ/ conj obgleich, obwohl

altitude /ˈæltɪtjuːd/ n Höhe f

altogether /ɔːltəˈgɛðə(r)/ adv insgesamt; (on the whole) alles in allem

aluminium /æljʊˈmɪnɪəm/ n, (Amer) **aluminum** n Aluminium nt

always /ˈɔːlweɪz/ adv immer

am /æm/ see **be**

a.m. abbr (ante meridiem) vormittags

amass /əˈmæs/ vt anhäufen

amateur /ˈæmətə(r)/ n Amateur m ●attrib Amateur-; (Theat) Laien-. ~ish adj laienhaft

amaze /əˈmeɪz/ vt erstaunen. ~d adj erstaunt. ~ment n Erstaunen nt

amazing /əˈmeɪzɪŋ/ adj erstaunlich

ambassador /æmˈbæsədə(r)/ n Botschafter m

amber /ˈæmbə(r)/ n Bernstein m ●adj (colour) gelb

ambigu|ity /æmbɪˈgjuːəti/ n Zweideutigkeit f. ~ous adj -ly adv zweideutig

ambiti|on /æmˈbɪʃn/ n Ehrgeiz m; (aim) Ambition f. ~ous adj ehrgeizig

a

amble /'æmbl/ vi schlendern

ambulance /'æmbjʊləns/ n Krankenwagen m. ~ **man** n Sanitäter m

ambush /'æmbʊʃ/ n Hinterhalt m ● vt aus dem Hinterhalt überfallen

amen /ɑː'men/ int amen

amend /ə'mend/ vt ändern. ~**ment** n Änderung f

amenities /ə'miːnətiz/ npl Einrichtungen pl

America /ə'merɪkə/ n Amerika nt. ~**n** adj amerikanisch ● n Amerikaner(in) m(f). ~**nism** n Amerikanismus m

> **American dream** Der Glaube, dass Amerika das Land unbegrenzter Möglichkeiten ist, in dem jeder sein Leben erfolgreich gestalten kann. Für Minderheiten und Einwanderer bedeutet der Traum weitgehende Toleranz und Anspruch auf eigene freie Lebensgestaltung. Der American dream verkörpert eine optimistische allgemeine Grundhaltung mit auf Erfolg gerichtetem Denken und Handeln.

amiable /'eɪmɪəbl/ adj nett

amicable /'æmɪkəbl/ adj, **-bly** adv freundschaftlich; (agreement) gütlich

amid[st] /ə'mɪd[st]/ prep inmitten (+ gen)

ammonia /ə'məʊnɪə/ n Ammoniak nt

ammunition /æmjʊ'nɪʃn/ n Munition f

amnesty /'æmnəstɪ/ n Amnestie f

among[st] /ə'mʌŋ[st]/ prep unter (+ dat/acc); ~ **yourselves** untereinander

amoral /eɪ'mɒrəl/ adj amoralisch

amorous /'æmərəs/ adj zärtlich

amount /ə'maʊnt/ n Menge f;

(sum of money) Betrag m; (total) Gesamtsumme f ● vi ~ **to** sich belaufen auf (+ acc); (fig) hinauslaufen auf (+ acc)

amphibi|an /æm'fɪbɪən/ n Amphibie f. ~**ous** adj amphibisch

amphitheatre /'æmfɪ-/ n Amphitheater nt

ample /'æmpl/ adj (-r,-st) reichlich; (large) füllig

amplif|ier /'æmplɪfaɪə(r)/ n Verstärker m. ~**y** vt (pt/pp -ied) weiter ausführen; verstärken (sound)

amputat|e /'æmpjʊteɪt/ vt amputieren. ~**ion** n Amputation f

amuse /ə'mjuːz/ vt amüsieren, belustigen; (entertain) unterhalten. ~**ment** n Belustigung f; Unterhaltung f

amusing /ə'mjuːzɪŋ/ adj amüsant

an /ən/, betont /æn/ see a

anaem|ia /ə'niːmɪə/ n Blutarmut f, Anämie f. ~**ic** adj blutarm

anaesthetic /ænəs'θetɪk/ n Narkosemittel nt, Betäubungsmittel nt; under [an] ~ in Narkose

anaesthetist /ə'niːsθətɪst/ n Narkosearzt m

analogy /ə'nælədʒɪ/ n Analogie f

analyse /'ænəlaɪz/ vt analysieren

analysis /ə'næləsɪs/ n Analyse f

analyst /'ænəlɪst/ n Chemiker(in) m(f); (psychologist) Analytiker m

analytical /ænə'lɪtɪkl/ adj analytisch

anarch|ist /'ænəkɪst/ n Anarchist m. ~**y** n Anarchie f

anatom|ical /ænə'tɒmɪkl/ adj anatomisch. ~**y** n Anatomie f

ancest|or /'ænsestə(r)/ n Vorfahr m. ~**ry** n Abstammung f

anchor /'æŋkə(r)/ n Anker m ● vi ankern ● vt verankern

ancient /'eɪnʃənt/ adj alt

and /ənd/, betont /ænd/ conj und;
~ so on und so weiter; six hundred ~ two sechshundertzwei;
more ~ more immer mehr; nice
~ warm schön warm

anecdote /ˈænɪkdəʊt/ n Anekdote f

angel /ˈeɪndʒl/ n Engel m. ~**ic** adj
engelhaft

anger /ˈæŋgə(r)/ n Zorn m ●vt
zornig machen

angle /ˈæŋgl/ n Winkel m; (fig)
Standpunkt m; at an ~ schräg

angler /ˈæŋglə(r)/ n Angler m

Anglican /ˈæŋglɪkən/ adj anglikanisch ●n Anglikaner(in) m(f)

Anglo-Saxon /æŋgləʊˈsæksn/
adj angelsächsisch ●n (Lang) Angelsächsisch nt

angry /ˈæŋgrɪ/ adj, **-ily** adv zornig;
be ~ with böse sein auf (+ acc)

anguish /ˈæŋgwɪʃ/ n Qual f

angular /ˈæŋgjʊlə(r)/ adj eckig;
(features) kantig

animal /ˈænɪml/ n Tier nt ●adj
tierisch

animat|e /ˈænɪmeɪt/ vt beleben.
~**ed** adj lebhaft

animosity /ænɪˈmɒsɪtɪ/ n Feindseligkeit f

ankle /ˈæŋkl/ n [Fuß]knöchel m

annex[e] /ˈæneks/ n Nebengebäude nt; (extension) Anbau m

annihilate /əˈnaɪəleɪt/ vt vernichten

anniversary /ænɪˈvɜːsərɪ/ n Jahrestag m

annotate /ˈænəteɪt/ vt kommentieren

announce /əˈnaʊns/ vt bekannt
geben; (over loudspeaker) durchsagen; (at reception) ankündigen;
(Radio, TV) ansagen; (in newspaper)
anzeigen. ~**ment** n Bekanntgabe f,

Bekanntmachung f; Durchsage f;
Ansage f; Anzeige f. ~**r** n Ansager(in) m(f)

annoy /əˈnɔɪ/ vt ärgern; (pester)
belästigen; get ~**ed** sich ärgern.
~**ance** n Ärger m. ~**ing** adj ärgerlich

annual /ˈænjʊəl/ adj jährlich ●n
(book) Jahresalbum nt

anonymous /əˈnɒnɪməs/ adj
anonym

anorak /ˈænəræk/ n Anorak m

anorexia /ænəˈreksɪə/ n Magersucht f; be ~**c** an Magersucht
leiden

another /əˈnʌðə(r)/ adj & pron ein
anderer/eine andere/ein anderes;
(additional) noch ein(e); ~ [one]
noch einer/eine/eins; ~ time ein
andermal; one ~ einander

answer /ˈɑːnsə(r)/ n Antwort f;
(solution) Lösung f ●vt antworten
(s.o. jdm); beantworten (question,
letter); ~ the door/telephone an
die Tür/ans Telefon gehen ●vi antworten; (Teleph) sich melden; ~
back eine freche Antwort geben.
~**ing machine** n (Teleph) Anrufbeantworter m

ant /ænt/ n Ameise f

antagonis|m /ænˈtægənɪzm/ n
Antagonismus m. ~**tic** adj
feindselig

Antarctic /ænˈtɑːktɪk/ n Antarktis f

antelope /ˈæntɪləʊp/ n Antilope f

antenatal /æntɪˈneɪtl/ adj ~ **care**
Schwangerschaftsfürsorge f

antenna /ænˈtenə/ n Fühler m;
(Amer: aerial) Antenne f

anthem /ˈænθəm/ n Hymne f

anthology /ænˈθɒlədʒɪ/ n Anthologie f

anthrax /ˈænθræks/ n Milzbrand
m, Anthrax m

a **anthropology** /ænθrə'pɒlədʒɪ/ n Anthropologie f

antibiotic /æntɪbaɪ'ɒtɪk/ n Antibiotikum nt

anticipat|e /æn'tɪsɪpeɪt/ vt vorhersehen; (forestall) zuvorkommen (+ dat); (expect) erwarten. ~**ion** n Erwartung f

anti'climax n Enttäuschung f

anti'clockwise adj & adv gegen den Uhrzeigersinn

antics /'æntɪks/ npl Mätzchen pl

antidote /'æntɪdəʊt/ n Gegengift nt

'antifreeze n Frostschutzmittel nt

antipathy /æn'tɪpəθɪ/ n Abneigung f, Antipathie f

antiquated /'æntɪkweɪtɪd/ adj veraltet

antique /æn'tiːk/ adj antik ● n Antiquität f. ~ **dealer** n Antiquitätenhändler m

antiquity /æn'tɪkwɪtɪ/ n Altertum nt

anti'septic adj antiseptisch ● n Antiseptikum nt

anti'social adj asozial; 🗓 ungesellig

antlers /'æntləz/ npl Geweih nt

anus /'eɪnəs/ n After m

anvil /'ænvɪl/ n Amboss m

anxiety /æŋ'zaɪətɪ/ n Sorge f

anxious /'æŋkʃəs/ adj ängstlich; (worried) besorgt; be ~ to do sth etw gerne machen wollen

any /'enɪ/ adj irgendein(e); pl irgendwelche; (every) jede(r,s); pl alle; (after negative) kein(e); pl keine; ~ colour/number you like eine beliebige Farbe/Zahl; have you ~ wine/apples? haben Sie Wein/Äpfel? ● pron [irgend]einer/eine/eins; pl [irgend]welche; (some) welche(r,s); pl welche; (all) alle pl; (negative) kei-

ner/keine/keins; pl keine; I don't want ~ of it ich will nichts davon; there aren't ~ es gibt keine ● adv noch; ~ quicker/slower noch schneller/langsamer; is it ~ better? geht es etwas besser? would you like ~ more? möchten Sie noch [etwas]? I can't eat ~ more ich kann nichts mehr essen

'anybody pron [irgend]jemand; (after negative) niemand; ~ can do that das kann jeder

'anyhow adv jedenfalls; (nevertheless) trotzdem; (badly) irgendwie

'anyone pron = anybody

'anything pron [irgend]etwas; (after negative) nichts; (everything) alles

'anyway adv jedenfalls; (in any case) sowieso

'anywhere adv irgendwo; (after negative) nirgendwo; (be, live) überall; (go) überallhin

apart /ə'pɑːt/ adv auseinander; live ~ getrennt leben; ~ **from** abgesehen von

apartment /ə'pɑːtmənt/ n Zimmer nt; (flat) Wohnung f

ape /eɪp/ n [Menschen]affe m ● vt nachäffen

aperitif /ə'perɪtiːf/ n Aperitif m

apologetic /əpɒlə'dʒetɪk/ adj, **-ally** adv entschuldigend; be ~ sich entschuldigen

apologize /ə'pɒlədʒaɪz/ vi sich entschuldigen (to bei)

apology /ə'pɒlədʒɪ/ n Entschuldigung f

apostle /ə'pɒsl/ n Apostel m

apostrophe /ə'pɒstrəfɪ/ n Apostroph m

appal /ə'pɔːl/ vt (pt/pp appalled) entsetzen. ~**ling** adj entsetzlich

apparatus /æpə'reɪtəs/ n Apparatur f; (Sport) Geräte pl; (single piece)

Gerät nt

apparent /ə'pærənt/ adj offenbar; (seeming) scheinbar. ~ly adv offenbar, anscheinend

appeal /ə'pi:l/ vi Appell m, Aufruf m; (request) Bitte f; (attraction) Reiz m; (Jur) Berufung f ● vi appellieren (to an + acc); (ask) bitten (for um); (be attractive) zusagen (to dat); (Jur) Berufung einlegen. ~ing adj ansprechend

appear /ə'pɪə(r)/ vi erscheinen; (seem) scheinen; (Theat) auftreten. ~ance n Erscheinen nt; (look) Aussehen nt; to all ~ances allem Anschein nach

appendicitis /əpendɪ'saɪtɪs/ n Blinddarmentzündung f

appendix /ə'pendɪks/ n (pl -ices -ɪsi:z/) (of book) Anhang m ● (pl -es) (Anat) Blinddarm m

appetite /'æpɪtaɪt/ n Appetit m

appetizing /'æpɪtaɪzɪŋ/ adj appetitlich

applau|d /ə'plɔːd/ vt/i Beifall klatschen (+ dat). ~se n Beifall m

apple /'æpl/ n Apfel m

appliance /ə'plaɪəns/ n Gerät nt

applicable /'æplɪkəbl/ adj anwendbar (to auf + acc); (on form) not ~ nicht zutreffend

applicant /'æplɪkənt/ n Bewerber(in) m(f)

application /æplɪ'keɪʃn/ n Anwendung f; (request) Antrag m; (for job) Bewerbung f; (diligence) Fleiß m

applied /ə'plaɪd/ adj angewandt

apply /ə'plaɪ/ vt (pt/pp -ied) auftragen (paint); anwenden (force, rule) ● vi zutreffen (to auf + acc); ~ for beantragen; sich bewerben um (job)

appoint /ə'pɔɪnt/ vt ernennen; (fix) festlegen. ~ment n Ernennung f; (meeting) Verabredung f; (at

doctor's, hairdresser's) Termin m; (job) Posten m; make an ~ment sich anmelden

appreciable /ə'pri:ʃəbl/ adj merklich; (considerable) beträchtlich

appreciat|e /ə'pri:ʃɪeɪt/ vt zu schätzen wissen; (be grateful for) dankbar sein für; (enjoy) schätzen; (understand) verstehen ● vi (increase in value) im Wert steigen. ~ion n (gratitude) Dankbarkeit f. ~ive adj dankbar

apprehens|ion /æprɪ'henʃn/ n (fear) Angst f. ~ive adj ängstlich

apprentice /ə'prentɪs/ n Lehrling m. ~ship n Lehre f

approach /ə'prəʊtʃ/ n Näherkommen nt; (of time) Nahen nt; (access) Zugang m; (road) Zufahrt f ● vi sich nähern; (time:) nahen ● vt sich nähern (+ dat); (with request) herantreten an (+ acc); (set about) sich heranmachen an (+ acc). ~able adj zugänglich

appropriate /ə'prəʊprɪət/ adj angebracht, angemessen

approval /ə'pru:vl/ n Billigung f; on ~ zur Ansicht

approv|e /ə'pru:v/ vt billigen ● vi ~e of sth/s.o. mit etw/jdm einverstanden sein. ~ing adj anerkennend

approximate /ə'prɒksɪmət/ adj, -ly adv ungefähr

approximation /əprɒksɪ'meɪʃn/ n Schätzung f

apricot /'eɪprɪkɒt/ n Aprikose f

April /'eɪprəl/ n April m; make an ~ fool of in den April schicken

apron /'eɪprən/ n Schürze f

apt /æpt/ adj passend; be ~ to do sth dazu neigen, etw zu tun

aqualung /'ækwəlʌŋ/ n Tauchgerät nt

aquarium /əˈkweəriəm/ n Aquarium nt

aquatic /əˈkwætɪk/ adj Wasser-

Arab /ˈærəb/ adj arabisch ● n Araber(in) m(f). **~ian** adj arabisch

Arabic /ˈærəbɪk/ adj arabisch

arbitrary /ˈɑːbɪtrərɪ/ adj, **-ily** adv willkürlich

arbitrat|e /ˈɑːbɪtreɪt/ vi schlichten. **~ion** n Schlichtung f

arc /ɑːk/ n Bogen m

arcade /ɑːˈkeɪd/ n Laubengang m; (shops) Einkaufspassage f

arch /ɑːtʃ/ n Bogen m; (of foot) Gewölbe nt ● vt ~ its back (cat:) einen Buckel machen

archaeological /ɑːkɪəˈlɒdʒɪkl/ adj archäologisch

archaeolog|ist /ɑːkɪˈɒlədʒɪst/ n Archäologe m/-login f. **~y** n Archäologie f

archaic /ɑːˈkeɪɪk/ adj veraltet

arch'bishop /ɑːtʃ-/ n Erzbischof m

archer /ˈɑːtʃə(r)/ n Bogenschütze m. **~y** n Bogenschießen nt

architect /ˈɑːkɪtekt/ n Architekt(in) m(f). **~ural** adj architektonisch

architecture /ˈɑːkɪtektʃə(r)/ n Architektur f

archives /ˈɑːkaɪvz/ npl Archiv nt

archway /ˈɑːtʃweɪ/ n Torbogen m

Arctic /ˈɑːktɪk/ adj arktisch ● n the ~ die Arktis

ardent /ˈɑːdənt/ adj leidenschaftlich

ardour /ˈɑːdə(r)/ n Leidenschaft f

arduous /ˈɑːdjʊəs/ adj mühsam

are /ɑː(r)/ see be

area /ˈeərɪə/ n (surface) Fläche f; (Geometry) Flächeninhalt m; (region) Gegend f; (fig) Gebiet nt

arena /əˈriːnə/ n Arena f

Argentina /ɑːdʒənˈtiːnə/ n Argentinien nt

Argentin|e /ˈɑːdʒəntaɪn/, **~ian** /-ˈtɪnɪən/ adj argentinisch

argue /ˈɑːgjuː/ vi streiten (about über + acc); (two people:) sich streiten; (debate) diskutieren; **don't ~!** keine Widerrede! ● vt (debate) diskutieren; (reason) ~ **that** argumentieren, dass

argument /ˈɑːgjʊmənt/ n Streit m, Auseinandersetzung f; (reasoning) Argument nt; **have an ~** sich streiten. **~ative** adj streitlustig

aria /ˈɑːrɪə/ n Arie f

arise /əˈraɪz/ vi (pt arose, pp arisen) sich ergeben (from aus)

aristocracy /ærɪˈstɒkrəsɪ/ n Aristokratie f

aristocrat /ˈærɪstəkræt/ n Aristokrat(in) m(f). **~ic** adj aristokratisch

arithmetic /əˈrɪθmətɪk/ n Rechnen nt

arm /ɑːm/ n Arm m; (of chair) Armlehne f; ~**s** pl (weapons) Waffen pl; (Heraldry) Wappen nt ● vt bewaffnen

armament /ˈɑːməmənt/ n Bewaffnung f; ~**s** pl Waffen pl

armchair n Sessel m

armed /ɑːmd/ adj bewaffnet; ~ **forces** Streitkräfte pl

armour /ˈɑːmə(r)/ n Rüstung f. **~ed** adj Panzer-

'armpit n Achselhöhle f

army /ˈɑːmɪ/ n Heer nt; (specific) Armee f; **join the ~** zum Militär gehen

aroma /əˈrəʊmə/ n Aroma nt, Duft m. **~tic** adj aromatisch

arose /əˈrəʊz/ see arise

around /əˈraʊnd/ adv [all] ~ rings herum; **he's not ~** er ist nicht da; **travel ~** herumreisen ● prep um (+ acc) ... herum; (approximately, nearly) gegen

arouse /əˈraʊz/ vt aufwecken; (excite) erregen

arrange /əˈreɪndʒ/ vt arrangieren; anordnen (furniture, books); (settle) abmachen. ~**ment** n Anordnung f; (agreement) Vereinbarung f; (of flowers) Gesteck nt; make ~ments Vorkehrungen treffen

arrest /əˈrest/ n Verhaftung f; under ~ verhaftet ● vt verhaften

arrival /əˈraɪvl/ n Ankunft f; new ~s pl Neuankömmlinge pl

arrive /əˈraɪv/ vi ankommen; ~ at (fig) gelangen zu

arrogan|ce /ˈærəgəns/ n Arroganz f. ~t adj arrogant

arrow /ˈærəʊ/ n Pfeil m

arse /ɑːs/ n (vulgar) Arsch m

arson /ˈɑːsn/ n Brandstiftung f. ~**ist** n Brandstifter m

art /ɑːt/ n Kunst f; work of ~ Kunstwerk nt; ~s and crafts pl Kunstgewerbe nt; **A**~s pl (Univ) Geisteswissenschaften pl

artery /ˈɑːtəri/ n Schlagader f, Arterie f

'**art gallery** n Kunstgalerie f

arthritis /ɑːˈθraɪtɪs/ n Arthritis f

artichoke /ˈɑːtɪtʃəʊk/ n Artischocke f

article /ˈɑːtɪkl/ n Artikel m; (object) Gegenstand m; ~ of clothing Kleidungsstück nt

artificial /ɑːtɪˈfɪʃl/ adj künstlich

artillery /ɑːˈtɪləri/ n Artillerie f

artist /ˈɑːtɪst/ n Künstler(in) m(f)

artiste /ɑːˈtiːst/ n (Theat) Artist(in) m(f)

artistic /ɑːˈtɪstɪk/ adj, **-ally** adv künstlerisch

as /æz/ conj (because) da; (when) als; (while) während ● prep als; as a child/foreigner als Kind/Ausländer

● adv as well auch; as soon as sobald; as much as so viel wie; as quick as you so schnell wie du; as you know wie Sie wissen; as far as I'm concerned was mich betrifft

asbestos /æzˈbestɒs/ n Asbest m

ascend /əˈsend/ vi [auf]steigen ● vt besteigen (throne)

ascent /əˈsent/ n Aufstieg m

ascertain /æsəˈteɪn/ vt ermitteln

ash[1] /æʃ/ n (tree) Esche f

ash[2] n Asche f

ashamed /əˈʃeɪmd/ adj beschämt; be ~ sich schämen (of über + acc)

ashore /əˈʃɔː(r)/ adv an Land

'**ashtray** n Aschenbecher m

Asia /ˈeɪʃə/ n Asien nt. ~n adj asiatisch ● n Asiat(in) m(f). ~**tic** adj asiatisch

aside /əˈsaɪd/ adv beiseite

ask /ɑːsk/ vt/i fragen; stellen (question); (invite) einladen; ~ for bitten um; verlangen (s.o.); ~ after sich erkundigen nach; ~ s.o. in jdn hereinbitten; ~ s.o. to do sth jdn bitten, etw zu tun

asleep /əˈsliːp/ adj be ~ schlafen; fall ~ einschlafen

asparagus /əˈspærəgəs/ n Spargel m

aspect /ˈæspekt/ n Aspekt m

asphalt /ˈæsfælt/ n Asphalt m

aspire /əˈspaɪə(r)/ vi ~ to streben nach

ass /æs/ n Esel m

assail /əˈseɪl/ vt bestürmen. ~**ant** n Angreifer(in) m(f)

assassin /əˈsæsɪn/ n Mörder(in) m(f). ~**ate** vt ermorden. ~**ation** n [politischer] Mord m

assault /əˈsɔːlt/ n (Mil) Angriff m; (Jur) Körperverletzung f ● vt [tätlich] angreifen

assemble /əˈsembl/ vi sich ver-

a sammeln ● vt versammeln; (Techn)
montieren

assembly /əˈsemblɪ/ n Versammlung f; (Sch) Andacht f; (Techn)
Montage f. ～ **line** n Fließband nt

assent /əˈsent/ n Zustimmung f

assert /əˈsɜːt/ vt behaupten; ～
oneself sich durchsetzen. ～**ion** n
Behauptung f

assess /əˈses/ vt bewerten; (fig &
for tax purposes) einschätzen; schätzen (value). ～**ment** n Einschätzung
f; (of tax) Steuerbescheid m

asset /ˈæset/ n Vorteil m; ～**s** pl
(money) Vermögen nt; (Comm) Aktiva pl

assign /əˈsaɪn/ vt zuweisen (to
dat). ～**ment** n (task) Aufgabe f

assist /əˈsɪst/ vt/i helfen (+ dat).
～**ance** n Hilfe f. ～**ant** adj Hilfs-
● n Assistent(in) m(f); (in shop)
Verkäufer(in) m(f)

associat|**e**[1] /əˈsəʊʃɪeɪt/ vt verbinden; (Psychology) assoziieren ● vi
～ with verkehren mit. ～**ion** n Verband m

associate[2] /əˈsəʊʃɪət/ adj assoziiert ● n Kollege m/-gin f

assort|**ed** /əˈsɔːtɪd/ adj gemischt.
～**ment** n Mischung f

assume /əˈsjuːm/ vt annehmen;
übernehmen (office). ～**ing that** angenommen, dass

assumption /əˈsʌmpʃn/ n Annahme f; **on the** ～ **that** in der Annahme
(that dass)

assurance /əˈʃʊərəns/ n Versicherung f; (confidence) Selbstsicherheit f

assure /əˈʃʊə(r)/ vt versichern (s.o.
jdm); **I** ～ **you [of that]** das versichere ich Ihnen. ～**d** adj sicher

asterisk /ˈæstərɪsk/ n Sternchen nt

asthma /ˈæsmə/ n Asthma nt

astonish /əˈstɒnɪʃ/ vt erstaunen.
～**ing** adj erstaunlich. ～**ment** n Erstaunen nt

astray /əˈstreɪ/ adv **go** ～ verloren
gehen; (person:) sich verlaufen

astride /əˈstraɪd/ adv rittlings
● prep rittlings auf (+ dat/acc)

astrolog|**er** /əˈstrɒlədʒə(r)/ n
Astrologe m/-gin f. ～**y** n Astrologie f

astronaut /ˈæstrənɔːt/ n Astronaut(in) m(f)

astronom|**er** /əˈstrɒnəmə(r)/ n
Astronom m. ～**ical** adj astronomisch. ～**y** n Astronomie f

astute /əˈstjuːt/ adj scharfsinnig

asylum /əˈsaɪləm/ n Asyl nt; [lunatic] ～ Irrenanstalt f. ～**-seeker** n
Asylbewerber(in) m(f)

---

at /æt/, unbetont /ət/

● preposition

····▸ (expressing place) an (+ dat).
at the station am Bahnhof. **at
the end** am Ende. **at the corner**
an der Ecke. **at the same place**
an der gleichen Stelle

····▸ (at s.o.'s house or shop) bei (+
dat). **at Lisa's** bei Lisa. **at my
uncle's** bei meinem Onkel. **at
the baker's/butcher's** beim Bäcker/Fleischer

····▸ (inside a building) in (+ dat).
at the theatre/supermarket im
Theater/Supermarkt. **we spent
the night at a hotel** wir übernachteten in einem Hotel. **he is
still at the office** er ist noch im
Büro

····▸ (expressing time) (with clock
time) um; (with main festivals)
zu. **at six o'clock** um sechs Uhr.
at midnight um Mitternacht. **at
midday** um zwölf Uhr mittags.
at Christmas/Easter zu

ate | audition

Weihnachten/Ostern
····➤ *(expressing age)* mit. at [the age of] forty mit vierzig; im Alter von vierzig
····➤ *(expressing price)* zu. at £2.50 [each] zu *od* für [je] 2,50 Pfund
····➤ *(expressing speed)* mit. at 30 m.p.h. mit dreißig Meilen pro Stunde
····➤ *(in phrases)* good/bad at languages gut/schlecht in Sprachen. two at a time zwei auf einmal. at that *(at that point)* dabei; *(at that provocation)* daraufhin; *(moreover)* noch dazu

ate /et/ *see* eat
atheist /'eɪθɪɪst/ *n* Atheist(in) *m(f)*.
athlet|e /'æθliːt/ *n* Athlet(in) *m(f)*. ~**ic** *adj* sportlich. ~**ics** *n* Leichtathletik *f*
Atlantic /ət'læntɪk/ *adj* & *n* the ~ [Ocean] der Atlantik
atlas /'ætləs/ *n* Atlas *m*
atmosphere /'ætməsfɪə(r)/ *n* Atmosphäre *f*
atom /'ætəm/ *n* Atom *nt*. ~ **bomb** *n* Atombombe *f*
atomic /ə'tɒmɪk/ *adj* Atom-
atrocious /ə'trəʊʃəs/ *adj* abscheulich
atrocity /ə'trɒsətɪ/ *n* Gräueltat *f*
attach /ə'tætʃ/ *vt* befestigen (to an + *dat*); beimessen *(importance)* (to *dat*); be ~ed to *(fig)* hängen an (+ *dat*). ~**ment** *n (to email)* Anhang *m*
attack /ə'tæk/ *n* Angriff *m; (Med)* Anfall *m* ●*vt/i* angreifen. ~**er** *n* Angreifer *m*
attain /ə'teɪn/ *vt* erreichen. ~**able** *adj* erreichbar
attempt /ə'tempt/ *n* Versuch *m* ●*vt* versuchen
attend /ə'tend/ *vt* anwesend sein bei; *(go regularly to)* besuchen; *(take* part in) teilnehmen an (+ *dat); (accompany)* begleiten; *(doctor:)* behandeln ●*vi* anwesend sein; *(pay attention)* aufpassen; ~ to sich kümmern um; *(in shop)* bedienen. ~**ance** *n* Anwesenheit *f; (number)* Besucherzahl *f*. ~**ant** *n* Wärter(in) *m(f); (in car park)* Wächter *m*
attention /ə'tenʃn/ *n* Aufmerksamkeit *f*; ~! *(Mil)* stillgestanden! pay ~ aufpassen; pay ~ to beachten, achten auf (+ *acc*)
attentive /ə'tentɪv/ *adj* aufmerksam
attic /'ætɪk/ *n* Dachboden *m*
attitude /'ætɪtjuːd/ *n* Haltung *f*
attorney /ə'tɜːnɪ/ *n (Amer: lawyer)* Rechtsanwalt *m*; power of ~ Vollmacht *f*
attract /ə'trækt/ *vt* anziehen; erregen *(attention)*; ~ s.o.'s attention jds Aufmerksamkeit auf (*acc*) lenken. ~**ion** *n* Anziehungskraft *f; (charm)* Reiz *m; (thing)* Attraktion *f*. ~**ive** *adj*, **-ly** *adv* attraktiv
attribute /ə'trɪbjuːt/ *vt* zuschreiben (to *dat*)
aubergine /'əʊbəʒiːn/ *n* Aubergine *f*
auburn /'ɔːbən/ *adj* kastanienbraun
auction /'ɔːkʃn/ *n* Auktion *f* Versteigerung *f* ●*vt* versteigern. ~**eer** *n* Auktionator *m*
audaci|ous /ɔː'deɪʃəs/ *adj* verwegen *(charm)*. ~**ty** *n* Verwegenheit *f; (impudence)* Dreistigkeit *f*
audible /'ɔːdəbl/ *adj*, **-bly** *adv* hörbar
audience /'ɔːdɪəns/ *n* Publikum *nt; (Theat, TV)* Zuschauer *pl; (Radio)* Zuhörer *pl; (meeting)* Audienz *f*
audit /'ɔːdɪt/ *n* Bücherrevision *f* ●*vt (Comm)* prüfen
audition /ɔː'dɪʃn/ *n (Theat)* Vorsprechen *nt; (Mus)* Vorspielen *nt*

(for singer) Vorsingen nt • vi vorsprechen; vorspielen; vorsingen

auditor /'ɔ:dɪtə(r)/ n Buchprüfer m

auditorium /ɔ:dɪ'tɔ:rɪəm/ n Zuschauerraum m

August /'ɔ:gəst/ n August m

aunt /ɑ:nt/ n Tante f

au pair /əʊ'peə(r)/ n ~ [girl] Au-pair-Mädchen nt

aura /'ɔ:rə/ n Fluidum nt

auspicious /ɔ:'spɪʃəs/ adj günstig; (occasion) freudig

auster|e /ɒ'stɪə(r)/ adj streng; (simple) nüchtern. ~ity n Strenge f; (hardship) Entbehrung f

Australia /ɒ'streɪlɪə/ n Australien nt. ~n adj australisch • n Australier(in) m(f)

Austria /'ɒstrɪə/ n Österreich nt ~n adj österreichisch • n Österreicher(in) m(f)

authentic /ɔ:'θentɪk/ adj echt, authentisch. ~ate vt beglaubigen. ~ity n Echtheit f

author /'ɔ:θə(r)/ n Schriftsteller m, Autor m; (of document) Verfasser m

authoritarian /ɔ:θɒrɪ'teərɪən/ adj autoritär

authoritative /ɔ:'θɒrɪtətɪv/ adj maßgebend

authority /ɔ:'θɒrətɪ/ n Autorität f; (public) Behörde f; in ~ verantwortlich

authorization /ɔ:θəraɪ'zeɪʃn/ n Ermächtigung f

authorize /'ɔ:θəraɪz/ vt ermächtigen (s.o.); genehmigen (sth)

autobi'ography /ɔ:tə-/ n Autobiographie f

autograph /'ɔ:tə-/ n Autogramm nt

automatic /ɔ:tə'mætɪk/ adj, -ally adv automatisch

automation /ɔ:tə'meɪʃn/ n Auto-

mation f

automobile /'ɔ:təməbi:l/ n Auto nt

autonom|ous /ɔ:'tɒnəməs/ adj autonom. ~y n Autonomie f

autumn /'ɔ:təm/ n Herbst m. ~al adj herbstlich

auxiliary /ɔ:g'zɪlɪərɪ/ adj Hilfs- • n Helfer(in) m(f), Hilfskraft f

avail /ə'veɪl/ n to no ~ vergeblich

available /ə'veɪləbl/ adj verfügbar; (obtainable) erhältlich

avalanche /'ævəlɑ:nʃ/ n Lawine f

avenge /ə'vendʒ/ vt rächen

avenue /'ævənju:/ n Allee f

average /'ævərɪdʒ/ adj Durchschnitts-, durchschnittlich • n Durchschnitt m; on ~ im Durchschnitt, durchschnittlich • vt durchschnittlich schaffen

averse /ə'vɜ:s/ adj not be ~e to sth etw (dat) nicht abgeneigt sein

avert /ə'vɜ:t/ vt abwenden

aviary /'eɪvɪərɪ/ n Vogelhaus nt

aviation /eɪvɪ'eɪʃn/ n Luftfahrt f

avocado /ævə'kɑ:dəʊ/ n Avocado f

avoid /ə'vɔɪd/ vt vermeiden; ~ s.o. jdm aus dem Weg gehen. ~able adj vermeidbar. ~ance n Vermeidung f

await /ə'weɪt/ vt warten auf (+ acc)

awake /ə'weɪk/ adj wach; wide ~ hellwach • vi (pt awoke, pp awoken) erwachen

awaken /ə'weɪkn/ vt wecken • vi erwachen. ~ing n Erwachen nt

award /ə'wɔ:d/ n Auszeichnung f; (prize) Preis m • vt zuerkennen (to s.o. dat); verleihen (prize)

aware /ə'weə(r)/ adj become ~ gewahr werden of (gen); be ~ that wissen, dass. ~ness nt Bewusstsein nt

away /ə'weɪ/ adv weg, fort; (absent) abwesend; four kilometres ~ vier Kilometer entfernt; play ~ (Sport) auswärts spielen. ~ **game** n Auswärtsspiel nt

awful /'ɔːfl/ adj furchtbar

awkward /'ɔːkwəd/ adj schwierig; (clumsy) ungeschickt; (embarrassing) peinlich; (inconvenient) ungünstig. ~**ly** adv ungeschickt; (embarrassedly) verlegen

awning /'ɔːnɪŋ/ n Markise f

awoke(n) /ə'wəʊk(n)/ see awake

axe /æks/ n Axt f ● vt (pres p axing) streichen

axle /'æksl/ n (Techn) Achse f

Bb

B /biː/ n (Mus) H nt

baboon /bə'buːn/ n Pavian m

baby /'beɪbɪ/ n Baby nt; (Amer, ⑪) Schätzchen nt

baby: ~**ish** adj kindisch. ~**sit** vi babysitten. ~**sitter** n Babysitter m

bachelor /'bætʃələ(r)/ n Junggeselle m

back /bæk/ n Rücken m; (reverse) Rückseite f; (of chair) Rückenlehne f; (Sport) Verteidiger m; at/(Auto) in the ~ hinten; on the ~ auf der Rückseite; ~ to front verkehrt ● adj Hinter- ● adv zurück; here/ there hier/da hinten; ~ at home zu Hause; go/pay ~ zurückgehen/ -zahlen ● vt (support) unterstützen; (with money) finanzieren; (Auto) zurücksetzen; (Betting) [Geld] setzen auf (+ acc); (cover the back of) mit einer Verstärkung versehen ● vi (Auto) zurücksetzen. ~ **down** vi

klein beigeben. ~ **in** vi rückwärts hineinfahren. ~ **out** vi rückwärts hinaus-/herausfahren; (fig) aussteigen (of aus). ~ **up** vt unterstützen; (confirm) bestätigen ● vi (Auto) zurücksetzen

back: ~**ache** n Rückenschmerzen pl. ~**biting** n gehässiges Gerede nt. ~**bone** n Rückgrat nt. ~**date** vt rückdatieren; ~**dated to** rückwirkend von. ~**door** n Hintertür f

backer /'bækə(r)/ n Geldgeber m

back: ~**fire** vi (Auto) fehlzünden; (fig) fehlschlagen. ~**ground** n Hintergrund m; **family** ~**ground** Familienverhältnisse pl. ~**hand** n (Sport) Rückhand f. ~**handed** adj (compliment) zweifelhaft

backing /'bækɪŋ/ n (support) Unterstützung f; (material) Verstärkung f

back: ~**lash** n (fig) Gegenschlag m. ~**log** n Rückstand m (of an + dat). ~**pack** n Rucksack m. ~'**seat** n Rücksitz m. ~**side** n ⑪ Hintern m. ~**stroke** n Rückenschwimmen nt. ~**up** n Unterstützung f; (Amer: traffic jam) Stau m

backward /'bækwəd/ adj zurückgeblieben; (country) rückständig ● adv rückwärts. ~**s** rückwärts; ~**s and forwards** hin und her

back'yard n Hinterhof m; **not in my** ~**yard** ⑪ nicht vor meiner Haustür

bacon /'beɪkn/ n [Schinken]speck m

bacteria /bæk'tɪərɪə/ npl Bakterien pl

bad /bæd/ adj (worse, worst) schlecht; (serious) schwer, schlimm; (naughty) unartig; ~ **language** gemeine Ausdrucksweise f; **feel** ~ sich schlecht fühlen; (feel guilty) ein schlechtes Gewissen haben

badge /bædʒ/ n Abzeichen nt

badger /'bædʒə(r)/ n Dachs m ● vt plagen

badly /'bædlɪ/ adv schlecht; (seriously) schwer; ~ off schlecht gestellt; ~ behaved unerzogen; want ~ sich (dat) sehnsüchtig wünschen; need ~ dringend brauchen

bad-'mannered adj mit schlechten Manieren

badminton /'bædmɪntən/ n Federball m

bad-'tempered adj schlecht gelaunt

baffle /'bæfl/ vt verblüffen

bag /bæg/ n Tasche f; (of paper) Tüte f; (pouch) Beutel m; ~s of 🔢 jede Menge ● vt (🔢: reserve) in Beschlag nehmen

baggage /'bægɪdʒ/ n [Reise]gepäck nt

baggy /'bægɪ/ adj (clothes) ausgebeult

'bagpipes npl Dudelsack m

bail /beɪl/ n Kaution f; on ~ gegen Kaution ● vt ~ s.o. out jdn gegen Kaution freibekommen; (fig) jdm aus der Patsche helfen

bait /beɪt/ n Köder m ● vt mit einem Köder versehen; (fig: torment) reizen

bake /beɪk/ vt/i backen

baker /'beɪkə(r)/ n Bäcker m; ~'s [shop] Bäckerei f. ~y n Bäckerei f

baking /'beɪkɪŋ/ n Backen nt. ~-powder n Backpulver nt

balance /'bæləns/ n (equilibrium) Gleichgewicht nt, Balance f; (scales) Waage f; (Comm) Saldo m; (outstanding sum) Restbetrag m; [bank] ~ Kontostand m; in the ~ (fig) in der Schwebe ● vt balancieren; (equalize) ausgleichen; (Comm) abschließen (books) ● vi balancieren;

(fig & Comm) sich ausgleichen. ~d adj ausgewogen

balcony /'bælkənɪ/ n Balkon m

bald /bɔːld/ adj (-er, -est) kahl; (person) kahlköpfig

bald|ly adv unverblümt. ~ness n Kahlköpfigkeit f

ball¹ /bɔːl/ n Ball m; (Billiards, Croquet) Kugel f; (of yarn) Knäuel m & nt; on the ~ 🔢 auf Draht

ball² n (dance) Ball m

ball-'bearing n Kugellager nt

ballerina /bælə'riːnə/ n Ballerina f

ballet /'bæleɪ/ n Ballett nt. ~ dancer n Ballettänzer(in) m(f)

balloon /bə'luːn/ n Luftballon m; (Aviat) Ballon m

ballot /'bælət/ n [geheime] Wahl f; (on issue) [geheime] Abstimmung f. ~-box n Wahlurne f. ~-paper n Stimmzettel m

ball: ~point ['pen] n Kugelschreiber m. ~room n Ballsaal m

balm /bɑːm/ n Balsam m

balmy /'bɑːmɪ/ adj sanft

Baltic /'bɔːltɪk/ adj & n the ~ [Sea] die Ostsee

bamboo /bæm'buː/ n Bambus m

ban /bæn/ n Verbot nt ● vt (pt/pp banned) verbieten

banal /bə'nɑːl/ adj banal. ~ity n Banalität f

banana /bə'nɑːnə/ n Banane f

band /bænd/ n Band nt; (stripe) Streifen m; (group) Schar f; (Mus) Kapelle f

bandage /'bændɪdʒ/ n Verband m; (for support) Bandage f ● vt verbinden; bandagieren (limb)

b. & b. abbr bed and breakfast

bandit /'bændɪt/ n Bandit m

band: ~stand n Musikpavillon m. ~wagon n jump on the ~wagon

(fig) sich einer erfolgreichen Sache anschließen

bang /bæŋ/ n (noise) Knall m; (blow) Schlag m ● vi go ~ knallen ● int bums! peng! ● vt knallen; (shut noisily) zuknallen; (strike) schlagen auf (+ acc); ~ one's head sich (dat) den Kopf stoßen (on an + acc) ● vi schlagen; (door:) zuknallen

banger /bæŋə(r)/ n (firework) Knallfrosch m; (🔲: sausage) Wurst f; old ~ (🔲: car) Klapperkiste f

bangle /bæŋgl/ n Armreifen m

banish /bænɪʃ/ vt verbannen

banisters /bænɪstəz/ npl [Treppen]geländer nt

banjo /bænʤəʊ/ n Banjo nt

bank[1] /bæŋk/ n (of river) Ufer nt; (slope) Hang m ● vi (Aviat) in die Kurve gehen

bank[2] n Bank f ● ~ on vt sich verlassen auf (+ acc)

'bank account n Bankkonto nt

banker /bæŋkə(r)/ n Bankier m

bank: ~ holiday n gesetzlicher Feiertag m. ~ing n Bankwesen nt. ~note n Banknote f

bankrupt /bæŋkrʌpt/ adj bankrott; go ~ Bankrott machen ● n Bankrotteur m ● vt Bankrott machen. ~cy n Bankrott m

banner /bænə(r)/ n Banner nt; (carried by demonstrators) Transparent nt, Spruchband nt

banquet /bæŋkwɪt/ n Bankett nt

baptism /bæptɪzm/ n Taufe f

baptize /bæptaɪz/ vt taufen

bar /bɑ:(r)/ n Stange f; (of cage) [Gitter]stab m; (of gold) Barren m; (of chocolate) Tafel f; (of soap) Stück nt; (long) Riegel m; (café) Bar f; (counter) Theke f; (Mus) Takt m; (fig: obstacle) Hindernis nt; parallel ~s (Sport) Barren m; behind ~s 🔲 hin-

ter Gittern ● vt (pt/pp barred) versperren (way, door); ausschließen (person)

barbar|ic /bɑ:ˈbærɪk/ adj barbarisch. ~ity n Barbarei f. ~ous adj barbarisch

barbecue /bɑ:bɪkju:/ n Grill m; (party) Grillfest nt ● vt [im Freien] grillen

barbed /bɑ:bd/ adj ~ wire Stacheldraht m

barber /bɑ:bə(r)/ n [Herren]friseur m

'bar code n Strichkode m

bare /beə(r)/ adj (-r, -st) nackt, bloß; (tree) kahl; (empty) leer; (mere) bloß ● vt freilegen; zeigen (teeth); one's teeth die Zähne zeigen; ~ one's head den Hut abnehmen

bare: ~back adv ohne Sattel. ~faced adj schamlos. ~foot adv barfuß. ~headed adj mit unbedecktem Kopf

barely /beəlɪ/ adv kaum

bargain /bɑ:gɪn/ n (agreement) Geschäft nt; (good buy) Gelegenheitskauf m; into the ~ noch dazu; make a ~ sich einigen ● vi handeln; (haggle) feilschen; ~ for (expect) rechnen mit

barge /bɑ:ʤ/ n Lastkahn m; (towed) Schleppkahn m ● vi ~ in 🔲 hereinplatzen

baritone /bærɪtəʊn/ n Bariton m

bark[1] /bɑ:k/ n (of tree) Rinde f

bark[2] n Bellen nt ● vi bellen

barley /bɑ:lɪ/ n Gerste f

bar: ~maid n Schankmädchen nt. ~man n Barmann m

barmy /bɑ:mɪ/ adj 🔲 verrückt

barn /bɑ:n/ n Scheune f

barometer /bəˈrɒmɪtə(r)/ n Barometer nt

baron /bærn/ n Baron m. ~ess n Baronin f

barracks /'bærəks/ npl Kaserne f

barrage /'bærɑ:ʒ/ n (in river) Wehr nt; (Mil) Sperrfeuer nt; (fig) Hagel m

barrel /'bærl/ n Fass nt; (of gun) Lauf m; (of cannon) Rohr nt. ~**organ** n Drehorgel f

barren /'bærn/ adj unfruchtbar; (landscape) öde

barricade /bærɪ'keɪd/ n Barrikade f ● vt verbarrikadieren

barrier /'bærɪə(r)/ n Barriere f; (across road) Schranke f; (Rail) Sperre f; (fig) Hindernis nt

barrow /'bærəʊ/ n Karre f, Karren m

base /beɪs/ n Fuß m; (fig) Basis f; (Mil) Stützpunkt m ● vt stützen (on auf + acc); be ~d on basieren auf (+ dat)

base: ~**ball** n Baseball m. ~**less** adj unbegründet. ~**ment** n Kellergeschoss nt

bash /bæʃ/ n Schlag m; have a ~! ⊞ probier es mal! ● vt hauen

basic /'beɪsɪk/ adj Grund-; (fundamental) grundlegend; (essential) wesentlich; (unadorned) einfach; the ~s das Wesentliche. ~**ally** adv grundsätzlich

basin /'beɪsn/ n Becken nt; (for washing) Waschbecken nt; (for food) Schüssel f

basis /'beɪsɪs/ n (pl -ses /-siːz/) Basis f

bask /bɑːsk/ vi sich sonnen

basket /'bɑːskɪt/ n Korb m. ~**ball** n Basketball m

Basle /bɑːl/ n Basel nt

bass /beɪs/ adj Bass-; ~ **voice** Bassstimme f ● n Bass m; (person) Bassist m

bassoon /bə'suːn/ n Fagott nt

bastard /'bɑːstəd/ n ⊠ Schuft m

bat¹ /bæt/ n Schläger m; off one's own ~ ⊞ auf eigene Faust ● vt (pt/pp batted) schlagen; not ~ an eyelid (fig) nicht mit der Wimper zucken

bat² n (Zool) Fledermaus f

batch /bætʃ/ n (of people) Gruppe f; (of papers) Stoß m; (of goods) Sendung f; (of bread) Schub m

bath /bɑːθ/ n (pl ~s /bɑːðz/) Bad nt; (tub) Badewanne f; ~s pl Badeanstalt f; have a ~ baden

bathe /beɪð/ n Bad nt ● vt/i baden. ~**r** n Badende(r) m/f

bathing /'beɪðɪŋ/ n Baden nt. ~**cap** n Bademütze f. ~**costume** n Badeanzug m

bath: ~**mat** n Badematte f. ~**room** n Badezimmer nt. ~**towel** n Badetuch nt

battalion /bə'tælɪən/ n Bataillon nt

batter /'bætə(r)/ n (Culin) flüssiger Teig m ● vt schlagen. ~**ed** adj (car) verbeult; (wife) misshandelt

battery /'bætərɪ/ n Batterie f

battle /'bætl/ n Schlacht f; (fig) Kampf m ● vi (fig) kämpfen (for um)

battle: ~**field** n Schlachtfeld nt. ~**ship** n Schlachtschiff nt

batty /'bætɪ/ adj ⊞ verrückt

Bavaria /bə'veərɪə/ n Bayern nt. ~**n** adj bayrisch ● n Bayer(in) m(f)

bawl /bɔːl/ n vt/i brüllen

bay¹ /beɪ/ n (Geog) Bucht f; (in room) Erker m

bay² n (Bot) [echter] Lorbeer m. ~**leaf** n Lorbeerblatt nt

bayonet /'beɪənet/ n Bajonett nt

bay 'window n Erkerfenster nt

bazaar /bə'zɑː(r)/ n Basar m

BC abbr (before Christ) v.Chr.

be /biː/

(*pres* am, are, is, *pl* are; *pt* was, *pl* were; *pp* been)

● *intransitive verb*

····▸ (*expressing identity, nature, state, age etc.*) sein. he is a teacher er ist Lehrer. she is French sie ist Französin. he is very nice er ist sehr nett. I am tall ich bin groß. you are thirty du bist dreißig. it was very cold es war sehr kalt

····▸ (*expressing general position*) sein; (*lie*) liegen; (*stand*) stehen. where is the bank? wo ist die Bank? the book is on the table das Buch liegt auf dem Tisch. the vase is on the shelf die Vase steht auf dem Brett

····▸ (*feel*) I am cold/hot mir ist kalt/heiß. I am ill ich bin krank. I am well mir geht es gut. how are you? wie geht es Ihnen?

····▸ (*date*) it is the 5th today heute haben wir den Fünften

····▸ (*go, come, stay*) sein. I have been to Vienna ich bin in Wien gewesen. have you ever been to London? bist du schon einmal in London gewesen? has the postman been? war der Briefträger schon da? I've been here for an hour ich bin seit einer Stunde hier

····▸ (*origin*) where are you from? woher stammen *od* kommen Sie? she is from Australia sie stammt *od* ist aus Australien

····▸ (*cost*) kosten. how much are the eggs? was kosten die Eier?

····▸ (*in calculations*) two threes are six zweimal drei ist *od* sind sechs

····▸ (*exist*) there is/are es gibt (+ acc). there's no fish left es gibt keinen Fisch mehr

● *auxiliary verb*

····▸ (*forming continuous tenses: not translated*) I'm working ich arbeite. I'm leaving morgen ich reise morgen [ab]. they were singing sie sangen. they will be coming on Tuesday sie kommen am Dienstag

····▸ (*forming passive*) werden. the child was found das Kind wurde gefunden. German is spoken here hier wird Deutsch gesprochen; hier spricht man Deutsch

····▸ (*expressing arrangement, obligation, destiny*) sollen. I am to go/inform you ich soll gehen/Sie unterrichten. they were to fly today sie sollten heute fliegen. you are to do that immediately das sollst du sofort machen. you are not to ... (*prohibition*) du darfst nicht ... they were never to meet again (*destiny*) sie sollten sich nie wieder treffen

····▸ (*in short answers*) Are you disappointed? — Yes I am Bist du enttäuscht? — Ja. (*negating previous statement*) Aren't you coming? — Yes I am! Kommst du nicht? — Doch!

····▸ (*in tag questions*) isn't it? wasn't she? aren't they? *etc.* nicht wahr, it's a beautiful house, isn't it? das Haus ist sehr schön, nicht wahr?

beach /biːtʃ/ *n* Strand *m*

bead /biːd/ *n* Perle *f*

beak /biːk/ *n* Schnabel *m*

beam /biːm/ n Balken m; (of light) Strahl m ● vi strahlen. ~ing adj [freude]strahlend

bean /biːn/ n Bohne f

bear¹ /beə(r)/ n Bär m

bear² vt/i (pt bore, pp borne) tragen; (endure) ertragen; gebären (child); ~ right sich rechts halten. ~able adj erträglich

beard /bɪəd/ n Bart m. ~ed adj bärtig

bearer /'beərə(r)/ n Träger m; (of news, cheque) Überbringer m; (of passport) Inhaber(in) m(f)

bearing /'beərɪŋ/ n Haltung f; (Techn) Lager nt; get one's ~s sich orientieren

beast /biːst/ n Tier nt; (🗊: person) Biest nt

beastly /'biːstlɪ/ adj 🗊 scheußlich; (person) gemein

beat /biːt/ n Schlag m; (of policeman) Runde f; (rhythm) Takt m ● vt/i (pt beat, pp beaten) schlagen; (thrash) verprügeln; klopfen (carpet); (hammer) hämmern (on an + acc); ~ it! 🗊 hau ab! it ~s me das begreife ich nicht. ~ up vt zusammenschlagen

beat|en /biːtn/ adj off the ~en track abseits. ~ing n Prügel pl

beauti|ful /'bjuːtɪfl/ adj schön. ~fy vt (pt/pp -ied) verschönern

beauty /'bjuːtɪ/ n Schönheit f. ~ parlour n Kosmetiksalon m. ~ spot n Schönheitsfleck m; (place) landschaftlich besonders reizvolles Fleckchen nt.

beaver /'biːvə(r)/ n Biber m

became /bɪ'keɪm/ see become

because /bɪ'kɒz/ conj weil ● adv ~ of wegen (+ gen)

become /bɪ'kʌm/ vt/i (pt became, pp become) werden. ~ing adj (clothes) kleidsam

bed /bed/ n Bett nt; (layer) Schicht f; (of flowers) Beet nt; in ~ im Bett; go to ~ ins od zu Bett gehen; ~ and breakfast Zimmer mit Frühstück. ~clothes npl, ~ding n Bettzeug nt. ~room n Schlafzimmer nt

'bedside n at his ~ an seinem Bett. ~ lamp n Nachttischlampe f. ~ 'table n Nachttisch m

bed: ~'sitter n, ~-'sitting-room n Wohnschlafzimmer nt. ~spread n Tagesdecke f. ~time n at ~time vor dem Schlafengehen

bee /biː/ n Biene f

beech /biːtʃ/ n Buche f

beef /biːf/ n Rindfleisch nt. ~burger n Hamburger m

bee: ~hive n Bienenstock m. ~line n make a ~line for 🗊 zusteuern auf (+ acc)

been /biːn/ see be

beer /bɪə(r)/ n Bier nt

beet /biːt/ n (Amer: beetroot) rote Bete f; [sugar] ~ Zuckerrübe f

beetle /'biːtl/ n Käfer m

'beetroot n rote Bete f

before /bɪ'fɔː(r)/ prep vor (+ dat/ acc); the day ~ yesterday vorgestern; ~ long bald ● adv vorher; (already) schon; never ~ noch nie; ~ that davor ● conj (time) ehe,

beg | bent

bevor. ~hand adv vorher, im Voraus

beg /beg/ v (pt/pp begged) ● vi betteln ● vt (entreat) anflehen; (ask) bitten (for um)

began /brˈgæn/ see begin

beggar /ˈbegə(r)/ n Bettler(in) m(f); 🗆 Kerl m

begin /brˈgɪn/ vt/i (pt began, pp begun, pres p beginning) anfangen, beginnen; to ~ with anfangs. ~ner n Anfänger(in) m(f). ~ning n Anfang m, Beginn m

begun /brˈgʌn/ see begin

behalf /brˈhɑːf/ n on ~ of im Namen von; on my ~ meinetwegen

behave /brˈheɪv/ vi sich verhalten; ~ oneself sich benehmen

behaviour /brˈheɪvjə(r)/ n Verhalten nt; good/bad ~ gutes/schlechtes Benehmen nt

behind /brˈhaɪnd/ prep hinter (+ dat/acc); be ~ sth hinter etw (dat) stecken ● adv hinten; (late) im Rückstand; a long way ~ weit zurück ● n 🗆 Hintern m. ~hand adv im Rückstand

beige /beɪʒ/ adj beige

being /ˈbiːɪŋ/ n Dasein nt; living ~ Lebewesen nt; come into ~ entstehen

belated /brˈleɪtɪd/ adj verspätet

belfry /ˈbelfrɪ/ n Glockenstube f; (tower) Glockenturm m

Belgian /ˈbeldʒən/ adj belgisch ● n Belgier(in) m(f)

Belgium /ˈbeldʒəm/ n Belgien nt

belief /brˈliːf/ n Glaube m

believable /brˈliːvəbl/ adj glaubhaft

believe /brˈliːv/ vt/i glauben (s.o. jdm; in an + acc). ~r n (Relig) Gläubige(r) m/f

belittle /brˈlɪtl/ vt herabsetzen

bell /bel/ n Glocke f; (on door) Klingel f

bellow /ˈbeləʊ/ vt/i brüllen

belly /ˈbelɪ/ n Bauch m

belong /brˈlɒŋ/ vi gehören (to dat); (be member) angehören (to dat). ~ings npl Sachen pl

beloved /brˈlʌvɪd/ adj geliebt ● n Geliebte(r) m/f

below /brˈləʊ/ prep unter (+ dat/ acc) ● adv unten; (Naut) unter Deck

belt /belt/ n Gürtel m; (area) Zone f; (Techn) [Treib]riemen m ● vi (🗆: rush) rasen ● vt (🗆: hit) hauen

bench /bentʃ/ n Bank f; (work-) Werkbank f

bend /bend/ n Biegung f; (in road) Kurve f; round the ~ 🗆 verrückt ● v (pt/pp bent) ● vt biegen; beugen (arm, leg) ● vi sich bücken; (thing:) sich biegen; (road:) eine Biegung machen. ~ down vi sich bücken. ~ over vi sich vornüberbeugen

beneath /brˈniːθ/ prep unter (+ dat/acc); ~ him (fig) unter seiner Würde ● adv darunter

benefactor /ˈbenɪfæktə(r)/ n Wohltäter(in) m(f)

beneficial /benɪˈfɪʃl/ adj nützlich

benefit /ˈbenɪfɪt/ n Vorteil m; (allowance) Unterstützung f; (insurance) Leistung f; sickness ~ Krankengeld nt ● v (pt/pp -fited, pres p -fiting) ● vt nützen (+ dat) ● vi profitieren (from von)

benevolen|ce /brˈnevələns/ n Wohlwollen nt. ~t adj wohlwollend

bent /bent/ see bend ● adj (person) gebeugt; (distorted) verbogen; (🗆: dishonest) korrupt; be ~ on doing sth darauf erpicht sein, etw zu tun ● n Hang m, Neigung f (for zu); artistic ~ künstlerische Ader f

bequeath /bɪ'kwi:ð/ vt vermachen (to dat)

bereave|d /bɪ'ri:vd/ n the ~d pl die Hinterbliebenen

beret /'beret/ n Baskenmütze f

Berne /bɜ:n/ n Bern nt

berry /'berɪ/ n Beere f

berth /bɜ:θ/ n (on ship) [Schlaf]koje f; (ship's anchorage) Liegeplatz m; give a wide ~ to 🔲 einen großen Bogen machen um

beside /bɪ'saɪd/ prep neben (+ dat/acc); ~ oneself außer sich (dat)

besides /bɪ'saɪdz/ prep außer (+ dat) ● adv außerdem

besiege /bɪ'si:dʒ/ vt belagern

best /best/ adj & n (the r,s); the ~ der/die/das Beste; at ~ bestenfalls; all the ~! alles Gute! do one's ~ sein Bestes tun; the ~ part of a year fast ein Jahr; to the ~ of my knowledge so viel ich weiß; make the ~ of it das Beste daraus machen ● adv am besten; as ~ I could so gut ich konnte. '~man ≈ Trauzeuge m. '~seller n Bestseller m

bet /bet/ n Wette f ● v (pt/pp bet or betted) ● vt ~ s.o. £5 mit jdm um £5 wetten ● vi wetten; ~ on [Geld] setzen auf (+ acc)

betray /bɪ'treɪ/ vt verraten. ~al n Verrat m

better /'betə(r)/ adj besser; get ~ sich bessern; (after illness) sich erholen ● adv besser; ~ off besser dran; ~ not lieber nicht; all the ~ umso besser; the sooner the ~ je eher, desto besser; think ~ of sth sich eines Besseren besinnen; you'd ~ stay du bleibst am besten hier ● vt verbessern; (do better than) übertreffen; ~ oneself sich verbessern

between /bɪ'twi:n/ prep zwischen (+ dat/acc); ~ you and me unter

uns; ~ us (together) zusammen ● adv [in] ~ dazwischen

beware /bɪ'weə(r)/ vi sich in Acht nehmen (of vor + dat); ~ of the dog! Vorsicht, bissiger Hund!

bewilder /bɪ'wɪldə(r)/ vt verwirren. ~ment n Verwirrung f

bewitch /bɪ'wɪtʃ/ vt verzaubern; (fig) bezaubern

beyond /bɪ'jɒnd/ prep über (+ acc) ... hinaus; (further) weiter als; ~ reach außer Reichweite; ~ doubt ohne jeden Zweifel; it's ~ me 🔲 das geht über meinen Horizont ● adv darüber hinaus

bias /'baɪəs/ n Voreingenommenheit f; (preference) Vorliebe f; (Jur) Befangenheit f ● vt (pt/pp biased) (influence) beeinflussen. ~ed adj voreingenommen; (Jur) befangen

bib /bɪb/ n Lätzchen nt

Bible /'baɪbl/ n Bibel f

biblical /'bɪblɪkl/ adj biblisch

bibliography /bɪblɪ'ɒgrəfɪ/ n Bibliographie f

bicycle /'baɪsɪkl/ n Fahrrad nt ● vi mit dem Rad fahren

bid /bɪd/ n Gebot nt; (attempt) Versuch m ● vt/i (pt/pp bid, pres p bidding) bieten (for auf + acc); (Cards) reizen

bidder /'bɪdə(r)/ n Bieter(in) m(f)

bide /baɪd/ vt ~ one's time den richtigen Moment abwarten

big /bɪg/ adj (bigger, biggest) groß ● adv talk ~ 🔲 angeben

bigam|ist /'bɪgəmɪst/ n Bigamist m. ~y n Bigamie f

big-'headed adj 🔲 eingebildet

bigot /'bɪgət/ n Eiferer m. ~ed adj engstirnig

'bigwig n 🔲 hohes Tier nt

bike /baɪk/ n 🔲 [Fahr]rad nt

bikini /bɪ'ki:nɪ/ n Bikini m

bile | blacken

bile /baɪl/ n Galle f

bilingual /baɪˈlɪŋgwəl/ adj zweisprachig

bilious /ˈbɪljəs/ adj (Med) ~ attack verdorbener Magen m

bill¹ /bɪl/ n Rechnung f; (poster) Plakat nt; (Pol) Gesetzentwurf m; (Amer: note) Banknote f; ~ of exchange Wechsel m f; ~ eine Rechnung schicken (+ dat)

bill² n (beak) Schnabel m

'billfold n (Amer) Brieftasche f

billiards /ˈbɪljədz/ n Billard nt

billion /ˈbɪljən/ n (thousand million) Milliarde f; (million million) Billion f

bin /bɪn/ n Mülleimer m

bind /baɪnd/ vt (pt/pp bound) binden (to an + acc); (bandage) verbinden; (Jur) verpflichten; (cover the edge of) einfassen. ~ing adj verbindlich ●n Einband m; (braid) Borte f; (on ski) Bindung f

binge /bɪndʒ/ n ⊞ go on the ~ eine Sauftour machen

binoculars /bɪˈnɒkjʊləz/ npl [pair of] ~ Fernglas nt

bio'chemistry /baɪəʊ-/ n Biochemie f. ~degradable adj biologisch abbaubar

biofuel /ˈbaɪəʊfjuːəl/ n Biokraftstoff m

biograph|er /baɪˈɒgrəfə(r)/ n Biograph(in) m(f). ~y n Biographie f

biological /baɪəˈlɒdʒɪkl/ adj biologisch

biolog|ist /baɪˈɒlədʒɪst/ n Biologe m. ~y n Biologie f

bio'terrorism /baɪəʊ-/ n Bioterrorismus m

birch /bɜːtʃ/ n Birke f; (whip) Rute f

bird /bɜːd/ n Vogel m; (⊞: girl) Mädchen nt; kill two ~s with one stone zwei Fliegen mit einer Klappe schlagen

Biro ® /ˈbaɪrəʊ/ n Kugel-

schreiber m

birth /bɜːθ/ n Geburt f

birth: ~ **certificate** n Geburtsurkunde f. ~**-control** n Geburtenregelung f. ~**day** n Geburtstag m. ~**-rate** n Geburtenziffer f

biscuit /ˈbɪskɪt/ n Keks m

bishop /ˈbɪʃəp/ n Bischof m

bit¹ /bɪt/ n Stückchen nt; (for horse) Gebiss nt; (Techn) Bohreinsatz m; a ~ ein bisschen; ~ by ~ nach und nach; a ~ of bread ein bisschen Brot; do one's ~ sein Teil tun

bit² see bite

bitch /bɪtʃ/ n Hündin f; ⊠ Luder nt. ~**y** adj gehässig

bit|e /baɪt/ n Biss m; [insect] ~ Stich m; (mouthful) Bissen m ●vt/i (pt bit, pp bitten) beißen; (insect:) stechen; kauen (one's nails). ~**ing** adj beißend

bitten /ˈbɪtn/ see bite

bitter /ˈbɪtə(r)/ adj bitter; ~**ly cold** bitterkalt ●n bitteres Bier nt. ~**ness** n Bitterkeit f

bitty /ˈbɪtɪ/ adj zusammengestoppelt

bizarre /bɪˈzɑː(r)/ adj bizarr

black /blæk/ adj (-er, -est) schwarz; **be** ~**and blue** grün und blau sein ●n Schwarz nt; (person) Schwarze(r) m/f ●vt schwärzen; boykottieren (goods)

black: ~**berry** n Brombeere f. ~**bird** n Amsel f. ~**board** n (Sch) [Wand]tafel f. ~'**currant** n schwarze Johannisbeere f

blacken vt/i schwärzen

black: ~'**eye** n blaues Auge nt. **B** ~ '**Forest** n Schwarzwald m. ~ '**ice** n Glatteis nt. ~**list** vt auf die schwarze Liste setzen. ~**mail** n Erpressung f ●vt erpressen. ~**mailer** n Erpresser(in) m(f). ~ '**market** n schwarzer Markt m. ~'**out** n have a ~-out (Med) das Bewusstsein verlieren. ~ 'pudding n Blutwurst f

bladder /'blædə(r)/ n (Anat) Blase f

blade /bleɪd/ n Klinge f; (of grass) Halm m

blame /bleɪm/ n Schuld f ● vt die Schuld geben (+ dat); no one is to ~ keiner ist schuld daran. ~less adj schuldlos

bland /blænd/ adj (-er, -est) mild

blank /blæŋk/ adj leer; (look) ausdruckslos ● n Lücke f; (cartridge) Platzpatrone f. ~ 'cheque n Blankoscheck m

blanket /'blæŋkɪt/ n Decke f; wet ~ 🗵 Spielverderber(in) m(f)

blare /bleə(r)/ vt/i schmettern

blasé /'blɑːzeɪ/ adj blasiert

blast /blɑːst/ n (gust) Luftstoß m; (sound) Schmettern nt; (of horn) Tuten nt ● vt sprengen ● int 🗵 verdammt. ~ed adj 🗵 verdammt

blatant /'bleɪtənt/ adj offensichtlich

blaze /bleɪz/ n Feuer nt ● vi brennen

blazer /'bleɪzə(r)/ n Blazer m

bleach /bliːtʃ/ n Bleichmittel nt ● vt/i bleichen

bleak /bliːk/ adj (-er, -est) öde; (fig) trostlos

bleary-eyed /'blɪərɪ-/ adj mit trüben/(on waking up) verschlafenen Augen

bleat /bliːt/ vi blöken

bleed /bliːd/ v (pt/pp bled) ● vi bluten ● vt entlüften (radiator)

bleep /bliːp/ n Piepton m ● vi piepsen ● vt mit dem Piepser rufen. ~er n Piepser m

blemish /'blemɪʃ/ n Makel m

blend /blend/ n Mischung f ● vt mischen ● vi sich vermischen

bless /bles/ vt segnen. ~ed adj heilig; 🗵 verflixt. ~ing n Segen m

blew /bluː/ see blow²

blight /blaɪt/ n (Bot) Brand m

blind /blaɪnd/ adj blind; (corner) unübersichtlich; ~ man/woman Blinde(r) m/f ● n (roller) ~ Rouleau nt ● vt blenden

blind: ~ 'alley n Sackgasse f. ~fold adj & adv mit verbundenen Augen ● n Augenbinde f ● vt die Augen verbinden (+ dat). ~ly adv blindlings. ~ness n Blindheit f

blink /blɪŋk/ vi blinzeln; (light:) blinken

bliss /blɪs/ n Glückseligkeit f. ~ful adj glücklich

blister /'blɪstə(r)/ n (Med) Blase f

blitz /blɪts/ n 🗵 Großaktion f

blizzard /'blɪzəd/ n Schneesturm m

bloated /'bləʊtɪd/ adj aufgedunsen

blob /blɒb/ n Klecks m

block /blɒk/ n Block m; (of wood) Klotz m; (of flats) [Wohn]block m ● vt blockieren. ~ up vt zustopfen

blockade /blɒ'keɪd/ n Blockade f ● vt blockieren

blockage /'blɒkɪdʒ/ n Verstopfung f

block: ~head n 🗵 Dummkopf m. ~ letters npl Blockschrift f

blog /blɒg/ n Online-Tagebuch nt, Blog f/m

bloke /bləʊk/ n 🗵 Kerl m

blonde /blɒnd/ adj blond ● n Blondine f

blood /blʌd/ n Blut nt

blood: ~-curdling adj markerschütternd. ~ donor n Blutspender m. ~ group n Blutgruppe f. ~hound n Bluthund m. ~-poisoning n Blutvergiftung f. ~ pressure n Blutdruck m. ~shed n Blutvergießen nt. ~shot adj blutunterlaufen. ~ **sports** npl Jagdsport m. ~**stained** adj blutbefleckt. ~**test** n Blutprobe f. ~**thirsty** adj blutdürstig. ~-**vessel** n Blutgefäß nt

bloody /ˈblʌdɪ/ adj blutig; ⊠ verdammt. ~-**minded** adj ⊠ stur

bloom /bluːm/ n Blüte f ● vi blühen

blossom /ˈblɒsəm/ n Blüte f ● vi blühen

blot /blɒt/ n [Tinten]klecks m; (fig) Fleck m ● ~ **out** vt (fig) auslöschen

blotch /blɒtʃ/ n Fleck m. ~**y** adj fleckig

'**blotting-paper** n Löschpapier nt

blouse /blaʊz/ n Bluse f

blow[1] /bləʊ/ n Schlag m

blow[2] v (pt blew, pp blown) ● vt blasen; (fam; squander) verpulvern; ~ **one's nose** sich (dat) die Nase putzen ● vi blasen; (fuse:) durchbrennen. ~ **away** vt wegblasen ● vi wegfliegen. ~ **down** vt umwehen ● vi umfallen. ~ **out** vt (extinguish) ausblasen. ~ **over** vi umfallen; (fig: die down) vorübergehen. ~ **up** vt (inflate) aufblasen; (enlarge) vergrößern; (shatter by explosion) sprengen ● vi explodieren

'**blowlamp** n Lötlampe f

blown /bləʊn/ see blow[2]

'**blowtorch** n (Amer) Lötlampe f

'**blowy** /ˈbləʊɪ/ adj windig

blue /bluː/ adj (-r, -st) blau; **feel** ~ deprimiert sein ● n Blau nt; **have the** ~**s** deprimiert sein; **out of the** ~ aus heiterem Himmel

blue: ~**bell** n Sternhyazinthe f. ~**berry** n Heidelbeere f. ~**bottle** n Schmeißfliege f. ~**film** n Pornofilm m. ~**print** n (fig) Entwurf m

bluff /blʌf/ n Bluff m ● vi bluffen

blunder /ˈblʌndə(r)/ n Schnitzer m

● vi einen Schnitzer machen

blunt /blʌnt/ adj stumpf; (person) geradeheraus. ~**ly** adv unverblümt, geradeheraus

blur /blɜː(r)/ n **it's all a** ~ alles ist verschwommen ● vt (pt/pp blurred) verschwommen machen; ~**red** verschwommen

blush /blʌʃ/ n Erröten nt ● vi erröten

bluster /ˈblʌstə(r)/ n Großtuerei f. ~**y** adj windig

boar /bɔː(r)/ n Eber m

board /bɔːd/ n Brett nt; (for notices) schwarzes Brett nt; (committee) Ausschuss m; (of directors) Vorstand m; **on** ~ an Bord; **full** ~ Vollpension f; ~ **and lodging** Unterkunft und Verpflegung f ● vt einsteigen in (+ acc); (Naut, Aviat) besteigen ● vi an Bord gehen. ~ **up** vt mit Brettern verschlagen

boarder /ˈbɔːdə(r)/ n Pensionsgast m; (Sch) Internatsschüler/in m(f)

board: ~-**game** n Brettspiel nt. ~**ing-house** n Pension f. ~**ing-school** n Internat nt

boast /bəʊst/ vi sich rühmen (+ gen) ● vi prahlen (about mit). ~**ful** adj prahlerisch

boat /bəʊt/ n Boot nt; (ship) Schiff nt

Boat Race Seit 1829 findet jährlich (meist am Samstag vor Ostern) auf der Themse in London statt. Die Achterrennen wird von den Rudermannschaften der Universitäten Oxford und Cambridge ausgetragen. Im Gegensatz zu anderen sportlichen Universitätswettbewerben wird dieses Ruderrennen landesweit im Fernsehen übertragen.

bob /bɒb/ vi (pt/pp **bobbed**) ~ **up** and down sich auf und ab bewegen

'bob-sleigh n Bob m

bodily /'bɒdɪlɪ/ adj körperlich ● adv (forcibly) mit Gewalt

body /'bɒdɪ/ n Körper m; (corpse) Leiche f; (corporation) Körperschaft f. ~**guard** n Leibwächter m. ~ **part** n Leichenteil nt. ~**work** n (Auto) Karosserie f

bog /bɒg/ n Sumpf m

bogus /'bəʊgəs/ adj falsch

boil¹ /bɔɪl/ n Furunkel m

boil² /bɔɪl/ n bring/come to the ~ zum Kochen bringen/kommen ● vt/i kochen; ~ed **potatoes** Salzkartoffeln pl. ~ **down** vi (fig) hinauslaufen (to auf + acc). ~ **over** vi überkochen

boiler /'bɔɪlə(r)/ n Heizkessel m

'boiling point n Siedepunkt m

boisterous /'bɔɪstərəs/ adj übermütig

bold /bəʊld/ adj (-er, -est) kühn; (Printing) fett. ~**ness** f Kühnheit f

bolster /'bəʊlstə(r)/ n Nackenrolle f ● vt ~ **up** Mut machen (+ dat)

bolt /bəʊlt/ n Riegel m; (Techn) Bolzen m ● vt schrauben (to an + acc); verriegeln (door); hinunterschlingen (food) ● vi abhauen; (horse:) durchgehen

bomb /bɒm/ n Bombe f ● vt bombardieren

bombard /bɒm'bɑːd/ vt beschießen; (fig) bombardieren

bombastic /bɒm'bæstɪk/ adj bombastisch

bomber /'bɒmə(r)/ n (Aviat) Bomber m; (person) Bombenleger(in) m(f)

bond /bɒnd/ n (fig) Band nt; (Comm) Obligation f

bone /bəʊn/ n Knochen m; (of fish) Gräte f ● vt von den Knochen lösen (meat); entgräten (fish). ~-'**dry** adj knochentrocken

bonfire /'bɒn-/ n Gartenfeuer nt; (celebratory) Freudenfeuer nt

bonus /'bəʊnəs/ n Prämie f; (gratuity) Gratifikation f; (fig) Plus nt

bony /'bəʊnɪ/ adj knochig; (fish) grätig

boo /buː/ int buh! ● vt ausbuhen ● vi buhen

boob /buːb/ n (fam: mistake) Schnitzer m

book /bʊk/ n Buch nt; (of tickets) Heft nt; keep the ~s (Comm) die Bücher führen ● vt/i buchen; (reserve) [vor]bestellen; (for offence) aufschreiben

book: ~**case** n Bücherregal nt. ~**ends** npl Buchstützen pl. ~**ing-office** n Fahrkartenschalter m. ~**keeping** n Buchführung f. ~**let** n Broschüre f. ~**maker** n Buchmacher m. ~**mark** n Lesezeichen nt. ~**seller** n Buchhändler(in) m(f). ~**shop** n Buchhandlung f. ~**stall** n Bücherstand m

boom /buːm/ n (Comm) Hochkonjunktur f; (upturn) Aufschwung m ● vi dröhnen; (fig) blühen

boon /buːn/ n Segen m

boost /buːst/ n Auftrieb m ● vt Auftrieb geben (+ dat)

boot /buːt/ n Stiefel m; (Auto) Kofferraum m

booth /buːð/ n Bude f; (cubicle) Kabine f

booty /'buːtɪ/ n Beute f

booze /buːz/ n (fam) Alkohol m ● vi (fam) saufen

border /'bɔːdə(r)/ n Rand m; (frontier) Grenze f; (in garden) Rabatte f ● vi ~ **on** grenzen an (+ acc). ~**line case** n Grenzfall m

bore | **boy**

bore¹ /bɔː(r)/ *see* bear²

bor|e² n (*of gun*) Kaliber nt; (*person*) langweiliger Mensch m; (*thing*) langweilige Sache f ● vt langweilen; be ~ed sich langweilen. ~edom /-dəm/ n Langeweile f. ~ing adj langweilig

born /bɔːn/ pp be ~ geboren werden ● adj geboren

borne /bɔːn/ *see* bear²

borrow /ˈbɒrəʊ/ vt [sich (dat)] borgen od leihen (from von)

bosom /ˈbʊzm/ n Busen m

boss /bɒs/ n 🗍 Chef m ● vt herumkommandieren. ~y adj herrschsüchtig

botanical /bəˈtænɪkl/ adj botanisch

botan|ist /ˈbɒtənɪst/ n Botaniker(in) m(f). ~y n Botanik f

both /bəʊθ/ adj & pron beide; ~[of] the children beide Kinder; ~ of them beide [von ihnen] ● adv ~ men and women sowohl Männer als auch Frauen

bother /ˈbʊðə(r)/ n Mühe f; (*minor trouble*) Ärger m ● int 🗍 verflixt! ● vt belästigen; (*disturb*) stören ● vi sich kümmern (about um)

bottle /ˈbɒtl/ n Flasche f ● vt Flaschen abfüllen; (*preserve*) einmachen

bottle: ~-neck n (*fig*) Engpass m. ~-opener n Flaschenöffner m

bottom /ˈbɒtəm/ adj unterste(r,s) ● n (*of container*) Boden m; (*of river*) Grund m; (*of page, hill*) Fuß m; (*buttocks*) Hintern m; at the ~ unten; get to the ~ of sth (*fig*) hinter etw (acc) kommen

bought /bɔːt/ *see* buy

bounce /baʊns/ vi [auf]springen; (*cheque*) 🗍 nicht gedeckt sein ● vt aufspringen lassen (ball)

bouncer /ˈbaʊnsə(r)/ n 🗍 Rausschmeißer m

bound¹ /baʊnd/ n Sprung m ● vi springen

bound² *see* bind ● adj ~ for (ship) mit Kurs auf (+ acc); be ~ to do sth etw bestimmt machen; (*obliged*) verpflichtet sein, etw zu machen

boundary /ˈbaʊndərɪ/ n Grenze f

bounds /baʊndz/ npl (*fig*) Grenzen pl; out of ~ verboten

bouquet /bʊˈkeɪ/ n [Blumen]strauß m; (*of wine*) Bukett nt

bourgeois /ˈbʊəʒwɑː/ adj (*pej*) spießbürgerlich

bout /baʊt/ n (*Med*) Anfall m; (*Sport*) Kampf m

bow¹ /bəʊ/ n (*weapon & Mus*) Bogen m; (*knot*) Schleife f

bow² /baʊ/ n Verbeugung f ● vi sich verbeugen ● vt neigen (*head*)

bow³ /baʊ/ n (*Naut*) Bug m

bowel /ˈbaʊəl/ n Darm m. ~s pl Eingeweide pl

bowl¹ /bəʊl/ n Schüssel f; (*shallow*) Schale f

bowl² n (*ball*) Kugel f ● vt/i werfen. ~ over vt umwerfen

bowler /ˈbəʊlə(r)/ n (*Sport*) Werfer m

bowling /ˈbəʊlɪŋ/ n Kegeln nt. ~-alley n Kegelbahn f

bowls /bəʊlz/ n Bowlsspiel nt

bow-'tie /bəʊ-/ n Fliege f

box¹ /bɒks/ n Schachtel f; (*wooden*) Kiste f; (*cardboard*) Karton m; (*Theat*) Loge f

box² vt/i (*Sport*) boxen

box|er /ˈbɒksə(r)/ n Boxer m. ~ing n Boxen nt. B~ing Day n zweiter Weihnachtstag m

box: ~-office n (*Theat*) Kasse f. ~-room n Abstellraum m

boy /bɔɪ/ n Junge m. ~ band n Jungenband f

b

boycott /'bɔɪkɒt/ n Boykott m ● vt boykottieren

boy: ~**friend** n Freund m. ~**ish** adj jungenhaft

bra /bra:/ n BH m

brace /breɪs/ n Strebe f, Stütze f; (dental) Zahnspange f; ~**s** npl Hosenträger mpl

bracelet /'breɪslɪt/ n Armband nt

bracing /'breɪsɪŋ/ adj stärkend

bracket /'brækɪt/ n Konsole f; (group) Gruppe f; (Printing) round/square ~**s** runde/eckige Klammern ● vt einklammern

brag /bræg/ vi (pt/pp bragged) prahlen (about mit)

braille /breɪl/ n Blindenschrift f

brain /breɪn/ n Gehirn nt; ~**s** (fig) Intelligenz f

brain: ~**less** adj dumm. ~**wash** vt einer Gehirnwäsche unterziehen. ~**wave** n Geistesblitz m

brainy /'breɪnɪ/ adj klug

brake /breɪk/ n Bremse f ● vt/i bremsen. ~**light** n Bremslicht nt

bramble /'bræmbl/ n Brombeerstrauch m

branch /brɑːntʃ/ n Ast m; (fig) Zweig m; (Comm) Zweigstelle f; (shop) Filiale f ● vi sich gabeln

brand /brænd/ n Marke f ● vt (fig) brandmarken als

brandish /'brændɪʃ/ vt schwingen

brand-'new adj nagelneu

brandy /'brændɪ/ n Weinbrand m

brash /bræʃ/ adj nassforsch

brass /brɑːs/ n Messing nt; (Mus) Blech nt; ~ top ~ ① hohe Tiere pl. ~ **band** n Blaskapelle f

brassy /'brɑːsɪ/ adj ① ordinär

brat /bræt/ n (pej) Balg m

bravado /brə'vɑːdəʊ/ n Forschheit f

brave /breɪv/ adj (-r, -st) tapfer

● vt die Stirn bieten (+ dat). ~**ry** n Tapferkeit f

bravo /brɑː'vəʊ/ int bravo!

brawl /brɔːl/ n Schlägerei f

brawn /brɔːn/ n (Culin) Sülze f

brawny /'brɔːnɪ/ adj muskulös

bray /breɪ/ vi iahen

brazen /'breɪzn/ adj unverschämt

Brazil /brə'zɪl/ n Brasilien nt. ~**ian** adj brasilianisch. ~ **nut** n Paranuss f

breach /briːtʃ/ n Bruch m; (Mil & fig) Bresche f; ~ **of contract** Vertragsbruch m

bread /bred/ n Brot nt; **slice of** ~ **and butter** Butterbrot nt. ~**crumbs** npl Brotkrümel pl; (Culin) Paniermehl nt

breadth /bredθ/ n Breite f

break /breɪk/ n Bruch m; (interval) Pause f; (interruption) Unterbrechung f; (①: chance) Chance f ● v (pt broke, pp broken) ● vt brechen; (smash) zerbrechen; (damage) kaputtmachen ①; (interrupt) unterbrechen; ~ **one's arm** sich (dat) den Arm brechen ● vi brechen; (day:) anbrechen; (storm:) losbrechen; (thing:) kaputtgehen ①; (rope, thread:) reißen; (news:) bekannt werden; **his voice is** ~**ing** er ist im Stimmbruch. ~ **away** vi sich reißen/(fig) sich absetzen (from von). ~ **down** vi zusammenbrechen; (Techn) eine Panne haben; (negotiations:) scheitern ● vt aufbrechen (door); aufgliedern (figures). ~ **in** vi einbrechen. ~ **off** vt/i abbrechen; lösen (engagement). ~ **out** vi ausbrechen. ~ **up** vt zerbrechen ● vi (crowd:) sich zerstreuen; (marriage, couple:) auseinander gehen; (Sch) Ferien bekommen

break|able /'breɪkəbl/ adj zerbrechlich. ~**age** n Bruch m. ~**down** n (Techn) Panne f; (Med)

Zusammenbruch m; (of figures) Aufgliederung f. ~**er** n (wave) Brecher m

breakfast /'brekfəst/ n Frühstück nt

break: ~**through** n Durchbruch m. ~**water** n Buhne f

breast /brest/ n Brust f. ~**bone** n Brustbein nt. ~**feed** vt stillen. ~**stroke** n Brustschwimmen nt

breath /breθ/ n Atem m; out of ~ außer Atem; under one's ~ vor sich (acc) hin

breathe /bri:ð/ vt/i atmen. ~ **in** vt/i einatmen. ~ **out** vt/i ausatmen

breathing n Atmen nt

breath: ~**less** adj atemlos. ~**taking** adj atemberaubend

bred /bred/ see breed

breed /bri:d/ n Rasse f ● vt (pt/pp bred) ● vt züchten; (give rise to) erzeugen ● vi sich vermehren. ~**er** n Züchter m. ~**ing** n Zucht f; (fig) [gute] Lebensart f

breez|**e** /bri:z/ n Lüftchen nt; (Naut) Brise f. ~**y** adj windig

brevity /'brevətɪ/ n Kürze f

brew /bru:/ n Gebräu nt ● vt brauen; kochen (tea). ~**er** n Brauer m. ~**ery** n Brauerei f

bribe /braɪb/ n (money) Bestechungsgeld nt ● vt bestechen. ~**ry** n Bestechung f

brick /brɪk/ n Ziegelstein m, Backstein m

'**bricklayer** n Maurer m

bridal /'braɪdl/ adj Braut-

bride /braɪd/ n Braut f. ~**groom** n Bräutigam m. ~**smaid** n Brautjungfer f

bridge[1] /brɪdʒ/ n Brücke f; (of nose) Nasenrücken m; (of spectacles) Steg m

bridge[2] n (Cards) Bridge nt

bridle /'braɪdl/ n Zaum m

brief[1] /bri:f/ adj (-er, -est) kurz; be ~ (person:) sich kurz fassen

brief[2] n Instruktionen pl; (Jur: case) Mandat nt. ~**case** n Aktentasche f

brief|**ing** /'bri:fɪŋ/ n Informationsgespräch n. ~**ly** adv kurz. ~**ness** n Kürze f

briefs /bri:fs/ npl Slip m

brigade /brɪ'geɪd/ n Brigade f

bright /braɪt/ adj (-er, -est) hell; (day) heiter; ~ red hellrot

bright|**en** /braɪtn/ v ~**en** [up] ● vt aufheitern ● vi sich aufheitern. ~**ness** n Helligkeit f

brilliance /'brɪljəns/ n Glanz m; (of person) Scharfsinn m

brilliant /'brɪljənt/ adj glänzend; (person) genial

brim /brɪm/ n Rand m; (of hat) Krempe f

bring /brɪŋ/ vt (pt/pp brought) bringen; ~ them with you bring sie mit; I can't b~ myself to do it ich bringe es nicht fertig. ~ **about** vt verursachen. ~ **along** vt mitbringen. ~ **back** vt zurückbringen. ~ **down** vt herunterbringen; senken (price). ~ **off** vt vollbringen. ~ **on** vt (cause) verursachen. ~ **out** vt herausbringen. ~ **round** vt vorbeibringen; (persuade) überreden; (un-conscious person). ~ **up** vt heraufbringen; (vomit) erbrechen; aufziehen (children); erwähnen (question)

brink /brɪŋk/ n Rand m

brisk /brɪsk/ adj (-er, -est,) -ly adv lebhaft; (quick) schnell

bristle /'brɪsl/ n Borste f

Brit|**ain** /'brɪtn/ n Großbritannien nt. ~**ish** adj britisch; the ~**ish** die Briten pl. ~ n Brite m/Britin f

Brittany /'brɪtənɪ/ n die Bretagne

brittle /'brɪtl/ adj brüchig, spröde

broad /brɔːd/ adj (-er, -est) breit; (hint) deutlich; in ~ daylight am hellichten Tag. ~ **beans** npl dicke Bohnen pl

broadband /'brɔːdbænd/ n Breitband nt

'broadcast n Sendung f • vt/i (pt/pp -cast) senden. ~**er** n Rundfunk- und Fernsehpersönlichkeit f. ~**ing** n Funk und Fernsehen pl

broaden /'brɔːdn/ vt verbreitern; (fig) erweitern • vi sich verbreitern

broadly /'brɔːdlɪ/ adv breit; ~ speaking allgemein gesagt

broad'minded adj tolerant

broccoli /'brɒkəlɪ/ n inv Brokkoli m

brochure /'brəʊʃə(r)/ n Broschüre f

broke /brəʊk/ see break • adj 🔢 pleite

broken /'brəʊkn/ see break • adj zerbrochen, 🔢 kaputt. ~-**hearted** adj untröstlich

broker /'brəʊkə(r)/ n Makler m

brolly /'brɒlɪ/ n 🔢 Schirm m

bronchitis /brɒŋ'kaɪtɪs/ n Bronchitis f

bronze /brɒnz/ n Bronze f

brooch /brəʊtʃ/ n Brosche f

brood /bruːd/ n; (fig) grübeln

broom /bruːm/ n Besen m; (Bot) Ginster m

broth /brɒθ/ n Brühe f

brothel /'brɒθl/ n Bordell nt

brother /'brʌðə(r)/ n Bruder m

brother: ~-**in-law** n (pl -s-in-law) Schwager m. ~**ly** adj brüderlich

brought /brɔːt/ see bring

brow /braʊ/ n Augenbraue f; (forehead) Stirn f; (of hill) [Berg]kuppe f

brown /braʊn/ adj (-er, -est) braun; ~ 'paper Packpapier nt • n Braun nt • vt bräunen • vi braun werden

browse /braʊz/ vi (read) schmökern; (in shop) sich umsehen. ~**r** n (Computing) Browser m

bruise /bruːz/ n blauer Fleck m • vt beschädigen (fruit); ~ one's arm sich (dat) den Arm quetschen

brunette /bruː'net/ n Brünette f

brush /brʌʃ/ n Bürste f; (with handle) Handfeger m; (for paint, pastry) Pinsel m; (bushes) Unterholz nt; (fig: conflict) Zusammenstoß m • vt bürsten; putzen (teeth); ~ against streifen [gegen]. ~ **aside** (fig) abtun. ~ **off** vt abbürsten. ~ **up** vt/i (fig) ~ **up** [on] auffrischen

brusque /brʊsk/ adj brüsk

Brussels /'brʌslz/ n Brüssel nt. ~ **sprouts** npl Rosenkohl m

brutal /'bruːtl/ adj brutal. ~**ity** n Brutalität f

brute /bruːt/ n Unmensch m. ~ **force** n rohe Gewalt f

BSE abbr (bovine spongiform encephalopathy) BSE f

bubble /'bʌbl/ n [Luft]blase f • vi sprudeln

buck[1] /bʌk/ n (deer & Gym) Bock m; (rabbit) Rammler m • vi (horse): bocken

buck[2] n (Amer 🔢) Dollar m

buck[3] n pass the ~ die Verantwortung abschieben

bucket /'bʌkɪt/ n Eimer m

buckle /'bʌkl/ n Schnalle f • vt zuschnallen • vi sich verbiegen

bud /bʌd/ n Knospe f

buddy /'bʌdɪ/ n 🔢 Freund m

budge /bʌdʒ/ vt bewegen • vi sich [von der Stelle] rühren

budget /'bʌdʒɪt/ n Budget nt; (Pol) Haushaltsplan m; (money available)

buff | burden

Etat m ● vi (pt/pp budgeted) ~ for sth etw einkalkulieren

buff /bʌf/ adj (colour) sandfarben ● n Sandfarbe f; 🔲 Fan m ● vt polieren

buffalo /'bʌfələʊ/ n (inv or pl -es) Büffel m

buffer /'bʌfə(r)/ n (Rail) Puffer m

buffet[1] /'bʊfeɪ/ n Büfett nt; (on station) Imbissstube f

buffet[2] /'bʌfɪt/ vt (pt/pp buffeted) hin und her werfen

bug /bʌg/ n Wanze f; (🔲: virus) Bazillus m; (🔲: device) Abhörgerät m, 🔲 Wanze f ● vt (pt/pp bugged) 🔲 verwanzen (room); abhören (telephone); (Amer: annoy) ärgern

bugle /'bjuːgl/ n Signalhorn nt

build /bɪld/ n (of person) Körperbau m ● vt/i (pt/pp built) bauen. ~ **on** vt anbauen (to an + acc). ~ **up** vt aufbauen ● vi zunehmen

builder /'bɪldə(r)/ n Bauunternehmer m

building /'bɪldɪŋ/ n Gebäude nt. ~ **site** n Baustelle f. ~ **society** n Bausparkasse f

built /bɪlt/ see **build**. ~-**in** adj eingebaut. ~-**in cupboard** n Einbauschrank m. ~-**up area** n bebautes Gebiet nt; (Auto) geschlossene Ortschaft f

bulb /bʌlb/ n [Blumen]zwiebel f; (Electr) Glüh]birne f

bulbous /'bʌlbəs/ adj bauchig

Bulgaria /bʌl'geərɪə/ n Bulgarien nt

bulge /bʌldʒ/ n Ausbauchung f ● vi sich ausbauchen. ~**ing** adj prall; (eyes) hervorquellend

bulk /bʌlk/ n Masse f; (greater part) Hauptteil m. ~**y** adj sperrig; (large) massig

bull /bʊl/ n Bulle m, Stier m

bulldog n Bulldogge f

bulldozer /'bʊldəʊzə(r)/ n Planierraupe f

bullet /'bʊlɪt/ n Kugel f

bulletin /'bʊlɪtɪn/ n Bulletin nt

'bullet-proof adj kugelsicher

'bullfight n Stierkampf m. ~**er** n Stierkämpfer m

'bullfinch n Dompfaff m

bullock /'bʊlək/ n Ochse m

bull: ~**ring** n Stierkampfarena f. ~'s-**eye** n score a ~'s-eye ins Schwarze treffen

bully /'bʊlɪ/ n Tyrann m ● vt tyrannisieren

bum /bʌm/ n 🔲 Hintern m

bumble-bee /'bʌmbl-/ n Hummel f

bump /bʌmp/ n Bums m; (swelling) Beule f; (in road) holperige Stelle f ● vt stoßen; ~ **into** stoßen gegen; (meet) zufällig treffen. ~ **off** vt 🔲 um die Ecke bringen

bumper /'bʌmpə(r)/ adj Rekord- ● n (Auto) Stoßstange f

bumpy /'bʌmpɪ/ adj holperig

bun /bʌn/ n Milchbrötchen nt; (hair) [Haar]knoten m

bunch /bʌntʃ/ n (of flowers) Strauß m; (of radishes, keys) Bund m; (of people) Gruppe f; ~ **of grapes** [ganze] Weintraube f

bundle /'bʌndl/ n Bündel nt ● vt ~ [up] bündeln

bungalow /'bʌŋgələʊ/ n Bungalow m

bungle /'bʌŋgl/ vt verpfuschen

bunk /bʌŋk/ n [Schlaf]koje f. ~-**beds** npl Etagenbett nt

bunker /'bʌŋkə(r)/ n Bunker m

bunny /'bʌnɪ/ n 🔲 Kaninchen nt

buoy /bɔɪ/ n Boje f

buoyan|cy /'bɔɪənsɪ/ n Auftrieb m. ~**t** adj be ~t schwimmen

burden /'bɜːdn/ n Last f

bureau | buzz

bureau /ˈbjʊərəʊ/ n (pl -x or ∼s) (desk) Sekretär m; (office) Büro nt

bureaucracy /bjʊəˈrɒkrəsɪ/ n Bürokratie f

bureaucratic /bjʊərəˈkrætɪk/ adj bürokratisch

burger /ˈbɜːgə(r)/ n Hamburger m

burglar /ˈbɜːglə(r)/ n Einbrecher m. ∼ **alarm** n Alarmanlage f

burglary /ˈbɜːglərɪ/ n Einbruch m

burgle /ˈbɜːgl/ vt einbrechen in (+ acc); they have been ∼d bei ihnen ist eingebrochen worden

burial /ˈberɪəl/ n Begräbnis nt

burly /ˈbɜːlɪ/ adj stämmig

Burma /ˈbɜːmə/ n Birma nt. ∼**ese** adj birmanisch

burn /bɜːn/ n Verbrennung f; (on skin) Brandwunde f; (on material) Brandstelle f ● v (pt/pp burnt or burned) ● vt verbrennen ● vi brennen; (food:) anbrennen. ∼ **down** vt/i niederbrennen

burner /ˈbɜːnə(r)/ n Brenner m

burnt /bɜːnt/ see burn

burp /bɜːp/ vi 🔲 aufstoßen

burrow /ˈbʌrəʊ/ n Bau m ● vi wühlen

burst /bɜːst/ n Bruch m; (surge) Ausbruch m ● v (pt/pp burst) ● vt platzen machen ● vi platzen; (bud:) aufgehen; ∼ **into tears** in Tränen ausbrechen

bury /ˈberɪ/ vt (pt/pp -ied) begraben; (hide) vergraben

bus /bʌs/ n [Auto]bus m

bush /bʊʃ/ n Strauch m; (land) Busch m. ∼**y** adj buschig

busily /ˈbɪzɪlɪ/ adv eifrig

business /ˈbɪznɪs/ n Angelegenheit f; (Comm) Geschäft nt; on ∼ geschäftlich; he has no ∼ to er hat kein Recht (to zu); mind one's own ∼ sich um seine eigenen Angelegenheiten kümmern; that's none of your ∼ das geht Sie nichts an. ∼**-like** adj geschäftsmäßig. ∼**man** n Geschäftsmann m

'bus-stop n Bushaltestelle f

bust[1] /bʌst/ n Büste f

bust[2] adj 🔲 kaputt; go ∼ Pleite gehen ● v (pt/pp busted or bust) 🔲 ● vt kaputtmachen ● vi kaputtgehen

busy /ˈbɪzɪ/ adj beschäftigt; (day) voll; (street) belebt; (with traffic) stark befahren; (Amer Teleph) besetzt; be ∼ zu tun haben ● vt ∼ oneself sich beschäftigen (with mit)

but /bʌt/, unbetont /bət/ conj aber; (after negative) sondern ● prep außer (+ dat); ∼ **for** (without) ohne (+ acc); **the last** ∼ **one** der/die/das vorletzte; **the next** ∼ **one** der/die/das übernächste ● adv nur

butcher /ˈbʊtʃə(r)/ n Fleischer m, Metzger m; ∼**'s [shop]** Fleischerei f, Metzgerei f ● vt [ab]schlachten

butler /ˈbʌtlə(r)/ n Butler m

butt /bʌt/ n (of gun) [Gewehr]kolben m; (fig: target) Zielscheibe f; (of cigarette) Stummel m; (for water) Regentonne f ● vi ∼ **in** unterbrechen

butter /ˈbʌtə(r)/ n Butter f ● vt mit Butter bestreichen. ∼ **up** vt 🔲 schmeicheln (+ dat)

butter: ∼**cup** n Butterblume f, Hahnenfuß m. ∼**fly** n Schmetterling m

buttocks /ˈbʌtəks/ npl Gesäß nt

button /ˈbʌtn/ n Knopf m ● vt ∼ [**up**] zuknöpfen. ∼**hole** n Knopfloch nt

buy /baɪ/ n Kauf m ● vt (pt/pp bought) kaufen. ∼**er** n Käufer(in) m(f)

buzz /bʌz/ n Summen nt ● vi

summen

buzzer /'bʌzə(r)/ n Summer m

by /baɪ/ prep (close to) bei (+ dat); (next to) neben (+ dat/acc); (past) an (+ dat) ... vorbei; (to the extent of) um (+ acc); (at the latest) bis; (by means of) durch; by Mozart/ Dickens von Mozart/Dickens; ~ oneself allein; ~ the sea am Meer; ~ car/bus mit dem Auto/Bus; ~ sea mit dem Schiff; ~ day/night bei Tag/Nacht; ~ the hour pro Stunde; ~ the metre meterweise; six metres ~ four sechs mal vier Meter; win ~ a length mit einer Länge Vorsprung gewinnen; miss the train ~ a minute den Zug um eine Minute verpassen ● adv ~ and large im Großen und Ganzen; put ~ beiseite legen; go/pass ~ vorbeigehen

bye /baɪ/ int 🛈 tschüs

by: ~-election n Nachwahl f. ~pass n Umgehungsstraße f; (Med) Bypass m ● vt umfahren. ~-product n Nebenprodukt m. ~stander n Zuschauer(in) m(f)

Cc

cab /kæb/ n Taxi nt; (of lorry, train) Führerhaus nt

cabaret /'kæbəreɪ/ n Kabarett nt

cabbage /'kæbɪdʒ/ n Kohl m

cabin /'kæbɪn/ n Kabine f; (hut) Hütte f

cabinet /'kæbɪnɪt/ n Schrank m; [display] ~ Vitrine f; C~ (Pol) Kabinett nt

cable /'keɪbl/ n Kabel nt; (rope) Tau nt. ~ railway n Seilbahn f. ~

'**television** n Kabelfernsehen nt

cackle /'kækl/ vi gackern

cactus /'kæktəs/ n (pl -ti or -tuses) Kaktus m

cadet /kə'det/ n Kadett m

cadge /kædʒ/ vt/i 🛈 schnorren

Caesarean /sɪ'zeərɪən/ adj & n ~ [section] Kaiserschnitt m

café /'kæfeɪ/ n Café nt

cafeteria /kæfə'tɪərɪə/ n Selbstbedienungsrestaurant nt

cage /keɪdʒ/ n Käfig m

cagey /'keɪdʒɪ/ adj 🛈 be ~ mit der Sprache nicht herauswollen

cake /keɪk/ n Kuchen m; (of soap) Stück nt. ~d adj verkrustet (with mit)

calamity /kə'læmətɪ/ n Katastrophe f

calculat|e /'kælkjʊleɪt/ vt berechnen; (estimate) kalkulieren. ~ing adj (fig) berechnend. ~ion n Rechnung f, Kalkulation f. ~or n Rechner m

calendar /'kælɪndə(r)/ n Kalender m

calf[1] /kɑːf/ n (pl calves) Kalb nt

calf[2] n (pl calves) (Anat) Wade f

calibre /'kælɪbə(r)/ n Kaliber nt

call /kɔːl/ n Ruf m; (Teleph) Anruf m; (visit) Besuch m ● vt rufen; (Teleph) anrufen; (wake) wecken; ausrufen (strike) (name) nennen; be ~ed heißen vi rufen; ~ [in or round] vorbeikommen. ~ back vt zurückrufen ● vi noch einmal vorbeikommen. ~ for vt rufen nach; (demand) verlangen; (fetch) abholen. ~ off vt zurückrufen (dog); (cancel) absagen. ~ on vt bitten (for um); (appeal to) appellieren an (+ acc); (visit) besuchen. ~ out vt rufen; aufrufen (names) ● vi rufen. ~ up vt (Mil) einberufen; (Teleph) anrufen

call: ~-box n Telefonzelle f. ~

centre n Callcenter nt. **~er** n Besucher m; (Teleph) Anrufer m. **~ing** n Berufung f. **~-up** n (Mil) Einberufung f

calm /kɑːm/ adj (-er, -est) ruhig ● n Ruhe f ● vt ~ [down] beruhigen ● vi ~ down sich beruhigen. **~ness** n Ruhe f; (of sea) Stille f

calorie /ˈkælərɪ/ n Kalorie f

calves /kɑːvz/ npl see calf¹ & ²

camcorder /ˈkæmkɔːdə(r)/ n Camcorder m

came /keɪm/ see come

camel /ˈkæml/ n Kamel nt

camera /ˈkæmərə/ n Kamera f

camouflage /ˈkæməflɑːʒ/ n Tarnung f ● vt tarnen

camp /kæmp/ n Lager nt ● vi campen; (Mil) kampieren

campaign /kæmˈpeɪn/ n Feldzug m; (Comm, Pol) Kampagne f ● vi (Pol) im Wahlkampf arbeiten

camp: ~-bed n Feldbett nt. **~er** n Camper m; (Auto) Wohnmobil nt. **~ing** n Camping nt. **~site** n Campingplatz m

can¹ /kæn/ n (for petrol) Kanister m; (tin) Dose f, Büchse f; a ~ of beer eine Dose Bier

---

can² /kæn/, unbetont /kən/

pres **can**, pt **could**

● modal verb

····▸ (be able to) können. I can't or cannot go ich kann nicht gehen. she couldn't or could not go (was unable to) sie konnte nicht gehen; (would not be able to) sie könnte nicht gehen. he could go if he had time er könnte gehen, wenn er Zeit hätte. if I could go wenn ich gehen könnte. that cannot

be true das kann nicht stimmen

····▸ (know how to) können. can you swim? können Sie schwimmen? she can drive sie kann Auto fahren

····▸ (be allowed to) dürfen. you can't smoke here hier dürfen Sie nicht rauchen. can I go? kann ich gehen?

····▸ (in requests) können. can I have a glass of water, please? kann ich ein Glas Wasser haben, bitte? could you ring me tomorrow? könnten Sie mich morgen anrufen?

····▸ could (expressing possibility) könnte. that could be so das könnte od kann sein. I could have killed him ich hätte ihn umbringen können

Canada /ˈkænədə/ n Kanada nt. **~ian** adj kanadisch ● n Kanadier(in) m(f)

canal /kəˈnæl/ n Kanal m

canary /kəˈneərɪ/ n Kanarienvogel m

cancel /ˈkænsl/ vt/i (pt/pp cancelled) absagen; abbestellen (newspaper); (Computing) abbrechen; be **~led** ausfallen. **~lation** n Absage f

cancer /ˈkænsə(r)/ n (also Astrology) C~ Krebs m. **~ous** adj krebsig

candid /ˈkændɪd/ adj offen

candidate /ˈkændɪdət/ n Kandidat(in) m(f)

candle /ˈkændl/ n Kerze f. **~stick** n Kerzenständer m, Leuchter m

candy /ˈkændɪ/ n (Amer) Süßigkeiten pl; [piece of] ~ Bonbon m

cane /keɪn/ n Rohr nt; (stick) Stock m ● vt mit dem Stock züchtigen

canine /ˈkeɪnaɪn/ adj Hunde-. **~ tooth** n Eckzahn m

cannabis /'kænəbɪs/ n Haschisch nt

canned /kænd/ adj Dosen-, Büchsen-

cannibal /'kænɪbl/ n Kannibale m. **~ism** n Kannibalismus m

cannon /'kænən/ n inv Kanone f

cannot /'kænɒt/ see can²

canoe /kə'nu:/ n Paddelboot nt; (Sport) Kanu m

'can-opener n Dosenöffner m

can't /kɑ:nt/ = cannot. See can²

canteen /kæn'ti:n/ n Kantine f; ~ of cutlery Besteckkasten m

canter /'kæntə(r)/ n Kanter m ●vi kantern

canvas /'kænvəs/ n Segeltuch nt; (Art) Leinwand f; (painting) Gemälde nt

canvass /'kænvəs/ vi um Stimmen werben

canyon /'kænjən/ n Cañon m

cap /kæp/ n Kappe f, Mütze f; (nurse's) Haube f; (top, lid) Verschluss m

capability /keɪpə'bɪlətɪ/ n Fähigkeit f

capable /'keɪpəbl/ adj, **-bly** adv fähig; be ~ of doing sth fähig sein, etw zu tun

capacity /kə'pæsətɪ/ n Fassungsvermögen nt; (ability) Fähigkeit f; in my ~ as in meiner Eigenschaft als

cape¹ /keɪp/ n (cloak) Cape nt

cape² n (Geog) Kap nt

capital /'kæpɪtl/ adj (letter) groß ●n (town) Hauptstadt f; (money) Kapital nt; (letter) Großbuchstabe m

capital|ism /'kæpɪtəlɪzm/ n Kapitalismus m. **~ist** adj kapitalistisch ●n Kapitalist m. **'letter** n Großbuchstabe m. **~ 'punishment** n Todesstrafe f

capsize /kæp'saɪz/ vi kentern ●vt zum Kentern bringen

captain /'kæptɪn/ n Kapitän m; (Mil) Hauptmann m ●vt anführen (team)

caption /'kæpʃn/ n Überschrift f; (of illustration) Bildtext m

captivate /'kæptɪveɪt/ vt bezaubern

captiv|e /'kæptɪv/ adj hold/take ~e gefangen halten/nehmen ●n Gefangene(r) m/f. **~ity** n Gefangenschaft f

capture /'kæptʃə(r)/ n Gefangennahme f ●vt gefangen nehmen; [ein]fangen (animal); (Mil) einnehmen (town)

car /kɑ:(r)/ n Auto nt, Wagen m; by ~ mit dem Auto od Wagen

caramel /'kærəmel/ n Karamell m

carat /'kærət/ n Karat nt

caravan /'kærəvæn/ n Wohnwagen m; (procession) Karawane f

carbon /'kɑ:bən/ n Kohlenstoff m; (copy) Durchschlag m

carbon: ~ **copy** n Durchschlag m. ~ **footprint** n CO_2-Fußabdruck m. ~ **paper** n Kohlepapier nt

carburettor /kɑ:bjʊ'retə(r)/ n Vergaser m

carcase /'kɑ:kəs/ n Kadaver m

card /kɑ:d/ n Karte f

'cardboard n Pappe f, Karton m. ~ **'box** n Pappschachtel f; (large) [Papp]karton m

'card-game n Kartenspiel nt

cardigan /'kɑ:dɪgən/ n Strickjacke f

cardinal /'kɑ:dɪnl/ adj Kardinal-

● *n* (*Relig*) Kardinal *m*

card 'index *n* Kartei *f*

care /keə(r)/ *n* Sorgfalt *f*; (*caution*) Vorsicht *f*; (*protection*) Obhut *f*; (*looking after*) Pflege *f*; (*worry*) Sorge *f*; ~ of (*on letter abbr* c/o) bei; **take** ~ vorsichtig sein; **take into** ~ in Pflege nehmen; **take** ~ of sich kümmern um ● *vi* ~ for (*like*) mögen; (*look after*) betreuen; **I don't** ~ das ist mir gleich

career /kə'rɪə(r)/ *n* Laufbahn *f*; (*profession*) Beruf *m* ● *vi* rasen

care: ~**free** *adj* sorglos. ~**ful** *adj* sorgfältig; (*cautious*) vorsichtig. ~**less** *adj* nachlässig. ~**lessness** *n* Nachlässigkeit *f*. ~**r** *n* Pflegende(r) *mf*

'caretaker *n* Hausmeister *m*

'car ferry *n* Autofähre *f*

cargo /'kɑ:gəʊ/ *n* (*pl* -es) Ladung *f*

Caribbean /kærɪ'bi:ən/ *n* **the** ~ die Karibik

caricature /'kærɪkətʊə(r)/ *n* Karikatur *f* ● *vt* karikieren

caring /'keərɪŋ/ *adj* (*parent*) liebevoll; (*profession, attitude*) sozial

carnation /kɑ:'neɪʃn/ *n* Nelke *f*

carnival /'kɑ:nɪvl/ *n* Karneval *m*

carol /'kærl/ *n* (*Christmas*) ~ Weihnachtslied *nt*

carp[1] /kɑ:p/ *n* inv Karpfen *m*

carp[2] *vi* nörgeln

'car park *n* Parkplatz *m*; (*multistorey*) Parkhaus *nt*; (*underground*) Tiefgarage *f*

carpent|er /'kɑ:pɪntə(r)/ *n* Zimmermann *m*; (*joiner*) Tischler *m*. ~**ry** *n* Tischlerei *f*

carpet /'kɑ:pɪt/ *n* Teppich *m*

carriage /'kærɪdʒ/ *n* Kutsche *f*; (*Rail*) Wagen *m*; (*of goods*) Beförderung *f*; (*cost*) Frachtkosten *pl*; (*bearing*) Haltung *f*

carrier /'kærɪə(r)/ *n* Träger(in) *m*(*f*); (*Comm*) Spediteur *m*; ~ [-**bag**] Tragetasche *f*

carrot /'kærət/ *n* Möhre *f*, Karotte *f*

carry /'kærɪ/ *vt*/*i* (*pt*/*pp* -**ied**) tragen; **be carried away** I hingerissen sein. ~ **off** *vt* wegtragen; gewinnen (*prize*). ~ **on** *vi* weitermachen; ~ **on with** I eine Affäre haben mit ● *vt* führen; (*continue*) fortführen. ~ **out** *vt* hinaus-/heraustragen; (*perform*) ausführen

cart /kɑ:t/ *n* Karren *m*; **put the** ~ **before the horse** das Pferd beim Schwanz aufzäumen ● *vt* karren; (I: *carry*) schleppen

carton /'kɑ:tn/ *n* [Papp]karton *m*; (*for drink*) Tüte *f*; (*of cream, yoghurt*) Becher *m*

cartoon /kɑ:'tu:n/ *n* Karikatur *f*; (*joke*) Witzzeichnung *f*; (*strip*) Comic Strips *pl*; (*film*) Zeichentrickfilm *m*. ~**ist** *n* Karikaturist *m*

cartridge /'kɑ:trɪdʒ/ *n* Patrone *f*; (*for film*) Kassette *f*

carve /kɑ:v/ *vt* schnitzen; (*in stone*) hauen; (*Culin*) aufschneiden

carving /'kɑ:vɪŋ/ *n* Schnitzerei *f*. ~-**knife** *n* Tranchiermesser *nt*

'car wash *n* Autowäsche *f*; (*place*) Autowaschanlage *f*

case[1] /keɪs/ *n* Fall *m*; **in any** ~ auf jeden Fall; **just in** ~ für alle Fälle; **in** ~ **he comes** falls er kommt

case[2] *n* Kasten *m*; (*crate*) Kiste *f*; (*for spectacles*) Etui *nt*; (*suitcase*) Koffer *m*; (*for display*) Vitrine *f*

cash /kæʃ/ *n* Bargeld *nt*; **pay [in]** ~ [**in**] bar bezahlen; ~ **on delivery** per Nachnahme ● *vt* einlösen (*cheque*). ~ **desk** *n* Kasse *f*

cashier /kæ'ʃɪə(r)/ *n* Kassierer(in) *m*(*f*)

cash: ~**point [machine]** *n* Geld-

automat m. ~ **register** n Registrierkasse f

cassette /kə'set/ n Kassette f. ~ **recorder** n Kassettenrecorder m

cast /kɑːst/ n (mould) Form f; (model) Abguss m; (Theat) Besetzung f; [plaster] ~ (Med) Gipsverband m ● vt (pt/pp cast) (throw) werfen; (shed) abwerfen; abgeben (vote); gießen (metal); (Theat) besetzen (role). ~ **off** vi (Naut) ablegen

castle /ˈkɑːsl/ n Schloss nt; (fortified) Burg f; (Chess) Turm m

'cast-offs npl abgelegte Kleidung f

castor /ˈkɑːstə(r)/ n (wheel) [Lauf]rolle f

'castor sugar n Streuzucker m

casual /ˈkæʒʊəl/ adj (chance) zufällig; (offhand) lässig; (informal) zwanglos; (not permanent) Gelegenheits-; ~ **wear** Freizeitbekleidung f

casualty /ˈkæʒʊəltɪ/ n [Todes]opfer nt; (injured person) Verletzte(r) m/f; ~ **[department]** Unfallstation f

cat /kæt/ n Katze f

catalogue /ˈkætəlɒg/ n Katalog m ● vt katalogisieren

catapult /ˈkætəpʌlt/ n Katapult nt ● vt katapultieren

cataract /ˈkætərækt/ n (Med) grauer Star m

catarrh /kə'tɑː(r)/ n Katarrh m

catastroph|e /kə'tæstrəfɪ/ n Katastrophe f. ~**ic** adj katastrophal

catch /kætʃ/ n (of fish) Fang m; (fastener) Verschluss m; (on door) Klinke f; (Ⅱ: snag) Haken m ● v (pt/pp caught) vt fangen; (be in time for) erreichen; (travel by) fahren mit; bekommen (illness); ~ **a cold** sich erkälten; ~ **sight of** erblicken; ~ s.o. **stealing** jdn beim Stehlen erwischen; ~ **one's finger in the**

door sich (dat) den Finger in der Tür [ein]klemmen ● vi (burn) anbrennen; (get stuck) klemmen. ~ **on** vi (Ⅰ: understand) kapieren; (become popular) sich durchsetzen. ~ **up** vt einholen ● vi einholen; ~ **up with** einholen (s.o.); nachholen (work)

catching /ˈkætʃɪŋ/ adj ansteckend

catch: ~phrase n, ~**word** n Schlagwort nt

catchy /ˈkætʃɪ/ adj einprägsam

categor|ical /kætɪˈgɒrɪkl/ adj kategorisch. ~**y** n Kategorie f

cater /ˈkeɪtə(r)/ vi ~ **for** beköstigen; (firm) das Essen liefern für (party); (fig) eingestellt sein auf (+ acc). ~**ing** n (trade) Gaststättengewerbe nt

caterpillar /ˈkætəpɪlə(r)/ n Raupe f

cathedral /kə'θiːdrl/ n Dom m, Kathedrale f

Catholic /ˈkæθəlɪk/ adj katholisch ● n Katholik(in) m(f). **C**~**ism** n Katholizismus m

cattle /ˈkætl/ npl Vieh nt

catty /ˈkætɪ/ adj boshaft

caught /kɔːt/ see **catch**

cauliflower /ˈkɒlɪ-/ n Blumenkohl m

cause /kɔːz/ n Ursache f; (reason) Grund m; **good** ~ gute Sache f ● vt verursachen; ~ **s.o. to do sth** jdn veranlassen, etw zu tun

caution /ˈkɔːʃn/ n Vorsicht f; (warning) Verwarnung f ● vt (Jur) verwarnen

cautious /ˈkɔːʃəs/ adj vorsichtig

cavalry /ˈkævəlrɪ/ n Kavallerie f

cave /keɪv/ n Höhle f ● vi ~ **in** einstürzen

cavern /ˈkævən/ n Höhle f

caviare /ˈkævɪɑː(r)/ n Kaviar m

cavity /'kævətɪ/ n Hohlraum m; (in tooth) Loch nt

CCTV abbr (closed-circuit television) CCTV nt; (surveillance) Videoüberwachung f

CD abbr (compact disc) CD f; ~-ROM CD-ROM f

cease /si:s/ vt/i aufhören. ~-fire n Waffenruhe f. ~less adj unaufhörlich

cedar /'si:də(r)/ n Zeder f

ceiling /'si:lɪŋ/ n [Zimmer]decke f; (fig) oberste Grenze f

celebrat|e /'selɪbreɪt/ vt/i feiern. ~ed adj berühmt (for wegen). ~ion n Feier f

celebrity /sɪ'lebrətɪ/ n Berühmtheit f

celery /'selərɪ/ n [Stangen]sellerie m & f

cell /sel/ n Zelle f

cellar /'selə(r)/ n Keller m

cellist /'tʃelɪst/ n Cellist(in) m(f)

cello /'tʃeləʊ/ n Cello nt

cellphone /'selfəʊn/ n Handy nt

Celsius /'selsɪəs/ adj Celsius

Celt /kelt/ n Kelte m/ Keltin f. ~ic adj keltisch

cement /sɪ'ment/ n Zement m; (adhesive) Kitt m

cemetery /'semətrɪ/ n Friedhof m

censor /'sensə(r)/ n Zensor m ● vt zensieren. ~ship n Zensur f

census /'sensəs/ n Volkszählung f

cent /sent/ n Cent m

centenary /sen'ti:nərɪ/ n, (Amer) **centennial** n Hundertjahrfeier f

center /'sentə(r)/ n (Amer) = centre

centi|grade /'sentɪ-/ adj Celsius. ~metre n Zentimeter m & nt

central /'sentrəl/ adj zentral. ~ 'heating n Zentralheizung f. ~ize vt zentralisieren

centre /'sentə(r)/ n Zentrum nt; (middle) Mitte f ● v (pt/pp centred) ● vt zentrieren. ~-'forward n Mittelstürmer m

century /'sentʃərɪ/ n Jahrhundert nt

ceramic /sɪ'ræmɪk/ adj Keramik-

cereal /'sɪərɪəl/ n Getreide nt; (breakfast food) Frühstücksflocken pl

ceremon|ial /serɪ'məʊnɪəl/ adj zeremoniell, feierlich ● n Zeremoniell nt. ~ious adj formell

ceremony /'serɪmənɪ/ n Zeremonie f, Feier f

certain /'sɜ:tn/ adj sicher; (not named) gewiss; for ~ mit Bestimmtheit; make ~ (check) sich vergewissern (that dass); (ensure) dafür sorgen (that dass); he is ~ to win er wird ganz bestimmt siegen. ~ly adv bestimmt, sicher; ~ly not! auf keinen Fall! ~ty n Sicherheit f, Gewissheit f; it's a ~ty es ist sicher

certificate /sə'tɪfɪkət/ n Bescheinigung f; (Jur) Urkunde f; (Sch) Zeugnis nt

certify /'sɜ:tɪfaɪ/ vt (pt/pp -ied) bescheinigen; (declare insane) für geisteskrank erklären

cf. abbr (compare) vgl.

chafe /tʃeɪf/ vt wund reiben

chaffinch /'tʃæfɪntʃ/ n Buchfink m

chain /tʃeɪn/ n Kette f ● vt ketten (to an + acc). ~ up vt anketten

chain: ~ re'action n Kettenreaktion f. ~-smoker n Kettenraucher m. ~ store n Kettenladen m

chair /tʃeə(r)/ n Stuhl m; (Univ) Lehrstuhl m; (Adm) Vorsitzende(r) m/f. ~-lift n Sessellift m. ~-man n Vorsitzende(r) m/f

chalet /'ʃæleɪ/ n Chalet nt

chalk /tʃɔ:k/ n Kreide f

challeng|e /'tʃælɪndʒ/ n Herausforderung f; (Mil) Anruf m ● vt herausfordern; (Mil) anrufen; (fig) anfechten (statement). ~er n Herausforderer m. ~ing adj herausfordernd; (demanding) anspruchsvoll

chamber /'tʃeɪmbə(r)/ n Kammer f; C~ of Commerce Handelskammer f. ~ **music** n Kammermusik f

chamois /'ʃæmɪ/ n ~[-leather] Ledertuch nt

champagne /ʃæm'peɪn/ n Champagner m

champion /'tʃæmpɪən/ n (Sport) Meister(in) m (f); (of cause) Verfechter m ● vt sich einsetzen für. ~**ship** n (Sport) Meisterschaft f

chance /tʃɑːns/ n Zufall m; (prospect) Chancen pl; (likelihood) Aussicht f; (opportunity) Gelegenheit f; by ~ zufällig; take a ~ ein Risiko eingehen; give s.o. a ~ jdm eine Chance geben ● attrib zufällig ● vt ~ it es riskieren

chancellor /'tʃɑːnsələ(r)/ n Kanzler m; (Univ) Rektor m

chancy /'tʃɑːnsɪ/ adj riskant

change /tʃeɪndʒ/ n Veränderung f; (alteration) Änderung f; (money) Wechselgeld nt; for a ~ zur Abwechslung ● v/ wechseln; (alter) ändern; (exchange) umtauschen (for gegen); (transform) verwandeln; trocken legen (baby); ~ one's clothes sich umziehen; ~ trains umsteigen ● vi sich verändern; (~ clothes) sich umziehen; (~ trains) umsteigen; all ~! alles aussteigen!

changeable /'tʃeɪndʒəbl/ adj wechselhaft

'**changing-room** n Umkleideraum m

channel /'tʃænl/ n Rinne f; (Radio, TV) Kanal m; (fig) Weg m; the [English] C~ der Ärmelkanal; the C~ Islands die Kanalinseln

chant /tʃɑːnt/ vt singen; (demonstrators:) skandieren

chao|s /'keɪɒs/ n Chaos nt. ~**tic** adj chaotisch

chap /tʃæp/ n ① Kerl m

chapel /'tʃæpl/ n Kapelle f

chaplain /'tʃæplɪn/ n Geistliche(r) m

chapped /tʃæpt/ adj (skin) aufgesprungen

chapter /'tʃæptə(r)/ n Kapitel nt

character /'kærɪktə(r)/ n Charakter m; (in novel, play) Gestalt f; (Printing) Schriftzeichen nt; out of ~ uncharakteristisch; quite a ~ ① ein Original

characteristic /kærɪktə'rɪstɪk/ adj, **-ally** adv charakteristisch (of für) ● n Merkmal nt

characterize /'kærɪktəraɪz/ vt charakterisieren

charge /tʃɑːdʒ/ n (price) Gebühr f; (Electr) Ladung f; (attack) Angriff m; (Jur) Anklage f; free of ~ kostenlos; be in ~ verantwortlich sein (of für); take ~ die Aufsicht übernehmen (of über + acc) ● vt berechnen (fee); (Electr) laden; (attack) angreifen; (Jur) anklagen (with gen); ~ s.o. for sth jdm etw berechnen

charitable /'tʃærɪtəbl/ adj wohltätig; (kind) wohlwollend

charity /'tʃærətɪ/ n Nächstenliebe f; (organization) wohltätige Einrichtung f; for ~ zu Wohltätigkeitszwecke

charm /tʃɑːm/ n Reiz m; (of person) Charme f; (object) Amulett nt ● vt bezaubern. ~**ing** adj reizend; (person, smile) charmant

chart /tʃɑːt/ n Karte f; (table) Tabelle f

charter /'tʃɑːtə(r)/ n ~ [flight] Charterflug m ● vt chartern; ~**ed accountant** Wirtschaftsprüfer,

Wirtschaftsprüferin m(f)

chase /tʃeɪs/ n Verfolgungsjagd f
● vt jagen, verfolgen. ∼ away or
off vt wegjagen

chassis /'ʃæsɪ/ n (pl chassis)
Chassis nt

chaste /tʃeɪst/ adj keusch

chat /tʃæt/ n Plauderei f; have a ∼
with plaudern mit ● vi (pt/pp chat-
ted) plaudern. ∼ show n Talkshow f

chatter /'tʃætə(r)/ n Geschwätz nt
● vi schwatzen; (child:) plappern;
(teeth:) klappern. ∼box n ⊞ Plapper-
maul nt

chatty /'tʃætɪ/ adj geschwätzig

chauffeur /'ʃəʊfə(r)/ n
Chauffeur m

cheap /tʃiːp/ adj & adv (-er, -est)
billig. ∼en vt entwürdigen

cheat /tʃiːt/ n Betrüger(in) m(f);
(at games) Mogler m ● vt betrügen
● vi (at games) mogeln ⊞

check[1] /tʃek/ adj (squared) kariert
● n Karo nt

check[2] n Überprüfung f; (inspection) Kontrolle f; (Chess) Schach nt;
(Amer: bill) Rechnung f; (Amer:
cheque) Scheck m; (Amer: tick)
Haken m; keep a ∼ on kontrollieren ● vt [über]prüfen; (inspect) kontrollieren; (restrain) hemmen; (stop)
aufhalten ● vi [go and] ∼ nachsehen. ∼ in vi sich anmelden; (Aviat)
einchecken ● vt abfertigen; einchecken. ∼ out vi sich abmelden. ∼
up vi prüfen, kontrollieren; ∼ up
on überprüfen

checked /tʃekt/ adj kariert

check: ∼out n Kasse f. ∼room n
(Amer) Garderobe f. ∼up n (Med)
[Kontroll]untersuchung f

cheek /tʃiːk/ n Backe f; (impudence) Frechheit f. ∼y adj, -ily
adv frech

cheer /tʃɪə(r)/ n Beifallsruf m;
three ∼s ein dreifaches Hoch (for
auf + acc); ∼s! prost! (goodbye)
tschüs! ● vt zujubeln (+ dat) ● vi ju-
beln. ∼ up vt aufmuntern; aufheitern ● vi munterer werden. ∼ful
adj fröhlich. ∼fulness n Fröhlichkeit f

cheerio /tʃɪərɪ'əʊ/ int ⊞ tschüs!

cheese /tʃiːz/ n Käse m. ∼cake n
Käsekuchen m

chef /ʃef/ n Koch m

chemical /'kemɪkl/ adj chemisch
● n Chemikalie f

chemist /'kemɪst/ n (pharmacist)
Apotheker(in) m(f); (scientist) Che-
miker(in) m(f); ∼'s [shop] Drogerie f; (dispensing) Apotheke f. ∼ry n
Chemie f

cheque /tʃek/ n Scheck m.
∼book n Scheckbuch nt. ∼ card n
Scheckkarte f

cherish /'tʃerɪʃ/ vt lieben;
(fig) hegen

cherry /'tʃerɪ/ n Kirsche f ● attrib
Kirsch-

chess /tʃes/ n Schach nt

chess: ∼board n Schachbrett nt.
∼man n Schachfigur f

chest /tʃest/ n Brust f; (box) Truhe f

chestnut /'tʃesnʌt/ n Esskastanie
f, Marone f; (horse-) [Ross]kastanie f

chest of 'drawers n
Kommode f

chew /tʃuː/ vt kauen. ∼ing-gum n
Kaugummi m

chick /tʃɪk/ n Küken nt

chicken /'tʃɪkɪn/ n Huhn nt
● attrib Hühner- ● adj ⊞ feige

chief /tʃiːf/ adj Haupt- ● n Chef m;
(of tribe) Häuptling m. ∼ly adv
hauptsächlich

child /tʃaɪld/ n (pl ∼ren) Kind nt

child: ∼birth n Geburt f. ∼hood

n Kindheit *f*. **~ish** *adj* kindisch.
~less *adj* kinderlos. **~like** *adj* kindlich. **~minder** *n* Tagesmutter *f*

children /'tʃɪldrən/ *npl see* child

Chile /'tʃɪli/ *n* Chile *nt*

chill /tʃɪl/ *n* Kälte *f*; (*illness*) Erkältung *f* ● *vt* kühlen

chilly /'tʃɪlɪ/ *adj* kühl; I felt ~ mich fröstelte [es]

chime /tʃaɪm/ *vi* läuten; (*clock:*) schlagen

chimney /'tʃɪmnɪ/ *n* Schornstein *m*. **~-pot** *n* Schornsteinaufsatz *m*. **~-sweep** *n* Schornsteinfeger *m*

chin /tʃɪn/ *n* Kinn *nt*

china /'tʃaɪnə/ *n* Porzellan *nt*

Chin|a /'tʃaɪnə/ *n* China *nt*. **~ese** *adj* chinesisch ● *n* (*Lang*) Chinesisch *nt*; **the ~ese** *pl* die Chinesen

chink[1] /tʃɪŋk/ *n* (*slit*) Ritze *f*

chink[2] *n* Geklirr *nt* ● *vi* klirren; (*coins:*) klimpern

chip /tʃɪp/ *n* (*fragment*) Span *m*; (*in china, paintwork*) angeschlagene Stelle *f*; (*Computing, Gambling*) Chip *m*; **~s** *pl* (*Culin*) Pommes frites *pl*; (*Amer: crisps*) Chips *pl* ● *vt* (*pt/pp* chipped) (*damage*) anschlagen. **~ped** *adj* angeschlagen

chirp /tʃɜːp/ *vi* zwitschern; (*cricket:*) zirpen. **~y** *adj* 𝔻 munter

chit /tʃɪt/ *n* Zettel *m*

chocolate /'tʃɒkələt/ *n* Schokolade *f*; (*sweet*) Praline *f*

choice /tʃɔɪs/ *n* Wahl *f*; (*variety*) Auswahl *f* ● *adj* auserlesen

choir /'kwaɪə(r)/ *n* Chor *m*. **~boy** *n* Chorknabe *m*

choke /tʃəʊk/ *n* (*Auto*) Choke *m* ● *vt* würgen; (*to death*) erwürgen ● *vi* sich verschlucken; **~ on** [fast] ersticken an (+ *dat*)

choose /tʃuːz/ *vt/i* (*pt* chose, *pp* chosen) wählen; (*select*) sich (*dat*)

aussuchen; **~ to** do/go [freiwillig] tun/gehen; **as you ~** wie Sie wollen

choos[e]y /'tʃuːzɪ/ *adj* 𝔻 wählerisch

chop /tʃɒp/ *n* (*blow*) Hieb *m*; (*Culin*) Kotelett *nt* ● *vt* (*pt/pp* chopped) hacken. **~ down** *vt* abhacken; fällen (*tree*). **~ off** *vt* abhacken

chop|per /'tʃɒpə(r)/ *n* Beil *nt*; 𝔻 Hubschrauber *m*. **~py** *adj* kabbelig

'chopsticks *npl* Essstäbchen *pl*

choral /'kɔːrəl/ *adj* Chor-

chord /kɔːd/ *n* (*Mus*) Akkord *m*

chore /tʃɔː(r)/ *n* lästige Pflicht *f*; [household] **~s** Hausarbeit *f*

chorus /'kɔːrəs/ *n* Chor *m*; (*of song*) Refrain *m*

chose, chosen *see* choose

Christ /kraɪst/ *n* Christus *m*

christen /'krɪsn/ *vt* taufen

Christian /'krɪstʃən/ *adj* christlich ● *n* Christ(in) *m(f)*. **~ity** *n* Christentum *nt*. **~ name** *n* Vorname *m*

Christmas /'krɪsməs/ *n* Weihnachten *nt*. **~ card** *n* Weihnachtskarte *f*. **~ 'Day** *n* erster Weihnachtstag *m*. **~ 'Eve** *n* Heiligabend *m*. **~ tree** *n* Weihnachtsbaum *m*

chrome /krəʊm/ *n*, **chromium** /'krəʊmɪəm/ *n* Chrom *nt*

chronic /'krɒnɪk/ *adj* chronisch

chronicle /'krɒnɪkl/ *n* Chronik *f*

chrysanthemum /krɪ'sænθəməm/ *n* Chrysantheme *f*

chubby /'tʃʌbɪ/ *adj* mollig

chuck /tʃʌk/ *vt* 𝔻 schmeißen. **~ out** *vt* 𝔻 rausschmeißen

chuckle /'tʃʌkl/ *vi* in sich (*acc*) hineinlachen

chum /tʃʌm/ *n* Freund(in) *m(f)*

chunk /tʃʌŋk/ *n* Stück *nt*

church /tʃɜːtʃ/ *n* Kirche *f*. **~yard** *n* Friedhof *m*

churn /tʃɜːn/ vt ~ **out** am laufenden Band produzieren

cider /'saɪdə(r)/ n ≈ Apfelwein m

cigar /sɪ'gɑː(r)/ n Zigarre f

cigarette /sɪgə'ret/ n Zigarette f

cine-camera /'sɪnɪ-/ n Filmkamera f

cinema /'sɪnɪmə/ n Kino nt

cinnamon /'sɪnəmən/ n Zimt m

circle /'sɜːkl/ n (Theat) Rang m • vt umkreisen • vi kreisen

circuit /'sɜːkɪt/ n Runde f; (racetrack) Rennbahn f; (Electr) Stromkreis m. ~**ous** adj ~ **route** Umweg m

circular /'sɜːkjʊlə(r)/ adj kreisförmig • n Rundschreiben nt. ~ **saw** n Kreissäge f. ~ **tour** n Rundfahrt f

circulat|e /'sɜːkjʊleɪt/ vt in Umlauf setzen • vi zirkulieren. ~**ion** n Kreislauf m; (of newspaper) Auflage f

circumference /sə'kʌmfərəns/ n Umfang m

circumstance /'sɜːkəmstəns/ n Umstand m; ~**s** pl Umstände pl; (financial) Verhältnisse pl

circus /'sɜːkəs/ n Zirkus m

cistern /'sɪstən/ n (tank) Wasserbehälter m; (of WC) Spülkasten m

cite /saɪt/ vt zitieren

citizen /'sɪtɪzn/ n Bürger(in) m(f). ~**ship** n Staatsangehörigkeit f

citrus /'sɪtrəs/ n ~ [**fruit**] Zitrusfrucht f

city /'sɪtɪ/ n [Groß]stadt f

City The City of London ist das Gebiet innerhalb der alten Stadtgrenzen von London. Heute ist es das Geschäfts- und Finanzzentrum Londons und viele Banken und andere Geldinstitute haben dort ihre Hauptquellen. Wenn Leute über die *City* sprechen, beziehen sie sich oft auf diese Institutionen und nicht auf den Ort.

---

civic /'sɪvɪk/ adj Bürger-

civil /'sɪvl/ adj bürgerlich; (aviation, defence) zivil; (polite) höflich. ~ en**gineering** n Hoch- und Tiefbau m

civilian /sɪ'vɪljən/ adj Zivil-; in ~ **clothes** in Zivil • n Zivilist m

civilization /sɪvəlaɪ'zeɪʃn/ n Zivilisation f. ~**e** vt zivilisieren

civil: ~**partnership** n Lebenspartnerschaft f. ~**servant** n Beamte(r) m/Beamtin f. **C~ 'Service** n Staatsdienst m

claim /kleɪm/ n Anspruch m; (application) Antrag m; (demand) Forderung f; (assertion) Behauptung f • vt beanspruchen; (apply for) beantragen; (demand) fordern; (assert) behaupten; (collect) abholen

clam /klæm/ n Klaffmuschel f

clamber /'klæmbə(r)/ vi klettern

clammy /'klæmɪ/ adj feucht

clamour /'klæmə(r)/ n Geschrei nt • vi ~ **for** schreien nach

clamp /klæmp/ n Klammer f; [wheel] ~ Parkkralle f • vt [ein]spannen • vi ① ~ **down** on vorgehen gegen

clan /klæn/ n Clan m

clang /klæŋ/ n Schmettern nt. ~**er** n ① Schnitzer m

clank /klæŋk/ vi klirren

clap /klæp/ n **give s.o. a** ~ jdm Beifall klatschen; ~ **of thunder** Donnerschlag m • vt/i (pt/pp clapped) Beifall klatschen (+ dat); ~ **one's hands** [in die Hände] klatschen

clari|fication /klærɪfɪ'keɪʃn/ n Klärung f. ~**fy** vt/i (pt/pp -ied) klären

clarinet /klærɪ'net/ n Klarinette f

clarity /'klærətɪ/ n Klarheit f

clash /klæʃ/ n Geklirr nt; (fig) Konflikt m ● vi klirren; (colours:) sich beißen; (events:) ungünstig zusammenfallen

clasp /klɑːsp/ n Verschluss m ● vt ergreifen; (hold) halten

class /klɑːs/ n Klasse f; **travel first/ second ~** erster/zweiter Klasse reisen ● vt einordnen

classic /'klæsɪk/ adj klassisch ● n Klassiker m. **~al** adj klassisch

classi|fication /klæsɪfɪ'keɪʃn/ n Klassifikation f. **~fy** vt (pt/pp -ied) klassifizieren

'classroom n Klassenzimmer nt

classy /'klɑːsɪ/ adj 🗈 schick

clatter /'klætə(r)/ n Geklapper nt ● vi klappern

clause /klɔːz/ n Klausel f; (Gram) Satzteil m

claw /klɔː/ n Kralle f; (of bird of prey & Techn) Klaue f; (of crab, lobster) Schere f ● vt kratzen

clay /kleɪ/ n Lehm m; (pottery) Ton m

clean /kliːn/ adj (-er, -est) sauber ● adv glatt ● vt sauber machen; putzen (shoes, windows); **~ one's teeth** sich (dat) die Zähne putzen; **have sth ~ed** etw reinigen lassen. **~ up** vt sauber machen

cleaner /'kliːnə(r)/ n Putzfrau f; (substance) Reinigungsmittel nt; [dry] **~'s** chemische Reinigung f

cleanliness /'klenlɪnɪs/ n Sauberkeit f

cleanse /klenz/ vt reinigen

clear /klɪə(r)/ adj (-er, -est) klar; (obvious) eindeutig; (distinct) deutlich; (conscience) rein; (without obstacles) frei; **make sth ~** etw klarmachen (to dat) ● adv stand **~** zurücktreten; **keep ~ of** aus dem Wege gehen (+ dat) ● vt räumen; abräumen (table); (acquit) freispre-

chen; (authorize) genehmigen; (jump over) überspringen; **~ one's throat** sich räuspern ● vi (fog:) sich auflösen. **~ away** vt wegräumen. **~ off** vi 🗈 abhauen. **~ out** vt ausräumen ● vi 🗈 abhauen. **~ up** vt (tidy) aufräumen; (solve) aufklären ● vi (weather): sich auflösen

clearance /'klɪərəns/ n Räumung f; (authorization) Genehmigung f; (customs) [Zoll]abfertigung f; (Techn) Spielraum m. **~ sale** n Räumungsverkauf m

clench /klentʃ/ vt **~ one's fist** die Faust ballen; **~ one's teeth** die Zähne zusammenbeißen

clergy /'klɜːdʒɪ/ npl Geistlichkeit f. **~man** n Geistliche(r) m

clerk /klɑːk/, Amer. /klɜːk/ n Büroangestellte(r) m/f; (Amer: shop assistant) Verkäufer(in) m(f)

clever /'klevə(r)/ adj (-er, -est), -ly adv klug; (skilful) geschickt

cliché /'kliːʃeɪ/ n Klischee nt

click /klɪk/ vi klicken

client /'klaɪənt/ n Kunde m/ Kundin f; (Jur) Klient(in) m(f)

cliff /klɪf/ n Kliff nt

climat|e /'klaɪmət/ n Klima nt. **~e change** n Klimawandel m

climax /'klaɪmæks/ n Höhepunkt m

climb /klaɪm/ n Aufstieg m ● vt besteigen (mountain); steigen auf (+ acc) (ladder, tree) ● vi klettern; (rise) steigen; (road:) ansteigen. **~ down** vi hinunter-/herunterklettern; (from ladder, tree) heruntersteigen; 🗈 nachgeben

climber /'klaɪmə(r)/ n Bergsteiger m; (plant) Kletterpflanze f

cling /klɪŋ/ vi (pt/pp clung) sich klammern (to an + acc); (stick) haften (to an + dat). **~ film** n Sichtfolie f mit Hafteffekt

clinic /'klɪnɪk/ n Klinik f. **~al** adj

klinisch

clink /klɪŋk/ vi klirren

clip¹ /klɪp/ n Klammer f; (jewellery) Klipp m ● vt (pt/pp **clipped**) anklammern (to an + acc)

clip² n (extract) Ausschnitt m ● vt schneiden; knipsen (ticket). ~**ping** n (extract) Ausschnitt m

cloak /kləʊk/ n Umhang m. ~**room** n Garderobe f; (toilet) Toilette f

clobber /'klɒbə(r)/ n 𝕀 Zeug nt ● vt (𝕀: hit, defeat) schlagen

clock /klɒk/ n Uhr f; (𝕀: speedometer) Tacho m ● vi ~ **in/out** stechen

clock: ~**wise** adj & adv im Uhrzeigersinn. ~**work** n Uhrwerk nt; (of toy) Aufziehmechanismus m; like ~**work** 𝕀 wie am Schnürchen

clod /klɒd/ n Klumpen m

clog /klɒg/ vt/i (pt/pp **clogged**) ~ [**up**] verstopfen

cloister /'klɔɪstə(r)/ n Kreuzgang m

clone /kləʊn/ n Klon m ● vt klonen

close¹ /kləʊs/ adj (-r, -st) nah[e] (to dat); (friend) eng; (weather) schwül; have a ~ **shave** 𝕀 mit knapper Not davonkommen ● adv nahe ● n (street) Sackgasse f

close² /kləʊz/ n Ende nt; draw to a ~ sich dem Ende nähern ● vt zumachen, schließen; (bring to an end) beenden; sperren (road) ● vi sich schließen; (shop:) schließen, zumachen; (end) enden. ~ **down** ● vt schließen; stilllegen (factory) ● vi schließen; (factory:) stillgelegt werden

closely /'kləʊslɪ/ adv eng, nah[e]; (with attention) genau

closet /'klɒzɪt/ n (Amer) Schrank m

close-up /'kləʊs-/ n Nahaufnahme f

closure /'kləʊʒə(r)/ n Schließung f; (of factory) Stilllegung f; (of road) Sperrung f

clot /klɒt/ n [Blut]gerinnsel nt; (𝕀: idiot) Trottel m

cloth /klɒθ/ n Tuch nt

clothe /kləʊð/ vt kleiden

clothes /kləʊðz/ npl Kleider pl. ~**line** n Wäscheleine f

clothing /'kləʊðɪŋ/ n Kleidung f

cloud /klaʊd/ n Wolke f ● vi ~ **over** sich bewölken

cloudy /'klaʊdɪ/ adj wolkig, bewölkt; (liquid) trübe

clout /klaʊt/ n Schlag m; (influence) Einfluss m

clove /kləʊv/ n [Gewürz]nelke f; ~ **of garlic** Knoblauchzehe f

clover /'kləʊvə(r)/ n Klee m. ~**leaf** n Kleeblatt nt

clown /klaʊn/ n Clown m ● vi ~ [**about**] herumalbern

club /klʌb/ n Klub m; (weapon) Keule f; (Sport) Schläger m; ~**s** pl (Cards) Kreuz nt, Treff nt

clue /kluː/ n Anhaltspunkt m; (in crossword) Frage f; **I haven't a** ~ 𝕀 ich habe keine Ahnung

clump /klʌmp/ n Gruppe f

clumsiness /'klʌmzɪnɪs/ n Ungeschicklichkeit f

clumsy /'klʌmzɪ/ adj, **-ily** adv ungeschickt; (unwieldy) unförmig

clung /klʌŋ/ see **cling**

clutch /klʌtʃ/ n Griff m; (Auto) Kupplung f; **be in s.o.'s** ~**es** 𝕀 in jds Klauen sein ● vt festhalten; (grab) ergreifen ● vi ~ **at** greifen nach

clutter /'klʌtə(r)/ n Kram m ● vt ~ [**up**] vollstopfen

c/o abbr (care of) bei

coach /kəʊtʃ/ n [Reise]bus m; (Rail) Wagen m; (horse-drawn) Kutsche f;

(Sport) Trainer m ● vt Nachhilfestunden geben (+ dat); (Sport) trainieren

coal /kəʊl/ n Kohle f

coalition /kəʊə'lɪʃn/ n Koalition f

'coal-mine n Kohlenbergwerk nt

coarse /kɔːs/ adj (-r, -st) grob

coast /kəʊst/ n Küste f ● vi (freewheel) im Freilauf fahren; (Auto) im Leerlauf fahren. **~er** n (mat) Untersatz m

coast: **~guard** n Küstenwache f. **~line** n Küste f

coat /kəʊt/ n Mantel m; (of animal) Fell nt; (of paint) Anstrich m; **~ of arms** Wappen nt ● vt überziehen; (with paint) streichen. **~hanger** n Kleiderbügel m. **~hook** n Kleiderhaken m

coating /'kəʊtɪŋ/ n Überzug m, Schicht f; (of paint) Anstrich m

coax /kəʊks/ vt gut zureden (+ dat)

cobble[1] /'kɒbl/ n Kopfstein m; **~s** pl Kopfsteinpflaster nt

cobble[2] vt flicken. **~r** n Schuster m

cobweb /'kɒb-/ n Spinnengewebe nt

cock /kɒk/ n Hahn m; (any male bird) Männchen nt ● vt (animal:) **~ its ears** die Ohren spitzen; **~ the gun** den Hahn spannen

cockerel /'kɒkərəl/ n [junger] Hahn m

cockney /'kɒknɪ/ n (dialect) Cockney nt; (person) Cockney m

cock: **~pit** n (Aviat) Cockpit nt. **~roach** /-rəʊtʃ/ n Küchenschabe f. **~tail** n Cocktail m. **~-up** n ⚡ **make a ~-up** Mist bauen (of bei)

cocky /'kɒkɪ/ adj ⚡ eingebildet

cocoa /'kəʊkəʊ/ n Kakao m

coconut /'kəʊkənʌt/ n Kokosnuß f

cod /kɒd/ n inv Kabeljau m

COD abbr (cash on delivery) per

Nachnahme

coddle /'kɒdl/ vt verhätscheln

code /kəʊd/ n Kode m; (Computing) Code m; (set of rules) Kodex m. **~d** adj verschlüsselt

coerc|e /kəʊ'ɜːs/ vt zwingen. **~ion** n Zwang m

coffee /'kɒfɪ/ n Kaffee m

coffee: **~-grinder** n Kaffeemühle f. **~-pot** n Kaffeekanne f. **~-table** n Couchtisch m

coffin /'kɒfɪn/ n Sarg m

cogent /'kəʊdʒənt/ adj überzeugend

coherent /kəʊ'hɪərənt/ adj zusammenhängend; (comprehensible) verständlich

coil /kɔɪl/ n Rolle f; (Electr) Spule f; (one ring) Windung f ● vt **~[up]** zusammenrollen

coin /kɔɪn/ n Münze f ● vt prägen

coincide /kəʊɪn'saɪd/ vi zusammenfallen; (agree) übereinstimmen

coinciden|ce /kəʊ'ɪnsɪdəns/ n Zufall m. **~tal** adj zufällig

coke /kəʊk/ n Koks m

Coke (R) n (drink) Cola f

cold /kəʊld/ adj (-er, -est) kalt; **I am** or **feel ~** mir ist kalt ● n Kälte f; (Med) Erkältung f

cold: **~-'blooded** adj kaltblütig. **~-'hearted** adj kaltherzig. **~ly** adv (fig) kühl. **~ness** n Kälte f

collaborat|e /kə'læbəreɪt/ vi zusammenarbeiten (with mit); **~e on sth** mitarbeiten bei etw. **~ion** n Zusammenarbeit f, Mitarbeit f; (with enemy) Kollaboration f. **~or** n Mitarbeiter(in) m(f); Kollaborateur m

collaps|e /kə'læps/ n Zusammenbruch m, Kollaps m ● vi zusammenbrechen; (roof, building) einstürzen. **~ible** adj zusammenklappbar

collar /'kɒlə(r)/ n Kragen m; (for

animal) Halsband nt. ~-**bone** n Schlüsselbein nt

colleague /ˈkɒliːg/ n Kollege m/Kollegin f

collect /kəˈlekt/ vt sammeln; (*fetch*) abholen; einsammeln; (*tickets*) einziehen (*taxes*) ●vi sich [an]sammeln ●adv call ~ (*Amer*) ein R-Gespräch führen

collection /kəˈlekʃn/ n Sammlung f; (*in church*) Kollekte f; (*of post*) Leerung f; (*designer's*) Kollektion f

collector /kəˈlektə(r)/ n Sammler(in) m(f)

college /ˈkɒlɪdʒ/ n College nt

collide /kəˈlaɪd/ vi zusammenstoßen

colliery /ˈkɒlɪərɪ/ n Kohlengrube f

collision /kəˈlɪʒn/ n Zusammenstoß m

colloquial /kəˈləʊkwɪəl/ adj umgangssprachlich

Cologne /kəˈləʊn/ n Köln nt

colon /ˈkəʊlən/ n Doppelpunkt m

colonel /ˈkɜːnl/ n Oberst m

colonial /kəˈləʊnɪəl/ adj Kolonial-

colony /ˈkɒlənɪ/ n Kolonie f

colossal /kəˈlɒsl/ adj riesig

colour /ˈkʌlə(r)/ n Farbe f; (*complexion*) Gesichtsfarbe f; (*race*) Hautfarbe f; **off** ~ 🄳 nicht ganz auf der Höhe ●vt färben; ~ **[in]** ausmalen

colour: ~-**blind** adj farbenblind. ~**ed** adj farbig ●n (*person*) Farbige(r) m/f. ~**fast** adj farbecht. ~ **film** n Farbfilm m. ~**ful** adj farbenfroh. ~**less** adj farblos. ~ **photo- [graph]** n Farbaufnahme f. ~ **television** n Farbfernsehen nt

column /ˈkɒləm/ n Säule f; (*of soldiers, figures*) Kolonne f; (*Printing*) Spalte f; (*newspaper*) Kolumne f

comb /kəʊm/ n Kamm m ●vt kämmen; (*search*) absuchen; ~

one's hair sich (*dat*) [die Haare] kämmen

combat /ˈkɒmbæt/ n Kampf m

combination /kɒmbɪˈneɪʃn/ n Kombination f

combine[1] /kəmˈbaɪn/ vt verbinden ●vi sich verbinden; (*people:*) sich zusammenschließen

combine[2] /ˈkɒmbaɪn/ n (*Comm*) Konzern m

combustion /kəmˈbʌstʃn/ n Verbrennung f

come /kʌm/ vi (*pt* came, *pp* come) kommen; (*reach*) reichen (to an + acc); that ~ s to £10 das macht £10; ~ **into** money zu Geld kommen; ~ **true** wahr werden; ~ in two sizes in zwei Größen erhältlich sein; the years to ~ die kommenden Jahre; how ~? 🄳 wie das? ~ **about** vi geschehen. ~ **across** vi herüberkommen; 🄳 klar werden ●vt stoßen auf (+ acc). ~ **apart** vi sich auseinander nehmen lassen; (*accidentally*) auseinander gehen. ~ **away** vi wegkommen; (*thing:*) abgehen. ~ **back** vi zurückkommen. ~ **by** vi vorbeikommen ●vt (*obtain*) bekommen. ~ **in** vi hereinkommen. ~ **off** vi abgehen; (*take place*) stattfinden; (*succeed*) klappen 🄳. ~ **out** vi herauskommen; (*book:*) erscheinen; (*stain:*) herausgehen. ~ **round** vi vorbeikommen; (*after fainting*) [wieder] zu sich kommen; (*change one's mind*) sich umstimmen lassen. ~ **to** vi [wieder] zu sich kommen. ~ **up** vi heraufkommen; (*plant:*) aufgehen; (*reach*) reichen (to bis); ~ **up with** sich (*dat*) einfallen lassen

'**come-back** n Comeback nt

comedian /kəˈmiːdɪən/ n Komiker m

'**come-down** n Rückschritt m

comedy /ˈkɒmədɪ/ n Komödie f

comet /'kɒmɪt/ n Komet m

comfort /'kʌmfət/ n Bequemlichkeit f; (consolation) Trost m ● vt trösten

comfortable /'kʌmfətəbl/ adj, **-bly** adv bequem

'comfort station n (Amer) öffentliche Toilette f

comfy /'kʌmfɪ/ adj 1 bequem

comic /'kɒmɪk/ adj komisch ● n Komiker m; (periodical) Comic-Heft m

coming /'kʌmɪŋ/ adj kommend ● n Kommen nt

comma /'kɒmə/ n Komma nt

command /kə'mɑːnd/ n Befehl m; (Mil) Kommando nt; (mastery) Beherrschung f ● vt befehlen (+ dat); kommandieren (army)

command|er /kə'mɑːndə(r)/ n Befehlshaber m. **~ing officer** n Befehlshaber m

commemorat|e /kə'meməreɪt/ vt gedenken (+ gen). **~ion** n Gedenken nt

commence /kə'mens/ vt/i anfangen, beginnen

commend /kə'mend/ vt loben; (recommend) empfehlen (to dat)

comment /'kɒment/ n Bemerkung f; no ~ kein Kommentar! ● vi sich äußern (on zu); ~ on (an event) kommentieren

commentary /'kɒməntrɪ/ n Kommentar m; [running] ~ (Radio, TV) Reportage f

commentator /'kɒməntəɪtə(r)/ n Kommentator m; (Sport) Reporter m

commerce /'kɒmɜːs/ n Handel m

commercial /kə'mɜːʃl/ adj kommerziell ● n (Radio, TV) Werbespot m

commission /kə'mɪʃn/ n (order for work) Auftrag m; (body of

people) Kommission f; (payment) Provision f; (Mil) [Offiziers]patent nt; out of ~ außer Betrieb ● vt beauftragen (s.o.); in Auftrag geben (thing); (Mil) zum Offizier ernennen

commit /kə'mɪt/ vt (pt/pp committed) begehen; (entrust) anvertrauen (to dat); (consign) einweisen (to in + acc); ~ oneself sich festlegen; (involve oneself) sich engagieren. **~ment** n Verpflichtung f; (involvement) Engagement nt. **~ted** adj engagiert

committee /kə'mɪtɪ/ n Ausschuss m, Komitee nt

common /'kɒmən/ adj (-er, -est) gemeinsam; (frequent) häufig; (ordinary) gewöhnlich; (vulgar) ordinär ● n Gemeindeland nt; have in ~ gemeinsam haben; House of C~s Unterhaus nt

common: **~ly** adv allgemein. **C~ 'Market** n Gemeinsamer Markt m. **~place** adj häufig. **~-room** n Aufenthaltsraum m. **~ 'sense** n gesunder Menschenverstand m

Commonwealth Seit 1931 ist das Commonwealth die Gemeinschaft der 53 unabhängigen Staaten des ehemaligen britischen Weltreichs. Die Mitgliedsländer, die jetzt bildungs- und kulturpolitisch miteinander verbunden sind, nehmen alle zwei Jahre an den Commonwealth-Konferenzen teil. Alle vier Jahre finden die Commonwealth-Spiele statt. In den USA ist Commonwealth die offizielle Bezeichnung der vier US-Staaten: Kentucky, Massachusetts, Pennsylvania und Virginia.

commotion /kə'məʊʃn/ n Tumult m

communal /ˈkɒmjʊnl/ adj gemeinschaftlich

communicate /kəˈmjuːnɪkeɪt/ vt mitteilen (to dat); übertragen (disease) ●vi sich verständigen

communication /kəmjuːnɪ-ˈkeɪʃn/ n Verständigung f; (contact) Verbindung f; (message) Mitteilung f; ~s pl (technology) Nachrichtenwesen nt

communicative /kəˈmjuː-nɪkətɪv/ adj mitteilsam

Communion /kəˈmjuːnɪən/ n [Holy] ~ das [heilige] Abendmahl; (Roman Catholic) die [heilige] Kommunion

communis|m /ˈkɒmjʊnɪzm/ n Kommunismus m. ~t adj kommunistisch ●n Kommunist(in) m(f)

community /kəˈmjuːnəti/ n Gemeinschaft f; local ~ Gemeinde f

commute /kəˈmjuːt/ vi pendeln. ~r n Pendler(in) m(f)

compact /kəmˈpækt/ adj kompakt

companion /kəmˈpænjən/ n Begleiter(in) m(f). ~ship n Gesellschaft f

company /ˈkʌmpəni/ n Gesellschaft f; (firm) Firma f; (Mil) Kompanie f; (🔲 : guests) Besuch m. ~ car n Firmenwagen m

comparable /ˈkɒmpərəbl/ adj vergleichbar

comparative /kəmˈpærətɪv/ adj vergleichend; (relative) relativ ●n (Gram) Komparativ m. ~ly adv verhältnismäßig

compare /kəmˈpeə(r)/ vt vergleichen (with/to mit) ●vi sich vergleichen lassen

comparison /kəmˈpærɪsn/ n Vergleich m

compartment /kəmˈpɑːtmənt/ n Fach nt; (Rail) Abteil nt

compass /ˈkʌmpəs/ n Kompass m

compassion /kəmˈpæʃn/ n Mitleid nt. ~ate adj mitfühlend

compatible /kəmˈpætəbl/ adj vereinbar; (drugs) verträglich; (Techn) kompatibel; be ~ (people:) [gut] zueinander passen

compatriot /kəmˈpætrɪət/ n Landsmann m /-männin f

compel /kəmˈpel/ vt (pt/pp compelled) zwingen

compensat|e /ˈkɒmpənseɪt/ vt entschädigen. ~ion n Entschädigung f; (fig) Ausgleich m

compete /kəmˈpiːt/ vi konkurrieren; (take part) teilnehmen (in an + dat)

competen|ce /ˈkɒmpɪtəns/ n Fähigkeit f. ~t adj fähig

competition /kɒmpəˈtɪʃn/ n Konkurrenz f; (contest) Wettbewerb m; (in newspaper) Preisausschreiben nt

competitive /kəmˈpetɪtɪv/ adj (Comm) konkurrenzfähig

competitor /kəmˈpetɪtə(r)/ n Teilnehmer m; (Comm) Konkurrent m

compile /kəmˈpaɪl/ vt zusammenstellen

complacen|cy /kəmˈpleɪsənsɪ/ n Selbstzufriedenheit f. ~t adj selbstzufrieden

complain /kəmˈpleɪn/ vi klagen (about/of über + acc); (formally) sich beschweren. ~t n Klage f; (formal) Beschwerde f; (Med) Leiden nt

complement¹ /ˈkɒmplɪmənt/ n Ergänzung f; full ~ volle Anzahl f

complement² /ˈkɒmplɪment/ vt ergänzen

complete /kəmˈpliːt/ adj vollständig; (finished) fertig; (utter) völlig ●vt vervollständigen; (finish) abschließen; (fill in) ausfüllen. ~ly adv völlig

completion /kəmˈpliːʃn/ n Vervollständigung f; (end) Abschluss m

complex /'kɒmpleks/ adj komplex ● n Komplex m

complexion /kəm'plekʃn/ n Teint m; (colour) Gesichtsfarbe f

complexity /kəm'pleksəti/ n Komplexität f

complicat|e /'kɒmplɪkeɪt/ vt komplizieren. ~ed adj kompliziert. ~ion n Komplikation f

compliment /'kɒmplɪmənt/ n Kompliment nt; ~s pl Grüße pl ● vt ein Kompliment machen (+ dat). ~ary adj schmeichelhaft; (given free) Frei-

comply /kəm'plaɪ/ vi (pt/pp -ied) ~ with nachkommen (+ dat)

compose /kəm'pəʊz/ vt verfassen; (Mus) komponieren; be ~d of sich zusammensetzen aus. ~r n Komponist m

composition /kɒmpə'zɪʃn/ n Komposition f; (essay) Aufsatz m

compost /'kɒmpɒst/ n Kompost m

composure /kəm'pəʊʒə(r)/ n Fassung f

compound /'kɒmpaʊnd/ adj zusammengesetzt; (fracture) kompliziert ● n (Chemistry) Verbindung f; (Gram) Kompositum nt

comprehen|d /kɒmprɪ'hend/ vt begreifen, verstehen. ~sible adj, -bly adv verständlich. ~sion n Verständnis m

comprehensive /kɒmprɪ'hensɪv/ adj & n umfassend; ~ [school] Gesamtschule f. ~ **insurance** n (Auto) Vollkaskoversicherung f

compress /kəm'pres/ vt zusammenpressen; ~ed air Druckluft f

comprise /kəm'praɪz/ vt umfassen, bestehen aus

compromise /'kɒmprəmaɪz/ n Kompromiss m ● vt kompromittie-

ren (person) ● vi einen Kompromiss schließen

compuls|ion /kəm'pʌlʃn/ n Zwang m. ~ive adj zwanghaft. ~ory adj obligatorisch

comput|e /kəm'pju:t/ vb berechnen. ~er Computer m. ~er game n Computerspiel. ~erize vt computerisieren (data); auf Computer umstellen (firm). ~-'literate adj mit Computern vertraut. ~ing n Computertechnik f

comrade /'kɒmreɪd/ n Kamerad m; (Pol) Genosse m/Genossin f

con[1] /kɒn/ see pro

con[2] n ⓘ Schwindel m ● vt (pt/pp conned) ⓘ beschwindeln

concave /'kɒŋkeɪv/ adj konkav

conceal /kən'si:l/ vt verstecken; (keep secret) verheimlichen

concede /kən'si:d/ vt zugeben; (give up) aufgeben

conceit /kən'si:t/ n Einbildung f. ~ed adj eingebildet

conceivable /kən'si:vəbl/ adj denkbar

conceive /kən'si:v/ vt (child) empfangen; (fig) sich (dat) ausdenken ● vi schwanger werden

concentrat|e /'kɒnsəntreɪt/ vt konzentrieren ● vi sich konzentrieren. ~ion n Konzentration f

concern /kən'sɜ:n/ n Angelegenheit f; (worry) Sorge f; (Comm) Unternehmen nt ● vt (be about, affect) betreffen; (worry) kümmern; be ~ed about besorgt sein um; ~ oneself with sich beschäftigen mit; as far as I am ~ed was mich angeht od betrifft. ~ing prep bezüglich (+ gen)

concert /'kɒnsət/ n Konzert nt

concerto /kən'tʃeətəʊ/ n Konzert nt

concession /kən'seʃn/ n Zugeständnis nt; (Comm) Konzession f; (reduction) Ermäßigung f

concise /kən'saɪs/ adj kurz

conclude /kən'kluːd/ vt/i schließen

conclusion /kən'kluːʒn/ n Schluss m; **in** ~ abschließend, zum Schluss

conclusive /kən'kluːsɪv/ adj schlüssig

concoct /kən'kɒkt/ vt zusammenstellen; (fig) fabrizieren. ~**ion** n Zusammenstellung f; (drink) Gebräu nt

concrete /'kɒnkriːt/ adj konkret ● n Beton m● vt betonieren

concurrently /kən'kʌrəntlɪ/ adv gleichzeitig

concussion /kən'kʌʃn/ n Gehirnerschütterung f

condemn /kən'dem/ vt verurteilen; (declare unfit) für untauglich erklären. ~**ation** n Verurteilung f

condensation /kɒnden'seɪʃn/ n Kondensation f

condense /kən'dens/ vt zusammenfassen

condescend /kɒndɪ'send/ vi sich herablassen (to zu). ~**ing** adj herablassend

condition /kən'dɪʃn/ n Bedingung f; (state) Zustand m; ~**s** pl Verhältnisse pl; on ~ **that** unter der Bedingung, dass ● vt (mentally) konditionieren. ~**al** adj bedingt ● n (Gram) Konditional m. ~**er** n Pflegespülung f; (for fabrics) Weichspüler m

condolences /kən'dəʊlənsɪz/ npl Beileid nt

condom /'kɒndəm/ n Kondom nt

condominium /kɒndə'mɪnɪəm/ n (Amer) ≈ Eigentumswohnung f

conduct[1] /'kɒndʌkt/ n Verhalten nt; (Sch) Betragen nt

conduct[2] /kən'dʌkt/ vt führen; (Phys) leiten; (Mus) dirigieren. ~**or** n Dirigent m; (of bus) Schaffner m;

(Phys) Leiter m

cone /kəʊn/ n Kegel m; (Bot) Zapfen m; (for ice-cream) [Eis]tüte f; (Auto) Leitkegel m

confectioner /kən'fekʃənə(r)/ n Konditor m. ~**y** n Süßwaren pl

conference /'kɒnfərəns/ n Konferenz f

confess /kən'fes/ vt/i gestehen; (Relig) beichten. ~**ion** n Geständnis nt; (Relig) Beichte f

confetti /kən'fetɪ/ n Konfetti nt

confide /kən'faɪd/ vt anvertrauen ● vi ~ **in** s.o. sich jdm anvertrauen

confidence /'kɒnfɪdəns/ n (trust) Vertrauen nt; (self-assurance) Selbstvertrauen nt; (secret) Geheimnis nt; in ~ im Vertrauen. ~ **trick** n Schwindel m

confident /'kɒnfɪdənt/ adj zuversichtlich; (self-assured) selbstsicher

confidential /kɒnfɪ'denʃl/ adj vertraulich

configuration /kənfɪgə'reɪʃn/ n Anordnung f, Konfiguration f

confine /kən'faɪn/ vt beschränken (to auf + acc). ~**d** adj (narrow) eng

confirm /kən'fɜːm/ vt bestätigen; (Relig) konfirmieren; (Roman Catholic) firmen. ~**ation** n Bestätigung f; Konfirmation f; Firmung f

confiscat|e /'kɒnfɪskeɪt/ vt beschlagnahmen. ~**ion** n Beschlagnahme f

conflict[1] /'kɒnflɪkt/ n Konflikt m

conflict[2] /kən'flɪkt/ vi im Widerspruch stehen (with zu). ~**ing** adj widersprüchlich

conform /kən'fɔːm/ vi (person:) sich anpassen; (thing:) entsprechen (to dat). ~**ist** n Konformist m

confounded /kən'faʊndɪd/ adj 🔲 verflixt

confront /kən'frʌnt/ vt konfrontieren. ~**ation** n Konfrontation f

confus|e /kənˈfjuːz/ vt verwirren; (*mistake for*) verwechseln (with mit). **~ing** adj verwirrend. **~ion** n Verwirrung f; (*muddle*) Durcheinander nt

congenial /kənˈdʒiːnɪəl/ adj angenehm

congest|ed /kənˈdʒestɪd/ adj verstopft; (*with people*) überfüllt. **~ion** n Verstopfung f; Überfüllung f

congratulat|e /kənˈɡrætjʊleɪt/ vt gratulieren (+ dat) (on zu). **~ions** npl Glückwünsche pl; **~ions!** [ich] gratuliere!

congregation /kɒŋɡrɪˈɡeɪʃn/ n (*Relig*) Gemeinde f

congress /ˈkɒŋɡres/ n Kongress m. **~man** n Kongressabgeordnete(r) m

> **Congress** Die nationale gesetzgebende Versammlung in den Vereinigten Staaten. Der Kongress tritt im ▸CAPITOL zusammen und besteht aus zwei Kammern, dem Senat und dem Repräsentantenhaus. Der Kongress erlässt Gesetze, die von beiden Kammern angenommen und anschließend vom Präsidenten verabschiedet werden.

conical /ˈkɒnɪkl/ adj kegelförmig

conifer /ˈkɒnɪfə(r)/ n Nadelbaum m

conjecture /kənˈdʒektʃə(r)/ n Mutmaßung f

conjunction /kənˈdʒʌŋkʃn/ n Konjunktion f; **in ~ with** zusammen mit

conjur|e /ˈkʌndʒə(r)/ vi zaubern ● vt **~e up** heraufbeschwören. **~or** n Zauberkünstler m

conk /kɒŋk/ vi **~ out** 🔲 (*machine:*) kaputtgehen

conker /ˈkɒŋkə(r)/ n 🔲 Kastanie f

'con-man n 🔲 Schwindler m

connect /kəˈnekt/ vt verbinden (to mit); (*Electr*) anschließen (to an + acc) ● vi verbunden sein (with mit); (*train:*) Anschluss haben (with an + acc); **be ~ed with** zu tun haben mit; (*be related to*) verwandt sein mit

connection /kəˈnekʃn/ n Verbindung f; (*Rail, Electr*) Anschluss m; **in ~ with** in Zusammenhang mit. **~s** npl Beziehungen pl

connoisseur /kɒnəˈsɜː(r)/ n Kenner m

conquer /ˈkɒŋkə(r)/ vt erobern; (*fig*) besiegen. **~or** n Eroberer m

conquest /ˈkɒŋkwest/ n Eroberung f

conscience /ˈkɒnʃəns/ n Gewissen nt

conscientious /kɒnʃɪˈenʃəs/ adj gewissenhaft

conscious /ˈkɒnʃəs/ adj bewusst; [**fully**] **~** bei [vollem] Bewusstsein; **be/become ~ of** sich (dat) etw (gen) bewusst sein/werden. **~ness** n Bewusstsein nt

conscript /ˈkɒnskrɪpt/ n Einberufene(r) m

consecrat|e /ˈkɒnsɪkreɪt/ vt weihen; einweihen (*church*). **~ion** n Weihe f; Einweihung f

consecutive /kənˈsekjʊtɪv/ adj aufeinanderfolgend. **-ly** adv fortlaufend

consent /kənˈsent/ n Einwilligung f, Zustimmung f ● vi einwilligen (to in + acc), zustimmen (to dat)

consequen|ce /ˈkɒnsɪkwəns/ n Folge f. **~t** adj daraus folgend. **~tly** adv folglich

conservation /kɒnsəˈveɪʃn/ n Erhaltung f, Bewahrung f. **~ist** n Umweltschützer m

conservative /kənˈsɜːvətɪv/ adj konservativ; (*estimate*) vorsichtig.

C~ (Pol) adj konservativ ● n Konservativ(er) m/f

conservatory /kən'sɜ:vətrɪ/ n Wintergarten m

conserve /kən'sɜ:v/ vt erhalten, bewahren; sparen (energy)

consider /kən'sɪdə(r)/ vt erwägen; (think over) sich (dat) überlegen; (take into account) berücksichtigen; (regard as) betrachten als; ~ doing sth erwägen, etw zu tun. ~able adj, ~ably adv erheblich

consider|ate /kən'sɪdərət/ adj rücksichtsvoll. ~ation n Erwägung f; (thoughtfulness) Rücksicht f; (payment) Entgelt nt; take into ~ation berücksichtigen. ~ing prep wenn man bedenkt (that dass)

consist /kən'sɪst/ vi ~ of bestehen aus

consisten|cy /kən'sɪstənsɪ/ n Konsequenz f; (density) Konsistenz f. ~t adj konsequent; (unchanging) gleichbleibend. ~tly adv konsequent; (constantly) ständig

consolation /kɒnsə'leɪʃn/ n Trost m. ~ prize n Trostpreis m

console /kən'səʊl/ vt trösten

consonant /'kɒnsənənt/ n Konsonant m

conspicuous /kən'spɪkjʊəs/ adj auffällig

conspiracy /kən'spɪrəsɪ/ n Verschwörung f

constable /'kʌnstəbl/ n Polizist m

constant /'kɒnstənt/ adj beständig; (continuous) ständig

constipat|ed /'kɒnstɪpeɪtɪd/ adj verstopft. ~ion n Verstopfung f

constituency /kən'stɪtjʊənsɪ/ n Wahlkreis m

constitut|e /'kɒnstɪtju:t/ vt bilden. ~ion n (Pol) Verfassung f; (of person) Konstitution f

constraint /kən'streɪnt/ n Zwang

m; (restriction) Beschränkung f; (strained manner) Gezwungenheit f

construct /kən'strʌkt/ vt bauen. ~ion n Bau m; (Gram) Konstruktion f; (interpretation) Deutung f; under ~ion im Bau

consul /'kɒnsl/ n Konsul m. ~ate n Konsulat nt

consult /kən'sʌlt/ vt [um Rat] fragen; konsultieren (doctor); nachschlagen in (+ dat) (book). ~ant n Berater m; (Med) Chefarzt m. ~ation n Beratung f; (Med) Konsultation f

consume /kən'sju:m/ vt verzehren; (use) verbrauchen. ~r n Verbraucher m

consumption /kən'sʌmpʃn/ n Konsum m; (use) Verbrauch m

contact /'kɒntækt/ n Kontakt m; (person) Kontaktperson f ● vt sich in Verbindung setzen mit. ~ lenses npl Kontaktlinsen pl

contagious /kən'teɪdʒəs/ adj direkt übertragbar

contain /kən'teɪn/ vt enthalten; (control) beherrschen. ~er n Behälter m; (Comm) Container m

contaminat|e /kən'tæmɪneɪt/ vt verseuchen. ~ion n Verseuchung f

contemplat|e /'kɒntəmpleɪt/ vt betrachten; (meditate) nachdenken über (+ acc). ~ion n Betrachtung f; Nachdenken nt

contemporary /kən'tempərərɪ/ adj zeitgenössisch ● n Zeitgenosse m/-genossin f

contempt /kən'tempt/ n Verachtung f; beneath ~ verabscheuungswürdig. ~ible adj verachtenswert. ~uous adj verächtlich

content¹ /'kɒntent/ n (also contents) pl Inhalt m

content² /kən'tent/ adj zufrieden ● n to one's heart's ~ nach Herzenslust ● *vt* ~ oneself sich begnügen (with mit). ~ed *adj* zufrieden

contentment /kən'tentmənt/ *n* Zufriedenheit *f*

contest /'kɒntest/ *n* Kampf *m*; (*competition*) Wettbewerb *m*. ~**ant** *n* Teilnehmer *m*

context /'kɒntekst/ *n* Zusammenhang *m*

continent /'kɒntɪnənt/ *n* Kontinent *m*

continental /kɒntɪ'nentl/ *adj* Kontinental-. ~ **breakfast** *n* kleines Frühstück *nt*. ~ **quilt** *n* Daunendecke *f*

continual /kən'tɪnjʊəl/ *adj* dauernd

continuation /kəntɪnjʊ'eɪʃn/ *n* Fortsetzung *f*

continue /kən'tɪnjuː/ *vt* fortsetzen; ~ doing *or* to do sth fortfahren, etw zu tun; to be ~d Fortsetzung folgt ● *vi* weitergehen; (*doing sth*) weitermachen; (*speaking*) fortfahren; (*weather*) anhalten

continuity /kɒntɪ'njuːətɪ/ *n* Kontinuität *f*

continuous /kən'tɪnjʊəs/ *adj* anhaltend, ununterbrochen

contort /kən'tɔːt/ *vt* verzerren. ~**ion** *n* Verzerrung *f*

contour /'kɒntʊə(r)/ *n* Kontur *f*; (*line*) Höhenlinie *f*

contracep|tion /kɒntrə'sepʃn/ *n* Empfängnisverhütung *f*. ~**tive** *n* Empfängnisverhütungsmittel *nt*

contract[1] /'kɒntrækt/ *n* Vertrag *m*

contract[2] /kən'trækt/ *vi* sich zusammenziehen. ~**or** *n* Unternehmer *m*

contradict /kɒntrə'dɪkt/ *vt* widersprechen (+ *dat*). ~**ion** *n* Widerspruch *m*. ~**ory** *adj* widersprüchlich

contralto /kən'træltəʊ/ *n* Alt *m*;

(*singer*) Altistin *f*

contraption /kən'træpʃn/ *n*[!] Apparat *m*

contrary /'kɒntrərɪ/ *adj & adv* entgegengesetzt; ~ **to** entgegen (+ *dat*) ● *n* Gegenteil *nt*; on the ~ im Gegenteil

contrast[1] /'kɒntrɑːst/ *n* Kontrast *m*

contrast[2] /kən'trɑːst/ *vt* gegenüberstellen (with *dat*) ● *vi* einen Kontrast bilden (with zu). ~**ing** *adj* gegensätzlich; (*colour*) Kontrast-

contribut|e /kən'trɪbjuːt/ *vt*/*i* beitragen; beisteuern (*money*); (*donate*) spenden. ~**ion** *n* Beitrag *m*; (*donation*) Spende *f*. ~**or** *n* Beitragende(r) *m*/*f*

contrivance /kən'traɪvns/ *n* Vorrichtung *f*

control /kən'trəʊl/ *n* Kontrolle *f*; (*mastery*) Beherrschung *f*; (Techn) Regler *m*; ~**s** *pl* (of car, plane) Steuerung *f*; get out of ~ außer Kontrolle geraten ● *vt* (pt/pp controlled) kontrollieren; (*restrain*) unter Kontrolle halten; ~ oneself sich beherrschen

controvers|ial /kɒntrə'vɜːʃl/ *adj* umstritten. ~**y** *n* Kontroverse *f*

convalesce /kɒnvə'les/ *vi* sich erholen. ~**nce** *n* Erholung *f*

convalescent /kɒnvə'lesnt/ *adj* ~ **home** *n* Erholungsheim *nt*

convenience /kən'viːnɪəns/ *n* Bequemlichkeit *f*; [public] ~ öffentliche Toilette *f*; with all modern ~s mit allem Komfort

convenient /kən'viːnɪənt/ *adj* günstig; be ~ for s.o. jdm gelegen sein *od* jdm passen; if it is ~ [for you] wenn es Ihnen passt

convent /'kɒnvənt/ *n* [Nonnen]-kloster *nt*

convention /kən'venʃn/ *n* (*cus-*

tom) Brauch m, Sitte f. **~al** adj konventionell

converge /kən'vɜːdʒ/ vi zusammenlaufen

conversation /kɒnvə'seɪʃn/ n Gespräch nt; (Sch) Konversation f

conversion /kən'vɜːʃn/ n Umbau m; (Relig) Bekehrung f; (calculation) Umrechnung f

convert[1] /'kɒnvɜːt/ n Bekehrte(r) m/f, Konvertit m

convert[2] /kən'vɜːt/ vt bekehren (person); (change) umwandeln (into in + acc); umbauen (building); (calculate) umrechnen; (Techn) umstellen. **~ible** a verwandelbar • n (Auto) Kabrio[lett] nt

convex /'kɒnveks/ adj konvex

convey /kən'veɪ/ vt befördern; vermitteln (idea, message). **~or belt** n Förderband nt

convict[1] /'kɒnvɪkt/ n Sträfling m

convict[2] /kən'vɪkt/ vt verurteilen (of wegen). **~ion** n Verurteilung f; (belief) Überzeugung f; previous **~ion** Vorstrafe f

convinc|e /kən'vɪns/ vt überzeugen. **~ing** adj überzeugend

convoy /'kɒnvɔɪ/ n Konvoi m

convulse /kən'vʌls/ vt be **~ed** sich krümmen (with vor + dat)

coo /kuː/ vi gurren

cook /kʊk/ n Koch m/ Köchin f • vt/i kochen; is it **~ed**? ist es gar? **~ the books** 🔲 die Bilanz frisieren. **~book** n Kochbuch nt

cooker /'kʊkə(r)/ n [Koch]herd m; (apple) Kochapfel m. **~y** n Kochen nt. **~y book** n Kochbuch nt

cookie /'kʊkɪ/ n (Amer) Keks m

cool /kuːl/ adj (-er, -est) kühl • n Kühle f • vt kühlen • vi abkühlen. **~-box** n Kühlbox f. **~ness** n Kühle f

coop /kuːp/ vt **~ up** einsperren

co-operat|e /kəʊ'ɒpəreɪt/ vi zusammenarbeiten. **~ion** n Kooperation f

co-operative /kəʊ'ɒpərətɪv/ adj hilfsbereit • n Genossenschaft f

cop /kɒp/ n 🔲 Polizist m

cope /kəʊp/ vi 🔲 zurechtkommen; **~ with** fertig werden mit

copious /'kəʊpɪəs/ adj reichlich

copper[1] /'kɒpə(r)/ n Kupfer nt • adj kupfern

copper[2] n 🔲 Polizist m

copper 'beech n Blutbuche f

coppice /'kɒpɪs/ n, **copse** n Gehölz nt

copy /'kɒpɪ/ n Kopie f; (book) Exemplar m • vt (pt/pp -ied) kopieren; (imitate) nachahmen; (Sch) abschreiben

copy: **~right** n Copyright nt. **~-writer** n Texter m

coral /'kɒrəl/ n Koralle f

cord /kɔːd/ n Schnur f; (fabric) Cordsamt m; **~s** pl Cordhose f

cordial /'kɔːdɪəl/ adj herzlich • n Fruchtsirup m

cordon /'kɔːdn/ n Kordon f • vt **~ off** absperren

corduroy /'kɔːdərɔɪ/ n Cordsamt m

core /kɔː(r)/ n Kern m; (of apple, pear) Kerngehäuse nt

cork /kɔːk/ n Kork m; (for bottle) Korken m. **~screw** n Korkenzieher m

corn[1] /kɔːn/ n Korn nt; (Amer: maize) Mais m

corn[2] n (Med) Hühnerauge nt

corned beef /kɔːnd'biːf/ n Cornedbeef nt

corner /'kɔːnə(r)/ n Ecke f; (bend) Kurve f; (football) Eckball m • vt (fig) in die Enge treiben; (Comm) monopolisieren (market). **~-stone**

n Eckstein m

cornet /'kɔːnɪt/ n (Mus) Kornett nt; (for ice-cream) [Eis]tüte f

corn: ~**flour** n, (Amer) ~**starch** n Stärkemehl nt

corny /'kɔːnɪ/ adj 🗉 abgedroschen

coronation /kɒrə'neɪʃn/ n Krönung f

coroner /'kɒrənə(r)/ n Beamte(r) m, der verdächtige Todesfälle untersucht

corporal /'kɔːpərəl/ n (Mil) Stabsunteroffizier m

corps /kɔː(r)/ n (pl corps /kɔːz/) Korps nt

corpse /kɔːps/ n Leiche f

correct /kə'rekt/ adj richtig; (proper) korrekt ● vt verbessern; (text, school work) korrigieren. ~**ion** n Verbesserung f; (Typ) Korrektur f

correspond /kɒrɪ'spɒnd/ vi entsprechen (to dat); (two things:) sich entsprechen; (write) korrespondieren. ~**ence** n Briefwechsel m; (Comm) Korrespondenz f. ~**ent** n Korrespondent(in) m(f). ~**ing** adj entsprechend

corridor /'kɒrɪdɔː(r)/ n Gang m; (Pol, Aviat) Korridor m

corro|de /kə'rəʊd/ vt zerfressen ● vi rosten. ~**sion** n Korrosion f

corrugated /'kɒrəgeɪtɪd/ adj gewellt. ~ **iron** n Wellblech nt

corrupt /kə'rʌpt/ adj korrupt ● vt korrumpieren; (spoil) verderben. ~**ion** n Korruption f

corset /'kɔːsɪt/ n Korsett nt

Corsica /'kɔːsɪkə/ n Korsika nt

cosh /kɒʃ/ n Totschläger m

cosmetic /kɒz'metɪk/ adj kosmetisch ● n ~s pl Kosmetika pl

cosset /'kɒsɪt/ vt verhätscheln

cost /kɒst/ n Kosten pl; ~s pl (Jur) Kosten; at all ~s um jeden Preis

● vt (pt/pp cost) kosten; it ~ me £20 es hat mich £20 gekostet ● vt (pt/pp costed) ~ [out] die Kosten kalkulieren für

costly /'kɒstlɪ/ adj teuer

cost: ~ of 'living n Lebenshaltungskosten pl. ~ price n Selbstkostenpreis m

costume /'kɒstjuːm/ n Kostüm nt; (national) Tracht f. ~ jewellery n Modeschmuck m

cosy /'kəʊzɪ/ adj gemütlich ● n (tea-, egg-) Wärmer m

cot /kɒt/ n Kinderbett nt; (Amer: camp bed) Feldbett nt

cottage /'kɒtɪdʒ/ n Häuschen nt. ~ 'cheese n Hüttenkäse m

cotton /'kɒtn/ n Baumwolle f; (thread) Nähgarn nt ● adj baumwollen ● vi ~ on 🗉 kapieren

cotton 'wool n Watte f

couch /kaʊtʃ/ n Liege f

couchette /kuː'ʃet/ n (Rail) Liegeplatz m

cough /kɒf/ n Husten m ● vi husten. ~ **up** vt/i husten; (🗉: pay) blechen

'cough mixture n Hustensaft m

could /kʊd, unbetont /kəd/ see can²

council /'kaʊnsl/ n Rat m; (Admin) Stadtverwaltung f; (rural) Gemeindeverwaltung f. ~ house n ≈ Sozialwohnung f

councillor /'kaʊnsələ(r)/ n Ratsmitglied nt

'council tax n Gemeindesteuer f

count¹ /kaʊnt/ n Graf m

count² n Zählung f; keep ~ zählen ● vt/i zählen. ~ on vt rechnen auf (+ acc)

counter¹ /'kaʊntə(r)/ n (in shop) Ladentisch m; (in bank) Schalter m; (in café) Theke f; (Games)

Spielmarke f

counter² adj Gegen- ● vt/i kontern

counter'act vt entgegenwirken (+ dat)

'counterfeit /-fɪt/ adj gefälscht

'counterfoil n Kontrollabschnitt m

'counterpart n Gegenstück nt

counter-pro'ductive adj be ~ das Gegenteil bewirken

'countersign vt gegenzeichnen

countess /'kaʊntɪs/ n Gräfin f

countless /'kaʊntlɪs/ adj unzählig

country /'kʌntrɪ/ n Land nt; (native land) Heimat f; (countryside) Landschaft f; in the ~ auf dem Lande. ~man n [fellow] ~man n Landsmann m. ~side n Landschaft f

county /'kaʊntɪ/ n Grafschaft f

coup /kuː/ n (Pol) Staatsstreich m

couple /'kʌpl/ n Paar nt; a ~ of (two) zwei ● vt verbinden

coupon /'kuːpɒn/ n Kupon m; (voucher) Gutschein m; (entry form) Schein m

courage /'kʌrɪdʒ/ n Mut m. ~ous adj mutig

courgettes /kʊə'ʒets/ npl Zucchini pl

courier /'kʊrɪə(r)/ n Bote m; (diplomatic) Kurier m; (for tourists) Reiseleiter(in) m(f)

course /kɔːs/ n (Naut, Sch) Kurs m; (Culin) Gang m; (for golf) Platz m; ~ of treatment (Med) Kur f; of ~ natürlich, selbstverständlich; in the ~ of im Lauf[e] (+ gen)

court /kɔːt/ n Hof m; (Sport) Platz m; (Jur) Gericht nt

courteous /'kɜːtɪəs/ adj höflich

courtesy /'kɜːtəsɪ/ n Höflichkeit f

court: ~ 'martial n (pl ~s mar-

tial) Militärgericht nt. ~-yard n Hof m

cousin /'kʌzn/ n Vetter m, Cousin m; (female) Kusine f

cove /kəʊv/ n kleine Bucht f

cover /'kʌvə(r)/ n Decke f; (of cushion) Bezug m; (of umbrella) Hülle f; (of typewriter) Haube f; (of book, lid) Deckel m; (of magazine) Umschlag m; (protection) Deckung f, Schutz m; take ~ Deckung nehmen; under separate ~ mit getrennter Post ● vt bedecken; beziehen (cushion); decken (costs, needs); zurücklegen (distance); berichten über (+ acc) event; (insure) versichern. ~ up zudecken; (fig) vertuschen

coverage /'kʌvərɪdʒ/ n (Journalism) Berichterstattung f (of über + acc)

cover: ~ing n Decke f; (for floor) Belag m. ~-up n Vertuschung f

cow /kaʊ/ n Kuh f

coward /'kaʊəd/ n Feigling m. ~ice n Feigheit f. ~ly adj feige

'cowboy n Cowboy m; 🔲 unsolider Handwerker m

cower /'kaʊə(r)/ vi sich [ängstlich] ducken

'cowshed n Kuhstall m

cox /kɒks/ n, **coxswain** n Steuermann m

coy /kɔɪ/ adj (-er, -est) gespielt schüchtern

crab /kræb/ n Krabbe f

crack /kræk/ n Riss m; (in china, glass) Sprung m; (noise) Knall m; (🔲: joke) Witz m; (🔲: attempt) Versuch m ● adj 🔲 erstklassig ● vt knacken (nut, code); einen Sprung machen in (+ acc) (china, glass); 🔲 reißen (joke); 🔲 lösen (problem) ● vi (china, glass:) springen; (whip:) knallen. ~ down vi 🔲 durchgreifen

cracked /krækt/ adj gesprungen; (rib) angebrochen; (🔟: crazy) verrückt

cracker /'krækə(r)/ n (biscuit) Kräcker m; (firework) Knallkörper m; [Christmas] ~ Knallbonbon m. **~s** adj be ~s 🔟 einen Knacks haben

crackle /'krækl/ vi knistern

cradle /'kreidl/ n Wiege f

craft /krɑːft/ n Handwerk nt; (technique) Fertigkeit f. **~sman** n Handwerker m

crafty /'krɑːftɪ/ adj , -ily adv gerissen

crag /kræg/ n Felszacken m

cram /kræm/ v (pt/pp crammed) ●vt hineinstopfen (into in + acc); vollstopfen (with mit) ●vi (for exams) pauken

cramp /kræmp/ n Krampf m. **~ed** adj eng

cranberry /'krænbərɪ/ n (Culin) Preiselbeere f

crane /krein/ n Kran m; (bird) Kranich m

crank /kræŋk/ n 🔟 Exzentriker m

'crankshaft n Kurbelwelle f

crash /kræʃ/ n (noise) Krach m; (Auto) Zusammenstoß m; (Aviat) Absturz m ●vi krachen (into gegen); (cars:) zusammenstoßen; (plane:) abstürzen ●vt einen Unfall haben mit (car)

crash: **~-helmet** n Sturzhelm m. **~-landing** n Bruchlandung f

crate /kreit/ n Kiste f

crater /'kreitə(r)/ n Krater m

crawl /krɔːl/ n (Swimming) Kraul nt; do the ~ kraulen; at a ~ im Kriechtempo ●vi kriechen; (baby:) krabbeln; ~ with wimmeln von

crayon /'kreiən/ n Wachsstift m; (pencil) Buntstift m

craze /kreiz/ n Mode f

crazy /'kreizi/ adj verrückt; be ~ about verrückt sein nach

creak /kriːk/ vi knarren

cream /kriːm/ n Sahne f; (Cosmetic, Med, Culin) Creme f ●adj (colour) cremefarben ●vt (Culin) cremig rühren. **~y** adj sahnig; (smooth) cremig

crease /kriːs/ n Falte f; (unwanted) Knitterfalte f ●vt falten; (accidentally) zerknittern ●vi knittern

creat|e /kriːˈeit/ vt schaffen. **~ion** n Schöpfung f. **~ive** adj schöpferisch. **~or** n Schöpfer m

creature /'kriːtʃə(r)/ n Geschöpf nt

crèche /kreʃ/ n Kinderkrippe f

credibility /kredə'biləti/ n Glaubwürdigkeit f

credible /'kredəbl/ adj glaubwürdig

credit /'kredit/ n Kredit m; (honour) Ehre f ●vt glauben; ~ s.o. with sth (Comm) jdm etw gutschreiben; (fig) jdm etw zuschreiben. **~able** adj lobenswert

credit: **~ card** n Kreditkarte f. **~or** n Gläubiger m

creep /kriːp/ vi (pt/pp crept) schleichen (up 🔟 fieser Kerl m; it gives me the ~s es ist mir unheimlich. **~er** n Kletterpflanze f. **~y** adj gruselig

cremat|e /kri'meit/ vt einäschern. **~ion** n Einäscherung f

crêpe /kreip/ n Krepp m. ~ **paper** n Kreppapier m

crept /krept/ see creep

crescent /'kresənt/ n Halbmond m

cress /kres/ n Kresse f

crest /krest/ n Kamm m; (coat of arms) Wappen nt

crew /kruː/ n Besatzung f; (gang) Bande f. ~ **cut** n Bürstenschnitt m

crib[1] /krɪb/ n Krippe f

crib[2] vt/i (pt/pp **cribbed**) 🔲 abschreiben

cricket /'krɪkɪt/ n Kricket nt. **~er** n Kricketspieler m

crime /kraɪm/ n Verbrechen nt; (rate) Kriminalität f

criminal /'krɪmɪnl/ adj kriminell, verbrecherisch; (law, court) Straf- ● n Verbrecher m

crimson /'krɪmzn/ adj purpurrot

crinkle /'krɪŋkl/ vt/i knittern

cripple /'krɪpl/ n Krüppel m ● vt zum Krüppel machen; (fig) lahmlegen. **~d** adj verkrüppelt

crisis /'kraɪsɪs/ n (pl **-ses** /-si:z/) Krise f

crisp /krɪsp/ adj (-er, -est) knusprig. **~bread** n Knäckebrot nt. **~s** npl Chips pl

criss-cross /'krɪs-/ adj schräg gekreuzt

criterion /kraɪ'tɪərɪən/ n (pl **-ria** /-rɪə/) Kriterium nt

critic /'krɪtɪk/ n Kritiker m. **~al** adj kritisch. **~ally** adv kritisch; **~ally ill** schwer krank

criticism /'krɪtɪsɪzm/ n Kritik f

criticize /'krɪtɪsaɪz/ vt kritisieren

croak /krəʊk/ vi krächzen; (frog:) quaken

crockery /'krɒkərɪ/ n Geschirr nt

crocodile /'krɒkədaɪl/ n Krokodil nt

crocus /'krəʊkəs/ n (pl **-es**) Krokus m

crony /'krəʊnɪ/ n Kumpel m

crook /krʊk/ n (stick) Stab m; (🔲: criminal) Schwindler m, Gauner m

crooked /'krʊkɪd/ adj schief; (bent) krumm; (🔲: dishonest) unehrlich

crop /krɒp/ n Feldfrucht f; (harvest) Ernte f ● v (pt/pp **cropped**) ● vt

stutzen ● vi **~ up** 🔲 zur Sprache kommen; (occur) dazwischenkommen

croquet /'krəʊkeɪ/ n Krocket nt

cross /krɒs/ adj (annoyed) böse (with auf + acc); **talk at ~ purposes** aneinander vorbeireden ● n Kreuz nt; (Bot, Zool) Kreuzung f ● vt kreuzen (cheque, animals); überqueren (road); **~ oneself** sich bekreuzigen; **~ one's arms** die Arme verschränken; **~ one's legs** die Beine übereinander schlagen; **keep one's fingers ~ed for s.o.** jdm die Daumen drücken; **it ~ed my mind** es fiel mir ein ● vi (go across) hinübergehen/-fahren; (lines:) sich kreuzen. **~ out** vt durchstreichen

cross: **~'country** n (Sport) Crosslauf m. **~'eyed** adj schielend; **be ~-eyed** schielen. **~fire** n Kreuzfeuer nt. **~ing** n Übergang m; (sea journey) Überfahrt f. **~'section** n [Straßen]kreuzung f. **~'section** n Querschnitt m. **~wise** adv quer. **~word** n **~word** [puzzle] Kreuzworträtsel n

crotchety /'krɒtʃɪtɪ/ adj griesgrämig

crouch /kraʊtʃ/ vi kauern

crow /krəʊ/ n Krähe f; **as the ~ flies** Luftlinie

crowd /kraʊd/ n [Menschen]menge f ● vi sich drängen. **~ed** adj [gedrängt] voll

crown /kraʊn/ n Krone f ● vt krönen; überkronen (tooth)

crucial /'kru:ʃl/ adj höchst wichtig; (decisive) entscheidend (to für)

crude /kru:d/ adj (-r, -st) primitiv; (raw) roh

cruel /kru:əl/ adj (crueller, cruellest) grausam (to gegen). **~ty** n Grausamkeit f

cruis|e /kru:z/ n Kreuzfahrt f ● vi

kreuzen; (*car:*) fahren. **~er** n (*Mil*) Kreuzer m; (*motor boat*) Kajütboot nt

crumb /krʌm/ n Krümel m

crumb|le /'krʌmbl/ vt/i krümeln; (*collapse*) einstürzen

crumple /'krʌmpl/ vt zerknittern ● vi knittern

crunch /krʌntʃ/ n ⊞ when it comes to the ~ wenn es [wirklich] drauf ankommt ● vt mampfen ● vi knirschen

crusade /kruː'seɪd/ n Kreuzzug m; (*fig*) Kampagne f. **~r** n Kreuzfahrer m; (*fig*) Kämpfer m

crush /krʌʃ/ n (*crowd*) Gedränge nt ● vt zerquetschen; zerknittern (*clothes*); (*fig: subdue*) niederschlagen

crust /krʌst/ n Kruste f

crutch /krʌtʃ/ n Krücke f

cry /kraɪ/ n Ruf m; (*shout*) Schrei m; a far ~ from (*fig*) weit entfernt von ● vi (*pt/pp* cried) (*weep*) weinen; (*baby:*) schreien; (*call*) rufen

crypt /krɪpt/ n Krypta f. **~ic** adj rätselhaft

crystal /'krɪstl/ n Kristall m; (*glass*) Kristall nt

cub /kʌb/ n (*Zool*) Junge(s) nt

Cuba /'kjuːbə/ n Kuba nt

cubby-hole /'kʌbɪ-/ n Fach nt

cub|e /kjuːb/ n Würfel m. **~ic** adj Kubik-

cubicle /'kjuːbɪkl/ n Kabine f

cuckoo /'kuːkuː/ n Kuckuck m. **~ clock** n Kuckucksuhr f

cucumber /'kjuːkʌmbə(r)/ n Gurke f

cuddl|e /'kʌdl/ vt herzen ● vi **~e up to** sich kuscheln an (+ *acc*). **~y** adj kuschelig

cue[1] /kjuː/ n Stichwort nt

cue[2] n (*Billiards*) Queue nt

cuff /kʌf/ n Manschette f; (*Amer: turn-up*) [Hosen]aufschlag m; (*blow*) Klaps m; **off the ~** ⊞ aus dem Stegreif. **~-link** n Manschettenknopf m

cul-de-sac /'kʌldəsæk/ n Sackgasse f

culinary /'kʌlɪnərɪ/ adj kulinarisch

culprit /'kʌlprɪt/ n Täter m

cult /kʌlt/ n Kult m

cultivate /'kʌltɪveɪt/ vt anbauen (*crop*); bebauen (*land*)

cultural /'kʌltʃərəl/ adj kulturell

culture /'kʌltʃə(r)/ n Kultur f. **~d** adj kultiviert

cumbersome /'kʌmbəsəm/ adj hinderlich; (*unwieldy*) unhandlich

cunning /'kʌnɪŋ/ adj listig ● n List f

cup /kʌp/ n Tasse f; (*prize*) Pokal m

cupboard /'kʌbəd/ n Schrank m

Cup 'Final n Pokalendspiel nt

curable /'kjʊərəbl/ adj heilbar

curate /'kjʊərət/ n Vikar m; (*Roman Catholic*) Kaplan m

curb /kɜːb/ vt zügeln

curdle /'kɜːdl/ vi gerinnen

cure /kjʊə(r)/ n [Heil]mittel nt ● vt heilen; (*salt*) pökeln; (*smoke*) räuchern; gerben (*skin*)

curiosity /kjʊərɪ'ɒsətɪ/ n Neugier f; (*object*) Kuriosität f

curious /'kjʊərɪəs/ adj neugierig; (*strange*) merkwürdig, seltsam

curl /kɜːl/ n Locke f ● vt locken ● vi sich locken

curly /'kɜːlɪ/ adj lockig

currant /'kʌrənt/ n (*dried*) Korinthe f

currency /'kʌrənsɪ/ n Geläufigkeit f; (*money*) Währung f; **foreign ~** Devisen pl

current /'kʌrənt/ adj augenblicklich, gegenwärtig; (*in general use*) geläufig, gebräuchlich • n Strömung f; (Electr) Strom m. ~ affairs or events npl Aktuelle(s) nt. ~ly adv zurzeit

curriculum /kə'rɪkjʊləm/ n Lehrplan m. ~ vitae n Lebenslauf m

curry /'kʌrɪ/ n Curry m & m; (meal) Currygericht nt

curse /kɜːs/ n Fluch m • vt verfluchen • vi fluchen

cursor /'kɜːsə(r)/ n Cursor m

cursory /'kɜːsərɪ/ adj flüchtig

curt /kɜːt/ adj barsch

curtain /'kɜːtn/ n Vorhang m

curtsy /'kɜːtsɪ/ n Knicks m • vi (pt/pp -ied) knicksen

curve /kɜːv/ n Kurve f • vi einen Bogen machen; ~ to the right/left nach rechts/links biegen. ~d adj gebogen

cushion /'kʊʃn/ n Kissen nt • vt dämpfen; (protect) beschützen

cushy /'kʊʃɪ/ adj 𝕋 bequem

custard /'kʌstəd/ n Vanillesoße f

custom /'kʌstəm/ n Brauch m; (habit) Gewohnheit f; (Comm) Kundschaft f. ~ary adj üblich; (habitual) gewohnt. ~er n Kunde m/Kundin f

customs /'kʌstəmz/ npl Zoll m. ~ officer n Zollbeamte(r) m

cut /kʌt/ n Schnitt m; (Med) Schnittwunde f; (reduction) Kürzung f; (in price) Senkung f; ~ [of meat] [Fleisch]stück nt • vt/i (pt/pp cut, pres p cutting) schneiden; (mow) mähen; abheben (cards); (reduce) kürzen; senken (price); ~ one's finger sich in den Finger schneiden; ~ s.o.'s hair jdm die Haare schneiden; ~ short abkürzen. ~ back vt zurückschneiden; (fig) einschränken, kürzen. ~ down vt fällen; (fig) einschränken. ~ off vt abschneiden; (disconnect) abstellen; be ~ off (Teleph) unterbrochen werden. ~

out vt ausschneiden; (delete) streichen; be ~ out for 𝕋 geeignet sein zu. ~ up vt zerschneiden; (slice) aufschneiden

'cut-back n Kürzung f

cute /kjuːt/ adj (-r, -st) 𝕋 niedlich

cut 'glass n Kristall nt

cutlery /'kʌtlərɪ/ n Besteck nt

cutlet /'kʌtlɪt/ n Kotelett nt

'cut-price adj verbilligt

cutting /'kʌtɪŋ/ adj (remark) bissig • n (from newspaper) Ausschnitt m; (of plant) Ableger m

CV abbr curriculum vitae

cyberspace /'saɪbəspeɪs/ n Cyberspace m

cycl|e /'saɪkl/ n Zyklus m; (bicycle) [Fahr]rad nt • vi mit dem Rad fahren. ~ing n Radfahren nt. ~ist n Radfahrer(in) m(f)

cylinder /'sɪlɪndə(r)/ n Zylinder m. ~rical adj zylindrisch

cynic /'sɪnɪk/ n Zyniker m. ~al adj zynisch. ~ism n Zynismus m

Cyprus /'saɪprəs/ n Zypern nt

Czech /tʃek/ adj tschechisch; ~ Republic Tschechische Republik f • n Tscheche m/ Tschechin f

Dd

dab /dæb/ n Tupfer m; (of butter) Klecks m

dabble /'dæbl/ vi ~ in sth (fig) sich nebenbei mit etw befassen

dachshund /'dækshʊnd/ n Dackel m

dad[dy] /'dæd[ɪ]/ n 𝕋 Vati m

daddy-'long-legs n [Kohl]schnake f; (Amer: spider) Weberknecht m

daffodil /ˈdæfədɪl/ n Osterglocke f, gelbe Narzisse f

daft /dɑːft/ adj (-er, -est) dumm

dagger /ˈdægə(r)/ n Dolch m

dahlia /ˈdeɪlɪə/ n Dahlie f

Dáil Éireann Das Repräsentantenhaus, der *Dáil Éireann* (ausgesprochen daːl'ern) ist das Unterhaus und gesetzgebende Organ des irischen Parlaments in der Republik Irland. Es setzt sich aus 166 Abgeordneten zusammen, die für fünf Jahre durch allgemeine Wahlen (Verhältniswahlsystem) bestimmt werden. Die Verfassung sorgt dafür, dass ein Abgeordneter je 20- bis 30 000 Einwohner vertritt.

daily /ˈdeɪlɪ/ adj & adv täglich

dainty /ˈdeɪntɪ/ adj zierlich

dairy /ˈdeərɪ/ n Molkerei f; (shop) Milchgeschäft nt. ~ **products** pl Milchprodukte pl

daisy /ˈdeɪzɪ/ n Gänseblümchen nt

dam /dæm/ n [Stau]damm m ● vt (pt/pp dammed) eindämmen

damag|e /ˈdæmɪdʒ/ n Schaden m (to an + dat); ~**es** pl (Jur) Schadenersatz m ● vt beschädigen; (fig) beeinträchtigen

damn /dæm/ adj, int & adv 🗆 verdammt ● n I don't care or give a 🗆 ich schere mich einen Dreck darum ● vt verdammen. ~**ation** n Verdammnis f

damp /dæmp/ adj (-er, -est) feucht ● n Feuchtigkeit f

damp|en vt anfeuchten; (fig) dämpfen. ~**ness** n Feuchtigkeit f

dance /dɑːns/ n Tanz m; (function) Tanzveranstaltung f ● vt/i tanzen. ~ **music** n Tanzmusik f

dancer /ˈdɑːnsə(r)/ n Tänzer(in) m(f)

dandelion /ˈdændɪlaɪən/ n Löwenzahn m

dandruff /ˈdændrʌf/ n Schuppen pl

Dane /deɪn/ n Däne m/Dänin f

danger /ˈdeɪndʒə(r)/ n Gefahr f; in/out of ~ in/außer Gefahr. ~**ous** adj gefährlich; ~**ously** ill schwer erkrankt

dangle /ˈdæŋgl/ vi baumeln ● vt baumeln lassen

Danish /ˈdeɪnɪʃ/ adj dänisch. ~ **'pastry** n Hefeteilchen nt

Danube /ˈdænjuːb/ n Donau f

dare /deə(r)/ vt/i (challenge) herausfordern (to zu); ~ [to] do sth [es] wagen, etw zu tun. ~**devil** n Draufgänger m

daring /ˈdeərɪŋ/ adj verwegen ● n Verwegenheit f

dark /dɑːk/ adj (-er, -est) dunkel; ~ blue/brown dunkelblau/-braun; ~ **horse** (fig) stilles Wasser nt ● n Dunkelheit f; after ~ nach Einbruch der Dunkelheit; in the ~ im Dunkeln

dark|en /ˈdɑːkn/ vt verdunkeln ● vi dunkler werden. ~**ness** n Dunkelheit f

'dark-room n Dunkelkammer f

darling /ˈdɑːlɪŋ/ adj allerliebst ● n Liebling m

darn /dɑːn/ vt stopfen

dart /dɑːt/ n Pfeil m; ~**s** sg (game) [Wurf]pfeil m ● vi flitzen

dash /dæʃ/ n (Printing) Gedankenstrich m; a ~ of milk ein Schuss Milch ● vi rennen ● vt schleudern. ~ **off** vi losstürzen ● vt (write quickly) hinwerfen

'dashboard n Armaturenbrett nt

data /ˈdeɪtə/ npl & sg Daten pl. ~ **processing** n Datenverarbeitung f

date[1] /deɪt/ n (fruit) Dattel f

date[2] /deɪt/ n Datum nt; 🛈 Verabredung f; **to ~** bis heute; **out of ~** überholt; (expired) ungültig; **be up to ~** auf dem Laufenden sein ●vt/i datieren; (Amer, fam: go out with) ausgehen mit

dated /deɪtɪd/ adj altmodisch

dative /deɪtɪv/ adj & n (Gram) ~ [case] Dativ m

daub /dɔ:b/ vt beschmieren (with mit); schmieren (paint)

daughter /dɔ:tə(r)/ n Tochter f. ~-in-law n (pl ~s-in-law) Schwiegertochter f

dawdle /dɔ:dl/ vi trödeln

dawn /dɔ:n/ n Morgendämmerung f; **at ~** bei Tagesanbruch ●vi anbrechen; **it ~ed on me** (fig) es ging mir auf

day /deɪ/ n Tag m; **~ by ~** Tag für Tag; **~ after ~** Tag um Tag; **these ~s** heutzutage; **in those ~s** zu der Zeit

day: **~-dream** n Tagtraum m ●vi [mit offenen Augen] träumen. **~light** n Tageslicht nt. **~time** n in the **~time** am Tage

daze /deɪz/ n in a **~** wie benommen. **~d** adj benommen

dazzle /dæzl/ vt blenden

dead /ded/ adj tot; (flower) verwelkt; (numb) taub; **~ body** Leiche f; **~ centre** genau in der Mitte ●adv **~ tired** todmüde; **~ slow** sehr langsam ●n **the ~** pl die Toten; **in the ~ of night** mitten in der Nacht

deaden /dedn/ vt dämpfen (sound); betäuben (pain)

dead: **~ end** n Sackgasse f. **~ heat** n totes Rennen nt. **~ line** n [letzter] Termin m

deadly /dedlɪ/ adj tödlich; (🛈: dreary) sterbenslangweilig

deaf /def/ adj (-er, -est) taub; **~ and dumb** taubstumm

deaf|**en** /defn/ vt betäuben; (permanently) taub machen. **~ening** adj ohrenbetäubend. **~ness** n Taubheit f

deal /di:l/ n (transaction) Geschäft nt; **whose ~?** (Cards) wer gibt? **a good or great ~** eine Menge; **get a raw ~** 🛈 schlecht wegkommen ●v (pt/pp dealt /delt/) ●vt (Cards) geben; **~ out** austeilen ●vi **~ in** handeln mit; **~ with** zu tun haben mit; (handle) sich befassen mit; (cope with) fertig werden mit; (be about) handeln von; **that's been dealt with** das ist schon erledigt

deal|**er** /di:lə(r)/ n Händler m

dean /di:n/ n Dekan m

dear /dɪə(r)/ adj (-er, -est) lieb; (expensive) teuer; (in letter) liebe(r,s) / (formal) sehr geehrte(r,s) ●n Liebe(r) m/f ●int oh ~! o je! ●**~ly** adv (love) sehr; (pay) teuer

death /deθ/ n Tod m; **three ~s** drei Todesfälle. **~ certificate** n Sterbeurkunde f

deathly adj **~ silence** Totenstille f ●adv **~ pale** totenblass

death: **~ penalty** n Todesstrafe f. **~-trap** n Todesfalle f

debatable /dɪbeɪtəbl/ adj strittig

debate /dɪbeɪt/ n Debatte f ●vt/i debattieren

debauchery /dɪbɔ:tʃərɪ/ n Ausschweifung f

debit /debɪt/ n [side] Soll nt ●vt (pt/pp debited) belasten; abbuchen (sum)

debris /debri:/ n Trümmer pl

debt /det/ n Schuld f; **in ~** verschuldet. **~or** n Schuldner m

début /deɪbu:/ n Debüt nt

decade /dekeɪd/ n Jahrzehnt nt

decadence /dekədəns/ n Dekadenz f. ~t adj dekadent

decaffeinated /diːˈkæfɪneɪtɪd/ adj koffeinfrei

decay /dɪˈkeɪ/ n Verfall m; (rot) Verwesung f; (of tooth) Zahnfäule f ● vi verfallen; (rot) verwesen; (tooth:) schlecht werden

deceased /dɪˈsiːsd/ adj verstorben ● the ~d der/die Verstorbene

deceit /dɪˈsiːt/ n Täuschung f. ~ful adj unaufrichtig

deceive /dɪˈsiːv/ vt täuschen; (be unfaithful to) betrügen

December /dɪˈsembə(r)/ n Dezember m

decency /ˈdiːsənsɪ/ n Anstand m

decent /ˈdiːsənt/ adj anständig

deception /dɪˈsepʃn/ n Täuschung f; (fraud) Betrug m. ~ive adj täuschend

decide /dɪˈsaɪd/ vt entscheiden ● vi sich entscheiden (on für)

decided /dɪˈsaɪdɪd/ adj entschieden

decimal /ˈdesɪml/ adj Dezimal- ● n Dezimalzahl f. ~ 'point n Komma nt

decipher /dɪˈsaɪfə(r)/ vt entziffern

decision /dɪˈsɪʒn/ n Entscheidung f; (firmness) Entschlossenheit f

decisive /dɪˈsaɪsɪv/ adj ausschlaggebend; (firm) entschlossen

deck[1] /dek/ vt schmücken

deck[2] n (Naut) Deck nt; on ~ an Deck; ~ of cards (Amer) [Karten]-spiel nt. ~-chair n Liegestuhl m

declaration /deklaˈreɪʃn/ n Erklärung f

declare /dɪˈkleə(r)/ vt erklären; angeben (goods); anything to ~? etwas zu verzollen?

decline /dɪˈklaɪn/ n Rückgang m; (in health) Verfall m ● vt ablehnen; (Gram) deklinieren ● vi ablehnen;

(fall) sinken; (decrease) nachlassen

decommission /diːkəˈmɪʃn/ vt stilllegen; außer Dienst stellen (Schiff)

décor /ˈdeɪkɔː(r)/ n Ausstattung f

decorat|e /ˈdekəreɪt/ vt (adorn) schmücken; verzieren (cake); (paint) streichen; (wallpaper) tapezieren; (award medal) einen Orden verleihen (+ dat). ~ion n Verzierung f; (medal) Orden m; ~ions pl Schmuck m. ~ive adj dekorativ. ~or n painter and ~or Maler und Tapezierer m

decoy /ˈdiːkɔɪ/ n Lockvogel m

decrease[1] /ˈdiːkriːs/ n Verringerung f; (in number) Rückgang m

decrease[2] /dɪˈkriːs/ vt verringern; herabsetzen (price) ● vi sich verringern; (price:) sinken

decrepit /dɪˈkrepɪt/ adj altersschwach

dedicat|e /ˈdedɪkeɪt/ vt widmen; (Relig) weihen. ~ed adj hingebungsvoll; (person) aufopfernd. ~ion n Hingabe f; (in book) Widmung f

deduce /dɪˈdjuːs/ vt folgern (from aus)

deduct /dɪˈdʌkt/ vt abziehen

deduction /dɪˈdʌkʃn/ n Abzug m; (conclusion) Folgerung f

deed /diːd/ n Tat f; (Jur) Urkunde f

deep /diːp/ adj (-er, -est) tief; go off the ~ end 🄳 auf die Palme gehen ● adv tief

deepen /ˈdiːpn/ vt vertiefen

deep-freeze n Gefriertruhe f; (upright) Gefrierschrank m

deer /dɪə(r)/ n inv Hirsch m; (roe) Reh nt

deface /dɪˈfeɪs/ vt beschädigen

default /dɪˈfɔːlt/ n win by ~ (Sport) kampflos gewinnen

defeat /dɪˈfiːt/ n Niederlage f; (defeating) Besiegung f; (rejection) Ablehnung f ●vt besiegen; ablehnen; (frustrate) vereiteln

defect /ˈdiːfɛkt/ n Fehler m; (Techn) Defekt m. ~**ive** adj fehlerhaft; (Techn) defekt

defence /dɪˈfɛns/ n Verteidigung f. ~**less** adj wehrlos

defend /dɪˈfɛnd/ vt verteidigen; (justify) rechtfertigen. ~**ant** n (Jur) Beklagte(r) m/f; (in criminal court) Angeklagte(r) m/f

defensive /dɪˈfɛnsɪv/ adj defensiv

defer /dɪˈfɜː(r)/ vt (pt/pp deferred) (postpone) aufschieben

deferen|ce /ˈdɛfərəns/ n Ehrerbietung f. ~**tial** adj ehrerbietig

defian|ce /dɪˈfaɪəns/ n Trotz m; **in ~ce of** zum Trotz (+ dat). ~**t** adj aufsässig

deficien|cy /dɪˈfɪʃənsɪ/ n Mangel m. ~**t** adj mangelhaft

deficit /ˈdɛfɪsɪt/ n Defizit nt

define /dɪˈfaɪn/ vt bestimmen; definieren (word)

definite /ˈdɛfɪnɪt/ adj bestimmt; (certain) sicher

definition /dɛfɪˈnɪʃn/ n Definition f; (Phot, TV) Schärfe f

definitive /dɪˈfɪnɪtɪv/ adj endgültig; (authoritative) maßgeblich

deflat|e /dɪˈfleɪt/ vt die Luft auslassen aus. ~**ion** n (Comm) Deflation f

deflect /dɪˈflɛkt/ vt ablenken

deform|ed /dɪˈfɔːmd/ adj missgebildet. ~**ity** n Missbildung f

defraud /dɪˈfrɔːd/ vt betrügen (of um)

defray /dɪˈfreɪ/ vt bestreiten

defrost /diːˈfrɒst/ vt entfrosten; abtauen (fridge); auftauen (food)

deft /dɛft/ adj (-er, -est) geschickt. ~**ness** n Geschicklichkeit f

defuse /diːˈfjuːz/ vt entschärfen

defy /dɪˈfaɪ/ vt (pt/pp -ied) trotzen (+ dat); widerstehen (+ dat) (attempt)

degrading /dɪˈgreɪdɪŋ/ adj entwürdigend

degree /dɪˈgriː/ n Grad m; (Univ) akademischer Grad m; **20 ~s** 20 Grad

de-ice /diːˈaɪs/ vt enteisen

deity /ˈdiːɪtɪ/ n Gottheit f

dejected /dɪˈdʒɛktɪd/ adj niedergeschlagen

delay /dɪˈleɪ/ n Verzögerung f; (of train, aircraft) Verspätung f; **without ~** unverzüglich ●vt aufhalten; (postpone) aufschieben ●vi zögern

delegate[1] /ˈdɛlɪgət/ n Delegierte(r) m/f

delegat|e[2] /ˈdɛlɪgeɪt/ vt delegieren. ~**ion** n Delegation f

delet|e /dɪˈliːt/ vt streichen. ~**ion** n Streichung f

deliberate /dɪˈlɪbərət/ adj absichtlich; (slow) bedächtig

delicacy /ˈdɛlɪkəsɪ/ n Feinheit f; Zartheit f; (food) Delikatesse f

delicate /ˈdɛlɪkət/ adj fein; (fabric, health) zart; (situation) heikel; (mechanism) empfindlich

delicatessen /dɛlɪkəˈtɛsn/ n Delikatessengeschäft nt

delicious /dɪˈlɪʃəs/ adj köstlich

delight /dɪˈlaɪt/ n Freude f ●vt entzücken ●vi **~ in** sich erfreuen an (+ dat). ~**ed** adj hocherfreut; **be ~ed** sich sehr freuen. ~**ful** adj reizend

delinquent /dɪˈlɪŋkwənt/ adj straffällig ●n Straffällige(r) m/f

deli|rious /dɪˈlɪrɪəs/ adj **be ~rious** im Delirium sein. ~**rium** n Delirium nt

deliver /dɪˈlɪvə(r)/ vt liefern; zustellen (*post, newspaper*); halten (*speech*); überbringen (*message*); versetzen (*blow*); (*set free*) befreien; ~ **a baby** ein Kind zur Welt bringen. ~**y** n Lieferung f; (*of post*) Zustellung f; (*Med*) Entbindung f; **cash on** ~**y** per Nachnahme

delta /'deltə/ n Delta nt

deluge /'delju:dʒ/ n Flut f; (*heavy rain*) schwerer Guss m

delusion /dɪ'lu:ʒn/ n Täuschung f

de luxe /də'lʌks/ adj Luxus-

demand /dɪ'mɑ:nd/ n Forderung f; (*Comm*) Nachfrage f; **in** ~ gefragt; **on** ~ auf Verlangen ● vt verlangen, fordern (*of/from* von). ~**ing** adj anspruchsvoll

demented /dɪ'mentɪd/ adj verrückt

demister /di:'mɪstə(r)/ n (*Auto*) Defroster m

demo /'deməʊ/ n (pl ~s) Ⅰ Demonstration f

democracy /dɪ'mɒkrəsɪ/ n Demokratie f

democrat /'deməkræt/ n Demokrat m. ~**ic** adj, ~**ally** adv demokratisch

demo|lish /dɪ'mɒlɪʃ/ vt abbrechen; (*destroy*) zerstören. ~**lition** n Abbruch m

demon /'di:mən/ n Dämon m

demonstrat|e /'demənstreɪt/ vt beweisen; vorführen (*appliance*) ● vi (*Pol*) demonstrieren. ~**ion** n (*Pol*) Demonstration f

demonstrator /'demənstreɪtə(r)/ n Vorführer m; (*Pol*) Demonstrant m

demoralize /dɪ'mɒrəlaɪz/ vt demoralisieren

demote /dɪ'məʊt/ vt degradieren

demure /dɪ'mjʊə(r)/ adj sittsam

den /den/ n Höhle f; (*room*) Bude f

denial /dɪ'naɪəl/ n Leugnen nt; official ~ Dementi nt

denim /'denɪm/ n Jeansstoff m; ~**s** pl Jeans pl

Denmark /'denmɑ:k/ n Dänemark nt

denounce /dɪ'naʊns/ vt denunzieren; (*condemn*) verurteilen

dens|e /dens/ adj (-r, -st) dicht; (Ⅰ: *stupid*) blöd[e]. ~**ity** n Dichte f

dent /dent/ n Delle f, Beule f ● vt einbeulen; ~**ed** verbeult

dental /'dentl/ adj Zahn-; (*treatment*) zahnärztlich. ~ **floss** n Zahnseide f. ~ **surgeon** n Zahnarzt m

dentist /'dentɪst/ n Zahnarzt m/-ärztin f. ~**ry** n Zahnmedizin f

denture /'dentʃə(r)/ n Zahnprothese f; ~**s** pl künstliches Gebiss nt

deny /dɪ'naɪ/ vt (pt/pp -ied) leugnen; (*officially*) dementieren; ~ **s.o. sth** jdm etw verweigern

deodorant /di:'əʊdərənt/ n Deodorant nt

depart /dɪ'pɑ:t/ vi abfahren; (*Aviat*) abfliegen; (*go away*) weggehen/-fahren; (*deviate*) abweichen (*from* von)

department /dɪ'pɑ:tmənt/ n Abteilung f; (*Pol*) Ministerium nt. ~ **store** n Kaufhaus nt

departure /dɪ'pɑ:tʃə(r)/ n Abfahrt f; (*Aviat*) Abflug m; (*from rule*) Abweichung f

depend /dɪ'pend/ vi abhängen (**on** von); (*rely*) sich verlassen (**on** auf + acc); **it all** ~**s** das kommt darauf an. ~**able** adj zuverlässig. ~**ant** n Abhängige(r) m/f. ~**ence** n Abhängigkeit f. ~**ent** adj abhängig (**on** von)

depict /dɪ'pɪkt/ vt darstellen

deplor|able /dɪ'plɔ:rəbl/ adj bedauerlich. ~**e** vt bedauern

deploy /dɪ'plɔɪ/ vt (*Mil*) einsetzen

depopulate /diːˈpɒpjʊleɪt/ vt entvölkern

deport /dɪˈpɔːt/ vt deportieren, ausweisen. **~ation** n Ausweisung f

depose /dɪˈpəʊz/ vt absetzen

deposit /dɪˈpɒzɪt/ n Anzahlung f; (against damage) Kaution f; (on bottle) Pfand nt; (sediment) Bodensatz m; (Geology) Ablagerung f ● vt (pt/pp deposited) legen; (for safety) deponieren; (Geology) ablagern. **~ account** n Sparkonto nt

depot /ˈdepəʊ/ n Depot nt; (Amer: railway station) Bahnhof m

deprav|e /dɪˈpreɪv/ vt verderben. **~ed** adj verkommen

depreciat|e /dɪˈpriːʃɪeɪt/ vi an Wert verlieren. **~ion** n Wertminderung f; (Comm) Abschreibung f

depress /dɪˈpres/ vt deprimieren; (press down) herunterdrücken. **~ed** adj deprimiert. **~ing** adj deprimierend. **~ion** n Vertiefung f; (Med) Depression f; (weather) Tiefdruckgebiet nt

deprivation /deprɪˈveɪʃn/ n Entbehrung f

deprive /dɪˈpraɪv/ vt **~ s.o. of sth** jdm etw entziehen. **~d** adj benachteiligt

depth /depθ/ n Tiefe f; **in ~** gründlich; **in the ~s of winter im tiefsten Winter**

deputize /ˈdepjʊtaɪz/ vi **~ for** vertreten

deputy /ˈdepjʊtɪ/ n Stellvertreter m ● attrib stellvertretend

derail /dɪˈreɪl/ vt **be ~ed** entgleisen. **~ment** n Entgleisung f

derelict /ˈderɪlɪkt/ adj verfallen; (abandoned) verlassen

derisory /dɪˈraɪsərɪ/ adj höhnisch; (offer) lächerlich

derivation /derɪˈveɪʃn/ n Ableitung f

derivative /dɪˈrɪvətɪv/ adj abgeleitet ● n Ableitung f

derive /dɪˈraɪv/ vt/i (obtain) gewinnen (from aus); **be ~d from** (word:) hergeleitet sein aus

derogatory /dɪˈrɒgətrɪ/ adj abfällig

derv /dɜːv/ n Diesel[kraftstoff] m

descend /dɪˈsend/ vt/i hinunter-/heruntergehen; (vehicle, lift:) hinunter-/herunterfahren; **be ~ed from** abstammen von. **~ant** n Nachkomme m

descent /dɪˈsent/ n Abstieg m; (lineage) Abstammung f

describe /dɪˈskraɪb/ vt beschreiben

descrip|tion /dɪˈskrɪpʃn/ n Beschreibung f; (sort) Art f. **~tive** adj beschreibend; (vivid) anschaulich

desecrate /ˈdesɪkreɪt/ vt entweihen

desert¹ /ˈdezət/ n Wüste f. **~ island** n verlassene Insel f

desert² /dɪˈzɜːt/ vt verlassen ● vt desertieren. **~ed** adj verlassen. **~er** n (Mil) Deserteur m. **~ion** n Fahnenflucht f

deserve /dɪˈzɜːv/ vt verdienen. **~edly** adv verdientermaßen. **~ing** adj verdienstvoll

design /dɪˈzaɪn/ n Entwurf m; (pattern) Muster nt; (construction) Konstruktion f; (aim) Absicht f ● vt entwerfen; (construct) konstruieren; **be ~ed for** bestimmt sein für

designer /dɪˈzaɪnə(r)/ n Designer m; (Techn) Konstrukteur m; (Theat) Bühnenbildner m

desirable /dɪˈzaɪrəbl/ adj wünschenswert; (sexually) begehrenswert

desire /dɪˈzaɪə(r)/ n Wunsch m; (longing) Verlangen nt (for nach); (sexual) Begierde f ● vt [sich (dat)] wünschen; (*sexually*) begehren

desk /desk/ n Schreibtisch m; (*Sch*) Pult nt

desolat|e /ˈdesələt/ adj trostlos. **~ion** n Trostlosigkeit f

despair /dɪˈspeə(r)/ n Verzweiflung f; in **~** verzweifelt ● vi verzweifeln

desperat|e /ˈdespərət/ adj verzweifelt; (*urgent*) dringend; be **~e** for dringend brauchen. **~ion** n Verzweiflung f

despicable /dɪˈspɪkəbl/ adj verachtenswert

despise /dɪˈspaɪz/ vt verachten

despite /dɪˈspaɪt/ prep trotz (+ *gen*)

despondent /dɪˈspɒndənt/ adj niedergeschlagen

dessert /dɪˈzɜːt/ n Dessert nt, Nachtisch m. **~ spoon** n Dessertlöffel m

destination /destɪˈneɪʃn/ n [Reise]ziel nt; (*of goods*) Bestimmungsort m

destiny /ˈdestɪnɪ/ n Schicksal nt

destitute /ˈdestɪtjuːt/ adj völlig mittellos

destroy /dɪˈstrɔɪ/ vt zerstören; (*totally*) vernichten. **~er** n (*Naut*) Zerstörer m

destruc|tion /dɪˈstrʌkʃn/ n Zerstörung f; Vernichtung f. **-tive** adj zerstörerisch; (*fig*) destruktiv

detach /dɪˈtætʃ/ vt abnehmen; (*tear off*) abtrennen. **~able** adj abnehmbar. **~ed** adj **~ed house** Einzelhaus nt

detail /ˈdiːteɪl/ n Einzelheit f, Detail nt; in **~** ausführlich ● vt einzeln aufführen. **~ed** adj ausführlich

detain /dɪˈteɪn/ vt aufhalten; (*police:*) in Haft behalten; (*take into custody*) in Haft nehmen

detect /dɪˈtekt/ vt entdecken; (*perceive*) wahrnehmen. **~ion** n Ent-

deckung f

detective /dɪˈtektɪv/ n Detektiv m. **~ story** n Detektivroman m

detention /dɪˈtenʃn/ n Haft f; (*Sch*) Nachsitzen nt

deter /dɪˈtɜː(r)/ vt (*pt/pp deterred*) abschrecken; (*prevent*) abhalten

detergent /dɪˈtɜːdʒənt/ n Waschmittel nt

deteriorat|e /dɪˈtɪərɪəreɪt/ vi sich verschlechtern. **~ion** n Verschlechterung f

determination /dɪtɜːmɪˈneɪʃn/ n Entschlossenheit f

determine /dɪˈtɜːmɪn/ vt bestimmen. **~d** adj entschlossen

deterrent /dɪˈterənt/ n Abschreckungsmittel nt

detest /dɪˈtest/ vt verabscheuen. **~able** adj abscheulich

detonate /ˈdetəneɪt/ vt zünden

detour /ˈdiːtʊə(r)/ n Umweg m

detract /dɪˈtrækt/ vi **~ from** beeinträchtigen

detriment /ˈdetrɪmənt/ n to the **~** (of) zum Schaden (+ *gen*). **~al** adj schädlich (to *dat*)

deuce /djuːs/ n (*Tennis*) Einstand m

devaluation /diːvæljʊˈeɪʃn/ n Abwertung f

de'value vt abwerten (*currency*)

devastat|e /ˈdevəsteɪt/ vt verwüsten. **~ing** adj verheerend. **~ion** n Verwüstung f

develop /dɪˈveləp/ vt entwickeln; bekommen (*illness*); erschließen (*area*) ● vi sich entwickeln (into zu). **~er** n (*property*) **~er** Bodenspekulant m

development /dɪˈveləpmənt/ n Entwicklung f

deviat|e /ˈdiːvɪeɪt/ vi abweichen. **~ion** n Abweichung f

device /dɪˈvaɪs/ n Gerät nt; (*fig*)

Mittel nt

devil /'devl/ n Teufel m. ~**ish** adj teuflisch

devious /'di:vɪəs/ adj verschlagen

devise /dɪ'vaɪz/ vt sich (dat) ausdenken

devot|e /dɪ'vəʊt/ vt widmen (to dat). ~**ed** adj ergeben; (care) liebevoll; be ~**ed** to s.o. sehr an jdm hängen

devotion /dɪ'vəʊʃn/ n Hingabe f

devour /dɪ'vaʊə(r)/ vt verschlingen

devout /dɪ'vaʊt/ adj fromm

dew /dju:/ n Tau m

dexterity /dek'sterətɪ/ n Geschicklichkeit f

diabet|es /daɪə'bi:ti:z/ n Zuckerkrankheit f. ~**ic** /ˈɪk/ n Diabetiker(in) m(f)

diabolical /daɪə'bɒlɪkl/ adj teuflisch

diagnose /daɪəg'nəʊz/ vt diagnostizieren

diagnosis /daɪəg'nəʊsɪs/ n (pl -oses /-si:z/) Diagnose f

diagonal /daɪ'ægənl/ adj diagonal ● n Diagonale f

diagram /'daɪəgræm/ n Diagramm nt

dial /'daɪəl/ n (of clock) Zifferblatt nt; (Techn) Skala f; (Teleph) Wählscheibe f ● vt/i (pt/pp dialled) (Teleph) wählen; ~ **direct** durchwählen

dialect /'daɪəlekt/ n Dialekt m

dialling: ~ **code** n Vorwahlnummer f. ~ **tone** n Amtszeichen nt

dialogue /'daɪəlɒg/ n Dialog m

diameter /daɪ'æmɪtə(r)/ n Durchmesser m

diamond /'daɪəmənd/ n Diamant m; (cut) Brillant m; (shape) Raute f; ~**s** pl (Cards) Karo nt

diaper /'daɪəpə(r)/ n (Amer)

Windel f

diarrhoea /daɪə'ri:ə/ n Durchfall m

diary /'daɪərɪ/ n Tagebuch nt; (for appointments) [Termin]kalender m

dice /daɪs/ n inv Würfel m.

dictat|e /dɪk'teɪt/ vt/i diktieren. ~**ion** n Diktat nt

dictator /dɪk'teɪtə(r)/ n Diktator m. ~**ial** adj diktatorisch. ~**ship** n Diktatur f

dictionary /'dɪkʃənrɪ/ n Wörterbuch nt

did /dɪd/ see do

didn't /'dɪdnt/ = did not

die¹ /daɪ/ n (Techn) Prägestempel m; (metal mould) Gussform f

die² vi (pres p dying) sterben (of an + dat); (plant, animal:) eingehen (flower:) verwelken; be dying to do sth 🖬 darauf brennen, etw zu tun; be dying for sth 🖬 sich nach etw sehnen. ~ **down** vi nachlassen; (fire:) herunterbrennen. ~ **out** vi aussterben

diesel /'di:zl/ n Diesel m. ~ **engine** n Dieselmotor m

diet /'daɪət/ n Kost f; (restricted) Diät f; (for slimming) Schlankheitskur f; be on a ~ Diät leben; eine Schlankheitskur machen ● vi Diät leben; eine Schlankheitskur machen

differ /'dɪfə(r)/ vi sich unterscheiden; (disagree) verschiedener Meinung sein

differ|ence /'dɪfrəns/ n Unterschied m; (disagreement) Meinungsverschiedenheit f. ~**t** adj andere(r,s); (various) verschiedene; be ~**t** anders sein (from als)

differential /dɪfə'renʃl/ adj Differenzial- ● n Unterschied m; (Techn) Differenzial nt

differentiate /dɪfə'renʃɪeɪt/ vt/i unterscheiden (between zwischen + dat)

differently /ˈdɪfrəntlɪ/ adv anders

difficult /ˈdɪfɪkəlt/ adj schwierig, schwer. ~**y** n Schwierigkeit f

diffiden|ce /ˈdɪfɪdəns/ n Zaghaftigkeit f. ~**t** adj zaghaft

dig /dɪg/ n (poke) Stoß m; (remark) spitze Bemerkung f; (archaeological) Ausgrabung f ● vt/i (pt/pp dug, pres p digging) graben; umgraben (garden). ~ **out** vt ausgraben. ~ **up** vt ausgraben; umgraben (garden); aufreißen (street)

digest /dɪˈdʒest/ vt verdauen. ~**ible** adj verdaulich. ~**ion** n Verdauung f

digit /ˈdɪdʒɪt/ n Ziffer f; (finger) Finger m; (toe) Zehe f. ~**ize** vt digitalisieren

digital /ˈdɪdʒɪtl/ adj Digital-; ~ **camera** n Digitalkamera f; ~ **television** n Digitalfernsehen nt

dignified /ˈdɪgnɪfaɪd/ adj würdevoll

dignity /ˈdɪgnɪtɪ/ n Würde f

dilapidated /dɪˈlæpɪdeɪtɪd/ adj baufällig

dilatory /ˈdɪlətərɪ/ adj langsam

dilemma /dɪˈlemə/ n Dilemma nt

dilettante /dɪlɪˈtæntɪ/ n Dilettant(in) m(f)

diligen|ce /ˈdɪlɪdʒəns/ n Fleiß m. ~**t** adj fleißig

dilute /daɪˈluːt/ vt verdünnen

dim /dɪm/ adj (dimmer, dimmest). -**ly** adv (weak) schwach; (dark) trüb[e]; (indistinct) undeutlich; (🄸: stupid) dumm, 🄸 doof ● vt (pt/pp dimmed) ✶ dämpfen

dime /daɪm/ n (Amer) Zehncentstück nt

dimension /daɪˈmenʃn/ n Dimension f; ~**s** pl Maße pl

diminutive /dɪˈmɪnjʊtɪv/ adj winzig ● n Verkleinerungsform f

dimple /ˈdɪmpl/ n Grübchen nt

din /dɪn/ n Krach m, Getöse nt

dine /daɪn/ vi speisen. ~**r** n Speisende(r) m/f; (Amer: restaurant) Esslokal nt

dinghy /ˈdɪŋgɪ/ n Dinghi nt; (inflatable) Schlauchboot nt

dingy /ˈdɪndʒɪ/ adj trübe

dining /ˈdaɪnɪŋ/: ~**car** n Speisewagen m. ~**room** n Esszimmer nt. ~**table** n Esstisch m

dinner /ˈdɪnə(r)/ n Abendessen nt; (at midday) Mittagessen nt; (formal) Essen nt. ~**jacket** n Smoking m

dinosaur /ˈdaɪnəsɔː(r)/ n Dinosaurier m

diocese /ˈdaɪəsɪs/ n Diözese f

dip /dɪp/ n (in ground) Senke f; (Culin) Dip m ● v (pt/pp dipped) vt [ein]tauchen; ~ **one's headlights** (Auto) [die Scheinwerfer] abblenden ● vi sich senken

diploma /dɪˈpləʊmə/ n Diplom nt

diplomacy /dɪˈpləʊməsɪ/ n Diplomatie f

diplomat /ˈdɪpləmæt/ n Diplomat m. ~**ic** adj, -**ally** adv diplomatisch

'dip-stick n (Auto) Ölmessstab m

dire /ˈdaɪə(r)/ adj (-r, -st) bitter; (consequences) furchtbar

direct /dɪˈrekt/ adj & adv direkt ● vt (aim) richten (at auf / (fig) an + acc); (control) leiten; (order) anweisen; ~ **a film/play** bei einem Film/Theaterstück Regie führen

direction /dɪˈrekʃn/ n Richtung f; (control) Leitung f; (of play, film) Regie f; ~**s** pl Anweisungen pl; ~**s for use** Gebrauchsanweisung f

directly /dɪˈrektlɪ/ adv direkt; (at once) sofort

director /dɪˈrektə(r)/ n (Comm) Direktor m; (of play, film) Regisseur m, Regisseurin f

directory /dɪˈrektərɪ/ n Verzeichnis nt; (Teleph) Telefonbuch nt

dirt /dɜːt/ n Schmutz m; (soil) Erde f; ~ **cheap** 🗉 spottbillig

dirty /ˈdɜːtɪ/ adj schmutzig

disˈability /dɪs-/ n Behinderung f. **~abled** adj [körper]behindert

disadˈvantage n Nachteil m; at a ~ im Nachteil. **~d** adj benachteiligt

disaˈgree vi nicht übereinstimmen (with mit); I ~ ich bin anderer Meinung; oysters ~ with me Austern bekommen mir nicht

disaˈgreeable adj unangenehm

disaˈgreement n Meinungsverschiedenheit f

disapˈpear vi verschwinden. **~ance** n Verschwinden nt

disapˈpoint vt enttäuschen. **~ment** n Enttäuschung f

disapˈproval n Missbilligung f

disapˈprove vi dagegen sein; ~ of missbilligen

disˈarm vt entwaffnen ● vi (Mil) abrüsten. **~ament** n Abrüstung f. **~ing** adj entwaffnend

disastˈer /dɪˈzɑːstə(r)/ n Katastrophe f; (accident) Unglück nt. **~rous** adj katastrophal

disbeˈlief n Ungläubigkeit f; in ~ ungläubig

disc /dɪsk/ n Scheibe f; (record) [Schall]platte f; (CD) CD f

discard /dɪˈskɑːd/ vt ablegen; (throw away) wegwerfen

discerning /dɪˈsɜːnɪŋ/ adj anspruchsvoll

ˈdischarge[1] n Ausstoßen nt; (Naut, Electr) Entladung f; (dismissal) Entlassung f; (Jur) Freispruch m; (Med) Ausfluss m

disˈcharge[2] vt ausstoßen; (Naut,

Electr) entladen; (dismiss) entlassen; (Jur) freisprechen (accused)

disciplinary /ˈdɪsɪplɪnərɪ/ adj disziplinarisch

discipline /ˈdɪsɪplɪn/ n Disziplin f ● vt Disziplin beibringen (+ dat); (punish) bestrafen

ˈdisc jockey n Diskjockey m

disˈclaim vt abstreiten. **~er** n Verzichterklärung f

disˈclosˈe vt enthüllen. **~ure** n Enthüllung f

disco /ˈdɪskəʊ/ n 🗉 Disko f

disˈcolour vt verfärben ● vi sich verfärben

disˈcomfort n Beschwerden pl; (fig) Unbehagen nt

disconˈnect vt trennen; (Electr) ausschalten; (cut supply) abstellen

disconˈtent n Unzufriedenheit f. **~ed** adj unzufrieden

disconˈtinue vt einstellen; (Comm) nicht mehr herstellen

disˈcord n Zwietracht f; (Mus & fig) Missklang m

discothèque /ˈdɪskətek/ n Diskothek f

ˈdiscount n Rabatt m

disˈcourage vt entmutigen; (dissuade) abraten (+ dat)

disˈcourteous adj unhöflich

disˈcover vt entdecken. **~y** n Entdeckung f

disˈcreet /dɪˈskriːt/ adj diskret

discretion /dɪˈskreʃn/ n Diskretion f; (judgement) Ermessen nt

discriminatˈe /dɪˈskrɪmɪneɪt/ vi unterscheiden (between zwischen + dat); ~e against diskriminieren. **~ing** adj anspruchsvoll. **~ion** n Diskriminierung f

discus /ˈdɪskəs/ n Diskus m

discuss /dɪˈskʌs/ vt besprechen; (examine critically) diskutieren.

~**ion** *n* Besprechung *f*; Diskussion *f*

disdain /dɪs'deɪn/ *n* Verachtung *f*

disease /dɪ'ziːz/ *n* Krankheit *f*

disem'bark *vi* an Land gehen

disen'chant *vt* ernüchtern

disen'gage *vt* losmachen

disen'tangle *vt* entwirren

dis'figure *vt* entstellen

dis'grace *n* Schande *f*; **in ~ in** Ungnade ●*vt* Schande machen (+ *dat*). **~ful** *adj* schändlich

disgruntled /dɪs'grʌntld/ *adj* verstimmt

disguise /dɪs'gaɪz/ *n* Verkleidung *f*; **in ~** verkleidet ●*vt* verkleiden; verstellen (*voice*)

disgust /dɪs'gʌst/ *n* Ekel *m*; **in ~** empört ●*vt* anekeln; (*appal*) empören. **~ing** *adj* eklig; (*appalling*) abscheulich

dish /dɪʃ/ *n* Schüssel *f*; (*shallow*) Schale *f*; (*small*) Schälchen *nt*; (*food*) Gericht *nt*. **~ out** austeilen. **~ up** *vt* auftragen

'dishcloth *n* Spültuch *nt*

dis'hearten *vt* entmutigen

dis'honest *adj* **-ly** *adv* unehrlich. **~y** *n* Unehrlichkeit *f*

dis'honour *n* Schande *f*. **~able** *adj*, **-bly** *adv* unehrenhaft

'dishwasher *n* Geschirrspülmaschine *f*

disil'lusion *vt* ernüchtern. **~ment** *n* Ernüchterung *f*

disin'fect *vt* desinfizieren. **~ant** *n* Desinfektionsmittel *nt*

disin'herit *vt* enterben

disin'tegrate *vi* zerfallen

dis'jointed *adj* unzusammenhängend

disk /dɪsk/ *n* = **disc**

dis'like *n* Abneigung *f* ●*vt* nicht mögen

dislocate /'dɪsləkeɪt/ *vt* ausrenken

dis'lodge *vt* entfernen

dis'loyal *adj* illoyal. **~ty** *n* Illoyalität *f*

dismal /'dɪzml/ *adj* trüb[e]; (*person*) trübselig

dismantle /dɪs'mæntl/ *vt* auseinander nehmen; (*take down*) abbauen

dis'may *n* Bestürzung *f*. **~ed** *adj* bestürzt

dis'miss *vt* entlassen; (*reject*) zurückweisen. **~al** *n* Entlassung *f*; Zurückweisung *f*

diso'bedien|ce *n* Ungehorsam *m*. **~t** *adj* ungehorsam

diso'bey *vt*/*i* nicht gehorchen (+ *dat*); nicht befolgen (*rule*)

dis'order *n* Unordnung *f*; (*Med*) Störung *f*. **~ly** *adj* unordentlich

dis'organized *adj* unorganisiert

dis'own *vt* verleugnen

disparaging /dɪs'pærɪdʒɪŋ/ *adj* abschätzig

dispassionate /dɪs'pæʃənət/ *adj* gelassen; (*impartial*) unparteiisch

dispatch /dɪs'pætʃ/ *n* (*Comm*) Versand *m*; (*Mil*) Nachricht *f*; (*report*) Bericht *m* ●*vt* [ab]senden; (*kill*) töten

dispel /dɪ'spel/ *vt* (*pt/pp* dispelled) vertreiben

dispensary /dɪ'spensərɪ/ *n* Apotheke *f*

dispense /dɪ'spens/ *vt* austeilen; **~ with** verzichten auf (+ *acc*). **~r** *n* (*device*) Automat *m*

disperse /dɪ'spɜːs/ *vt* zerstreuen ●*vi* sich zerstreuen

dispirited /dɪ'spɪrɪtɪd/ *adj* entmutigt

display /dɪ'spleɪ/ *n* Ausstellung *f*; (*Comm*) Auslage *f*; (*performance*) Vorführung *f* ●*vt* zeigen; ausstellen (*goods*)

dis'please vt missfallen (+ dat)

dis'pleasure n Missfallen nt

disposable /dɪ'spəʊzəbl/ adj Wegwerf-; (income) verfügbar

disposal /dɪ'spəʊzl/ n Beseitigung f; be at s.o.'s ~ jdm zur Verfügung stehen

dispose /dɪ'spəʊz/ vi ~ of beseitigen; (deal with) erledigen

disposition /dɪspə'zɪʃn/ n Veranlagung f; (nature) Wesensart f

disproportionate /dɪsprə'pɔːʃənət/ adj unverhältnismäßig

dis'prove vt widerlegen

dispute /dɪ'spjuːt/ n Disput m; (quarrel) Streit m ● vt bestreiten

disqualifi'cation n Disqualifikation f

dis'qualify vt disqualifizieren; ~ s.o. from driving jdm den Führerschein entziehen

disre'gard vt nicht beachten

disre'pair n fall into ~ verfallen

dis'reputable adj verrufen

disre'pute n Verruf m

disre'spect n Respektlosigkeit f. ~ful adj respektlos

disrupt /dɪs'rʌpt/ vt stören. ~ion n Störung f

dissatis'faction n Unzufriedenheit f

dis'satisfied adj unzufrieden

dissect /dɪ'sekt/ vt zergliedern; (Med) sezieren. ~ion n Zergliederung f; (Med) Sektion f

dissent /dɪ'sent/ n Nichtübereinstimmung f ● vi nicht übereinstimmen

dissident /'dɪsɪdənt/ n Dissident m

dis'similar adj unähnlich (to dat)

dissociate /dɪ'səʊʃɪeɪt/ vt ~ oneself sich distanzieren (from von)

dissolute /'dɪsəluːt/ adj zügellos; (life) ausschweifend

dissolve /dɪ'zɒlv/ vt auflösen ● vi sich auflösen

dissuade /dɪ'sweɪd/ vt abbringen (from von)

distance /'dɪstəns/ n Entfernung f; long/short ~ lange/kurze Strecke f; in the/from a ~ in/aus der Ferne

distant /'dɪstənt/ adj fern; (aloof) kühl; (relative) entfernt

dis'tasteful adj unangenehm

distil /dɪ'stɪl/ vt (pt/pp distilled) brennen; (Chemistry) destillieren. ~lery n Brennerei f

distinct /dɪ'stɪŋkt/ adj deutlich; (different) verschieden. ~ion n Unterschied m; (Sch) Auszeichnung f. ~ive adj kennzeichnend; (unmistakable) unverwechselbar. ~ly adv deutlich

distinguish /dɪ'stɪŋgwɪʃ/ vt/i unterscheiden; (make out) erkennen; ~ oneself sich auszeichnen. ~ed adj angesehen; (appearance) distinguiert

distort /dɪ'stɔːt/ vt verzerren; (fig) verdrehen. ~ion n Verzerrung f; (fig) Verdrehung f

distract /dɪ'strækt/ vt ablenken. ~ion n Ablenkung f; (despair) Verzweiflung f

distraught /dɪ'strɔːt/ adj [völlig] aufgelöst

distress /dɪ'stres/ n Kummer m; (pain) Schmerz m; (poverty, danger) Not f ● vt Kummer/Schmerz bereiten (+ dat); (sadden) bekümmern; (shock) erschüttern. ~ing adj schmerzlich; (shocking) erschütternd

distribut|e /dɪ'strɪbjuːt/ vt verteilen; (Comm) vertreiben. ~ion n Verteilung f; Vertrieb m. ~or n Verteiler m

district /'dɪstrɪkt/ n Gegend f; (Admin) Bezirk m

dis'trust n Misstrauen nt ● vt misstrauen (+ dat). **~ful** adj misstrauisch

disturb /dɪˈstɜ:b/ vt stören; (perturb) beunruhigen; (touch) anrühren. **~ance** n Unruhe f; (interruption) Störung f. **~ed** adj beunruhigt; (mentally) ~ed geistig gestört. **~ing** adj beunruhigend

dis'used adj stillgelegt; (empty) leer

ditch /dɪtʃ/ n Graben m ● vt (🄘: abandon) fallen lassen (plan)

dither /ˈdɪðə(r)/ vi zaudern

ditto /ˈdɪtəʊ/ n dito; (🄣) ebenfalls

dive /daɪv/ n (Kopf)sprung m; (Aviat) Sturzflug m; (🄘: place) Spelunke f ● vi einen Kopfsprung machen; (when in water) tauchen; (Aviat) einen Sturzflug machen; (🄘: rush) stürzen

diver /ˈdaɪvə(r)/ n Taucher m; (Sport) [Kunst]springer m

diverse /daɪˈvɜ:s/ adj verschieden

diversify /daɪˈvɜ:sɪfaɪ/ vt/i (pt/pp -ied) variieren; (Comm) diversifizieren

diversion /daɪˈvɜ:ʃn/ n Umleitung f; (distraction) Ablenkung f

diversity /daɪˈvɜ:sətɪ/ n Vielfalt f

divert /daɪˈvɜ:t/ vt umleiten; ablenken (attention); (entertain) unterhalten

divide /dɪˈvaɪd/ vt teilen; (separate) trennen; (Math) dividieren (by durch) ● vi sich teilen

dividend /ˈdɪvɪdend/ n Dividende f

divine /dɪˈvaɪn/ adj göttlich

diving /ˈdaɪvɪŋ/ n (Sport) Kunstspringen nt. **~board** n Sprungbrett nt

divinity /dɪˈvɪnətɪ/ n Göttlichkeit f; (subject) Theologie f

division /dɪˈvɪʒn/ n Teilung f; (sep-

aration) Trennung f; (Math, Mil) Division f; (Parl) Hammelsprung m; (line) Trennlinie f; (group) Abteilung f

divorce /dɪˈvɔ:s/ n Scheidung f ● vt sich scheiden lassen von. **~d** adj geschieden; get **~d** sich scheiden lassen

DIY abbr do-it-yourself

dizziness /ˈdɪzɪnɪs/ n Schwindel m

dizzy /ˈdɪzɪ/ adj schwindlig; I feel ~ mir ist schwindlig

---

do /du:/, unbetont /də/

3 sg pres tense **does**; *pt* **did**; *pp* **done**

● *transitive verb*

·····▸ (perform) machen (homework, housework, exam, handstand etc); tun (duty, favour, something, nothing); vorführen (trick, dance); durchführen (test). what are you doing? was tust od machst du? what can I do for you? was kann ich für Sie tun? do something! tu doch etwas! have you nothing better to do? hast du nichts Besseres zu tun? do the washing-up /cleaning abwaschen/ sauber machen

·····▸ (as job) what does your father do? was macht dein Vater?; was ist dein Vater von Beruf?

·····▸ (clean) putzen; (arrange) [zurecht]machen (hair)

·····▸ (cook) kochen; (roast, fry) braten. well done (meat) durch[gebraten]. the potatoes aren't ready yet die Kartoffeln sind noch nicht richtig durch

·····▸ (solve) lösen (problem, riddle); machen (puzzle)

····▸ (🎯: *swindle*) reinlegen. do s.o. out of sth jdn um etw bringen

● **intransitive verb**

····▸ (*with* as *or adverb*) es tun; es machen. do as they do mach es wie sie. he can do as he likes er kann tun *od* machen, was er will. you did well du hast es gut gemacht

····▸ (*get on*) vorankommen; (*in exams*) abschneiden. do well/badly at school gut/schlecht in der Schule sein. how are you doing? wie geht's dir? how do you do? (*formal*) guten Tag!

····▸ will do (*serve purpose*) es tun; (*suffice*) [aus]reichen; (*be suitable*) gehen. that won't do das geht nicht. that will do! jetzt aber genug!

● **auxiliary verb**

····▸ (*in questions*) do you know him? kennst du ihn? what does he want? was will er?

····▸ (*in negation*) I don't or do not wish to take part ich will nicht teilnehmen. don't be so noisy! seid [doch] nicht so laut!

····▸ (*as verb substitute*) you mustn't act as he does du darfst nicht so wie er handeln. come in, do! komm doch herein!

····▸ (*in tag questions*) don't you, doesn't he *etc*. nicht wahr. you went to Paris, didn't you? du warst in Paris, nicht wahr?

····▸ (*in short questions*) Does he live in London? — Yes, he does Wohnt er in London? — Ja, stimmt

····▸ (*for special emphasis*) I do love Greece Griechenland gefällt mir wirklich gut

····▸ (*for inversion*) little did he know that ... er hatte keine Ahnung, dass ...

● **noun**

pl **do's** *or* **dos** /duːz/

····▸ (🎯: *celebration*) Feier f

● **phrasal verbs**

● **do away with** *vt* abschaffen. ● **do for** *vt* 🎯: do for s.o. jdn fertig machen 🎯; be done for erledigt sein. ● **do in** *vt* (*sl*: *kill*) kaltmachen 🎯. ● **do up** *vt* (*fasten*) zumachen; binden (*shoe-lace, bow-tie*); (*wrap*) einpacken; (*renovate*) renovieren. ● **do with** *vt*: I could do with ... ich brauche .... ● **do without** *vt*: do without sth auf etw (*acc*) verzichten; *vi* darauf verzichten

docile /ˈdəʊsaɪl/ *adj* fügsam

dock[1] /dɒk/ *n* (*Jur*) Anklagebank f

dock[2] *n* Dock *nt* ● *vi* anlegen. ~**er** *n* Hafenarbeiter m. ~**yard** *n* Werft f

doctor /ˈdɒktə(r)/ *n* Arzt m/ Ärztin f; (*Univ*) Doktor m ● *vt* kastrieren; (*spay*) sterilisieren

doctrine /ˈdɒktrɪn/ *n* Lehre f

document /ˈdɒkjʊmənt/ *n* Dokument *nt*. ~**ary** *adj* Dokumentar- ● *n* Dokumentarbericht m; (*film*) Dokumentarfilm m

dodge /dɒdʒ/ *n* Trick m, Kniff m ● *vt/i* ausweichen (+ *dat*)

dodgy /ˈdɒdʒɪ/ *adj* 🎯 (*awkward*) knifflig; (*dubious*) zweifelhaft

doe /dəʊ/ *n* Ricke f; (*rabbit*) [Kaninchen]weibchen *nt*

does /dʌz/ *see* **do**

doesn't /ˈdʌznt/ = does not

dog /dɒg/ *n* Hund m

dog: ~**-biscuit** *n* Hundekuchen m.

~-collar n Hundehalsband nt; (*Relig*, 🔲) Kragen m eines Geistlichen. **~-eared** adj be ~-eared Eselsohren haben

dogged /'dɒgɪd/ adj beharrlich

dogma /'dɒgmə/ n Dogma nt. **~tic** adj dogmatisch

do-it-yourself /duːɪtjə'self/ n Heimwerken nt. ~ **shop** n Heimwerkerladen m

doldrums /'dɒldrəmz/ npl be in the ~ niedergeschlagen sein; (*business*:) daniederliegen

dole /dəʊl/ n Stempelgeld nt; be on the ~ arbeitslos sein ● vt ~ out austeilen

doll /dɒl/ n Puppe ● vt 🔲 ~ one-self up sich herausputzen

dollar /'dɒlə(r)/ n Dollar m

dolphin /'dɒlfɪn/ n Delphin m

domain /də'meɪn/ n Gebiet nt

dome /dəʊm/ n Kuppel m

domestic /də'mestɪk/ adj häuslich; (*Pol*) Innen-; (*Comm*) Binnen-. ~ **animal** n Haustier m. ~ **flight** n Inlandflug m

domestic flight n Inlandflug m

dominant /'dɒmɪnənt/ adj vorherrschend

dominat|e /'dɒmɪneɪt/ vt beherrschen ● vi dominieren. ~**ion** n Vorherrschaft f

domineering /dɒmɪ'nɪərɪŋ/ adj herrschsüchtig

domino /'dɒmɪnəʊ/ n (pl -es) Dominostein m; ~**es** sg (*game*) Domino nt

donat|e /dəʊ'neɪt/ vt spenden. ~**ion** n Spende f

done /dʌn/ see do

donkey /'dɒŋkɪ/ n Esel m; ~'s years 🔲 eine Ewigkeit. ~**-work** n Routinearbeit f

donor /'dəʊnə(r)/ n Spender m,

Spenderin f

don't /dəʊnt/ = do not

doom /duːm/ n Schicksal nt; (*ruin*) Verhängnis nt

door /dɔː(r)/ n Tür f; out of ~s im Freien

door: **~man** n Portier m. **~mat** n [Fuß]abtreter m. **~step** n Türschwelle f; on the ~step vor der Tür. **~way** n Türöffnung f

dope /dəʊp/ n 🔲 Drogen pl; (🔲: *information*) Informationen pl; (🔲: *idiot*) Trottel m ● vt betäuben; (*Sport*) dopen

dormant /'dɔːmənt/ adj ruhend

dormitory /'dɔːmɪtərɪ/ n Schlafsaal m

dormouse /'dɔː-/ n Haselmaus f

dosage /'dəʊsɪdʒ/ n Dosierung f

dose /dəʊs/ n Dosis f

dot /dɒt/ n Punkt m; on the ~ pünktlich

dote /dəʊt/ vi ~ on vernarrt sein in (+ acc)

dotted /'dɒtɪd/ adj ~ line punktierte Linie f; be ~ with bestreut sein mit

dotty /'dɒtɪ/ adj 🔲 verdreht

double /'dʌbl/ adj & adv doppelt; (*bed, chin*) Doppel-; (*flower*) gefüllt ● n das Doppelte; (*person*) Doppelgänger m; ~**s** pl (*Tennis*) Doppel nt; ● vt verdoppeln; (*fold*) falten ● vi sich verdoppeln. ~ **up** vi sich krümmen (with vor + dat)

double: ~-'**bass** n Kontrabass m. ~-**breasted** adj zweireihig. ~-**click** vt/i doppelklicken (on auf + acc). ~-'**cross** vt ein Doppelspiel treiben mit. ~-**decker** n Doppeldecker m. ~ **glazing** n Doppelverglasung f. ~ **room** n Doppelzimmer nt

doubly /'dʌblɪ/ adv doppelt

doubt /daʊt/ n Zweifel m ● vt bezweifeln. ~**ful** adj zweifelhaft; (*dis-*

believing) skeptisch. **~less** *adv* zweifellos

dough /dəʊ/ *n* [fester] Teig *m*; (⊞: *money*) Pinke *f*. **~nut** *n* Berliner [Pfannkuchen] *m*

dove /dʌv/ *n* Taube *f*

dowdy /ˈdaʊdɪ/ *adj* unschick

down[1] /daʊn/ *n* (*feathers*) Daunen *pl*

down[2] *adv* unten; (*with movement*) nach unten; **go ~** hinuntergehen; **come ~** herunterkommen; **~ there** da unten; £50 **~** £50 Anzahlung; **~!** (*to dog*) Platz! **~ with ...!** nieder mit ...! ●*prep* **~ the road/stairs** die Straße/Treppe hinunter; **~ the river** den Fluss abwärts ●*vt* ⊞ (*drink*) runterkippen; **~ tools** die Arbeit niederlegen

down: **~cast** *adj* niedergeschlagen. **~fall** *n* Sturz *m*; (*ruin*) Ruin *m*. **~'hearted** *adj* entmutigt. **~hill** *adv* bergab. **~load** *vt* herunterladen. **~ payment** *n* Anzahlung *f*. **~pour** *n* Platzregen *m*. **~right** *adj* & *adv* ausgesprochen. **~size** *vt* verschlanken ● *vi* abspecken. **~'stairs** *adv* unten; (*go*) nach unten ●*adj* im Erdgeschoss. **~stream** *adv* stromabwärts. **~to-'earth** *adj* sachlich. **~town** *adv* (*Amer*) im Stadtzentrum. **~ward** *adj* nach unten; (*slope*) abfallend ●*adv* **~[s]** abwärts, nach unten

doze /dəʊz/ *n* Nickerchen *nt* ●*vi* dösen. **~ off** *vi* einnicken

dozen /ˈdʌzn/ *n* Dutzend *nt*

Dr *abbr* doctor

draft[1] /drɑːft/ *n* Entwurf *m*; (*Comm*) Tratte *f*; (*Amer Mil*) Einberufung *f* ●*vt* entwerfen; (*Amer Mil*) einberufen

draft[2] *n* (*Amer*) = **draught**

drag /dræg/ *n* **in ~** ⊞ (*man*) als Frau gekleidet ●*vt* (*pt/pp* **dragged**) schleppen; absuchen (*river*). **~ on** *vi* sich in die Länge ziehen

dragon /ˈdrægən/ *n* Drache *m*. **~fly** *n* Libelle *f*

drain /dreɪn/ *n* Abfluss *m*; (*underground*) Kanal *m*; **the ~s** die Kanalisation ●*vt* entwässern (*land*); ablassen (*liquid*); das Wasser ablassen aus (*tank*); abgießen (*vegetables*); austrinken (*glass*) ●*vi* **~ [away]** ablaufen

drain|age /ˈdreɪnɪdʒ/ *n* Kanalisation *f*; (*of land*) Dränage *f*. **~ing board** *n* Abtropfbrett *nt*. **~-pipe** *n* Abflussrohr *nt*

drake /dreɪk/ *n* Enterich *m*

drama /ˈdrɑːmə/ *n* Drama *nt*

dramatic /drəˈmætɪk/ *adj*, **-ally** *adv* dramatisch

dramat|ist /ˈdræmətɪst/ *n* Dramatiker *m*. **~ize** *vt* für die Bühne bearbeiten; (*fig*) dramatisieren

drank /dræŋk/ *see* **drink**

drape /dreɪp/ *n* (*Amer*) Vorhang *m* ●*vt* drapieren

drastic /ˈdræstɪk/ *adj*, **-ally** *adv* drastisch

draught /drɑːft/ *n* [Luft]zug *m*; **~s** *sg* (*game*) Damespiel *nt*; **there is a ~** es zieht

draught beer *n* Bier *nt* vom Fass

draughty /ˈdrɑːftɪ/ *adj* zugig

draw /drɔː/ *n* Attraktion *f*; (*Sport*)

Unentschieden nt; (in lottery) Ziehung f ●v (pt drew, pp drawn) ●vt ziehen; (attract) anziehen; zeichnen (picture); abheben (money); ~ the curtains die Vorhänge zuziehen (back) aufziehen ●vi (Sport) unentschieden spielen. ~ back vt zurückziehen ●vi (recoil) zurückweichen. ~ in vt einziehen ●vi einfahren. ~ out vt herausziehen; abheben (money) ●vi ausfahren. ~ up vt aufsetzen (document); herrücken (chair) ●vi [an]halten.

draw: ~back n Nachteil m. ~bridge n Zugbrücke f

drawer /drɔ:(r)/ n Schublade f

drawing /'drɔ:ɪŋ/ n Zeichnung f

drawing: ~-board n Reißbrett nt. ~-pin n Reißzwecke f. ~-room n Wohnzimmer nt

drawl /drɔ:l/ n schleppende Aussprache f

drawn /drɔ:n/ see draw

dread /dred/ n Furcht f (of vor + dat) ●vt fürchten. ~ful adj, -fully adv fürchterlich

dream /dri:m/ n Traum m ●vt/i (pt/pp dreamt or dreamed) träumen (about/of von)

dreary /'drɪərɪ/ adj trüb[e]; (boring) langweilig

dregs /dregz/ npl Bodensatz m

drench /drentʃ/ vt durchnässen

dress /dres/ n Kleid nt; (clothing) Kleidung f ●vt anziehen; (Med) verbinden; ~ oneself, get ~ed sich anziehen ●vi sich anziehen. ~ up vi sich schön anziehen; (in disguise) sich verkleiden (as als)

dress: ~ circle n (Theat) erster Rang m. ~er n (furniture) Anrichte f; (Amer: dressing-table) Frisiertisch m

dressing n (Culin) Soße f; (Med) Verband m

dressing: ~-gown n Morgenmantel m. ~-room n (Theat) [Künstler]garderobe f. ~-table n Frisiertisch m

dress: ~maker n Schneiderin f. ~ rehearsal n Generalprobe f

drew /dru:/ see draw

dried /draɪd/ adj getrocknet; ~ fruit Dörrobst nt

drier /'draɪə(r)/ n Trockner m

drift /drɪft/ n Abtrieb f; (of snow) Schneewehe f; (meaning) Sinn m ●vi treiben; (off course) abtreiben; (snow:) Wehen bilden; (fig) (person:) sich treiben lassen

drill /drɪl/ n Bohrer m; (Mil) Drill m ●vt/i bohren (for nach); (Mil) drillen

drily /'draɪlɪ/ adv trocken

drink /drɪŋk/ n Getränk nt; (alcoholic) Drink m; (alcohol) Alkohol m ●vt/i (pt drank, pp drunk) trinken. ~ up vt/i austrinken

drink|able /'drɪŋkəbl/ adj trinkbar. ~er n Trinker m

'drinking-water n Trinkwasser nt

drip /drɪp/ n Tropfen m; (drop) Tropfen m; (Med) Tropf m; (I: person) Niete f ●vi (pt/pp dripped) tropfen

drive /draɪv/ n (Auto)fahrt f; (entrance) Einfahrt f; (energy) Elan m; (Psychology) Trieb m; (Pol) Aktion f; (Sport) Treibschlag m; (Techn) Antrieb m ●v (pt drove, pp driven) ●vt treiben; fahren (car); (Sport: hit) schlagen; (Techn) antreiben; ~ s.o. mad I jdn verrückt machen; what are you driving at? I worauf willst du hinaus? ●vi fahren. ~ away vt vertreiben ●vi abfahren. ~ off vt vertreiben ●vi abfahren. ~ on vi weiterfahren. ~ up vi vorfahren

drivel /'drɪvl/ n ▣ Quatsch m

driven /'drɪvn/ see **drive**

driver /'draɪvə(r)/ n Fahrer(in) m(f); (of train) Lokführer m

driving: ~ **lesson** n Fahrstunde f. ~ **licence** n Führerschein m. ~ **school** n Fahrschule f. ~ **test** Fahrprüfung f

drizzle /'drɪzl/ n Nieselregen m ● vi nieseln

drone /drəʊn/ n (sound) Brummen nt

droop /druːp/ vi herabhängen

drop /drɒp/ n Tropfen m; (fall) Fall m; (in price, temperature) Rückgang m ● v (pt/pp dropped) ● vt fallen lassen; abwerfen (bomb); (omit) auslassen; (give up) aufgeben ● vi fallen; (fall lower) sinken; (wind:) nachlassen. ~ **in** vi vorbeikommen. ~ **off** vt absetzen (person) ● vi abfallen; (fall asleep) einschlafen. ~ **out** vi herausfallen; (give up) aufgeben

drought /draʊt/ n Dürre f

drove /drəʊv/ see **drive**

drown /draʊn/ vi ertrinken ● vt ertränken; übertönen (noise); be ~ed ertrinken

drowsy /'draʊzɪ/ adj schläfrig

drudgery /'drʌdʒərɪ/ n Plackerei f

drug /drʌg/ n Droge f ● vt (pt/pp drugged) betäuben

drug: ~ **addict** n Drogenabhängige(e) m/f. ~**store** n (Amer) Drogerie f; (dispensing) Apotheke f

drum /drʌm/ n Trommel f; (for oil) Tonne f ● v (pt/pp drummed) ● vi trommeln ● vt ~**s.th into** s.o. ▣ jdm etw einbläuen. ~**mer** n Trommler m; (in pop-group) Schlagzeuger m. ~**stick** n Trommelschlegel m; (Culin) Keule f

drunk /drʌŋk/ see **drink** ● adj betrunken; get ~ sich betrinken ● n Betrunkene(r) m

drunk|ard /'drʌŋkəd/ n Trinker m. ~**en** adj betrunken

dry /draɪ/ adj (drier, driest) trocken ● vt/i trocknen. ~ **up** vt/i austrocknen

dry: ~-'**clean** vt chemisch reinigen. ~-'**cleaner's** n (shop) chemische Reinigung f. ~**ness** n Trockenheit f

dual /'djuːəl/ adj doppelt

dual 'carriageway n ≈ Schnellstraße f

dubious /'djuːbɪəs/ adj zweifelhaft

duchess /'dʌtʃɪs/ n Herzogin f

duck /dʌk/ n Ente f ● vt (in water) untertauchen ● vi sich ducken

duct /dʌkt/ n Rohr nt; (Anat) Gang m

dud /dʌd/ adj ▣ nutzlos; (coin) falsch; (cheque) ungedeckt; (forged) gefälscht

due /djuː/ adj angemessen; be ~ fällig sein; (baby:) erwartet werden; (train:) planmäßig ankommen; ~ **to** (owing to) wegen (+ gen); be ~ **to** zurückzuführen sein auf (+ acc) ● adv ~ **west** genau westlich

duel /'djuːəl/ n Duell nt

duet /dju:'et/ n Duo nt; (vocal) Duett nt

dug /dʌg/ see **dig**

duke /djuːk/ n Herzog m

dull /dʌl/ adj (-er, -est) (overcast, not bright) trüb[e]; (not shiny) matt; (sound) dumpf; (boring) langweilig; (stupid) schwerfällig

duly /'djuːlɪ/ adv ordnungsgemäß

dumb /dʌm/ adj (-er, -est) stumm. ~ **down** vt/i verflachen

dummy /'dʌmɪ/ n (tailor's) [Schneider]puppe f; (for baby) Schnuller m; (Comm) Attrappe f

dump /dʌmp/ n Abfallhaufen m; (for refuse) Müllhalde f, Deponie f; (▣: town) Kaff nt; be down in the

~s 🔢 deprimiert sein ●vt abladen
dumpling /'dʌmplɪŋ/ n Kloß m
dunce /dʌns/ n Dummkopf m
dune /dju:n/ n Düne f
dung /dʌŋ/ n Mist m
dungarees /dʌŋgə'ri:z/ npl Latzhose f
dungeon /'dʌndʒən/ n Verlies nt
dunk /dʌŋk/ vt eintunken
duo /'dju:əʊ/ n Paar nt; (Mus) Duo nt
dupe /dju:p/ n Betrogene(r) m/f ●vt betrügen
duplicate[1] /'dju:plɪkət/ n Doppel nt; in ~ in doppelter Ausfertigung f
duplicat|e[2] /'dju:plɪkeɪt/ vt kopieren; (do twice) zweimal machen
durable /'djʊərəbl/ adj haltbar
duration /djʊə'reɪʃn/ n Dauer f
during /'djʊərɪŋ/ prep während (+ gen)
dusk /dʌsk/ n (Abend)dämmerung f
dust /dʌst/ n Staub m ●vt abstauben; (sprinkle) bestäuben (with mit) ●vi Staub wischen
dust: ~**bin** n Mülltonne f. ~**cart** n Müllwagen m. ~**er** n Staubtuch nt. ~**jacket** n Schutzumschlag m. ~**man** n Müllmann m. ~**pan** n Kehrschaufel f
dusty /'dʌstɪ/ adj staubig
Dutch /dʌtʃ/ adj holländisch ●n (Lang) Holländisch nt; **the** ~ pl die Holländer. ~**man** n Holländer m
dutiful /'dju:tɪfl/ adj pflichtbewusst
duty /'dju:tɪ/ n Pflicht f; (task) Aufgabe f; (tax) Zoll m; be on ~ Dienst haben. ~-**free** adj zollfrei
duvet /'du:veɪ/ n Steppdecke f
DVD abbr (digital versatile disc) DVD f
dwarf /dwɔ:f/ n (pl -s or dwarves) Zwerg m

dwell /dwel/ vi (pt/pp dwelt); ~ **on** (fig) verweilen bei. ~**ing** n Wohnung f
dwindle /'dwɪndl/ vi abnehmen, schwinden
dye /daɪ/ n Farbstoff m ●vt (pres p dyeing) färben
dying /'daɪɪŋ/ see die[2]
dynamic /daɪ'næmɪk/ adj dynamisch
dynamite /'daɪnəmaɪt/ n Dynamit nt
dynamo see dynamite
dyslex|ia /dɪs'leksɪə/ n Legasthenie f. ~**ic** adj legasthenisch; be ~**ic** Legastheniker sein

·····································

Ee

·····································

each /i:tʃ/ adj & pron jede(r,s); (per) je; ~ **other** einander; £1 ~ £1 pro Person; (for thing) pro Stück
eager /'i:gə(r)/ adj eifrig; be ~ **to do** sth etw gerne machen wollen. ~**ness** n Eifer m
eagle /'i:gl/ n Adler m
ear n Ohr nt. ~**ache** n Ohrenschmerzen pl. ~-**drum** n Trommelfell nt
earl /ɜ:l/ n Graf m
early /'ɜ:lɪ/ adj & adv (-ier, -iest) früh; (reply) baldig; be ~ früh dran sein
earn /ɜ:n/ vt verdienen
earnest /'ɜ:nɪst/ adj ernsthaft ●n in ~ im Ernst
earnings /'ɜ:nɪŋz/ npl Verdienst m
ear: ~**phones** npl Kopfhörer pl. ~-**ring** n Ohrring m; (clip-on) Ohrklips m. ~**shot** n within/out of ~**shot** in/außer Hörweite

earth /ɜːθ/ n Erde f; (of fox) Bau m
● vt (Electr) erden

earthenware /ˈɜːθn-/ n Tonwaren pl

earthly /ˈɜːθlɪ/ adj irdisch; be no ~ use 🗅 völlig nutzlos sein

'**earthquake** n Erdbeben nt

earthy /ˈɜːθɪ/ adj erdig; (coarse) derb

ease /iːz/ n Leichtigkeit f ● vt erleichtern; lindern (pain) ● vi (pain:) nachlassen; (situation:) sich entspannen

easily /ˈiːzɪlɪ/ adv leicht, mit Leichtigkeit

east /iːst/ n Osten m; to the ~ of östlich von ● adj Ost-, ost- ● adv nach Osten

Easter /ˈiːstə(r)/ n Ostern nt ● attrib Oster-. ~ **egg** n Osterei nt

east|erly /ˈiːstəlɪ/ adj östlich. ~**ern** adj östlich. ~**ward[s]** adv nach Osten

easy /ˈiːzɪ/ adj leicht; take it ~ 🗅 sich schonen; go ~ with 🗅 sparsam umgehen mit

easy: ~ **chair** n Sessel m. ~**going** adj gelassen

eat /iːt/ vt/i (pt ate, pp eaten) essen; (animal:) fressen. ~ **up** vt aufessen

eatable /ˈiːtəbl/ adj genießbar

eau-de-Cologne /əʊdəkəˈləʊn/ n Kölnisch Wasser nt

eaves /iːvz/ npl Dachüberhang m. ~**drop** vi (pt/pp ~ dropped) [heimlich] lauschen

ebb /eb/ n (tide) Ebbe f ● vi zurückgehen; (fig) verebben

ebony /ˈebənɪ/ n Ebenholz nt

EC abbr (European Community) EG f

eccentric /ɪkˈsentrɪk/ adj exzentrisch ● n Exzentriker m

ecclesiastical /ɪkliːzɪˈæstɪkl/ adj kirchlich

echo /ˈekəʊ/ n (pl -es) Echo nt, Widerhall m ● v (pt/pp echoed, pres p echoing) ● vi widerhallen (with von)

eclipse /ɪˈklɪps/ n (Astronomy) Finsternis f

ecolog|ical /iːkəˈlɒdʒɪkl/ adj ökologisch. ~**y** n Ökologie f

e-commerce /ˈiːkɒmɜːs/ n E-Commerce m

economic /iːkəˈnɒmɪk/ adj wirtschaftlich. ~**al** adj sparsam. ~**ally** adv wirtschaftlich; (thriftily) sparsam. ~ **refugee** n Wirtschaftsflüchtling m. ~**s** n Volkswirtschaft f

economist /ɪˈkɒnəmɪst/ n Volkswirt m; (Univ) Wirtschaftswissenschaftler m

economize /ɪˈkɒnəmaɪz/ vi sparen (on an + dat)

economy /ɪˈkɒnəmɪ/ n Wirtschaft f; (thrift) Sparsamkeit f

ecstasy /ˈekstəsɪ/ n Ekstase f

ecstatic /ɪkˈstætɪk/ adj, -**ally** adv ekstatisch

eczema /ˈeksɪmə/ n Ekzem nt

eddy /ˈedɪ/ n Wirbel m

edge /edʒ/ n Rand m; (of table, lawn) Kante f; (of knife) Schneide f; on ~ 🗅 nervös ● vt einfassen. ~ **forward** vi sich nach vorn schieben

edgy /ˈedʒɪ/ adj 🗅 nervös

edible /ˈedɪbl/ adj essbar

edifice /ˈedɪfɪs/ n [großes] Gebäude nt

ziehen Besucher aus aller Welt an. Ergänzt wird das Programm durch das gleichzeitig stattfindende *Edinburgh Festival Fringe*, das ein Forum für unbekannte Künstler, experimentelle Kunst und alternative Veranstaltungen ist.

edit /ˈedɪt/ *vt* (*pt/pp* edited) redigieren; herausgeben (*anthology, dictionary*); schneiden (*film, tape*)

edition /ɪˈdɪʃn/ *n* Ausgabe *f*; (*impression*) Auflage *f*

editor /ˈedɪtə(r)/ *n* Redakteur *m*; (*of anthology, dictionary*) Herausgeber *m*; (*of newspaper*) Chefredakteur *m*; (*of film*) Cutter(in) *m* (*f*)

editorial /edɪˈtɔːrɪəl/ *adj* redaktionell, Redaktions- ● *n* (*in newspaper*) Leitartikel *m*

educate /ˈedjʊkeɪt/ *vt* erziehen. **~d** *adj* gebildet

education /edjʊˈkeɪʃn/ *n* Erziehung *f*; (*culture*) Bildung *f*. **~al** *adj* pädagogisch; (*visit*) kulturell

eel /iːl/ *n* Aal *m*

eerie /ˈɪərɪ/ *adj* unheimlich

effect /ɪˈfekt/ *n* Wirkung *f*, Effekt *m*; take **~** in Kraft treten

effective /ɪˈfektɪv/ *adj* wirksam, effektiv; (*striking*) wirkungsvoll, effektvoll; (*actual*) tatsächlich. **~ness** *n* Wirksamkeit *f*

effeminate /ɪˈfemɪnət/ *adj* unmännlich

effervescent /efəˈvesnt/ *adj* sprudelnd

efficiency /ɪˈfɪʃənsɪ/ *n* Tüchtigkeit *f*; (*of machine, organization*) Leistungsfähigkeit *f*

efficient /ɪˈfɪʃnt/ *adj* tüchtig; (*machine, organization*) leistungsfähig; (*method*) rationell. **~ly** *adv* gut; (*function*) rationell

effort /ˈefət/ *n* Anstrengung *f*;

make an **~** sich (*dat*) Mühe geben. **~less** *adj* mühelos

e.g. *abbr* (exempli gratia) z.B.

egalitarian /ɪɡælɪˈteərɪən/ *adj* egalitär

egg *n* Ei *nt*. **~-cup** *n* Eierbecher *m*. **~shell** *n* Eierschale *f*

ego /ˈiːɡəʊ/ *n* Ich *nt*. **~ism** *n* Egoismus *m*. **~ist** *n* Egoist *m*. **~tism** *n* Ichbezogenheit *f*. **~tist** *n* ichbezogener Mensch *m*

Egypt /ˈiːdʒɪpt/ *n* Ägypten *nt*. **~ian** *adj* ägyptisch ● *n* Ägypter(in) *m* (*f*)

eiderdown /ˈaɪdə-/ *n* (*quilt*) Daunendecke *f*

eigh|t /eɪt/ *adj* acht ● *n* Acht *f*; (*boat*) Achter *m*. **~teen** *adj* achtzehn. **~teenth** *adj* achtzehnte(r,s)

eighth /eɪtθ/ *adj* achte(r,s) ● *n* Achtel *nt*

eightieth /ˈeɪtɪɪθ/ *adj* achtzigste(r,s)

eighty /ˈeɪtɪ/ *adj* achtzig

either /ˈaɪðə(r)/ *adj & pron* ~ [of them] einer von [den] beiden; (*both*) beide; on ~ side auf beiden Seiten ● *adv* I don't ~ ich auch nicht ● *conj* ~ ... or entweder ... oder

eject /ɪˈdʒekt/ *vt* hinauswerfen

elaborate /ɪˈlæbərət/ *adj* kunstvoll; (*fig*) kompliziert

elapse /ɪˈlæps/ *vi* vergehen

elastic /ɪˈlæstɪk/ *adj* elastisch. ~ 'band *n* Gummiband *nt*

elasticity /ɪlæsˈtɪsətɪ/ *n* Elastizität *f*

elated /ɪˈleɪtɪd/ *adj* überglücklich

elbow /ˈelbəʊ/ *n* Ellbogen *m*

elder[1] /ˈeldə(r)/ *n* Holunder *m*

eld|er[2] *adj* ältere(r,s) ● *n* the ~er der/die Ältere. **~erly** *adj* alt. **~est** *adj* älteste(r,s) ● *n* the ~est der/die Älteste

elect /ɪ'lekt/ vt wählen. **∼ion** n Wahl f

elector /ɪ'lektə(r)/ n Wähler(in) m(f). **∼ate** n Wählerschaft f

electric /ɪ'lektrɪk/ adj, **-ally** adv elektrisch

electrical /ɪ'lektrɪkl/ adj elektrisch; **∼ engineering** Elektrotechnik f

electric: **∼ 'blanket** n Heizdecke f. **∼ 'fire** n elektrischer Heizofen m

electrician /ɪlek'trɪʃn/ n Elektriker m

electricity /ɪlek'trɪsəti/ n Elektrizität f; (supply) Strom m

electrify /ɪ'lektrɪfaɪ/ vt (pt/pp -ied) elektrifizieren. **∼ing** adj (fig) elektrisierend

electrocute /ɪ'lektrəkju:t/ vt durch einen elektrischen Schlag töten

electrode /ɪ'lektrəʊd/ n Elektrode f

electronic /ɪlek'trɒnɪk/ adj elektronisch. **∼s** n Elektronik f

elegance /'elɪgəns/ n Eleganz f

elegant /'elɪgənt/ adj elegant

elegy /'elɪdʒɪ/ n Elegie f

element /'elɪmənt/ n Element nt. **∼ary** adj elementar

elephant /'elɪfənt/ n Elefant m

elevate /'elɪveɪt/ vt heben; (fig) erheben. **∼ion** n Erhebung f

elevator /'elɪveɪtə(r)/ n (Amer) Aufzug m, Fahrstuhl m

eleven /ɪ'levn/ adj elf ● n Elf f. **∼th** adj elfte(r,s); **at the ∼th hour** ⊤ in letzter Minute

eligible /'elɪdʒəbl/ adj berechtigt

eliminate /ɪ'lɪmɪneɪt/ vt ausschalten

élite /eɪ'li:t/ n Elite f

elm /elm/ n Ulme f

elocution /elə'kju:ʃn/ n Sprecherziehung f

elope /ɪ'ləʊp/ vi durchbrennen ⊤

eloquen|ce /'eləkwəns/ n Beredsamkeit f. **∼t** adj, **∼ly** adv beredt

else /els/ adv sonst; **nothing ∼** sonst nichts; **or ∼** oder; (otherwise) sonst; **someone/somewhere ∼** jemand/irgendwo anders; **anyone ∼** jeder andere; (as question) sonst noch jemand? **anything ∼** alles andere; (as question) sonst noch etwas? **∼where** adv woanders

elucidate /ɪ'lu:sɪdeɪt/ vt erläutern

elusive /ɪ'lu:sɪv/ adj **be ∼** schwer zu fassen sein

emaciated /ɪ'meɪsɪeɪtɪd/ adj abgezehrt

e-mail /'i:meɪl/ n E-Mail f ● vt per E-Mail übermitteln (Ergebnisse, Datei usw.); **∼ s.o.** jdm eine E-Mail schicken. **∼ address** n E-Mail-Adresse f. **∼ message** n E-Mail f

emancipat|ed /ɪ'mænsɪpeɪtɪd/ adj emanzipiert. **∼ion** n Emanzipation f; (of slaves) Freilassung f

embankment /ɪm'bæŋkmənt/ n Böschung f; (of railway) Bahndamm m

embark /ɪm'bɑ:k/ vi sich einschiffen. **∼ation** n Einschiffung f

embarrass /ɪm'bærəs/ vt in Verlegenheit bringen. **∼ed** adj verlegen. **∼ing** adj peinlich. **∼ment** n Verlegenheit f

embassy /'embəsi/ n Botschaft f

embellish /ɪm'belɪʃ/ vt verzieren; (fig) ausschmücken

embezzle /ɪm'bezl/ vt unterschlagen. **∼ment** n Unterschlagung f

emblem /'embləm/ n Emblem nt

embodiment /ɪm'bɒdɪmənt/ n Verkörperung f

embody /ɪm'bɒdɪ/ vt (pt/pp -ied) verkörpern; (include) enthalten

embrace /ɪm'breɪs/ n Umarmung f ● vt umarmen; (fig) umfassen ● vi sich umarmen

embroider /ɪm'brɔɪdə(r)/ vt besticken; sticken (design) ● vi sticken. ~y n Stickerei f

embryo /'embrɪəʊ/ n Embryo m

emerald /'emərəld/ n Smaragd m

emer|ge /ɪ'mɜːdʒ/ vi auftauchen (from aus); (become known) sich herausstellen; (come into being) entstehen. ~gence n Auftauchen nt; Entstehung f

emergency /ɪ'mɜːdʒənsɪ/ n Notfall m. ~ exit n Notausgang m

emigrant /'emɪgrənt/ n Auswanderer m

emigrat|e /'emɪgreɪt/ vi auswandern. ~ion n Auswanderung f

eminent /'emɪnənt/ adj eminent

emission /ɪ'mɪʃn/ n Ausstrahlung f; (of pollutant) Emission f

emit /ɪ'mɪt/ vt (pt/pp emitted) ausstrahlen (light, heat); ausstoßen (smoke, fumes, cry)

emotion /ɪ'məʊʃn/ n Gefühl nt. ~al adj emotional; become ~al sich erregen

empathy /'empəθɪ/ n Einfühlungsvermögen m

emperor /'empərə(r)/ n Kaiser m

emphasis /'emfəsɪs/ n Betonung f

emphasize /'emfəsaɪz/ vt betonen

emphatic /ɪm'fætɪk/ adj, -ally adv nachdrücklich

empire /'empaɪə(r)/ n Reich nt

employ /ɪm'plɔɪ/ vt beschäftigen; (appoint) einstellen; (fig) anwenden. ~ee n Beschäftigte m/f; (in contrast to employer) Arbeitnehmer m. ~er n Arbeitgeber m. ~ment n Beschäftigung f; (work) Arbeit f. ~ment agency n Stellenvermittlung f

empress /'emprɪs/ n Kaiserin f

emptiness /'emptɪnɪs/ n Leere f

empty /'emptɪ/ adj leer ● vt leeren; ausleeren (container) ● vi sich leeren

emulsion /ɪ'mʌlʃn/ n Emulsion f

enable /ɪ'neɪbl/ vt ~ s.o. to es jdm möglich machen, zu

enact /ɪ'nækt/ vt (Theat) aufführen

enamel /ɪ'næml/ n Email nt; (on teeth) Zahnschmelz m; (paint) Lack m

enchant /ɪn'tʃɑːnt/ vt bezaubern. ~ing adj bezaubernd. ~ment n Zauber m

encircle /ɪn'sɜːkl/ vt einkreisen

enclos|e /ɪn'kləʊz/ vt einschließen; (in letter) beilegen (with dat). ~ure n (at zoo) Gehege nt; (in letter) Anlage f

encore /'ɒŋkɔː(r)/ n Zugabe f ● int bravo!

encounter /ɪn'kaʊntə(r)/ n Begegnung f ● vt begegnen (+ dat); (fig) stoßen auf (+ acc)

encourage /ɪn'kʌrɪdʒ/ vt ermutigen; (promote) fördern. ~ment n Ermutigung f. ~ing adj ermutigend

encroach /ɪn'krəʊtʃ/ vi ~ on eindringen in (+ acc) (land)

encyclopaed|ia /ɪnsaɪklə'piːdɪə/ n Enzyklopädie f, Lexikon nt. ~ic adj enzyklopädisch

end /end/ n Ende nt; (purpose) Zweck m; in the ~ schließlich; at the ~ of May Ende Mai; on ~ hochkant; for days on ~ tagelang; make ~s meet [] [gerade] auskommen; no ~ of [] unheimlich viel(e) ● vt beenden ● vi enden; ~ up in ([]: arrive at) landen in (+ dat)

endanger /ɪn'deɪndʒə(r)/ vt gefährden

endeavour /ɪn'devə(r)/ n Bemühung f ● vi sich bemühen (to zu)

ending /'endɪŋ/ n Schluss m, Ende nt; (Gram) Endung f

endless /'endlɪs/ adj endlos

endorse /en'dɔːs/ vt (Comm) indossieren; (confirm) bestätigen. ~ment n (Comm) Indossament nt; (fig) Bestätigung f; (on driving licence) Strafvermerk m

endow /ɪn'daʊ/ vt stiften; be ~ed with (fig) haben

endurance /ɪn'djʊərəns/ n Durchhaltevermögen nt

endure /ɪn'djʊə(r)/ vt ertragen

enemy /'enəmɪ/ n Feind m ● attrib feindlich

energetic /enə'dʒetɪk/ adj tatkräftig; be ~ voller Energie sein

energy /'enədʒɪ/ n Energie f. ~-efficient adj energieeffizient

enforce /ɪn'fɔːs/ vt durchsetzen. ~d unfreiwillig

engage /ɪn'geɪdʒ/ vt einstellen (staff); (Theat) engagieren; (Auto) einlegen (gear) ● vi sich beteiligen (in an + dat); (Techn) ineinandergreifen. ~d adj besetzt; (person) beschäftigt; (to be married) verlobt; get ~d sich verloben (to mit). ~ment n Verlobung f; (appointment) Verabredung f; (Mil) Gefecht nt

engaging /ɪn'geɪdʒɪŋ/ adj einnehmend

engine /'endʒɪn/ n Motor m; (Naut) Maschine f; (Rail) Lokomotive f; (of jet plane) Triebwerk nt. ~-driver n Lokomotivführer m

engineer /endʒɪ'nɪə(r)/ n Ingenieur m; (service, installation) Techniker m; (Naut) Maschinist m; (Amer) Lokomotivführer m. ~ing n [mechanical] ~ing Maschinenbau m

England /'ɪŋglənd/ n England nt

English /'ɪŋglɪʃ/ adj englisch; the ~ Channel der Ärmelkanal ● n

(Lang) Englisch nt; in ~ auf Englisch; into ~ ins Englische; the ~ pl die Engländer. ~man n Engländer m. ~woman n Engländerin f

engrave /ɪn'greɪv/ vt eingravieren. ~ing n Stich m

enhance /ɪn'hɑːns/ vt verschönern; (fig) steigern

enigma /ɪ'nɪgmə/ n Rätsel nt. ~tic adj rätselhaft

enjoy /ɪn'dʒɔɪ/ vt genießen; ~ oneself sich amüsieren; ~ cooking gern kochen; I ~ed it es hat mir gut gefallen; (food:) geschmeckt. ~able adj angenehm, nett. ~ment n Vergnügen nt

enlarge /ɪn'lɑːdʒ/ vt vergrößern. ~ment n Vergrößerung f

enlist /ɪn'lɪst/ vt (Mil) einziehen; ~ s.o.'s help jdn zur Hilfe heranziehen ● vi (Mil) sich melden

enliven /ɪn'laɪvn/ vt beleben

enmity /'enmətɪ/ n Feindschaft f

enormity /ɪ'nɔːmətɪ/ n Ungeheuerlichkeit f

enormous /ɪ'nɔːməs/ adj riesig

enough /ɪ'nʌf/ a, adv & n genug; be ~ reichen; funnily ~ komischerweise

enquir|e /ɪn'kwaɪə(r)/ vi sich erkundigen (about nach). ~y n Erkundigung f; (investigation) Untersuchung f

enrage /ɪn'reɪdʒ/ vt wütend machen

enrich /ɪn'rɪtʃ/ vt bereichern

enrol /ɪn'rəʊl/ v (pt/pp -rolled) ● vt einschreiben ● vi sich einschreiben

ensemble /ɒn'sɒmbl/ n (clothing & Mus) Ensemble nt

enslave /ɪn'sleɪv/ vt versklaven

ensue /ɪn'sjuː/ vi folgen; (result) sich ergeben (from aus)

ensure /ɪnˈʃʊə(r)/ vt sicherstellen; ~ that dafür sorgen, dass

entail /ɪnˈteɪl/ vt erforderlich machen; what does it ~? was ist damit verbunden?

entangle /ɪnˈtæŋgl/ vt get ~d sich verfangen (in in + dat)

enter /ˈentə(r)/ vt eintreten in (+ acc); (vehicle:) einfahren in (+ acc); einreisen in (+ acc) (country); (register) eintragen; sich anmelden zu (competition) ●vi eintreten; (vehicle:) einfahren; (Theat) auftreten; (register as competitor) sich anmelden; (take part) sich beteiligen (in an + dat)

enterpris|e /ˈentəpraɪz/ n Unternehmen nt; (quality) Unternehmungsgeist m. ~ing adj unternehmend

entertain /entəˈteɪn/ vt unterhalten; (invite) einladen; (to meal) bewirten (guest) ●vi unterhalten; (have guests) Gäste haben. ~er n Unterhalter m. ~ment n Unterhaltung f

enthral /ɪnˈθrɔːl/ vt (pt/pp enthralled) be ~led gefesselt sein (by von)

enthuse /ɪnˈθjuːz/ vi ~ over schwärmen von

enthusias|m /ɪnˈθjuːzɪæzm/ n Begeisterung f. ~t n Enthusiast m. ~tic adj, ~ally adv begeistert

entice /ɪnˈtaɪs/ vt locken. ~ment n Anreiz m

entire /ɪnˈtaɪə(r)/ adj ganz. ~ly adv ganz, völlig. ~ty n in its ~ty in seiner Gesamtheit

entitle /ɪnˈtaɪtl/ vt berechtigen; ~d ... mit dem Titel ...; be ~d to sth das Recht auf etw (acc) haben. ~ment n Berechtigung f; (claim) Anspruch m (to auf + acc)

entrance /ˈentrəns/ n Eintritt m; (Theat) Auftritt m; (way in) Eingang

m; (for vehicle) Einfahrt f. ~ fee n Eintrittsgebühr f

entrant /ˈentrənt/ n Teilnehmer(in) m (f)

entreat /ɪnˈtriːt/ vt anflehen (for um)

entrust /ɪnˈtrʌst/ vt ~ s.o. with sth, ~ sth to s.o. jdm etw anvertrauen

entry /ˈentrɪ/ n Eintritt m; (into country) Einreise f; (on list) Eintrag m; no ~ Zutritt! (Auto) Einfahrt verboten

envelop /ɪnˈveləp/ vt (pt/pp enveloped) einhüllen

envelope /ˈenvələʊp/ n [Brief]umschlag m

enviable /ˈenvɪəbl/ adj beneidenswert

envious /ˈenvɪəs/ adj neidisch (of auf + acc)

environment /ɪnˈvaɪərənmənt/ n Umwelt f

environmental /ɪnvaɪərən- ˈmentl/ adj Umwelt-. ~ist n Umweltschützer m. ~ly adv ~ly friendly umweltfreundlich

envisage /ɪnˈvɪzɪdʒ/ vt sich (dat) vorstellen

envoy /ˈenvɔɪ/ n Gesandte(r) m

envy /ˈenvɪ/ n Neid m ●vt (pt/pp -ied) ~ s.o. sth jdn um etw beneiden

epic /ˈepɪk/ adj episch ●n Epos nt

epidemic /epɪˈdemɪk/ n Epidemie f

epilep|sy /ˈepɪlepsɪ/ n Epilepsie f. ~tic adj epileptisch ●n Epileptiker(in) m (f)

epilogue /ˈepɪlɒg/ n Epilog m

episode /ˈepɪsəʊd/ n Episode f; (instalment) Folge f

epitome /ɪˈpɪtəmɪ/ n Inbegriff m

epoch /ˈiːpɒk/ n Epoche f. ~-making adj epochemachend

equal /ˈiːkwl/ adj gleich (to dat); be ~ to a task einer Aufgabe gewachsen sein ● n Gleichgestellte(r) m/f ● vt (pt/pp equalled) gleichen (+ dat); (fig) gleichkommen (+ dat). ~ity n Gleichheit f

equalize /ˈiːkwəlaɪz/ vt/i ausgleichen

equally /ˈiːkwəli/ adv gleich; (divide) gleichmäßig; (just as) genauso

equate /ɪˈkweɪt/ vt gleichsetzen (with mit). ~ion n (Math) Gleichung f

equator /ɪˈkweɪtə(r)/ n Äquator m

equestrian /ɪˈkwestrɪən/ adj Reit-

equilibrium /iːkwɪˈlɪbrɪəm/ n Gleichgewicht nt

equinox /ˈiːkwɪnɒks/ n Tagundnachtgleiche f

equip /ɪˈkwɪp/ vt (pt/pp equipped) ausrüsten; (furnish) ausstatten. ~ment n Ausrüstung f; Ausstattung f

equity /ˈekwəti/ n Gerechtigkeit f

equivalent /ɪˈkwɪvələnt/ adj gleichwertig; (corresponding) entsprechend ● n Äquivalent nt; (value) Gegenwert m; (counterpart) Gegenstück nt

era /ˈɪərə/ n Ära f, Zeitalter nt

eradicate /ɪˈrædɪkeɪt/ vt ausrotten

erase /ɪˈreɪz/ vt ausradieren; (from tape) löschen

erect /ɪˈrekt/ adj aufrecht ● vt errichten. ~ion n Errichtung f; (building) Bau m; (Physiology) Erektion f

erode /ɪˈrəʊd/ vt (water:) auswaschen; (acid:) angreifen. ~sion n Erosion f

erotic /ɪˈrɒtɪk/ adj erotisch

errand /ˈerənd/ n Botengang m

erratic /ɪˈrætɪk/ adj unregelmäßig;

(person) unberechenbar

erroneous /ɪˈrəʊnɪəs/ adj falsch; (belief, assumption) irrig

error /ˈerə(r)/ n Irrtum m; (mistake) Fehler m; in ~ irrtümlicherweise

erupt /ɪˈrʌpt/ vi ausbrechen. ~ion n Ausbruch m

escalat|e /ˈeskəleɪt/ vt/i eskalieren. ~or n Rolltreppe f

escape /ɪˈskeɪp/ n Flucht f; (from prison) Ausbruch m; have a narrow ~ gerade noch davonkommen ● vi flüchten; (prisoner:) ausbrechen; entkommen (from aus; from s.o. jdm); (gas:) entweichen ● vt the name ~s me der Name entfällt mir

escapism /ɪˈskeɪpɪzm/ n Eskapismus m

escort¹ /ˈeskɔːt/ n (of person) Begleiter m; (Mil) Eskorte f

escort² /ɪˈskɔːt/ vt begleiten; (Mil) eskortieren

Eskimo /ˈeskɪməʊ/ n Eskimo m

esoteric /esəˈterɪk/ adj esoterisch

especially /ɪˈspeʃəlɪ/ adv besonders

espionage /ˈespɪɑːnɑːʒ/ n Spionage f

essay /ˈeseɪ/ n Aufsatz m

essence /ˈesns/ n Wesen nt; (Chemistry, Culin) Essenz f

essential /ɪˈsenʃl/ adj wesentlich; (indispensable) unentbehrlich ● n the ~s das Wesentliche; (items) das Nötigste. ~ly adv im Wesentlichen

establish /ɪˈstæblɪʃ/ vt gründen; (form) bilden; (prove) beweisen

estate /ɪˈsteɪt/ n Gut nt; (possessions) Besitz m; (after death) Nachlass m; (housing) [Wohn]siedlung f. ~ agent n Immobilienmakler m. ~ car n Kombi[wagen] m

esteem /ɪˈstiːm/ n Achtung f ● vt hochschätzen

estimate¹ /ˈestɪmət/ n Schätzung f; (Comm) [Kosten]voranschlag m; at a rough ~ grob geschätzt

estimat|e² /ˈestɪmeɪt/ vt schätzen. ~ion n Einschätzung f

estuary /ˈestjʊərɪ/ n Mündung f

etc. /etˈsetərə/ abbr (et cetera) und so weiter, usw.

eternal /ɪˈtɜːnl/ adj ewig

eternity /ɪˈtɜːnətɪ/ n Ewigkeit f

ethical /ˈeθɪkl/ adj ethisch; (morally correct) moralisch einwandfrei. ~s n Ethik f

Ethiopia /iːθɪˈəʊpɪə/ n Äthiopien nt

ethnic /ˈeθnɪk/ adj ethnisch. ~ **cleansing** n ethnische Säuberung

etiquette /ˈetɪket/ n Etikette f

EU abbr (European Union) EU f

eulogy /ˈjuːlədʒɪ/ n Lobrede f

euphemis|m /ˈjuːfəmɪzm/ n Euphemismus m. ~**tic** adj, -ally adv verhüllend

euro /ˈjʊərəʊ/ n Euro m. E~**cheque** n Euroscheck m. E~**land** n Euroland nt

Europe /ˈjʊərəp/ n Europa nt

European /jʊərəˈpiːən/ adj europäisch; ~ **Union** Europäische Union f ●n Europäer(in) m(f)

eurosceptic /ˈjʊərəʊskeptɪk/ n Euroskeptiker(in) m(f)

evacuat|e /ɪˈvækjʊeɪt/ vt evakuieren; räumen (building, area). ~**ion** n Evakuierung f; Räumung f

evade /ɪˈveɪd/ vt sich entziehen (+ dat); hinterziehen (taxes)

evaluat|e /ɪˈvæljʊeɪt/ vt einschätzen. ~**ion** n Beurteilung f, Einschätzung f

evange|lical /iːvænˈdʒelɪkl/ adj evangelisch. ~**list** n Evangelist m

evaporat|e /ɪˈvæpəreɪt/ vi verdunsten. ~**ion** n Verdampfung f

evasion /ɪˈveɪʒn/ n Ausweichen nt; tax ~ Steuerhinterziehung f

evasive /ɪˈveɪsɪv/ adj ausweichend; be ~ ausweichen

even /ˈiːvn/ adj (level) eben; (same, equal) gleich; (regular) gleichmäßig; (number) gerade; get ~ with 🄸 es jdm heimzahlen ●adv sogar, selbst; ~ so trotzdem; not ~ nicht einmal ●vt ~ the score ausgleichen

evening /ˈiːvnɪŋ/ n Abend m; this ~ heute Abend; in the ~ abends, am Abend. ~ **class** n Abendkurs m

evenly /ˈiːvnlɪ/ adv gleichmäßig

event /ɪˈvent/ n Ereignis nt; (function) Veranstaltung f; (Sport) Wettbewerb m. ~**ful** adj ereignisreich

eventual /ɪˈventjʊəl/ adj his ~ success der Erfolg, der ihm schließlich zuteil wurde. ~**ly** adv schließlich

ever /ˈevə(r)/ adv je[mals]; not ~ nie; for ~ für immer; hardly ~ fast nie; ~ since seitdem

'evergreen n immergrüner Strauch m; (tree) Baum m

ever'lasting adj ewig

every /ˈevrɪ/ adj jede(r,s); ~ **one** jede(r,s) Einzelne; ~ **other day** jeden zweiten Tag

every: ~**body** pron jeder[mann]; alle pl. ~**day** adj alltäglich. ~ **one** pron jeder[mann]; alle pl. ~**thing** pron alles. ~**where** adv überall

evict /ɪˈvɪkt/ vt [aus der Wohnung] hinausweisen. ~**ion** n Ausweisung f

eviden|ce /ˈevɪdəns/ n Beweise pl; (Jur) Beweismaterial nt; (testimony) Aussage f; give ~ce aussagen. ~**t** adj offensichtlich

evil /ˈiːvl/ adj böse ●n Böse nt

evoke /ɪˈvəʊk/ vt heraufbeschwören

evolution /iːvəˈluːʃn/ n Evolution f

evolve /ɪˈvɒlv/ vt entwickeln • vi sich entwickeln

ewe /juː/ n Schaf nt

exact /ɪgˈzækt/ adj genau; not ~ly nicht gerade. ~ness n Genauigkeit f

exaggerat|e /ɪgˈzædʒəreɪt/ vt/i übertreiben. ~ion n Übertreibung f

exam /ɪgˈzæm/ n Ⓣ Prüfung f

examination /ɪgzæmɪˈneɪʃn/ n Untersuchung f; (Sch) Prüfung f

examine /ɪgˈzæmɪn/ vt untersuchen; (Sch) prüfen

example /ɪgˈzɑːmpl/ n Beispiel nt (of für); for ~ zum Beispiel; make an ~ of ein Exempel statuieren an (+ dat)

exasperat|e /ɪgˈzæspəreɪt/ vt zur Verzweiflung treiben. ~ion n Verzweiflung f

excavat|e /ˈekskəveɪt/ vt ausschachten; ausgraben (site). ~ion n Ausgrabung f

exceed /ɪkˈsiːd/ vt übersteigen. ~ingly adv äußerst

excel /ɪkˈsel/ v (pt/pp excelled) vi sich auszeichnen • vt ~ oneself sich selbst übertreffen

excellen|ce /ˈeksələns/ n Vorzüglichkeit f. ~t adj ausgezeichnet, vorzüglich

except /ɪkˈsept/ prep außer (+ dat); ~ for abgesehen von • vt ausnehmen

exception /ɪkˈsepʃn/ n Ausnahme f. ~al adj außergewöhnlich

excerpt /ˈeksɜːpt/ n Auszug m

excess /ɪkˈses/ n Übermaß nt (of an + dat); (surplus) Überschuss m; ~es pl Exzesse pl

excessive /ɪkˈsesɪv/ adj übermäßig

exchange /ɪksˈtʃeɪndʒ/ n Austausch m; (Teleph) Fernsprechamt nt; (Comm) [Geld]wechsel m; in ~

dafür • vt austauschen (for gegen); tauschen (places). ~ rate n Wechselkurs m

excitable /ɪkˈsaɪtəbl/ adj [leicht] erregbar

excit|e /ɪkˈsaɪt/ vt aufregen; (cause) erregen. ~ed adj aufgeregt; get ~ed sich aufregen. ~ement n Aufregung f; Erregung f. ~ing adj aufregend; (story) spannend

exclaim /ɪkˈskleɪm/ vt/i ausrufen

exclamation /ekskləˈmeɪʃn/ n Ausruf m. ~ mark n, (Amer) ~ point n Ausrufezeichen nt

exclu|de /ɪkˈskluːd/ vt ausschließen. ~ding prep ausschließlich (+ gen). ~sion n Ausschluss m

exclusive /ɪkˈskluːsɪv/ adj ausschließlich; (select) exklusiv

excrement /ˈekskrɪmənt/ n Kot m

excrete /ɪkˈskriːt/ vt ausscheiden

excruciating /ɪkˈskruːʃɪeɪtɪŋ/ adj grässlich

excursion /ɪkˈskɜːʃn/ n Ausflug m

excusable /ɪkˈskjuːzəbl/ adj entschuldbar

excuse¹ /ɪkˈskjuːs/ n Entschuldigung f; (pretext) Ausrede f

excuse² /ɪkˈskjuːz/ vt entschuldigen; ~ me! Entschuldigung!

ex-di'rectory adj be ~ nicht im Telefonbuch stehen

execute /ˈeksɪkjuːt/ vt ausführen; (put to death) hinrichten

execution /eksɪˈkjuːʃn/ n Ausführung f; Hinrichtung f

executive /ɪgˈzekjʊtɪv/ adj leitend • n leitende(r) Angestellte(r) m/f; (Pol) Exekutive f

exemplary /ɪgˈzemplərɪ/ adj beispielhaft

exemplify /ɪgˈzemplɪfaɪ/ vt (pt/pp -ied) veranschaulichen

exempt /ɪgˈzempt/ adj befreit ● vt befreien (from von). **∼ion** n Befreiung f

exercise /ˈeksəsaɪz/ n Übung f; physical ∼ körperliche Bewegung f ● vt (use) ausüben; bewegen (horse) ● vi sich bewegen. ∼ **book** n [Schul]heft nt

exert /ɪgˈzɜːt/ vt ausüben; ∼ oneself sich anstrengen. **∼ion** n Anstrengung f

exhale /eksˈheɪl/ vt/i ausatmen

exhaust /ɪgˈzɔːst/ n (Auto) Auspuff m; (fumes) Abgase pl ● vt erschöpfen. **∼ed** adj erschöpft. **∼ing** adj anstrengend. **∼ion** n Erschöpfung f. **∼ive** adj (fig) erschöpfend

exhibit /ɪgˈzɪbɪt/ n Ausstellungsstück nt; (Jur) Beweisstück n ● vt ausstellen

exhibition /eksɪˈbɪʃn/ n Ausstellung f; (Univ) Stipendium nt. **∼ist** n Exhibitionist(in) m(f)

exhibitor /ɪgˈzɪbɪtə(r)/ n Aussteller m

exhilarat|ing /ɪgˈzɪləreɪtɪŋ/ adj berauschend. **∼ion** n Hochgefühl nt

exhume /ɪgˈzjuːm/ vt exhumieren

exile /ˈeksaɪl/ n Exil nt; (person) im Exil Lebende(r) m/f ● vt ins Exil schicken

exist /ɪgˈzɪst/ vi bestehen, existieren. **∼ence** n Existenz f; be in ∼ence existieren

exit /ˈeksɪt/ n Ausgang m; (Auto) Ausfahrt f; (Theat) Abgang m

exorbitant /ɪgˈzɔːbɪtənt/ adj übermäßig hoch

exotic /ɪgˈzɒtɪk/ adj exotisch

expand /ɪkˈspænd/ vt ausdehnen; (explain better) weiter ausführen ● vi sich ausdehnen; (Comm) expandieren

expans|e /ɪkˈspæns/ n Weite f.

∼ion n Ausdehnung f; (Techn, Pol, Comm) Expansion f

expect /ɪkˈspekt/ vt erwarten; (suppose) annehmen; I ∼ so wahrscheinlich

expectan|cy /ɪkˈspektənsɪ/ n Erwartung f. **∼t** adj erwartungsvoll; **∼t mother** werdende Mutter f

expectation /ekspekˈteɪʃn/ n Erwartung f

expedient /ɪkˈspiːdɪənt/ adj zweckdienlich

expedite /ˈekspɪdaɪt/ vt beschleunigen

expedition /ekspɪˈdɪʃn/ n Expedition f

expel /ɪkˈspel/ vt (pt/pp expelled) ausweisen (from aus); (from school) von der Schule verweisen

expenditure /ɪkˈspendɪtʃə(r)/ n Ausgaben pl

expense /ɪkˈspens/ n Kosten pl; business ∼s pl Spesen pl; at my ∼ auf meine Kosten

expensive /ɪkˈspensɪv/ adj teuer

experience /ɪkˈspɪərɪəns/ n Erfahrung f; (event) Erlebnis n ● vt erleben. **∼d** adj erfahren

experiment /ɪkˈsperɪmənt/ n Versuch m, Experiment nt ● /-ment/ vi experimentieren. **∼al** adj experimentell

expert /ˈekspɜːt/ adj fachmännisch ● n Fachmann m, Experte m

expertise /ekspɜːˈtiːz/ n Sachkenntnis f

expire /ɪkˈspaɪə(r)/ vi ablaufen

expiry /ɪkˈspaɪərɪ/ n Ablauf m

explain /ɪkˈspleɪn/ vt erklären

explana|tion /ekspləˈneɪʃn/ n Erklärung f. **∼tory** adj erklärend

explicit /ɪkˈsplɪsɪt/ adj deutlich

explode /ɪkˈspləʊd/ vi explodieren ● vt zur Explosion bringen

e

exploit[1] /'eksploit/ n [Helden]tat f

exploit[2] /ik'sploit/ vt ausbeuten. ~**ation** n Ausbeutung f

exploration /eksplə'reiʃn/ n Erforschung f

explore /ik'splɔ:(r)/ vt erforschen. ~**r** n Forschungsreisende(r) m

explos|ion /ik'spləuʒn/ n Explosion f. ~**ive** adj explosiv ● n Sprengstoff m

export[1] /'ekspɔ:t/ n Export m, Ausfuhr f

export[2] /ik'spɔ:t/ vt exportieren, ausführen. ~**er** n Exporteur m

expos|e /ik'spəuz/ vt freilegen; (to danger) aussetzen (to dat); (reveal) aufdecken; (Phot) belichten. ~**ure** n Aussetzung f; (Med) Unterkühlung f; (Phot) Belichtung f; **24 ~ures** 24 Aufnahmen

express /ik'spres/ adv (send) per Eilpost ● n (train) Schnellzug m ● vt ausdrücken; ~ **oneself** sich ausdrücken. ~**ion** n Ausdruck m. ~**ive** adj ausdrucksvoll. ~**ly** adv ausdrücklich

expulsion /ik'spʌlʃn/ n Ausweisung f; (Sch) Verweisung f von der Schule

exquisite /ek'skwizit/ adj erlesen

extend /ik'stend/ vt verlängern; (stretch out) ausstrecken; (enlarge) vergrößern ● vi sich ausdehnen; (table:) sich ausziehen lassen

extension /ik'stenʃn/ n Verlängerung f; (to house) Anbau m; (Teleph) Nebenanschluss m

extensive /ik'stensiv/ adj weit; (fig) umfassend. ~**ly** adv viel

extent /ik'stent/ n Ausdehnung f; (scope) Ausmaß nt, Umfang m; **to a certain ~** in gewissem Maße

exterior /ik'stiəriə(r)/ adj äußere(r,s) ● n the ~ das Äußere

exterminat|e /ik'stɜ:mineit/ vt

ausrotten. ~**ion** n Ausrottung f

external /ik'stɜ:nl/ adj äußere(r,s); **for ~ use only** (Med) nur äußerlich. ~**ly** adv äußerlich

extinct /ik'stiŋkt/ adj ausgestorben; (volcano) erloschen. ~**ion** n Aussterben nt

extinguish /ik'stiŋgwiʃ/ vt löschen. ~**er** n Feuerlöscher m

extort /ik'stɔ:t/ vt erpressen. ~**ion** n Erpressung f

extortionate /ik'stɔ:ʃənət/ adj übermäßig hoch

extra /'ekstrə/ adj zusätzlich ● adv extra; (especially) besonders ● n (Theat) Statist(in) m(f); ~**s** pl Nebenkosten pl; (Auto) Extras pl

extract[1] /'ekstrækt/ n Auszug m

extract[2] /ik'strækt/ vt herausziehen; ziehen (tooth)

extraordinary /ik'strɔ:dinəri/ adj, **-ily** adv außerordentlich; (strange) seltsam

extravagan|ce /ik'strævəgəns/ n Verschwendung f; **an ~ce** ein Luxus m. ~**t** adj verschwenderisch

extrem|e /ik'stri:m/ adj äußerste(r,s); (fig) extrem ● n Extrem nt; **in the ~e** im höchsten Grade. ~**ely** adv äußerst. ~**ist** n Extremist m

extricate /'ekstrikeit/ vt befreien

extrovert /'ekstrəvɜ:t/ n extravertierter Mensch m

exuberant /ig'zju:bərənt/ adj überglücklich

exude /ig'zju:d/ vt absondern; (fig) ausstrahlen

exult /ig'zʌlt/ vi frohlocken

eye /ai/ n Auge nt; (of needle) Öhr nt; (for hook) Öse f; **keep an ~ on** aufpassen auf (+ acc) ● vt (pt/pp eyed, pres p ey[e]ing) ansehen

eye: ~**brow** n Augenbraue f. ~**lash** n Wimper f. ~**lid** n Augenlid

nt. **~-shadow** n Lidschatten m.
~sight n Sehkraft f; **~sore** n 🔟
Schandfleck m. **~witness** n Augenzeuge m

....

Ff

....

fable /ˈfeɪbl/ n Fabel f

fabric /ˈfæbrɪk/ n Stoff m

fabrication /fæbrɪˈkeɪʃn/ n Erfindung f

fabulous /ˈfæbjʊləs/ adj 🔟 phantastisch

façade /fəˈsɑːd/ n Fassade f

face /feɪs/ n Gesicht nt; (surface)
Fläche f; (of clock) Zifferblatt nt; pull
~s Gesichter schneiden; in the **~**
of angesichts (+ gen); on the **~** of
it allem Anschein nach ● vt/i gegenüberstehen (+ dat); **~** north
(house:) nach Norden liegen; **~** the
fact that sich damit abfinden, dass

face: ~-flannel n Waschlappen m.
~less adj anonym. **~-lift** n Gesichtsstraffung f

facet /ˈfæsɪt/ n Facette f; (fig)
Aspekt m

facetious /fəˈsiːʃəs/ adj spöttisch

facial /ˈfeɪʃl/ adj Gesichts-

facile /ˈfæsaɪl/ adj oberflächlich

facilitate /fəˈsɪlɪteɪt/ vt erleichtern

facility /fəˈsɪlɪtɪ/ n Leichtigkeit f;
(skill) Gewandtheit f; **~ies** pl Einrichtungen pl

facsimile /fækˈsɪmɪlɪ/ n Faksimile nt

fact /fækt/ n Tatsache f; **in ~** tatsächlich; (actually) eigentlich

faction /ˈfækʃn/ n Gruppe f

factor /ˈfæktə(r)/ n Faktor m

factory /ˈfæktərɪ/ n Fabrik f

factual /ˈfæktʃʊəl/ adj sachlich

faculty /ˈfækəltɪ/ n Fähigkeit f;
(Univ) Fakultät f

fad /fæd/ n Fimmel m

fade /feɪd/ vi verblassen; (material:)
verbleichen; (sound:) abklingen;
(flower:) verwelken

fag /fæg/ n (chore) Plage f; (🔟: cigarette) Zigarette f

fail /feɪl/ n **without ~** unbedingt
● vi (attempt:) scheitern; (grow
weak) nachlassen; (break down) versagen; (in exam) durchfallen; **~ to**
do sth etw nicht tun ● vt nicht bestehen (exam); durchfallen lassen
(candidate); (disappoint) enttäuschen

failing /ˈfeɪlɪŋ/ n Fehler m

failure /ˈfeɪljə(r)/ n Misserfolg m;
(breakdown) Versagen nt; (person)
Versager m

faint /feɪnt/ adj (-er, -est) schwach;
I feel~ mir ist schwach ● n Ohnmacht f ● vi ohnmächtig werden.
~ness n Schwäche f

fair¹ /feə(r)/ n Jahrmarkt m;
(Comm) Messe f

fair² /feə(r)/ adj (-er, -est) (hair) blond;
(skin) hell; (weather) heiter; (just)
gerecht, fair; (quite good) ziemlich
gut; (Sch) genügend ● adv play **~ fair** sein.
~ly adv gerecht; (rather) ziemlich.
~ness n Blondheit f; Helle f; Gerechtigkeit f; (Sport) Fairness f

fairy /ˈfeərɪ/ n Elfe f; good/wicked
~ gute/böse Fee f. **~ story,**
~-tale n Märchen nt

faith /feɪθ/ n Glaube m; (trust) Vertrauen nt (in zu)

faithful /ˈfeɪθfl/ adj treu; (exact)
genau; Yours **~ly** Hochachtungsvoll. **~ness** n Treue f; Genauigkeit f

fake /feɪk/ adj falsch ● n Fälschung
f; (person) Schwindler m ● vt fäl-

e
f

schen; (*pretend*) vortäuschen

falcon /ˈfɔːlkən/ n Falke m

fall /fɔːl/ n Fall m; (*heavy*) Sturz m; (*in prices*) Fallen nt; (*Amer: autumn*) Herbst m; have a ~ fallen ● vi (*pt* fell, *pp* fallen) fallen; (*heavily*) stürzen; (*night:*) anbrechen; ~ in love sich verlieben; ~ **back on** zurückgreifen auf (+ acc); ~ **for s.o.** [!] sich in jdn verlieben; ~ **for sth** auf etw (acc) hereinfallen. ~ **about** vi (*with laughter*) sich [vor Lachen] kringeln. ~ **down** vi umfallen; (*thing:*) herunterfallen; (*building:*) einstürzen. ~ **in** vi hineinfallen; (*collapse*) einfallen; (*Mil*) antreten; ~ **in with** sich anschließen (+ *dat*). ~ **off** vi herunterfallen; (*diminish*) abnehmen. ~ **out** vi herausfallen; (*hair:*) ausfallen; (*quarrel*) sich überwerfen. ~ **over** vi hinfallen. ~ **through** vi durchfallen; (*plan:*) ins Wasser fallen

fallacy /ˈfæləsɪ/ n Irrtum m

fallible /ˈfæləbl/ adj fehlbar

'fall-out n [radioaktiver] Niederschlag m

false /fɔːls/ adj falsch; (*artificial*) künstlich. ~**hood** n Unwahrheit f. ~**ly** adv falsch

false 'teeth npl [künstliches] Gebiss nt

falsify /ˈfɔːlsɪfaɪ/ vt (*pt/pp* -ied) fälschen

falter /ˈfɔːltə(r)/ vi zögern

fame /feɪm/ n Ruhm m.

familiar /fəˈmɪljə(r)/ adj vertraut; (*known*) bekannt; too ~ familiär. ~**ity** n Vertrautheit f. ~**ize** vt vertraut machen (with mit)

family /ˈfæmɪlɪ/ n Familie f

family: ~ **'doctor** n Hausarzt m. ~ **'life** n Familienleben nt. ~ **'planning** n Familienplanung f. ~ **'tree** n Stammbaum m

famine /ˈfæmɪn/ n Hungersnot f

famished /ˈfæmɪʃt/ adj sehr hungrig

famous /ˈfeɪməs/ adj berühmt

fan¹ /fæn/ n Fächer m; (*Techn*) Ventilator m

fan² n (*admirer*) Fan m

fanatic /fəˈnætɪk/ n Fanatiker m. ~**al** adj fanatisch. ~**ism** n Fanatismus m

fanciful /ˈfænsɪfl/ adj phantastisch; (*imaginative*) phantasiereich

fancy /ˈfænsɪ/ n Phantasie f; I have taken a real ~ **to him** er hat es mir angetan ● adj ausgefallen ● vt (*believe*) meinen; (*imagine*) sich (*dat*) einbilden; ([!]: *want*) Lust haben auf (+ acc); ~ **that!** stell dir vor! (*really*) tatsächlich! ~ **'dress** n Kostüm nt

fanfare /ˈfænfeə(r)/ n Fanfare f

fang /fæŋ/ n Fangzahn m

'fan heater n Heizlüfter m

fantas|ize /ˈfæntəsaɪz/ vi phantasieren. ~**tic** adj phantastisch. ~**y** n Phantasie f

far /fɑː(r)/ adv weit; (*much*) viel; by ~ bei weitem; ~ **away** weit weg; as ~ as I know soviel ich weiß; as ~ as the church bis zur Kirche ● adj at the ~ **end** am anderen Ende; the F~ **East** der Ferne Osten

farc|e /fɑːs/ n Farce f. ~**ical** adj lächerlich

fare /feə(r)/ n Fahrpreis m; (*money*) Fahrgeld nt; (*food*) Kost f; **air** ~ Flugpreis m

farewell /feəˈwel/ int (*literary*) lebe wohl! ● n Lebewohl nt

far-'fetched adj weit hergeholt

farm /fɑːm/ n Bauernhof m ● vi Landwirtschaft betreiben ● vt bewirtschaften (*land*). ~**er** n Landwirt m

farm: ~**house** n Bauernhaus nt. ~**ing** n Landwirtschaft f.

~**yard** n Hof m

far: ~-'**reaching** adj weit reichend; ~-'**sighted** adj (fig) umsichtig; (Amer: long-sighted) weitsichtig

farther /'fɑːðə(r)/ adv weiter; ~ **off** weiter entfernt

fascinat|e /'fæsɪnɛɪt/ vt faszinieren. ~**ing** adj faszinierend. ~**ion** n Faszination f

fascis|m /'fæʃɪzm/ n Faschismus m. ~**t** n Faschist m ● adj faschistisch

fashion /'fæʃn/ n Mode f; (manner) Art f. ~**able** adj, -**bly** adv modisch

fast /fɑːst/ adj & adv (-er, -est) schnell; (firm) fest; (colour) waschecht; be ~ (clock:) vorgehen; be ~ **asleep** fest schlafen

fasten /'fɑːsn/ vt zumachen; (fix) befestigen (to an + dat). ~**er** n, ~**ing** n Verschluss m

fastidious /fə'stɪdɪəs/ adj wählerisch; (particular) penibel

fat /fæt/ adj (fatter, fattest) dick; (meat) fett ● n Fett nt

fatal /'feɪtl/ adj tödlich; (error) verhängnisvoll. ~**ity** n Todesopfer nt. ~**ly** adv tödlich

fate /feɪt/ n Schicksal nt. ~**ful** adj verhängnisvoll

'**fat-head** n ⓘ Dummkopf m

father /'fɑːðə(r)/ n Vater m; F~ **Christmas** der Weihnachtsmann ● vt zeugen

father: ~**hood** n Vaterschaft f. ~-**in-law** n (pl ~**s-in-law**) Schwiegervater m. ~**ly** adj väterlich

fathom /'fæðəm/ n (Naut) Faden m ● vt verstehen

fatigue /fə'tiːg/ n Ermüdung f

fatten /'fætn/ vt mästen (animal)

fatty /'fætɪ/ adj fett; (foods) fetthaltig

fatuous /'fætjʊəs/ adj albern

fault /fɔːlt/ n Fehler m; (Techn) Defekt m; (Geology) Verwerfung f; **at** ~ im Unrecht; **find** ~ **with** etwas auszusetzen haben an (+ dat); **it's your** ~ du bist schuld. ~**less** adj fehlerfrei

faulty /'fɔːltɪ/ adj fehlerhaft

favour /'feɪvə(r)/ n Gunst f; **I am in** ~ **ich** bin dafür; **do s.o. a** ~ jdm einen Gefallen tun ● vt begünstigen; (prefer) bevorzugen. ~**able** adj, -**bly** adv günstig; (reply) positiv

favourit|e /'feɪvərɪt/ adj Lieblings- ● n Liebling m; (Sport) Favorit(in) m(f). ~**ism** n Bevorzugung f

fawn /fɔːn/ adj rehbraun ● n Hirschkalb nt

fax /fæks/ n Fax nt ● vt faxen (s.o. jdm). ~ **machine** n Faxgerät nt

fear /fɪə(r)/ n Furcht f, Angst f (of vor + dat) ● vt/i fürchten

fear|ful /'fɪəfl/ adj besorgt; (awful) furchtbar. ~**less** adj furchtlos

feas|ibility /fiːzə'bɪlətɪ/ n Durchführbarkeit f. ~**ible** adj durchführbar; (possible) möglich

feast /fiːst/ n Festmahl nt; (Relig) Fest nt ● vi ~ [**on**] schmausen

feat /fiːt/ n Leistung f

feather /'feðə(r)/ n Feder f

feature /'fiːtʃə(r)/ n Gesichtszug m; (quality) Merkmal nt; (article) Feature nt ● vt darstellen

February /'febrʊərɪ/ n Februar m

fed /fed/ see **feed** ● adj **be** ~ **up** ⓘ die Nase voll haben (with von)

federal /'fedərəl/ adj Bundes-

federation /fedə'reɪʃn/ n Föderation f

fee /fiː/ n Gebühr f; (professional) Honorar nt

feeble /'fiːbl/ adj (-r, -st), -**bly** adv schwach

feed /fiːd/ n Futter nt; (for baby)
Essen nt ● v (pt/pp fed) ● vt füttern; (support) ernähren; (into machine) eingeben; speisen (computer)
● vi sich ernähren (on von)

'**feedback** n Feedback nt

feel /fiːl/ v (pt/pp felt) ● vt fühlen;
(experience) empfinden; (think) meinen ● vi sich fühlen; ~ soft/hard
sich weich/hart anfühlen; I ~ hot/ill
mir ist heiß/schlecht; ~**ing** n Gefühl nt; no hard ~**ings** nichts
für ungut

feet /fiːt/ see **foot**

feline /fiːlaɪn/ adj Katzen-; (catlike)
katzenartig

fell[1] /fel/ vt fällen

fell[2] see **fall**

fellow /feləʊ/ n (fam: man) Kerl m

fellow: ~'**countryman** n Landsmann m. ~**men** pl Mitmenschen pl

felt[1] /felt/ see **feel**

felt[2] n Filz m. ~**[-tipped]** '**pen** n
Filzstift m

female /fiːmeɪl/ adj weiblich ● nt
Weibchen nt; (pej: woman) Weib nt

femin|ine /femmnɪn/ adj weiblich
● n (Gram) Femininum nt. ~**inity** n
Weiblichkeit f. ~**ist** adj feministisch
● n Feminist(in) m(f)

fenc|e /fens/ n Zaun m; (fam: per-
son) Hehler m ● vi (Sport) fechten
● vt ~**e** in einzäunen. ~**er** n Fech-
ter m. ~**ing** n Zaun m; (Sport)
Fechten nt

fender /fendə(r)/ n Kaminvorset-
zer m; (Naut) Fender m; (Amer:
wing) Kotflügel m

ferment /fəˈment/ vi gären ● vt
gären lassen

fern /fɜːn/ n Farn m

ferocious /fəˈrəʊʃəs/ adj wild.
~**ity** n Wildheit f

ferry /ferɪ/ n Fähre f

fertil|e /fɜːtaɪl/ adj fruchtbar. ~**ity**
n Fruchtbarkeit f

fertilize /fɜːtəlaɪz/ vt befruchten;
düngen (land). ~**r** n Dünger m

fervent /fɜːvənt/ adj leidenschaftlich

fervour /fɜːvə(r)/ n Leidenschaft f

festival /festɪvl/ n Fest nt; (Mus,
Theat) Festspiele pl

festive /festɪv/ adj festlich.
~**ities** npl Feierlichkeiten pl

festoon /feˈstuːn/ vt behängen
(with mit)

fetch /fetʃ/ vt holen; (collect) abholen; (be sold for) einbringen

fetching /fetʃɪŋ/ adj anziehend

fête /feɪt/ n Fest nt ● vt feiern

feud /fjuːd/ n Fehde f

feudal /fjuːdl/ adj Feudal-

fever /fiːvə(r)/ n Fieber nt. ~**ish**
adj fiebrig; (fig) fieberhaft

few /fjuː/ adj (-er, -est) wenige;
every ~ days alle paar Tage ● n a
~ ein paar; quite a ~ ziemlich viele

fiancé /fiˈɒnseɪ/ n Verlobte(r) m. **fiancée** n Verlobte f

fiasco /fiˈæskəʊ/ n Fiasko nt

fib /fɪb/ n kleine Lüge

fibre /faɪbə(r)/ n Faser f

fiction /fɪkʃn/ n Erfindung f;
[works of] ~ Erzählungsliteratur f.
~**al** adj erfunden

fictitious /fɪkˈtɪʃəs/ adj [frei] erfunden

fiddle /fɪdl/ n (fam) Geige f; (cheat-
ing) Schwindel m ● vi herumspielen
(with mit) ● vt (fam) frisieren (accounts)

fiddly /fɪdlɪ/ adj knifflig

fidelity /fɪˈdelətɪ/ n Treue f

fidget /fɪdʒɪt/ vi zappeln. ~**y** adj
zappelig

field /fiːld/ n Feld nt; (meadow)

Wiese f; (subject) Gebiet nt

field: ~ **events** npl Sprung- und Wurfdisziplinen pl. **F~** '**Marshal** n Feldmarschall m

fiendish /'fi:ndɪʃ/ adj teuflisch

fierce /fɪəs/ adj (-r, -st) wild; (fig) heftig. ~**ness** n Wildheit f; (fig) Heftigkeit f

fiery /'faɪərɪ/ adj feurig

fifteen /fɪf'ti:n/ adj fünfzehn ●n Fünfzehn f. ~**th** adj fünfzehnte(r,s)

fifth /fɪfθ/ adj fünfte(r,s)

fiftieth /'fɪftɪθ/ adj fünfzigste(r,s)

fifty /'fɪftɪ/ adj fünfzig

fig /fɪg/ n Feige f

fight /faɪt/ n Kampf m; (brawl) Schlägerei f; (between children, dogs) Rauferei f ●v (pt/pp fought) ●vt kämpfen gegen; (fig) bekämpfen ●vi kämpfen; (brawl) sich schlagen; (children, dogs) sich raufen. ~**er** n Kämpfer m; (Aviat) Jagdflugzeug nt. ~**ing** n Kampf m

figurative /'fɪgjərətɪv/ adj bildlich, übertragen

figure /'fɪgə(r)/ n (digit) Ziffer f; (number) Zahl f; (sum) Summe f; (carving, sculpture, woman's) Figur f; (form) Gestalt f; (illustration) Abbildung f; **good at** ~**s** gut im Rechnen ●vi (appear) erscheinen ●vt (Amer: think) glauben

filch /fɪltʃ/ vt Ⓣ klauen

file[1] /faɪl/ n Akte f; (for documents) [Akten]ordner m ●vt ablegen (documents); (Jur) einreichen

file[2] n (line) Reihe f; **in single** ~ im Gänsemarsch

file[3] n (Techn) Feile f ●vt feilen

fill /fɪl/ n **eat one's** ~ sich satt essen ●vt füllen; plombieren (tooth) ●vi sich füllen. ~ **in** vt auffüllen; ausfüllen (form). ~ **out** vt ausfüllen (form). ~ **up** vi sich füllen ●vt vollfüllen; (Auto) volltanken; ausfüllen

(questionnaire)

fillet /'fɪlɪt/ n Filet nt ●vt (pt/pp filleted) entgräten

filling /'fɪlɪŋ/ n Füllung f; (of tooth) Plombe f. ~ **station** n Tankstelle f

filly /'fɪlɪ/ n junge Stute f

film /fɪlm/ n Film m ●vt/i filmen; verfilmen (book). ~ **star** n Filmstar m

filter /'fɪltə(r)/ n Filter m ●vt filtern

filth /fɪlθ/ n Dreck m. ~**y** adj dreckig

fin /fɪn/ n Flosse f

final /'faɪnl/ adj letzte(r,s); (conclusive) endgültig ●n (Sport) Endspiel nt; ~**s** pl (Univ) Abschlussprüfung f

finale /fɪ'nɑ:lɪ/ n Finale nt

final|ist /'faɪnəlɪst/ n Finalist(in) m(f)

final|ize /'faɪnəlaɪz/ vt endgültig festlegen. ~**ly** adv schließlich

finance /faɪ'næns/ n Finanz f ●vt finanzieren

financial /faɪ'nænʃl/ adj finanziell

find /faɪnd/ n Fund m ●vt (pt/pp found) finden; (establish) feststellen; **go and** ~ holen; **try to** ~ suchen. ~ **out** vt herausfinden; (learn) erfahren ●vi (enquire) sich erkundigen

fine[1] /faɪn/ n Geldstrafe f ●vt zu einer Geldstrafe verurteilen

fine[2] adj (-r, -st,) ~**ly** adv fein; (weather) schön; **he's** ~ es geht ihm gut ●adv gut; **cut it** ~ Ⓣ sich (dat) wenig Zeit lassen

finesse /fɪ'nes/ n Gewandtheit f

finger /'fɪŋgə(r)/ n Finger m ●vt anfassen

finger: ~**nail** n Fingernagel m. ~**print** n Fingerabdruck m. ~**tip** n Fingerspitze f

finicky /'fɪnɪkɪ/ adj knifflig; (choosy) wählerisch

finish /'fɪnɪʃ/ n Schluss m; (Sport)

Finish nt; (line) Ziel nt; (of product) Ausführung f ● vt beenden; (use up) aufbrauchen; ~ one's drink austrinken; ~ **reading** zu Ende lesen ● vi fertig werden; (performance:) zu Ende sein; (runner:) durchs Ziel gehen

Finland /ˈfɪnlənd/ n Finnland nt

Finn /fɪn/ n Finne m/ Finnin f. ~**ish** adj finnisch

fir /fɜː(r)/ n Tanne f.

fire /ˈfaɪə(r)/ n Feuer nt; (forest, house) Brand m; **be on** ~ brennen; **catch** ~ Feuer fangen; **set** ~ **to** anzünden; (arsonist:) in Brand stecken; **under** ~ unter Beschuss ● vt brennen; (pottery:) abfeuern (shot); schießen mit (gun); (fig: dismiss) feuern ● vi schießen (**at** auf + acc); (engine:) anspringen

fire: ~ **alarm** n Feuermelder m. ~**brigade** n Feuerwehr f. ~**engine** n Löschfahrzeug nt. ~ **extinguisher** n Feuerlöscher m. ~**man** n Feuerwehrmann m. ~**place** n Kamin m. ~**side** n by or at the ~**side** am Kamin. ~ **station** n Feuerwache f. ~**wood** n Brennholz nt. ~**work** n Feuerwerkskörper m; ~**works** pl (display) Feuerwerk nt

firm¹ /fɜːm/ n Firma f

firm² adj (-er, -est) fest; (resolute) entschlossen; (strict) streng

first /fɜːst/ adj u a erste(r,s); **at** ~ zuerst; **at** ~ **sight** auf den ersten Blick; **from the** ~ von Anfang an ● adv zuerst; (firstly) erstens

first: ~ **aid** n erste Hilfe. ~**'aid kit** n Verbandskasten m. ~**class** adj erstklassig; (Rail) erster Klasse ● /-'-/ adv (travel) erster Klasse. ~**floor** n erster Stock; (Amer: ground floor) Erdgeschoss nt. ~**ly** adv erstens. ~**name** n Vorname m. ~**rate** adj erstklassig

fish /fɪʃ/ n Fisch m ● vt/i fischen;

(with rod) angeln

fish: ~**bone** n Gräte f. ~**erman** n Fischer m. ~ **'finger** n Fischstäbchen nt

fishing /ˈfɪʃɪŋ/ n Fischerei f. ~**boat** n Fischerboot nt. ~**rod** n Angel[rute] f

fish: ~**monger** /-mʌŋgə(r)/ n Fischhändler m. ~**y** adj Fisch-; (fig: suspicious) verdächtig

fission /ˈfɪʃn/ n (Phys) Spaltung f

fist /fɪst/ n Faust f

fit¹ /fɪt/ n (attack) Anfall m

fit² adj (fitter, fittest) (suitable) geeignet; (healthy) gesund; (Sport) fit; ~ **to eat** essbar

fit³ n (of clothes) Sitz m; **be a good** ~ gut passen ● v (pt/pp fitted) ● v (be the right size) passen ● vt anbringen (**to** an + dat); (install) einbauen; ~ **with** versehen mit. ~ **in** vi hineinpassen; (adapt) sich einfügen (**with** in + acc) ● vt (accommodate) unterbringen

fit|ness n Eignung f; [**physical**] ~**ness** Gesundheit f; (Sport) Fitness f. ~**ted** adj eingebaut; (garment) tailliert

fitted: ~ **'carpet** n Teppichboden m. ~ **'kitchen** n Einbauküche f. ~ **'sheet** n Spannlaken f

fitting /ˈfɪtɪŋ/ adj passend ● n (of clothes) Anprobe f; (of shoes) Weite f; (Techn) Zubehörteil nt. ~**s** pl Zubehör nt

five /faɪv/ adj fünf ● n Fünf f. ~**r** n Fünfpfundschein m

fix /fɪks/ n (sl: drugs) Fix m; **be in a** ~ (fig) in der Klemme sitzen ● vt befestigen (**to** an + dat); (arrange) festlegen; (repair) reparieren; (Phot) fixieren; ~ **a meal** Essen machen

fixed /fɪkst/ adj fest

fixture /ˈfɪkstʃə(r)/ n (Sport) Veranstaltung f. ~**s and fittings** zu einer Wohnung gehörende Einrichtungen pl

fizz /fɪz/ vi sprudeln

fizzle /ˈfɪzl/ vi ~ **out** verpuffen

fizzy /ˈfɪzi/ adj sprudelnd. ~ **drink** n Brause[limonade] f

flabbergasted /ˈflæbəɡɑːstɪd/ adj **be** ~ platt sein 🔲

flabby /ˈflæbɪ/ adj schlaff

flag /flæɡ/ n Fahne f; (Naut) Flagge f

'**flag-pole** n Fahnenstange f

flagrant /ˈfleɪɡrənt/ adj flagrant

'**flagstone** n [Pflaster]platte f

flair /fleə(r)/ n Begabung f

flake /fleɪk/ n Flocke f ● vi ~[off] abblättern

flamboyant /flæmˈbɔɪənt/ adj extravagant

flame /fleɪm/ n Flamme f

flan /flæn/ n [fruit] ~ Obsttorte f

flank /flæŋk/ n Flanke f

flannel /ˈflænl/ n Flanell m; (for washing) Waschlappen m

flap /flæp/ n Klappe f; **in a** ~ 🔲 aufgeregt ● vi (pt/pp flapped) vi flattern; 🔲 sich aufregen ● vt ~ **its wings** mit den Flügeln schlagen

flare /fleə(r)/ n Leuchtsignal nt. ● vi ~ **up** auflodern; (🔲: get angry) aufbrausen

flash /flæʃ/ n Blitz m; **in a** ~ 🔲 im Nu ● vi blitzen; (repeatedly) blinken; ~ **past** vorbeirasen

flash: ~**back** n Rückblende f. ~**er** n (Auto) Blinker m. ~**light** n (Phot) Blitzlicht nt; (Amer: torch) Taschenlampe f. ~**y** adj auffällig

flask /flɑːsk/ n Flasche f

flat /flæt/ adj (flatter, flattest) flach; (surface) eben; (refusal) glatt; (beer) schal; (battery) verbraucht/ (Auto) leer; (tyre) platt; (Mus) A ~ As nt; B ~ B nt ● n Wohnung f;

(🔲: puncture) Reifenpanne f

flat: ~**ly** adv (refuse) glatt. ~ **rate** n Einheitspreis m

flatten /ˈflætn/ vt platt drücken

flatter /ˈflætə(r)/ vt schmeicheln (+ dat). ~**y** n Schmeichelei f

flat 'tyre n Reifenpanne f

flaunt /flɔːnt/ vt prunken mit

flautist /ˈflɔːtɪst/ n Flötist(in) m(f)

flavour /ˈfleɪvə(r)/ n Geschmack m ● vt abschmecken. ~**ing** n Aroma nt

flaw /flɔː/ n Fehler m. ~**less** adj tadellos; (complexion) makellos

flea /fliː/ n Floh m

fleck /flek/ n Tupfen m

fled /fled/ see **flee**

flee /fliː/ v (pt/pp fled) ● vi fliehen (from vor + dat) ● vt flüchten aus

fleec|e /fliːs/ n Vlies nt ● vt 🔲 schröpfen

fleet /fliːt/ n Flotte f; (of cars) Wagenpark m

fleeting /ˈfliːtɪŋ/ adj flüchtig

Flemish /ˈflemɪʃ/ adj flämisch

flesh /fleʃ/ n Fleisch nt

flew /fluː/ see **fly²**

flex¹ /fleks/ vt anspannen (muscle)

flex² n (Electr) Schnur f

flexi|bility /fleksəˈbɪlɪti/ n Biegsamkeit f; (fig) Flexibilität f. ~**le** adj biegsam; (fig) flexibel

flick /flɪk/ vt schnippen

flicker /ˈflɪkə(r)/ vi flackern

flier /ˈflaɪə(r)/ n = **flyer**

flight¹ /flaɪt/ n (fleeing) Flucht f

flight² n (flying) Flug m; ~ **of stairs** Treppe f

'**flight recorder** n Flugschreiber m

flimsy /ˈflɪmzɪ/ adj dünn; (excuse) fadenscheinig

flinch /flɪntʃ/ vi zurückzucken

fling /flɪŋ/ vt (pt/pp flung) schleudern

flint /flɪnt/ n Feuerstein m

flip /flɪp/ vt/i schnippen; ~ through durchblättern

flippant /'flɪpənt/ adj leichtfertig

flirt /flɜːt/ n kokette Frau f ● vi flirten

flirtat|ion /flɜːˈteɪʃn/ n Flirt m. ~ious adj kokett

flit /flɪt/ vi (pt/pp flitted) flattern

float /fləʊt/ n Schwimmer m; (in procession) Festwagen m; (money) Wechselgeld nt ● vi (thing:) schwimmen; (person:) sich treiben lassen; (in air) schweben

flock /flɒk/ n Herde f; (of birds) Schwarm m ● vi strömen

flog /flɒg/ vt (pt/pp flogged) auspeitschen; (ᵭ: sell) verklopfen

flood /flʌd/ n Überschwemmung f; (fig) Flut f ● vt überschwemmen

floodlight n Flutlicht nt ● vt (pt/pp floodlit) anstrahlen

floor /flɔː(r)/ n Fußboden m; (storey) Stock m

floor: ~ board n Dielenbrett nt. ~polish n Bohnerwachs nt. ~show n Kabarettvorstellung f

flop /flɒp/ n (ᵭ: failure) Reinfall m; (Theat) Durchfall m ● vi (pt/pp flopped) ᵭ (fail) durchfallen

floppy /'flɒpɪ/ adj schlapp. ~ 'disc n Diskette f

floral /'flɔːrl/ adj Blumen-

florid /'flɒrɪd/ adj (complexion) gerötet; (style) blumig

florist /'flɒrɪst/ n Blumenhändler(in) m(f)

flounder /'flaʊndə(r)/ vi zappeln

flour /'flaʊə(r)/ n Mehl nt

flourish /'flʌrɪʃ/ n große Geste f; (scroll) Schnörkel m ● vi gedeihen; (fig) blühen ● vt schwenken

flout /flaʊt/ vt missachten

flow /fləʊ/ n Fluss m; (of traffic, blood) Strom m ● vi fließen

flower /'flaʊə(r)/ n Blume f ● vi blühen

flower: ~-bed n Blumenbeet nt. ~pot n Blumentopf m. ~y adj blumig

flown /fləʊn/ see fly²

flu /fluː/ n ᵭ Grippe f

fluctuat|e /'flʌktjʊeɪt/ vi schwanken. ~ion n Schwankung f

fluent /'fluːənt/ adj fließend

fluff /flʌf/ n Fusseln pl; (down) Flaum m. ~y adj flauschig

fluid /'fluːɪd/ adj flüssig, (fig) veränderlich ● n Flüssigkeit f

fluke /fluːk/ n [glücklicher] Zufall m

flung /flʌŋ/ see fling

fluorescent /flʊəˈresnt/ adj fluoreszierend

fluoride /'flʊəraɪd/ n Fluor nt

flush /flʌʃ/ n (blush) Erröten nt ● vi rot werden ● vt spülen ● adj in einer Ebene (with mit); (ᵭ: affluent) gut bei Kasse

flustered /'flʌstəd/ adj nervös

flute /fluːt/ n Flöte f

flutter /'flʌtə(r)/ n Flattern nt ● vi flattern

fly¹ /flaɪ/ n (pl flies) Fliege f

fly² /flaɪ/ v (pt flew, pp flown) ● vi fliegen; (flag:) wehen; (rush) sausen ● vt fliegen; führen (flag)

fly³ n & flies pl (on trousers) Hosenschlitz m

flyer /'flaɪə(r)/ n Flieger(in) m(f); (leaflet) Flugblatt nt

foal /fəʊl/ n Fohlen nt

foam /fəʊm/ n Schaum m; (synthetic) Schaumstoff m ● vi schäumen

fob /fɒb/ vt (pt/pp fobbed) ~ sth off etw andrehen (on s.o. jdm); ~

s.o. off jdn abspeisen (with mit)

focal /ˈfəʊkl/ n Brenn-

focus /ˈfəʊkəs/ n Brennpunkt m; in ~ scharf eingestellt ● v (pt/pp focused or focussed) ● vt einstellen (on auf + acc) ● vi (fig) sich konzentrieren (on auf + acc)

fog /fɒg/ n Nebel m

foggy /ˈfɒgɪ/ adj (foggier, foggiest) neblig

'fog-horn n Nebelhorn nt

foible /ˈfɔɪbl/ n Eigenart f

foil[1] /fɔɪl/ n Folie f; (Culin) Alufolie f

foil[2] vt (thwart) vereiteln

foil[3] n (Fencing) Florett nt

fold /fəʊld/ n Falte f; (in paper) Kniff m ● vt falten; ~ one's arms die Arme verschränken ● vi sich falten lassen; (fail) eingehen. ~ **up** vt zusammenfalten; zusammenklappen (chair) ● vi sich zusammenfalten/-klappen lassen; (ᴛ business:) eingehen

fold|er /ˈfəʊldə(r)/ n Mappe f. ~ing adj Klapp-

foliage /ˈfəʊlɪʤ/ n Blätter pl; (of tree) Laub nt

folk /fəʊk/ npl Leute pl

folk: ~**dance** n Volkstanz m. ~**song** n Volkslied nt

follow /ˈfɒləʊ/ vt/i folgen (+ dat); (pursue) verfolgen; (in vehicle) nachfahren (+ dat). ~ **up** vt nachgehen (+ dat)

follow|er /ˈfɒləʊə(r)/ n Anhänger(in) m(f). ~ing adj folgend ● n Folgende(s) nt; (supporters) Anhängerschaft f ● prep im Anschluss an (+ acc)

folly /ˈfɒlɪ/ n Torheit f

fond /fɒnd/ adj (-er, -est) liebevoll; be ~ of gern haben; gern essen (food)

fondle /ˈfɒndl/ vt liebkosen

fondness /ˈfɒndnɪs/ n Liebe f

(for zu)

food /fuːd/ n Essen nt; (for animals) Futter nt; (groceries) Lebensmittel pl. ~ **poisoning** n Lebensmittelvergiftung f

food poisoning n Lebensmittelvergiftung f

fool[1] /fuːl/ n (Culin) Fruchtcreme f

fool[2] n Narr m; make a ~ of oneself sich lächerlich machen ● vt hereinlegen ● vi ~ **around** herumalbern

'fool|hardy adj tollkühn. ~ish adj dumm. ~ishness n Dummheit f. ~proof adj narrensicher

foot /fʊt/ n (pl feet) Fuß m; (measure) Fuß m (30.48 cm); (of bed) Fußende nt; on ~ zu Fuß; on one's feet auf den Beinen; put one's ~ in it ᴛ ins Fettnäpfchen treten

foot: ~**-and-'mouth [disease]** n Maul- und Klauenseuche f. ~**ball** n Fußball m. ~**baller** n Fußballspieler m. ~**ball pools** npl Fußballtoto nt. ~**bridge** n Fußgängerbrücke f. ~**hills** npl Vorgebirge nt. ~**hold** n Halt m. ~**ing** n Halt m. ~**lights** npl Rampenlicht nt. ~**note** n Fußnote f. ~**path** n Fußweg m. ~**print** n Fußabdruck m. ~**step** n Schritt m; follow in s.o.'s ~steps (fig) in jds Fußstapfen treten. ~**wear** n Schuhwerk nt

for /fɔː(r)/, unstressed /fə(r)/
● preposition
⋯▸ (on behalf of; in place of; in favour of) für (+ acc). I did it for you ich habe es für dich gemacht. I work for him/for a bank ich arbeite für ihn/für eine Bank. be for doing sth dafür sein, etw zu tun. cheque/bill for £5 Scheck/Rechnung über 5 Pfund. for nothing umsonst.

what have you got for a cold? was haben Sie gegen Erkältungen?

····▸ (expressing reason) wegen (+ gen); (with emotion) aus. famous for these wines berühmt wegen dieser Weine od für diese Weine. he was sentenced to death for murder er wurde wegen Mordes zum Tode verurteilt. were it not for you/your help ohne dich/deine Hilfe. for fear/love of aus Angst vor (+ dat)/aus Liebe zu (+ dat)

····▸ (expressing purpose) (with action, meal) zu (+ dat); (with object) für (+ acc). it's for washing the car es ist zum Autowaschen. we met for a discussion wir trafen uns zu einer Besprechung. for pleasure zum Vergnügen. meat for lunch Fleisch zum Mittagessen. what is that for? wofür od wozu ist das? a dish for nuts eine Schale für Nüsse

····▸ (expressing direction) nach (+ dat); (less precise) in Richtung. the train for Oxford der Zug nach Oxford. they were heading or making for London sie fuhren in Richtung London

····▸ (expressing time) (completed process) ... lang; (continuing process) seit (+ dat). I lived there for two years ich habe zwei Jahre [lang] dort gewohnt. I have been living here for two years ich wohne hier seit zwei Jahren. we are staying for a week wir werden eine Woche bleiben

····▸ (expressing difficulty, impossibility, embarrassment etc.) + dat. it's impossible/inconvenient for her es ist ihr unmöglich/ungelegen. it was embarrassing for our teacher unserem Lehrer war es peinlich

● conjunction

····▸ denn. he's not coming for he has no money er kommt nicht mit, denn er hat kein Geld

forbade /fə'bæd/ see **forbid**

forbid /fə'bɪd/ vt (pt forbade, pp forbidden) verbieten (s.o. jdm). ∼ding adj bedrohlich; (stern) streng

force /fɔːs/ n Kraft f; (of blow) Wucht f; (violence) Gewalt f; in ∼ gültig; (in large numbers) in großer Zahl; come into ∼ in Kraft treten; the ∼s pl die Streitkräfte pl ● vt zwingen; (break open) aufbrechen

forced /fɔːst/ adj gezwungen; ∼ landing Notlandung f

force: ∼-**feed** vt (pt/pp -fed) zwangsernähren. ∼**ful** adj energisch

forceps /'fɔːseps/ n inv Zange f

forcible /'fɔːsəbl/ adj gewaltsam

ford /fɔːd/ n Furt f ● vt durchwaten; (in vehicle) durchfahren

fore /fɔː(r)/ adj vordere(r,s)

fore: ∼**arm** n Unterarm m. ∼**cast** n Voraussage f; (for weather) Vorhersage f ● vt (pt/pp ∼cast) voraussagen, vorhersagen. ∼**finger** n Zeigefinger m. ∼**gone** adj be a ∼gone conclusion von vornherein feststehen. ∼**ground** n Vordergrund m. ∼**head** /'fɒrɪd/ n Stirn f. ∼**hand** n Vorhand f

foreign /'fɒrən/ adj ausländisch; (country) fremd; he is ∼ er ist Ausländer. ∼ **currency** n Devisen pl. ∼**er** n Ausländer(in) m(f). ∼ **language** n Fremdsprache f

Foreign: ∼ **Office** n ≈ Außenministerium nt. ∼ **'Secretary** n ≈ Außenminister m

fore: ∼**leg** n Vorderbein nt. ∼**man**

foresee | forward

n Vorarbeiter m. ~**most** a führend
● adv first and ~most zuallererst.
~**name** n Vorname m. ~**runner** n
Vorläufer m

fore'see vt (pt -saw, pp -seen)
voraussehen, vorhersehen. ~**able**
adj in the ~able future in absehbarer Zeit

foresight n Weitblick m

forest /'fɒrɪst/ n Wald m. ~**er** n
Förster m

forestry /'fɒrɪstrɪ/ n Forstwirtschaft f

foretaste n Vorgeschmack m

forever /fə'revə(r)/ adv für immer

fore'warn vt vorher warnen

foreword /'fɔːwɜːd/ n Vorwort nt

forfeit /'fɔːfɪt/ n (in game) Pfand nt
● vt verwirken

forgave /fə'geɪv/ see forgive

forge /fɔːdʒ/ n Schmiede f ● vt
schmieden; (counterfeit) fälschen.
~**r** n Fälscher m. ~**ry** n Fälschung f

forget /fə'get/ vt/i (pt -got, pp
-gotten) vergessen; verlernen (language, skill). ~**ful** adj vergesslich.
~**fulness** n Vergesslichkeit f.
~**-me-not** n Vergissmeinnicht nt

forgive /fə'gɪv/ vt (pt -gave, pp
-given) ~ s.o. for sth jdm etw vergeben od verzeihen

forgot(ten) /fə'gɒt(n)/ see forget

fork /fɔːk/ n Gabel f; (in road) Gabelung f ● vi (road:) sich gabeln; ~
right rechts abzweigen

fork-lift 'truck n Gabelstapler m

forlorn /fə'lɔːn/ adj verlassen;
(hope) schwach

form /fɔːm/ n Form f; (document)
Formular nt; (bench) Bank f; (Sch)
Klasse f; come (into zu); (create) bilden ● vi sich bilden; (idea:)
Gestalt annehmen

formal /'fɔːml/ adj formell, förm-

lich. ~**ity** n Förmlichkeit f; (requirement) Formalität f

format /'fɔːmæt/ n Format nt ● vt
formatieren

formation /fɔː'meɪʃn/ n Formation f

former /'fɔːmə(r)/ adj ehemalig;
the ~ der/die/das Erstere. ~**ly** adv
früher

formidable /'fɔːmɪdəbl/ adj gewaltig

formula /'fɔːmjʊlə/ n (pl -ae or -s)
Formel f

formulate /'fɔːmjʊleɪt/ vt formulieren

forsake /fə'seɪk/ vt (pt -sook
/-sʊk/, pp -saken) verlassen

fort /fɔːt/ n (Mil) Fort nt

forth /fɔːθ/ adv back and ~ hin
und her; and so ~ und so weiter

forth: ~**coming** adj bevorstehend; (⊡: communicative) mitteilsam. ~**right** adj direkt

fortieth /'fɔːtɪɪθ/ adj vierzigste(r,s)

fortification /fɔːtɪfɪ'keɪʃn/ n Befestigung f

fortify /'fɔːtɪfaɪ/ vt (pt/pp -ied) befestigen; (fig) stärken

fortnight /'fɔːt-/ n vierzehn Tage
pl. ~**ly** adj vierzehntäglich ● adv
alle vierzehn Tage

fortress /'fɔːtrɪs/ n Festung f

fortunate /'fɔːtʃʊnət/ adj glücklich; be ~ Glück haben. ~**ly** adv
glücklicherweise

fortune /'fɔːtʃuːn/ n Glück nt;
(money) Vermögen nt. ~**-teller** n
Wahrsagerin f

forty /'fɔːtɪ/ adj vierzig

forward /'fɔːwəd/ adv vorwärts;
(to the front) nach vorn ● adj Vorwärts-; (presumptuous) anmaßend
● n (Sport) Stürmer m ● vt nachsenden (letter). ~**s** adv vorwärts

fossil /ˈfɒsl/ n Fossil nt

foster /ˈfɒstə(r)/ vt fördern; in Pflege nehmen (child). **~-child** n Pflegekind nt. **~-mother** n Pflegemutter f

fought /fɔːt/ see **fight**

foul /faʊl/ adj (-er, -est) widerlich; (language) unflätig; ~ **play** (Jur) Mord m ● n (Sport) Foul nt ● vt verschmutzen; (obstruct) blockieren; (Sport) foulen

found[1] /faʊnd/ see **find**

found[2] vt gründen

foundation /faʊnˈdeɪʃn/ n (basis) Grundlage f; (charitable) Stiftung f; **~s** pl Fundament nt

founder[1] /ˈfaʊndə(r)/ n Gründer(in) m (f)

foundry /ˈfaʊndri/ n Gießerei f

fountain /ˈfaʊntɪn/ n Brunnen m

four /fɔː(r)/ adj vier ● n Vier f

four: **~teen** adj vierzehn ● n Vierzehn f. **~teenth** adj vierzehnte(r,s)

fourth /fɔːθ/ adj vierte(r,s)

fowl /faʊl/ n Geflügel nt

fox /fɒks/ n Fuchs m ● vt (puzzle) verblüffen

foyer /ˈfɔɪeɪ/ n Foyer nt; (in hotel) Empfangshalle f

fraction /ˈfrækʃn/ n Bruchteil m; (Math) Bruch m

fracture /ˈfræktʃə(r)/ n Bruch m ● vt/i brechen

fragile /ˈfrædʒaɪl/ adj zerbrechlich

fragment /ˈfrægmənt/ n Bruchstück nt, Fragment nt

fragran|ce /ˈfreɪɡrəns/ n Duft m. **~t** adj duftend

frail /freɪl/ adj (-er, -est) gebrechlich

frame /freɪm/ n Rahmen m; (of spectacles) Gestell nt; (Anat) Körperbau m ● vt einrahmen; (fig) formulieren; ⊠ ein Verbrechen anhängen

(+ dat). **~work** n Gerüst nt; (fig) Gerippe nt

franc /fræŋk/ n (French, Belgian) Franc m; (Swiss) Franken m

France /frɑːns/ n Frankreich nt

franchise /ˈfræntʃaɪz/ n (Pol) Wahlrecht nt; (Comm) Franchise f

frank[1] /fræŋk/ adj offen

frankfurter /ˈfræŋkfɜːtə(r)/ n Frankfurter f

frantic /ˈfræntɪk/ adj, **-ally** adv verzweifelt; außer sich (dat) (with vor)

fraternal /frəˈtɜːnl/ adj brüderlich

fraud /frɔːd/ n Betrug m; (person) Betrüger(in) m (f)

fray[1] /freɪ/ vi ausfransen

freak /friːk/ n Missbildung f; (person) Missgeburt f ● adj anormal

freckle /ˈfrekl/ n Sommersprosse f

free /friː/ adj (freer, freest) frei; (ticket, copy, time) Frei-; (lavish) freigebig; ~ [of charge] kostenlos; set ~ (rescue) befreien ● vt (pt/pp freed) freilassen; (rescue) befreien; (disentangle) freibekommen

free: **~dom** n Freiheit f. **~hold** n [freier] Grundbesitz m. **~lance** adj & adv freiberuflich. **~ly** adv frei; (voluntarily) freiwillig; (generously) großzügig. **F~mason** n Freimaurer m. **~-range** adj **~-range eggs** Landeier pl. **~ sample** n Gratisprobe f. **~style** n Freistil m. **~way** n (Amer) Autobahn f

freeze /friːz/ vt (pt froze, pp frozen) einfrieren; stoppen (wages) ● vi it's ~ing es friert.

freez|er /ˈfriːzə(r)/ n Gefriertruhe f; (upright) Gefrierschrank m. **~ing** adj eiskalt ● n five degrees below **~ing** fünf Grad unter Null

freight /freɪt/ n Fracht f. **~er** n Frachter m. **~ train** ~ Güterzug m

French /frentʃ/ adj französisch ●n (Lang) Französisch nt; **the ~** pl die Franzosen

French: **~ 'beans** npl grüne Bohnen pl. **~ 'bread** n Stangenbrot m. **~' fries** npl Pommes frites pl. **~man** n Franzose m. **~ 'window** n Terrassentür f. **~woman** n Französin f

frenzy /'frenzɪ/ n Raserei f

frequency /'fri:kwənsɪ/ n Häufigkeit f; (Phys) Frequenz f

frequent¹ /'fri:kwənt/ adj häufig

frequent² /frɪ'kwent/ vt regelmäßig besuchen

fresh /freʃ/ adj (-er, -est) frisch; (new) neu; (cheeky) frech

freshness /'freʃnɪs/ n Frische f

'freshwater adj Süßwasser-

fret /fret/ vi (pt/pp fretted) sich grämen. **~ful** adj weinerlich

'fretsaw n Laubsäge f

friction /'frɪkʃn/ n Reibung f; (fig) Reibereien pl

Friday /'fraɪdeɪ/ n Freitag m

fridge /frɪdʒ/ n Kühlschrank m

fried /fraɪd/ see fry² ●adj gebraten; **~ egg** Spiegelei nt

friend /frend/ n Freund(in) m(f). **~liness** n Freundlichkeit f. **~ly** adj freundlich; **~ly with** befreundet mit. **~ship** n Freundschaft f

fright /fraɪt/ n Schreck m

frighten /'fraɪtn/ vt Angst machen (+ dat); (startle) erschrecken; **be ~ed** Angst haben (of vor + dat). **~ing** adj Angst erregend

frightful /'fraɪtfl/ adj schrecklich

frigid /'frɪdʒɪd/ adj frostig; (sexually) frigide. **~ity** n Frostigkeit f; Frigidität f

frill /frɪl/ n Rüsche f; (paper) Man-

schette f. **~y** adj rüschenbesetzt

fringe /frɪndʒ/ n Fransen pl; (of hair) Pony m; (fig: edge) Rand m

frisk /frɪsk/ vi herumspringen ●vt (search) durchsuchen

frisky /'frɪskɪ/ adj lebhaft

fritter /'frɪtə(r)/ vt ~ [away] verplempern 🔲

frivol|ity /frɪ'vɒlətɪ/ n Frivolität f. **~ous** adj frivol, leichtfertig

fro /frəʊ/ see to

frock /frɒk/ n Kleid nt

frog /frɒg/ n Frosch m. **~man** n Froschmann m

frolic /'frɒlɪk/ vi (pt/pp frolicked) herumtollen

from /frɒm/ prep von (+ dat); (out of) aus (+ dat); (according to) nach (+ dat); **~ Monday** ab Montag; **~ that day** seit dem Tag

front /frʌnt/ n Vorderseite f; (fig) Fassade f; (of garment) Vorderteil nt; (sea~) Strandpromenade f; (Mil, Pol, Meteorol) Front f; **in ~ of** vor; **in or at the ~** vorne; **to the ~** nach vorne ●adj vordere(r,s); (page, row) erste(r,s). (tooth, wheel) Vorder-

front: **~ 'door** n Haustür f. **~ 'garden** n Vorgarten m

frontier /'frʌntɪə(r)/ n Grenze f

frost /frɒst/ n Frost m; (hoar-~) Raureif m; **ten degrees of ~** zehn Grad Kälte. **~bite** n Erfrierung f. **~bitten** adj erfroren

frost|ed /'frɒstɪd/ adj **~ed glass** Mattglas nt. **~ing** n (Amer Culin) Zuckerguss m. **~y** adj, **-ily** adv frostig

froth /frɒθ/ n Schaum m ●vi schäumen. **~y** adj schaumig

frown /fraʊn/ n Stirnrunzeln nt ●vi die Stirn runzeln

froze /frəʊz/ see freeze

frozen /'frəʊzn/ see freeze ●adj

gefroren; (Culin) tiefgekühlt; **I'm ~**
🄸 mir ist eiskalt. **~ food** n Tief-
kühlkost f

frugal /ˈfruːgl/ adj sparsam; (meal)
frugal

fruit /fruːt/ n Frucht f; (collectively)
Obst nt. **~ cake** n englischer [Tee-
]kuchen m

fruitful adj fruchtbar

fruit: **~ juice** n Obstsaft m. **~less**
adj fruchtlos. **~'salad** n Obst-
salat m

fruity /ˈfruːtɪ/ adj fruchtig

frustrat|e /frʌˈstreɪt/ vt vereiteln;
(Psychology) frustrieren. **~ion** n Fru-
stration f

fry /fraɪ/ vt/i (pt/pp fried) [in der
Pfanne] braten. **~ing-pan** n Brat-
pfanne f

fuel /ˈfjuːəl/ n Brennstoff m; (for
car) Kraftstoff m; (for aircraft) Treib-
stoff m

fugitive /ˈfjuːdʒɪtɪv/ n
Flüchtling m

fulfil /fʊlˈfɪl/ vt (pt/pp -filled) erfüllen. **~ment** n Erfüllung f

full /fʊl/ adj & adv (-er, -est) voll;
(detailed) ausführlich; (skirt) weit; **~**
of voll von (+ dat), voller (+ gen); **at
~ speed** in voller Fahrt ● n **in ~**
vollständig

full: **~ 'moon** n Vollmond m.
~-scale adj (model) in Original-
größe; (rescue, alert) großangelegt.
~ 'stop n Punkt m. **~-time** adj
ganztägig ● adv ganztags

fully /ˈfʊlɪ/ adv völlig; (in detail)
ausführlich

fumble /ˈfʌmbl/ vi herumfummeln
(with an + dat)

fume /fjuːm/ vi vor Wut schäumen

fumes /fjuːmz/ npl Dämpfe pl;
(from car) Abgase pl

fun /fʌn/ n Spaß m; **for ~** aus od
zum Spaß; **make ~ of** sich lustig

machen über (+ acc); **have ~!**
viel Spaß!

function /ˈfʌŋkʃn/ n Funktion f;
(event) Veranstaltung f ● vi funktionieren; (serve) dienen (as als). **~al**
adj zweckmäßig

fund /fʌnd/ n Fonds m; (fig) Vorrat
m; **~s** pl Geldmittel pl ● vt finanzieren

fundamental /fʌndəˈmentl/ adj
grundlegend; (essential) wesentlich

funeral /ˈfjuːnərl/ n Beerdigung f;
(cremation) Feuerbestattung f

funeral: **~ march** n Trauermarsch
m. **~ service** n Trauergottes-
dienst m

'funfair n Jahrmarkt m

fungus /ˈfʌŋgəs/ n (pl -gi /-gaɪ/)
Pilz m

funnel /ˈfʌnl/ n Trichter m; (on
ship, train) Schornstein m

funnily /ˈfʌnɪlɪ/ adv komisch; **~
enough** komischerweise

funny /ˈfʌnɪ/ adj komisch

fur /fɜː(r)/ n Fell nt; (for clothing)
Pelz m; (in kettle) Kesselstein m. **~
'coat** n Pelzmantel m

furious /ˈfjʊərɪəs/ adj wütend
(with auf + acc)

furnace /ˈfɜːnɪs/ n (Techn) Ofen m

furnish /ˈfɜːnɪʃ/ vt einrichten;
(supply) liefern. **~ed** adj **~ed room**
möbliertes Zimmer nt. **~ings** npl
Einrichtungsgegenstände pl

furniture /ˈfɜːnɪtʃə(r)/ n Möbel pl

further /ˈfɜːðə(r)/ adj weitere(r,s);
at the ~ end am anderen Ende;
until ~ notice bis auf weiteres
● adv weiter; **~ off** weiter entfernt
● vt fördern

furthermore /fɜːðəˈmɔː(r)/ adv
außerdem

furthest /ˈfɜːðɪst/ adj am weitesten entfernt ● adv am weitesten

fury /ˈfjʊərɪ/ n Wut f

fuse[1] /fjuːz/ n (of bomb) Zünder m; (cord) Zündschnur f

fuse[2] n (Electr) Sicherung f • vt/i verschmelzen; **the lights have ~d** die Sicherung [für das Licht] ist durchgebrannt. **~box** n Sicherungskasten m

fuselage /ˈfjuːzəlɑːʒ/ n (Aviat) Rumpf m

fuss /fʌs/ n Getue nt; **make a ~ of** verwöhnen; (caress) liebkosen • vi Umstände machen

fussy /ˈfʌsɪ/ adj wählerisch; (particular) penibel

futil|e /ˈfjuːtaɪl/ adj zwecklos. **~ity** n Zwecklosigkeit f

future /ˈfjuːtʃə(r)/ adj zukünftig • n Zukunft f; (Gram) [erstes] Futur nt

futuristic /fjuːtʃəˈrɪstɪk/ adj futuristisch

fuzzy /ˈfʌzɪ/ adj (hair) kraus; (blurred) verschwommen

Gg

gabble /ˈɡæbl/ vi schnell reden

gable /ˈɡeɪbl/ n Giebel m

gadget /ˈɡædʒɪt/ n [kleines] Gerät nt

Gaelic /ˈɡeɪlɪk/ n Gälisch nt

gag /ɡæɡ/ n Knebel m; (joke) Witz m; (Theat) Gag m • vt (pt/pp gagged) knebeln

gaiety /ˈɡeɪətɪ/ n Fröhlichkeit f

gaily /ˈɡeɪlɪ/ adv fröhlich

gain /ɡeɪn/ n Gewinn m; (increase) Zunahme f • vt gewinnen; (obtain) erlangen; **~ weight** zunehmen • vi

(clock:) vorgehen

gait /ɡeɪt/ n Gang m

gala /ˈɡɑːlə/ n Fest nt • attrib Gala-

galaxy /ˈɡæləksɪ/ n Galaxie f; **the G~** die Milchstraße

gale /ɡeɪl/ n Sturm m

gallant /ˈɡælənt/ adj tapfer; (chivalrous) galant. **~ry** n Tapferkeit f

'gall-bladder n Gallenblase f

gallery /ˈɡælərɪ/ n Galerie f

galley /ˈɡælɪ/ n (ship's kitchen) Kombüse f; **~ [proof]** [Druck-]fahne f

gallon /ˈɡælən/ n Gallone f (= 4,5 l; Amer = 3,785 l)

gallop /ˈɡæləp/ n Galopp m • vi galoppieren

gallows /ˈɡæləʊz/ n Galgen m

galore /ɡəˈlɔː(r)/ adv in Hülle und Fülle

gamble /ˈɡæmbl/ n (risk) Risiko nt • vi [um Geld] spielen; **~ on** (rely) sich verlassen auf (+ acc). **~r** n Spieler(in) m(f)

game /ɡeɪm/ n Spiel nt; (animals, birds) Wild nt; **~s** (Sch) Sport m • adj (brave) tapfer; (willing) bereit (for zu). **~keeper** n Wildhüter m

gammon /ˈɡæmən/ n [geräucherter] Schinken m

gang /ɡæŋ/ n Bande f; (of workmen) Kolonne f

gangling /ˈɡæŋɡlɪŋ/ adj schlaksig

gangmaster /ˈɡæŋmɑːstə(r)/ n Aufseher(in) m(f) von (meist illegalen) Gelegenheitsarbeitern

gangrene /ˈɡæŋɡriːn/ n Wundbrand m

gangster /ˈɡæŋstə(r)/ n Gangster m

gangway /ˈɡæŋweɪ/ n Gang m; (Naut, Aviat) Gangway f

gaol /dʒeɪl/ n Gefängnis nt • vt ins Gefängnis sperren. **~er** n

Gefängniswärter m

gap /gæp/ n Lücke f; (interval) Pause f; (difference) Unterschied m

gap|e /geɪp/ vi gaffen; ~e at anstarren. ~ing adj klaffend

> **gap year** Britische Schulabsolventen legen vor Universitätsbeginn oft eine einjährige Pause ein. In diesem gap year jobben sie, um Arbeitserfahrung zu erwerben oder Geld für ihr Studium zu verdienen. Viele reisen um die Welt, lernen die Kultur anderer Länder kennen, sammeln Auslandserfahrungen, belegen Sprachkurse oder arbeiten ehrenamtlich in Entwicklungsländern.

garage /'gæraːʒ/ n Garage f; (for repairs) Werkstatt f; (for petrol) Tankstelle f

garbage /'gaːbɪdʒ/ n Müll m. ~ can n (Amer) Mülleimer m

garbled /'gaːbld/ adj verworren

garden /'gaːdn/ n Garten m; [public] ~s pl [öffentliche] Anlagen pl ● vi im Garten arbeiten. ~er n Gärtner(in) m(f). ~ing n Gartenarbeit f

gargle /'gaːgl/ n (liquid) Gurgelwasser nt ● vi gurgeln

garish /'geərɪʃ/ adj grell

garland /'gaːlənd/ n Girlande f

garlic /'gaːlɪk/ n Knoblauch m

garment /'gaːmənt/ n Kleidungsstück nt

garnet /'gaːnɪt/ n Granat m

garnish /'gaːnɪʃ/ n Garnierung f ● vt garnieren

garrison /'gærɪsn/ n Garnison f

garrulous /'gærʊləs/ adj geschwätzig

garter /'gaːtə(r)/ n Strumpfband nt; (Amer: suspender) Strumpfhalter m

gas /gæs/ n Gas nt; (Amer, fam: petrol) Benzin nt ● v (pt/pp gassed) ● vt vergasen ● vi ⊞ schwatzen. ~-cooker n Gasherd m. ~ 'fire n Gasofen m

gash /gæʃ/ n Schnitt m; (wound) klaffende Wunde f

gasket /'gæskɪt/ n (Techn) Dichtung f

gas: ~ mask n Gasmaske f. ~-meter n Gaszähler m

gasoline /'gæsəliːn/ n (Amer) Benzin nt

gasp /gaːsp/ vi keuchen; (in surprise) hörbar die Luft einziehen

'gas station n (Amer) Tankstelle f

gastric /'gæstrɪk/ adj Magen-

gastronomy /gæ'strɒnəmɪ/ n Gastronomie f

gate /geɪt/ n Tor nt; (to field) Gatter nt; (barrier) Schranke f; (at airport) Flugsteig m

gate: ~crasher n ungeladener Gast m. ~way n Tor nt

gather /'gæðə(r)/ vt sammeln; (pick) pflücken; (conclude) folgern (from aus) ● vi sich versammeln; (storm) sich zusammenziehen. ~ing n family ~ing Familientreffen nt

gaudy /'gɔːdɪ/ adj knallig

gauge /geɪdʒ/ n Stärke f; (Rail) Spurweite f; (device) Messinstrument nt

gaunt /gɔːnt/ adj hager

gauze /gɔːz/ n Gaze f

gave /geɪv/ see give

gawky /'gɔːkɪ/ adj schlaksig

gay /geɪ/ adj (-er, -est) fröhlich; (homosexual) homosexuell

gaze /geɪz/ n [langer] Blick m ● vi sehen; ~ at ansehen

GB abbr Great Britain

gear /gɪə(r)/ n Ausrüstung f; (Techn) Getriebe nt; (Auto) Gang m; change ~ schalten

gear: ~**box** n (Auto) Getriebe nt. ~**-lever** n, (Amer) ~**-shift** n Schalthebel m

geese /giːs/ see **goose**

gel /dʒel/ n Gel nt

gelatine /ˈdʒelətiːn/ n Gelatine f

gem /dʒem/ n Juwel nt

gender /ˈdʒendə(r)/ n (Gram) Geschlecht nt

gene /dʒiːn/ n Gen nt

genealogy /dʒiːnɪˈælədʒɪ/ n Genealogie f

general /ˈdʒenrəl/ adj allgemein ● n General m; in ~ im Allgemeinen. ~ e'**lection** n allgemeine Wahlen pl

generaliz|ation /dʒenrəlaɪˈzeɪʃn/ n Verallgemeinerung f. ~**e** vi verallgemeinern

generally /ˈdʒenrəlɪ/ adv im Allgemeinen

general prac'titioner n praktischer Arzt m

generate /ˈdʒenəreɪt/ vt erzeugen

generation /dʒenəˈreɪʃn/ n Generation f

generator /ˈdʒenəreɪtə(r)/ n Generator m

generosity /dʒenəˈrɒsɪtɪ/ n Großzügigkeit f

generous /ˈdʒenərəs/ adj großzügig

genetic /dʒəˈnetɪk/ adj, -**ally** adv genetisch. ~**ally modified** gentechnisch verändert; genmanipuliert. ~ **engineering** n Gentechnologie f

Geneva /dʒɪˈniːvə/ n Genf nt

genial /ˈdʒiːnɪəl/ adj freundlich

genitals /ˈdʒenɪtlz/ pl [äußere] Geschlechtsteile pl

genitive /ˈdʒenɪtɪv/ adj & n ~

[case] Genitiv m

genius /ˈdʒiːnɪəs/ n (pl -uses) Genie nt; (quality) Genialität f

genome /ˈdʒiːnəʊm/ n Genom nt

genre /ˈʒãrə/ n Gattung f, Genre nt

gent /dʒent/ n 🄸 Herr m; **the ~s** sg die Herrentoilette f

genteel /dʒenˈtiːl/ adj vornehm

gentle /ˈdʒentl/ adj (-r, -st) sanft

gentleman /ˈdʒentlmən/ n Herr m; (well-mannered) Gentleman m

gent|leness /ˈdʒentlnɪs/ n Sanftheit f. ~**ly** adv sanft

genuine /ˈdʒenjʊɪn/ adj echt; (sincere) aufrichtig. ~**ly** adv (honestly) ehrlich

geograph|ical /dʒɪəˈgræfɪkl/ adj geographisch. ~**y** n Geographie f, Erdkunde f

geological /dʒɪəˈlɒdʒɪkl/ adj geologisch

geolog|ist /dʒɪˈɒlədʒɪst/ n Geologe m/-gin f. ~**y** n Geologie f

geometr|ic(al) /dʒɪəˈmetrɪk(l)/ adj geometrisch. ~**y** n Geometrie f

geranium /dʒəˈreɪnɪəm/ n Geranie f

geriatric /dʒerɪˈætrɪk/ adj geriatrisch ● n geriatrischer Patient m

germ /dʒɜːm/ n Keim m; ~**s** pl 🄸 Bazillen pl

German /ˈdʒɜːmən/ adj deutsch ● n (person) Deutsche(r) m/f; (Lang) Deutsch nt; in ~ auf Deutsch; into ~ ins Deutsche

Germanic /dʒɜːˈmænɪk/ adj germanisch

Germany /ˈdʒɜːmənɪ/ n Deutschland nt

germinate /ˈdʒɜːmɪneɪt/ vi keimen

gesticulate /dʒeˈstɪkjʊleɪt/ vi gestikulieren

gesture /ˈdʒestʃə(r)/ n Geste f

get | get

get /get/ v

pt **got**, *pp* **got** (*Amer also* **gotten**), *pres p* **getting**

● *transitive verb*

·····> (*obtain, receive*) bekommen; Ⓣ kriegen; (*procure*) besorgen; (*buy*) kaufen; (*fetch*) holen. **get a job/taxi for s.o.** jdm einen Job verschaffen/ein Taxi besorgen. **I must get some bread** ich muss Brot holen. **get permission** die Erlaubnis erhalten. **I couldn't get her on the phone** ich konnte sie nicht telefonisch erreichen

·····> (*prepare*) machen (*meal*). **he got the breakfast** er machte das Frühstück

·····> (*cause*) **get s.o. to do sth** jdn dazu bringen, etw zu tun. **get one's hair cut** sich (*dat*) die Haare schneiden lassen. **get one's hands dirty** sich (*dat*) die Hände schmutzig machen

·····> **get the bus/train.** (*travel by*) den Bus/Zug nehmen; (*be in time for, catch*) den Bus/Zug erreichen

·····> **have got** (Ⓣ: *have*) haben. **I've got a cold** ich habe eine Erkältung

·····> **have got to do sth** etw tun müssen. **I've got to hurry** ich muss mich beeilen

·····> (Ⓣ: *understand*) kapieren Ⓣ. **I don't get it** ich kapiere nicht

● *intransitive verb*

·····> (*become*) werden. **get older** älter werden. **the weather got worse** das Wetter wurde schlechter. **get to** kommen zu /nach (*town*); (*reach*)

erreichen. **get dressed** sich anziehen. **get married** heiraten.

● *phrasal verbs*

● **get about** *vi* (*move*) sich bewegen; (*travel*) herumkommen; (*spread*) sich verbreiten. ● **get at** *vt* (*have access*) herankommen an (+ *acc*); (Ⓣ: *criticize*) anmachen Ⓣ. (*mean*) **what are you getting at?** worauf willst du hinaus? ● **get away** *vi* (*leave*) wegkommen; (*escape*) entkommen. ● **get back** *vi* zurückkommen; *vt* (*recover*) zurückbekommen; **get one's own back** sich revanchieren. ● **get by** *vi* vorbeikommen; (*manage*) sein Auskommen haben. ● **get down** *vi* heruntersteigen; *vt* (*depress*) deprimieren; **get down to** sich [heran]machen an (+ *acc*). ● **get in** *vi* (*into bus*) einsteigen; *vt* (*fetch*) hereinholen. ● **get off** *vi* (*dismount*) absteigen; (*from bus*) aussteigen; (*leave*) wegkommen; (*Jur*) freigesprochen werden; *vt* (*remove*) abbekommen. ● **get on** *vi* (*mount*) aufsteigen; (*to bus*) einsteigen; (*be on good terms*) gut auskommen (*with* mit + *dat*); (*make progress*) Fortschritte machen; **how are you getting on?** wie geht's? ● **get out** *vi* herauskommen; (*of car*) aussteigen; **get out of** (*avoid doing*) sich drücken um; *vt* (*take out*) herausholen; herausbekommen (*cork, stain*). ● **get over** *vi* hinübersteigen; *vt* (*fig*) hinwegkommen über (+ *acc*). ● **get round** *vi* herumkommen; **I never get round to it** ich komme nie dazu; *vt* herumkriegen; (*avoid*) umgehen. ● **get through** *vi* durchkommen. ● **get up** *vi* aufstehen

get: ~**away** n Flucht f. ~**-up** n Aufmachung f

ghastly /ˈgɑːstlɪ/ adj grässlich; (pale) blass

gherkin /ˈgɜːkɪn/ n Essiggurke f

ghost /gəʊst/ n Geist m, Gespenst nt. ~**ly** adj geisterhaft

ghoulish /ˈguːlɪʃ/ adj makaber

giant /ˈdʒaɪənt/ n Riese m ● adj riesig

gibberish /ˈdʒɪbərɪʃ/ n Kauderwelsch nt

giblets /ˈdʒɪblɪts/ npl Geflügelklein nt

giddiness /ˈgɪdɪnɪs/ n Schwindel m

giddy /ˈgɪdɪ/ adj schwindlig

gift /gɪft/ n Geschenk nt; (to charity) Gabe f; (talent) Begabung f. ~**ed** adj begabt

gigantic /dʒaɪˈgæntɪk/ adj riesig, riesengroß

giggle /ˈgɪgl/ n Kichern nt ● vi kichern

gild /gɪld/ vt vergolden

gilt /gɪlt/ adj vergoldet ● n Vergoldung f. ~**-edged** adj (Comm) mündelsicher

gimmick /ˈgɪmɪk/ n Trick m

gin /dʒɪn/ n Gin m

ginger /ˈdʒɪndʒə(r)/ adj rotblond; (cat) rot ● n Ingwer m. ~**bread** n Pfefferkuchen m

gingerly /ˈdʒɪndʒəlɪ/ adv vorsichtig

gipsy /ˈdʒɪpsɪ/ n = gypsy

giraffe /dʒɪˈrɑːf/ n Giraffe f

girder /ˈgɜːdə(r)/ n (Techn) Träger m

girl /gɜːl/ n Mädchen nt; (young woman) junge Frau f. ~ **band** n Mädchenband f. ~**friend** n Freundin f. ~**ish** adj mädchenhaft

gist /dʒɪst/ n the ~ das

Wesentliche

give /gɪv/ n Elastizität f ● v (pt gave, pp given) ● vt geben/(as present) schenken (to dat); (donate) spenden; (lecture) halten; (one's name) angeben ● vi geben; (yield) nachgeben. ~ **away** vt verschenken; (betray) verraten; (distribute) verteilen. ~ **back** vt zurückgeben. ~ **in** vt einreichen ● vi (yield) nachgeben. ~ **off** vt abgeben. ~ **up** vt/i aufgeben; ~ oneself up sich stellen. ~ **way** vi nachgeben; (Auto) die Vorfahrt beachten

glacier /ˈglæsɪə(r)/ n Gletscher m

glad /glæd/ adj froh (of über + acc)

gladly /ˈglædlɪ/ adv gern[e]

glamorous /ˈglæmərəs/ adj glanzvoll; (film star) glamourös

glamour /ˈglæmə(r)/ n [betörender] Glanz m

glance /glɑːns/ n [flüchtiger] Blick m ● vi ~ at einen Blick werfen auf (+ acc). ~ **up** vi aufblicken

gland /glænd/ n Drüse f

glare /gleə(r)/ n grelles Licht nt; (look) ärgerlicher Blick m ● vi ~ at böse ansehen

glaring /ˈgleərɪŋ/ adj grell; (mistake) krass

glass /glɑːs/ n Glas nt; (mirror) Spiegel m; ~es pl (spectacles) Brille f. ~**y** adj glasig

glaze /gleɪz/ n Glasur f

gleam /gliːm/ n Schein m ● vi glänzen

glib /glɪb/ adj (pej) gewandt

glid|e /glaɪd/ vi gleiten; (through the air) schweben. ~**er** n Segelflugzeug nt. ~**ing** n Segelfliegen nt

glimmer /ˈglɪmə(r)/ n Glimmen nt ● vi glimmen

glimpse /glɪmps/ vt flüchtig sehen

glint /glɪnt/ n Blitzen nt ● vi blitzen

g

glisten /'glɪsn/ vi glitzern

glitter /'glɪtə(r)/ vi glitzern

global /'gləʊbl/ adj global

globaliz|e /'gləʊbalaɪz/ vt globalisieren. **~ation** n Globalisierung f

globe /gləʊb/ n Kugel f; (map) Globus m

gloom /gluːm/ n Düsterkeit f; (fig) Pessimismus m

gloomy /'gluːmɪ/ adj, -ily adv düster; (fig) pessimistisch

glorif|y /'glɔːrɪfaɪ/ vt (pt/pp -ied) verherrlichen

glorious /'glɔːrɪəs/ adj herrlich; (deed, hero) glorreich

glory /'glɔːrɪ/ n Ruhm m; (splendour) Pracht f ● vi ~ in genießen

gloss /glɒs/ n Glanz m ● adj Glanz- ● vi ~ over beschönigen

glossary /'glɒsərɪ/ n Glossar nt

glossy /'glɒsɪ/ adj glänzend

glove /glʌv/ n Handschuh m

glow /gləʊ/ n Glut f; (of candle) Schein m ● vi glühen; (candle:) scheinen. **~ing** adj glühend; (account) begeistert

glucose /'gluːkəʊs/ n Traubenzucker m, Glukose f

glue /gluː/ n Klebstoff m ● vt (pres p gluing) kleben (to an + acc)

glum /glʌm/ adj (glummer, glummest) niedergeschlagen

glut /glʌt/ n Überfluss m (of an + dat)

glutton /'glʌtən/ n Vielfraß m

GM abbr (genetically modified); ~ crops/food gentechnisch veränderte Feldfrüchte/Nahrungsmittel

gnash /næʃ/ vt ~ one's teeth mit den Zähnen knirschen

gnat /næt/ n Mücke f

gnaw /nɔː/ vt/i nagen (at an + dat)

---

go /gəʊ/

3 sg pres tense goes; pt went; pp gone

● intransitive verb

····▸ gehen; (in vehicle) fahren. go by air fliegen. where are you going? wo gehst du hin? I'm going to France ich fahre nach Frankreich. go to the doctor's/dentist's zum Arzt/Zahnarzt gehen. go to the theatre/cinema ins Theater/Kino gehen. I must go to Paris/to the doctor's ich muss nach Paris/zum Arzt. go shopping einkaufen gehen. go swimming schwimmen gehen. go to see s.o. jdn besuchen [gehen]

····▸ (leave) weggehen; (on journey) abfahren. I must go now ich muss jetzt gehen. we're going on Friday wir fahren am Freitag

····▸ (work, function) (engine, clock) gehen

····▸ (become) werden. go deaf taub werden. go mad verrückt werden. he went red er wurde rot

····▸ (pass) (time) vergehen

····▸ (disappear) weggehen; (coat, hat, stain) verschwinden. my headache/my coat/the stain has gone mein Kopfweh/mein Mantel/der Fleck ist weg

····▸ (turn out, progress) gehen; verlaufen. everything's going very well alles geht od verläuft sehr gut. how did the party go? wie war die Party? go smoothly/according to plan reibungslos/planmäßig verlaufen

····▸ (*match*) zusammenpassen.
the two colours don't go
[together] die beiden Farben
passen nicht zusammen

····▸ (*cease to function*) kaputtgehen; (*fuse*) durchbrennen. his
memory is going sein Gedächtnis lässt nach

● *auxiliary verb*

····▸ be going to werden + *inf.*
it's going to rain es wird regnen. I'm not going to ich werde
es nicht tun

● *noun*

pl goes

····▸ (*turn*) it's your go du bist
jetzt an der Reihe *od* dran

····▸ (*attempt*) Versuch. have a
go at doing sth versuchen,
etw zu tun. have another go!
versuch's noch mal!

····▸ (*energy, drive*) Energie

····▸ (*in phrases*) on the go auf
Trab. make a go of sth das
Beste aus etw machen

● *phrasal verbs*

● **go across** *vi* hinübergehen/-
fahren; *vt* überqueren. ● **go
after** *vt* (*pursue*) jagen. ● **go
away** *vi* weggehen/-fahren; (*on
holiday or business*) verreisen.
● **go back** *vi* zurückgehen/-fah-
ren. ● **go back on** *vt* nicht
[ein]halten (*promise*). ● **go by**
vi vorbeigehen/-fahren; (*time*)
vergehen. ● **go down** *vi* hinun-
tergehen/-fahren; (*sun, ship*)
untergehen; (*prices*) fallen;
(*temperature, swelling*) zurückgehen. ● **go for** *vt* holen; (⊞:
attack) losgehen auf (+ *acc*).
● **go in** *vi* hineingehen/-fahren;
● **go in for** teilnehmen an (+
dat) (*competition*); (*take up*)

sich verlegen auf (+ *acc*). ● **go
off** *vi* weggehen/-fahren; (*alarm
clock*) klingeln; (*alarm, gun,
bomb*) losgehen; (*light*) ausgehen; (*go bad*) schlecht werden;
vt: go off sth von etw abkommen. ● **go off well** gut verlaufen. ● **go on** *vi* weitergehen/-
fahren; (*light*) angehen; (*talking*) fortfahren; (*happen*) vorgehen. ● **go on at** ⊞ herumnör-
geln an (+ *dat*). ● **go out** *vi*
(*from home*) ausgehen; (*leave*)
hinausgehen/-fahren; (*fire,
light*) ausgehen; go out to
work/for a meal arbeiten/
essen gehen; go out with s.o.
(⊞: *date s.o.*) mit jdm gehen
⊞. ● **go over** *vi* hinüberge-
hen/-fahren; *vt* (*rehearse*)
durchgehen. ● **go round** *vi*
herumgehen/-fahren; (*visit*) vorbeigehen; (*turn*) sich drehen;
(*be enough*) reichen. ● **go
through** *vi* durchgehen/-fah-
ren; *vt* (*suffer*) durchmachen;
(*rehearse*) durchgehen; (*bags*)
durchsuchen. ● **go through
with** *vt* zu Ende machen. ● **go
under** *vi* untergehen/-fahren;
(*fail*) scheitern. ● **go up** *vi* hin-
aufgehen/-fahren; (*lift*) hoch-
fahren; (*prices*) steigen. ● **go
without** *vt*: go without sth
auf etw (*acc*) verzichten; *vi* darauf verzichten

'**go-ahead** *adj* fortschrittlich; (*en-
terprising*) unternehmend ● *n* (*fig*)
grünes Licht *nt*

goal /gəʊl/ *n* Ziel *nt*; (*sport*) Tor *nt*.
~**keeper** *n* Torwart *m*. ~**post** *n*
Torpfosten *m*

goat /gəʊt/ *n* Ziege *f*

gobble /'gɒbl/ *vt* hinunterschlingen

God, god /gɒd/ *n* Gott *m*

god: ~**child** n Patenkind nt.
~**daughter** n Patentochter f.
~**dess** n Göttin f. ~**father** n Pate
m. ~**mother** n Patin f. ~**parents**
npl Paten pl. ~**send** n Segen m.
~**son** n Patensohn m

goggles /'gɒglz/ npl Schutzbrille f

going /'gəʊɪŋ/ adj (price, rate) gängig; (concern) gut gehend ● n **it is
hard** ~ es ist schwierig

gold /gəʊld/ n Gold nt ● adj golden

golden /'gəʊldn/ adj golden. ~'
wedding n goldene Hochzeit f

gold: ~**fish** n inv Goldfisch m.
~**mine** n Goldgrube f. ~**-plated**
adj vergoldet. ~**smith** n Gold-
schmied m

golf /gɒlf/ n Golf nt

golf: ~**-club** n Golfklub m; (implement) Golfschläger m. ~**course** n
Golfplatz m. ~**er** m Golfspiele-
r(in) m(f)

gone /gɒn/ see go

good /gʊd/ adj (better, best) gut;
(well-behaved) brav, artig; ~ at gut
in (+ dat); a ~ deal ziemlich viel; ~
morning/evening guten Morgen/
Abend ● n for ~ für immer; do ~
Gutes tun; do s.o. ~ jdm gut tun;
it's no ~ es ist nutzlos; (hopeless)
da ist nichts zu machen

goodbye /gʊd'baɪ/ int auf Wiedersehen; (Teleph, Radio) auf Wieder-
hören

good: G~ '**Friday** n Karfreitag m.
~-'**looking** adj gut aussehend.
~-'**natured** adj gutmütig

goodness /'gʊdnɪs/ n Güte f;
thank ~! Gott sei Dank!

goods /gʊdz/ npl Waren pl. ~
train n Güterzug m

good'will n Wohlwollen nt;
(Comm) Goodwill m

gooey /'gu:ɪ/ adj ⓘ klebrig

google /'gu:gl/ ⊛ vt, vi googeln

goose /gu:s/ n (pl geese) Gans f

gooseberry /'gʊzbərɪ/ n Stachel-
beere f

goose: /gu:s/ ~**-flesh** n, ~**-pimp-
les** npl Gänsehaut f

gorge /gɔːdʒ/ n (Geog) Schlucht f
● vt ~ oneself sich vollessen

gorgeous /'gɔːdʒəs/ adj prachtvoll; ⓘ herrlich

gorilla /gə'rɪlə/ n Gorilla m

gormless /'gɔːmlɪs/ adj ⓘ doof

gorse /gɔːs/ n inv Stechginster m

gory /'gɔːrɪ/ adj blutig; (story) blut-
rünstig

gosh /gɒʃ/ int ⓘ Mensch!

gospel /'gɒspl/ n Evangelium nt

gossip /'gɒsɪp/ n Klatsch m; (person) Klatschbase f ● vi klatschen

got /gɒt/ see get; **have** ~ haben;
have ~ **to** müssen; **have** ~ **to do**
sth etw tun müssen

Gothic /'gɒθɪk/ adj gotisch

gotten /'gɒtn/ see get

goulash /'gu:læʃ/ n Gulasch m

gourmet /'gʊəmeɪ/ n Feinschme-
cker m

govern /'gʌvn/ vt/i regieren; (determine) bestimmen

government /'gʌvnmənt/ n Regierung f

governor /'gʌvnə(r)/ n Gouver-
neur m; (on board) Vorstandsmit-
glied nt; (of prison) Direktor m; (ⓘ:
boss) Chef m

gown /gaʊn/ n [elegantes] Kleid
nt; (Univ, Jur) Talar m

GP abbr general practitioner

GPS abbr (Global Positioning System) GPS nt

grab /græb/ vt (pt/pp grabbed) ergreifen; ~ [hold of] packen

grace /greɪs/ n Anmut f; (before
meal) Tischgebet nt; **three days'** ~
drei Tage Frist. ~**ful** adj anmutig

gracious /'greɪʃəs/ adj gnädig; (elegant) vornehm

grade /greɪd/ n Stufe f; (Comm) Güteklasse f; (Sch) Note f; (Amer, Sch: class) Klasse f; (Amer) = gradient ● vt einstufen; (Comm) sortieren. **~ crossing** n (Amer) Bahnübergang m

gradient /'greɪdɪənt/ n Steigung f; (downward) Gefälle nt

gradual /'grædʒʊəl/ adj allmählich

graduate /'grædʒʊət/ n Akademiker(in) m(f)

graffiti /grə'fiːti/ npl Graffiti pl

graft /grɑːft/ n (Bot) Pfropfreis nt; (Med) Transplantat nt; (𝕀: hard work) Plackerei f

grain /greɪn/ n (sand, salt, rice) Korn nt; (cereals) Getreide nt; (in wood) Maserung f

gram /græm/ n Gramm nt

grammar /'græmə(r)/ n Grammatik f. **~ school** n ≈ Gymnasium nt

grammatical /grə'mætɪkl/ adj grammatisch

grand /grænd/ adj (-er, -est) großartig

grandad /'grændæd/ n 𝕀 Opa m

grandchild n Enkelkind nt

granddaughter n Enkelin f

grandeur /'grændʒə(r)/ n Pracht f

grandfather n Großvater m. **~ clock** n Standuhr f

grandiose /'grændɪəʊs/ adj grandios

grand: ~mother n Großmutter f. **~parents** npl Großeltern pl. **~piano** n Flügel m. **~son** n Enkel m. **~stand** n Tribüne f

granite /'grænɪt/ n Granit m

granny /'grænɪ/ n 𝕀 Oma f

grant /grɑːnt/ n Subvention f; (Univ) Studienbeihilfe f ● vt gewähren; (admit) zugeben; take sth for

~ed etw als selbstverständlich hinnehmen

grape /greɪp/ n [Wein]traube f; bunch of **~s** [ganze] Weintraube f

grapefruit /'greɪp-/ n invar Grapefruit f

graph /grɑːf/ n grafische Darstellung f

graphic /'græfɪk/ adj, **-ally** adv grafisch; (vivid) anschaulich

'graph paper n Millimeterpapier nt

grapple /'græpl/ vi ringen

grasp /grɑːsp/ n Griff m ● vt ergreifen; (understand) begreifen. **~ing** adj habgierig

grass /grɑːs/ n Gras nt; (lawn) Rasen m. **~hopper** n Heuschrecke f

grassy /'grɑːsɪ/ adj grasig

grate¹ /greɪt/ n Feuerrost m; (hearth) Kamin m

grate² vt (Culin) reiben

grateful /'greɪtfl/ adj dankbar (to dat)

grater /'greɪtə(r)/ n (Culin) Reibe f

gratify /'grætɪfaɪ/ vt (pt/pp -ied) befriedigen. **~ing** adj erfreulich

gratis /'grɑːtɪs/ adv gratis

gratitude /'grætɪtjuːd/ n Dankbarkeit f

gratuitous /grə'tjuːɪtəs/ adj (uncalled for) überflüssig

grave¹ /greɪv/ adj (-r, -st) ernst; **~ly ill** schwer krank

grave² n Grab nt. **~-digger** n Totengräber m

gravel /'grævl/ n Kies m

grave: ~stone n Grabstein m. **~yard** n Friedhof m

gravity /'grævɪtɪ/ n Ernst m; (force) Schwerkraft f

gravy /'greɪvɪ/ n [Braten]soße f

gray /greɪ/ adj (Amer) = grey

graze¹ /greɪz/ vi (animal:) weiden

graze² n Schürfwunde f ● vt (car) streifen; (knee) aufschürfen

grease /griːs/ n Fett nt; (lubricant) Schmierfett nt ● vt einfetten; (lubricate) schmieren

greasy /griːsɪ/ adj fettig

great /greɪt/ adj (-er, -est) groß; (Ⅱ: marvellous) großartig

great: ∼'aunt n Großtante f. G∼ 'Britain n Großbritannien nt. ∼'grandchildren npl Urenkel pl. ∼'grandfather n Urgroßvater m. ∼'grandmother n Urgroßmutter f

great|ly /greɪtlɪ/ adv sehr. ∼ness n Größe f

great-'uncle n Großonkel m

Greece /griːs/ n Griechenland nt

greed /griːd/ n [Hab]gier f

greedy /griːdɪ/ adj , -ily adv gierig

Greek /griːk/ adj griechisch ● n Grieche m/Griechin f; (Lang) Griechisch nt

green /griːn/ adj (-er, -est) grün; (fig) unerfahren ● n Grün nt; (grass) Wiese f; ∼s pl Kohl m; **the G∼s** pl (Pol) die Grünen pl

---

green card Ein offizielles Dokument, das nichtamerikanische Bürger zur Erwerbstätigkeit in den USA berechtigt. Die green card braucht jeder, der beabsichtigt, eine feste Stelle in den USA anzutreten. In Europa ist die grüne Karte ein vom Versicherungsverband ausgestellter grüner Ausweis, mit dem ein Kraftfahrer beim Grenzübertritt nachweist, dass er haftpflichtversichert ist.

---

greenery /griːnərɪ/ n Grün nt

green: ∼fly n Blattlaus f. ∼grocer n Obst- und Gemüsehändler m. ∼house n Gewächshaus nt

Greenland /griːnlənd/ n Grönland nt

greet /griːt/ vt grüßen; (welcome) begrüßen. ∼ing n Gruß m; (welcome) Begrüßung f

grew /gruː/ see grow

grey /greɪ/ adj (-er, -est) grau ● n Grau nt ● vi grau werden. ∼hound n Windhund m

grid /grɪd/ n Gitter nt

grief /griːf/ n Trauer f

grievance /griːvəns/ n Beschwerde f

grieve /griːv/ vi trauern (for um)

grill /grɪl/ n Gitter nt; (Culin) Grill m; mixed ∼ Gemischtes nt vom Grill ● vt/i grillen; (interrogate) [streng] verhören

grille /grɪl/ n Gitter nt

grim /grɪm/ adj (grimmer, grimmest) ernst; (determination) verbissen

grimace /grɪˈmeɪs/ n Grimasse f ● vi Grimassen schneiden

grime /graɪm/ n Schmutz m

grimy /graɪmɪ/ adj schmutzig

grin /grɪn/ n Grinsen nt ● vi (pt/pp grinned) grinsen

grind /graɪnd/ n (Ⅱ: hard work) Plackerei f ● vt (pt/pp ground) mahlen; (smooth, sharpen) schleifen; (Amer: mince) durchdrehen

grip /grɪp/ n Griff m; (bag) Reisetasche f ● vt (pt/pp gripped) ergreifen; (hold) festhalten

gripping /grɪpɪŋ/ adj fesselnd

grisly /grɪzlɪ/ adj grausig

gristle /grɪsl/ n Knorpel m

grit /grɪt/ n [grober] Sand m; (for roads) Streugut nt; (courage) Mut m ● vt (pt/pp gritted) streuen (road)

groan /grəʊn/ n Stöhnen nt ● vi stöhnen

grocer /grəʊsə(r)/ n Lebensmittel-

groin | guilty

händler m; ~'s [shop] Lebensmittelgeschäft nt. ~**ies** npl Lebensmittel pl

groin /grɔɪn/ n (Anat) Leiste f

groom /gru:m/ n Bräutigam m; (for horse) Pferdepfleger(in) m(f) ● vt striegeln (horse)

groove /gru:v/ n Rille f

grope /grəʊp/ vi tasten (for nach)

gross /grəʊs/ adj (-er, -est) fett; (coarse) derb; (glaring) grob; (Comm) brutto; (salary, weight) Brutto-. ~**ly** adv (very) sehr

grotesque /grəʊˈtesk/ adj grotesk

ground[1] /gratzn/ see grind

ground[2] n Boden m; (terrain) Gelände nt; (reason) Grund m; (Amer, Electr) Erde f. ~**s** pl (park) Anlagen pl; (of coffee) Satz m

ground: ~ **floor** n Erdgeschoss nt. ~**ing** n Grundlage f. ~**less** adj grundlos. ~**sheet** n Bodenplane f. ~**work** n Vorarbeiten fpl

group /gru:p/ n Gruppe f ● vt gruppieren ● vi sich gruppieren

grouse[1] vi 🔢 meckern

grovel /ˈgrɒvl/ vi (pt/pp grovelled) kriechen

grow /grəʊ/ v (pt grew, pp grown) ● vi wachsen; (become) werden; (increase) zunehmen ● vt anbauen. ~ **up** vi aufwachsen; (town:) entstehen

growl /graʊl/ n Knurren nt ● vi knurren

grown /grəʊn/ see grow. ~-**up** adj erwachsen ● n Erwachsene(r) m/f

growth /grəʊθ/ n Wachstum nt; (increase) Zunahme f; (Med) Gewächs nt

grub /grʌb/ n (larva) Made f; (🔢 food) Essen nt

grubby /ˈgrʌbɪ/ adj schmuddelig

grudg|e /grʌdʒ/ n Groll m ● vt ~e s.o. sth jdm etw missgönnen. ~**ing** adj widerwillig

gruelling /ˈgruːəlɪŋ/ adj strapaziös

gruesome /ˈgruːsəm/ adj grausig

gruff /grʌf/ adj barsch

grumble /ˈgrʌmbl/ vi schimpfen (at mit)

grumpy /ˈgrʌmpɪ/ adj griesgrämig

grunt /grʌnt/ n Grunzen nt ● vi grunzen

guarantee /gærənˈtiː/ n Garantie f; (document) Garantieschein m ● vt garantieren; garantieren für (quality, success)

guard /gɑːd/ n Wache f; (security) Wächter m; (on train) ≈ Zugführer m; (Techn) Schutz m; **be on** ~ Wache stehen; **on one's** ~ auf der Hut ● vt bewachen; (protect) schützen ● vi ~ **against** sich hüten vor (+ dat). ~-**dog** n Wachhund m

guarded /ˈgɑːdɪd/ adj vorsichtig

guardian /ˈgɑːdɪən/ n Vormund m

guess /ges/ n Vermutung f ● vt erraten ● vi raten; (Amer: believe) glauben. ~**work** n Vermutung f

guest /gest/ n Gast m. ~-**house** n Pension f

guidance /ˈgaɪdəns/ n Führung f, Leitung f; (advice) Beratung f

guide /gaɪd/ n Führer(in) m(f); (book) Führer m; [**Girl**] **G**~ Pfadfinderin f ● vt führen, leiten. ~**book** n Führer m

guided /ˈgaɪdɪd/ adj ~ **tour** Führung f

guide: ~-**dog** n Blindenhund m. ~**lines** npl Richtlinien pl

guilt /gɪlt/ n Schuld f. ~**ily** adv schuldbewusst

guilty /ˈgɪltɪ/ adj adj schuldig (of gen); (look) schuldbewusst; (conscience) schlecht

g

guinea-pig /'gɪnɪ-/ n Meerschweinchen nt; (person) Versuchskaninchen nt

guitar /gɪ'tɑː(r)/ n Gitarre f. **~ist** n Gitarrist(in) m(f)

gulf /gʌlf/ n (Geog) Golf m; (fig) Kluft f

gull /gʌl/ n Möwe f

gullible /'gʌlɪbl/ adj leichtgläubig

gully /'gʌlɪ/ n Schlucht f; (drain) Rinne f

gulp /gʌlp/ n Schluck m ● vi schlucken ● vt **~ down** hinunterschlucken

gum¹ /gʌm/ n (also pl -s) (Anat) Zahnfleisch nt

gum² n Gummi[harz] nt; (glue) Klebstoff m; (chewing gum) Kaugummi m

gummed /gʌmd/ ● adj (label) gummiert

gun /gʌn/ n Schusswaffe f; (pistol) Pistole f; (rifle) Gewehr nt; (cannon) Geschütz nt

gun: ~fire n Geschützfeuer nt. **~man** bewaffneter Bandit m

gunner /'gʌnə(r)/ n Artillerist m

gunpowder n Schießpulver nt

gurgle /'gɜːgl/ vi gluckern; (of baby) glucksen

gush /gʌʃ/ vi strömen; (enthuse) schwärmen (over von)

gust /gʌst/ n (of wind) Windstoß m; (Naut) Bö f

gusto /'gʌstəʊ/ n **with ~** mit Schwung

gusty /'gʌstɪ/ adj böig

gut /gʌt/ n Darm m; **~s** pl Eingeweide pl; (▯: courage) Schneid m ● vt (pt/pp gutted) (Culin) ausnehmen; **~ted by fire** ausgebrannt

gutter /'gʌtə(r)/ n Rinnstein m; (fig) Gosse f; (on roof) Dachrinne f

guy /gaɪ/ n ▯ Kerl m

guzzle /'gʌzl/ vt/i schlingen; (drink) schlürfen

gym /dʒɪm/ n ▯ Turnhalle f; (gymnastics) Turnen nt

gymnasium /dʒɪm'neɪzɪəm/ n Turnhalle f

gymnast /'dʒɪmnæst/ n Turner(in) m(f). **~ics** n Turnen nt

gym shoes pl Turnschuhe pl

gynaecolog|ist /gaɪnɪ'kɒlədʒɪst/ n Frauenarzt m/-ärztin f. **~y** n Gynäkologie f

gypsy /'dʒɪpsɪ/ n Zigeuner(in) m(f)

Hh

habit /'hæbɪt/ n Gewohnheit f; (Relig: costume) Ordenstracht f; **be in the ~** die Angewohnheit haben (of zu)

habitat /'hæbɪtæt/ n Habitat nt

habitation /hæbɪ'teɪʃn/ n **unfit for human ~** für Wohnzwecke ungeeignet

habitual /hə'bɪtjʊəl/ adj gewohnt; (inveterate) gewohnheitsmäßig. **~ly** adv gewohnheitsmäßig; (constantly) ständig

hack¹ /hæk/ n (writer) Schreiberling m; (hired horse) Mietpferd nt

hack² vt hacken; **~ to pieces** zerhacken

hackneyed /'hæknɪd/ adj abgedroschen

'hacksaw n Metallsäge f

had /hæd/ see have

haddock /'hædək/ n inv Schellfisch m

haggard /'hægəd/ adj abgehärmt

haggle /'hægl/ vi feilschen

(over um)

hail¹ /heɪl/ vt begrüßen; herbeirufen (taxi) ● vi ~ from kommen aus

hail² n Hagel m ● vi hageln.
~**stone** n Hagelkorn nt

hair /heə(r)/ n Haar nt; wash one's ~ sich (dat) die Haare waschen

hair: ~**brush** n Haarbürste f. ~**cut** n Haarschnitt m; have a ~**cut** sich (dat) die Haare schneiden lassen.
~**do** n 🗓 Frisur f. ~**dresser** n Friseur m/Friseuse f. ~**drier** n Haartrockner m; (hand-held) Föhn m.
~**pin** n Haarnadel f. ~**pin 'bend** n Haarnadelkurve f. ~**-raising** adj haarsträubend. ~**style** n Frisur f

hairy /heərɪ/ adj behaart; (excessively) haarig; (🗓 frightening) brenzlig

hake /heɪk/ n inv Seehecht m

half /haːf/ n (pl halves) Hälfte f; cut in ~ halbieren; one and a ~ eineinhalb, anderthalb; ~ a dozen ein halbes Dutzend; an hour eine halbe Stunde ● adj & adv halb; ~ past two halb drei; [at] ~ price zum halben Preis

half: ~**-hearted** adj lustlos.
~**-term** n schulfreie Tage nach dem halben Trimester. ~**-'timbered** adj Fachwerk-. ~**-'time** n (Sport) Halbzeit f. ~**-'way** adj the ~**-way mark/stage** die Hälfte ● adv auf halbem Weg

halibut /hælɪbət/ n inv Heilbutt m

hall /hɔːl/ n Halle f; (room) Saal m; (Sch) Aula f; (entrance) Flur m; (mansion) Gutshaus nt; ~ of residence (Univ) Studentenheim nt

'hallmark n [Feingehalts]stempel m; (fig) Kennzeichen nt (of für)

hallo /hə'ləʊ/ int [guten] Tag! 🗓 hallo!

hallucination /həluːsɪ'neɪʃn/ n Halluzination f

halo /heɪləʊ/ n (pl -es) Heiligenschein m; (Astronomy) Hof m

halt /hɔːlt/ n Halt m; come to a ~ stehen bleiben; (traffic:) zum Stillstand kommen ● vi Halt machen; ~! halt! ~**ing** adj, ~**ly** adv zögernd

halve /haːv/ vt halbieren; (reduce) um die Hälfte reduzieren

ham /hæm/ n Schinken m

hamburger /hæmbɜːgə(r)/ n Hamburger m

hammer /hæmə(r)/ n Hammer m ● vt/i hämmern (at an + acc)

hammock /hæmək/ n Hängematte f

hamper¹ vt behindern

hamster /hæmstə(r)/ n Hamster m

hand /hænd/ n Hand f; (of clock) Zeiger m; (writing) Handschrift f; (worker) Arbeiter(in) m(f); (Cards) Blatt nt; on the one/other ~ einer-/andererseits; out of ~ außer Kontrolle; (summarily) kurzerhand; in ~ unter Kontrolle; (available) verfügbar; give s.o. a ~ jdm behilflich sein ● vt reichen (to dat). ~ **in** vt abgeben. ~ **out** vt austeilen. ~ **over** vt überreichen

hand: ~**bag** n Handtasche f. ~**brake** n Handbremse f. ~**book** n Handbuch nt. ~**cuffs** npl Handschellen pl. ~**ful** n Handvoll f; be [quite] a ~**ful** 🗓 nicht leicht zu haben sein

handicap /hændɪkæp/ n Behinderung f; (Sport & fig) Handikap nt.
~**ped** adj mentally/physically ~**ped** geistig/körperlich behindert

handkerchief /hæŋkətʃɪf/ n (pl ~s & -chieves) Taschentuch nt

handle /hændl/ n Griff m; (of door) Klinke f; (of cup) Henkel m; (of broom) Stiel m ● vt handhaben; (treat) umgehen mit; (touch) anfas-

h

sen. ∼**bars** *npl* Lenkstange *f*

hand: ∼**made** *adj* handgemacht. ∼**shake** *n* Händedruck *m*

handsome /'hænsəm/ *adj* gut aussehend; (*generous*) großzügig; (*large*) beträchtlich

hand: ∼**writing** *n* Handschrift *f*. ∼**'written** *adj* handgeschrieben

handy /'hændɪ/ *adj* handlich; (*person*) geschickt; **have/keep** ∼ griffbereit haben/halten

hang /hæŋ/ *vt/i* (*pt/pp* hung) hängen; ∼ **wallpaper** tapezieren ●*vt* (*pt/pp* hanged) hängen (*criminal*) ●**n get the** ∼ **of it** 𝕀 den Dreh herauskriegen. ∼ **about** *vi* sich herumdrücken. ∼ **on** *vi* sich festhalten (**to** an + *dat*); (𝕀: *wait*) warten. ∼ **out** *vi* heraushängen; (𝕀: *live*) wohnen ●*vt* draußen aufhängen (*washing*). ∼ **up** *vt/i* aufhängen

hangar /'hæŋə(r)/ *n* Flugzeughalle *f*

hanger /'hæŋə(r)/ *n* [Kleider]bügel *m*

hang: ∼**glider** *n* Drachenflieger *m*. ∼**gliding** *n* Drachenfliegen *nt*. ∼**man** *n* Henker *m*. ∼**over** *n* 𝕀 Kater *m* 𝕀. ∼**up** *n* 𝕀 Komplex *m*

hanker /'hæŋkə(r)/ *vi* ∼ **after sth** sich (*dat*) etw wünschen

hanky /'hæŋkɪ/ *n* 𝕀 Taschentuch *nt*

haphazard /hæp'hæzəd/ *adj* planlos

happen /'hæpn/ *vi* geschehen, passieren; **I** ∼**ed to be there** ich war zufällig da; **what has** ∼**ed to him?** was ist mit ihm? (*become of*) was ist aus ihm geworden? ∼**ing** *n* Ereignis *nt*

happily /'hæpɪlɪ/ *adv* glücklich; (*fortunately*) glücklicherweise. ∼**ness** *n* Glück *nt*

happy /'hæpɪ/ *adj* glücklich.

∼-**go-'lucky** *adj* sorglos

harass /'hærəs/ *vt* schikanieren. ∼**ed** *adj* abgehetzt. ∼**ment** *n* Schikane *f*; (*sexual*) Belästigung *f*

harbour /'hɑːbə(r)/ *n* Hafen *m*

hard /hɑːd/ *adj* (-**er**, -**est**) hart; (*difficult*) schwer; ∼ **of hearing** schwerhörig ●*adv* hart; (*work*) schwer; (*pull*) kräftig; (*rain, snow*) stark; **be** ∼ **up** 𝕀 knapp bei Kasse sein

hard: ∼**back** *n* gebundene Ausgabe *f*. ∼**board** *n* Hartfaserplatte *f*. ∼-**boiled** *adj* hart gekocht ∼**disk** *n* Festplatte *f*

harden /'hɑːdn/ *vi* hart werden

hard-'hearted *adj* hartherzig

hard|ly /'hɑːdlɪ/ *adv* kaum; ∼**ly ever** kaum [jemals]. ∼**ness** *n* Härte *f*. ∼**ship** *n* Not *f*

hard: ∼ **'shoulder** *n* (*Auto*) Randstreifen *m*. ∼**ware** *n* Haushaltswaren *pl*; (*Computing*) Hardware *f*. ∼-**'wearing** *adj* strapazierfähig. ∼-**'working** *adj* fleißig

hardy /'hɑːdɪ/ *adj* abgehärtet; (*plant*) winterhart

hare /heə(r)/ *n* Hase *m*

harm /hɑːm/ *n* Schaden *m*; **it won't do any** ∼ **es kann nichts schaden** ●*vt* **s.o.** jdm etwas antun. ∼**ful** *adj* schädlich. ∼**less** *adj* harmlos

harmonious /hɑː'məʊnɪəs/ *adj* harmonisch

harmon|ize /'hɑːmənaɪz/ *vi* (*fig*) harmonieren. ∼**y** *n* Harmonie *f*

harness /'hɑːnɪs/ *n* Geschirr *nt*; (*of parachute*) Gurtwerk *nt* ●*vt* anschirren (*horse*); (*use*) nutzbar machen

harp /hɑːp/ *n* Harfe *f*. ∼**ist** *n* Harfenist(in) *m(f)*

harpsichord /'hɑːpsɪkɔːd/ *n* Cembalo *nt*

harrowing /'hærəʊŋ/ *adj*

grauenhaft

harsh /hɑːʃ/ *adj* (-er, -est) hart; (*voice*) rau; (*light*) grell. **∼ness** *n* Härte *f*; Rauheit *f*

harvest /ˈhɑːvɪst/ *n* Ernte *f* ● *vt* ernten

has /hæz/ *see* have

hassle /ˈhæsl/ *n* ① Ärger *m* ● *vt* schikanieren

haste /heɪst/ *n* Eile *f*

hasten /ˈheɪsn/ *vi* sich beeilen (to zu); (*go quickly*) eilen ● *vt* beschleunigen

hasty /ˈheɪstɪ/ *adj* , **-ily** *adv* hastig; (*decision*) voreilig

hat /hæt/ *n* Hut *m*; (*knitted*) Mütze *f*

hatch[1] /hætʃ/ *n* (*for food*) Durchreiche *f*; (*Naut*) Luke *f*

hatch[2] *vi* ∼[out] ausschlüpfen ● *vt* ausbrüten

'hatchback *n* (*Auto*) Modell *nt* mit Hecktür

hate /heɪt/ *n* Hass *m* ● *vt* hassen. **∼ful** *adj* abscheulich

hatred /ˈheɪtrɪd/ *n* Hass *m*

haughty /ˈhɔːtɪ/ *adj* , **-ily** *adv* hochmütig

haul /hɔːl/ *n* (*loot*) Beute *f* ● *vt/i* ziehen (on an + *dat*)

haunt /hɔːnt/ *n* Lieblingsaufenthalt *m* ● *vt* umgehen in (+ *dat*); **this house is ∼ed** in diesem Haus spukt es

---

have /hæv/, *unbetont* /həv/, /əv/

3 *sg pres tense* **has**; *pt and pp* **had**

● *transitive verb*
····▸ (*possess*) haben. he has [got] a car er hat ein Auto. she has [got] a brother sie

hat einen Bruder. we have [got] five minutes wir haben fünf Minuten

····▸ (*eat*) essen; (*drink*) trinken; (*smoke*) rauchen. have a cup of tea eine Tasse Tee trinken. have a pizza eine Pizza essen. have a cigarette eine Zigarette rauchen. have breakfast/dinner/lunch frühstücken/zu Abend essen/zu Mittag essen

····▸ (*take esp. in shop, restaurant*) nehmen. I'll have the soup/the red dress ich nehme die Suppe/das rote Kleid. have a cigarette! nehmen Sie eine Zigarette!

····▸ (*get, receive*) bekommen. I had a letter from her ich bekam einen Brief von ihr. have a baby ein Baby bekommen

····▸ (*suffer*) haben (*illness, pain, disappointment*); erleiden (*shock*)

····▸ (*organize*) have a party eine Party veranstalten. have a meeting sie hielten eine Versammlung ab

····▸ (*take part in*) have a game of football Fußball spielen. have a swim schwimmen

····▸ (*as guest*) have s.o. to stay jdn zu Besuch haben

····▸ have had it ① (*thing*) ausgedient haben; (*person*) geliefert sein. you've had it now jetzt ist es aus

····▸ have sth done etw machen lassen. we had the house painted wir haben das Haus malen lassen. have a dress made sich (*dat*) ein Kleid machen lassen. have a tooth out sich (*dat*) einen Zahn ziehen lassen. have one's hair cut sich (*dat*) die Haare schneiden lassen

····▸ have to do sth etw tun

h

müssen. I have to go now ich muss jetzt gehen

● **auxiliary verb**

····▸ (forming perfect and past perfect tenses) haben; (with verbs of motion and some others) sein. I have seen him ich habe ihn gesehen. he has never been there er ist nie da gewesen. I had gone ich war gegangen. if I had known ... wenn ich gewusst hätte ...

····▸ (in tag questions) nicht wahr. you've met her, haven't you? du kennst sie, nicht wahr?

····▸ (in short answers) Have you seen the film? — Yes, I have Hast du den Film gesehen? — Ja [, stimmt]

● **have on** vt (be wearing) anhaben; (dupe) anführen

havoc /ˈhævək/ n Verwüstung f

hawk /hɔːk/ n Falke m

hawthorn /ˈhɔː-/ n Hagedorn m

hay /heɪ/ n Heu nt. ~ **fever** n Heuschnupfen m. ~ **stack** n Heuschober m

hazard /ˈhæzəd/ n Gefahr f; (risk) Risiko nt ● vt riskieren. ~**ous** adj gefährlich; (risky) riskant

haze /heɪz/ n Dunst m

hazel /ˈheɪzl/ n Haselbusch m. ~**nut** n Haselnuss f

hazy /ˈheɪzɪ/ adj dunstig; (fig) unklar

he /hiː/ pron er

head /hed/ n Kopf m; (chief) Oberhaupt nt; (of firm) Chef(in) m(f); (of school) Schulleiter(in) m(f); (on beer) Schaumkrone f; (of bed) Kopfende nt; ~ **first** kopfüber ● vt anführen; (Sport) köpfen (ball) ● vi ~ **for** zusteuern auf (+ acc). ~**ache** n Kopfschmerzen pl

head|er /ˈhedə(r)/ n Kopfball m; (dive) Kopfsprung m. ~**ing** n Überschrift f

head: ~**lamp**, ~**light** n (Auto) Scheinwerfer m. ~**line** n Schlagzeile f. ~**long** adv kopfüber. ~**master** n Schulleiter m. ~**mistress** n Schulleiterin f. ~**on** adj & adv frontal. ~**phones** npl Kopfhörer m. ~**quarters** npl Hauptquartier nt; (Pol) Zentrale f. ~**rest** n Kopfstütze f. ~**room** n lichte Höhe f. ~**scarf** n Kopftuch nt. ~**strong** adj eigenwillig. ~**way** n make ~**way** Fortschritte machen. ~**word** n Stichwort nt

heady /ˈhedɪ/ adj berauschend

heal /hiːl/ vt/i heilen

health /helθ/ n Gesundheit f

health: ~ **farm** n Schönheitsfarm f. ~ **foods** npl Reformkost f. ~**food shop** n Reformhaus nt. ~ **insurance** n Krankenversicherung f

healthy /ˈhelθɪ/ adj , -**ily** adv gesund

heap /hiːp/ n Haufen m; ~**s** 🆒 jede Menge ● vt ~ [up] häufen

hear /hɪə(r)/ vt/i (pt/pp heard) hören; ~,~! hört, hört! he would not ~ of it er ließ es nicht zu

hearing /ˈhɪərɪŋ/ n Gehör nt; (Jur) Verhandlung f. ~**aid** n Hörgerät nt

hearse /hɜːs/ n Leichenwagen m

heart /hɑːt/ n Herz nt; (courage) Mut m; ~**s** pl (Cards) Herz nt; by ~ auswendig

heart: ~**ache** n Kummer m. ~**attack** n Herzanfall m. ~**beat** n Herzschlag m. ~**breaking** adj herzzerreißend. ~**broken** adj untröstlich. ~**burn** n Sodbrennen nt. ~**en** vt ermutigen. ~**felt** adj herzlich[st]

hearth /hɑːθ/ n Herd m; (fireplace) Kamin m

heart|ily /ˈhɑːtɪlɪ/ adv herzlich;

heat | heresy

(eat) viel. **~less** adj herzlos. **~y** adj
herzlich; (meal) groß; (person) bur-
schikos

heat /hiːt/ n Hitze f; (Sport) Vorlauf
m ● vt heiß machen; heizen (room).
~ed adj geheizt; (swimming pool)
beheizt; (discussion) hitzig. **~er** n
Heizgerät nt; (Auto) Heizanlage f

heath /hiːθ/ n Heide f

heathen /'hiːðn/ adj heidnisch ● n
Heide m/Heidin f

heather /'heðə(r)/ n Heidekraut nt

heating /'hiːtɪŋ/ n Heizung f

heat wave n Hitzewelle f

heave /hiːv/ vt/i ziehen; (lift)
heben; (🔲: throw) schmeißen

heaven /hevn/ n Himmel m. **~ly**
adj himmlisch

heavy /'hevɪ/ adj, **-ily** adv schwer;
(traffic, rain) stark. **~weight** n
Schwergewicht nt

heckle /'hekl/ vt [durch Zwischen-
rufe] unterbrechen. **~r** n Zwischen-
rufer m

hectic /'hektɪk/ adj hektisch

hedge /hedʒ/ n Hecke f. **~hog** n
Igel m

heed /hiːd/ vt beachten

heel¹ /hiːl/ n Ferse f; (of shoe) Absatz m; **down at ~** heruntergekommen

heel² vi **~ over** (Naut) sich auf die
Seite legen

hefty /'heftɪ/ adj kräftig; (heavy)
schwer

height /haɪt/ n Höhe f; (of person)
Größe f. **~en** vt (fig) steigern

heir /eə(r)/ n Erbe m. **~ess** n Erbin
f. **~loom** n Erbstück nt

held /held/ see hold²

helicopter /'helɪkɒptə(r)/ n Hubschrauber m

hell /hel/ n Hölle f; **go to ~!** 🔲
geh zum Teufel! ● int verdammt!

hello /hə'ləʊ/ int [guten] Tag!
hallo!

helm /helm/ n [Steuer]ruder nt

helmet /'helmɪt/ n Helm m

help /help/ n Hilfe f; (employees)
Hilfskräfte pl; that's no **~** das nützt
nichts ● vt/i helfen (s.o. jdm); **~**
oneself to sth sich (dat) etw nehmen; **~ yourself** (at table) greif zu;
I could not **~** laughing ich musste
lachen; it cannot be **~ed** es lässt
sich nicht ändern; I can't **~** it ich
kann nichts dafür

help|er /'helpə(r)/ n Helfer(in)
m (f). **~ful** adj, **-ly** adv hilfsbereit;
(advice) nützlich. **~ing** n Portion f.
~less adj hilflos

hem /hem/ n Saum m ● vt (pt/pp
hemmed) säumen; **~ in** umzingeln

hemisphere /'hemɪ-/ n Hemisphäre f

'hem-line n Rocklänge f

hen /hen/ n Henne f; (any female
bird) Weibchen nt

hence /hens/ adv daher; five years
~ in fünf Jahren. ~forth adv von
nun an

'henpecked adj **~ husband** Pan-
toffelheld m

her /hɜː(r)/ adj ihr ● pron (acc) sie;
(dat) ihr

herald /'herəld/ vt verkünden.
~ry n Wappenkunde f

herb /hɜːb/ n Kraut nt

herbaceous /hɜː'beɪʃəs/ adj **~**
border Staudenrabatte f

herd /hɜːd/ n Herde f. **~ together**
vt zusammentreiben

here /hɪə(r)/ adv hier; (to this place)
hierher; in **~** hier drinnen; come/
bring **~** herkommen/herbringen

hereditary /hə'redɪtərɪ/ adj
erblich

here|sy /'herəsɪ/ n Ketzerei f. **~tic**
n Ketzer(in) m (f)

h

here'with adv (Comm) beiliegend

heritage /'herɪtɪdʒ/ n Erbe nt. ~ **tourism** n Kulturtourismus m

hero /'hɪərəʊ/ n (pl -es) Held m

heroic /hɪ'rəʊɪk/ adj, **-ally** adv heldenhaft

heroin /'herəʊɪn/ n Heroin nt

hero|ine /'herəʊɪn/ n Heldin f. ~**ism** n Heldentum nt

heron /'hern/ n Reiher m

herring /'herɪŋ/ n Hering m

hers /hɜːz/ poss pron ihre(r), ihrs; a friend of ~ ein Freund von ihr; that is ~ das gehört ihr

her'self pron selbst; (reflexive) sich; by ~ allein

hesitant /'hezɪtənt/ adj zögernd

hesitat|e /'hezɪteɪt/ vi zögern. ~**ion** n Zögern nt; without ~**ion** ohne zu zögern

hexagonal /hek'sægənl/ adj sechseckig

heyday /'heɪ-/ n Glanzzeit f

hi /haɪ/ int he! (hallo) Tag!

hiatus /haɪ'eɪtəs/ n (pl -tuses) Lücke f

hibernat|e /'haɪbəneɪt/ vi Winterschlaf halten. ~**ion** n Winterschlaf m

hiccup /'hɪkʌp/ n Hick m; (🔟: hitch) Panne f; have the ~s den Schluckauf haben ● vi hick machen

hid /hɪd/, **hidden** see hide[2]

hide v (pt hid, pp hidden) ● vt verstecken; (keep secret) verheimlichen ● vi sich verstecken

hideous /'hɪdɪəs/ adj hässlich; (horrible) grässlich

'hide-out n Versteck nt

hiding[1] /'haɪdɪŋ/ n 🔟 give s.o. a ~ jdn verdreschen

hiding[2] n go into ~ untertauchen

hierarchy /'haɪərɑːkɪ/ n Hierarchie f

high /haɪ/ adj (-er, -est) hoch; attrib hohe(r,s); (meat) angegangen; (wind) stark; (on drugs) high; it's ~ time es ist höchste Zeit ● adv hoch; ~ and low überall ● n Hoch nt; (temperature) Höchsttemperatur f

high: ~**brow** adj intellektuell. ~**chair** n Kinderhochstuhl m. ~'-**handed** adj selbstherrlich. ~'-**heeled** adj hochhackig. ~ **jump** n Hochsprung m

'highlight n (fig) Höhepunkt m; ~s pl (in hair) helle Strähnen pl ● vt (emphasize) hervorheben

highly /'haɪlɪ/ adv hoch; speak ~ of loben; think ~ of sehr schätzen. ~'-**strung** adj nervös

Highness /'haɪnɪs/ n Hoheit f

high school Eine weiterführende Schule in den USA, normalerweise für Schüler von vierzehn bis achtzehn Jahren. Schüler erwerben einen Highschoolabschluss durch Nachweis von credits (Punkten) in bestimmten Pflicht- und Wahlkursen. Der Abschluss ist Voraussetzung zum Besuch einer Hochschule. Auch in Großbritannien werden einige weiterführende Schulen als high schools bezeichnet.

---

high: ~ **season** n Hochsaison f. ~ **street** n Hauptstraße f. ~ **'tide** n Hochwasser nt. ~**way** n public ~**way** öffentliche Straße f

hijack /'haɪdʒæk/ vt entführen. ~**er** n Entführer m

hike /haɪk/ n Wanderung f ● vi wandern. ~**r** n Wanderer m

hilarious /hɪ'leərɪəs/ adj sehr komisch

hill /hɪl/ n Berg m; (mound) Hügel m; (slope) Hang m

hill: ~**side** n Hang m. ~**y** adj

hügelig

him /hɪm/ pron (acc) ihn; (dat) ihm. **~'self** pron selbst; (reflexive) sich; by **~self** allein

hind /haɪnd/ adj Hinter-

hind|er /'hɪndə(r)/ vt hindern. **~rance** n Hindernis nt

hindsight /'haɪnd-/ n with **~** rückblickend

Hindu /'hɪnduː/ n Hindu m ● adj Hindu-. **~ism** n Hinduismus m

hinge /hɪndʒ/ n Scharnier nt; (on door) Angel f

hint /hɪnt/ n Wink m, Andeutung f; (advice) Hinweis m; (trace) Spur f ● vi **~ at** anspielen auf (+ acc)

hip /hɪp/ n Hüfte f

hip 'pocket n Gesäßtasche f

hippopotamus /hɪpə'pɒtəməs/ n (pl -muses or -mi -maɪ/) Nilpferd nt

hire /'haɪə(r)/ vt mieten (car); leihen (suit); einstellen (person); **~[out]** vermieten; verleihen

his /hɪz/ adj sein ● poss pron seine(r), seins; a friend of **~** ein Freund von ihm; that is **~** das gehört ihm

hiss /hɪs/ n Zischen nt ● vt/i zischen

historian /hɪ'stɔːrɪən/ n Historiker(in) m(f)

historic /hɪ'stɒrɪk/ adj historisch. **~al** adj geschichtlich, historisch

history /'hɪstərɪ/ n Geschichte f

hit /hɪt/ n (blow) Schlag m; (I: success) Erfolg m; direct **~** Volltreffer m ● vt/i (pt/pp hit, pres p hitting) schlagen; (knock against, collide with, affect) treffen; **~ the target** das Ziel treffen; **~** on (fig) kommen auf (+ acc); **~ it off** gut auskommen (with mit); **~ one's head on sth** sich (dat) den Kopf an etw (dat) stoßen

hitch /hɪtʃ/ n Problem nt; technical **~** Panne f ● vt festmachen (to an + dat); **~ up** hochziehen. **~-hike** vi I trampen. **~-hiker** n Anhalter(in) m(f)

hive /haɪv/ n Bienenstock m

hoard /hɔːd/ n Hort m ● vt horten, hamstern

hoarding /'hɔːdɪŋ/ n Bauzaun m; (with advertisements) Reklamewand f

hoar-frost /'hɔː-/ n Raureif m

hoarse /hɔːs/ adj (-r, -st) heiser. **~ness** n Heiserkeit f

hoax /həʊks/ n übler Scherz m; (false alarm) blinder Alarm m

hobble /'hɒbl/ vi humpeln

hobby /'hɒbɪ/ n Hobby nt. **~-horse** n (fig) Lieblingsthema nt

hockey /'hɒkɪ/ n Hockey nt

hoe /həʊ/ n Hacke f ● vt (pres p hoeing) hacken

hog /hɒg/ vt (pt/pp hogged) I mit Beschlag belegen

hoist /hɔɪst/ n Lastenaufzug m ● vt hochziehen; hissen (flag)

hold¹ /həʊld/ n (Naut) Laderaum m

hold² n Halt m; (Sport) Griff m; (fig: influence) Einfluss m; get **~** of fassen; (I: contact) erreichen ● v (pt/pp held) ● vt halten; (container:) fassen; (believe) meinen; (possess) haben; anhalten (breath) ● vi (rope:) halten; (weather:) sich halten. **~ back** vt zurückhalten ● vi zögern. **~ on** vi (wait) warten; (on telephone) am Apparat bleiben; **~ on to** (keep) behalten; (cling to) sich festhalten an (+ dat). **~ out** vt hinhalten ● vi (resist) aushalten. **~ up** vt hochhalten; (delay) aufhalten; (rob) überfallen

'hold|all n Reisetasche f. **~er** n Inhaber(in) m(f); (container) Halter m. **~-up** n Verzögerung f; (attack) Überfall m

hole /həʊl/ n Loch nt

holiday /'hɒlədeɪ/ n Urlaub m; (Sch) Ferien pl; (public) Feiertag m; (day off) freier Tag m; go on ~ in Urlaub fahren

holiness /'həʊlɪnɪs/ n Heiligkeit f

Holland /'hɒlənd/ n Holland nt

hollow /'hɒləʊ/ adj hohl; (promise) leer ● n Vertiefung f; (in ground) Mulde f. ~ out vt aushöhlen

holly /'hɒlɪ/ n Stechpalme f

holster /'həʊlstə(r)/ n Pistolentasche f

holy /'həʊlɪ/ adj (-ier, -est) heilig. H~ Ghost or Spirit n Heiliger Geist m

homage /'hɒmɪdʒ/ n Huldigung f; pay ~ to huldigen (+ dat)

home /həʊm/ n Zuhause nt (house) Haus nt; (institution) Heim nt; (native land) Heimat f ● adv at ~ zu Hause; come/go ~ nach Hause kommen/gehen

home: ~ ad'dress n Heimatanschrift f. ~ game n Heimspiel nt. ~ help n Haushaltshilfe f. ~land n Heimatland nt. ~land security n innere Sicherheit f. ~less adj obdachlos

homely /'həʊmlɪ/ adj adj gemütlich; (Amer: ugly) unscheinbar

home: ~-'made adj selbst gemacht. H~ Office n Innenministerium nt. ~ page n Homepage f. H~ 'Secretary n Innenminister m. ~sick adj be ~sick Heimweh haben (for nach). ~sickness n Heimweh nt. ~'town n Heimatstadt f. ~work n (Sch) Hausaufgaben pl

homo'sexual adj homosexuell ● n Homosexuelle(r) m/f

honest /'ɒnɪst/ adj ehrlich. ~y n Ehrlichkeit f

honey /'hʌnɪ/ n Honig m (🔊: darling) Schatz m

honey: ~comb n Honigwabe f. ~moon n Flitterwochen pl; (journey) Hochzeitsreise f

honorary /'ɒnərərɪ/ adj ehrenamtlich; (member, doctorate) Ehren-

honour /'ɒnə(r)/ n Ehre f ● vt ehren; honorieren (cheque). ~able adj. ~bly adv ehrenhaft

hood /hʊd/ n Kapuze f; (of car, pram) [Klapp]verdeck nt; (over cooker) Abzugshaube f; (Auto, Amer) Kühlerhaube f

hoof /huːf/ n (pl ~s or hooves) Huf m

hook /hʊk/ n Haken m ● vt festhaken (to an + acc)

hook|ed /hʊkt/ adj ~ed nose Hakennase f. ~ed on 🔊 abhängig von; (keen on) besessen von. ~er n (Amer, 🔊) Nutte f

hookey /'hʊkɪ/ n play ~ (Amer, 🔊) schwänzen

hooligan /'huːlɪgən/ n Rowdy m. ~ism n Rowdytum nt

hooray /hʊ'reɪ/ int & n = hurrah

hoot /huːt/ n Ruf m; ~s of laughter schallendes Gelächter nt ● vi (owl:) rufen; (car:) hupen; (jeer) johlen. ~er n (of factory) Sirene f; (Auto) Hupe f

hoover /'huːvə(r)/ n H~ ® Staubsauger m ● vt/i [staub]saugen

hop¹ /hɒp/ n, & ~s pl Hopfen m

hop² vi (pt/pp hopped) hüpfen; ~ it! 🔊 hau ab!

hope /həʊp/ n Hoffnung f; (prospect) Aussicht f (of auf + acc) ● vt/i hoffen (for auf + acc); I ~ so hoffentlich

hope|ful /'həʊpfl/ adj hoffnungsvoll; be ~ful that hoffen, dass. ~fully adv hoffnungsvoll; (it is hoped) hoffentlich. ~less adj hoffnungslos; (useless) nutzlos; (incompetent) untauglich

horde /hɔːd/ n Horde f

horizon /hə'raɪzn/ n Horizont m

horizontal /hɒrɪ'zɒntl/ adj horizontal. ~**bar** n Reck nt

horn /hɔːn/ n Horn nt; (Auto) Hupe f

hornet /'hɔːnɪt/ n Hornisse f

horoscope /'hɒrəskəʊp/ n Horoskop nt

horrible /'hɒrɪbl/ adj, -**bly** adv schrecklich

horrid /'hɒrɪd/ adj grässlich

horrific /hə'rɪfɪk/ adj entsetzlich

horrify /'hɒrɪfaɪ/ vt (pt/pp -ied) entsetzen

horror /'hɒrə(r)/ n Entsetzen nt

hors-d'œuvre /ɔː'dɜːvr/ n Vorspeise f

horse /hɔːs/ n Pferd nt

horse: ~**back** n on ~back zu Pferde. ~**man** n Reiter m. ~**power** n Pferdestärke f. ~**racing** n Pferderennen nt. ~**radish** n Meerrettich m. ~**shoe** n Hufeisen nt

'horticulture n Gartenbau m

hose /həʊz/ n (pipe) Schlauch m ● vt ~ **down** abspritzen

hosiery /'həʊzɪərɪ/ n Strumpfwaren pl

hospitable /hɒ'spɪtəbl/ adj, -**bly** adv gastfreundlich

hospital /'hɒspɪtl/ n Krankenhaus nt

hospitality /hɒspɪ'tælɪtɪ/ n Gastfreundschaft f

host[1] /həʊst/ n Gastgeber m

hostage /'hɒstɪdʒ/ n Geisel f

hostel /'hɒstl/ n [Wohn]heim nt

hostess /'həʊstɪs/ n Gastgeberin f

hostile /'hɒstaɪl/ adj feindlich; (unfriendly) feindselig

hostilit|y /hɒ'stɪlətɪ/ n Feindschaft f; ~**ies** pl Feindseligkeiten pl

hot /hɒt/ adj (hotter, hottest) heiß;

(meal) warm; (spicy) scharf; **I am** or **feel** ~ mir ist heiß

hotel /həʊ'tel/ n Hotel nt

hot: ~**head** n Hitzkopf m. ~**house** n Treibhaus nt. ~**ly** adv (fig) heiß, heftig. ~**plate** n Tellerwärmer m; (of cooker) Kochplatte f. ~**tap** n Warmwasserhahn m. ~**tempered** adj jähzornig. ~'**waterbottle** n Wärmflasche f

hound /haʊnd/ n Jagdhund m ● vt (fig) verfolgen

hour /'aʊə(r)/ n Stunde f. ~**ly** adj & adv stündlich

house[1] /haʊs/ n Haus nt; **at my** ~ bei mir

house[2] /haʊz/ vt unterbringen

house: /haʊs/ ~**breaking** n Einbruch m. ~**hold** n Haushalt m. ~**holder** n Hausinhaber(in) m(f). ~**keeper** n Haushälterin f. ~**keeping** n Hauswirtschaft f; (money) Haushaltsgeld nt. ~**plant** n Zimmerpflanze f. ~**trained** adj stubenrein. ~**warming** n have a ~warming party Einstand feiern. ~**wife** n Hausfrau f. ~**work** n Hausarbeit f

housing /'haʊzɪŋ/ n Wohnungen pl; (Techn) Gehäuse nt

hovel /'hɒvl/ n elende Hütte f

hover /'hɒvə(r)/ vi schweben. ~**craft** n Luftkissenfahrzeug nt

how /haʊ/ adv how ~ do you do? guten Tag!; and ~! und ob!

how'ever adv (in question) wie; (nevertheless) jedoch, aber; ~ **small** wie klein es auch sein mag

howl /haʊl/ n Heulen nt ● vi heulen; (baby:) brüllen

hub /hʌb/ n Nabe f

huddle /'hʌdl/ vi ~ **together** sich zusammendrängen

huff /hʌf/ n in a ~ beleidigt

hug /hʌg/ n Umarmung f ● vt (pt/

h

pp hugged) umarmen

huge /hjuːdʒ/ *adj* riesig

hull /hʌl/ *n* (Naut) Rumpf *m*

hullo /hə'ləʊ/ *int* = hallo

hum /hʌm/ *n* Summen *nt*; Brummen *nt* ●*vt/i* (pt/pp hummed) summen; (motor:) brummen

human /'hjuːmən/ *adj* menschlich ●*n* Mensch *m*. ~ 'being *n* Mensch *m*

humane /hjuː'meɪn/ *adj* human

humanitarian /hjuːmænɪ 'teərɪən/ *adj* humanitär

humanity /hjuː'mænətɪ/ *n* Menschheit *f*

humble /'hʌmbl/ *adj* (-r, -st), **-bly** *adv* demütig ●*vt* demütigen

'humdrum *adj* eintönig

humid /'hjuːmɪd/ *adj* feucht. ~**ity** *n* Feuchtigkeit *f*

humiliat|e /hjuː'mɪlɪeɪt/ *vt* demütigen. ~**ion** *n* Demütigung *f*

humility /hjuː'mɪlətɪ/ *n* Demut *f*

humorous /'hjuːmərəs/ *adj* humorvoll; (story) humoristisch

humour /'hjuːmə(r)/ *n* Humor *m*; (mood) Laune *f*; have a sense of ~ Humor haben

hump /hʌmp/ *n* Buckel *m*; (of camel) Höcker *m* ●*vt* schleppen

hunch /hʌntʃ/ *n* (idea) Ahnung *f*

'hunchback *n* Bucklige(r) *m/f*

hundred /'hʌndrəd/ *adj* one ~a [ein]hundert ●*n* Hundert *nt*; (written figure) Hundert *f*. ~**th** *adj* hundertste(r,s) ●*n* Hundertstel *nt*. ~**weight** *n* ≈ Zentner *m*

hung /hʌŋ/ *see* hang

Hungarian /hʌŋ'geərɪən/ *adj* ungarisch ●*n* Ungar(in) *m(f)*

Hungary /'hʌŋgərɪ/ *n* Ungarn *nt*

hunger /'hʌŋgə(r)/ *n* Hunger *m*. ~**-strike** *n* Hungerstreik *m*

hungry /'hʌŋgrɪ/ *adj*, **-ily** *adv*

hungrig; be ~ Hunger haben

hunt /hʌnt/ *n* Jagd *f*; (for criminal) Fahndung *f* ●*vt/i* jagen; fahnden nach (criminal). ~ **for** suchen. ~**er** *n* Jäger *m*; (horse) Jagdpferd *nt*. ~**ing** *n* Jagd *f*

hurdle /'hɜːdl/ *n* (Sport & fig) Hürde *f*

hurl /hɜːl/ *vt* schleudern

hurrah /hʊ'rɑː/, **hurray** /hʊ'reɪ/ *int* hurra! ●*n* Hurra *nt*

hurricane /'hʌrɪkən/ *n* Orkan *m*

hurried /'hʌrɪd/ *adj* eilig; (superficial) flüchtig

hurry /'hʌrɪ/ *n* Eile *f*; be in a ~ es eilig haben ●*vi* (pt/pp -ied) sich beeilen; (go quickly) eilen. ~ **up** *vi* sich beeilen ●*vt* antreiben

hurt /hɜːt/ *n* Schmerz *m* ●*vt/i* (pt/pp hurt) weh tun (+ dat); (injure) verletzen; (offend) kränken

hurtle /'hɜːtl/ *vi* ~ along rasen

husband /'hʌzbənd/ *n* [Ehe]mann *m*

hush /hʌʃ/ *n* Stille *f* ●*vt* ~ **up** vertuschen. ~**ed** *adj* gedämpft

husky /'hʌskɪ/ *adj* heiser; (burly) stämmig

hustle /'hʌsl/ *vt* drängen ●*n* Gedränge *nt*

hut /hʌt/ *n* Hütte *f*

hutch /hʌtʃ/ *n* [Kaninchen]stall *m*

hybrid /'haɪbrɪd/ *adj* hybrid ●*n* Hybride *f*

hydraulic /haɪ'drɔːlɪk/ *adj*, **-ally** *adv* hydraulisch

hydroe'lectric /haɪdrəʊ-/ *adj* hydroelektrisch

hydrogen /'haɪdrədʒən/ *n* Wasserstoff *m*

hygien|e /'haɪdʒiːn/ *n* Hygiene *f*. ~**ic** *adj*, **-ally** *adv* hygienisch

hymn /hɪm/ *n* Kirchenlied *nt*. ~**-book** *n* Gesangbuch *nt*

hyphen /ˈhaɪfn/ n Bindestrich m. **~ate** vt mit Bindestrich schreiben

hypno|sis /hɪpˈnəʊsɪs/ n Hypnose f. **~tic** adj hypnotisch

hypno|tism /ˈhɪpnətɪzm/ n Hypnotik f. **~tist** n Hypnotiseur m. **~tize** vt hypnotisieren

hypochondriac /haɪpəˈkɒndrɪæk/ n Hypochonder m

hypocrisy /hɪˈpɒkrəsɪ/ n Heuchelei f

hypocrit|e /ˈhɪpəkrɪt/ n Heuchler(in) m(f)

hypodermic /haɪpəˈdɜːmɪk/ adj & n **~** [syringe] Injektionsspritze f

hypothe|sis /haɪˈpɒθəsɪs/ n Hypothese f. **~tical** adj hypothetisch

hyster|ia /hɪˈstɪərɪə/ n Hysterie f. **~ical** adj hysterisch. **~ics** npl hysterischer Anfall m

Ii

I /aɪ/ pron ich

ice /aɪs/ n Eis nt ● vt mit Zuckerguss überziehen (cake)

ice: **~berg** /-bɜːg/ n Eisberg m. **~box** n (Amer) Kühlschrank m. **~-'cream** n [Speise]eis nt. **~-cube** n Eiswürfel m

Iceland /ˈaɪslənd/ n Island nt

ice: **~lolly** n Eis nt am Stiel. **~rink** n Eisbahn f

icicle /ˈaɪsɪkl/ n Eiszapfen m

icing /ˈaɪsɪŋ/ n Zuckerguss m. **~ sugar** n Puderzucker m

icon /ˈaɪkɒn/ n Ikone f

icy /ˈaɪsɪ/ adj , **-ily** adv eisig; (road) vereist

idea /aɪˈdɪə/ n Idee f; (conception)

Vorstellung f; I have no **~**! ich habe keine Ahnung!

ideal /aɪˈdɪəl/ adj ideal ● n Ideal nt. **~ism** n Idealismus m. **~ist** n Idealist(in) m(f). **~istic** adj idealistisch. **~ize** vt idealisieren. **~ly** adv ideal; (in ideal circumstances) idealerweise

identical /aɪˈdentɪkl/ adj identisch; (twins) eineiig

identi|fication /aɪdentɪfɪˈkeɪʃn/ n Identifizierung f; (proof of identity) Ausweispapiere pl. **~fy** vt (pt/pp -ied) identifizieren

identity /aɪˈdentɪtɪ/ n Identität f. **~ card** n [Personal]ausweis m. **~ theft** Identitätsdiebstahl m

idiom /ˈɪdɪəm/ n [feste] Redewendung f. **~atic** adj, **-ally** adv idiomatisch

idiosyncrasy /ɪdɪəˈsɪŋkrəsɪ/ n Eigenart f

idiot /ˈɪdɪət/ n Idiot m. **~ic** adj idiotisch

idle /ˈaɪdl/ adj (-r, -st) untätig; (lazy) faul; (empty) leer; (machine) nicht in Betrieb ● vi faulenzen; (engine:) leer laufen. **~ness** n Untätigkeit f; Faulheit f

idol /ˈaɪdl/ n Idol m. **~ize** vt vergöttern

idyllic /ɪˈdɪlɪk/ adj idyllisch

i.e. abbr (id est) d.h.

if /ɪf/ conj wenn; (whether) ob; as if als ob

ignition /ɪgˈnɪʃn/ n (Auto) Zündung f. **~ key** n Zündschlüssel m

ignoramus /ɪgnəˈreɪməs/ n Ignorant m

ignoran|ce /ˈɪgnərəns/ n Unwissenheit f. **~t** adj unwissend

ignore /ɪgˈnɔː(r)/ vt ignorieren

ill /ɪl/ adj krank; (bad) schlecht; feel **~** at ease sich unbehaglich fühlen ● adv schlecht

illegal /ɪˈliːgl/ adj illegal

h
i

illegible /ɪˈledʒəbl/ adj, **-bly** adv unleserlich

illegitimate /ɪlɪˈdʒɪtɪmət/ adj unehelich; (claim) unberechtigt

illicit /ɪˈlɪsɪt/ adj illegal

illiterate /ɪˈlɪtərət/ adj be ~te nicht lesen und schreiben können

illness /ˈɪlnɪs/ n Krankheit f

illogical /ɪˈlɒdʒɪkl/ adj unlogisch

ill-treat /ɪlˈtriːt/ vt misshandeln. ~ment n Misshandlung f

illuminate /ɪˈluːmɪneɪt/ vt beleuchten. ~ion n Beleuchtung f

illusion /ɪˈluːʒn/ n Illusion f; be under the ~ that sich (dat) einbilden, dass

illustrate /ˈɪləstreɪt/ vt illustrieren. ~ion n Illustration f

illustrious /ɪˈlʌstrɪəs/ adj berühmt

image /ˈɪmɪdʒ/ n Bild nt; (statue) Standbild nt; (exact likeness) Ebenbild nt; (public) ~ Image nt

imagin|able /ɪˈmædʒɪnəbl/ adj vorstellbar. ~ary adj eingebildet

imagination /ɪmædʒɪˈneɪʃn/ n Phantasie f; (fancy) Einbildung f. ~ive adj phantasievoll; (full of ideas) einfallsreich

imagine /ɪˈmædʒɪn/ vt sich (dat) vorstellen; (wrongly) sich (dat) einbilden

im'balance n Unausgeglichenheit f

imbecile /ˈɪmbəsiːl/ n Schwachsinnige(r) m/f; (pej) Idiot m

imitat|e /ˈɪmɪteɪt/ vt nachahmen, imitieren. ~ion n Nachahmung f, Imitation f

immaculate /ɪˈmækjʊlət/ adj tadellos; (Relig) unbefleckt

imma'ture adj unreif

immediate /ɪˈmiːdɪət/ adj sofortig; (nearest) nächste(r,s). ~ly adv

sofort; ~ly next to unmittelbar neben ● conj sobald

immemorial /ɪməˈmɔːrɪəl/ adj from time ~ seit Urzeiten

immense /ɪˈmens/ adj riesig; 🛈 enorm

immerse /ɪˈmɜːs/ vt untertauchen

immigrant /ˈɪmɪgrənt/ n Einwanderer m

immigration /ɪmɪˈgreɪʃn/ n Einwanderung f

imminent /ˈɪmɪnənt/ adj be ~ unmittelbar bevorstehen

immobil|e /ɪˈməʊbaɪl/ adj unbeweglich. ~ize vt (fig) lähmen; (Med) ruhig stellen. ~izer n (Auto) Wegfahrsperre f

immodest /ɪˈmɒdɪst/ adj unbescheiden

immoral /ɪˈmɒrəl/ adj unmoralisch. ~ity n Unmoral f

immortal /ɪˈmɔːtl/ adj unsterblich. ~ity n Unsterblichkeit f. ~ize vt verewigen

immune /ɪˈmjuːn/ adj immun (to/from gegen)

immunity /ɪˈmjuːnətɪ/ n Immunität f

imp /ɪmp/ n Kobold m

impact /ˈɪmpækt/ n Aufprall m; (collision) Zusammenprall m; (of bomb) Einschlag m; (fig) Auswirkung f

impair /ɪmˈpeə(r)/ vt beeinträchtigen

impart /ɪmˈpɑːt/ vt übermitteln (to dat); vermitteln (knowledge)

im'parti|al adj unparteiisch. ~ality n Unparteilichkeit f

im'passable adj unpassierbar

impassioned /ɪmˈpæʃnd/ adj leidenschaftlich

im'passive adj unbeweglich

im'patien|ce n Ungeduld f. ~t

adj ungeduldig

impeccable /ɪm'pekəbl/ *adj*, **-bly** *adv* tadellos

impede /ɪm'piːd/ *vt* behindern

impediment /ɪm'pedɪmənt/ *n* Hindernis *nt*; (*in speech*) Sprachfehler *m*

impel /ɪm'pel/ *vt* (*pt/pp* impelled) treiben

impending /ɪm'pendɪŋ/ *adj* bevorstehend

impenetrable /ɪm'penɪtrəbl/ *adj* undurchdringlich

imperative /ɪm'perətɪv/ *adj* be ~ dringend notwendig sein ● *n* (*Gram*) Imperativ *m*

imper'ceptible *adj* nicht wahrnehmbar

im'perfect *adj* unvollkommen; (*faulty*) fehlerhaft ● *n* (*Gram*) Imperfekt *nt*. **~ion** *n* Unvollkommenheit *f*; (*fault*) Fehler *m*

imperial /ɪm'pɪərɪəl/ *adj* kaiserlich. **~ism** *n* Imperialismus *m*

im'personal *adj* unpersönlich

impersonat|e /ɪm'pɜːsəneɪt/ *vt* sich ausgeben als; (*Theat*) nachahmen, imitieren. **~or** *n* Imitator *m*

impertinen|ce /ɪm'pɜːtɪnəns/ *n* Frechheit *f*. **~t** *adj* frech

imperturbable /ɪmpə'tɜːbəbl/ *adj* unerschütterlich

impetuous /ɪm'petjʊəs/ *adj* ungestüm

impetus /'ɪmpɪtəs/ *n* Schwung *m*

implacable /ɪm'plækəbl/ *adj* unerbittlich

im'plant *vt* einpflanzen

implement¹ /'ɪmplɪmənt/ *n* Gerät *nt*

implement² /'ɪmplɪment/ *vt* ausführen. **~ation** *n* Ausführung *f*, Durchführung *f*

implication /ɪmplɪ'keɪʃn/ *n* Verwicklung *f*; **~s** *pl* Auswirkungen *pl*; **by ~** implizit

implicit /ɪm'plɪsɪt/ *adj* unausgesprochen; (*absolute*) unbedingt

implore /ɪm'plɔː(r)/ *vt* anflehen

imply /ɪm'plaɪ/ *vt* (*pt/pp* -ied) andeuten; what are you **~ing**? was wollen Sie damit sagen?

impo'lite *adj* unhöflich

import¹ /'ɪmpɔːt/ *n* Import *m*, Einfuhr *f*

import² /ɪm'pɔːt/ *vt* importieren, einführen

importan|ce /ɪm'pɔːtns/ *n* Wichtigkeit *f*. **~t** *adj* wichtig

importer /ɪm'pɔːtə(r)/ *n* Importeur *m*

impos|e /ɪm'pəʊz/ *vt* auferlegen (on *dat*) ● *vi* sich aufdrängen (on *dat*). **~ing** *adj* eindrucksvoll

impossi'bility *n* Unmöglichkeit *f*

im'possible *adj*, **-bly** *adv* unmöglich

impostor /ɪm'pɒstə(r)/ *n* Betrüger(in) *m(f)*

impoten|ce /'ɪmpətəns/ *n* Machtlosigkeit *f*; (*Med*) Impotenz *f*. **~t** *adj* machtlos; (*Med*) impotent

impoverished /ɪm'pɒvərɪʃt/ *adj* verarmt

im'practicable *adj* undurchführbar

im'practical *adj* unpraktisch

impre'cise *adj* ungenau

im'press *vt* beeindrucken; **sth** [up]on s.o. jdm etw einprägen

impression /ɪm'preʃn/ *n* Eindruck *m*; (*imitation*) Nachahmung *f*; (*edition*) Auflage *f*. **~ism** *n* Impressionismus *m*

impressive /ɪm'presɪv/ *adj* eindrucksvoll

im'prison *vt* gefangen halten; (*put in prison*) ins Gefängnis sperren

i

im'probable adj unwahrscheinlich

impromptu /ɪmˈprɒmptjuː/ adj
improvisiert ● adv aus dem Stegreif

im'proper adj inkorrekt; (indecent)
unanständig

impro'priety n Unkorrektheit f

improve /ɪmˈpruːv/ vt verbessern;
verschönern (appearance) ● vi sich
bessern; ~ [up]on übertreffen.
~ment n Verbesserung f; (in
health) Besserung f

improvise /ˈɪmprəvaɪz/ vt/i improvisieren

im'prudent adj unklug

impuden|ce /ˈɪmpjʊdəns/ n
Frechheit f. ~t adj frech

impulse /ˈɪmpʌls/ n Impuls m; on
[an] ~e impulsiv. ~ive adj impulsiv

im'pur|e adj unrein. ~ity n Un-
reinheit f

in /ɪn/ prep in (+ dat/into) + acc);
sit in the garden im Garten sitzen;
go in the garden in den Garten
gehen; in May im Mai; in 1992 [im
Jahre] 1992; in this heat bei dieser
Hitze; in the evening am Abend; in
the sky am Himmel; in the world
auf der Welt; in the street auf der
Straße; deaf in one ear auf einem
Ohr taub; in the army beim Militär;
in English/German auf Englisch/
Deutsch; in ink/pencil mit Tinte/
Bleistift; in a soft/loud voice mit
leiser/lauter Stimme; in doing this,
he ... indem er das tut/tat, ... er
● adv (at home) zu Hause; (indoors)
drinnen; he's not in yet er ist noch
nicht da; all in alles inbegriffen; (🅸:
exhausted) kaputt; day in, day out
tagaus, tagein; have it in for s.o.
🅸 es auf jdn abgesehen haben;
send/go in hineinschicken/-gehen;
come/bring in hereinkommen/-
bringen ● adj (🅸: in fashion) in ● n

the ins and outs alle Einzelheiten pl

ina'bility n Unfähigkeit f

inac'cessible adj unzugänglich

inac'curacy n Ungenauigkeit f.
~te adj ungenau

in'ac|tive adj untätig. ~tivity n
Untätigkeit f

in'adequate adj unzulänglich

inad'missable adj unzulässig

inadvertently /ɪnədˈvɜːtəntlɪ/
adv versehentlich

inad'visable adj nicht ratsam

inane /ɪˈneɪn/ adj albern

in'animate adj unbelebt

in'applicable adj nicht zutreffend

inap'propriate adj unangebracht

inar'ticulate adj undeutlich; be
~ sich nicht gut ausdrücken
können

inat'tentive adj unaufmerksam

in'audible adj, -bly adv unhörbar

inaugural /ɪˈnɔːgjʊrl/ adj Antritts-

inau'spicious adj ungünstig

inborn /ˈɪnbɔːn/ adj angeboren

inbred /ɪnˈbred/ adj angeboren

incalculable /ɪnˈkælkjʊləbl/ adj
nicht berechenbar; (fig) unabsehbar

in'capable adj unfähig; be ~ of
doing sth nicht fähig sein, etw
zu tun

incapacitate /ɪnkəˈpæsɪteɪt/ vt
unfähig machen

incarnation /ɪnkɑːˈneɪʃn/ n In-
karnation f

incendiary /ɪnˈsendɪərɪ/ adj & n
~ [bomb] Brandbombe f

incense¹ /ˈɪnsens/ n Weihrauch m

incense² /ɪnˈsens/ vt wütend
machen

incentive /ɪnˈsentɪv/ n Anreiz m

incessant /ɪnˈsesnt/ adj unaufhörlich

incest /ˈɪnsest/ n Inzest m,

Blutschande *f*

inch /ɪntʃ/ *n* Zoll *m* • *vi* ~ forward sich ganz langsam vorwärts schieben

incident /'ɪnsɪdənt/ *n* Zwischenfall *m*

incidental /ɪnsɪ'dentl/ *adj* nebensächlich; (*remark*) beiläufig; (*expenses*) Neben-. ~**ly** *adv* übrigens

incinerat|e /ɪn'sɪnəreɪt/ *vt* verbrennen

incision /ɪn'sɪʒn/ *n* Einschnitt *m*

incisive /ɪn'saɪsɪv/ *adj* scharfsinnig

incite /ɪn'saɪt/ *vt* aufhetzen. ~**ment** *n* Aufhetzung *f*

in'clement *adj* rau

inclination /ɪnklɪ'neɪʃn/ *n* Neigung *f*

incline /ɪn'klaɪn/ *vt* neigen; be ~d to do sth dazu neigen, etw zu tun • *vi* sich neigen

inclu|de /ɪn'kluːd/ *vt* einschließen; (*contain*) enthalten; (*incorporate*) aufnehmen (in in + *acc.*). ~**ding** *prep* einschließlich (+ *gen*). ~**sion** *n* Aufnahme *f*

inclusive /ɪn'kluːsɪv/ *adj* Inklusiv-; ~ of einschließlich (+ *gen*)

incognito /ɪnkɒg'niːtəʊ/ *adv* inkognito

inco'herent *adj* zusammenhanglos; (*incomprehensible*) unverständlich

income /'ɪnkəm/ *n* Einkommen *n*. ~ **tax** *n* Einkommensteuer *f*

'incoming *adj* ankommend; (*mail, call*) eingehend

in'comparable *adj* unvergleichlich

incom'patible *adj* unvereinbar; be ~ (*people:*) nicht zueinander passen

in'competen|ce *n* Unfähigkeit *f*. ~**t** *adj* unfähig

incom'plete *adj* unvollständig

incompre'hensible *adj* unverständlich

incon'ceivable *adj* undenkbar

incon'clusive *adj* nicht schlüssig

incongruous /ɪn'kɒŋgrʊəs/ *adj* unpassend

incon'siderate *adj* rücksichtslos

incon'sistent *adj* widersprüchlich; (*illogical*) inkonsequent; be ~ nicht übereinstimmen

inconsolable /ɪnkən'səʊləbl/ *adj* untröstlich

incon'spicuous *adj* unauffällig

inconting|ce /ɪn'kɒntɪnəns/ *n* Inkontinenz *f*. ~**t** *adj* inkontinent

incon'venien|ce *n* Unannehmlichkeit *f*; (*drawback*) Nachteil *m*. ~**t** *adj* ungünstig; be ~**t** for s.o. jdm nicht passen

incorporate /ɪn'kɔːpəreɪt/ *vt* aufnehmen; (*contain*) enthalten

incor'rect *adj* inkorrekt

incorrigible /ɪn'kɒrɪdʒəbl/ *adj* unverbesserlich

incorruptible /ɪnkə'rʌptəbl/ *adj* unbestechlich

increase¹ /'ɪnkriːs/ *n* Zunahme *f*; (*rise*) Erhöhung *f*; be on the ~ zunehmen

increas|e² /ɪn'kriːs/ *vt* vergrößern; (*raise*) erhöhen • *vi* zunehmen; (*rise*) sich erhöhen. ~**ing** *adj* zunehmend

in'cred|ible *adj*, -**bly** *adv* unglaublich

incredulous /ɪn'kredjʊləs/ *adj* ungläubig

incriminate /ɪn'krɪmɪneɪt/ *vt* (*Jur*) belasten

incur /ɪn'kɜː(r)/ *vt* (*pt/pp* incurred) sich (*dat*) zuziehen; machen (*debts*)

in'cura|ble *adj*, -**bly** *adv* unheilbar

indebted /ɪn'detɪd/ *adj* verpflichtet (to *dat*)

in'decent adj unanständig

inde'cision n Unentschlossenheit f

inde'cisive adj ergebnislos; (person) unentschlossen

indeed /ɪnˈdiːd/ adv in der Tat, tatsächlich; very much ~ sehr

indefatigable /ɪndɪˈfætɪgəbl/ adj unermüdlich

in'definite adj unbestimmt. ~ly adv unbegrenzt; (postpone) auf unbestimmte Zeit

indent /ɪnˈdent/ vt (Printing) einrücken. ~ation n Einrückung f; (notch) Kerbe f

inde'penden|ce n Unabhängigkeit f; (self-reliance) Selbstständigkeit f. ~t adj unabhängig; selbstständig

indescriba|ble /ɪndɪˈskraɪbəbl/ adj, -bly adv unbeschreiblich

indestructible /ɪndɪˈstrʌktəbl/ adj unzerstörbar

indeterminate /ɪndɪˈtɜːmɪnət/ adj unbestimmt

index /ˈɪndeks/ n Register nt

index: ~ card n Karteikarte f. ~ finger n Zeigefinger m. ~-linked adj (pension) dynamisch

India /ˈɪndɪə/ n Indien nt. ~n adj indisch; (American) indianisch ● n Inder(in) m(f); (American) Indianer(in) m(f)

Indian 'summer n Nachsommer m

indicat|e /ˈɪndɪkeɪt/ vt zeigen; (point at) zeigen auf (+ acc); (hint) andeuten; (register) anzeigen ● vi (Auto) blinken. ~ion n Anzeichen nt

indicative /ɪnˈdɪkətɪv/ n (Gram) Indikativ m

indicator /ˈɪndɪkeɪtə(r)/ n (Auto) Blinker m

in'differen|ce n Gleichgültigkeit f. ~t adj gleichgültig; (not good) mittelmäßig

indi'gest|ible adj unverdaulich; (difficult to digest) schwer verdaulich. ~ion n Magenverstimmung f

indigna|nt /ɪnˈdɪgnənt/ adj entrüstet, empört. ~tion n Entrüstung f, Empörung f

in'dignity n Demütigung f

indi'rect adj indirekt

indi'screet adj indiskret

indis'cretion n Indiskretion f

indi'spensable adj unentbehrlich

indisposed /ɪndɪˈspəʊzd/ adj indisponiert

indisputable /ɪndɪˈspjuːtəbl/ adj, -bly adv unbestreitbar

indi'stinct adj undeutlich

indistinguishable /ɪndɪˈstɪŋgwɪʃəbl/ adj be ~ nicht zu unterscheiden sein

individual /ɪndɪˈvɪdjʊəl/ adj individuell; (single) einzeln ● n Individuum nt. ~ity n Individualität f

indi'visible adj unteilbar

indoctrinate /ɪnˈdɒktrɪneɪt/ vt indoktrinieren

indolen|ce /ˈɪndələns/ n Faulheit f. ~t adj faul

indomitable /ɪnˈdɒmɪtəbl/ adj unbeugsam

indoor /ˈɪndɔː(r)/ adj Innen-; (clothes) Haus-; (plant) Zimmer-; (Sport) Hallen-. ~s adv im Haus, drinnen; go ~s ins Haus gehen

indulge /ɪnˈdʌldʒ/ vt frönen (+ dat); verwöhnen (child) ● vi ~ in frönen (+ dat). ~nce n Nachgiebigkeit f; (leniency) Nachsicht f. ~nt adj [zu] nachgiebig; nachsichtig

industrial /ɪnˈdʌstrɪəl/ adj Industrie-. ~ist n Industrielle(r) m

industr|ious /ɪnˈdʌstrɪəs/ adj fleißig. ~y n Industrie f; (zeal) Fleiß m

inebriated /ɪˈniːbrɪeɪtɪd/ adj

betrunken

in'edible *adj* nicht essbar

inef'fective *adj* unwirksam; (*person*) untauglich

inef'ficient *adj* unfähig; (*organization*) nicht leistungsfähig; (*method*) nicht rationell

in'eligible *adj* nicht berechtigt

inept /ɪ'nept/ *adj* ungeschickt

ine'quality *n* Ungleichheit *f*

inertia /ɪ'nɜ:ʃə/ *n* Trägheit *f*

inescapable /ɪnɪ'skeɪpəbl/ *adj* unvermeidlich

inestimable /ɪn'estɪməbl/ *adj* unschätzbar

inevitab|le /ɪn'evɪtəbl/ *adj* unvermeidlich. ~**ly** *adv* zwangsläufig

ine'xact *adj* ungenau

inex'cusable *adj* unverzeihlich

inexhaustible /ɪnɪg'zɔ:stəbl/ *adj* unerschöpflich

inex'pensive *adj* preiswert

inex'perience *n* Unerfahrenheit *f*. ~**d** *adj* unerfahren

inexplicable /ɪnɪk'splɪkəbl/ *adj* unerklärlich

in'fallible *adj* unfehlbar

infamous /'ɪnfəməs/ *adj* niederträchtig; (*notorious*) berüchtigt

infan|cy /'ɪnfənsɪ/ *n* frühe Kindheit *f*; (*fig*) Anfangsstadium *nt*. ~**t** *n* Kleinkind *nt*. ~**tile** *adj* kindisch

infantry /'ɪnfəntrɪ/ *n* Infanterie *f*

infatuated /ɪn'fætjʊeɪtɪd/ *adj* vernarrt (**with** *in* + *acc*)

infect /ɪn'fekt/ *vt* anstecken, infizieren; **become** ~**ed** (*wound.*) sich infizieren. ~**ion** *n* Infektion *f*. ~**ious** *adj* ansteckend

inferior /ɪn'fɪərɪə(r)/ *adj* minderwertig; (*in rank*) untergeordnet ● *n* Untergebene(r) *m/f*

inferiority /ɪnfɪərɪ'ɒrɪtɪ/ *n* Minderwertigkeit *f*. ~ **complex** *n* Min-

derwertigkeitskomplex *m*

infern|al /ɪn'fɜ:nl/ *adj* höllisch. ~**o** *n* flammendes Inferno *nt*

in'fertile *adj* unfruchtbar

infest /ɪn'fest/ *vt* **be** ~**ed with** befallen sein von; (*place*) verseucht sein mit

infi'delity *n* Untreue *f*

infighting /'ɪnfaɪtɪŋ/ *n* (*fig*) interne Machtkämpfe *pl*

infinite /'ɪnfɪnət/ *adj* unendlich

infinitive /ɪn'fɪnətɪv/ *n* (*Gram*) Infinitiv *m*

infinity /ɪn'fɪnətɪ/ *n* Unendlichkeit *f*

inflame /ɪn'fleɪm/ *vt* entzünden. ~**d** *adj* entzündet

in'flammable *adj* feuergefährlich

inflammation /ɪnflə'meɪʃn/ *n* Entzündung *f*

inflammatory /ɪn'flæmətrɪ/ *adj* aufrührerisch

inflat|e /ɪn'fleɪt/ *vt* aufblasen; (*with pump*) aufpumpen. ~**ion** *n* Inflation *f*. ~**ionary** *adj* inflationär

in'flexible *adj* starr; (*person*) unbeugsam

inflict /ɪn'flɪkt/ *vt* zufügen (**on** *dat*); versetzen (*blow*) (**on** *dat*)

influen|ce /'ɪnfluəns/ *n* Einfluss *m* ● *vt* beeinflussen. ~**tial** *adj* einflussreich

influenza /ɪnflu'enzə/ *n* Grippe *f*

inform /ɪn'fɔ:m/ *vt* benachrichtigen; (*officially*) informieren; ~ **s.o. of sth** jdm etw mitteilen; **keep s.o.** ~**ed** jdn auf dem Laufenden halten ● *vi* ~ **against** denunzieren

in'formal *adj* zwanglos; (*unofficial*) inoffiziell. ~'**mality** *n* Zwanglosigkeit *f*

informant /ɪn'fɔ:mənt/ *n* Gewährsmann *m*

information /ɪnfə'meɪʃn/ *n* Auskunft f; a piece of ~ion eine Auskunft. ~ive adj aufschlussreich; (instructive) lehrreich

informer /ɪnˈfɔːmə(r)/ n Spitzel m; (Pol) Denunziant m

infra-'red /ɪnfrə-/ adj infrarot

in'frequent adj selten

infringe /ɪnˈfrɪndʒ/ vt/i ~ [on] verstoßen gegen. ~ment n Verstoß m

infuriate /ɪnˈfjʊərɪeɪt/ vt wütend machen. ~ing adj ärgerlich

ingenious /ɪnˈdʒiːnɪəs/ adj erfinderisch; (thing) raffiniert

ingenuity /ɪndʒɪˈnjuːətɪ/ n Geschicklichkeit f

ingrained /ɪnˈɡreɪnd/ adj eingefleischt; be ~ (dirt:) tief sitzen

ingratiate /ɪnˈɡreɪʃɪeɪt/ vt ~ oneself sich einschmeicheln (with bei)

in'gratitude n Undankbarkeit f

ingredient /ɪnˈɡriːdɪənt/ n (Culin) Zutat f

ingrowing /ˈɪnɡrəʊɪŋ/ adj (nail) eingewachsen

inhabit /ɪnˈhæbɪt/ vt bewohnen. ~ant n Einwohner(in) m(f)

inhale /ɪnˈheɪl/ vt/i einatmen; (Med & when smoking) inhalieren

inherent /ɪnˈhɪərənt/ adj natürlich

inherit /ɪnˈherɪt/ vt erben. ~ance n Erbschaft f, Erbe nt

inhibit|ed /ɪnˈhɪbɪtɪd/ adj gehemmt. ~ion n Hemmung f

inho'spitable adj ungastlich

in'human adj unmenschlich

inimitable /ɪˈnɪmɪtəbl/ adj unnachahmlich

initial /ɪˈnɪʃl/ adj anfänglich, Anfangs- ● n Anfangsbuchstabe m; my ~s meine Initialen. ~ly adv anfangs, am Anfang

initiate /ɪˈnɪʃɪeɪt/ vt einführen.

~ion n Einführung f

initiative /ɪˈnɪʃətɪv/ n Initiative f

inject /ɪnˈdʒekt/ vt einspritzen, injizieren. ~ion n Spritze f, Injektion f

injur|e /ˈɪndʒə(r)/ vt verletzen. ~y n Verletzung f

in'justice n Ungerechtigkeit f; do s.o. an ~ jdm unrecht tun

ink /ɪŋk/ n Tinte f

inlaid /ɪnˈleɪd/ adj eingelegt

inland /ˈɪnlənd/ adj Binnen- ● adv landeinwärts. I~ Revenue (UK) ≈ Finanzamt nt

in-laws /ˈɪnlɔːz/ npl 🗓 Schwiegereltern pl

inlay /ˈɪnleɪ/ n Einlegearbeit f

inlet /ˈɪnlet/ n schmale Bucht f; (Techn) Zuleitung f

inmate /ˈɪnmeɪt/ n Insasse m

inn /ɪn/ n Gasthaus nt

innate /ɪˈneɪt/ adj angeboren

inner /ˈɪnə(r)/ adj innere(r,s). ~most adj innerste(r,s)

innocen|ce /ˈɪnəsəns/ n Unschuld f. ~t adj unschuldig. ~tly adv in aller Unschuld

innocuous /ɪˈnɒkjʊəs/ adj harmlos

innovat|ion /ɪnəˈveɪʃn/ n Neuerung f. ~ive adj innovativ. ~or n Neuerer m

innumerable /ɪˈnjuːmərəbl/ adj unzählig

inoculat|e /ɪˈnɒkjʊleɪt/ vt impfen. ~ion n Impfung f

inof'fensive adj harmlos

in'operable adj nicht operierbar

in'opportune adj unpassend

inor'ganic adj anorganisch

'in-patient n [stationär behandelter] Krankenhauspatient m

input /ˈɪnpʊt/ n Input m & nt

inquest /ˈɪnkwest/ n gerichtliche Untersuchung f der Todesursache

inquir|e /ɪnˈkwaɪə(r)/ vi sich erkundigen (about nach); ~e **into** untersuchen ● vt sich erkundigen nach. ~**y** n Erkundigung f; (*investigation*) Untersuchung f

inquisitive /ɪnˈkwɪzətɪv/ adj neugierig

in'sane adj geisteskrank; (*fig*) wahnsinnig

in'sanitary adj unhygienisch

in'sanity n Geisteskrankheit f

insatiable /ɪnˈseɪʃəbl/ adj unersättlich

inscription /ɪnˈskrɪpʃn/ n Inschrift f

inscrutable /ɪnˈskruːtəbl/ adj unergründlich; (*expression*) undurchdringlich

insect /ˈɪnsekt/ n Insekt nt. ~**icide** n Insektenvertilgungsmittel nt

inse'cur|e adj nicht sicher; (*fig*) unsicher. ~**ity** n Unsicherheit f

in'sensitive adj gefühllos; ~ **to** unempfindlich gegen

in'separable adj untrennbar; (*people*) unzertrennlich

insert¹ /ˈɪnsɜːt/ n Einsatz m

insert² /ɪnˈsɜːt/ vt einfügen, einsetzen; einstecken (key); einwerfen (coin). ~**ion** n (insert) Einsatz m; (in text) Einfügung f

inside /ɪnˈsaɪd/ n Innenseite f; (of house) Innere(s) nt ● attrib Innen- ● adv innen; (indoors) drinnen; go ~ hineingehen; (come ~ hereinkommen; ~ **out** links [herum]; know sth ~ **out** etw in- und auswendig kennen ● prep ~ [of] in (+ dat/(into) + acc)

insight /ˈɪnsaɪt/ n Einblick m (into in + acc); (understanding) Einsicht f

insig'nificant adj unbedeutend

insin'cere adj unaufrichtig

insinuat|e /ɪnˈsɪnjʊeɪt/ vt andeuten. ~**ion** n Andeutung f

insipid /ɪnˈsɪpɪd/ adj fade

insist /ɪnˈsɪst/ vi darauf bestehen; ~ **on** bestehen auf (+ dat) ● vt ~ **that** darauf bestehen, dass. ~**ence** n Bestehen nt. ~**ent** adj beharrlich; be ~**ent** darauf bestehen

'insole n Einlegesohle f

insolen|ce /ˈɪnsələns/ n Unverschämtheit f. ~**t** adj unverschämt

in'soluble adj unlöslich; (fig) unlösbar

in'solvent adj zahlungsunfähig

insomnia /ɪnˈsɒmnɪə/ n Schlaflosigkeit f

inspect /ɪnˈspekt/ vt inspizieren; (test) prüfen; kontrollieren (ticket). ~**ion** n Inspektion f. ~**or** n Inspektor m; (of tickets) Kontrolleur m

inspiration /ɪnspəˈreɪʃn/ n Inspiration f

inspire /ɪnˈspaɪə(r)/ vt inspirieren

insta'bility n Unbeständigkeit f; (of person) Labilität f

install /ɪnˈstɔːl/ vt installieren. ~**ation** n Installation f

instalment /ɪnˈstɔːlmənt/ n (Comm) Rate f; (of serial) Fortsetzung f; (Radio, TV) Folge f

instance /ˈɪnstəns/ n Fall m; (example) Beispiel nt; in the first ~ zunächst; for ~ zum Beispiel

instant /ˈɪnstənt/ adj sofortig; (Culin) Instant- ● n Augenblick m, Moment m. ~**aneous** adj unverzüglich, unmittelbar

instant 'coffee n Pulverkaffee m

instantly /ˈɪnstəntlɪ/ adv sofort

instead /ɪnˈsted/ adv statt dessen; ~ **of** statt (+ gen), anstelle von; ~ **of me** an meiner Stelle; ~ **of going** anstatt zu gehen

'instep n Spann m, Rist m

instigat|e /ˈɪnstɪgeɪt/ vt anstiften; einleiten (proceedings). ~**ion** n Anstiftung f; at his ~**ion** auf seine

Veranlassung

instil /ɪnˈstɪl/ vt (pt/pp instilled) einprägen (into s.o. jdm)

instinct /ˈɪnstɪŋkt/ n Instinkt m. **~ive** adj instinktiv

institut|e /ˈɪnstɪtjuːt/ n Institut nt. **~ion** n Institution f; (home) Anstalt f

instruct /ɪnˈstrʌkt/ vt unterrichten; (order) anweisen. **~ion** n Unterricht m; Anweisung f. **~ions** pl for use Gebrauchsanweisung f. **~ive** adj lehrreich. **~or** n Lehrer(in) m(f); (Mil) Ausbilder m

instrument /ˈɪnstrəmənt/ n Instrument nt. **~al** adj Instrumental-

insubordinate adj ungehorsam. **~nation** n Ungehorsam m; (Mil) Insubordination f

insufficient adj nicht genügend

insulat|e /ˈɪnsjʊleɪt/ vt isolieren. **~ing tape** n Isolierband nt. **~ion** n Isolierung f

insult¹ /ˈɪnsʌlt/ n Beleidigung f

insult² /ɪnˈsʌlt/ vt beleidigen

insur|ance /ɪnˈʃʊərəns/ n Versicherung f. **~e** vt versichern

intact /ɪnˈtækt/ adj unbeschädigt; (complete) vollständig

'intake n Aufnahme f

in'tangible adj nicht greifbar

integral /ˈɪntɪɡrl/ adj wesentlich

integrat|e /ˈɪntɪɡreɪt/ vt integrieren ●vi sich integrieren. **~ion** n Integration f

integrity /ɪnˈteɡrəti/ n Integrität f

intellect /ˈɪntəlekt/ n Intellekt m. **~ual** adj intellektuell

intelligen|ce /ɪnˈtelɪdʒəns/ n Intelligenz f; (Mil) Nachrichtendienst m; (information) Meldungen pl. **~t** adj intelligent

intelligible /ɪnˈtelɪdʒəbl/ adj verständlich

intend /ɪnˈtend/ vt beabsichtigen;

be **~ed** for bestimmt sein für

intense /ɪnˈtens/ adj intensiv; (pain) stark. **~ly** adv äußerst; (study) intensiv

intensif|y /ɪnˈtensɪfaɪ/ v (pt/pp -ied) ●vt intensivieren ●vi zunehmen

intensity /ɪnˈtensəti/ n Intensität f

intensive /ɪnˈtensɪv/ adj intensiv; be in **~ care** auf der Intensivstation sein

intent /ɪnˈtent/ adj aufmerksam; **~ on** (absorbed in) vertieft in (+ acc) ●n Absicht f

intention /ɪnˈtenʃn/ n Absicht f. **~al** adj absichtlich

inter'acti|on n Wechselwirkung f. **~ve** adj interactiv

intercede /ɪntəˈsiːd/ vi Fürsprache einlegen (on behalf of für)

intercept /ɪntəˈsept/ vt abfangen

'interchange n Austausch m; (Auto) Autobahnkreuz nt

intercom /ˈɪntəkɒm/ n [Gegen]-sprechanlage f

'intercourse n (sexual) Geschlechtsverkehr m

interest /ˈɪntrəst/ n Interesse nt; (Comm) Zinsen pl ●vt interessieren; be **~ed** sich interessieren (in für). **~ing** adj interessant. **~ rate** n Zinssatz m

interface /ˈɪntəfeɪs/ n Schnittstelle f

interfere /ɪntəˈfɪə(r)/ vi sich einmischen. **~nce** n Einmischung f; (Radio, TV) Störung f

interim /ˈɪntərɪm/ adj Zwischen-; (temporary) vorläufig

interior /ɪnˈtɪərɪə(r)/ adj innere(r,s), Innen- ●n Innere(s) nt

interject /ɪntəˈdʒekt/ vt einwerfen. **~ion** n Interjektion f; (remark) Einwurf m

interlude /ˈɪntəluːd/ n Pause f;

(*performance*) Zwischenspiel nt

inter'marry vi untereinander heiraten; (*different groups:*) Mischehen schließen

intermediary /ɪntəˈmiːdɪərɪ/ n Vermittler(in) m(f)

intermediate /ɪntəˈmiːdɪət/ adj Zwischen-

interminable /ɪnˈtɜːmɪnəbl/ adj endlos [lang]

intermittent /ɪntəˈmɪtənt/ adj in Abständen auftretend

internal /ɪnˈtɜːnl/ adj innere(r,s); (*matter, dispute*) intern. **I∼ Revenue** (USA) ≈ Finanzamt nt. **∼ly** adv innerlich; (*deal with*) intern

inter'national adj international ●n Länderspiel nt; (*player*) Nationalspieler(in) m(f)

'Internet n Internet nt; **on the ∼** im Internet

internment /ɪnˈtɜːnmənt/ n Internierung f

'interplay n Wechselspiel nt

interpolate /ɪnˈtɜːpəleɪt/ vt einwerfen

interpret /ɪnˈtɜːprɪt/ vt interpretieren; auslegen (*text*); deuten (*dream*); (*translate*) dolmetschen ●vi dolmetschen. **∼ation** n Interpretation f. **∼er** n Dolmetscher(in) m(f)

interrogat|e /ɪnˈterəgeɪt/ vt verhören. **∼ion** n Verhör nt

interrogative /ɪntəˈrɒgətɪv/ adj & n ∼ [**pronoun**] Interrogativpronomen nt

interrupt /ɪntəˈrʌpt/ vt/i unterbrechen; **don't ∼!** red nicht dazwischen! **∼ion** n Unterbrechung f

intersect /ɪntəˈsekt/ vi sich kreuzen; (*of lines*) sich schneiden. **∼ion** n Kreuzung f

interspersed /ɪntəˈspɜːst/ ∼ **with** durchsetzt mit

inter'twine vi sich ineinanderschlingen

interval /ˈɪntəvl/ n Abstand m; (*Theat*) Pause f; (*Mus*) Intervall nt; **at hourly ∼s** alle Stunde; **bright ∼s** pl Aufheiterungen pl

interven|e /ɪntəˈviːn/ vi eingreifen; (*occur*) dazwischenkommen. **∼tion** n Eingreifen nt; (*Mil, Pol*) Intervention f

interview /ˈɪntəvjuː/ n (*in media*) Interview nt; (*for job*) Vorstellungsgespräch nt ●vt interviewen; ein Vorstellungsgespräch führen mit. **∼er** n Interviewer(in) m(f)

intimacy /ˈɪntɪməsɪ/ n Vertrautheit f; (*sexual*) Intimität f

intimate /ˈɪntɪmət/ adj vertraut; (*friend*) eng; (*sexually*) intim

intimidat|e /ɪnˈtɪmɪdeɪt/ vt einschüchtern. **∼ion** n Einschüchterung f

in'tolerable adj unerträglich

in'toleran|ce n Intoleranz f. **∼t** adj intolerant

intonation /ɪntəˈneɪʃn/ n Tonfall m

intoxicat|ed /ɪnˈtɒksɪkeɪtɪd/ adj betrunken; (*fig*) berauscht. **∼ion** n Rausch m

intransigent /ɪnˈtrænsɪdʒənt/ adj unnachgiebig

in'transitive adj intransitiv

intrepid /ɪnˈtrepɪd/ adj kühn, erschrocken

intricate /ˈɪntrɪkət/ adj kompliziert

intrigue /ɪnˈtriːg/ n Intrige f ●vt faszinieren. **∼ing** adj faszinierend

intrinsic /ɪnˈtrɪnsɪk/ adj ∼ **value** Eigenwert m

introduce /mtrə'dju:s/ vt vorstellen; (bring in, insert) einführen

introduct|ion /mtrə'dʌkʃn/ n Einführung f; (to person) Vorstellung f; (to book) Einleitung f. ~ory adj einleitend

introvert /'mtrəvɜ:t/ n introvertierter Mensch m

intru|de /m'tru:d/ vi stören. ~der n Eindringling m. ~sion n Störung f

intuit|ion /mtju:'ɪʃn/ n Intuition f. ~ive adj intuitiv

inundate /'mʌndeɪt/ vt überschwemmen

invade /m'veɪd/ vt einfallen in (+ acc). ~r n Angreifer m

invalid¹ /'mvəlɪd/ n Kranke(r) m/f

invalid² /m'vælɪd/ adj ungültig

in'valuable adj unschätzbar; (person) unersetzlich

in'variab|le adj unveränderlich. ~ly adv immer

invasion /m'veɪʒn/ n Invasion f

invent /m'vent/ vt erfinden. ~ion n Erfindung f. ~ive adj erfinderisch. ~or n Erfinder m

inventory /'mvəntrɪ/ n Bestandsliste f

invert /m'vɜ:t/ vt umkehren. ~ed commas npl Anführungszeichen pl

invest /m'vest/ vt investieren, anlegen; ~ in (fig: buy) sich (dat) zulegen

investigat|e /m'vestɪgeɪt/ vt untersuchen. ~ion n Untersuchung f

invest|ment /m'vestmənt/ n Anlage f; be a good ~ment (fig) sich bezahlt machen. ~or n Kapitalanleger m

invidious /m'vɪdɪəs/ adj unerfreulich; (unfair) ungerecht

invincible /m'vɪnsəbl/ adj unbesiegbar

inviolable /m'vaɪələbl/ adj

unantastbar

in'visible adj unsichtbar

invitation /mvɪ'teɪʃn/ n Einladung f

invit|e /m'vaɪt/ vt einladen. ~ing adj einladend

invoice /'mvɔɪs/ n Rechnung f ● vt ~ s.o. jdm eine Rechnung schicken

in'voluntary adj, -ily adv unwillkürlich

involve /m'vɒlv/ vt beteiligen; (affect) betreffen; (implicate) verwickeln; (entail) mit sich bringen; (mean) bedeuten; be ~d in beteiligt sein an (+ dat); (implicated) verwickelt sein in (+ acc); get ~d with s.o. sich mit jdm einlassen. ~d adj kompliziert. ~ment n Verbindung f

in'vulnerable adj unverwundbar; (position) unangreifbar

inward /'mwəd/ adj innere(r,s). ~s adv nach innen

iodine /'aɪədi:n/ n Jod nt

IOU abbr Schuldschein m

Iran /ɪ'rɑ:n/ n der Iran

Iraq /ɪ'rɑ:k/ n der Irak

irascible /ɪ'ræsəbl/ adj aufbrausend

irate /aɪ'reɪt/ adj wütend

Ireland /'aɪələnd/ n Irland nt

iris /'aɪərɪs/ n (Anat) Regenbogenhaut f, Iris f; (Bot) Schwertlilie f

Irish /'aɪərɪʃ/ adj irisch ● n the ~ pl die Iren. ~man n Ire m. ~woman n Irin f

iron /'aɪən/ adj Eisen-; (fig) eisern ● n Eisen nt; (appliance) Bügeleisen nt ● vt/i bügeln

ironic[al] /aɪ'rɒnɪk[l]/ adj ironisch

ironing /'aɪənɪŋ/ n Bügeln nt; (articles) Bügelwäsche f. ~-board n Bügelbrett nt

ironmonger /'-mʌŋɡə(r)/ n ~'s [shop] Haushaltswarengeschäft nt

irony /ˈaɪərənɪ/ n Ironie f

irrational /ɪˈræʃənl/ adj irrational

irreconcilable /ɪˈrekənsaɪləbl/ adj unversöhnlich

irrefutable /ɪrɪˈfjuːtəbl/ adj unwiderlegbar

irregular /ɪˈregjʊlə(r)/ adj unregelmäßig; (against rules) regelwidrig. **~ity** n Unregelmäßigkeit f; Regelwidrigkeit f

irrelevant /ɪˈreləvənt/ adj irrelevant

irreparable /ɪˈrepərəbl/ adj nicht wieder gutzumachen

irreplaceable /ɪrɪˈpleɪsəbl/ adj unersetzlich

irrepressible /ɪrɪˈpresəbl/ adj unverwüstlich; be ~ (person): nicht unterzukriegen sein

irresistible /ɪrɪˈzɪstəbl/ adj unwiderstehlich

irresolute /ɪˈrezəluːt/ adj unentschlossen

irrespective /ɪrɪˈspektɪv/ adj ~ of ungeachtet (+ gen)

irresponsible /ɪrɪˈspɒnsəbl/ adj. **-bly** adv unverantwortlich; (person) verantwortungslos

irreverent /ɪˈrevərənt/ adj respektlos

irrevocable /ɪˈrevəkəbl/ adj, **-bly** adv unwiderruflich

irrigat|e /ˈɪrɪgeɪt/ vt bewässern. **~ion** n Bewässerung f

irritable /ˈɪrɪtəbl/ adj reizbar

irritant /ˈɪrɪtənt/ n Reizstoff m

irritat|e /ˈɪrɪteɪt/ vt irritieren; (Med) reizen. **~ion** n Ärger m; (Med) Reizung f

is /ɪz/ see **be**

Islam /ˈɪzlɑːm/ n der Islam. **~ic** adj islamisch

island /ˈaɪlənd/ n Insel f. **~er** n Inselbewohner(in) m(f)

isolat|e /ˈaɪsəleɪt/ vt isolieren.

~ed adj (remote) abgelegen; (single) einzeln. **~ion** n Isoliertheit f; (Med) Isolierung f

Israel /ˈɪzreɪl/ n Israel nt. **~i** adj israelisch **●** n Israeli m/f

issue /ˈɪʃuː/ n Frage f; (outcome) Ergebnis nt; (of magazine) Ausgabe f; (offspring) Nachkommen pl **●** vt ausgeben; ausstellen (passport); erteilen (order); herausgeben (book); be ~d with sth etw erhalten

---

it /ɪt/

● pronoun

····► (as subject) er (m), sie (f), es (nt); (in impersonal sentence) es. where is the spoon? it's on the table wo ist der Löffel? Er liegt auf dem Tisch. it was very kind of you es war sehr nett von Ihnen. it's five o'clock es ist fünf Uhr

····► (as direct object) ihn (m), sie (f), es (nt). that's my pencil — give it to me das ist mein Bleistift — gib ihn mir.

····► (as dative object) ihm (m), ihr (f), ihm (nt). he found a track and followed it er fand eine Spur und folgte ihr.

····► (after prepositions)

! Combinations such as with it, from it, to it are translated by the prepositions with the prefix da- (damit, davon, dazu). Prepositions beginning with a vowel insert an 'r' (daran, darauf, darüber). I can't do anything with it ich kann nichts damit anfangen. don't lean on it! lehn dich nicht daran!

····► (the person in question) es.

it's me ich bin's. is it you,
Dad? bist du es, Vater? who is
it? wer ist da?

Italian /ɪˈtæljən/ adj italienisch ● n
Italiener(in) m(f); (Lang) Italienisch nt

italics /ɪˈtælɪks/ npl Kursivschrift f;
in ~s kursiv

Italy /ˈɪtəlɪ/ n Italien nt

itch /ɪtʃ/ n Juckreiz m; I have an ~
es juckt mich ● vi jucken; I'm ~ing
🔟 es juckt mich (to zu). ~y adj be
~y jucken

item /ˈaɪtəm/ n Gegenstand m;
(Comm) Artikel m; (on agenda)
Punkt m; (on invoice) Posten m;
(act) Nummer f

itinerary /aɪˈtɪnərərɪ/ n [Reise]-
route f

its /ɪts/ poss pron sein; (f) ihr

it's = it is, it has

itself /ɪtˈsɛlf/ pron selbst; (reflexive)
sich; by ~ von selbst; (alone) allein

ivory /ˈaɪvərɪ/ n Elfenbein nt
● attrib Elfenbein-

ivy /ˈaɪvɪ/ n Efeu m

Ivy League Amerikanische
Universitäten sind in
Gruppen von Institutio-
nen aufgeteilt, die untereinander
sportliche Veranstaltungen durchführen. Die exklusivste Gruppe ist
die Ivy League im Nordosten der
USA. (Efeuliga, nach den mit Efeu
bewachsenen, alten Universitätsge-
bäuden.) Harvard und Yale haben
den besten akademischen Ruf der
acht Eliteuniversitäten. Viele amerikanische Politiker haben an einer
Ivy-League Universität studiert.

Jj

jab /dʒæb/ n Stoß m; (🔟: injection)
Spritze f ● vt (pt/pp jabbed) stoßen

jabber /ˈdʒæbə(r)/ vi plappern

jack /dʒæk/ n (Auto) Wagenheber
m; (Cards) Bube m ● vt ~ up (Auto)
aufbocken

jacket /ˈdʒækɪt/ n Jacke f; (of book)
Schutzumschlag m

jackpot n hit the ~ das große
Los ziehen

jade /dʒeɪd/ n Jade m

jagged /ˈdʒæɡɪd/ adj zackig

jail /dʒeɪl/ = gaol

jam[1] /dʒæm/ n Marmelade f

jam[2] n Gedränge nt; (Auto) Stau m;
(fam. difficulty) Klemme f ● vt (pt/pp
jammed) ● vt klemmen (in in +
acc); stören (broadcast) ● vi
klemmen

Jamaica /dʒəˈmeɪkə/ n Jamaika nt

jangle /ˈdʒæŋɡl/ vi klimpern ● vt
klimpern mit

January /ˈdʒænjʊərɪ/ n Januar m

Japan /dʒəˈpæn/ n Japan nt. ~ese
adj japanisch ● n Japaner(in) m(f);
(Lang) Japanisch nt

jar[1] /dʒɑː(r)/ n Glas nt; (earthenware)
Topf m

jargon /ˈdʒɑːɡən/ n Jargon m

jaunt /dʒɔːnt/ n Ausflug m

jaunty /ˈdʒɔːntɪ/ adj -ily adv keck

javelin /ˈdʒævlɪn/ n Speer m

jaw /dʒɔː/ n Kiefer m

jazz /dʒæz/ n Jazz m. ~y adj knallig

jealous /ˈdʒɛləs/ adj eifersüchtig
(of auf + acc). ~y n Eifersucht f

jeans /dʒiːnz/ npl Jeans pl

jeer /dʒɪə(r)/ vi johlen; ~ at

verhöhnen

jelly /'dʒelɪ/ n Gelee nt; (dessert) Götterspeise f. ~**fish** n Qualle f

jeopar|dize /'dʒepədaɪz/ vt gefährden. ~**dy** n in ~**dy** gefährdet

jerk /dʒɜːk/ n Ruck m • vt stoßen; (pull) reißen • vi rucken; (limb, muscle) zucken. ~**ily** adv ruckweise. ~**y** adj ruckartig

jersey /'dʒɜːzɪ/ n Pullover m; (Sport) Trikot nt; (fabric) Jersey m

jest /dʒest/ n **in** ~ im Spaß

jet /dʒet/ n (of water) [Wasser]strahl m; (nozzle) Düse f; (plane) Düsenflugzeug nt

jet: ~-**black** adj pechschwarz. ~-**pro'pelled** adj mit Düsenantrieb

jetty /'dʒetɪ/ n Landesteg m; (breakwater) Buhne f

Jew /dʒuː/ n Jude m Jüdin f

jewel /'dʒuːəl/ n Edelstein m; (fig) Juwel nt. ~**ler** n Juwelier m; ~**ler's [shop]** Juweliergeschäft nt. ~**lery** n Schmuck m

Jew|ess /'dʒuːɪs/ n Jüdin f. ~**ish** adj jüdisch

jib /dʒɪb/ vi (pt/pp jibbed) (fig) sich sträuben (**at** gegen)

jigsaw /'dʒɪgsɔː/ n ~ [puzzle] Puzzlespiel nt

jilt /dʒɪlt/ vt sitzen lassen

jingle /'dʒɪŋgl/ n (rhyme) Verschen nt • vi klimpern

jinx /dʒɪŋks/ n it's got a ~ on it es ist verhext

jittery /'dʒɪtərɪ/ adj 🔢 nervös

job /dʒɒb/ n Aufgabe f; (post) Stelle f, 🔢 Job m; **be a** ~ 🔢 nicht leicht sein; **it's a good** ~ **that** es ist [nur] gut, dass. ~**less** adj arbeitslos

jockey /'dʒɒkɪ/ n Jockei m

jocular /'dʒɒkjʊlə(r)/ adj spaßhaft

jog /dʒɒg/ n Stoß m • v (pt/pp jogged) • vt anstoßen; ~ **s.o.'s**

memory jds Gedächtnis nachhelfen • vi (Sport) joggen. ~**ging** n Jogging nt

john /dʒɒn/ n (Amer, 🔢) Klo nt

join /dʒɔɪn/ n Nahtstelle f • vt verbinden (**to** mit); sich anschließen (+ dat) (person); (become member of) beitreten (+ dat); eintreten in (+ acc) (firm) • vi (roads): sich treffen. ~ **in** vi mitmachen. ~ **up** vi (Mil) Soldat werden • vt zusammenfügen

joint /dʒɔɪnt/ adj gemeinsam • n Gelenk nt; (in wood, brickwork) Fuge f; (Culin) Braten m; (🔢: bar) Lokal nt

jok|e /dʒəʊk/ n Scherz m; (funny story) Witz m; (trick) Streich m • vi scherzen. ~**er** n Witzbold m; (Cards) Joker m. ~**ing** n ~**ing apart** Spaß beiseite. ~**ingly** adv im Spaß

jolly /'dʒɒlɪ/ adj lustig • adv 🔢 sehr

jolt /dʒəʊlt/ n Ruck m • vt einen Ruck versetzen (+ dat) • vi holpern

Jordan /'dʒɔːdn/ n Jordanien nt

jostle /'dʒɒsl/ vt anrempeln

jot /dʒɒt/ vt (pt/pp jotted) ~ [**down**] sich (dat) notieren

journal /'dʒɜːnl/ n Zeitschrift f; (diary) Tagebuch nt. ~**ese** n Zeitungsjargon m. ~**ism** n Journalismus m. ~**ist** n Journalist(in) m(f)

journey /'dʒɜːnɪ/ n Reise f

jovial /'dʒəʊvɪəl/ adj lustig

joy /dʒɔɪ/ n Freude f. ~**ful** adj freudig, froh. ~**ride** n 🔢 Spritztour f [im gestohlenen Auto]

jubil|ant /'dʒuːbɪlənt/ adj überglücklich. ~**ation** n Jubel m

jubilee /'dʒuːbɪliː/ n Jubiläum nt

judder /'dʒʌdə(r)/ vi rucken

judge /dʒʌdʒ/ n Richter m; (of competition) Preisrichter m • vt beurteilen; (estimate) [ein]schätzen • vi urteilen (**by** nach). ~**ment** n Beurteilung f; (Jur) Urteil nt; (fig)

Urteilsvermögen nt

judic|ial /dʒuːˈdɪʃl/ adj gerichtlich.
~**ious** adj klug

jug /dʒʌg/ n Kanne f; (small) Kännchen nt; (for water, wine) Krug m

juggle /ˈdʒʌgl/ vi jonglieren. ~**r** n Jongleur m

juice /dʒuːs/ n Saft m

juicy /ˈdʒuːsɪ/ adj saftig; 🔲 (story) pikant

juke-box /ˈdʒuːk-/ n Musikbox f

July /dʒuˈlaɪ/ n Juli m

jumble /ˈdʒʌmbl/ n Durcheinander nt ●vt ~ [up] durcheinander bringen. ~ **sale** n [Wohltätigkeits]-basar m

jump /dʒʌmp/ n Sprung m; (in prices) Anstieg m; (in horse racing) Hindernis m ●vi springen; (start) zusammenzucken; **make s.o.** ~ jdn erschrecken; ~ **at** (fig) sofort zugreifen bei (offer); ~ **to conclusions** voreilige Schlüsse ziehen ●vt überspringen. ~ **up** vi aufspringen

jumper /ˈdʒʌmpə(r)/ n Pullover m, Pulli m

jumpy /ˈdʒʌmpɪ/ adj nervös

junction /ˈdʒʌŋkʃn/ n Kreuzung f; (Rail) Knotenpunkt m

June /dʒuːn/ n Juni m

jungle /ˈdʒʌŋgl/ n Dschungel m

junior /ˈdʒuːnɪə(r)/ adj jünger; (in rank) untergeordnet; (Sport) Junioren- ●n Junior m

junk /dʒʌŋk/ n Gerümpel nt, Trödel m

junkie /ˈdʒʌŋkɪ/ n 🔀 Fixer m

'junk-shop n Trödelladen m

jurisdiction /dʒʊərɪsˈdɪkʃn/ n Gerichtsbarkeit f

jury /ˈdʒʊərɪ/ n the ~ die Geschworenen pl; (for competition) die Jury

just /dʒʌst/ adj gerecht ●adv ge-

rade; (only) nur; (simply) einfach; (exactly) genau; ~ **as tall** ebenso groß; **I'm** ~ **going** ich gehe schon

justice /ˈdʒʌstɪs/ n Gerechtigkeit f; **do** ~ **to gerecht werden** (+ dat)

justifiab|le /ˈdʒʌstɪfaɪəbl/ adj berechtigt. ~**ly** adv berechtigterweise

justi|fication /dʒʌstɪfɪˈkeɪʃn/ n Rechtfertigung f. ~**fy** vt (pt/pp -ied) rechtfertigen

justly /ˈdʒʌstlɪ/ adv zu Recht

jut /dʒʌt/ vi (pt/pp jutted) ~ **out** vorstehen

juvenile /ˈdʒuːvənaɪl/ adj jugendlich; (childish) kindisch ●n Jugendliche(r) m/f. ~ **delinquency** n Jugendkriminalität f

Kk

kangaroo /kæŋgəˈruː/ n Känguru nt

kebab /kɪˈbæb/ n Spießchen nt

keel /kiːl/ n Kiel m ●vi ~ **over** umkippen; (Naut) kentern

keen /kiːn/ adj (-er, -est) (sharp) scharf; (intense) groß; (eager) eifrig, begeistert; ~ **on** 🔲 erpicht auf (+ acc); ~ **on s.o.** von jdm sehr angetan; **be** ~ **to do** sth etw gerne machen wollen. ~**ly** adv tief. ~**ness** n Eifer m, Begeisterung f

keep /kiːp/ n (maintenance) Unterhalt m; (of castle) Bergfried m; **for** ~**s** für immer ●v (pt/pp kept) ●vt behalten; (store) aufbewahren; (not throw away) aufheben; (support) unterhalten; (detain) aufhalten; freihalten (seat); halten (promise, animals); führen, haben (shop); einhalten (law, rules); ~ **s.o. waiting** jdn warten lassen; ~ sth to oneself etw nicht weitersagen ● vi (remain) bleiben; (food:) sich halten; ~ left/right sich links/rechts halten; ~ on doing sth etw weitermachen; (repeatedly) etw dauernd machen; ~ in with sich gut stellen mit. ~ **up** vi Schritt halten ● vt (continue) weitermachen

keep|er /'kiːpə(r)/ n Wärter(in) m(f). ~**ing** n be in ~ing with passen zu

kennel /'kenl/ n Hundehütte f; ~**s** pl (boarding) Hundepension f; (breeding) Zwinger m

Kenya /'kenjə/ n Kenia nt

kept /kept/ see keep

kerb /kɜːb/ n Bordstein m

kernel /'kɜːnl/ n Kern m

ketchup /'ketʃəp/ n Ketschup m

kettle /'ketl/ n [Wasser]kessel m; put the ~ on Wasser aufsetzen

key /kiː/ n Schlüssel m; (Mus) Tonart f; (of piano, typewriter) Taste f ● vt ~ **in** eintasten

key: ~**board** n Tastatur f; (Mus) Klaviatur f. ~**hole** n Schlüsselloch nt. ~**ring** n Schlüsselring m

khaki /'kɑːkɪ/ adj khakifarben ● n Khaki nt

kick /kɪk/ n [Fuß]tritt m; for ~s 🔢 zum Spaß ● vt treten; ~ **the bucket** 🔢 abkratzen ● vi (animal) ausschlagen

kid /kɪd/ n (🔢: child) Kind nt ● vt (pt/pp kidded) 🔢 ~ s.o. jdm etwas vormachen

kidnap /'kɪdnæp/ vt (pt/pp -napped) entführen. ~**per** n Entführer m. ~**ping** n Entführung f

kidney /'kɪdnɪ/ n Niere f

kill /kɪl/ vt töten; 🔢 totschlagen (time); ~ **two birds with one stone** zwei Fliegen mit einer Klappe schlagen. ~**er** n Mörder(in) m(f)

~**ing** n Tötung f; (murder) Mord m

killjoy n Spielverderber m

kilo /'kiːləʊ/ n Kilo nt

kilo: /'kɪlə/ ~**gram** n Kilogramm nt. ~**metre** n Kilometer m. ~**watt** n Kilowatt nt

kilt /kɪlt/ n Schottenrock m

kind¹ /kaɪnd/ n Art f; (brand, type) Sorte f; **what** ~ **of car?** was für ein Auto? ~ **of** 🔢 irgendwie

kind² adj (-er, -est) nett ● **to animals** gut zu Tieren

kind|ly /'kaɪndlɪ/ adj nett ● adv netterweise; (if you please) gefälligst. ~**ness** n Güte f; (favour) Gefallen m

king /kɪŋ/ n König m; (Draughts) Dame f. ~**dom** n Königreich nt; (fig & Relig) Reich nt

king: ~**fisher** n Eisvogel m. ~**-sized** adj extragroß

kink /kɪŋk/ n Knick m. ~**y** adj 🔢 pervers

kiosk /'kiːɒsk/ n Kiosk m

kip /kɪp/ n have a ~ 🔢 pennen ● vi (pt/pp kipped) 🔢 pennen

kipper /'kɪpə(r)/ n Räucherhering m

kiss /kɪs/ n Kuss m ● vt/i küssen

kit /kɪt/ n Ausrüstung f; (tools) Werkzeug nt; (construction ~) Bausatz m ● vt (pt/pp kitted) ~**out** ausrüsten

kitchen /'kɪtʃɪn/ n Küche f ● attrib Küchen-. ~**ette** n Kochnische f

kitchen: ~**garden** n Gemüsegarten m. ~**sink** n Spülbecken nt

kite /kaɪt/ n Drachen m

kitten /'kɪtn/ n Kätzchen nt

kitty /'kɪtɪ/ n (money) [gemeinsame] Kasse f

knack /næk/ n Trick m, Dreh m

knead /niːd/ vt kneten

knee /niː/ n Knie nt. ~**cap** n

k

Kniescheibe f

kneel /ni:l/ vi (pt/pp knelt) knien; ~ [down] sich [nieder]knien

knelt /nelt/ see kneel

knew /nju:/ see know

knickers /'nɪkəz/ npl Schlüpfer m

knife /naɪf/ n (pl knives) Messer nt ●vt einen Messerstich versetzen (+ dat)

knight /naɪt/ n Ritter m; (Chess) Springer m ●vt adeln

knit /nɪt/ vt/i (pt/pp knitted) stricken; ~ one's brow die Stirn runzeln. ~ting n Stricken nt; (work) Strickzeug nt. ~ting-needle n Stricknadel f. ~wear n Strickwaren pl

knives /naɪvz/ npl see knife

knob /nɒb/ n Knopf m; (on door) Knauf m; (small lump) Beule f. ~bly adj knorrig; (bony) knochig

knock /nɒk/ n Klopfen nt; (blow) Schlag m; there was a ~ es klopfte ●vt anstoßen; (☐: criticize) heruntermachen; ~ a hole in sth ein Loch in etw (acc) schlagen; ~ one's head sich (dat) den Kopf stoßen (on an + dat) ●vi klopfen. ~ about vt schlagen ●vi (☐) herumkommen. ~ down vt herunterwerfen; (with fist) schlagen; (in car) anfahren; (demolish) abreißen; (☐: reduce) herabsetzen. ~ off vt herunterwerfen; (☐: steal) klauen; (☐: complete quickly) hinhauen ●vi (☐: cease work) Feierabend machen. ~ out vt ausschlagen; (make unconscious) bewusstlos schlagen; (Boxing) k.o. schlagen. ~ over vt umwerfen; (in car) anfahren

knock: ~-down adj ~-down prices Schleuderpreise pl. ~er n Türklopfer m. ~-out n (Boxing) K.o. m

knot /nɒt/ n Knoten m ●vt (pt/pp

knotted) knoten

know /nəʊ/ vt/i (pt knew, pp known) wissen; kennen (person); können (language); get to ~ kennen lernen ●n in the ~ ☐ im Bild

know: ~-all n ☐ Alleswisser m. ~-how n ☐ [Sach]kenntnis f. ~ing adj wissend. ~ingly adv wissend; (intentionally) wissentlich

knowledge /'nɒlɪdʒ/ n Kenntnis f (of von/gen); (general) Wissen nt; (specialized) Kenntnisse pl. ~able adj be ~able viel wissen

knuckle /'nʌkl/ n [Finger]knöchel m; (Culin) Hachse f

kosher /'kəʊʃə(r)/ adj koscher

kudos /'kju:dɒs/ n ☐ Prestige nt

Ll

lab /læb/ n ☐ Labor nt

label /'leɪbl/ n Etikett nt ●vt (pt/pp labelled) etikettieren

laboratory /lə'bɒrətrɪ/ n Labor nt

laborious /lə'bɔːrɪəs/ adj mühsam

labour /'leɪbə(r)/ n Arbeit f; (workers) Arbeitskräfte pl; (Med) Wehen pl; L~ (Pol) die Labourpartei ●attrib Labour- ●vi arbeiten ●vt (fig) sich lange auslassen über (+ acc). ~er n Arbeiter m

¹labour-saving adj arbeitssparend

lace /leɪs/ n Spitze f; (of shoe) Schnürsenkel m ●vt schnüren

lack /læk/ n Mangel m (of an + dat) ●vt I ~ the time mir fehlt die Zeit ●vi be ~ing fehlen

laconic /lə'kɒnɪk/ adj, -ally adv lakonisch

lacquer /ˈlækə(r)/ n Lack m; (for hair) [Haar]spray m

lad /læd/ n Junge m

ladder /ˈlædə(r)/ n Leiter f; (in fabric) Laufmasche f

ladle /ˈleɪdl/ n [Schöpf]kelle f ● vt schöpfen

lady /ˈleɪdɪ/ n Dame f; (title) Lady f

lady: ~**bird** n, (Amer) ~**bug** n Marienkäfer m. ~**like** adj damenhaft

lag¹ /læg/ vi (pt/pp lagged) ~ behind zurückbleiben; (fig) nachhinken

lag² vt (pt/pp lagged) umwickeln (pipes)

lager /ˈlɑːgə(r)/ n Lagerbier nt

laid /leɪd/ see lay³

lain /leɪn/ see lie²

lake /leɪk/ n See m

lamb /læm/ n Lamm nt

lame /leɪm/ adj (-r, -st) lahm

lament /ləˈment/ n Klage f; (song) Klagelied nt ● vt beklagen ● vi klagen

laminated /ˈlæmɪneɪtɪd/ adj laminiert

lamp /læmp/ n Lampe f; (in street) Laterne f. ~**post** n Laternenpfahl m. ~**shade** n Lampenschirm m

lance /lɑːns/ vt (Med) aufschneiden

land /lænd/ n Land nt; plot of ~ Grundstück nt ● vt/i landen; ~ s.o. with sth 🗊 jdm etw aufhalsen

landing /ˈlændɪŋ/ n Landung f; (top of stairs) Treppenflur m. ~**stage** n Landesteg m

land: ~**lady** n Wirtin f. ~**lord** n Wirt m; (of land) Grundbesitzer m; (of building) Hausbesitzer m. ~**mark** n Erkennungszeichen nt; (fig) Meilenstein m. ~**owner** n Grundbesitzer m. ~**scape** /-skeɪp/ n Landschaft f. ~**slide** n Erdrutsch m

lane /leɪn/ n kleine Landstraße f; (Auto) Spur f; (Sport) Bahn f; 'get in ~' (Auto) 'bitte einordnen'

language /ˈlæŋgwɪdʒ/ n Sprache f; (speech, style) Ausdrucksweise f

languid /ˈlæŋgwɪd/ adj träge

languish /ˈlæŋgwɪʃ/ vi schmachten

lanky /ˈlæŋkɪ/ adj schlaksig

lantern /ˈlæntən/ n Laterne f

lap¹ /læp/ n Schoß m

lap² n (Sport) Runde f; (of journey) Etappe f ● vi (pt/pp lapped) plätschern (against gegen)

lap³ vt (pt/pp lapped) ~ up aufschlecken

lapel /ləˈpel/ n Revers nt

lapse /læps/ n Fehler m; (moral) Fehltritt m; (of time) Zeitspanne f ● vi (expire) erlöschen; ~ into verfallen in (+ acc)

laptop /ˈlæptɒp/ n Laptop m

lard /lɑːd/ n [Schweine]schmalz m

larder /ˈlɑːdə(r)/ n Speisekammer f

large /lɑːdʒ/ adj (-r, -st) & adv groß; by and ~ im Großen und Ganzen; at ~ auf freiem Fuß. ~**ly** adv großenteils

lark¹ /lɑːk/ n (bird) Lerche f

lark² n (joke) Jux m ● vi ~ about herumalbern

laryngitis /lærɪnˈdʒaɪtɪs/ n Kehlkopfentzündung f

larynx /ˈlærɪŋks/ n Kehlkopf m

laser /ˈleɪzə(r)/ n Laser m

lash /læʃ/ n Peitschenhieb m; (eyelash) Wimper f ● vt peitschen; (tie) festbinden (to an + acc). ~ **out** vi um sich schlagen; (spend) viel Geld ausgeben (on für)

lass /læs/ n Mädchen nt

lasso /ləˈsuː/ n Lasso nt

last /lɑːst/ adj & n letzte(r,s); ~ night heute od gestern Nacht;

latch | layer

(*evening*) gestern Abend; at ~ endlich; for the ~ time zum letzten Mal; the ~ but one der/die/das vorletzte ● *adv* zuletzt; (*last time*) das letzte Mal; he/she went ~ er-/sie ging als Letzter/Letzte ● *vi* dauern; (*weather:*) sich halten; (*relationship:*) halten. ~**ing** *adj* dauerhaft. ~**ly** *adv* schließlich, zum Schluss

latch /lætʃ/ n [einfache] Klinke f

late /leɪt/ *adj* & *adv* (-r, -st) spät; (*delayed*) verspätet; (*deceased*) verstorben; the ~**st news** die neuesten Nachrichten; **stay up** ~ bis spät aufbleiben; **arrive** ~ zu spät ankommen; **I am** ~ ich komme zu spät *od* habe mich verspätet; the **train is** ~ der Zug hat Verspätung. ~**comer** n Zuspätkommende(r) m/f. ~**ly** *adv* in letzter Zeit. ~**ness** n Zuspätkommen nt; (*delay*) Verspätung f

later /ˈleɪtə(r)/ *adj* & *adv* später; ~ **on** nachher

lateral /ˈlætərəl/ *adj* seitlich

lather /ˈlɑːðə(r)/ n [Seifen]schaum m

Latin /ˈlætɪn/ *adj* lateinisch ● n Latein nt. ~ **A'merica** n Lateinamerika nt

latitude /ˈlætɪtjuːd/ n (*Geog*) Breite f; (*fig*) Freiheit f

latter /ˈlætə(r)/ *adj* & n **the** ~ der/die/das Letztere

Latvia /ˈlætvɪə/ n Lettland nt

laudable /ˈlɔːdəbl/ *adj* lobenswert

laugh /lɑːf/ n Lachen nt; **with a** ~ lachend ● *vi* lachen (**at/about** über + *acc*); ~ **at s.o.** (*mock*) jdn auslachen. ~**able** *adj* lachhaft, lächerlich

laughter /ˈlɑːftə(r)/ n Gelächter nt

launch[1] /lɔːntʃ/ n (*boat*) Barkasse f

launch[2] n Stapellauf m; (*of rocket*) Abschuss m; (*of product*) Lancierung f ● *vt* vom Stapel lassen (*ship*); zu

Wasser lassen (*lifeboat*); abschießen (*rocket*); starten (*attack*); (*Comm*) lancieren (*product*)

laund(e)rette /lɔːndret/ n Münzwäscherei f

laundry /ˈlɔːndrɪ/ n Wäscherei f; (*clothes*) Wäsche f

laurel /ˈlɒrl/ n Lorbeer m

lava /ˈlɑːvə/ n Lava f

lavatory /ˈlævətrɪ/ n Toilette f

lavender /ˈlævəndə(r)/ n Lavendel m

lavish /ˈlævɪʃ/ *adj* großzügig; (*wasteful*) verschwenderisch ● *vt* ~ **sth on s.o.** jdn mit etw überschütten

law /lɔː/ n Gesetz nt; (*system*) Recht nt; **study** ~ Jura studieren; ~ **and order** Recht und Ordnung

law: ~**abiding** *adj* gesetzestreu. ~**court** n Gerichtshof m. ~**ful** *adj* rechtmäßig. ~**less** *adj* gesetzlos

lawn /lɔːn/ n Rasen m. ~**mower** n Rasenmäher m

lawyer /ˈlɔːjə(r)/ n Rechtsanwalt m -anwältin f

lax /læks/ *adj* lax, locker

laxative /ˈlæksətɪv/ n Abführmittel nt

laxity /ˈlæksətɪ/ n Laxheit f

lay[1] /leɪ/ *see* **lie**[2]

lay[2] *vt* (*pt/pp* laid) legen; decken (*table*); ~ **a trap** eine Falle stellen. ~ **down** *vt* hinlegen; festlegen (*rules, conditions*). ~ **off** *vt* entlassen (*workers*) ● *vi* (□: *stop*) aufhören. ~ **out** *vt* hinlegen; aufbahren (*corpse*); anlegen (*garden*); (*Typography*) gestalten

lay-by n Parkbucht f

layer /ˈleɪə(r)/ n Schicht f

lay: ~**man** n Laie m. ~**out** n Anordnung f; (*design*) Gestaltung f; (*Typography*) Layout nt

laze /leɪz/ vi ~**about**) faulenzen

laziness /'leɪzɪnɪs/ n Faulheit f

lazy /'leɪzɪ/ adj faul. ~**bones** n Faulenzer m

lead¹ /led/ n Blei nt; (of pencil) [Bleistift]mine f

lead² /liːd/ n Führung f; (leash) Leine f; (flex) Schnur f; (clue) Hinweis m, Spur f; (Theat) Hauptrolle f; (distance ahead) Vorsprung m; be in the ~ in Führung liegen ● vt/i (pt/pp led) führen; leiten (team); (induce) bringen; (at cards) ausspielen; ~ the way vorangehen; ~ up to sth (fig) etw (dat) vorangehen

leader /'liːdə(r)/ n Führer m; (of expedition, group) Leiter(in) m(f); (of orchestra) Konzertmeister m; (in newspaper) Leitartikel m. ~**ship** n Führung f; Leitung f

leading /'liːdɪŋ/ adj führend; ~ lady Hauptdarstellerin f

leaf /liːf/ n (pl leaves) Blatt nt; ~ through sth etw durchblättern. ~**let** n Merkblatt nt; (advertising) Reklameblatt nt; (political) Flugblatt nt

league /liːg/ n Liga f

leak /liːk/ n (hole) undichte Stelle f; (Naut) Leck nt; (of gas) Gasausfluss m ● vi undicht sein; (ship:) leck sein, lecken; (liquid:) auslaufen; (gas:) ausströmen ● vt auslaufen lassen; ~ sth to s.o. (fig) jdm etw zuspielen. ~**y** adj undicht; (Naut) leck

lean¹ /liːn/ adj (-er, -est) mager

lean² /liːn/ v (pt/pp leaned or leant) /lent/ ● vt lehnen (against/on an + acc) ● vi (person) sich lehnen (against/on an + acc); (not be straight) sich neigen; be ~ing against lehnen an (+ dat). ~ **back** vi sich zurücklehnen. ~ **forward** vi sich vorbeugen. ~ **out** vi sich hinauslehnen. ~ **over** vi sich vorbeugen

leaning /'liːnɪŋ/ adj schief ● n Neigung f

leap /liːp/ n Sprung m ● vi (pt/pp leapt or leaped) springen; he leapt at it 🅣 er griff sofort zu. ~ **year** n Schaltjahr nt

learn /lɜːn/ vt/i (pt/pp learnt or learned) lernen; (hear) erfahren; ~ to swim schwimmen lernen

learn|ed /'lɜːnɪd/ adj gelehrt. ~**er** n Anfänger m; ~**er** [driver] Fahrschüler(in) m(f). ~**ing** n Gelehrsamkeit f; ~**ing curve** Lernkurve f

lease /liːs/ n Pacht f; (contract) Mietvertrag m ● vt pachten

leash /liːʃ/ n Leine f

least /liːst/ adj geringste(r,s) ● n the ~ das wenigste; at ~ wenigstens, mindestens; not in the ~ nicht im Geringsten ● adv am wenigsten

leather /'leðə(r)/ n Leder nt

leave /liːv/ n Erlaubnis f; (holiday) Urlaub m; on ~ auf Urlaub; take one's ~ sich verabschieden ● v (pt/pp left) ● vt lassen; (go out of, abandon) verlassen; (forget) liegen lassen; (bequeath) vermachen (to dat); ~ it to me! überlassen Sie es mir! there is nothing left es ist nichts mehr übrig ● vi (weg)gehen/-fahren; (train, bus:) abfahren. ~ **behind** vt zurücklassen; (forget) liegen lassen. ~ **out** vt liegen lassen; (leave outside) draußen lassen; (omit) auslassen

leaves /liːvz/ see leaf

Lebanon /'lebənən/ n Libanon m

lecherous /'letʃərəs/ adj lüstern

lecture /'lektʃə(r)/ n Vortrag m; (Univ) Vorlesung f; (reproof) Strafpredigt f ● vi einen Vortrag/eine Vorlesung halten (on über + acc) ● vt ~ s.o. jdm eine Strafpredigt halten. ~**r** n Vortragende(r) m/f;

(*Univ*) Dozent(in) *m*(*f*)

led /led/ *see* lead²

ledge /ledʒ/ *n* Leiste *f*; (*shelf, of window*) Sims *m*; (*in rock*) Vorsprung *m*

ledger /'ledʒə(r)/ *n* Hauptbuch *nt*

leech /liːtʃ/ *n* Blutegel *m*

leek /liːk/ *n* Stange *f* Porree; ~s *pl* Porree *m*

left¹ /left/ *see* leave

left² /left/ linke(r,s) ● *adv* links; (*go*) nach links ● *n* linke Seite *f*; on the ~ links; from/to the ~ von/nach links; the ~ (*Pol*) die Linke

left: ~-**handed** *adj* linkshändig. ~-**luggage [office]** *n* Gepäckaufbewahrung *f*. ~**overs** *npl* Reste *pl*. ~-**wing** *adj* (*Pol*) linke(r,s)

leg /leg/ *n* Bein *nt*; (*Culin*) Keule *f*; (*of journey*) Etappe *f*

legacy /'legəsɪ/ *n* Vermächtnis *nt*, Erbschaft *f*

legal /'liːgl/ *adj* gesetzlich; (*matters*) rechtlich; (*department, position*) Rechts-; be ~ [gesetzlich] erlaubt sein

legality /lɪ'gælətɪ/ *n* Legalität *f*

legend /'ledʒənd/ *n* Legende *f*. ~**ary** *adj* legendär

legible /'ledʒəbl/ *adj*, **-bly** *adv* leserlich

legion /'liːdʒn/ *n* Legion *f*

legislat|e /'ledʒɪsleɪt/ *vi* Gesetze erlassen. ~**ion** *n* Gesetzgebung *f*; (*laws*) Gesetze *pl*

legislative /'ledʒɪslətɪv/ *adj* gesetzgebend

legitimate /lɪ'dʒɪtɪmət/ *adj* rechtmäßig; (*justifiable*) berechtigt

leisure /'leʒə(r)/ *n* Freizeit *f*; at your ~ wenn Sie Zeit haben. ~**ly** *adj* gemächlich

lemon /'lemən/ *n* Zitrone *f*. ~**ade** *n* Zitronenlimonade *f*

lend /lend/ *vt* (*pt/pp* lent) leihen (s.o. sth jdm etw)

length /leŋθ/ *n* Länge *f*; (*piece*) Stück *nt*; (*of wallpaper*) Bahn *f*; (*of time*) Dauer *f*

length|en /'leŋθən/ *vt* länger machen ● *vi* länger werden. ~**ways** *adv* der Länge nach

lengthy /'leŋθɪ/ *adj* langwierig

lenient /'liːnɪənt/ *adj* nachsichtig

lens /lenz/ *n* Linse *f*; (*Phot*) Objektiv *nt*; (*of spectacles*) Glas *nt*

lent /lent/ *see* lend

Lent *n* Fastenzeit *f*

lentil /'lentl/ *n* (*Bot*) Linse *f*

leopard /'lepəd/ *n* Leopard *m*

leotard /'liːətɑːd/ *n* Trikot *nt*

lesbian /'lezbɪən/ *adj* lesbisch ● *n* Lesbierin *f*

less /les/ *a, adv, n & prep* weniger; ~ and ~ immer weniger

lessen /'lesn/ *vt* verringern ● *vi* nachlassen; (*value:*) abnehmen

lesser /'lesə(r)/ *adj* geringere(r,s)

lesson /'lesn/ *n* Stunde *f*; (*in textbook*) Lektion *f*; (*Relig*) Lesung *f*; teach s.o. a ~ (*fig*) jdm eine Lehre erteilen

lest /lest/ *conj* (*literary*) damit ... nicht

let /let/ *vt* (*pt/pp* let, *pres p* letting) lassen; (*rent*) vermieten; ~ **alone** (*not to mention*) geschweige denn; ~ us go gehen wir; ~ me know sagen Sie mir Bescheid; ~ **oneself** in for sth 🔢 sich (*dat*) etw einbrocken. ~ **down** *vt* hinunter-/herunterlassen; (*lengthen*) länger machen; ~ s.o. **down** 🔢 jdn im Stich lassen; (*disappoint*) jdn enttäuschen. ~ **in** *vt* hereinlassen. ~ **off** *vt* abfeuern (*gun*); hochgehen lassen (*firework, bomb*); (*emit*) ausstoßen; (*excuse from*) befreien von; (*not punish*) frei ausgehen lassen. ~ **out** *vt* hinaus-/

herauslassen; (make larger) auslassen. ~ **through** vt durchlassen. ~ **up** vi 🔟 nachlassen

'**let-down** n Enttäuschung f, 🔟 Reinfall m

lethal /'liːθl/ adj tödlich

letharg|ic /lɪ'θɑːdʒɪk/ adj lethargisch. ~**y** n Lethargie f

letter /'letə(r)/ n Brief m; (of alphabet) Buchstabe m. ~**box** n Briefkasten m. ~**head** n Briefkopf m. ~**ing** n Beschriftung f

lettuce /'letɪs/ n [Kopf]salat m

'**let-up** n 🔟 Nachlassen nt

level /'levl/ adj eben; (horizontal) waagerecht; (in height) auf gleicher Höhe; (spoonful) gestrichen; one's ~ **best** sein Möglichstes ● n Höhe f; (fig) Ebene f, Niveau nt; (stage) Stufe f; on the ~ 🔟 ehrlich ● vt (pt/pp levelled) einebnen

level '**crossing** n Bahnübergang m

lever /'liːvə(r)/ n Hebel m ● vt ~ up mit einem Hebel anheben. ~**age** n Hebelkraft f

lewd /ljuːd/ adj (-er, -est) anstößig

liabilit|y /laɪə'bɪlətɪ/ n Haftung f; ~**ies** pl Verbindlichkeiten pl

liable /'laɪəbl/ adj haftbar; be ~ to do sth etw leicht tun können

liaise /lɪ'eɪz/ vi 🔟 Verbindungsperson sein

liaison /lɪ'eɪzɒn/ n Verbindung f; (affair) Verhältnis nt

liar /'laɪə(r)/ n Lügner(in) m(f)

libel /'laɪbl/ n Verleumdung f ● vt (pt/pp libelled) verleumden. ~**lous** adj verleumderisch

liberal /'lɪbərl/ adj tolerant; (generous) großzügig. L~ adj (Pol) liberal ● n Liberale(r) m/f

liberat|e /'lɪbəreɪt/ vt befreien. ~**ed** adj (woman) emanzipiert. ~**ion** n Befreiung f. ~**or** n Be-

freier m

liberty /'lɪbətɪ/ n Freiheit f; take liberties sich (dat) Freiheiten erlauben

librarian /laɪ'breərɪən/ n Bibliothekar(in) m(f)

library /'laɪbrərɪ/ n Bibliothek f

Libya /'lɪbɪə/ n Libyen nt

lice /laɪs/ see louse

licence /'laɪsns/ n Genehmigung f; (Comm) Lizenz f; (for TV) ~ Fernsehgebühr f; (for driving) Führerschein m; (for alcohol) Schankkonzession f

license /'laɪsns/ vt eine Genehmigung/(Comm) Lizenz erteilen (+ dat); be ~**d** (car:) zugelassen sein; (restaurant:) Schankkonzession haben. ~**plate** n (Amer) Nummernschild nt

lick /lɪk/ n Lecken nt; a ~ of paint ein bisschen Farbe ● vt lecken; (🔟: defeat) schlagen

lid /lɪd/ n Deckel m; (of eye) Lid nt

lie¹ /laɪ/ n Lüge f; tell a ~ lügen ● vi (pt/pp lied, pres p lying) lügen; ~ **to** belügen

lie² /laɪ/ vi (pt lay, pp lain, pres p lying) liegen; here ~**s** ... hier ruht ... ~ **down** vi sich hinlegen

'**lie-in** n have a ~ [sich] ausschlafen

lieu /ljuː/ n in ~ of statt (+ gen)

lieutenant /lef'tenənt/ n Oberleutnant m

life /laɪf/ n (pl lives) Leben nt; lose one's ~ ums Leben kommen

life: ~**boat** n Rettungsboot nt. ~**coach** n Lebensberater(in) m(f). ~**guard** n Lebensretter m. ~**jacket** n Schwimmweste f. ~**less** adj leblos. ~**like** adj naturgetreu. ~**long** adj lebenslang. ~**preserver** n (Amer) Rettungsring m. ~**size(d)** adj ... in Lebensgröße.

~time n Leben nt; in s.o.'s ~time zu jds Lebzeiten; the chance of a ~time eine einmalige Gelegenheit

lift /lɪft/ n Aufzug m, Lift m; give s.o. a ~ jdn mitnehmen; get a ~ mitgenommen werden ● vt heben; aufheben (restrictions) ● vi (fog:) sich lichten. ~ **up** vt hochheben

light[1] /laɪt/ adj (-er, -est) (not dark) hell; ~ **blue** hellblau ● n Licht nt; (lamp) Lampe f; have you [got] a ~? haben Sie Feuer? ● vt (pt/pp lit or lighted) anzünden (fire, cigarette); (illuminate) beleuchten. ~ **up** vi (face:) sich erhellen

light[2] adj (-er, -est) (not heavy) leicht; ~ **sentence** milde Strafe f ● adv travel ~ mit wenig Gepäck reisen

'**light-bulb** n Glühbirne f

lighten[1] /ˈlaɪtn/ vt heller machen

lighten[2] vt leichter machen (load)

lighter /ˈlaɪtə(r)/ n Feuerzeug nt

light: ~-'**hearted** adj unbekümmert. ~**house** n Leuchtturm m. ~**ing** n Beleuchtung f. ~**ly** adv leicht; get off ~**ly** glimpflich davonkommen

lightning /ˈlaɪtnɪŋ/ n Blitz m

'**lightweight** adj leicht ● n (Boxing) Leichtgewicht nt

like[1] /laɪk/ adj ähnlich; (same) gleich ● prep wie; (similar to) ähnlich (+ dat); ~ **this** so; what's he ~? wie ist er denn? ● conj (🗆: as) wie; (Amer: as if) als ob

like[2] vt mögen; I should/would ~ ich möchte; I ~ the car das Auto gefällt mir; ~ dancing/singing gern tanzen/singen ● n ~s and dislikes pl Vorlieben und Abneigungen pl

like|able /ˈlaɪkəbl/ adj sympathisch. ~**lihood** n Wahrscheinlichkeit f. ~**ly** adj & adv wahrscheinlich;

not ~**ly!** 🗆 auf gar keinen Fall!

'**like-minded** adj gleich gesinnt

liken /ˈlaɪkən/ vt vergleichen (to with)

like|ness /ˈlaɪknɪs/ n Ähnlichkeit f. ~**wise** adv ebenso

liking /ˈlaɪkɪŋ/ n Vorliebe f; is it to your ~? gefällt es Ihnen?

lilac /ˈlaɪlək/ n Flieder m

lily /ˈlɪlɪ/ n. Lilie f

limb /lɪm/ n Glied nt

lime[1] /laɪm/ n (fruit) Limone f; (tree) Linde f. ~**light** n be in the ~**light** im Rampenlicht stehen

limit /ˈlɪmɪt/ n Grenze f; (limitation) Beschränkung f; that's the ~! 🗆 das ist doch die Höhe! ● vt beschränken (to auf + acc). ~**ation** n Beschränkung f. ~**ed** adj beschränkt. ~**ed company** Gesellschaft f mit beschränkter Haftung

limousine /ˈlɪməziːn/ n Limousine f

limp[1] /lɪmp/ n Hinken nt ● vi hinken

limp[2] adj (-er -est) schlaff

limpid /ˈlɪmpɪd/ adj klar

line[1] /laɪn/ n Linie f; (length of rope, cord) Leine f; (Teleph) Leitung f; (of writing) Zeile f; (row) Reihe f; (wrinkle) Falte f; (of business) (Amer: queue) Schlange f; in ~ with gemäß (+ dat) ● vt säumen (street)

line[2] vt füttern (garment); (Techn) auskleiden

lined[1] /laɪnd/ adj (wrinkled) faltig; (paper) liniert

lined[2] (garment) gefüttert

'**line dancing** n Linedance-Tanzen m

linen /ˈlɪnɪn/ n Leinen nt; (articles) Wäsche f

liner /ˈlaɪnə(r)/ n Passagierschiff nt

'**linesman** n (-men) (Sport)

Linienrichter *m*

linger /'lɪŋɡə(r)/ *vi* [zurück]bleiben

lingerie /'læˈʒəri/ *n* Damenunterwäsche *f*

linguist /'lɪŋɡwɪst/ *n* Sprachkundige(r) *m/f*

linguistic /lɪŋˈgwɪstɪk/ *adj*, **-ally** *adv* sprachlich

lining /'laɪnɪŋ/ *n* (of garment) Futter *nt*; (Techn) Auskleidung *f*

link /lɪŋk/ *n* (of chain) Glied *nt* (fig) Verbindung *f* ●*vt* verbinden; ~ arms sich unterhaken

links /lɪŋks/ *n or npl* Golfplatz *m*

lint /lɪnt/ *n* Verbandstoff *m*

lion /'laɪən/ *n* Löwe *m*; ~'s share (fig) Löwenanteil *m*. ~**ess** *n* Löwin *f*

lip /lɪp/ *n* Lippe *f*; (edge) Rand *m*; (of jug) Schnabel *m*

lip: ~**-reading** *n* Lippenlesen *nt*. ~**-service** *n* pay ~**-service** ein Lippenbekenntnis ablegen (to zu). ~**stick** *n* Lippenstift *m*

liqueur /lɪ'kjʊə(r)/ *n* Likör *m*

liquid /'lɪkwɪd/ *n* Flüssigkeit *f* ●*adj* flüssig

liquidation /lɪkwɪ'deɪʃn/ *n* Liquidation *f*

liquidize /'lɪkwɪdaɪz/ *vt* [im Mixer] pürieren. ~**r** *n* Mixer *m*

liquor /'lɪkə(r)/ *n* Alkohol *m*. ~ **store** *n* (Amer) Spirituosengeschäft *nt*

lisp /lɪsp/ *n* Lispeln *nt* ●*vt/i* lispeln

list¹ /lɪst/ *n* Liste *f* ●*vt* aufführen

list² *vi* (ship): Schlagseite haben

listen /'lɪsn/ *vi* zuhören (to dat); ~ to the radio Radio hören. ~**er** *n* Zuhörer(in) *m(f)*; (Radio) Hörer(in) *m(f)*

listless /'lɪstlɪs/ *adj* lustlos

lit /lɪt/ see **light¹**

literacy /'lɪtərəsɪ/ *n* Lese- und Schreibfertigkeit *f*

literal /'lɪtərl/ *adj* wörtlich. ~**ly** *adv* buchstäblich

literary /'lɪtərəri/ *adj* literarisch

literate /'lɪtərət/ *adj* be ~ lesen und schreiben können

literature /'lɪtrətʃə(r)/ *n* Literatur *f*; 🄳 Informationsmaterial *nt*

lithe /laɪð/ *adj* geschmeidig

Lithuania /lɪθjʊ'eɪnɪə/ *n* Litauen *nt*

litre /'liːtə(r)/ *n* Liter *m* & *nt*

litter /'lɪtə(r)/ *n* Abfall *m*; (Zool) Wurf *m*. ~**-bin** *n* Abfalleimer *m*

little /'lɪtl/ *adj* klein; (not much) wenig ●*adv* & *n* wenig; a ~ ein bisschen/wenig; ~ by ~ nach und nach

live¹ /laɪv/ *adj* lebendig; (ammunition) scharf; ~ broadcast Live-Sendung *f*; be ~ (Electr) unter Strom stehen

live² /lɪv/ *vi* leben; (reside) wohnen. ~ on *vt* leben von; (eat) sich ernähren von ●*vi* weiterleben

liveli|hood /'laɪvlɪhʊd/ *n* Lebensunterhalt *m*. ~**ness** *n* Lebendigkeit *f*

lively /'laɪvlɪ/ *adj* lebhaft, lebendig

liver /'lɪvə(r)/ *n* Leber *f*

lives /laɪvz/ see **life**

livid /'lɪvɪd/ *adj* 🄳 wütend

living /'lɪvɪŋ/ *adj* lebend ●*n* earn one's ~ seinen Lebensunterhalt verdienen. ~**-room** *n* Wohnzimmer *nt*

lizard /'lɪzəd/ *n* Eidechse *f*

load /ləʊd/ *n* Last *f*; (quantity) Ladung *f*; (Electr) Belastung *f*; ~**s of** 🄳 jede Menge ●*vt* laden (goods, gun); beladen (vehicle); ~ a camera einen Film in eine Kamera einlegen. ~**ed** *adj* beladen; (🄳: rich) steinreich

loaf /ləʊf/ *n* (pl loaves) Brot *nt*

loan /ləʊn/ n Leihgabe f; (money) Darlehen nt; **on ~** geliehen • vt leihen (to dat)

loath /ləʊθ/ adj **be ~ to do sth** etw ungern tun

loath|e /ləʊð/ vt verabscheuen. **~ing** n Abscheu m

loaves /ləʊvz/ see **loaf**[1]

lobby /'lɒbɪ/ n Foyer nt; (anteroom) Vorraum m; (Pol) Lobby f

lobster /'lɒbstə(r)/ n Hummer m

local /'ləʊkl/ adj hiesig; (time, traffic) Orts-; **~ anaesthetic** örtliche Betäubung; **I'm not ~** ich bin nicht von hier • n Hiesige(r) m/f; (🔲: public house) Stammkneipe f. **~ call** n (Teleph) Ortsgespräch nt

locality /ləʊ'kælətɪ/ n Gegend f

localization /ləʊkəlaɪ'zeɪʃn/ n Lokalisierung f

locally /'ləʊkəlɪ/ adv am Ort

locat|e /ləʊ'keɪt/ vt ausfindig machen; **be ~ed** sich befinden. **~ion** n Lage f; **filmed on ~ion** als Außenaufnahme gedreht

lock[1] /lɒk/ n (hair) Strähne f

lock[2] n (on door) Schloss nt; (on canal) Schleuse f • vt abschließen • vi sich abschließen lassen. **~ in** vt einschließen. **~ out** vt ausschließen. **~ up** vt abschließen; einsperren (person)

locker /lɒkə(r)/ n Schließfach nt; (Mil) Spind m

lock|: ~out n Aussperrung f. **~smith** n Schlosser m

locomotive /ləʊkə'məʊtɪv/ n Lokomotive f

locum /'ləʊkəm/ n Vertreter(in) m(f)

locust /'ləʊkəst/ n Heuschrecke f

lodge /lɒdʒ/ n (porter's) Pförtnerhaus nt • vt (submit) einreichen; (deposit) deponieren • vi zur Untermiete wohnen (with bei); (become

fixed) stecken bleiben. **~r** n Untermieter(in) m(f)

lodging /'lɒdʒɪŋ/ n Unterkunft f. **~s** npl möbliertes Zimmer nt

loft /lɒft/ n Dachboden m

lofty /'lɒftɪ/ adj hoch

log /lɒɡ/ n Baumstamm m; (for fire) [Holz]scheit nt; **sleep like a ~** 🔲 wie ein Murmeltier schlafen • vi **~ off** sich abmelden; **~ on** sich anmelden

loggerheads /'lɒɡə-/ npl **be at ~** 🔲 sich in den Haaren liegen

logic /'lɒdʒɪk/ n Logik f. **~al** adj logisch

logo /'ləʊɡəʊ/ n Symbol nt, Logo nt

loiter /'lɔɪtə(r)/ vi herumlungern

loll /lɒl/ vi sich lümmeln

loll|ipop /'lɒlɪpɒp/ n Lutscher m. **~y** n Lutscher m; (🔲: money) Moneten pl

London /'lʌndən/ n London nt • attrib Londoner. **~er** n Londoner(in) m(f)

lone /ləʊn/ adj einzeln. **~liness** n Einsamkeit f

lonely /'ləʊnlɪ/ adj einsam

lone|r /'ləʊnə(r)/ n Einzelgänger m. **~some** adj einsam

long[1] /lɒŋ/ adj (-er /-ɡə(r)/, -est /'lɒŋɡɪst/) lang; (journey) weit; **a ~ time** lange; **a ~ way** weit; **in the ~ run** auf lange Sicht; (in the end) letzten Endes • adv lange; **all day ~** den ganzen Tag; **not ~ ago** vor kurzem; **before ~** bald; **no ~er** nicht mehr; **as ~ as** or **so ~ as** solange; **so ~!** 🔲 tschüs!

long[2] vi **~ for** sich sehnen nach

long-'distance adj Fern-; (Sport) Langstrecken-

longing /'lɒŋɪŋ/ adj sehnsüchtig • n Sehnsucht f

longitude /'lɒŋɡɪtjuːd/ n

(Geog) Länge f.

long: ~ **jump** n Weitsprung m. ~-**lived** /-lıvd/ adj langlebig. ~-**range** adj (Mil, Aviat) Langstrecken-; (forecast) langfristig. ~-**sighted** adj weitsichtig. ~-**sleeved** adj langärmelig. ~-**suffering** adj langmütig. ~-**term** adj langfristig. ~-**wave** n Langwelle. ~-**winded** /-'wındıd/ adj langatmig

loo /luː/ n 🔢 Klo nt

look /lʊk/ n Blick m; (appearance) Aussehen nt; [good] ~**s** pl [gutes] Aussehen nt; have a ~ at sich (dat) ansehen; go and have a ~ sieh mal nach ● vi sehen; (search) nachsehen; (seem) aussehen; don't ~ sieh hin; here! hören Sie mal! ~ at ansehen; ~ for suchen; ~ forward to sich freuen auf (+ acc); ~ in on vorbeischauen bei; ~ into (examine) nachgehen (+ dat); ~ like aussehen wie; ~ on to (room:) gehen auf (+ acc). ~ after vt betreuen. ~ down vi hinuntersehen; ~ down on s.o. (fig) auf jdn herabsehen. ~ out vi hinaus-/heraussehen; (take care) aufpassen; ~ out for Ausschau halten nach; ~ out! Vorsicht! ~ round vi sich umsehen. ~ up vi aufblicken; ~ up to s.o. (fig) zu jdm aufsehen ● vt nachschlagen (word)

'**look-out** n Wache f; (prospect) Aussicht f; be on the ~ for Ausschau halten nach

loom¹ /luːm/ n Webstuhl m

loom² vi auftauchen

loony /'luːnı/ adj 🔢 verrückt

loop /luːp/ n Schlinge f; (in road) Schleife f. ~**hole** n Hintertürchen nt; (in the law) Lücke f

loose /luːs/ adj (-r, -st) lose; (not tight enough) locker; (inexact) frei; be at a ~ end nichts zu tun haben. ~ '**change** n Kleingeld nt

loosen /'luːsn/ vt lockern

loot /luːt/ n Beute f ● vt/i plündern. ~**er** n Plünderer m

lop /lɒp/ vt (pt/pp lopped) stutzen

lop'sided adj schief

lord /lɔːd/ n Herr m; (title) Lord m; House of L~s ≈ Oberhaus nt; the L~'s Prayer das Vaterunser

lorry /'lɒrı/ n Last[kraft]wagen m

lose /luːz/ v (pt/pp lost) ● vt verlieren; (miss) verpassen ● vi verlieren; (clock:) nachgehen; get lost verloren gehen; (person) sich verlaufen. ~**r** n Verlierer m

loss /lɒs/ n Verlust m; be at a ~ nicht mehr weiter wissen

lost /lɒst/ see **lose**. ~ '**property office** n Fundbüro nt

lot¹ /lɒt/ Los m; (at auction) Posten m; draw ~**s** losen (for um)

lot² n the ~ alle; (everything) alles; a ~ [of] viel; (many) viele; ~**s of** 🔢 eine Menge; it has changed a ~ es hat sich sehr verändert

lotion /'ləʊʃn/ n Lotion f

lottery /'lɒtərı/ n Lotterie f. ~ **ticket** n Los nt

loud /laʊd/ adj (-er, -est) laut; (colours) grell ● adv [out] ~ laut. ~ '**speaker** n Lautsprecher m

lounge /laʊndʒ/ n Wohnzimmer nt; (in hotel) Aufenthaltsraum m. ● vi sich lümmeln

louse /laʊs/ n (pl **lice**) Laus f

lousy /'laʊzı/ adj 🔢 lausig

lout /laʊt/ n Flegel m, Lümmel m

lovable /'lʌvəbl/ adj liebenswert

love /lʌv/ n Liebe f; (Tennis) null; in ~ verliebt ● vt lieben; ~ **doing sth** etw sehr gerne machen. ~-**affair** n Liebesverhältnis nt. ~ **letter** n Liebesbrief m

lovely /'lʌvlı/ adj schön

lover /'lʌvə(r)/ n Liebhaber m

love: ~ **song** n Liebeslied nt. ~ **story** n Liebesgeschichte f

loving /ˈlʌvɪŋ/ adj liebevoll

low /ləʊ/ adj (-er, -est) niedrig; (cloud, note) tief; (voice) leise; (depressed) niedergeschlagen ● adv niedrig; (fly, sing) tief; (speak) leise ● n (weather) Tief nt; (fig) Tiefstand m

low: ~**brow** adj geistig anspruchslos. ~-**cut** adj (dress) tief ausgeschnitten

lower /ˈləʊə(r)/ adj & adv see **low** ● vt niedriger machen; (let down) herunterlassen; (reduce) senken

low: ~-**fat** adj fettarm. ~**lands** /-ləndz/ npl Tiefland nt. ~ **tide** n Ebbe f

loyal /ˈlɔɪəl/ adj treu. ~**ty** n Treue f. ~**ty card** n Treuekarte f

lozenge /ˈlɒzɪndʒ/ n Pastille f

Ltd abbr (Limited) GmbH

lubricant /ˈluːbrɪkənt/ n Schmiermittel nt

lubricat|e /ˈluːbrɪkeɪt/ vt schmieren. ~**ion** n Schmierung f

lucid /ˈluːsɪd/ adj klar. ~**ity** n Klarheit f

luck /lʌk/ n Glück nt; bad ~ Pech nt; good ~! viel Glück! ~**ily** adv glücklicherweise, zum Glück

lucky /ˈlʌkɪ/ adj glücklich; (day, number) Glücks-; be ~ Glück haben; (thing:) Glück bringen

lucrative /ˈluːkrətɪv/ adj einträglich

ludicrous /ˈluːdɪkrəs/ adj lächerlich

lug /lʌg/ vt (pt/pp lugged) 🄵 schleppen

luggage /ˈlʌgɪdʒ/ n Gepäck nt. **luggage:** ~**rack** in Gepäckablage f. ~-**van** n Gepäckwagen m

lukewarm /ˈluːk-/ adj lauwarm

lull /lʌl/ n Pause f ● vt ~ to sleep einschläfern

lullaby /ˈlʌləbaɪ/ n Wiegenlied nt

lumber /ˈlʌmbə(r)/ n Gerümpel nt; (Amer: timber) Bauholz nt ● vt ~ s.o. with sth jdm etw aufhalsen. ~**jack** n (Amer) Holzfäller m

luminous /ˈluːmɪnəs/ adj leuchtend

lump /lʌmp/ n Klumpen m; (of sugar) Stück nt; (swelling) Beule f; (in breast) Knoten m; (tumour) Geschwulst f; a ~ in one's throat 🄵 ein Kloß im Hals

lump: ~ **sugar** n Würfelzucker m. ~ **sum** n Pauschalsumme f

lumpy /ˈlʌmpɪ/ adj klumpig

lunacy /ˈluːnəsɪ/ n Wahnsinn m

lunar /ˈluːnə(r)/ adj Mond-

lunatic /ˈluːnətɪk/ n Wahnsinnige(r) m/f

lunch /lʌntʃ/ n Mittagessen nt ● vi zu Mittag essen

luncheon /ˈlʌntʃn/ n Mittagessen nt. ~ **voucher** n Essensbon m

lunch: ~-**hour** n Mittagspause f. ~-**time** n Mittagszeit f

lung /lʌŋ/ n Lungenflügel m; ~**s** pl Lunge f

lunge /lʌndʒ/ vi sich stürzen (at auf + acc)

lurch[1] /lɜːtʃ/ n leave in the ~ 🄵 im Stich lassen

lurch[2] vi (person:) torkeln

lure /ljʊə(r)/ vt locken

lurid /ˈlʊərɪd/ adj grell; (sensational) reißerisch

lurk /lɜːk/ vi lauern

luscious /ˈlʌʃəs/ adj lecker, köstlich

lush /lʌʃ/ adj üppig

lust /lʌst/ n Begierde f. ~**ful** adj lüstern

lustre /ˈlʌstə(r)/ n Glanz m

lusty /ˈlʌsti/ *adj* kräftig
luxuriant /lʌgˈʒʊəriənt/ *adj* üppig
luxurious /lʌgˈʒʊəriəs/ *adj* luxuriös
luxury /ˈlʌkʃəri/ *n* Luxus *m*
● *attrib* Luxus-
lying /ˈlaɪɪŋ/ *see* lie¹, lie²
lynch /lɪntʃ/ *vt* lynchen
lyric /ˈlɪrɪk/ *adj* lyrisch. **~al** *adj* lyrisch; (*enthusiastic*) schwärmerisch. **~ poetry** *n* Lyrik *f*. **~s** *npl* [Lied]text *m*

Mm

mac /mæk/ *n* 🔲 Regenmantel *m*
macabre /məˈkɑːbr/ *adj* makaber
macaroni /mækəˈrəʊni/ *n* Makkaroni *pl*
machinations /mækɪˈneɪʃnz/ *pl* Machenschaften *pl*
machine /məˈʃiːn/ *n* Maschine *f*
● *vt* (*sew*) mit der Maschine nähen; (*Techn*) maschinell bearbeiten. **~-gun** *n* Maschinengewehr *nt*
machinery /məˈʃiːnəri/ *n* Maschinerie *f*
mackerel /ˈmækrl/ *n inv* Makrele *f*
mackintosh /ˈmækɪntɒʃ/ *n* Regenmantel *m*
mad /mæd/ *adj* (madder, maddest) verrückt; (*dog*) tollwütig; (🔲: *angry*) böse (at auf + *acc*)
madam /ˈmædəm/ *n* gnädige Frau *f*
mad 'cow disease *n* 🔲 Rinderwahnsinn *m*
madden /ˈmædn/ *vt* (*make angry*) wütend machen
made /meɪd/ *see* make; **~ to**

measure maßgeschneidert
mad|ly /ˈmædli/ *adv* 🔲 wahnsinnig. **~man** *n* Irre(r) *m*. **~ness** *n* Wahnsinn *m*
madonna /məˈdɒnə/ *n* Madonna *f*
magazine /mægəˈziːn/ *n* Zeitschrift *f*; (*Mil, Phot*) Magazin *nt*
maggot /ˈmægət/ *n* Made *f*
magic /ˈmædʒɪk/ *n* Zauber *m*; (*tricks*) Zauberkunst *f* ● *adj* magisch; (*word, wand*) Zauber-. **~al** *adj* zauberhaft
magician /məˈdʒɪʃn/ *n* Zauberer *m*; (*entertainer*) Zauberkünstler *m*
magistrate /ˈmædʒɪstreɪt/ *n* ≈ Friedensrichter *m*
magnet /ˈmægnɪt/ *n* Magnet *m*. **~ic** *adj* magnetisch. **~ism** *n* Magnetismus *m*
magnification /mægnɪfɪˈkeɪʃn/ *n* Vergrößerung *f*
magnificen|ce /mægˈnɪfɪsəns/ *n* Großartigkeit *f*. **~t** *adj* großartig
magnify /ˈmægnɪfaɪ/ *vt* (*pt/pp* -ied) vergrößern; (*exaggerate*) übertreiben. **~ing glass** *n* Vergrößerungsglas *nt*
magnitude /ˈmægnɪtjuːd/ *n* Größe *f*; (*importance*) Bedeutung *f*
magpie /ˈmægpaɪ/ *n* Elster *f*
mahogany /məˈhɒgəni/ *n* Mahagoni *nt*
maid /meɪd/ *n* Dienstmädchen *nt*; old ~ (*pej*) alte Jungfer *f*
maiden /ˈmeɪdn/ *adj* (*speech, voyage*) Jungfern-. **~ name** *n* Mädchenname *m*
mail /meɪl/ *n* Post *f* ● *vt* mit der Post schicken
mail: **~bag** *n* Postsack *m*. **~box** *n* (*Amer*) Briefkasten *m*. **~ing list** *n* Postversandliste *f*. **~man** *n* (*Amer*) Briefträger *m*. **~-order firm** *n* Versandhaus *nt*

maim /meɪm/ vt verstümmeln

main /meɪn/ adj Haupt- ● n (water, gas, electricity) Hauptleitung f

main: ~**land** /-lænd/ n Festland nt. ~**ly** adv hauptsächlich. ~**stay** n (fig) Stütze f. ~ **street** n Hauptstraße f

maintain /meɪn'teɪn/ vt aufrechterhalten; (keep in repair) instand halten; (support) unterhalten; (claim) behaupten

maintenance /'meɪntənəns/ n Aufrechterhaltung f; (care) Instandhaltung f; (allowance) Unterhalt m

maize /meɪz/ n Mais m

majestic /mə'dʒestɪk/ adj, -ally adv majestätisch

majesty /'mædʒəsti/ n Majestät f

major /'meɪdʒə(r)/ adj größer ● n (Mil) Major m; (Mus) Dur nt ● vi ~ in als Hauptfach studieren

majority /mə'dʒɒrəti/ n Mehrheit f; in the ~ in der Mehrzahl

major road n Hauptverkehrsstraße f

make /meɪk/ n (brand) Marke f ● v (pt/pp made). ● vt machen; (force) zwingen; (earn) verdienen; halten (speech); treffen (decision); erreichen (destination) ● vi ~ **do** vi zurechtkommen (with mit). ~ **for** vi zusteuern auf (+ acc). ~ **off** vi sich davonmachen (with mit). ~ **out** vt (distinguish) ausmachen; (write out) ausstellen; (assert) behaupten. ~ **up** vt (constitute) bilden; (invent) erfinden; (apply cosmetics to) schminken; ~ **up one's mind** sich entschließen ● vi sich versöhnen. ~ **up for** sth etw wieder gutmachen; ~ **up for lost time** verlorene Zeit aufholen

'make-believe n Phantasie f

maker /'meɪkə(r)/ n Hersteller m

make: ~ **shift** adj behelfsmäßig

● n Notbehelf m. ~**-up** n Make-up m

maladjusted /mælə'dʒʌstɪd/ adj verhaltensgestört

male /meɪl/ adj männlich ● n Mann m; (animal) Männchen nt. ~ **nurse** n Krankenpfleger m. ~ **voice 'choir** n Männerchor m

malice /'mælɪs/ n Bosheit f

malicious /mə'lɪʃəs/ adj böswillig

malign /mə'laɪn/ vt verleumden

malignant /mə'lɪgnənt/ adj bösartig

mallet /'mælɪt/ n Holzhammer m

malnu'trition /mæl-/ n Unterernährung f

malt /mɔːlt/ n Malz nt

mal'treat /mæl-/ vt misshandeln. ~**ment** n Misshandlung f

mammal /'mæml/ n Säugetier nt

mammoth /'mæməθ/ adj riesig

man /mæn/ n (pl men) Mann m; (mankind) der Mensch; (chess) Figur f; (draughts) Stein m ● vt (pt/pp manned) bemannen (ship); bedienen (pump); besetzen (counter)

manage /'mænɪdʒ/ vt leiten; verwalten (estate); (cope with) fertig werden mit; ~ **to do** sth es schaffen, etw zu tun ● vi zurechtkommen; ~ **on** auskommen mit. ~**able** adj (tool) handlich; (person) fügsam. ~**ment** n Leitung f; the ~**ment** die Geschäftsleitung f

manager /'mænɪdʒə(r)/ n Geschäftsführer m; (of bank) Direktor m; (of estate) Verwalter m; (Sport) [Chef]trainer m. ~**ess** n Geschäftsführerin f. ~**ial** adj ~**ial staff** Führungskräfte pl

managing /'mænɪdʒɪŋ/ adj ~ **director** Generaldirektor m

mandate /'mændeɪt/ n Mandat nt. ~**ory** adj obligatorisch

mane /meɪn/ n Mähne f

manful /'mænfl/ adj mannhaft

man: ~**handle** vt grob behandeln (person). ~**hole** n Kanalschacht m. ~**hood** n Mannesalter nt; (quality) Männlichkeit f. ~**hour** n Arbeitsstunde f. ~**hunt** n Fahndung f

man|ia /'meɪnɪə/ n Manie f; ~**iac** n Wahnsinnige(r) m/f

manicure /'mænɪkjʊə(r)/ n Maniküre f ●vt maniküren

manifest /'mænɪfest/ adj offensichtlich

manifesto /mænɪ'festəʊ/ n Manifest nt

manifold /'mænɪfəʊld/ adj mannigfaltig

manipulat|e /mə'nɪpjʊleɪt/ vt handhaben; (pej) manipulieren. ~**ion** n Manipulation f

man'kind n die Menschheit

manly /'mænlɪ/ adj männlich

'man-made adj künstlich. ~ **fibre** n Kunstfaser f

manner /'mænə(r)/ n Weise f; (kind, behaviour) Art f; (good/bad) ~**s** [gute/schlechte] Manieren pl. ~**ism** n Angewohnheit f

manœuvrable /mə'nu:vrəbl/ adj manövrierfähig

manœuvre /mə'nu:və(r)/ n Manöver nt ●vt/i manövrieren

manor /'mænə(r)/ n Gutshof m; (house) Gutshaus nt

'manpower n Arbeitskräfte pl

mansion /'mænʃn/ n Villa f

'manslaughter n Totschlag m

mantelpiece /'mæntl-/ n Kaminsims m & nt

manual /'mænjʊəl/ adj Hand- n Handbuch nt

manufacture /mænjʊ'fæktʃə(r)/ vt herstellen ●n Herstellung f. ~**r** n Hersteller m

manure /mə'njʊə(r)/ n Mist m

manuscript /'mænjʊskrɪpt/ n Manuskript nt

many /'menɪ/ adj viele ●n a good/ great ~ sehr viele

map /mæp/ n Landkarte f; (of town) Stadtplan m

maple /'meɪpl/ n Ahorn m

mar /mɑː/ vt (pt/pp marred) verderben

marathon /'mærəθən/ n Marathon m

marble /'mɑːbl/ n Marmor m; (for game) Murmel f

March /mɑːtʃ/ n März m

march n Marsch m ●vi marschieren ●vt marschieren lassen; ~ s.o. off jdn abführen

mare /meə(r)/ n Stute f

margarine /mɑːdʒə'riːn/ n Margarine f

margin /'mɑːdʒɪn/ n Rand m; (leeway) Spielraum m; (Comm) Spanne f. ~**al** adj geringfügig

marigold /'mærɪɡəʊld/ n Ringelblume f

marina /mə'riːnə/ n Jachthafen m

marine /mə'riːn/ adj Meeres- ●n Marine f; (sailor) Marineinfanterist m

marital /'mærɪtl/ adj ehelich. ~ **status** n Familienstand m

maritime /'mærɪtaɪm/ adj See-

mark[1] /mɑːk/ n (former German currency) Mark f

mark[2] n Fleck m; (sign) Zeichen nt; (trace) Spur f; (target) Ziel nt; (Sch) Note f ●vt markieren; (spoil) beschädigen; (characterize) kennzeichnen; (Sch) korrigieren; (Sport) decken; ~ **time** (Mil) auf der Stelle treten; (fig) abwarten. ~ **out** vt markieren

marked /mɑːkt/ adj, ~**ly** adv deutlich; (pronounced) ausgeprägt

m

market /ˈmɑːkɪt/ n Markt m ● vt
vertreiben; (*launch*) auf den Markt
bringen. **~ing** n Marketing nt. **~**
reˈsearch n Marktforschung f

marking /ˈmɑːkɪŋ/ n Markierung
f; (*on animal*) Zeichnung f

marksman /ˈmɑːksmən/ n Scharf-
schütze m

marmalade /ˈmɑːməleɪd/ n Oran-
genmarmelade f

maroon /məˈruːn/ adj dunkelrot

marooned /məˈruːnd/ adj (*fig*)
von der Außenwelt abgeschnitten

marquee /mɑːˈkiː/ n Festzelt nt

marquetry /ˈmɑːkɪtrɪ/ n Einlegearbeit f

marriage /ˈmærɪdʒ/ n Ehe f; (*wedding*) Hochzeit f. **~able** adj hei-
ratsfähig

married /ˈmærɪd/ *see* marry ● adj
verheiratet. **~** life n Eheleben nt

marrow /ˈmærəʊ/ n (*Anat*) Mark
nt; (*vegetable*) Kürbis m

marr|y /ˈmærɪ/ vt/i (*pt/pp* mar-
ried) heiraten; (*unite*) trauen; get
~ied heiraten

marsh /mɑːʃ/ n Sumpf m

marshal /ˈmɑːʃl/ n Marschall m;
(*steward*) Ordner m

marshy /ˈmɑːʃɪ/ adj sumpfig

martial /ˈmɑːʃl/ adj kriegerisch. **~**
law n Kriegsrecht nt

martyr /ˈmɑːtə(r)/ n Märtyrer(in)
m(f). **~dom** n Martyrium nt

marvel /ˈmɑːvl/ n Wunder nt ● vi
(*pt/pp* marvelled) staunen (at über
+ acc). **~lous** a, **-ly** adv wunderbar

Marxis|m /ˈmɑːksɪzm/ n Marxis-
mus m. **~t** adj marxistisch ● n Mar-
xist(in) m(f)

marzipan /ˈmɑːzɪpæn/ n Marzipan nt

mascot /ˈmæskət/ n Maskott-
chen nt

masculin|e /ˈmæskjʊlɪn/ adj
männlich ● n (*Gram*) Maskulinum
nt. **~ity** n Männlichkeit f

mash /mæʃ/ n ①, **~ed potatoes**
npl Kartoffelpüree nt

mask /mɑːsk/ n Maske f ● vt maskieren

masochis|m /ˈmæsəkɪzm/ n Ma-
sochismus m. **~t** n Masochist m

mason /ˈmeɪsn/ n Steinmetz m.
~ry n Mauerwerk nt

mass[1] /mæs/ n (*Relig*) Messe f

mass[2] n Masse f ● vi sich sammeln;
(*Mil*) sich massieren

massacre /ˈmæsəkə(r)/ n Massaker nt ● vt niedermetzeln

massage /ˈmæsɑːʒ/ n Massage f
● vt massieren

masseu|r /mæˈsɜː(r)/ n Masseur
m. **~se** n Masseuse f

massive /ˈmæsɪv/ adj massiv;
(*huge*) riesig

mass: **~ 'media** npl Massenme-
dien pl. **~proˈduce** vt in Massenproduktion herstellen. **~proˈduc**
tion n Massenproduktion f

mast /mɑːst/ n Mast m

master /ˈmɑːstə(r)/ n Herr m;
(*teacher*) Lehrer m; (*craftsman, artist*) Meister m; (*of ship*) Kapitän m
● vt meistern; beherrschen
(*language*)

master: **~ly** adj meisterhaft.
~-mind n führender Kopf m ● vt
der führende Kopf sein von.
~piece n Meisterwerk nt. **~y** n (*of
subject*) Beherrschung f

mat /mæt/ n Matte f; (*on table*) Untersatz m

match[1] /mætʃ/ n Wettkampf m;
(*in ball games*) Spiel nt; (*Tennis*)
Match nt; (*marriage*) Heirat f; be a
good **~** (*colours*) gut zusammenpassen; be no **~** for s.o. jdm nicht
gewachsen sein ● vt (*equal*) gleich-

match | mayonnaise

kommen (+ dat); (be like) passen zu; (find sth similar) etwas Passendes finden zu ●vi zusammenpassen

match² n Streichholz nt. **~box** n Streichholzschachtel f

mate¹ /meɪt/ n Kumpel m; (assistant) Gehilfe m; (Naut) Maat m; (Zool) Männchen nt; (female) Weibchen nt ●vi sich paaren

mate² n (Chess) Matt nt

material /məˈtɪərɪəl/ n Material nt; (fabric) Stoff m; raw **~s** Rohstoffe pl ●adj materiell

materialism /məˈtɪərɪəlɪzm/ n Materialismus m. **~istic** adj materialistisch. **~ize** vi sich verwirklichen

maternal /məˈtɜːnl/ adj mütterlich

maternity /məˈtɜːnɪtɪ/ n Mutterschaft f. **~ clothes** npl Umstandskleidung f. **~ ward** n Entbindungsstation f

mathematical /mæθəˈmætɪkl/ adj mathematisch. **~ian** n Mathematiker(in) m(f)

mathematics /mæθəˈmætɪks/ n Mathematik f

maths /mæθs/ n ① Mathe f

matinée /ˈmætɪneɪ/ n (Theat) Nachmittagsvorstellung f

matrimony /ˈmætrɪmənɪ/ n Ehe f

matron /ˈmeɪtrən/ n (of hospital) Oberin f; (of school) Hausmutter f

matt /mæt/ adj matt

matted /ˈmætɪd/ adj verfilzt

matter /ˈmætə(r)/ n (affair) Sache f; (Phys: substance) Materie f; money **~s** Geldangelegenheiten pl; what is the **~**? was ist los? ●vi wichtig sein; **~ to s.o.** jdm etwas ausmachen; it doesn't **~** es macht nichts. **~-of-fact** adj sachlich

mattress /ˈmætrɪs/ n Matratze f

mature /məˈtjʊə(r)/ adj reif; (Comm) fällig ●vi reifen; (person:) reifer werden; (Comm) fällig werden

●vt reifen lassen. **~ity** n Reife f; (Comm) Fälligkeit f

mauve /məʊv/ adj lila

maximum /ˈmæksɪməm/ adj maximal ●n (pl -ima) Maximum nt. **~ speed** n Höchstgeschwindigkeit f

---

may /meɪ/

pres may, pt might

● modal verb

····▸ (expressing possibility) können. she may come es kann sein, dass sie kommt; es ist möglich, dass sie kommt. she might come (more distant possibility) sie könnte kommen. it may/might rain es könnte regnen. I may be wrong vielleicht irre ich mich. he may have missed his train vielleicht hat er seinen Zug verpasst

····▸ (expressing permission) dürfen. may I come in? darf ich reinkommen? you may smoke Sie dürfen rauchen

····▸ (expressing wish) may the best man win! auf dass der Beste gewinnt!

····▸ (expressing concession) he may be slow but he's accurate mag od kann sein, dass er langsam ist, aber dafür ist er auch genau

····▸ may/might as well können. we may/might as well go wir könnten eigentlich ebensogut gehen; we might as well give up da können wir gleich aufgeben

---

May n Mai m

maybe /ˈmeɪbɪ/ adv vielleicht

'May Day n der Erste Mai

mayonnaise /meɪəˈneɪz/ n

Mayonnaise f

mayor /'meə(r)/ n Bürgermeister m. **~ess** n Bürgermeisterin f; (wife of mayor) Frau Bürgermeister f

maze /meɪz/ n Irrgarten m; (fig) Labyrinth nt

me /miː/ pron (acc) mich; (dat) mir; it's **~** 🔲 ich bin es

meadow /'medəʊ/ n Wiese f

meagre /'miːɡə(r)/ adj dürftig

meal /miːl/ n Mahlzeit f; (food) Essen nt; (grain) Schrot m

mean¹ /miːn/ adj (-er, -est) (miserly) geizig; (unkind) gemein; (poor) schäbig

mean² adj mittlere(r,s) ● n (average) Durchschnitt m

mean³ vt (pt/pp meant) heißen; (signify) bedeuten; (intend) beabsichtigen; I **~** it das ist mein Ernst; **~** well es gut meinen; be meant for (present:) bestimmt sein für; (remark:) gerichtet sein an (+ acc)

meaning /'miːnɪŋ/ n Bedeutung f. **~ful** adj bedeutungsvoll. **~less** adj bedeutungslos

means /miːnz/ n Möglichkeit f, Mittel nt; **~** of transport Verkehrsmittel nt; by **~** of durch; by all **~**! aber natürlich! by no **~** keineswegs ● npl (resources) [Geld]mittel pl

meant /ment/ see mean³

'meantime n the **~** in der Zwischenzeit ● adv inzwischen

'meanwhile adv inzwischen

measles /'miːzlz/ n Masern pl

measure /'meʒə(r)/ n Maß nt; (action) Maßnahme f ● vt/i messen; **~** up to (fig) herankommen an (+ acc). **~d** adj gemessen. **~ment** n Maß nt

meat /miːt/ n Fleisch nt

mechanic /mɪ'kænɪk/ n Mechaniker m. **~ical** adj mechanisch. **~ical engineering** Maschinenbau m

mechanism /'mekənɪzm/ n Mechanismus m. **~ize** vt mechanisieren

medal /'medl/ n Orden m; (Sport) Medaille f

medallist /'medəlɪst/ n Medaillengewinner(in) m(f)

meddle /'medl/ vi sich einmischen (in in + acc); (tinker) herumhantieren (with an + acc)

media /'miːdɪə/ see medium ● n pl the **~** die Medien pl

mediate /'miːdɪeɪt/ vi vermitteln. **~or** n Vermittler(in) m(f)

medical /'medɪkl/ adj medizinisch; (treatment) ärztlich ● n ärztliche Untersuchung f. **~ insurance** n Krankenversicherung f. **~ student** n Medizinstudent m

medicated /'medɪkeɪtɪd/ adj medizinisch. **~ion** n (drugs) Medikamente pl

medicinal /mɪ'dɪsɪnl/ adj medizinisch; (plant) heilkräftig

medicine /'medsɪn/ n Medizin f; (preparation) Medikament nt

medieval /medɪ'iːvl/ adj mittelalterlich

mediocre /miːdɪ'əʊkə(r)/ adj mittelmäßig. **~ity** n Mittelmäßigkeit f

meditate /'medɪteɪt/ vi nachdenken (on über + acc). **~ion** n Meditation f

Mediterranean /medɪtə'reɪnɪən/ n Mittelmeer nt ● adj Mittelmeer-

medium /'miːdɪəm/ adj mittlere(r,s); (steak) medium; of **~** size von mittlerer Größe ● n (pl media) Medium nt; (means) Mittel nt

medium: ~-sized adj mittelgroß. **~ wave** n Mittelwelle f

medley /'medlɪ/ n Gemisch nt; (Mus) Potpourri nt

meek /miːk/ adj (-er, -est) sanftmütig; (unprotesting, compliant) widerspruchslos

meet /miːt/ v (pt/pp **met**) ● vt treffen; (by chance) begegnen (+ dat); (at station) abholen; (make the acquaintance of) kennen lernen; stoßen auf (+ acc) (problem); bezahlen (bill); erfüllen (requirements) ● vi sich treffen; (for the first time) sich kennen lernen

meeting /ˈmiːtɪŋ/ n Treffen nt; (by chance) Begegnung f; (discussion) Besprechung f; (of committee) Sitzung f; (large) Versammlung f

megalomania /meɡələˈmeɪnɪə/ n Größenwahnsinn m

megaphone /ˈmeɡəfəʊn/ n Megaphon nt

melancholy /ˈmelənkəlɪ/ adj melancholisch ● n Melancholie f

mellow /ˈmeləʊ/ adj(-er, -est) (fruit) ausgereift; (sound, person) sanft ● vi reifer werden

melodious /mɪˈləʊdɪəs/ adj melodiös

melodramatic /melədrəˈmætɪk/ adj, -ally adv melodramatisch

melody /ˈmelədɪ/ n Melodie f

melon /ˈmelən/ n Melone f

melt /melt/ vt/i schmelzen

member /ˈmembə(r)/ n Mitglied nt; (of family) Angehörige(r) m/f; M~ of Parliament Abgeordnete(r) m/f. ~ship n Mitgliedschaft f; (members) Mitgliederzahl f

memento /mɪˈmentəʊ/ n Andenken nt

memo /ˈmeməʊ/ n Mitteilung f

memoirs /ˈmemwɑːz/ n pl Memoiren pl

memorable /ˈmemərəbl/ adj denkwürdig

memorial /mɪˈmɔːrɪəl/ n Denkmal nt. ~ service n Gedenkfeier f

memorize /ˈmeməraɪz/ vt sich (dat) einprägen

memory /ˈmemərɪ/ n Gedächtnis nt; (thing remembered) Erinnerung f; (of computer) Speicher m; from ~ auswendig; in ~ of zur Erinnerung an (+ acc). ~ stick n Memory-stick m

men /men/ see **man**

menace /ˈmenɪs/ n Drohung f; (nuisance) Plage f ● vt bedrohen. ~ing adj. ~ly adv drohend

mend /mend/ vt reparieren; (patch) flicken; ausbessern (clothes)

menfolk n pl Männer pl

menial /ˈmiːnɪəl/ adj niedrig

menopause /ˈmenə-/ n Wechseljahre pl

mental /ˈmentl/ adj geistig; (🗇: mad) verrückt. ~ a'rithmetic n Kopfrechnen nt. ~ illness n Geisteskrankheit f

mentality /menˈtælətɪ/ n Mentalität f

mention /ˈmenʃn/ n Erwähnung f ● vt erwähnen; don't ~ it keine Ursache; bitte

menu /ˈmenjuː/ n Speisekarte f

merchandise /ˈmɜːtʃəndaɪz/ n Ware f

merchant /ˈmɜːtʃənt/ n Kaufmann m; (dealer) Händler m. ~ 'navy n Handelsmarine f

merci|ful /ˈmɜːsɪfl/ adj barmherzig. ~fully adv 🗇 glücklicherweise. ~less adj erbarmungslos

mercury /ˈmɜːkjʊrɪ/ n Quecksilber nt

mercy /ˈmɜːsɪ/ n Barmherzigkeit f, Gnade f; be at s.o.'s ~ jdm ausgeliefert sein

mere /mɪə(r)/ adj bloß

merest /ˈmɪərɪst/ adj kleinste(r,s)

merge /mɜːdʒ/ vt/i zusammenlaufen; (Comm) fusionieren

merger /ˈmɜːdʒə(r)/ n Fusion f

meringue /məˈræŋ/ n Baiser nt

merit /'merɪt/ n Verdienst nt; (advantage) Vorzug m; (worth) Wert m ●vt verdienen

merry /'merɪ/ adj fröhlich

merry-go-round n Karussell nt

mesh /meʃ/ n Masche f

mesmerized /'mezmǝraɪzd/ adj (fig) [wie] gebannt

mess /mes/ n Durcheinander nt; (trouble) Schwierigkeiten pl; (something spilt) Bescherung f 🟦; (Mil) Messe f; make a ~ of (botch) verpfuschen ●vt ~ up in Unordnung bringen; (botch) verpfuschen ●vi ~ about with etw herumalbern; (tinker) herumspielen (with mit)

message /'mesɪdʒ/ n Nachricht f; give s.o. a ~ jdm etwas ausrichten

messenger /'mesɪndʒǝ(r)/ n Bote m

Messrs /'mesǝz/ n pl see Mr; (on letter) ~ Smith Firma Smith

messy /'mesɪ/ adj schmutzig; (untidy) unordentlich

met /met/ see meet

metal /'metl/ n Metall nt ●adj Metall-. ~**lic** adj metallisch

metaphor /'metǝfǝ(r)/ n Metapher f. ~**ical** adj metaphorisch

meteor /'miːtɪǝ(r)/ n Meteor m. ~**ic** adj kometenhaft

meteorological /miːtɪǝrǝ 'lɒdʒɪkl/ adj Wetter-

meteorolog|ist /miːtɪǝ 'rɒlǝdʒɪst/ n Meteorologe m/ -gin f. ~**y** n Meteorologie f

meter[1] /'miːtǝ(r)/ n Zähler m

meter[2] n (Amer) = metre

method /'meθǝd/ n Methode f; (Culin) Zubereitung f

methodical /mɪ'θɒdɪkl/ adj systematisch, methodisch

methylated /'meθɪleɪtɪd/ adj ~ spirit[s] Brennspiritus m

meticulous /mɪ'tɪkjʊlǝs/ adj sehr genau

metre /'miːtǝ(r)/ n Meter m & nt; (rhythm) Versmaß nt

metric /'metrɪk/ adj metrisch

metropolis /mɪ'trɒpǝlɪs/ n Metropole f

metropolitan /metrǝ'pɒlɪtǝn/ adj haupstädtisch; (international) weltstädtisch

mew /mjuː/ n Miau nt ●vi miauen

Mexican /'meksɪkǝn/ adj mexikanisch ●n Mexikaner(in) m(f). '**Mexico** n Mexiko nt

miaow /mɪ'aʊ/ n Miau nt ●vi miauen

mice /maɪs/ see mouse

micro: ~**film** n Mikrofilm m. ~**light** [aircraft] n Ultraleichtflugzeug nt. ~**phone** n Mikrofon nt. ~**scope** /-skǝʊp/ n Mikroskop nt. ~**scopic** /-'skɒpɪk/ adj mikroskopisch. ~**wave** [oven] n Mikrowellenherd m

mid /mɪd/ adj ~ May Mitte Mai; in ~ air in der Luft

midday /'mɪddeɪ/ n Mittag m

middle /'mɪdl/ adj mittlere(r,s); the M~ Ages das Mittelalter; the ~ class[es] der Mittelstand; the M~ East der Nahe Osten ●n Mitte f; in the ~ of the night mitten in der Nacht

middle: ~-**aged** adj mittleren Alters. ~-**class** adj bürgerlich

midge /mɪdʒ/ n [kleine] Mücke f

midget /'mɪdʒɪt/ n Liliputaner(in) m(f)

Midlands /'mɪdlǝndz/ npl the ~ Mittelengland n

midnight /'mɪdnaɪt/ n Mitternacht f

midriff /'mɪdrɪf/ n 🟦 Taille f

midst /mɪdst/ n in the ~ of mitten in (+ dat); in our ~ unter uns

mid: ~**summer** n Hochsommer m. ~**way** adv auf halbem Wege. ~**wife** n Hebamme f. '~**winter** n Mitte f des Winters

might[1] /mart/ modal verb I ~ vielleicht; it ~ be true es könnte wahr sein; he asked if he ~ go er fragte, ob er gehen dürfte; you ~ have drowned du hättest ertrinken können

might[2] n Macht f

mighty /'martɪ/ adj mächtig

migraine /'mi:greɪn/ n Migräne f

migrat|e /mar'greɪt/ vi abwandern; (birds:) ziehen. ~**ion** n Wanderung f. (of birds) Zug m

mike /maɪk/ n 🅘 Mikrofon nt

mild /maɪld/ adj (-er, -est) mild

mild|ly /'maɪldlɪ/ adv leicht; to put it ~ly gelinde gesagt. ~**ness** n Milde f

mile /maɪl/ n Meile f (= 1,6 km); ~**s too big** 🅘 viel zu groß

mile|age /-ɪdʒ/ n Meilenzahl f; (of car) Meilenstand m

militant /'mɪlɪtənt/ adj militant

military /'mɪlɪtrɪ/ adj militärisch. ~ **service** n Wehrdienst m

milk /mɪlk/ n Milch f ● vt melken

milk: ~**man** n Milchmann m. ~**shake** n Milchmixgetränk nt. ~**tooth** n Milchzahn m

milky /'mɪlkɪ/ adj milchig. **M~ Way** n (Astronomy) Milchstraße f

mill /mɪl/ n Mühle f; (factory) Fabrik f

millennium /mɪ'lenɪəm/ n Jahrtausend nt

milli|gram /'mɪlɪ-/ n Milligramm nt. ~**metre** n Millimeter m & nt

million /'mɪljən/ n Million f; a ~ pounds eine Million Pfund. ~**aire** n Millionär(in) m (f)

mime /maɪm/ n Pantomime f ● vt

pantomimisch darstellen

mimic /'mɪmɪk/ n Imitator m ● vt (pt/pp mimicked) nachahmen

mince /mɪns/ n Hackfleisch nt ● vt (Culin) durchdrehen; not ~ words kein Blatt vor den Mund nehmen

mince: ~**meat** n Masse f aus Korinthen, Zitronat usw; make ~**meat of** (fig) vernichtend schlagen. ~**pie** n mit 'mincemeat' gefülltes Pastetchen nt

mincer /'mɪnsə(r)/ n Fleischwolf m

mind /maɪnd/ n Geist m; (sanity) Verstand m; give s.o. a piece of one's ~ jdm gehörig die Meinung sagen; make up one's ~ sich entschließen; be out of one's ~ nicht bei Verstand sein; have sth in mind etw im Sinn haben; bear sth in ~ an etw (acc) denken; have a good ~ to große Lust haben, zu; I have changed my ~ ich habe es mir anders überlegt ● vt aufpassen auf (+ acc); I don't ~ the noise der Lärm stört mich nicht; ~ the step! Achtung Stufe! ● vi (care) sich kümmern (about um); I don't ~ mir macht es nichts aus; never ~! macht nichts! do you ~ if? haben Sie etwas dagegen, wenn? ~ **out** vi aufpassen

'**mindless** adj geistlos

mine[1] /maɪn/ poss pron meine(r), meins; a friend of ~ ein Freund von mir; that is ~ das gehört mir

mine[2] n Bergwerk nt; (explosive) Mine f ● vt abbauen; (Mil) verminen

miner /'maɪnə(r)/ n Bergarbeiter m

mineral /'mɪnərl/ n Mineral nt. ~**water** n Mineralwasser nt

minesweeper /'maɪn-/ n Minenräumboot nt

mingle /'mɪŋgl/ vi ~ with sich mischen unter (+ acc)

miniature /'mɪnɪtʃə(r)/ adj Klein-

● *n* Miniatur *f*

mini|bus /'mɪnɪ-/ *n* Kleinbus *m*.
~**cab** *n* Kleintaxi *nt*

minim|al /'mɪnɪməl/ *adj* minimal.
~**um** *n* (*pl* -**ima**) Minimum *nt* ● *adj*
Mindest-

mining /'maɪnɪŋ/ *n* Bergbau *m*

miniskirt /'mɪnɪ-/ *n* Minirock *m*

minist|er /'mɪnɪstə(r)/ *n* Minister
m; (*Relig*) Pastor *m*. ~**erial** *adj* mi-
nisteriell

ministry /'mɪnɪstrɪ/ *n* (*Pol*) Ministerium *nt*

mink /mɪŋk/ *n* Nerz *m*

minor /'maɪnə(r)/ *adj* kleiner; (*less
important*) unbedeutend ● *n* Min-
derjährige(r) *m/f*; (*Mus*) Moll *nt*

minority /maɪ'nɒrətɪ/ *n* Minderheit *f*

minor road *n* Nebenstraße *f*

mint¹ /mɪnt/ *n* Münzstätte *f* ● *adj*
(*stamp*) postfrisch; **in ~ condition**
wie neu ● *vt* prägen

mint² *n* (*herb*) Minze *f*; (*sweet*)
Pfefferminzbonbon *m* & *nt*

minus /'maɪnəs/ *prep* minus, weniger; (ɪ: *without*) ohne

minute¹ /'mɪnɪt/ *n* Minute *f*; **in a
~** (*shortly*) gleich; ~**s** *pl* (*of meeting*) Protokoll *nt*

minute² /maɪ'njuːt/ *adj* winzig

miracl|e /'mɪrəkl/ *n* Wunder *nt*.
~**ulous** *adj* wunderbar

mirror /'mɪrə(r)/ *n* Spiegel *m* ● *vt*
widerspiegeln

mirth /mɜːθ/ *n* Heiterkeit *f*

misad'venture /mɪs-/ *n* Missgeschick *nt*

misappre'hension *n* Missverständnis *nt*; **be under a ~**
sich irren

misbe'hav|e *vi* sich schlecht be-
nehmen. ~**iour** *n* schlechtes Benehmen *nt*

mis'calcu|late *vt* falsch berech-
nen ● *vi* sich verrechnen. ~**lation**
n Fehlkalkulation *f*

'miscarriage *n* Fehlgeburt *f*

miscellaneous /mɪsə'leɪnɪəs/ *adj*
vermischt

mischief /'mɪstʃɪf/ *n* Unfug *m*

mischievous /'mɪstʃɪvəs/ *adj*
schelmisch; (*malicious*) boshaft

miscon'ception *n* falsche Vorstellung *f*

mis'conduct *n* unkorrektes Verhalten *nt*; (*adultery*) Ehebruch *m*

miser /'maɪzə(r)/ *n* Geizhals *m*

miserable /'mɪzrəbl/ *adj*, -**bly** *adv*
unglücklich; (*wretched*) elend

miserly /'maɪzəlɪ/ *adv* geizig

misery /'mɪzərɪ/ *n* Elend *nt*; (ɪ:
person) Miesepeter *m*

mis'fire *vi* fehlzünden; (*go wrong*)
fehlschlagen

'misfit *n* Außenseiter(in) *m(f)*

mis'fortune *n* Unglück *nt*

mis'givings *npl* Bedenken *pl*

mis'guided *adj* töricht

mishap /'mɪshæp/ *n* Missgeschick *nt*

misin'form *vt* falsch unterrichten

misin'terpret *vt* missdeuten

mis'judge *vt* falsch beurteilen

mis'lay *vt* (*pt/pp* -**laid**) verlegen

mis'lead *vt* (*pt/pp* -**led**) irreführen.
~**ing** *adj* irreführend

mis'manage *vt* schlecht verwalten. ~**ment** *n* Misswirtschaft *f*

misnomer /mɪs'nəʊmə(r)/ *n* Fehl-
bezeichnung *f*

'misprint *n* Druckfehler *m*

mis'quote *vt* falsch zitieren

misrepre'sent *vt* falsch darstellen

miss /mɪs/ *n* Fehltreffer *m* ● *vt* verpassen; (*fail to hit or find*) verfeh-

len; (*fail to attend*) versäumen; (*fail to notice*) übersehen; (*feel the loss of*) vermissen ●*vi* (*fail to hit*) nicht treffen. ~ **out** *vt* auslassen

Miss *n* (*pl* -es) Fräulein *nt*

missile /ˈmɪsaɪl/ *n* [Wurf]geschoss *nt*; (Mil) Rakete *f*

missing /ˈmɪsɪŋ/ *adj* fehlend; (*lost*) verschwunden; (Mil) vermisst; be ~ fehlen

mission /ˈmɪʃn/ *n* Auftrag *m*; (Mil) Einsatz *m*; (Relig) Mission *f*

missionary /ˈmɪʃənrɪ/ *n* Missionar(in) *m(f)*

mis'spell *vt* (*pt/pp* -spelt or -spelled) falsch schreiben

mist /mɪst/ *n* Dunst *m*; (fog) Nebel *m*; (on window) Beschlag *m* ●*vi* ~ **up** beschlagen

mistake /mɪˈsteɪk/ *n* Fehler *m*; by ~ aus Versehen ●*vt* (*pt* mistook, *pp* mistaken); ~ **for** verwechseln mit

mistaken /mɪˈsteɪkən/ *adj* falsch; be ~ sich irren. ~**ly** *adv* irrtümlicherweise

mistletoe /ˈmɪsltəʊ/ *n* Mistel *f*

mistress /ˈmɪstrɪs/ *n* Herrin *f*; (teacher) Lehrerin *f*; (lover) Geliebte *f*

mis'trust *n* Misstrauen *nt* ●*vt* misstrauen (+ *dat*)

misty /ˈmɪstɪ/ *adj* dunstig; (foggy) neblig; (fig) unklar

misunder'stand *vt* (*pt/pp* -stood) missverstehen. ~**ing** *nt* Missverständnis *nt*

misuse[1] /mɪsˈjuːz/ *vt* missbrauchen

misuse[2] /mɪsˈjuːs/ *n* Missbrauch *m*

mitigating /ˈmɪtɪɡeɪtɪŋ/ *adj* mildernd

mix /mɪks/ *n* Mischung *f* ●*vt* mischen ●*vi* sich mischen; ~ **with** (associate with) verkehren mit. ~ **up** *vt* mischen; (muddle) durchein-

ander bringen; (*mistake for*) verwechseln (with with)

mixed /mɪkst/ *adj* gemischt; be ~ **up** durcheinander sein

mixer /ˈmɪksə(r)/ *n* Mischmaschine *f*; (Culin) Küchenmaschine *f*

mixture /ˈmɪkstʃə(r)/ *n* Mischung *f*; (medicine) Mixtur *f*; (Culin) Teig *m*

'mix-up *n* Durcheinander *nt*; (confusion) Verwirrung *f*; (mistake) Verwechslung *f*

moan /məʊn/ *n* Stöhnen *nt* ●*vi* stöhnen; (complain) jammern

mob /mɒb/ *n* Horde *f*; (rabble) Pöbel *m*; (🔲: gang) Bande *f* ●*vt* (*pt/pp* mobbed) herfallen über (+ *acc*); belagern (celebrity)

mobile /ˈməʊbaɪl/ *adj* beweglich ●*n* Mobile *nt*; (telephone) Handy *nt*. ~ **'home** *n* Wohnwagen *m*. ~ **'phone** *n* Handy *nt*

mobility /məˈbɪlətɪ/ *n* Beweglichkeit *f*

mock /mɒk/ *adj* Schein- ●*vt* verspotten. ~**ery** *n* Spott *m*

'mock-up *n* Modell *nt*

mode /məʊd/ *n* [Art und] Weise *f*; (fashion) Mode *f*

model /ˈmɒdl/ *n* Modell *nt*; (example) Vorbild *nt*; [fashion] ~ Mannequin *nt* ●*adj* Modell-; (exemplary) Muster- ●*v* (*pt/pp* modelled) ●*vt* formen, modellieren; vorführen (clothes) ●*vi* Mannequin sein; (for artist) Modell stehen

moderate[1] /ˈmɒdəreɪt/ *vt* mäßigen

moderate[2] /ˈmɒdərət/ *adj* mäßig; (opinion) gemäßigt. ~**ly** *adv* mäßig; (fairly) einigermaßen

moderation /mɒdəˈreɪʃn/ *n* Mäßigung *f*; in ~ mit Maß[en]

modern /ˈmɒdn/ *adj* modern. ~**ize** *vt* modernisieren. ~ **'languages** *npl* neuere Sprachen *pl*

modest /'mɒdɪst/ adj bescheiden; (decorous) schamhaft. ~y n Bescheidenheit f

modif|ication /mɒdɪfɪ'keɪʃn/ n Abänderung f. ~y vt (pt/pp -fied) abändern

module /'mɒdjuːl/ n Element nt; (of course) Kurseinheit f

moist /mɔɪst/ adj (-er, -est) feucht

moisten /'mɔɪsn/ vt befeuchten

moistur|e /'mɔɪstʃə(r)/ n Feuchtigkeit f. ~izer n Feuchtigkeitscreme f

molar /'məʊlə(r)/ n Backenzahn m

mole[1] /məʊl/ n Leberfleck m

mole[2] n (Zool) Maulwurf m

molecule /'mɒlɪkjuːl/ n Molekül n

molest /mə'lest/ vt belästigen

mollify /'mɒlɪfaɪ/ vt (pt/pp -ied) besänftigen

mollycoddle /'mɒlɪkɒdl/ vt verzärteln

molten /'məʊltən/ adj geschmolzen

mom /mɒm/ n (Amer fam) Mutti f

moment /'məʊmənt/ n Moment m, Augenblick m; at the ~ im Augenblick, augenblicklich. ~ary adj vorübergehend

momentous /mə'mentəs/ adj bedeutsam

momentum /mə'mentəm/ n Schwung m

monarch /'mɒnək/ n Monarch(in) m(f). ~y n Monarchie f

monastery /'mɒnəstrɪ/ n Kloster nt

Monday /'mʌndeɪ/ n Montag m

money /'mʌnɪ/ n Geld nt

money: ~-box n Sparbüchse f. ~-lender n Geldverleiher m. ~ order n Zahlungsanweisung f

mongrel /'mʌŋgrəl/ n Promena-

denmischung f

monitor /'mɒnɪtə(r)/ n (Techn) Monitor m ● vt überwachen (progress); abhören (broadcast)

monk /mʌŋk/ n Mönch m

monkey /'mʌŋkɪ/ n Affe m

mono /'mɒnəʊ/ n Mono nt

monogram /'mɒnəgræm/ n Monogramm nt

monologue /'mɒnəlɒg/ n Monolog m

monopol|ize /mə'nɒpəlaɪz/ vt monopolisieren. ~y n Monopol nt

monosyllable /'mɒnəsɪləbl/ n einsilbiges Wort nt

monotone /'mɒnətəʊn/ n in a ~ mit monotoner Stimme

monoton|ous /mə'nɒtənəs/ adj eintönig, monoton; (tedious) langweilig. ~y n Eintönigkeit f, Monotonie f

monster /'mɒnstə(r)/ n Ungeheuer nt; (cruel person) Unmensch m

monstrosity /mɒn'strɒsətɪ/ n Monstrosität f

monstrous /'mɒnstrəs/ adj ungeheuer; (outrageous) ungeheuerlich

month /mʌnθ/ n Monat m. ~ly adj & adv monatlich ● n (periodical) Monatszeitschrift f

monument /'mɒnjʊmənt/ n Denkmal nt. ~al adj (fig) monumental

moo /muː/ n Muh nt ● vi (pt/pp mooed) muhen

mood /muːd/ n Laune f; be in a good/bad ~ gute/schlechte Laune haben

moody /'muːdɪ/ adj launisch

moon /muːn/ n Mond m; over the ~ 🗊 überglücklich

moon: ~light n Mondschein m. ~lighting n 🗊 ≈ Schwarzarbeit f

~**lit** adj mondhell

moor¹ /mʊə(r)/ n Moor nt

moor² vt (Naut) festmachen ●vi anlegen

mop /mɒp/ n Mopp m; ~ of hair Wuschelkopf m ●vt (pt/pp mopped) wischen. ~ **up** vt aufwischen

moped /ˈməʊped/ n Moped nt

moral /ˈmɒrl/ adj moralisch, sittlich; (virtuous) tugendhaft ●n Moral f; ~**s** pl Moral f

morale /məˈrɑːl/ n Moral f

morality /məˈrælətɪ/ n Sittlichkeit f

morbid /ˈmɔːbɪd/ adj krankhaft; (gloomy) trübe

more /mɔː(r)/ a, adv & n mehr; (in addition) noch; a few ~ noch ein paar; any ~ noch etwas; once ~ noch einmal; ~ or less mehr oder weniger; some ~ tea? noch etwas Tee? ~ interesting interessanter; ~ [and ~] quickly [immer] schneller

moreover /mɔːˈrəʊvə(r)/ adv außerdem

morgue /mɔːg/ n Leichenschauhaus nt

morning /ˈmɔːnɪŋ/ n Morgen m; in the ~ morgens, am Morgen; (tomorrow) morgen früh

Morocco /məˈrɒkəʊ/ n Marokko nt

moron /ˈmɔːrɒn/ n 🔢 Idiot m

morose /məˈrəʊs/ adj mürrisch

morsel /ˈmɔːsl/ n Happen m

mortal /ˈmɔːtl/ adj sterblich; (fatal) tödlich ●n Sterbliche(r) m/f. ~**ity** n Sterblichkeit f. ~**ly** adv tödlich

mortar /ˈmɔːtə(r)/ n Mörtel m

mortgage /ˈmɔːgɪdʒ/ n Hypothek f ●vt hypothekarisch belasten

mortuary /ˈmɔːtjʊərɪ/ n Leichenhalle f; (public) Leichenschauhaus nt; (Amer: undertaker's) Bestattungsinstitut nt

mosaic /məʊˈzeɪɪk/ n Mosaik nt

Moscow /ˈmɒskəʊ/ n Moskau nt

mosque /mɒsk/ n Moschee f

mosquito /mɒsˈkiːtəʊ/ n (pl -es) [Stech]mücke f, Schnake f; (tropical) Moskito m

moss /mɒs/ n Moos nt. ~**y** adj moosig

most /məʊst/ adj der/die/das meiste; (majority) die meisten; the ~ part zum größten Teil ●adv am meisten; (very) höchst; the ~ interesting day der interessanteste Tag; ~ unlikely höchst unwahrscheinlich ●n das meiste; ~ of them die meisten [von ihnen]; at [the] ~ höchstens; ~ of the time die meiste Zeit. ~**ly** adv meist

MOT n ≈ TÜV m

motel /məʊˈtel/ n Motel nt

moth /mɒθ/ n Nachtfalter m; [clothes-] ~ Motte f

'mothball n Mottenkugel f

mother /ˈmʌðə(r)/ n Mutter f

mother: ~**hood** n Mutterschaft f. ~**-in-law** n (pl ~**s-in-law**) Schwiegermutter f. ~**land** n Mutterland nt. ~**ly** adj mütterlich. ~**-of-pearl** n Perlmutter f. ~**-to-be** n werdende Mutter f

mothproof /ˈmɒθ-/ adj mottenfest

motif /məʊˈtiːf/ n Motiv nt

motion /ˈməʊʃn/ n Bewegung f; (proposal) Antrag m. ~**less** adj bewegungslos

motivat|e /ˈməʊtɪveɪt/ vt motivieren. ~**ion** n Motivation f

motive /ˈməʊtɪv/ n Motiv nt

motor /ˈməʊtə(r)/ n Motor m; (car) Auto nt ●adj Motor-; (Anat) moto-

m

risch ● *vi* [mit dem Auto] fahren

motor- ~**bike** *n* Motorrad *nt*. ~ **boat** *n* Motorboot *nt*. ~ **car** *n* Auto *nt*, Wagen *m*. ~ **cycle** *n* Motorrad *nt*. ~**-cyclist** *n* Motorradfahrer *m*. ~**ing** *n* Autofahren *nt*. ~**ist** *n* Kraftfahrer(in) *m(f)*. ~ **vehicle** *n* Kraftfahrzeug *nt*. ~**way** *n* Autobahn *f*

mottled /'mɒtld/ *adj* gesprenkelt

motto /'mɒtəʊ/ *n* (*pl* -es) Motto *nt*

mould¹ /məʊld/ *n* (*fungus*) Schimmel *m*

mould² *n* Form *f* ● *vt* formen (into zu). ~**ing** *n* (*decorative*) Fries *m*

mouldy /'məʊldɪ/ *adj* schimmelig; (🗉: *worthless*) schäbig

mound /maʊnd/ *n* Hügel *m*; (*of stones*) Haufen *m*

mount *n* (*animal*) Reittier *nt*; (*of jewel*) Fassung *f*; (*of photo, picture*) Passepartout *nt* ● *vt* (*on* steigen auf (+ *acc*); (*on pedestal*) montieren auf (+ *acc*); besteigen (*horse*); fassen (*jewel*); aufziehen (*photo, picture*) ● *vi* aufsteigen; (*tension:*) steigen. ~ **up** *vi* sich häufen; (*add up*) sich anhäufen

mountain /'maʊntɪn/ *n* Berg *m*

mountaineer /maʊntɪ'nɪə(r)/ *n* Bergsteiger(in) *m(f)*. ~**ing** *n* Bergsteigen *nt*

mountainous /'maʊntɪnəs/ *adj* bergig, gebirgig

mourn /mɔːn/ *vt* betrauern ● *vi* trauern (for um). ~**er** *n* Trauernde(r) *m/f*. ~**ful** *adj* trauervoll. ~**ing** *n* Trauer *f*

mouse /maʊs/ *n* (*pl* mice) Maus *f*. ~**trap** *n* Mausefalle *f*

moustache /mə'stɑːʃ/ *n* Schnurrbart *m*

mouth¹ /maʊð/ *vt* ~ sth etw lautlos mit den Lippen sagen

mouth² /maʊθ/ *n* Mund *m*; (*of ani-*

mal) Maul *nt*; (*of river*) Mündung *f*

mouth: ~**ful** *n* Mundvoll *m*; (*bite*) Bissen *m*. ~**organ** *n* Mundharmonika *f*. ~**wash** *n* Mundwasser *nt*

movable /'muːvəbl/ *adj* beweglich

move /muːv/ *n* Bewegung *f*; (*fig*) Schritt *m*; (*moving house*) Umzug *m*; (*in board game*) Zug *m*; on the ~ unterwegs; get a ~ on 🗉 sich beeilen ● *vt* bewegen; (*emotionally*) rühren; (*move along*) rücken; (*in board game*) ziehen; (*take away*) wegnehmen; wegfahren (car); (*rearrange*) umstellen; (*transfer*) versetzen (*person*); verlegen (*office*); (*propose*) beantragen; ~ house umziehen ● *vi* sich bewegen; (*moving house*) umziehen; don't ~! stillhalten! (stop) stillstehen! ~ **along** *vt/i* weiterrücken. ~ **away** *vt/i* wegrücken; (*move house*) wegziehen. ~ **in** *vi* einziehen. ~ **off** *vi* (vehicle:) losfahren. ~ **out** *vi* ausziehen. ~ **over** *vt/i* [zur Seite] rücken. ~ **up** *vi* aufrücken

movement /'muːvmənt/ *n* Bewegung *f*; (*Mus*) Satz *m*; (*of clock*) Uhrwerk *nt*

movie /'muːvɪ/ *n* (*Amer*) Film *m*; go to the ~s ins Kino gehen

moving /'muːvɪŋ/ *adj* beweglich; (*touching*) rührend

mow /məʊ/ *vt* (*pt* mowed, *pp* mown or mowed) mähen

mower /'məʊə(r)/ *n* Rasenmäher *m*

MP *abbr* Member of Parliament

Mr /'mɪstə(r)/ *n* (*pl* Messrs) Herr *m*

Mrs /'mɪsɪz/ *n* Frau *f*

Ms /mɪz/ *n* Frau *f*

much /mʌtʃ/ *a, adv & n* viel; as ~ as so viel wie; ~ loved sehr geliebt

muck /mʌk/ *n* Mist *m*; (🗉: *filth*) Dreck *m*. ~ **about** *vi* herumalbern; (*tinker*) herumspielen (with mit). ~

out *vt* ausmisten. **~ up** *vt* T vermasseln; (*make dirty*) schmutzig machen

mucky /'mʌkɪ/ *adj* dreckig

mud /mʌd/ *n* Schlamm *m*

muddle /'mʌdl/ *n* Durcheinander *nt*; (*confusion*) Verwirrung *f* ● *vt* ~ [up] durcheinander bringen

muddy /'mʌdɪ/ *adj* schlammig; (*shoes*) schmutzig

'**mudguard** *n* Kotflügel *m*; (*on bicycle*) Schutzblech *nt*

muffle /'mʌfl/ *vt* dämpfen

muffler /'mʌflə(r)/ *n* Schal *m*; (*Amer, Auto*) Auspufftopf *m*

mug[1] /mʌg/ *n* Becher *m*; (*for beer*) Bierkrug *m*; (T: *face*) Visage *f*; (T: *simpleton*) Trottel *m*

mug[2] *vt* (*pt/pp* mugged) überfallen. **~ger** *n* Straßenräuber *m*. **~ging** *n* Straßenraub *m*

muggy /'mʌgɪ/ *adj* schwül

mule /mjuːl/ *n* Maultier *nt*

mulled /mʌld/ *adj* ~ wine Glühwein *m*

multi /'mʌltɪ/: **~coloured** *adj* vielfarbig, bunt. **~lingual** *adj* mehrsprachig. **~national** *adj* multinational

multiple /'mʌltɪpl/ *adj* vielfach; (*with pl*) mehrere ● *n* Vielfache(s) *nt*

multiplication /mʌltɪplɪ'keɪʃn/ *n* Multiplikation *f*

multiply /'mʌltɪplaɪ/ *v* (*pt/pp* -ied) ● *vt* multiplizieren (by mit) ● *vi* sich vermehren

multistorey *adj* ~ car park Parkhaus *nt*

mum /mʌm/ *n* T Mutti *f*

mumble /'mʌmbl/ *vt/i* murmeln

mummy[1] /'mʌmɪ/ *n* T Mutti *f*

mummy[2] *n* (*Archaeology*) Mumie *f*

mumps /mʌmps/ *n* Mumps *m*

munch /mʌntʃ/ *vt/i* mampfen

municipal /mjuː'nɪsɪpl/ *adj* städtisch

munitions /mjuː'nɪʃnz/ *npl* Kriegsmaterial *nt*

mural /'mjʊərəl/ *n* Wandgemälde *nt*

murder /'mɜːdə(r)/ *n* Mord *m* ● *vt* ermorden. **~er** *n* Mörder *m*. **~ess** *n* Mörderin *f*. **~ous** *adj* mörderisch

murky /'mɜːkɪ/ *adj* düster

murmur /'mɜːmə(r)/ *n* Murmeln *nt* ● *vt/i* murmeln

muscle /'mʌsl/ *n* Muskel *m*

muscular /'mʌskjʊlə(r)/ *adj* Muskel-; (*strong*) muskulös

museum /mjuː'zɪəm/ *n* Museum *nt*

mushroom /'mʌʃrʊm/ *n* [essbarer] Pilz *m*, *esp* Champignon *m* ● *vi* (*fig*) wie Pilze aus dem Boden schießen

mushy /'mʌʃɪ/ *adj* breiig

music /'mjuːzɪk/ *n* Musik *f*; (*written*) Noten *pl*; set to ~ vertonen

musical /'mjuːzɪkl/ *adj* musikalisch ● *n* Musical *nt*. **~ box** *n* Spieldose *f*. **~ instrument** *n* Musikinstrument *nt*

musician /mjuː'zɪʃn/ *n* Musiker(in) *m*(*f*)

'**music-stand** *n* Notenständer *m*

Muslim /'mʊzlɪm/ *adj* mohammedanisch ● *n* Mohammedaner(in) *m*(*f*)

must /mʌst/ *modal verb* (*nur Präsens*) müssen; (*with negative*) dürfen ● *n* a ~ T ein Muss *nt*

mustard /'mʌstəd/ *n* Senf *m*

musty /'mʌstɪ/ *adj* muffig

mute /mjuːt/ *adj* stumm

mutilat|e /'mjuːtɪleɪt/ *vt* verstümmeln. **~ion** *n* Verstümmelung *f*

mutin|ous /'mjuːtɪnəs/ *adj* meuterisch. **~y** *n* Meuterei *f* ● *vi* (*pt/pp*

m

-ied) meutern

mutter /'mʌtə(r)/ n Murmeln nt
● vt/i murmeln

mutton /'mʌtn/ n Hammel-
fleisch nt

mutual /'mjuːtjʊəl/ adj gegenseitig; (Ⅱ: common) gemeinsam. ~ly
adv gegenseitig

muzzle /'mʌzl/ n (of animal)
Schnauze f; (of firearm) Mündung f;
(for dog) Maulkorb m

my /maɪ/ adj mein

myself /maɪ'self/ pron selbst; (reflexive) mich; by ~ allein; I thought
to ~ ich habe mir gedacht

mysterious /mɪ'stɪərɪəs/ adj ge-
heimnisvoll; (puzzling) mysteriös,
rätselhaft

mystery /'mɪstəri/ n Geheimnis
nt; (puzzle) Rätsel nt; ~ [story]
Krimi m

mysti|c[al] /'mɪstɪk[l]/ adj my-
stisch. ~cism n Mystik f

mystified /'mɪstɪfaɪd/ adj be ~
vor einem Rätsel stehen

mystique /mɪ'stiːk/ n geheimnis-
voller Zauber m

myth /mɪθ/ n Mythos m; (Ⅱ: untruth) Märchen nt. ~ical adj my-
thisch; (fig) erfunden

mythology /mɪ'θɒlədʒɪ/ n Mytho-
logie f

. . . .

Nn

. . . .

nab /næb/ vt (pt/pp nabbed) Ⅱ erwischen

nag¹ /næg/ n (horse) Gaul m

nag² /næg/ vt/i (pp/pp nagged) herum-
nörgeln (s.o. an jdm)

nail /neɪl/ n (Anat, Techn) Nagel m;
on the ~ Ⅱ sofort ● vt nageln (to
an + acc)

nail: ~-brush n Nagelbürste f.
~-file n Nagelfeile f. ~ scissors
npl Nagelschere f. ~ varnish n Na-
gellack m

naïve /naɪ'iːv/ adj naiv. ~ty n Nai-
vität f

naked /'neɪkɪd/ adj nackt; (flame)
offen; with the ~ eye mit bloßem
Auge. ~ness n Nacktheit f

name /neɪm/ n Name m; (reputation) Ruf m; by ~ dem Namen
nach; by the ~ of namens; call s.o.
~ Ⅱ jdn beschimpfen ● vt nennen; (give a name to) einen Namen
geben (+ dat); (announce publicly)
den Namen bekannt geben von.
~less adj namenlos. ~ly adv
nämlich

name: ~-plate n Namensschild nt.
~sake n Namensvetter
m/Namensschwester f

nanny /'nænɪ/ n Kindermädchen nt

nap /næp/ n Nickerchen nt

napkin /'næpkɪn/ n Serviette f

nappy /'næpɪ/ n Windel f

narcotic /nɑː'kɒtɪk/ n (drug)
Rauschgift nt

narrat|e /nə'reɪt/ vt erzählen.
~ion n Erzählung f

narrative /'nærətɪv/ n Erzählung f

narrator /nə'reɪtə(r)/ n Erzähl-
er(in) m(f)

narrow /'nærəʊ/ adj (-er, -est)
schmal; (restricted) eng; (margin,
majority) knapp; have a ~ escape
mit knapper Not davonkommen ● vi
sich verengen. ~-'minded adj engstirnig

nasal /'neɪzl/ adj nasal; (Med &
Anat) Nasen-

nasty /'nɑːstɪ/ adj übel; (unpleasant) unangenehm; (unkind) boshaft;

(serious) schlimm

nation /ˈneɪʃn/ n Nation f; (people) Volk nt

national /ˈnæʃənl/ adj national; (newspaper) überregional; (campaign) landesweit ● n Staatsbürger(in) m(f)

national: ~ 'anthem n Nationalhymne f. N~ 'Health Service n staatlicher Gesundheitsdienst m. N~ In'surance n Sozialversicherung f

nationalism /ˈnæʃənəlɪzm/ n Nationalismus m

nationality /næʃəˈnælətɪ/ n Staatsangehörigkeit f

national|ization /næʃənəlaɪˈzeɪʃn/ n Verstaatlichung f. ~ize vt verstaatlichen

native /ˈneɪtɪv/ adj einheimisch; (innate) angeboren ● n Eingeborene(r) m/f; (local inhabitant) Einheimische(r) m/f; a ~ of Vienna ein gebürtiger Wiener

native: ~ 'land n Heimatland nt. ~ 'language n Muttersprache f

natter /ˈnætə(r)/ vi 🗔 schwatzen

natural /ˈnætʃrəl/ adj natürlich; ~[-coloured] naturfarben

natural: ~ 'gas n Erdgas nt. ~ 'history n Naturkunde f

naturalist /ˈnætʃrəlɪst/ n Naturforscher m

natural|ization /nætʃrəlaɪˈzeɪʃn/ n Einbürgerung f. ~ize vt einbürgern

nature /ˈneɪtʃə(r)/ n Natur f; (kind) Art f; by ~ von Natur aus. ~ reserve n Naturschutzgebiet nt

naughty /ˈnɔːtɪ/ adj, ~ily adv unartig; (slightly indecent) gewagt

nausea /ˈnɔːzɪə/ n Übelkeit f

nautical /ˈnɔːtɪkl/ adj nautisch. ~ mile n Seemeile f

naval /ˈneɪvl/ adj Marine-

nave /neɪv/ n Kirchenschiff nt

navel /ˈneɪvl/ n Nabel m

navigable /ˈnævɪɡəbl/ adj schiffbar

navigat|e /ˈnævɪɡeɪt/ vi navigieren ● vt befahren (river). ~ion n Navigation f

navy /ˈneɪvɪ/ n [Kriegs]marine f ● adj ~ [blue] marineblau

near /nɪə(r)/ adj (-er, -est) nah[e]; the ~est bank die nächste Bank ● adv nahe; draw ~ sich nähern ● prep nahe an (+ dat/acc); in der Nähe von

near: ~by adj nahe gelegen, nahe liegend. ~ly adv fast, beinahe; not ~ly bei weitem nicht. ~ness n Nähe f. ~ side n Beifahrerseite f. ~sighted adj (Amer) kurzsichtig

neat /niːt/ adj (-er, -est) adrett; (tidy) ordentlich; (clever) geschickt; (undiluted) pur. ~ness n Ordentlichkeit f

necessarily /ˈnesəsərəlɪ/ adv notwendigerweise; not ~ nicht unbedingt

necessary /ˈnesəsərɪ/ adj nötig, notwendig

necessit|ate /nɪˈsesɪteɪt/ vt notwendig machen. ~y n Notwendigkeit f; work from ~y arbeiten, weil man es nötig hat

neck /nek/ n Hals m; ~ and ~ Kopf an Kopf

necklace /'neklɪs/ n Halskette f

neckline n Halsausschnitt m

née /neɪ/ adj ~ X geborene X

need /niːd/ n Bedürfnis nt; (*misfortune*) Not f; be in ~ of brauchen; in case of ~ notfalls; if ~ be wenn nötig; there is a ~ for es besteht ein Bedarf an (+ *dat*); there is no ~ for that das ist nicht nötig ● *vt* brauchen; you ~ not go du brauchst nicht zu gehen; ~ I come? muss ich kommen? I ~ to know ich muss ich wissen

needle /'niːdl/ n Nadel f

needless /'niːdlɪs/ adj unnötig; ~ to say selbstverständlich, natürlich

needlework n Nadelarbeit f

needy /'niːdɪ/ adj bedürftig

negation /nɪ'geɪʃn/ n Verneinung f

negative /'negətɪv/ adj negativ ● n Verneinung f; (*photo*) Negativ nt

neglect /nɪ'glekt/ n Vernachlässigung f ● *vt* vernachlässigen; (*omit*) versäumen (to zu). ~ed adj verwahrlost. ~ful adj nachlässig

negligen|ce /'neglɪdʒəns/ n Nachlässigkeit f. ~t adj nachlässig

negligible /'neglɪdʒəbl/ adj unbedeutend

negotiat|e /nɪ'gəʊʃɪeɪt/ *vt* aushandeln; (*Auto*) nehmen (*bend*) ● *vi* verhandeln. ~ion n Verhandlung f. ~or n Unterhändler(in) m(f)

Negro /'niːgrəʊ/ adj Neger- ● n (*pl* -es) Neger m

neigh /neɪ/ *vi* wiehern

neighbour /'neɪbə(r)/ n Nachbar(in) m(f). ~hood n Nachbarschaft f. ~ing adj Nachbar-. ~ly adj [gut]nachbarlich

neither /'naɪðə(r)/ adj & pron keine(r, s) [von beiden] ● *adv* ~...nor weder ... noch ● *conj* auch nicht

neon /'niːɒn/ n Neon nt

nephew /'nevjuː/ n Neffe m

nepotism /'nepətɪzm/ n Vetternwirtschaft f

nerve /nɜːv/ n Nerv m; (🏳: *courage*) Mut m; (🏳: *impudence*) Frechheit f. ~-**racking** adj nervenaufreibend

nervous /'nɜːvəs/ adj (*afraid*) ängstlich; (*highly strung*) nervös; (*Anat, Med*) Nerven-. ~ '**breakdown** n Nervenzusammenbruch m. ~ness Ängstlichkeit f

nervy /'nɜːvɪ/ adj nervös; (*Amer: impudent*) frech

nest /nest/ n Nest nt ● *vi* nisten

nestle /'nesl/ *vi* sich schmiegen (against an + *acc*)

net¹ /net/ n Netz nt; (*curtain*) Store m

net² adj netto; (*salary, weight*) Netto-

'netball n ≈ Korbball m

Netherlands /'neðələndz/ npl the ~ die Niederlande pl

nettle /'netl/ n Nessel f

'network n Netz nt

neurolog|ist /njʊə'rɒlədʒɪst/ n Neurologe m; -gin f. ~y n Neurologie f

neur|osis /njʊə'rəʊsɪs/ n (*pl* -oses /-siːz/) Neurose f. ~otic adj neurotisch

neuter /'njuːtə(r)/ adj (*Gram*) sächlich ● n (*Gram*) Neutrum nt ● *vt* kastrieren; (*spay*) sterilisieren

neutral /'njuːtrl/ adj neutral ● n in ~ (*Auto*) im Leerlauf. ~ity n Neutralität f

never /'nevə(r)/ adv nie, niemals; (🏳: *not*) nicht; ~ mind macht nichts; well I ~! ja so was! ~**-ending** adj endlos

nevertheless /nevəðə'les/ adv dennoch, trotzdem

new /nju:/ adj (-er, -est) neu

new: ~**comer** n Neuankömmling m. ~**fangled** /-'fæŋgld/ adj (pej) neumodisch. ~**laid** adj frisch gelegt

'**newly** adv frisch. ~**-weds** npl Jungverheiratete pl

new: ~ '**moon** n Neumond m. ~**ness** n Neuheit f

news /nju:z/ n Nachricht f; (Radio, TV) Nachrichten pl; piece of ~ Neuigkeit f

news: ~**agent** n Zeitungshändler m. ~**bulletin** n Nachrichtensendung f. ~**letter** n Mitteilungsblatt nt. ~**paper** n Zeitung f; (material) Zeitungspapier nt. ~**reader** n Nachrichtensprecher(in) m(f)

New: ~ Year's 'Day n Neujahr nt. ~ Year's 'Eve n Silvester nt. ~ Zealand /'zi:lənd/ n Neuseeland nt

next /nekst/ adj & n nächste(r, s); who's ~? wer kommt als Nächster dran? the ~ best das nächstbeste; ~ door nebenan; my ~ of kin mein nächster Verwandter; ~ to nothing fast gar nichts; the week after ~ übernächste Woche ●adv als Nächstes; ~ to neben

nib /nɪb/ n Feder f.

nibble /'nɪbl/ vt/i knabbern (at an + dat)

nice /naɪs/ adj (-r, -st) nett; (day, weather) schön; (food) gut; (distinction) fein. ~**ly** adv nett; (well) gut

niche /ni:ʃ/ n Nische f; (fig) Platz m

nick /nɪk/ n Kerbe f; (🔲: prison) Knast m; (🔲: police station) Revier nt; in good ~ 🔲 in gutem Zustand ●vt einkerben; (steal) klauen; (🔲:

---

neverthless | nobility

arrest) schnappen

nickel /'nɪkl/ n Nickel nt; (Amer) Fünfcentstück nt

'**nickname** n Spitzname m

nicotine /'nɪkəti:n/ n Nikotin nt

niece /ni:s/ n Nichte f

Nigeria /naɪ'dʒɪərɪə/ n Nigeria nt. ~**n** adj nigerianisch ●n Nigerianer(in) m(f)

night /naɪt/ n Nacht f; (evening) Abend m; at ~ nachts

night: ~**-club** n Nachtklub m. ~**dress** n Nachthemd nt. ~**fall** n at ~fall bei Einbruch der Dunkelheit. ~**gown** n, 🔲 ~**ie** /'naɪtɪ/ n Nachthemd nt

nightingale /'naɪtɪŋgeɪl/ n Nachtigall f

night: ~**-life** n Nachtleben nt. ~**ly** adj nächtlich ●adv jede Nacht. ~**mare** n Albtraum m. ~**-time** n at ~-time bei Nacht

nil /nɪl/ n null

nimble /'nɪmbl/ adj (-r, -st), **-bly** adv flink

nine /naɪn/ adj neun ●n Neun f. ~**teen** adj neunzehn. ~**teenth** adj neunzehnte(r, s)

ninetieth /'naɪntɪɪθ/ adj neunzigste(r, s)

ninety /'naɪntɪ/ adj neunzig

ninth /naɪnθ/ adj neunte(r, s)

nip /nɪp/ vt kneifen; (bite) beißen; ~ in the bud (fig) im Keim ersticken ●vi (🔲: run) laufen

nipple /'nɪpl/ n Brustwarze f; (Amer: on bottle) Sauger m

nitwit /'nɪtwɪt/ n 🔲 Dummkopf m

no /nəʊ/ adj nein ●n (pl noes) Nein nt ●adj keine; (pl) keine; in no time [sehr] schnell; no parking/smoking Parken/Rauchen verboten; no one = nobody

nobility /nəʊ'bɪlətɪ/ n Adel m

noble /ˈnəʊbl/ adj (-r, -st) edel; (*aristocratic*) adlig. ~**man** n Adlige(r) m

nobody /ˈnəʊbədɪ/ pron niemand, keiner ● n a ~ ein Niemand m

nocturnal /nɒkˈtɜːnl/ adj nächtlich; (*animal, bird*) Nacht-

nod /nɒd/ n Nicken nt ● v (pt/pp nodded) ● vi nicken ● vt ~ one's head mit dem Kopf nicken

noise /nɔɪz/ n Geräusch nt; (*loud*) Lärm m. ~**less** adj geräuschlos

noisy /ˈnɔɪzɪ/ adj , -ily adv laut; (*eater*) geräuschvoll

nomad /ˈnəʊmæd/ n Nomade m. ~**ic** adj nomadisch; (*life, tribe*) Nomaden-

nominal /ˈnɒmɪnl/ adj nominell

nominat|e /ˈnɒmɪneɪt/ vt nominieren, aufstellen; (*appoint*) ernennen. ~**ion** n Nominierung f; Ernennung f

nominative /ˈnɒmɪnətɪv/ adj & n (Gram) ~[case] Nominativ m

nonchalant /ˈnɒnʃələnt/ adj nonchalant; (*gesture*) lässig

nondescript /ˈnɒndɪskrɪpt/ adj unbestimmbar; (*person*) unscheinbar

none /nʌn/ pron keine(r)/keins; ~ of it/this nichts davon ● adv ~ too nicht gerade; ~ too soon [um] keine Minute zu früh; ~ the less dennoch

nonentity /nɒˈnentətɪ/ n Null f

non-ex'istent adj nicht vorhanden

non-'fiction n Sachliteratur f

nonplussed /nɒnˈplʌst/ adj verblüfft

nonsens|e /ˈnɒnsəns/ n Unsinn m. ~**ical** adj unsinnig

non-'smoker n Nichtraucher m

non-'stop adv ununterbrochen;

(*fly*) nonstop

non-'swimmer n Nichtschwimmer m

non-'violent adj gewaltlos

noodles /ˈnuːdlz/ npl Bandnudeln pl

noon /nuːn/ n Mittag m; at ~ um 12 Uhr mittags

noose /nuːs/ n Schlinge f

nor /nɔː(r)/ adv noch ● conj auch nicht

Nordic /ˈnɔːdɪk/ adj nordisch

norm /nɔːm/ n Norm f

normal /ˈnɔːml/ adj normal. ~**ity** n Normalität f. ~**ly** adv normal; (*usually*) normalerweise

north /nɔːθ/ n Norden m; to the ~ of nördlich von ● adj Nord-, nord- ● adv nach Norden

north: N~ **America** n Nordamerika nt. ~-**east** n Nordost- ● Nordosten m

norther|ly /ˈnɔːðəlɪ/ adj nördlich. ~**n** adj nördlich. N~**n Ireland** n Nordirland nt

north: N~ **Pole** n Nordpol m. N~ **Sea** n Nordsee f. ~**ward[s]** /-wəd[z]/ adv nach Norden. ~-**west** adj Nordwest- ● n Nordwesten m

Nor|way /ˈnɔːweɪ/ n Norwegen nt. ~**wegian** adj norwegisch ● n Norweger(in) m(f)

nose /nəʊz/ n Nase f

'nosebleed n Nasenbluten nt

nostalg|ia /nɒˈstældʒɪə/ n Nostalgie f. ~**ic** adj nostalgisch

nostril /ˈnɒstrəl/ n Nasenloch nt

nosy /ˈnəʊzɪ/ adj ① neugierig

not /nɒt/
● adverb
••••▸ nicht. I don't know ich weiß nicht. isn't she pretty? ist sie nicht hübsch?

····▸ **not** a kein. **he is not a doctor** er ist kein Arzt. **she didn't wear a hat** sie trug keinen Hut. **there was not a person to be seen** es gab keinen Menschen zu sehen. **not a thing** gar nichts. **not a bit** kein bisschen

····▸ *(in elliptical phrases)* **I hope not** ich hoffe nicht. **of course not** natürlich nicht. **not at all** überhaupt nicht; *(in polite reply to thanks)* keine Ursache; gern geschehen. **certainly not!** auf keinen Fall! **not I** ich nicht

····▸ **not ... but ... nicht ... sondern ....** **it was not a small town but a big one** es war keine kleine Stadt, sondern eine große

notab|le /'nəʊtəbl/ adj bedeutend; *(remarkable)* bemerkenswert. **~ly** adv insbesondere

notation /nəʊ'teɪʃn/ n Notation f; *(Mus)* Notenschrift f

notch /nɒtʃ/ n Kerbe f

note /nəʊt/ n *(written comment)* Notiz f, Anmerkung f; *(short letter)* Briefchen nt, Zettel m; *(bank ~)* Banknote f, Schein m; *(Mus)* Note f; *(sound)* Ton m; *(on piano)* Taste f; **half/whole ~** *(Amer)* halbe/ganze Note f; **of ~** von Bedeutung; **make a ~ of** notieren ● vt beachten; *(notice)* bemerken *(that dass)*

'**notebook** n Notizbuch nt

noted /'nəʊtɪd/ adj bekannt *(for für)*

note: **~paper** n Briefpapier nt. **~worthy** adj beachtenswert

nothing /'nʌθɪŋ/ n, pron & adv nichts; **for ~** umsonst; **~ but** nichts als; **~ much** nicht viel; **~ interesting** nichts Interessantes

notice /'nəʊtɪs/ n *(on board)* An-

schlag m, Bekanntmachung f; *(announcement)* Anzeige f; *(review)* Kritik f; *(termination of lease, employment)* Kündigung f; **give [in one's] ~** kündigen; **give s.o. ~** jdm kündigen; **take no ~ of** ignorieren es! ● vt bemerken. **~able** /-əbl/, adj, **-bly** adv merklich. **~board** n Anschlagbrett nt

noti|fication /nəʊtɪfɪ'keɪʃn/ n Benachrichtigung f. **~fy** vt *(pt/pp -ied)* benachrichtigen

notion /'nəʊʃn/ n Idee f

notorious /nəʊ'tɔːrɪəs/ adj berüchtigt

notwith'standing prep trotz (+ gen) ● adv trotzdem, dennoch

nought /nɔːt/ n Null f

noun /naʊn/ n Substantiv nt

nourish /'nʌrɪʃ/ vt nähren. **~ing** adj nahrhaft. **~ment** n Nahrung f

novel /'nɒvl/ adj neu[artig] ● n Roman m. **~ist** n Romanschriftsteller(in) m(f). **~ty** n Neuheit f

November /nəʊ'vembə(r)/ n November m

novice /'nɒvɪs/ n Neuling m; *(Relig)* Novize m/Novizin f

now /naʊ/ adv & conj jetzt; **~ [that]** jetzt, wo; **just ~** gerade, eben; **right ~** sofort; **~ and again** hin und wieder; **now, now!** na, na!

'**nowadays** adv heutzutage

nowhere /'nəʊ-/ adv nirgendwo, nirgends

nozzle /'nɒzl/ n Düse f

nuance /'njuːɑ̃s/ n Nuance f

nuclear /'njuːklɪə(r)/ adj Kern-. **~ de'terrent** n nukleares Abschreckungsmittel nt

nucleus /'njuːklɪəs/ n *(pl* **-lei** /-lɪaɪ/*)* Kern m

nude /njuːd/ adj nackt ● n *(Art)* Akt m; **in the ~** nackt

nudge /nʌdʒ/ vt stupsen

nud|ist /'njuːdɪst/ n Nudist m. **~ity** n Nacktheit f

nuisance /'njuːsns/ n Ärgernis nt; (pest) Plage f; **be a ~** ärgerlich sein

null /nʌl/ adj **~ and void** null und nichtig

numb /nʌm/ adj gefühllos, taub ● vt betäuben

number /'nʌmbə(r)/ n Nummer f; (amount) Anzahl f; (Math) Zahl f ● vt nummerieren; (include) zählen (among zu). **~-plate** n Nummernschild nt

numeral /'njuːmərl/ n Ziffer f

numerical /njuː'merɪkl/ adj numerisch; **in ~ order** zahlenmäßig geordnet

numerous /'njuːmərəs/ adj zahlreich

nun /nʌn/ n Nonne f

nurse /nɜːs/ n [Kranken]schwester f; (male) Krankenpfleger m; children's ~ Kindermädchen nt ● vt pflegen

nursery /'nɜːsərɪ/ n Kinderzimmer nt; (for plants) Gärtnerei f. [day] ~ Kindertagesstätte f. ~ **rhyme** n Kinderreim m. ~-**school** n Kindergarten m

nursing /'nɜːsɪŋ/ n Krankenpflege f. ~ **home** n Pflegeheim nt

nut /nʌt/ n Nuss f; (Techn) [Schrauben]mutter f; (⊞: head) Birne f⊞; **be ~s** ⊞ spinnen ⊞. ~-**crackers** npl Nussknacker m. ~**meg** n Muskat m

nutrient /'njuːtrɪənt/ n Nährstoff m

nutri|tion /nju'trɪʃn/ n Ernährung f. ~**ious** adj nahrhaft

'nutshell n Nussschale f; **in a ~** (fig) kurz gesagt

nylon /'naɪlɒn/ n Nylon nt

Oo

O /əʊ/ n (Teleph) null

oak /əʊk/ n Eiche f

OAP abbr (old-age pensioner) Rentner(in) m(f)

oar /ɔː(r)/ n Ruder nt. ~**sman** n Ruderer m

oasis /əʊ'eɪsɪs/ n (pl oases /-siːz/) Oase f

oath /əʊθ/ n Eid m; (swear-word) Fluch m

oatmeal /'əʊt-/ n Hafermehl nt

oats /əʊts/ npl Hafer m; (Culin) [rolled] ~ Haferflocken pl

obedien|ce /ə'biːdɪəns/ n Gehorsam m. ~**t** adj gehorsam

obey /ə'beɪ/ vt gehorchen (+ dat); befolgen (instructions, rules)

obituary /ə'bɪtjʊərɪ/ n Nachruf m; (notice) Todesanzeige f

object[1] /'ɒbdʒɪkt/ n Gegenstand m; (aim) Zweck m; (intention) Absicht f; (Gram) Objekt nt; **money is no ~** Geld spielt keine Rolle

object[2] /əb'dʒekt/ vi Einspruch erheben (to gegen); (be against) etwas dagegen haben

objection /əb'dʒekʃn/ n Einwand m; **have no ~** nichts dagegen haben. ~**able** adj anstößig; (person) unangenehm

objectiv|e /əb'dʒektɪv/ adj objektiv ● n Ziel nt. ~**ity** n Objektivität f

objector /əb'dʒektə(r)/ n Gegner m

obligation /ɒblɪ'geɪʃn/ n Pflicht f; **without ~** unverbindlich

obligatory /ə'blɪgətrɪ/ adj obligatorisch; **be ~** Vorschrift sein

oblige /ə'blaɪdʒ/ vt verpflichten;

(compel) zwingen; (do a small service) einen Gefallen tun (+ dat). ~ing adj entgegenkommend

oblique /əˈbliːk/ adj schräg; (angle) schief; (fig) indirekt

obliterate /əˈblɪtəreɪt/ vt auslöschen

oblivion /əˈblɪvɪən/ n Vergessenheit f

oblivious /əˈblɪvɪəs/ adj be ~ sich (dat) nicht bewusst sein (of gen)

oblong /ˈɒblɒŋ/ adj rechteckig ● n Rechteck nt

obnoxious /əbˈnɒkʃəs/ adj widerlich

oboe /ˈəʊbəʊ/ n Oboe f

obscen|e /əbˈsiːn/ adj obszön. ~ity n Obszönität f

obscur|e /əbˈskjʊə(r)/ adj dunkel; (unknown) unbekannt ● vt verdecken; (confuse) verwischen. ~ity n Dunkelheit f; Unbekanntheit f

observa|nce /əbˈzɜːvns/ n (of custom) Einhaltung f. ~nt adj aufmerksam. ~tion n Beobachtung f; (remark) Bemerkung f

observatory /əbˈzɜːvətrɪ/ n Sternwarte f

observe /əbˈzɜːv/ vt beobachten; (say, notice) bemerken; (keep, celebrate) feiern; (obey) einhalten. ~r n Beobachter m

obsess /əbˈses/ vt be ~ed by besessen sein von. ~ion n Besessenheit f; (persistent idea) fixe Idee f. ~ive adj zwanghaft

obsolete /ˈɒbsəliːt/ adj veraltet

obstacle /ˈɒbstəkl/ n Hindernis nt

obstina|cy /ˈɒbstɪnəsɪ/ n Starrsinn m. ~te adj starrsinnig; (refusal) hartnäckig

obstruct /əbˈstrʌkt/ vt blockieren; (hinder) behindern. ~ion n Blockierung f; Behinderung f; (obstacle)

Hindernis nt. ~ive adj be ~ive Schwierigkeiten bereiten

obtain /əbˈteɪn/ vt erhalten. ~able adj erhältlich

obtrusive /əbˈtruːsɪv/ adj aufdringlich; (thing) auffällig

obtuse /əbˈtjuːs/ adj begriffsstutzig

obvious /ˈɒbvɪəs/ adj offensichtlich, offenbar

occasion /əˈkeɪʒn/ n Gelegenheit f; (time) Mal nt; (event) Ereignis nt; (cause) Anlass m, Grund m; on the ~ of anlässlich (+ gen)

occasional /əˈkeɪʒənl/ adj gelegentlich. ~ly adv gelegentlich, hin und wieder

occult /ɒˈkʌlt/ adj okkult

occupant /ˈɒkjʊpənt/ n Bewohner(in) m(f); (of vehicle) Insasse m

occupation /ɒkjʊˈpeɪʃn/ n Beschäftigung f; (job) Beruf m; (Mil) Besetzung f; (period) Besatzung f. ~al adj Berufs-. ~al therapy n Beschäftigungstherapie f

occupier /ˈɒkjʊpaɪə(r)/ n Bewohner(in) m(f)

occupy /ˈɒkjʊpaɪ/ vt (pt/pp occupied) besetzen (seat, Mil: country); einnehmen (space); in Anspruch nehmen (time); (live in) bewohnen; (fig) bekleiden (office); (keep busy) beschäftigen

occur /əˈkɜː(r)/ vi (pt/pp occurred) geschehen; (exist) vorkommen, auftreten; it ~red to me that es fiel mir ein, dass. ~rence n Auftreten nt; (event) Ereignis nt

ocean /ˈəʊʃn/ n Ozean m

o'clock /əˈklɒk/ adv [at] 7 ~ [um] 7 Uhr

octagonal /ɒkˈtæɡənl/ adj achteckig

October /ɒkˈtəʊbə(r)/ n Oktober m

octopus /ˈɒktəpəs/ n (pl -puses)

o

Tintenfisch m

odd /ɒd/ adj (-er, -est) seltsam, merkwürdig; (number) ungerade; (not of set) einzeln; forty ~ über vierzig; ~ jobs Gelegenheitsarbeiten pl; the ~ one out die Ausnahme; at ~ moments zwischendurch

odd|ity /'ɒdɪtɪ/ n Kuriosität f. ~ly adv merkwürdig; ~ly enough merkwürdigerweise. ~ment n (of fabric) Rest m

odds /ɒdz/ npl (chances) Chancen pl; at ~ uneinig; ~ and ends Kleinkram m

ode /əʊd/ n Ode f

odious /'əʊdɪəs/ adj widerlich

odour /'əʊdə(r)/ n Geruch m. ~less adj geruchlos

of /ɒv/, unbetont /əv/
● preposition

····▸ (indicating belonging, origin) von (+ dat); genitive. the mother of twins die Mutter von Zwillingen. the mother of the twins die Mutter der Zwillinge or von den Zwillingen. the Queen of England die Königin von England. a friend of mine ein Freund von mir. a friend of the teacher's ein Freund des Lehrers. the brother of her father der Bruder ihres Vaters. the works of Shakespeare Shakespeares Werke. it was nice of him es war nett von ihm

····▸ (made of) aus (+ dat). a dress of cotton ein Kleid aus Baumwolle

····▸ (following number) five of us fünf von uns. the two of us wir zwei. there were four of us waiting wir waren vier, die warteten

····▸ (followed by number, description) von (+ dat). a girl of ten ein Mädchen von zehn Jahren. a distance of 50 miles eine Entfernung von 50 Meilen. a man of character ein Mann von Charakter. a woman of exceptional beauty eine Frau von außerordentlicher Schönheit. a person of strong views ein Mensch mit festen Ansichten

! of is not translated after measures and in some other cases: a pound of apples ein Pfund Äpfel; a cup of tea eine Tasse Tee; a glass of wine ein Glas Wein; the city of Chicago die Stadt Chicago; the fourth of January der vierte Januar

off /ɒf/ prep von (+ dat); ~ the coast vor der Küste; get ~ the ladder/bus von der Leiter/aus dem Bus steigen ● adv weg; (button, lid, handle) ab; (light) aus; (brake) los; (machine) abgeschaltet; (tap) zu; (on appliance) 'off' 'aus'; 2 kilometres ~ 2 Kilometer entfernt; a long way ~ weit weg; (time) noch lange hin; ~ and on hin und wieder; with his hat/coat ~ ohne Hut/Mantel; 20% ~ 20% Nachlass; be ~ (leave) [weg]gehen; (Sport) starten; (food:) schlecht sein; be well ~ gut dran sein; (financially) wohlhabend sein; have a day ~ einen freien Tag haben

offal /'ɒfl/ n (Culin) Innereien pl

gewann nach 1952 an Bedeutung. Viele junge Intendanten sind nicht an kommerziellen Aufführungen interessiert, und ihre Inszenierungen finden in alten Lagerhäusern abseits des *Broadway*, der großen New Yorker Theaterstraße, statt.

offence /ə'fens/ n (*illegal act*) Vergehen *nt*; **give/take ~** Anstoß erregen/nehmen (**at** an + *dat*)

offend /ə'fend/ vt beleidigen. **~er** n (*Jur*) Straftäter *m*

offensive /ə'fensiv/ adj anstößig; (*Mil, Sport*) offensiv ● n Offensive *f*

offer /'ɒfə(r)/ n Angebot *nt*; **on** (**special**) im Sonderangebot ● vt anbieten (**to** *dat*); leisten (*resistance*); **~ to do** sth sich anbieten, etw zu tun. **~ing** n Gabe *f*

off'hand adj brüsk; (*casual*) lässig

office /'ɒfɪs/ n Büro *nt*; (*post*) Amt *nt*

officer /'ɒfɪsə(r)/ n Offizier *m*; (*official*) Beamte(r) *m*/Beamtin *f*; (*police*) Polizeibeamte(r) *m*/-beamtin *f*

official /ə'fɪʃl/ adj offiziell, amtlich ● n Beamte(r) *m*/Beamtin *f*. (*Sport*) Funktionär *m*. **~ly** adv offiziell

officious /ə'fɪʃəs/ adj übereifrig

'off-licence n Wein- und Spirituosenhandlung *f*

off-'load vt ausladen

'off-putting adj [I] abstoßend

off-'set vt (*pt/pp* -set, *pres p* -setting) ausgleichen

'offshoot n Schössling *m*; (*fig*) Zweig *m*

'offshore adj (*oil field*) im Meer; (*breeze*) vom Land kommend ● adv im/ins Ausland

off'side adj (*Sport*) abseits

off'stage adv hinter den Kulissen

off-'white adj fast weiß

often /'ɒfn/ adv oft; **every so ~** von Zeit zu Zeit

oh /əʊ/ int oh! ach! oh dear! o weh!

oil /ɔɪl/ n Öl *nt*; (*petroleum*) Erdöl *nt* ● vt ölen

oil: ~field n Ölfeld *nt*. **~-painting** n Ölgemälde *nt*. **~ refinery** n [Erd]ölraffinerie *f*. **~-tanker** n Öltanker *m*. **~ well** n Ölquelle *f*

oily /'ɔɪlɪ/ adj ölig

ointment /'ɔɪntmənt/ n Salbe *f*

OK /əʊ'keɪ/ adj & int [I] in Ordnung; okay ● adv (*well*) gut ● vt (*auch* okay) (*pt/pp* okayed) genehmigen

old /əʊld/ adj (-er, -est) alt; (*former*) ehemalig

old: ~ age n Alter *nt*. **~-age 'pensioner** n Rentner(in) *m(f)*. **~ boy** n ehemaliger Schüler. **~-fashioned** adj altmodisch. **~ girl** n ehemalige Schülerin *f*

olive /'ɒlɪv/ n Olive *f*; (*colour*) Oliv *nt* ● adj olivgrün. **~ 'oil** n Olivenöl *nt*

Olympic /ə'lɪmpɪk/ adj olympisch ● n the **~s** die Olympischen Spiele *pl*

omelette /'ɒmlɪt/ n Omelett *nt*

ominous /'ɒmɪnəs/ adj bedrohlich

omission /ə'mɪʃn/ n Auslassung *f*; (*failure to do*) Unterlassung *f*

omit /ə'mɪt/ vt (*pt/pp* omitted)

o

auslassen; ~ to do sth es unterlassen, etw zu tun

omnipotent /ɒmˈnɪpətənt/ adj allmächtig

on /ɒn/ prep auf (+ dat/(on to) + acc); (on vertical surface) an (+ dat/(on to) + acc); (about) über (+ acc); on Monday [am] Montag; on Mondays montags; on the first of May am ersten Mai; on arriving as ich ankam; on one's finger an Finger; on the right/left rechts/links; on the Rhine am Rhein; on the radio/television in Radio/Fernsehen; on the bus/train in Bus/Zug; go on the bus/train mit dem Bus/Zug fahren; on me (with me) bei mir; it's on me Ⓣ das spendiere ich ● adv (further on) weiter; (switched on) an; (brake) angezogen; (machine) eingeschaltet; (on appliance) 'on' 'ein'; with/without my hat/coat on mit/ohne Hut/Mantel; be on (film:) laufen; (event:) stattfinden; be on at Ⓣ bedrängen (zu to); it's not on Ⓣ das geht nicht; on and on immer weiter; on and off hin und wieder; and so on und so weiter

once /wʌns/ adv einmal; (formerly) früher; at ~ sofort; (at the same time) gleichzeitig; ~ and for all ein für alle Mal ● conj wenn; (with past tense) als

oncoming adj ~ traffic Gegenverkehr m

one /wʌn/ adj ein(e); (only) einzig; not ~ kein(e); ~ day/evening eines Tages/Abends ● n Eins f ● pron eine(r)/eins; (impersonal) man; which ~ welche(r,s); ~ another einander; ~ by ~ einzeln; ~ never knows man kann nie wissen

one: ~-parent 'family n Einelternfamilie f. ~'self pron selbst; (reflexive) sich; by ~self allein. ~-sided

adj einseitig. ~-way adj (street) Einbahn-; (ticket) einfach

onion /ˈʌnjən/ n Zwiebel f.

on-'line adv online

'onlooker n Zuschauer(in) m(f)

only /ˈəʊnlɪ/ adj einzige(r,s); an ~ child ein Einzelkind nt ● adv & conj nur; ~ just gerade erst; (barely) gerade noch

onset n Beginn m; (of winter) Einsetzen nt

'on-shore adj (oil field) an Land; (breeze) vom Meer kommend

onward[s] /ˈɒnwəd[z]/ adv vorwärts; from then ~ von der Zeit an

ooze /uːz/ vi sickern

opaque /əʊˈpeɪk/ adj undurchsichtig

open /ˈəʊpən/ adj offen; be ~ (shop:) geöffnet sein; in the ~ air im Freien ● n in the ~ im Freien ● vt öffnen, aufmachen; (start, set up) eröffnen ● vi sich öffnen; (flower:) aufgehen; (shop:) öffnen, aufmachen; (be started) eröffnet werden. ~ up vt öffnen, aufmachen

'open day n Tag m der offenen Tür

opener /ˈəʊpənə(r)/ n Öffner m

opening /ˈəʊpənɪŋ/ n Öffnung f; (beginning) Eröffnung f; (job) Einstiegsmöglichkeit f. ~ hours npl Öffnungszeiten pl

open: ~-'minded adj aufgeschlossen. ~ 'sandwich n belegtes Brot nt

---

ⓘ **Open University - OU** Eine britische Fernuniversität, die 1969 gegründet wurde und vor allem Berufstätigen im Fernstudium Kurse auf verschiedenem Niveau bietet. Studenten jeder Altersgruppe, selbst

opera | order

solche ohne die erforderlichen Schulabschlüsse, können das Studium mit dem *Bachelor's degree* und dem *Master's degree* abschließen. Teilnehmer studieren von zu Hause und können auch an Direktunterricht teilnehmen.

opera /'ɒpərə/ n Oper f. ~ **glasses** pl Opernglas n ~-**house** n Opernhaus nt. ~-**singer** n Opernsänger(in) m(f)

operate /'ɒpəreɪt/ vt bedienen (*machine, lift*); betätigen (*lever, brake*); (*fig: run*) betreiben ● vi (*Techn*) funktionieren; (*be in action*) in Betrieb sein; (*Mil & fig*) operieren; ~ **[on]** (*Med*) operieren

operatic /ɒpə'rætɪk/ adj Opern-

operation /ɒpə'reɪʃn/ n (*see operate*) Bedienung f; Betätigung f; Operation f; in ~ (*Techn*) in Betrieb; **come into** ~ (*fig*) in Kraft treten; **have an** ~ (*Med*) operiert werden. ~**al** adj einsatzbereit; be ~**al** in Betrieb sein; (*law:*) in Kraft sein

operative /'ɒpərətɪv/ adj wirksam

operator /'ɒpəreɪtə(r)/ n (*user*) Bedienungsperson f; (*Teleph*) Vermittlung f

operetta /ɒpə'retə/ n Operette f

opinion /ə'pɪnjən/ n Meinung f; **in my** ~ meiner Meinung nach. ~**ated** adj rechthaberisch

opponent /ə'pəʊnənt/ n Gegner(in) m(f)

opportun|e /'ɒpətju:n/ adj günstig. ~**ist** n Opportunist m

opportunity /ɒpə'tju:nətɪ/ n Gelegenheit f

oppos|e /ə'pəʊz/ vt Widerstand leisten (+ dat); (*argue against*) sprechen gegen; **be** ~**ed** to sth gegen etw sein; **as** ~**ed** to im Gegensatz zu. ~**ing** adj gegnerisch

opposite /'ɒpəzɪt/ adj entgegengesetzt; (*house, side*) gegenüberliegend; ~ **number** (*fig*) Gegenstück nt; **the** ~ **sex** das andere Geschlecht ● n Gegenteil nt ● adv gegenüber ● prep gegenüber (+ dat)

opposition /ɒpə'zɪʃn/ n Widerstand m; (*Pol*) Opposition f

oppress /ə'pres/ vt unterdrücken. ~**ion** n Unterdrücken f. ~**ive** adj tyrannisch; (*heat*) drückend

opt /ɒpt/ vi ~ **for** sich entscheiden für

optical /'ɒptɪkl/ adj optisch

optician /ɒp'tɪʃn/ n Optiker m

optimis|m /'ɒptɪmɪzm/ n Optimismus m. ~**t** n Optimist m. ~**tic** adj, -ally adv optimistisch

optimum /'ɒptɪməm/ adj optimal

option /'ɒpʃn/ n Wahl f; (*Comm*) Option f. ~**al** adj auf Wunsch erhältlich; (*subject*) wahlfrei

opulen|ce /'ɒpjʊləns/ n Prunk m. ~**lent** adj prunkvoll

or /ɔ:(r)/ conj oder; (*after negative*) noch; **or** [**else**] sonst; **in a year or two** in ein bis zwei Jahren

oral /'ɔ:rl/ adj mündlich; (*Med*) oral ● n Mündliche(s) f

orange /'ɒrɪndʒ/ n Apfelsine f, Orange f; (*colour*) Orange nt ● adj orangefarben

oratorio /ɒrə'tɔ:rɪəʊ/ n Oratorium nt

oratory /'ɒrətərɪ/ n Redekunst f

orbit /'ɔ:bɪt/ n Umlaufbahn f ● vt umkreisen

orchard /'ɔ:tʃəd/ n Obstgarten m

orchestra /'ɔ:kɪstrə/ n Orchester nt. ~**tral** adj Orchester-. ~**trate** orchestrieren

ordeal /ɔ:'di:l/ n (*fig*) Qual f

order /'ɔ:də(r)/ n Ordnung f; (*se-*

o

quence) Reihenfolge f; (condition)
Zustand m; (command) Befehl m;
(in restaurant) Bestellung f; (Comm)
Auftrag m; (Relig, medal) Orden m;
out of ~ (machine) außer Betrieb;
in ~ that damit; in ~ to help um
zu helfen ● vt (put in ~) ordnen;
(command) befehlen (+ dat);
(Comm, in restaurant) bestellen; (prescribe) verordnen

orderly /'ɔːdəlɪ/ adj ordentlich;
(not unruly) friedlich ● n (Mil, Med)
Sanitäter m

ordinary /'ɔːdɪnərɪ/ adj gewöhnlich, normal

ore /ɔː(r)/ n Erz nt

organ /'ɔːgən/ n (Biology) Organ nt;
(Mus) Orgel f

organic /ɔː'gænɪk/ adj, **-ally** adv
organisch; (without chemicals) biodynamisch; (crop) biologisch angebaut; (food) Bio-. **~ farming** n
biologischer Anbau m

organism /'ɔːgənɪzm/ n Organismus m

organist /'ɔːgənɪst/ n Organist m

organization /ɔːgənaɪ'zeɪʃn/ n
Organisation f

organize /'ɔːgənaɪz/ vt organisieren; veranstalten (event). **~r** n Organisator m; Veranstalter m

orgy /'ɔːdʒɪ/ n Orgie f

Orient /'ɔːrɪənt/ n Orient m. **o~al** adj orientalisch ● n Orientale
m/Orientalin f

orientation /ɔːrɪən'teɪʃn/ n Orientierung f

origin /'ɒrɪdʒɪn/ n Ursprung m; (of
person, goods) Herkunft f

original /ə'rɪdʒənl/ adj ursprünglich; (not copied) original; (new) originell ● n Original nt. **~ity** n Originalität f. **~ly** adv ursprünglich

originate /ə'rɪdʒɪneɪt/ vi entstehen

ornament /'ɔːnəmənt/ n Ziergegenstand m; (decoration) Verzierung
f. **~al** adj dekorativ

ornate /ɔː'neɪt/ adj reich verziert

ornithology /ɔːnɪ'θɒlədʒɪ/ n Vogelkunde f

orphan /'ɔːfn/ n Waisenkind nt,
Waise f. **~age** n Waisenhaus nt

orthodox /'ɔːθədɒks/ adj orthodox

ostensible /ɒ'stensəbl/ adj, **-bly**
adv angeblich

ostentat|ion /ɒsten'teɪʃn/ n Protzerei f 🔟. **~ious** adj protzig 🔟

osteopath /'ɒstɪəpæθ/ n Osteopath m

ostrich /'ɒstrɪtʃ/ n Strauß m

other /'ʌðə(r)/ adj, pron & n andere(r,s); the ~ [one] der/die/das andere; the ~ two die zwei anderen;
no ~s sonst keine; any ~ questions? sonst noch Fragen? every ~
day jeden zweiten Tag; the ~ evening neulich
abends; someone/something or ~
irgendjemand/-etwas ● adv anders;
~ than him außer ihm; somehow/
somewhere or ~ irgendwie/irgendwo

'otherwise adv sonst; (differently)
anders

ought /ɔːt/ modal verb I/we ~ to
stay ich sollte/wir sollten eigentlich
bleiben; he ~ not to have done it
er hätte es nicht machen sollen

ounce /aʊns/ n Unze f (28,35 g)

our /'aʊə(r)/ adj unser

ours /'aʊəz/ poss pron unsere(r,s); a
friend of ~ ein Freund von uns;
that is ~ das gehört uns

ourselves /aʊə'selvz/ pron selbst;
(reflexive) uns; by ~ allein

out /aʊt/ adv (not at home) weg;
(outside) draußen; (not alight) aus;
(unconscious) bewusstlos; be ~

(sun:) scheinen; (flower) blühen; (workers) streiken; (calculation:) nicht stimmen; (Sport) aus sein; (fig: not feasible) nicht infrage kommen; ~ and about unterwegs; have it ~ with s.o. 🔲 jdn zur Rede stellen; get ~! 🔲 raus! ~ with it! 🔲 heraus damit! ●prep ~ of aus (+dat); go ~ (of) the door zur Tür hinausgehen; be ~ of bed/ the room nicht im Bett/im Zimmer sein; ~ of breath/danger außer Atem/Gefahr; ~ of work arbeitslos; nine ~ of ten neun von zehn; be ~ of sugar keinen Zucker mehr haben

'outboard adj ~ motor Außenbordmotor m

'outbreak n Ausbruch m

'outbuilding n Nebengebäude nt

'outburst n Ausbruch m

'outcast n Ausgestoßene(r) m/f

'outcome n Ergebnis nt

'outcry n Aufschrei m [der Entrüstung]

out'dated adj überholt

out'do vt (pt -did, pp -done) übertreffen

'outdoor adj (life, sports) im Freien; ~ swimming pool Freibad nt

out'doors adv draußen; go ~ nach draußen gehen

'outer adj äußere(r,s)

'outfit n Ausstattung f; (clothes) Ensemble nt; (🔲: organization) Laden m

'outgoing adj ausscheidend; (mail) ausgehend; (sociable) kontaktfreudig, ~s npl Ausgaben pl

out'grow vi (pt -grew, pp -grown) herauswachsen aus

'outing /'aʊtɪŋ/ n Ausflug m

'outlaw n Geächtete(r) m/f ●vt

ächten

'outlay n Auslagen pl

'outlet n Abzug m; (for water) Abfluss m; (fig) Ventil nt; (Comm) Absatzmöglichkeit f

'outline n Umriss m; (summary) kurze Darstellung f ●vt umreißen

out'live vt überleben

'outlook n Aussicht f; (future prospect) Aussichten pl; (attitude) Einstellung f

out'moded adj überholt

out'number vt zahlenmäßig überlegen sein (+dat)

'out-patient n ambulanter Patient m

'outpost n Vorposten m

'output n Leistung f; Produktion f

'outrage n Gräueltat f; (fig) Skandal m; (indignation) Empörung f. ~ous adj empörend

'outright¹ adj völlig, total; (refusal) glatt

out'right² adv ganz; (at once) sofort; (frankly) offen

'outset n Anfang m

'outside¹ adj äußere(r,s); ~ wall Außenwand f ●n Außenseite f; from the ~ von außen; at the ~ höchstens

out'side² adv außen; (out of doors) draußen; go ~ nach draußen gehen ●prep außerhalb (+gen); (in front of) vor (+dat/acc)

out'sider n Außenseiter m

'outsize adj übergroß

'outskirts npl Rand m

out'spoken adj offen; be ~ kein Blatt vor den Mund nehmen

out'standing adj hervorragend; (conspicuous) bemerkenswert; (Comm) ausstehend

'outstretched adj ausgestreckt

o

outvote | overlook

out'vote vt überstimmen

'outward /-wəd/ adj äußerlich; ~ journey Hinreise f ● adv nach außen. **~ly** adv nach außen hin, äußerlich. **~s** adv nach außen

out'wit vt (pt/pp -witted) überlisten

oval /'əʊvl/ adj oval ● n Oval nt

> **Oval Office** Das Oval Office ist das Büro des amerikanischen Präsidenten. Es befindet sich im westlichen Flügel des Weißen Hauses und sein Name bezieht sich auf die ovale Form des Raumes. George Washington (1. Präsident der USA) bestand auf ein ovales Büro, damit er bei Besprechungen allen Anwesenden in die Augen sehen konnte.

ovation /əʊ'veɪʃn/ n Ovation f

oven /'ʌvn/ n Backofen m

over /'əʊvə(r)/ prep über (+ acc/ dat); ~ dinner beim Essen; ~ the phone am Telefon; ~ the page auf der nächsten Seite ● adv (remaining) übrig; (ended) zu Ende; ~ again noch einmal; ~ and ~ immer wieder; ~ here/there hier/da drüben; all ~ (everywhere) überall; it's all ~ es ist vorbei; I ache all ~ mir tut alles weh

overall¹ /'əʊvərɔːl/ n Kittel m; **~s** pl Overall m

overall² /əʊvər'ɔːl/ adj gesamt; (general) allgemein ● adv insgesamt

over'balance vi das Gleichgewicht verlieren

over'bearing adj herrisch

'overboard adv (Naut) über Bord

'overcast adj bedeckt

over'charge vt ~ s.o. jdm zu viel berechnen ● vi zu viel verlangen

'overcoat n Mantel m

over'come vt (pt -came, pp -come) überwinden; be ~ by überwältigt werden von

over'crowded adj überfüllt

over'do vt (pt -did, pp -done) übertreiben; (cook too long) zu lange kochen; ~ it (🛈: do too much) sich übernehmen

'overdose n Überdosis f

'overdraft n [Konto]überziehung f; have an ~ sein Konto überzogen haben

over'due adj überfällig

over'estimate vt überschätzen

'overflow¹ n Überschuss m; (outlet) Überlauf m; ~ car park zusätzlicher Parkplatz m

over'flow² vi überlaufen

over'grown adj (garden) überwachsen

'overhang¹ n Überhang m

over'hang² vt/i (pt/pp -hung) überhängen (über + acc)

'overhaul¹ n Überholung f

over'haul² vt (Techn) überholen

over'head¹ adv oben

'overhead² adj Ober-; (ceiling) Decken-. **~s** npl allgemeine Unkosten pl

over'hear vt (pt/pp -heard) mit anhören (conversation)

over'heat vi zu heiß werden

over'joyed adj überglücklich

'overland adj & adv /--'-/ auf dem Landweg; ~ route Landroute f

over'lap vi (pt/pp -lapped) sich überschneiden

over'leaf adv umseitig

over'load vt überladen

over'look vt überblicken; (fail to see, ignore) übersehen

over'night[1] *adv* über Nacht; stay ~ übernachten

'overnight[2] *adj* Nacht-; ~ stay Übernachtung *f*

'overpass *n* Überführung *f*

over'pay *vt* (*pt/pp* -**paid**) überbezahlen

over'populated *adj* übervölkert

over'power *vt* überwältigen. ~**ing** *adj* überwältigend

over'priced *adj* zu teuer

over'rated *adj* überbewertet

over're'act *vi* überreagieren. ~**ion** *n* Überreaktion *f*

over'riding *adj* Haupt-

over'rule *vt* ablehnen; we were ~d wir wurden überstimmt

over'run *vt* (*pt* -**ran**, *pp* -**run**, *pres p* -**running**) überrennen; überschreiten (*time*); be ~ **with** überlaufen sein von

over'seas[1] *adv* in Übersee; go ~ nach Übersee gehen

'overseas[2] *adj* Übersee-

over'see *vt* (*pt* -**saw**, *pp* -**seen**) beaufsichtigen

over'shadow *vt* überschatten

over'shoot *vt* (*pt/pp* -**shot**) hinausschießen über (+ *acc*)

'oversight *n* Versehen *nt*

over'sleep *vi* (*pt/pp* -**slept**) [sich] verschlafen

over'step *vt* (*pt/pp* -**stepped**) überschreiten

overt /əʊˈvɜːt/ *adj* offen

over'take *vt/i* (*pt* -**took**, *pp* -**taken**) überholen

over'throw *vt* (*pt* -**threw**, *pp* -**thrown**) (*Pol*) stürzen

'overtime *n* Überstunden *pl* ● *adv* work ~ Überstunden machen

over'tired *adj* übermüdet

overture /ˈəʊvətjʊə(r)/ *n* (*Mus*) Ouvertüre *f*; ~**s** *pl* (*fig*) Annäherungsversuche *pl*

over'turn *vt* umstoßen ● *vi* umkippen

over'weight *adj* übergewichtig; be ~ Übergewicht haben

over'whelm /-ˈwelm/ *vt* überwältigen. ~**ing** *adj* überwältigend

over'work *n* Überarbeitung *f* ● *vt* überfordern ● *vi* sich überarbeiten

over'wrought *adj* überreizt

ow|e /əʊ/ *vt* schulden; (*fig*) verdanken ([to] s.o. jdm); ~**e** s.o. sth jdm etw schuldig sein. '~**ing** *to* prep wegen (+ *gen*)

owl /aʊl/ *n* Eule *f*

own[1] /əʊn/ *adj* & *pron* eigen; it's my ~ es gehört mir; a car of my ~ mein eigenes Auto; on one's ~ allein; get one's ~ **back** 🄵 sich revanchieren

own[2] *vt* besitzen; I don't ~ it es gehört mir nicht. ~ **up** *vi* es zugeben

owner /ˈəʊnə(r)/ *n* Eigentümer(in) *m*(*f*), Besitzer(in) *m*(*f*); (*of shop*) Inhaber(in) *m*(*f*). ~**ship** *n* Besitz *m*

Oxbridge Eine Wortbildung aus den Namen Oxford und Cambridge. Diese umgangssprachliche Zusammensetzung wird als Sammelbegriff für die zwei Eliteuniversitäten in England verwendet, um sie von anderen Hochschulen zu unterscheiden. Oxford und Cambridge sind die ältesten britischen Universitäten mit dem besten akademischen Ruf. Oxbridge-Absolventen werden häufig von Arbeitgebern bevorzugt.

oxygen /ˈɒksɪdʒən/ *n* Sauerstoff *m*

oyster /ˈɔɪstə(r)/ *n* Auster *f*

o

Pp

pace /peɪs/ n Schritt m; (speed)
Tempo nt; **keep ~ with** Schritt halten mit ● vi ~ **up and down** auf
und ab gehen. **~-maker** n (Sport &
Med) Schrittmacher m

Pacific /pə'sɪfɪk/ adj & n **the ~**
[Ocean] der Pazifik

pacifist /'pæsɪfɪst/ n Pazifist m

pacify /'pæsɪfaɪ/ vt (pt/pp -ied) beruhigen

pack /pæk/ n Packung f; (Mil) Tornister m; (of cards) [Karten]spiel nt;
(gang) Bande f; (of hounds) Meute f;
(of wolves) Rudel nt; **a ~ of lies** ein
Haufen Lügen ● vt/i packen, einpacken (article); **be ~ed** (crowded)
[gedrängt] voll sein. ~ **up** vt einpacken ● vi 𝕀 (machine:) kaputtgehen

package /'pækɪdʒ/ n Paket nt. ~
holiday n Pauschalreise f

packet /'pækɪt/ n Päckchen nt

packing /'pækɪŋ/ n Verpackung f

pact /pækt/ n Pakt m

pad /pæd/ n Polster nt; (for writing)
[Schreib]block m ● vt (pt/pp padded) polstern

padding /'pædɪŋ/ n Polsterung f;
(in written work) Füllwerk nt

paddle¹ /'pædl/ n Paddel nt ● vt
(row) paddeln

paddle² vi waten

paddock /'pædək/ n Koppel f

padlock /'pædlɒk/ n Vorhängeschloss nt ● vt mit einem Vorhängeschloss verschließen

paediatrician /piːdɪə'trɪʃn/ n
Kinderarzt m /-ärztin f

pagan /'peɪgən/ adj heidnisch ● n
Heide m/Heidin f

page¹ /peɪdʒ/ n Seite f

page² n (boy) Page m ● vt ausrufen
(person)

paid /peɪd/ see **pay** ● adj bezahlt;
put ~ to 𝕀 zunichte machen

pail /peɪl/ n Eimer m

pain /peɪn/ n Schmerz m; **be in ~**
Schmerzen haben; **take ~s** sich
(dat) Mühe geben; **~ in the neck**
𝕀 Nervensäge f

pain: **~ful** adj schmerzhaft; (fig)
schmerzlich. **~killer** n schmerzstil-
lendes Mittel nt. **~less** adj
schmerzlos

painstaking /'peɪnzteɪkɪŋ/ adj
sorgfältig

paint /peɪnt/ n Farbe f ● vt/i streichen; (artist:) malen. **~brush** n Pinsel m. **~er** n Maler m; (decorator)
Anstreicher m. **~ing** n Malerei f;
(picture) Gemälde nt

pair /peə(r)/ n Paar nt; **~ of trousers** Hose f ● vi ~ **off** Paare bilden

pajamas /pə'dʒɑːməz/ n pl (Amer)
Schlafanzug m

Pakistan /pɑːkɪ'stɑːn/ n Pakistan
nt. **~i** adj pakistanisch ● n Pakista-
ner(in) m(f)

pal /pæl/ n Freund(in) m(f)

palace /'pælɪs/ n Palast m

palatable /'pælətəbl/ adj
schmackhaft

palate /'pælət/ n Gaumen m

palatial /pə'leɪʃl/ adj palastartig

pale adj (-r, -st) blass ● vi blass
werden. **~ness** n Blässe f

Palestine /'pælɪstaɪn/ n Palästina
nt. **~ian** adj palästinensisch ● n Pa-
lästinenser(in) m(f)

palette /'pælɪt/ n Palette f

palm /pɑːm/ n Handfläche f; (tree,
symbol) Palme f ● vt ~ **sth off on
s.o.** jdm etw andrehen. **P~Sunday**
n Palmsonntag m

palpable /'pælpǝbl/ adj tastbar; (perceptible) spürbar

palpitations /pælpɪ'teɪʃnz/ npl Herzklopfen nt

paltry /'pɔːltrɪ/ adj armselig

pamper /'pæmpǝ(r)/ vt verwöhnen

pamphlet /'pæmflɪt/ n Broschüre f

pan /pæn/ n Pfanne f; (saucepan) Topf m; (of scales) Schale f

panacea /pænǝ'siːǝ/ n Allheilmittel nt

'pancake n Pfannkuchen m

panda /'pændǝ/ n Panda m

pandemonium /pændɪ'mǝʊnɪǝm/ n Höllenlärm m

pane /peɪn/ n [Glas]scheibe f

panel /'pænl/ n Tafel f, Platte f; ~ of experts Expertenrunde f; ~ of judges Jury f. ~ling n Täfelung f

pang /pæŋ/ n ~s of hunger Hungergefühl nt; ~s of conscience Gewissensbisse pl

panic /'pænɪk/ n Panik f ● vi (pt/pp panicked) in Panik geraten. ~-stricken adj von Panik ergriffen

panorama /pænǝ'rɑːmǝ/ n Panorama nt. ~ic adj Panorama-

pansy /'pænzɪ/ n Stiefmütterchen nt

pant /pænt/ vi keuchen; (dog:) hecheln

panther /'pænθǝ(r)/ n Panther m

panties /'pæntɪz/ npl [Damen]slip m

pantomime /'pæntǝmaɪm/ n [zu Weihnachten aufgeführte] Märchenvorstellung f

pantry /'pæntrɪ/ n Speisekammer f

pants /pænts/ npl Unterhose f; (woman's) Schlüpfer m; (trousers) Hose f

'pantyhose n (Amer) Strumpfhose f

paper /'peɪpǝ(r)/ n Papier nt; (newspaper) Zeitung f; (exam~) Testbogen m; (exam) Klausur f; (treatise) Referat nt; ~s pl (documents) Unterlagen pl; (for identification) [Ausweis]papiere pl ● vt tapezieren

paper: ~back n Taschenbuch nt. ~-clip n Büroklammer f. ~weight n Briefbeschwerer m. ~work n Schreibarbeit f

par /pɑː(r)/ n (Golf) Par nt; on a ~ gleichwertig (with dat)

parable /'pærǝbl/ n Gleichnis nt

parachut|e /'pærǝʃuːt/ n Fallschirm m ● vi [mit dem Fallschirm] abspringen. ~ist n Fallschirmspringer m

parade /pǝ'reɪd/ n Parade f; (procession) Festzug m ● vt (show off) zur Schau stellen

paradise /'pærǝdaɪs/ n Paradies nt

paradox /'pærǝdɒks/ n Paradox nt. ~ical adj paradox

paraffin /'pærǝfɪn/ n Paraffin nt

paragraph /'pærǝgrɑːf/ n Absatz m

parallel /'pærǝlel/ adj & adv parallel ● n (Geog) Breitenkreis m; (fig) Parallele f

Paralympics /pærǝ'lɪmpɪks/ npl the ~ die Paralympics pl

paralyse /'pærǝlaɪz/ vt lähmen; (fig) lahmlegen

paralysis /pǝ'rælǝsɪs/ n (pl -ses /-siːz/) Lähmung f

paramedic /pærǝ'medɪk/ n Rettungssanitäter(in) m(f)

parameter /pǝ'ræmɪtǝ(r)/ n Parameter m, Rahmen m

paranoid /'pærǝnɔɪd/ adj [krankhaft] misstrauisch

parapet /'pærǝpɪt/ n Brüstung f

paraphernalia /pærəfə'neɪlɪə/ n Kram m

parasite /'pærəsaɪt/ n Parasit m, Schmarotzer m

paratrooper /'pærətru:pə(r)/ n Fallschirmjäger m

parcel /'pɑ:sl/ n Paket nt

parch /pɑ:tʃ/ vt austrocknen; be ~ed (person:) einen furchtbaren Durst haben

parchment /'pɑ:tʃmənt/ n Pergament m

pardon /'pɑ:dn/ n Verzeihung f; (Jur) Begnadigung f; ~? 🅸 bitte? I beg your ~ wie bitte? (sorry) Verzeihung! ● vt verzeihen; (Jur) begnadigen

parent /'peərənt/ n Elternteil m; ~s pl Eltern pl. ~al /pə'rentl/ adj elterlich

parenthesis /pə'renθəsɪs/ n (pl -ses /-si:z/) Klammer f

parish /'pærɪʃ/ n Gemeinde f. ~ioner n Gemeindemitglied nt

park /pɑ:k/ n Park m ● vt/i parken. ~-and-ride n Park-and-ride-Platz m

parking /'pɑ:kɪŋ/ n Parken nt; 'no ~' 'Parken verboten'. ~-lot n (Amer) Parkplatz m. ~-meter n Parkuhr f. ~ space n Parkplatz m

parliament /'pɑ:ləmənt/ n Parlament nt. ~ary adj parlamentarisch

Parliament Das britische Parlament ist die oberste gesetzgebende Gewalt in Großbritannien und besteht aus dem Souverän (dem König oder der Königin), dem House of Lords (Oberhaus) und dem House of Commons (Unterhaus). Die Partei mit der Mehrheit im Unterhaus bildet die Regierung. ▷DÁIL ÉIREANN, ▷SCOTTISH PARLIAMENT, ▷WELSH ASSEMBLY.

parochial /pə'rəʊkɪəl/ adj Ge-

meinde-; (fig) beschränkt

parody /'pærədɪ/ n Parodie f ● vt (pt/pp -ied) parodieren

parole /pə'rəʊl/ n on ~ auf Bewährung

parquet /'pɑ:keɪ/ n ~ floor Parkett nt

parrot /'pærət/ n Papagei m

parsley /'pɑ:slɪ/ n Petersilie f

parsnip /'pɑ:snɪp/ n Pastinake f

parson /'pɑ:sn/ n Pfarrer m

part /pɑ:t/ n Teil m; (Techn) Teil nt; (area) Gegend f; (Theat) Rolle f; (Mus) Part m; spare ~ Ersatzteil nt; for my ~ meinerseits; on the ~ of vonseiten (+ gen); take s.o.'s ~ für jdn Partei ergreifen; take ~ in teilnehmen an (+ dat) ● adv teils ● vt trennen; scheiteln (hair) ● vi (people:) sich trennen; ~ with sich trennen von

partial /'pɑ:ʃl/ adj Teil-; be ~ to mögen. ~ly adv teilweise

participant /pɑ:'tɪsɪpənt/ n Teilnehmer(in) m(f). ~ate vi teilnehmen (in an + dat). ~ation n Teilnahme f

particle /'pɑ:tɪkl/ n Körnchen nt; (Phys) Partikel nt; (Gram) Partikel f

particular /pə'tɪkjʊlə(r)/ adj besondere(r,s); (precise) genau; (fastidious) penibel; in ~ besonders. ~ly adv besonders. ~s npl nähere Angaben pl

parting /'pɑ:tɪŋ/ n Abschied m; (in hair) Scheitel m

partition /pɑ:'tɪʃn/ n Trennwand f; (Pol) Teilung f ● vt teilen

partly /'pɑ:tlɪ/ adv teilweise

partner /'pɑ:tnə(r)/ n Partner(in) m(f); (Comm) Teilhaber m. ~ship n Partnerschaft f; (Comm) Teilhaberschaft f

partridge /'pɑ:trɪdʒ/ n Rebhuhn nt

part-time | patriot

part-'time *adj & adv* Teilzeit-; **be or work** ~ Teilzeitarbeit machen

party /'pɑːtɪ/ *n* Party *f*, Fest *nt*; (*group*) Gruppe *f*; (*Pol, Jur*) Partei *f*

pass /pɑːs/ *n* Ausweis *m*; (*Geog, Sport*) Pass *m*; (*Sch*) ≈ ausreichend; **get a** ~ bestehen ● *vt* vorbeigehen/-fahren an (+ *dat*); (*overtake*) überholen; (*hand*) reichen; (*Sport*) abgeben, abspielen; (*approve*) annehmen; (*exceed*) übersteigen; bestehen (*exam*); machen (*remark*); fällen (*judgement*); (*Jur*) verhängen (*sentence*); ~ **the time** sich (*dat*) die Zeit vertreiben; ~ **one's hand over sth** mit der Hand über etw (*acc*) fahren ● *vi* vorbeigehen/-fahren; (*get by*) vorbeikommen; (*overtake*) überholen; (*time:*) vergehen; (*in exam*) bestehen; ~ **away** *vi* sterben; ~ **down** *vt* herunterreichen; (*fig*) weitergeben. ~ **out** *vi* ohnmächtig werden. ~ **round** *vt* herumreichen; ~ **up** *vt* heraufreichen; (□: *miss*) vorübergehen lassen

passable /'pɑːsəbl/ *adj* (*road*) befahrbar; (*satisfactory*) passabel

passage /'pæsɪdʒ/ *n* Durchgang *m*; (*corridor*) Gang *m*; (*voyage*) Überfahrt *f*; (*in book*) Passage *f*

passenger /'pæsɪndʒə(r)/ *n* Fahrgast *m*; (*Naut, Aviat*) Passagier *m*; (*in car*) Mitfahrer *m*. ~ **seat** *n* Beifahrersitz *m*

passer-by /pɑːsə'baɪ/ *n* (*pl* -s-by) Passant(in) *m*(*f*)

passion /'pæʃn/ *n* Leidenschaft *f*. ~**ate** *adj* leidenschaftlich

passive /'pæsɪv/ *adj* passiv ● *n* Passiv *nt*

pass: ~**port** *n* [Reise]pass *m*. ~**word** *n* Kennwort *nt*; (*Mil*) Losung *f*

past /pɑːst/ *adj* vergangene(r,s); (*former*) ehemalig; **that's all** ~ das

ist jetzt vorbei ● *n* Vergangenheit *f* ● *prep* an (+ *dat*) ... vorbei; (*after*) nach; **at ten** ~ **two** um zehn nach zwei ● *adv* vorbei; **go** ~ vorbeigehen

pasta /'pæstə/ *n* Nudeln *pl*

paste /peɪst/ *n* Brei *m*; (*adhesive*) Kleister *m*; (*jewellery*) Strass *m* ● *vt* kleistern

pastel /'pæstl/ *n* Pastellfarbe *f*; (*drawing*) Pastell *nt* ● *attrib* Pastell-

pastime /'pɑːstaɪm/ *n* Zeitvertreib *m*

pastry /'peɪstrɪ/ *n* Teig *m*; **cakes and** ~**ies** Kuchen und Gebäck

pasture /'pɑːstʃə(r)/ *n* Weide *f*

pasty[1] /'pæstɪ/ *n* Pastete *f*

pat /pæt/ *n* Klaps *m*; (*of butter*) Stückchen *nt* ● *vt* (*pt/pp* patted) tätscheln; ~ **s.o. on the back** jdm auf die Schulter klopfen

patch /pætʃ/ *n* Flicken *m*; (*spot*) Fleck *m*; **not a** ~ **on** □ gar nicht zu vergleichen mit ● *vt* flicken. ~ **up** *vt* [zusammen]flicken; beilegen (*quarrel*)

patchy /'pætʃɪ/ *adj* ungleichmäßig

patent /'peɪtnt/ *n* Patent *nt* ● *vt* patentieren. ~ **leather** *n* Lackleder *nt*

paternal /pə'tɜːnl/ *adj* väterlich

path /pɑːθ/ *n* (*pl* ~**s** /pɑːðz/) [Fuß]weg *m*, Pfad *m*; (*orbit, track*) Bahn *f*; (*fig*) Weg *m*

pathetic /pə'θetɪk/ *adj* mitleiderregend; (*attempt*) erbärmlich

patience /'peɪʃns/ *n* Geduld *f*; (*game*) Patience *f*

patient /'peɪʃnt/ *adj* geduldig ● *n* Patient(in) *m*(*f*)

patio /'pætɪəʊ/ *n* Terrasse *f*

patriot /'pætrɪət/ *n* Patriot(in) *m*(*f*). ~**ic** *adj* patriotisch. ~**ism** *n* Patriotismus *m*

P

patrol /pə'trəʊl/ n Patrouille f • vt/i patrouillieren [in (+ dat)]; (police) auf Streife gehen/fahren [in (+ dat)]. ~ **car** n Streifenwagen m

patron /'peɪtrən/ n Gönner m; (of charity) Schirmherr m; (of the arts) Mäzen m; (customer) Kunde m/Kundin f; (Theat) Besucher m. ~**age** n Schirmherrschaft f

patronize /'pætrənaɪz/ vt (fig) herablassend behandeln. ~**ing** adj gönnerhaft

patter n (speech) Gerede nt

pattern /'pætn/ n Muster nt

paunch /pɔ:ntʃ/ n [Schmer]bauch m

pause /pɔ:z/ n Pause f • vi innehalten

pave /peɪv/ vt pflastern; ~ the way den Weg bereiten (for dat). ~**ment** n Bürgersteig m

paw /pɔ:/ n Pfote f; (of large animal) Pranke f, Tatze f

pawn[1] /pɔ:n/ n (Chess) Bauer m; (fig) Schachfigur f

pawn[2] vt verpfänden. ~ **broker** n Pfandleiher m

pay /peɪ/ n Lohn m; (salary) Gehalt nt; be in the ~ of bezahlt werden von • v (pt/pp paid) • vt bezahlen; zahlen (money); ~ s.o. a visit jdm einen Besuch abstatten; ~ s.o. a compliment jdm ein Kompliment machen • vi zahlen; (be profitable) sich bezahlt machen; (fig) sich lohnen; ~ for sth etw bezahlen. ~ **back** vt zurückzahlen. ~ **in** vt einzahlen. ~ **off** vt abzahlen (debt) • vi (fig) sich auszahlen

payable /'peɪəbl/ adj zahlbar; make ~ to ausstellen auf (+ acc)

payment /'peɪmənt/ n Bezahlung f; (amount) Zahlung f

pea /pi:/ n Erbse f

peace /pi:s/ n Frieden m; for my

~ **of mind** zu meiner eigenen Beruhigung

peace|**ful** adj friedlich. ~**maker** n Friedensstifter m

peach /pi:tʃ/ n Pfirsich m

peacock /'pi:kɒk/ n Pfau m

peak /pi:k/ n Gipfel m; (fig) Höhepunkt m. ~**ed 'cap** n Schirmmütze f. ~ **hours** npl Hauptbelastungszeit f; (for traffic) Hauptverkehrszeit f

peal /pi:l/ n (of bells) Glockengeläut nt; ~**s of laughter** schallendes Gelächter nt

'peanut n Erdnuss f

pear /peə(r)/ n Birne f

pearl /pɜ:l/ n Perle f

peasant /'peznt/ n Bauer m

peat /pi:t/ n Torf m

pebble /'pebl/ n Kieselstein m

peck /pek/ n Schnabelhieb m; (kiss) flüchtiger Kuss m • vt/i picken/(nip) hacken (at nach)

peculiar /pɪ'kju:lɪə(r)/ adj eigenartig, seltsam; ~ **to** eigentümlich (+ dat). ~**ity** n Eigenart f

pedal /'pedl/ n Pedal nt • vt fahren (bicycle) • vi treten

pedantic /pɪ'dæntɪk/ adj, ~**ally** adv pedantisch

pedestal /'pedɪstl/ n Sockel m

pedestrian /pɪ'destrɪən/ n Fußgänger(in) m(f) • adj (fig) prosaisch. ~ **'crossing** n Fußgängerüberweg m. ~ **'precinct** n Fußgängerzone f

pedigree /'pedɪgri:/ n Stammbaum m • attrib (animal) Rassehund m

pedlar /'pedlə(r)/ n Hausierer m

peek /pi:k/ vi 🔢 gucken

peel /pi:l/ n Schale f • vt schälen; • vi (skin) sich schälen; (paint) abblättern. ~ **ings** npl Schalen pl

peep /pi:p/ n kurzer Blick m • vi gucken. ~**hole** n Guckloch m

peer¹ /pɪə(r)/ vi ~ at forschend ansehen

peer² n Peer m; **his** ~**s** pl seinesgleichen

peg /peg/ n (hook) Haken m; (for tent) Pflock m, Hering m; (for clothes) [Wäsche]klammer f; off the ~ ① von der Stange

pejorative /prɪˈdʒɒrətɪv/ adj abwertend

pelican /ˈpelɪkən/ n Pelikan m

pellet /ˈpelɪt/ n Kügelchen nt

pelt¹ /pelt/ n (skin) Pelz m, Fell nt

pelt² vt bewerfen ● vi ~ [down] (rain:) [hernieder]prasseln

pelvis /ˈpelvɪs/ n (Anat) Becken nt

pen¹ /pen/ n (for animals) Hürde f

pen² n Federhalter m; (ballpoint) Kugelschreiber m

penal /ˈpiːnl/ adj Straf-. ~**ize** vt bestrafen; (fig) benachteiligen

penalty /ˈpenltɪ/ n Strafe f; (fine) Geldstrafe f; (Sport) Strafstoß m; (Football) Elfmeter m

penance /ˈpenəns/ n Buße f

pence /pens/ see penny

pencil /ˈpensɪl/ n Bleistift m ● vt (pt/pp pencilled) mit Bleistift schreiben. ~**-sharpener** n Bleistiftspitzer m

pendulum /ˈpendjʊləm/ n Pendel nt

penetrat|e /ˈpenɪtreɪt/ vt durchdringen; ~**e into** eindringen in (+ acc). ~**ing** adj durchdringend. ~**ion** n Durchdringen nt

'**penfriend** n Brieffreund(in) m(f)

penguin /ˈpeŋgwɪn/ n Pinguin m

penicillin /penɪˈsɪlɪn/ n Penizillin nt

peninsula /pəˈnɪnsʊlə/ n Halbinsel f

penis /ˈpiːnɪs/ n Penis m

penitentiary /penɪˈtenʃərɪ/ n (Amer) Gefängnis nt

pen-knife n Taschenmesser nt. ~**-name** n Pseudonym nt

penniless /ˈpenɪlɪs/ adj mittellos

penny /ˈpenɪ/ n (pl pence; single coins pennies) Penny m; (Amer) Centstück nt; the ~'**s dropped** ① der Groschen ist gefallen

pension /ˈpenʃn/ n Rente f; (of civil servant) Pension f. ~**er** n Rentner(in) m(f); Pensionär(in) m(f)

pensive /ˈpensɪv/ adj nachdenklich

pent-up /ˈpentʌp/ adj angestaut

penultimate /peˈnʌltɪmət/ adj vorletzte(r,s)

people /ˈpiːpl/ npl Leute pl, Menschen pl; (citizens) Bevölkerung f; the ~ das Volk; English ~ die Engländer; ~ **say** man sagt; **for four** ~ für vier Personen ● vt bevölkern

pepper /ˈpepə(r)/ n Pfeffer m; (vegetable) Paprika m

pepper-mint n Pfefferminz nt; (Bot) Pfefferminze f. ~**pot** n Pfefferstreuer m

per /pɜː(r)/ prep pro; ~ **cent** Prozent nt

percentage /pəˈsentɪdʒ/ n Prozentsatz m; (part) Teil m

perceptible /pəˈseptəbl/ adj wahrnehmbar

percept|ion /pəˈsepʃn/ n Wahrnehmung f. ~**ive** adj feinsinnig

perch¹ /pɜːtʃ/ n Stange f ● vi (bird:) sich niederlassen

perch² n inv (fish) Barsch m

percussion /pəˈkʌʃn/ n Schlagzeug m. ~ **instrument** n Schlaginstrument nt

perennial /pəˈreniəl/ adj (problem) immer wiederkehrend ● n (Bot) mehrjährige Pflanze f

perfect¹ /ˈpɜːfɪkt/ adj perfekt, vollkommen; (①: utter) völlig ● n

(*Gram*) Perfekt nt

perfect² /pəˈfekt/ vt vervollkommnen. **~ion** n Vollkommenheit f; to ~ion perfekt

perfectly /ˈpɜːfɪktlɪ/ adv perfekt; (*completely*) vollkommen, völlig

perforated /ˈpɜːfəreɪtɪd/ adj perforiert

perform /pəˈfɔːm/ vt ausführen; erfüllen (*duty*); (*Theat*) aufführen (*play*); spielen (*role*) ●vi (*Theat*) auftreten; (*Techn*) laufen. **~ance** n Aufführung f; (*at theatre, cinema*) Vorstellung f; (*Techn*) Leistung f. **~er** n Künstler(in) m(f)

perfume /ˈpɜːfjuːm/ n Parfüm nt; (*smell*) Duft m

perhaps /pəˈhæps/ adv vielleicht

perilous /ˈperələs/ adj gefährlich

perimeter /pəˈrɪmɪtə(r)/ n [äußere] Grenze f; (*Geometry*) Umfang m

period /ˈpɪərɪəd/ n Periode f; (*Sch*) Stunde f; (*full stop*) Punkt m ●attrib (*costume*) zeitgenössisch; (*furniture*) antik. **~ic** adj, **~ally** adv periodisch. **~ical** n Zeitschrift f

peripheral /pəˈrɪfərl/ adj nebensächlich. **~y** n Peripherie f

perish /ˈperɪʃ/ vi (*rubber:*) verrotten; (*food:*) verderben; (*to die*) ums Leben kommen. **~able** adj leicht verderblich. **~ing** adj (🄸: *cold*) eiskalt

perjur|e /ˈpɜːdʒə(r)/ vt **~e** oneself einen Meineid leisten. **~y** n Meineid m

perk¹ /pɜːk/ n 🄸 [Sonder]vergünstigung f

perk² vi **~ up** munter werden

perm /pɜːm/ n Dauerwelle f ●vt **~ s.o.'s** hair jdm eine Dauerwelle machen

permanent /ˈpɜːmənənt/ adj ständig; (*job, address*) fest. **~ly** adv

ständig; (*work, live*) dauernd, permanent; (*employed*) fest

permissible /pəˈmɪsəbl/ adj erlaubt

permission /pəˈmɪʃn/ n Erlaubnis f

permit¹ /pəˈmɪt/ vt (*pt/pp* -mitted) erlauben (s.o. jdm)

permit² /ˈpɜːmɪt/ n Genehmigung f

perpendicular /pɜːpən-ˈdɪkjʊlə(r)/ adj senkrecht ●n Senkrechte f

perpetual /pəˈpetjʊəl/ adj ständig, dauernd

perpetuate /pəˈpetjʊeɪt/ vt bewahren; verewigen (*error*)

perplex /pəˈpleks/ vt verblüffen. **~ed** adj verblüfft

persecut|e /ˈpɜːsɪkjuːt/ vt verfolgen. **~ion** n Verfolgung f

perseverance /pɜːsɪˈvɪərəns/ n Ausdauer f

persevere /pɜːsɪˈvɪə(r)/ vi beharrlich weitermachen

Persia /ˈpɜːʃə/ n Persien nt

Persian /ˈpɜːʃn/ adj persisch; (*cat, carpet*) Perser-

persist /pəˈsɪst/ vi beharrlich weitermachen; (*continue*) anhalten; (*view:*) weiter bestehen; **~ in** doing sth dabei bleiben, etw zu tun. **~ence** n Beharrlichkeit f. **~ent** adj beharrlich; (*continuous*) anhaltend

person /ˈpɜːsn/ n Person f; **in ~** persönlich

personal /ˈpɜːsənl/ adj persönlich. **~ hygiene** n Körperpflege f

personality /pɜːsəˈnælətɪ/ n Persönlichkeit f

personify /pəˈsɒnɪfaɪ/ vt (*pt/pp* -ied) personifizieren, verkörpern

personnel /pɜːsəˈnel/ n Personal nt

perspective /pəˈspektɪv/ n Perspektive f

persp|iration /pəːspɪˈreɪʃn/ n Schweiß m. ~**ire** vi schwitzen

persua|de /pəˈsweɪd/ vt überreden; (convince) überzeugen. ~**sion** n Überredung f; (powers of ~sion) Überredungskunst f

persuasive /pəˈsweɪsɪv/ adj beredsam; (convincing) überzeugend

pertinent /ˈpəːtɪnənt/ adj relevant (to für)

perturb /pəˈtəːb/ vt beunruhigen

peruse /pəˈruːz/ vt lesen

perverse /pəˈvəːs/ adj eigensinnig. ~**ion** n Perversion f

pervert[1] /pəˈvəːt/ vt verdrehen; verführen (person)

pervert[2] /ˈpəːvəːt/ n Perverse(r) m

pessimis|m /ˈpesɪmɪzm/ n Pessimismus m. ~**t** n Pessimist m. ~**tic** adj, **-ally** adv pessimistisch

pest /pest/ n Schädling m; ((I): person) Nervensäge f

pester /ˈpestə(r)/ vt belästigen

pesticide /ˈpestɪsaɪd/ n Schädlingsbekämpfungsmittel nt

pet /pet/ n Haustier nt; (favourite) Liebling m ● vt (pt/pp petted) liebkosen

petal /ˈpetl/ n Blütenblatt nt

peter /ˈpiːtə(r)/ vi ~ out allmählich aufhören

petition /pəˈtɪʃn/ n Bittschrift f

pet 'name n Kosename m

petrified /ˈpetrɪfaɪd/ adj vor Angst wie versteinert

petrol /ˈpetrl/ n Benzin nt

petroleum /pɪˈtrəʊlɪəm/ n Petroleum nt

petrol: ~**pump** n Zapfsäule f. ~ **station** n Tankstelle f. ~ **tank** n Benzintank m

petticoat /ˈpetɪkəʊt/ n Un-

terrock m

petty /ˈpetɪ/ adj kleinlich. ~ **'cash** n Portokasse f

petulant /ˈpetjʊlənt/ adj gekränkt

pew /pjuː/ n [Kirchen]bank f

pharmaceutical /faːməˈsjuːtɪkl/ adj pharmazeutisch

pharmac|ist /ˈfaːməsɪst/ n Apotheker(in) m(f). ~**y** n Pharmazie f; (shop) Apotheke f

phase /feɪz/ n Phase f ● vt ~ in/out allmählich einführen/abbauen

Ph.D. (abbr Doctor of Philosophy) Dr. phil.

pheasant /ˈfeznt/ n Fasan m

phenomen|al /fɪˈnɒmɪnl/ adj phänomenal. ~**on** n (pl -na) Phänomen nt

philharmonic /fɪləˈmɒnɪk/ n (orchestra) Philharmoniker pl

Philippines /ˈfɪlɪpiːnz/ npl Philippinen pl

philistine /ˈfɪlɪstaɪn/ n Banause m

philosoph|er /fɪˈlɒsəfə(r)/ n Philosoph m. ~**ical** adj philosophisch. ~**y** n Philosophie f

phlegmatic /flegˈmætɪk/ adj phlegmatisch

phobia /ˈfəʊbɪə/ n Phobie f

phone /fəʊn/ n Telefon nt; be on the ~ Telefon haben; (be phoning) telefonieren ● vt anrufen ● vi telefonieren. ~ **back** vt/i zurückrufen. ~ **book** n Telefonbuch nt. ~ **box** n Telefonzelle f. ~ **card** n Telefonkarte f. ~**in** n (Radio) Hörersendung f. ~ **number** n Telefonnummer f

phonetic /fəˈnetɪk/ adj phonetisch. ~**s** n Phonetik f

phoney /ˈfəʊnɪ/ adj falsch; (forged) gefälscht

photo /ˈfəʊtəʊ/ n Foto nt, Aufnahme f. ~**copier** n Fotokopiergerät nt. ~**copy** n Fotokopie f ● vt fotokopieren

photogenic /fəʊtəʊˈdʒenɪk/ adj fotogen

photograph /ˈfəʊtəgrɑːf/ n Fotografie f, Aufnahme f ● vt fotografieren

photograph|er /fəˈtɒgrəfə(r)/ n Fotograf(in) m(f). ~**ic** adj, ~**ally** adv fotografisch. ~**y** n Fotografie f

phrase /freɪz/ n Redensart f ● vt formulieren. ~-**book** n Sprachführer m

physical /ˈfɪzɪkl/ adj körperlich

physician /fɪˈzɪʃn/ n Arzt m/ Ärztin f

physic|ist /ˈfɪzɪsɪst/ n Physiker(in) m(f). ~**s** n Physik f

physio·therap|ist /fɪziəʊ-/ n Physiotherapeut(in) m(f). ~**y** n Physiotherapie f

physique /fɪˈziːk/ n Körperbau m

pianist /ˈpɪənɪst/ n Klavierspieler(in) m(f). (professional) Pianist(in) m(f)

piano /pɪˈænəʊ/ n Klavier nt

pick[1] /pɪk/ n Spitzhacke f

pick[2] n Auslese f; take one's ~ sich (dat) aussuchen ● vt/i (pluck) pflücken; (select) wählen, sich (dat) aussuchen; ~ and choose wählerisch sein; ~ a quarrel einen Streit anfangen; ~ holes in ⊞ kritisieren; ~ at one's food im Essen herumstochern. ~ **on** vt wählen; (⊞: find fault with) herumhacken auf (+ dat). ~ **up** vt in die Hand nehmen; (off the ground) aufheben; hochnehmen (baby); (learn) lernen; (acquire) erwerben; (buy) kaufen; (Teleph) abnehmen (receiver); (collect) abholen; aufnehmen (passengers); (police) aufgreifen (criminal); sich holen (illness). ⊞

aufgabeln (girl); ~ oneself up aufstehen ● vi (improve) sich bessern

'pickaxe n Spitzhacke f

picket /ˈpɪkɪt/ n Streikposten m

pickle /ˈpɪkl/ n (Amer: gherkin) Essiggurke f; ~**s** pl [Mixed] Pickles pl ● vt einlegen

pick: ~**pocket** n Taschendieb m. ~-**up** n (truck) Lieferwagen m

picnic /ˈpɪknɪk/ n Picknick nt ● vi (pt/pp -nicked) picknicken

picture /ˈpɪktʃə(r)/ n Bild nt; (film) Film m; as pretty as a ~ bildhübsch; put s.o. in the ~ (fig) jdn ins Bild setzen ● vt (imagine) sich (dat) vorstellen

picturesque /pɪktʃəˈresk/ adj malerisch

pie /paɪ/ n Pastete f; (fruit) Kuchen m

piece /piːs/ n Stück nt; (of set) Teil nt; (in game) Stein m; (writing) Artikel m; a ~ of bread/paper ein Stück Brot/Papier; a ~ of news/advice eine Nachricht/ein Rat; take to ~**s** auseinander nehmen ● vt ~ together zusammenfügen; (fig) zusammenstückeln. ~**meal** adv stückweise

pier /pɪə(r)/ n Pier m; (pillar) Pfeiler m

pierc|e /pɪəs/ vt durchstechen. ~**ing** adj durchdringend

pig /pɪg/ n Schwein nt

pigeon /ˈpɪdʒɪn/ n Taube f. ~-**hole** n Fach nt

piggy·back /ˈpɪgɪbæk/ n give s.o. a ~**back** jdn huckepack tragen. ~**bank** n Sparschwein nt

pig·headed adj ⊞ starrköpfig

pigment /ˈpɪgmənt/ n Pigment nt

pig: ~**skin** n Schweinsleder nt. ~**sty** n Schweinestall m. ~**tail** n ⊞ Zopf m

pilchard /ˈpɪltʃəd/ n Sardine f

pile[1] /paɪl/ n (of fabric) Flor m

pile[2] n Haufen m ●vt ~ sth on to sth etw auf etw (acc) häufen. ~ **up** vt häufen ●vi sich häufen

piles /paɪlz/ npl Hämorrhoiden pl

'pile-up n Massenkarambolage f

pilgrim /ˈpɪlɡrɪm/ n Pilger(in) m(f). ~**age** n Pilgerfahrt f, Wallfahrt f

pill /pɪl/ n Pille f

pillar /ˈpɪlə(r)/ n Säule f. ~**-box** n Briefkasten m

pillow /ˈpɪləʊ/ n Kopfkissen nt. ~**case** n Kopfkissenbezug m

pilot /ˈpaɪlət/ n Pilot m; (Naut) Lotse m ●vt fliegen (plane); lotsen (ship). ~**light** n Zündflamme f

pimple /ˈpɪmpl/ n Pickel m

pin /pɪn/ n Stecknadel f; (Techn) Bolzen m, Stift m; (Med) Nagel m; I have ~s and needles in my leg 🄸 mein Bein ist eingeschlafen ●vt (pt/ pp pinned) anstecken (to/on an + acc); (sewing) stecken; (hold down) festhalten

PIN /pɪn/ n PIN f, Geheimnummer f

pinafore /ˈpɪnəfɔː(r)/ n Schürze f. ~ **dress** n Kleiderrock m

pincers /ˈpɪnsəz/ npl Kneifzange f; (Zool) Scheren pl

pinch /pɪntʃ/ n Kniff m; (of salt) Prise f; at a ~ 🄸 zur Not ●vt kneifen, zwicken; (fam: steal) klauen; ~ one's finger sich (dat) den Finger klemmen ●vi (shoe) drücken

pine[1] /paɪn/ n (tree) Kiefer f

pine[2] vi ~ for sich sehnen nach

pineapple /ˈpaɪn-/ n Ananas f.

pink /pɪŋk/ adj rosa

pinnacle /ˈpɪnəkl/ n Gipfel m; (on roof) Turmspitze f

pin: ~**point** vt genau festlegen. ~**stripe** n Nadelstreifen m

pint /paɪnt/ n Pint nt (0,57 l,

Amer: 0,47 l)

pioneer /paɪəˈnɪə(r)/ n Pionier m. ●vt bahnbrechende Arbeit leisten für

pious /ˈpaɪəs/ adj fromm

pip[1] /pɪp/ n (seed) Kern m

pip[2] n (sound) Tonsignal nt

pipe /paɪp/ n Pfeife f; (for water, gas) Rohr nt ●vt in Rohren leiten; (Culin) spritzen

pipe: ~**dream** n Luftschloss nt. ~**line** n Pipeline f; in the ~**line** 🄸 in Vorbereitung

piping /ˈpaɪpɪŋ/ adj ~ **hot** kochend heiß

pirate /ˈpaɪərət/ n Pirat m

piss /pɪs/ vi 🆇 pissen

pistol /ˈpɪstl/ n Pistole f

piston /ˈpɪstən/ n (Techn) Kolben m

pit /pɪt/ n Grube f; (for orchestra) Orchestergraben m; (for audience) Parkett nt; (motor racing) Box f

pitch[1] /pɪtʃ/ n (steepness) Schräge f; (of voice) Stimmlage f; (of sound) [Ton]höhe f; (Sport) Feld nt; (of street-trader) Standplatz m; (fig: degree) Grad m ●vt werfen; aufschlagen (tent) ●vi fallen

pitch[2] n (tar) Pech nt. ~**'black** adj pechschwarz. ~**'dark** adj stockdunkel

piteous /ˈpɪtɪəs/ adj erbärmlich

pitfall n (fig) Falle f

pith /pɪθ/ n (Bot) Mark nt; (of orange) weiße Haut f

pithy /ˈpɪθɪ/ adj (fig) prägnant

piti|ful /ˈpɪtɪfl/ adj bedauernswert. ~**less** adj mitleidslos

'pit stop n Boxenstopp m

pittance /ˈpɪtns/ n Hungerlohn m

pity /ˈpɪtɪ/ n Mitleid nt, Erbarmen nt; [what a] ~! [wie] schade! take ~ on sich erbarmen über (+ acc) ●vt bemitleiden

pivot /ˈpɪvət/ n Drehzapfen m ● vi sich drehen (on um)

pizza /ˈpiːtsə/ n Pizza f

placard /ˈplækɑːd/ n Plakat nt

placate /pləˈkeɪt/ vt beschwichtigen

place /pleɪs/ n Platz m; (spot) Stelle f; (town, village) Ort m; (☐: house) Haus nt; out of ~ fehl am Platze; take ~ stattfinden ● vt setzen; (upright) stellen; (flat) legen; (remember) unterbringen ☐; ~ an order eine Bestellung aufgeben ☐; be ~d (in race) sich platzieren. **~-mat** n Set nt

placid /ˈplæsɪd/ adj gelassen

plague /pleɪɡ/ n Pest f ● vt plagen

plaice /pleɪs/ n inv Scholle f

plain /pleɪn/ adj (-er, -est) klar; (simple) einfach; (not pretty) nicht hübsch; (not patterned) einfarbig; (chocolate) zartbitter; in ~ clothes in Zivil ● adv (simply) einfach ● n Ebene f. **~ly** adv klar, deutlich; (simply) einfach; (obviously) offensichtlich

p **plaintiff** /ˈpleɪntɪf/ n Kläger(in) m(f)

plait /plæt/ n Zopf m ● vt flechten

plan /plæn/ n Plan m ● vt (pt/pp planned) planen; (intend) vorhaben

plane¹ /pleɪn/ n (tree) Platane f

plane² n Flugzeug nt; (Geometry & fig) Ebene f

plane³ n (Techn) Hobel m ● vt hobeln

planet /ˈplænɪt/ n Planet m

plank /plæŋk/ n Brett nt; (thick) Planke f

planning /ˈplænɪŋ/ n Planung f

plant /plɑːnt/ n Pflanze f; (Techn) Anlage f; (factory) Werk nt ● vt pflanzen; (place in position) setzen; ~ oneself sich hinstellen. **~ation** n Plantage f

plaque /plɑːk/ n (Gedenk)tafel f; (on teeth) Zahnbelag m

plaster /ˈplɑːstə(r)/ n Verputz m; (sticking ~) Pflaster nt; ~ [of Paris] Gips m ● vt verputzen (wall); (cover) bedecken mit

plastic /ˈplæstɪk/ n Kunststoff m, Plastik nt ● adj Kunststoff-, Plastik-; (malleable) formbar, plastisch

plastic ˈsurgery n plastische Chirurgie f

plate /pleɪt/ n Teller m; (flat sheet) Platte f; (with name, number) Schild nt; (gold and silverware) vergoldete/ versilberte Ware f; (in book) Tafel f ● vt (with gold) vergolden; (with silver) versilbern

platform /ˈplætfɔːm/ n Plattform f; (stage) Podium nt; (Rail) Bahnsteig m; ~ 5 Gleis 5

platinum /ˈplætɪnəm/ n Platin nt

platitude /ˈplætɪtjuːd/ n Plattitüde f

plausible /ˈplɔːzəbl/ adj plausibel

play /pleɪ/ n Spiel nt; [Theater]stück nt; (Radio) Hörspiel nt; (TV) Fernsehspiel nt; ~ on words Wortspiel nt ● vt/i spielen; ausspielen (card); ~ safe sichergehen. ~ **down** vt herunterspielen. ~ **up** vi ☐ Mätzchen machen

play: ~**er** n Spieler(in) m(f). ~**ful** adj verspielt. ~**ground** n Spielplatz m; (Sch) Schulhof m. ~**group** n Kindergarten m

playing: ~**card** n Spielkarte f. ~**field** n Sportplatz m

play: ~**mate** n Spielkamerad m. ~**thing** n Spielzeug nt. ~**wright** /-raɪt/ n Dramatiker m

plc abbr (public limited company) ≈ GmbH

plea /pliː/ n Bitte f; make a ~ for bitten um

plead /pliːd/ vi flehen (for um); ~

guilty sich schuldig bekennen; ~ with s.o. jdn anflehen

pleasant /'plezənt/ adj angenehm; (person) nett. ~**ly** adv angenehm; (say, smile) freundlich

pleas|e /pli:z/ adv bitte ● vt gefallen (+ dat); ~ s.o. jdn eine Freude machen; ~e oneself tun, was man will. ~**ed** adj erfreut; be ~ed with/about sth sich über etw (acc) freuen. ~**ing** adj erfreulich

pleasure /'pleʒə(r)/ n Vergnügen nt; (joy) Freude f; with ~ gern[e]

pleat /pli:t/ n Falte f ● vt fälteln

pledge /pledʒ/ n Versprechen nt ● vt verpfänden; versprechen

plentiful /'plentɪfl/ adj reichlich

plenty /'plentɪ/ n eine Menge; (enough) reichlich; ~ of money/ people viel Geld/viele Leute

pliable /'plaɪəbl/ adj biegsam

pliers /'plaɪəz/ npl [Flach]zange f

plight /plaɪt/ n [Not]lage f

plinth /plɪnθ/ n Sockel m

plod /plɒd/ vi (pt/pp plodded) trotten; (work) sich abmühen

plonk /plɒŋk/ n 🔢 billiger Wein m

plot /plɒt/ n Komplott nt; (of novel) Handlung f; ~ of land Stück n Land ● vt einzeichnen ● vi ein Komplott schmieden

plough /plaʊ/ n Pflug m ● vt/i pflügen

ploy /plɔɪ/ n 🔢 Trick m

pluck /plʌk/ n Mut m ● vt zupfen; rupfen (bird); pflücken (flower); ~ up courage Mut fassen

plucky /'plʌkɪ/ adj tapfer, mutig

plug /plʌg/ n Stöpsel m; (wood) Zapfen m; (cotton wool) Bausch m; (Electr) Stecker m; (Auto) Zündkerze f; (🔢: advertisement) Schleichwerbung f ● vt zustopfen; (🔢: advertise) Schleichwerbung machen für. ~ **in**

vt (Electr) einstecken

plum /plʌm/ n Pflaume f

plumage /'plu:mɪdʒ/ n Gefieder nt

plumb|er /'plʌmə(r)/ n Klempner m. ~**ing** n Wasserleitungen f

plume /plu:m/ n Feder f

plump /plʌmp/ adj (-er, -est) mollig, rundlich ● vt ~ for wählen

plunge /plʌndʒ/ n Sprung m; take the ~ 🔢 den Schritt wagen ● vt/i tauchen

plural /'plʊərl/ adj pluralisch ● n Mehrzahl f, Plural m

plus /plʌs/ prep plus (+ dat) ● adj Plus- ● n Pluszeichen nt; (advantage) Plus nt

plush[y] /'plʌʃ[ɪ]/ adj luxuriös

ply /plaɪ/ vt (pt/pp plied) ausüben (trade); ~ s.o. with drink jdm ein Glas nach dem anderen eingießen. ~**wood** n Sperrholz nt

p.m. adv abbr (post meridiem) nachmittags

pneumatic /nju:'mætɪk/ adj pneumatisch. ~ **drill** n Pressluft-hammer m

pneumonia /nju:'məʊnɪə/ n Lungenentzündung f

poach /pəʊtʃ/ vt (Culin) pochieren; (steal) wildern. ~**er** n Wilddieb m

pocket /'pɒkɪt/ n Tasche f; be out of ~ [an einem Geschäft] verlieren ● vt einstecken. ~**book** n Notiz-buch nt; (wallet) Brieftasche f. ~-**money** n Taschengeld nt

pod /pɒd/ n Hülse f

poem /'pəʊɪm/ n Gedicht nt

poet /'pəʊɪt/ n Dichter(in) m(f). ~**ic** adj dichterisch

poetry /'pəʊɪtrɪ/ n Dichtung f

poignant /'pɔɪnjənt/ adj ergreifend

point /pɔɪnt/ n Punkt m; (sharp end) Spitze f; (meaning) Sinn m;

(*purpose*) Zweck m; (*Electr*) Steckdose f; ~s pl (*Rail*) Weiche f; ~ of view Standpunkt m; good/bad ~s gute/schlechte Seiten; what is the ~? wozu? the ~ is es geht darum; up to a ~ bis zu einem gewissen Grade; be on the ~ of doing sth im Begriff sein, etw zu tun ●vt richten (at auf + acc); ausfügen (*brickwork*) ●vi deuten (at/to auf + acc); (*with finger*) mit dem Finger zeigen. ~ out vt zeigen auf (+ acc); ~ sth out to s.o. jdn auf etw (acc) hinweisen

point-'blank adj aus nächster Entfernung; (*fig*) rundweg

point|ed /'pɔɪntɪd/ adj spitz; (*question*) gezielt. ~less adj zwecklos, sinnlos

poise /pɔɪz/ n Haltung f

poison /'pɔɪzn/ n Gift nt ●vt vergiften. ~ous adj giftig

poke /pəʊk/ n Stoß m ●vt stoßen; schüren (*fire*); (*put*) stecken

poker[1] /'pəʊkə(r)/ n Schüreisen nt

poker[2] n (*Cards*) Poker nt

poky /'pəʊki/ adj eng

Poland /'pəʊlənd/ n Polen nt

polar /'pəʊlə(r)/ adj Polar-. ~'bear n Eisbär m

Pole /pəʊl/ n Pole m/Polin f

pole[1] n Stange f

pole[2] n (*Geog, Electr*) Pol m

'pole-vault n Stabhochsprung m

police /pə'liːs/ npl Polizei f

police: ~man n Polizist m. ~ station n Polizeiwache f. ~woman n Polizistin f

policy[1] /'pɒlɪsɪ/ n Politik f

policy[2] n (*insurance*) Police f

Polish /'pɒlɪʃ/ adj polnisch

polish /'pɒlɪʃ/ n (*shine*) Glanz m; (*for shoes*) [Schuh]creme f; (*for floor*) Bohnerwachs m; (*for furni-*

ture) Politur f; (*for silver*) Putzmittel nt; (*for nails*) Lack m; (*fig*) Schliff m ●vt polieren; bohnern (*floor*). ~ off ⊕ vt verputzen (*food*); erledigen (*task*)

polite /pə'laɪt/ adj höflich. ~ness n Höflichkeit f

politic|al /pə'lɪtɪkl/ adj politisch. ~ian n Politiker(in) m(f)

politics /'pɒlətɪks/ n Politik f

poll /pəʊl/ n Abstimmung f; (*election*) Wahl f; [opinion] ~ [Meinungs]umfrage f

pollen /'pɒlən/ n Blütenstaub m, Pollen m

polling /'pəʊlɪŋ/: ~-booth n Wahlkabine f. ~-station n Wahllokal nt

pollut|e /pə'luːt/ vt verschmutzen. ~ion n Verschmutzung f

polo /'pəʊləʊ/ n Polo nt. ~-neck n Rollkragen m

polystyrene /pɒlɪ'staɪriːn/ n Polystyrol nt; (*for packing*) Styropor® nt

polythene /'pɒlɪθiːn/ n Polyäthylen nt. ~ bag n Plastiktüte f

pomp /pɒmp/ n Pomp m

pompous /'pɒmpəs/ adj großspurig

pond /pɒnd/ n Teich m

ponder /'pɒndə(r)/ vi nachdenken

ponderous /'pɒndərəs/ adj schwerfällig

pony /'pəʊnɪ/ n Pony nt. ~-tail n Pferdeschwanz m

poodle /'puːdl/ n Pudel m

pool /puːl/ n [Schwimm]becken nt; (*pond*) Teich m; (*of blood*) Lache f; (*common fund*) [gemeinsame] Kasse f; ~s pl [Fußball]toto nt ●vt zusammenlegen

poor /pʊə(r)/ adj (-er, -est) arm; (*not good*) schlecht; in ~ health nicht gesund. **~ly** *adj* be **~ly** krank sein ● *adv* ärmlich; (*badly*) schlecht

pop¹ /pɒp/ *n* Knall *m* ● *v* (*pt/pp* popped) ● *vt* 🗓 *put*) stecken (**in** + *acc*) ● *vi* knallen; (*burst*) platzen. **~ in** *vi* 🗓 reinschauen. **~ out** *vi* 🗓 kurz rausgehen

pop² *n* 🗓 Popmusik *f*, Pop *m* ● *attrib* Pop-

'popcorn *n* Puffmais *m*

pope /pəʊp/ *n* Papst *m*

poplar /'pɒplə(r)/ *n* Pappel *f*

poppy /'pɒpɪ/ *n* Mohn *m*

popular /'pɒpjʊlə(r)/ *adj* beliebt, populär; (*belief*) volkstümlich. **~ity** *n* Beliebtheit *f*, Popularität *f*

populat|e /'pɒpjʊleɪt/ *vt* bevölkern. **~ion** *n* Bevölkerung *f*

pop-up /'pɒpʌp/ *n* Pop-up-Werbefenster *nt*

porcelain /'pɔːsəlɪn/ *n* Porzellan *nt*

porch /pɔːtʃ/ *n* Vorbau *m*; (*Amer*) Veranda *f*

porcupine /'pɔːkjʊpaɪn/ *n* Stachelschwein *nt*

pore /pɔː(r)/ *n* Pore *f*

pork /pɔːk/ *n* Schweinefleisch *nt*

porn /pɔːn/ *n* 🗓 Porno *m*

pornograph|ic /pɔːnə'græfɪk/ *adj* pornographisch. **~y** *n* Pornographie *f*

porridge /'pɒrɪdʒ/ *n* Haferbrei *m*

port¹ /pɔːt/ *n* Hafen *m*; (*town*) Hafenstadt *f*

port² *n* (*Naut*) Backbord *nt*

port³ *n* (*wine*) Portwein *m*

portable /'pɔːtəbl/ *adj* tragbar

porter /'pɔːtə(r)/ *n* Portier *m*; (*for luggage*) Gepäckträger *m*

'porthole *n* Bullauge *nt*

portion /'pɔːʃn/ *n* Portion *f*; (*part, share*) Teil *nt*

portrait /'pɔːtrɪt/ *n* Porträt *nt*

portray /pɔː'treɪ/ *vt* darstellen. **~al** *n* Darstellung *f*

Portug|al /'pɔːtjʊɡl/ *n* Portugal *nt*. **~uese** *adj* portugiesisch ● *n* Portugiese *m*/-giesin *f*

pose /pəʊz/ *n* Pose *f* ● *vt* aufwerfen (*problem*); stellen (*question*) ● *vi* posieren; (*for painter*) Modell stehen

posh /pɒʃ/ *adj* 🗓 feudal

position /pə'zɪʃn/ *n* Platz *m*; (*posture*) Haltung *f*; (*job*) Stelle *f*; (*situation*) Lage *f*, Situation *f*; (*status*) Stellung *f* ● *vt* platzieren; **~ oneself** sich stellen

positive /'pɒzətɪv/ *adj* positiv; (*definite*) eindeutig; (*real*) ausgesprochen ● *n* Positiv *nt*

possess /pə'zes/ *vt* besitzen. **~ion** *n* Besitz *m*; **~ions** *pl* Sachen *pl*

possess|ive /pə'zesɪv/ *adj* Possessiv-; be **~ive about s.o.** zu sehr an jdm hängen

possibility /pɒsə'bɪlətɪ/ *n* Möglichkeit *f*

possib|le /'pɒsəbl/ *adj* möglich. **~ly** *adv* möglicherweise; **not ~ly** unmöglich

post¹ /pəʊst/ *n* (*pole*) Pfosten *m*

post² *n* (*place of duty*) Posten *m*; (*job*) Stelle *f*

post³ *n* (*mail*) Post *f*; **by ~** mit der Post ● *vt* aufgeben (*letter*); (*send by ~*) mit der Post schicken; **keep s.o. ~ed** jdn auf dem Laufenden halten

postage /'pəʊstɪdʒ/ *n* Porto *nt*

postal /'pəʊstl/ *adj* Post-. **~ order** *n* ≈ Geldanweisung *f*

post: **~box** *n* Briefkasten *m*. **~card** *n* Postkarte *f*; (*picture*) Ansichtskarte *f*. **~code** *n* Postleitzahl *f*. **~'date** *vt* vordatieren

poster /'pəʊstə(r)/ *n* Plakat *nt*

posterity /pɒ'sterətɪ/ *n* Nachwelt *f*

posthumous /'pɒstjʊməs/ *adj*

postum

post: ~**man** n Briefträger m. ~**mark** n Poststempel m

post-mortem /-'mɔːtəm/ n Obduktion f

'**post office** n Post f

postpone /pəʊst'pəʊn/ vt aufschieben; ~ until verschieben auf (+ acc). ~**ment** n Verschiebung f

postscript /'pəʊstskrɪpt/ n Nachschrift f

posture /'pɒstʃə(r)/ n Haltung f

pot /pɒt/ n Topf m; (for tea, coffee) Kanne f; ~s of money ① eine Menge Geld

potato /pə'teɪtəʊ/ n (pl -es) Kartoffel f

potent /'pəʊtənt/ adj stark

potential /pə'tenʃl/ adj potenziell ●n Potenzial nt

pot: ~**hole** n Höhle f; (in road) Schlagloch nt. ~**shot** n take a ~**shot** at schießen auf (+ acc)

potter[1] /'pɒtə(r)/ n Töpfer(in) m(f). ~**y** n Töpferei f; (articles) Töpferwaren pl

potty /'pɒtɪ/ adj ① verrückt ●n Töpfchen nt

pouch /paʊtʃ/ n Beutel m

poultry /'pəʊltrɪ/ n Geflügel nt

pounce /paʊns/ vi zuschlagen; ~ on sich stürzen auf (+ acc)

pound[1] /paʊnd/ n (money & 0,454 kg) Pfund nt

pound[2] vi (heart): hämmern; (run heavily) stampfen

pour /pɔː(r)/ vt gießen; einschenken (drink) ●vi strömen; (with rain) gießen. ~ **out** vi ausströmen; einschenken (drink)

pout /paʊt/ vi einen Schmollmund machen

poverty /'pɒvətɪ/ n Armut f

powder /'paʊdə(r)/ n Pulver nt;

(cosmetic) Puder m ●vt pudern

power /'paʊə(r)/ n Macht f; (strength) Kraft f; (Electr) Strom m; (nuclear) Energie f; (Math) Potenz f. ~ **cut** n Stromsperre f. ~**ed** adj betrieben (by mit); ~**ed** by electricity mit Elektroantrieb. ~**ful** adj mächtig; (strong) stark. ~**less** adj machtlos. ~**station** n Kraftwerk nt

practicable /'præktɪkəbl/ adj durchführbar, praktikabel

practical /'præktɪkl/ adj praktisch. ~ '**joke** n Streich m

practice /'præktɪs/ n Praxis f; (custom) Brauch m; (habit) Gewohnheit f; (exercise) Übung f; (Sport) Training nt; **in** ~ (in reality) in der Praxis; **out of** ~ außer Übung; **put into** ~ ausführen

practise /'præktɪs/ vt üben; (carry out) praktizieren; ausüben (profession) ●vi üben; (doctor:) praktizieren. ~**d** adj geübt

praise /preɪz/ n Lob nt ●vt loben. ~**worthy** adj lobenswert

pram /præm/ n Kinderwagen m

prank /præŋk/ n Streich m

prawn /prɔːn/ n Garnele f, Krabbe f

pray /preɪ/ vi beten. ~**er** n Gebet nt

preach /priːtʃ/ vt/i predigen. ~**er** n Prediger m

pre-ar'range /priː-/ vt im Voraus arrangieren

precarious /prɪ'keərɪəs/ adj unsicher

precaution /prɪ'kɔːʃn/ n Vorsichtsmaßnahme f

precede /prɪ'siːd/ vt vorangehen (+ dat)

preceden|ce /'presɪdəns/ n Vorrang m. ~**t** n Präzedenzfall m

preceding /prɪ'siːdɪŋ/ adj vorhergehend

precinct /ˈpriːsɪŋkt/ n Bereich m; (traffic-free) Fußgängerzone f; (Amer: district) Bezirk m

precious /ˈprɛʃəs/ adj kostbar; (style) preziös ● adv ⨪ ~ **little** recht wenig

precipice /ˈprɛsɪpɪs/ n Steilabfall m

precipitation /prɪsɪpɪˈteɪʃn/ n (rain) Niederschlag m

precis|e /prɪˈsaɪs/ adj genau. ~**ion** n Genauigkeit f

precocious /prɪˈkəʊʃəs/ adj frühreif

pre|con'ceived /priː-/ adj vorgefasst. ~**con'ception** n vorgefasste Meinung f

predator /ˈprɛdətə(r)/ n Raubtier nt

predecessor /ˈpriːdɪsɛsə(r)/ n Vorgänger(in) m(f)

predicat|e /ˈprɛdɪkət/ n (Gram) Prädikat nt. ~**ive** adj prädikativ

predict /prɪˈdɪkt/ vt voraussagen. ~**able** adj voraussehbar; (person) berechenbar. ~**ion** n Voraussage f

pre'domin|ant /prɪ-/ adj vorherrschend. ~**antly** adv hauptsächlich, überwiegend. ~**ate** vi vorherrschen

preen /priːn/ vt putzen

pre'fab /ˈpriːfæb/ n ⨪ [einfaches] Fertighaus nt. ~'**fabricated** adj vorgefertigt

preface /ˈprɛfɪs/ n Vorwort nt

prefect /ˈpriːfɛkt/ n Präfekt m

prefer /prɪˈfɜː(r)/ vt (pt/pp preferred) vorziehen; I ~ **to walk** ich gehe lieber zu Fuß; I ~ **wine** ich trinke lieber Wein

prefera|ble /ˈprɛfərəbl/ adj be ~**ble** vorzuziehen sein (to dat). ~**bly** adv vorzugsweise

preferen|ce /ˈprɛfərəns/ n Vorzug m. ~**tial** adj bevorzugt

pregnan|cy /ˈprɛgnənsɪ/ n Schwangerschaft f. ~**t** adj schwanger; (animal) trächtig

prehi'storic /priː-/ adj prähistorisch

prejudice /ˈprɛdʒʊdɪs/ n Vorurteil nt; (bias) Voreingenommenheit f ● vt einnehmen (against gegen). ~**d** adj voreingenommen

preliminary /prɪˈlɪmɪnərɪ/ adj Vor-

prelude /ˈprɛljuːd/ n Vorspiel nt

premature /ˈprɛmətjʊə(r)/ adj vorzeitig; (birth) Früh-. ~**ly** adv zu früh

pre'meditated /priː-/ adj vorsätzlich

premier /ˈprɛmɪə(r)/ adj führend ● n (Pol) Premier[minister] m

première /ˈprɛmɪeə(r)/ n Premiere f

premise /ˈprɛmɪs/ n Prämisse f, Voraussetzung f

premises /ˈprɛmɪsɪz/ npl Räumlichkeiten pl; on the ~ im Haus

premium /ˈpriːmɪəm/ n Prämie f; be at a ~ hoch im Kurs stehen

premonition /prɛməˈnɪʃn/ n Vorahnung f

preoccupied /prɪˈɒkjʊpaɪd/ adj [in Gedanken] beschäftigt

preparation /prɛpəˈreɪʃn/ n Vorbereitung f; (substance) Präparat nt

preparatory /prɪˈpærətrɪ/ adj Vor-

prepare /prɪˈpeə(r)/ vt vorbereiten; anrichten (meal) ● vi sich vorbereiten (for auf + acc); ~**d** to be reit zu

preposition /prɛpəˈzɪʃn/ n Präposition f

preposterous /prɪˈpɒstərəs/ adj absurd

prerequisite /priːˈrɛkwɪzɪt/ n

P

Voraussetzung f

Presbyterian /prezbɪ'tɪərɪən/ adj presbyterianisch ● n Presbyterianer(in) m(f)

prescribe /prɪ'skraɪb/ vt vorschreiben; (Med) verschreiben

prescription /prɪ'skrɪpʃn/ n (Med) Rezept nt

presence /'prezns/ n Anwesenheit f, Gegenwart f; ~ of mind Geistesgegenwart f

present¹ /'preznt/ adj gegenwärtig; be ~ anwesend sein; (occur) vorkommen ● n Gegenwart f; (Gram) Präsens nt; at ~ zurzeit; for the ~ vorläufig

present² (gift) Geschenk nt

present³ /prɪ'zent/ vt überreichen; (show) vorlegen (cheque); (introduce) vorstellen; ~ s.o. with sth jdm etw überreichen. ~able adj be ~able sich zeigen lassen können

presentation /prezn'teɪʃn/ n Überreichung f

presently /'prezntlɪ/ adv nachher; (Amer: now) zurzeit

preservation /prezə'veɪʃn/ n Erhaltung f

preservative /prɪ'zɜːvətɪv/ n Konservierungsmittel nt

preserve /prɪ'zɜːv/ vt erhalten; (Culin) konservieren; (bottle) einmachen ● n (Hunting & fig) Revier nt; (jam) Konfitüre f

preside /prɪ'zaɪd/ vi den Vorsitz haben (over bei)

presidency /'prezɪdənsɪ/ n Präsidentschaft f

president /'prezɪdənt/ n Präsident m; (Amer: chairman) Vorsitzende(r) m/f. ~ial adj Präsidenten-; (election) Präsidentschafts-

press /pres/ n Presse f ● vt/i drücken; drücken auf (+ acc) (button); pressen (flower); (iron) bügeln; (urge) bedrängen; ~ for drängen auf (+ acc); be ~ed for time in Zeitdruck sein. ~ on vi weitergehen/-fahren; (fig) weitermachen

press: ~ cutting n Zeitungsausschnitt m. ~ing adj dringend

pressure /'preʃə(r)/ n Druck m. ~-cooker n Schnellkochtopf m

pressurize /'preʃəraɪz/ vt Druck ausüben auf (+ acc). ~d adj Druck-

prestig|e /pre'stiːʒ/ n Prestige nt. ~ious adj Prestige-

presumably /prɪ'zjuːməblɪ/ adv vermutlich

presume /prɪ'zjuːm/ vt vermuten

presumpt|ion /prɪ'zʌmpʃn/ n Vermutung f; (boldness) Anmaßung f. ~uous adj anmaßend

pretence /prɪ'tens/ n Verstellung f; (pretext) Vorwand m

pretend /prɪ'tend/ vt (claim) vorgeben; ~ that so tun, als ob; ~ to be sich ausgeben als

pretentious /prɪ'tenʃəs/ adj protzig

pretext /'priːtekst/ n Vorwand m

prett|y /'prɪtɪ/ adj , ~ily adv hübsch ● adv (🗉: fairly) ziemlich

prevail /prɪ'veɪl/ vi siegen; (custom) vorherrschen; ~ on s.o. to do sth jdn dazu bringen, etw zu tun

prevalen|ce /'prevələns/ n Häufigkeit f. ~t adj vorherrschend

prevent /prɪ'vent/ vt verhindern, verhüten; ~ s.o. [from] doing sth jdn daran hindern, etw zu tun. ~ion n Verhinderung f, Verhütung f. ~ive adj vorbeugend

preview /'priːvjuː/ n Voraufführung f

previous /'priːvɪəs/ adj vorhergehend; ~ to vor (+ *dat*). ~ly *adv* vorher, früher

prey /preɪ/ *n* Beute *f*; bird of ~ Raubvogel *m*

price /praɪs/ *n* Preis *m* ● *vt* (*Comm*) auszeichnen. ~less *adj* unschätzbar; (*fig*) unbezahlbar

prick /prɪk/ *n* Stich *m* ● *vt/i* stechen

prickl|e /ˈprɪkl/ *n* Stachel *m*; (*thorn*) Dorn *m*. ~y *adj* stachelig; (*sensation*) stechend

pride /praɪd/ *n* Stolz *m*; (*arrogance*) Hochmut *m* ● *vt* ~ oneself on stolz sein auf (+ *acc*)

priest /priːst/ *n* Priester *m*

prim /prɪm/ *adj* (primmer, primmest) prüde

primarily /ˈpraɪmərɪlɪ/ *adv* hauptsächlich, in erster Linie

primary /ˈpraɪmərɪ/ *adj* Haupt-. ~ **school** *n* Grundschule *f*

prime[1] /praɪm/ *adj* Haupt-; (*firstrate*) erstklassig

prime[2] *vt* scharf machen (*bomb*); grundieren (*surface*)

Prime Minister /praɪˈmɪnɪstə(r)/ *n* Premierminister(in) *m(f)*

primitive /ˈprɪmɪtɪv/ *adj* primitiv

primrose /ˈprɪmrəʊz/ *n* gelbe Schlüsselblume *f*

prince /prɪns/ *n* Prinz *m*

princess /prɪnˈses/ *n* Prinzessin *f*

principal /ˈprɪnsəpl/ *adj* Haupt- ● *n* (*Sch*) Rektor(in) *m(f)*

principally /ˈprɪnsəplɪ/ *adv* hauptsächlich

principle /ˈprɪnsəpl/ *n* Prinzip *nt*, Grundsatz *m*; in/on ~ im/aus Prinzip

print /prɪnt/ *n* Druck *m*; (*Phot*) Abzug *m*; in ~ gedruckt; (*available*)

erhältlich; out of ~ vergriffen ● *vt* drucken; (*write in capitals*) in Druckschrift schreiben; (*Computing*) ausdrucken; (*Phot*) abziehen. ~ed **matter** *n* Drucksache *f*

print|er /ˈprɪntə(r)/ *n* Drucker *m*. ~ing *n* Druck *m*.

printout *n* (*Computing*) Ausdruck *m*

prior /ˈpraɪə(r)/ *adj* frühere(r,s); ~ **to** vor (+ *dat*)

priority /praɪˈɒrətɪ/ *n* Priorität *f*, Vorrang *m*

prise /praɪz/ *vt* ~ open/up aufstemmen/hochstemmen

prison /ˈprɪzn/ *n* Gefängnis *nt*. ~er *n* Gefangene(r) *m/f*

privacy /ˈprɪvəsɪ/ *n* Privatsphäre *f*; have no ~ nie für sich sein

private /ˈpraɪvət/ *adj* privat; (*confidential*) vertraulich; (*car, secretary, school*) Privat- ● *n* (*Mil*) [einfacher] Soldat *m*; in ~ privat; (*confidentially*) vertraulich

privation /praɪˈveɪʃn/ *n* Entbehrung *f*

privilege /ˈprɪvəlɪdʒ/ *n* Privileg *nt*. ~d *adj* privilegiert

prize /praɪz/ *n* Preis *m* ● *vt* schätzen

pro /prəʊ/ *n* ① Profi *m*; the ~s and cons das Für und Wider

probability /prɒbəˈbɪlətɪ/ *n* Wahrscheinlichkeit *f*

proba|ble /ˈprɒbəbl/ *adj*, **-bly** *adv* wahrscheinlich

probation /prəˈbeɪʃn/ *n* (*Jur*) Bewährung *f*

probe /prəʊb/ *n* Sonde *f*; (*fig: investigation*) Untersuchung *f*

problem /ˈprɒbləm/ *n* Problem *nt*; (*Math*) Textaufgabe *f*. ~atic *adj* problematisch

procedure /prəˈsiːdʒə(r)/ *n*

Verfahren nt

proceed /prəˈsiːd/ vi gehen; (in vehicle) fahren; (continue) weitergehen/-fahren; (speaking) fortfahren; (act) verfahren

proceedings /prəˈsiːdɪŋz/ npl Verfahren nt; (Jur) Prozess m

proceeds /ˈprəʊsiːdz/ npl Erlös m

process /ˈprəʊses/ n Prozess m; (procedure) Verfahren nt; in the ~ dabei ● vt verarbeiten; (Admin) bearbeiten; (Phot) entwickeln

procession /prəˈseʃn/ n Umzug m, Prozession f

processor /ˈprəʊsesə(r)/ n Prozessor m

proclaim /prəˈkleɪm/ vt ausrufen

proclamation /prɒkləˈmeɪʃn/ n Proklamation f

procure /prəˈkjʊə(r)/ vt beschaffen

prod /prɒd/ n Stoß m ● vt stoßen

prodigy /ˈprɒdɪdʒɪ/ n [infant] ~ Wunderkind nt

produce[1] /ˈprɒdjuːs/ n landwirtschaftliche Erzeugnisse pl

produce[2] /prəˈdjuːs/ vt erzeugen, produzieren; (manufacture) herstellen; (bring out) hervorholen; (cause) hervorrufen; inszenieren. (play); (Radio, TV) redigieren. ~r n Erzeuger m, Produzent m; Hersteller m; (Theat) Regisseur m; (Radio, TV) Redakteur(in) m(f)

product /ˈprɒdʌkt/ n Erzeugnis nt, Produkt nt. ~ion n Produktion f; (Theat) Inszenierung f

productive /prəˈdʌktɪv/ adj produktiv; (land, talks) fruchtbar. ~ity n Produktivität f

profession /prəˈfeʃn/ n Beruf m. ~al adj beruflich; (not amateur) Berufs-; (expert) fachmännisch; (Sport) professionell ● n Fachmann m;

(Sport) Profi m

professor /prəˈfesə(r)/ n Professor m

proficien|cy /prəˈfɪʃnsɪ/ n Können nt. ~t adj be ~t in beherrschen

profile /ˈprəʊfaɪl/ n Profil nt; (character study) Porträt nt

profit /ˈprɒfɪt/ n Gewinn m, Profit m ● vi ~ from profitieren von. ~able adj, -bly adv gewinnbringend; (fig) nutzbringend

profound /prəˈfaʊnd/ adj tief

program /ˈprəʊgræm/ n Programm nt; ● vt (pt/pp programmed) programmieren

programme /ˈprəʊgræm/ n Programm nt; (Radio, TV) Sendung f. ~r n (Computing) Programmierer(in) m(f)

progress[1] /ˈprəʊgres/ n Vorankommen nt, (fig) Fortschritt m; in ~ im Gange; make ~ (fig) Fortschritte machen

progress[2] /prəˈgres/ vi vorankommen; (fig) fortschreiten. ~ion n Folge f; (development) Entwicklung f

progressive /prəˈgresɪv/ adj fortschrittlich. ~ly adv zunehmend

prohibit /prəˈhɪbɪt/ vt verbieten (s.o. jdm). ~ive adj unerschwinglich

project[1] /ˈprɒdʒekt/ n Projekt nt; (Sch) Arbeit f

project[2] /prəˈdʒekt/ vt projizieren (film); (plan) planen ● vi (jut out) vorstehen

projector /prəˈdʒektə(r)/ n Projektor m

prolific /prəˈlɪfɪk/ adj fruchtbar; (fig) produktiv

prologue /ˈprəʊlɒg/ n Prolog m

prolong /prəˈlɒŋ/ vt verlängern

promenade /prɒməˈnɑːd/ n Pro-

505

menade f ● vi spazieren gehen

prominent /'prɒmɪnənt/ adj vorstehend; (*important*) prominent; (*conspicuous*) auffällig

promiscuous /prə'mɪskjʊəs/ adj be ~ous häufig den Partner wechseln

promis|e /'prɒmɪs/ n Versprechen nt ● vt/i versprechen (s.o. jdm). ~ing adj viel versprechend

promot|e /prə'məʊt/ vt befördern; (*advance*) fördern; (*publicize*) Reklame machen für; be ~ed (*Sport*) aufsteigen. ~ion n Beförderung f; (*Sport*) Aufstieg m; (*Comm*) Reklame f

prompt /prɒmpt/ adj prompt, unverzüglich; (*punctual*) pünktlich ● adv pünktlich ● vt veranlassen (to zu); (*Theat*) soufflieren (+ dat). ~er n Souffleur m/Souffleuse f. ~ly adv prompt

Proms Die Proms, offiziell *BBC Henry Wood Promenade Concerts*, finden jeden Sommer in der Londoner Royal Albert Hall statt. Bei den Promenadenkonzerten steht ein Teil des Publikums vor dem Orchester. In den USA bezeichnet *Prom* einen Ball, den eine ▸HIGH SCHOOL veranstaltet, um das Ende des Schuljahrs zu feiern.

prone /prəʊn/ adj be or lie ~ auf dem Bauch liegen; be ~ to neigen zu

pronoun /'prəʊnaʊn/ n Fürwort nt, Pronomen nt

pronounce /prə'naʊns/ vt aussprechen; (*declare*) erklären. ~d adj ausgeprägt; (*noticeable*) deutlich. ~ment n Erklärung f

pronunciation /prənʌnsɪ'eɪʃn/ n Aussprache f

---

prominent | prosecute

proof /pruːf/ n Beweis m; (*Typography*) Korrekturbogen m. ~-reader n Korrektor m

prop¹ /prɒp/ n Stütze f ● vt (*pt/pp* propped) ~ against lehnen an (+ *acc*). ~ up vt stützen

prop² n (*Theat*, 🔢) Requisit nt

propaganda /prɒpə'gændə/ n Propaganda f

propel /prə'pel/ vt (*pt/pp* propelled) [an]treiben. ~ler n Propeller m

proper /'prɒpə(r)/ adj richtig; (*decent*) anständig

property /'prɒpətɪ/ n Eigentum nt; (*quality*) Eigenschaft f; (*Theat*) Requisit nt; (*land*) [Grund]besitz m; (*house*) Haus nt

prophecy /'prɒfəsɪ/ n Prophezeiung f

prophesy /'prɒfɪsaɪ/ vt (*pt/pp* -ied) prophezeien

prophet /'prɒfɪt/ n Prophet m. ~ic adj prophetisch

proportion /prə'pɔːʃn/ n Verhältnis nt; (*share*) Teil m; ~s pl Proportionen; (*dimensions*) Maße. ~al adj proportional

proposal /prə'pəʊzl/ n Vorschlag m; (*of marriage*) [Heirats]antrag m

propose /prə'pəʊz/ vt vorschlagen; (*intend*) vorhaben, einbringen (*motion*) ● vi einen Heiratsantrag machen

proposition /prɒpə'zɪʃn/ n Vorschlag m

proprietor /prə'praɪətə(r)/ n Inhaber(in) m(f)

propriety /prə'praɪətɪ/ n Korrektheit f; (*decorum*) Anstand m

prose /prəʊz/ n Prosa f

prosecut|e /'prɒsɪkjuːt/ vt strafrechtlich verfolgen. ~ion n strafrechtliche Verfolgung f; the ~ion die Anklage. **~or** n [Public] P~or Staatsanwalt m

prospect /'prɒspekt/ n Aussicht f

prospect|ive /prə'spektɪv/ adj (future) zukünftig. **~or** n Prospektor m

prospectus /prə'spektəs/ n Prospekt m

prosper /'prɒspə(r)/ vi gedeihen, florieren; (person) Erfolg haben. **~ity** n Wohlstand m

prosperous /'prɒspərəs/ adj wohlhabend

prostitut|e /'prɒstɪtjuːt/ n Prostituierte f. **~ion** n Prostitution f

prostrate /'prɒstreɪt/ adj ausgestreckt

protagonist /prəʊ'tægənɪst/ n Kämpfer m; (fig) Protagonist m

protect /prə'tekt/ vt schützen (from vor + dat); beschützen (person). **~ion** n Schutz m. **~ive** adj Schutz-; (fig) beschützend. **~or** n Beschützer m

protein /'prəʊtiːn/ n Eiweiß nt

protest¹ /'prəʊtest/ n Protest m

protest² /prə'test/ vi protestieren

Protestant /'prɒtɪstənt/ adj protestantisch ●n Protestant(in) m(f)

protester /prə'testə(r)/ n Protestierende(r) m/f

prototype /'prəʊtə-/ n Prototyp m

protrude /prə'truːd/ vi [her]vorstehen

proud /praʊd/ adj stolz (of auf + acc)

prove /pruːv/ vt beweisen ●vi **~to** be sich erweisen als

proverb /'prɒvɜːb/ n Sprichwort nt

provide /prə'vaɪd/ vt zur Verfügung stellen; spenden (shade); **~** s.o. with sth jdn mit etw versorgen

of versehen ●vi **~** for sorgen für

provided /prə'vaɪdɪd/ conj **~** [that] vorausgesetzt [dass]

providen|ce /'prɒvɪdəns/ n Vorsehung f. **~tial** adj be **~tial** ein Glück sein

provinc|e /'prɒvɪns/ n Provinz f; (fig) Bereich m. **~ial** adj provinziell

provision /prə'vɪʒn/ n Versorgung f (of mit); **~s** pl Lebensmittel pl. **~al** adj vorläufig

provocat|ion /prɒvə'keɪʃn/ n Provokation f. **~ive** adj provozierend; (sexually) aufreizend

provoke /prə'vəʊk/ vt provozieren; (cause) hervorrufen

prow /praʊ/ n Bug m

prowl /praʊl/ vi herumschleichen

proximity /prɒk'sɪmətɪ/ n Nähe f

pruden|ce /'pruːdns/ n Umsicht f. **~t** adj umsichtig; (wise) klug

prudish /'pruːdɪʃ/ adj prüde

prune¹ /pruːn/ n Backpflaume f

prune² vt beschneiden

pry /praɪ/ vi (pt/pp pried) neugierig sein

psalm /sɑːm/ n Psalm m

psychiatric /saɪkɪ'ætrɪk/ adj psychiatrisch

psychiatr|ist /saɪ'kaɪətrɪst/ n Psychiater(in) m(f). **~y** n Psychiatrie f

psychic /'saɪkɪk/ adj übersinnlich

psycho|a'nalysis /saɪkəʊ-/ n Psychoanalyse f. **~'analyst** Psychoanalytiker(in) m(f)

psychological /saɪkə'lɒdʒɪkl/ adj psychologisch; (illness) psychisch

psycholog|ist /saɪ'kɒlədʒɪst/ n Psychologe m/ -login f. **~y** n Psychologie f

P.T.O. abbr (please turn over) b.w.

pub /pʌb/ n 🔢 Kneipe f

pub Ein *pub*, kurz für *public house*, ist ein englisches Wirtshaus. *Pubs* sind bei allen Schichten der britischen Gesellschaft beliebt und Gäste haben oft eine Stammkneipe, wo sie Bier trinken und Darts oder Pool spielen. Öffnungszeiten sind meist von 11–23 Uhr und in vielen *pubs* kann man auch essen. *i*

puberty /'pju:bətɪ/ n Pubertät f

public /'pʌblɪk/ adj öffentlich; make ~ publik machen • n the ~ die Öffentlichkeit

publican /'pʌblɪkən/ n [Gast]wirt m

publication /pʌblɪ'keɪʃn/ n Veröffentlichung f

public: ~ 'holiday n gesetzlicher Feiertag m. ~ 'house n [Gast]wirtschaft f

publicity /pʌb'lɪsətɪ/ n Publicity f; (advertising) Reklame f

publicize /'pʌblɪsaɪz/ vt Reklame machen für

public: ~ 'school n Privatschule f; (Amer) staatliche Schule f. ~-'spirited adj je ~s-spirited Gemeinsinn haben

public school Eine Privatschule in England und Wales für Schüler im Alter von dreizehn bis achtzehn Jahren. Die meisten *public schools* sind Internate, normalerweise entweder für Jungen oder Mädchen. Die Eltern zahlen Schulgeld für die Ausbildung ihrer Kinder. In Schottland und den USA ist eine *public school* eine staatliche Schule. *i*

publish /'pʌblɪʃ/ vt veröffentlichen. ~er n Verleger(in) m(f); (firm) Verlag m. ~ing n Verlagswesen nt

pudding /'pʊdɪŋ/ n Pudding m; (course) Nachtisch m

puddle /'pʌdl/ n Pfütze f

puff /pʌf/ n (of wind) Hauch m; (of smoke) Wölkchen nt • vt blasen, pusten; ~ out ausstoßen. • vi keuchen; ~ at paffen an (+ dat) (pipe). ~ed adj (out of breath) außer der Puste. ~ pastry n Blätterteig m

pull /pʊl/ n Zug m; (jerk) Ruck m; (fig: influence) Einfluss m • vt ziehen; ~ a muscle sich (dat) einen Muskel zerren; ~ oneself together sich zusammennehmen; ~ one's weight tüchtig mitarbeiten; ~ s.o.'s leg jdn auf den Arm nehmen. ~ down vt herunterziehen; (demolish) abreißen. ~ in vt hereinziehen • vi (Auto) einscheren. ~ off vt abziehen; (fig) schaffen. ~ out vt herausziehen • vi (Auto) ausscheren. ~ through vi durchziehen • vi (recover) durchkommen. ~ up vt heraufziehen; ausziehen (plant) • vi (Auto) anhalten

pullover /'pʊləʊvə(r)/ n Pullover m

pulp /pʌlp/ n Brei m; (of fruit) [Frucht]fleisch m

pulpit /'pʊlpɪt/ n Kanzel f

pulse /pʌls/ n Puls m

pulses /'pʌlsɪz/ npl Hülsenfrüchte pl

pummel /'pʌml/ vt (pt/pp pummelled) mit den Fäusten bearbeiten

pump /pʌmp/ n Pumpe f • vt pumpen; (fig) aushorchen. ~ up vt (inflate) aufpumpen

pumpkin /'pʌmpkɪn/ n Kürbis m

pun /pʌn/ n Wortspiel nt

punch¹ /pʌntʃ/ n Faustschlag m; (device) Locher m • vt boxen; lochen (ticket); stanzen (hole)

punch² n (drink) Bowle f

punctual /'pʌŋktjʊəl/ adj pünktlich. ~**ity** n Pünktlichkeit f

punctuat|e /'pʌŋktjʊeɪt/ vt mit Satzzeichen versehen. ~**ion** n Interpunktion f

puncture /'pʌŋktʃə(r)/ n Loch nt; (tyre) Reifenpanne f ● vt durchstechen

punish /'pʌnɪʃ/ vt bestrafen. ~**able** adj strafbar. ~**ment** n Strafe f

punt /pʌnt/ n (boat) Stechkahn m

puny /'pjuːnɪ/ adj mickerig

pup /pʌp/ n = puppy

pupil /'pjuːpl/ n Schüler(in) m(f); (of eye) Pupille f

puppet /'pʌpɪt/ n Puppe f; (fig) Marionette f

puppy /'pʌpɪ/ n junger Hund m

purchase /'pɜːtʃəs/ n Kauf m; (leverage) Hebelkraft f ● vt kaufen. ~**r** n Käufer m

pure /pjʊə(r)/ adj (-r, -st,) -**ly** adv rein

purge /pɜːdʒ/ n (Pol) Säuberungsaktion f ● vt reinigen

purification /pjʊərɪfɪ'keɪʃn/ n Reinigung f. ~**fy** vt (pt/pp -ied) reinigen

puritanical /pjʊərɪ'tænɪkl/ adj puritanisch

purity /'pjʊərɪtɪ/ n Reinheit f

purple /'pɜːpl/ adj (dunkel)lila

purpose /'pɜːpəs/ n Zweck m; (intention) Absicht f; (determination) Entschlossenheit f; on ~ absichtlich. ~**ful** adj entschlossen. ~**ly** adv absichtlich

purr /pɜː(r)/ vi schnurren

purse /pɜːs/ n Portemonnaie nt; (Amer: handbag) Handtasche f

pursue /pə'sjuː/ vt verfolgen; (fig) nachgehen (+ dat). ~**r** n

Verfolger(in) m(f)

pursuit /pə'sjuːt/ n Verfolgung f; Jagd f; (pastime) Beschäftigung f

pus /pʌs/ n Eiter m

push /pʊʃ/ n Stoß m; get the ~ 🔲 hinausfliegen ● vt/i schieben; (press) drücken; (roughly) stoßen. ~ **off** vt hinunterstoßen ● vi (🔲: leave) abhauen. ~ **on** vi (continue) weitergehen/-fahren; (with activity) weitermachen. ~ **up** vt hochschieben; hochtreiben (price)

push: ~**button** n Druckknopf m. ~**chair** n [Kinder]sportwagen m

pushy /'pʊʃɪ/ adj 🔲 aufdringlich

puss /pʊs/, **pussy** n Mieze f

put /pʊt/ vt (pt/pp put, pres p putting) tun; (place) setzen; (upright) stellen; (flat) legen; (express) ausdrücken; (say) sagen; (estimate) schätzen (at auf + acc); ~ **aside** or by beiseite legen ● vi ~ to sea auslaufen ● adj stay ~ dableiben. ~ **away** vt wegräumen. ~ **back** vt wieder zurückstellen/-legen; zurückstellen (clock). ~ **down** vt hinsetzen/-stellen/-legen; (suppress) niederschlagen; (kill) töten; (write) niederschreiben; (attribute) zuschreiben (to dat). ~ **forward** vt vorbringen; vorstellen (clock). ~ **in** vt hineinsetzen/-stellen/-legen; (insert) einstecken; (submit) einreichen ● vi ~ **in for** beantragen. ~ **off** vt ausmachen (light); (postpone) verschieben; ~ **s.o. off** jdn abbestellen; (disconnect) jdn aus der Fassung bringen. ~ **on** vt anziehen (clothes, brake); sich (dat) aufsetzen (hat); (Culin) aufsetzen; anmachen (light); aufführen (play); annehmen (accent); ~ **on weight** zunehmen. ~ **out** vt hinaussetzen/-stellen/-legen; ausmachen (fire, light); ausstrecken (hand); (disconcert) aus der Fassung bringen. ~ **s.o./oneself out** jdm/

sich Umstände machen. ~
through vt durchstecken; (*Teleph*)
verbinden (to mit). ~ **up** vt errichten (*building*); aufschlagen (*tent*);
aufspannen (*umbrella*); anschlagen
(*notice*); erhöhen (*price*); unterbringen (*guest*) ● vi (at hotel) absteigen
in (+ dat); ~ **up with** sth sich (*dat*)
etw bieten lassen

putrid /'pju:trɪd/ faulig

putt /pʌt/ n Putt m

putty /'pʌtɪ/ n Kitt m

puzzl|e /'pʌzl/ n Rätsel nt; (*jigsaw*)
Puzzlespiel nt ● vt it ~es me es ist
mir rätselhaft. **~ing** adj rätselhaft

pyjamas /pə'dʒɑːməz/ npl Schlafanzug m

pylon /'paɪlən/ n Mast m

pyramid /'pɪrəmɪd/ n Pyramide f

python /'paɪθn/ n Python-
schlange f

Qq

quack /kwæk/ n Quaken nt; (*doctor*) Quacksalber m ● vi quaken

quadrangle /'kwɒdræŋgl/ n Viereck nt; (*court*) Hof m

quadruped /'kwɒdruped/ n Vier-
füßer m

quadruple /'kwɒdrupl/ adj vier-
fach ● vt vervierfachen ● vi sich
vierfachen

quaint /kweɪnt/ adj (-er, -est) malerisch; (*odd*) putzig

quake /kweɪk/ n 🔲 Erdbeben nt
● vi beben; (*with fear*) zittern

qualif|ication /kwɒlɪfɪ'keɪʃn/ n
Qualifikation f; (*reservation*) Einschränkung f. **~ied** adj qualifiziert;

(*trained*) ausgebildet; (*limited*)
bedingt

qualify /'kwɒlɪfaɪ/ v (pt/pp -ied)
● vt qualifizieren; (*entitle*) berechtigen; (*limit*) einschränken ● vi sich
qualifizieren

quality /'kwɒlɪtɪ/ n Qualität f;
(*characteristic*) Eigenschaft f

qualm /kwɑːm/ n Bedenken pl

quantity /'kwɒntɪtɪ/ n Quantität
f, Menge f; **in** ~ in großen Mengen

quarantine /'kwɒrəntiːn/ n Quarantäne f

quarrel /'kwɒrl/ n Streit m ● vi
(pt/pp quarrelled) sich streiten.
~some adj streitsüchtig

quarry[1] /'kwɒrɪ/ n (*prey*) Beute f

quarry[2] n Steinbruch m

quart /kwɔːt/ n Quart nt

quarter /'kwɔːtə(r)/ n Viertel nt;
(*of year*) Vierteljahr nt; (*Amer*)
25-Cent-Stück nt; **~s** pl Quartier nt;
at ¼ **to** six um Viertel vor
sechs ● vt vierteln; (*Mil*) einquartie-
ren (on bei). **~-final** n Viertelfi-
nale nt

quarterly /'kwɔːtəlɪ/ adj & adv
vierteljährlich

quartet /kwɔː'tet/ n Quartett nt

quartz /kwɔːts/ n Quarz m

quay /kiː/ n Kai m

queasy /'kwiːzɪ/ adj I feel ~ mir
ist übel

queen /kwiːn/ n Königin f; (*Cards,
Chess*) Dame f

queer /kwɪə(r)/ adj (-er, -est) eigenartig; (*dubious*) zweifelhaft; (*ill*)
unwohl

quell /kwel/ vt unterdrücken

quench /kwentʃ/ vt löschen

query /'kwɪərɪ/ n Frage f; (*question
mark*) Fragezeichen n ● vt (pt/pp
-ied) infrage stellen; reklamieren
(*bill*)

quest /kwest/ n Suche f (for nach)

question /'kwestʃn/ n Frage f; (for discussion) Thema nt; out of the ~ ausgeschlossen; the person in ~ die fragliche Person •vt infrage stellen; ~ s.o. jdn ausfragen; (police:) jdn verhören. **~able** adj zweifelhaft. **~ mark** n Fragezeichen nt

questionnaire /kwestʃə'neə(r)/ n Fragebogen m

queue /kju:/ n Schlange f •vi ~ [up] Schlange stehen, sich anstellen (for nach)

quibble /'kwɪbl/ vi Haarspalterei treiben

quick /kwɪk/ adj (-er, -est) schnell; be ~! mach schnell! • adv schnell. **~en** vt beschleunigen •vi sich beschleunigen

quick: ~sand n Treibsand m. **~-tempered** adj aufbrausend

quid /kwɪd/ n inv 🆒 Pfund nt

quiet /'kwaɪət/ adj (-er, -est) still; (calm) ruhig; (soft) leise; keep ~ about 🆒 nichts sagen von • n Stille f; Ruhe f

quiet|en /'kwaɪətn/ vt beruhigen •vi ~en down ruhig werden. **~ness** n Stille f; Ruhe f

quilt /kwɪlt/ n Steppdecke f. **~ed** adj Stepp-

quintet /kwɪn'tet/ n Quintett nt

quirk /kwɜ:k/ n Eigenart f

quit /kwɪt/ v (pt/pp quitted or quit) •vt verlassen; (give up) aufgeben; ~ doing sth aufhören, etw zu tun •vi gehen

quite /kwaɪt/ adv ganz; (really) wirklich; ~ [so]! genau!; a few ziemlich viele

quits /kwɪts/ adj quitt

quiver /'kwɪvə(r)/ vi zittern

quiz /kwɪz/ n Quiz nt •vt (pt/pp quizzed) ausfragen. **~zical** adj fragend

quota /'kwəʊtə/ n Anteil m; (Comm) Kontingent nt

quotation /kwəʊ'teɪʃn/ n Zitat nt; (price) Kostenvoranschlag m; (of shares) Notierung f. **~ marks** npl Anführungszeichen pl

quote /kwəʊt/ n 🆒 = quotation; in ~s in Anführungszeichen •vt/i zitieren

Rr

rabbi /'ræbaɪ/ n Rabbiner m; (title) Rabbi m

rabbit /'ræbɪt/ n Kaninchen nt

rabid /'ræbɪd/ adj fanatisch; (animal) tollwütig

rabies /'reɪbi:z/ n Tollwut f

race¹ /reɪs/ n Rasse f

race² n Rennen nt; (fig) Wettlauf m •vi [am Rennen] teilnehmen; (athlete, horse:) laufen; (🆒: rush) rasen •vt um die Wette laufen mit; an einem Rennen teilnehmen lassen (horse)

race: ~course n Rennbahn f. **~horse** n Rennpferd nt. **~track** n Rennbahn f

racial /'reɪʃl/ adj rassisch; (discrimination) Rassen-

racing /'reɪsɪŋ/ n Rennsport m; (horse-) Pferderennen nt. ~ **car** n Rennwagen m. ~ **driver** n Rennfahrer m

racis|m /'reɪsɪzm/ n Rassismus m. **~t** adj rassistisch • n Rassist m

rack¹ /ræk/ n Ständer m; (for plates) Gestell nt •vt ~ one's brains sich (dat) den Kopf zerbrechen

rack² *n* go to ∼ and ruin verfallen; (*fig*) herunterkommen

racket /'rækɪt/ *n* (*Sport*) Schläger *m*; (*din*) Krach *m*; (*swindle*) Schwindelgeschäft *nt*

racy /'reɪsɪ/ *adj* schwungvoll; (*risqué*) gewagt

radar /'reɪdɑː(r)/ *n* Radar *m*

radian|ce /'reɪdɪəns/ *n* Strahlen *nt*. ∼**t** *adj* strahlend

radiat|e /'reɪdɪeɪt/ *vt* ausstrahlen ●*vi* (*heat:*) ausgestrahlt werden; (*roads:*) strahlenförmig ausgehen. ∼**ion** *n* Strahlung *f*

radiator /'reɪdɪeɪtə(r)/ *n* Heizkörper *m*; (*Auto*) Kühler *m*

radical /'rædɪkl/ *adj* radikal ●*n* Radikale(r) *m/f*

radio /'reɪdɪəʊ/ *n* Radio *nt*; by ∼ über Funk ●*vt* funken (*message*)

radio'active *adj* radioaktiv. ∼**ac'tivity** *n* Radioaktivität *f*

radish /'rædɪʃ/ *n* Radieschen *nt*

radius /'reɪdɪəs/ *n* (*pl* **-dii** /-dɪaɪ/) Radius *m*, Halbmesser *m*

raffle /'ræfl/ *n* Tombola *f*

raft /rɑːft/ *n* Floß *nt*

rafter /'rɑːftə(r)/ *n* Dachsparren *m*

rag /ræg/ *n* Lumpen *m*; (*pej: newspaper*) Käseblatt *nt*

rage /reɪdʒ/ *n* Wut *f*; all the ∼ 🄳 der letzte Schrei ●*vi* rasen

ragged /'rægɪd/ *adj* zerlumpt; (*edge*) ausgefranst

raid /reɪd/ *n* Überfall *m*; (*Mil*) Angriff *m*; (*police*) Razzia *f* ●*vt* überfallen; (*Mil*) angreifen; (*police*) eine Razzia durchführen in (+ *dat*); (*break in*) eindringen in (+ *acc*). ∼**er** *n* Eindringling *m*; (*of bank*) Bankräuber *m*

rail /reɪl/ *n* Schiene *f*; (*pole*) Stange *f*; (*hand*∼) Handlauf *m*; (*Naut*) Reling *f*; by ∼ mit der Bahn

railings /'reɪlɪŋz/ *npl* Geländer *nt*

'railroad *n* (*Amer*) = railway

'railway *n* [Eisen]bahn *f*. ∼ **station** *n* Bahnhof *m*

rain /reɪn/ *n* Regen *m* ●*vi* regnen

rain: ∼**bow** *n* Regenbogen *m*. ∼**coat** *n* Regenmantel *m*. ∼**fall** *n* Niederschlag *m*

rainy /'reɪnɪ/ *adj* regnerisch

raise /reɪz/ *n* (*Amer*) Lohnerhöhung *f* ●*vt* erheben; (*upright*) aufrichten; (*make higher*) erhöhen; (*lift*) [hoch]heben; aufziehen (*child, animal*); aufwerfen (*question*); aufbringen (*money*)

raisin /'reɪzn/ *n* Rosine *f*

rake /reɪk/ *n* Harke *f*, Rechen *m* ●*vt* harken, rechen

rally /'rælɪ/ *n* Versammlung *f*; (*Auto*) Rallye *f*; (*Tennis*) Ballwechsel *m* ●*vt* sammeln

ram /ræm/ *n* Schafbock *m* ●*vt* (*pt/pp* **rammed**) rammen

rambl|e /'ræmbl/ *n* Wanderung *f* ●*vi* wandern; (*in speech*) irrereden. ∼**er** *n* Wanderer *m*; (*rose*) Kletterrose *f*. ∼**ing** *adj* weitschweifig; (*club*) Wander-

ramp /ræmp/ *n* Rampe *f*; (*Aviat*) Gangway *f*

rampage¹ /'ræmpeɪdʒ/ *n* be/go on the ∼ randalieren

rampage² /ræm'peɪdʒ/ *vi* randalieren

ramshackle /'ræmʃækl/ *adj* baufällig

ran /ræn/ *see* run

ranch /rɑːntʃ/ *n* Ranch *f*

random /'rændəm/ *adj* willkürlich; a ∼ sample eine Stichprobe ●*n* at ∼ aufs Geratewohl; (*choose*) willkürlich

rang /ræŋ/ *see* ring²

range /reɪndʒ/ *n* Serie *f*, Reihe *f*;

r

(*Comm*) Auswahl f, Angebot nt (of an + dat); (of mountains) Kette f; (*Mus*) Umfang m; (distance) Reichweite f; (for shooting) Schießplatz m; (stove) Kohlenherd m ● vi reichen; ~ from ... to gehen von ... bis. ~r n Aufseher m

rank /ræŋk/ n (row) Reihe f; (*Mil*) Rang m; (social position) Stand m; the ~ and file die breite Masse ● vt/i einstufen; ~ among zählen zu

ransack /ˈrænsæk/ vt durchwühlen; (pillage) plündern

ransom /ˈrænsəm/ n Lösegeld nt; hold s.o. to ~ Lösegeld für jdn fordern

rape /reɪp/ n Vergewaltigung f ● vt vergewaltigen

rapid /ˈræpɪd/ adj schnell. ~ity n Schnelligkeit f

rapist /ˈreɪpɪst/ n Vergewaltiger m

rapture /ˈræptʃə(r)/ n Entzücken nt. ~ous adj begeistert

rare[1] /reə(r)/ adj (-r, -st) selten

rare[2] adj (Culin) englisch gebraten

rarefied /ˈreərɪfaɪd/ adj dünn

rarity /ˈreərətɪ/ n Seltenheit f

rascal /ˈrɑːskl/ n Schlingel m

rash[1] /ræʃ/ n (Med) Ausschlag m

rash[2] adj (-er, -est) voreilig

rasher /ˈræʃə(r)/ n Speckscheibe f

raspberry /ˈrɑːzbərɪ/ n Himbeere f

rat /ræt/ n Ratte f; (🗌: person) Schuft m; smell a ~ 🗌 Lunte riechen

rate /reɪt/ n Rate f; (speed) Tempo nt; (of payment) Satz m; (of exchange) Kurs m; ~s pl (taxes) ≈ Grundsteuer f; at any ~ auf jeden Fall; at this ~ auf diese Weise ● vt einschätzen; ~ among zählen zu ● vi ~ as gelten als

rather /ˈrɑːðə(r)/ adv lieber; (fairly) ziemlich; ~! und ob!

rating /ˈreɪtɪŋ/ n Einschätzung f; (class) Klasse f; (sailor) [einfacher] Matrose m; ~s pl (Radio, TV) ≈ Einschaltquote f

ratio /ˈreɪʃɪəʊ/ n Verhältnis nt

ration /ˈræʃn/ n Ration f ● vt rationieren

rational /ˈræʃənl/ adj rational. ~ize vt/i rationalisieren

rattle /ˈrætl/ n Rasseln nt; (of windows) Klappern nt; (toy) Klapper f ● vi rasseln; klappern ● vt rasseln mit

raucous /ˈrɔːkəs/ adj rau

rave /reɪv/ vi toben; ~ about schwärmen von

raven /ˈreɪvn/ n Rabe m

ravenous /ˈrævənəs/ adj heißhungrig

ravine /rəˈviːn/ n Schlucht f

raving /ˈreɪvɪŋ/ adj ~ mad 🗌 total verrückt

ravishing /ˈrævɪʃɪŋ/ adj hinreißend

raw /rɔː/ adj (-er, -est) roh; (not processed) Roh-; (skin) wund; (weather) nasskalt; (inexperienced) unerfahren; get a ~ deal 🗌 schlecht wegkommen. ~ ma'terials npl Rohstoffe pl

ray /reɪ/ n Strahl m

razor /ˈreɪzə(r)/ n Rasierapparat m. ~ blade n Rasierklinge f

re /riː/ prep betreffs (+ gen)

reach /riːtʃ/ n Reichweite f; (of river) Strecke f; within/out of ~ in/außer Reichweite ● vt erreichen; (arrive at) ankommen in (+ dat); (~ as far as) reichen bis zu; kommen zu (decision, conclusion); (pass) reichen ● vi reichen (to bis zu); ~ for greifen nach

re'act /riːˈækt/ vi reagieren

(to auf + acc)

re'action /rɪ-/ n Reaktion f. ~ary adj reaktionär

reactor /rɪ'æktə(r)/ n Reaktor m

read /riːd/ vt/i (pt/pp read /red/) lesen; (aloud) vorlesen (to dat); (Univ) studieren; ablesen (meter). ~ out vt vorlesen

readable /'riːdəbl/ adj lesbar

reader /'riːdə(r)/ n Leser(in) m(f); (book) Lesebuch nt

readily /'redɪlɪ/ adv bereitwillig; (easily) leicht

reading /'riːdɪŋ/ n Lesen nt; (Pol, Relig) Lesung f

rea'djust /riː-/ vt neu einstellen ● vi sich umstellen (to auf + acc)

ready /'redɪ/ adj fertig; (willing) bereit; (quick) schnell; get ~ sich fertig machen; (prepare to) sich bereitmachen

ready: ~-'made adj fertig. ~-to--'wear adj Konfektions-

real /rɪəl/ adj wirklich; (genuine) echt; (actual) eigentlich ● adv (Amer, ▯) echt. ~ estate n Immobilien pl

realis|m /'rɪəlɪzm/ n Realismus m. ~t n Realist m. ~tic adj, -ally adv realistisch

reality /rɪ'ælɪtɪ/ n Wirklichkeit f

realization /rɪəlaɪ'zeɪʃn/ n Erkenntnis f

realize /'rɪəlaɪz/ vt einsehen; (become aware) gewahr werden; verwirklichen (hopes, plans); einbringen (price)

really /'rɪəlɪ/ adv wirklich; (actually) eigentlich

realm /relm/ n Reich nt

realtor /'riːəltə(r)/ n (Amer) Immobilienmakler m

reap /riːp/ vt ernten

reap'pear /riː-/ vi wiederkommen

rear¹ /rɪə(r)/ adj Hinter-; (Auto) Heck-. ● n die ~ der hintere Teil; from the ~ von hinten

rear² vt aufziehen ● vi ~ [up] (horse:) sich aufbäumen

rear'range /riː-/ vt umstellen

reason /'riːzn/ n Grund m; (good sense) Vernunft f; (ability to think) Verstand m; within ~ in vernünftigen Grenzen ● vi argumentieren; ~ with vernünftig reden mit. ~able adj vernünftig; (not expensive) preiswert. ~ably adv (fairly) ziemlich

reas'surance /riː-/ n Beruhigung f; Versicherung f. ~e vt beruhigen; ~e s.o. of sth jdm etw (gen) versichern

rebel¹ /'rebl/ n Rebell m

rebel² /rɪ'bel/ vi (pt/pp rebelled) rebellieren. ~lion n Rebellion f. ~lious adj rebellisch

re'bound¹ /rɪ-/ vi abprallen

'rebound² /riː-/ n Rückprall m

re'build /riː-/ vt (pt/pp -built) wieder aufbauen

rebuke /rɪ'bjuːk/ n Tadel m ● vt tadeln

re'call /rɪ-/ n Erinnerung f ● vt zurückrufen; abberufen (diplomat); (remember) sich erinnern an (+ acc)

recant /rɪ'kænt/ vi widerrufen

recap /'riːkæp/ vt/i ▯ = recapitulate

recapitulate /riːkə'pɪtjʊleɪt/ vt/i zusammenfassen; rekapitulieren

re'capture /riː-/ vt wieder gefangen nehmen (person); wieder einfangen (animal)

reced|e /rɪ'siːd/ vi zurückgehen. ~ing adj (forehead, chin) fliehend

receipt /rɪ'siːt/ n Quittung f; (receiving) Empfang m; ~s pl (Comm) Einnahmen pl

receive /rɪ'siːv/ vt erhalten, bekommen; empfangen (guests). ~r n

(*Teleph*) Hörer m; (*of stolen goods*) Hehler m

recent /ˈriːsənt/ adj kürzlich erfolgte(r,s). ∼**ly** adv vor kurzem

receptacle /rɪˈseptəkl/ n Behälter m

reception /rɪˈsepʃn/ n Empfang m; ∼ [**desk**] (*in hotel*) Rezeption f; ∼**ist** n Empfangsdame f

receptive /rɪˈseptɪv/ adj aufnahmefähig; ∼ **to** empfänglich für

recess /rɪˈses/ n Nische f; (*holiday*) Ferien pl

recession /rɪˈseʃn/ n Rezession f

re'charge /riː-/ vt [wieder] aufladen

recipe /ˈresəpɪ/ n Rezept nt

recipient /rɪˈsɪpɪənt/ n Empfänger m

recital /rɪˈsaɪtl/ n (*of poetry, songs*) Vortrag m; (*on piano*) Konzert nt

recite /rɪˈsaɪt/ vt aufsagen; (*before audience*) vortragen

reckless /ˈreklɪs/ adj leichtsinnig; (*careless*) rücksichtslos. ∼**ness** n Leichtsinn m; Rücksichtslosigkeit f

reckon /ˈrekən/ vt rechnen; (*consider*) glauben ● vi ∼ **on/with** rechnen mit

re'claim /rɪ-/ vt zurückfordern; zurückgewinnen (*land*)

recline /rɪˈklaɪn/ vi liegen. ∼**ing** seat n Liegesitz m

recluse /rɪˈkluːs/ n Einsiedler(in) m(f)

recognition /rekəgˈnɪʃn/ n Erkennen nt; (*acknowledgement*) Anerkennung f; **in** ∼ **as** Anerkennung (*of gen*)

recognize /ˈrekəgnaɪz/ vt erkennen; (*know again*) wieder erkennen; (*acknowledge*) anerkennen

re'coil /rɪ-/ vi zurückschnellen; (*in fear*) zurückschrecken

recollect /rekəˈlekt/ vt sich erinnern an (+ acc). ∼**ion** n Erinnerung f

recommend /rekəˈmend/ vt empfehlen. ∼**ation** n Empfehlung f

recon|cile /ˈrekənsaɪl/ vt versöhnen; ∼**cile** oneself to sich abfinden mit. ∼**ciliation** n Versöhnung f

reconnaissance /rɪˈkɒnɪsns/ n (*Mil*) Aufklärung f

reconnoitre /rekəˈnɔɪtə(r)/ vi (*pres p* -**tring**) auf Erkundung ausgehen

recon'sider /riː-/ vt sich (*dat*) noch einmal überlegen

recon'struct /riː-/ vt wieder aufbauen; rekonstruieren (*crime*)

record[1] /rɪˈkɔːd/ vt aufzeichnen; (*register*) registrieren; (*on tape*) aufnehmen

record[2] /ˈrekɔːd/ n Aufzeichnung f; (*Jur*) Protokoll nt; (*Mus*) [Schall]platte f; (*Sport*) Rekord m; ∼**s** pl Unterlagen pl; **off the** ∼ inoffiziell; **have a** [**criminal**] ∼ vorbestraft sein

recorder /rɪˈkɔːdə(r)/ n (*Mus*) Blockflöte f

recording /rɪˈkɔːdɪŋ/ n Aufnahme f

re-'count[1] /riː-/ vt nachzählen

're-count[2] /riː-/ n (*Pol*) Nachzählung f

recover /rɪˈkʌvə(r)/ vt zurückbekommen ● vi sich erholen. ∼**y** n Wiedererlangung f; (*of health*) Erholung f

recreation /rekrɪˈeɪʃn/ n Erholung f; (*hobby*) Hobby nt. ∼**al** adj Freizeit-; **be** ∼**al** erholsam sein

recruit /rɪˈkruːt/ n (*Mil*) Rekrut m; **new** ∼ (*member*) neues Mitglied nt; (*worker*) neuer Mitarbeiter m ● vt rekrutieren; anwerben (*staff*). ∼**ment** n Rekrutierung f;

Anwerbung f

rectang|le /'rektæŋgl/ n Rechteck nt. ~**ular** adj rechteckig

rectify /'rektɪfaɪ/ vt (pt/pp -ied) berichtigen

rector /'rektə(r)/ n Pfarrer m; (Univ) Rektor m. ~**y** n Pfarrhaus nt

recur /rɪ'kɜː(r)/ vi (pt/pp recurred) sich wiederholen; (illness:) wiederkehren

recurren|ce /rɪ'kʌrəns/ n Wiederkehr f. ~**t** adj wiederkehrend

recycle /riː'saɪkl/ vt wieder verwerten

red /red/ adj (redder, reddest) rot ● n Rot nt

redd|en /'redn/ vt röten ● vi rot werden. ~**ish** adj rötlich

re'decorate /riː-/ vt renovieren; (paint) neu streichen; (wallpaper) neu tapezieren

redeem /rɪ'diːm/ vt einlösen; (Relig) erlösen

redemption /rɪ'dempʃn/ n Erlösung f

red: ~-**haired** adj rothaarig. ~-'**handed** adj catch s.o. ~-**handed** jdn auf frischer Tat ertappen. ~'**herring** n falsche Spur f. ~-**hot** adj glühend heiß. ~-'**light** n (Auto) rote Ampel f. ~**ness** f Röte f

re'do /riː-/ vt (pt -did, pp -done) noch einmal machen

re'double /riː-/ vt verdoppeln

red 'tape ① Bürokratie f

reduc|e /rɪ'djuːs/ vt verringern, vermindern; (in size) verkleinern; ermäßigen (costs); herabsetzen (price, goods); (Culin) einkochen lassen. ~**tion** n Verringerung f; (in price) Ermäßigung f; (in size) Verkleinerung f

redundan|cy /rɪ'dʌndənsɪ/ n Beschäftigungslosigkeit f. ~**t** adj über-

flüssig; make ~**t** entlassen; be made ~**t** beschäftigungslos werden

reed /riːd/ n [Schilf]rohr nt; ~**s** pl Schilf nt

reef /riːf/ n Riff nt

reek /riːk/ vi riechen (of nach)

reel /riːl/ n Rolle f, Spule f ● vi (stagger) taumeln ● vt ~ **off** (fig) herunterrasseln

refectory /rɪ'fektərɪ/ n Refektorium nt; (Univ) Mensa f

refer /rɪ'fɜː(r)/ v (pt/pp referred) ● vt verweisen (to an + acc); übergeben, weiterleiten (matter) (to an + acc) ● vi ~ **to** sich beziehen auf (+ acc); (mention) erwähnen; (concern) betreffen; (consult) sich wenden an (+ acc); nachschlagen in (+ dat) (book); are you ~**ring** to me? meinen Sie mich?

referee /refə'riː/ n Schiedsrichter m; (Boxing) Ringrichter m; (for job) Referenz f ● vt/i (pt/pp refereed) Schiedsrichter/Ringrichter sein (bei)

reference /'refərəns/ n Erwähnung f; (in book) Verweis m; (for job) Referenz f; **with** ~ **to** in Bezug auf (+ acc); **make** [a] ~ **to** erwähnen. ~ **book** n Nachschlagewerk nt

referendum /refə'rendəm/ n Volksabstimmung f

re'fill /riː-/ vt nachfüllen

'refill /riː-/ n (for pen) Ersatzmine f

refine /rɪ'faɪn/ vt raffinieren. ~**d** adj fein, vornehm. ~**ment** n Vornehmheit f; (Techn) Verfeinerung f. ~**ry** n Raffinerie f

reflect /rɪ'flekt/ vt reflektieren; (mirror:) [wider]spiegeln; **be ~ed in** sich spiegeln in (+ dat) ● vi nachdenken (on über + acc). ~**ion** n Reflexion f; (image) Spiegelbild nt; **on** ~**ion** nach nochmaliger Überlegung. ~**or** n Rückstrahler m

r

reflex /'ri:fleks/ n Reflex m

reflexive /rɪ'fleksɪv/ adj reflexiv

reform /rɪ'fɔ:m/ n Reform f ●vt reformieren ●vi sich bessern

refrain[1] /rɪ'freɪn/ n Refrain m

refrain[2] vi ~ from doing sth etw nicht tun

refresh /rɪ'freʃ/ vt erfrischen. ~ing adj erfrischend. ~ments npl Erfrischungen pl

refrigerat|e /rɪ'frɪdʒəreɪt/ vt kühlen. ~or n Kühlschrank m

re'fuel /ri:-/ vt/i (pt/pp -fuelled) auftanken

refuge /'refju:dʒ/ n Zuflucht f; take ~ Zuflucht nehmen

refugee /refju'dʒi:/ n Flüchtling m

'refund[1] /ri:-/ n get a ~ sein Geld zurückbekommen

re'fund[2] /rɪ-/ vt zurückerstatten

refusal /rɪ'fju:zl/ n (see refuse[1]) Ablehnung f; Weigerung f

refuse[1] /rɪ'fju:z/ vt ablehnen; (not grant) verweigern; ~ to do sth sich weigern, etw zu tun ●vi ablehnen; sich weigern

refuse[2] /'refju:s/ n Müll m

refute /rɪ'fju:t/ vt widerlegen

re'gain /rɪ-/ vt wiedergewinnen

regal /'ri:gl/ adj königlich

regard /rɪ'gɑ:d/ n (heed) Rücksicht f; (respect) Achtung f; ~s pl Grüße pl; with ~ to in Bezug auf (+ acc) ●vt ansehen, betrachten (as als). ~ing prep bezüglich (+ gen). ~less adv ohne Rücksicht (of auf + acc)

regatta /rɪ'gætə/ n Regatta f

regime /reɪ'ʒi:m/ n Regime nt

regiment /'redʒɪmənt/ n Regiment nt. ~al adj Regiments-

region /'ri:dʒən/ n Region f; in the ~ of (fig) ungefähr. ~al adj regional

register /'redʒɪstə(r)/ n Register

nt; (Sch) Anwesenheitsliste f ●vt registrieren; (report) anmelden; einschreiben (letter); aufgeben (luggage) ●vi (report) sich anmelden

registrar /redʒɪ'strɑ:(r)/ n Standesbeamte(r) m

registration /redʒɪ'streɪʃn/ n Registrierung f; Anmeldung f. ~ number n Autonummer f

registry office /'redʒɪstrɪ-/ n Standesamt nt

regret /rɪ'gret/ n Bedauern nt ●vt (pt/pp regretted) bedauern. ~fully adv mit Bedauern

regrettab|le /rɪ'gretəbl/ adj bedauerlich. ~ly adv bedauerlicherweise

regular /'regjʊlə(r)/ adj regelmäßig; (usual) üblich ●n (in pub) Stammgast m; (in shop) Stammkunde m. ~ity n Regelmäßigkeit f

regulat|e /'regjʊleɪt/ vt regulieren. ~ion n (rule) Vorschrift f

rehearsal /rɪ'hɜ:sl/ n (Theat) Probe f. ~e vt proben

reign /reɪn/ n Herrschaft f ●vi herrschen, regieren

rein /reɪn/ n Zügel m

reindeer /'reɪndɪə(r)/ n inv Rentier nt

reinforce /ri:ɪn'fɔ:s/ vt verstärken. ~ment n Verstärkung f; send ~ments Verstärkung schicken

reiterate /ri:'ɪtəreɪt/ vt wiederholen

reject /rɪ'dʒekt/ vt ablehnen. ~ion n Ablehnung f

rejects /'ri:dʒekts/ npl (Comm) Ausschussware f

rejoic|e /rɪ'dʒɔɪs/ vi (literary) sich freuen. ~ing n Freude f

re'join /rɪ-/ vt sich wieder anschließen (+ dat); wieder beitreten (+ dat) (club, party)

rejuvenate /rɪ'dʒu:vəneɪt/ vt

verjüngen

relapse /rɪ'læps/ n Rückfall m ● vi einen Rückfall erleiden

relate /rɪ'leɪt/ vt (tell) erzählen; (connect) verbinden

relation /rɪ'leɪʃn/ n Beziehung f; (person) Verwandte(r) m/f. **~ship** n Beziehung f; (link) Verbindung f; (blood tie) Verwandtschaft f; (affair) Verhältnis nt

relative /'relətɪv/ n Verwandte(r) m/f ● adj relativ; (Gram) Relativ-. **~ly** adv relativ, verhältnismäßig

relax /rɪ'læks/ vt lockern, entspannen ● vi sich lockern, sich entspannen. **~ation** n Entspannung f. **~ing** adj entspannend

relay¹ /riː'leɪ/ vt (pt/pp -layed) weitergeben; (Radio, TV) übertragen

relay² /'riːleɪ/ n. ~ **[race]** n Staffel f

release /rɪ'liːs/ n Freilassung f, Entlassung f; (Techn) Auslöser m ● vt freilassen; (let go of) loslassen; (Techn) auslösen; veröffentlichen (information)

relent /rɪ'lent/ vi nachgeben. **~less** adj erbarmungslos; (unceasing) unaufhörlich

relevan|ce /'reləvəns/ n Relevanz f. **~t** adj relevant (to für)

reliab|ility /rɪlaɪə'bɪlətɪ/ n Zuverlässigkeit f. **~le** adj zuverlässig

relian|ce /rɪ'laɪəns/ n Abhängigkeit f (on von). **~t** adj angewiesen (on auf + acc)

relic /'relɪk/ n Überbleibsel nt; (Relig) Reliquie f

relief /rɪ'liːf/ n Erleichterung f; (assistance) Hilfe f; (replacement) Ablösung f; (Art) Relief nt

relieve /rɪ'liːv/ vt erleichtern; (take over from) ablösen; ~ of entlasten von

religion /rɪ'lɪdʒən/ n Religion f

religious /rɪ'lɪdʒəs/ adj religiös

relinquish /rɪ'lɪŋkwɪʃ/ vt loslassen; (give up) aufgeben

relish /'relɪʃ/ n Genuss m; (Culin) Würze f ● vt genießen

reluctan|ce /rɪ'lʌktəns/ n Widerstreben m. **~t** adj widerstrebend; be ~t zögern (to zu). **~tly** adv ungern, widerstrebend

rely /rɪ'laɪ/ vi (pt/pp -ied) ~ on sich verlassen auf (+ acc); (be dependent on) angewiesen sein auf (+ acc)

remain /rɪ'meɪn/ vi bleiben; (be left) übrig bleiben. **~der** n Rest m. **~ing** adj restlich. **~s** npl Reste pl; (mortal) ~s (sterbliche) Überreste pl

remand /rɪ'mɑːnd/ n on ~ in Untersuchungshaft ● vt ~ in custody in Untersuchungshaft schicken

remark /rɪ'mɑːk/ n Bemerkung f ● vt bemerken. **~able** adj, **-bly** adv bemerkenswert

re|marry /riː-/ vi wieder heiraten

remedy /'remədɪ/ n [Heil]mittel nt (for gegen); (fig) Abhilfe f ● vt (pt/pp -ied) abhelfen (+ dat); beheben (fault)

rememb|er /rɪ'membə(r)/ vt sich erinnern an (+ acc); **~er to do sth** daran denken, etw zu tun ● vi sich erinnern

remind /rɪ'maɪnd/ vt erinnern (of an + acc). **~er** n Andenken nt; (letter, warning) Mahnung f

reminisce /remɪ'nɪs/ vi sich seinen Erinnerungen hingeben. **~nces** npl Erinnerungen pl. **~nt** adj be ~nt of erinnern an (+ acc)

remnant /'remnənt/ n Rest m

remorse /rɪ'mɔːs/ n Reue f. **~ful** adj reumütig. **~less** adj unerbittlich

remote /rɪ'məʊt/ adj fern; (isolated) abgelegen; (slight) gering. ~

con'trol n Fernsteuerung f; (for TV) Fernbedienung f

remotely /rɪˈməʊtlɪ/ adv entfernt; not ~ nicht im Entferntesten

re'movable /rɪ-/ adj abnehmbar

removal /rɪˈmuːvl/ n Entfernung f; (from house) Umzug m. ~ **van** n Möbelwagen m

remove /rɪˈmuːv/ vt entfernen; (take off) abnehmen; (take out) herausnehmen

render /ˈrendə(r)/ vt machen; erweisen (service); (translate) wiedergeben; (Mus) vortragen

renegade /ˈrenɪɡeɪd/ n Abtrünnige(r) m/f

renew /rɪˈnjuː/ vt erneuern; verlängern (contract). ~**al** n Erneuerung f; Verlängerung f

renounce /rɪˈnaʊns/ vt verzichten auf (+ acc)

renovat|e /ˈrenəveɪt/ vt renovieren. ~**ion** n Renovierung f

renown /rɪˈnaʊn/ n Ruf m. ~**ed** adj berühmt

rent /rent/ n Miete f ● vt mieten; (hire) leihen; ~ [out] vermieten; verleihen. ~**al** n Mietgebühr f; Leihgebühr f

renunciation /rɪnʌnsɪˈeɪʃn/ n Verzicht m

re'open /riː-/ vt/i wieder aufmachen

re'organize /riː-/ vt reorganisieren

rep /rep/ n 🔲 Vertreter m

repair /rɪˈpeə(r)/ n Reparatur f; in good/bad ~ in gutem/schlechtem Zustand ● vt reparieren

repatriat|e /riːˈpætrɪeɪt/ vt repatriieren

re'pay /riː-/ vt (pt/pp -paid) zurückzahlen; ~ s.o. for sth jdm etw zurückzahlen. ~**ment** n Rückzahlung f

repeal /rɪˈpiːl/ n Aufhebung f ● vt aufheben

repeat /rɪˈpiːt/ n Wiederholung f ● vt/i wiederholen; ~ after me sprechen Sie mir nach. ~**ed** adj wiederholt

repel /rɪˈpel/ vt (pt/pp repelled) abwehren; (fig) abstoßen. ~**lent** adj abstoßend

repent /rɪˈpent/ vi Reue zeigen. ~**ance** n Reue f. ~**ant** adj reuig

repercussions /riːpəˈkʌʃnz/ npl Auswirkungen pl

repertoire /ˈrepətwɑː(r)/, **repertory** n Repertoire nt

repetit|ion /repɪˈtɪʃn/ n Wiederholung f. ~**ive** adj eintönig

re'place /rɪ-/ vt zurücktun; (take the place of) ersetzen; (exchange) austauschen. ~**ment** n Ersatz m.

'replay /riː-/ n (Sport) Wiederholungsspiel nt; (action) ~ Wiederholung f

replenish /rɪˈplenɪʃ/ vt auffüllen (stocks); (refill) nachfüllen

replica /ˈreplɪkə/ n Nachbildung f

reply /rɪˈplaɪ/ n Antwort f (to auf + acc) ● vt/i (pt/pp replied) antworten

report /rɪˈpɔːt/ n Bericht m; (Sch) Zeugnis nt; (rumour) Gerücht nt; (of gun) Knall m ● vt berichten; (notify) melden; ~ s.o. to the police jdn anzeigen ● vi berichten (on über + acc); (present oneself) sich melden (to bei). ~**er** n Reporter(in) m(f)

reprehensible /reprɪˈhensəbl/ adj tadelnswert

represent /reprɪˈzent/ vt darstellen; (act for) vertreten, repräsentieren. ~**ation** n Darstellung f

representativ /reprɪˈzentətɪv/ adj repräsentativ (of für) ● n Bevollmächtigte(r) m(f); (Comm) Vertreter(in) m(f); (Amer, Politics) Abgeordnete(r) m(f)

Abgeordnete(r) *m/f*

repress /rɪˈpres/ *vt* unterdrücken. **∼ion** *n* Unterdrückung *f*. **∼ive** *adj* repressiv

reprieve /rɪˈpriːv/ *n* Begnadigung *f*; (*fig*) Gnadenfrist *f* ● *vt* begnadigen

reprimand /ˈreprɪmɑːnd/ *n* Tadel *m* ● *vt* tadeln

'reprint[1] /riː-/ *n* Nachdruck *m*

re'print[2] /riː-/ *vt* neu auflegen

reprisal /rɪˈpraɪzl/ *n* Vergeltungsmaßnahme *f*

reproach /rɪˈprəʊtʃ/ *n* Vorwurf *m* ● *vt* Vorwürfe *pl* machen (+ *dat*). **∼ful** *adj* vorwurfsvoll

repro'duc|e /riː-/ *vt* wiedergeben, reproduzieren ● *vi* sich fortpflanzen. **∼tion** *n* Reproduktion *f*; (*Biology*) Fortpflanzung *f*

reptile /ˈreptaɪl/ *n* Reptil *nt*

republic /rɪˈpʌblɪk/ *n* Republik *f*. **∼an** *adj* republikanisch ● *n* Republikaner(in) *m(f)*

repugnan|ce /rɪˈpʌɡnəns/ *n* Widerwille *m*. **∼t** *adj* widerlich

repuls|ion /rɪˈpʌlʃn/ *n* Widerwille *m*. **∼ive** *adj* abstoßend, widerlich

reputable /ˈrepjʊtəbl/ *adj* (*firm*) von gutem Ruf; (*respectable*) anständig

reputation /repjʊˈteɪʃn/ *n* Ruf *m*

request /rɪˈkwest/ *n* Bitte *f* ● *vt* bitten

require /rɪˈkwaɪə(r)/ *vt* (*need*) brauchen; (*demand*) erfordern; be **∼d** to do sth etw tun müssen. **∼ment** *n* Bedürfnis *nt*; (*condition*) Erfordernis *nt*

re'sale /riː-/ *n* Weiterverkauf *m*

rescue /ˈreskjuː/ *n* Rettung *f* ● *vt* retten. **∼r** *n* Retter *m*

research /rɪˈsɜːtʃ/ *n* Forschung *f* ● *vt* erforschen; (*in media*) recher-

chieren. **∼er** *n* Forscher *m*; (*for media*) Rechercheur *m*

resem|blance /rɪˈzembləns/ *n* Ähnlichkeit *f*. **∼ble** *vt* ähneln (+ *dat*)

resent /rɪˈzent/ *vt* übel nehmen; einen Groll hegen gegen (*person*). **∼ful** *adj* verbittert. **∼ment** *n* Groll *m*

reservation /rezəˈveɪʃn/ *n* Reservierung *f*; (*doubt*) Vorbehalt *m*; (*enclosure*) Reservat *nt*

reserve /rɪˈzɜːv/ *n* Reserve *f*; (*for animals*) Reservat *nt*; (*Sport*) Reservespieler(in) *m(f)* ● *vt* reservieren; (*client:*) reservieren lassen; (*keep*) aufheben; sich (*dat*) vorbehalten (*right*). **∼d** *adj* reserviert

reservoir /ˈrezəvwɑː(r)/ *n* Reservoir *nt*

re'shuffle /riː-/ *n* (*Pol*) Umbildung *f* ● *vt* (*Pol*) umbilden

residence /ˈrezɪdəns/ *n* Wohnsitz *m*; (*official*) Residenz *f*; (*stay*) Aufenthalt *m*

resident /ˈrezɪdənt/ *adj* ansässig (in in + *dat*); (*housekeeper, nurse*) im Haus wohnend ● *n* Bewohner(in) *m(f)*; (*of street*) Anwohner *m*. **∼ial** *adj* Wohn-

residue /ˈrezɪdjuː/ *n* Rest *m*; (*Chemistry*) Rückstand *m*

resign /rɪˈzaɪn/ *vt* ∼ oneself to sich abfinden mit ● *vi* kündigen; (*from public office*) zurücktreten. **∼ation** *n* Resignation *f*; (*from job*) Kündigung *f*; Rücktritt *m*. **∼ed** *adj* resigniert

resilient /rɪˈzɪlɪənt/ *adj* federnd; (*fig*) widerstandsfähig

resin /ˈrezɪn/ *n* Harz *nt*

resist /rɪˈzɪst/ *vt/i* sich widersetzen (+ *dat*, (*fig*) widerstehen (+ *dat*). **∼ance** *n* Widerstand *m*. **∼ant** *adj* widerstandsfähig

r

resolut|e /'rezəluːt/ adj entschlossen. **~ion** n Entschlossenheit f; (intention) Vorsatz m; (Pol) Resolution f

resolve /rɪ'zɒlv/ n Entschlossenheit f; (decision) Beschluss m ● vt beschließen; (solve) lösen

resort /rɪ'zɔːt/ n (place) Urlaubsort m; as a last ~ wenn alles andere fehlschlägt ● vi ~ to (fig) greifen zu

resound /rɪ'zaʊnd/ vi widerhallen

resource /rɪ'zɔːs/ n ~s pl Ressourcen pl. **~ful** adj findig

respect /rɪ'spekt/ n Respekt m, Achtung f (for vor + dat); (aspect) Hinsicht f; with ~ to in Bezug auf (+ acc) ● vt respektieren, achten

respect|able /rɪ'spektəbl/ adj, **-bly** adv ehrbar; (decent) anständig; (considerable) ansehnlich. **~ful** adj respektvoll

respective /rɪ'spektɪv/ adj jeweilig. **~ly** adv beziehungsweise

respiration /respə'reɪʃn/ n Atmung f

respite /'respaɪt/ n [Ruhe]pause f; (delay) Aufschub m

respond /rɪ'spɒnd/ vi antworten; (react) reagieren (to auf + acc)

response /rɪ'spɒns/ n Antwort f, Reaktion f

responsibility /rɪspɒnsɪ'bɪlətɪ/ n Verantwortung f; (duty) Verpflichtung f

responsib|le /rɪ'spɒnsəbl/ adj verantwortlich; (trustworthy) verantwortungsvoll. **~ly** adv verantwortungsbewusst

rest¹ /rest/ n Ruhe f; (holiday) Erholung f; (interval & Mus) Pause f; have a ~ eine Pause machen; (rest) sich ausruhen ● vt (lean) lehnen (on an/auf + acc) ● vi ruhen; (have a rest) sich ausruhen

rest² n der ~ der Rest; (people) die Übrigen pl ● vi it ~s with you es ist an Ihnen (to zu)

restaurant /'rest(ə)rɒnt/ n Restaurant nt, Gaststätte f

restful /'restfl/ adj erholsam

restive /'restɪv/ adj unruhig

restless /'restlɪs/ adj unruhig

restoration /restə'reɪʃn/ n (of building) Restaurierung f

restore /rɪ'stɔː(r)/ vt wiederherstellen; restaurieren (building)

restrain /rɪ'streɪn/ vt zurückhalten; ~ oneself sich beherrschen. **~ed** adj zurückhaltend. **~t** n Zurückhaltung f

restrict /rɪ'strɪkt/ vt einschränken; ~ to beschränken auf (+ acc). **~ion** n Einschränkung f; Beschränkung f. **~ive** adj einschränkend

'rest room n (Amer) Toilette f

result /rɪ'zʌlt/ n Ergebnis nt, Resultat nt; (consequence) Folge f; as a ~ als Folge (of gen) ● vi sich ergeben (from aus); ~ in enden in (+ dat); (lead to) führen zu

resume /rɪ'zjuːm/ vt wieder aufnehmen ● vi wieder beginnen

résumé /'rezjumeɪ/ n Zusammenfassung f

resumption /rɪ'zʌmpʃn/ n Wiederaufnahme f

resurrect /rezə'rekt/ vt (fig) wieder beleben. **~ion** n the R~ion (Relig) die Auferstehung

resuscitat|e /rɪ'sʌsɪteɪt/ vt wieder beleben. **~ion** n Wiederbelebung f

retail /'riːteɪl/ n Einzelhandel m ● adj Einzelhandels- ● adv im Einzelhandel ● vt im Einzelhandel verkaufen ● vi ~ at im Einzelhandel kosten. **~er** n Einzelhändler m

retain /rɪ'teɪn/ vt behalten

retaliat|e /rɪ'tælɪeɪt/ vi zurückschlagen. **~ion** n Vergeltung f; in

~ion als Vergeltung

retarded /rɪˈtɑːdɪd/ *adj* zurückgeblieben

reticen|ce /ˈretɪsns/ *n* Zurückhaltung *f*. ~t *adj* zurückhaltend

retina /ˈretɪnə/ *n* Netzhaut *f*

retinue /ˈretɪnjuː/ *n* Gefolge *nt*

retire /rɪˈtaɪə(r)/ *vi* in den Ruhestand treten; (*withdraw*) sich zurückziehen. ~d *adj* im Ruhestand. ~ment *n* Ruhestand *m*

retiring /rɪˈtaɪərɪŋ/ *adj* zurückhaltend

retort /rɪˈtɔːt/ *n* scharfe Erwiderung *f*; (*Chemistry*) Retorte *f* ● *vt* scharf erwidern

re'trace /riː-/ *vt* ~ one's steps denselben Weg zurückgehen

re'train /riː-/ *vt* umschulen ● *vi* umgeschult werden

retreat /rɪˈtriːt/ *n* Rückzug *m*; (*place*) Zufluchtsort *m* ● *vi* sich zurückziehen

re'trial /riː-/ *n* Wiederaufnahmeverfahren *nt*

retrieve /rɪˈtriːv/ *vt* zurückholen; (*from wreckage*) bergen; (*Computing*) wieder auffinden

retrograde /ˈretrəgreɪd/ *adj* rückschrittlich

retrospect /ˈretrəspekt/ *n* in ~ rückblickend. ~ive *adj* rückwirkend; (*looking back*) rückblickend

return /rɪˈtɜːn/ *n* Rückkehr *f*; (*giving back*) Rückgabe *f*; (*Comm*) Ertrag *m*; (*ticket*) Rückfahrkarte *f*; (*Aviat*) Rückflugschein *m*; by ~ [of post] postwendend; in ~ dafür; in ~ for; many happy ~s! herzlichen Glückwunsch zum Geburtstag! ● *vt* zurückgehen/-fahren; (*come back*) zurückkommen ● *vt* zurückgeben; (*put back*) zurückstellen/-legen; (*send back*) zurückschicken

return ticket *n* Rückfahrkarte *f*;

(*Aviat*) Rückflugschein *m*

reunion /riːˈjuːnɪən/ *n* Wiedervereinigung *f*; (*social gathering*) Treffen *nt*

reunite /riːjuːˈnaɪt/ *vt* wieder vereinigen

re'use *vt* wieder verwenden

rev /rev/ *n* (*Auto*, ⊡) Umdrehung *f* ● *vt/i* ~ [up] den Motor auf Touren bringen

reveal /rɪˈviːl/ *vt* zum Vorschein bringen; (*fig*) enthüllen. ~ing *adj* (*fig*) aufschlussreich

revel /ˈrevl/ *vi* (*pt/pp* revelled) ~ in sth etw genießen

revelation /revəˈleɪʃn/ *n* Offenbarung *f*, Enthüllung *f*

revenge /rɪˈvendʒ/ *n* Rache *f*; (*fig & Sport*) Revanche *f* ● *vt* rächen

revenue /ˈrevənjuː/ *n* [Staats]einnahmen *pl*

revere /rɪˈvɪə(r)/ *vt* verehren. ~nce *n* Ehrfurcht *f*

Reverend /ˈrevərənd/ *adj* the ~ X Pfarrer X; (*Catholic*) Hochwürden X

reverent /ˈrevərənt/ *adj* ehrfürchtig

reversal /rɪˈvɜːsl/ *n* Umkehrung *f*

reverse /rɪˈvɜːs/ *adj* umgekehrt ● *n* Gegenteil *nt*; (*back*) Rückseite *f*; (*Auto*) Rückwärtsgang *m* ● *vt* umkehren; (*Auto*) zurücksetzen ● *vi* zurücksetzen

re'vert /rɪˈvɜːt/ *vi* ~ to zurückfallen an (+ *acc*)

review /rɪˈvjuː/ *n* Rückblick *m* (of auf + *acc*); (*re-examination*) Überprüfung *f*; (*Mil*) Truppenschau *f*; (*of book, play*) Kritik *f*, Rezension *f* ● *vt* zurückblicken auf (+ *acc*); überprüfen (*situation*); rezensieren (*book, play*). ~er *n* Kritiker *m*, Rezensent *m*

revis|e /rɪˈvaɪz/ *vt* revidieren; (*for*

exam) wiederholen. **~ion** n Revision f; Wiederholung f

revival /rɪˈvaɪvl/ n Wiederbelebung f

revive /rɪˈvaɪv/ vt wieder beleben; (*fig*) wieder aufleben lassen ● vi wieder aufleben

revolt /rɪˈvəʊlt/ n Aufstand m ● vi rebellieren ● vt anwidern. **~ing** adj widerlich, eklig

revolution /revəˈluːʃn/ n Revolution f; (*Auto*) Umdrehung f. **~ary** adj revolutionär. **~ize** vt revolutionieren

revolve /rɪˈvɒlv/ vi sich drehen; **~ around** kreisen um

revolver /rɪˈvɒlvə(r)/ n Revolver m. **~ing** adj Dreh-

revue /rɪˈvjuː/ n Revue f; (*satirical*) Kabarett nt

revulsion /rɪˈvʌlʃn/ n Abscheu m

reward /rɪˈwɔːd/ n Belohnung f ● vt belohnen. **~ing** adj lohnend

re'write /riː-/ vt (pt rewrote, pp rewritten) noch einmal [neu] schreiben; (*alter*) umschreiben

rhetoric /ˈretərɪk/ n Rhetorik f. **~al** adj rhetorisch

rheumatism /ˈruːmətɪzm/ n Rheumatismus m, Rheuma nt

Rhine /raɪn/ n Rhein m

rhinoceros /raɪˈnɒsərəs/ n Nashorn nt, Rhinozeros nt

rhubarb /ˈruːbɑːb/ n Rhabarber m

rhyme /raɪm/ n Reim m ● vt reimen ● vi sich reimen

rhythm /ˈrɪðm/ n Rhythmus m. **~ic[al]** adj, **-ally** adv rhythmisch

rib /rɪb/ n Rippe f

ribbon /ˈrɪbən/ n Band nt; (*for typewriter*) Farbband nt

rice /raɪs/ n Reis m

rich /rɪtʃ/ adj (-er, -est) reich; (*food*) gehaltvoll; (*heavy*) schwer

● n **the ~** pl die Reichen; **~es** pl Reichtum m

ricochet /ˈrɪkəʃeɪ/ vi abprallen

rid /rɪd/ vt (pt/pp rid, pres p ridding) befreien (of von); **get ~ of** loswerden

riddance /ˈrɪdns/ n **good ~!** auf Nimmerwiedersehen!

ridden /ˈrɪdn/ see ride

riddle /ˈrɪdl/ n Rätsel nt

riddled /ˈrɪdld/ adj **~ with** durchlöchert mit

ride /raɪd/ n Ritt m; (*in vehicle*) Fahrt f; **take s.o. for a ~** ⚠ jdn reinlegen ● v (pt rode, pp ridden) ● vt reiten (*horse*); fahren mit (*bicycle*) ● vi reiten; (*in vehicle*) fahren. **~r** n Reiter(in) m(f); (*on bicycle*) Fahrer(in) m(f)

ridge /rɪdʒ/ n Erhebung f; (*on roof*) First m; (*of mountain*) Grat m, Kamm m

ridicule /ˈrɪdɪkjuːl/ n Spott m ● vt verspotten, spotten über (+ acc)

ridiculous /rɪˈdɪkjʊləs/ adj lächerlich

riding /ˈraɪdɪŋ/ n Reiten nt ● attrib Reit-

riff-raff /ˈrɪfræf/ n Gesindel nt

rifle /ˈraɪfl/ n Gewehr nt ● vt plündern; **~ through** durchwühlen

rift /rɪft/ n Spalt m; (*fig*) Riss m

rig /rɪg/ n Ölbohrturm m; (*at sea*) Bohrinsel f ● vt (pt/pp rigged) **~ out** ausrüsten; **~ up** aufbauen

right /raɪt/ adj richtig; (*not left*) rechte(r,s); **be ~** (*person:*) Recht haben; (*clock:*) richtig gehen; **put ~** wieder in Ordnung bringen; (*fig*) richtig stellen; **that's ~!** das stimmt! ● adv richtig; (*directly*) direkt; (*completely*) ganz; (*not left*) rechts; (*go*) nach rechts; **~ away** sofort ● n Recht nt; (*not left*) Seite f; **on the ~** rechts; **from/to**

the ~ von/nach rechts; be in the ~ Recht haben; by ~s eigentlich; the R~ (Pol) die Rechte. ~ angle n rechter Winkel m

rightful /'raɪtfl/ adj rechtmäßig

right-'handed adj rechtshändig

rightly /'raɪtlɪ/ adv mit Recht

right-'wing adj (Pol) rechte(r,s)

rigid /'rɪdʒɪd/ adj starr (strict) streng. ~ity n Starrheit f; Strenge f

rigorous /'rɪgərəs/ adj streng

rigour /'rɪgə(r)/ n Strenge f

rim /rɪm/ n Rand m; (of wheel) Felge f

rind /raɪnd/ n (on fruit) Schale f; (on cheese) Rinde f; (on bacon) Schwarte f

ring¹ /rɪŋ/ n Ring m; (for circus) Manege f; stand in a ~ im Kreis stehen ● vt umringen

ring² n Klingeln nt; give s.o. a ~ (Teleph) jdn anrufen ● v (pt rang, pp rung) ● vt läuten; ~ [up] (Teleph) anrufen ● vi (bells:) läuten; (telephone:) klingeln. ~ **back** vt/i (Teleph) zurückrufen

ring: ~**leader** n Rädelsführer m. ~ **road** n Umgehungsstraße f

rink /rɪŋk/ n Eisbahn f

rinse /rɪns/ n Spülung f; (hair colour) Tönung f ● vt spülen

riot /'raɪət/ n Aufruhr m; ~s Unruhen pl; run ~ randalieren ● vi randalieren. ~**er** n Randalierer m. ~**ous** adj aufrührerisch; (boisterous) wild

rip /rɪp/ n Riss m ● vt/i (pt/pp ripped) zerreißen; ~ **open** aufreißen. ~ **off** vt 🗊 neppen

ripe /raɪp/ adj (-r, -st) reif

ripen /'raɪpn/ vi reifen ● vt reifen lassen

ripeness /'raɪpnɪs/ n Reife f

'rip-off n 🗊 Nepp m

ripple /'rɪpl/ n kleine Welle f

rise /raɪz/ n Anstieg m; (fig) Aufstieg m; (increase) Zunahme f; (in wages) Lohnerhöhung f; (in salary) Gehaltserhöhung f; give ~ to Anlass geben zu ● vi (pt rose, pp risen) steigen; (ground:) ansteigen; (sun, dough:) aufgehen; (river:) entspringen; (get up) aufstehen; (fig) aufsteigen (to zu). ~**r** n early ~**r** Frühaufsteher m

rising /'raɪzɪŋ/ adj steigend; (sun) aufgehend ● n (revolt) Aufstand m

risk /rɪsk/ n Risiko nt; at one's own ~ auf eigene Gefahr ● vt riskieren

risky /'rɪskɪ/ adj riskant

rite /raɪt/ n Ritus m

ritual /'rɪtjʊəl/ adj rituell ● n Ritual nt

rival /'raɪvl/ adj rivalisierend ● n Rivale m/Rivalin f. ~**ry** n Rivalität f; (Comm) Konkurrenzkampf m

river /'rɪvə(r)/ n Fluss m

rivet /'rɪvɪt/ n Niete f ● vt [ver]nieten; ~**ed by** (fig) gefesselt von

road /rəʊd/ n Straße f; (fig) Weg m

road: ~-**map** n Straßenkarte f. ~ **safety** n Verkehrssicherheit f. ~**side** n Straßenrand m. ~**way** n Fahrbahn f. ~-**works** npl Straßenarbeiten pl. ~**worthy** adj verkehrssicher

roam /rəʊm/ vi wandern

roar /rɔ:(r)/ n Gebrüll nt; ~s of laughter schallendes Gelächter nt ● vi brüllen; (with laughter) schallend lachen. ~**ing** adj (fire) prasselnd; do a ~**ing trade** 🗊 ein Bombengeschäft machen

roast /rəʊst/ adj gebraten, Brat-; ~ **beef/pork** Rinder-/Schweinebraten m ● n Braten m ● vt/i braten; rösten (coffee, chestnuts)

rob /rɒb/ vt (pt/pp robbed) berauben (of gen); ausrauben (bank). ∼ber n Räuber m. ∼bery n Raub m

robe /rəʊb/ n Robe f; (Amer: bathrobe) Bademantel m

robin /'rɒbɪn/ n Rotkehlchen n

robot /'rəʊbɒt/ n Roboter m

robust /rəʊ'bʌst/ adj robust

rock¹ /rɒk/ n Fels m; on the ∼s (ship) aufgelaufen; (marriage) kaputt; (drink) mit Eis

rock² vt/i schaukeln

rock³ n (Mus) Rock m

rockery /'rɒkərɪ/ n Steingarten m

rocket /'rɒkɪt/ n Rakete f

rocking: ∼chair n Schaukelstuhl m. ∼horse n Schaukelpferd n

rocky /'rɒkɪ/ adj felsig; (unsteady) wackelig

rod /rɒd/ n Stab m; (stick) Rute f; (for fishing) Angel[rute] f

rode /rəʊd/ see ride

rodent /'rəʊdnt/ n Nagetier nt

rogue /rəʊg/ n Gauner m

role /rəʊl/ n Rolle f

roll /rəʊl/ n Rolle f; (bread) Brötchen nt; (list) Liste f; (of drum) Wirbel m ●vi rollen; be ∼ing in money 🄳 Geld wie Heu haben ●vt rollen; walzen (lawn); ausrollen (pastry). ∼ over vi sich auf die andere Seite rollen. ∼ up vt aufrollen; hochkrempeln (sleeves) ●vi 🄳 auftauchen

roller /'rəʊlə(r)/ n Rolle f; (lawn, road) Walze f; (hair) Lockenwickler m. ∼ blind n Rollo nt. R∼blades® npl Rollerblades® mpl. ∼coaster n Berg-und-Talbahn f. ∼skate n Rollschuh m

'rolling-pin n Teigrolle f

Roman /'rəʊmən/ adj römisch ●n Römer(in) m(f)

romance /rə'mæns/ n Romantik f;

(love-affair) Romanze f; (book) Liebesgeschichte f

Romania /rəʊ'meɪnɪə/ n Rumänien nt. ∼n adj rumänisch ●n Rumäne m/-nin f

romantic /rəʊ'mæntɪk/ adj, -ally adv romantisch. ∼ism n Romantik f

Rome /rəʊm/ n Rom nt

romp /rɒmp/ vi [herum]tollen

roof /ruːf/ n Dach nt; (of mouth) Gaumen m ●vt ∼ [over] überdachen. ∼top n Dach nt

rook /rʊk/ n Saatkrähe f; (Chess) Turm m

room /ruːm/ n Zimmer nt; (for functions) Saal m; (space) Platz m. ∼y adj geräumig

roost /ruːst/ n Hühnerstange f

root¹ /ruːt/ n Wurzel f; take ∼ anwachsen ●vi Wurzeln schlagen. ∼ out vt (fig) ausrotten

root² vi ∼ about wühlen; ∼ for s.o. 🄰 für jdn sein

rope /rəʊp/ n Seil nt; know the ∼s 🄳 sich auskennen. ∼ in vt 🄳 einspannen

rose¹ /rəʊz/ n Rose f; (of wateringcan) Brause f

rose² see rise

rostrum /'rɒstrəm/ n Podium nt

rosy /'rəʊzɪ/ adj rosig

rot /rɒt/ n Fäulnis f; (🄳: nonsense) Quatsch m ●vi (pt/pp rotted) [ver]faulen

rota /'rəʊtə/ n Dienstplan m

rotary /'rəʊtərɪ/ adj Dreh-; (Techn) Rotations-

rotate /rəʊ'teɪt/ vt drehen ●vi sich drehen; (Techn) rotieren. ∼ion n Drehung f; in ∼ion im Wechsel

rote /rəʊt/ n by ∼ auswendig

rotten /'rɒtn/ adj faul; 🄳 mies; (person) fies

rough /rʌf/ adj (-er, -est) rau; (*uneven*) uneben; (*coarse, not gentle*) grob; (*brutal*) roh; (*turbulent*) stürmisch; (*approximate*) ungefähr ●adv sleep ~ im Freien übernachten ●vi ~ it primitiv leben. ~ **out** vt im Groben entwerfen

roughage /ˈrʌfɪdʒ/ n Ballaststoffe pl

rough 'draft n grober Entwurf

rough|ly /ˈrʌflɪ/ adv (see rough) rau; grob; roh; ungefähr. ~**ness** n Rauheit f

'rough paper n Konzeptpapier nt

round /raʊnd/ adj (-er, -est) rund ●n Runde f; (*slice*) Scheibe f; do one's ~s seine Runde machen ●prep um (+ acc); ~ the clock rund um die Uhr ●adv all ~ ringsherum; ask s.o. ~ jdn einladen ●vt biegen um (*corner*). ~ **off** vt abrunden. ~ **up** vt aufrunden; zusammentreiben (*animals*); festnehmen (*criminals*)

roundabout /ˈraʊndəbaʊt/ adj ~ route Umweg m ●n Karussell nt; (*for traffic*) Kreisverkehr m

round 'trip n Rundreise f

rous|e /raʊz/ vt wecken; (*fig*) erregen. ~**ing** adj mitreißend

route /ruːt/ n Route f; (*of bus*) Linie f

routine /ruːˈtiːn/ adj routinemäßig ●n Routine f; (*Theat*) Nummer f

row¹ /rəʊ/ n (line) Reihe f

row² vt/i rudern

row³ /raʊ/ n 🄸 Krach m ●vi 🄸 sich streiten

rowdy /ˈraʊdɪ/ adj laut

rowing boat /ˈrəʊɪŋ-/ n Ruderboot nt

royal /ˈrɔɪəl/ adj königlich

royal|ty /ˈrɔɪəltɪ/ n Königtum nt; (*persons*) Mitglieder pl der königlichen Familie; **-ies** pl (*payments*) Tantiemen pl

RSI abbr (repetitive strain injury) chronisches Überlastungssyndrom nt

rub /rʌb/ vt (pt/pp rubbed) reiben; (*polish*) polieren; don't ~ it in 🄸 reib es mir nicht unter die Nase. ~ **off** vt abreiben ●vi abgehen. ~ **out** vt ausradieren

rubber /ˈrʌbə(r)/ n Gummi m; (*eraser*) Radiergummi m. ~ **band** n Gummiband nt

rubbish /ˈrʌbɪʃ/ n Abfall m, Müll m; (🄸 *nonsense*) Quatsch m; (🄸 *junk*) Plunder m. ~ **bin** n Abfalleimer m. ~ **dump** n Abfallhaufen m; (*official*) Müllhalde f

rubble /ˈrʌbl/ n Trümmer pl

ruby /ˈruːbɪ/ n Rubin m

rudder /ˈrʌdə(r)/ n [Steuer]ruder nt

rude /ruːd/ adj (-r, -st) unhöflich; (*improper*) unanständig. ~**ness** n Unhöflichkeit f

rudimentary /ruːdɪˈmentərɪ/ adj elementar; (*Biology*) rudimentär

ruffian /ˈrʌfɪən/ n Rüpel m

ruffle /ˈrʌfl/ vt zerzausen

rug /rʌg/ n Vorleger m, [kleiner] Teppich m; (*blanket*) Decke f

rugged /ˈrʌgɪd/ adj (*coastline*) zerklüftet

ruin /ˈruːɪn/ n Ruine f; (*fig*) Ruin m ●vt ruinieren

rule /ruːl/ n Regel f; (*control*) Herrschaft f; (*government*) Regierung f; (*for measuring*) Lineal nt; as a ~ in der Regel ●vt regieren, herrschen über (+ acc); (*fig*) beherrschen; (*decide*) entscheiden; ziehen (*line*) ●vi regieren, herrschen. ~ **out** vt ausschließen

ruled /ruːld/ adj (*paper*) liniert

ruler /'ruːlə(r)/ n Herrscher(in) m(f); (measure) Lineal nt

ruling /'ruːlɪŋ/ adj herrschend; (factor) entscheidend; (Pol) regierend • n Entscheidung f

rum /rʌm/ n Rum m

rumble /'rʌmbl/ n Grollen nt • vi grollen; (stomach:) knurren

rummage /'rʌmɪdʒ/ vi wühlen; ~ through durchwühlen

rumour /'ruːmə(r)/ n Gerücht nt • vt it is ~ed that es geht das Gerücht, dass

rump /rʌmp/ n Hinterteil nt. ~ steak n Rumpsteak nt

run /rʌn/ n Lauf m; (journey) Fahrt f; (series) Serie f, Reihe f; (Theat) Laufzeit f; (Skiing) Abfahrt f; (enclosure) Auslauf m; (Amer: ladder) Laufmasche f; ~ of bad luck Pechsträhne f; be on the ~ flüchtig sein; in the long ~ auf lange Sicht • v (pt ran, pp run, pres p running) • vi laufen; (flow) fließen; (eyes:) tränen; (bus:) verkehren; (butter, ink:) zerfließen; (colours:) [ab]färben; (in election) kandidieren • vt laufen lassen; einlaufen lassen (bath); (manage) führen, leiten; (drive) fahren; (eingehen (risk); (Journalism) bringen (story); ~ one's hand over sth mit der Hand über etw (acc) fahren. ~ away vi weglaufen. ~ down vi hinunter-/herunterlaufen; (clockwork:) ablaufen; (stocks:) sich verringern • vt (run over) überfahren; (reduce) verringern; (II: criticize) heruntermachen. ~ in vi hinein-/hereinlaufen. ~ off vi weglaufen • vt abziehen (copies). ~ out vi hinaus-/herauslaufen; (supplies, money:) ausgehen; I've ~ out of sugar ich habe keinen Zucker mehr. ~ over vt überfahren. ~ up vi hinauf-/herauflaufen; (towards) hinlaufen • vt machen (debts); auf-

laufen lassen (bill); (sew) schnell nähen

'runaway n Ausreißer m

run-'down adj (area) verkommen

rung¹ /rʌŋ/ n (of ladder) Sprosse f

rung² see ring²

runner /'rʌnə(r)/ n Läufer m; (Bot) Ausläufer m; (on sledge) Kufe f. ~ bean n Stangenbohne f. ~-up n Zweite(r) m/f

running /'rʌnɪŋ/ adj laufend; (water) fließend; four times ~ viermal nacheinander • n Laufen nt; (management) Führung f, Leitung f; be/not be in the ~ eine/keine Chance haben

runny /'rʌnɪ/ adj flüssig

run: ~-up n (Sport) Anlauf m; (to election) Zeit f vor der Wahl. ~way n Start- und Landebahn f

rupture /'rʌptʃə(r)/ n Bruch m • vt/i brechen

rural /'rʊərəl/ adj ländlich

ruse /ruːz/ n List f

rush¹ /rʌʃ/ n (Bot) Binse f

rush² n Hetze f; in a ~ in Eile • vi sich hetzen; (run) rasen; (water:) rauschen • vt hetzen, drängen. ~-hour n Hauptverkehrszeit f, Stoßzeit f

Russia /'rʌʃə/ n Russland nt. ~n adj russisch • n Russe m/Russin f; (Lang) Russisch nt

rust /rʌst/ n Rost m • vi rosten

rustle /'rʌsl/ vi rascheln • vt rascheln mit; (Amer) stehlen (cattle). ~ up vt I improvisieren

'rustproof adj rostfrei

rusty /'rʌstɪ/ adj rostig

rut /rʌt/ n Furche f

ruthless /'ruːθlɪs/ adj rücksichtslos. ~ness n Rücksichtslosigkeit f

rye /raɪ/ n Roggen m

Ss

sabbath /'sæbəθ/ n Sabbat m

sabot|age /'sæbətɑːʒ/ n Sabotage f ● vt sabotieren

sachet /'sæʃeɪ/ n Beutel m; (scented) Kissen nt

sack n Sack m; **get the** [T] rausgeschmissen werden ● vt [T] rausschmeißen

sacred /'seɪkrɪd/ adj heilig

sacrifice /'sækrɪfaɪs/ n Opfer nt ● vt opfern

sacrilege /'sækrɪlɪdʒ/ n Sakrileg nt

sad /sæd/ adj (sadder, saddest) traurig; (loss, death) schmerzlich. **~den** vt traurig machen

saddle /'sædl/ n Sattel m ● vt satteln; **~ s.o. with sth** [T] jdm etw aufhalsen

sadist /'seɪdɪst/ n Sadist m. **~ic** adj, **-ally** adv sadistisch

sad|ly /'sædlɪ/ adv traurig; (unfortunately) leider. **~ness** n Traurigkeit f

safe /seɪf/ adj (-r, -st) sicher; (journey) gut; (not dangerous) ungefährlich; **~ and sound** gesund und wohlbehalten ● n Safe m. **~guard** n Schutz m ● vt schützen. **~ly** adv sicher; (arrive) gut

safety /'seɪftɪ/ n Sicherheit f. **~-belt** n Sicherheitsgurt m. **~-pin** n Sicherheitsnadel f. **~-valve** n [Sicherheits]ventil nt

sag /sæg/ vi (pt/pp sagged) durchhängen

saga /'sɑːgə/ n Saga f; (fig) Geschichte f

said /sed/ see say

sail /seɪl/ n Segel nt; (trip) Segelfahrt f ● vi segeln; (on liner) fahren; (leave) abfahren (for nach) ● vt segeln mit

sailing /'seɪlɪŋ/ n Segelsport m. **~-boat** n Segelboot nt. **~-ship** n Segelschiff nt

sailor /'seɪlə(r)/ n Seemann m; (in navy) Matrose m

saint /seɪnt/ n Heilige(r) m/f. **~ly** adj heilig

sake /seɪk/ n **for the ~ of** um ... (gen) willen; **for my/your ~** um meinet-/deinetwillen

salad /'sæləd/ n Salat m. **~-dressing** n Salatsoße f

salary /'sælərɪ/ n Gehalt nt

sale /seɪl/ n Verkauf m; (event) Basar m; (at reduced prices) Schlussverkauf m; **for ~** zu verkaufen

sales|man n Verkäufer m. **~woman** n Verkäuferin f

saliva /sə'laɪvə/ n Speichel m

salmon /'sæmən/ n Lachs m

saloon /sə'luːn/ n Salon m; (Auto) Limousine f; (Amer: bar) Wirtschaft f

salt /sɔːlt/ n Salz nt ● adj salzig; (water, meat) Salz- ● vt salzen; (cure) pökeln; streuen (road). **~-cellar** n Salzfass nt. **~ 'water** n Salzwasser nt. **~y** adj salzig

salute /sə'luːt/ n (Mil) Gruß m ● vt/i (Mil) grüßen

salvage /'sælvɪdʒ/ n (Naut) Bergung f ● vt bergen

salvation /sæl'veɪʃn/ n Rettung f; (Relig) Heil nt

same /seɪm/ adj & pron **the ~** der/die/das gleiche; (pl) die gleichen; (identical) der-/die-/dasselbe; (pl) dieselben ● adv **the ~** gleich; **all the ~** trotzdem

sample /'sɑːmpl/ n Probe f; (Comm) Muster nt ● vt probieren; kosten (food)

sanatorium /sænə'tɔːrɪəm/ n

Sanatorium nt

sanction /'sæŋkʃn/ n Sanktion f
● vt sanktionieren

sanctuary /'sæŋktjʊərɪ/ n (Relig)
Heiligtum nt; (refuge) Zuflucht f;
(for wildlife) Tierschutzgebiet nt

sand /sænd/ n Sand m ● vt ~
[down] [ab]schmirgeln

sandal /'sændl/ n Sandale f

sand: ~**bank** n Sandbank f.
~**paper** n Sandpapier nt. ~**pit** n
Sandkasten m

sandwich /'sænwɪdʒ/ n; Sandwich
m ● vt ~ed between eingeklemmt
zwischen

sandy /'sændɪ/ adj sandig; (beach,
soil) Sand-; (hair) rotblond

sane /seɪn/ adj (-r, -st) geistig normal; (sensible) vernünftig

sang /sæŋ/ see sing

sanitary /'sænɪtərɪ/ adj hygie-
nisch; (system) sanitär. ~ **napkin** n
(Amer), ~ **towel** n [Damen]binde f

sanitation /sænɪ'teɪʃn/ n Kanalisation und Abfallbeseitigung pl

sanity /'sænɪtɪ/ n [gesunder] Verstand m

sank /sæŋk/ see sink

sap /sæp/ n (Bot) Saft m ● vt (pt/pp
sapped) schwächen

sarcas|m /'sɑːkæzm/ n Sarkasmus
m. ~**tic** adj, **-ally** adv sarkastisch

sardine /sɑː'diːn/ n Sardine f

sash /sæʃ/ n Schärpe f

sat /sæt/ see sit

satchel /'sætʃl/ n Ranzen m

satellite /'sætəlaɪt/ n Satellit m.
~**television** n Satellitenfern-
sehen nt

satin /'sætɪn/ n Satin m

satire /'sætaɪə(r)/ n Satire f

satirical /sə'tɪrɪkl/ adj satirisch

satirist /'sætɪrɪst/ n Satirike-
r(in) m(f)

satisfaction /sætɪs'fækʃn/ n Be-
friedigung f; to my ~ zu meiner
Zufriedenheit

satisfactory /sætɪs'fæktərɪ/ adj,
-ily adv zufrieden stellend

satisf|y /'sætɪsfaɪ/ vt (pt/pp -fied)
befriedigen; zufrieden stellen (customer); (convince) überzeugen; be
~ied zufrieden sein. ~**ying** adj befriedigend; (meal) sättigend

satphone /'sætfəʊn/ n Satelliten-
telefon nt

saturate /'sætʃəreɪt/ vt durchträn-
ken; (Chemistry & fig) sättigen

Saturday /'sætədeɪ/ n Samstag m

sauce /sɔːs/ n Soße f; (cheek)
Frechheit f. ~**pan** n Kochtopf m

saucer /'sɔːsə(r)/ n Untertasse f

saucy /'sɔːsɪ/ adj frech

Saudi Arabia /saʊdɪə'reɪbɪə/ n
Saudi-Arabien n

sauna /'sɔːnə/ n Sauna f

saunter /'sɔːntə(r)/ vi schlendern

sausage /'sɒsɪdʒ/ n Wurst f

savage /'sævɪdʒ/ adj wild; (fierce)
scharf; (brutal) brutal ● n Wilde(r)
m/f. ~**ry** n Brutalität f

save /seɪv/ n (Sport) Abwehr f ● vt
retten (from + dat); (keep) aufheben; (not waste) sparen; (collect)
sammeln; (avoid) ersparen; (Sport)
verhindern (goal) ● vi ~ [up]
sparen

saver /'seɪvə(r)/ n Sparer m

saving /'seɪvɪŋ/ n (see save) Rettung f; Sparen nt; Ersparnis f. ~**s** pl
(money) Ersparnisse pl

savour /'seɪvə(r)/ n Geschmack m
● vt auskosten. ~**y** adj würzig

saw[1] /sɔː/ see see

saw[2] n Säge f ● vt/i (pt sawed, pp
sawn or sawed) sägen

saxophone /'sæksəfəʊn/ n Saxophon nt

say /seɪ/ n Mitspracherecht nt; have one's ~ seine Meinung sagen ● vt/i (pt/pp said) sagen; sprechen (prayer); that is to ~ das heißt; that goes without ~ing das versteht sich von selbst. ~ing n Redensart f

scab /skæb/ n Schorf m; (pej) Streikbrecher m

scaffolding /'skæfəldɪŋ/ n Gerüst nt

scald /skɔːld/ vt verbrühen

scale¹ /skeɪl/ n (of fish) Schuppe f

scale² n Skala f; (Mus) Tonleiter f; (ratio) Maßstab m ● vt (climb) erklettern. ~ **down** vt verkleinern

scales /skeɪlz/ npl (for weighing) Waage f

scalp /skælp/ n Kopfhaut f

scamper /'skæmpə(r)/ vi huschen

scan /skæn/ n (Med) Szintigramm nt ● v (pt/pp scanned) ● vt absuchen; (quickly) flüchtig ansehen; (Med) szintigraphisch untersuchen

scandal /'skændl/ n Skandal m; (gossip) Skandalgeschichten pl. ~**ize** vt schockieren. ~**ous** adj skandalös

Scandinavia /skændɪ'neɪvɪə/ n Skandinavien nt. ~**n** adj skandinavisch ● n Skandinavier(in) m(f)

scanner /'skænə(r)/ n Scanner m

scanty /'skæntɪ/ adj, **-ily** adv spärlich; (clothing) knapp

scapegoat /'skeɪp-/ n Sündenbock m

scar /skɑː(r)/ n Narbe f

scarce /skeəs/ adj (-r, -st) knapp; make oneself ~ 🄸 sich aus dem Staub machen. ~**ely** adv kaum. ~**ity** n Knappheit f

scare /skeə(r)/ n Schreck m; (panic) [allgemeine] Panik f ● vt Angst machen (+ dat); be ~d Angst haben (of vor + dat)

scarf /skɑːf/ n (pl scarves) Schal m; (square) Tuch nt

scarlet /'skɑːlət/ adj scharlachrot

scary /'skeərɪ/ adj unheimlich

scathing /'skeɪðɪŋ/ adj bissig

scatter /'skætə(r)/ vt verstreuen; (disperse) zerstreuen ● vi sich zerstreuen. ~**ed** adj verstreut; (showers) vereinzelt

scatty /'skætɪ/ adj 🄸 verrückt

scene /siːn/ n Szene f; (sight) Anblick m; (place of event) Schauplatz m; behind the ~s hinter den Kulissen

scenery /'siːnərɪ/ n Landschaft f; (Theat) Szenerie f

scenic /'siːnɪk/ adj landschaftlich schön

scent /sent/ n Duft m; (trail) Fährte f; (perfume) Parfüm nt. ~**ed** adj parfümiert

scepti|cal /'skeptɪkl/ adj skeptisch. ~**ism** n Skepsis f

schedule /'ʃedjuːl/ n Programm nt; (of work) Zeitplan m; (timetable) Fahrplan m; behind ~ im Rückstand; according to ~ planmäßig ● vt planen

scheme /skiːm/ n Programm nt; (plan) Plan m; (plot) Komplott nt ● vi Ränke schmieden

schizophrenic /skɪtsə'frenɪk/ adj schizophren

scholar /'skɒlə(r)/ n Gelehrte(r) m/f. ~**ly** adj gelehrt. ~**ship** n Gelehrtheit f; (grant) Stipendium nt

school /skuːl/ n Schule f; (Univ) Fakultät f ● vt schulen

school: ~**boy** n Schüler m. ~**girl** n Schülerin f. ~**ing** n Schulbildung f. ~**master** n Lehrer m. ~**mistress** n Lehrerin f. ~**teacher** n Lehrer(in) m(f)

scien|ce /'saɪəns/ n Wissenschaft f. ~**tific** adj wissenschaftlich. ~**tist** n

Wissenschaftler(in) m(f)

scissors /'sɪzəz/ npl Schere f; a pair of ~ eine Schere

scoff[1] /skɒf/ vi ~ at spotten über (+ acc)

scoff[2] vt 🗓 verschlingen

scold /skəʊld/ vt ausschimpfen

scoop /skuːp/ n Schaufel f; (Culin) Portionierer m; (story) Exklusivmeldung f ● vt ~ out aushöhlen; (remove) auslöffeln

scooter /skuːtə(r)/ n Roller m

scope /skəʊp/ n Bereich m; (opportunity) Möglichkeiten pl

scorch /skɔːtʃ/ vt versengen. ~ing adj glühend heiß

score /skɔː(r)/ n [Spiel]stand m; (individual) Punktzahl f; (Mus) Partitur f; (Cinema) Filmmusik f; on that ~ was das betrifft ● vt erzielen; schießen (goal); (cut) einritzen ● vi Punkte erzielen; (Sport) ein Tor schießen; (keep score) Punkte zählen. ~r n Punktezähler m; (of goals) Torschütze m

scorn /skɔːn/ n Verachtung f ● vt verachten. ~ful adj verächtlich

Scot /skɒt/ n Schotte m/Schottin f

Scotch /skɒtʃ/ adj schottisch ● n (whisky) Scotch m

Scot|land /'skɒtlənd/ n Schottland nt. ~s, ~tish adj schottisch

nach dem Verhältniswahlrecht bestimmt.

scoundrel /'skaʊndrl/ n Schurke m

scour /'skaʊə(r)/ vt (search) absuchen; (clean) scheuern

scout /skaʊt/ n (Mil) Kundschafter m; [Boy] S~ Pfadfinder m

scowl /skaʊl/ n böser Gesichtsausdruck m ● vi ein böses Gesicht machen

scram /skræm/ vi 🗓 abhauen

scramble /'skræmbl/ n Gerangel nt ● vi klettern; ~ for sich drängen nach. ~d egg[s] n[pl] Rührei nt

scrap[1] /skræp/ n (🗓: fight) Rauferei f ● vi sich raufen

scrap[2] n Stückchen nt; (metal) Schrott m; ~s pl Reste; not a ~ kein bisschen ● vt (pt/pp scrapped) aufgeben

'scrapbook n Sammelalbum nt

scrape /skreɪp/ vt schaben; (clean) abkratzen; (damage) [ver]schrammen. ~ through vi gerade noch durchkommen. ~ together vt zusammenkriegen

scrappy /'skræpɪ/ adj lückenhaft

'scrapyard n Schrottplatz m

scratch /skrætʃ/ n Kratzer m; start from ~ von vorne anfangen; not be up to ~ zu wünschen übrig lassen ● vt/i kratzen; (damage) zerkratzen

scrawl /skrɔːl/ n Gekrakel nt ● vt/i krakeln

scream /skriːm/ n Schrei m ● vt/i schreien

screech /skriːtʃ/ n Kreischen nt ● vt/i kreischen

screen /skriːn/ n Schirm m; (Cinema) Leinwand f; (TV) Bildschirm m ● vt verdecken; (conceal) verdecken; vorführen (film); (examine) überprüfen; (Med) untersuchen

screw /skruː/ n Schraube f ●vt schrauben. ~ **up** vt festschrauben; (crumple) zusammenknüllen; zusammenkneifen (eyes); (sl: bungle) vermasseln

'**screwdriver** n Schraubenzieher m

scribble /'skrɪbl/ n Gekritzel nt ●vt/i kritzeln

script /skrɪpt/ n Schrift f; (of speech, play) Text m; (Radio, TV) Skript nt; (of film) Drehbuch nt

scroll /skrəʊl/ n Rolle f ● vt ~ up/down nach oben/unten rollen. ~ **bar** n Rollbalken m

scrounge /skraʊndʒ/ vt/i schnorren. ~r n Schnorrer m

scrub¹ /skrʌb/ n (land) Buschland nt, Gestrüpp nt

scrub² vt/i (pt/pp scrubbed) schrubben

scruff /skrʌf/ n by the ~ of the neck beim Genick

scruffy /'skrʌfɪ/ adj vergammelt

scrum /skrʌm/ n Gedränge nt

scruple /'skruːpl/ n Skrupel m

scrupulous /'skruːpjʊləs/ adj gewissenhaft

scuffle /'skʌfl/ n Handgemenge nt

sculpt|or /'skʌlptə(r)/ n Bildhauer(in) m(f). ~**ure** n Bildhauerei f; (piece of work) Skulptur f, Plastik f

scum /skʌm/ n Schmutzschicht f; (people) Abschaum m

scurry /'skʌrɪ/ vi (pt/pp -ied) huschen

scuttle¹ /'skʌtl/ vt versenken (ship)

scuttle² vi schnell krabbeln

sea /siː/ n Meer nt, See f; at ~ auf See; by ~ mit dem Schiff. ~**food** n Meeresfrüchte pl. ~**gull** n Möwe f

seal¹ /siːl/ n (Zool) Seehund m

seal² n Siegel nt ●vt versiegeln;

(fig) besiegeln. ~ **off** vt abriegeln

'**sea-level** n Meeresspiegel m

seam /siːm/ n Naht f; (of coal) Flöz nt

'**seaman** n Seemann m; (sailor) Matrose m

seance /'seɪɑːns/ n spiritistische Sitzung f

search /sɜːtʃ/ n Suche f; (official) Durchsuchung f ●vt durchsuchen; absuchen (area) ●vi suchen (for nach). ~ **engine** n Suchmaschine f. ~**ing** adj prüfend, forschend. ~**light** n [Such]scheinwerfer m. ~-**party** n Suchmannschaft f

sea: ~**sick** adj seekrank. ~**side** n at/to the ~side am/ans Meer

season /'siːzn/ n Jahreszeit f; (social, tourist, sporting) Saison f ●vt (flavour) würzen. ~**al** adj Saison-. ~**ing** n Gewürze pl

'**season ticket** n Dauerkarte f

seat /siːt/ n Sitz m; (place) Sitzplatz m; (bottom) Hintern m; take a ~ Platz nehmen ●vt setzen; (have seats for) Sitzplätze bieten (+ dat); remain ~ed sitzen bleiben. ~**belt** n Sicherheitsgurt m; fasten one's ~-belt sich anschnallen

sea: ~**weed** n [See]tang m. ~**worthy** adj seetüchtig

seclu|ded /sɪ'kluːdɪd/ adj abgelegen. ~**sion** n Zurückgezogenheit f

second /'sekənd/ adj zweite(r,s); on ~ thoughts nach weiterer Überlegung ●n Sekunde f; (Sport) Sekundant m; ~s pl (goods) Waren zweiter Wahl ●adv (in race) an zweiter Stelle ●vt unterstützen (proposal)

secondary /'sekəndrɪ/ adj zweitrangig; (Phys) Sekundär-. ~ **school** n höhere Schule f

second: ~-**best** adj zweitbeste(r,s). ~ '**class** adv (travel, send) zweiter Klasse. ~-**class** adj zweit-klassig

'**second hand** n (on clock) Sekun-denzeiger m

second-'hand adj gebraucht ● adv aus zweiter Hand

secondly /'sekəndlı/ adv zweitens

second-'rate adj zweitklassig

secrecy /'si:krəsı/ n Heimlichkeit f

secret /'si:krıt/ adj geheim; (agent, police) Geheim-; (drinker, lover) heimlich ● n Geheimnis nt

secretarial /sekrə'teərıəl/ adj Se-kretärinnen-; (work, staff) Sekreta-riats-

secretary /'sekrətərı/ n Sekretär-r(in) m (f)

secretive /'si:krətıv/ adj geheim-tuerisch

secretly /'si:krıtlı/ adv heimlich

sect /sekt/ n Sekte f

section /'sekʃn/ n Teil m; (of text) Abschnitt m; (of firm) Abteilung f; (of organization) Sektion f

sector /'sektə(r)/ n Sektor m

secular /'sekjʊlə(r)/ adj weltlich

secure /sı'kjʊə(r)/ adj sicher; (firm) fest; (emotionally) geborgen ● vt sichern; (fasten) festmachen; (obtain) sich (dat) sichern

secur|ity /sı'kjʊərətı/ n Sicherheit f; (emotional) Geborgenheit f. ~ies pl Wertpapiere pl

sedan /sı'dæn/ n (Amer) Li-mousine f

sedate /sı'deıt/ adj gesetzt

sedative /'sedətıv/ adj beruhigend ● n Beruhigungsmittel nt

sediment /'sedımənt/ n [Boden]-satz m

seduce /sı'dju:s/ vt verführen

seduct|ion /sı'dʌkʃn/ n Verfüh-rung f. ~ive /-tıv/ adj verführerisch

see /si:/ v (pt saw, pp seen) ● vt sehen; (understand) einsehen; (im-agine) sich (dat) vorstellen; (escort) begleiten; go and ~ nachsehen; (visit) besuchen; ~ **you later!** bis nachher! ~ing that da ● vi sehen; (check) nachsehen; ~ **about** sich kümmern um. ~ **off** vt verabschie-den; (chase away) vertreiben. ~ **through** vt (fig) durchschauen (person)

seed /si:d/ n Samen m; (of grape) Kern m; (fig) Saat f; (Tennis) gesetz-ter Spieler m; **go to** ~ Samen bil-den; (fig) herunterkommen. ~**ed** adj (Tennis) gesetzt

seedy /'si:dı/ adj schäbig; (area) heruntergekommen

seek /si:k/ vt (pt/pp sought) suchen

seem /si:m/ vi scheinen

seen /si:n/ see see[1]

seep /si:p/ vi sickern

seethe /si:ð/ vi ~ **with anger** vor Wut schäumen

'see-through adj durchsichtig

segment /'segmənt/ n Teil m; (of worm) Segment m; (of orange) Spalte f

segregat|e /'segrıgeıt/ vt trennen. ~**ion** n Trennung f

seize /si:z/ vt ergreifen; (Jur) be-schlagnahmen; ~ **s.o. by the arm** jdn am Arm packen. ~ **up** vi (Techn) sich festfressen

seldom /'seldəm/ adv selten

select /sı'lekt/ adj ausgewählt; (ex-clusive) exklusiv ● vt auswählen; auf-stellen (team). ~**ion** n Auswahl f

self /self/ n (pl selves) Ich nt

self: ~-**as'surance** n Selbstsicher-heit f. ~-**as'sured** adj selbstsicher. ~-**'catering** n Selbstversorgung f. ~-**'centred** adj egozentrisch. ~-**'confidence** n Selbstbewusstsein nt, Selbstvertrauen nt. ~-**'confi-**

dent adj selbstbewusst. ~·**'conscious** adj befangen. ~·**con'tained** adj (flat) abgeschlossen. ~·**con'trol** n Selbstbeherrschung f. ~·**de'fence** n Selbstverteidigung f; (Jur) Notwehr f. ~·**em'ployed** selbstständig. ~·**e'steem** n Selbstachtung f. ~·**evident** adj offensichtlich. ~·**in'dulgent** adj maßlos. ~·**interest** n Eigennutz m

self|ish /ˈselfɪʃ/ adj egoistisch, selbstsüchtig. ~**less** adj selbstlos

self: ~·**'pity** n Selbstmitleid nt. ~·**'portrait** n Selbstporträt nt. ~·**re'spect** n Selbstachtung f. ~·**'righteous** adj selbstgerecht. ~·**'sacrifice** n Selbstaufopferung f. ~·**'satisfied** adj selbstgefällig. ~·**'service** n Selbstbedienung f ● attrib Selbstbedienungs-. ~·**'sufficient** adj selbstständig

sell /sel/ v (pt/pp sold) ● vt verkaufen; be sold out ausverkauft sein ● vi sich verkaufen. ~ **off** vt verkaufen

seller /ˈselə(r)/ n Verkäufer m

Sellotape® /ˈseləʊ-/, n ≈ Tesafilm® m

'sell-out n be a ~ ausverkauft sein; (⊞: betrayal) Verrat sein

selves /selvz/ see self

semester /sɪˈmestə(r)/ n Semester nt

semi|breve /ˈsemɪbriːv/ n (Mus) ganze Note f. ~·**circle** n Halbkreis m. ~·**circular** adj halbkreisförmig. ~·**colon** n Semikolon nt. ~·**detached** adj & n ~·**detached** [house] Doppelhaushälfte f. ~·**final** n Halbfinale nt

seminar /ˈsemɪnɑː(r)/ n Seminar nt

senat|e /ˈsenət/ n Senat m. ~**or** n Senator m

send /send/ vt/i (pt/pp sent) schi-

cken; ~ for kommen lassen (person); sich (dat) schicken lassen (thing). ~·**er** n Absender m. ~·**off** n Verabschiedung f

senil|e /ˈsiːnaɪl/ adj senil. ~**ity** n senil

senior /ˈsiːnɪə(r)/ adj älter; (in rank) höher ● n Ältere(r) m/f; (in rank) Vorgesetzte(r) m/f. ~ **citizen** n Senior(in) m(f)

seniority /siːnɪˈɒrɪtɪ/ n höheres Alter nt; (in rank) höherer Rang m

sensation /senˈseɪʃn/ n Sensation f; (feeling) Gefühl nt. ~**al** adj sensationell

sense /sens/ n Sinn m; (feeling) Gefühl nt; (common ~) Verstand m; make ~ Sinn ergeben ● vt spüren. ~**less** adj sinnlos; (unconscious) bewusstlos

sensible /ˈsensəbl/ adj, **-bly** adv vernünftig; (suitable) zweckmäßig

sensitiv|e /ˈsensɪtɪv/ adj empfindlich; (understanding) einfühlsam. ~**ity** n Empfindlichkeit f

sensual /ˈsensjʊəl/ adj sinnlich. **-ity** n Sinnlichkeit f

sensuous /ˈsensjʊəs/ adj sinnlich

sent /sent/ see send

sentence /ˈsentəns/ n Satz m; (Jur) Urteil nt; (punishment) Strafe f ● vt verurteilen

sentiment /ˈsentɪmənt/ n Gefühl nt; (opinion) Meinung f; (sentimentality) Sentimentalität f ~**al** adj sentimental. ~**ality** n Sentimentalität f

sentry /ˈsentrɪ/ n Wache f

separable /ˈsepərəbl/ adj trennbar

separate[1] /ˈsepərət/ adj getrennt, separat

separat|e[2] /ˈsepəreɪt/ vt trennen ● vi sich trennen. ~**ion** n Trennung f

September /sepˈtembə(r)/ n September m

septic /ˈseptɪk/ adj vereitert

s

sequel /'si:kwl/ n Folge f; (fig) Nachspiel nt

sequence /'si:kwəns/ n Reihenfolge f

serenade /serə'neɪd/ n Ständchen nt ● vt ~ s.o. jdm ein Ständchen bringen

seren|e /sɪ'ri:n/ adj gelassen. ~ity n Gelassenheit f

sergeant /'sa:dʒənt/ n (Mil) Feldwebel m; (in police) Polizeimeister m

serial /'sɪərɪəl/ n Fortsetzungsgeschichte f; (Radio, TV) Serie f. ~ize vt in Fortsetzungen veröffentlichen/(Radio, TV) senden

series /'sɪəri:z/ n inv Serie f

serious /'sɪərɪəs/ adj ernst; (illness, error) schwer. ~ness n Ernst m

sermon /'sa:mən/ n Predigt f

servant /'sa:vənt/ n Diener(in) m(f)

serve /sa:v/ n (Tennis) Aufschlag m ● vt dienen (+ dat); bedienen (customer, guest); servieren (food); verbüßen (sentence); it ~s you right! das geschieht dir recht! ● vi dienen; (Tennis) aufschlagen. ~r n (Computing) Server m

service /'sa:vɪs/ n Dienst m; (Relig) Gottesdienst m; (in shop, restaurant) Bedienung f; (transport) Verbindung f; (maintenance) Wartung f; (set of crockery) Service nt; (Tennis) Aufschlag m; ~s pl Dienstleistungen pl; (on motorway) Tankstelle und Raststätte f; in the ~s beim Militär; out of/in ~ (machine:) außer/ in Betrieb ● vt (Techn) warten

service: ~ area n Tankstelle und Raststätte f. ~ charge n Bedienungszuschlag m. ~man n Soldat m. ~ station n Tankstelle f

serviette /sa:vɪ'et/ n Serviette f

servile /'sa:vaɪl/ adj unterwürfig

session /'seʃn/ n Sitzung f

set /set/ n Satz m; (of crockery) Service nt; (of cutlery) Garnitur f; (TV, Radio) Apparat m; (Math) Menge f; (Theat) Bühnenbild nt; (Cinema) Szenenaufbau m; (of people) Kreis m ● adj (ready) fertig, bereit; (rigid) fest; (book) vorgeschrieben; be ~ on doing sich entschlossen sein, etw zu tun ● v (pt/pp set, pres p setting) ● vt setzen; (adjust) einstellen; stellen (task, alarm clock); festsetzen, festlegen (date, limit); aufgeben (homework); zusammenstellen (questions); [ein]fassen (gem); einrichten (bone); legen (hair); decken (table) ● vi (sun:) untergehen; (become hard) fest werden. ~ back vt zurücksetzen; (hold up) aufhalten; (☐: cost) kosten. ~ off vi losfahren; (in vehicle) losfahren ● vt auslösen (alarm); explodieren lassen (bomb). ~ out vi losgehen; (in vehicle) losfahren ● vt auslegen; (state) darlegen. ~ up vt aufbauen; (fig) gründen

settee /se'ti:/ n Sofa nt, Couch f

setting /'setɪŋ/ n Rahmen m; (surroundings) Umgebung f

settle /'setl/ v (decide) entscheiden; (agree) regeln; fix festsetzen; (calm) beruhigen; (pay) bezahlen ● vi sich niederlassen; (snow, dust:) liegen bleiben; (subside) sich senken; (sediment:) sich absetzen. ~ down vi sich beruhigen; (permanently) sesshaft werden. ~ up vi abrechnen

settlement /'setlmənt/ n (see settle) Entscheidung f; Regelung f; Bezahlung f; (Jur) Vergleich m; (colony) Siedlung f

settler /'setlə(r)/ n Siedler m

'set-up n System nt

seven /'sevn/ adj sieben. ~teen adj siebzehn. ~teenth adj siebzehnte(r,s)

seventh /ˈsevnθ/ adj siebte(r,s)
seventieth /ˈsevntɪɪθ/ adj siebzigste(r,s)
seventy /ˈsevntɪ/ adj siebzig
several /ˈsevrl/ adj & pron mehrere, einige
sever|e /sɪˈvɪə(r)/ adj (-r, -st,) **-ly** adv streng; (pain) stark; (illness) schwer. **~ity** n Strenge f; Schwere f
sew /səʊ/ vt/i (pt **sewed**, pp **sewn** or **sewed**) nähen
sewage /ˈsuːɪdʒ/ n Abwasser nt
sewer /ˈsuːə(r)/ n Abwasserkanal m
sewing /ˈsəʊɪŋ/ n Nähen nt, (work) Näharbeit f. **~ machine** n Nähmaschine f
sewn /səʊn/ see **sew**
sex /seks/ n Geschlecht nt; (sexuality, intercourse) Sex m. **~ist** adj sexistisch
sexual /ˈseksjʊal/ adj sexuell. **~ 'intercourse** n Geschlechtsverkehr m
sexuality /seksjʊˈælɪtɪ/ n Sexualität f
sexy /ˈseksɪ/ adj sexy
shabby /ˈʃæbɪ/ adj, **-ily** adv schäbig
shack /ʃæk/ n Hütte f
shade /ʃeɪd/ n Schatten m; (of colour) [Farb]ton m; (for lamp) [Lampen]schirm m; (Amer: windowblind) Jalousie f ● vt beschatten
shadow /ˈʃædəʊ/ n Schatten m ● vt (follow) beschatten
shady /ˈʃeɪdɪ/ adj schattig; (□: disreputable) zwielichtig
shaft /ʃɑːft/ n Schaft m; (Techn) Welle f; (of light) Strahl m; (of lift) Schacht m
shaggy /ˈʃægɪ/ adj zottig
shake /ʃeɪk/ n Schütteln nt ● v (pt **shook**, pp **shaken**) ● vt schütteln; (shock) erschüttern; **~ hands with**

s.o. jdm die Hand geben ● vi wackeln; (tremble) zittern. **~ off** vt abschütteln
shaky /ˈʃeɪkɪ/ adj wackelig; (hand, voice) zittrig
shall /ʃæl/ v aux **we ~ see** wir werden sehen; **what ~ I do?** was soll ich machen?
shallow /ˈʃæləʊ/ adj (-er, -est) seicht; (dish) flach; (fig) oberflächlich
sham /ʃæm/ adj unecht ● n Heuchelei f ● vt (pt/pp **shammed**) vortäuschen
shambles /ˈʃæmblz/ n Durcheinander nt
shame /ʃeɪm/ n Scham f; (disgrace) Schande f; **be a ~** schade sein; **what a ~!** wie schade!
shame|ful /ˈʃeɪmfl/ adj schändlich. **~less** adj schamlos
shampoo /ʃæmˈpuː/ n Shampoo nt ● vt schamponieren
shan't /ʃɑːnt/ = **shall not**
shape /ʃeɪp/ n Form f; (figure) Gestalt f ● vt formen (into zu). **~less** adj formlos; (clothing) unförmig
share /ʃeə(r)/ n (Comm) Aktie f ● vt/i teilen. **~holder** n Aktionär(in) m (f)
shark /ʃɑːk/ n Hai[fisch] m
sharp /ʃɑːp/ adj (-er, -est) scharf; (pointed) spitz; (severe) heftig; (sudden) steil; (alert) clever; (unscrupulous) gerissen ● adv scharf; (Mus) zu hoch; **at six o'clock ~** Punkt sechs Uhr ● n (Mus) Kreuz nt. **~en** vt schärfen; [an]spitzen (pencil)
shatter /ˈʃætə(r)/ vt zertrümmern; (fig) zerstören; **~ed** (person:) erschüttert; (□: exhausted) kaputt ● vi zersplittern
shave /ʃeɪv/ n Rasur f; **have a ~** sich rasieren ● vt rasieren ● vi sich rasieren. **~r** n Rasierapparat m

s

shawl /ʃɔːl/ n Schultertuch nt

she /ʃiː/ pron sie

shears /ʃɪəz/ npl [große] Schere f

shed[1] /ʃed/ n Schuppen m

shed[2] vt (pt/pp shed, pres p shedding) verlieren; vergießen (blood, tears); ~ light on Licht bringen in (+ acc)

sheep /ʃiːp/ n inv Schaf nt. ~-dog n Hütehund m

sheepish /ʃiːpɪʃ/ adj verlegen

sheer /ʃɪə(r)/ adj rein; (steep) steil; (transparent) hauchdünn

sheet /ʃiːt/ n Laken nt, Betttuch nt; (of paper) Blatt nt; (of glass, metal) Platte f

shelf /ʃelf/ n (pl shelves) Brett nt, Bord nt; (set of shelves) Regal nt

shell /ʃel/ n Schale f; (of snail) Haus nt; (of tortoise) Panzer m; (on beach) Muschel f; (Mil) Granate f ● vt pellen; enthülsen (peas); (Mil) [mit Granaten] beschießen. ~ out vi 🄸 blechen

'shellfish n inv Schalentiere pl; (Culin) Meeresfrüchte pl

shelter /ʃeltə(r)/ n Schutz m; (air-raid ~) Luftschutzraum m ● vt schützen (from vor + dat) ● vi sich unterstellen. ~ed adj geschützt; (life) behütet

shelve /ʃelv/ vt auf Eis legen; (abandon) aufgeben

shelving /ʃelvɪŋ/ n (shelves) Regale pl

shepherd /ʃepəd/ n Schäfer m ● vt führen

sherry /ʃerɪ/ n Sherry m

shield /ʃiːld/ n Schild m; (for eyes) Schirm m; (Techn & fig) Schutz m ● vt schützen (from vor + dat)

shift /ʃɪft/ n Verschiebung f; (at work) Schicht f ● vt rücken; (take away) wegnehmen; (rearrange) umstellen; schieben (blame) (on to auf

+ acc) ● vi sich verschieben; (🄸: rush) rasen

shifty /ʃɪftɪ/ adj (pej) verschlagen

shimmer /ʃɪmə(r)/ n Schimmer m ● vi schimmern

shin /ʃɪn/ n Schienbein nt

shine /ʃaɪn/ n Glanz m ● v (pt/pp shone) ● vi leuchten; (reflect light) glänzen; (sun:) scheinen ● vt ~ a light on beleuchten

shingle /ʃɪŋgl/ n (pebbles) Kiesel pl

shiny /ʃaɪnɪ/ adj glänzend

ship /ʃɪp/ n Schiff nt ● vt (pt/pp shipped) verschiffen

ship: ~building n Schiffbau m. ~ment n Sendung f. ~per n Spediteur m. ~ping n Versand m; (traffic) Schifffahrt f. ~shape adj & adv in Ordnung. ~wreck n Schiffbruch m. ~wrecked adj schiffbrüchig. ~yard n Werft f

shirt /ʃɜːt/ n [Ober]hemd nt; (for woman) Hemdbluse f

shit /ʃɪt/ n (vulgar) Scheiße f ● vi (pt/pp shit) (vulgar) scheißen

shiver /ʃɪvə(r)/ n Schauder m ● vi zittern

shoal /ʃəʊl/ n (fish) Schwarm m

shock /ʃɒk/ n Schock m; (Electr) Schlag m; (impact) Erschütterung f ● vt einen Schock versetzen (+ dat); (scandalize) schockieren. ~ing adj schockierend; (🄸: bad) fürchterlich

shoddy /ʃɒdɪ/ adj minderwertig

shoe /ʃuː/ n Schuh m; (of horse) Hufeisen nt ● vt (pt/pp shod, pres p shoeing) beschlagen (horse)

shoe: ~horn n Schuhanzieher m. ~-lace n Schnürsenkel m. ~-string n on a ~-string 🄸 mit ganz wenig Geld

shone /ʃɒn/ see shine

shoo /ʃuː/ vt scheuchen ● int sch!

shook /ʃʊk/ *see* shake

shoot /ʃuːt/ n (Bot) Trieb m; (hunt) Jagd f ●v (pt/pp shot) ●vt schießen; (kill) erschießen; drehen (film) ●vi schießen. ~ **down** vt abschießen. ~ **out** vi (rush) herausschießen. ~ **up** vi (grow) in die Höhe schießen/(prices:) schnellen

shop /ʃɒp/ n Laden m, Geschäft nt; (workshop) Werkstatt f; **talk** ~ ⓘ fachsimpeln ●vi (pt/pp shopped, pres p shopping) einkaufen; go ~**ping** einkaufen gehen

shop: ~ **assistant** n Verkäufer(in) m(f). ~**keeper** n Ladenbesitzer(in) m(f). ~**lifter** n Ladendieb m. ~**lifting** n Ladendiebstahl m

shopping /ʃɒpɪŋ/ n Einkaufen nt; (articles) Einkäufe pl; do the ~ einkaufen. ~ **bag** n Einkaufstasche f. ~ **centre** n Einkaufszentrum nt. ~ **trolley** n Einkaufswagen m

shop-'window n Schaufenster nt

shore /ʃɔː(r)/ n Strand m; (of lake) Ufer nt

short /ʃɔːt/ (er, -est) kurz; (person) klein; (curt) schroff; a ~ time ago vor kurzem; be ~ of zu wenig ... haben; be in ~ supply knapp sein ●adv kurz; (abruptly) plötzlich; (curtly) kurz angebunden; in ~ kurzum; ~ of (except) außer; go ~ Mangel leiden

shortage /ʃɔːtɪdʒ/ n Mangel m (of an + dat); (scarcity) Knappheit f

short: ~**bread** n ≈ Mürbekekse pl. ~ **circuit** n Kurzschluss m. ~**coming** n Fehler m. ~ **'cut** n Abkürzung f

shorten /ʃɔːtn/ vt [ab]kürzen; kürzer machen (garment)

short: ~**hand** n Kurzschrift f, Stenographie f. ~ **list** n engere Auswahl f

short|ly /ʃɔːtlɪ/ adv in Kürze; ~ly before/after kurz vorher/danach. ~**ness** n Kürze f; (of person) Kleinheit f

shorts /ʃɔːts/ npl Shorts pl

short: ~**sighted** adj kurzsichtig. ~**sleeved** adj kurzärmelig. ~**story** n Kurzgeschichte f. ~**tempered** adj aufbrausend. ~**term** adj kurzfristig. ~ **wave** n Kurzwelle f

shot /ʃɒt/ see shoot ●n Schuss m; (pellets) Schrot m; (person) Schütze m; (Phot) Aufnahme f; (injection) Spritze f; (ⓘ: attempt) Versuch m; like a ~ ⓘ sofort. ~**gun** n Schrotflinte f. ~**put** n (Sport) Kugelstoßen nt

should /ʃʊd/ modal verb you ~ go du solltest gehen; I ~ have seen him ich hätte ihn sehen sollen; I ~ like ich möchte; this ~ be enough das müsste eigentlich reichen; if he ~ be there falls er da sein sollte

shoulder /ʃəʊldə(r)/ n Schulter f ●vt schultern; (fig) auf sich (acc) nehmen. ~**blade** n Schulterblatt nt

shout /ʃaʊt/ n Schrei m ●vt/i schreien. ~ **down** vt niederschreien

shouting /ʃaʊtɪŋ/ n Geschrei nt

●**shove** /ʃʌv/ n Stoß m ●vt stoßen; (ⓘ: put) tun ●vi drängeln. ~ **off** vi ⓘ abhauen

shovel /ʃʌvl/ n Schaufel f ●vt (pt/pp shovelled) schaufeln

show /ʃəʊ/ n (display) Pracht f; (exhibition) Ausstellung f, Schau f; (performance) Vorstellung f (Theat, TV) Show f; on ~ ausgestellt ●v (pt showed, pp shown) vt zeigen; (put on display) ausstellen; vorführen (film) ●vi sichtbar sein; (film:) gezeigt werden. ~ **in** vt hereinführen. ~ **off** vi ⓘ angeben ●vt vorführen; (flaunt) angeben mit. ~ **up** vi [deutlich] zu sehen sein; (ⓘ: arrive) auftauchen • vt deutlich zeigen; (🔲: *embarrass*) blamieren

shower /'ʃaʊə(r)/ n Dusche f; (*of rain*) Schauer m; have a ∼ duschen • vt ∼ with überschütten mit • vi duschen

'show-jumping n Springreiten nt

shown /ʃəʊn/ *see* show

show: ∼**-off** n Angeber(in) m(f). ∼**room** n Ausstellungsraum m

showy /'ʃəʊɪ/ adj protzig

shrank /ʃræŋk/ *see* shrink

shred /ʃred/ n Fetzen m; (*fig*) Spur f • vt (*pt/pp* shredded) zerkleinern; (*Culin*) schnitzeln. ∼**der** n Reißwolf m; (*Culin*) Schnitzelwerk nt

shrewd /ʃruːd/ adj (-er, -est) klug. ∼**ness** n Klugheit f

shriek /ʃriːk/ n Schrei m • vt/i schreien

shrill /ʃrɪl/ adj, **-y** adv schrill

shrimp /ʃrɪmp/ n Garnele f, Krabbe f

shrine /ʃraɪn/ n Heiligtum nt

shrink /ʃrɪŋk/ vi (*pt* shrank, *pp* shrunk) schrumpfen; (*garment:*) einlaufen; (*draw back*) zurückschrecken (from vor + dat)

shrivel /'ʃrɪvl/ vi (*pt/pp* shrivelled) verschrumpeln

Shrove /ʃrəʊv/ n ∼ Tuesday Fastnachtsdienstag m

shrub /ʃrʌb/ n Strauch m

shrug /ʃrʌg/ n Achselzucken nt • vt/i (*pt/pp* shrugged) ∼ [one's shoulders] die Achseln zucken

shrunk /ʃrʌŋk/ *see* shrink

shudder /'ʃʌdə(r)/ n Schauder m • vi schaudern; (*tremble*) zittern

shuffle /'ʃʌfl/ vi schlurfen • vt mischen (*cards*)

shun /ʃʌn/ vt (*pt/pp* shunned) meiden

shunt /ʃʌnt/ vt rangieren

shut /ʃʌt/ v (*pt/pp* shut, *pres p* shutting) • vt zumachen, schließen • vi sich schließen; (*shop:*) schließen, zumachen. ∼ **down** vt schließen; stilllegen (*factory*) • vi schließen. ∼ **up** vt abschließen; (*lock in*) einsperren • vi 🔲 den Mund halten

shutter /'ʃʌtə(r)/ n [Fenster]laden m; (*Phot*) Verschluss m

shuttle /'ʃʌtl/ n (*textiles*) Schiffchen nt

shuttle service n Pendelverkehr m

shy /ʃaɪ/ adj (-er, -est) schüchtern; (*timid*) scheu. ∼**ness** n Schüchternheit f

siblings /'sɪblɪŋz/ npl Geschwister pl

Sicily /'sɪsɪlɪ/ n Sizilien nt

sick /sɪk/ adj krank; (*humour*) makaber; be ∼ (*vomit*) sich übergeben; be ∼ of sth 🔲 etw satt haben; I feel ∼ mir ist schlecht

sick|ly /'sɪklɪ/ adj kränklich. ∼**ness** n Krankheit f; (*vomiting*) Erbrechen nt

side /saɪd/ n Seite f; on the ∼ (*as sideline*) nebenbei; ∼ by ∼ nebeneinander; (*fig*) Seite an Seite; take ∼s Partei ergreifen (with für) • attrib Seiten- • vi ∼ with Partei ergreifen für

side: ∼**board** n Anrichte f. ∼**-effect** n Nebenwirkung f. ∼**lights** npl Standlicht nt. ∼**line** n Nebenbeschäftigung f. ∼**-show** n Nebenattraktion f. ∼**-step** vt ausweichen (+ dat). ∼**walk** n (*Amer*) Bürgersteig m. ∼**ways** adv seitwärts

siding /'saɪdɪŋ/ n Abstellgleis nt

siege /siːdʒ/ n Belagerung f; (*by police*) Umstellung f

sieve /sɪv/ n Sieb nt • vt sieben

sift /sɪft/ vt sieben; (*fig*) durchsehen

sigh /saɪ/ n Seufzer m ●vi seufzen

sight /saɪt/ n Sicht f; (faculty) Sehvermögen nt; (spectacle) Anblick m; (on gun) Visier nt; ~**s** pl Sehenswürdigkeiten pl; at first ~ auf den ersten Blick; lose ~ of aus dem Auge verlieren; know by ~ vom Sehen kennen ● vt sichten

'sightseeing n go ~ die Sehenswürdigkeiten besichtigen

sign /saɪn/ n Zeichen nt; (notice) Schild nt ●vt/i unterschreiben; (author, artist) signieren. ~ **on** vi (as unemployed) sich arbeitslos melden; (Mil) sich verpflichten

signal /'sɪgnl/ n Signal nt ●vt/i (pt/pp signalled) signalisieren; ~ **to** s.o. jdm ein Signal geben

signature /'sɪgnətʃə(r)/ n Unterschrift f; (of artist) Signatur f

significan|ce /sɪg'nɪfɪkəns/ n Bedeutung f. ~**t** adj (important) bedeutend

signify /'sɪgnɪfaɪ/ vt (pt/pp -ied) bedeuten

signpost /'saɪn-/ n Wegweiser m

silence /'saɪləns/ n Stille f; (of person) Schweigen nt ●vt zum Schweigen bringen. ~**r** n (on gun) Schalldämpfer m; (Auto) Auspufftopf m

silent /'saɪlənt/ adj still; (without speaking) schweigend; remain ~ schweigen

silhouette /sɪlu:'et/ n Silhouette f; (picture) Schattenriss m ●vt be ~**d** sich als Silhouette abheben

silicon /'sɪlɪkən/ n Silizium nt

silk /sɪlk/ n Seide f ●attrib Seiden-

silky /'sɪlkɪ/ adj seidig

sill /sɪl/ n Sims m & nt

silly /'sɪlɪ/ adj dumm, albern

silver /'sɪlvə(r)/ adj silbern; (coin, paper) Silber- ● n Silber nt

silver: ~**plated** adj versilbert. ~**ware** n Silber nt

SIM card n SIM-Karte f

similar /'sɪmɪlə(r)/ adj ähnlich. ~**ity** n Ähnlichkeit f

simmer /'sɪmə(r)/ vi leise kochen, ziehen ●vt kochen lassen

simple /'sɪmpl/ adj (-r, -st) einfach; (person) einfältig. ~**-minded** adj einfältig

simplicity /sɪm'plɪsətɪ/ n Einfachheit f

simpli|fication /sɪmplɪfɪ'keɪʃn/ n Vereinfachung f. ~**fy** vt (pt/pp -ied) vereinfachen

simply /'sɪmplɪ/ adv einfach

simulat|e /'sɪmjʊleɪt/ vt vortäuschen; (Techn) simulieren

simultaneous /sɪml'teɪnɪəs/ adj gleichzeitig

sin /sɪn/ n Sünde f ●vi (pt/pp sinned) sündigen

---

since /sɪns/

● preposition

····▸ seit (+ dat). he's been living here since 1991 er wohnt* seit 1991 hier. I had been waiting since 8 o'clock ich wartete* [schon] seit 8 Uhr. since seeing you seit ich dich gesehen habe. how long is it since your interview? wie lange ist es seit deinem Vorstellungsgespräch?

● adverb

····▸ seitdem. I haven't spoken to her since seitdem habe ich mit ihr nicht gesprochen. the house has been empty ever since das Haus steht seitdem leer. he has since remarried er hat danach wieder geheiratet. long since vor langer Zeit

● conjunction

····▸ seit. since she has been living in Germany seit sie in Deutschland wohnt*. since they

s

had been in London **seit sie in London waren***. **how long is it since he left?** wie lange ist es her, dass er weggezogen ist? **it's a year since he left** es ist ein Jahr her, dass er weggezogen ist

┈┈▸ (*because*) da. **since she was ill, I had to do it** da sie krank war, musste ich es tun

! *Note the different tenses in German

sincere /sɪnˈsɪə(r)/ adj aufrichtig; (*heartfelt*) herzlich. ~**ly** adv aufrichtig; **Yours** ~**ly** Mit freundlichen Grüßen

sincerity /sɪnˈserətɪ/ n Aufrichtigkeit f

sinful /ˈsɪnfl/ adj sündhaft

sing /sɪŋ/ vt/i (pt sang, pp sung) singen

singe /sɪndʒ/ vt (pres p singeing) versengen

singer /ˈsɪŋə(r)/ n Sänger(in) m(f)

single /ˈsɪŋgl/ adj einzeln; (one only) einzig; (unmarried) ledig; (ticket) einfach; (room, bed) Einzel- ● n (ticket) einfache Fahrkarte f; (record) Single f; ~s pl (Tennis) Einzel nt ● vt ~**out** auswählen

single: ~**-handed** adj & adv allein. ~ '**parent** n Alleinerziehende/r m/f

singly /ˈsɪŋglɪ/ adv einzeln

singular /ˈsɪŋgjʊlə(r)/ adj eigenartig; (*Gram*) im Singular ● n Singular m

sinister /ˈsɪnɪstə(r)/ adj finster

sink /sɪŋk/ n Spülbecken nt ● v (pt sank, pp sunk) ● vi sinken ● vt versenken (ship); senken (shaft). ~ **in** vi einsinken; (🄵: be understood) kapiert werden

sinner /ˈsɪnə(r)/ n Sünder(in) m(f)

sip /sɪp/ n Schlückchen nt ● vt (pt/pp sipped) in kleinen Schlucken trinken

siphon /ˈsaɪfn/ n (bottle) Siphon m. ~ **off** vt mit einem Saugheber ablassen

sir /sɜː(r)/ n mein Herr; **S**~ (title) Sir; **Dear S**~**s** Sehr geehrte Herren

siren /ˈsaɪrən/ n Sirene f

sister /ˈsɪstə(r)/ n Schwester f; (nurse) Oberschwester f. ~**-in-law** n Schwägerin f

sit /sɪt/ v (pt/pp sat, pres p sitting) ● vi sitzen; (sit down) sich setzen; (committee:) tagen ● vt setzen; machen (exam). ~ **back** vi sich zurücklehnen. ~ **down** vi sich setzen. ~ **up** vi [aufrecht] sitzen; (rise) sich aufsetzen; (not slouch) gerade sitzen

site /saɪt/ n Gelände nt; (for camping) Platz m; (Archaeology) Stätte f

sitting /ˈsɪtɪŋ/ n Sitzung f; (for meals) Schub m

situate /ˈsɪtjʊeɪt/ vt legen; **be** ~**d** liegen. ~**ion** /-ˈeɪʃn/ n Lage f; (circumstances) Situation f; (job) Stelle f

six /sɪks/ adj sechs. ~**teen** adj sechzehn. ~**teenth** adj sechzehnte(r,s)

sixth /sɪksθ/ adj sechste(r,s)

sixtieth /ˈsɪkstɪɪθ/ adj sechzigste(r,s)

sixty /ˈsɪkstɪ/ adj sechzig

size /saɪz/ n Größe f

sizzle /ˈsɪzl/ vi brutzeln

skate /skeɪt/ n Schlittschuh m ● vi Schlittschuh laufen. ~**board** n Skateboard nt ● vi Skateboard fahren. ~**boarding** n Skateboardfahren nt. ~**r** n Eisläufer(in) m(f)

skating /ˈskeɪtɪŋ/ n Eislaufen nt. ~**-rink** n Eisbahn f

skeleton /ˈskelɪtn/ n Skelett nt. ~ '**key** n Dietrich m

sketch /sketʃ/ n Skizze f; (Theat) Sketch m ● vt skizzieren

sketchy /'sketʃɪ/ adj , -ily adv skizzenhaft

ski /skiː/ n Ski m ● vi (pt/pp skied, pres p skiing) Ski fahren or laufen

skid /skɪd/ n Schleudern f ● vi (pt/pp skidded) schleudern

skier /'skiːə(r)/ n Skiläufer(in) m(f)

skiing /'skiːɪŋ/ n Skilaufen nt

skilful /'skɪlfl/ adj geschickt

skill /skɪl/ n Geschick nt. ~ed adj geschickt; (trained) ausgebildet

skim /skɪm/ vt (pt/pp skimmed) entrahmen (milk)

skimp /skɪmp/ vt sparen an (+ dat)

skimpy /'skɪmpɪ/ adj knapp

skin /skɪn/ n Haut f; (on fruit) Schale f ● vt (pt/pp skinned) häuten; schälen (fruit)

skin: ~-deep adj oberflächlich. ~-diving n Sporttauchen nt

skinny /'skɪnɪ/ adj dünn

skip¹ /skɪp/ n Container m

skip² n Hüpfer m ● vi (pt/pp skipped) vi hüpfen; (with rope) seilspringen ● vt überspringen

skipper /'skɪpə(r)/ n Kapitän m

'skipping-rope n Sprungseil nt

skirmish /'skɜːmɪʃ/ n Gefecht nt

skirt /skɜːt/ n Rock m ● vt herumgehen um

skittle /'skɪtl/ n Kegel m

skive /skaɪv/ vi 🅣 blaumachen

skull /skʌl/ n Schädel m

sky /skaɪ/ n Himmel m. ~light n Dachluke f. ~ marshal n bewaffneter Flugbegleiter m. ~scraper n Wolkenkratzer m

slab /slæb/ n Platte f; (slice) Scheibe f; (of chocolate) Tafel f

slack /slæk/ adj (-er, -est) schlaff, locker; (person) nachlässig; (Comm) flau ● vi bummeln

slacken /'slækn/ vi sich lockern; (diminish) nachlassen ● vt lockern; (diminish) verringern

slain /sleɪn/ see slay

slam /slæm/ n 🅣 slammed) ● vt zuschlagen; (put) knallen 🅣; (🅣: criticize) verreißen ● vi zuschlagen

slander /'slɑːndə(r)/ n Verleumdung f ● vt verleumden

slang /slæŋ/ n Slang m. ~y adj salopp

slant /slɑːnt/ n Schräge f; on the ~ schräg ● vt abschrägen; (fig) färben (report) ● vi sich neigen

slap /slæp/ n Schlag m ● vt (pt/pp slapped) schlagen; (put) knallen 🅣 ● adv direkt

slapdash adj 🅣 schludrig

slash /slæʃ/ n Schlitz m ● vt aufschlitzen; (drastically) reduzieren (prices)

slat /slæt/ n Latte f

slate /sleɪt/ n Schiefer m ● vt 🅣 heruntermachen; verreißen (performance)

slaughter /'slɔːtə(r)/ n Schlachten nt; (massacre) Gemetzel nt ● vt schlachten; abschlachten (men)

Slav /slɑːv/ adj slawisch ● n Slawe m, Slawin f

slave /sleɪv/ n Sklave m, Sklavin f ● vi ~ [away] schuften

slavery /'sleɪvərɪ/ n Sklaverei f

slay /sleɪ/ vt (pt slew, pp slain) ermorden

sledge /sledʒ/ n Schlitten m

sleek /sliːk/ adj (-er, -est) seidig; (well-fed) wohlgenährt

sleep /sliːp/ n Schlaf m; go to ~ einschlafen; put to ~ einschläfern ● v (pt/pp slept) ● vi schlafen ● vt (accommodate) Unterkunft bieten für. ~er n Schläfer(in) m(f); (Rail) Schlafwagen m; (on track)

s

Schwelle f
sleeping: ~**-bag** n Schlafsack m.
~**-pill** n Schlaftablette f
sleep: ~**less** adj schlaflos. ~**-wal**
king n Schlafwandeln nt
sleepy /'sliːpɪ/ adj , **-ily** adv
schläfrig
sleet /sliːt/ n Schneeregen m
sleeve /sliːv/ n Ärmel m; (for record) Hülle f. ~**less** adj ärmellos
sleigh /sleɪ/ n [Pferde]schlitten m
slender /'slendə(r)/ adj schlank;
(fig) gering
slept /slept/ see sleep
slew see slay
slice /slaɪs/ n Scheibe f ● vt in
Scheiben schneiden
slick /slɪk/ adj clever
slid|e /slaɪd/ n Rutschbahn f; (for
hair) Spange f; (Phot) Dia nt ● v (pt/
pp slid) ● vi rutschen ● vt schieben.
~**ing** adj gleitend; (door, seat)
Schiebe-
slight /slaɪt/ adj (-er, -est) leicht;
(importance) gering; (acquaintance)
flüchtig; (slender) schlank; not in
the ~**est** nicht im Geringsten; ~**ly**
better ein bisschen besser ● vt
kränken, beleidigen ● n Beleidigung f
slim /slɪm/ adj (slimmer, slim-
mest) schlank; (volume) schmal;
(fig) gering ● vi eine Schlankheitskur machen
slim|e /slaɪm/ n Schleim m. ~**y** adj
schleimig
sling /slɪŋ/ n (Med) Schlinge f ● vt
(pt/pp slung) 🔲 schmeißen
slip /slɪp/ n (mistake) Fehler m, 🔲
Patzer m; (petticoat) Unterrock m;
(paper) Zettel m; give s.o. the ~
🔲 jdm entwischen; ~ of the
tongue Versprecher m ● v (pt/pp
slipped) ● vi rutschen; (fall) ausrutschen; (go quickly) schlüpfen ● vt

schieben; ~ s.o.'s mind jdm entfallen. ~ **away** vi sich fortschleichen.
~ **up** vi 🔲 einen Schnitzer machen
slipper /'slɪpə(r)/ n Hausschuh m
slippery /'slɪpərɪ/ adj glitschig;
(surface) glatt
slipshod /'slɪpʃɒd/ adj schludrig
'**slip-up** n 🔲 Schnitzer m
slit /slɪt/ n Schlitz m ● vt (pt/pp
slit) aufschlitzen
slither /'slɪðə(r)/ vi rutschen
slog /slɒg/ n [hard] ~ Schinderei f
● vi (pt/pp slogged) schuften
slogan /'sləʊgən/ n Schlagwort nt;
(advertising) Werbespruch m
slop|e /sləʊp/ n Hang m; (inclin-
ation) Neigung f ● vi sich neigen.
~**ing** adj schräg
sloppy /'slɒpɪ/ adj schludrig; (sentimental) sentimental
slosh /slɒʃ/ vi 🔲 schwappen
slot /slɒt/ n Schlitz m; (TV) Sende-
zeit f ● v (pt/pp slotted) ● vt einfügen ● vi sich einfügen (in in + acc)
'**slot-machine** n Münzautomat
m; (for gambling) Spielautomat m
slouch /slaʊtʃ/ vi sich schlecht
halten
slovenly /'slʌvnlɪ/ adj schlampig
slow /sləʊ/ adj (-er, -est) langsam;
be ~ (clock:) nachgehen; in ~ motion in Zeitlupe ● adv langsam ● vt
verlangsamen; ~ **down**, ~ **up**
langsamer werden. ~**ness** n Lang-
samkeit f
sludge /slʌdʒ/ n Schlamm m
slug /slʌg/ n Nacktschnecke f
sluggish /'slʌgɪʃ/ adj träge
sluice /sluːs/ n Schleuse f
slum /slʌm/ n Elendsviertel nt
slumber /'slʌmbə(r)/ n Schlummer m ● vi schlummern
slump /slʌmp/ n Sturz m ● vi fallen; (crumple) zusammensacken;

(prices:) stürzen; (sales:) zurückgehen

slung /slʌŋ/ see sling

slur /slɜː(r)/ vt (pt/pp slurred) undeutlich sprechen

slurp /slɜːp/ vt/i schlürfen

slush /slʌʃ/ n [Schnee]matsch m; (fig) Kitsch m

slut /slʌt/ n Schlampe f 🗆

sly /slaɪ/ adj (-er, -est) verschlagen ● n on the ~ heimlich

smack /smæk/ n Schlag m, Klaps m ● vt schlagen ● adv 🗆 direkt

small /smɔːl/ adj (-er, -est) klein ● adv chop up ~ klein hacken ● n ~ of the back Kreuz nt

small: ~ **ads** npl Kleinanzeigen pl. ~ '**change** n Kleingeld nt. ~**pox** n Pocken pl. ~ **talk** n leichte Konversation f

smart /smɑːt/ adj (-er, -est) schick; (clever) schlau, clever; (brisk) flott; (Amer, fam: cheeky) frech ● vi brennen

smarten /ˈsmɑːtn/ vt ~ oneself up mehr auf sein Äußeres achten

smash /smæʃ/ n Krach m; (collision) Zusammenstoß m; (Tennis) Schmetterball m ● vt zerschlagen; (strike) schlagen; (Tennis) schmettern ● vi zerschmettern; (crash) krachen (into gegen). ~**ing** adj 🗆 toll

smear /smɪə(r)/ n verschmierter Fleck m; (Med) Abstrich m; (fig) Verleumdung f ● vt schmieren; (coat) beschmieren (with mit); (fig) verleumden ● vi schmieren

smell /smel/ n Geruch m; (sense) Geruchssinn m ● vt/i (pt/pp smelt or smelled) vt riechen; (sniff) riechen an (+ dat) ● vi riechen (of nach)

smelly /ˈsmelɪ/ adj übel riechend

smelt /smelt/ see smell

smile /smaɪl/ n Lächeln nt ● vi lä-

cheln; ~ at anlächeln

smirk /smɜːk/ vi feixen

smith /smɪθ/ n Schmied m

smock /smɒk/ n Kittel m

smog /smɒg/ n Smog m

smoke /sməʊk/ n Rauch m ● vt/i rauchen; (Culin) räuchern. ~**less** adj rauchfrei; (fuel) rauchlos

smoker /ˈsməʊkə(r)/ n Raucher m; (Rail) Raucherabteil nt

smoking /ˈsməʊkɪŋ/ n Rauchen nt; 'no ~' 'Rauchen verboten'

smoky /ˈsməʊkɪ/ adj verraucht; (taste) rauchig

smooth /smuːð/ adj (-er, -est) glatt ● vt glätten. ~ **out** vt glatt streichen

smother /ˈsmʌðə(r)/ vt ersticken; (cover) bedecken; (suppress) unterdrücken

smoulder /ˈsməʊldə(r)/ vi schwelen

smudge /smʌdʒ/ n Fleck m ● vt verwischen ● vi schmieren

smug /smʌg/ adj (smugger, smuggest) selbstgefällig

smuggl|e /ˈsmʌgl/ vt schmuggeln. ~**er** n Schmuggler m. ~**ing** n Schmuggel m

snack /snæk/ n Imbiss m. ~-**bar** n Imbissstube f

snag /snæg/ n Schwierigkeit f, 🗆 Haken m

snail /sneɪl/ n Schnecke f; at a ~'s pace im Schneckentempo

snake /sneɪk/ n Schlange f

snap /snæp/ n Knacken nt; (photo) Schnappschuss m ● attrib (decision) plötzlich ● v (pt/pp snapped) ● vi [entzwei]brechen; ~ at (bite) schnappen nach; (speak sharply) [scharf] anfahren ● vt zerbrechen; (say) fauchen; (Phot) knipsen. ~ **up** vt wegschnappen

snappy /'snæpɪ/ *adj* (*smart*) flott; make it ~! ein bisschen schnell!

'snapshot *n* Schnappschuss *m*

snare /sneə(r)/ *n* Schlinge *f*

snarl /snɑːl/ *vi* [mit gefletschten Zähnen] knurren

snatch /snætʃ/ *n* (*fragment*) Fetzen *pl* • *vt* schnappen; (*steal*) klauen; entführen (*child*); ~ **sth** from s.o. jdm etw entreißen

sneak /sniːk/ *n* 🄵 Petze *f* • *vi* schleichen; (🄵: *tell tales*) petzen • *vt* (*take*) mitgehen lassen • *vi* ~ **in/out** sich hinein-/hinausschleichen

sneakers /'sniːkəz/ *npl* (*Amer*) Turnschuhe *pl*

sneer /snɪə(r)/ *vi* höhnisch lächeln; (*mock*) spotten

sneeze /sniːz/ *n* Niesen *nt* • *vi* niesen

snide /snaɪd/ *adj* 🄵 abfällig

sniff /snɪf/ *vi* schnüffeln • *vt* schnüffeln an (+ *dat*)

snigger /'snɪgə(r)/ *vi* [boshaft] kichern

snip /snɪp/ *n* Schnitt *m* • *vt/i* ~ [**at**] schnippeln an (+ *dat*)

snippet /'snɪpɪt/ *n* Schnipsel *m*; (*of information*) Bruchstück *nt*

snivel /'snɪvl/ *vi* (*pt/pp* snivelled) flennen

snob /snɒb/ *n* Snob *m*. **~bery** *n* Snobismus *m*. **~bish** *adj* snobistisch

snoop /snuːp/ *vi* 🄵 schnüffeln

snooty /'snuːtɪ/ *adj* 🄵 hochnäsig

snooze /snuːz/ *n* Nickerchen *nt* • *vi* dösen

snore /snɔː(r)/ *vi* schnarchen

snorkel /'snɔːkl/ *n* Schnorchel *m*

snort /snɔːt/ *vi* schnauben

snout /snaʊt/ *n* Schnauze *f*

snow /snəʊ/ *n* Schnee *m* • *vi* schneien; **~ed under with** (*fig*) überhäuft mit

snow: **~ball** *n* Schneeball *m*. **~board** *n* Snowboard *nt*. **~drift** *n* Schneewehe *f*. **~drop** *n* Schneeglöckchen *nt*. **~fall** *n* Schneefall *m*. **~flake** *n* Schneeflocke *f*. **~man** *n* Schneemann *m*. **~plough** *n* Schneepflug *m*

snub /snʌb/ *n* Abfuhr *f* • *vt* (*pt/pp* snubbed) brüskieren

'snub-nosed *adj* stupsnasig

snuffle /'snʌfl/ *vi* schnüffeln

snug /snʌg/ *adj* (snugger, snuggest) behaglich, gemütlich

snuggle /'snʌgl/ *vi* sich kuscheln (up to an + *acc*)

so /səʊ/ *adv* so; so am I ich auch; so I see das sehe ich; that is so das stimmt; so much the better umso besser; if so wenn ja; so as to um zu; so long! 🄵 tschüs! I hope so hoffentlich; I think so ich glaube schon; I'm afraid so leider ja; so saying/doing, he/she ... indem er/sie das sagte/tat, ... • *con* (*therefore*) also; so that damit; so what! na und! so you see wie du siehst

soak /səʊk/ *vt* nass machen; (*steep*) einweichen; (🄵: *fleece*) schröpfen • *vi* weichen; (*liquid:*) sickern. **~ up** *vt* aufsaugen

soaking /'səʊkɪŋ/ *adj & adv* ~ [**wet**] patschnass 🄵

soap /səʊp/ *n* Seife *f*. **~ opera** *n* Seifenoper *f*. **~ powder** *n* Seifenpulver *nt*

soapy /'səʊpɪ/ *adj* seifig

soar /sɔː(r)/ *vi* aufsteigen; (*prices:*) in die Höhe schnellen

sob /sɒb/ *n* Schluchzer *m* • *vi* (*pt/pp* sobbed) schluchzen

sober /'səʊbə(r)/ *adj* (*serious*) ernst; (*colour*) gedeckt. **~ up** *vi* nüchtern werden

'so-called adj sogenannt

soccer /'sɒkə(r)/ n Ⓔ Fußball m

sociable /'səʊʃəbl/ adj gesellig

social /'səʊʃl/ adj gesellschaftlich; (Admin, Pol, Zool) sozial

socialis|m /'səʊʃəlɪzm/ n Sozialismus m. ~t adj sozialistisch ●n Sozialist m

socialize /'səʊʃəlaɪz/ vi [gesellschaftlich] verkehren

socially /'səʊʃəlɪ/ adv gesellschaftlich; know ~ privat kennen

social: ~ **security** n Sozialhilfe f. ~ **worker** n Sozialarbeiter(in) m(f)

society /sə'saɪətɪ/ n Gesellschaft f; (club) Verein m

sociolog|ist /səʊsɪ'ɒlədʒɪst/ n Soziologe m. ~**y** n Soziologie f

sock /sɒk/ n Socke f; (kneelength) Kniestrumpf m

socket /'sɒkɪt/ n (of eye) Augenhöhle f; (of joint) Gelenkpfanne f; (wall plug) Steckdose f

soda /'səʊdə/ n Soda nt; (Amer) Limonade f. ~ **water** n Sodawasser nt

sodden /'sɒdn/ adj durchnässt

sofa /'səʊfə/ n Sofa nt. ~ **bed** n Schlafcouch f

soft /sɒft/ adj (-er, -est) weich; (quiet) leise; (gentle) sanft; (Ⓔ silly) dumm. ~ **drink** n alkoholfreies Getränk nt

soften /'sɒfn/ vt weich machen; (fig) mildern ●vi weich werden

soft: ~ **toy** n Stofftier nt. ~**ware** n Software f

soggy /'sɒgɪ/ adj aufgeweicht

soil[1] /sɔɪl/ n Erde f, Boden m

soil[2] vt verschmutzen

solar /'səʊlə(r)/ adj Sonnen-

sold /səʊld/ see **sell**

soldier /'səʊldʒə(r)/ n Soldat m ●vi ~ **on** [unbeirrbar] weiter-

machen

sole[1] /səʊl/ n Sohle f

sole[2] n (fish) Seezunge f

sole[3] adj einzig. ~**ly** adv einzig und allein

solemn /'sɒləm/ adj feierlich; (serious) ernst

solicitor /sə'lɪsɪtə(r)/ n Rechtsanwalt m/-anwältin f

solid /'sɒlɪd/ adj fest; (sturdy) stabil; (not hollow, of same substance) massiv; (unanimous) einstimmig; (complete) ganz

solidarity /sɒlɪ'dærətɪ/ n Solidarität f

solidify /sə'lɪdɪfaɪ/ vi (pt/pp -ied) fest werden

solitary /'sɒlɪtərɪ/ adj einsam; (sole) einzig

solitude /'sɒlɪtjuːd/ n Einsamkeit f

solo /'səʊləʊ/ n Solo nt ●adj Solo-; (flight) Allein- ●adv solo. ~**ist** n Solist(in) m(f)

solstice /'sɒlstɪs/ n Sonnenwende f

soluble /'sɒljʊbl/ adj löslich

solution /sə'luːʃn/ n Lösung f

solvable /'sɒlvəbl/ adj lösbar

solve /sɒlv/ vt lösen

solvent /'sɒlvənt/ n Lösungsmittel nt

sombre /'sɒmbə(r)/ adj dunkel; (mood) düster

some /sʌm/ adj & pron etwas; (a little) ein bisschen; (with pl noun) einige; (a few) ein paar; (certain) manche(r,s); (one or the other) [irgend]ein; ~ **day** eines Tages; I want ~ ich möchte etwas; (pl) welche; will you have ~ **wine?** möchten Sie Wein? do ~ **shopping** einkaufen

some: ~**body** /-bədɪ/ pron & n jemand; (emphatic) irgendjemand. ~**how** adv irgendwie. ~**one** pron & n = **somebody**

somersault /'sʌməsɔːlt/ n Purzelbaum m 🖽; (Sport) Salto m; turn a ~ einen Purzelbaum schlagen/einen Salto springen

'something pron & adv etwas; (emphatic) irgendetwas; ~ different etwas anderes; ~ like this so etwas [wie das]

some: ~**time** adv irgendwann ● adj ehemalig. ~**times** adv manchmal. ~**what** adv ziemlich. ~**where** adv irgendwo; (go) irgendwohin

son /sʌn/ n Sohn m

song /sɒŋ/ n Lied nt. ~**bird** n Singvogel m

'son-in-law n (pl ~s-in-law) Schwiegersohn m

soon /suːn/ adv (-er, -est) bald; (quickly) schnell; too ~ zu früh; as ~ as possible so bald wie möglich; ~er or later früher oder später; no ~er had I arrived than ... kaum war ich angekommen, da ...; I would ~er stay ich würde lieber bleiben

soot /sʊt/ n Ruß m

sooth|e /suːð/ vt beruhigen; lindern (pain). ~**ing** adj beruhigend; lindernd

sophisticated /sə'fɪstɪkeɪtɪd/ adj weltgewandt; (complex) hoch entwickelt

sopping /'sɒpɪŋ/ adj & adv ~[wet] durchnässt

soppy /'sɒpɪ/ adj 🖽 rührselig

soprano /sə'prɑːnəʊ/ n Sopran m; (woman) Sopranistin f

sordid /'sɔːdɪd/ adj schmutzig

sore /sɔː(r)/ adj (-r, -st) wund; (painful) schmerzhaft; have a ~ throat Halsschmerzen haben ● n wunde Stelle f. ~**ly** adv sehr

sorrow /'sɒrəʊ/ n Kummer m

sorry /'sɒrɪ/ adj (sad) traurig;

(wretched) erbärmlich; I am ~ es tut mir Leid; she is or feels ~ for him er tut ihr Leid; I am ~ to say leider; ~! Entschuldigung!

sort /sɔːt/ n Art f; (brand) Sorte f; he's a good ~ 🖽 er ist in Ordnung ● vt sortieren. ~ **out** vt sortieren; (fig) klären

sought /sɔːt/ see **seek**

soul /səʊl/ n Seele f

sound[1] /saʊnd/ adj (-er, -est) gesund; (sensible) vernünftig; (secure) solide; (thorough) gehörig ● adv be ~ asleep fest schlafen

sound[2] n (strait) Meerenge f

sound[3] n Laut m; (noise) Geräusch nt; (Phys) Schall m; (Radio, TV) Ton m; (of bells, music) Klang m; I don't like the ~ of it 🖽 das hört sich nicht gut an ● vi [er]tönen; (seem) sich anhören ● vt (pronounce) aussprechen; schlagen (alarm); (Med) abhorchen (chest)

soundly /'saʊndlɪ/ adv solide; (sleep) fest; (defeat) vernichtend

'soundproof adj schalldicht

soup /suːp/ n Suppe f

sour /'saʊə(r)/ adj (-er, -est) sauer; (bad-tempered) griesgrämig, verdrießlich

source /sɔːs/ n Quelle f

south /saʊθ/ n Süden m; to the ~ of südlich von ● adj Süd-, südlich ● adv nach Süden

south: S~ **'Africa** n Südafrika nt. S~ **A'merica** n Südamerika nt. ~**'east** n Südosten m

southerly /'sʌðəlɪ/ adj südlich

southern /'sʌðən/ adj südlich

'southward[s] /-wəd[z]/ adv nach Süden

souvenir /suːvə'nɪə(r)/ n Andenken nt, Souvenir nt

Soviet /'səʊvɪət/ adj (History) sowjetisch; ~ **Union** Sowjetunion f

sow[1] /saʊ/ n Sau f

sow[2] /səʊ/ vt (pt sowed, pp sown or sowed) säen

soya /'sɔɪə/ n ~ bean Sojabohne f

spa /spɑ:/ n Heilbad nt

space /speɪs/ n Raum m; (gap) Platz m; (Astronomy) Weltraum m ●vt ~ [out] [in Abständen] verteilen

space: ~**craft** n Raumfahrzeug nt. ~**ship** n Raumschiff nt

spacious /'speɪʃəs/ adj geräumig

spade /speɪd/ n Spaten m; (for child) Schaufel f; ~**s** pl (Cards) Pik nt

Spain /speɪn/ n Spanien nt

span[1] /spæn/ n Spanne f; (of arch) Spannweite f ●vt (pt/pp spanned) überspannen; umspannen

span[2] see **spick**

Span|**iard** /'spænjəd/ n Spanier(in) m(f). ~**ish** adj spanisch ●n (Lang) Spanisch nt; **the** ~**ish** pl die Spanier

spank /spæŋk/ vt verhauen

spanner /'spænə(r)/ n Schraubenschlüssel m

spare /speə(r)/ adj (surplus) übrig; (additional) zusätzlich; (seat, time) frei; (room) Gäste-; (bed, cup) Extra- ●n (part) Ersatzteil nt ●vt ersparen; (not hurt) verschonen; (do without) entbehren; (afford to give) erübrigen. ~ '**wheel** n Reserverad nt

sparing /'speərɪŋ/ adj sparsam

spark /spɑ:k/ n Funke m. ~[**ing**]-**plug** n (Auto) Zündkerze f

sparkl|**e** /'spɑ:kl/ n Funkeln nt ●vi funkeln. ~**ing** adj funkelnd; (wine) Schaum-

sparrow /'spærəʊ/ n Spatz m

sparse /spɑ:s/ adj spärlich. ~**ly** adv spärlich; (populated) dünn

spasm /'spæzm/ n Anfall m;

(cramp) Krampf m. ~**odic** adj, -**ally** adv sporadisch

spastic /'spæstɪk/ adj spastisch [gelähmt] ●n Spastiker(in) m(f)

spat /spæt/ see **spit**[2]

spatter /'spætə(r)/ vt spritzen; ~ **with** bespritzen mit

spawn /spɔ:n/ n Laich m ●vt (fig) hervorbringen

speak /spi:k/ vi (pt spoke, pp spoken) ●vi sprechen (to mit) ~**ing!** (Teleph) am Apparat! ●vt sprechen; sagen (truth). ~ **up** vi lauter sprechen; ~ **up for oneself** seine Meinung äußern

speaker /'spi:kə(r)/ n Sprecher(in) m(f); (in public) Redner(in) m(f); (loudspeaker) Lautsprecher m

spear /spɪə(r)/ n Speer m ●vt aufspießen

spec /spek/ n **on** ~ 🄸 auf gut Glück

special /'speʃl/ adj besondere(r,s), speziell. ~**ist** n Spezialist m; (Med) Facharzt m/-ärztin f. ~**ity** n Spezialität f

special|**ize** /'speʃəlaɪz/ vi sich spezialisieren (in auf + acc). ~**ly** adv speziell; (particularly) besonders

species /'spi:ʃi:z/ n Art f

specific /spə'sɪfɪk/ adj bestimmt; (precise) genau; (Phys) spezifisch. ~**ally** adv ausdrücklich

specification /spesɪfɪ'keɪʃn/ n (also ~**s**) pl genaue Angaben pl

specify /'spesɪfaɪ/ vt (pt/pp -ied) [genau] angeben

specimen /'spesɪmən/ n Exemplar nt; (sample) Probe f; (of urine) Urinprobe f

speck /spek/ n Fleck m

speckled /'spekld/ adj gesprenkelt

spectacle /'spektəkl/ n (show) Schauspiel nt; (sight) Anblick m. ~**s** npl Brille f

spectacular /spek'tækjʊlə(r)/ adj spektakulär

spectator /spek'teɪtə(r)/ n Zuschauer(in) m(f)

speculat|e /'spekjʊleɪt/ vi spekulieren. **∼ion** n Spekulation f. **∼or** n Spekulant m

sped /sped/ see speed

speech /spiːtʃ/ n Sprache f; (address) Rede f. **∼less** adj sprachlos

speed /spiːd/ n Geschwindigkeit f; (rapidity) Schnelligkeit f ● vi (pt/pp sped) schnell fahren ● (pt/pp speeded) (go too fast) zu schnell fahren. **∼ up** (pt/pp speeded up) ● vt/i beschleunigen

speed: **∼boat** n Rennboot nt. **∼-camera** n Geschwindigkeitsüberwachungskamera f. **∼ dating** n Speeddating nt. **∼ing** n Geschwindigkeitsüberschreitung f. **∼ limit** n Geschwindigkeitsbeschränkung f

speedometer /spiːˈdɒmɪtə(r)/ n Tachometer m

speedy /'spiːdɪ/ adj , **-ily** adv schnell

spell¹ /spel/ n (of weather) Periode f

spell² v (pt/pp spelled or spelt) ● vt schreiben; (aloud) buchstabieren; (fig: mean) bedeuten ● vi richtig schreiben; (aloud) buchstabieren. **∼ out** vt buchstabieren; (fig) genau erklären

spell³ n Zauber m; (words) Zauberspruch m. **∼bound** adj wie verzaubert

'spell checker n Rechtschreibprogramm nt

spelling /'spelɪŋ/ n (of a word) Schreibweise f; (orthography) Rechtschreibung f

spelt /spelt/ see spell²

spend /spend/ vt/i (pt/pp spent) ausgeben; verbringen (time)

spent /spent/ see spend

sperm /spɜːm/ n Samen m

sphere /sfɪə(r)/ n Kugel f; (fig) Sphäre f

spice /spaɪs/ n Gewürz nt; (fig) Würze f

spicy /'spaɪsɪ/ adj würzig, pikant

spider /'spaɪdə(r)/ n Spinne f

spik|e /spaɪk/ n Spitze f; (Bot, Zool) Stachel m; (on shoe) Spike m. **∼y** adj stachelig

spill /spɪl/ v (pt/pp spilt or spilled) ● vt verschütten ● vi überlaufen

spin /spɪn/ v (pt/pp spun, pres p spinning) ● vt drehen; spinnen (wool); schleudern (washing) ● vi sich drehen

spinach /'spɪnɪdʒ/ n Spinat m

spindl|e /'spɪndl/ n Spindel f. **∼y** adj spindeldürr

spin-'drier n Wäscheschleuder f

spine /spaɪn/ n Rückgrat nt; (of book) [Buch]rücken m; (Bot, Zool) Stachel m. **∼less** adj (fig) rückgratlos

'spin-off n Nebenprodukt nt

spinster /'spɪnstə(r)/ n ledige Frau f

spiral /'spaɪrl/ adj spiralig ● n Spirale f ● vi (pt/pp spiralled) sich hochwinden. **∼ 'staircase** n Wendeltreppe f

spire /'spaɪə(r)/ n Turmspitze f

spirit /'spɪrɪt/ n Geist m; (courage) Mut m; **∼s** pl (alcohol) Spirituosen pl; in low **∼s** niedergedrückt. **∼ away** vt verschwinden lassen

spirited /'spɪrɪtɪd/ adj lebhaft; (courageous) beherzt

spiritual /'spɪrɪtjʊəl/ adj geistig; (Relig) geistlich

spit¹ /spɪt/ n (for roasting) [Brat]spieß m

spit² n Spucke f ● vt/i (pt/pp spat,

pres p spitting) spucken; (*cat:*) fauchen; (*fat:*) spritzen; it's ~ting with rain es tröpfelt

spite /spaɪt/ *n* Boshaftigkeit *f*; in ~ of trotz (+ *gen*) ● *vt* ärgern. ~ful *adj* gehässig

splash /splæʃ/ *n* Platschen *nt*; (ɪ: *drop*) Schuss *m*; ~ of colour Farbfleck *m* ● *vt* spritzen; ~ s.o. with sth jdn mit etw bespritzen ● *vi* spritzen. ~ about *vi* planschen

splendid /'splendɪd/ *adj* herrlich, großartig

splendour /'splendə(r)/ *n* Pracht *f*

splint /splɪnt/ *n* (Med) Schiene *f*

splinter /'splɪntə(r)/ *n* Splitter *m* ● *vi* zersplittern

split /splɪt/ *n* Spaltung *f*; (*Pol*) Bruch *m*; (*tear*) Riss *m* ● *v* (*pt/pp* split, *pres p* splitting) ● *vt* spalten; (*share*) teilen; (*tear*) zerreißen ● *vi* sich spalten; (*tear*) zerreißen; ~ on s.o. ɪ jdn verpfeifen. ~ up *vt* aufteilen ● *vi* (*couple:*) sich trennen

splutter /'splʌtə(r)/ *vi* prusten

spoil /spɔɪl/ *n* ~s *pl* Beute *f* ● *v* (*pt/pp* spoilt or spoiled) ● *vt* verderben; verwöhnen (*person*) ● *vi* verderben. ~sport *n* Spielverderber *m*

spoke[1] /spəʊk/ *n* Speiche *f*

spoke[2], **spoken** *see* speak

'spokesman *n* Sprecher *m*

sponge /spʌndʒ/ *n* Schwamm *m* ● *vt* abwaschen ● *vi* ~ on schmarotzen bei. ~bag *n* Waschbeutel *m*. ~cake *n* Biskuitkuchen *m*

sponsor /'spɒnsə(r)/ *n* Sponsor *m*; (*godparent*) Pate *m*/Patin *f* ● *vt* sponsern

spontaneous /spɒn'teɪnɪəs/ *adj* spontan

spoof /spu:f/ *n* ɪ Parodie *f*

spooky /'spu:kɪ/ *adj* ɪ gespenstisch

spool /spu:l/ *n* Spule *f*

spoon /spu:n/ *n* Löffel *m* ● *vt* löffeln. ~ful *n* Löffel *m*

sporadic /spə'rædɪk/ *adj*, **-ally** *adv* sporadisch

sport /spɔ:t/ *n* Sport *m* ● *vt* [stolz] tragen. ~ing *adj* sportlich

sports: ~car *n* Sportwagen *m*. ~coat *n*, ~jacket *n* Sakko *m*. ~man *n* Sportler *m*. ~woman *n* Sportlerin *f*

sporty /'spɔ:tɪ/ *adj* sportlich

spot /spɒt/ *n* Fleck *m*; (*place*) Stelle *f* (*dot*) Punkt *m*; (*drop*) Tropfen *m*; (*pimple*) Pickel *m*; ~s *pl* (*rash*) Ausschlag *m*; on the ~ auf der Stelle ● *vt* (*pt/pp* spotted) entdecken

spot: ~'check *n* Stichprobe *f*. ~less *adj* makellos; (ɪ: *very clean*) blitzsauber. ~light *n* Scheinwerfer *m*; (*fig*) Rampenlicht *nt*

spotted /'spɒtɪd/ *adj* gepunktet

spouse /spaʊz/ *n* Gatte *m*/Gattin *f*

spout /spaʊt/ *n* Schnabel *m*, Tülle *f* ● *vi* schießen (from aus)

sprain /spreɪn/ *n* Verstauchung *f* ● *vt* verstauchen

sprang /spræŋ/ *see* spring[2]

sprawl /sprɔ:l/ *vi* sich ausstrecken

spray[1] /spreɪ/ *n* (*of flowers*) Strauß *m*

spray[2] *n* Sprühnebel *m*; (*from sea*) Gischt *m*; (*device*) Spritze *f*; (*container*) Sprühdose *f*; (*preparation*) Spray *nt* ● *vt* spritzen; (*with aerosol*) sprühen

spread /spred/ *n* Verbreitung *f*; (*paste*) Aufstrich *m*; (ɪ: *feast*) Festessen *nt* ● *v* (*pt/pp* spread) ● *vt* ausbreiten; streichen (*butter, jam*); bestreichen (*bread, surface*); streuen (*sand, manure*); verbreiten (*news, disease*); verteilen (*payments*) ● *vi* sich ausbreiten. ~ out *vt* ausbreiten; (*space out*) verteilen ● *vi* sich verteilen

spree /spri:/ n 🔢 go on a shopping ~ groß einkaufen gehen

sprightly /'spraɪtlɪ/ adj rüstig

spring¹ /sprɪŋ/ n Frühling m ● attrib Frühlings-

spring² n (jump) Sprung m; (water) Quelle f; (device) Feder f; (elasticity) Elastizität f ● vi (pt sprang, pp sprung) ● vi springen; (arise) entspringen (from dat) ● vt ~ sth on s.o. jdn mit etw überfallen

spring: ~-'cleaning n Frühjahrsputz m. ~time n Frühling m

sprinkl|e /'sprɪŋkl/ vt sprengen; (scatter) streuen; bestreuen (surface). ~ing n dünne Schicht f

sprint /sprɪnt/ n Sprint m ● vi rennen; (Sport) sprinten. ~er n Kurzstreckenläufer(in) m(f)

sprout /spraʊt/ n Trieb m; [Brussels] ~s pl Rosenkohl m ● vi sprießen

sprung /sprʌŋ/ see spring²

spud /spʌd/ n 🔢 Kartoffel f

spun /spʌn/ see spin

spur /spɜ:(r)/ n Sporn m; (stimulus) Ansporn m; on the ~ of the moment ganz spontan ● vt (pt/pp spurred) ~ [on] (fig) anspornen

spurn /spɜ:n/ vt verschmähen

spurt /spɜ:t/ n (Sport) Spurt m; put on a ~ spurten ● vi spritzen

spy /spaɪ/ n Spion(in) m(f) ● vi spionieren; ~ on s.o. jdm nachspionieren; ~ sth (🔢: see) sehen

spying /'spaɪɪŋ/ n Spionage f

squabble /'skwɒbl/ n Zank m ● vi sich zanken

squad /skwɒd/ n Gruppe f; (Sport) Mannschaft f

squadron /'skwɒdrən/ n (Mil) Geschwader nt

squalid /'skwɒlɪd/ adj schmutzig

squall /skwɔ:l/ n Bö f ● vi brüllen

squalor /'skwɒlə(r)/ n Schmutz m

squander /'skwɒndə(r)/ vt vergeuden

square /skweə(r)/ adj quadratisch; (metre, mile) Quadrat-; (meal) anständig; all ~ 🔢 quitt ● n Quadrat nt; (area) Platz m; (on chessboard) Feld n ● vt (settle) klären; (Math) quadrieren

squash /skwɒʃ/ n Gedränge nt; (drink) Fruchtsaftgetränk nt; (Sport) Squash nt ● vt zerquetschen; (suppress) niederschlagen. ~y adj weich

squat /skwɒt/ adj gedrungen ● vi (pt/pp squatted) hocken; ~ in a house ein Haus besetzen. ~ter n Hausbesetzer m

squawk /skwɔ:k/ vi krächzen

squeak /skwi:k/ n Quieken nt; (of hinge, brakes) Quietschen nt ● vi quieken; quietschen

squeal /skwi:l/ n Kreischen nt ● vi kreischen

squeamish /'skwi:mɪʃ/ adj empfindlich

squeeze /skwi:z/ n Druck m; (crush) Gedränge nt ● vt drücken; (to get juice) ausdrücken; (force) zwängen

squiggle /'skwɪgl/ n Schnörkel m

squint /skwɪnt/ n Schielen nt ● vi schielen

squirm /skwɜ:m/ vi sich winden

squirrel /'skwɪrl/ n Eichhörnchen nt

squirt /skwɜ:t/ n Spritzer m ● vt/i spritzen

St abbr (Saint) St.; (Street) Str.

stab /stæb/ n Stich m; (🔢: attempt) Versuch m ● vt (pt/pp stabbed) stechen; (to death) erstechen

stability /stə'bɪlətɪ/ n Stabilität f

stable[1] /'steɪbl/ adj (-r, -st) stabil

stable[2] n Stall m; (establishment) Reitstall m

stack /stæk/ n Stapel m; (of chimney) Schornstein m ● vt stapeln

stadium /'steɪdɪəm/ n Stadion nt

staff /stɑːf/ n (stick & Mil) Stab m ● (& pl) (employees) Personal nt; (Sch) Lehrkräfte pl ● vt mit Personal besetzen. **~-room** n (Sch) Lehrerzimmer nt

stag /stæg/ n Hirsch m

stage /steɪdʒ/ n Bühne f; (in journey) Etappe f; (in process) Stadium nt; by or in ~s in Etappen ● vt aufführen; (arrange) veranstalten

stagger /'stægə(r)/ vi taumeln ● vt staffeln (holidays); versetzt anordnen (seats); I was ~ed es hat mir die Sprache verschlagen. **~ing** adj unglaublich

stagnant /'stægnənt/ adj stehend; (fig) stagnierend

stagnate /stæg'neɪt/ vi (fig) stagnieren

stain /steɪn/ n Fleck m; (for wood) Beize f ● vt färben; beizen (wood); **~ed glass** farbiges Glas nt. **~less** adj (steel) rostfrei

stair /steə(r)/ n Stufe f; ~s pl Treppe f. **~case** n Treppe f

stake /steɪk/ n Pfahl m; (wager) Einsatz m; (Comm) Anteil m; **be at ~** auf dem Spiel stehen ● vt ~ **a claim to sth** Anspruch auf etw (acc) erheben

stale /steɪl/ adj (-r, -st) alt; (air) verbraucht. **~mate** n Patt nt

stalk[1] /stɔːk/ n Stiel m, Stängel m

stall /stɔːl/ n Stand m; ~s pl (Theat) Parkett nt ● vi (engine:) stehen bleiben; (fig) ausweichen ● vt abwürgen (engine)

stalwart /'stɔːlwət/ adj treu ● n treuer Anhänger m

stamina /'stæmɪnə/ n Ausdauer f

stammer /'stæmə(r)/ n Stottern nt ● vt/i stottern

stamp /stæmp/ n Stempel m; (postage ~) [Brief]marke f ● vt stempeln; (impress) prägen; (put postage on) frankieren ● vi stampfen. ~ **out** vt [aus]stanzen; (fig) ausmerzen

stampede /stæm'piːd/ n wilde Flucht f ● vi in Panik fliehen

stance /stɑːns/ n Haltung f

stand /stænd/ n Stand m; (rack) Ständer m; (pedestal) Sockel m; (Sport) Tribüne f; (fig) Einstellung f ● v (pt/pp stood) ● vi stehen; (rise) aufstehen; (be candidate) kandidieren; (stay valid) gültig bleiben; ~ **still** stillstehen; ~ **firm** (fig) festbleiben; ~ **to reason** logisch sein; ~ **in for** vertreten; ~ **for** (mean) bedeuten ● vt stellen; (withstand) standhalten (+ dat); (endure) ertragen; vertragen (climate); (put up with) aushalten; haben (chance); ~ **s.o. a beer** jdm ein Bier spendieren; **I can't ~ her** 🔊 ich kann sie nicht ausstehen. ~ **by** vi daneben stehen; (be ready) sich bereithalten ● vt ~ **by s.o.** (fig) zu jdm stehen. ~ **down** vi (retire) zurücktreten. ~ **out** vi hervorstehen; (fig) herausragen. ~ **up** vi aufstehen; ~ **up for** eintreten für; ~ **up to** sich wehren gegen

standard /'stændəd/ adj Normal- ● n Maßstab m; (Techn) Norm f; (level) Niveau nt; (flag) Standarte f. ~s pl (morals) Prinzipien pl. **~ize** vt standardisieren; (Techn) normen

'stand-in n Ersatz m

standing /'stændɪŋ/ adj (erect) stehend; (permanent) ständig ● n Rang m; (duration) Dauer f. **~-room** n Stehplätze pl

stand: **~-offish** /stænd'ɒfɪʃ/ adj

distanziert. ~point n Standpunkt m. ~still n Stillstand m; come to a ~still zum Stillstand kommen

stank /stæŋk/ see stink

staple¹ /'sterpl/ adj Grund-

staple² n Heftklammer f ● vt heften. ~r n Heftmaschine f

star /stɑ:(r)/ n Stern m; (asterisk) Sternchen nt; (Theat, Sport) Star m ● vi (pt/pp starred) die Hauptrolle spielen

starboard /'stɑ:bəd/ n Steuerbord nt

starch /stɑ:tʃ/ n Stärke f ● vt stärken. ~y adj stärkehaltig; (fig) steif

stare /steə(r)/ n Starren nt ● vt starren; ~ at anstarren

stark /stɑ:k/ adj (-er, -est) scharf; (contrast) krass

starling /'stɑ:lɪŋ/ n Star m

start /stɑ:t/ n Anfang m, Beginn m; (departure) Aufbruch m; (Sport) Start m; from the ~ von Anfang an; for a ~ erstens ● vi anfangen, beginnen; (set out) aufbrechen; (engine:) anspringen; (Auto, Sport) starten; (jump) aufschrecken; to ~ with zuerst ● vt anfangen, beginnen; (cause) verursachen; (found) gründen; starten (car, race); in Umlauf setzen (rumour). ~er n (Culin) Vorspeise f; (Auto, Sport) Starter m. ~ing-point n Ausgangspunkt m

startle /'stɑ:tl/ vt erschrecken

starvation /stɑ:'veɪʃn/ n Verhungern nt

starve /stɑ:v/ vi hungern; (to death) verhungern ● vt verhungern lassen

state /steɪt/ n Zustand m; (Pol) Staat m; ~ of play Spielstand m; be in a ~ (person:) aufgeregt sein ● attrib Staats-, staatlich ● vt erklären; (specify) angeben

stately /'steɪtlɪ/ adj stattlich. ~

'**home** n Schloss nt

statement /'steɪtmənt/ n Erklärung f; (Jur) Aussage f; (Banking) Auszug m

'**statesman** n Staatsmann m

static /'stætɪk/ adj statisch; remain ~ unverändert bleiben

station /'steɪʃn/ n Bahnhof m; (police) Wache f; (radio) Sender m; (space, weather) Station f; (Mil) Posten m; (status) Rang m ● vt stationieren; (post) postieren. ~ary adj stehend; be ~ary stehen

stationery /'steɪʃənrɪ/ n Briefpapier nt; (writing materials) Schreibwaren pl

'**station-wagon** n (Amer) Kombi[wagen] n

statistic /stə'tɪstɪk/ n statistische Tatsache f. ~al adj statistisch. ~s n & pl Statistik f

statue /'stætju:/ n Statue f

stature /'stætʃə(r)/ n Statur f; (fig) Format n

status /'steɪtəs/ n Status m, Rang m

statut|e /'stætju:t/ n Statut nt. ~ory adj gesetzlich

staunch /stɔ:ntʃ/ adj (-er, -est) treu

stave /steɪv/ vt ~ off abwenden

stay /steɪ/ n Aufenthalt m ● vi bleiben; (reside) wohnen; ~ the night übernachten. **~ behind** vi zurückbleiben. **~ in** vi zu Hause bleiben; (Sch) nachsitzen. **~ up** vi (person:) aufbleiben

steadily /'stedɪlɪ/ adv fest; (continually) stetig

steady /'stedɪ/ adj fest; (not wobbly) stabil; (hand) ruhig; (regular) regelmäßig; (dependable) zuverlässig

steak /steɪk/ n Steak nt

steal /stiːl/ vt/i (pt stole, pp stolen) stehlen (from dat). **~ in/out** vi sich hinein-/hinausstehlen

stealthy /'stelθɪ/ adj heimlich

steam /stiːm/ n Dampf m ● vt (Culin) dämpfen, dünsten ● vi dampfen. **~ up** vi beschlagen

'steam engine n Dampfmaschine f; (Rail) Dampflokomotive f

steamer /'stiːmə(r)/ n Dampfer m

steamy /'stiːmɪ/ adj dampfig

steel /stiːl/ n Stahl m

steep /stiːp/ adj steil; (fig: exorbitant) gesalzen

steeple /'stiːpl/ n Kirchturm m

steer /stɪə(r)/ vt/i (Auto) lenken; (Naut) steuern; **~ clear of s.o./sth** jdm/ etw aus dem Weg gehen. **~ing** n (Auto) Lenkung f. **~ing-wheel** n Lenkrad nt

stem[1] /stem/ n Stiel m; (of word) Stamm m

stem[2] vt (pt/pp stemmed) eindämmen; stillen (bleeding)

stench /stentʃ/ n Gestank m

stencil /'stensl/ n Schablone f

step /step/ n Schritt m; (stair) Stufe f; **~s** pl (ladder) Trittleiter f; **in ~** im Schritt; **~ by ~** Schritt für Schritt; **take ~s** (fig) Schritte unternehmen ● vi (pt/pp stepped) treten; **~ in** (fig) eingreifen. **~ up** vt (increase) erhöhen, steigen; verstärken (efforts)

step: ~brother n Stiefbruder m. **~child** n Stiefkind nt. **~daughter** n Stieftochter f. **~father** n Stiefvater m. **~ladder** n Trittleiter f. **~mother** n Stiefmutter f. **~sister** n Stiefschwester f. **~son** n Stiefsohn m

stereo /'sterɪəʊ/ n Stereo nt; (equipment) Stereoanlage f. **~phonic** adj stereophon

stereotype /'sterɪətaɪp/ n stereotype Figur f

steril|e /'steraɪl/ adj steril. **~ize** vt sterilisieren

sterling /'stɜːlɪŋ/ adj Sterling-; (fig) gediegen ● n Sterling m

stern[1] /stɜːn/ adj (-er, -est) streng

stern[2] n (of boat) Heck nt

stew /stjuː/ n Eintopf m; **in a ~** 🇮🇹 aufgeregt ● vt/i schmoren; **~ed fruit** Kompott n

steward /'stjuːəd/ n Ordner m; (on ship, aircraft) Steward m. **~ess** n Stewardess f

stick[1] /stɪk/ n Stock m; (of chalk) Stück m; (of rhubarb) Stange f; (Sport) Schläger m

stick[2] v (pt/pp stuck) ● vt stecken; (stab) stechen; (glue) kleben; (🇮🇹 put) tun; (🇮🇹 endure) aushalten ● vi stecken; (adhere) kleben, haften (to an + dat); (jam) klemmen; **~ at it** 🇮🇹 dranbleiben; **~ up for** 🇮🇹 eintreten für; **be stuck** nicht weiterkönnen; (vehicle:) festsitzen, festgefahren sein; (drawer:) klemmen; **be stuck with sth** 🇮🇹 etw am Hals haben. **~ out** vi abstehen; (project) vorstehen ● vt hinausstrecken; herausstrecken (tongue)

sticker /'stɪkə(r)/ n Aufkleber m

'sticking plaster n Heftpflaster nt

sticky /'stɪkɪ/ adj klebrig; (adhesive) Klebe-

stiff /stɪf/ adj (-er, -est) steif; (brush) hart; (dough) fest; (difficult) schwierig; (penalty) schwer; be bored ~ 🔲 sich zu Tode langweilen. ~en vt steif machen ● vi steif werden. ~ness n Steifheit f

stifl|e /'staɪfl/ vt ersticken; (fig) unterdrücken. ~ing adj be ~ing zum Ersticken sein

still /stɪl/ adj still; (drink) ohne Kohlensäure; keep ~ stillhalten; stand ~ stillstehen ● adv noch; (emphatic) immer noch; (nevertheless) trotzdem; ~ not immer noch nicht

'stillborn adj tot geboren

still 'life n Stilleben nt

stilted /'stɪltɪd/ adj gestelzt, geschraubt

stimulant /'stɪmjʊlənt/ n Anregungsmittel nt

stimulat|e /'stɪmjʊleɪt/ vt anregen. ~ion n Anregung f

stimulus /'stɪmjʊləs/ n (pl -li /-laɪ/) Reiz m

sting /stɪŋ/ n Stich m; (from nettle, jellyfish) Brennen nt; (organ) Stachel m ● v (pt/pp stung) ● vt stechen ● vi brennen; (insect:) stechen

stingy /'stɪndʒɪ/ adj geizig, 🔲 knauserig

stink /stɪŋk/ n Gestank m ● vi (pt stank, pp stunk) stinken (of nach)

stipulat|e /'stɪpjʊleɪt/ vt vorschreiben. ~ion n Bedingung f

stir /stɜː(r)/ n (commotion) Aufregung f ● v (pt/pp stirred) vt rühren ● vi sich rühren

stirrup /'stɪrəp/ n Steigbügel m

stitch /stɪtʃ/ n Stich m; (Knitting) Masche f; (pain) Seitenstechen nt; be in ~es 🔲 sich kaputtlachen ● vt nähen

stock /stɒk/ n Vorrat m (of an + dat); (in shop) [Waren]bestand m; (livestock) Vieh nt; (lineage) Abstam-

mung f; (Finance) Wertpapiere pl; (Culin) Brühe f; (plant) Levkoje f; in/out of ~ vorrätig/nicht vorrätig; take ~ (fig) Bilanz ziehen ● adj Standard-. ● vt (shop:) führen; auffüllen (shelves). ~ **up** vi sich eindecken (with mit)

stock: ~**broker** n Börsenmakler m. **S~ Exchange** n Börse f

stocking /'stɒkɪŋ/ n Strumpf m

stock: ~**market** n Börse f. ~**taking** n (Comm) Inventur f

stocky /'stɒkɪ/ adj untersetzt

stodgy /'stɒdʒɪ/ adj pappig [und schwer verdaulich]

stoke /stəʊk/ vt heizen

stole /stəʊl/, **stolen** see **steal**

stomach /'stʌmək/ n Magen m. ~**ache** n Magenschmerzen pl

stone /stəʊn/ n Stein m; (weight) 6,35kg ● adj steinern; (wall, Age) Stein- ● vt mit Steinen bewerfen; entsteinen (fruit). ~**-cold** adj eiskalt. ~'**deaf** adj 🔲 stocktaub

stony /'stəʊnɪ/ adj steinig

stood /stʊd/ see **stand**

stool /stuːl/ n Hocker m

stoop /stuːp/ n walk with a ~ gebeugt gehen ● vi sich bücken

stop /stɒp/ n Halt m; (break) Pause f; (for bus) Haltestelle f; (for train) Station f; (Gram) Punkt m; (on organ) Register nt; come to a ~ stehen bleiben; put a ~ to etw (dat) ein Ende setzen ● v (pt/pp stopped) ● vt anhalten, stoppen; (switch off) abstellen; (plug, block) zustopfen; (prevent) verhindern; ~ s.o. doing sth jdn daran hindern, etw zu tun; ~ doing sth aufhören, etw zu tun; ~ that! hör auf damit! ● vi anhalten; (cease) aufhören; (clock:) stehen bleiben ● int halt!

stop: ~**gap** n Notlösung f. ~**over** n (Aviat) Zwischenlandung f

stoppage /'stɒpɪdʒ/ n Unterbrechung f; (strike) Streik m

stopper /'stɒpə(r)/ n Stöpsel m

stop-watch n Stoppuhr f

storage /'stɔːrɪdʒ/ n Aufbewahrung f; (in warehouse) Lagerung f; (Computing) Speicherung f

store /stɔː/ n (stock) Vorrat m; (shop) Laden m; (department ~) Kaufhaus nt; (depot) Lager nt; in ~ auf Lager; be in ~ for s.o. (fig) jdm bevorstehen ●vt aufbewahren; (in warehouse) lagern; (Computing) speichern. ~room n Lagerraum m

storey /'stɔːrɪ/ n Stockwerk nt

stork /stɔːk/ n Storch m

storm /stɔːm/ n Sturm m; (with thunder) Gewitter nt ●vt/i stürmen. ~y adj stürmisch

story /'stɔːrɪ/ n Geschichte f; (in newspaper) Artikel m; (𝕀: lie) Märchen nt

stout /staʊt/ adj (-er, -est) beleibt; (strong) fest

stove /stəʊv/ n Ofen m; (for cooking) Herd m

stow /stəʊ/ vt verstauen. ~away n blinder Passagier m

straggle /'strægl/ vi hinterherhinken. ~er n Nachzügler m. ~y adj strähnig

straight /streɪt/ adj (-er, -est) gerade; (direct) direkt; (clear) klar; (hair) glatt; (drink) pur; be ~ (tidy) in Ordnung sein ●adv gerade; (directly) direkt, geradewegs; (clearly) klar; ~ away sofort; ~ on or ahead geradeaus; ~ out (fig) geradeheraus; sit/stand up ~ gerade sitzen/stehen

straighten /'streɪtn/ vt gerade machen; (put straight) gerade richten ●vi gerade werden; ~ [up] (person:) sich aufrichten. ~ out vt gerade biegen

straightforward adj offen; (simple) einfach

strain¹ /streɪn/ n Belastung f; ~s pl (of music) Klänge pl ●vt belasten; (overexert) überanstrengen; (injure) zerren (muscle); (Culin) durchseihen; abgießen (vegetables). ~ed adj (relations) gespannt. ~er n Sieb nt

strait /streɪt/ n Meerenge f; in dire ~s in großen Nöten

strand¹ /strænd/ n (of thread) Faden m; (of hair) Strähne f

strand² vt be ~ed festsitzen

strange /streɪndʒ/ adj (-r, -st) fremd; (odd) seltsam, merkwürdig. ~ly adv seltsam, merkwürdig; ~ enough seltsamerweise. ~r n Fremde(r) m/f

strangle /'stræŋgl/ vt erwürgen; (fig) unterdrücken

strap /stræp/ n Riemen m; (for safety) Gurt m; (to grasp in vehicle) Halteriemen m; (of watch) Armband nt; (shoulder~) Träger m ●vt (pt/pp strapped) schnallen

strapping /'stræpɪŋ/ adj stramm

strategic /strə'tiːdʒɪk/ adj, **-ally** adv strategisch

strategy /'strætədʒɪ/ n Strategie f

straw /strɔː/ n Stroh nt; (single piece, drinking) Strohhalm m; that's the last ~ jetzt reicht's aber

strawberry /'strɔːbərɪ/ n Erdbeere f

stray /streɪ/ adj streunend ●n streunendes Tier nt ●vi sich verirren; (deviate) abweichen

streak /striːk/ n Streifen m; (in hair) Strähne f; (fig: trait) Zug m

stream /striːm/ n Bach m; (flow) Strom m; (current) Strömung f; (Sch) Parallelzug m ●vi strömen

streamline vt (fig) rationalisieren. ~d adj stromlinienförmig

street /striːt/ n Straße f. ~car n

strength | structure

556

(Amer) Straßenbahn f. ~lamp n Straßenlaterne f

strength /streŋθ/ n Stärke f; (power) Kraft f; on the ~ of auf Grund (+ gen). ~en vt stärken; (reinforce) verstärken

strenuous /'strenjʊəs/ adj anstrengend

stress /stres/ n (emphasis) Betonung f; (strain) Belastung f; (mental) Stress m ● vt betonen; (put a strain on) belasten. ~ful adj stressig 🔟

stretch /stretʃ/ n (of road) Strecke f; (elasticity) Elastizität f; at a ~ ohne Unterbrechung; have a ~ sich strecken ● vt strecken; (widen) dehnen; (spread) ausbreiten; fordern (person); ~ one's legs sich (dat) die Beine vertreten ● vi sich erstrecken; (become wider) sich dehnen; (person:) sich strecken. ~er n Tragbahre f

strict /strɪkt/ adj (-er, -est) streng; ~ly speaking streng genommen

stride /straɪd/ n [großer] Schritt m; take sth in one's ~ mit etw gut fertig werden ● vi (pt strode, pp stridden) [mit großen Schritten] gehen

strident /'straɪdnt/ adj schrill; (colour) grell

strife /straɪf/ n Streit m

strike /straɪk/ n Streik m; (Mil) Angriff m; be on ~ streiken ● v (pt/pp struck) ● vt schlagen; (knock against, collide with) treffen; anzünden (match); stoßen auf (+ acc) (oil, gold); abbrechen (camp); (impress) beeindrucken; (occur to) einfallen (+ dat); ~ s.o. a blow jdm einen Schlag versetzen ● vi (lightning:) einschlagen; (clock:) schlagen; (attack) zuschlagen; (workers:) streiken

striker /'straɪkə(r)/ n Streikende(r) m/f

striking /'straɪkɪŋ/ adj auffallend

string /strɪŋ/ n Schnur f; (thin) Bindfaden m; (of musical instrument, racket) Saite f; (of bow) Sehne f; (of pearls) Kette f; the ~s (Mus) die Streicher pl; pull ~s 🔟 seine Beziehungen spielen lassen ● vt (pt/pp strung) (thread) aufziehen (beads)

stringent /'strɪndʒnt/ adj streng

strip /strɪp/ n Streifen m ● v (pt/pp stripped) ● vt ablösen; ausziehen (person, clothes); abziehen (bed); abbeizen (wood, furniture); auseinander nehmen (machine); (deprive) berauben (of gen); ~ sth off sth etw von etw entfernen ● vi (undress) sich ausziehen

stripe /straɪp/ n Streifen m. ~d adj gestreift

stripper /'strɪpə(r)/ n Stripperin f; (male) Stripper m

strive /straɪv/ n (pt strove, pp striven) sich bemühen (to zu); ~ for streben nach

strode /strəʊd/ see stride

stroke[1] /strəʊk/ n Schlag m; (of pen) Strich m; (Swimming) Zug m; (style) Stil m; (Med) Schlaganfall m; ~ of luck Glücksfall m

stroke[2] ● vt streicheln

stroll /strəʊl/ n Bummel m 🔟 ● vi bummeln 🔟. ~er n (Amer: pushchair) [Kinder]sportwagen m

strong /strɒŋ/ adj (-er /-gə(r)/, -est /-gɪst/) stark; (powerful, healthy) kräftig; (severe) streng; (sturdy) stabil; (convincing) gut

strong: ~hold n Festung f; (fig) Hochburg f. ~-room n Tresorraum m

strove /strəʊv/ see strive

struck /strʌk/ see strike

structural /'strʌktʃərl/ adj baulich

structure /'strʌktʃə(r)/ n Struktur

f; (building) Bau m

struggle /'strʌgl/ n Kampf m; with a ~ mit Mühe ● vt kämpfen; ~ to do sth sich abmühen, etw zutun

strum /strʌm/ v (pt/pp strummed) ● vt klimpern auf (+ dat) ● vi klimpern

strung /strʌŋ/ see string

strut[1] /strʌt/ n Strebe f

strut[2] vi (pt/pp strutted) stolzieren

stub /stʌb/ n Stummel m; (counterfoil) Abschnitt m. ~ **out** vt (pt/pp stubbed) ausdrücken (cigarette)

stubble /'stʌbl/ n Stoppeln pl

stubborn /'stʌbən/ adj starrsinnig; (refusal) hartnäckig

stubby /'stʌbɪ/ adj, (-ier, -iest) kurz und dick

stuck /stʌk/ see stick[2]. ~-'**up** adj 🔟 hochnäsig

stud[1] /stʌd/ n Nagel m; (on clothes) Niete f; (for collar) Kragenknopf m; (for ear) Ohrstecker m

student /'stjuːdnt/ n Student(in) m(f); (Sch) Schüler(in) m(f)

studio /'stjuːdɪəʊ/ n Studio nt; (for artist) Atelier nt

studious /'stjuːdɪəs/ adj lerneifrig; (earnest) ernsthaft

stud|y /'stʌdɪ/ n Studie f; (room) Arbeitszimmer nt; (investigation) Untersuchung f; ~**ies** pl Studium nt ● v (pt/pp studied) ● vt studieren; (examine) untersuchen ● vi lernen; (at university) studieren

stuff /stʌf/ n Stoff m; (🔟: things) Zeug nt ● vt vollstopfen; (with padding, Culin) füllen; ausstopfen (animal); (cram) [hinein]stopfen. ~**ing** n Füllung f

stuffy /'stʌfɪ/ adj stickig; (old-fashioned) spießig

stumbl|e /'stʌmbl/ vi stolpern; ~**e across** zufällig stoßen auf (+ acc).

~**ing-block** n Hindernis nt

stump /stʌmp/ n Stumpf m ● ~ **up** vt/i 🔟 blechen. ~**ed** adj 🔟 überfragt

stun /stʌn/ vt (pt/pp stunned) betäuben

stung /stʌŋ/ see sting

stunk /stʌŋk/ see stink

stunning /'stʌnɪŋ/ adj 🔟 toll

stunt[1] /stʌnt/ n 🔟 Kunststück nt

stupendous /stjuː'pendəs/ adj enorm

stupid /'stjuːpɪd/ adj dumm. ~**ity** n Dummheit f. ~**ly** adv dumm; ~**ly** [enough] dummerweise

sturdy /'stɜːdɪ/ adj stämmig; (furniture) stabil; (shoes) fest

stutter /'stʌtə(r)/ n Stottern nt ● vt/i stottern

sty /staɪ/ n (pl sties) Schweinestall m

style /staɪl/ n Stil m; (fashion) Mode f; (sort) Art f; (hair~) Frisur f; in ~ in großem Stil

stylish /'staɪlɪʃ/ adj, ~**ly** adv stilvoll

stylist /'staɪlɪst/ n Friseur m/ Friseuse f. ~**ic** adj, ~**ally** adv stilistisch

suave /swɑːv/ adj (pej) gewandt

sub'conscious /sʌb-/ adj unterbewusst ● n Unterbewusstsein nt

subdi'vide /sʌb-/ vt unterteilen. ~**sion** n Unterteilung f

subdue /səb'djuː/ vt unterwerfen. ~**d** adj gedämpft; (person) still

subject[1] /'sʌbdʒɪkt/ adj be ~ to sth etw dat unterworfen sein ● n Staatsbürger(in) m(f); (of ruler) Untertan m; (theme) Thema nt; (of investigation) Gegenstand m; (Sch) Fach nt; (Gram) Subjekt nt

subject[2] /səb'dʒekt/ vt unterwerfen (to dat); (expose) aussetzen (to dat)

subjective /səb'dʒektɪv/ adj

subjektiv

subjunctive /səb'dʒʌŋktɪv/ n
Konjunktiv m

sublime /sə'blaɪm/ adj erhaben

subma'rine n Unterseeboot nt

submerge /səb'mɜːdʒ/ vt untertauchen; be ~d unter Wasser stehen ● vi tauchen

submission /səb'mɪʃn/ n Unterwerfung f

submit /səb'mɪt/ v (pt/pp -mitted, pres p -mitting) ● vt vorlegen (to dat); (hand in) einreichen ● vi sich unterwerfen (to dat)

subordinate[1] /sə'bɔːdɪnət/ adj untergeordnet ● n Untergebene(r) m/f

subordinate[2] /sə'bɔːdɪneɪt/ vt unterordnen (to dat)

subscribe /səb'skraɪb/ vi spenden; ~ to (fig) abonnieren (newspaper). ~r n Spender m; Abonnent m

subscription /səb'skrɪpʃn/ n (to club) [Mitglieds]beitrag m; (to newspaper) Abonnement nt; by ~ mit Spenden; (buy) im Abonnement

subsequent /'sʌbsɪkwənt/ adj folgend; (later) später

subside /səb'saɪd/ vi sinken; (ground:) sich senken; (storm:) nachlassen

subsidiary /səb'sɪdɪərɪ/ adj untergeordnet ● n Tochtergesellschaft f

subsid|ize /'sʌbsɪdaɪz/ vt subventionieren. ~y n Subvention f

substance /'sʌbstəns/ n Substanz f

sub'standard adj unzulänglich; (goods) minderwertig

substantial /səb'stænʃl/ adj solide; (meal) reichhaltig; (considerable) beträchtlich. ~ly adv solide; (essentially) im Wesentlichen

substitut|e /'sʌbstɪtjuːt/ n Ersatz m; (Sport) Ersatzspieler(in) m(f) ● vt

~e A for B B durch A ersetzen ● vi
~e for s.o. jdn vertreten. ~ion n
Ersetzung f

subterranean /sʌbtə'reɪnɪən/ adj
unterirdisch

'subtitle n Untertitel m

subtle /'sʌtl/ adj (-r, -st), **-tly** adv
fein; (fig) subtil

subtract /səb'trækt/ vt abziehen,
subtrahieren. ~ion n Subtraktion f

suburb /'sʌbɜːb/ n Vorort m. ~an
adj Vorort-. ~ia n die Vororte pl

'subway n Unterführung f; (Amer:
railway) U-Bahn f

succeed /sək'siːd/ vi Erfolg haben;
(plan:) gelingen; (follow) nachfolgen
(+ dat); I ~ed es ist mir gelungen;
he ~ed in escaping es gelang ihm
zu entkommen ● vt folgen (+ dat)

success /sək'ses/ n Erfolg m. ~ful
adj. ~ly adv erfolgreich

succession /sək'seʃn/ n Folge f;
(series) Serie f; (to title, office) Nachfolge f; (to throne) Thronfolge f; in
~ hintereinander

successive /sək'sesɪv/ adj aufeinander folgend

successor /sək'sesə(r)/ n Nachfolger(in) m(f)

succumb /sə'kʌm/ vi erliegen
(to dat)

such /sʌtʃ/

● adjective

⸱⸱⸱▸ (of that kind) solch. such a
book ein solches Buch; so ein
Buch [T]. such a person ein solcher Mensch; so ein Mensch [T].
such people solche Leute. such
a thing so etwas. no such example kein solches Beispiel.
there is no such thing so etwas
gibt es nicht; das gibt es gar
nicht. there is no such person

eine solche Person gibt es nicht. such writers as Goethe and Schiller Schriftsteller wie Goethe und Schiller

····▸ (so great) solch; derartig. I've got such a headache! ich habe solche Kopfschmerzen! it was such fun! das machte solchen Spaß! I got such a fright that ... ich bekam einen derartigen od 🔲 so einen Schrecken, dass ...

····▸ (with adjective) so. such a big house ein so großes Haus. he has such lovely blue eyes or hat so schöne blaue Augen. a long time so lange

● pronoun

····▸ as such als solcher/solche/ solches. the thing as such die Sache als solche. (strictly speaking) this is not a promotion as such dies ist im Grunde genommen keine Beförderung

····▸ such is: such is life so ist das Leben. such is not the case das ist nicht der Fall

····▸ such as wie [zum Beispiel]

suchlike /'sʌtʃlaɪk/ pron 🔲 dergleichen

suck /ʃʌk/ vt/i saugen; lutschen (sweet). ~ **up** vt aufsaugen ● vi ~ up to s.o. 🔲 sich bei jdm einschmeicheln

suction /'sʌkʃn/ n Saugwirkung f

sudden /'sʌdn/ adj plötzlich; (abrupt) jäh ● n all of a ~ auf einmal

sue /su:/ vt (pres p suing) verklagen (for auf + acc) ● vi klagen

suede /sweɪd/ n Wildleder nt

suet /'su:ɪt/ n [Nieren]talg m

suffer /'sʌfə(r)/ vi leiden (from an + dat) ● vt erleiden; (tolerate) dulden

suffice /sə'faɪs/ vi genügen

sufficient /sə'fɪʃnt/ adj genug, genügend; be ~ genügen

suffocat|e /'sʌfəkeɪt/ vt/i ersticken. ~**ion** n Ersticken nt

sugar /'ʃʊgə(r)/ n Zucker m ● vt zuckern; (fig) versüßen. ~ **basin**, ~**bowl** n Zuckerschale f. ~**y** adj süß; (fig) süßlich

suggest /sə'dʒest/ vt vorschlagen; (indicate, insinuate) andeuten. ~**ion** n Vorschlag m; Andeutung f; (trace) Spur f. ~**ive** adj anzüglich

suicidal /su:ɪ'saɪdl/ adj selbstmörderisch

suicide /'su:ɪsaɪd/ n Selbstmord m

suit /su:t/ n Anzug m; (woman's) Kostüm nt; (Cards) Farbe f; (Jur) Prozess m ● vt (adapt) anpassen (to dat); (be convenient for) passen (+ dat); (go with) passen zu; (clothing:) stehen (s.o. jdm); be ~ed for geeignet sein für; ~ yourself! wie du willst!

suit|able /'su:təbl/ adj geeignet; (convenient) passend; (appropriate) angemessen; (for weather, activity) zweckmäßig. ~**ably** adv angemessen; zweckmäßig

'suitcase n Koffer m

suite /swi:t/ n Suite f; (of furniture) Garnitur f

sulk /sʌlk/ vi schmollen. ~**y** adj schmollend

sullen /'sʌlən/ adj mürrisch

sultry /'sʌltrɪ/ adj (-ier, -iest) (weather) schwül

sum /sʌm/ n Summe f; (Sch) Rechenaufgabe f ● vt/i (pt/pp summed) ~ up zusammenfassen; (assess) einschätzen

summar|ize /'sʌməraɪz/ vt zusammenfassen. ~**y** n Zusammenfassung f ● adj. -**ily** adv summarisch; (dismissal) fristlos

s

summer /'sʌmə(r)/ n Sommer m. **~time** n Sommer m

summer camp Amerikanische Feriencamps haben eine lange Tradition. Sie bieten ein umfassendes Fitnessprogramm, und Schulkinder haben die Möglichkeit, alle erdenklichen Sportarten und Spiele in den Sommerferien auszuprobieren. Hier erhalten die Teilnehmer Survival-Training und lernen außerdem Unabhängigkeit und Führungseigenschaften. Tausende von Studenten arbeiten während der Sommermonate als Betreuer in den Feriencamps.

summery /'sʌməri/ adj sommerlich

summit /'sʌmɪt/ n Gipfel m. **~ conference** n Gipfelkonferenz f

summon /'sʌmən/ vt rufen; holen (help); (Jur) vorladen

summons /'sʌmənz/ n (Jur) Vorladung f ● vt vorladen

sumptuous /'sʌmptjʊəs/ adj prunkvoll; (meal) üppig

sun /sʌn/ n Sonne f ● vt (pt/pp sunned) **~ oneself** sich sonnen

sun: ~bathe vi sich sonnen. **~bed** n Sonnenbank f. **~burn** n Sonnenbrand m

Sunday /'sʌndeɪ/ n Sonntag m

'sunflower n Sonnenblume f

sung /sʌŋ/ see sing

'sunglasses npl Sonnenbrille f

sunk /sʌŋk/ see sink

sunny /'sʌnɪ/ adj (-ier, -iest) sonnig

sun: ~rise n Sonnenaufgang m. **~roof** n (Auto) Schiebedach nt. **~set** n Sonnenuntergang m. **~shade** n Sonnenschirm m.

~shine n Sonnenschein m. **~stroke** n Sonnenstich m. **~tan** n [Sonnen]bräune f. **~tanned** adj braun [gebrannt]. **~tan oil** n Sonnenöl nt

super /'suːpə(r)/ adj 🅣 prima, toll

superb /sʊ'pɜːb/ adj erstklassig

superficial /suːpə'fɪʃl/ a oberflächlich

superfluous /sʊ'pɜːflʊəs/ adj überflüssig

superintendent /suːpərɪn'tendənt/ n (of police) Kommissar m

superior /suː'pɪərɪə(r)/ a überlegen; (in rank) höher ● n Vorgesetzte(r) m/f. **~ity** n Überlegenheit f

superlative /suː'pɜːlətɪv/ a unübertrefflich ● n Superlativ m

'supermarket n Supermarkt m

super'natural adj übernatürlich

supersede /suːpə'siːd/ vt ersetzen

superstiti|on /suːpə'stɪʃn/ n Aberglaube m. **~ous** adj abergläubisch

supervis|e /'suːpəvaɪz/ vt beaufsichtigen; überwachen (work). **~ion** n Aufsicht f; Überwachung f. **~or** n Aufseher(in) m(f)

supper /'sʌpə(r)/ n Abendessen nt

supple /'sʌpl/ adj geschmeidig

supplement /'sʌplɪmənt/ n Ergänzung f; (addition) Zusatz m; (to fare) Zuschlag m; (book) Ergänzungsband m; (to newspaper) Beilage f ● vt ergänzen. **~ary** a zusätzlich

supplier /sə'plaɪə(r)/ n Lieferant m

supply /sə'plaɪ/ n Vorrat m; **supplies** pl (Mil) Nachschub m ● vt (pt/pp -ied) liefern; **~ s.o. with sth** jdn mit etw versorgen

support /sə'pɔːt/ n Stütze f; (fig) Unterstützung f ● vt stützen; (bear weight of) tragen; (keep) ernähren; (give money to) unterstützen; (speak *in favour of*) befürworten; (*Sport*) Fan sein von. ~**er** *n* Anhänger(in) *m(f)*; (*Sport*) Fan *m*

suppose /səˈpəʊz/ *vt* annehmen; (*presume*) vermuten; (*imagine*) sich (*dat*) vorstellen; **be** ~**d to** do sth etw tun sollen; **not be** ~**d to** 🇬🇧 nicht dürfen; **I** ~ so vermutlich. ~**dly** *adv* angeblich

supposition /sʌpəˈzɪʃn/ *n* Vermutung *f*

suppress /səˈpres/ *vt* unterdrücken. ~**ion** *n* Unterdrückung *f*

supremacy /suːˈpreməsɪ/ *n* Vorherrschaft *f*

supreme /suːˈpriːm/ *adj* höchste(r,s); (*court*) oberste(r,s)

sure /ʃʊə(r)/ *adj* (-r, -st) sicher; **make** ~ sich vergewissern (*of gen*); (*check*) nachprüfen ● *adv* (*Amer*, 🇬🇧) klar; ~ **enough** tatsächlich. ~**ly** *adv* sicher; (*for emphasis*) doch; (*Amer*: *gladly*) gern

surf /sɜːf/ *n* Brandung *f* ● *vi* surfen

surface /ˈsɜːfɪs/ *n* Oberfläche *f* ● *vi* (*emerge*) auftauchen

'surfboard /ˈsɜːf-/ *n* Surfbrett *nt*

surfing /ˈsɜːfɪŋ/ *n* Surfen *nt*

surge /sɜːdʒ/ *n* (*of sea*) Branden *nt*; (*fig*) Welle *f* ● *vi* branden; ~ **forward** nach vorn drängen

surgeon /ˈsɜːdʒən/ *n* Chirurg(in) *m(f)*

surgery /ˈsɜːdʒərɪ/ *n* Chirurgie *f*; (*place*) Praxis *f*; (*room*) Sprechzimmer *nt*; (*hours*) Sprechstunde *f*; **have** ~ operiert werden

surgical /ˈsɜːdʒɪkl/ *adj* chirurgisch

surly /ˈsɜːlɪ/ *adj* mürrisch

surname /ˈsɜːneɪm/ *n* Nachname *m*

surpass /səˈpɑːs/ *vt* übertreffen

surplus /ˈsɜːpləs/ *adj* überschüssig ● *n* Überschuss *m* (*of an* + *dat*)

surprise /səˈpraɪz/ *n* Überraschung *f* ● *vt* überraschen; **be** ~**ed** sich wundern (**at** über + *acc*). ~**ing** *adj* überraschend

surrender /səˈrendə(r)/ *n* Kapitulation *f* ● *vi* sich ergeben; (*Mil*) kapitulieren ● *vt* aufgeben

surround /səˈraʊnd/ *vt* umgeben; (*encircle*) umzingeln; **be** ~**ed by** umgeben von. ~**ing** *adj* umliegend. ~**ings** *npl* Umgebung *f*

surveillance /səˈveɪləns/ *n* Überwachung *f*; **be under** ~ überwacht werden

survey¹ /ˈsɜːveɪ/ *n* Überblick *m*; (*poll*) Umfrage *f*; (*investigation*) Untersuchung *f*; (*of land*) Vermessung *f*; (*of house*) Gutachten *nt*

survey² /səˈveɪ/ *vt* betrachten; vermessen (*land*); begutachten (*building*). ~**or** *n* Landvermesser *m*; Gutachter *m*

survival /səˈvaɪvl/ *n* Überleben *nt*; (*of tradition*) Fortbestand *m*

surviv|e /səˈvaɪv/ *vt* überleben ● *vi* überleben; (*tradition*:) erhalten bleiben. ~**or** *n* Überlebende(r) *m/f*; **be a** ~**or** nicht unterzukriegen sein

susceptible /səˈseptəbl/ *adj* empfänglich; (*Med*) anfällig (**to** für)

suspect¹ /səˈspekt/ *vt* verdächtigen; (*assume*) vermuten; **he** ~**s** nothing *or* ahnt nichts

suspect² /ˈsʌspekt/ *adj* verdächtig ● *n* Verdächtige(r) *m/f*

suspend /səˈspend/ *vt* aufhängen; (*stop*) [vorläufig] einstellen; (*from duty*) vorläufig beurlauben. ~**ders** *npl* (*Amer*: *braces*) Hosenträger *pl*

suspense /səˈspens/ *n* Spannung *f*

suspension /səˈspenʃn/ *n* (*Auto*) Federung *f*. ~ **bridge** *n* Hängebrücke *f*

suspici|on /səˈspɪʃn/ *n* Verdacht *m*; (*mistrust*) Misstrauen *nt*; (*trace*)

Spur f. ~ous adj misstrauisch; (arousing suspicion) verdächtig

sustain /sə'steɪn/ vt tragen; (fig) aufrechterhalten; erhalten (life); erleiden (injury)

sustenance /'sʌstɪnəns/ n Nahrung f

swagger /'swægə(r)/ vi stolzieren

swallow[1] /'swɒləʊ/ vt/i schlucken. ~ up vt verschlucken; verschlingen (resources)

swallow[2] n (bird) Schwalbe f

swam /swæm/ see swim

swamp /swɒmp/ n Sumpf m • vt überschwemmen

swan /swɒn/ n Schwan m

swank /swæŋk/ vi 🗆 angeben

swap /swɒp/ n 🗆 Tausch m • vt/i (pt/pp swapped) 🗆 tauschen (for gegen)

swarm /swɔːm/ n Schwarm m • vi schwärmen; be ~ing with wimmeln von

swat /swɒt/ vt (pt/pp swatted) totschlagen

sway /sweɪ/ vi schwanken; (gently) sich wiegen • vt (influence) beeinflussen

swear /sweə(r)/ v (pt swore, pp sworn) • vt schwören • vi schwören (by auf + acc); (curse) fluchen. ~-word n Kraftausdruck m

sweat /swet/ n Schweiß m • vi schwitzen

sweater /'swetə(r)/ n Pullover m

Swed|e /swiːd/ n Schwede m/Schwedin f. ~en n Schweden nt. ~ish adj schwedisch

sweep /swiːp/ n Schornsteinfeger m; (curve) Bogen m; (movement) ausholende Bewegung f • v (pt/pp swept) • vt fegen, kehren • vi (go swiftly) rauschen; (wind:) fegen

sweeping /'swiːpɪŋ/ adj aushollend; (statement) pauschal; (changes) weit reichend

sweet /swiːt/ adj (-er, -est) süß; have a ~ tooth gern Süßes mögen • n Bonbon m & nt; (dessert) Nachtisch m

sweeten /'swiːtn/ vt süßen

sweet: ~heart n Schatz m. ~ness n Süße f. ~ pea n Wicke f. ~-shop n Süßwarenladen m

swell /swel/ n Dünung f • v (pt swelled, pp swollen or swelled) • vi [an]schwellen; (wood:) aufquellen • vt anschwellen lassen; (increase) vergrößern. ~ing n Schwellung f

swelter /'sweltə(r)/ vi schwitzen

swept /swept/ see sweep

swerve /swɜːv/ vi einen Bogen machen

swift /swɪft/ adj (-er, -est) schnell

swig /swɪg/ n 🗆 Schluck m

swim /swɪm/ n have a ~ schwimmen • vi (pt swam, pp swum) schwimmen; my head is ~ming mir dreht sich der Kopf. ~mer n Schwimmer(in) m(f)

swimming /'swɪmɪŋ/ n Schwimmen nt. ~-baths npl Schwimmbad nt. ~-pool n Schwimmbecken nt; (private) Swimmingpool m

'swimsuit n Badeanzug m

swindle /'swɪndl/ n Schwindel m, Betrug m • vt betrügen. ~r n Schwindler m

swine /swaɪn/ n (pej) Schwein nt

swing /swɪŋ/ n Schwung m; (shift) Schwenk m; (seat) Schaukel f; in full ~ in vollem Gange • (pt/pp swung) • vi schwingen; (on swing) schaukeln; (dangle) baumeln; (turn) schwenken • vt schwingen; (influence) beeinflussen

swipe /swaɪp/ n 🗆 Schlag m • vt 🗆 knallen; (steal) klauen

swirl /swɜːl/ n Wirbel m ●vt/i
wirbeln

Swiss /swɪs/ adj Schweizer-,
schweizerisch ●n Schweizer(in)
m(f); **the** ~ pl die Schweizer. ~
'**roll** n Biskuitrolle f

switch /swɪtʃ/ n Schalter m;
(change) Wechsel m; (Amer, Rail)
Weiche f ●vt wechseln; (exchange)
tauschen ●vi wechseln; ~ to umstellen auf (+ acc). ~ **off** vt ausschalten; abschalten (engine). ~ **on**
vt einschalten

switchboard n [Telefon]zen-
trale f

Switzerland /ˈswɪtsələnd/ n die
Schweiz

swivel /ˈswɪvl/ v (pt/pp swivelled)
●vt drehen ●vi sich drehen

swollen /ˈswəʊlən/ see swell

swoop /swuːp/ n (by police) Razzia
f ●vi ~ **down** herabstoßen

sword /sɔːd/ n Schwert nt

swore /swɔː(r)/ see swear

sworn /swɔːn/ see swear

swot /swɒt/ n 🄸 Streber m ●vt
(pt/pp swotted) 🄸 büffeln

swum /swʌm/ see swim

swung /swʌŋ/ see swing

syllable /ˈsɪləbl/ n Silbe f

syllabus /ˈsɪləbəs/ n Lehrplan m;
(for exam) Studienplan m

symbol /ˈsɪmbl/ n Symbol nt (of
für). ~**ic** adj, **-ally** adv symbolisch
~**ism** n Symbolik f. ~**ize** vt sym-
bolisieren

symmetr|ical /sɪˈmetrɪkl/ adj
symmetrisch. ~**y** n Symmetrie f

sympathetic /sɪmpəˈθetɪk/ adj,
-ally adv mitfühlend; (likeable) sympathisch

sympathize /ˈsɪmpəθaɪz/ vi mitfühlen

sympathy /ˈsɪmpəθɪ/ n Mitgefühl

nt; (condolences) Beileid nt

symphony /ˈsɪmfənɪ/ n Sinfonie f

symptom /ˈsɪmptəm/ n Symptom nt

synagogue /ˈsɪnəɡɒɡ/ n Synagoge f

synchronize /ˈsɪŋkrənaɪz/ vt synchronisieren

synonym /ˈsɪnənɪm/ n Synonym
nt. ~**ous** adj synonym

synthesis /ˈsɪnθəsɪs/ n (pl **-ses**
/-siːz/) Synthese f

synthetic /sɪnˈθetɪk/ adj syn-
thetisch

Syria /ˈsɪrɪə/ n Syrien nt

syringe /sɪˈrɪndʒ/ n Spritze f

syrup /ˈsɪrəp/ n Sirup m

system /ˈsɪstəm/ n System nt.
~**atic** adj, **-ally** adv systematisch

Tt

tab /tæb/ n (projecting) Zunge f;
(with name) Namensschild nt; (loop)
Aufhänger m; **pick up the** ~ 🄸 bezahlen

table /ˈteɪbl/ n Tisch m; (list) Tabelle f; **at** [**the**] ~ bei Tisch. ~
-cloth n Tischdecke f. ~**spoon** n
Servierlöffel m

tablet /ˈtæblɪt/ n Tablette f; (of
soap) Stück nt

'**table tennis** n Tischtennis nt

tabloid /ˈtæblɔɪd/ n kleinformatige
Zeitung f; (pej) Boulevardzeitung f

taciturn /ˈtæsɪtɜːn/ adj wortkarg

tack /tæk/ n (nail) Stift m; (stitch)
Heftstich m; (Naut & fig) Kurs m
●vt festnageln; (sew) heften ●vi
(Naut) kreuzen

tackle /'tækl/ n Ausrüstung f ● vt angehen (*problem*); (*Sport*) angreifen

tact /tækt/ n Takt m, Taktgefühl nt. ~**ful** adj taktvoll

tactic|al /'tæktɪkl/ adj taktisch. ~**s** npl Taktik f

tactless /'tæktlɪs/ adj taktlos. ~**ness** n Taktlosigkeit f

tag /tæg/ n (*label*) Schild nt ● vi (*pt/pp* tagged) ~ **along** mitkommen

tail /teɪl/ n Schwanz m; ~**s** pl (*tailcoat*) Frack m; **heads or ~s?** Kopf oder Zahl? ● vt [⊥] (*follow*) beschatten ● vi ~ **off** zurückgehen

tail: ~**back** n Rückstau m. ~ **light** n Rücklicht nt

tailor /'teɪlə(r)/ n Schneider m. ~-**made** adj maßgeschneidert

taint /teɪnt/ vt verderben

take /teɪk/ v (*pt* took, *pp* taken) ● vt nehmen; (*with one*) mitnehmen; (*take to a place*) bringen; (*steal*) stehlen; (*win*) gewinnen; (*capture*) einnehmen; (*require*) brauchen; (*last*) dauern; (*teach*) geben; machen (*exam, subject, holiday, photograph*); messen (*pulse, temperature*); ~ **sth to the cleaner's** etw in die Reinigung bringen; be ~**n ill** krank werden; ~ **sth calmly** etw gelassen aufnehmen ● vi (*plant:*) angehen; ~ **after** s.o. ähnlich sein; (*in looks*) jdm ähnlich sehen; ~ **to** (*like*) mögen; (*as a habit*) sich (*dat*) angewöhnen. ~ **away** vt wegbringen; (*remove*) wegnehmen; (*subtract*) abziehen; '**to** ~ **away**' 'zum Mitnehmen'. ~ **back** vt zurücknehmen; (*return*) zurückbringen. ~ **down** vt herunternehmen; (*remove*) abnehmen; (*write down*) aufschreiben. ~ **in** vt hineinbringen; (*bring indoors*) hereinholen; (*to one's home*) aufnehmen; (*under-*

stand) begreifen; (*deceive*) hereinlegen; (*make smaller*) enger machen. ~ **off** vt abnehmen; ablegen (*coat*); sich (*dat*) ausziehen (*clothes*); (*deduct*) abziehen; (*mimic*) nachmachen ● vi (*Aviat*) starten. ~ **on** vt annehmen; (*undertake*) übernehmen; (*engage*) einstellen; (*as opponent*) antreten gegen. ~ **out** vt hinausbringen; (*for pleasure*) ausgehen mit; ausführen (*dog*); (*remove*) herausnehmen; (*withdraw*) abheben (*money*); (*from library*) ausleihen; ~ **it out on** s.o. [⊥] seinen Ärger an jdm auslassen. ~ **over** vt hinüberbringen; übernehmen (*firm, control*) ● vi ~ **over from** s.o. jdn ablösen. ~ **up** vt hinaufbringen; annehmen (*offer*); ergreifen (*profession*); sich (*dat*) zulegen (*hobby*); in Anspruch nehmen (*time*); einnehmen (*space*); aufreißen (*floorboards*); ~ **sth up with** s.o. mit jdm über etw (*acc*) sprechen

take: ~-**away** n Essen nt zum Mitnehmen; (*restaurant*) Restaurant nt mit Straßenverkauf. ~-**off** n (*Aviat*) Start m, Abflug m. ~-**over** n Übernahme f

takings /'teɪkɪŋz/ npl Einnahmen pl

talcum /'tælkəm/ n ~ [**powder**] Körperpuder m

tale /teɪl/ n Geschichte f

talent /'tælənt/ n Talent nt

talk /tɔːk/ n Gespräch nt; (*lecture*) Vortrag m ● vi reden, sprechen (**to/** **with** mit) ● vt reden; ~ **s.o. into** sth jdn zu etw überreden. ~ **over** vt besprechen

talkative /'tɔːkətɪv/ adj gesprächig

tall /tɔːl/ adj (-**er**, -**est**) groß; (*building, tree*) hoch. ~ **story** n übertriebene Geschichte f

tally /'tælɪ/ vi übereinstimmen

tame /teɪm/ adj (-r, -st) zahm; (dull) lahm 🔟 ● vt zähmen. **~r** n Dompteur m

tamper /'tæmpə(r)/ vi ~ with sich (dat) zu schaffen machen an (+ dat)

tampon /'tæmpɒn/ n Tampon m

tan /tæn/ adj gelbbraun ● n Gelbbraun nt; (from sun) Bräune f ● v (pt/pp tanned) ● vt gerben (hide) ● vi braun werden

tang /tæŋ/ n herber Geschmack m; (smell) herber Geruch m

tangible /'tændʒɪbl/ adj greifbar

tangle /'tæŋgl/ n Gewirr nt; (in hair) Verfilzung f ● vt ~ [up] verheddern ● vi sich verhedderen

tank /tæŋk/ n Tank m; (Mil) Panzer m

tanker /'tæŋkə(r)/ n Tanker m; (lorry) Tank[last]wagen m

tantrum /'tæntrəm/ n Wutanfall m

tap /tæp/ n Hahn m; (knock) Klopfen nt; on ~ zur Verfügung ● v (pt/pp tapped) ● vt klopfen an (+ acc); anzapfen (barrel, tree); erschließen (resources); abhören (telephone) ● vi klopfen. **~-dance** n Step[tanz] m ● vi Stepp tanzen, steppen

tape /teɪp/ n Band nt; (adhesive) Klebstreifen m; (for recording) Tonband nt ● vt mit Klebstreifen zukleben; (record) auf Band aufnehmen

'tape-measure n Bandmaß nt

taper /'teɪpə(r)/ vi sich verjüngen

'tape recorder n Tonbandgerät nt

tar /tɑː(r)/ n Teer m ● vt (pt/pp tarred) teeren

target /'tɑːgɪt/ n Ziel nt; (board) [Ziel]scheibe f

tarnish /'tɑːnɪʃ/ vi anlaufen

tarpaulin /tɑː'pɔːlɪn/ n Plane f

tart¹ /tɑːt/ adj (-er, -est) sauer

tart² n ≈ Obstkuchen m; (individual) Törtchen nt; (sl: prostitute) Nutte f ● vt ~ oneself up 🔟 sich auftakeln

tartan /'tɑːtn/ n Schottenmuster nt; (cloth) Schottenstoff m

task /tɑːsk/ n Aufgabe f; take s.o. to ~ jdm Vorhaltungen machen. **~ force** n Sonderkommando nt

tassel /'tæsl/ n Quaste f

taste /teɪst/ n Geschmack m; (sample) Kostprobe f ● vt kosten, probieren; schmecken (flavour) ● vi schmecken (of nach). **~ful** adj (fig) geschmackvoll. **~less** adj geschmacklos

tasty /'teɪstɪ/ adj lecker

tat /tæt/ see **tit²**

tatters /'tætəz/ npl in ~s in Fetzen

tattoo /tə'tuː/ n Tätowierung f ● vt tätowieren

tatty /'tætɪ/ adj schäbig; (book) zerfleddert

taught /tɔːt/ see **teach**

taunt /tɔːnt/ n höhnische Bemerkung f ● vt verhöhnen

taut /tɔːt/ adj straff

tawdry /'tɔːdrɪ/ adj billig und geschmacklos

tax /tæks/ n Steuer f ● vt besteuern; (fig) strapazieren. **~able** adj steuerpflichtig. **~ation** n Besteuerung f

taxi /'tæksɪ/ n Taxi nt ● vi (pt/pp taxied, pres p taxiing) (aircraft:) rollen. **~ driver** n Taxifahrer m. **~ rank** n Taxistand m

'taxpayer n Steuerzahler m

tea /tiː/ n Tee m. **~-bag** n Teebeutel m. **~-break** n Teepause f

teach /tiːtʃ/ vt/i (pt/pp taught) unterrichten; **~ s.o. sth** jdm etw beibringen. **~er** n Lehrer(in) m(f). **~ing** n Unterrichten nt

tea: **~-cloth** n (for drying) Geschirrtuch nt. **~cup** n Teetasse f

teak /tiːk/ n Teakholz nt

team /tiːm/ n Mannschaft f; (fig) Team nt; (of animals) Gespann nt

'teapot n Teekanne f

tear¹ /teə(r)/ n Riss m ●v (pt tore, pp torn) ●vt reißen; (damage) zerreißen; **~** oneself away sich losreißen ●vi [zer]reißen; (run) rasen. **~ up** vt zerreißen

tear² /tɪə(r)/ n Träne f. **~ful** adj weinend. **~fully** adv unter Tränen. **~gas** n Tränengas nt

tease /tiːz/ vt necken

tea: **~-set** n Teeservice nt. **~ shop** n Café nt. **~spoon** n Teelöffel m

teat /tiːt/ n Zitze f; (on bottle) Sauger m

'tea-towel n Geschirrtuch nt

technical /'teknɪkl/ adj technisch; (specialized) fachlich. **~ity** n technisches Detail nt; (Jur) Formfehler m. **~ly** adv technisch; (strictly) streng genommen. **~ term** n Fachausdruck m

technician /tek'nɪʃn/ n Techniker m

technique /tek'niːk/ n Technik f

technological /teknə'lɒdʒɪkl/ adj technologisch

technology /tek'nɒlədʒɪ/ n Technik f

teddy /'tedɪ/ n **~** [bear] Teddybär m

tedious /'tiːdɪəs/ adj langweilig

tedium /'tiːdɪəm/ n Langeweile f

teenage /'tiːneɪdʒ/ adj Teenager-; **~ boy/girl** Junge m/Mädchen nt im Teenageralter. **~r** n Teenager m

teens /tiːnz/ npl the **~** die Teenagerjahre pl

teeter /'tiːtə(r)/ vi schwanken

teeth /tiːθ/ see tooth

teeth|e /tiːð/ vi zahnen. **~ing**

troubles npl (fig) Anfangsschwierigkeiten pl

teetotal /tiː'təʊtl/ adj abstinent. **~ler** n Abstinenzler m

telebanking /'telɪbæŋkɪŋ/ n Telebanking nt

telecommunications /telɪkəmjuːnɪ'keɪʃnz/ npl Fernmeldewesen nt

telegram /'telɪgræm/ n Telegramm nt

telegraph /'telɪgrɑːf/ **~ pole** n Telegrafenmast m

telephone /'telɪfəʊn/ n Telefon nt; be on the **~** Telefon haben; (be telephoning) telefonieren ●vt anrufen ●vi telefonieren

telephone: **~ booth** n, **~ box** n Telefonzelle f. **~ directory** n Telefonbuch nt. **~ number** n Telefonnummer f

tele'photo /telɪ-/ adj **~ lens** Teleobjektiv nt

telescop|e /'telɪskəʊp/ n Teleskop nt, Fernrohr nt. **~ic** adj (collapsible) ausziehbar

televise /'telɪvaɪz/ vt im Fernsehen übertragen

television /'telɪvɪʒn/ n Fernsehen nt; watch **~** fernsehen; **~ [set]** Fernseher m 🅣

teleworking /'telɪwɜːkɪŋ/ n Telearbeit f

tell /tel/ vt/i (pt/pp told) sagen (s.o. jdm); (relate) erzählen; (know) wissen; (distinguish) erkennen; **~** the time die Uhr lesen; time will **~** das wird man erst sehen; his age is beginning to **~** sein Alter macht sich bemerkbar. **~ off** vt ausschimpfen

telly /'telɪ/ n 🅣 = television

temp /temp/ n 🅣 Aushilfssekretärin f

temper /'tempə(r)/ n (disposition)

Naturell *nt*; (*mood*) Laune *f*; (*anger*) Wut *f*; lose one's ~ wütend werden ● *vt* (*fig*) mäßigen

temperament /'temprəmənt/ *n* Temperament *nt*. ~al *adj* temperamentvoll; (*moody*) launisch

temperate /'tempərət/ *adj* gemäßigt

temperature /'temprətʃə(r)/ *n* Temperatur *f*; have or run a ~ Fieber haben

temple¹ /'templ/ *n* Tempel *m*

temple² *n* (*Anat*) Schläfe *f*

tempo /'tempəʊ/ *n* Tempo *nt*

temporary /'tempərəri/ *adj*, **-ily** *adv* vorübergehend; (*measure, building*) provisorisch

tempt /tempt/ *vt* verleiten; (*Relig*) versuchen; herausfordern (*fate*); (*entice*) [ver]locken; be ~ed versucht sein (to zu). ~**ation** *n* Versuchung *f*. ~**ing** *adj* verlockend

ten /ten/ *adj* zehn

tenaci|ous /tɪ'neɪʃəs/ *adj*, **-ly** *adv* hartnäckig. ~**ty** *n* Hartnäckigkeit *f*

tenant /'tenənt/ *n* Mieter(in) *m(f)*; (*Comm*) Pächter(in) *m(f)*

tend /tend/ *vi* ~ to do sth dazu neigen, etw zu tun

tendency /'tendənsɪ/ *n* Tendenz *f*; (*inclination*) Neigung *f*

tender /'tendə(r)/ *adj* zart; (*loving*) zärtlich; (*painful*) empfindlich. ~**ly** *adv* zärtlich. ~**ness** *n* Zartheit *f*; Zärtlichkeit *f*

tendon /'tendən/ *n* Sehne *f*

tenner /'tenə(r)/ *n* 🔟 Zehnpfundschein *m*

tennis /'tenɪs/ *n* Tennis *nt*. ~**-court** *n* Tennisplatz *m*

tenor /'tenə(r)/ *n* Tenor *m*

tense¹ /tens/ *n* (*Gram*) Zeitform *f*

tense² *adj* (**-r**, **-st**) gespannt ● *vt* anspannen (*muscle*)

tension /'tenʃn/ *n* Spannung *f*

tent /tent/ *n* Zelt *nt*

tentative /'tentətɪv/ *adj*, **-ly** *adv* vorläufig; (*hesitant*) zaghaft

tenterhooks /'tentəhʊks/ *npl* be on ~ wie auf glühenden Kohlen sitzen

tenth /tenθ/ *adj* zehnte(r,s) ● *n* Zehntel *nt*

tenuous /'tenjʊəs/ *adj* schwach

tepid /'tepɪd/ *adj* lauwarm

term /tɜːm/ *n* Zeitraum *m*; (*Sch*) ≈ Halbjahr *nt*; (*Univ*) ≈ Semester *nt*; (*expression*) Ausdruck *m*; ~**s** *pl* (*conditions*) Bedingungen *pl*; in the short/long ~ kurz-/langfristig; be on good/bad ~**s** gut/nicht gut miteinander auskommen

terminal /'tɜːmɪnl/ *adj* End-; (*Med*) unheilbar ● *n* (*Aviat*) Terminal *m*; (*of bus*) Endstation *f*; (*on battery*) Pol *m*; (*Computing*) Terminal *nt*

terminat|e /'tɜːmɪneɪt/ *vt* beenden; lösen (*contract*); unterbrechen (*pregnancy*) ● *vi* enden

terminology /tɜːmɪ'nɒlədʒɪ/ *n* Terminologie *f*

terminus /'tɜːmɪnəs/ *n* (*pl* **-ni** /-naɪ/) Endstation *f*

terrace /'terəs/ *n* Terrasse *f*; (*houses*) Häuserreihe *f*. ~**d house** *n* Reihenhaus *nt*

terrain /te'reɪn/ *n* Gelände *nt*

terrible /'terəbl/ *adj*, **-bly** *adv* schrecklich

terrific /tə'rɪfɪk/ *adj* 🔟 (*excellent*) sagenhaft; (*huge*) riesig

terri|fy /'terɪfaɪ/ *vt* (*pt/pp* -ied) Angst machen (+ *dat*); be ~**fied** Angst haben. ~**fying** *adj* Furcht erregend

territorial /terɪ'tɔːrɪəl/ *adj* Territorial-

territory /'terɪtərɪ/ *n* Gebiet *nt*

terror /'terə(r)/ *n* [panische] Angst *f*; (*Pol*) Terror *m*. ~**ism** *n* Terrorismus *m*. ~**ist** *n* Terrorist(in) *m(f)*

~**ize** vt terrorisieren

terse /tɜːs/ adj kurz, knapp

test /test/ n Test m; (Sch) Klassenarbeit f; put to the ~ auf die Probe stellen ● vt prüfen; (examine) untersuchen (for auf + acc)

testament /'testəmənt/ n Testament nt

testify /'testɪfaɪ/ v (pt/pp -ied) ● vt beweisen; ~ that bezeugen, dass ● vi aussagen

testimonial /testɪ'məʊnɪəl/ n Zeugnis nt

testimony /'testɪmənɪ/ n Aussage f

'**test-tube** n Reagenzglas nt

tether /'teðə(r)/ n be at the end of one's ~ am Ende seiner Kraft sein ● vt anbinden

text /tekst/ n Text m ● vt/i texten. ~**book** n Lehrbuch nt

textile /'tekstaɪl/ adj Textil- ● n ~s pl Textilien pl

'**text message** n SMS-Nachricht f

texture /'tekstʃə(r)/ n Beschaffenheit f; (of cloth) Struktur f

Thai /taɪ/ adj thailändisch. ~**land** n Thailand nt

Thames /temz/ n Themse f

than /ðæn, betont ðæn/ conj als

thank /θæŋk/ vt danken (+ dat); ~ you [very much] danke [schön]. ~**ful** adj dankbar. ~**less** adj undankbar

thanks /θæŋks/ npl Dank m; ~! ⊡ danke! ~ to dank (+ dat or gen)

---

that /ðæt/

pl **those**

● adjective

···▸ der (m), die (f), das (nt),

die (pl); (just seen or experienced) dieser (m), diese (f), dieses (nt), diese (pl). I'll never forget that day den Tag werde ich nie vergessen. I liked that house dieses Haus hat mir so gut gefallen

● pronoun

···▸ der (m), die (f), das (nt), die (pl). that is not true das ist nicht wahr. who is that in the garden? wer ist das [da im Garten? I'll take that ich nehme den/die/das. I don't like those die mag ich nicht. is that you? bist du es? that is why deshalb

···▸ like that so. don't be like that! sei doch nicht so! a man like that ein solcher Mann; so ein Mann ⊡

···▸ (after prepositions) da .... after that danach. with that damit. apart from that außerdem

···▸ (relative pronoun) der (m), die (f), das (nt), die (pl). the book that I'm reading das Buch, das ich lese. the people that you got it from die Leute, von denen du es bekommen hast. everyone that I know jeder, den ich kenne. that is all that I have das ist alles, was ich habe

● adverb

···▸ so. he's not 'that stupid so blöd ist er [auch wieder] nicht. it wasn't 'that bad so schlecht war es auch nicht. a nail about 'that long ein etwa so langer Nagel

···▸ (relative adverb) der (m), die (f), das (nt), die (pl). the day that I first met her der Tag, an dem ich sie zum ersten Mal sah. at the speed that he was going bei der Geschwindigkeit, die er hatte

● conjunction

····▸ dass. I don't think that he'll come ich denke nicht, dass er kommt. we know that you're right wir wissen, dass du Recht hast. I'm so tired that I can hardly walk ich bin so müde, dass ich kaum gehen kann

····▸ so that (purpose) damit; (result) sodass. he came earlier so that they would have more time er kam früher, damit sie mehr Zeit hatten. it was late, so that I had to catch the bus es war spät, sodass ich den Bus nehmen musste

thatch /θætʃ/ n Strohdach nt. ~ed adj strohgedeckt

thaw /θɔː/ n Tauwetter nt ● vt/i auftauen; it's ~ing es taut

the /ðə/, vor einem Vokal /ðiː/ def art der/die/das; (pl) die; play ~ piano/ violin Klavier/Geige spielen ● adv ~ more ~ better je mehr, desto besser; all ~ better umso besser

theatre /ˈθɪətə(r)/ n Theater nt; (Med) Operationssaal m

theatrical /θɪˈætrɪkl/ adj Theater-; (showy) theatralisch

theft /θeft/ n Diebstahl m

their /ðeə(r)/ adj ihr

theirs /ðeəz/ poss pron ihre(r), ihrs; a friend of ~ ein Freund von ihnen; those are ~ die gehören ihnen

them /ðem/ pron (acc) sie; (dat) ihnen

theme /θiːm/ n Thema nt. ~ park n Themenpark m

them'selves pron selbst; (reflexive) sich; by ~ allein

then /ðen/ adv dann; (at that time in past) damals; by ~ bis dahin;

since ~ seitdem; before ~ vorher; from ~ on von da an; now and ~ dann und wann; there and ~ auf der Stelle ● adj damalig

theology /θɪˈɒlədʒɪ/ n Theologie f

theoretical /θɪəˈretɪkl/ adj theoretisch

theory /ˈθɪərɪ/ n Theorie f; in ~ theoretisch

therap|**ist** /ˈθerəpɪst/ n Therapeut(in) m(f). ~**y** n Therapie f

there /ðeə(r)/ adv da; (with movement) dahin, dorthin; down/up ~ da unten/oben; ~ is/are da ist/ sind; (in existence) es gibt ● int ~, ~! nun, nun!

there: ~**abouts** adv da [in der Nähe]; or ~abouts (roughly) ungefähr. ~**fore** /-fɔː(r)/ adv deshalb, also

thermometer /θəˈmɒmɪtə(r)/ n Thermometer nt

Thermos ® /ˈθɜːməs/ n ~ [flask] Thermosflasche ® f

thermostat /ˈθɜːməstæt/ n Thermostat m

these /ðiːz/ see this

thesis /ˈθiːsɪs/ n (pl -ses /-siːz/) Dissertation f; (proposition) These f

they /ðeɪ/ pron sie; ~ say (generalizing) man sagt

thick /θɪk/ adj (-er, -est) dick; (dense) dicht; (liquid) dickflüssig; (🔲: stupid) dumm ● adv dick ● n in the ~ of mitten in (+ dat). ~**en** vt dicker machen; eindicken (sauce) ● vi dicker werden; (fog:) dichter werden; (plot:) komplizierter werden. ~**ness** n Dicke f; Dichte f; Dickflüssigkeit f

thief /θiːf/ n (pl thieves) Dieb(in) m(f)

thigh /θaɪ/ n Oberschenkel m

thimble /ˈθɪmbl/ n Fingerhut m

thin /θɪn/ adj (thinner, thinnest) dünn ● adv dünn ● v (pt/pp thinned) ● vt verdünnen (liquid) ● vi sich lichten

thing /θɪŋ/ n Ding nt; (subject, affair) Sache f; ∼s pl (belongings) Sachen pl; for one ∼ erstens; just the ∼! genau das Richtige! how are ∼s? wie geht's? the latest ∼ 🔲 der letzte Schrei

think /θɪŋk/ vt/i (pt/pp thought) denken (about/of an + acc); (believe) meinen; (consider) nachdenken; (regard as) halten für; I ∼ so ich glaube schon; what do you ∼ of it? was halten Sie davon? ∼ over vt sich (dat) überlegen. ∼ up vt sich (dat) ausdenken

third /θɜːd/ adj dritte(r,s) ● n Drittel nt. ∼ly adv drittens. ∼-rate adj drittrangig

thirst /θɜːst/ n Durst m. ∼y adj, -ily adv durstig; be ∼y Durst haben

thirteen /θɜːˈtiːn/ adj dreizehn. ∼th adj dreizehnte(r,s)

thirtieth /ˈθɜːtɪɪθ/ adj dreißigste(r,s)

thirty /ˈθɜːtɪ/ adj dreißig

this /ðɪs/ adj (pl these) diese(r,s); (pl) diese; ∼ one diese(r,s); I'll take ∼ ich nehme diesen/diese/dieses; ∼ evening/morning heute Abend/Morgen; these days heutzutage ● pron (pl these) dies, dies[es]; (pl) die, diese; ∼ and that dies und das; ∼ or that dieses oder das da; like ∼ so; ∼ is Peter das ist Peter; (Teleph) hier [spricht] Peter; who is ∼? wer ist das? (Teleph, Amer) wer ist am Apparat?

thistle /ˈθɪsl/ n Distel f

thorn /θɔːn/ n Dorn m

thorough /ˈθʌrə/ adj gründlich

thoroughbred n reinrassiges Tier nt; (horse) Rassepferd nt

thorough|ly /ˈθʌrəlɪ/ adv gründlich; (completely) völlig; (extremely) äußerst. ∼ness n Gründlichkeit f

those /ðəʊz/ see that

though /ðəʊ/ conj obgleich, obwohl; as ∼ als ob ● adv 🔲 doch

thought /θɔːt/ see think ● n Gedanke m; (thinking) Denken nt. ∼ful adj nachdenklich; (considerate) rücksichtsvoll. ∼less adj gedankenlos

thousand /ˈθaʊznd/ adj one/a ∼ [ein]tausend ● n Tausend nt. ∼th adj tausendste(r,s) ● n Tausendstel nt

thrash /θræʃ/ vt verprügeln; (defeat) [vernichtend] schlagen

thread /θred/ n Faden m; (of screw) Gewinde nt ● vt einfädeln; auffädeln (beads). ∼bare adj fadenscheinig

threat /θret/ n Drohung f; (danger) Bedrohung f

threaten /ˈθretn/ vt drohen (+ dat); (with weapon) bedrohen; ∼ s.o. with sth jdm etw androhen ● vi drohen. ∼ing adj drohend; (ominous) bedrohlich

three /θriː/ adj drei. ∼fold adj & adv dreifach

thresh /θreʃ/ vt dreschen

threshold /ˈθreʃəʊld/ n Schwelle f

threw /θruː/ see throw

thrift /θrɪft/ n Sparsamkeit f. ∼y adj sparsam

thrill /θrɪl/ n Erregung f; 🔲 Nervenkitzel m ● vt (excite) erregen; be ∼ed with sich sehr freuen über (+ acc). ∼er n Thriller m. ∼ing adj erregend

thrive /θraɪv/ vi (pt thrived or throve, pp thrived or thriven /ˈθrɪvn/) gedeihen (on bei); (business) florieren

throat /θrəʊt/ *n* Hals *m*; **cut s.o.'s ~** jdm die Kehle durchschneiden

throb /θrɒb/ *n* Pochen *nt* ● *vi* (*pt*/*pp* throbbed) pochen; (*vibrate*) vibrieren

throes /θrəʊz/ *npl* **in the ~ of** (*fig*) mitten in (+ *dat*)

throne /θrəʊn/ *n* Thron *m*

throttle /ˈθrɒtl/ *vt* erdrosseln

through /θruː/ *prep* durch (+ *acc*); (*during*) während (+ *gen*); (*Amer: up to & including*) bis einschließlich ● *adv* durch; **wet ~** durch und durch nass; **read sth ~** etw durchlesen ● *adj* (*train*) durchgehend; **be ~** (*finished*) fertig sein; (*Teleph*) durch sein

throughout /θruːˈaʊt/ *prep* **~ the country** im ganzen Land; **~ the night** die Nacht durch ● *adv* ganz; (*time*) die ganze Zeit

throve /θrəʊv/ *see* **thrive**

throw /θrəʊ/ *n* Wurf *m* ● *vt* (*pt* threw, *pp* **thrown**) werfen; schütten (*liquid*); betätigen (*switch*); abwerfen (*rider*); ([!]: *disconcert*) aus der Fassung bringen; [!] geben (*party*); **~ sth to s.o.** jdm etw zuwerfen. **~ away** *vt* wegwerfen. **~ out** *vt* hinauswerfen; (**~** *away*) wegwerfen; verwerfen (*plan*). **~ up** *vt* hochwerfen ● *vi* sich übergeben

ˈthrow-away *adj* Wegwerf-

thrush /θrʌʃ/ *n* Drossel *f*

thrust /θrʌst/ *n* Stoß *m*; (*Phys*) Schub *m* ● *vt* (*pt*/*pp* **thrust**) stoßen; (*insert*) stecken

thud /θʌd/ *n* dumpfer Schlag *m*

thug /θʌg/ *n* Schläger *m*

thumb /θʌm/ *n* Daumen *m* ● *vt* **~ a lift** [!] per Anhalter fahren. **~tack** *n* (*Amer*) Reißzwecke *f*

thump /θʌmp/ *n* Schlag *m*; (*noise*) dumpfer Schlag *m* ● *vt* schlagen ● *vi* hämmern; (*heart:*) pochen

thunder /ˈθʌndə(r)/ *n* Donner *m* ● *vi* donnern. **~clap** *n* Donnerschlag *m*. **~stòrm** *n* Gewitter *nt*. **~y** *adj* gewittrig

Thursday /ˈθɜːzdeɪ/ *n* Donnerstag *m*

thus /ðʌs/ *adv* so

thwart /θwɔːt/ *vt* vereiteln; **~ s.o.** jdm einen Strich durch die Rechnung machen

tick¹ /tɪk/ *n* **on ~** [!] auf Pump

tick² *n* (*sound*) Ticken *nt*; (*mark*) Häkchen *nt*; ([!]: *instant*) Sekunde *f* ● *vi* ticken ● *vt* abhaken. **~ off** *vt* abhaken; [!] rüffeln

ticket /ˈtɪkɪt/ *n* Karte *f*; (*for bus, train*) Fahrschein *m*; (*Aviat*) Flugschein *m*; (*for lottery*) Los *nt*; (*for article deposited*) Schein *m*; (*label*) Schild *nt*; (*for library*) Lesekarte *f*; (*fine*) Strafzettel *m*. **~ collector** *n* Fahrkartenkontrolleur *m*. **~ office** *n* Fahrkartenschalter *m*; (*for entry*) Kasse *f*

tick|le /ˈtɪkl/ *n* Kitzeln *nt* ● *vt*/*i* kitzeln. **~lish** *adj* kitzlig

tidal /ˈtaɪdl/ *adj* **~ wave** Flutwelle *f*

tide /taɪd/ *n* Gezeiten *pl*; (*of events*) Strom *m*; **the ~ is in/out** es ist Flut/Ebbe ● *vt* **~ s.o. over** jdm über die Runden helfen

tidiness /ˈtaɪdɪnɪs/ *n* Ordentlichkeit *f*

tidy /ˈtaɪdɪ/ *adj* , **-ily** *adv* ordentlich ● *vt* **~ [up]** aufräumen

tie /taɪ/ *n* Krawatte *f*; Schlips *m*; (*cord*) Schnur *f*; (*fig: bond*) Band *nt*; (*restriction*) Bindung *f*; (*Sport*) Unentschieden *nt*; (*in competition*) Punktgleichheit *f* ● *v* (*pres p* **tying**) ● *vt* binden; machen (*knot*) ● *vi* (*Sport*) unentschieden spielen; (*have equal scores, votes*) punktgleich sein.

~ **up** vt festbinden; verschnüren (parcel); fesseln (person); be ~d up (busy) beschäftigt sein

tier /tɪə(r)/ n Stufe f; (of cake) Etage f; (in stadium) Rang m

tiger /ˈtaɪgə(r)/ n Tiger m

tight /taɪt/ adj (-er, -est) fest; (taut) straff; (clothes) eng; (control) streng; (🔡: drunk) blau ● adv fest

tighten /ˈtaɪtn/ vt fester ziehen; straffen (rope); anziehen (screw); verschärfen (control) ● vi sich spannen

tightrope n Hochseil nt

tights /taɪts/ npl Strumpfhose f

tile /taɪl/ n Fliese f; (on wall) Kachel f; (on roof) [Dach]ziegel m ● vt mit Fliesen auslegen; kacheln (wall); decken (roof)

till[1] /tɪl/ prep & conj = until

till[2] n Kasse f

tilt /tɪlt/ n Neigung f ● vt kippen; [zur Seite] neigen (head) ● vi sich neigen

timber /ˈtɪmbə(r)/ n [Nutz]holz nt

time /taɪm/ n Zeit f; (occasion) Mal nt; (rhythm) Takt m; (Math) mal; at ~s manchmal; ~ and again immer wieder; two at a ~ zwei auf einmal; on ~ pünktlich; in ~ rechtzeitig; (eventually) mit der Zeit; in no ~ im Handumdrehen; in a year's ~ in einem Jahr; behind ~ verspätet; behind the ~s rückständig; for the ~ being vorläufig; what is the ~? wie spät ist es? wie viel Uhr ist es? did you have a nice ~? hat es dir gut gefallen? ● vt stoppen (race); be well ~d gut abgepaßt sein

time: ~ **bomb** n Zeitbombe f. ~**less** adj zeitlos. ~**ly** adj rechtzeitig. ~**switch** n Zeitschalter m. ~-**table** n Fahrplan m; (Sch) Stundenplan m

timid /ˈtɪmɪd/ adj scheu; (hesitant) zaghaft

timing /ˈtaɪmɪŋ/ n (Sport, Techn) Timing nt

tin /tɪn/ n Zinn nt; (container) Dose f ● vt (pt/pp tinned) in Dosen konservieren. ~ **foil** n Stanniol nt; (Culin) Alufolie f

tinge /tɪndʒ/ n Hauch m

tingle /ˈtɪŋgl/ vi kribbeln

tinker /ˈtɪŋkə(r)/ vi herumbasteln (with an + dat)

tinkle /ˈtɪŋkl/ n Klingeln nt ● vi klingeln

tinned /tɪnd/ adj Dosen-

'tin opener n Dosenöffner m

tinsel /ˈtɪnsl/ n Lametta nt

tint /tɪnt/ n Farbton m ● vt tönen

tiny /ˈtaɪnɪ/ adj winzig

tip[1] /tɪp/ n Spitze f

tip[2] n (money) Trinkgeld nt; (advice) Rat m, 🔡 Tipp m; (for rubbish) Müllhalde f ● vt (pt/pp tipped) ● vt (tilt) kippen; (reward) Trinkgeld geben (s.o. jdm) ● vi kippen. ~ **out** vt auskippen. ~ **over** vt/i umkippen

tipped /tɪpt/ adj Filter-

tipsy /ˈtɪpsɪ/ adj beschwipst

tiptoe /ˈtɪptəʊ/ n on ~ auf Zehenspitzen

tiptop /tɪpˈtɒp/ adj 🔡 erstklassig

tire /ˈtaɪə(r)/ vt/i ermüden. ~**d** adj müde; be ~d of sth etw satt haben; ~d out [völlig] erschöpft. ~**less** adj unermüdlich. ~**some** adj lästig

tiring /ˈtaɪərɪŋ/ adj ermüdend

tissue /ˈtɪʃuː/ n Gewebe nt; (handkerchief) Papiertaschentuch nt

tit /tɪt/ n (bird) Meise f

'titbit n Leckerbissen m

title /ˈtaɪtl/ n Titel m

to /tuː/, unbetont /tə/
● *preposition*
····▸ *(destinations: most cases)* zu (+ dat.). go to work/the station zur Arbeit/zum Bahnhof gehen. from house to house von Haus zu Haus. go/come to s.o. zu jdm gehen/kommen
····▸ *(with name of place or points of compass)* nach. go to Paris/Germany nach Paris/Deutschland. to Switzerland in die Schweiz. from East to West von Osten nach Westen. I've never been to Berlin ich war noch nie in Berlin
····▸ *(to cinema, theatre, bed)* in (+ acc). to bed with you! ins Bett mit dir!
····▸ *(to wedding, party, university, the toilet)* auf (+ acc).
····▸ *(up to)* bis (+ dat). to the end bis zum Schluss. to this day bis heute. 5 to 6 pounds 5 bis 6 Pfund
····▸ *(give, say, write)* + dat. give/say sth to s.o. jdm etw geben/sagen. she wrote to him/the firm sie hat ihm/an die Firma geschrieben
····▸ *(address, send, fasten)* an (+ acc). she sent it to her brother sie schickte es an ihren Bruder
····▸ *(in telling the time)* vor. five to eight fünf vor acht. a quarter to ten Viertel vor zehn
● *before infinitive*
····▸ *(after modal verb)* *(not translated)*. I want to go ich will gehen. he is learning to swim er lernt schwimmen. you have to do you must [es tun]
····▸ *(after adjective)* zu. it is easy to forget es ist leicht zu vergessen

····▸ *(expressing purpose, result)* um ... zu. he did it to annoy me er tat es, um mich zu ärgern. she was too tired to go sie war zu müde um zu gehen
● *adverb*
····▸ be to *(door, window)* angelehnt sein. pull a door to eine Tür anlehnen
····▸ **to and fro** hin und her

toad /təʊd/ n Kröte f

toast /təʊst/ n Toast m ● vt toasten *(bread)*; *(drink a ~ to)* trinken auf (+ acc). **~er** n Toaster m

tobacco /tə'bækəʊ/ n Tabak m. **~nist's [shop]** n Tabakladen m

toboggan /tə'bɒgən/ n Schlitten m ● vi Schlitten fahren

today /tə'deɪ/ n & adv heute; ~ week heute in einer Woche

toddler /'tɒdlə(r)/ n Kleinkind nt

toe /təʊ/ n Zeh m; *(of footwear)* Spitze f ● vt ~ the line spuren. **~nail** n Zehennagel m

toffee /'tɒfɪ/ n Karamell m & nt

together /tə'geðə(r)/ adv zusammen; *(at the same time)* gleichzeitig

toilet /'tɔɪlɪt/ n Toilette f. ~ **bag** n Kulturbeutel m. ~ **paper** n Toilettenpapier nt

toiletries /'tɔɪltrɪz/ npl Toilettenartikel pl

token /'təʊkən/ n Zeichen nt; *(counter)* Marke f; *(voucher)* Gutschein m ● attrib symbolisch

told /təʊld/ see **tell** ● adj **all** ~ insgesamt

tolerable /'tɒlərəbl/ adj, **-bly** adv erträglich; *(not bad)* leidlich

toleran|ce /'tɒlərəns/ n Toleranz f. **~t** adj tolerant

tolerate /'tɒləreɪt/ vt dulden, tolerieren; *(bear)* ertragen

toll /təʊl/ n Gebühr f; (for road) Maut f (Aust); death ~ Zahl f der Todesopfer

tomato /təˈmɑːtəʊ/ n (pl -es) Tomate f

tomb /tuːm/ n Grabmal nt

'tombstone n Grabstein m

'tom-cat n Kater m

tomorrow /təˈmɒrəʊ/ n & adv morgen; ~ **morning** morgen früh; **the day after** ~ übermorgen; see **you** ~! bis morgen!

ton /tʌn/ n Tonne f; ~**s of** 🔟 jede Menge

tone /təʊn/ n Ton m; (colour) Farbton m ● vt ~ **down** dämpfen; (fig) mäßigen. ~ **up** vt kräftigen; straffen (muscles)

tongs /tɒŋz/ npl Zange f

tongue /tʌŋ/ n Zunge f; ~ **in cheek** 🔟 nicht ernst

tonic /ˈtɒnɪk/ n Tonikum nt; (for hair) Haarwasser nt; (fig) Wohltat f; ~ [**water**] Tonic nt

tonight /təˈnaɪt/ n & adv heute Nacht; (evening) heute Abend

tonne /tʌn/ n Tonne f

tonsil /ˈtɒnsl/ n (Anat) Mandel f. ~**litis** /-ˈlaɪtɪs/ n Mandelentzündung f

too /tuː/ adv auch; (also) auch; ~ **much/little** zu viel/zu wenig

took /tʊk/ see **take**

tool /tuːl/ n Werkzeug nt; (for gardening) Gerät nt. ~**bar** n Werkzeugleiste f

tooth /tuːθ/ n (pl teeth) Zahn m

'tooth|ache n Zahnschmerzen pl. ~**brush** n Zahnbürste f. ~**less** adj zahnlos. ~**paste** n Zahnpasta f. ~**pick** n Zahnstocher m

top[1] /tɒp/ n (toy) Kreisel m.

top[2] n oberer Teil m; (apex) Spitze f; (summit) Gipfel m; (Sch) Erste(r) m/f; (top part or half) Oberteil m;

(head) Kopfende nt; (of road) oberes Ende nt; (upper surface) Oberfläche f; (lid) Deckel m; (of bottle) Verschluss m; (garment) Top nt; **at the/on** ~ oben; **on** ~ **of** oben auf (+ dat); **on** ~ **of that** (besides) obendrein; **from** ~ **to bottom** von oben bis unten ● adj oberste(r,s); (highest) höchste(r,s); (best) beste(r,s) ● vt (pt/pp **topped**) an erster Stelle stehen auf (+ dat) (list); (exceed) übersteigen; (remove the ~ of) die Spitze abschneiden von. ~ **up** vt nachfüllen, auffüllen

top: ~ '**hat** n Zylinder[hut] m. ~**-heavy** adj kopflastig

topic /ˈtɒpɪk/ n Thema nt. ~**al** adj aktuell

topple /ˈtɒpl/ vt/i umstürzen

torch /tɔːtʃ/ n Taschenlampe f; (flaming) Fackel f

tore /tɔː(r)/ see **tear**[1]

torment[1] /ˈtɔːment/ n Qual f

torment[2] /tɔːˈment/ vt quälen

torn /tɔːn/ see **tear**[1] ● adj zerrissen

torpedo /tɔːˈpiːdəʊ/ n (pl -es) Torpedo m ● vt torpedieren

torrent /ˈtɒrənt/ n reißender Strom m. ~**ial** adj (rain) wolkenbruchartig

tortoise /ˈtɔːtəs/ n Schildkröte f. ~**shell** n Schildpatt m

tortuous /ˈtɔːtjʊəs/ adj verschlungen; (fig) umständlich

torture /ˈtɔːtʃə(r)/ n Folter f; (fig) Qual f ● vt foltern; (fig) quälen

toss /tɒs/ vt werfen; (into the air) hochwerfen; (shake) schütteln; (in seat) abwerfen; mischen (salad); wenden (pancake); ~ **a coin** mit einer Münze losen ● vi ~ **and turn** (in bed) sich [schlaflos] im Bett wälzen

tot[1] /tɒt/ n kleines Kind nt; (🔟: of liquor) Gläschen nt

|

tot² vt (pt/pp **totted**) ~ **up** 🔢 zusammenzählen

total /'təʊtl/ adj gesamt; (complete) völlig, total ●n Gesamtzahl f; (sum) Gesamtsumme f ●vt (pt/pp totalled); (amount to) sich belaufen auf (+ acc)

totalitarian /təʊtælɪ'teərɪən/ adj totalitär

totally /'təʊtəlɪ/ adv völlig, total

totter /'tɒtə(r)/ vi taumeln

touch /tʌtʃ/ n Berührung f; (sense) Tastsinn m; (Mus) Anschlag m; (contact) Kontakt m; (trace) Spur f; (fig) Anflug m; **get/be in** ~ sich in Verbindung setzen/in Verbindung stehen (with mit) ●vt berühren; (get hold of) anfassen; (lightly) tippen auf/an (+ acc); (brush against) streifen [gegen]; (fig: move) rühren; anrühren (food, subject); **don't** ~ **that!** fass das nicht an! ●vi sich berühren; ~ **on** (fig) berühren; ~ **down** vi (Aviat) landen. ~ **up** vt ausbessern

touch|ing /'tʌtʃɪŋ/ adj rührend. ~ **y** adj empfindlich

tough /tʌf/ adj (-er, -est) zäh; (severe, harsh) hart; (difficult) schwierig; (durable) strapazierfähig

toughen /'tʌfn/ vt härten; ~ **up** abhärten

tour /tʊə(r)/ n Reise f, Tour f; (of building, town) Besichtigung f; (Theat, Sport) Tournee f; (of duty) Dienstzeit f ●vt fahren durch ●vi herumreisen

touris|m /'tʊərɪzm/ n Tourismus m, Fremdenverkehr m. ~**t** n Tourist(in) m(f) ●attrib Touristen-. ~**t office** n Fremdenverkehrsbüro nt

tournament /'tʊənəmənt/ n Turnier nt

'tour operator n Reiseveranstalter m

tousle /'taʊzl/ vt zerzausen

tow /təʊ/ n give s.o./a car a ~ jdn/ein Auto abschleppen ●vt schleppen; ziehen (trailer)

toward[s] /tə'wɔːd(z)/ prep zu (+ dat); (with time) gegen (+ acc); (with respect to) gegenüber (+ dat)

towel /'taʊəl/ n Handtuch nt. ~**ling** n (cloth) Frottee nt

tower /'taʊə(r)/ n Turm m ●vi ~ **above** überragen. ~ **block** n Hochhaus nt. ~**ing** adj hoch aufragend

town /taʊn/ n Stadt f. ~ **'hall** n Rathaus nt

'tow-rope n Abschleppseil nt

toxic /'tɒksɪk/ adj giftig

toy /tɔɪ/ n Spielzeug nt ●vi ~ **with** spielen mit; stochern in (+ dat) (food). ~**shop** n Spielwarengeschäft nt

trac|e /treɪs/ n Spur f ●vt folgen (+ dat); (find) finden; (draw) zeichnen; (with tracing-paper) durchpausen

track /træk/ n Spur f; (path) [unbefestigter] Weg m; (Sport) Bahn f; (Rail) Gleis nt; **keep** ~ **of** im Auge behalten ●vt verfolgen. ~ **down** vt aufspüren; (find) finden

'tracksuit n Trainingsanzug m

tractor /'træktə(r)/ n Traktor m

trade /treɪd/ n Handel m; (line of business) Gewerbe nt; (business) Geschäft nt; (craft) Handwerk nt; **by** ~ von Beruf ●vt tauschen; ~ **in** (give in part exchange) in Zahlung geben ●vi handeln (in mit)

'trade mark n Warenzeichen nt

'trader /'treɪdə(r)/ n Händler m

trade: ~ 'union n Gewerkschaft f. ~ **'unionist** n Gewerkschaftler(in) m(f)

trading /'treɪdɪŋ/ n Handel m

tradition /trə'dɪʃn/ n Tradition f. ~**al** adj traditionell

traffic /'træfɪk/ n Verkehr m; (*trading*) Handel m

traffic: ~ **circle** n (*Amer*) Kreisverkehr m. ~ **jam** n [Verkehrs]stau m. ~ **lights** npl [Verkehrs]ampel f. ~ **warden** n ≈ Hilfspolizist m; (*woman*) Politesse f

tragedy /'trædʒədɪ/ n Tragödie f

tragic /'trædʒɪk/ adj, **-ally** adv tragisch

trail /treɪl/ n Spur f; (*path*) Weg m, Pfad m ● vi schleifen; (*plant:*) sich ranken ● vt verfolgen, folgen (+ *dat*); (*drag*) schleifen

trailer /'treɪlə(r)/ n (*Auto*) Anhänger m; (*Amer: caravan*) Wohnwagen m; (*film*) Vorschau f

train /treɪn/ n Zug m; (*of dress*) Schleppe f ● vt ausbilden; (*Sport*) trainieren; (*aim*) richten auf (+ *acc*); erziehen (*child*); abrichten/(*to do tricks*) dressieren (*animal*); ziehen (*plant*) ● vi eine Ausbildung machen; (*Sport*) trainieren. ~**ed** adj ausgebildet

trainee /treɪ'niː/ n Auszubildende(r) m/f; (*Techn*) Praktikant(in) m(f)

train|er /'treɪnə(r)/ n (*Sport*) Trainer m; (*in circus*) Dompteur m; ~**ers** pl Trainingsschuhe pl. ~**ing** n Ausbildung f; (*Sport*) Training nt; (*of animals*) Dressur f

trait /treɪt/ n Eigenschaft f

traitor /'treɪtə(r)/ n Verräter m

tram /træm/ n Straßenbahn f

tramp /træmp/ n Landstreicher m ● vi stapfen; (*walk*) marschieren

trample /'træmpl/ vt/i trampeln

trance /trɑːns/ n Trance f

tranquil /'træŋkwɪl/ adj ruhig. ~**lity** n Ruhe f

tranquillizer /'træŋkwɪlaɪzə(r)/ n Beruhigungsmittel nt

transaction /træn'zækʃn/ n Transaktion f

transcend /træn'send/ vt übersteigen

transfer[1] /'trænsfɜː(r)/ n (*see* transfer[2]) Übertragung f; Verlegung f; Versetzung f; Überweisung f; (*Sport*) Transfer m; (*design*) Abziehbild nt

transfer[2] /træns'fɜː(r)/ v (*pt/pp* transferred*) ● vt übertragen; verlegen (*firm, prisoners*); versetzen (*employee*); überweisen (*money*); (*Sport*) transferieren ● vi [über]wechseln; (*when travelling*) umsteigen

transform /træns'fɔːm/ vt verwandeln. ~**ation** n Verwandlung f. ~**er** n Transformator m

transfusion /træns'fjuːʒn/ n Transfusion f

transistor /træn'zɪstə(r)/ n Transistor m

transit /'trænsɪt/ n Transit m; (*of goods*) Transport m; **in** ~ (*goods*) auf dem Transport

transition /træn'sɪʒn/ n Übergang m. ~**al** adj Übergangs-

translat|e /træns'leɪt/ vt übersetzen. ~**ion** n Übersetzung f. ~**or** n Übersetzer(in) m(f)

transmission /trænz'mɪʃn/ n Übertragung f

transmit /trænz'mɪt/ vt (*pt/pp* transmitted*) übertragen. ~**ter** n Sender m

transparen|cy /træns'pærənsɪ/ n (*Phot*) Dia nt. ~**t** adj durchsichtig

transplant[1] /'trænsplɑːnt/ n Verpflanzung f, Transplantation f

transplant[2] /træns'plɑːnt/ vt umpflanzen; (*Med*) verpflanzen

transport[1] /'trænspɔːt/ n Transport m

transport[2] /træn'spɔːt/ vt transportieren. ~**ation** n Transport m

transpose /træns'pəʊz/ vt

umstellen

trap /træp/ n Falle f; (🔲: mouth) Klappe f; pony and ~ Einspänner m ● vt (pt/pp trapped) [mit einer Falle] fangen; (jam) einklemmen; be ~ped festsitzen; (shut in) eingeschlossen sein. ~'door n Falltür f

trash /træʃ/ n Schund m; (rubbish) Abfall m; (nonsense) Quatsch m. ~can n (Amer) Mülleimer m. ~y adj Schund-

trauma /'trɔːmə/ n Trauma nt. ~tic adj traumatisch

travel /'trævl/ n Reisen nt ● v (pt/pp travelled) ● vi reisen; (go in vehicle) fahren; (light, sound:) sich fortpflanzen; (Techn) sich bewegen ● vt bereisen; fahren (distance). ~ agency n Reisebüro nt. ~ agent n Reisebürokaufmann m

traveller /'trævələ(r)/ n Reisende(r) m/f; (Comm) Vertreter m; ~s pl (gypsies) Zigeuner pl. ~'s cheque n Reisescheck m

trawler /'trɔːlə(r)/ n Fischdampfer m

tray /treɪ/ n Tablett nt; (for baking) [Back]blech nt; (for documents) Ablagekorb m

treacher|ous /'tretʃərəs/ adj treulos; (dangerous, deceptive) tückisch. ~y n Verrat m

tread /tred/ n Schritt m; (step) Stufe f; (of tyre) Profil nt ● v (pt trod, pp trodden) ● vi (walk) gehen; ~ on/in treten auf/ in (+ acc) ● vt treten

treason /'triːzn/ n Verrat m

treasure /'treʒə(r)/ n Schatz m ● vt in Ehren halten. ~r n Kassenwart m

treasury /'treʒərɪ/ n Schatzkammer f; the T~ das Finanzministerium

treat /triːt/ n [besonderes] Vergnü-

gen nt ● vt behandeln; ~ s.o. to sth jdm etw spendieren

treatment /'triːtmənt/ n Behandlung f

treaty /'triːtɪ/ n Vertrag m

treble /'trebl/ adj dreifach; ~ the amount dreimal so viel ● n (Mus) Diskant m; (voice) Sopran m ● vt verdreifachen ● vi sich verdreifachen

tree /triː/ n Baum m

trek /trek/ n Marsch m ● vi (pt/pp trekked) latschen

trellis /'trelɪs/ n Gitter nt

tremble /'trembl/ vi zittern

tremendous /trɪ'mendəs/ adj gewaltig; (🔲: excellent) großartig

tremor /'tremə(r)/ n Zittern nt; [earth] ~ Beben nt

trench /trentʃ/ n Graben m; (Mil) Schützengraben m

trend /trend/ n Tendenz f; (fashion) Trend m. ~y adj 🔲 modisch

trepidation /trepɪ'deɪʃn/ n Beklommenheit f

trespass /'trespəs/ vi ~ on unerlaubt betreten

trial /'traɪəl/ n (Jur) [Gerichts]verfahren nt, Prozess m; (test) Probe f; (ordeal) Prüfung f; be on ~ auf Probe sein; (Jur) angeklagt sein (for wegen); by ~ and error durch Probieren

triang|le /'traɪæŋgl/ n Dreieck nt; (Mus) Triangel m. ~ular adj dreieckig

tribe /traɪb/ n Stamm m

tribunal /traɪ'bjuːnl/ n Schiedsgericht nt

tributary /'trɪbjʊtərɪ/ n Nebenfluss m

tribute /'trɪbjuːt/ n Tribut m; pay ~ Tribut zollen (to dat)

trick /trɪk/ n Trick m; (joke) Streich m; (Cards) Stich m; (feat of skill)

t

Kunststück nt ●vt täuschen, ⊞ hereinlegen

trickle /'trɪkl/ vi rinnen

trick|ster /'trɪkstə(r)/ n Schwindler m. ~y adj adj schwierig

tricycle /'traɪsɪkl/ n Dreirad nt

tried /traɪd/ see try

trifl|e /'traɪfl/ n Kleinigkeit f; (Culin) Trifle nt. ~ing adj unbedeutend

trigger /'trɪgə(r)/ n Abzug m; (fig) Auslöser m ●vt ~ [off] auslösen

trim /trɪm/ adj (trimmer, trimmest) gepflegt ●n (cut) Nachschneiden nt; (decoration) Verzierung f; (condition) Zustand m ●vt schneiden; (decorate) besetzen. ~ming n Besatz m; ~mings npl (accessories) Zubehör nt; (decorations) Verzierungen pl

trio /'triːəʊ/ n Trio nt

trip /trɪp/ n Reise f; (excursion) Ausflug m ●v (pt/pp tripped) ●vt ~ s.o. up jdm ein Bein stellen ●vi stolpern (on/over über + acc)

tripe /traɪp/ n Kaldaunen pl; (nonsense) Quatsch m

triple /'trɪpl/ adj dreifach ●vt verdreifachen ●vi sich verdreifachen

triplets /'trɪplɪts/ npl Drillinge pl

triplicate /'trɪplɪkət/ n in ~ in dreifacher Ausfertigung

tripod /'traɪpɒd/ n Stativ nt

tripper /'trɪpə(r)/ n Ausflügler m

trite /traɪt/ adj banal

triumph /'traɪʌmf/ n Triumph m ●vi triumphieren (over über + acc). ~ant adj triumphierend

trivial /'trɪvɪəl/ adj belanglos. ~ity n Belanglosigkeit f

trod, trodden see tread

trolley /'trɒlɪ/ n (for food) Servierwagen m; (for shopping) Einkaufswagen m; (for luggage) Kofferkuli m; (Amer: tram) Straßenbahn f

trombone /trɒm'bəʊn/ n Posaune f

troop /truːp/ n Schar f; ~s pl Truppen pl

trophy /'trəʊfɪ/ n Trophäe f; (in competition) ≈ Pokal m

tropics /'trɒpɪks/ npl Tropen pl. ~al adj tropisch; (fruit) Süd-

trot /trɒt/ n Trab m ●vi (pt/pp trotted) traben

trouble /'trʌbl/ n Ärger m; (difficulties) Schwierigkeiten pl; (inconvenience) Mühe f; (conflict) Unruhe f; (Med) Beschwerden pl; (Techn) Probleme pl; get into ~ Ärger bekommen; take ~ sich (dat) Mühe geben ●vt (disturb) stören; (worry) beunruhigen ●vi sich bemühen. ~-maker n Unruhestifter m. ~some adj schwierig; (flies, cough) lästig

trough /trɒf/ n Trog m

troupe /truːp/ n Truppe f

trousers /'traʊzəz/ npl Hose f

trousseau /'truːsəʊ/ n Aussteuer f

trout /traʊt/ n inv Forelle f

trowel /'traʊəl/ n Kelle f

truant /'truːənt/ n play ~ die Schule schwänzen

truce /truːs/ n Waffenstillstand m

truck /trʌk/ n Last[kraft]wagen m; (Rail) Güterwagen m

trudge /trʌdʒ/ vi latschen

true /truː/ adj (-r, -st) wahr; (loyal) treu; (genuine) echt; come ~ in Erfüllung gehen; is that ~? stimmt das?

truly /'truːlɪ/ adv wirklich; (faithfully) treu; Yours ~ mit freundlichen Grüßen

trump /trʌmp/ n (Cards) Trumpf m ●vt übertrumpfen

trumpet /'trʌmpɪt/ n Trompete f. ~er n Trompeter m

truncheon /ˈtrʌntʃn/ n Schlagstock m

trunk /trʌŋk/ n (Baum)stamm m; (body) Rumpf m; (of elephant) Rüssel m; (for travelling) (Übersee)koffer m; (Amer: of car) Kofferraum m; ~s pl Badehose f

trust /trʌst/ n Vertrauen nt; (group of companies) Trust m; (organization) Treuhandgesellschaft f; (charitable) Stiftung f • vt trauen (+ dat), vertrauen (+ dat); (hope) hoffen • vi vertrauen (in/to auf + acc)

trustee /trʌsˈtiː/ n Treuhänder m

trust|ful /ˈtrʌstfl/ adj, ~ly adv, ~ing adj vertrauensvoll. ~worthy adj vertrauenswürdig

truth /truːθ/ n (pl -s /truːðz/) Wahrheit f. ~ful adj ehrlich

try /traɪ/ n Versuch m • v (pt/pp tried) • vt versuchen; (sample, taste) probieren; (be a strain on) anstrengen; (Jur) vor Gericht stellen; verhandeln (case) • vi versuchen; (make an effort) sich bemühen. ~ on vt anprobieren; aufprobieren (hat). ~ out vt ausprobieren

trying /ˈtraɪɪŋ/ adj schwierig

T-shirt /ˈtiː-/ n T-Shirt nt

tub /tʌb/ n Kübel m; (carton) Becher m; (bath) Wanne f

tuba /ˈtjuːbə/ n (Mus) Tuba f

tubby /ˈtʌbɪ/ adj rundlich

tube /tjuːb/ n Röhre f; (pipe) Rohr nt; (flexible) Schlauch m; (of toothpaste) Tube f; (Rail, 🄴) U-Bahn f

tuberculosis /tjuːbɜːkjʊˈləʊsɪs/ n Tuberkulose f

tubular /ˈtjuːbjʊlə(r)/ adj röhrenförmig

tuck /tʌk/ n Saum m; (decorative) Biese f • vt (put) stecken. ~ in vt hineinstecken; ~ s.o. in or up jdn zudecken • vi (🄴: eat) zulangen

Tuesday /ˈtjuːzdeɪ/ n Dienstag m

tuft /tʌft/ n Büschel nt

tug /tʌg/ n Ruck m; (Naut) Schleppdampfer m • v (pt/pp tugged) • vt ziehen • vi zerren (at an + dat)

tuition /tjuːˈɪʃn/ n Unterricht m

tulip /ˈtjuːlɪp/ n Tulpe f

tumble /ˈtʌmbl/ n Sturz m • vi fallen. ~down adj verfallen. ~drier n Wäschetrockner m

tumbler /ˈtʌmblə(r)/ n Glas nt

tummy /ˈtʌmɪ/ n 🄴 Bauch m

tumour /ˈtjuːmə(r)/ n Tumor m

tumult /ˈtjuːmʌlt/ n Tumult m

tuna /ˈtjuːnə/ n Thunfisch m

tune /tjuːn/ n Melodie f; out of ~ (instrument) verstimmt • vt stimmen; (Techn) einstellen. ~ in vt einstellen • vi ~ in to a station einen Sender einstellen. ~ up vi (Mus) stimmen

tuneful /ˈtjuːnfl/ adj melodisch

Tunisia /tjuːˈnɪzɪə/ n Tunesien nt

tunnel /ˈtʌnl/ n Tunnel m • vi (pt/pp tunnelled) einen Tunnel graben

turban /ˈtɜːbən/ n Turban m

turbine /ˈtɜːbaɪn/ n Turbine f

turbulen|ce /ˈtɜːbjʊləns/ n Turbulenz f. ~t adj stürmisch

turf /tɜːf/ n Rasen m; (segment) Rasenstück nt

Turk /tɜːk/ n Türke m/Türkin f

turkey /ˈtɜːkɪ/ n Truthahn m

Turk|ey n die Türkei. ~ish adj türkisch

turmoil /ˈtɜːmɔɪl/ n Aufruhr m; (confusion) Durcheinander m

turn /tɜːn/ n (rotation) Drehung f; (bend) Kurve f; (change of direction) Wende f; (Theat) Nummer f; (🄴: attack) Anfall m; do s.o. a good ~ jdm einen guten Dienst erweisen; take ~s abwechseln; in ~ der Reihe nach; out of ~ außer der Reihe; it's your ~ du bist an der

t

Reihe ● vt drehen; (~ over) wenden; (reverse) wenden; (Techn) drechseln (wood); ~ the page umblättern; ~ the corner um die Ecke biegen ● vi sich drehen; (~ round) sich umdrehen; (car:) wenden; (leaves:) sich drehen (weather:) umschlagen; (become) werden; ~ right/left nach rechts/links abbiegen; ~ to s.o. sich an jdn wenden. ~ away vt abweisen ● vi sich abwenden. ~ down vt herunterschlagen (collar); herunterdrehen (heat, gas); leiser stellen (sound); (reject) ablehnen; abweisen (person). ~ in vt einschlagen (edges) ● vi (car:) einbiegen; (🔲: go to bed) ins Bett gehen. ~ off vt zudrehen (tap); ausschalten (light, radio); abstellen (water, gas, engine, machine) ● vi abbiegen. ~ on vt aufdrehen (tap); einschalten (light, radio); anstellen (water, gas, engine, machine). ~ out vt (expel) vertreiben, 🔲 hinauswerfen; ausschalten (light); abdrehen (gas); (produce) produzieren; (empty) ausleeren; [gründlich] aufräumen (room, cupboard) ● vi (go out) hinausgehen; (transpire) sich herausstellen. ~ over vt umdrehen. ~ up vt hochschlagen (collar); aufdrehen (heat, gas); lauter stellen (sound, radio) ● vi auftauchen

turning /ˈtɜːnɪŋ/ n Abzweigung f. **~point** n Wendepunkt m

turnip /ˈtɜːnɪp/ n weiße Rübe f

turn: **~out** n (of people) Beteiligung f. **~over** n (Comm) Umsatz m; (of staff) Personalwechsel m. **~pike** n (Amer) gebührenpflichtige Autobahn f. **~table** n Drehscheibe f; (on record player) Plattenteller m. **~up** n [Hosen]aufschlag m

turquoise /ˈtɜːkwɔɪz/ adj türkis[farben] ● n (gem) Türkis m

turret /ˈtʌrɪt/ n Türmchen n

turtle /ˈtɜːtl/ n Seeschildkröte f

tusk /tʌsk/ n Stoßzahn m

tutor /ˈtjuːtə(r)/ n [Privat]lehrer m

tuxedo /tʌkˈsiːdəʊ/ n (Amer) Smoking m

TV /tiːˈviː/ abbr television

tweed /twiːd/ n Tweed m

tweezers /ˈtwiːzəz/ npl Pinzette f

twelfth /twelfθ/ adj zwölfter(r,s)

twelve /twelv/ adj zwölf

twentieth /ˈtwentɪθ/ adj zwanzigste(r,s)

twenty /ˈtwentɪ/ adj zwanzig

twice /twaɪs/ adv zweimal

twig /twɪg/ n Zweig m

twilight /ˈtwaɪ-/ n Dämmerlicht n

twin /twɪn/ n Zwilling m ● attrib Zwillings-

twine /twaɪn/ n Bindfaden m

twinge /twɪndʒ/ n Stechen nt; ~ of conscience Gewissensbisse pl

twinkle /ˈtwɪŋkl/ n Funkeln nt ● vi funkeln

twin 'town n Partnerstadt f

twirl /twɜːl/ vt/i herumwirbeln

twist /twɪst/ n Drehung f; (curve) Kurve f; (unexpected occurrence) überraschende Wendung f ● vt drehen; (distort) verdrehen; (🔲: swindle) beschummeln ● vi sich drehen; ~ one's ankle sich (dat) den Knöchel verrenken ● vi sich drehen; (road:) sich winden. **~er** n 🔲 Schwindler m

twit /twɪt/ n 🔲 Trottel m

twitch /twɪtʃ/ n Zucken nt ● vi zucken

twitter /ˈtwɪtə(r)/ n Zwitschern nt ● vi zwitschern

two /tuː/ adj zwei

two: **~faced** adj falsch. **~piece** adj zweiteilig. **~way** adj ~-way traffic Gegenverkehr m

tycoon /taɪˈkuːn/ n Magnat m

tying /'taɪŋ/ *see* tie

type /taɪp/ n Art f, Sorte f; (*person*) Typ m; (*printing*) Type f ● vt mit der Maschine schreiben, 🔤 tippen ● vi Maschine schreiben, 🔤 tippen.
~**writer** n Schreibmaschine f.
~**written** adj maschinengeschrieben

typical /'tɪpɪkl/ adj typisch (of für)

typify /'tɪpɪfaɪ/ vt (*pt/pp* -ied) typisch sein für

typing /'taɪpɪŋ/ n Maschineschreiben nt

typist /'taɪpɪst/ n Schreibkraft f

tyrannical /tɪ'rænɪkl/ adj tyrannisch

tyranny /'tɪrənɪ/ n Tyrannei f

tyrant /'taɪrənt/ n Tyrann m

tyre /'taɪə(r)/ n Reifen m

Uu

ugl|iness /'ʌglɪnɪs/ n Hässlichkeit f. ~**y** adj hässlich; (*nasty*) übel

UK abbr United Kingdom

ulcer /'ʌlsə(r)/ n Geschwür nt

ultimate /'ʌltɪmət/ adj letzte(r,s); (*final*) endgültig; (*fundamental*) grundlegend, eigentlich. ~**ly** adv schließlich

ultimatum /ʌltɪ'meɪtəm/ n Ultimatum nt

ultra'violet adj ultraviolett

umbrella /ʌm'brelə/ n [Regen-] schirm m

umpire /'ʌmpaɪə(r)/ n Schiedsrichter m ● vt/i Schiedsrichter sein (bei)

umpteen /ʌmp'tiːn/ adj zig.
~**th** 🔤 zigste(r,s)

un'able /ʌn-/ adj be ~ to do sth

etw nicht tun können

una'bridged adj ungekürzt

unac'companied adj ohne Begleitung; (*luggage*) unbegleitet

unac'countable adj unerklärlich

unac'customed adj ungewohnt; be ~ to sth etw (*acc*) nicht gewohnt sein

un'aided adj ohne fremde Hilfe

unanimous /juː'nænɪməs/ adj einmütig; (*vote, decision*) einstimmig

un'armed adj unbewaffnet

unas'suming adj bescheiden

unat'tended adj unbeaufsichtigt

un'authorized adj unbefugt

una'voidable adj unvermeidlich

una'ware adj be ~ of sth sich (*dat*) etw (*gen*) nicht bewusst sein. ~**s** adv catch s.o. ~**s** jdn überraschen

un'bearable adj, **-bly** adv unerträglich

unbeat|able /ʌn'biːtəbl/ adj unschlagbar. ~**en** adj ungeschlagen; (*record*) ungebrochen

unbe'lievable adj unglaublich

un'biased adj unvoreingenommen

un'block vt frei machen

un'bolt vt aufriegeln

un'breakable adj unzerbrechlich

un'button vt aufknöpfen

uncalled-for /ʌn'kɔːldfɔː(r)/ adj unangebracht

un'canny adj unheimlich

un'ceasing adj unaufhörlich

un'certain adj (*doubtful*) ungewiss; (*origins*) unbestimmt; be ~ nicht sicher sein. ~**ty** n Ungewissheit f

un'changed adj unverändert

un'charitable adj lieblos

uncle /'ʌŋkl/ n Onkel m

Uncle Sam Eine Bezeich- ⓘ
nung für die USA und ihre
Einwohner. Meist darge-
stellt durch einen mit Frack und
Zylinder und in den Farben und mit
den Sternen der Nationalflagge be-
kleideten hageren Mann mit
weißen Haaren und Backenbart.
Die Bezeichnung ist besonders
durch das Poster von 1917 zur Rekrutierung von Soldaten 'I want
you' bekannnt geworden.

un'comforta|ble adj, -bly adv
unbequem; feel ∼ (fig) sich nicht
wohl fühlen

un'common adj ungewöhnlich

un'compromising adj kompro-
misslos

uncon'ditional adj, ∼ly adv be-
dingungslos

un'conscious adj bewusstlos;
(unintended) unbewusst; be ∼ of
sth sich (dat) etw (gen) nicht bewusst sein. ∼ly adv unbewusst

uncon'ventional adj unkonven-
tionell

unco'operative adj nicht hilfsbereit

un'cork vt entkorken

uncouth /ʌn'kuːθ/ adj ungehobelt

un'cover vt aufdecken

unde'cided adj unentschlossen;
(not settled) nicht entschieden

undeniable /ʌndɪ'naɪəbl/ adj,
-bly adv unbestreitbar

under /'ʌndə(r)/ prep unter (+ dat/
acc); ∼ it darunter; ∼ there da
drunter; ∼ repair in Reparatur; ∼
construction im Bau; ∼ age minderjährig ● adv darunter

'undercarriage n (Aviat) Fahr-
werk nt, Fahrgestell nt

'underclothes npl Unterwäsche f

under'cover adj geheim

'undercurrent n Unterströmung
f; (fig) Unterton m

'underdog n Unterlegene(r) m

under'done adj nicht gar; (rare)
nicht durchgebraten

under'estimate vt unter-
schätzen

under'fed adj unterernährt

under'foot adv am Boden

under'go vt (pt -went, pp -gone)
durchmachen; sich unterziehen (+
dat) (operation, treatment)

under'graduate n Stu-
dent(in) m(f)

'underground¹ adv unter der
Erde; (mining) unter Tage

'underground² adj unterirdisch;
(secret) Untergrund-. ● n (railway)
U-Bahn f. ∼ car park n Tiefgarage f

'undergrowth n Unterholz nt

'underhand adj hinterhältig

under'lie vt (pt -lay, pp -lain, pres
p -lying) zugrunde liegen (+ dat)

under'line vt unterstreichen

under'lying adj eigentlich

under'mine vt (fig) untermini-
eren, untergraben

underneath /ʌndə'niːθ/ prep
unter (+ dat/acc) ● adv darunter

'underpants npl Unterhose f

'underpass n Unterführung f

under'privileged adj unterprivi-
legiert

under'rate vt unterschätzen

'undershirt n (Amer) Unter-
hemd nt

under'stand vt/i (pt/pp -stood)
verstehen; I ∼ that ... (have heard)
ich habe gehört, dass ... ∼able adj
verständlich. ∼ably adv verständli-
cherweise

under'standing adj verständnis-
voll ● n Verständnis nt; (agreement)

Vereinbarung f; reach an ~ sich verständigen

'**understatement** n Untertreibung f

under'**take** vt (pt -**took**, pp -**taken**) unternehmen; ~ to do sth sich verpflichten, etw zu tun

under'**taker** n Leichenbestatter m; [firm of] ~s Bestattungsinstitut n

under'**taking** n Unternehmen nt; (promise) Versprechen n

'**undertone** n (fig) Unterton m; in an ~ mit gedämpfter Stimme

under'**value** vt unterbewerten

'**underwater**[1] adj Unterwasser-

under'**water**[2] adv unter Wasser

'**underwear** n Unterwäsche f

under'**weight** adj untergewichtig; be ~ Untergewicht haben

'**underworld** n Unterwelt f

unde'**sirable** adj unerwünscht

un'**dignified** adj würdelos

un'**do** vt (pt -**did**, pp -**done**) aufmachen; (fig) ungeschehen machen

un'**done** adj offen; (not accomplished) unerledigt

un'**doubted** adj unzweifelhaft. ~ly adv zweifellos

un'**dress** vt ausziehen; get ~ed sich ausziehen ● vi sich ausziehen

un'**due** adj übermäßig

und'**uly** adv übermäßig

un'**earth** vt ausgraben; (fig) zutage bringen. ~ly adj unheimlich; at an ~ly hour 🄘 in aller Herrgottsfrühe

un'**easy** adj unbehaglich

uneco'**nomic** adj, -**ally** adv unwirtschaftlich

unem'**ployed** adj arbeitslos ● npl the ~ die Arbeitslosen

unem'**ployment** n Arbeitslosigkeit f

un'**ending** adj endlos

un'**equal** adj unterschiedlich; (struggle) ungleich; ~**ly** adv ungleichmäßig

une**quivocal** /ʌnɪ'kwɪvəkl/ adj eindeutig

un'**ethical** adj unmoralisch; be ~ gegen das Berufsethos verstoßen

un'**even** adj uneben; (unequal) ungleich; (not regular) ungleichmäßig; (number) ungerade

unex'**pected** adj unerwartet

un'**fair** adj ungerecht, unfair. ~**ness** n Ungerechtigkeit f

un'**faithful** adj untreu

unfa'**miliar** adj ungewohnt; (unknown) unbekannt

un'**fasten** vt aufmachen; (detach) losmachen

un'**favourable** adj ungünstig

un'**feeling** adj gefühllos

un'**fit** adj ungeeignet; (incompetent) unfähig; (Sport) nicht fit; ~ for work arbeitsunfähig

un'**fold** vt auseinander falten, entfalten; (spread out) ausbreiten ● vi sich entfalten

unfore'**seen** adj unvorhergesehen

unfor**gettable** /ʌnfə'getəbl/ adj unvergesslich

unfor**givable** /ʌnfə'gɪvəbl/ adj unverzeihlich

un'**fortunate** adj unglücklich; (unfavourable) ungünstig; (regrettable) bedauerlich; be ~ (person:) Pech haben. ~ly adv leider

un'**founded** adj unbegründet

un'**furl** vt entrollen

un'**furnished** adj unmöbliert

un'**gainly** /ʌn'geɪnlɪ/ adj unbeholfen

un'**grateful** adj undankbar

un'**happiness** n Kummer m

un'**happy** adj unglücklich; (not

u

content) unzufrieden

un'harmed adj unverletzt
un'healthy adj ungesund
un'hurt adj unverletzt
unification /ˌjuːnɪfɪˈkeɪʃn/ n Einigung f
uniform /ˈjuːnɪfɔːm/ adj einheitlich ● n Uniform f
unify /ˈjuːnɪfaɪ/ vt (pt/pp -ied) einigen
uni'lateral /juːnɪ-/ adj einseitig
uni'maginable adj unvorstellbar
unim'portant adj unwichtig
unin'habited adj unbewohnt
unin'tentional adj unabsichtlich
union /ˈjuːnjən/ n Vereinigung f; (Pol) Union f; (trade ~) Gewerkschaft f
unique /juːˈniːk/ adj einzigartig. **~ly** adv einmalig
unison /ˈjuːnɪsn/ n in ~ einstimmig
unit /ˈjuːnɪt/ n Einheit f; (Math) Einer m; (of furniture) Teil nt, Element nt
unite /juːˈnaɪt/ vt vereinigen ● vi sich vereinigen
united /juːˈnaɪtɪd/ adj einig. **U~ 'Kingdom** n Vereinigtes Königreich nt. **U~ 'Nations** n Vereinte Nationen pl. **U~ States [of America]** n Vereinigte Staaten pl [von Amerika]
unity /ˈjuːnɪtɪ/ n Einheit f; (harmony) Einigkeit f
universal /juːnɪˈvɜːsl/ adj allgemein
universe /ˈjuːnɪvɜːs/ n [Welt]all nt, Universum nt
university /juːnɪˈvɜːsɪtɪ/ n Universität f ● attrib Universitäts-
un'just adj ungerecht
un'kind adj unfreundlich; (harsh) hässlich
un'known adj unbekannt

un'lawful adj gesetzwidrig
unleaded /ʌnˈledɪd/ adj bleifrei
un'leash vt (fig) entfesseln
unless /anˈles/ conj wenn ... nicht; ~ I am mistaken wenn ich mich nicht irre
un'like prep im Gegensatz zu (+ dat)
un'likely adj unwahrscheinlich
un'limited adj unbegrenzt
un'load vt entladen; ausladen (luggage)
un'lock vt aufschließen
un'lucky adj unglücklich; (day, number) Unglücks-; be ~ Pech haben; (thing:) Unglück bringen
un'married adj unverheiratet. **~ 'mother** n ledige Mutter f
un'mask vt (fig) entlarven
unmistakable /ʌnmɪˈsteɪkəbl/ adj, **-bly** adv unverkennbar
un'natural adj unnatürlich; (not normal) nicht normal
un'necessary adj, **-ily** adv unnötig
un'noticed adj unbemerkt
unob'tainable adj nicht erhältlich
unob'trusive adj unaufdringlich; (thing) unauffällig
unof'ficial adj inoffiziell
un'pack vt/i auspacken
un'paid adj unbezahlt
un'pleasant adj unangenehm
un'plug vt (pt/pp -plugged) den Stecker herausziehen von
un'popular adj unbeliebt
un'precedented adj beispiellos
unpre'dictable adj unberechenbar
unpre'pared adj nicht vorbereitet
unpre'tentious adj bescheiden
un'profitable adj unrentabel

un'qualified adj unqualifiziert; (fig: absolute) uneingeschränkt

un'questionable adj unbezweifelbar; (right) unbestreitbar

unravel /ʌnˈrævl/ vt (pt/pp -ravelled) entwirren; (Knitting) aufziehen

un'real adj unwirklich

un'reasonable adj unvernünftig

unre'lated adj unzusammenhängend; be ~ nicht verwandt sein; (events:) nicht miteinander zusammenhängen

unre'liable adj unzuverlässig

un'rest n Unruhen pl

un'rivalled adj unübertroffen

un'roll vt aufrollen ● vi sich aufrollen

unruly /ʌnˈruːlɪ/ adj ungebärdig

un'safe adj nicht sicher

unsatis'factory adj unbefriedigend

un'savoury adj unangenehm; (fig) unerfreulich

unscathed /ʌnˈskeɪðd/ adj unversehrt

un'screw vt abschrauben

un'scrupulous adj skrupellos

un'seemly adj unschicklich

un'selfish adj selbstlos

un'settled adj ungeklärt; (weather) unbeständig; (bill) unbezahlt

unshakeable /ʌnˈʃeɪkəbl/ adj unerschütterlich

unshaven /ʌnˈʃeɪvn/ adj unrasiert

unsightly /ʌnˈsaɪtlɪ/ adj unansehnlich

un'skilled adj ungelernt; (work) unqualifiziert

un'sociable adj ungesellig

unso'phisticated adj einfach

un'sound adj krank, nicht gesund; (building) nicht sicher; (advice) unzu-

verlässig; (reasoning) nicht stichhaltig

un'stable adj nicht stabil; (mentally) labil

un'steady adj, -ily adv unsicher; (wobbly) wackelig

un'stuck adj come ~ sich lösen; (☐: fail) scheitern

unsuc'cessful adj erfolglos; be ~ keinen Erfolg haben

un'suitable adj ungeeignet; (inappropriate) unpassend; (for weather, activity) unzweckmäßig

unthinkable /ʌnˈθɪŋkəbl/ adj unvorstellbar

un'tidiness n Unordentlichkeit f

un'tidy adj, -ily adv unordentlich

un'tie vt aufbinden; losbinden (person, boat, horse)

until /ʌnˈtɪl/ prep bis (+ acc); not ~ erst; ~ the evening bis zum Abend ● conj bis; not ~ erst wenn; (in past) erst als

un'told adj unermesslich

un'true adj unwahr; that's ~ das ist nicht wahr

unused¹ /ʌnˈjuːzd/ adj unbenutzt; (not utilized) ungenutzt

unused² /ʌnˈjuːst/ adj be ~ to sth etw nicht gewohnt sein

un'usual adj ungewöhnlich

un'veil vt enthüllen

un'wanted adj unerwünscht

un'welcome adj unwillkommen

un'well adj be or feel ~ sich nicht wohl fühlen

unwieldy /ʌnˈwiːldɪ/ adj sperrig

un'willing adj widerwillig; be ~ to do sth etw nicht tun wollen

un'wind v (pt/pp unwound) ● vt abwickeln ● vi sich abwickeln; (☐: relax) sich entspannen

un'wise adj unklug

un'worthy adj unwürdig

un'wrap vt (pt/pp -wrapped) auswickeln; auspacken (*present*)

un'written *adj* ungeschrieben

up /ʌp/ *adv* oben; (*with movement*) nach oben; (*not in bed*) auf; (*road*) aufgerissen; (*price*) gestiegen; be up for sale zu verkaufen sein; up there da oben; up to (*as far as*) bis; time's up die Zeit ist um; what's up? 🔲 was ist los? what's he up to? 🔲 was hat er vor? I don't feel up to it ich fühle mich dem nicht gewachsen; go up hinaufgehen; come up heraufkommen ●*prep* be up on sth [oben] auf etw (*dat*) sein; up the mountain oben am Berg; (*movement*) den Berg hinauf; be up the tree oben im Baum sein; up the road die Straße entlang; up the river stromaufwärts; go up the stairs die Treppe hinaufgehen

'upbringing *n* Erziehung *f*

up'date *vt* auf den neuesten Stand bringen

up'grade *vt* aufstufen

upheaval /ʌpˈhiːvl/ *n* Unruhe *f*; (*Pol*) Umbruch *m*

up'hill *adj* (*fig*) mühsam ●*adv* bergauf

up'hold *vt* (*pt/pp* upheld) unterstützen; bestätigen (*verdict*)

upholster /ʌpˈhəʊlstə(r)/ *vt* polstern. **~y** *n* Polsterung *f*

'upkeep *n* Unterhalt *m*

up'market *adj* anspruchsvoll

upon /əˈpɒn/ *prep* auf (+ *dat*/*acc*)

upper /ˈʌpə(r)/ *adj* obere(r,s); (*deck, jaw, lip*) Ober-; have the ~ hand die Oberhand haben ●*n* (*of shoe*) Obermaterial *nt*

upper class *n* Oberschicht *f*

'upright *adj* aufrecht

'uprising *n* Aufstand *m*

'uproar *n* Aufruhr *m*

up'set¹ *vt* (*pt/pp* upset, *pres p* up-setting) umstoßen; (*spill*) verschüt-

ten; durcheinander bringen (*plan*); (*distress*) erschüttern; (*food*) nicht bekommen (+ *dat*); get ~ about sth sich über etw (*acc*) aufregen

'upset² *n* Aufregung *f*; have a stomach ~ einen verdorbenen Magen haben

'upshot *n* Ergebnis *nt*

upside 'down *adv* verkehrt herum; turn ~ umdrehen

up'stairs¹ *adv* (*go*) nach oben

'upstairs² *adj* im Obergeschoss

'upstart *n* Emporkömmling *m*

up'stream *adv* stromaufwärts

'uptake *n* slow on the ~ schwer von Begriff; be quick on the ~ schnell begreifen

'upturn *n* Aufschwung *m*

upward /ˈʌpwəd/ *adj* nach oben; (*movement*) Aufwärts-; ~ slope Steigung *f* ●*adv* ~[s] aufwärts, nach oben

uranium /jʊˈreɪnɪəm/ *n* Uran *nt*

urban /ˈɜːbən/ *adj* städtisch

urge /ɜːdʒ/ *n* Trieb *m*, Drang *m* ●*vt* drängen; ~ on antreiben

urgen|cy /ˈɜːdʒənsɪ/ *n* Dringlichkeit *f*. **~t** *adj* dringend

urine /ˈjʊərɪn/ *n* Urin *m*, Harn *m*

us /ʌs/ *pron* uns; it's us wir sind es

US[A] *abbr* USA *pl*

usable /ˈjuːzəbl/ *adj* brauchbar

usage /ˈjuːsɪdʒ/ *n* Brauch *m*; (*of word*) [Sprach]gebrauch *m*

use¹ /juːs/ *n* (*see* use²) Benutzung *f*; Verwendung *f*; Gebrauch *m*; be (of) no ~ nichts nützen; it is no ~ es hat keinen Zweck; what's the ~? wozu?

use² /juːz/ *vt* benutzen (*implement, room, lift*); verwenden (*ingredient, method, book, money*); gebrauchen (*words, force, brains*); ~ [up] aufbrauchen

used[1] /juːzd/ adj gebraucht; (towel) benutzt; (car) Gebraucht-

used[2] /juːst/ pt be ~ to sth an etw (acc) gewöhnt sein; get ~ to sich gewöhnen an (+ acc); he ~ to say er hat immer gesagt; he ~ to live here er hat früher hier gewohnt

useful /ˈjuːsfl/ adj nützlich. ~ness n Nützlichkeit f

useless /ˈjuːslɪs/ adj nutzlos; (not usable) unbrauchbar; (pointless) zwecklos

user /ˈjuːzə(r)/ n Benutzer(in) m(f)

usher /ˈʌʃə(r)/ n Platzanweiser m; (in court) Gerichtsdiener m

usherette /ʌʃəˈret/ n Platzanweiserin f

USSR abbr (History) UdSSR f

usual /ˈjuːʒʊəl/ adj üblich. ~ly adv gewöhnlich

utensil /juːˈtensl/ n Gerät nt

utility /juːˈtɪlətɪ/ adj Gebrauchs-

utilize /ˈjuːtɪlaɪz/ vt nutzen

utmost /ˈʌtməʊst/ adj äußerste(r,s), größte(r,s) ● n do one's ~ sein Möglichstes tun

utter[1] /ˈʌtə(r)/ adj völlig

utter[2] vt von sich geben (sigh, sound); sagen (word)

U-turn /ˈjuː-/ n (fig) Kehrtwendung f; 'no ~s' (Auto) 'Wenden verboten'

Vv

vacan|cy /ˈveɪkənsɪ/ n (job) freie Stelle f; (room) freies Zimmer nt; 'no ~cies' 'belegt'. ~t adj frei; (look) [gedanken]leer

vacate /vəˈkeɪt/ vt räumen

vacation /vəˈkeɪʃn/ n (Univ & Amer) Ferien pl

vaccinat|e /ˈvæksɪneɪt/ vt impfen. ~ion n Impfung f

vaccine /ˈvæksiːn/ n Impfstoff m

vacuum /ˈvækjʊəm/ n Vakuum nt, luftleerer Raum m ● vt saugen. ~ cleaner n Staubsauger m

vagina /vəˈdʒaɪnə/ n (Anat) Scheide f

vague /veɪg/ adj (-r,-st) vage; (outline) verschwommen

vain /veɪn/ adj (-er,-est) eitel; (hope, attempt) vergeblich; in ~ vergeblich. ~ly adv vergeblich

valiant /ˈvælɪənt/ adj tapfer

valid /ˈvælɪd/ adj gültig; (claim) berechtigt; (argument) stichhaltig; (reason) triftig. ~ity n Gültigkeit f

valley /ˈvælɪ/ n Tal nt

valour /ˈvælə(r)/ n Tapferkeit f

valuable /ˈvæljʊəbl/ adj wertvoll. ~s npl Wertsachen pl

valuation /væljʊˈeɪʃn/ n Schätzung f

value /ˈvæljuː/ n Wert m; (usefulness) Nutzen m ● vt schätzen. ~ 'added tax n Mehrwertsteuer f

valve /vælv/ n Ventil nt; (Anat) Klappe f; (Electr) Röhre f

van /væn/ n Lieferwagen m

vandal /ˈvændl/ n Rowdy m. ~ism n mutwillige Zerstörung f. ~ize vt demolieren

vanilla /vəˈnɪlə/ n Vanille f

vanish /ˈvænɪʃ/ vi verschwinden

vanity /ˈvænətɪ/ n Eitelkeit f

vapour /ˈveɪpə(r)/ n Dampf m

variable /ˈveərɪəbl/ adj unbeständig; (Math) variabel; (adjustable) regulierbar

variant /ˈveərɪənt/ n Variante f

variation /veərɪˈeɪʃn/ n Variation f; (difference) Unterschied m

u
v

varied /ˈveərɪd/ adj vielseitig; (diet:) abwechslungsreich

variety /vəˈraɪətɪ/ n Abwechslung f; (quantity) Vielfalt f; (Comm) Auswahl f; (type) Art f; (Bot) Abart f; (Theat) Varieté nt

various /ˈveərɪəs/ adj verschieden. ~ly adv unterschiedlich

varnish /ˈvɑːnɪʃ/ n Lack m ● vt lackieren

vary /ˈveərɪ/ v (pt/pp -ied) ● vi sich ändern; (be different) verschieden sein ● vt [ver]ändern; (add variety to) abwechslungsreicher gestalten

vase /vɑːz/ n Vase f

vast /vɑːst/ adj riesig; (expanse) weit. ~ly adv gewaltig

vat /væt/ n Bottich m

VAT /viːeɪˈtiː, væt/ abbr (value added tax) Mehrwertsteuer f, MwSt.

vault[1] /vɔːlt/ n (roof) Gewölbe nt; (in bank) Tresor m; (tomb) Gruft f

vault[2] n Sprung m ● vt/i ~ [over] springen über (+ acc)

VDU abbr (visual display unit) Bildschirmgerät nt

veal /viːl/ n Kalbfleisch nt ● attrib Kalbs-

veer /vɪə(r)/ vi sich drehen; (Auto) ausscheren

vegetable /ˈvedʒtəbl/ n Gemüse nt; ~s pl Gemüse nt ● attrib Gemüse-; (oil, fat) Pflanzen-

vegetarian /vedʒɪˈteərɪən/ adj vegetarisch ● n Vegetarier(in) m(f)

vegetation /vedʒɪˈteɪʃn/ n Vegetation f

vehement /ˈviːəmənt/ adj heftig

vehicle /ˈviːɪkl/ n Fahrzeug nt

veil /veɪl/ n Schleier m ● vt verschleiern

vein /veɪn/ n Ader f; (mood) Stim-

mung f; (manner) Art f

velocity /vɪˈlɒsətɪ/ n Geschwindigkeit f

velvet /ˈvelvɪt/ n Samt m

vending-machine /ˈvendɪŋ-/ n [Verkaufs]automat m

vendor /ˈvendə(r)/ n Verkäufer(in) m(f)

veneer /vəˈnɪə(r)/ n Furnier nt; (fig) Tünche f. ~ed adj furniert

venerable /ˈvenərəbl/ adj ehrwürdig

Venetian /vəˈniːʃn/ adj venezianisch. v~ blind n Jalousie f

vengeance /ˈvendʒəns/ n Rache f; with a ~ gewaltig

Venice /ˈvenɪs/ n Venedig nt

venison /ˈvenɪsn/ n (Culin) Reh(fleisch) nt

venom /ˈvenəm/ n Gift nt; (fig) Hass m. ~ous adj giftig

vent /vent/ n Öffnung f

ventilat|e /ˈventɪleɪt/ vt belüften. ~ion n Belüftung f; (installation) Lüftung f. ~or n (ventilation) Lüftungsvorrichtung f; (Med) Beatmungsgerät nt

ventriloquist /venˈtrɪləkwɪst/ n Bauchredner m

venture /ˈventʃə(r)/ n Unternehmung f ● vt wagen ● vi sich wagen

venue /ˈvenjuː/ n (for event) Veranstaltungsort m

veranda /vəˈrændə/ n Veranda f

verb /vɜːb/ n Verb nt. ~al adj mündlich; (Gram) verbal

verbose /vɜːˈbəʊs/ adj weitschweifig

verdict /ˈvɜːdɪkt/ n Urteil nt

verge /vɜːdʒ/ n Rand m ● vi ~ on (fig) grenzen an (+ acc)

verify /ˈverɪfaɪ/ vt (pt/pp -ied) überprüfen; (confirm) bestätigen

vermin /ˈvɜːmɪn/ n Ungeziefer nt

vermouth /ˈvɜːməθ/ n Wermut m

versatil|e /ˈvɜːsətaɪl/ adj vielseitig. ~ity n Vielseitigkeit f

verse /vɜːs/ n Strophe f; (of Bible) Vers m; (poetry) Lyrik f

version /ˈvɜːʃn/ n Version f; (translation) Übersetzung f; (model) Modell nt

versus /ˈvɜːsəs/ prep gegen (+ acc)

vertical /ˈvɜːtɪkl/ adj senkrecht • n Senkrechte f

vertigo /ˈvɜːtɪgəʊ/ n (Med) Schwindel m

verve /vɜːv/ n Schwung m

very /ˈverɪ/ adv sehr; ~ much sehr; (quantity) sehr viel; ~ probably höchstwahrscheinlich; at the ~ most allerhöchstens • adj (mere) bloß; the ~ first der/die/das allererste; the ~ thing genau das Richtige; at the ~ end/beginning ganz am Ende/Anfang; only a ~ little nur ein ganz kleines bisschen

vessel /ˈvesl/ n Schiff nt; (receptacle & Anat) Gefäß nt

vest /vest/ n [Unter]hemd nt; (Amer: waistcoat) Weste f

vestige /ˈvestɪdʒ/ n Spur f

vestry /ˈvestrɪ/ n Sakristei f

vet /vet/ n Tierarzt m /-ärztin f • vt (pt/pp vetted) überprüfen

veteran /ˈvetərən/ n Veteran m

veterinary /ˈvetərɪnərɪ/ adj tierärztlich. ~ surgeon n Tierarzt m /-ärztin f

veto /ˈviːtəʊ/ n (pl -es) Veto nt

VHF abbr (very high frequency) UKW

via /ˈvaɪə/ prep über (+ acc)

viable /ˈvaɪəbl/ adj lebensfähig; (fig) realisierbar; (firm) rentabel

viaduct /ˈvaɪədʌkt/ n Viadukt m

vibrat|e /vaɪˈbreɪt/ vi vibrieren.

~ion n Vibrieren nt

vicar /ˈvɪkə(r)/ n Pfarrer m. ~age n Pfarrhaus nt

vice[1] /vaɪs/ n Laster nt

vice[2] n (Techn) Schraubstock m

vice[3] adj Vize-; ~ 'chairman stellvertretender Vorsitzender m

vice versa /vaɪsɪˈvɜːsə/ adv umgekehrt

vicinity /vɪˈsɪnɪtɪ/ n Umgebung f; in the ~ in der Nähe von

vicious /ˈvɪʃəs/ adj boshaft; (animal) bösartig

victim /ˈvɪktɪm/ n Opfer nt. ~ize vt schikanieren

victor /ˈvɪktə(r)/ n Sieger m

victor|ious /vɪkˈtɔːrɪəs/ adj siegreich. ~y n Sieg m

video /ˈvɪdɪəʊ/ n Video nt; (recorder) Videorecorder m • attrib Video-

video: ~ cas'sette n Videokassette f. ~ game n Videospiel nt. ~ recorder n Videorecorder m

Vienn|a /vɪˈenə/ n Wien nt. ~ese adj Wiener

view /vjuː/ n Sicht f; (scene) Aussicht f, Blick m; (picture, opinion) Ansicht f; in my ~ meiner Ansicht nach; in ~ of angesichts (+ gen); be on ~ besichtigt werden können • vt sich (dat) ansehen; besichtigen (house); (consider) betrachten • vi (TV) fernsehen. ~er n (TV) Zuschauer(in) m(f)

view: ~finder n (Phot) Sucher m. ~point n Standpunkt m

vigilan|ce /ˈvɪdʒɪləns/ n Wachsamkeit f. ~t adj wachsam

vigorous /ˈvɪgərəs/ adj kräftig; (fig) heftig

vigour /ˈvɪgə(r)/ n Kraft f; (fig) Heftigkeit f

vile /vaɪl/ adj abscheulich

villa /ˈvɪlə/ n (for holidays) Ferienhaus nt

village /ˈvɪlɪdʒ/ n Dorf nt. **~r** n Dorfbewohner(in) m(f)

villain /ˈvɪlən/ n Schurke m; (in story) Bösewicht m

vindicat|e /ˈvɪndɪkeɪt/ vt rechtfertigen. **~ion** n Rechtfertigung f

vindictive /vɪnˈdɪktɪv/ adj nachtragend

vine /vaɪn/ n Weinrebe f

vinegar /ˈvɪnɪɡə(r)/ n Essig m

vineyard /ˈvɪnjɑːd/ n Weinberg m

vintage /ˈvɪntɪdʒ/ adj erlesen ● n (year) Jahrgang m. **~ 'car** n Oldtimer m

viola /vɪˈəʊlə/ n (Mus) Bratsche f

violat|e /ˈvaɪəleɪt/ vt verletzen; (break) brechen; (disturb) stören; (defile) schänden. **~ion** n Verletzung f; Schändung f

violen|ce /ˈvaɪələns/ n Gewalt f; (fig) Heftigkeit f. **~t** adj gewalttätig; (fig) heftig. **~tly** adv brutal; (fig) heftig

violet /ˈvaɪələt/ adj violett ● n (flower) Veilchen nt

violin /vaɪəˈlɪn/ n Geige f, Violine f. **~ist** n Geiger(in) m(f)

VIP abbr (very important person) Prominente(r) m/f

viper /ˈvaɪpə(r)/ n Kreuzotter f

virgin /ˈvɜːdʒɪn/ adj unberührt ● n Jungfrau f. **~ity** n Unschuld f

viril|e /ˈvɪraɪl/ adj männlich. **~ity** n Männlichkeit f

virtual /ˈvɜːtjʊəl/ adj a **~ ...** praktisch ein **...** /y adv praktisch

virtue /ˈvɜːtjuː/ n Tugend f; (advantage) Vorteil m; by or in **~e** of auf Grund (+ gen)

virtuoso /vɜːtjʊˈəʊzəʊ/ n (pl **-si** /-ziː/) Virtuose m

virtuous /ˈvɜːtjʊəs/ adj tugendhaft

virus /ˈvaɪərəs/ n Virus nt

visa /ˈviːzə/ n Visum nt

visibility /vɪzəˈbɪlɪti/ n Sichtbarkeit f; (range) Sichtweite f

visi|ble /ˈvɪzəbl/ adj, **-bly** adv sichtbar

vision /ˈvɪʒn/ n Vision f; (sight) Sehkraft f; (foresight) Weitblick m

visit /ˈvɪzɪt/ n Besuch m ● vt besuchen; besichtigen (town, building). **~or** n Besucher(in) m(f); (in hotel) Gast m; have **~ors** Besuch haben

visor /ˈvaɪzə(r)/ n Schirm m; (Auto) [Sonnen]blende f

vista /ˈvɪstə/ n Aussicht f

visual /ˈvɪzjʊəl/ adj visuell. **~ display unit** n Bildschirmgerät nt

visualize /ˈvɪzjʊəlaɪz/ vt sich (dat) vorstellen

vital /ˈvaɪtl/ adj unbedingt notwendig; (essential to life) lebenswichtig. **~ity** n Vitalität f. **~ly** adv äußerst

vitamin /ˈvɪtəmɪn/ n Vitamin nt

vivaci|ous /vɪˈveɪʃəs/ adj lebhaft. **~ty** n Lebhaftigkeit f

vivid /ˈvɪvɪd/ adj lebhaft; (description) lebendig

vocabulary /vəˈkæbjʊləri/ n Wortschatz m; (list) Vokabelverzeichnis nt; learn **~** Vokabeln lernen

vocal /ˈvəʊkl/ adj stimmlich; (vociferous) lautstark

vocalist /ˈvəʊkəlɪst/ n Sänger(in) m(f)

vocation /vəˈkeɪʃn/ n Berufung f. **~al** adj Berufs-

vociferous /vəˈsɪfərəs/ adj lautstark

vodka /ˈvɒdkə/ n Wodka m

vogue /vəʊɡ/ n Mode f

voice /vɔɪs/ n Stimme f ● vt zum

Ausdruck bringen. ~ **mail** n Voicemail f

void /vɔɪd/ adj leer; (not valid) ungültig; ~ **of** ohne ●n Leere f

volatile /'vɒlətaɪl/ adj flüchtig; (person) sprunghaft

volcanic /vɒl'kænɪk/ adj vulkanisch

volcano /vɒl'keɪnəʊ/ n Vulkan m

volley /'vɒlɪ/ n (of gunfire) Salve f; (Tennis) Volley m

volt /vəʊlt/ n Volt nt. ~**age** n (Electr) Spannung f

voluble /'vɒljʊbl/ adj, -**bly** adv redselig; (protest) wortreich

volume /'vɒljuːm/ n (book) Band m; (Geometry) Rauminhalt m; (amount) Ausmaß nt; (Radio, TV) Lautstärke f

voluntary /'vɒləntərɪ/ adj, -**ily** adv freiwillig

volunteer /vɒlən'tɪə(r)/ n Freiwillige/r m/f ●vt anbieten; geben (information) ●vi sich freiwillig melden

vomit /'vɒmɪt/ n Erbrochene(s) nt ●vt erbrechen ●vi sich übergeben

voracious /və'reɪʃəs/ adj gefräßig; (appetite) unbändig

vot|e /vəʊt/ n Stimme f; (ballot) Abstimmung f; (right) Wahlrecht nt ●vi abstimmen; (in election) wählen. ~**er** n Wähler(in) m(f)

vouch /vaʊtʃ/ vi ~ **for** sich verbürgen für. ~**er** n Gutschein m

vowel /'vaʊəl/ n Vokal m

voyage /'vɔɪɪdʒ/ n Seereise f; (in space) Reise f, Flug m

vulgar /'vʌlgə(r)/ adj vulgär, ordinär. ~**ity** n Vulgarität f

vulnerable /'vʌlnərəbl/ adj verwundbar

vulture /'vʌltʃə(r)/ n Geier m

Ww

wad /wɒd/ n Bausch m; (bundle) Bündel nt. ~**ding** n Wattierung f

waddle /'wɒdl/ vi watscheln

wade /weɪd/ vi waten

wafer /'weɪfə(r)/ n Waffel f

waffle[1] /'wɒfl/ vi 🆒 schwafeln

waffle[2] n (Culin) Waffel f

waft /wɒft/ vt/i wehen

wag /wæg/ v (pt/pp wagged) ●vt wedeln mit ●vi wedeln

wage /weɪdʒ/ n (also ~**s**) pl Lohn m

wager /'weɪdʒə(r)/ n Wette f

wagon /'wægən/ n Wagen m; (Rail) Waggon m

wail /weɪl/ n [klagender] Schrei m ●vi heulen; (lament) klagen

waist /weɪst/ n Taille f. ~**coat** n Weste f. ~**line** n Taille f

wait /weɪt/ n Wartezeit f; lie in ~ **for** auflauern (+ dat) ●vi warten (for auf + acc); (at table) servieren; ~ **on** bedienen ●vt ~ one's **turn** warten, bis man an der Reihe ist

waiter /'weɪtə(r)/ n Kellner m; ~! Herr Ober!

waiting: ~**list** n Warteliste f. ~**room** n Warteraum m; (doctor's) Wartezimmer nt

waitress /'weɪtrɪs/ n Kellnerin f

waive /weɪv/ vt verzichten auf (+ acc)

wake[1] /weɪk/ n Totenwache f ●v (pt woke, pp woken) ~ [**up**] ●vt [auf]wecken ●vi aufwachen

wake[2] n (Naut) Kielwasser nt; in the ~ **of** im Gefolge (+ gen)

Wales /weɪlz/ n Wales nt

walk /wɔ:k/ n Spaziergang m; (gait) Gang m; (path) Weg m; go for a ~ spazieren gehen ● vi gehen; (not ride) laufen, zu Fuß gehen; (ramble) wandern; learn to ~ laufen lernen ● vt ausführen (dog). ~ **out** vi hinausgehen; (workers:) in den Streik treten; ~ **out on** s.o. jdn verlassen

walker /'wɔ:kə(r)/ n Spaziergänger(in) m(f); (rambler) Wanderer m/Wanderin f

walking /'wɔ:kɪŋ/ n Gehen nt; (rambling) Wandern nt. ~**stick** n Spazierstock m

wall /wɔ:l/ n Wand f; (external) Mauer f; drive s.o. up the ~ 🗊 jdn auf die Palme bringen ● vt ~ **up** zumauern

wallet /'wɒlɪt/ n Brieftasche f

'**wallflower** n Goldlack m

wallop /'wɒləp/ vt (pt/pp walloped) 🗊 schlagen

wallow /'wɒləʊ/ vi sich wälzen; (fig) schwelgen

'**wallpaper** n Tapete f ● vt tapezieren

walnut /'wɔ:lnʌt/ n Walnuss f

waltz /wɔ:lts/ n Walzer m ● vi Walzer tanzen

wander /'wɒndə(r)/ vi umherwandern, 🗊 bummeln; (fig: digress) abschweifen. ~ **about** vi umherwandern

wangle /'wæŋgl/ vt 🗊 organisieren

want /wɒnt/ n Mangel m (of an + dat); (hardship) Not f; (desire) Bedürfnis nt ● vt wollen; (need) brauchen; ~ [to have] sth etw haben wollen; ~ to do sth etw tun wollen; I ~ you to go ich will, dass du gehst; it ~s painting es müsste gestrichen werden ● vi he doesn't ~ for anything ihm fehlt es an

nichts. ~**ed** adj (criminal) gesucht

war /wɔ:(r)/ n Krieg m; be at ~ sich im Krieg befinden

ward /wɔ:d/ n [Kranken]saal m; (unit) Station f; (of town) Wahlbezirk m; (child) Mündel nt ● vt ~ **off** abwehren

warden /'wɔ:dn/ n (of hostel) Heimleiter(in) m(f); (of youth hostel) Herbergsvater m; (supervisor) Aufseher(in) m(f)

warder /'wɔ:də(r)/ n Wärter(in) m(f)

wardrobe /'wɔ:drəʊb/ n Kleiderschrank m; (clothes) Garderobe f

warehouse /'weəhaʊs/ n Lager nt; (building) Lagerhaus nt

wares /weəz/ npl Waren pl

war: ~**fare** n Krieg m. ~**like** adj kriegerisch

warm /wɔ:m/ adj (-er, -est) warm; (welcome) herzlich; I am ~ mir ist warm ● vt wärmen. ~ **up** vt aufwärmen ● vi warm werden; (Sport) sich aufwärmen. ~**hearted** adj warmherzig

warmth /wɔ:mθ/ n Wärme f

warn /wɔ:n/ vt warnen (of vor + dat). ~**ing** n Warnung f; (advance notice) Vorwarnung f; (caution) Verwarnung f

warp /wɔ:p/ vt verbiegen ● vi sich verziehen

warrant /'wɒrənt/ n (for arrest) Haftbefehl m; (for search) Durchsuchungsbefehl m ● vt (justify) rechtfertigen; (guarantee) garantieren

warranty /'wɒrənti/ n Garantie f

warrior /'wɒrɪə(r)/ n Krieger m

'**warship** n Kriegsschiff nt

wart /wɔ:t/ n Warze f

'**wartime** n Kriegszeit f

war|y /'weərɪ/ adj, -**ily** adv vorsichtig; (suspicious) misstrauisch

was /wɒz/ *see* be

wash /wɒʃ/ *n* Wäsche *f*; (*Naut*) Wellen *pl*; **have a ~** sich waschen ● *vt* waschen; spülen (*dishes*); aufwischen (*floor*); **~ one's hands** (*dat*) die Hände waschen ● *vi* sich waschen. **~ out** *vt* auswaschen; ausspülen (*mouth*). **~ up** *vt/i* abwaschen, spülen ● *vi* (*Amer*) sich waschen

washable /ˈwɒʃəbl/ *adj* waschbar

wash-basin *n* Waschbecken *nt*

washer /ˈwɒʃə(r)/ *n* (*Techn*) Dichtungsring *m*; (*machine*) Waschmaschine *f*

washing /ˈwɒʃɪŋ/ *n* Wäsche *f*. **~-machine** *n* Waschmaschine *f*. **~-powder** *n* Waschpulver *nt*. **~-up** *n* Abwasch *m*; **do the ~-up** abwaschen, spülen. **~-'up liquid** *n* Spülmittel *nt*

wasp /wɒsp/ *n* Wespe *f*

waste /weɪst/ *n* Verschwendung *f*; (*rubbish*) Abfall *m*; **~s** *pl* Öde *f* ● *adj* (*product*) Abfall- ● *vt* verschwenden ● *vi* **~ away** immer mehr abmagern

waste: **~ful** *adj* verschwenderisch. **~ land** *n* Ödland *nt*. **~ 'paper** *n* Altpapier *nt*. **~-'paper basket** *n* Papierkorb *m*

watch /wɒtʃ/ *n* Wache *f*; (*timepiece*) [Armband]uhr *f* ● *vt* beobachten; sich (*dat*) ansehen (*film, match*); (*keep an eye on*) achten auf (+ *acc*); **~ television** fernsehen ● *vi* zusehen. **~ out** *vi* Ausschau halten (*for nach*); (*be careful*) aufpassen

watch: **~-dog** *n* Wachhund *m*. **~ful** *adj* wachsam. **~man** *n* Wachmann *m*

water /ˈwɔːtə(r)/ *n* Wasser *nt*; **~s** *pl* Gewässer *nt* ● *vt* gießen (*garden, plant*); (*dilute*) verdünnen ● *vi* (*eyes*) tränen; **my mouth was ~ing** mir lief das Wasser im Munde zusam-

men. **~ down** *vt* verwässern

water: **~-colour** *n* Wasserfarbe *f*; (*painting*) Aquarell *nt*. **~cress** *n* Brunnenkresse *f*. **~fall** *n* Wasserfall *m*

'watering-can *n* Gießkanne *f*

water: **~-lily** *n* Seerose *f*. **~logged** *adj* **be ~logged** (*ground*:) unter Wasser stehen. **~ polo** *n* Wasserball *m*. **~proof** *adj* wasserdicht. **~-skiing** *n* Wasserskilaufen *nt*. **~tight** *adj* wasserdicht. **~way** *n* Wasserstraße *f*

watery /ˈwɔːtərɪ/ *adj* wässrig

watt /wɒt/ *n* Watt *nt*

wave /weɪv/ *n* Welle *f*; (*gesture*) Handbewegung *f*; (*as greeting*) Winken *nt* ● *vt* winken mit; (*brandish*) schwingen; wellen (*hair*); **~ one's hand** winken ● *vi* winken (*to dat*); (*flag*:) wehen. **~length** *n* Wellenlänge *f*

waver /ˈweɪvə(r)/ *vi* schwanken

wavy /ˈweɪvɪ/ *adj* wellig

wax /wæks/ *n* Wachs *nt*; (*in ear*) Schmalz *nt* ● *vt* wachsen. **~works** *n* Wachsfigurenkabinett *nt*

way /weɪ/ *n* Weg *m*; (*direction*) Richtung *f*; (*respect*) Hinsicht *f*; (*manner*) Art *f*; (*method*) Art und Weise *f*; **~s** *pl* Gewohnheiten *pl*; **on the ~** auf dem Weg (*to zu*); (*under way*) unterwegs; **a little/long ~** ein kleines/ganzes Stück; **a long ~ off** weit weg; **this ~** hierher; (*like this*) so; **which ~** in welche Richtung; (*how*) wie; **by the ~** übrigens; **in some ~s** in gewisser Hinsicht; **either ~** so oder so; **in this ~** auf diese Weise; **in a ~** in gewisser Weise; **lead the ~** vorausgehen; **make ~** Platz machen (*for dat*); **'give ~'** (*Auto*) 'Vorfahrt beachten'; **go out of one's ~** (*fig*) sich (*dat*) besondere Mühe geben (*to zu*); **get one's [own] ~** seinen Willen

durchsetzen ●*adv* weit; ~ **behind**
weit zurück. ~ **in** *n* Eingang *m*

way 'out *n* Ausgang *m*; (*fig*) Ausweg *m*

WC *abbr* WC *nt*

we /wiː/ *pron* wir

weak /wiːk/ *adj* (-er, -est)
schwach; (*liquid*) dünn. ~**en** *vt*
schwächen ●*vi* schwächer werden.
~**ling** *n* Schwächling *m*. ~**ness** *n*
Schwäche *f*

wealth /welθ/ *n* Reichtum *m*; (*fig*)
Fülle *f* (of an + *dat*). ~**y** *adj* reich

weapon /ˈwepən/ *n* Waffe *f*. ~**s**
of mass destruction Massenvernichtungswaffen *pl*

wear /weə(r)/ *n* (*clothing*) Kleidung
f; ~ **and tear** Abnutzung *f*, Verschleiß *m* ●*v* (*pt* **wore**, *pp* **worn**) *vt*
tragen; (*damage*) abnutzen; **what**
shall I ~? was soll ich anziehen?
●*vi* sich abnutzen; (*last*) halten. ~
off *vi* abgehen; (*effect*) nachlassen. ~
out *vt* abnutzen; (*exhaust*) erschöpfen ●*vi* sich abnutzen

weary /ˈwɪərɪ/ *adj*, **-ily** *adv* müde

weather /ˈweðə(r)/ *n* Wetter *nt*;
in this ~ bei diesem Wetter; **under**
the ~ (*fig*) nicht ganz auf dem Posten ●*vt* abwettern (*storm*). (*fig*)
überstehen

weather-: ~**beaten** *adj* verwittert; wettergegerbt (*face*). ~**fore-**
cast *n* Wettervorhersage *f*

weave[1] /wiːv/ *vi* (*pt/pp* **weaved**)
sich schlängeln (**through** durch)

weave[2] *n* (of cloth) Bindung *f* ●*vt*
(*pt* **wove**, *pp* **woven**) weben. ~**r** *n*
Weber *m*

web /web/ *n* Netz *nt*; **the W~** des
Web. ~**master** *n* Webmaster *m*. ~
page *n* Webseite *f*. ~**site** *n* Website *f*

wed /wed/ *vt/i* (*pt/pp* **wedded**) heiraten. ~**ding** *n* Hochzeit *f*

wedding: ~ **day** *n* Hochzeitstag
m. ~ **dress** *n* Hochzeitskleid *nt*.
~**ring** *n* Ehering *m*, Trauring *m*

wedge /wedʒ/ *n* Keil *m* ●*vt* festklemmen

Wednesday /ˈwenzdeɪ/ *n* Mittwoch *m*

wee /wiː/ *adj* 🄸 klein ●*vi* Pipi
machen

weed /wiːd/ *n* Unkraut *nt* ●*vt/i*
jäten. ~ **out** *vt* (*fig*) aussieben

'weedkiller *n* Unkrautvertilgungsmittel *nt*

weedy /ˈwiːdɪ/ *adj* 🄸 spillerig

week /wiːk/ *n* Woche *f*. ~**day** *n*
Wochentag *m*. ~**end** *n* Wochenende *nt*

weekly /ˈwiːklɪ/ *adj* & *adv* wöchentlich ●*n* Wochenzeitschrift *f*

weep /wiːp/ *vi* (*pt/pp* **wept**)
weinen

weigh /weɪ/ *vt/i* wiegen. ~ **down**
vt (*fig*) niederdrücken. ~ **up** *vt*
(*fig*) abwägen

weight /weɪt/ *n* Gewicht *nt*; **put**
on/lose ~ zunehmen/abnehmen

'weight-lifting *n* Gewichtheben *nt*

weighty /ˈweɪtɪ/ *adj* schwer; (*important*) gewichtig

weir /wɪə(r)/ *n* Wehr *nt*.

weird /wɪəd/ *adj* (-er, -est) unheimlich; (*bizarre*) bizarr

welcome /ˈwelkəm/ *adj* willkommen; **you're ~!** nichts zu danken!
you're ~ to (**have**) **it** das können
Sie gerne haben ●*n* Willkommen *nt*
●*vt* begrüßen

weld /weld/ *vt* schweißen. ~**er** *n*
Schweißer *m*

welfare /ˈwelfeə(r)/ *n* Wohl *nt*;
(*Admin*) Fürsorge *f*. **W~ State** *n*
Wohlfahrtsstaat *m*

well[1] /wel/ *n* Brunnen *m*;

(oil ∼) Quelle f

well² /wel/ adv (better, best) gut; as ∼ auch; as ∼ as (in addition) sowohl ... als auch; ∼ done! gut gemacht! ● adj gesund; he is not ∼ es geht ihm nicht gut; get ∼ soon! gute Besserung! ● int nun, na

well: ∼**-behaved** adj artig. ∼**-being** n Wohl nt

wellingtons /'welɪŋtənz/ npl Gummistiefel pl

well: ∼**-known** adj bekannt. ∼**-off** adj wohlhabend; be ∼**-off** gut dransein. ∼**-to-do** adj wohlhabend

Welsh /welʃ/ adj walisisch ● n (Lang) Walisisch nt; **the** ∼ pl die Waliser. ∼ **man** n Waliser m

---

> **ⓘ**
> **Welsh Assembly** Das walisische Parlament, dessen Mitglieder in der Hauptstadt Cardiff zusammentreten. Es wurde 1999 (nach einer Volksabstimmung) eröffnet und verleiht Wales eine größere Autonomie gegenüber dem britischen Parlament in London. Das Parlament setzt sich aus 60 Mitgliedern zusammen, 40 sind direkt gewählt, die restlichen Abgeordneten nach dem Verhältniswahlrecht.

---

went /went/ see go

wept /wept/ see weep

were /wɜː(r)/ see be

west /west/ n Westen m; to the ∼ of westlich von ● adv westlich nach Westen. west- ● adv westlich nach Westen. ∼**erly** adj westlich. ∼**ern** adj westlich ● n Western m

West: ∼ '**Germany** n Westdeutschland nt. ∼ '**Indian** adj westindisch ● n Westinder(in) m (f). ∼ '**Indies** /-'ɪndɪz/ npl Westindische

Inseln pl

'**westward[s]** /-wəd[z]/ adv nach Westen

wet /wet/ adj (wetter, wettest) nass; (fam: person) weichlich, lasch; '∼ **paint** 'frisch gestrichen' ● vt (pt/pp wet or wetted) nass machen

whack /wæk/ vt 🔢 schlagen. ∼**ed** adj 🔢 kaputt

whale /weɪl/ n Wal m

wharf /wɔːf/ n Kai m

---

what /wɒt/

● pronoun

····▶ (in questions) was. what is it? was ist das? what do you want? was wollen Sie? what is your name? wie heißen Sie? what? (🔢: say that again) wie?; was? what is the time? wie spät ist es? (indirect) I didn't know what to do ich wusste nicht, was ich machen sollte

---

> **❗** The equivalent of a preposition with what in English is a special word in German beginning with **wo-** (**wor-** before a vowel): for what? what for? = wofür? wozu? from what? wovon? on what? worauf? worüber? under what? worunter? with what? womit? etc. what do you want the money for? wozu willst du das Geld? what is he talking about? wovon redet er?

····▶ (relative pronoun) was. do what I tell you tu, was ich dir sage. give me what you can gib mir, so viel du kannst. what little I know das bisschen, das ich weiß. I don't agree with what you are

w

saying ich stimme dem nicht zu, was Sie sagen

····▸ (in phrases) what about me? was ist mit mir? what about a cup of coffee? wie wäre es mit einer Tasse Kaffee? what if she doesn't come? was ist, wenn sie nicht kommt? what of it? was ist dabei?

● adjective

····▸ (asking for selection) welcher (m), welche (f), welches (nt), welche (pl). what book do you want? welches Buch willst du haben? what colour are the walls? welche Farbe haben die Wände? I asked him what train to take ich habe ihn gefragt, welchen Zug ich nehmen soll

····▸ (asking how much/many) what money does he have? wie viel Geld hat er? what time is it? wie spät ist es? what time does it start? um wie viel Uhr fängt es an?

····▸ what kind of ...? was für [ein(e)]? what kind of man is he? was für ein Mensch ist er?

····▸ (in exclamations) was für [e nom]. what a fool you are! was für ein Dummkopf du doch bist! what cheek/luck! was für eine Frechheit/ein Glück! what a huge house! was für ein riesiges Haus! what a lot of people! was für viele Leute!

what'ever adj [egal] welche(r,s) ● pron was ... auch; ~ is it? was ist das bloß?; ~ he does was er auch tut; nothing ~ überhaupt nichts

whatso'ever pron & adj ≈ whatever

wheat /wi:t/ n Weizen m

wheel /wi:l/ n Rad nt; (pottery) Töpferscheibe f; (steering ~) Lenk-

rad nt; at the ~ am Steuer ● vt (push) schieben ● vi kehrtmachen; (circle) kreisen

wheel: ~barrow n Schubkarre f. ~chair n Rollstuhl m. ~-clamp n Parkkralle f

when /wen/ adv wann; the day ~ der Tag, an dem ● conj wenn; (in the past) als; (although) wo ... doch; ~ swimming/reading beim Schwimmen/Lesen

when'ever conj & adv (immer) wenn; (at whatever time) immer; ~ did it happen? wann ist das bloß passiert?

where /weə(r)/ adv & conj wo; ~ [to] wohin; ~ [from] woher

whereabouts¹ /weərə'bauts/ adv wo

'whereabouts² n Verbleib m; (of person) Aufenthaltsort m

where'as conj während; (in contrast) wohingegen

whereu'pon adv worauf[hin]

wher'ever conj & adv wo immer; (to whatever place) wohin immer; (from whatever place) woher immer; (everywhere) überall wo; ~ possible wenn irgend möglich

whether /'weðə(r)/ conj ob

which /wɪtʃ/

● adjective

····▸ (in questions) welcher (m), welche (f), welches (nt), welche (pl). which book do you need? welches Buch brauchst du? which one? welcher/welche/welches? which ones? welche? which one of you did it? wer von euch hat es getan? which way? (which direction) welche Richtung? (where) wohin?; (how) wie?

····▸ (relative) he always comes at

one at which time I'm having lunch/by which time I've finished er kommt immer um ein Uhr; dann esse ich gerade zu Mittag/bis dahin bin ich schon fertig

● *pronoun*

⇢ (*in questions*) welcher (m), welche (f), welches (nt), welche (pl). **which is which?** welcher/welche/welches ist welcher/welche/welches? **which of you?** wer von euch?

⇢ (*relative*) der (m), die (f), das (nt), die (pl); (*genitive*) dessen (m, nt), deren (f, pl); (*dative*) dem (m, nt), der (f), denen (pl); (*referring to a clause*) was. **the book which I gave you** das Buch, das ich dir gab. **the trial, the result of which we are expecting** der Prozess, dessen Ergebnis wir erwarten. **the house of which I was speaking** das Haus, von dem *od* wovon ich redete. **after which** wonach; **on which** worauf; **on which we parked the car** auf dem. **the shop opposite which we parked the car** den Laden, gegenüber dem wir parkten. **everything which I tell you** alles, was ich dir sage

which'ever adj & pron [egal] welche(r,s); ~ **it was** es war, wie es auch ist

while /waɪl/ n Weile f; **a long** ~ lange; **be worth** ~ sich lohnen; **it's worth my** ~ es lohnt sich für mich ● *conj* während; (*as long as*) solange; (*although*) obgleich ● vt ~ **away sth** (*dat*) vertreiben

whilst /waɪlst/ conj während

whim /wɪm/ n Laune f

whimper /'wɪmpə(r)/ vi wimmern; (*dog:*) winseln

whine /waɪn/ vi winseln

whip /wɪp/ n Peitsche f; (Pol) Einpeitscher m ● vt (pt/pp **whipped**) peitschen; (Culin) schlagen. ~**ped 'cream** n Schlagsahne f

whirl /wɜːl/ vt/i wirbeln. ~**pool** n Strudel m. ~**wind** n Wirbelwind m

whirr /wɜː(r)/ vi surren

whisk /wɪsk/ n (Culin) Schneebesen m ● vt (Culin) schlagen

whisker /'wɪskə(r)/ n Schnurrhaar n

whisky /'wɪskɪ/ n Whisky m

whisper /'wɪspə(r)/ n Flüstern nt ● vt/i flüstern

whistle /'wɪsl/ n Pfiff m; (*instrument*) Pfeife f ● vt/i pfeifen

white /waɪt/ adj (-r, -st) weiß ● n Weiß nt; (*of egg*) Eiweiß nt; (*person*) Weiße(r) m/f

white: ~ **'coffee** n Kaffee m mit Milch. ~**'collar worker** n Angestellte(r) m. ~**'lie** n Notlüge f

whiten /'waɪtn/ vt weiß machen ● vi weiß werden

whiteness /'waɪtnɪs/ n Weiß nt

Whitsun /'wɪtsn/ n Pfingsten nt

whiz[z] /wɪz/ vi (pt/pp **whizzed**) zischen. ~**kid** n Ⓣ Senkrechtstarter m

who /huː/ pron wer; (*acc*) wen; (*dat*) wem ● *rel pron* der/die/das, (*pl*) die

who'ever pron wer [immer]; ~ **he is** wer er auch ist; ~ **is it?** wer ist das bloß?

whole /həʊl/ adj ganz; (*truth*) voll ● n Ganze(s) nt; **as a** ~ als Ganzes; **on the** ~ im Großen und Ganzen; **the** ~ **of Germany** ganz Deutschland

whole: ~**food** n Vollwertkost f. ~**'hearted** adj rückhaltlos. ~**meal** adj Vollkorn-

'wholesale adj Großhandels- ● adv en gros; (*fig*) in Bausch und

W

Bogen. **~r** n Großhändler m

wholly /ˈhəʊlɪ/ adv völlig

whom /huːm/ pron wen; to ~ wem ● rel pron den/die/das, (pl) die; (dat) dem/der/dem, (pl) denen

whopping /ˈwɒpɪŋ/ adj 🖪 Riesen-

whore /hɔː(r)/ n Hure f

whose /huːz/ pron wessen; ~ is that? wem gehört das? ● rel pron dessen/deren/dessen, (pl) deren

why /waɪ/ adv warum; (for what purpose) wozu; that's ~ darum

wick /wɪk/ n Docht m

wicked /ˈwɪkɪd/ adj böse; (mischievous) frech, boshaft

wicker /ˈwɪkə(r)/ n Korbgeflecht nt ● attrib Korb-

wide /waɪd/ adj (-r,-st) weit; (broad) breit; (fig) groß ● adv weit; (off target) daneben; ~ awake hellwach; far and ~ weit und breit. **~ly** adv weit; (known, accepted) weithin; (differ) stark

widen /ˈwaɪdn/ vt verbreitern; (fig) erweitern ● vi sich verbreitern

widespread adj weit verbreitet

widow /ˈwɪdəʊ/ n Witwe f. **~ed** adj verwitwet. **~er** n Witwer m

width /wɪdθ/ n Weite f; (breadth) Breite f

wield /wiːld/ vt schwingen; ausüben (power)

wife /waɪf/ n (pl wives) [Ehe]frau f

wig /wɪɡ/ n Perücke f

wiggle /ˈwɪɡl/ vi wackeln ● vt wackeln mit

wild /waɪld/ adj (-er, -est) wild; (animal) wild lebend; (flower) wild wachsend; (furious) wütend ● adv wild; run ~ frei herumlaufen ● n in the ~ wild; **the ~s** pl die Wildnis f

wilderness /ˈwɪldənɪs/ n Wildnis f; (desert) Wüste f

wildlife n Tierwelt f

will[1] /wɪl/
● **modal verb**

past would

····▸ (expressing the future) werden. she will arrive tomorrow sie wird morgen ankommen. he will be there by now er wird jetzt schon da sein

····▸ (expressing intention) (present tense) will you go? gehst du? I promise I won't do it again ich verspreche, ich machs nicht noch mal

····▸ (in requests) will/would you please tidy up? würdest du bitte aufräumen? will you be quiet! willst du ruhig sein!

····▸ (in invitations) will you have/would you like some wine? wollen Sie/möchten Sie Wein?

····▸ (negative: refuse to) nicht wollen. they won't help me sie wollen mir nicht helfen. the car won't start das Auto will nicht anspringen

····▸ (in tag questions) nicht wahr. you'll be back soon, won't you? du kommst bald wieder, nicht wahr? you will help me, won't you? du hilfst ihr doch, nicht wahr?

····▸ (in short answers) Will you be there? — Yes I will Wirst du da sein? — Ja

will[2] n Wille m; (document) Testament nt

willing /ˈwɪlɪŋ/ adj willig; (eager) bereitwillig; be ~ bereit sein. **~ly** adv bereitwillig; (gladly) gern. **~ness** n Bereitwilligkeit f

willow /'wɪləʊ/ n Weide f

'will-power n Willenskraft f

wilt /wɪlt/ vi welk werden, welken

wily /'waɪlɪ/ adj listig

win /wɪn/ n Sieg m ● v (pt/pp won; pres p winning) ● vt gewinnen; bekommen (scholarship) ● vi gewinnen; (in battle) siegen. ~ **over** vt auf seine Seite bringen

wince /wɪns/ vi zusammenzucken

winch /wɪntʃ/ n Winde f ● vt ~ **up** hochwinden

wind[1] /wɪnd/ n Wind m; (1: flatulence) Blähungen pl ● vt ~ s.o. jdm den Atem nehmen

wind[2] /waɪnd/ v (pt/pp wound) ● vt (wrap) wickeln; (move by turning) kurbeln; aufziehen (clock) ● vi (road:) sich winden. ~ **up** vt aufziehen (clock); schließen (proceedings)

wind: ~ **farm** n Windpark m. ~ **instrument** n Blasinstrument nt. ~ **mill** n Windmühle f

window /'wɪndəʊ/ n Fenster nt; (of shop) Schaufenster nt

window: ~ **box** n Blumenkasten m. ~ **cleaner** n Fensterputzer m. ~ **pane** n Fensterscheibe f. ~ **shopping** n Schaufensterbummel m. ~ **sill** n Fensterbrett nt

'windpipe n Luftröhre f

'windscreen n, (Amer) **'windshield** n Windschutzscheibe f. ~ **wiper** n Scheibenwischer m

wind surfing n Windsurfen nt

windy /'wɪndɪ/ adj windig

wine /waɪn/ n Wein m

wine: ~ **bar** n Weinstube f. ~ **glass** n Weinglas nt. ~ **list** n Weinkarte f

winery /'waɪnərɪ/ n (Amer) Weingut nt

'wine-tasting n Weinprobe f

wing /wɪŋ/ n Flügel m; (Auto) Kot-

flügel m; ~**s** pl (Theat) Kulissen pl

wink /wɪŋk/ n Zwinkern nt; not sleep a ~ kein Auge zutun ● vi zwinkern; (light:) blinken

winner /'wɪnə(r)/ n Gewinner(in) m(f)

winning /'wɪnɪŋ/ adj siegreich; (smile) gewinnend. ~ **post** n Zielpfosten m. ~**s** npl Gewinn m

wint|er /'wɪntə(r)/ n Winter m. ~**ry** adj winterlich

wipe /waɪp/ n give sth a ~ etw abwischen ● vt abwischen; aufwischen (floor); (dry) abtrocknen. ~ **out** vt (cancel) löschen; (destroy) ausrotten. ~ **up** vt aufwischen

wire /'waɪə(r)/ n Draht m

wiring /'waɪərɪŋ/ n [elektrische] Leitungen pl

wisdom /'wɪzdəm/ n Weisheit f; (prudence) Klugheit f. ~ **tooth** n Weisheitszahn m

wise /waɪz/ adj (-r, -st) weise; (prudent) klug

wish /wɪʃ/ n Wunsch m ● vt wünschen; ~ s.o. well jdm alles Gute wünschen; I ~ you could stay ich wünschte, du könntest hier bleiben ● vi sich (dat) etwas wünschen. ~ **ful** adj ~ ful thinking Wunschdenken nt

wistful /'wɪstfl/ adj wehmütig

wit /wɪt/ n Geist m, Witz m; (intelligence) Verstand m; (person) geistreicher Mensch m; be at one's ~**s'** end sich (dat) keinen Rat mehr wissen

witch /wɪtʃ/ n Hexe f. ~ **craft** n Hexerei f

with /wɪð/ prep mit (+ dat); ~ fear/cold vor Angst/Kälte; ~ it damit; I'm going ~ you ich gehe mit; take it ~ you nimm es mit; I haven't got it ~ me ich habe es nicht bei mir

W

with'draw v (pt -drew, pp -drawn) ● vi sich zurückziehen; abheben (money) ● vi sich zurückziehen. ~al n Zurückziehen nt; (of money) Abhebung f; (from drugs) Entzug m

wither /'wɪðə(r)/ vi [ver]welken

with'hold vt (pt/pp -held) vorenthalten (from s.o. jdm)

with'in prep innerhalb (+ gen) ● adv innen

with'out prep ohne (+ acc); ~ my noticing it ohne dass ich es merkte

with'stand vt (pt/pp -stood) standhalten (+ dat)

witness /'wɪtnɪs/ n Zeuge m/ Zeugin f ● vt Zeuge/Zeugin sein (+ gen); bestätigen (signature)

witticism /'wɪtɪsɪzm/ n geistreicher Ausspruch m

witty /'wɪtɪ/ adj witzig, geistreich

wives /waɪvz/ see wife

wizard /'wɪzəd/ n Zauberer m

wizened /'wɪznd/ adj verhutzelt

wobb|le /'wɒbl/ vi wackeln. ~ly adj wackelig

woke, woken /wəʊk, 'wəʊkn/ see wake¹

wolf /wʊlf/ n (pl wolves /wʊlvz/) Wolf m

woman /'wʊmən/ n (pl women) Frau f. ~izer n Schürzenjäger m

womb /wu:m/ n Gebärmutter f

women /'wɪmɪn/ npl see woman

won /wʌn/ see win

wonder /'wʌndə(r)/ n Wunder nt; (surprise) Staunen nt ● vt/i sich fragen; (be surprised) sich wundern; I ~ da frage ich mich; I ~ whether she is ill ob sie wohl krank ist? ~ful adj wunderbar

won't /wəʊnt/ = will not

wood /wʊd/ n Holz nt; (forest) Wald m; touch ~! unberufen!

wood: ~ed /-ɪd/ adj bewaldet.

~en adj Holz-; (fig) hölzern. ~pecker n Specht m. ~wind n Holzbläser pl. ~work n (wooden parts) Holzteile pl; (craft) Tischlerei f. ~worm n Holzwurm m

wool /wʊl/ n Wolle f ● attrib Woll-. ~len adj wollen

woolly /'wʊlɪ/ adj wollig; (fig) unklar

word /wɜ:d/ n Wort nt; (news) Nachricht f; by ~ of mouth mündlich; have a ~ with sprechen mit; have ~s einen Wortwechsel haben. ~ing n Wortlaut m. ~ processor n Textverarbeitungssystem nt

wore /wɔ:(r)/ see wear

work /wɜ:k/ n Arbeit f; (Art, Literature) Werk nt; ~s pl (factory, mechanism) Werk nt; at ~ bei der Arbeit; out of ~ arbeitslos ● vi arbeiten; (machine, system:) funktionieren; (have effect) wirken; (study) lernen; it won't ~ (fig) es klappt nicht ● vt arbeiten lassen; bedienen (machine); betätigen (lever). ~ off vt abarbeiten. ~ out vt ausrechnen; (solve) lösen ● vi gut gehen, 🇹 klappen. ~ up vt aufbauen; sich (dat) holen (appetite); get ~ed up sich aufregen

workable /'wɜ:kəbl/ adj (feasible) durchführbar

worker /'wɜ:kə(r)/ n Arbeiter(in) m(f)

working /'wɜ:kɪŋ/ adj berufstätig; (day, clothes) Arbeits-; be in ~ order funktionieren. ~ class n Arbeiterklasse f

work: ~man n Arbeiter m; (craftsman) Handwerker m. ~manship n Arbeit f. ~shop n Werkstatt f

world /wɜ:ld/ n Welt f; in the ~ auf der Welt; think the ~ of s.o. große Stücke auf jdn halten. ~ly adj weltlich; (person) weltlich gesinnt. ~-**wide** adj & adv /·'·/ weltweit

worm /wɜːm/ n Wurm m

worn /wɔːn/ see wear ● adj abgetragen. ~-**out** adj abgetragen; (carpet) abgenutzt; (person) erschöpft

worried /'wʌrɪd/ adj besorgt

worry /'wʌrɪ/ n Sorge f ● v (pt/pp worried) ● vt beunruhigen; (bother) stören ● vi sich beunruhigen, sich (dat) Sorgen machen. ~**ing** adj beunruhigend

worse /wɜːs/ adj & adv schlechter; (more serious) schlimmer ● n Schlechtere(s) nt; Schlimmere(s) nt

worsen /'wɜːsn/ vt verschlechtern ● vi sich verschlechtern

worship /'wɜːʃɪp/ n Anbetung f; (service) Gottesdienst m ● vt (pt/pp -shipped) anbeten

worst /wɜːst/ adj schlechteste(r,s); (most serious) schlimmste(r,s) ● adv am schlechtesten; am schlimmsten ● n the ~ das Schlimmste

worth /wɜːθ/ n Wert m; £10's ~ of petrol Benzin für £10 ● adj be ~ £5 £5 wert sein; be ~ it (fig) sich lohnen. ~**less** adj wertlos. ~**while** adj lohnend

worthy /'wɜːðɪ/ adj würdig

would /wʊd/ modal verb I ~ do it ich würde es tun, ich täte es; ~ you go? würdest du gehen? he said he ~n't er sagte, er würde es nicht tun; what ~ you like? was möchten Sie?

wound¹ /wuːnd/ n Wunde f ● vt verwunden

wound² /waʊnd/ see wind²

wove, woven see weave¹

wrangle /'ræŋgl/ n Streit m

wrap /ræp/ n Umhang m ● vt (pt/pp wrapped) ~ [up] wickeln; einpacken (present) ● vi ~ up warmly sich warm einpacken. ~**per** n Hülle f. ~**ping** n Verpackung f

wrath /rɒθ/ n Zorn m

wreath /riːθ/ n (pl ~s /-ðz/) Kranz m

wreck /rek/ n Wrack nt ● vt zerstören; zunichte machen (plans); zerrütten (marriage). ~**age** n Wrackteile pl; (fig) Trümmer pl

wren /ren/ n Zaunkönig m

wrench /rentʃ/ n Ruck m; (tool) Schraubenschlüssel m; be a ~ (fig) weh tun ● vt reißen; ~ sth from s.o. jdm etw entreißen

wrestl|e /'resl/ vi ringen. ~**er** n Ringer m. ~**ing** n Ringen nt

wretch /retʃ/ n Kreatur f. ~**ed** adj elend; (very bad) erbärmlich

wriggle /'rɪgl/ n Zappeln nt ● vi zappeln; (move forward) sich schlängeln; ~ out of sth 🛈 sich vor etw (dat) drücken

wring /rɪŋ/ vt (pt/pp wrung) wringen; (~ out) auswringen; umdrehen (neck); ringen (hands)

wrinkle /'rɪŋkl/ n Falte f; (on skin) Runzel f ● vt kräuseln ● vi sich kräuseln, sich falten. ~**d** adj runzlig

wrist /rɪst/ n Handgelenk n. ~-**watch** n Armbanduhr f

write /raɪt/ vt/i (pt wrote, pp written, pres p writing) schreiben. ~ **down** vt aufschreiben; zu Schrott fahren (car). ~ **off** vt abschreiben; zu Schrott fahren (car)

'write-off n ~ Totalschaden m

writer /'raɪtə(r)/ n Schreiber(in) m(f); (author) Schriftsteller(in) m(f)

writhe /raɪð/ vi sich winden

writing /'raɪtɪŋ/ n Schreiben nt; (handwriting) Schrift f; in ~ schriftlich. ~-**paper** n Schreibpapier nt

written /'rɪtn/ see write

wrong /rɒŋ/ adj falsch; (morally) unrecht; (not just) ungerecht; be ~ nicht stimmen; (person:) Unrecht haben; what's ~? was ist los? ● adv falsch; go ~ (person:) etwas falsch machen; (machine:) kaputtgehen; (*plan:*) schief gehen ●n Unrecht nt ●vt Unrecht tun (+ dat). ~ful adj ungerechtfertigt. ~fully adv (*accuse*) zu Unrecht

wrote /rəʊt/ *see* write

wrung /rʌŋ/ *see* wring

wry /raɪ/ adj (-er, -est) ironisch; (*humour*) trocken

. . . .

Xx

. . . .

Xmas /'krɪsməs, 'eksməs/ n 🗌 Weihnachten nt

X-ray /'eks-/ n (*picture*) Röntgenaufnahme f; ~s pl Röntgenstrahlen pl ●vt röntgen; durchleuchten (*luggage*)

. . . .

Yy

. . . .

yacht /jɒt/ n Jacht f; (*for racing*) Segeljacht f. ~ing n Segeln nt

yank /jæŋk/ vt 🗌 reißen

Yank n 🗌 Ami m 🗌

yap /jæp/ vi (*pt/pp* yapped) (*dog:*) kläffen

yard[1] /jɑːd/ n Hof m; (*for storage*) Lager nt

yard[2] n Yard nt (= 0,91 m)

yarn /jɑːn/ n Garn nt; (🗌: *tale*) Geschichte f

yawn /jɔːn/ n Gähnen nt ●vi gähnen

year /jɪə(r)/ n Jahr nt; (*of wine*) Jahrgang m; for ~s jahrelang. ~ly adj & adv jährlich

yearn /jɜːn/ vi sich sehnen (for

nach). ~ing n Sehnsucht f

yeast /jiːst/ n Hefe f

yell /jel/ n Schrei m ●vi schreien

yellow /'jeləʊ/ adj gelb ●n Gelb nt

yelp /jelp/ vi jaulen

yes /jes/ adv ja; (*contradicting*) doch ●n Ja nt

yesterday /'jestədeɪ/ n & adv gestern; ~'s paper die gestrige Zeitung; the day before ~ vorgestern

yet /jet/ adv noch; (*in question*) schon; (*nevertheless*) doch; as ~ bisher; not ~ noch nicht; the best ~ das bisher beste ●conj doch

Yiddish /'jɪdɪʃ/ n Jiddisch nt

yield /jiːld/ n Ertrag m ● vt bringen; abwerfen (*profit*) ● vi nachgeben; (*Amer, Auto*) die Vorfahrt beachten

yoga /'jəʊgə/ n Yoga m

yoghurt /'jɒgət/ n Joghurt m

yoke /jəʊk/ n Joch nt; (*of garment*) Passe f

yolk /jəʊk/ n Dotter m, Eigelb nt

you /juː/ pron du; (*acc*) dich; (*dat*) dir; (*pl*) ihr; (*acc, dat*) euch; (*formal*) (*nom & acc, sg & pl*) Sie; (*dat, sg & pl*) Ihnen; (*one*) man; (*acc*) einen; (*dat*) einem; all of ~ ihr/Sie alle; I know ~ ich kenne dich/euch/Sie; I'll give ~ the money ich gebe dir/euch/Ihnen das Geld; it does ~ good es tut einem gut; it's bad for ~ es ist ungesund

young /jʌŋ/ adj (-er /-gə(r)/, -est /-gɪst/) jung ●npl (*animals*) Junge pl; the ~ die Jugend f. ~ster n Jugendliche(r) m/f; (*child*) Kleine(r) m/f

your /jɔː(r)/ adj dein; (*pl*) euer; (*formal*) Ihr

yours /jɔːz/ poss pron deine(r), deins; (*pl*) eure(r), euers; (*formal, sg & pl*) Ihre(r), Ihr[e]s; a friend of ~ ein Freund von dir/Ihnen/euch; that is ~ das gehört dir/

Ihnen/euch

your'self *pron* (*pl* -selves) selbst; (*reflexive*) dich; (*dat*) dir; (*pl*) euch; (*formal*) sich; by ~ allein

youth /ju:θ/ *n* (*pl* youths /-ð:z/) Jugend *f*; (*boy*) Jugendliche(r) *m*. ~**ful** *adj* jugendlich. ~ **hostel** *n* Jugendherberge *f*

Yugoslavia /ju:gə'sla:vɪə/ *n* Jugoslawien *nt*

• •

Zz

• •

zeal /zi:l/ *n* Eifer *m*

zealous /'zeləs/ *adj* eifrig

zebra /'zebrə/ *n* Zebra *nt*. ~ '**crossing** *n* Zebrastreifen *m*

zero /'zɪərəʊ/ *n* Null *f*

zest /zest/ *n* Begeisterung *f*

zigzag /'zɪgzæg/ *n* Zickzack *m* • *vi* (*pt/pp* -zagged) im Zickzack laufen/ (*in vehicle*) fahren

zinc /zɪŋk/ *n* Zink *nt*

zip /zɪp/ *n* ~ [fastener] Reißverschluss *m* • *vt* ~ [up] den Reißverschluss zuziehen an (+ *dat*)

'**zip code** *n* (*Amer*) Postleitzahl *f*

zipper /'zɪpə(r)/ *n* Reißverschluss *m*

zodiac /'zəʊdɪæk/ *n* Tierkreis *m*

zone /zəʊn/ *n* Zone *f*

zoo /zu:/ *n* Zoo *m*

zoological /zu:ə'lɒdʒɪkl/ *adj* zoologisch

zoolog|ist /zu:'ɒlədʒɪst/ *n* Zoologe *m*/-gin *f*. ~**y** Zoologie *f*

zoom /zu:m/ *vi* sausen. ~ **lens** *n* Zoomobjektiv *nt*

German irregular verbs

1st, 2nd, and 3rd person present are given after the infinitive, and past subjunctive after the past indicative, where there is a change of vowel or any other irregularity.

Compound verbs are only given if they do not take the same forms as the corresponding simple verb, e.g. *befehlen*, or if there is no corresponding simple verb, e.g. *bewegen*.

An asterisk (*) indicates a verb which is also conjugated regularly.

Infinitive	Past tense	Past participle
abwägen	wog (wöge) ab	abgewogen
ausbedingen	bedang (bedänge) aus	ausbedungen
backen (du bäckst, er bäckt)	backte (backte)	gebacken
befehlen (du befiehlst, er befiehlt)	befahl (befähle)	befohlen
beginnen	begann (begänne)	begonnen
beißen (du/er beißt)	biss (bisse)	gebissen
bergen (du birgst, er birgt)	barg (bärge)	geborgen
bewegen²	bewog (bewöge)	bewogen
biegen	bog (böge)	gebogen
bieten	bot (böte)	geboten
binden	band (bände)	gebunden
bitten	bat (bäte)	gebeten
blasen (du/er bläst)	blies	geblasen
bleiben	blieb	geblieben
braten (du brätst, er brät)	briet	gebraten
brechen (du brichst, er bricht)	brach (bräche)	gebrochen
brennen	brannte (brennte)	gebrannt
bringen	brachte (brächte)	gebracht
denken	dachte (dächte)	gedacht
dreschen (du drischst, er drischt)	drosch (drösche)	gedroschen
dringen	drang (dränge)	gedrungen
dürfen (ich/er darf, du darfst)	durfte (dürfte)	gedurft
empfehlen (du empfiehlst, er empfiehlt)	empfahl (empföhle)	empfohlen

Infinitive	Past tense	Past participle
erlöschen (du erlischst, er erlischt)	erlosch (erlösche)	erloschen
erschrecken* (du erschrickst, er erschrickt)	erschrak (erschäke)	erschrocken
erwägen	erwog (erwöge)	erwogen
essen (du/er isst)	aß (äße)	gegessen
fahren (du fährst, er fährt)	fuhr (führe)	gefahren
fallen (du fällst, er fällt)	fiel	gefallen
fangen (du fängst, er fängt)	fing	gefangen
fechten (du fichtst, er ficht)	focht (föchte)	gefochten
finden	fand (fände)	gefunden
flechten (du flichtst, er flicht)	flocht (flöchte)	geflochten
fliegen	flog (flöge)	geflogen
fliehen	floh (flöhe)	geflohen
fließen (du/er fließt)	floss (flösse)	geflossen
fressen (du/er frisst)	fraß (fräße)	gefressen
frieren	fror (fröre)	gefroren
gären*	gor (göre)	gegoren
gebären (du gebierst, sie gebiert)	gebar (gebäre)	geboren
geben (du gibst, er gibt)	gab (gäbe)	gegeben
gedeihen	gedieh	gediehen
gehen	ging	gegangen
gelingen	gelang (gelänge)	gelungen
gelten (du giltst, er gilt)	galt (gälte)	gegolten
genesen (du/er genest)	genas (genäse)	genesen
genießen (du/er genießt)	genoss (genösse)	genossen
geschehen (es geschieht)	geschah (geschähe)	geschehen
gewinnen	gewann (gewänne)	gewonnen
gießen (du/er gießt)	goss (gösse)	gegossen
gleichen	glich	geglichen
gleiten	glitt	geglitten
glimmen	glomm (glömme)	geglommen
graben (du gräbst, er gräbt)	grub (grübe)	gegraben
greifen	griff	gegriffen
haben (du hast, er hat)	hatte (hätte)	gehabt
halten (du hältst, er hält)	hielt	gehalten
hängen²	hing	gehangen
hauen	haute	gehauen
heben	hob (höbe)	gehoben
heißen (du/er heißt)	hieß	geheißen

Infinitive	Past tense	Past participle
helfen (du hilfst, er hilft)	half (hülfe)	geholfen
kennen	kannte (kennte)	gekannt
klingen	klang (klänge)	geklungen
kneifen	kniff	gekniffen
kommen	kam (käme)	gekommen
können (ich/er kann, du kannst)	konnte (könnte)	gekonnt
kriechen	kroch (kröche)	gekrochen
laden (du lädst, er lädt)	lud (lüde)	geladen
lassen (du/er lässt)	ließ	gelassen
laufen (du läufst, er läuft)	lief	gelaufen
leiden	litt	gelitten
leihen	lieh	geliehen
lesen (du/er liest)	las (läse)	gelesen
liegen	lag (läge)	gelegen
lügen	log (löge)	gelogen
mahlen	mahlte	gemahlen
meiden	mied	gemieden
melken	molk (mölke)	gemolken
messen (du/er misst)	maß (mäße)	gemessen
misslingen	misslang (misslänge)	misslungen
mögen (ich/er mag, du magst)	mochte (möchte)	gemocht
müssen (ich/er muss, du musst)	musste (müsste)	gemusst
nehmen (du nimmst, er nimmt)	nahm (nähme)	genommen
nennen	nannte (nennte)	genannt
pfeifen	pfiff	gepfiffen
preisen (du/er preist)	pries	gepriesen
raten (du rätst, er rät)	riet	geraten
reiben	rieb	gerieben
reißen (du/er reißt)	riss	gerissen
reiten	ritt	geritten
rennen	rannte (rennte)	gerannt
riechen	roch (röche)	gerochen
ringen	rang (ränge)	gerungen
rinnen	rann (ränne)	geronnen
rufen	rief	gerufen
salzen* (du/er salzt)	salzte	gesalzen
saufen (du säufst, er säuft)	soff (söffe)	gesoffen
saugen*	sog (söge)	gesogen
schaffen[1]	schuf (schüfe)	geschaffen
scheiden	schied	geschieden
scheinen	schien	geschienen

Infinitive	Past tense	Past participle
scheißen (du/er scheißt)	schiss	geschissen
schelten (du schiltst, er schilt)	schalt (schölte)	gescholten
scheren[1]	schor (schöre)	geschoren
schieben	schob (schöbe)	geschoben
schießen (du/er schießt)	schoss (schösse)	geschossen
schlafen (du schläfst, er schläft)	schlief	geschlafen
schlagen (du schlägst, er schlägt)	schlug (schlüge)	geschlagen
schleichen	schlich	geschlichen
schleifen[2]	schliff	geschliffen
schließen (du/er schießt)	schloss (schlösse)	geschlossen
schlingen	schlang (schlänge)	geschlungen
schmeißen (du/er schmeißt)	schmiss (schmisse)	geschmissen
schmelzen (du/er schmilzt)	schmolz (schmölze)	geschmolzen
schneiden	schnitt	geschnitten
schrecken* (du schrickst, er schrickt)	schrak (schräke)	geschreckt
schreiben	schrieb	geschrieben
schreien	schrie	geschrie[e]n
schreiten	schritt	geschritten
schweigen	schwieg	geschwiegen
schwellen (du schwillst, er schwillt)	schwoll (schwölle)	geschwollen
schwimmen	schwamm (schwömme)	geschwommen
schwinden	schwand (schwände)	geschwunden
schwingen	schwang (schwänge)	geschwungen
schwören	schwor (schwüre)	geschworen
sehen (du siehst, er sieht)	sah (sähe)	gesehen
sein (ich bin, du bist, er ist, wir sind, ihr seid, sie sind)	war (wäre)	gewesen
senden[1]	sandte (sendete)	gesandt
sieden	sott (sötte)	gesotten
singen	sang (sänge)	gesungen
sinken	sank (sänke)	gesunken
sitzen (du/er sitzt)	saß (säße)	gesessen
sollen (ich/er soll, du sollst)	sollte	gesollt
spalten*	spaltete	gespalten
spinnen	spann (spänne)	gesponnen
sprechen (du sprichst, er spricht)	sprach (spräche)	gesprochen
sprießen (du/er sprießt)	spross (sprösse)	gesprossen
springen	sprang (spränge)	gesprungen

Infinitive	Past tense	Past participle
stechen (du stichst, er sticht)	stach (stäche)	gestochen
stehen	stand (stünde, stände)	gestanden `
stehlen (du stiehlst, er stiehlt)	stahl (stähle)	gestohlen
steigen	stieg	gestiegen
sterben (du stirbst, er stirbt)	starb (stürbe)	gestorben
stinken	stank (stänke)	gestunken
stoßen (du/er stößt)	stieß	gestoßen
streichen	strich	gestrichen
streiten	stritt	gestritten
tragen (du trägst, er trägt)	trug (trüge)	getragen
treffen (du triffst, er trifft)	traf (träfe)	getroffen
treiben	trieb	getrieben
treten (du trittst, er tritt)	trat (träte)	getreten
triefen*	troff (tröffe)	getroffen
trinken	trank (tränke)	getrunken
trügen	trog (tröge)	getrogen
tun (du tust, er tut)	tat (täte)	getan
verderben (du verdirbst, er verdirbt)	verdarb (verdürbe)	verdorben
vergessen (du/er vergisst)	vergaß (vergäße)	vergessen
verlieren	verlor (verlöre)	verloren
verzeihen	verzieh	verziehen
wachsen[1] (du wächst, er wächst)	wuchs (wüchse)	gewachsen
waschen (du wäschst, er wäscht)	wusch (wüsche)	gewaschen
wenden[2]*	wandte (wendete)	gewandt
werben (du wirbst, er wirbt)	warb (würbe)	geworben
werden (du wirst, er wird)	wurde (würde)	geworden
werfen (du wirfst, er wirft)	warf (würfe)	geworfen
wiegen[1]	wog (wöge)	gewogen
winden	wand (wände)	gewunden
wissen (ich/er weiß, du weißt)	wusste (wüsste)	gewusst
wollen (ich/er will, du willst)	wollte	gewollt
wringen	wrang (wränge)	gewrungen
ziehen	zog (zöge)	gezogen
zwingen	zwang (zwänge)	gezwungen

Englische unregelmäßige Verben

Infinitiv	Präteritum	2. Partizip	Infinitiv	Präteritum	2. Partizip
be	was	been	**drive**	drove	driven
bear	bore	borne	**eat**	ate	eaten
beat	beat	beaten	**fall**	fell	fallen
become	became	become	**feed**	fed	fed
begin	began	begun	**feel**	felt	felt
bend	bent	bent	**fight**	fought	fought
bet	bet,	bet,	**find**	found	found
	betted	betted	**flee**	fled	fled
bid	bade, bid	bidden, bid	**fly**	flew	flown
bind	bound	bound	**forecast**	forecast,	forecast,
bite	bit	bitten		forecasted	forecasted
bleed	bled	bled	**forget**	forgot	forgotten,
blow	blew	blown			forgot *US*
break	broke	broken	**freeze**	froze	frozen
breed	bred	bred	**get**	got	got, gotten *US*
bring	brought	brought	**give**	gave	given
build	built	built	**go**	went	gone
burn	burnt,	burnt,	**grow**	grew	grown
	burned	burned	**hang**	hung,	hung,
burst	burst	burst		hanged	hanged
buy	bought	bought	**have**	had	had
catch	caught	caught	**hear**	heard	heard
choose	chose	chosen	**hide**	hid	hidden
cling	clung	clung	**hit**	hit	hit
come	came	come	**hold**	held	held
cost	cost,	cost,	**hurt**	hurt	hurt
	costed (vt)	costed	**keep**	kept	kept
cut	cut	cut	**kneel**	knelt	knelt
deal	dealt	dealt	**know**	knew	known
dig	dug	dug	**lay**	laid	laid
do	did	done	**lead**	led	led
draw	drew	drawn	**lean**	leaned,	leaned,
dream	dreamt,	dreamt,		leant	leant
	dreamed	dreamed	**leap**	leaped,	leaped,
drink	drank	drunk		leapt	leapt

Infinitiv	Präteritum	2. Partizip	Infinitiv	Präteritum	2. Partizip
learn	learnt, learned	learnt, learned	**smell**	smelt, smelled	smelt, smelled
leave	left	left	**speak**	spoke	spoken
lend	lent	lent	**spell**	spelled, spelt	spelled, spelt
let	let	let			
lie	lay	lain	**spend**	spent	spent
lose	lost	lost	**spit**	spat	spat
make	made	made	**spoil**	spoilt, spoiled	spoilt, spoiled
mean	meant	meant			
meet	met	met	**spread**	spread	spread
pay	paid	paid	**spring**	sprang	sprung
put	put	put	**stand**	stood	stood
quit	quitted, quit	quitted, quit	**steal**	stole	stolen
			stick	stuck	stuck
read	read	read	**sting**	stung	stung
ride	rode	ridden	**stride**	strode	stridden
ring	rang	rung	**strike**	struck	struck
rise	rose	risen	**swear**	swore	sworn
run	ran	run	**sweep**	swept	swept
say	said	said	**swell**	swelled	swollen, swelled
see	saw	seen			
seek	sought	sought	**swim**	swam	swum
sell	sold	sold	**swing**	swung	swung
send	sent	sent	**take**	took	taken
set	set	set	**teach**	taught	taught
sew	sewed	sewn, sewed	**tear**	tore	torn
shake	shook	shaken	**tell**	told	told
shine	shone	shone	**think**	thought	thought
shoe	shod	shod	**throw**	threw	thrown
shoot	shot	shot	**thrust**	thrust	thrust
show	showed	shown	**tread**	trod	trodden
shut	shut	shut	**understand**	understood	understood
sing	sang	sung			
sink	sank	sunk	**wake**	woke	woken
sit	sat	sat	**wear**	wore	worn
sleep	slept	slept	**win**	won	won
sling	slung	slung	**write**	wrote	written

Abbreviations/Abkürzungen

adjective	*adj*	Adjektiv
abbreviation	*abbr*	Abkürzung
accusative	*acc*	Akkusativ
Administration	*Admin*	Administration
adverb	*adv*	Adverb
American	*Amer*	amerikanisch
Anatomy	*Anat*	Anatomie
attributive	*attrib*	attributiv
Austrian	*Aust*	österreichisch
Motor vehicles	*Auto*	Automobil
Aviation	*Aviat*	Luftfahrt
Botany	*Bot*	Botanik
collective	*coll*	Kollektivum
Commerce	*Comm*	Handel
conjunction	*conj*	Konjunktion
Cookery	*Culin*	Kochkunst
dative	*dat*	Dativ
definite article	*def art*	bestimmter Artikel
demonstrative	*dem*	Demonstrativ-
Electricity	*Electr*	Elektrizität
something	*etw*	etwas
feminine	*f*	Femininum
figurative	*fig*	figurativ
genitive	*gen*	Genitiv
Geography	*Geog*	Geographie
Grammar	*Gram*	Grammatik
impersonal	*impers*	unpersönlich
inseparable	*insep*	untrennbar
interjection	*int*	Interjektion
invariable	*inv*	unveränderlich
someone	*jd*	jemand
someone (dat)	*jdm*	jemandem
someone (acc)	*jdn*	jemanden
someone's	*jds*	jemandes
Law	*Jur*	Jura
Language	*Lang*	Sprache
masculine	*m*	Maskulinum